EVOLUTION/GENETICS

CULTURE/ETHNICI

Continued on Inside of Back Cover

IMPORTANT:

HERE IS YOUR REGISTRATION CODE TO ACCESS YOUR PREMIUM McGRAW-HILL ONLINE RESOURCES.

For key premium online resources you need THIS CODE to gain access. Once the code is entered, you will be able to use the Web resources for the length of your course.

If your course is using **WebCT** or **Blackboard**, you'll be able to use this code to access the McGraw-Hill content within your instructor's online course.

Access is provided if you have purchased a new book. If the registration code is missing from this book, the registration screen on our Website, and within your WebCT or Blackboard course, will tell you how to obtain your new code.

Registering for McGraw-Hill Online Resources

To gain access to your McGraw-Hill web resources simply follow the steps below:

1. USE YOUR WEB BROWSER TO GO TO: **www.mhhe.com/passer2**
2. CLICK ON **FIRST TIME USER**.
3. ENTER THE REGISTRATION CODE* PRINTED ON THE TEAR-OFF BOOKMARK ON THE RIGHT.
4. AFTER YOU HAVE ENTERED YOUR REGISTRATION CODE, CLICK **REGISTER**.
5. FOLLOW THE INSTRUCTIONS TO SET-UP YOUR PERSONAL UserID AND PASSWORD.
6. WRITE YOUR UserID AND PASSWORD DOWN FOR FUTURE REFERENCE. KEEP IT IN A SAFE PLACE.

TO GAIN ACCESS to the McGraw-Hill content in your instructor's **WebCT** or **Blackboard** course simply log in to the course with the UserID and Password provided by your instructor. Enter the registration code exactly as it appears in the box to the right when prompted by the system. You will only need to use the code the first time you click on McGraw-Hill content.

Thank you, and welcome to your McGraw-Hill online resources!

* YOUR REGISTRATION CODE CAN BE USED ONLY ONCE TO ESTABLISH ACCESS. IT IS NOT TRANSFERABLE.

0-07-294379-3 T/A PASSER: PSYCHOLOGY: THE SCIENCE OF MIND AND BEHAVIOR, 2/E

MCGRAW-HILL

ONLINE RESOURCES

REGISTRATION CODE

TEF8-C4ZC-9RN2-FC5G-P9B0

Mc Graw Hill Higher Education

PSYCHOLOGY

The Science of Mind and Behavior

SECOND EDITION

PSYCHOLOGY

The Science of Mind and Behavior

Michael W. Passer
University of Washington

Ronald E. Smith
University of Washington

Boston Burr Ridge, IL Dubuque, IA Madison, WI New York
San Francisco St. Louis Bangkok Bogotá Caracas Kuala Lumpur
Lisbon London Madrid Mexico City Milan Montreal New Delhi
Santiago Seoul Singapore Sydney Taipei Toronto

The McGraw·Hill Companies

PSYCHOLOGY: THE SCIENCE OF MIND AND BEHAVIOR, SECOND EDITION

Published by McGraw-Hill, a business unit of The McGraw-Hill Companies, Inc., 1221 Avenue of the Americas, New York, NY 10020.

2 3 4 5 6 7 8 9 0 VNH/VNH 0 9 8 7 6 5 4

Vice president and editor-in-chief: *Thalia Dorwick*
Publisher: *Steve Rutter*
Sponsoring editor: *John Wannemacher*
Senior development editor: *Elsa Peterson*
Marketing manager: *Melissa Caughlin*
Production supervisor: *Tandra Jorgensen*
Project manager: *David Sutton*
Art director: *Jeanne M. Schreiber*
Design manager: *Cassandra Chu*
Cover designer: *Yvo Riezebos*
Interior designer: *Susan Breitbard*
Art editor: *Robin Mouat*
Photo research coordinator: *Nora Agbayani*
Photo researcher: *David Tietz*
Typeface: 9.5/12 Palatino
Printer: Von Hoffmann Press
Cover image: © Bilderberg/Photonica

Psychology Advisory Group: *Sherree D'Amico, Stephen Day, Myron Flemming, Tim Haak, John Kindler, James Koch, Don Mason, Jeff Neel, Robert Edward Oakley, Dan Pellow, Terri Rowenhorst, Kathy Shackelford, Emily Sparano*

The credits for this book begin on page C-1, which constitutes a continuation of the copyright page.

Library of Congress Cataloging-in-Publication Data

Passer, Michael W.
Psychology: the science of mind and behavior / Michael W. Passer, Ronald E. Smith.— 2nd ed.
p. cm.
Includes bibliographical references and index.
ISBN 0-07-256330-3
1. Psychology. I. Smith, Ronald Edward, 1940– II. Title.

BF121.P348 2003
150—dc21

2003056236

www.mhhe.com

About the Authors

Michael W. Passer, Ph.D.

Michael Passer coordinates the introductory psychology program at the University of Washington, which enrolls about 2,500 students per year, and also is the faculty coordinator of training for new teaching assistants (TAs). He received his bachelor's degree from the University of Rochester and his Ph.D. in Psychology from the University of California, Los Angeles, with a specialization in social psychology. Dr. Passer has been a faculty member at the University of Washington since 1977. A former Danforth Foundation Fellow and University of Washington Distinguished Teaching Award finalist, Dr. Passer has had a career-long love of teaching. Each academic year he teaches introductory psychology twice and a required pre-major course in research methods. Dr. Passer developed and teaches a graduate course on the Teaching of Psychology, which prepares students for careers in the college classroom, and has also taught courses in social psychology and attribution theory. He has published over twenty scientific articles and chapters, primarily in the areas of attribution, stress, and anxiety, and has taught the introductory psychology course for over fifteen years.

Ronald E. Smith, Ph.D.

Ronald E. Smith is Professor of Psychology at the University of Washington, where he has served as Director of Clinical Psychology Training and as Head of the Social Psychology and Personality area. He received his bachelor's degree from Marquette University and his Ph.D. from Southern Illinois University, where he had dual specializations in clinical and physiological psychology. His major research interests are in anxiety, stress and coping, and in performance enhancement research and intervention. Dr. Smith is a Fellow of the American Psychological Association. He received a Distinguished Alumnus Award from the UCLA Neuropsychiatric Institute for his contributions to the field of mental health. He has published more than 140 scientific articles and book chapters in his areas of interest and has authored or co-authored 21 books on introductory psychology, human performance enhancement, and personality, including "*Introduction to Personality: Toward an Integration*," with Walter Mischel and Yuichi Shoda (Wiley, 2004). An award-winning teacher, he has more than fifteen years of experience in teaching the introductory psychology course.

To Bev and Kay, for their endless love and support.

Brief Contents

Contents

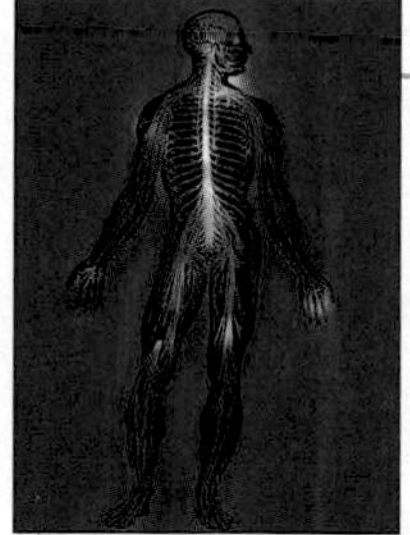

CHAPTER 3

CHAPTER 4

SENSATION AND PERCEPTION 108

CHAPTER 5

STATES OF CONSCIOUSNESS 154

CHAPTER 6

LEARNING AND ADAPTATION: THE ROLE OF EXPERIENCE 197

CHAPTER 7

MEMORY 238

CHAPTER 8

LANGUAGE, THINKING, AND INTELLIGENT BEHAVIOR 279

CHAPTER 9

MOTIVATION AND EMOTION 325

CHAPTER 10

DEVELOPMENT OVER THE LIFE SPAN 373

CHAPTER 11

PERSONALITY 418

CHAPTER 12

ADJUSTING TO LIFE: STRESS, COPING, AND HEALTH 463

CHAPTER 13

PSYCHOLOGICAL DISORDERS 505

CHAPTER 15

SOCIAL THINKING AND BEHAVIOR 590

Preface

Psychology: The Science of Mind and Behavior (2nd Edition)

—Michael W. Passer and Ronald E. Smith
University of Washington

Mind and behavior: There is nothing more fascinating in all the universe, but we didn't recognize this when we entered college. In fact, the study of psychology wasn't on either of our radar screens. Michael planned to major in physics, Ron in journalism. Then something unexpected occurred. Each of us took an introductory psychology course, and suddenly our life paths changed. Because of instructors who brought psychology to life, we were hooked, and that initial enthusiasm has never left us.

Now, through this textbook, we have the pleasure and privilege of sharing our enthusiasm with today's instructors and a new generation of students. We've endeavored to create a thoughtfully integrated book and multimedia package that strikes just the right balance between student friendliness and scientific integrity—a teaching tool that introduces students to psychology as a science while highlighting its relevance to their lives and to society. We want students to experience, as we did, the intellectual excitement of studying the mind and behavior. We also seek to help students sharpen their critical thinking skills, dispelling some commonly held myths. We have used clear prose, careful explanations, engaging examples, and supporting artwork to make the book and multimedia accessible to a wide range of students. All of this is done within a conceptual framework that emphasizes relations between biological, psychological, and environmental levels of analysis.

We are particularly excited about the unique way in which our second edition book is integrated with its supplements. This integration results in a learning package that "uses science to teach science." Specifically, we are impressed with research (e.g., Moreland et al., 1997; Pauk & Fiore, 2000) showing that recall of textual material is significantly enhanced by specific focus questions and learning objectives that serve as retrieval cues and that help students identify important information and assess their mastery of the material. Over the years, students in our own courses have profited greatly from focus questions we've prepared. Because of the research evidence and our own experiences as instructors, we have retained the Focus Questions that were a popular feature in the first edition—and taken them to the next level by using them as a comprehensive learning framework for the supplements.

What you will find in the supplements is a carefully developed integration of the in-text Focus Questions with Learning Objectives throughout the various elements of the package. Instructors and students alike will be guided by the Learning Objectives, as they form the cornerstone of the Instructor's Manual, Online Learning Center, Instructor's Resource CD-ROM, student Study Guide, In-Psych Plus CD-ROM including exclusive Discovery Channel$^{(TM)}$ video clips, and Test Banks. Items in the three Test Banks are keyed specifically to the Focus Questions and Learning Objectives. Students who are guided by the Focus Questions and Learning Objectives will be well prepared for questions taken from the test banks and should achieve at a high level.

Let's take a look at the features of our second edition.

ESTABLISHED FEATURES

- **Focus on Scientific Psychology:** Throughout the book we portray *psychology as a contemporary science* without becoming excessively formal or terminological. And because we live in an era in which students (along with everyone else) are bombarded with scientific information and misinformation, we focus not only on principles derived from research, but also on how good research is done.
- **Levels of Analysis: A Unifying Framework Students Will Remember:** To help students become more sophisticated in their everyday understanding of behavior, we present a simple framework that emphasizes how to study behavior at *biological, psychological, and environmental levels,* and how

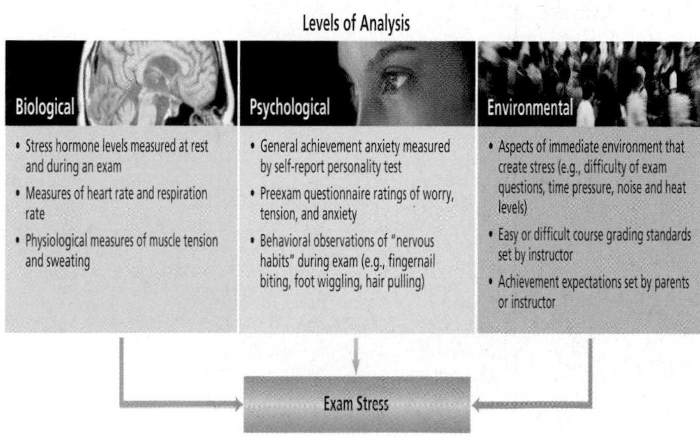

these explanations for behavior are related to one another. While we carry this Levels of Analysis framework throughout the book in textual discussion and *Understanding Behavior* schematics, we apply it selectively without being overly repetitious for students or confining for instructors.

- **Helping Students to Think Critically:** The Levels of Analysis framework reinforces the concept that behavior typically has multiple causes and encourages students to be wary of overly simplistic explanations. Moreover, the discussion section built into each *Research Close-Up* illustrates critical thinking about research results. Throughout the text we address critical thinking issues such as correlation and causation, noting that many faulty inferences—in everyday life as well as in science—are made by failing to understand the simple principle that correlation does not establish causation.
- **Focus on Relations Between Basic Science and Applications:** Whether in the context of their personal lives or of larger societal issues, we point out that many questions studied from a basic science perspective are inspired by real-world questions and issues, and that basic research findings often guide solutions to social and individual problems.
- **Integrated Coverage of Cultural and Gender Issues:** Cultural and gender issues are at the forefront of contemporary psychology, and rather than isolating this material within dedicated chapters we integrate it throughout the text. Our Levels of Analysis approach conceptualizes culture as an environmental factor and also as a psychological factor that reflects the internalization of cultural influences.
- **Thorough, Up-To-Date Coverage:** To portray our discipline with accuracy, we have made every effort to be the most current book on the market. As in our first edition, our emphasis on new research is balanced with thorough coverage of classic studies.
- **Research Close-Ups:** In each chapter this feature provides students with an inside look at research studies in a scientific journal format and engages students in a process of critical thinking about the research question.

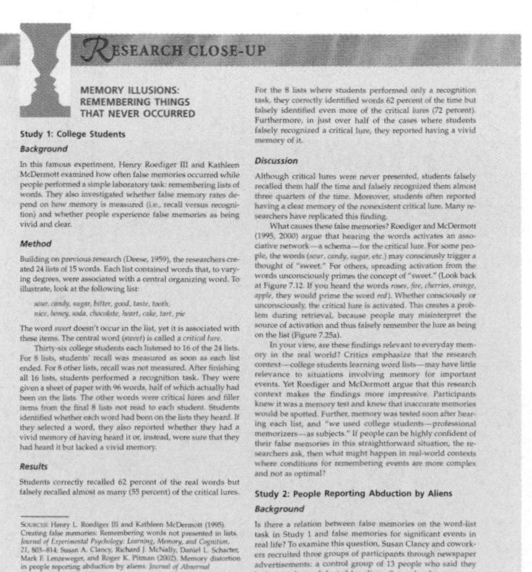

RESEARCH CLOSE-UP

MEMORY ILLUSIONS: REMEMBERING THINGS THAT NEVER OCCURRED

Study 1: College Students

Background

In this famous experiment, Henry Roediger III and Kathleen McDermott examined how often false memories occurred while people performed a simple laboratory task: remembering lists of words. They also investigated whether false memory rates depend on how memory is measured (i.e., recall versus recognition) and whether people experience false memories as being vivid and clear.

Method

Building on previous research (Deese, 1959), the researchers created 24 lists of 15 words. Each list contained words that, to varying degrees, were associated with a central organizing word. To illustrate, look at the following list:

sour, candy, sugar, bitter, good, taste, tooth, nice, honey, soda, chocolate, heart, cake, tart, pie

The word *sweet* doesn't occur in the list, yet it is associated with these items. The central word (*sweet*) is called a *critical lure.*

Thirty-six college students each listened to 16 of the 24 lists. For 8 lists, students' recall was measured as soon as each list ended. For 8 other lists, recall was not measured. After finishing all 16 lists, students performed a recognition task. They were given a sheet of paper with 96 words, half of which actually had been on the lists. The other words were critical lures and filler items from the final 8 lists not read to each student. Students identified whether each word had been on the lists they heard. If they selected a word, they also reported whether they had a vivid memory of having heard it or, instead, were sure that they had heard it but lacked a vivid memory.

Results

Students correctly recalled 62 percent of the real words but falsely recalled almost as many (55 percent) of the critical lures.

For the 8 lists where students performed only a recognition task, they correctly identified words 62 percent of the time but falsely identified even more of the critical lures (72 percent). Furthermore, in just over half of the cases where students falsely recognized a critical lure, they reported having a vivid memory of it.

Discussion

Although critical lures were never presented, students falsely recalled them half the time and falsely recognized them almost three quarters of the time. Moreover, students often reported having a clear memory of the nonexistent critical lure. Many researchers have replicated this finding.

What causes these false memories? Roediger and McDermott (1995, 2000) argue that hearing the words activates an associative network—a schema—for the critical lure. For some people, the words (*sour, candy, sugar,* etc.) may consciously trigger a thought of "sweet." For others, spreading activation from the words unconsciously primes the concept of "sweet." (Look back at Figure 7.12. If you heard the words *roses, fire, cherries, orange, apple,* they would prime the word *red*). Whether consciously or unconsciously, the critical lure is activated. This creates a problem during retrieval, because people may misinterpret the source of activation and thus falsely remember the lure as being on the list (Figure 7.25a).

In your view, are these findings relevant to everyday memory in the real world? Critics emphasize that the research context—college students learning word lists—may have little relevance to situations involving memory for important events. Yet Roediger and McDermott argue that this research context makes the findings more impressive. Participants knew it was a memory test and knew that inaccurate memories would be spotted. Further, memory was tested soon after hearing each list, and "we used college students—professional memorizers—as subjects." If people can be highly confident of their false memories in this straightforward situation, the researchers ask, then what might happen in real-world contexts where conditions for remembering events are more complex and not as optimal?

Study 2: People Reporting Abduction by Aliens

Background

Is there a relation between false memories on the word-list task in Study 1 and false memories for significant events in real life? To examine this question, Susan Clancy and coworkers recruited three groups of participants through newspaper advertisements: a control group of 13 people who said they had never been abducted by aliens, 9 people who were sure

SOURCES: Henry L. Roediger III and Kathleen McDermott (1995). Creating false memories: Remembering words not presented in lists. *Journal of Experimental Psychology: Learning, Memory, and Cognition*, 21, 803–814. Susan A. Clancy, Richard J. McNally, Daniel L. Schacter, Mark F. Lenzeweger, and Roger K. Pitman (2002). Memory distortion in people reporting abduction by aliens. *Journal of Abnormal Psychology*, 111, 455–461.

- **Applying Psychological Science:** In each chapter this feature brings a key concept into the realm of real-life application. Five of these *Applying Psychological Science* boxes throughout the book focus on important skills that can enhance students' learning and performance. In Chapter 1, this feature comprises a discussion of good study habits and other ways that students can enhance their learning. In Chapter 6, it focuses on behavioral self-regulation and breaking bad study habits. Other *APS* features emphasize memory enhancement (Chapter 7), systematic goal setting (Chapter 11), and stress management (Chapter 12).

BIOLOGICAL FOUNDATIONS OF BEHAVIOR: Evolution, Genetics, and the Brain 79

paralyzing the underlying muscles whose contraction causes them.

The opposite effect on ACh occurs with the bite of the black widow spider. The spider's venom triggers a torrent of ACh, resulting in violent muscle contractions, convulsions, and possible death. Some chemical agents, such as the deadly sarin gas released into the Tokyo subway system by terrorists in 1995, also raise havoc by allowing ACh to run wild in the nervous system. Sarin and similar nerve gas agents prevent the activity of an enzyme that normally degrades ACh at the synapse. The result is uncontrolled seizures and convulsions that can kill. Among antidotes issued to coalition troops during the Iraq War was a substance that inhibits nerve agents from preventing the action of the enzyme.

Most neurotransmitters have their excitatory or inhibitory effects only on specific neurons that have receptors for them. Others, called **neuromodulators,** *have a more widespread and generalized influence on synaptic transmission.* These substances circulate through the brain and either increase or decrease (i.e., modulate) the sensitivity of thousands, perhaps millions, of neurons to their specific transmitters. The best known neuromodulators are the *endorphins,* which travel through the brain's circulatory system and inhibit pain transmission while enhancing neural activity that produces pleasurable feelings. Other neuromodulators play important roles in functions such as eating, sleeping, and coping with stress.

Knowledge about neurotransmitter systems has many important applied implications. For one thing, it helps us understand the mechanisms that underlie the effects of **psychoactive drugs,** *chemicals that produce alterations in consciousness, emotion, and behavior.* The following *Applying Psychological Science* feature focuses on mechanisms of drug effects within the brain.

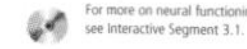
For more on neural functioning, see Interactive Segment 3.1.

▶ 13. How do agonist and antagonist functions underlie the neural and behavioral effects of psychoactive drugs?

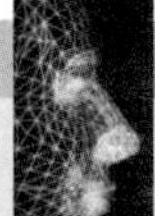

APPLYING PSYCHOLOGICAL SCIENCE

UNDERSTANDING HOW DRUGS AFFECT YOUR BRAIN

Drugs affect consciousness and behavior by influencing the activity of neurons. If you've had a soft drink or a cup of coffee, taken an aspirin or smoked a cigarette, you've ingested a drug. A recent survey of 55,000 students at 132 colleges in the United States revealed that in the past year, 47 percent had used tobacco; 84 percent, alcohol; 33.6 percent, marijuana; and 5 to 10 percent, cocaine, amphetamines, hallucinogenic drugs such as LSD, and designer drugs such as Ecstasy (Core Institute, 2002). Countless students ingest caffeine in coffee, chocolate, cocoa, and soft drinks. Perhaps you have wondered exactly how these drugs exert their diverse effects.

Most psychoactive drugs produce their effects by either increasing or decreasing the synthesis, storage, release, binding, or deactivation of neurotransmitters. An **agonist** *is a drug that increases the activity of a neurotransmitter.* Agonists may (1) enhance a neuron's ability to synthesize, store, or release neurotransmitters; (2) bind with and stimulate postsynaptic receptor sites; or (3) make it more difficult for neurotransmitters to be deactivated, such as by inhibiting reuptake.

An **antagonist** *is a drug that inhibits or decreases the action of a neurotransmitter.* An antagonist may (1) reduce a neuron's ability to synthesize, store, or release neurotransmitters; or (2) prevent a neurotransmitter from binding with the postsynaptic neuron by fitting into and blocking the receptor sites on the postsynaptic neuron.

With the distinction between agonist and antagonist functions in mind, let us consider how some commonly used drugs work within the brain. We will discuss drug effects on consciousness and behavior in greater detail in Chapter 5.

Alcohol is a depressant drug having both agonist and antagonist effects. As an agonist, it stimulates the activity of the inhibitory transmitter GABA, thereby depressing neural activity. As an antagonist, it decreases the activity of glutamate, an excitatory transmitter (Gonzalez & Jaworski, 1997). The double-barreled effect is a neural slowdown that inhibits normal brain functions of clear thinking, emotional control, and motor coordination. Sedative drugs, including barbiturates and tranquilizers, also increase GABA activity, and mixing them with alcohol intake can be a deadly combination when their depressant effects on neural activity are combined with those of alcohol.

Caffeine is a stimulant drug that increases the activity of neurons and other cells. It is an antagonist for the transmitter adenosine. Adenosine inhibits the release of excitatory transmitters. By reducing adenosine activity, caffeine helps produce higher rates of cellular activity and more available energy. Although caffeine is a stimulant, it is important to note that, contrary to popular belief, caffeine does *not* counteract the effects of alcohol

Continued

- **Additional Pedagogical Features:** A textbook should inspire students and help them master the material at hand. Our book incorporates many pedagogical features to accomplish these goals.
  - *Chapter opening vignettes* present interesting stories that capture students' attention, draw them into the material, and are used later in the chapter to reinforce important points.
  - *Focus Questions* occur in the margin of the book adjacent to important material. These are designed to function as study guides, retrieval cues, and self-tests.

▶ 22. What is meant by the term schizophrenia? What are its major cognitive, behavioral, emotional, and perceptual features?

Of all the psychological disorders, schizophrenia is the most bizzarre and, in many ways, the most puzzling. It is also one of the most challenging disorders to treat effectively (Hogarty, 2003). Despite many theories of schizophrenia and thousands of research studies, a complete understanding of this disorder continues to elude us.

- We have retained and, in some cases, improved other pedagogical features including *chapter outlines*, *boldfaced key terms* in the narrative, *summaries*, *Understanding Behavior schematics*, and an *end of chapter list of key terms*.

KEY TERMS AND CONCEPTS

Each term has been boldfaced and defined in the chapter on the page indicated in parentheses.

archetypes (p. 436)
behavioral assessment (p. 457)
behavioral signatures (p. 451)
behavior-outcome expectancy (p. 449)
cognitive-affective personality system (CAPS; p. 449)
collective unconscious (p. 436)
conditions of worth (p. 441)
congruence (p. 440)
defense mechanisms (p. 433)
ego (p. 432)
Electra complex (p. 435)
empirical approach (p. 458)
evolutionary personality theory (p. 430)
factor analysis (p. 421)
fixation (p. 434)
fully functioning persons (p. 441)
gender schemas (p. 455)
id (p. 432)
internal-external locus of control (p. 444)
Minnesota Multiphasic Personality Inventory-2 (MMPI-2; p. 458)
need for positive regard (p. 440)
need for positive self-regard (p. 441)
neoanalytic theorists (p. 435)
NEO-PI (p. 458)
object relations theories (p. 436)
Oedipus complex (p. 435)
personal unconscious (p. 436)
personality (p. 420)
personality trait (p. 421)
phenomenology (p. 439)
pleasure principle (p. 432)
projective tests (p. 459)
psychosexual stages (p. 434)
rational-theoretical approach (p. 458)
reality principle (p. 432)
reciprocal determinism (p. 444)
regression (p. 434)
remote behavior sampling (p. 457)
repression (p. 433)
Rorschach test (p. 459)
self (p. 439)
self-actualization (p. 439)
self-consistency (p. 440)
self-efficacy (p. 445)
self-enhancement (p. 442)
self-esteem (p. 441)
self-monitoring (p. 424)
self-reinforcement processes (p. 450)
self-verification (p. 442)
social-cognitive theory (p. 444)
structured interview (p. 456)
sublimation (p. 433)
superego (p. 432)
Thematic Apperception Test (p. 460)
threat (p. 440)
unconditional positive regard (p. 441)

NEW FEATURES

- **Multimedia Integration with the Text and Instructional Materials:** The Instructor's Manual, In-Psych Plus CD-ROM, Test Banks, and other supplements are built to support this book; in turn, the book supports them with the Focus Questions and multimedia icons that appear in its margins. The Focus Questions are streamlined from the Learning Objectives on which the Instructor's Manual is built, making it easy for instructors to use them in whatever way best supports their course, and to access Test Bank questions covering whichever Focus Questions they wish to emphasize. In addition, each multimedia segment—including McGraw-Hill's exclusive Discovery Channel(TM) video clips, additional videos, animation, and interactivities—has been chosen to support one or more Learning Objectives, is accompanied by its own pedagogy, and has Test Bank items and Instructor's Manual commentary associated with it. Further details about these multimedia materials appear below under "Supplements."
- **Revised Chapter Order and Structure of Topics:** In response to reviewer and user suggestions, the text now has 15 chapters, including a new chapter on *Stress and Health* and merged coverage of *Motivation and Emotion* within a single chapter. The former capstone chapter on *Psychology and Society* has been removed (its important components have been distributed into other chapters) and the chapter on social psychology now concludes the book.
- **A More Modular Approach:** To facilitate student understanding and instructor flexibility of assignments, chapters now feature fewer first-level sections, each one largely self-contained. At the end of each major section an interim summary (*In Review*) now breaks the content into more manageable modules or segments.

IN REVIEW

- *Somatoform disorders involve physical complaints that do not have a physiological explanation. They include hypochondriasis, pain disorders, and conversion disorders in which a physical symptom or disability occurs in the absence of physical pathology.*
- *Familial similarities in somatoform disorders may have a biological basis, or they may be the result of environmental shaping through attention and sympathy. Somatoform patients may be highly vigilant and reactive to somatic symptoms. Such disorders tend to occur with greater frequency in cultures that discourage open expression of negative emotions.*
- *Dissociative disorders involve losses of memory and personal identity. The major dissociative disorders are psychogenic amnesia, psychogenic fugue, and dissociative identity disorder (DID).*
- *The trauma-dissociation theory holds that DID emerges when children dissociate to defend themselves from severe physical or sexual abuse. This model has been challenged by other theorists who believe that multiple personalities result from role immersion and therapist suggestion.*

- **Increased Emphasis on Critical Thinking and Dispelling Misconceptions:** We now put more emphasis on critical thinking as a skill for students to learn and practice. Two new features, *Beneath the Surface* discussions and *What Do You Think?* exercises, challenge students to think critically in evaluating popular truisms, scientific and pseudoscientific claims, and psychology's relevance to their own lives.

BENEATH THE SURFACE

COLLEGE-AGE DRINKING: HARMLESS FUN OR RUSSIAN ROULETTE?

The harmful problems that result from the behaviors of alcoholics and drug addicts are self-evident. But because college students view themselves as different from these populations, many fail to realize the extent to which they place themselves in harm's way through their use of alcohol. Many students view parties featuring heavy drinking as a natural part of college life, like going to classes or athletic events. Studies have found that many heavy-drinking students, who average 40 to 50 drinks per week, do not view their behavior as either abnormal or problematic (Marlatt, 1998).

Beneath this surface of complacency lies evidence that heavy-drinking students are placing themselves at considerable risk. In one national study carried out by the Harvard School of Public Health, binge drinking was defined as having more than 4 (for women) or 5 (for men) drinks at a time on at least three occasions during the previous 2 weeks (Wechsler et al., 1994). Data from 18,000 students at 140 U.S. colleges revealed that 50 percent of the males and 40 percent of the women met this bingeing criterion, yet fewer than 1 percent saw themselves as having an alcohol problem. However, the dangerous consequences of their drinking became clear when binge drinkers were asked about alcohol-related problems (Table 12.6). Frequent binge drinkers were 7 to 10 times more likely than moderate drinkers to engage in unplanned and unprotected sexual intercourse, to suffer injuries, to drive under the influence of alcohol, to damage property, and to get into trouble with the law. At schools with the highest alcohol-consumption rates, nondrinkers and moderate drinkers were 2 to 3 times more likely to report physical assault, sexual harassment, destruction of their property, and interruption of their sleep and studying by heavy drinkers. Some college women (sound sleepers, apparently) complained that they woke up Sunday after Sunday to find a strange man in bed with their roommate (and all too frequently the heavy-drinking roommate didn't know him either). Common belief may have it that heavy drinking is harmless fun, but scientific findings suggest otherwise.

Table 12.6 Percentage of Binge-Drinking College Students Who Reported Drinking-Related Problems

Missed a class	61%
Forgot where they were or what they did	54%
Engaged in unplanned sex	41%
Got hurt	23%
Had unprotected sex	22%
Damaged property	22%
Got into trouble with campus or local police	11%
Had 5 or more alcohol-related problems in school year	47%

SOURCE: Based on Wechsler et al., 1994.

> **? What Do You Think?**
>
> **DO STRESSFUL EVENTS CAUSE PSYCHOLOGICAL DISTRESS?**
>
> A consistent statistical relation has been shown between stressful life events and psychological distress; the greater the number of stressful events people have experienced, the more distress they are likely to report. Based on these results, are you willing to accept the conclusion that life stress causes distress, or can you think of other possible reasons for this relation? Think about it, then see page 504 for a commentary.

- **Enhanced Coverage of Culture, Gender and Sexuality, and Aging:** We have expanded our coverage of these topics throughout the narrative and via features such as the *Research Close-Ups* and *What Do You Think?* exercises. Notable in this regard are new sections in Chapter 13 (Psychological Disorders) on disorders of childhood and old age and in Chapter 14 (Treatment of Psychological Disorders) on cultural and gender issues in psychotherapy.
- **Key Terms with Definitions:** Key terms are now presented in the text in boldface, followed by italicized definitions. This in-context presentation serves as an *integrated glossary* supplementing the list of key terms at chapter's end and the overall glossary in the back of the book.

Acquisition

Acquisition refers to the period during which a response is being learned. Suppose we wish to condition a dog to salivate to a tone. Sounding the tone initially may cause the dog to perk up its ears but not to salivate. At this time, the tone is a *neutral stimulus* because it does not elicit salivation (Figure 6.5). If, however, we place food in the dog's mouth, the dog will salivate. This salivation response to food is *reflexive*—it's what dogs do by nature. Because no learning is required for food to produce salivation, the food is an **unconditioned stimulus (UCS):** *a stimulus that elicits a reflexive or innate response (the UCR) without prior learning.* Salivation is an **unconditioned response (UCR):** *a reflexive or innate response that is elicited by a stimulus (the UCS) without prior learning.*

Next the tone and the food are paired—each pairing is called a *learning trial*—and the dog salivates. After several learning trials, if the tone is presented by itself, the dog salivates even though there is no food. The tone has now become a **conditioned stimulus (CS),** *a stimulus that, through association with a UCS, comes to elicit a conditioned response similar to the original UCR.* Because the dog is now salivating to the tone, salivation has become a **conditioned response (CR),** *a response elicited by a conditioned stimulus.* Notice that we have two terms for salivation: UCR and CR. When the dog salivates to food, this UCR is a natural, unlearned (unconditioned) reflex. But when it salivates to a tone, this CR represents a learned (conditioned) response.

During acquisition, a CS typically must be paired multiple times with a UCS to establish a strong CR (Figure 6.6). Pavlov also found that

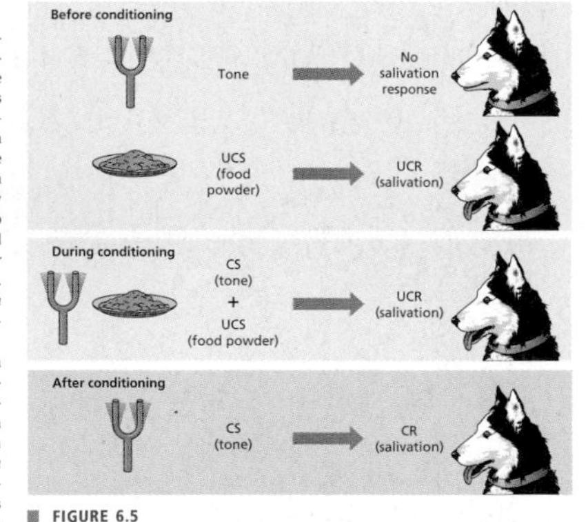

FIGURE 6.5

In classical conditioning, after a neutral stimulus such as a tone is repeatedly associated with food (unconditioned stimulus), the tone becomes a conditioned stimulus capable of eliciting a salivation response (conditioned response).

a tone became a CS more rapidly when it was followed by greater amounts of food. Indeed, when the UCS is intense and aversive—such as an electric shock or a traumatic event—conditioning may require only one CS-UCS pairing (Richard et al.,

- **New Art:** Approximately 30% of the photographs are new to this edition, and the line art program has been revised for improved conceptual clarity and visual appeal.
- **Updated coverage:** Our second edition is rich in discussions of research and new references—over 800 of the book's citations are from the years 2000 and beyond.

CONTENT CHANGES IN INDIVIDUAL CHAPTERS

Chapter 1: The Science of Psychology

- A new section on *The Scope of Psychology: From Brain to Culture* introduces the theme of multicausality early in the chapter and expands coverage of mind (brain)-body interactions and cultural influences.
- A new section on *Psychology's Intellectual Roots* condenses information previously spread throughout the chapter and provides a more integrated picture of how psychology became a science.
- Evolutionary psychology coverage is expanded and the positive psychology movement is discussed.
- New *What Do You Think?* exercises challenge students to think critically about alternative explanations for behavior (in this case, the phenomenon of "voodoo death") and apply concepts from the chapter to a real-life situation (an instructor whose students seem to be apathetic).
- *Beneath the Surface,* a new critical thinking feature, calls students' attention to common misconceptions about the field of psychology and about the introductory psychology course.

Chapter 2: Studying Behavior Scientifically

- A new *Research Close-Up* on *Very Happy People* is presented to illustrate the causal limitations of correlational research.
- *What Do You Think?* exercises enable students to demonstrate the pitfalls of after-the-fact reasoning, test their understanding of why correlation does not establish causation, and hypothesize about why people believe in the paranormal despite a lack of scientific evidence.

Chapter 3: Biological Foundations Of Behavior: Evolution, Genetics, And The Brain

- Completely reorganized, the chapter begins with a new section on evolution, followed by treatment of genetic influences on behavior and concluding with a section on behavioral neuroscience (nervous, endocrine, and immune systems).
- A new section on genetic engineering describes recent developments and their implications for altering behavior.
- A new *Applying Psychological Science* feature describes how psychoactive drugs (including "date rape" substances) affect behavior and experience by altering neurotransmitter processes.
- A new *Research Close-Up* feature describes an fMRI study on neural processes in the brains of violent murderers and

how such processes are affected by previous environmental experiences, illustrating brain-environment interactions.

- The *Beneath the Surface* feature challenges the widely stated conception that we use only 10 percent of our brain capacity.
- New material on neural plasticity, including recent research on neurogenesis and neural stem cell interventions.
- An updated treatment of research on reciprocal interactions among the nervous, endocrine, and immune systems.

Chapter 4: Sensation and Perception

- An integrated treatment of sensation and perception as overlapping phenomena.
- New research on subliminal influences on perception and aggressive behavior.
- Expanded coverage of sensory prosthetic devices, including cortical implants and the "seeing tongue" research of Bach-y-Rita.

Chapter 5: States of Consciousness

- A new chapter opening vignette on "sleepeating" replaces the vignette on dissociative identity disorder. (DID is now discussed in Chapter 13 on mental disorders).
- A new section on *Ecstasy (MDMA)* is added to the discussion of drugs.
- *Beneath the Surface* helps students think critically about the chance nature of so-called "psychic dreams."
- Hypnosis coverage includes a new section on *The Hypnotized Brain* and ends with a reorganized section—*I'm Intoxicated, No Matter What You Say*—that integrates views of hypnosis with other aspects of mind-body relations.

Chapter 6: Learning and Adaptation: The Role of Experience

- A revised chapter structure more clearly highlights evolutionary influences on learning.
- *What Do You Think?* exercises help students better understand why some classically conditioned responses fail to extinguish, and ask students to consider ethical issues surrounding the case of "Little Albert."
- *Beneath the Surface* explores whether "sparing the rod spoils the child" and is accompanied by an expanded discussion of punishment.

Chapter 7: Memory

- A new chapter opening vignette about a mnemonist, Rajan, now accompanies the vignette on the amnesia victim H.M.
- The discussion of mnemonic devices is expanded and a section on *Encoding and Exceptional Memory* is added.
- Coverage of how distinctiveness affects memory is updated and a new *Beneath the Surface* feature uses the September 11, 2001 attack on the World Trade Center as a framework to examine the accuracy of flashbulb memories and the relation between memory confidence and memory accuracy.
- *What Do You Think?* exercises ask students to consider whether perfect memory would indeed be a blessing, and to develop alternative explanations (beyond retrieval failure) for tip-of-the-tongue experiences.
- A new *Research Close-Up* ties in Roediger and McDermott's classic study of memory illusions with a recent study of memory illusions among people claiming to be alien abductees.
- Discussions of children's memory for traumatic events and of the repressed memory controversy are updated.
- A new section on *Culture and Memory Construction* is added.

Chapter 8: Language, Thinking, and Intelligent Behavior

- Linkages between language, thinking, and adaptive behavior are emphasized in this integrative chapter.
- Expanded treatment of language, including neural and environmental mechanisms of acquisition and sex differences in lateralization of language functions.
- Expanded coverage of psychometric principles underlying the development and evaluation of intelligence tests.
- Expanded treatment of cultural and sex differences in cognitive functions and their biological and social foundations.
- New research on neural processes underlying individual differences in intelligence.

Chapter 9: Motivation and Emotion

- This new chapter combines the motivation content from the first edition chapter on motivation (9) with the emotion section from the previous edition's "Emotion, Stress, and Coping" chapter (10).
- Coverage of cultural factors that affect many aspects of motivation has been expanded.
- Coverage of evolutionary and alternative explanations for male-female differences in sexual motivation is expanded.
- Treatment of emotion is based on an integrative conceptual model that specifies relations among situational, cognitive, physiological, and behavioral components.
- A new section explores the factors underlying happiness and the implications of a positive psychology that focuses

on human strengths, and *Applying Psychological Science* provides students with research-based guidelines for increasing their own subjective well-being.

Chapter 10: Development Over the Life Span

- Coverage of childhood includes a new section on the development of early emotions and emotion regulation.
- A new section on parenting-heredity interactions illustrates how children's home environment and genetic inheritance jointly affect their behavior. This section also emphasizes the bidirectional nature of parent-child influences.
- Coverage of gender identity and gender socialization is expanded.
- Coverage of moral development is now divided into sections on moral thinking and a new section on moral behavior.
- A new Research Close-Up on *The "Ups and Downs" of Adolescence: Does Emotion Change During the Teen Years?* enhances coverage of adolescents' social-emotional development.
- The already substantial coverage of cognitive changes in late adulthood is expanded to include recent data on the prevalence of cognitive impairment.
- *Beneath the Surface* explores the nature of wisdom and whether we become "older but wiser" throughout adulthood.
- Coverage of marriage and family issues now describes changes in American family structure across recent generations.

Chapter 11: Personality

- A theme of this chapter is the psychological profile of mass murderer Charles Whitman, whose records were made public for the first time in 2002. We open with a vignette of Whitman and use his personality as a springboard for discussing various theories of personality throughout the chapter.
- Extended treatment of biological factors in personality. A new section discusses incentive and threat reactivity, their biological bases, and their effects on behavior.
- Updated treatment of recent developments in social cognitive theory, including Mischel and Shoda's Cognitive-Affective Personality System (CAPS).

Chapter 12: Adjusting to Life: Stress, Coping, and Health

- A new chapter that combines stress and coping topics from the first edition's Emotion, Stress, and Coping chapter (10) with health psychology topics from the former capstone chapter on Psychology and Society (16).
- New material on Ann Masten's exploration of psychosocial factors that underlie resilience in children who grow up in highly stressful environments.
- New section on the physical stressor of pain explores biological, psychological and cultural factors.
- A new *Research Close-Up* focuses on a recent longitudinal study on attitudes toward aging and longevity, illustrating the role of psychological factors on physical well-being.
- *Beneath the Surface* focuses on new data on the dangers that attend heavy drinking among college students.

Chapter 13: Psychological Disorders

- New sections focus on disorders of childhood and old age.
- New *Research Close-Up* highlights a recent study that compares the effects of rape and nonsexual physical assault on the development and course of posttraumatic stress disorder in women.
- Updated material on scientific, legal, and social issues in psychiatric diagnosis.

Chapter 14: Treatment of Psychological Disorders

- New coverage of the use of VR (virtual reality) in exposure therapy for fear of flying is featured in the *Research Close-Up*.
- New material on cultural factors in seeking and remaining in therapy and on the training of culturally competent therapists.
- *Beneath the Surface* feature challenges the misconception that psychotherapy need be a long and expensive process by focusing on new 2002 and 2003 studies on the course of improvement and the efficacy of briefer forms of treatment.
- New PET-scan research showing that similar brain activation changes are found in phobics successfully treated with either drug or cognitive-behavioral treatments, indicating alternate methods for producing the same neurological changes.
- Expanded and updated treatment of preventive and community approaches to mental health.

Chapter 15: Social Thinking and Behavior

- This chapter is fully reorganized, incorporating coverage from the prior Chapter 12 (Behavior in a Social Context) as well as material on reducing prejudice from the prior Chapter 16 (Psychology and Society). The sequence of major sections now begins with Social Thinking and is followed by coverage of Social Influence and Social Relations.
- A major section on interpersonal attraction is updated from the prior Chapter 9 (Motivation) and now incorporated into the section on Social Relations.

- Coverage of how culture and general cognitive style influence attribution has been expanded.
- The discussion of compliance techniques (formerly under Social Thinking) is now in the module on Social Influence and is updated to include recent research examining compliance techniques used via e-mail.
- A *Beneath the Surface* feature on the effects of video game violence highlights recent experiments and the results of three comprehensive research reviews.

SUPPLEMENTS

A unique feature of our second edition supplements package is the comprehensive chapter-by-chapter list of Learning Objectives linked to the Focus Questions in the margins of the textbook. The Learning Objectives form the cornerstone of not only the Instructor's Manual, but also the Test Banks, multimedia CDs, and student Study Guide. Instructors may use the Learning Objectives as a guide to structuring the content of their courses, to preparing lectures, class activities, quizzes and exams. Students may use them to focus on key concepts before, during, and after the reading of the chapter; as well as to review and test their knowledge.

For the Instructor

Instructor's Manual

Written by Kevin Larkin of West Virginia University, this invaluable 500-page guide (ISBN 0-07-295228-8) contains a wealth of material that you can tailor to your teaching preferences and goals. For new instructors, it offers a master blueprint for organizing and structuring the introductory psychology course. Learning Objectives for each section of a chapter expand upon the Focus Questions found in the textbook's margins, and serve as the foundation upon which all instructor resources are built. These resources include: pre-class student assignments, material for lecture enhancement, in-class demonstrations and activities, suggestions for class discussions, a list of images available either as overhead transparencies or in digital formats, recommended guest presentations, an extensive array of handouts, and a complete list of the technology resources relevant to that portion of the text. Recommended strategies for evaluating student progress on mastery of the Learning Objectives cap off each section of a chapter. The Instructor's Manual incorporates the **In-Class Activities Manual for Instructors of Introductory Psychology** written by the Illinois State University team of Pat Jarvis, Cynthia Nordstrom, and Karen Williams.

Three Test Banks Featuring Over 7,200 Items

Consonant with our top-down media integration, all Test Bank questions are written to support the Learning Objectives and can be customized for instructor control and convenience.

- Test Bank 1, written by Donald S. Christensen, is revised and expanded over the previous edition, and now includes not only fact- and application-based questions but also more challenging conceptual items (33%). This comprehensive resource offers 4,133 items in all, including multiple choice, true-false, fill-in-the-blank, matching, and essay questions; there are also 3 questions for each multimedia segment (264 in all).
- Test Bank 2, written by P. Niels Christensen, comprises 2500 multiple choice items, of which 46% are conceptual in nature.
- Test Bank 3, written by Jacqueline E. Pickrell, offers 40 conceptual questions per chapter (600 in all). This unique resource is especially appealing to instructors who wish to challenge their students to think more conceptually.

As with other McGraw-Hill test banks, these are available in Brownstone, a dual platform computer testing system that lets you easily select questions and print tests and answer keys. You can also customize questions, headings, and instructions; add or import your own questions; and print tests in a choice of printer-supported fonts. The test items are also available in Word format (Rich text format) on the Instructor's Resource CD-ROM.

McGraw-Hill Media Resources for Teaching Psychology

McGraw-Hill and The Discovery Channel(TM) have formed an exclusive partnership to bring you video segments and interactivities for use in your psychology course. 48 video segments and 17 interactivities were chosen especially to support the Learning Objectives and are fully described in the Instructor's Manual. The majority of the video segments are timed at 5 minutes or less; the longest at 12 minutes. They are available either as a DVD + CD-ROM set (ISBN 0-07-293885-4) or as a set of two VHS videocassettes + CD-ROM (ISBN 0-07-293884-6).

Online Learning Center for Instructors

The instructor side of the Passer & Smith *Psychology* 2nd edition Web site at http://www.mhhe.com/passer2 contains all the material you need to design your course. Ask your local McGraw-Hill representative for your password.

- **PowerPoint Lecture Outlines** These presentations (also available as transparency masters) cover the key points of each chapter and include charts and graphs from the text. Helpful lecture guidelines are provided in the notes section for each slide. They can be used as-is or modified to meet your needs.
- **PowerWeb** This unique online reader at www.dushkin.com/powerweb provides readings, *New York Times* news feeds, weekly updates, curriculum-based

materials, refereed Web links; tools for research, study, and assessment; and interactive exercises. You will be excited by this powerful tool for helping keep your lectures up to date and timely.

- **Course Management Systems:**
  - **WebCT and Blackboard** Popular **WebCT** and **Blackboard** course cartridges are available for free upon adoption of a McGraw-Hill textbook. Contact your McGraw-Hill sales representative for details.
  - **PageOut** Build your own course web site in less than an hour. You don't have to be a computer whiz to create a Web site, especially with an exclusive McGraw-Hill product called PageOut. It requires no prior knowledge of HTML, no long hours of coding, and no design skills on your part. With PageOut, even the most inexperienced computer user can quickly and easily create a professional-looking course Web site. Simply fill in templates with your information and with content provided by McGraw-Hill, choose a design, and you've got a Web site specifically designed for your course. Best of all, it's FREE! Visit us at www.pageout.net to find out more.
  - **Knowledge Gateway** McGraw-Hill service is second to none. We offer a help desk that can be reached by phone, e-mail, or online with a special Web site called Knowledge Gateway. For larger adoptions, if hands-on training is necessary, we have a team of experts ready to train you on campus. This FREE service is available to support PageOut, WebCT, and BlackBoard users.
- **Image Banks** These files include all of the figures, tables, and photos from this textbook (more than 150 images in all) for which McGraw-Hill holds copyright.

Overhead Transparencies

These four-color transparency masters (ISBN 0-07-256336-2), which are also available in PowerPoint, include approximately 125 images from the text.

Instructor's Resource CD-ROM

This CD-ROM (ISBN 0-07-256335-4) conveniently contains the Instructor's Manual, Test Banks and Brownstone testing system, Image Bank, and PowerPoint lectures described above. *Also visit McGraw-Hill's Psychology Supersite at http://www.mhhe.com/psych This comprehensive web resource provides a superstructure that organizes and houses all of our psychology text websites.*

As a full service publisher of quality educational products, McGraw-Hill does much more than just sell textbooks to your students. We create and publish an extensive array of print, video, and digital supplements to support instruction on your campus. Orders of new (versus used) textbooks help us to defray the cost of developing such supplements, which is substantial. We have a broad range of other supplements in psychology that you may wish to tap for your introductory psychology course. Ask your local McGraw-Hill representative about the availability of these and other supplements that may help you with your course design.

For The Student

In-Psych Plus Student CD-ROM

In-Psych Plus sets a new standard for introductory psychology multimedia through its total integration with the textbook and Learning Objectives. Each CD-ROM icon in the margin of the textbook guides students to the multimedia item on the CD (video, animation, or interactive segment) pertaining to the topic under discussion. Each multimedia segment includes a pre-test, follow-up discussion questions, and Web resources. In-Psych Plus also includes chapter quizzes, a student research guide, and an interactive timeline that puts events, key figures, and research in psychology in historical perspective. Teachers may choose to test students on any of these items.

For more on sleep stages, see Interactive Segment 5.1.

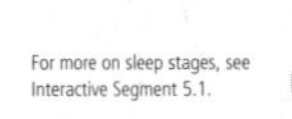

Although each cycle through the sleep stages takes an average of about 90 minutes, Figure 5.12 shows that as the hours pass, stage 4 and stage 3 drop out and REM periods become longer.

Study Guide

The Study Guide (ISBN 0-07-256340-0) is built upon the same list of chapter-by-chapter Learning Objectives that forms the cornerstone of many of the instructor supplements, encouraging students to focus on the same key concepts that they are learning from the textbook and in class lectures and activities. New to this edition of the Study Guide is the "Analyze This" feature, in which students examine an assertion based on information in the text by using a series of critical thinking questions. Critical thinking is also promoted by the essay questions at the end of each chapter, which challenge students to apply concepts from the chapter to issues of ethics, social policy, and their own personal lives.

Online Learning Center for Students

The Passer & Smith, *Psychology* 2nd edition, Website at http://www.mhhe.com/passer2 gives students access to *New York Times* news feeds, chapter outlines, practice quizzes, key term flashcards, interactive exercises, Internet activities, Web Links to relevant psychology sites, drag-and-drop labeling exercises, Internet primer, a career appendix, and a statistics primer, and our PowerWeb Online Reader.

PowerWeb

A PowerWeb passcard is included free with each new copy of the book—students should be sure to save it so that they can benefit from this unique online reader. Here they will find readings, *New York Times* news feeds, weekly updates, curriculum-based materials, refereed Web links; tools for research, study, and assessment; and interactive exercises.

GradeSummit

GradeSummit is an online assessment tool used by students to identify their understanding of course concepts and offers a guide for further study. This focuses their study efforts on the materials they haven't learned and helps them make their study time more useful. Instructors can also view the student's progress, without needing to upload or download data. Visit the Web site at http://www.gradesummit.com for more information.

ACKNOWLEDGMENTS

A project having the scope of an introductory psychology text is truly a team enterprise, and we have been the fortunate recipients of a great team effort. We wish to thank and acknowledge the contributions of the many people who made this book possible, beginning with Steve Rutter, McGraw-Hill Higher Education's Publisher for Psychology. We are indebted to Steve for his strong faith in this project and his unwavering support for putting together the best introductory psychology textbook package in the market. We are also grateful to the editors who have helped bring this second edition to fruition: Melissa Mashburn, John Wannemacher, and especially Ken King, for his invaluable guidance throughout the past year and a half. We have been blessed with a superlative Developmental Editor, Elsa Peterson, who helped shape the textbook in so many important ways and who coordinated numerous aspects of this project. Similarly, our Copy Editor, Andrea McCarrick, was splendid, and her input went well beyond the normal call of duty.

On the production end, thanks go to our Project Manager, David Sutton, for coordinating the endless production details, and to Cassandra Chu, our Designer, and Robin Mouat, our Art Editor, for creating the fabulous cover and attractive layout of the book. David Tietz, our Photo Researcher, worked diligently to acquire many of the excellent and unique photos in this edition. We also thank Betty Johnson, who cheerfully helped us compile the long files of references, and Melissa Caughlin, our Marketing Manager who has worked tirelessly to create an imaginative marketing program.

In today's competitive market, outstanding supplements are a critical element in the success of any textbook, but our supplement authors have gone beyond excellence in implementing the total integration of the supplements with the text. We are in great debt to Kevin Larkin (West Virginia University) for developing an absolutely first-class Instructor's Manual that not only includes a wealth of useful material for novice and experienced instructors alike, but also coordinates outstanding audio/visual and electronic resources with the content of the textbook. David Jones (Westminster College) developed a highly effective, parsimonious set of Powerpoint slides that instructors can use to augment their lectures, and Elsa Peterson did a stellar job of enhancing the Student Study Guide for this edition. Finally, Donald S. Christensen (Tacoma Community College), P. Niels Christensen (San Diego State University) and Jacqueline E. Pickrell (Claremont College) crafted three excellent Test Banks that that are second to none in quality and breadth.

We also owe special thanks to the distinguished corps of colleagues who reviewed the manuscript of *Psychology: The Science of Mind and Behavior,* second edition. Many of the improvements in the book are the outgrowth of their comments about what they want in an introductory psychology textbook for their courses. In this regard, we sincerely appreciate the time and effort contributed by the following instructors:

Mark D. Alicke, Ohio University

Susan Baillet, University of Portland

Jeffrey Baker, Rochester Institute of Technology

Mark Brechtel, University of Florida

James F. Calhoun, University of Georgia

P. Niels Christensen, San Diego State University

M. Catherine DeSoto, University of Northern Iowa

William Fabricius, Arizona State University

Barry Fritz, Quinnipiac University

Ray Fuller, Trinity College of Dublin

Janet Gebelt, University of Portland

Andrew Getzfeld, New Jersey City University

Gary J. Greguras, Louisiana State University

Carlos Grijalva, University of California, Los Angeles

Michelle Haney, Berry College

Jason W. Hart, Indiana University of Pennsylvania

Deana Julka, University of Portland

Gary King, Rose State College

F. Scott Kraly, Colgate University

Kevin Larkin, West Virginia University

Estevan R. Limon, Hunter College, City University of New York

Mary Lee Meiners, Miramar College

Joseph Morrissey, State University of New York-Binghamton

Janice L. Rank, Portland Community College

Scott Ronis, University of Missouri

Richard Sandargas, University of Tennessee

William G. Shadel, University of Pittsburgh

Rebecca Shiner, Colgate University

Jennifer Siciliani, University of Missouri at St. Louis

Dawn L. Strongin, California State University, Stanislaus

David M. Todd, University of Massachusetts—Amherst

Joseph Troisi, Saint Anselm College

Kristin Vermillion, Rose State College

Alan S. W. Winton, Massey University—Palmerston North

Tricia Yurak, Rowan University

SUPPLEMENT REVIEWERS

Pat King, Del Mar College

Kathleen Malley-Morrison, Boston University

David McDonald, University of Missouri

Mary Lee Meiners, San Diego Miramar College

J. T. Ptacek, Whitman College

Stephan Saunders, Marquette University

We also wish to thank the distinguished colleagues who provided review assistance for our first edition:

Ute J. Bayen, University of North Carolina, Chapel Hill

David Burrows, Beloit College

James Calhoun, University of Georgia

Marc Carter, Hofstra University

Betty Davenport, Campbell University

Rochelle Diogenes, Montclair, NJ

Dean E. Frost, Portland State University

Shepard B. Gorman, Nassau Community College

Robert A. Johnston, College of William & Mary

Robert Kaleta, University of Wisconsin—Milwaukee

Rick Kasschau, University of Houston

Karen Kopera-Frye, Buchtel College of Arts and Sciences

Alan J. Lipman, Georgetown University

Laura Madson, New Mexico State University

Kathleen Malley-Morrison, Boston University

David McDonald, University of Missouri

Mary Lee Meiners, San Diego Miramar College

Kevin Moore, De Pauw University

Donald J. Polzella, University of Dayton

Gary Poole, Simon Fraser University

J. T. Ptacek, Bucknell University

Jacqueline T. Ralston, Columbia College

Stephen Saunders, Marquette University

Alice H. Skeens, University of Toledo

Steven M. Smith, Texas A&M University

Sheldon Solomon, Skidmore College

Mary Hellen Spear, Prince George's Community College

David Thomas, Oklahoma State University

David Uttal, Northwestern University

Lori Van Wallandael, University of North Carolina at Charlotte

Dennis Wanamaker, Bellevue College

Paul J. Watson, University of Tennessee

Clemens Weikert, Lund University

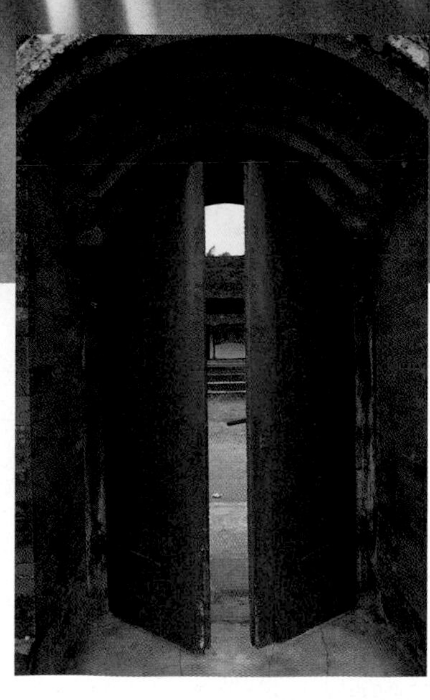

1

THE SCIENCE OF PSYCHOLOGY

CHAPTER OUTLINE

Perhaps the most fascinating and mysterious universe of all is the one within us.

—Carl Sagan

A young woman appeared in the emergency room of Baltimore City Hospital three days before her 23rd birthday, pleading for help. The story she told was a strange one indeed. She and two other girls had been delivered by the same midwife in Georgia's Okefenokee Swamp on a Friday the 13th. The midwife, a member of a voodoo cult, had placed a curse on all three babies. She proclaimed that the first would die before her 16th birthday, the second before her 21st birthday, and the third (the patient) before her 23rd birthday.

True to the midwife's prediction, the first died in an auto accident when she was 15 years old. The second was killed during a shooting in a nightclub where she was celebrating her 21st birthday. Now, the third woman waited in fear for her own death.

The emergency-room psychiatrist admitted her for observation and reassured the terrified woman that no harm would come to her in the hospital. Still, the woman believed that she was doomed. The next morning, two days before her 23rd birthday, she was found dead in her hospital bed. Doctors were unable to determine a physical cause for her death (Seligman, 1975).

■■■

Waiting in line at the theater, Ray put his arms around Kira and playfully kissed her cheek. "Remember that party where we met last year?" he asked. "You caught my eye the moment you walked into the room." "Maybe," Kira laughed, "but you were so shy. Your friends practically had to drag you over to talk to me! You're lucky I'm so outgoing."

Ray knew he was shy, especially around women, yet he wasn't sure why. He had been too nervous to enjoy the few dates he had gone on in high school. During his first semester at college he met a few women he really liked but was afraid to ask them out. He didn't make many male friends, either, and by winter the loneliness was getting to him. He became mildly depressed, couldn't sleep well, and his schoolwork suffered.

After a good visit with his family during spring break, Ray turned things around. He studied hard, did well on his tests, and made friends with some guys in the dorm. His mood improved, and toward the end of the semester he met Kira. Attracted to Ray and sensing his shyness, Kira asked Ray out. Now dating Kira for a year and doing well in school, Ray is happy and self-confident. He and Kira have even talked about getting married after they graduate.

THE NATURE OF PSYCHOLOGY

▶ 1. What is psychology's focus? In science and daily life, what does critical thinking involve and why is it important? (These Focus Questions will help you identify key concepts as you read, study, and review; they also tie in with the Learning Objectives in the supplements.)

Why are some individuals shy and others outgoing? What causes people, such as Kira and Ray, to become attracted to one another and fall in love? Can we predict which relationships will last? Why is it that we remember a first date from long ago yet forget information during a test that we studied for only hours before? Where in the brain are memories stored? What makes people happy? Why did Ray become depressed? Was it his lack of social life, or was something else going on? And in the case of the "cursed" woman, is it possible that a psychological factor—a culturally based belief in voodoo—could have affected her biological functioning and actually brought about her death?

Welcome to psychology, the discipline that studies all of these questions and countless more.

We can define **psychology** as *the scientific study of behavior and the mind*. The term *behavior* refers to actions and responses that we can directly observe, whereas the term *mind* refers to internal states and processes—such as thoughts and feelings—that cannot be seen directly and that must be inferred from observable, measurable responses. For example, we cannot see Ray's feeling of loneliness directly. Instead, we must infer how Ray feels based on his verbal statement that he is lonely. In searching for the causes of why people behave, think, and feel the way they do, psychologists take into account biological, psychological, and environmental factors.

Because behavior is so complex, its scientific study poses special challenges. As you become familiar with the kinds of evidence necessary to validate scientific conclusions, you will become a better-informed consumer of the many claims made in the name of psychology. For one thing, this course will teach you that many widely held beliefs about behavior are inaccurate. Can you distinguish the valid from invalid claims in Table 1.1?

Perhaps even more important than the concepts you learn in your introductory psychology course will be the habits of thought that you acquire—habits that involve what many people call *critical thinking*. Although critical thinking means different things to different people, it always involves taking an active role in understanding the world around us, rather than merely receiving information. It's important to reflect on what that information means, how it fits in with your experiences, and its implications for your own life and for society.

Critical thinking also means evaluating the validity of something presented to us as fact. For example, when someone tells you a new "fact," ask yourself the following questions:

What exactly are you asking me to believe?

How do you know? What is the evidence?

Are there other possible explanations?

What is the most reasonable conclusion?

We hope that after completing this course you will be more cautious about accepting psychological claims and less likely to form simplistic judgments about why people behave and think as they do. These critical-thinking skills will serve you well in many areas of your life.

In this book we hope to share with you our enthusiasm about psychology. As you will see, psychology relates to virtually every aspect of your life. Psychological research continues to push the frontiers of knowledge in many realms,

TABLE 1.1 Widely Held Beliefs About Behavior: Fact or Fiction?

Directions: Decide whether each statement is true or false.

1. Most people with exceptionally high IQs are well adjusted in other areas of their life.
2. In romantic relationships, opposites usually attract.
3. Overall, married adults are happier than adults who aren't married.
4. In general, we only use about 10 percent of our brain.
5. A person who is innocent of a crime has nothing to fear from a lie detector test.
6. People who commit suicide usually have signaled to others their intention to do so.
7. In small doses, alcohol stimulates the nervous system, which is why people may feel a "high" or a "buzz" after a few drinks.
8. On some types of mental tasks, people perform better when they are 70 years old than when they are 20 years old.
9. Usually, it is safe to awaken someone who is sleepwalking.
10. A schizophrenic is a person who has two or more distinct personalities, hence the term *split personality.*

Answers: Items 1, 3, 6, 8, and 9 are supported by psychological research. The remaining items are false. (If you correctly answered 9 or 10 of these items, you've done significantly better than random guessing.)

providing us with a greater understanding of ourselves and with powerful tools to improve our lives and promote human welfare.

Psychology as a Basic and Applied Science

▶ 2. How do basic and applied research differ? Explain how knowledge from basic research helps solve practical problems.

Science involves two types of research: **basic research,** *which reflects the quest for knowledge purely for its own sake*, and **applied research,** *which is designed to solve specific, practical problems*. For psychologists, most basic research examines how and why people behave, think, and feel the way they do. Basic research may be carried out in laboratories or real-world settings, with human participants or other species. Psychologists who study other species usually attempt to discover principles that ultimately will shed light on human behavior, but some study animal behavior for its own sake. Applied research often uses principles discovered through basic research to solve practical problems. Consider the following example.

Robber's Cave and the Jigsaw Classroom

How does hostility and prejudice develop between groups, and what can be done to reduce it? In today's multicultural world, where religious and ethnic groups often clash, this question has great importance.

To provide an answer, psychologists conduct basic research on factors that increase and reduce intergroup hostility. In one experiment, researchers divided 11-year-old boys into two groups when the boys arrived at a summer camp in Robber's Cave, Oklahoma (Sherif et al., 1961). The groups, named the "Eagles" and "Rattlers," lived in separate cabins but did all other activities together. Initially, they got along well.

To test the hypothesis that competition would breed intergroup hostility, the researchers began to pit the Eagles and Rattlers against one another in a series of athletic and other contests. As predicted, strong hostility and prejudice soon developed between the groups. Next the researchers examined whether conflict could be reduced by having the two groups interact under enjoyable circumstances, such as dining and watching movies together. Surprisingly, these activities only bred more taunting, name-calling, and fighting. The researchers then created several small emergencies to test a final hypothesis—that placing hostile groups in situations requiring cooperation to attain important, common goals will reduce intergroup conflict. In one "emergency," a heavy truck bringing food to the hungry boys supposedly stalled, forcing the Eagles and Rattlers to pool their strength and tow it with a rope to get it started. This and other cooperative experiences gradually dissolved the boundaries between the groups, and many new friendships developed.

▶ 3. Explain and illustrate the major goals and scope of psychology.

The Robber's Cave study, which has since become a classic (that is, an older but widely known and influential study), represents basic research because its goal was to discover general principles of intergroup conflict, not to solve some pre-existing problem. Prejudice between the Eagles and Rattlers did not exist from the outset; rather, the researchers created it. They showed that hostility could be bred by competition and reduced by making hostile groups dependent on one another to reach a common goal. But could this principle, derived from basic research, also be used in applied situations?

Years later, in the midst of a stormy desegregation of public schools in Texas, psychologist Elliot Aronson and his coworkers developed a classroom procedure called the "jigsaw program" (Aronson et al., 1978). This program, which is now widely used to foster cooperation among children, involves creating multiethnic groups of five or six children who are assigned to prepare for an upcoming test on, for example, the life of Abraham Lincoln. Within the groups, each child is given a "piece" of the total knowledge to be learned. One child has information about Lincoln's childhood, another about his political career, a third about his death, and so on. For group members to pass the test, they must fit their knowledge pieces together as if they were working on a jigsaw puzzle. Each child must teach the others his or her piece of knowledge. Like the children at Robber's Cave, the students learn that to succeed they must work together, and they come to appreciate one another (Figure 1.1).

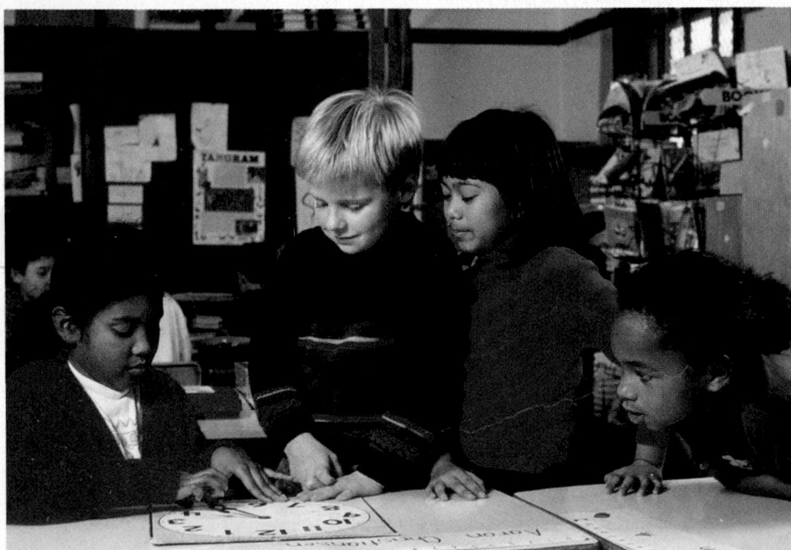

FIGURE 1.1

The jigsaw classroom, designed by psychologist Elliot Aronson, was inspired by basic research that showed how mutual dependence and cooperation can reduce intergroup hostility. Aronson's applied research had similar positive effects within racially integrated classrooms.

The jigsaw technique and other *cooperative learning programs* have been evaluated in hundreds of classrooms, with encouraging results (Aronson, 1997; Johnson, 2000). Across racial boundaries, children's liking for one another generally increases, prejudice decreases, and self-esteem and school achievement improve. Cooperative learning programs show how basic research, such as the Robber's Cave experiment, can be used as a foundation for designing an intervention program. We will see many other examples of how basic research provides knowledge that not only satisfies our desire to understand our world but also can be applied to solve practical problems.

The Goals of Psychology

As a science, psychology has five central goals:

1. to *describe* how people and other species behave
2. to *understand* the causes of these behaviors
3. to *predict* how people and animals will behave under certain conditions
4. to *influence* behavior through the control of its causes

5. to *apply* psychological knowledge in ways that enhance human welfare

In the Robber's Cave study, the researchers carefully observed the boys' behavior under various conditions (description). The researchers believed that competition is one cause of intergroup hostility and that cooperation could reduce such hostility (tentative understanding). To determine whether their understanding was correct, they predicted that competition would create hostility between the Eagles and Rattlers and that cooperation would reduce this hostility (prediction). Next they controlled the camp setting, first by pitting the Eagles and Rattlers against one another in contests and then by arranging situations that forced the groups to cooperate (influence). As predicted, competition produced hostility and cooperation reduced hostility. This suggested that the researchers' understanding of factors that cause and reduce hostility was correct. Later, when Aronson and his coworkers sought to reduce racial hostility and discrimination within newly integrated schools, they had a scientific basis for predicting what might work. They were able to apply their knowledge successfully in the form of the jigsaw program (application).

The Scope of Psychology: From Brain to Culture

Because we are biological creatures living in a complex social world, the scope of modern psychology stretches from the borders of medicine and the biological sciences to those of philosophy and the social sciences (Figure 1.2). To understand behavior we must consider our biological makeup, cultural influences, and all points in between.

Consider a behavior you engage in every day: eating. Various chemicals and neural circuits in your brain respond to signals from your body to help determine when you feel hungry and full. At the same time, your cultural upbringing influences many aspects of eating, such as what you eat (Figure 1.3). To most westerners, fish gills, duck feet, and solidified duck blood may not sound appetizing, but during a stay in China one of your authors discovered that his hosts considered them delicious. In between biology and culture lie many factors—our moods and thoughts, learning experiences, and environmental stimuli—that also affect eating. Do you ever eat when you're not hungry, perhaps because you feel stressed or bored? Can the aroma of freshly baked treats or the mere thought of food make your stomach growl?

Let's consider another example of how psychology's broad scientific scope furthers our understanding: the case of voodoo death described earlier. Voodoo is practiced in several regions of the world, including parts of the Caribbean, South America, Africa, and the United States. But how can we explain voodoo death without invoking supernatural powers? A possible answer focuses on what historically have been called *mind-body interactions*—the relations between mental processes in the brain and the functioning of other bodily systems.

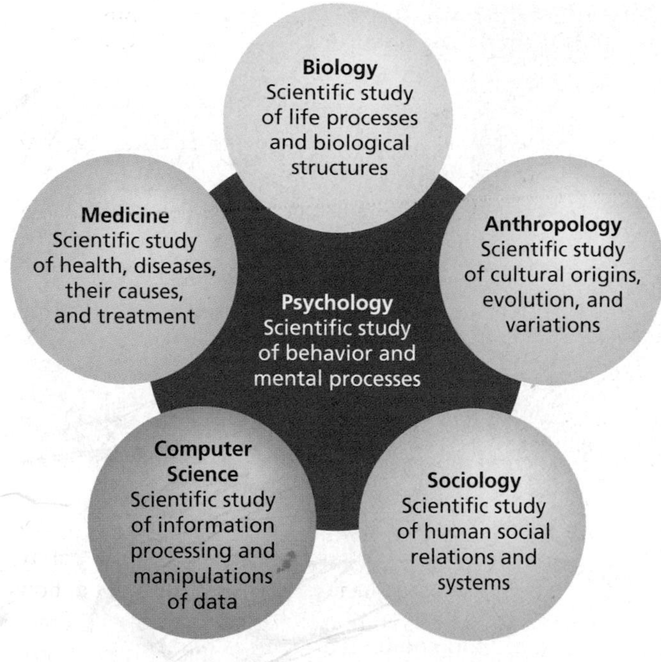

FIGURE 1.2

Psychology is the scientific study of behavior and mental processes; it draws from and overlaps with many other scientific disciplines.

Decades ago, physiologist Walter Cannon (1942) suggested a possible mechanism for death by "magic curses." Cannon drew on his own research on severe stress responses in animals, as well as eyewitness reports by cultural anthropologists of deaths by magic curses. One such account described placing a death curse by pointing a sacred bone at the victim:

> The man who discovers that he is being boned by any enemy is, indeed, a pitiable sight. He stands aghast, with his eyes staring at the treacherous pointer, and with his hands lifted as though to ward off the lethal medium, which he imagines is pouring into his body. His cheeks blanch and his eyes become glassy. . . . His body begins to tremble and the muscles twitch involuntarily . . . soon after he writhes as if in mortal agony. Unless help is forthcoming in the shape of a countercharm administered by the hands of the

FIGURE 1.3

(left) The role of the brain. This rat weighs 1,080 grams (2.38 pounds), about triple the weight of a normal rat. As we (or a rat) eat, hunger decreases as certain brain regions help regulate the sensation of becoming full. Those regions in this rat's brain have been damaged, causing it to overeat and become obese. (right) The role of culture. Does a plateful of big, juicy insects sound appetizing to you? Grubs, traditionally eaten by Australian Aboriginal peoples, are now served in some fine restaurants.

> Nangarri, or medicine-man, his death is only a matter of a comparatively short time. (Basedow, 1925, pp. 178–179)

Cannon noted that in cases of death by magic curses, the victim firmly believed (as did family, friends, and enemies) that he or she was doomed, a conviction unquestioned within the victim's culture. He speculated that the victim's beliefs triggered a profound and persistent stress response—a flood of stress hormones (chemicals released by glands in the body)—sending the victim into physiological shock. Cannon's own research had shown that one aspect of such shock is a rapid and often fatal drop in blood pressure as stress hormones allow fluid to leak out of veins and capillaries. He noted that normal autopsy procedures would not detect this mechanism of death, making it appear, as in the case of the young woman, that there was no natural cause. Cannon's hypothesis is a plausible alternative to supernatural explanations, and it is consistent with research showing that negative thoughts about a stressful situation can quickly trigger the secretion of stress hormones (Borod, 2000).

The study of mind-body interactions has a long history within psychology and remains one of its most exciting frontiers. Throughout this book you will see examples of how psychological processes interact with other bodily functions and are shaped by our environment and cultural learning experiences.

What Do You Think?

THE CASE OF VOODOO DEATH

Based on Cannon's hypothesis, why did the woman cursed by voodoo die? Do you believe that this hypothesis is reasonable? Can you think of other explanations for her death? (Think about it, then see page 28.)

IN REVIEW

- *Psychology is the scientific study of behavior and the mind. The term* behavior *refers to actions and responses that can be observed and measured directly. In contrast, mental processes such as thoughts and feelings must be inferred from directly observable responses.*
- *Basic research is the quest for knowledge for its own sake, whereas applied research involves the application of knowledge derived from basic research to solve practical problems.*
- *The primary goals of psychological science are to describe, understand, predict, and influence behavior and to apply psychological knowledge to enhance human welfare.*
- *To understand more fully why people behave, think, and feel as they do, psychologists study our biological makeup and mental processes, learning experiences, cultural influences, and other environmental factors.*

PERSPECTIVES ON BEHAVIOR

How did psychology's scope become so broad? In part, it happened because psychology has historical roots in such varied disciplines as philosophy, medicine, and the biological and physical sciences. As a result, different ways of viewing people became part of psychology's intellectual traditions. These diverse viewpoints, or *perspectives*, are vantage points for analyzing behavior (Figure 1.4).

If you have ever encountered someone who views the world very differently from the way you do, you know that perspectives matter. Like our own personal viewpoints, perspectives serve as lenses through which psychologists examine behavior. Perspectives influence the aspects of behavior that psychologists consider important, the questions they ask, and the methods they use to study behavior. In science, new perspectives are the lifeblood of progress. Advances occur as existing beliefs are challenged, a debate ensues, and scientists seek new evidence to resolve the debate. Sometimes, the best-supported elements of contrasting viewpoints are merged into a new framework, which in turn will be challenged when still newer viewpoints are proposed.

These perspectives address timeless questions about human nature and guide us through psychology's intellectual traditions. For a better understanding of how the perspectives of modern psychology evolved, let's briefly examine psychology's roots.

Psychology's Intellectual Roots

Humans have long sought to understand themselves, and at the center of this quest lies an issue that has tested the best minds of ages, the so-called *mind-body problem.* Is the mind—the inner agent of consciousness and thought—a spiritual entity separate from the body, or is it a part of our body's activities?

Many early philosophers held a position of **mind-body dualism,** *the belief that the mind is a spiritual entity not subject to physical laws that govern the body.* But if the mind is not composed of physical matter, how could it become aware of bodily sensations and how could its thoughts exert control over bodily functions? French philosopher, mathematician, and scientist René Descartes (1596–1650) proposed that the mind and body interact through the tiny pineal gland in the brain. Although Descartes placed the mind within the brain, he maintained that the mind was a spiritual, nonmaterial entity. Dualism implies that no amount of research on the physical body (including the brain) could ever hope to unravel the mysteries of the nonphysical mind.

An alternative view, **monism** (from the Greek word *monos,* meaning "one"), *holds that mind and body are one and that the mind is not a separate spiritual entity.* To monists, mental events are simply a product of physical events in the brain, a position advocated by English philosopher Thomas Hobbes (1588–1679). Monism helped set the stage for psychology because it implied that the mind could be studied by measuring physical processes within the brain. The stage was further set by John Locke (1632–1704) and other philosophers from the school of **British empiricism,** *which held that all ideas and knowledge are gained empirically—that is, through the senses.* According to the empiricists, observation is a more valid approach to knowledge than is reason, because reason is fraught with the potential for error. This idea bolstered the development of modern science, whose methods are rooted in empirical observation.

Discoveries from physiology (an area of biology that examines bodily functioning) and medicine also paved the way for psychology's emergence. By 1870, European researchers were electrically stimulating the brains of experimental animals and "mapping" the surface areas that controlled various body movements. During this same period, medical reports linked damage in specific areas of patients' brains with various behavioral and mental impairments. For example, on the brain's left side, damage to one region produced an inability to understand speech, whereas damage to a different area rendered a person incapable of producing coherent speech.

Mounting evidence of the relation between brain and behavior supported the view that empirical methods of the natural sciences could also be used to study mental processes. Indeed, by the mid-1800s, German scientists were measuring people's sensory experiences to many types of physical stimuli (for example, how the perceived loudness of a sound changes as its decibel level increases). Their experiments established a new field called *psychophysics,* the study of how psychologically experienced sensations depend on the characteristics of physical stimuli.

Around this same period, Charles Darwin's (1809–1882) theory of evolution generated shock waves that are still felt today. His theory, which we discuss later, met with vigorous opposition because it seemed to contradict philosophical and religious beliefs about the exalted nature of human beings. Evolution implied that the human mind was not a spiritual entity but rather the product of a biological continuity between humans and other species that could be studied scientifically. Moreover, Darwin's theory implied that scientists might gain insight into the nature of human behavior by studying the behavior of other species. By the late 1800s, a convergence of intellectual forces provided the impetus for psychology's birth.

FIGURE 1.4

Youth and beauty? Or maturity and wisdom? If you examine this drawing, you will see either a young woman or an old one. The images will alternate, particularly if you interpret the dark horizontal line in the lower half of the figure as either a necklace or a mouth. Like many aspects of our experience, what we perceive depends on our perspective. Still having trouble seeing both women? The "ear" of the young woman is the "eye" of the old woman.

▶ 4. Discuss psychology's philosophical and scientific roots, earliest schools of thought, and founders.

Early Schools: Structuralism and Functionalism

The infant science of psychology emerged in 1879, when Wilhelm Wundt (1832–1920) established the first laboratory of experimental psychology at the University of Leipzig in Germany. There he helped train the first generation of scientific psychologists (Figure 1.5). Wundt wanted to model the study of the mind after the natural sciences, and he believed that the mind could be studied by breaking it down into its basic components, as a chemist might do in studying a complex chemical compound. One of his graduate students, Englishman Edward Titchener (1867–1927), later established a psychological laboratory in the United States at Cornell University. Like Wundt, Titchener was a kind of mental chemist who attempted to identify the basic building blocks, or structures, of the mind. Wundt

FIGURE 1.5

Wilhelm Wundt (standing on the right) established a laboratory of experimental psychology at the University of Leipzig in 1879. This marked the first time that a major university officially recognized psychology as a separate academic discipline.

▶ 5. Describe the psychodynamic perspective. Contrast Freud's psychoanalytic theory with modern psychodynamic theories.

FIGURE 1.6

William James, a leader of functionalism, helped establish psychology in North America. His classic multivolume book Principles of Psychology *(1890) greatly expanded the scope of psychology.*

FIGURE 1.7

Mary Whiton Calkins founded a psychology laboratory at Wellesley College, where she taught for more than 30 years. She studied memory and dreams, wrote a popular introductory psychology textbook, and in 1905 became the first female president of the American Psychological Association.

and Titchener's approach came to be known as **structuralism,** *the analysis of the mind in terms of its basic elements.*

In their experiments, structuralists used the method of *introspection* ("looking within") to study sensations, which they considered the basic elements of consciousness. They exposed participants to all sorts of sensory stimuli—lights, sounds, tastes—and trained them to describe their inner experiences. Although this method of studying the mind died out after a few decades, the structuralists left an important mark on the infant science of psychology by establishing a scientific tradition for the study of mental processes.

In the United States, structuralism eventually gave way to an approach called **functionalism,** *which held that psychology should study the functions of consciousness rather than its structure.* Here's a rough analogy to explain the difference between structuralism and functionalism: Consider your arms and hands. A structuralist would try to explain their movement by examining the operation of muscles, tendons, and bones. In contrast, a functionalist would ask, "Why do we have arms and hands? How do they help us adapt to our environment?" The functionalists asked similar questions about mental processes and behavior. In part, functionalism was influenced by Darwin's evolutionary theory, which stressed the importance of adaptive behavior in helping organisms respond successfully to their environment and survive. Much of the early research on learning and problem solving was done by functionalists.

William James (1842–1910), a leader in the functionalist movement, was a "big-picture" person who taught courses in physiology, psychology, and philosophy at Harvard University (Figure 1.6). James's broad functionalist approach helped widen the scope of psychology to include the study of various biological processes, mental processes, and behaviors. Like Wundt, James helped train psychologists who went on to distinguished careers. Among them was Mary Whiton Calkins (1863–1930), who became the first female president of the American Psychological Association in 1905 (Figure 1.7). Had you been a college student a century ago, her textbook (*An Introduction to Psychology,* 1901) is one you might have read.

Although functionalism no longer exists as a school of thought within psychology, its tradition endures in two modern-day fields: *cognitive psychology,* which examines how the mind processes information and directs behavior, and *evolutionary psychology,* which emphasizes the adaptiveness of behavior.

The Psychodynamic Perspective: The Forces Within

Have you ever been mystified by why you behaved or felt a certain way? Recall the case of Ray, the student described at the beginning of the chapter who could not understand why he was so shy. The **psychodynamic perspective** *searches for the causes of behavior within the inner workings of our personality* (our unique pattern of traits, emotions, and motives), *emphasizing the role of unconscious processes and unresolved conflicts from the past.* Sigmund Freud (1856–1939) developed the first and most influential psychodynamic theory.

Psychoanalysis: Freud's Great Challenge

Late in the 19th century, as the intellectual aftershocks of Darwin's evolutionary theory were still being felt, Freud mounted another assault on the conception of human beings as exalted creatures. Unlike Darwin, Freud emphasized the role of complex psychological forces in controlling behavior (Figure 1.8). He called his theory **psychoanalysis**—*the analysis of internal and primarily unconscious psychological forces.*

As a young physician in Vienna, Freud was intrigued by the workings of the brain. He began to treat patients who experienced physical symptoms such as blindness, pain, or paralysis without any apparent bodily cause. Over time, he treated patients who had other problems, such as *phobias* (intense unrealistic fears). Because no disease or bodily malfunction could explain these conditions, Freud reasoned that the causes must be psychological. Moreover, if his patients were not producing their symptoms consciously, Freud reasoned that the causes must be hidden from awareness—they must be unconscious. At first Freud treated his patients by using hypnosis. Later he used a technique called *free association,* in which the patient expressed any thoughts that came to mind. To Freud's surprise, his patients eventually described painful and long-"forgotten" childhood experiences, often sexual in nature. After recalling and figuratively reliving these traumatic childhood experiences, the patients often found that their symptoms improved.

Freud became convinced that an unconscious part of the mind profoundly influences behavior. He also proposed that humans have powerful inborn sexual and aggressive drives and that our adult personality is largely determined by early childhood experiences. Freud speculated that because sexual desires and needs in childhood are punished, we learn to fear them and become anxious when we are aware of their presence. This leads us to develop **defense mechanisms,** *psychological techniques that help us cope with anxiety and the pain of traumatic experiences. Repression,* the most basic defense mechanism, protects us by keeping unacceptable impulses, feelings, and memories in the unconscious depths of the mind. There they remain as sources of energy, continually striving for release. All behavior, whether normal or "abnormal," reflects the largely unconscious and inevitable conflict between internal impulses and the defenses. This ongoing psychological struggle between conflicting energy forces is dynamic in nature, hence the term *psychodynamic.* To explain Ray's extreme shyness around women, Freud might have explored whether Ray is unconsciously afraid of his sexual impulses and therefore avoids putting himself into dating situations where he would have to confront those hidden impulses.

Freud was not a conventional scientist. He opposed laboratory research on psychoanalytic theory, believing that his clinical observations were more valid (Rosenzweig, 1992). Many contemporary psychologists view Freud's theory as difficult to test. Nevertheless, his ideas stimulated research on topics such as dreams, memory, aggression, psychological disorders, and therapy. A scholarly review of more than 3,000 scientific studies examining Freud's ideas found support for some aspects of his theory, whereas other aspects were unsupported or contradicted (Fisher & Greenberg, 1996). But even where Freud's theory was not supported, the research it inspired led to important discoveries.

Freud's work forever broadened the face of psychology to include the study and treatment of psychological disorders. The psychodynamic perspective dominated thinking on personality, mental disorders, and psychotherapy for nearly 50 years before gradually being overtaken by other perspectives.

Modern Psychodynamic Theory

Even in Freud's time, some of his followers strongly disagreed with aspects of his theory, especially its heavy emphasis on childhood sexuality. Modern psychodynamic theories continue to explore how the unconscious mind influences behavior, but they downplay the role of hidden sexual and aggressive motives and focus more on how early family relationships, other social factors, and our sense of "self" shape our personality (Kohut, 1977). To explain Ray's shyness, a modern psychodynamic psychologist might examine Ray's images of himself and his parents. Ray's shyness may stem from fear of rejection or fear of intimacy, of which he is unaware. These fears may be based on images that he developed of his parents as "rejecting" or "smothering," images that now unconsciously shape his expectations of how relationships with women will be.

Psychodynamic concepts continue to influence applied and academic psychology. Among American psychologists who provide therapy, 20 to 30 percent report their orientation as being psychodynamic. Psychoanalysis also remains a major force in European psychology (Norcross et al., 1995).

Links with psychodynamic concepts can be found within other areas of psychological science. For example, biologically oriented psychologists have identified brain mechanisms that can produce emotional reactions of which we are consciously unaware (LeDoux, 2000), and cognitive scientists have shown that many aspects of information processing occur outside of awareness (Chartrand & Bargh, 2002). Thus, while most contemporary psychological scientists reject Freud's version of the unconscious mind, many support the concept that behaviors can be triggered by nonconscious processes.

FIGURE 1.8

Sigmund Freud founded psychoanalysis and probed the unconscious mind. A physician trained in biology, Freud noted the value of a multiperspective approach when he wrote, "Let the biologists go as far as they can, and let us go as far as we can. One day the two will meet" (1900/1965, p. 276).

The Behavioral Perspective: The Power of the Environment

The **behavioral perspective** *focuses on the role of the external environment in governing our actions.* From this perspective, our behavior is jointly determined by habits we learned from previous life experiences and by stimuli in our immediate environment.

Origins of the Behavioral Perspective

The behavioral perspective is rooted in the philosophical school of British empiricism, which held that all ideas and knowledge are gained through the senses. According to John Locke, an early empiricist, at birth the human mind is a *tabula rasa*—a "blank tablet" or "slate"—upon which experiences are written. In this view, human nature is shaped purely by the environment.

In the early 1900s, experiments by Russian physiologist Ivan Pavlov (1849–1936) revealed one way in which the environment shapes behavior: through the association of events with one another. Pavlov found that dogs would "automatically" learn to salivate to the sound of a "new" stimulus, such as a tone, if that stimulus had first been repeatedly paired with food. Meanwhile, in the United States, Edward Thorndike (1874–1949) examined how organisms learn through the consequences of their actions. According to Thorndike's (1911) *law of*

FIGURE 1.9

John B. Watson founded the school of behaviorism. He published Psychology as a Behaviorist Views It *in 1913 and* Psychology from the Standpoint of a Behaviorist *in 1919.*

▶ 6. What are the behavioral perspective's origins and focus? Contrast radical behaviorism with cognitive behaviorism.

effect, responses followed by satisfying consequences become more likely to recur, and those followed by unsatisfying consequences become less likely to recur. Thus learning is the key to understanding how experience molds behavior.

Behaviorism

Behaviorism, *a school of thought that emphasizes environmental control of behavior through learning,* began to emerge in 1913. John B. Watson (1878–1958), who led the new movement, strongly opposed the "mentalism" of the structuralists, functionalists, and psychoanalysts (Figure 1.9). He argued that the proper subject matter of psychology was observable behavior, not unobservable inner consciousness. Human beings, he said, are products of their learning experiences. So passionately did Watson hold this position that in 1924 he issued the following challenge:

> Give me a dozen healthy infants, well-formed, and my own specialized world to bring them up in and I'll guarantee you to take any one of them at random and train him to become any type of specialist I might select—doctor, lawyer, artist, merchant-chief and, yes, even beggar-man and thief, regardless of his talents, penchants, tendencies, abilities, vocations, and race of his ancestors. (p. 82)

Behaviorists sought to discover the laws that govern learning, and in accord with Darwin's theory of evolution, they believed that the same basic principles of learning apply to all organisms. Their research with humans and other animals led to many discoveries and applications of learning principles.

B. F. Skinner (1904–1990) of Harvard University was the leading modern figure in behaviorism (Figure 1.10). Although Skinner did not deny that thoughts and feelings occur within us, he maintained that "No account of what is happening inside the human body, no matter how complete, will explain the origins of human behavior" (1989b, p. 18). Skinner believed that the real causes of behavior reside in the outer world and insisted that "A person does not act upon the world, the world acts upon him" (1971, p. 211). His research, based largely on studies of rats and pigeons under controlled laboratory conditions, examined how behavior is shaped by the rewarding and punishing consequences that it produces.

In the case of our college student, Ray, a behaviorist might look to explain Ray's shyness around women by examining his past dating experiences. In high school, the first time Ray invited a girl to a dance he was turned down. Later, he had a serious crush on a girl and went out with her twice, after which she spurned his attention. Though nervous, he asked out a few girls after that but was turned down each time. Such punishing consequences decreased the likelihood that Ray would ask someone out in the future. Fortunately, Kira asked Ray out. A behaviorist would note that the positive consequences Kira and Ray experienced on their first date reinforced their behavior, increasing the likelihood that they would go out again.

Skinner believed that society could harness the power of the environment to change behavior in beneficial ways and that the chief barrier to creating a better world through "social engineering" is an outmoded conception of people as free agents. Skinner's approach, known as *radical behaviorism,* was considered extreme by many psychologists, but he was esteemed for his scientific contributions and for focusing attention on how environmental forces could be used to enhance human welfare. In the 1960s, behaviorism inspired powerful techniques known collectively as *behavior modification.* These techniques, aimed at decreasing problem behaviors and increasing positive behaviors by manipulating environmental factors, are still used widely today (Green et al., 2002).

Behaviorism's insistence that psychology should focus only on externally observable stimuli and responses resonated with many who wanted this young science to model itself on the physical and biological sciences. Behaviorism dominated North American research on learning into the 1960s, but radical behaviorism's influence waned after the 1970s as interest in studying mental

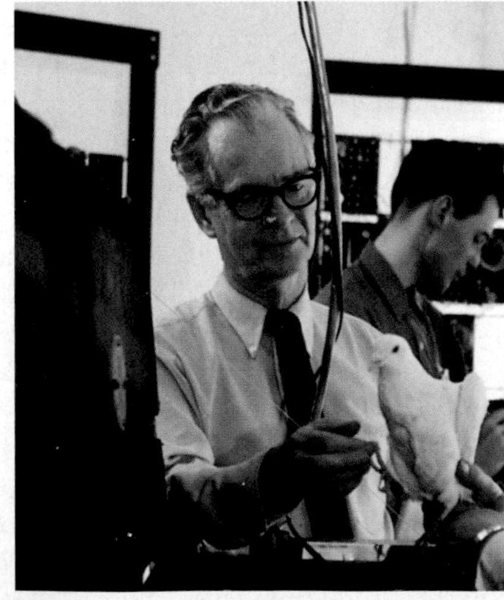

FIGURE 1.10

B. F. Skinner was a major figure in modern behaviorism. He argued that mentalistic concepts were not necessary to explain behavior and that learning principles could be used to enhance human welfare.

processes grew (Robins et al., 1999). Nevertheless, behaviorists continue to make important contributions to basic and applied psychology, and their discovery of the laws of learning was arguably the greatest contribution made by American psychology in the first half of the 20th century.

In recent decades some behaviorists have adopted a modified view called **cognitive behaviorism,** *which proposes that learning experiences influence our thoughts and expectations, which in turn guide how we behave* (Bandura, 1969, 2002). A cognitive behaviorist might say that Ray's past dating rejections were punishing and led him to expect that further attempts at romance would be doomed to fail. In turn, these negative expectations inhibited him from asking someone out.

What Do You Think?

ARE THE STUDENTS LAZY?

Imagine that you are a high school teacher. Whenever you try to engage your students in a class discussion, they gaze into space and hardly say anything. You start to think that they're "just a bunch of lazy kids." From a radical behavioral perspective, is your conclusion reasonable? How might you improve the situation? (Think about it, then see page 28).

The Humanistic Perspective: Self-Actualization and Positive Psychology

After the psychodynamic and behavioristic perspectives became firmly entrenched, a new psychological movement arose in the mid-20th century to challenge them both. Known as the **humanistic perspective** (or **humanism),** *it emphasized free will, innate tendencies toward growth, and the attempt to find ultimate meaning in one's existence.* Humanists rejected psychodynamic concepts of humans as being controlled by unconscious forces. They denied behaviorism's view of humans as mere reactors molded by the external environment. Instead, humanistic theorists such as Abraham Maslow (1908–1970) proposed that in each of us there is an active force toward growth and *self-actualization,* the reaching of one's individual potential (Figure 1.11). When the human personality develops in a supportive environment, the positive inner nature of a person emerges. Human misery and pathology, in contrast, are fostered by environments that frustrate our innate tendencies toward self-actualization. Humanistic theorists insisted that our existence and its meaning are squarely in our own hands, for we alone can decide what our attitudes and behaviors will be.

Thinking about Ray's shyness and loneliness, a humanist might say that no matter how many rejections Ray has had in the past, he must take personal responsibility for turning things around. A humanist also might wonder whether, in his freshman year, Ray's happiness and sense of self-worth were resting too heavily on his hope for a good romantic relationship. By focusing on building a few friendships first, Ray wisely found another way to satisfy what Maslow (1954) called "belongingness," our basic human need for social acceptance and companionship.

Although few early humanists were scientists, humanism inspired important areas of research. For example, humanist Carl Rogers (1902–1987) pioneered the scientific study of psychotherapy. In the 1940s and 1950s, his research group was the first to make audio recordings of counseling sessions and systematically analyze their content. This research identified important therapeutic processes that led to constructive personal change in their clients (Rogers, 1967).

Historically, humanism had a more limited impact on mainstream psychological science than did other perspectives, but its influence is clearly seen in several areas of contempary research. Studies of the self-concept have been one of the most active areas of personality research over the past 20 years, and much of this work incorporates humanistic ideas (Verplanken & Holland, 2002).

FIGURE 1.11

The humanistic perspective emphasizes the human ability to surmount obstacles in our drive toward self-actualization.

▶ 7. How does humanism's conception of human nature differ from that advanced by psychodynamic theory and behaviorism?

FIGURE 1.12

This painting illustrates the Gestalt principle that the whole is often greater than the sum of its parts. Once you have perceived the organized image of a portrait, you are less likely to perceive the sea creatures as separate elements. Water by Arcimboldo, from Kunsthistorisches Museum, Vienna.

Moreover, humanism's focus on self-actualization and growth is seen in today's growing **positive psychology movement,** *which emphasizes the study of human strengths, fulfillment, and optimal living* (Seligman, 2002). In contrast to psychology's long-standing and important focus on "what's wrong with our world" (e.g., mental disorders, conflict, crime, poverty, prejudice), positive psychology examines how we can nurture what is best within ourselves and society to create a happy, virtuous, and fulfilling life.

The Cognitive Perspective: The Thinking Human

▶ 8. Describe the focus and the origins of the cognitive perspective and some areas of modern cognitive science.

Derived from the Latin word *cogitare* ("to think"), the **cognitive perspective** *examines how we perceive, organize, and store information in our minds and how mental processes influence behavior.* In this view, humans are information processors and problem solvers whose actions are governed by thought and planning.

Origins of the Cognitive Perspective

When psychology was founded in the late 1800s, the study of cognition was at the forefront. The structuralists sought to identify the basic elements of consciousness, and the functionalists explored the purposes of consciousness. Other psychologists were studying the nature of memory.

Gestalt Psychology By the 1920s, German scientists had formed a school of thought known as Gestalt psychology. The word *gestalt* may be translated roughly as "whole" or "organization," and **Gestalt psychology** *was concerned with how elements of experience are organized into wholes.* Instead of trying to break consciousness down into its basic elements, as the structuralists strove to do, the Gestalt psychologists argued that our perceptions are organized so that "the whole is greater than the sum of its parts." Consider, for example, the painting in Figure 1.12. When you first looked at it, what did you see? Many people initially perceive it as a portrait of a person (albeit a strange-looking person) rather than a mosaic composed of individual sea creatures. The Gestalt psychologists believed that this tendency to perceive wholes is, like other forms of perceptual organization, built into our nervous system.

Wolfgang Köhler (1887–1967), a leader of Gestalt psychology, proposed that the ability to perceive relationships is the essence of what we call *intelligence.* He studied the problem-solving abilities of apes and observed examples of what he called *insight,* the sudden perception of a useful relationship or solution to a problem—a kind of "Aha!" experience. For example, unable to reach a banana that had been placed outside his cage, a chimpanzee named Sultan suddenly joined two sticks together to extend his range and snare his reward (Figure 1.13). Gestalt psychology eventually disappeared as a scientific school, but it stimulated new interest in cognitive topics such as perception, problem solving, and intelligence.

The Child's Mind, Language, and the Computer Behaviorism's rise pushed North American research on mental processes to the back burner, but some scientists continued to explore the nature of the mind. Swiss psychologist Jean Piaget (1896–1980) spent more than 50 years studying how children reason (Figure 1.14). He carefully observed children as they tried to solve problems and concluded that new stages of cognitive development—new ways of thinking and understanding the world—unfold naturally as children mature. His influential model of cognitive development spread to North America, sparking broader interest in the study of mental processes.

In the 1950s, a heated debate arose between behaviorists and linguists about how children acquire language. The behaviorists, led by B. F. Skinner, claimed that language, much like any other behavior, is acquired through basic principles of learning. The linguists, led by Noam Chomsky (b. 1928), argued that humans are biologically "preprogrammed" to acquire language and that children naturally come to understand language as a set of "mental rules." This debate, which we will examine further in Chapter 8, increased psychologists' interest in studying language and other processes (such as planning and problem solving) from a cognitive perspective.

Around this time, advances in computer technology opened many psychologists' eyes to a striking new metaphor: the human mind as a system, much like a computer, that processes, stores, and retrieves information. As you will learn in Chapter 7, there are flaws in this analogy, but it helped spark a booming interest in mental processes in the 1960s and 1970s—a period that many psychologists refer to as the "cognitive revolution."

Modern Cognitive Science

Modern cognitive science has links with computer science, linguistics, biology, and mathematics. Cognitive psychologists study how people produce and recognize speech and how they devise creative solutions to problems. Some, such as Elizabeth Loftus (b. 1944), have greatly expanded our understanding of the nature and fallibility of human memory (Figure 1.15). Cognitive psychologists continue to explore the nature of consciousness and have increasingly become interested in how nonconscious mental processes influence behavior. An important intersection of biological and cognitive perspectives has resulted in a new area called **cognitive neuroscience,** *which uses sophisticated electrical recording and brain-imaging techniques to examine brain activity as people engage in mental tasks* (Müller & Hübner, 2002).

One area of cognitive science, **artificial intelligence (AI),** *develops computer models of human thought and reasoning* (Wagman, 1997). AI researchers believe that by developing computer models that seem to duplicate natural mental processes, they will better understand how humans think.

Social constructivism, an influential cognitive viewpoint, *maintains that what we consider "reality" is largely our own mental creation,* the product of a shared way of thinking among members of social groups (Gergen, 2000). Constructivists would maintain, for example, that male and female sex roles are created not by biology but by the shared worldview that exists within social groups. Likewise, the long-standing conflict between Middle Eastern Jews and Arabs reflects radically different views of God's plan for them and of how to interpret the history of the land where they live (Rouhana & Bar-Tal, 1998). These two groups, though coexisting in the same place, live in vastly different subjective worlds.

From a cognitive perspective, Ray's thoughts about his past dating failures may hold the key to his shyness. Ray believes he was rejected because of his personal qualities ("I'm not attractive or interesting enough") and therefore expects that future dating attempts will also be unsuccessful. Had Ray attributed the rejections to some temporary or situational factor ("Clarissa must have been interested in someone else"), then he would not necessarily expect other women to reject him in the future. Ray's rosy recall of how he met Kira also is the province of cognitive psychology. Where and how are such memories stored in his brain? Are his memories accurate, or have they become distorted by his positive feelings about Kira?

FIGURE 1.13

A modern-day counterpart of Sultan demonstrates what Köhler believed was insight learning, by using a series of shorter sticks to pull in a stick that is long enough to reach the delicacy.

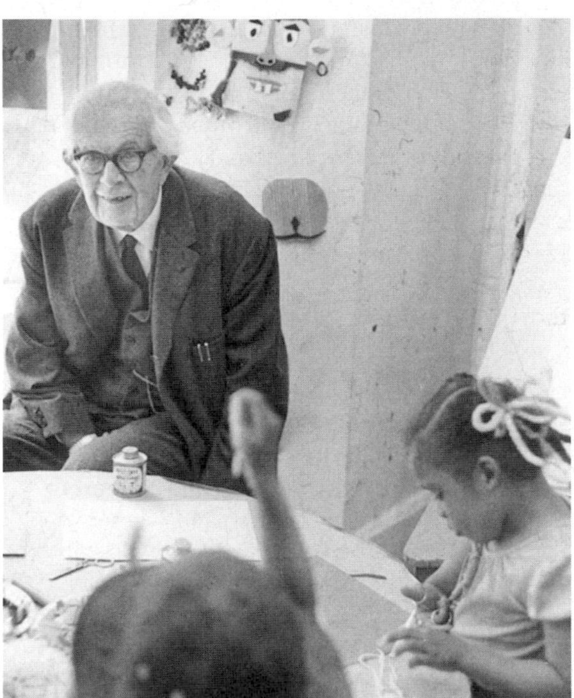

FIGURE 1.14

Swiss psychologist Jean Piaget was a master of observation. Many of his conclusions about cognitive development came from carefully watching children solve problems.

FIGURE 1.15

Cognitive psychologist Elizabeth Loftus studies the nature of human memory and how memories of events become distorted.

▶ 9. Explain the sociocultural perspective. What are culture, norms, socialization, and individualism-collectivism?

The Sociocultural Perspective: The Embedded Human

Humans are social creatures. Embedded within a culture, each of us encounters ever changing social settings that shape our actions and values, our sense of identity, our very conception of reality. The **sociocultural perspective** *examines how the social environment and cultural learning influence our behavior, thoughts, and feelings.*

Cultural Learning and Diversity

Culture *refers to the enduring values, beliefs, behaviors, and traditions that are shared by a large group of people and passed from one generation to the next.* All cultural groups develop their own social **norms,** *which are rules (often unwritten) that specify what behavior is acceptable and expected for members of that group.* Norms may involve rules for how to dress, respond to people higher in status, or act as a woman or man. For culture to endure, each new generation must internalize, or adopt, the norms and values of the group as their own. **Socialization** *is the process by which culture is transmitted to new members and internalized by them.*

In word if not in deed, psychologists have long recognized culture's impact in shaping who we are. Two influential behaviorists, John Dollard and Neil Miller, noted in 1941 that

> No psychologist would venture to predict the behavior of a rat without knowing [where in a maze] the feed or the shock is placed. It is no easier to predict the behavior of a human being without knowing the conditions of his "maze," i.e., the structure of his social environment. Culture . . . is a statement of the design of the human maze, of the type of reward involved, and of what responses are to be rewarded. (p. 5)

FIGURE 1.16

Psychologists Kenneth B. Clark and Mamie P. Clark studied the development of racial identity among African American children. Kenneth Clark also wrote books on the psychological impact of prejudice and discrimination.

Yet despite acknowledging culture's importance, throughout much of the 20th century psychological research largely ignored non-Western groups. This work usually was left to anthropologists, such as Margaret Mead (1901–1978), who in 1935 described three tribes in New Guinea that showed striking differences in behavior among men and women. Among the Arapesh, men and women were kind, sympathetic, and cooperative. Among the Mundugumor, men and women were fierce and aggressive. A third tribe, the Tchambuli, exhibited a reversal of traditional Western sex roles. The women were boisterous, shaved their heads, and took responsibility for obtaining the tribe's food. The men focused on art, their hairstyles, and gossip about the women (Mead, 1935). Mead's observations graphically illustrated how cultural norms affect behavior.

Even within Western societies, for decades participants in psychological research typically were white and came from middle- or upper-class backgrounds. This situation was so common that in 1976, African American psychologist Robert Guthrie published a book titled *Even the Rat Was White: A Historical View of Psychology*. There were important exceptions, however, such as research by Kenneth Clark (1914–2000) and Mamie Clark (1917–1983) and others examining how discrimination and prejudice influenced the personality development of African American children (Clark & Clark, 1947; Figure 1.16).

Over time, psychologists increasingly began to study diverse ethnic and cultural groups. Today the growing field of **cultural psychology** (sometimes called *cross-cultural psychology*) *explores how culture is transmitted to its members and examines psychological similarities and differences that occur between people from diverse cultures.*

One important difference among cultures is the extent to which they emphasize *individualism* versus *collectivism* (Triandis & Suh, 2002). Most industrialized cultures of northern Europe and North America promote **individualism,** *an emphasis on personal goals and self-identity based primarily on one's own attributes and achievements.* In contrast, many cultures in Asia, Africa, and South America nurture **collectivism,** *in which individual goals are subordinated to those of the group and personal identity is defined largely by the ties that bind one to the extended family and other social groups.*

This difference is created by social learning experiences that begin in childhood and continue in the form of social customs. Japan and the United States exemplify cultures that differ moderately on the individualism-collectivism dimension (Kagitçibasi, 1997). In school, for example, Japanese children more often work as part of a group having a common assignment, whereas American children more often work alone on individual assignments.

Thinking about Ray's lonely first year in college, the sociocultural perspective leads us to ask how his cultural upbringing and other social factors contributed to his shy behavior. Throughout his teen years, cultural norms for male assertiveness may have put pressure on Ray. His shyness may have evoked teasing and other negative reactions from his high school peers, increasing his feelings of inadequacy by the time he reached college. As for Ray and Kira's relationship, we might examine how norms differ across cultures regarding courtship and marriage. Our *Research Close-Up* examines this issue.

RESEARCH CLOSE-UP

LOVE AND MARRIAGE IN ELEVEN CULTURES

Background

Would you marry someone you did not love? According to one theory, people in individualistic cultures are more likely to view romantic love as a requirement for marriage because love is a matter of personal choice (Goode, 1959). In collectivistic cultures, concern for the extended family plays a larger role in marriage decisions.

Psychologist Richard Levine and his colleagues (1995) examined college students' views about love and marriage. Whereas previous research focused on American students, these authors studied students from 11 countries. They also examined whether students from collectivistic and economically poorer countries would be less likely to view love as a prerequisite to marriage.

Method

The researchers administered language-appropriate versions of the same questionnaire to 1,163 female and male college students from 11 countries. The key question was "If someone had all the other qualities you desired, would you marry this person if you were not in love with him/her?" The students responded, "No," "Yes," or "Not Sure." The researchers determined each country's economic status and collectivistic versus individualistic orientation from data gathered by previous cross-cultural investigators.

Results

Within each country, the views of female and male students did not differ significantly. In contrast, beliefs across countries varied strongly (Table 1.2). In India, Thailand, and Pakistan, most students said they would marry or at least consider marrying someone they did not love. In the Philippines and Japan, a sizeable minority—just over a third—felt the same way. In contrast, students from the other countries overwhelmingly rejected the notion of marrying somebody they did not love. Overall, students from collectivistic and economically poorer countries were less likely to view love as a prerequisite to marriage.

Table 1.2 Love and Marriage in Eleven Cultures

If someone had all the other qualities you desired, would you marry this person if you were not in love with him/her?

	Percentage		
Country	No	Yes	Not Sure
India	24	49	27
Thailand	34	19	47
Pakistan	39	50	11
Philippines	64	11	25
Japan	64	2	34
Hong Kong	78	6	16
Australia	80	5	15
Mexico	83	10	7
England	84	7	9
Brazil	86	4	10
United States	86	4	10

SOURCE: Levine et al., 1995.

Discussion

Among most of our own students, the notion that "you marry someone you love" is a truism. They are surprised—as perhaps you are—that many students in other countries would consider marrying someone they did not love. This study reminds us that, as members of a particular culture, it is easy to mistakenly assume that "our way" is the "normal" way.

As in all research, we must interpret the results carefully. For example, among those students who said they would marry someone without being in love, would it be accurate to conclude that they view love as irrelevant to marriage?

Not necessarily, because other research has found that "mutual attraction/love" is viewed across most cultures as a desirable quality in a mate (Buss, 1989). Thus, the results of the Levine et al. study suggest only that in some cultures love is not viewed as an *essential prerequisite* to enter into marriage.

SOURCE: Robert Levine, Suguru Sato, Tsukasa Hashimoto, and Jyoti Verma (1995). Love and marriage in eleven cultures. *Journal of Cross-Cultural Psychology, 26*, 554–571.

▶ 10. How does the *Research Close-Up* illustrate cultural psychology's goals and importance?

The Biological Perspective: The Brain, Genes, and Evolution

▶ 11. Describe the biological perspective and the goals of behavioral neuroscience and behavior genetics.

The **biological perspective** *examines how brain processes and other bodily functions regulate behavior.* Biological psychology has always been a prominent part of the field, but its influence has increased dramatically over recent decades.

Behavioral Neuroscience

Ray and Kira are in love. They often study and eat together; they often hold hands and kiss; each of them considers the other "my favorite person." Yet a year earlier, Ray was afraid to ask women out and became mildly depressed. What regions of the brain, what neural circuits and brain chemicals, enable us to feel love, pleasure, fear, and depression? To read, study, and feel hunger? To smell a perfume or recognize a familiar face? These questions are the province of **behavioral neuroscience** (also called *physiological psychology*), *which examines brain processes and other physiological functions that underlie our behavior, sensory experiences, emotions, and thoughts.*

The study of brain-behavior relations was in its infancy as psychology entered the 20th century. Two pioneers of biological psychology, American Karl Lashley (1890–1958) and Canadian Donald O. Hebb (1904–1985), studied the brain's role in learning. Lashley trained rats to run mazes and then measured how surgically produced lesions (damage) to various brain areas affected the rats' learning and memory. His research inspired other psychologists to map the brain regions involved in specific psychological functions (Figure 1.17).

FIGURE 1.17

Karl Lashley was a pioneer in the field of physiological psychology (behavioral neuroscience). He examined how damage to various brain regions affected rats' ability to learn and remember.

Hebb (1949) proposed that changes in the connections between nerve cells in the brain provide the biological basis for learning, memory, and perception. His influential theory inspired much research, continuing to this day, on how the brain's neural circuitry changes as we learn, remember, and perceive. This research led to the discovery of **neurotransmitters,** *which are chemicals released by nerve cells that allow them to communicate with one another.* The study of neurotransmitters' role in normal behavior and mental disorders represents an important area of current neuroscience research.

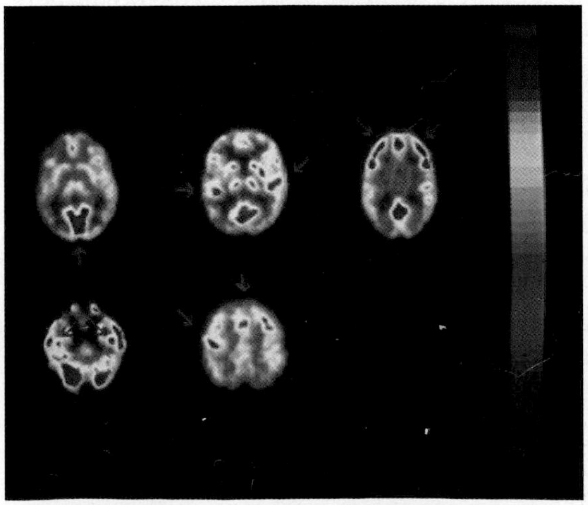

FIGURE 1.18

Behavioral neuroscientists use PET scans to measure brain activity as people perform various tasks. Viewed from above, each image pictures a horizontal slice of the brain with the front of brain at the top. Yellow and red indicate regions of greatest activity.
Top left: Visual task
Top center: Auditory task
Top right: Cognitive task
Bottom left: Memory task
Bottom right: Motor task

Because behavioral neuroscience focuses on processes that are largely invisible to the naked eye, its development has depended on scientific and technological advancements. Today, using computer-based brain-imaging techniques and devices that record people's brain waves, psychologists "watch" activity in specific brain areas as people experience emotions, perceive stimuli, and perform mental or physical tasks (Figure 1.18). These advances have forged new relations between the various psychological perspectives. One example, described earlier, is cognitive neuroscience, in which scientists representing the biological and cognitive perspectives join forces to discover the brain processes that underlie many kinds of mental activities.

Behavior Genetics

Psychologists have had a long-standing interest in **behavior genetics,** *the study of how behavioral tendencies are influenced by genetic factors* (Efran & Greene, 2000). Animals can be selectively bred not only for physical traits (Figure 1.19) but also for behavioral traits such as aggression or intelligence. This is done by allowing highly aggressive or very bright males and females to mate with one another over a number of generations. In Thailand, where gambling on fish fights has long been a national pastime, the selective breeding of winners has produced the highly aggressive Siamese fighting fish. The male of this species will instantly attack his own image in a mirror and can sometimes engage in fierce fighting contests that last up to six hours.

Human behavior also is influenced by genetic factors. Identical twins, who result from the splitting of a fertilized egg and therefore have the same genetic makeup, are far more similar to one another on many behavioral traits than are fraternal twins, who result from two different fertilized eggs and therefore are no more similar genetically than are nontwin siblings. This greater degree of similarity is found even when the identical twins have been reared in different homes and dissimilar environments (Plomin & Caspi, 1999).

Thinking about Ray, a behavior geneticist would consider the extent to which heredity contributes to differences among people in shyness.

Some infants display an extremely shy, inhibited emotional style that seems to be biologically based and persists through childhood into adulthood (Kagan, 1989; Newman et al., 1997). Perhaps Ray inherited a tendency to be shy, and dating rejections in high school reinforced his natural reluctance to ask women out.

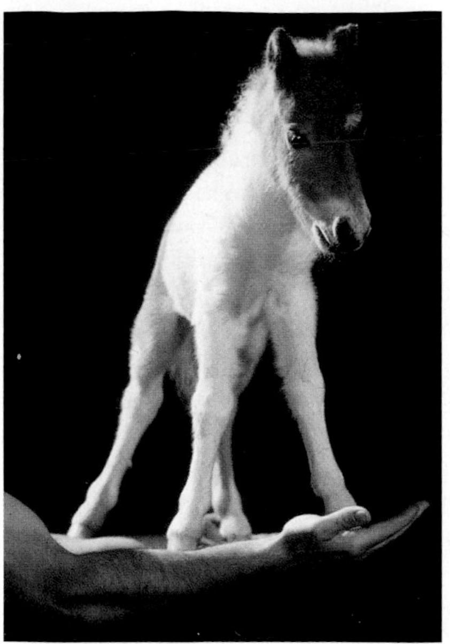

FIGURE 1.19

Selective breeding can produce physical and behavioral characteristics. This tiny horse was produced by selectively breeding smaller and smaller horses over a number of generations.

Evolutionary Psychology

As we noted earlier, in 1859 Charles Darwin published a theory of evolution that forever changed the scientific landscape (Figure 1.20). Darwin was not the first to suggest the evolution of animals, but his theory was the best documented. His ideas were stimulated by a five-year voyage aboard a British research vessel that explored coastal regions around the globe. Darwin was struck by the numerous differences between seemingly similar species who lived in different environments. He began to view these differences as ways in which each species had adapted to its unique environment.

Darwin noted that the individual members of given species differ naturally in many ways. Some possess specific traits to a greater extent than other members do. Through a process he called **natural selection,** *if an inherited trait gives certain members an advantage over others* (such as increasing their ability to attract mates, escape danger, or acquire food) *these members will be more likely to survive and pass these characteristics on to their offspring.* In this way, species evolve as the presence of adaptive traits increases within the population over generations. In contrast, traits that put certain members at a disadvantage tend to become less common within a species over time because members having these traits will be less likely to survive and reproduce. The adaptiveness of a trait, however, may increase or decrease if the environment changes. Thus, through natural selection, a species' biology evolves in response to environmental conditions (Figure 1.21).

Darwin did not know how inherited characteristics were passed across generations, but he did assume that the principle of natural selection could be applied to all living organisms, including humans. Later in the 19th century an Austrian monk, Gregor Mendel (1822–1884), conducted research on the hereditary transmission of characteristics in plants that would eventually lead to the discovery of genes.

Evolutionary psychology is a growing discipline that *seeks to explain how evolution shaped modern human behavior* (Caporael, 2000). Evolutionary psychologists stress that through natural selection, human mental abilities and behavioral tendencies evolved along with a changing body (Tooby & Cosmides, 1992). Consider how the brain evolved over millions of years, with the greatest growth occurring in brain regions involving higher mental processes.

According to one theory, as our humanlike ancestors developed new physical abilities (such as the ability to walk upright, thus freeing the use of the arms and hands), they began to use tools and weapons and to hunt and live in social groups (Pilbeam, 1984). Certain psychological abilities—memory, thought, language, and the capacity to learn and solve problems—became more important to survival as our ancestors had to adapt to new ways of living. Within any generation, genetically based variations in brain structure and functioning occur among individuals. Ancestors whose brain characteristics better supported adaptive mental abilities were more likely to survive and reproduce. Thus through natural selection, adaptations to new environmental demands contributed to the development of the brain, just as brain growth contributed to the further development of human behavior.

▶ 12. What is evolutionary psychology? Contrast evolutionary and sociocultural perspectives in explaining behavior.

The notion that the brain evolved in ways that allow us to learn, think, and communicate more effectively is generally accepted by scientists today. Many evolutionary theorists, however, propose a more controversial view that through natural selection, humans have become genetically predisposed to display various social traits such as aggression, dominance, and nurturance. According to one viewpoint, an organism's *genetic* survival (i.e., transmission of one's genes) is more important than its physical survival. This

FIGURE 1.20

Charles Darwin, a British naturalist, formulated a theory of evolution that revolutionalized scientific thinking.

FIGURE 1.21

Natural selection pressures result in physical changes. The peppered moth's natural color is that of the lighter insect. However, over many generations, peppered moths who live in polluted urban areas have become darker—not from the pollution but because moths who inherited slightly darker coloration blended better into their grimy environment. Thus they were more likely to survive predators and pass their "darker" genes on to their offspring. However, a trip into the countryside to visit their light-colored relatives could easily prove fatal for these darker urban insects.

principle is even used to explain certain altruistic behaviors, including giving up one's life to save children or relatives (Hamilton, 1964). Although such behavior is hardly in the survival interests of the individual, it serves a higher purpose: It keeps one's genes alive in the gene pool to live on in our descendants (Sober & Wilson, 1998).

Recall that when Ray and Kira first met, Kira accurately sensed Ray's shyness (as well as his interest in her), which led her to ask him out. While dating, Kira has continued to do a good job of reading Ray's emotions and seems slightly more tuned in to Ray's emotional state than he is to hers. Research has found that across many cultures, women are somewhat more accurate than men in judging facial expressions of emotion (Leppänen & Hietanen, 2001). Some evolutionary theorists propose that sex differences in social behavior result from males' predominant ancestral role of hunter-protector and women's role as bearer and caretaker of children, roles that created genetically based differences in men and women through a process of natural selection (Buss, 1991). Although reading emotions accurately is important for both men and women, it may have been especially adaptive for ancestral women. As the primary caregivers of infants and children, those who were more accurate in reading the emotional states of their mate and of their children stood an increased chance of helping their offspring survive, which increased the odds that their genes would be passed on to the next generation.

Many sociocultural theorists argue that evolutionary explanations for social behaviors and gender differences overemphasize the role of biological "predeterminism" and ignore the cultural norms and socialization experiences that dictate what men and women "should" be like (Eagly et al., 2000). Women's greater accuracy in reading emotional expressions may stem from cultural encouragement for women to be sensitive to others' emotions and to express their feelings openly. We will encounter this lively controversy between evolutionary and sociocultural viewpoints at several points throughout the book.

IN REVIEW

- *Several perspectives have shaped psychology's scientific growth. Each perspective views human nature differently and focuses on different causes of behavior.*
- *Psychology's intellectual roots lie in philosophy, biology, and medicine. In the late 1800s, Wundt and James helped found psychology.* Structuralism, *which examined the basic components of consciousness, and* functionalism, *which focused on the purposes of consciousness, were psychology's two earliest schools of thought.*
- *The* psychodynamic perspective *calls attention to unconscious motives, conflicts, and defense mechanisms that influence our personality and behavior. Freud's psychoanalytic theory emphasized unconscious sexual and aggressive impulses and early childhood experiences that shape personality. Modern psychodynamic theories focus more on how early family relationships and our sense of self unconsciously influence our current behavior.*
- *With roots in 18th-century British empiricism, the* behavioral perspective *emphasizes how the external environment and learning shape behavior. Behaviorists such as Watson and Skinner believed that psychology should only study observable stimuli and responses, not unobservable mental processes. They argued that to change behavior, the key is to modify the environment. Behaviorists discovered basic laws of learning through controlled research with laboratory animals and successfully applied these principles to enhance human welfare.*
- *Humanists reject the notion that people are controlled by unconscious forces or merely react to environmental stimuli. Instead, the* humanistic perspective *emphasizes personal freedom and choice, psychological growth, and self-actualization. Humanism has contributed to research on the self, the process of psychotherapy, and today's positive psychology movement.*
- *The* cognitive perspective *views humans as information processors who think, judge, and solve problems. Its roots lie in the early*

schools of structuralism, functionalism, and Gestalt psychology. Piaget's work on cognitive development, the study of linguistics, and the advent of computers sparked new interest in mental processes. Research in artificial intelligence develops computer models of human thought, whereas cognitive neuroscience studies brain processes that underlie mental activity. Social constructivism maintains that much of what we call reality is a creation of our own mental processes.

- *The* sociocultural perspective *examines how the social environment and cultural learning influence our behavior and thoughts. Cultural psychologists study how culture is transmitted to its members and examine similarities and differences among people from various cultures. An orientation toward individualism versus collectivism represents one of many ways in which cultures vary.*
- *With roots in physiology, medicine, and Darwin's theory of evolution, the* biological perspective *examines how bodily functions regulate behavior. Behavioral neuroscientists (or physiological psychologists) study brain processes and other physiological functions that underlie our behavior, sensory experiences, emotions, and thoughts. In contrast, behavior geneticists study how behavior is influenced by our genetic inheritance. Evolutionary psychologists examine behavior in terms of its adaptive functions and seek to explain how evolution has biologically predisposed modern humans toward certain ways of behaving.*

For more on identifying psychological perspectives, see Interactive Segment 1.1.

INTEGRATING THE PERSPECTIVES: THREE LEVELS OF ANALYSIS

▶ 13. Integrate psychology's perspectives within a 3-level framework. Use this framework to discuss causes of depression.

As summarized in Table 1.3, psychology's major perspectives provide us with differing conceptions of human nature. Fortunately, we can distill the essence of these perspectives into a simple, three-part framework for understanding behavior. This framework is called *levels of analysis*.

First, we can analyze behavior and its causes in terms of brain functioning and hormones, as well as genetic factors shaped over the course of evolution. This is the *biological level of analysis*. The biological level can tell us much, but not everything. For example, we may know that certain thoughts and emotions are associated with activity in particular brain regions, but this does not tell us what those thoughts and feelings are. Thus we must examine a second level, the *psychological level of analysis*. Here we might look to the cognitive perspective and analyze how thought, memory, planning, and problem solving influence behavior. Borrowing from the psychodynamic and humanistic perspectives, we also can examine how certain motives, desires, and personality characteristics influence behavior. Finally, we also consider the *environmental level of analysis*. Here, using concepts from the behavioral and sociocultural perspectives, we can examine how stimuli in the physical and social environment shape our behavior, thoughts, and feelings.

Realize that a full understanding of behavior often moves us back and forth between the three levels. For example, let's return once again to Ray and Kira. When we describe features of the culture in which Ray and Kira were raised, such as its religious values and social customs, we are operating at the environmental level of analysis. However, once Ray and Kira adopted those cultural values as their own, those values became an essential part of their identity and worldview, which represents the psychological level of analysis. Similarly, we might describe a family environment as highly abusive, but an abused child's tendency to worry and feel anxious—and the chemical changes in the brain that underlie this anxiety—move us to the psychological and biological levels of analysis.

An Example: Understanding Depression

To appreciate how the biological, psychological, and environmental levels of analysis can help us understand behavior, let's examine a common but complex psychological problem in our culture: depression. Most people experience sadness, grief, or the blues at some time in their lives. Recall that Ray was lonely during his first year at college and became mildly depressed for a short time. These feelings often are normal

Table 1.3 Comparison of Six Major Perspectives on Human Behavior

	Biological	Cognitive	Psychodynamic	Behavioral	Humanistic	Sociocultural
Conception of human nature	The human animal	The human as thinker and information processor	The human as controlled by inner forces and conflicts	The human as a reactor to the environment	The human as free agent, seeking self-actualization and personal meaning	The human as a social being embedded in a culture
Major causal factors in behavior	Genetic and evolutionary factors; brain and biochemical processes	Thought, anticipations, planning, perception, and memory processes	Unconscious motives, conflicts, and defenses; early childhood experiences and unresolved conflicts	Past learning experiences and the stimuli and behavioral consequences that exist in the current environment	Free will, choice, and innate drive toward self-actualization; search for personal meaning of existence	Social forces, including norms, social interactions, and group processes in one's culture and social environment
Predominant focus and methods of discovery	Study of brain-behavior relations; role of hormones and biochemical factors in behavior; behavior genetics research	Study of cognitive processes, usually under highly controlled laboratory conditions	Intensive observations of personality processes in clinical settings; some laboratory research	Study of learning processes in laboratory and real-world settings, with an emphasis on precise observation of stimuli and responses	Study of meaning, values, and purpose in life; study of self-concept and its role in thought, emotion, and behavior	Study of behavior and mental processes of people in different cultures; experiments examining people's responses to varying social stimuli and conditions

responses to negative events or meaningful losses that we have experienced. However, when these emotional responses are intense, persist over a long period, and are accompanied by thoughts of hopelessness and an inability to experience pleasure, we have crossed the boundary between a normal reaction and clinical depression (Rubin, 2000).

To better understand depression, let's begin at the biological level of analysis. First, genetic factors appear to predispose some people toward developing depression (Kendler et al., 2001). In one study, relatives of people who had developed major depression before age 20 were eight times more likely to become depressed at some point than were relatives of nondepressed people (Weissman et al., 1984).

Biochemical factors also play a role. Recall that neurotransmitters are chemicals that transmit signals between nerve cells within the brain. Depressed people often have an imbalance in the activity of certain neurotransmitters, and the most effective antidepressant drugs operate by restoring a normal chemical balance (Riedel et al., 2002).

From an evolutionary perspective, ancestors who developed effective ways to cope with environmental threats increased their chances of surviving and passing on their genes. At times, the psychological and physical ability to withdraw and conserve one's resources was undoubtedly the most adaptive defense against an environmental stressor, such as an unavoidable defeat or personal loss. Some evolutionary theorists view depression (and its accompanying disengagement and sense of hopelessness) as an exaggerated form of this normally adaptive, genetically based withdrawal process (Gilbert, 2001).

Moving to a psychological level of analysis sheds additional light on depression and its causes. For example, depression is associated with a particular thinking style in which the person interprets events in a pessimistic way (Seligman & Isaacowitz, 2000). Depressed people can find the black cloud that surrounds every silver lining. They tend to blame themselves for negative things that occur while taking no personal credit for the good things that happen in their lives; they generally view the future as bleak and may have perfectionistic expectations that inevitably lead to disappointment (Wiebe & McCabe, 2002).

Are some personality patterns more prone to depression than others? Many psychodynamic theorists believe that severe losses, rejections, or traumas in childhood help create a personality style that causes people to overreact to future setbacks, setting the stage for later depression. In support of this notion, studies show that depressed people are more likely than nondepressed people to have experienced parental rejection, sexual abuse, or the loss of a parent through death or separation during childhood (Bowlby, 2000a; Cheasty et al., 2002).

Finally, at the environmental level of analysis, behaviorists propose that depression is a reaction to a nonrewarding environment. A vicious cycle begins when the environment provides fewer rewards for the person. As depression intensifies, some people feel so badly that they stop doing things that ordinarily give them pleasure, which decreases environmental rewards still further. To make things worse, depressed people may complain a good deal and seek excessive reassurance and support from others. These behaviors eventually begin to alienate other people, causing them to shy away from the depressed person. The net result is a worsening environment with fewer rewards, reduced support from others, and the hopeless pessimism that characterizes chronic depression (Lewinsohn et al., 1985; Nezlek et al., 2000).

Sociocultural factors also affect depression. As noted above, abusive family environments and other traumatic social experiences increase children's risk for depression later in life. Moreover, although depression is found in virtually all cultures, its symptoms, causes, and prevalence may reflect cultural differences (Lopez & Guarnaccia, 2000). For reasons still unknown, in developed countries such as the United States, Canada, and other Western nations, women are about twice as likely as men to report feeling depressed, whereas no such sex difference is found in developing countries (Culbertson, 1997).

Figure 1.22 organizes the causal factors in depression into three classes: biological, psychological, and environmental. Keep in mind, however, that the specific causes of depression and the way in which they combine or interact may differ from case to case. **Interaction** *means that the way in which one factor influences behavior depends on the presence of another factor*. For example, someone who experiences a minor setback in life may become depressed if she or he has a strong biological predisposition for depression, whereas this same setback would barely faze a person with a weak biological predisposition for depression. Nothing short of a catastrophic loss might cause this other person to become depressed. In this instance, the intensity of life stress and strength of biological predisposition would interact to influence behavior. Just as boiling water softens celery and hardens an egg, the same environment can affect two people in different ways.

Nature *and* Nurture: Biology, Experience, and Behavior

▶ 14. What does the levels of analysis framework imply for understanding the nature versus nuture controversy?

The levels of analysis framework addresses a philosophical and scientific issue that has been debated since antiquity: Is our behavior primarily shaped by nature (our biological endowment) or by nurture (our environment and learning history)? A century ago, the biological emphasis predominated, and many scientists believed that human characteristics are genetically determined. With behaviorism's rise, by the 1950s and 1960s the pendulum had swung toward nurture, and most experts believed that humans are largely a product of their environment.

Growing interest in cultural influences and advances in behavior genetics and brain research

FIGURE 1.22

Understanding Behavior: Biological, psychological, and environmental factors in depression.

Levels of Analysis

Biological

- Genetic predisposition, as shown in identical vs. fraternal twin rates
- Chemical factors within brain, influenced by antidepressant drugs
- Possible exaggerated form of adaptive withdrawal mechanism shaped by evolution

Psychological

- Negative thought patterns and distortions, which may trigger depression
- Pessimistic personality style
- Susceptibility to loss and rejection, possibly linked to early life experiences

Environmental

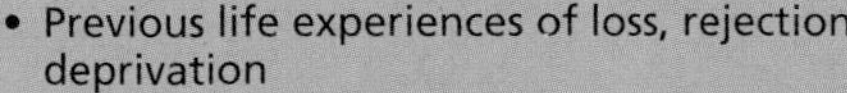

- Previous life experiences of loss, rejection, deprivation
- Current decreases in pleasurable experiences and/or increases in life stress
- Loss of social support due to own behaviors
- Cultural factors, including sex roles and cultural norms for reacting to negative events and expressing unhappiness

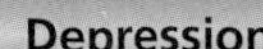

Depression

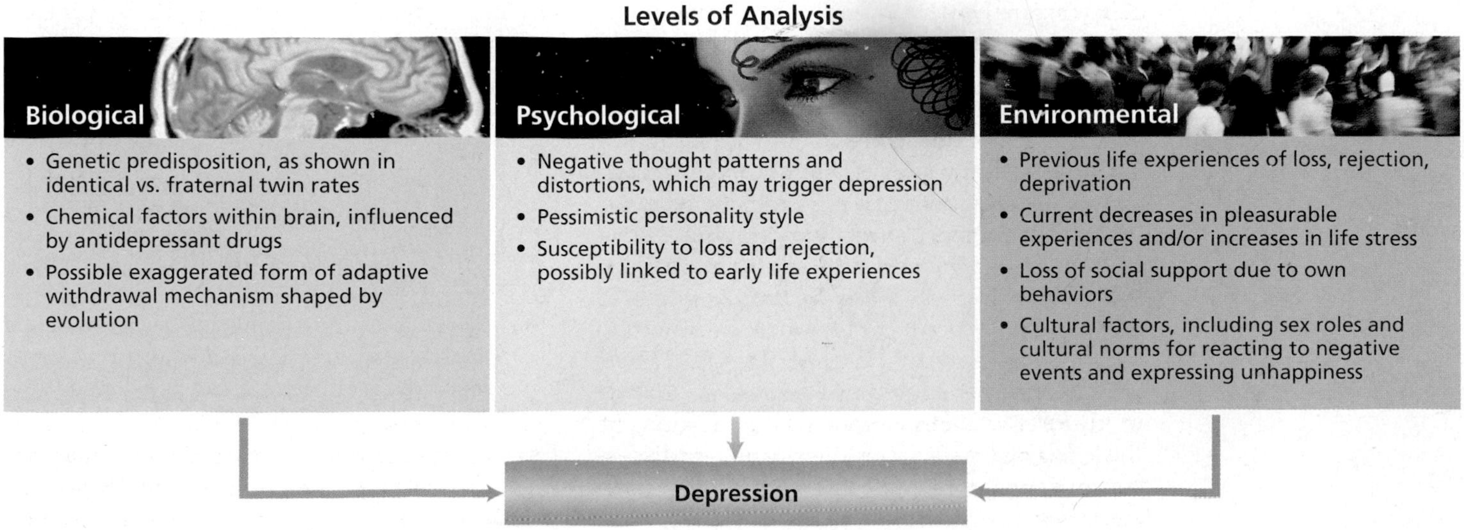

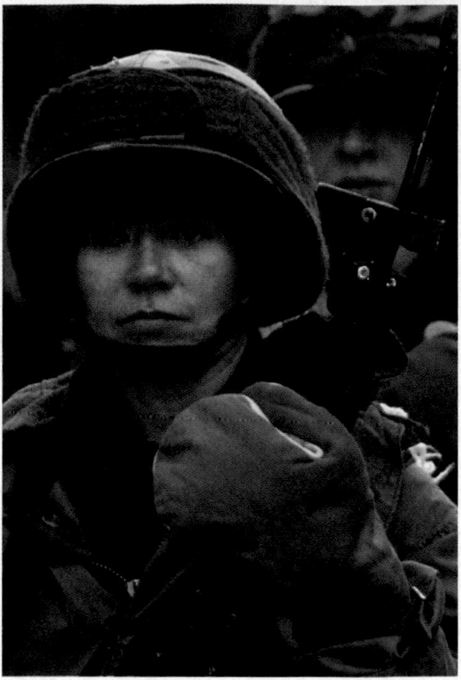

FIGURE 1.23

Social norms change over time. Today, competitive, even aggressive, behavior is seen as appropriate among female athletes and soldiers. Several generations ago, such behavior would have been highly inconsistent with sex role norms for women.

▶ 15. Discuss the six major themes identified in this chapter and provide an example of each.

are now keeping the pendulum in a more balanced position between nature and nurture. For example, returning to our earlier discussion of male-female differences, research continues to remind us that cultural norms and socialization processes powerfully shape gender behavior. At the same time, brain-imaging studies and other neuroscience research have found differences between the brains of men and women (Halpern, 2000; Shaywitz et al., 1995). Are these differences inborn, or do they result from different types of experiences that men and women have? The answer is not yet clear, but ultimately these findings should lead to new research that more fully explains the behavioral differences between the sexes (Figure 1.23).

Perhaps most important, modern research increasingly reveals that nature and nurture interact. Just as our biological capacities affect how we behave and experience the world, our experiences influence our biological capacities. Among humans and rats, exposing a fetus in the womb to alcohol, continually depriving a newborn of physical contact, or providing a newborn with an enriched environment in which to grow, can influence its brain functioning and biological development (Rosenzweig, 1984). Thus, while it may be tempting to take sides, "nature *or* nurture?" usually is the wrong question. As the levels of analysis framework and our discussion of depression imply, seldom does one or the other operate in isolation (Lippa, 2002). The challenge for psychologists is to sort out how nature *and* nurture influence behavior and affect one another.

Summary of Major Themes

Our excursion through psychology's major perspectives and levels of analysis reveals several principles that you will encounter repeatedly as we explore the realm of behavior:

- As a science, *psychology is empirical.* It favors direct observation over pure intuition or reasoning as a means of attaining knowledge about behavior.
- Although committed to studying behavior objectively, psychologists recognize that *our personal experience of the world is subjective* and is influenced by our thoughts, motives, and expectations.
- *Behavior is determined by multiple causal factors*, which increases the challenge of understanding behavior.
- *Nature and nurture jointly shape our behavior* and influence one another.
- *Behavior is a means of adapting to environmental demands; capacities have evolved* during each species' history because they facilitated adaptation and survival.
- *Behavior and mental processes are affected by the social and cultural environments* in which we develop and live.

BENEATH THE SURFACE

WHAT DID YOU EXPECT?

At this point in the chapter, we'd like you to reflect for a moment on a simple question: What have you learned thus far about psychology that differs from your expectations coming into the course? We ask you this question because, up to now, we've attempted to paint a picture of what psychology is. We would now like to point out what psychology *isn't*.

Perhaps like many of our own students you may have equated psychology with counseling or therapy. If so, then you have already seen that psychology, as the scientific study of behavior and the mind, is much more. Indeed, you may have been surprised by psychology's enormous scope. Many students do not expect psychologists to study brain processes, genetics, and other biological factors; others are surprised at the overlap between areas of psychology and disciplines such as sociology and anthropology. In the next section of the chapter, you will learn more about some of psychology's diverse subfields.

Perhaps you did not expect the rich diversity of theoretical perspectives within psychology. You may have heard of Sigmund Freud and psychoanalysis, or possibly of B. F. Skinner and behaviorism. Indeed, in popular cartoons, psychologists are often stereotyped either as therapists who—like Freud—analyze patients lying on couches, or as researchers in white lab coats studying rats in a maze. Now you know that several other major perspectives represent important parts of psychology's past and present.

Given psychology's theoretical diversity, perhaps you did not expect how environmental, psychological, and biological factors intertwine to influence behavior. And, with regard to influencing behavior, we hasten to dispel the notion that psychology is about "mind control." Psychology's goal is not to control people's minds in the sense that *control* means inducing people to think or do things against their will. Rather, psychologists conduct basic research to learn how people behave, think, and feel; many also seek to apply that research to promote positive changes for individuals, groups, and society as a whole.

We've observed that some students mistakenly expect psychology to be "just common sense." After all, each of us has spent much of our lives interacting with other people, and we all form notions about human behavior and why people act as they do. For many reasons (which we'll explore in later chapters), our common sense often misleads us. For example, we usually don't subject our commonsense notions to a careful test, and we tend to selectively remember only those instances that confirm our beliefs. Perhaps when you took the true-false test in Table 1.1 you found that some of your commonsense answers were not consistent with the scientific findings.

Finally, we have found that many students who believe that psychology is largely common sense tend to underestimate the amount of work required to succeed in this course. Indeed, even students who *don't* hold this view mistakenly expect introductory psychology to be easy. However, because of the breadth of topics and the nature of the concepts and information covered in this course, you may find that it takes a lot more effort than you anticipated to gain a true understanding of the material.

In the coming chapters, you will find many instances where research findings are likely to contradict your expectations and many popular misconceptions about behavior. We look forward to helping you explore our exciting and important branch of science.

IN REVIEW

- *Factors that influence behavior can be organized into three broad levels of analysis. The biological level of analysis focuses on brain processes, hormonal and genetic influences, and evolutionary adaptations that underlie behavior. The psychological level of analysis examines mental processes and psychological motives, and how they influence behavior. The environmental level of analysis calls attention to physical and social stimuli, including cultural factors, that shape our behavior and thoughts.*
- *To understand behavior, we often move back and forth between these levels of analysis. For example, when as children we are first exposed to cultural norms, those norms reflect a characteristic of our environment. However, once we adopt norms as our own, they become a part of our worldview and now represent the psychological level of analysis.*
- *Biological, psychological, and environmental factors contribute to the development of depression. These factors can also interact to influence a given behavior. It may take only a mild setback to trigger depression in a person who has a strong biological predisposition toward depression, whereas a person who does not have such a biological predisposition may become depressed only after suffering a severe setback.*

PSYCHOLOGY TODAY: A GLOBAL SCIENCE AND PROFESSION

▶ 16. Describe some of psychology's major subfields and professional organizations.

As a science and profession, psychology today is more diversified and robust than ever before. Because of psychology's enormous breadth, no psychologist can be an expert on all aspects of behavior, just as no physician can be an expert in all areas of medicine. As in other scholarly disciplines, many areas of specialization have emerged. Table 1.4 describes some of psychology's major subfields, but realize that psychological research often cuts across subfields. For example, developmental, social, clinical, and physiological psychologists might all study the causes of antisocial behavior among children.

TABLE 1.4 Major Specialty Areas Within Psychology

Specialty	Major Focus
Animal behavior (comparative)	Study of nonhuman species in natural or laboratory environments; includes genetics, brain processes, social behavior, evolutionary processes
Behavioral neuroscience	Examination of brain and hormonal processes that underlie behavior; behavior genetics and evolutionary psychology are sometimes grouped under behavioral neuroscience.
Clinical	Diagnosis and treatment of psychological disorders; research on causes of disorders and treatment effectiveness
Cognitive	Study of mental processes such as memory, problem solving, planning, consciousness, and language (psycholinguistics)
Counseling	Consultation with clients on issues of personal adjustment; vocational and career planning; interest and aptitude testing
Cultural/Cross-cultural	Study of cultural transmission, psychological similarities and differences among people from different cultures
Developmental	Study of physical, mental, emotional, and social development across the entire life span
Educational	Study of psychological aspects of the educational process; curriculum and instructional research; teacher training
Experimental	Research (typically laboratory experiments, often with nonhumans) on basic processes such as learning, perception, and motivation
Industrial/Organizational	Examination of behavior in work settings; study of factors related to employee morale and performance; development of tests to select job applicants; development of machines and tasks to fit human capabilities
Personality	Study of individual differences in personality and their effects on behavior; development of personality tests
Social	Examination of how the social environment—the presence of other people—influences an individual's behavior, thoughts, and feelings
Quantitative	Measurement issues and data analysis; development of mathematical models of behavior.

To many people, the term *psychologist* evokes the image of a therapist or counselor. Many psychologists are, in fact, *clinical psychologists*, who diagnose and treat people with psychological problems in clinics, hospitals, and in private practice. But as Table 1.4 indicates, there are many other types of psychologists who have no connection with therapy and who work as basic or applied researchers in their chosen subfield. Even within clinical psychology, many scientists conduct research on the causes of mental disorders and the effects of various kinds of treatment.

Modern psychology also is geographically, ethnically, and gender diversified. A century ago, psychological research was conducted almost entirely in Europe, North America, and Russia by White males. Today these regions remain scientific powerhouses, but you will find women and men from diverse backgrounds conducting psychological research and providing psychological services around the globe. Founded in 1951 to support psychology worldwide, the International Union of Psychological Science consists of major psychological organizations from nearly 70 countries (IUPsyS, 2003). From the sweltering summer heat of southeastern China to the frigid winter nights above the Arctic circle in Norway, you also will find college students of all nationalities eagerly studying psychology. In the United States, psychology ranks among the top five disciplines in the number of undergraduate degrees and doctoral degrees awarded annually (National Center for Education Statistics, 2001). By the early 1990s, over half of the doctoral degrees in psychology in the United States were earned by women (Pion et al., 1996).

The American Psychological Association (APA), founded in 1892, is the largest individual psychological association in the world. Its 155,000 members and 55 divisions represent not only the subfields shown in Table 1.4 but also areas that focus on psychology's relation to the arts, religion, the military, the environment, sports, social issues, the law, and the media (APA, 2003). The American Psychology Society (APS), a newer organization consisting primarily of researchers, has grown to 12,000 members in just two decades (APS, 2003). Both APA and APS have international members in dozens of countries.

A career in most of the subfields described in Table 1.4 requires a doctoral degree based on four to six years of training beyond the bachelor's degree. Graduate training in psychology includes broad exposure to the theories and body of knowledge in the field, concentrated study in one or more of the subfields, and extensive training in research methods. In some areas, such as clinical, counseling, school, and industrial/organizational psychology, an additional year or more of supervised practical experience in a hospital, clinic, school, or workplace setting is generally required. Please note, however, that psychologists who perform mental-health services are not the same as psychiatrists. *Psychiatrists* are medical doctors who, after completing their general training in medicine, receive additional training in diagnosing and treating mental disorders.

Besides its fascinating subject matter, psychology attracts many people with its rich variety of career options. Figure 1.24 shows the major settings in which psychologists work. Many psychologists teach, engage in research, or apply psychological principles and techniques to help solve personal or social problems. For more information on careers in psychology, visit the Online Learning Center (OLC) that accompanies this book.

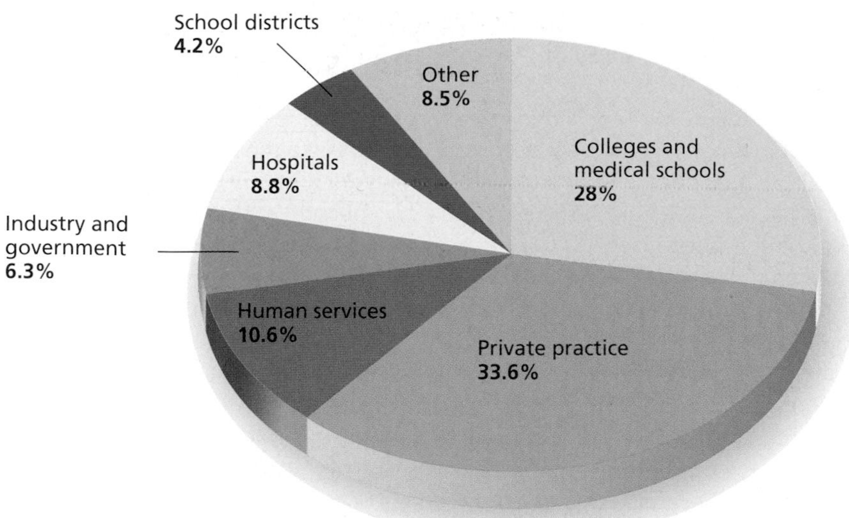

FIGURE 1.24

Work settings of psychologists. Source: Adapted from data in table, American Psychological Association Research Office, 2001.

▶ 17. Are psychiatrists the same as clinical psychologists? Explain.

Psychologists in all of the areas shown in Table 1.4 engage in basic research and applied work. Some do one or the other, some do both. As you will see throughout this book, principles discovered through basic psychological research can be applied to many areas of our lives and to solving important social problems. For example, research by cognitive and educational psychologists on learning and memory provides useful guidelines that can enhance your academic performance. Our first "Applying Psychological Science" feature describes some research-based pointers that can help you be more successful in your coursework.

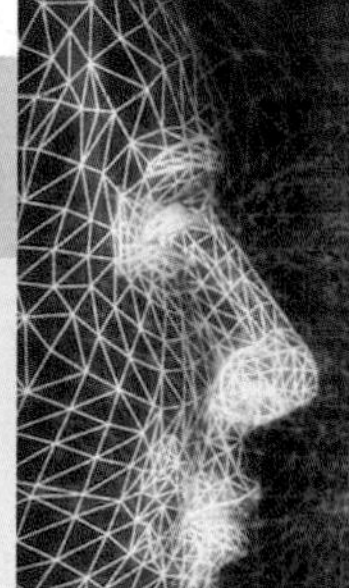

APPLYING PSYCHOLOGICAL SCIENCE

HOW TO ENHANCE YOUR ACADEMIC PERFORMANCE

College life presents many challenges, and working smart can be as important in meeting those challenges as working hard. The following strategies can help you increase your learning and academic performance (Figure 1.25).

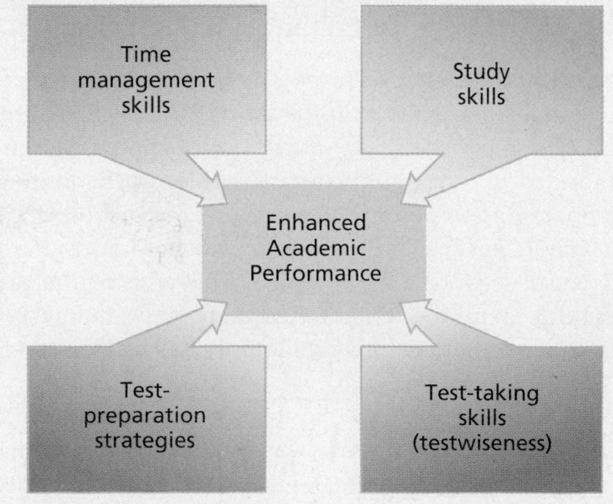

FIGURE 1.25

Academic performance-enhancement methods for students include strategies for managing and allocating time, studying more effectively, preparing for tests, and taking tests.

Effective Time Management

If you efficiently allocate the time needed for study, you will have a clear conscience when it's time for recreational activities and relaxation. First, *develop a written schedule*. This forces you to decide how to allocate your time and increases your commitment to the plan. Begin by writing in all of your class meetings and other responsibilities, such as your job schedule. Then block in periods of study, avoiding times when you are likely to be tired. Try to distribute your study times throughout the week, and schedule some study times immediately before enjoyable activities, which you can use as rewards for studying.

Continued

Second, *prioritize your tasks* (Lakein, 1973). Most of us tend to procrastinate by working on simple tasks while putting off the most demanding (and often the most disliked) tasks until later. Unfortunately, this can result in never getting to the major tasks (such as writing a term paper or studying for an exam) until it is too late to devote sufficient time. Ask yourself, each day, "What is the most important thing to get done?" Do that task first, then move to the second most important task, and so on.

Third, *break large tasks into smaller parts* that can be completed at specific times (Catambrone, 1998). Important tasks often are too big to complete all at once, so break them down and define each part in terms of a specific but realistic goal (e.g., number of pages to be read or amount of material to be studied). Successfully completing each goal is rewarding, strengthens your study skills, and increases your feelings of mastery.

Studying More Effectively

After planning your study time, use that time most effectively. *Choose a study place where you can concentrate, where there are no distracting influences, and where you do nothing but study*—a quiet library rather than the middle of a cafeteria. In time, you will learn to associate that location with study behaviors and it will become even easier to study there (Watson & Tharp, 1997).

How you study is vital to your academic success. Don't read material passively and hope that it will just soak in. Instead, *use an active approach to learning* (Glaser & Bassok, 1989). For example, when reading a textbook chapter, first look over the chapter outline, which will give you a good idea of the information you are going to be processing. As you read the material, think about how it applies to your life or how it relates to other information that you already know—information that you may have learned or may be learning in other courses, or that you have learned from your personal experiences.

Use Focus Questions to Enhance Active Learning

You can also increase active learning by taking advantage of the Focus Questions that appear in the margins of each chapter of this book. These questions call attention to some of the major concepts and facts you should know. Use these questions to help you anticipate certain points before you read a section, and use them as knowledge checks to test your understanding after you have read each section of the textbook. This will require you to stop and think about the content. Research shows that responding to these types of questions promotes better recall (Moreland et al., 1997; Pauk & Fiore, 2000).

Realize, however, that these questions focus on only a portion of the important material. We could have written many more questions, and just because some sections of a chapter don't have focus questions doesn't mean that they are unimportant or that you can skip the material. In fact, you will learn even more if you supplement our questions by writing questions of your own—especially for sections of the textbook that do not already have a focus question. Answering the focus questions and writing questions of your own will require more effort than passive reading does, but it will result in better learning (Estes & Vaughn, 1985).

Preparing for Tests

Contrary to what many students believe, introductory psychology is not an easy course. In fact, it can be demanding because of the sheer amount of material that is covered and the many new concepts that must be mastered. Many students who take the course are relatively new to college and don't realize that the academic demands of college far exceed those of high school. Moreover, many students are not aware of how hard high achievers actually work. In one study, researchers found that failing students were spending only one third as many hours studying as were A students (who were spending about two hours of active study for every hour spent in class). Yet the failing students *thought* they were studying as much as anyone else in the class, and many wondered why they were not doing as well as their high-achieving peers (Watson & Tharp, 1997).

The strategies we've discussed thus far can help you prepare for tests. First, a written study schedule helps distribute your learning of the material over time, and it helps avoid the need to cram at the last minute. Cramming is less effective because it is fatiguing, taxes your memory, and often increases test anxiety, which in turn interferes with learning and actual test performance (Sarason & Sarason, 1990). The ideal situation as you near an exam is to have a solid familiarity with the material through previous study and to use the time before the test to refine your knowledge. Second, the focus-question approach can pay big dividends in the final days before an exam.

Test-Taking Strategies

Some students are more effective test-takers than others. They know how to approach different types of tests (e.g., multiple-choice or essay) to maximize their performance. Such skills are called *testwiseness* (Fagley, 1987). Here are some strategies that testwise students use:

- Use time wisely. Check your progress occasionally during the test. Answer the questions you know first (and, on essay exams, the ones worth the most points). Do not get bogged down on a question you find difficult. Mark it and come back to it later.
- On essay exams, organize your answer before you begin writing. Outline the points you want to make, and try to cover the key points in enough detail to communicate what you know.
- On multiple-choice items, read each question and then try to answer it before reading the answer options. If you then find your answer among the alternatives, that alternative is probably the correct one. Nonetheless, read all the other alternatives to make sure that you chose the best one.

- Many students believe that they should not change answers on multiple-choice tests because the first guess is most likely to be correct. Research shows, however, that this belief is false (Benjamin et al., 1984). As you can see in Figure 1.26, changing an answer is far more likely to result in a wrong answer becoming a correct one than vice versa. One study found that, on average, three points are gained for each point lost because of changing answers (Geiger, 1991). Therefore don't be reluctant to change an answer if you are fairly sure that the alternative is better.
- Some multiple-choice questions have "all of the above" as an alternative. If one of the other answers is clearly incorrect, eliminate the "all of the above" option; if you are sure at least two of the other answers are correct but are not sure about the third, choose "all of the above."

Time management, study skills, test-preparation strategies, and testwiseness are not acquired overnight; they require effort and practice. Look ahead to the "Applying Psychological Science" features in the following chapters; they discuss additional principles that may help you enhance your academic performance:

Chapter 6: using operant principles to modify your behavior

Chapter 7: improving memory

Chapter 11: setting goals

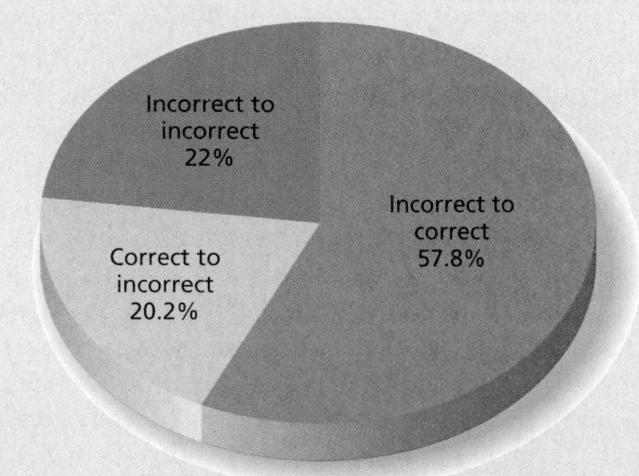

FIGURE 1.26

The combined results of 20 studies show that changing one's answers on multiple-choice examinations more often results in a correct answer. SOURCE: Based on Benjamin et al., 1984.

IN REVIEW

- *Psychologists specialize in numerous subfields and work in many settings. Their professional activities include teaching, research, clinical work, and application of psychological principles to solve personal and social problems.*
- *Psychologists today conduct research and provide services around the globe.*
- *You can use principles derived from psychological science to enhance your learning and increase your likelihood of performing well on tests. These include time management principles, strategies for studying more effectively, test-preparation strategies, and techniques for taking tests.*

▶ 18. Describe scientifically based strategies that can enhance students' learning and academic performance.

KEY TERMS AND CONCEPTS

Each term has been boldfaced and defined in the chapter on the page indicated in parentheses.

applied research (p. 3)
artificial intelligence (AI; p. 13)
basic research (p. 3)
behavior genetics (p. 16)
behavioral neuroscience (p. 16)
behavioral perspective (p. 9)
behaviorism (p. 10)
biological perspective (p. 16)
British empiricism (p. 7)
cognitive behaviorism (p. 11)
cognitive neuroscience (p. 13)
cognitive perspective (p. 12)
collectivism (p. 14)
cultural psychology (p. 14)
culture (p. 14)
defense mechanisms (p. 9)
evolutionary psychology (p. 17)
functionalism (p. 8)
Gestalt psychology (p. 12)
humanistic perspective (humanism; p. 11)
individualism (p. 14)
interaction (p. 21)
mind-body dualism (p. 7)
monism (p. 7)
natural selection (p. 17)
neurotransmitters (p. 16)
norms (p. 14)
positive psychology movement (p. 12)
psychoanalysis (p. 8)
psychodynamic perspective (p. 8)
psychology (p. 3)
social constructivism (p. 13)
socialization (p. 14)
sociocultural perspective (p. 14)
structuralism (p. 8)

What Do You Think?

THE CASE OF VOODOO DEATH p. 6

According to Cannon's hypothesis, the woman's belief in voodoo and knowledge that she had been "cursed" caused her to experience persistent, excessive stress. She became increasingly terrified as her 23rd birthday neared, and her stress response eventually triggered a fatal drop in blood pressure, producing shock and causing death.

Does this explanation seem reasonable to you? In forming your answer, one issue to consider is whether any good evidence supports Cannon's explanation. Cannon's research with animals suggested that a persistent, intense stress response could cause death in a way that would not be easily detectable upon autopsy, and more recent psychological and medical research points to negative effects that stress (caused by fear, worry, or other factors) can have on bodily functioning. However, we also need to consider other possible explanations for the woman's death.

First, in many cases, even ones that Cannon described, voodoo victims refuse all food and drink after they have been cursed, and prolonged severe dehydration may have caused their death (Barber, 1961). However, in other documented cases, food and drink restriction can be ruled out. Had the woman in our example been severely dehydrated, it seems unlikely that the hospital medical staff would have failed to notice this.

Second, voodoo victims often seem to "surrender" psychologically; they feel helpless and hopeless, believing that there is no place to hide from impending death (Cohen, 1985). Some scientists argue that this hopelessness increases victims' susceptibility to disease (especially if they refuse food and drink), which then leads to death (Lester, 1972). Others propose that this hopelessness has a more direct physiological effect, triggering bodily responses that eventually decrease one's heart rate and cause death (Richter, 1957). Realize that all of these explanations, although different from Cannon's, still support the more general point that psychological beliefs can trigger responses that—one way or another—impair health.

Finally, even without the voodoo curse, perhaps the woman would have died that night anyway. Sudden death at such a young age is rare, and the timing would have been an amazing coincidence, but we can't completely rule out the possibility that the woman suffered from a life-threatening medical condition that the physicians did not detect when performing the autopsy.

In our opinion, Cannon's explanation seems plausible, but as a critical thinker, you should keep the bottom line in mind: We can't say for sure why the woman died. For obvious ethical reasons, researchers don't expose people to voodoo curses in controlled experiments to carefully examine whether and how they die! Instead, scientists obtain clues from natural cases of voodoo death and from research on stress and mind-body interactions and then try to formulate the most plausible explanation. ■

ARE THE STUDENTS LAZY? p. 11

It may be tempting to blame the students' unresponsiveness on laziness, but a radical behaviorist would not focus on internal mental states to explain their inaction. First, to say that students are unresponsive *because* they're lazy doesn't explain anything. Consider this reasoning: How do we know that the students are lazy? Answer: because they are unresponsive. Therefore, if we say that students are lazy because they're unresponsive and then turn around and conclude that "students are unresponsive because they are lazy," all we are really saying is that "Students are unresponsive because they are unresponsive." This is not an explanation at all but rather an example of circular reasoning.

From a behavioral perspective, people's actions are shaped by the environment and learning experiences. Put yourself in the hypothetical role of the high school teacher: You may not realize it, but when you are lecturing you stop and glare at anyone who whispers to a neighbor. You pointedly ignore students who raise their hands to ask questions. When students sit quietly, you smile and seem more relaxed. When students do participate in class discussions, you are quick to criticize their ideas. In these ways you may have taught your students to behave passively.

To change their behavior, you need to modify their educational environment so that they will learn new responses. In particular, reward the behaviors that you want to see (raising hands and correctly answering questions, expressing interest in the material, and so on). For example, praise students not only for giving correct answers but also for participating. If a student's answer is incorrect or a comment is tangential, point this out in a nonpunitive way while still reinforcing the student's participation.

Modifying the environment to change behavior is often not as easy as it sounds, but this example illustrates one way a behaviorist might try to rearrange the environmental consequences rather than jump to the conclusion that the situation is hopeless. ■

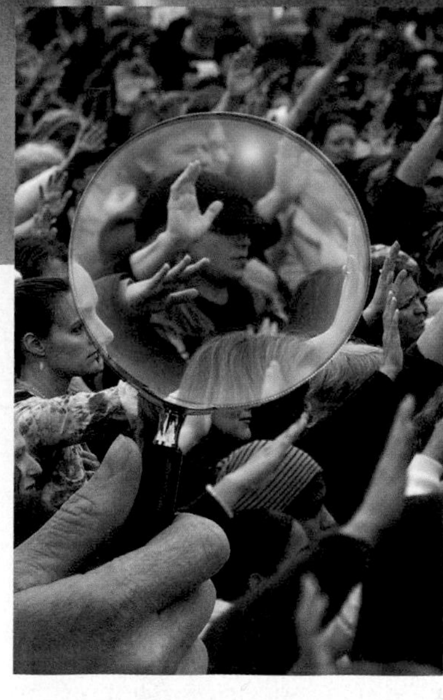

2

STUDYING BEHAVIOR SCIENTIFICALLY

CHAPTER OUTLINE

I have no special talents. I am only passionately curious.

—Albert Einstein

Winter was around the corner, and Teryl's Sunday morning drive to Oregon City was about to take an unexpected twist. The pickup truck in front of her hit a slick spot, veered off the road, and went over the edge. Teryl, who has paralyzed legs and only partial use of her arms, stopped her minivan, lowered herself into her wheelchair, and headed to the crash site. She then got out of her wheelchair, slid down the wet embankment, crawled to reach the bleeding, dazed driver, and administered first aid until the paramedics arrived. Said Teryl, "I think anybody would have done that. You see a car go down a ditch, and I can't imagine not stopping to help" (Seattle Times, *December 11, 1997). Yet three decades earlier, the unimaginable had occurred.*

■■■

In March of 1964 a young woman named Kitty Genovese was stabbed repeatedly and raped by a knife-wielding assailant as she returned from work to her New York City apartment at about 3 A.M. The attack lasted about 30 minutes, during which time her screams and pleas for help were heard by at least 38 of her neighbors. Many went to their windows to find out what was happening. Yet nobody assisted her, and by the time anyone called the police, she had died. The incident drew international attention from a shocked public, and commentators expressed outrage over "bystander apathy" and people's refusal to "get involved."

Science frequently has all the mystery and drama of a detective story. Consider the psychological puzzle of bystander intervention. If you were in an emergency and needed help from bystanders, would you receive it? Indeed, ordinary citizens like Teryl often take decisive action to help someone in need. But, as the Kitty Genovese murder (Figure 2.1) and similar tragedies illustrate, people do not always come to another's aid (Figure 2.2). Why do bystanders sometimes risk injury and death to assist a complete stranger, yet at other times fail to intervene—even when providing help or calling the police entails little personal risk? We will return to this puzzle shortly.

In this chapter we explore principles and methods that form the foundation of psychological science. These scientific principles also form the basis for a way of thinking—critical thinking—that can serve you well in many aspects of your life.

▶ 1. Describe three key scientific attitudes and how they guided Darley and Latané's response to the Genovese murder.

SCIENTIFIC PRINCIPLES IN PSYCHOLOGY

Science is about discovery. At its core, science is an approach to asking and answering questions about the universe around us (Klahr & Simon, 2001). Certainly, there are other ways we learn about our world and ourselves: through philosophy, reason, and logic; religious faith and spirituality; art, music, and literature; the teachings of family, friends, and others; and intuition and everyday common sense. What distinguishes science from these approaches is a general process guided by certain principles.

Scientific Attitudes

Curiosity, skepticism, and open-mindedness are driving forces behind scientific inquiry. Like a child who constantly asks "Why?" the good

FIGURE 2.1

Catherine ("Kitty") Genovese, a 28-year-old bar manager, was raped and murdered outside her New York City apartment building in 1964 when she came home from work at about 3 A.M. The attack lasted half an hour, and although 38 of her neighbors heard her screams, no one intervened or called the police until it was too late.

scientist has an insatiable curiosity. And like a master detective, the good scientist is an incurable skeptic. Each claim is met with the reply, "Show me your evidence." Even when a mystery appears to be solved, the good scientist asks, "Might there be another—maybe better—explanation?" Scientists also must remain open-minded to conclusions that are supported by facts, even if those conclusions refute their own beliefs.

Following the Kitty Genovese murder, two psychology professors in New York City, John Darley of New York University and Bibb Latané of Columbia University, met for dinner. Like everyone else, they wondered how 38 people could witness a violent crime and not even call the police. Their curiosity, however, was so strong that they decided to investigate further. Darley and Latané were skeptical of the "bystander apathy" explanation offered by social commentators; they believed it was unlikely that every one of the 38 bystanders could have been apathetic. As social psychologists, they understood that the immediate social environment powerfully influences behavior, even though people may be unaware of this influence. They noted that the bystanders could see that other neighbors had turned on their lights and were looking out their windows. Each bystander might have been concerned about Kitty Genovese's plight but assumed that someone else surely would help or call the police.

Darley and Latané reasoned that the presence of multiple bystanders produced a *diffusion of responsibility*, a psychological state in which each person feels decreased personal responsibility for

FIGURE 2.2

What determines whether a bystander will help a victim? (left) In Greece, as a rapidly advancing fire engulfs everything in its path, a woman risks her life to help an elderly man who has trouble walking. (right) In 1995, an enraged 19-year-old whose car had been hit by Deletha Word's caught up to her on a Detroit-area bridge. He smashed her car windows, dragged her out, ripped off most of her clothes, and beat her. As in the Kitty Genovese murder, none of the 40 bystanders intervened during this half-hour incident. Overcome with terror, Word escaped, jumped off the bridge, and drowned. Here at the bridge, Word's mother and loved ones mourn her death.

intervening. They performed several experiments to test their explanation but had to remain open-minded to the possibility that the findings would not support their point of view.

Gathering Evidence: Steps in the Scientific Process

▶ 2. Use Darley and Latané's research or another study to illustrate six major steps in the scientific process.

Science involves a continuous interplay between observing and explaining events. Figure 2.3 shows how the gathering of scientific evidence often proceeds. Curiosity sparks the first step: Scientists observe something noteworthy and ask a question about it. For Darley and Latané, the initial observation was that nobody helped Kitty Genovese, and the question became "Why?"

At the second step, scientists examine whether any studies, theories, and other information already exist that might help answer their question, and then they formulate a tentative explanation. Noting that many bystanders had been present and that each one probably knew that others were witnessing Genovese's plight, Darley and Latané combined these clues to arrive at a possible explanation: A diffusion of responsibility reduced the likelihood that any one bystander would feel responsible for helping. This tentative explanation is then translated into a **hypothesis:** *a specific prediction about some phenomenon* that often takes the form of an "If-Then" statement: "In an emergency, IF multiple bystanders are present, THEN the likelihood that any one bystander will intervene is reduced."

The third step is to test the hypothesis by conducting research. Darley and Latané (1968) staged an "emergency" in their experimental laboratory and observed people's responses. The participants were undergraduates who were told that they would be discussing "personal problems faced by normal college students." They were informed that to ensure privacy, they would be seated in separate rooms, communicate through an intercom system, and the experimenter would not listen to their conversation. Participants would take turns speaking for several rounds. In each round, a participant would have two minutes to speak, during which time the others would be unable to interrupt or be heard, because their microphones would be turned off.

As the discussion began over the intercom, a speaker described his difficulties adjusting to college life and disclosed that he suffered from seizures. During the next round of conversation, this same speaker began to gasp and stammer, saying: " '. . . Could somebody-er-er—help . . . [choking sounds] . . . I'm gonna die-er-er—I'm gonna die-er—help . . . seizure' [chokes, then silence]" (Darley & Latané, 1968, p. 379).

Unbeknownst to the participants, they were actually listening to a tape recording. This ensured that all of them were exposed to the identical "emergency." To test how the number of bystanders influences helping, Darley and Latané manipulated the number of other people that each participant believed to be present and listening over the intercom. The participants were assigned to one of three conditions on a random basis: In the first condition, participants were told that they were alone with the victim; in the second condition, participants were led to believe there was another listener present; in the third condition, they believed that four other listeners were present. The participants believed that the seizure was real and serious. But did they help?

At the fourth step of scientific inquiry, researchers analyze the information (called *data*) they collect and draw tentative conclusions. As

STEPS IN THE SCIENTIFIC PROCESS

1. Initial Observation or Question

Kitty Genovese incident. Why did no one help?

2. Gather Information and Form Hypothesis

A diffusion of responsibility may have occurred. Hypothesis: IF multiple bystanders are present, THEN each bystander's likelihood of intervening will decrease.

3. Test Hypothesis (Conduct Research)

- Create "emergency" in controlled setting.
- Manipulate perceived number of bystanders.
- Measure helping.

4. Analyze Data

Helping decreases as the perceived number of bystanders increases. The hypothesis is supported. (If data do not support the hypothesis, revise and retest.)

5. Further Research and Theory Building

Additional studies support the hypothesis. A Theory of Social Impact is developed based on these and other findings.

6. New Hypotheses Derived from Theory

The theory is tested directly by deriving new hypotheses and conducting new research.

FIGURE 2.3

This sequence represents one common path to scientific understanding. In other cases, scientists begin with an observation or question, gather background information, and proceed directly to research without testing hypotheses or trying to build theories.

Figure 2.4 shows, Darley and Latané found that 80 percent of the participants who thought they were alone with the victim helped within the first minute of the seizure and that 100 percent helped within three minutes. As the number of presumed bystanders increased, the proportion of actual participants who helped decreased, and those who did help took longer to respond. These findings support the diffusion-of-responsibility explanation and also demonstrate how scientific research can contradict commonsense adages, such as "There's safety in numbers." As you will see throughout this book, many commonsense beliefs have not survived the cutting edge of psychological research.

At the fifth step, the process of inquiry continues as scientists conduct more research. As additional evidence comes in, scientists attempt to build theories. A **theory** *is a set of formal statements that explains how and why certain events are related to one another.* Theories are broader than hypotheses. For example, dozens of additional experiments revealed that diffusion of responsibility occurred across a range of situations. Latané then combined the principle of diffusion of responsibility with other principles of group behavior to develop a broader *theory of social impact*, which he and others have since used to explain a variety of human social behaviors (Latané & Bourgeois, 2001).

Finally, at the sixth step, scientists use the theory to develop new hypotheses, which are then tested by conducting additional research and gathering new evidence. In this manner the scientific process becomes self-correcting. If research consistently supports the hypotheses derived from the theory, our confidence in the theory becomes stronger. If the predictions made by the theory are not supported, then it will need to be modified or, ultimately, discarded.

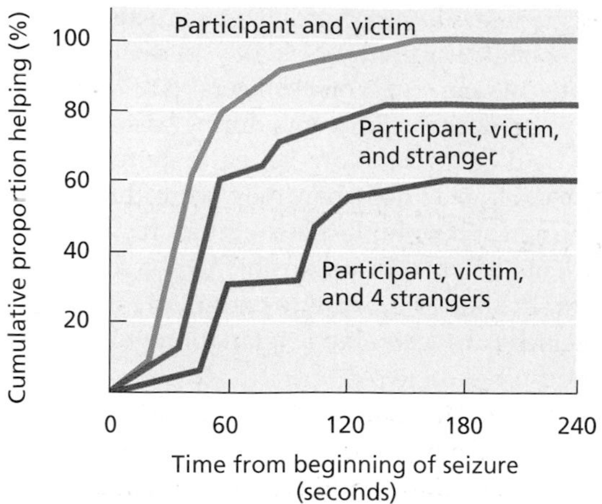

FIGURE 2.4

Some participants believed that they were alone with a student who presumably was having a seizure. Others believed that either one or four more bystanders were present. Participants who believed they were alone with the victim were more likely to intervene and did so more quickly. SOURCE: Adapted from Darley & Latané, 1968.

Two Approaches to Understanding Behavior

Humans have a strong desire to understand why things happen. Why do scientists favor the preceding step-by-step approach to understanding behavior over the approach typically involved in everyday common sense: hindsight, or after-the-fact, understanding?

Hindsight (After-the-Fact Understanding)

Many people erroneously believe that psychology is nothing more than common sense. "I knew that all along!" or "They had to do a study to find that out?" are common responses to findings from psychological research. For example, decades ago a *New York Times* book reviewer leveled criticism against a report titled *The American Soldier* (Stouffer et al., 1949a, 1949b), which summarized the results of a large-scale study of the goals, attitudes, and behavior of U.S. soldiers during World War II. The reviewer blasted the government for spending a lot of money to "tell us nothing we don't already know."

Consider the following statements. How would you account for each of them?

1. The motivation to become officers was higher among White soldiers than among Black soldiers.
2. During basic training, soldiers from rural backgrounds had higher morale and adapted better than soldiers from large cities.
3. Soldiers serving in Europe were more highly motivated to return home while the fighting was going on than they were after the war had ended.

You should have no difficulty arriving at psychological explanations for these results. A typical line of reasoning might go something like this: (1) Because of widespread prejudice, Black soldiers knew that their chances of becoming officers were remote. Why should they torment themselves wanting something that was unattainable? (2) It makes sense that the rigors of basic training would be more tolerable for people from farm settings, who were used to working hard and getting up at the crack of dawn. (3) Who in his right mind would not want to go home while bullets were flying and people were dying?

Did your explanations resemble these? If so, they are perfectly reasonable. There is one catch, however. The results of the actual study were the

▶ 3. Explain the major drawback of hindsight understanding. What approach to understanding do scientists prefer? Why?

exact *opposite* of the preceding statements. In fact, Black soldiers were more highly motivated than White soldiers to become officers; city boys had higher morale than farm boys during basic training; and soldiers were more eager to return home after the war ended than they were during the fighting. When told these actual results, our students quickly find plausible explanations for them. In short, it is easy to arrive at completely reasonable after-the-fact explanations for almost any result.

In everyday life, hindsight, or after-the-fact, explanation is probably our most common method of trying to understand behavior. In the words of the Danish philosopher Søren Kierkegaard, "Life is lived forwards, but understood backwards." The major limitation of relying solely on hindsight is that past events usually can be explained in many ways, and there is no sure way to determine which—if any—of the explanations is correct. But despite this drawback, after-the-fact understanding can provide valuable insights and is often the foundation on which further scientific inquiry is built. For example, Darley and Latané's diffusion-of-responsibility explanation was initially based on after-the-fact reasoning about the Kitty Genovese murder.

What Do You Think?

I KNEW IT ALL ALONG

Typically, when it comes to romantic partners, do "birds of a feather flock together" or do "opposites attract"? With *The American Soldier* exercise as a model, how might you use these contradictory commonsense adages to demonstrate the way people tend to use "I knew it all along" reasoning? Think about it, then see page 60.

Understanding Through Prediction, Control, and Theory Building

▶ 4. Describe some characteristics of a good theory.

Whenever possible, scientists prefer to test their understanding of "what causes what" more directly. If we truly understand the causes of a given behavior, then we should be able to predict the conditions under which that behavior will occur in the future. Furthermore, if we can control those conditions (e.g., in the laboratory), then we should be able to produce that behavior.

▶ 5. Why are operational definitions important? Identify four major ways to measure behavior and a limitation of each.

Darley and Latané's research illustrates this approach. They predicted that, due to a diffusion of responsibility, the presence of multiple bystanders during an emergency would reduce individual helping. Next, they carefully staged an emergency and controlled participants' beliefs about the number of bystanders present. Their prediction was supported. Understanding through prediction and control is a scientific alternative to after-the-fact understanding.

Theory building is the strongest test of scientific understanding, because good theories generate an integrated network of predictions. A good theory has several important characteristics.

- It incorporates existing facts and observations within a single broad framework; that is, it organizes information in a meaningful way.
- It is testable. It generates new hypotheses—new specific predictions—whose accuracy or inaccuracy can be evaluated by gathering new evidence (Figure 2.5).
- The predictions made by the theory are supported by the findings of new research.
- It conforms to the *law of parsimony:* If two theories can explain and predict the same phenomena equally well, the simpler theory is the preferred one.

Even when a theory is supported by many successful predictions, it is never regarded as an absolute truth. It is always possible that some future observation will contradict it or that a newer and more accurate theory will take its place. If this happens, scientists do not wring their hands in despair. Disproving established theories frequently opens up exciting new frontiers for investigation. The displacement of old beliefs and theoretical frameworks by new ones is the essence of scientific progress.

Finally, although scientists use prediction as a test of "understanding," this does not mean that prediction requires understanding. Based on experience, even a child can predict that thunder will follow lightning without knowing why it does so. But prediction based on understanding (i.e., theory building) has important advantages: It satisfies our curiosity, increases knowledge, and generates principles that can be applied to new situations that we have not yet directly experienced.

Defining and Measuring Variables

Psychologists study variables and the relations among them. A **variable**, quite simply, *is any characteristic or factor that can vary.* Gender is a variable: Some people are female, others male. People's age, grade point average, and typing speed

"IT MAY VERY WELL BRING ABOUT IMMORTALITY, BUT IT WILL TAKE FOREVER TO TEST IT."

FIGURE 2.5

Is the scientist's claim of discovering an "eternal life potion" a testable hypothesis? Yes, because it is possible to show the hypothesis to be false. If people drink it but still die at some point, then we have refuted the hypothesis. Therefore it is testable. It is, however, impossible to absolutely prove true. If a person drinks the potion, then no matter how long she or he lives—a thousand, million, or billion years—she or he might still die the next day. Thus, we cannot prove that the potion can make you live forever. © 2004 by Sidney Harris.

are variables, as are concepts such as intelligence, stress, and motivation. Because any particular variable (such as stress or intelligence) may mean different things to different people, it is important for scientists to define their terms clearly. When conducting research, scientists do this by defining their concepts operationally. An **operational definition** *defines a variable in terms of the specific procedures used to produce or measure it.* In essence, operational definitions translate an abstract term into something observable and measurable.

For example, as you may know all too well, taking exams can be stressful. Suppose we want to study the relation between stress and academic performance among college students. How shall we operationally define our concepts? "Academic performance" could mean a single test score, a course grade, or one's overall grade point average. So, for this particular study, let's define academic performance as students' final exam scores in an introductory chemistry course. As for "stress," before or during the exam we could measure students' level of muscle tension or stress hormones, or we could have them complete a questionnaire rating how worried they feel. During the test we might observe their frequency of nail biting and foot tapping. We also could define stress in terms of environmental conditions, such as whether the exam is easy or difficult or whether there is ample or too little time to complete it. Figure 2.6 summarizes how we might operationally define stress at biological, psychological, and environmental levels.

To define a concept operationally, we must be able to measure it. Measurement is challenging because psychologists study incredibly varied and complex processes. Some processes are directly observable, but others are not. Fortunately, psychologists have numerous measurement techniques at their disposal (Figure 2.7).

Self-Reports and Reports by Others

Self-report measures ask people to report on their own knowledge, attitudes, feelings, experiences, or behavior. This information can be gathered in

FIGURE 2.6

Understanding Behavior: When studying the effects of exam stress on academic performance, the concept of "exam stress" can be operationally defined at the biological, psychological, and environmental levels of analysis.

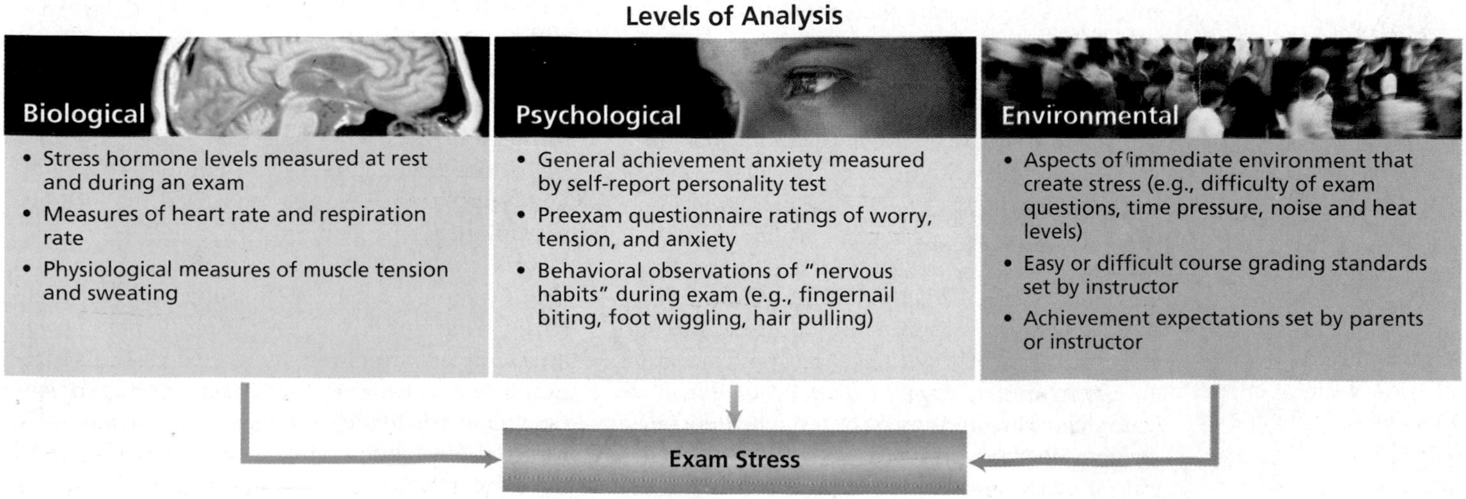

Levels of Analysis

Biological
- Stress hormone levels measured at rest and during an exam
- Measures of heart rate and respiration rate
- Physiological measures of muscle tension and sweating

Psychological
- General achievement anxiety measured by self-report personality test
- Preexam questionnaire ratings of worry, tension, and anxiety
- Behavioral observations of "nervous habits" during exam (e.g., fingernail biting, foot wiggling, hair pulling)

Environmental
- Aspects of immediate environment that create stress (e.g., difficulty of exam questions, time pressure, noise and heat levels)
- Easy or difficult course grading standards set by instructor
- Achievement expectations set by parents or instructor

Exam Stress

(a)

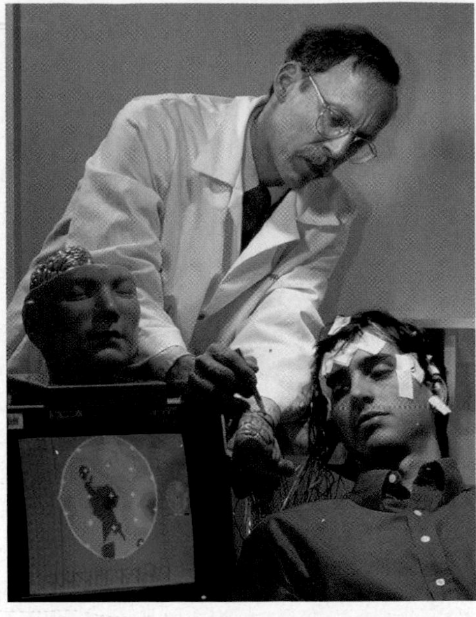

(b)

(c)

FIGURE 2.7

(a) Self-report, (b) physiological, and (c) behavioral measures are important scientific tools for psychologists.

several ways, such as through interviews or questionnaires. The accuracy of self-report measures hinges on people's ability and willingness to respond honestly. Especially when research questions focus on sensitive topics, such as sexual habits or drug use, participants' self-reports may be distorted by a *social desirability bias:* the tendency to respond in a socially acceptable manner rather than according to how one truly feels or behaves. Researchers try to minimize this bias by establishing rapport with participants and allowing them to respond confidentially or anonymously. Questionnaires can also be designed to reduce social desirability bias (Nederhof, 1985).

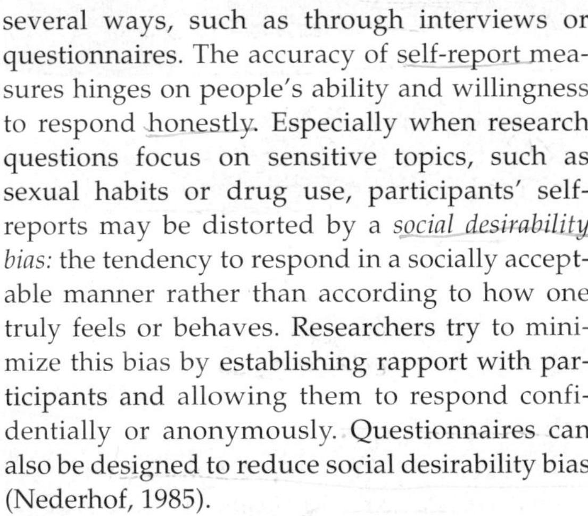

For more on self-report bias in surveys, see Interactive Segment 2.1.

We also can get important information about someone's behavior by obtaining *reports made by other people,* such as parents, spouses, and teachers who know the person. College students might be asked to rate their roommates' personality traits, and job supervisors might be asked to rate a worker's competence and motivation. As with self-reports, researchers try to maximize participants' honesty in reporting about other people.

Observations of Behavior

Another measurement approach is to *observe and record overt* (i.e., directly visible) *behavior.* In an animal learning experiment, we might measure how often a rat follows the correct path in a maze. In Darley and Latané's (1968) bystander emergency experiment, they recorded whether college students helped a seizure victim. Psychologists also develop *coding systems* to record different categories of behavior. Thus, if we observe how a parent behaves while a child tries to perform a task, we might code each instance of parental behavior into categories such as "praises child," "assists child," "criticizes child," "ignores child," and so forth. Once a coding system is developed, observers are rigorously trained to use it properly so that their measurements will be *reliable* (i.e., consistent). If two observers watching the same behaviors repeatedly disagree in their coding (e.g., one says the parent "praised" and another says the parent "assisted"), then the data are unreliable and of little use.

Humans and other animals may behave differently when they know they are being observed. To counter this problem, researchers in natural environments may camouflage themselves or use *unobtrusive measures,* which record behavior in a way that keeps participants unaware that they are being observed (Lee, 2000; Webb et al., 1966). For example, researchers from the Centers for Disease Control assessed the effects of a "safer sex" program by counting the number of used condoms that turned up in a Baltimore sewage treatment plant before and after the program. (No one promised that science would always be glamorous.)

Psychologists sometimes gather information about people's behavior by using **archival measures,** *which are records or documents that already exist.* For example, researchers assessing a program to reduce drunk driving could examine police records to measure how many people were arrested for driving while intoxicated before and after the program was implemented.

Psychological Tests

Psychologists develop and use specialized tests to measure many types of variables. For example, *personality tests,* which assess people's personality traits, often contain series of questions that ask how a person typically feels or behaves (e.g., "True or False: I prefer to spend time by myself rather than in large social gatherings."). In essence, such tests are a specialized type of self-report measure. In contrast, other personality tests present a series of ambiguous stimuli (e.g., pictures that could have different meanings), and personality traits are judged based on how a person interprets these stimuli.

Other psychological tests consist of performance tasks. For example, *intelligence tests* may ask people to assemble objects, arrange sequences of pictures, or solve arithmetic problems. *Neuropsychological tests* help diagnose normal and abnormal brain functioning by measuring how well people perform various mental and physical tasks, such as recalling lists of words or manipulating objects (Miller & Rohling, 2001). As you will learn in later chapters, developing a good psychological test takes a tremendous amount of technical work.

Physiological Measures

Although psychologists frequently depend on participants' self-reports to measure subjective experiences, they may also record objective physiological responses to assess what a person is experiencing. Measures of heart rate, blood pressure, respiration rate, hormonal secretions, and electrical and biochemical processes in the brain have long been the mainstay of researchers working within the biological perspective, but these measures have become increasingly important in many other areas of psychology.

Physiological responses can have their own interpretive problems, the main one being that we don't always understand what they mean. For example, if a person shows increased heart rate and brain activity in a particular situation, what emotion or thought is being expressed? The links between specific patterns of physiological activity and particular mental events are far from being completely understood.

In sum, psychologists can measure behavior in many ways, each with advantages and disadvantages. To gain greater confidence in their findings, researchers may use several types of measures within a single study.

IN REVIEW

- *Curiosity, skepticism, and open-mindedness are key scientific attitudes. The scientific process proceeds through several steps: (1) asking questions based on some type of observation; (2) formulating a tentative explanation and a testable hypothesis; (3) conducting research to test the hypothesis; (4) analyzing the data and drawing a tentative conclusion; (5) building a theory; and (6) using the theory to generate new hypotheses, which are tested by more research.*
- *In everyday life we typically use hindsight (after-the-fact understanding) to explain behavior. This approach is flawed because there may be countless possible explanations and no way to ascertain which is correct. Psychologists prefer to test their understanding through prediction, control, and building theories about the causes of behavior.*
- *A good theory organizes known facts, gives rise to additional hypotheses that are testable, is supported by the findings of new research, and is parsimonious.*
- *An operational definition defines a concept or variable in terms of the specific procedures used to produce or measure it.*
- *Psychologists assess behavior by obtaining participants' self-reports, gathering reports from others who know the participants, directly observing behavior, analyzing archival data, recording responses to specialized tests, and measuring physiological responses.*

METHODS OF RESEARCH

Like detectives searching for clues to solve a cas psychologists conduct research to gather eviden about behavior and its causes. The research metho chosen depends on the problem being studied, the investigator's objectives, and ethical principles.

Descriptive Research: Recording Events

▶ 6. Discuss three types of descriptive research, and explain the advantages and disadvantages of each.

The most basic goal of science is to describe phenomena. In psychology, **descriptive research** *seeks to identify how humans and other animals behave, particularly in natural settings.* It provides valuable information about the diversity of behavior, can be

FIGURE 2.8

Many Hmong refugees who escaped the ravages of war in their homeland experienced great stress and guilt when they resettled in North America. This stress, combined with cultural beliefs about angry spirits, may have contributed to the Hmong sudden death syndrome, which eventually claimed more than 40 lives.

used to test hypotheses, and may yield clues about potential cause-effect relations that are later tested experimentally. Case studies, naturalistic observation, and surveys are common descriptive methods.

Case Studies: The Hmong Sudden Death Syndrome

A **case study** *is an in-depth analysis of an individual, group, or event.* By studying a single case in great detail, the researcher typically hopes to discover principles of behavior that hold true for people or situations in general. Data may be gathered through observation, interviews, psychological tests, physiological recordings, or task performance.

One advantage of a case study is that when a rare phenomenon occurs, this method enables scientists to study the phenomenon intensively and collect a large amount of data. A second advantage is that a case study may challenge the validity of a theory or widely held scientific belief. Perhaps the biggest advantage of a case study is that it can be a vibrant source of new ideas that may subsequently be examined using other research methods. Consider the following example.

Vang is a former Hmong (Laotian) soldier who resettled in Chicago in 1980 after escaping the ravages of war in Laos. Vang had traumatic memories of death and destruction, as well as severe guilt about leaving his brothers and sisters behind when he fled with his wife and child (Figure 2.8). The culture shock created by moving from his rural Laotian home to Chicago's urban environment increased Vang's stress. According to a mental health team that reported on Vang's case, he experienced problems almost immediately:

> [He] could not sleep the first night in the apartment, nor the second, nor the third. After three days . . . Vang came to see his resettlement worker . . . Moua Lee. Vang told Moua that the first night he woke suddenly, short of breath, from a dream in which a cat was sitting on his chest. The second night . . . a figure, like a large black dog, came to his bed and sat on his chest . . . and he grew quickly and dangerously short of breath. The third night, a tall, white-skinned female spirit came into his bedroom . . . and lay on top of him. Her weight made it increasingly difficult for him to breathe. . . . He attempted to turn onto his side, but found he was pinned down. After 15 minutes, the spirit left him and he awoke, screaming. (Tobin & Friedman, 1983, p. 440)

Vang's report may not have attracted scientific interest had it not been for one fact: About 25 Laotian refugees in the United States had died of what was termed the "Hmong sudden death syndrome." The cases were strikingly similar to Vang's: A person in good health died in his or her sleep after exhibiting labored breathing, screams, and frantic movements. The U.S. Centers for Disease Control investigated these mysterious deaths. Unable to find a physical cause, the investigators concluded that the deaths were triggered by a combination of psychological factors: the stress of resettlement, guilt stemming from abandoning family in Laos, and the Hmong's cultural beliefs about angry spirits.

The authors of Vang's case study concluded that he might have been a survivor of the sudden death syndrome. The role of cultural beliefs in this syndrome is suggested by what happened next. Vang went for treatment to a Hmong woman regarded as a shaman (a person, acting as both doctor and priest, who is believed to work with spirits and the supernatural). She told him his problems were caused by unhappy spirits and performed the ceremonies needed to release the spirits. Vang encountered no further problems with nightmares or with his breathing during sleep.

Vang's case study—like the case of "voodoo death" described in Chapter 1—suggests that cultural beliefs and stress may have profound effects on physical well-being. This work was followed by other studies of Hmong immigrants in the United States and Canada and stimulated additional interest in the general relation between cultural beliefs and health (Johnson, 2002).

The most important limitation of a case study is that it is a poor method for determining cause-effect relations. Vang's case study cannot prove that the Hmong sudden death syndrome is a fatal stress response produced by cultural beliefs. In most case studies, explanations of behavior occur after the fact and there is little opportunity to rule out alternative explanations. Thus the fact that Vang's symptoms ended after seeing a shaman could have been pure coincidence; some other change in Vang's life could have been responsible.

A second potential drawback concerns the *generalizability* of the findings: Will the principles uncovered in a case study hold true for other people or in other situations? The question of generalizability pertains to all research methods, but drawing broad conclusions from one or several case studies can be particularly risky. The key issue is the degree to which the case under study is representative of other people or situations.

A third drawback of a case study is the possible lack of objectivity in the way the researcher gathers and interprets the data. Although such bias can occur in any type of research, case studies can be particularly worrisome because they are often based largely on the researcher's subjective impressions. In science a skeptical attitude requires that claims based on case studies be followed up by more comprehensive research methods before they are accepted. In everyday life we should adopt a similar skeptical view. When you encounter claims based on case examples or anecdotes, keep in mind that the case may be atypical or that the person making the claim may be biased. Try to seek out other evidence to support or refute the claim.

Naturalistic Observation: Chimpanzees, Tool Use, and Cultural Learning

In **naturalistic observation,** *the researcher observes behavior as it occurs in a natural setting*. Naturalistic observation is used extensively to study animal behavior (Figure 2.9). British researcher Jane Goodall gained worldwide fame for her extensive observations of African chimpanzees in the wild. Goodall (1986) and other researchers have found that chimpanzees display a variety of behaviors, such as making and using tools, that were formerly believed to lie only within the domain of human capabilities.

Swiss researcher Christophe Boesch (1991) has observed a "hammer/anvil" tool-use technique among wild African chimpanzees. A chimp places a nut on a hard surface (the anvil) and then hammers it several times with a stone or a fallen branch until it cracks. Some nuts with hard shells are tricky to open, and it may take several years for chimps to perfect their hammering. Especially fascinating is Boesch's observation that mothers seem to intentionally teach their young how to use this technique. Consider this interaction between a chimp named Ricci and her 5-year-old daughter, Nina:

> Nina . . . tried to open nuts with the only available hammer, which was of an irregular shape. As she struggled unsuccessfully . . . Ricci joined her and Nina immediately gave her the hammer. . . . Ricci, in a very deliberate manner, slowly rotated the hammer into the best position with which to pound the nut effectively. . . . With Nina watching her, she then proceeded to use the hammer to crack 10 nuts . . . then Ricci left and Nina resumed cracking. Now, by adopting the same hammer grip as her mother, she succeeded in opening four nuts in 15 min. . . . In this example the mother corrected an error in her daughter's behaviour. (Boesch, 1991, p. 532)

For evolutionary and cultural psychologists, naturalistic observations of animals can provide important clues about the possible origins of human behavior. As in human cultures, these chimpanzees have developed a unique method for using tools and appear to teach it to their young deliberately. These findings support the view that the mechanisms by which human cultures are formed and maintained—such as the intentional transmission of information across age generations—may have an evolutionary basis (Greenfield, 1997).

FIGURE 2.9

Researcher Jane Goodall uses naturalistic observation to study the behavior of wild chimpanzees.

The excerpt about Ricci and Nina illustrates how naturalistic observation can provide a rich description of behavior. Numerical data, such as the frequency of various behaviors, may be recorded and analyzed. Naturalistic observation is also used to study human behavior. For example, developmental psychologists observe children in natural settings to learn about their cooperative and competitive play, aggression, and problem-solving abilities.

Like case studies, naturalistic observation does not permit clear causal conclusions about the relations between variables. In the real world, many variables simultaneously influence behavior, and they cannot be disentangled with this research technique. There also is the possibility of bias in the way that researchers interpret the behaviors they observe. Finally, researchers must try to avoid influencing the participants being studied. Even the mere presence of a human observer may disrupt a person's or animal's behavior, at least initially. (As time passes, people and other animals typically adapt to and ignore the presence of an observer. This adaptation process is called *habituation*.)

Survey Research: How Well Do You Sleep?

▶ 7. What is random sampling and why do survey researchers use it? What problems can occur when sampling isn't random?

In **survey research,** *information about a topic is obtained by administering questionnaires or interviews to many people*. Survey questions typically ask about participants' attitudes, opinions, and behaviors. For example, do you sometimes have difficulty falling or staying asleep? Have you ever fallen asleep while driving? Are you ever so sleepy during the day that it interferes with your activities? The National Sleep Foundation (2002) recently conducted a nationwide survey of American adults' sleep problems. Almost 60 percent of the participants reported experiencing symptoms of insomnia a few nights or more per week. Astoundingly, 1 out of every 6 admitted to falling asleep while driving, and 37 percent reported that daytime sleepiness interfered with their daily activities at least a few times a month. This survey studied 1,010 Americans, ages 18 and older, who were interviewed by telephone. How is it possible to make an accurate estimate of the sleep problems of almost 200 million adults based on these data?

Two key concepts in survey research are population and sample. A **population** *consists of all the individuals that we are interested in drawing a conclusion about*, such as "American adults" in the sleep survey example. Unfortunately, it is often impractical to study the entire population. Therefore we would administer the survey to a **sample**, *which is a subset of individuals drawn from the larger population.*

To draw valid conclusions about a population from the results of a single survey, the sample must be representative: A **representative sample** *is one that reflects the important characteristics of the population* (Figure 2.10). A sample composed of 80 percent males would not be representative of the student body at a college where only 50 percent of the students are men. To obtain a representative sample, survey researchers typically use a procedure called **random sampling,** *in which every member of the population has an equal probability of being chosen to participate in the survey.* A common variation of this procedure, called *stratified random sampling*, is to divide the population into subgroups based on characteristics such as gender or ethnic identity. Suppose the population is 55 percent female. In this case, 55 percent of the spaces in the sample would be allocated to women and 45 percent to men. Random sampling is then used to select the individual women and men who will be in the survey.

When a representative sample is surveyed, we can be confident (though never completely certain) that the findings closely portray the population as a whole. This is the strongest advantage of survey research. Modern political opinion polls use such excellent sampling procedures that, just prior to elections, they can reasonably predict from a sample of about 1,000 people how a national election is going to turn out.

In contrast, unrepresentative samples can produce distorted results. It is better to have a smaller representative sample than a larger, unrepresentative one. In 1936, a mail survey of almost 2 million voters by *Literary Digest* magazine predicted that Republican presidential candidate Alf Landon would easily defeat Democratic candidate Franklin Roosevelt. When the election took place, Roosevelt won in a landslide!

How could a prediction based on 2 million people be wrong? The answer is that the sample selected for the poll was unrepresentative of the population that voted in the election. The researchers obtained names and addresses from telephone directories, automobile registration lists, and magazine subscription lists. In 1936, most poorer Americans did not have telephones, cars, or magazine subscriptions. Thus the sample underrepresented poorer socioeconomic groups and overrepresented wealthier people. Bad sample. Bad prediction. In sum, always consider the nature of the sample when interpreting survey results.

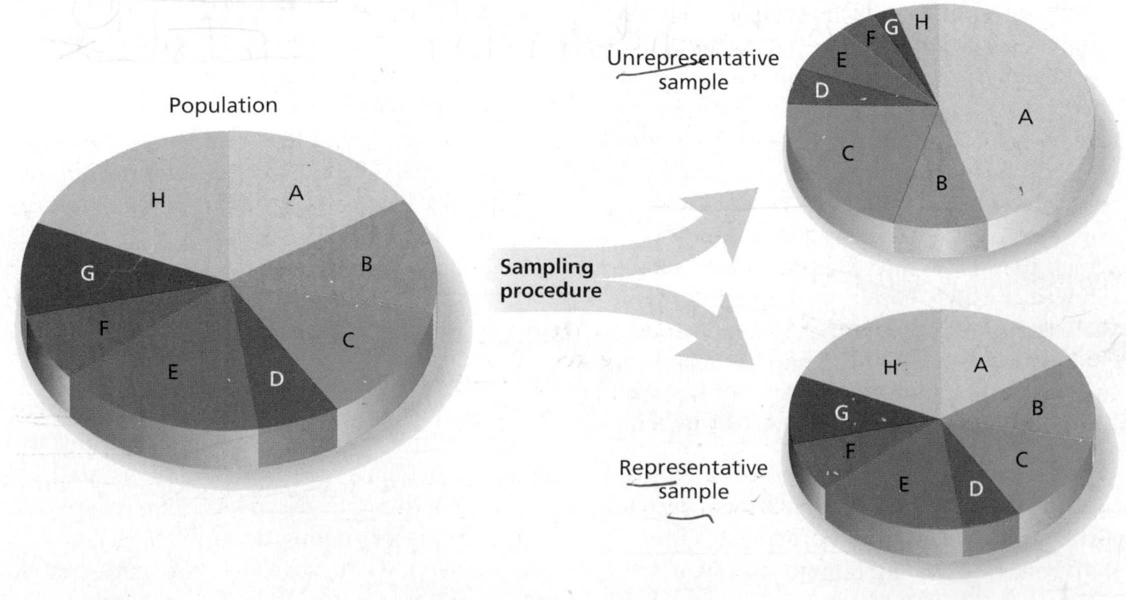

FIGURE 2.10

A representative sample possesses the important characteristics of the population in the same proportions. Data from a representative sample are more likely to generalize to the larger population than are data from an unrepresentative sample.

that represent the participants' responses). In our example, the researcher uses the multiple-choice test to measure whether the amount of learning differs in the noise condition versus the no-noise condition.

3. The researcher *attempts to control extraneous factors that might influence the outcome of the experiment*. For example, we would not want one group to do better because they had easier textbook material or test questions. So all the participants will read the same textbook pages and take the same test. Similarly, the room temperature and lighting will be kept constant, and the researcher will be equally courteous to everyone.

The logic behind this approach is straightforward:

- Start out with equivalent groups of participants.
- Treat them equally in all respects except for the variable that is of particular interest (in this case, noise).
- Isolate this variable and manipulate it (creating the presence or absence of noise).
- Measure how the groups respond (in this case, the amount they learn, as measured by their performance on the test).

If the groups respond differently, then the most likely explanation is that these differences were caused by the manipulated variable (Figure 2.14).

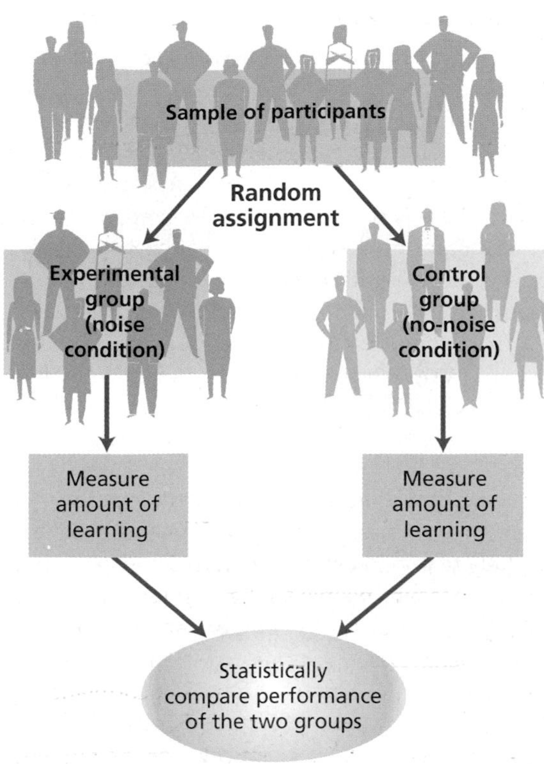

FIGURE 2.14

The logic of designing an experiment. The experimenter manipulates the amount of noise to which participants are exposed, measures their learning, and attempts to treat them equally in every other way. This creates an experimental group and a control group.

Independent and Dependent Variables

The term **independent variable** *refers to the factor that is manipulated by the experimenter*. In our example, noise is the independent variable. The **dependent variable** *is the factor that is measured by the experimenter and may be influenced by the independent variable*. In this experiment, the amount of learning is the dependent variable.

An easy way to keep this distinction clear is to remember that the dependent variable depends on the independent variable. Presumably, students' learning will depend on whether they were in a noisy or quiet room. The independent variable is the cause, and the dependent variable is the effect.

We have described the independent and dependent variables at a general level, but recall that when doing research we must also define our variables operationally. *Noise* could mean many things, from the roar of a jet engine to the annoying drip of a faucet. *Learning* could mean anything from memorizing a list of words to acquiring the skill to ride a bicycle. In our experiment, we could operationally define our independent and dependent variables as follows:

	Independent Variable (cause)	Dependent Variable (effect)
Conceptual Level	Noise	Learning
Operational Level	Recording of street sounds played at 60 decibels for 30 minutes (versus quiet room)	Number of multiple-choice questions, based on five pages of text, answered correctly

▶ 12. What are independent and dependent variables? Experimental and control groups?

Our noise experiment thus far has only one dependent variable, but we could have many. For example, we could measure how quickly participants read the material, their stress during the task, and so on. In this manner, we might gain more knowledge about how people are affected by noise. To test your understanding, think back to the Darley and Latané experiment on bystander helping in an emergency, discussed on pages 32–33. Can you identify the independent and dependent variables? (The answer appears in the margin on page 50.)

Experimental and Control Groups

The terms *experimental group* and *control group* are often used when discussing experiments. An **experimental group** *is the group that receives a* *treatment or an "active" level of the independent variable*. A **control group** *is not exposed to the treatment or receives a zero-level of the independent variable*. The purpose of the control group is to provide a standard of behavior to which our experimental group can be compared. In our experiment, the participants in the noise condition represent the experimental group (or experimental condition), and the participants in the no-noise condition represent the control group (or control condition).

Experiments often include several experimental groups. In our study on noise, we could play the recording of street noise at three different volume levels, creating high-noise, moderate-noise, and low-noise experimental conditions. The no-noise condition would still represent the control group. In some experiments, however, the concept of a control group does not apply. In a taste-test experiment in which participants taste and then rate how much they like Coca-Cola versus Pepsi-Cola, each drink represents an experimental condition, and participants simply make a direct comparison between the two drinks.

Two Basic Ways to Design an Experiment

▶ 13. How and why are random assignment and counterbalancing used to design experiments?

▶ 14. Explain the advantage of manipulating two independent variables in the same experiment? Provide an example.

One common way to design an experiment is to have different participants in each condition. To draw meaningful conclusions, the various groups of participants must be equivalent at the start of the study. For example, suppose that the noise group performs substantially worse on the multiple-choice test than the no-noise group. If the students in the noise group, on average, happened to be poorer readers or more anxious than the students in the no-noise group, then one of these factors—having nothing whatsoever to do with the noise—might have been the reason why they performed more poorly.

To address this issue, researchers typically use **random assignment**, *a procedure in which each participant has an equal likelihood of being assigned to any one group within an experiment*. Thus you would have a 50 percent chance of being in the noise group and a 50 percent chance of being in the no-noise group; that determination would be made randomly. This procedure does not eliminate the fact that participants differ from one another in reading ability, anxiety, or other characteristics. Instead, random assignment is used to balance these differences across the various conditions of the experiment. It increases our confidence that, at the start of an experiment, participants in the various conditions are equivalent overall.

A second way to design experiments is to expose each participant to all the conditions. We could measure how much the same people learn when exposed to noise and when the room is quiet. By doing so, factors such as the participants' reading ability and general anxiety are held constant across the no-noise and noise conditions, and therefore we can rule them out as alternative explanations for any results we obtain. However, this approach creates problems if not used properly.

For one thing, it would make little sense to have our participants read the same textbook pages and take the same multiple-choice questions twice. Instead, we would have to develop two equally difficult reading tasks and have participants perform each task only once. Most important, suppose that every participant was exposed to the no-noise condition first. If they then learned more poorly in the noise condition, what would be the cause? The noise? Perhaps. But it could be that participants were bored or fatigued by the time they performed the second task. A procedure called *counterbalancing* avoids this problem: The order of conditions is varied so that no condition has an overall advantage relative to the others. Half the participants would be exposed to the no-noise condition first and the noise condition second. For the remaining participants this order would be reversed.

Manipulating One Independent Variable: Effects of Environmental Stimulation on Brain Development

In a Miami hospital, a massage therapist gently strokes a tiny premature baby who was exposed to cocaine while in its mother's womb. This procedure is repeated several times each day. Why is the infant receiving this treatment?

The answer partially lies in landmark experiments by physiological psychologist Mark Rosenzweig (1984) and his coworkers at the University of California, Berkeley, who experimentally manipulated the degree of environmental stimulation to which infant rats (called *pups*) were exposed. This independent variable—environmental stimulation—was operationally defined by creating two conditions: an experimental condition in which some pups lived in a stimulating environment containing toys and other pups with whom they could interact, and a control condition in which other pups lived in standard laboratory cages (Figure 2.15). The pups came from several litters, so to create equivalent groups at the outset the researchers randomly assigned some pups from each litter to the enriched and standard environments.

After the rats had lived in these environments for several months, the dependent variable—brain development—was measured. Brain development was operationally defined by several measures, such as the weight of the rats' brains, the size of brain cells, and the concentrations of brain chemicals involved in learning and memory. The rats raised in the enriched environment were superior on each measure and also performed better on learning tasks than did the rats raised in the standard environment.

These experiments sparked a wave of research on how experience affects the brain. Across Canada, Europe, and the United States, researchers found that enriched environments and other types of stimulation, such as physical stroking and touch, enhanced rats' brain development and performance on learning and memory tasks (Meaney et al., 1991).

Developmental psychologist Tiffany Field and other University of Miami researchers have found that, like the rat pups, human infants benefit from special stimulation (Field, 2001). In one experiment, they studied premature infants exposed to cocaine by their mothers' drug use during pregnancy (Wheeden et al., 1993). The researchers manipulated one independent variable, randomly assigning infants either to receive three daily massage sessions for 10 days or to a control group receiving standard care and contact. Results showed that the massaged infants had fewer health complications, less stress, more mature movement patterns, and averaged 28 percent greater weight gain per day (Figure 2.16). Full-term infants and premature infants not exposed to cocaine also benefit from massage, and massaged infants display better development than infants who are simply held and rocked for the same amount of time. Moreover, because massaged premature infants are healthier and can leave the hospital sooner, health-care costs are reduced. Field (2001) estimates that if all premature infants received massage therapy, the national savings would be nearly $5 billion.

Over the past 20 years, this area of research has revolutionized scientists' thinking about the role of experience in brain development. It also demonstrates once again how basic scientific research—including animal experiments—can have important human applications.

Manipulating Two Independent Variables: Effects of Alcohol and Expectations on Sexual Arousal

As noted in Chapter 1, behavior is complex and has multiple causes. To better capture this complexity, researchers often examine several causal factors within a single experiment by manipulating two or more independent variables simultaneously. Researchers can examine the separate influence of each variable on behavior and also determine whether particular combinations of variables produce distinct effects.

Consider the widely held belief that alcohol is a sexual stimulant. Many men and women report that alcohol enhances their sexual arousal, and people who have been drinking are viewed by others as more responsive to sexual advances (George et al., 2000). Why might this be? Perhaps alcohol's chemical properties directly influence sexual arousal. Or maybe the cause is psychological—that is, if people simply believe that alcohol will enhance their sexual arousal, then perhaps this expectation by itself can bring about increased sexual responsiveness.

How can a researcher separate the purely physiological effects of drinking from the psychological ones? The answer emerged in the form of an ingenious experimental procedure developed more than 20 years ago (Rohsenow & Marlatt, 1981). The researchers created two drinks that people could not tell apart by taste: one with tonic water and a squirt of lime juice, the other with vodka added to this mix. Then they designed an experiment with two independent variables. The first independent variable manipulated participants' expectations: They were told either that their drink

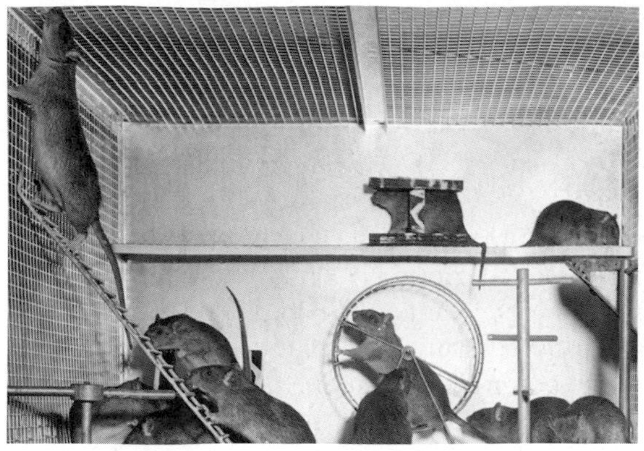

FIGURE 2.15

At birth, rat pups from several litters were randomly assigned to experimental and control groups. This photo illustrates the enriched environment of the experimental group, with toys and playmates. The control group was raised in standard laboratory cages. In this experiment, the difference in the environmental conditions represented the independent variable. Brain development was the main dependent variable.

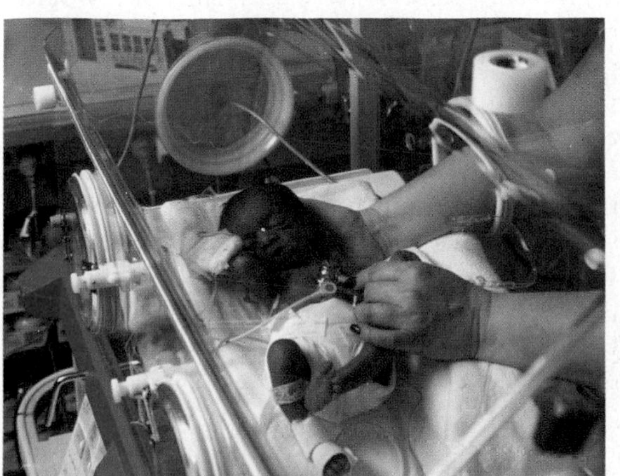

FIGURE 2.16

Experiments by psychologist Tiffany Field and others reveal that massage therapy improves the health and enhances the physical development of premature infants. By shortening their hospital stay, this also reduces medical costs.

contained alcohol or that it didn't. The second independent variable was whether participants received the alcoholic drink or the nonalcoholic drink.

As Figure 2.17a shows, when these two independent variables are combined within the same experiment, four different conditions are created. *Condition 1* is expect alcohol/receive alcohol. This is the normal state of affairs when people drink; they expect that they are drinking alcohol and actually are. Changes in sexual arousal that occur in this condition could reflect either the chemical effects of alcohol, psychological expectations, or a combination of both. *Condition 2* is expect no alcohol/receive alcohol. This condition assesses physiological effects alone. Because participants believe they are not receiving alcohol, changes in sexual arousal would presumably be due to alcohol's chemical effects. *Condition 3* is expect alcohol/receive no alcohol. Because no alcohol is consumed, changes in sexual arousal, if any, would have to be caused by participants' expectations about drinking alcohol. Finally, *Condition 4* is expect no alcohol/receive no alcohol. This condition creates a control group having neither alcohol nor alcohol expectations.

Participants in the four conditions are then shown identical sexually stimulating materials (e.g., slides or films) or are led to anticipate that they will be viewing such materials. The dependent variable, sexual arousal, may be assessed by self-report ratings on questionnaires or by physiological measures.

Most experiments have studied male participants. (In part, this is due to researchers' interest in the issue of alcohol consumption and rape, which overwhelmingly is committed by men. We will discuss the findings with women later in the chapter.) Overall, as Figure 2.17b shows, participants who are led to believe that they have consumed low to moderate doses of alcohol—regardless of whether they actually drink alcohol—feel more aroused and show greater physiological arousal to sexual stimuli than participants who believe that they have consumed only tonic water (Seto & Barbaree, 1995). Among men, *the mere expectation* that one is drinking alcohol also produces more intense sexual fantasies, weaker sexual inhibitions, and poorer judgment in recognizing coercive sexual behavior toward women (Gross et al., 2001).

Thus, at low to moderate doses that produce blood-alcohol levels of about .04 or less, men's expectations and beliefs about alcohol contribute significantly to the enhanced sexual arousal that they experience. But at higher doses, the chemical effects of alcohol take over and decrease—yes, decrease—men's sexual arousal (Kelly, 2001). This occurs because alcohol is a depressant drug; it suppresses neural activity. As blood-alcohol levels increase, men typically take longer to reach orgasm, report that orgasms are less intense and less pleasurable, or may be unable to reach orgasm.

This research illustrates how studying several independent variables simultaneously can help unravel some of the complexity of behavior. It also reinforces one of our main themes: Behavior

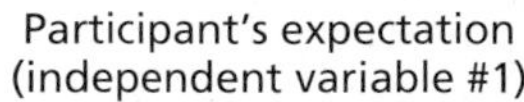

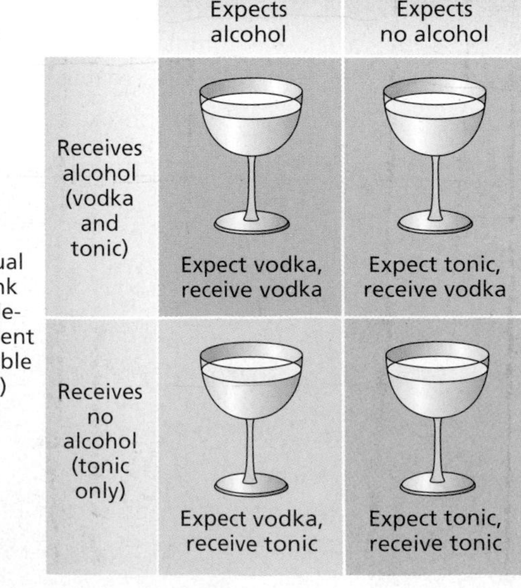

(a)

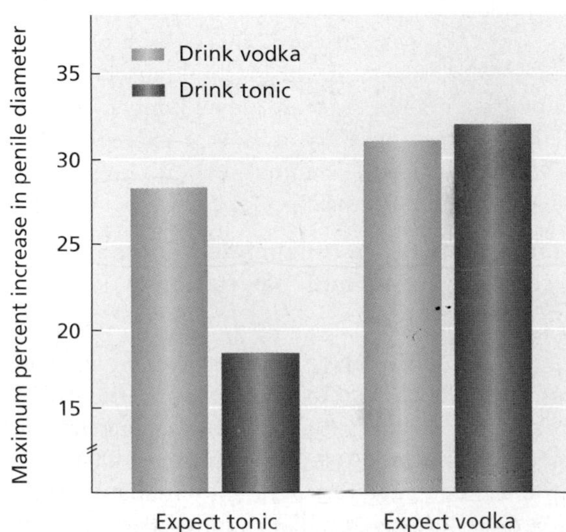

(b)

FIGURE 2.17

(a) Simultaneously manipulating two independent variables—participant's expectation and actual drink content—creates four conditions in this design. (b) In one experiment, male participants in these four conditions were shown sexually explicit films. The dependent variable, sexual arousal, was measured by a device that recorded changes in the size of each man's penis. Regardless of what they actually drank, men who believed they had consumed alcohol showed more sexual arousal than men who believed they had not consumed alcohol. Among men who believed they had consumed alcohol, those who drank only tonic were just as aroused as those who actually drank alcohol. SOURCE: Adapted from Wilson & Lawson, 1976.

(in this case, sexual arousal) results from an interplay of factors that are psychological (beliefs and expectations), environmental (the presence of sexual stimuli), and physiological (chemical effects of alcohol at certain doses).

Table 2.2 summarizes key features of the research methods we have discussed. (Limitations of experiments are discussed in the next section of the text.) Keep in mind that descriptive and correlational studies, though poorly suited for examining cause-effect relations, shine in other ways: They uncover exciting new phenomena, stimulate hypotheses for further research, and examine whether laboratory findings extend to real-world situations. And, like experiments, they are used to test hypotheses and build theories.

TABLE 2.2 An Overview of Research Methods

Method	Primary Features	Main Advantages	Main Disadvantages
Case study	An individual, group, or event is examined in detail, often using several techniques (e.g., observations, interviews, psychological tests).	Provides rich descriptive information, often suggesting hypotheses for further study. Can study rare phenomena in depth.	Poor method for establishing cause-effect relations. The person or event may not be representative. Often relies heavily on the researcher's subjective interpretations.
Naturalistic observation	Behavior is observed in the setting where it naturally occurs.	Can provide detailed information about the nature, frequency, and context of naturally occurring behaviors.	Poor method for establishing cause-effect relations. Observer's presence, if known, may influence participants' behavior.
Survey	Questions or tests are adminstered to a sample drawn from a larger population.	A properly selected, representative sample typically yields accurate information about the broader population.	Unrepresentative samples can provide misleading information about the population. Interviewer bias and social desirability bias can distort the findings.
Correlational study	Variables are measured and the strength of their association is determined. (Naturalistic observation and surveys are often used to examine associations between variables.)	Correlation allows prediction. May help establish how well findings from experiments generalize to more natural settings. Can examine issues that cannot be studied ethically or practically in experiments.	Correlation does not imply causation, due to the bidirectionality problem and third-variable problem
Experiment	Independent variables are manipulated and their effects on dependent variables are measured.	Optimal method for examining cause-effect relations. Ability to control extraneous factors helps rule out alternative explanations.	Confounding of variables, demand characteristics, placebo effects, and experimenter expectancies can threaten the validity of causal conclusions.

IN REVIEW

- *The goal of descriptive research is to identify how organisms behave, particularly in natural settings. Case studies involve the detailed study of a person, group, or event. Case studies often suggest important ideas for further research, but they are a poor method for establishing cause-effect relations.*
- *Naturalistic observation gathers information about behavior in real-life settings. It*

Continued

often yields rich descriptions of behavior and allows the examination of relations between variables. Researchers must be careful to avoid influencing the participants being observed and to interpret their observations objectively.

- *Surveys involve administering questionnaires or interviews to many people. Most surveys study a subset of people (a sample) that is randomly drawn from the larger population of people the researcher is interested in. A major advantage of surveys is that representative samples allow for reasonably accurate estimates of the opinions or behaviors of the entire population. Unrepresentative samples, however, can lead to inaccurate estimates. Survey results also can be distorted by interviewer bias or biases in the way participants report about themselves.*
- *Correlational research measures the relation between naturally occurring variables. A positive correlation means that higher scores on one variable are associated with higher scores on a second variable. A negative correlation occurs when higher scores on one variable are associated with lower scores on a second variable.*
- *Causal conclusions cannot be drawn from correlational data. Variable X may cause Y, Y may cause X, or some third variable (Z) may be the true cause of both X and Y. Nevertheless, if two variables are correlated, then knowing the scores of one variable will help predict the scores of the other.*
- *A well-designed experiment is the best way to examine cause-effect relations. Experiments have three essential characteristics: (1) one or more variables are manipulated; (2) their effects on other variables are measured; and (3) extraneous factors are eliminated or reduced so that cause-effect conclusions can be drawn.*
- *Each variable manipulated by the experimenter is an independent variable. Variables that are measured are dependent variables. The independent variable is viewed as the cause, the dependent variable as the effect. The experimental group receives a treatment or an active level of the independent variable, whereas the control group does not. The behavior of the control group sets a standard against which the behavior of the experimental group can be compared.*
- *In some experiments different participants are randomly assigned to each condition, creating experimental and control groups that are equivalent at the start of the study. In other experiments the same participants are exposed to all the conditions, but the order in which the conditions are presented is counterbalanced.*
- *Researchers often examine several causal factors within a single experiment by simultaneously manipulating two or more independent variables. They examine the separate influence of each variable on behavior and determine whether particular combinations of variables produce distinct effects.*

Answer to Question on page 45

Helping in an emergency. The independent variable in the Darley and Latané experiment was the number of other bystanders presumed to be present (0, 1, or 4). The dependent variables were the percentage of participants who aided the victim and the speed of response.

THREATS TO THE VALIDITY OF RESEARCH

▶ 15. What is internal validity? Why do confounding and demand characteristics decrease internal validity?

Although the experimental approach is a powerful tool for examining causality, researchers must avoid errors that can lead to faulty conclusions. **Internal validity** *represents the degree to which an experiment supports clear causal conclusions*. For example, because Darley and Latané's bystander experiment was conducted carefully and had proper controls, we can be confident that it was the independent variable (i.e., the number of bystanders) that caused the differences in the dependent variable (i.e., whether a bystander helped the victim). Therefore, the experiment had high internal validity. However, if an experiment contains important flaws—such as those we are about to describe—it will have low internal validity because we can no longer be sure what caused the differences in the dependent variable.

Confounding of Variables

Consider a (fictitious) laboratory experiment in which Dr. Starr examines how listening to different types of music influences people's feelings of relaxation. The independent variable is the type of music: new age, country, or rock. Sixty college students participate, with each student randomly assigned to listen to one of the three types of music for 20 minutes. Afterward, the students rate how relaxed they feel on a questionnaire.

Dr. Starr believes that the experiment will be more realistic to the students if the new age music is played at a low volume, the country music at a moderate volume, and the rock music at a loud volume. The results show that students who listened to the new age music felt most relaxed, while those who listened to the rock music felt least relaxed. Dr. Starr concludes that, of the three types of music tested, new age music is the most relaxing.

What is wrong with Dr. Starr's conclusion that the type of music caused the differences in how relaxed students felt? Stated differently, can you identify another major factor that could have produced these results? Perhaps the reason students who listened to new age music felt most relaxed was because their music was played at the lowest, most soothing volume. Had they listened to it at a high volume, maybe they would have felt no more relaxed than the students who listened to the rock music. We now have two variables that, like the strands of a rope, are intertwined: the independent variable (the type of music) that Dr. Starr really was interested in and a second variable (the volume level) that Dr. Starr was not interested in but foolishly did not keep constant.

Confounding of variables *means that two variables are intertwined in such a way that we cannot determine which one has influenced a dependent variable*. In this experiment the volume level of the music would be called a *confound* or a *confounding variable*.

	Group 1	Group 2	Group 3
Independent Variable (type of music)	New age	Country	Rock
Confounding Variable (volume level)	Low	Moderate	High

An essential point to remember is that this confounding of variables prevents Dr. Starr from drawing clear causal conclusions, and therefore it has ruined the internal validity of the experiment. The simplest way to eliminate this problem is keep the volume level constant across the three music conditions.

Demand Characteristics

When we enter unfamiliar situations, it is natural for us to search for clues about how we are expected to act. **Demand characteristics** *are cues that participants pick up about the hypothesis of a study or about how they are supposed to behave* (Orne, 1962). Consider the experiments on alcohol and sexual arousal discussed earlier. In one condition, participants are told that they are drinking alcohol but in reality are given nonalcoholic drinks. Suppose that after a few drinks a participant does not feel intoxicated and concludes that the drinks are nonalcoholic. At this point the researchers' statement that the drinks are alcoholic is a cue—a demand characteristic—that may tip off the participant about the hypothesis being tested ("Hmm, maybe they're trying to see how I behave if I simply believe I'm drinking alcohol.") This damages the internal validity of the experiment because it can distort participants' true responses (Orne, 1962). Most people are eager to be "good participants" and may try to respond in ways that they think the experimenter wants (Figure 2.18).

"WHAT IT COMES DOWN TO IS YOU HAVE TO FIND OUT WHAT REACTION THEY'RE LOOKING FOR, AND YOU GIVE THEM THAT REACTION."

FIGURE 2.18

Demand characteristics provide participants with clues about how they "should" behave during a study. This may cause participants to alter their natural responses, thereby ruining the internal validity of the experiment. © 2004 by Sidney Harris.

Skilled researchers try to anticipate demand characteristics and design studies to avoid them. For example, if careful procedures are used, participants given nonalcoholic drinks can be convinced that they have consumed moderate to high amounts of alcohol (MacDonald et al., 2000).

Placebo Effects

▶ 16. What are placebo effects and experimenter expectancy effects? How can they be minimized?

In medical research, the term **placebo** *refers to a substance that has no pharmacological effect*. In experiments testing the effectiveness of new drugs for treating diseases, one group of patients—the treatment group—receives the actual drug (e.g., through pills or injections). A second group, called a *placebo control group*, only receives a placebo (e.g., pills composed of inactive ingredients or injections

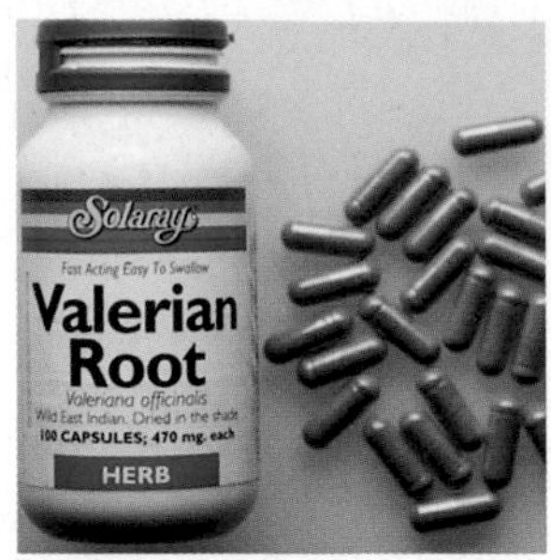

FIGURE 2.19

Throughout history, placebo effects have fostered the commercial success of many products that had no proven physiological benefit. Herbal medicines are one of today's health crazes. Do they really work? If so, is it because of placebo effects or the herbs' chemical properties? The best way to answer this question is through experiments that include placebo control groups.

of saline). Typically, patients who volunteer for this research are told that they will be given either a drug or a placebo, but they are not told which one they are receiving.

The rationale for using placebos is that patients' symptoms may improve solely because they expect that a drug will help them. If 40 percent of patients receiving the actual drug improve but 37 percent of the placebo-control patients show similar improvement, then we have evidence of a **placebo effect:** *People receiving a treatment show a change in behavior because of their expectations, not because the treatment itself had any specific benefit* (Ray, 2000; Figure 2.19).

Placebo effects decrease internal validity by providing an alternative explanation for why responses change after exposure to a treatment. For example, if patients improve after receiving psychotherapy, is this due to the therapy itself, or might it be a placebo effect? By carefully designing experiments to include placebo control conditions, researchers can determine whether behavior change is truly caused by the various interventions or whether a placebo effect might have played a role.

Experimenter Expectancy Effects

▶ 17. Contrast external and internal validity. Why is replication important? Apply these concepts to paranormal claims.

Researchers typically have a strong commitment to the hypothesis they are testing. In psychology, the term **experimenter expectancy effects** *refers to the subtle and unintentional ways researchers influence their participants to respond in a manner that is consistent with the researcher's hypothesis*. Scientists can take several steps to avoid experimenter expectancy effects. For example, researchers who interact with participants in a study or who record participants' responses are often "kept blind to" (i.e., not told about) the hypothesis or the specific condition to which a participant has been assigned. This makes it less likely that these researchers will develop expectations about how participants "should" behave.

The **double-blind procedure,** *in which both the participant and experimenter are kept blind as to which experimental condition the participant is in*, simultaneously minimizes participant placebo effects and experimenter expectancy effects. In research testing drug effects, each participant receives either a real drug or a placebo but does not know which. People who interact with the participants (e.g., those who dispense the drugs or measure participants' symptoms) also are kept unaware of which participants receive the drug or placebo. This procedure minimizes the likelihood that the researchers will behave differently toward the two groups of participants, and it

"IT WAS MORE OF A 'TRIPLE-BLIND' TEST. THE PATIENTS DIDN'T KNOW WHICH ONES WERE GETTING THE REAL DRUG, THE DOCTORS DIDN'T KNOW, AND I'M AFRAID, NOBODY KNEW."

FIGURE 2.20

Although the double-blind technique is a powerful tool for controlling participants' and researchers' expectations, scientists try to avoid the infamous "triple-blind procedure." © 2004 by Sidney Harris.

reduces the chance that participants' own expectations will influence the outcome of the experiment (Figure 2.20).

Replicating and Generalizing the Findings

Let's return to the experiment we designed on noise and learning. Suppose we find that college students learn textbook material more poorly in a noisy room than in a quiet room and that our experiment has high internal validity. Thus we are confident that it is the noise, and not some other factor, that causes poorer learning. There remains, however, another set of questions that we must ask. If this experiment were repeated in other laboratories, would we obtain the same finding? What if the participants were children, or adults not in college? Would noise impair learning in real-world settings? Would the results be the same if we examined other types of noise and learning tasks?

These questions focus on another type of validity: **External validity** *is the degree to which the results of a study can be generalized to other people, settings, and conditions*. Keep in mind that judgments about external validity typically do not focus on the exact responses of the participants. For example, the fact that students in noisy versus quiet rooms correctly answered, say, 48 percent versus 83 percent of the questions is not the issue. Rather, we are concerned about the external validity of the basic underlying principle of behavior: Does noise decrease learning?

Ultimately, to determine the external validity of our findings, either we or other scientists will need to replicate our experiment. **Replication** *is the process of repeating a study to determine whether the original findings can be duplicated.* If our findings are successfully replicated—especially in experiments that study other types of participants (e.g., schoolchildren), noise (e.g., jet airliners flying overhead), and learning tasks (e.g., learning math or how to play a musical instrument)—we become more confident in concluding that noise impairs learning. For example, researchers in Canada, Israel, Japan, and the United States attempted to replicate Darley and Latané's (1968) findings on bystander helping behavior. Some studies took place in subways, liquor stores, Internet chat rooms, and other real-life settings. The number of bystanders varied, and different types of helping behavior were measured. Both women and men were studied. Indeed, the vast majority of experiments replicated the original finding (Latané & Nida, 1981; Markey, 2000).

FIGURE 2.21

Cross-cultural replications help establish the generalizability of psychological principles. Among families in Denver (United States) and Bogota (Colombia), sensitive maternal caregiving was associated with closer emotional bonding by infants (Posada et al., 2002). More research will be needed to examine whether this relation occurs among other cultural groups.

Increasingly, psychologists are paying more attention to *cross-cultural replication.* In some cases, such as the bystander intervention research just mentioned, researchers attempt to replicate an earlier study in a different country or with different cultural groups. In other cases, psychologists attempt to build a cross-cultural replication directly into their research by studying several cultural groups simultaneously. For example, in a collaborative project by psychologists in the United States and Colombia, German Posada and his coworkers (2002) studied interactions between mothers and their infant girls and boys. Middle-class families from Denver and Bogota participated. In both samples, infants showed a closer emotional attachment (i.e., emotional bond) to mothers who were more sensitive and responsive to their baby's needs (Figure 2.21). Because this study was correlational, it does not demonstrate cause-effect relations. (Can you explain why? If you're having trouble, refer back to the causality problems illustrated in Figure 2.11). Nevertheless, replicating the findings across two cultural groups increases our confidence in the generalizability of a *potential* causal association between sensitive caregiving and infant attachment.

When research findings fail to replicate, such failures often lead to important discoveries. For example, we have seen that men's belief that they have consumed a few alcoholic drinks (even if the drinks are nonalcoholic) increases their sexual arousal to explicit sexual materials. But experiments with women yield a different finding. Women's expectation of having consumed a few alcoholic drinks does not increase their sexual responsiveness (Crowe & George, 1989; Norris, 1994). Scientists are still exploring why this gender difference occurs.

In contrast, when new studies consistently fail to replicate the original results of earlier research, this suggests that the original study may have been flawed or that the finding was a fluke. Even so, the scientific process has done its job and prevented us from getting caught in a blind alley. To see why replication is such an important component of the scientific process, let's take a look at *Beneath the Surface* on the next page.

What Do You Think?

WHY DO PEOPLE BELIEVE IN THE PARANORMAL?

Given the lack of clear scientific support for paranormal activity or psychic powers, can you explain why so many people continue to believe in the paranormal? Think about it, then see page 60.

Beneath the Surface

SCIENCE, PSYCHICS, AND THE PARANORMAL

Do you believe—or know of people who believe—in "psychic" phenomena, such as mental telepathy (transmitting thoughts between individuals) and precognition (foretelling the future)? Certainly, self-proclaimed psychics do (Figure 2.22). But surveys in countries around the world, including Brazil, Great Britain, India, New Zealand, Sweden, and the United States, also reveal widespread public belief in the paranormal (Newport & Strausberg, 2001; Zangari & Machado, 1996). Adopting a scientific attitude means we should approach this issue with open-minded skepticism; that is, we should apply rigorous standards of evaluation, as we do to all phenomena (Cardeña et al., 2000). The ability of independent investigators to replicate initial research findings is one of those standards.

Placed under controlled conditions in well-designed experiments and replications, claim after claim of psychic ability has evaporated. Consider claims of *dermo-optical perception (DOP),* which refers to the ability to use the skin (mainly on the forehead) as a visual sensor and therefore to be able to see while blindfolded. Many people who claimed this ability decades ago were discovered to be peeking through their blindfolds, but in 1996, medical researchers from two respected laboratories in Paris seemingly obtained evidence to support the existence of DOP. Yet when a subsequent team of French scientists (including psychologists and physicists) employed more rigorous procedures, they found no evidence of DOP (Benski et al., 1998).

A decade ago, a report in a major scientific journal presented evidence of mental telepathy from 11 studies using the *ganzfeld procedure* (Bem & Honorton, 1994). In this approach, a participant (the "receiver") listens to a hissing sound played through earphones and sees red light through translucent goggles. Parapsychologists believe this procedure makes the receiver more sensitive to mental telepathy signals. In another shielded room, the "sender" concentrates on one of four different visual forms presented in random order. In these studies, the receivers reported the correct form on 32 percent of the trials, a statistically significant increase above the chance level of 25 percent.

Does the ganzfeld procedure—which involves many rigorous controls—provide the first solid evidence of a psychic phenomenon? Some scientists suggest that the original ganzfeld studies may not have fully prevented the receivers from detecting extremely subtle cues that could have influenced their responses (Hyman, 1994). Although several parapsychology researchers have reported successful replications (Parker, 2000), psychologists Julie Milton and Richard Wiseman (1999) analyzed 30 ganzfeld studies conducted by seven independent laboratories and concluded that "the ganzfeld technique *does not* at present offer a replicable method for producing ESP in the laboratory" (p. 387, italics added). As newer studies are published, scientists continue to debate the status of the ganzfeld findings (Milton & Wiseman, 2001; Storm & Ertel, 2001).

FIGURE 2.22

Many people believe in the paranormal despite an overwhelming lack of reliable scientific evidence. Psychic readings, psychic hotlines, and popular science-fiction TV shows and movies dramatizing paranormal events illustrate the public's fascination.

In 1976, an organization called the Committee for the Scientific Investigation of Claims of the Paranormal was formed. It consists of psychologists, other scientists, philosophers, and magicians expert in the art of fakery. To conclude that a phenomenon is psychic, the committee requires that presently known natural physical or psychological explanations be ruled out. To date, it has not judged any psychic claims to be valid.

What about paranormal demonstrations by self-proclaimed psychics, such as using mental powers to bend spoons? Over 25 years ago, James Randi—a magician and expert in the art of psychic fraud—began offering $10,000 to anyone who could demonstrate paranormal ability under his scrutiny. Today the offer is $1 million, and still no one has collected. Predictions made by leading psychics in national newspapers also yield dismal results (Emery Jr., 2001). Accuracy rates range from a meager 4 percent to less than 1 percent (Blodgett, 1986).

Critical thinking requires us to have a reasoned skepticism that demands solid scientific evidence, but not a blind skepticism that rejects the unknown as impossible. In our opinion, at present there is no generally accepted scientific evidence to support the existence of paranormal phenomena. Research continues, and while the burden of proof lies with those who believe in the paranormal, evaluations of their claims should be based on scientific evidence rather than on preconceived positive or negative expectations.

Meta-Analysis: Combining the Results of Many Studies

▶ 18. Describe the purpose of meta-analysis.

As research on a topic accumulates, scientists must reach overall conclusions about how variables are related. Often experts on a topic will examine the number and quality of studies that support, or fail to support, a particular relation and then draw conclusions that they believe are best supported by the facts.

Increasingly, an approach called *meta-analysis* is being used to supplement these expert reviews. **Meta-analysis** *is a statistical procedure for combining the results of different studies that examine the same topic.* In a typical research study, the responses of each participant are analyzed. In a meta-analysis, however, each study is treated as a "single participant," and its overall results are analyzed with those of other studies. A meta-analysis will tell researchers about the direction and statistical strength of the relation between two variables.

Given that many people feel they have sleep problems (as indicated earlier by the National Sleep Foundation survey), let's consider whether exercising might help improve their sleep. Would you expect research to show that exercising during the day helps people sleep better at night? A meta-analysis combined the results of 38 studies on this topic and concluded that the overall relation is weak (Youngstedt et al., 1997). On average, people slept only about 10 minutes longer when they had exercised that day, and they fell asleep only about 1 minute faster. If they awakened during the night, they did not fall back asleep any sooner.

Although meta-analysis is a statistical procedure, a researcher must decide which studies to include and point out their common limitations. The authors of the meta-analysis on exercise and sleep cautioned that most studies examined young adults who slept well and did not focus on people with insomnia. Many researchers consider meta-analysis, when properly used, to be the most objective way to integrate the findings of various studies and reach overall conclusions about behavior.

IN REVIEW

- *An experiment has high internal validity when it is designed well and permits clear causal conclusions. Confounding occurs when the independent variable becomes mixed up with an uncontrolled variable. This ruins internal validity because we can no longer tell which variable caused the changes in the dependent variable.*
- *Internal validity is weakened by (1) demand characteristics, which are cues that tip off participants as to how they should behave; (2) placebo effects, in which the mere expectation of receiving a treatment produces a change in behavior; and (3) experimenter expectancy effects, which are the subtle ways a researcher's behavior influences participants to behave in a manner consistent with the hypothesis being tested. The double-blind procedure prevents placebo effects and experimenter expectancy effects from biasing research results.*
- *External validity is the degree to which the findings of a study can be generalized to other people, settings, and conditions. By replicating (repeating) a study under both similar and dissimilar circumstances, researchers can examine its external validity.*

ETHICAL PRINCIPLES IN RESEARCH

▶ 19. Identify the major ethical issues in human and animal research.

When conducting research, the knowledge and possible applications to be gained must always be weighed against potential risks to research participants. To safeguard the rights of participants, researchers must adhere to ethical standards based on government regulations and guidelines from national psychological organizations. Nonhuman (animal) subjects, too, must be treated in accord with established ethical guidelines (Figure 2.23). At academic and research institutions, special committees review the ethical issues involved in research proposals. If a proposed study is considered ethically questionable, it must be modified or the research cannot be conducted.

Ethical Standards in Human Research

According to the American Psychological Association (APA) guideline of **informed consent**, *when people agree to participate in research they should be*

- *given a full description of the procedures to be followed,*
- *informed about any risks that might be involved, and*
- *told that they are free to withdraw from a study at any time without penalty.*

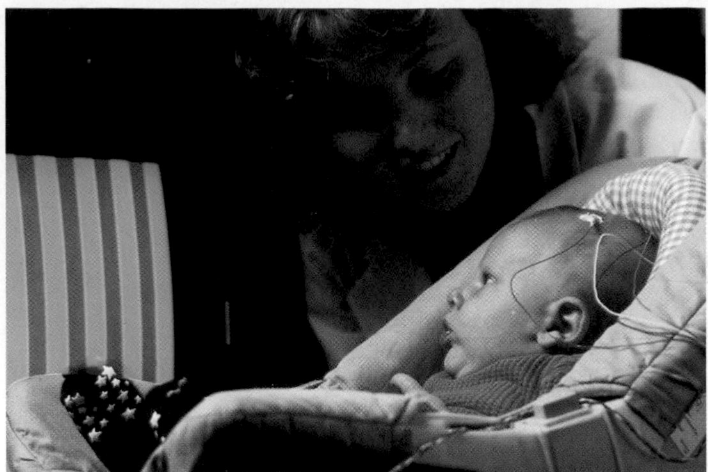

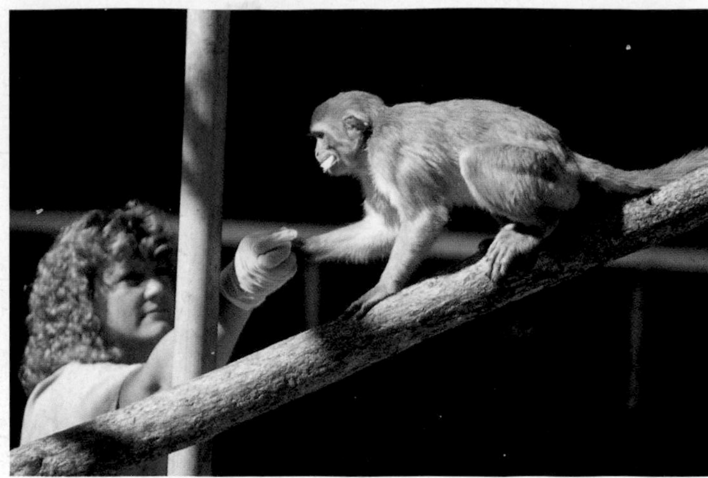

FIGURE 2.23

Ethical standards are designed to protect the welfare of both humans and non-humans in psychological research.

When children, seriously disturbed mental patients, or other people who are not able to give true informed consent are involved, consent must be obtained from their parents or guardians.

To safeguard a participant's *right to privacy*, researchers typically collect, store, and report data in ways the keep participants' identity anonymous or confidential. Two other considerations are *psychological risk*, which represents the degree to which the research procedures may expose someone to significant mental or emotional stress, and *social risk*, which involves information recorded about individual participants that could become known to others and, if so, might result in negative consequences for the participant.

Deception, which occurs when participants are misled about the nature of a study, is controversial. Consider the Darley and Latané (1968) bystander experiment. Participants were not told that the study was going to examine how they would respond to an emergency, nor were they informed that the procedure (someone presumably having a seizure) might cause them stress. Proponents of deception research argue that when studying certain types of behaviors, deception is the only way to obtain natural, spontaneous responses from participants. Darley and Latané's participants, for example, had to believe that the emergency was significant and real or else the experiment would have failed.

Deception, of course, violates the principle of informed consent. Guidelines currently permit deception only when no other feasible alternative is available and the study has scientific, educational, or applied benefits that clearly outweigh the ethical costs of deceiving participants. When deception is used, the true purpose of the study should be explained to participants after it is over. The overwhelming majority of psychological studies do not involve deception.

Ethical Standards in Animal Research

Animals frequently are subjects in psychological studies conducted in laboratory and naturalistic settings. National surveys find that the vast majority of psychologists and college psychology majors believe that animal research is necessary for scientific progress in psychology (Plous, 1996a, 1996b). As in medical research, however, some psychological studies expose animals to conditions considered too hazardous for humans. For example, should researchers be allowed to inject a drug into an animal in order to learn whether that drug might permanently impair memory?

APA and federal government guidelines require that animals be treated humanely and that the potential importance of the research justify the risks to which they are exposed. This determination, however, is not always easy to make, and people of good will can disagree. Before animal research can be conducted, it must reviewed and approved, often by panels that include nonscientists.

Animal research is debated, both outside and within the psychological community (Baldwin, 1993; Vonk, 1997). Psychologists agree that it is morally wrong to subject animals to needless suffering. Many scientists, however, do not agree with the head of the American Anti-Vivisection Society who maintained that animals should never be used in research "which is not for the benefit of the animals involved" (Goodman, 1982, p. 61). Proponents of animal research point to important medical and psychological advances made possible by animal research (Baldwin, 1993). For example, had Louis Pasteur not subjected some dogs to suffering, he could not have developed the rabies vaccine, which has saved the lives of countless animals as well as humans. They ask, "Does the prospect of finding a cure for cancer or identifying the causes of psychological disorders justify exposing some animals to harm?"

Although animal research has declined slightly in recent years, the ethical questions remain as vexing as ever (Petrinovich, 1999). What is most encouraging is that the welfare of animals in research is receiving the careful attention it deserves.

IN REVIEW

- *Psychological research follows extensive ethical guidelines. In human research, key issues are the use of informed consent, the participants' right to privacy, the degree of psychological and social risk, and the use of deception.*
- *Ethical guidelines require that animals be treated humanely and that the risks to which they are exposed be justified by the potential importance of the research. As in human research, before animal research can be conducted it must reviewed and approved, often by ethics review boards that include nonscientists.*

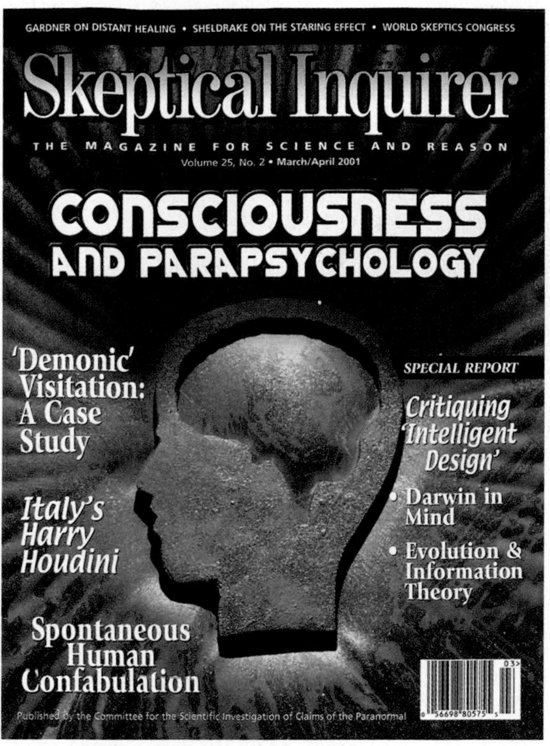

FIGURE 2.24

Modern society bombards us with scientific and pseudoscientific claims. A good dose of critical thinking often can help us tell good science from junk science. This journal, which promotes healthy skepticism and critical thinking, is published by the Committee for the Scientific Investigation of Claims of the Paranormal.

CRITICAL THINKING IN SCIENCE AND EVERYDAY LIFE

In today's world we are exposed to a great deal of scientific information about human behavior—some of which is accurate and much of which, intentionally or unintentionally, is not. Especially in the popular media, we encounter many oversimplifications and overgeneralizations, along with lots of *pseudoscientific misinformation*—bunk and psychobabble that is made to sound scientific. To be an informed consumer, you must be able to critically evaluate research and claims, and to identify factors that limit the validity of conclusions. Critical-thinking skills can also help you avoid being misled by claims made in everyday life, such as those in advertisements. Thus, enhancing your critical-thinking skills may be one of the most important benefits you derive from your psychology course.

Throughout this chapter you have seen how critical thinking, a healthy dose of skepticism, and the scientific method help scientists solve puzzles of mind and behavior. As critical thinkers, we should recognize that our beliefs and emotions can act as psychological blinders that allow us to accept inadequate evidence uncritically, especially when this evidence supports our current views. This does not mean that we should be so skeptical of everything that we end up believing nothing at all. Rather, we need to balance open-mindedness with a healthy skepticism and evaluate evidence for what it is worth (Figure 2.24).

▶ 20. What critical-thinking questions can be used to evaluate claims made in everyday life?

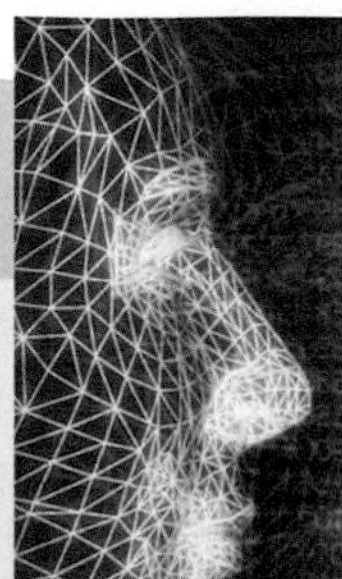

APPLYING PSYCHOLOGICAL SCIENCE

EVALUATING CLAIMS IN RESEARCH AND EVERYDAY LIFE

To exercise your critical-thinking skills, read the following brief descriptions of a research study, an advertisement, and a newspaper article. Have some fun and see if you agree with the claims made. Write down and compare your answers to ours. You can facilitate critical thinking by asking yourself the following questions:

- What claim is being made?
- What evidence is being presented to support this claim?

- What is the quality of the evidence? Are there any other plausible explanations for the conclusions being drawn?
- What additional evidence would be needed to reach a clearer conclusion?
- At present, what is the most reasonable conclusion to draw?

Some Interesting Claims

Example 1: A Lot of Bull

Deep inside the brain of humans and other mammals is a structure called the *caudate nucleus*. Years ago, a prominent researcher hypothesized that this part of the brain is responsible for turning off aggressive behavior. The scientist was so confident in his hypothesis that he bet his life on it. A microelectrode was implanted inside the caudate nucleus of a large, aggressive bull. The researcher stood before the bull and, like a Spanish matador, waved a cape to incite the bull to charge. As the bull thundered toward him, the researcher pressed a button on a radio transmitter that he held in his other hand. This sent a signal that caused the microelectrode to stimulate the bull's caudate nucleus. Suddenly, the bull broke off its charge and stopped. Each time this sequence was repeated, the bull stopped its charge. The researcher concluded that the caudate nucleus was the "aggression-off" center of the brain.

Stimulating the caudate nucleus caused the bull to stop charging, but does this demonstrate that the caudate nucleus is an aggression-off center? Why or why not? (*Hint*: What other bodily functions might the caudate nucleus help regulate that would cause the bull to stop charging?)

Example 2: Vacations and Burglaries

A newspaper advertisement appeared in several American cities. The headline "While You're on Vacation, Burglars go to Work" was followed by this statement: "According to FBI statistics, over 26 percent of home burglaries take place between Memorial Day and Labor Day" (U.S. holidays in late May and early September). The ad then offered a summer sale price for a home security system. In sum, the ad implied that burglaries are particularly likely to occur while people are away on summer vacation. How do you feel about this claim and its supporting evidence?

Example 3: Will Staying up Late Cause You to Forget What You Have Studied?

The headline of a newspaper article read, "Best Way to Retain Complex Information? Sleep on It, Researcher Says." The article began, "Students who study hard Monday through Friday and then party all night on weekends may lose much of what they learned during the week, according to a sleep researcher." The researcher was then quoted as saying, "It appears skewing the sleep cycle by just two hours can have this effect. Watching a long, late movie the night following a class and then sleeping in the next morning will make it so you're not learning what you thought. You'll not lose it all—just about 30 percent."

Next, the experiment was described. College students learned a complex logic game and then were assigned to one of four sleep conditions. Students in the control condition were allowed to have a normal night's sleep. Those in Condition 2 were not allowed to have any sleep, whereas students in Conditions 3 and 4 were awakened only when they went into a particular stage (phase) of sleep. (We'll learn about sleep stages in Chapter 5.) A week later everyone was tested again. Participants in Conditions 3 and 4 performed 30 percent worse than the other two groups.

Think about the claims reported in the first paragraph above, then examine the experimental conditions. Does anything seem wrong to you?

Critical Analyses of the Claims

Analysis 1: A Lot of Bull

Perhaps the caudate nucleus plays a role in vision, memory, or movement, and stimulating it momentarily caused the bull either to become blind, to forget what it was doing, or to alter its movement. Perhaps the bull simply became dizzy or experienced pain. These are all possible explanations for why the bull stopped charging. In fact, the caudate nucleus helps regulate movement; it is not an aggression-off center in the brain.

Analysis 2: Vacations and Burglaries

First, how much is "over 26 percent"? We don't know for sure, but can assume that it is less than 27 percent, because it would be to the advertiser's advantage to state the highest number possible. The key problem is that the time period between Memorial Day and Labor Day typically represents between 26 and 29 percent of the days of the year. Therefore about 26 percent of burglaries occur during about 26 percent of the year. Wow! Technically the ad is correct: Burglars do go to work in the summer while you're on vacation. But the ad also may have misled people. Burglars seem to be just as busy at other times of the year.

Analysis 3: Does Staying up Late Cause You to Forget What You Have Studied?

It could be true that going to bed and waking up later than usual might cause you to forget more of what you have studied. However, the article does not provide evidence for this claim. Look at the four conditions carefully. To test this claim, an experiment would need to include a condition in which participants went to bed later than usual, slept through the night, and then awakened later than usual. But in this experiment, the control group slept normally, and the three experimental conditions examined only the effects of getting no sleep or losing certain types of sleep.

When you read newspaper or magazine articles, look beyond the headlines and think about whether the claims are truly supported by the evidence. Were you able to pick out some flaws in these claims before you read the analyses? Critical thinking requires practice, and you will get better at it if you keep asking yourself the five critical-thinking questions listed earlier.

A Final Thought: How to See a UFO

About 300 strong, they scanned the dark night sky above the Nevada desert, awaiting the appearance of an alien spaceship. George Kresge, Jr., better known as The Amazing Kreskin, had predicted that a UFO (unidentified flying object) might appear. Kreskin, a magician, hypnotist, and self-proclaimed "mentalist," did not really expect to see a UFO. His goal was to plant the seed in people's minds, telling them, "It's going to be fulfilling. It will be real to you, but it will be subjective" (Manning, 2002, p. A8). And, indeed, many believers saw what they expected to see. Several reported seeing a strangely colored cloud. After spotting distant red and green blinking lights in the sky (the site was under a flight path, and planes were approaching), a woman pointed overhead and cried, "You may not be able to see anything, but I can feel its presence" (p. A8). Another exclaimed that she saw a green ship.

UFO believers, of course, aren't the only ones influenced by their expectations. It's part of being human, and scientists are not exempt. Experimenter expectancy effects can distort the results of a study, and the theoretical lenses through which researchers view behavior influence how they interpret their findings.

Because science is a human endeavor, it is subject to human frailties. But the beauty of science is that it attempts to build safeguards into the system. Research can be designed to minimize biases that may distort the findings. By publishing their findings, researchers give other scientists the opportunity to critically evaluate and disagree with their methods and interpretations. Such disagreement often breeds more sophisticated research. As further research replicates or fails to replicate, confidence in the original findings increases or decreases, blind alleys are avoided, and the scientific process ultimately does its job and becomes self-correcting.

IN REVIEW

- *Critical thinking is an important life skill. However, we should also be open-minded to ideas that are supported by solid evidence, even when they conflict with our preconceptions.*
- *There is no generally accepted, replicable scientific evidence to support the existence of paranormal phenomena. Even the ganzfeld procedure, initially supported by several highly controlled experiments, is controversial because it has often failed to replicate.*
- *In science and everyday life, critical thinking can prevent us from developing false impressions about how the world operates and from being duped in everyday life by unsubstantiated claims.*

KEY TERMS AND CONCEPTS

Each term has been boldfaced and defined in the chapter on the page indicated in parentheses.

archival measures (p. 36)
case study (p. 38)
confounding of variables (p. 51)
control group (p. 46)
correlation coefficient (p. 43)
correlational research (p. 41)
demand characteristics (p. 51)
dependent variable (p. 45)
descriptive research (p. 37)
double-blind procedure (p. 52)
experiment (p. 44)
experimental group (p. 45)
experimenter expectancy effects (p. 52)
external validity (p. 52)
hypothesis (p. 32)
independent variable (p. 45)
informed consent (p. 55)
internal validity (p. 50)
meta-analysis (p. 55)
naturalistic observation (p. 39)
negative correlation (p. 43)
operational definition (p. 35)
placebo (p. 51)
placebo effect (p. 52)
population (p. 40)
positive correlation (p. 43)
random assignment (p. 46)
random sampling (p. 40)
replication (p. 53)
representative sample (p. 40)
sample (p. 40)
scatterplot (p. 43)
survey research (p. 39)
theory (p. 33)
variable (p. 34)

What Do You Think?

I KNEW IT ALL ALONG p. 34

You may be able to think of couples in which the partners seem to be "opposites" in personality, attitudes, and so forth, but research consistently shows that "birds of a feather" is the norm. People typically are most attracted to, and pair up with, those who share similar characteristics.

Here's a simple way to demonstrate "I knew it all along" (after-the-fact) reasoning. Think of 6 to 10 people you know (the larger the sample, the better). Approach each person individually. In half the cases, tell them, "Research shows that in most romantic relationships, the adage 'opposites attract' is true. Does this surprise you, and can you explain why this would be so?" Tell the remaining people, "Research shows that in most romantic relationships, the adage 'birds of a feather flock together' is true. Does this surprise you, and can you explain why this would be so?" Just as in *The American Soldier* example, you should find that no matter what you tell people—the accurate statement or its opposite—most will say that they are not surprised and will easily come up with an explanation. By the way, after each person responds, you should explain the nature and purpose of this little exercise. ■

DOES EATING ICE CREAM CAUSE PEOPLE TO DROWN? p. 43

Just because two variables are correlated, we cannot conclude that they are causally related. First, consider the bidirectionality problem. We don't see any likely way that drownings could cause the rest of the public to eat more ice cream, so let's rule that out. Can we conclude, then, that more ice cream consumption causes more drownings? We suppose that in a few cases gorging on ice cream soon before swimming might enhance the risk of drowning. But nationally, how often is this likely to happen?

Now consider the third-variable problem. What other factors might cause people to eat more ice cream and also lead to an increase in drownings? The most obvious third variable that comes to mind is "daily temperature" (or even "month of the year"). Summer months bring hotter days, and people eat more ice cream in hot weather. Likewise, although the risk of an individual swimmer's drowning may remain the same, on hotter days drownings increase simply because so many more people go swimming. In short, the most reasonable conclusion is that the ice cream–drowning correlation really is due to a third variable. ■

WHY DO PEOPLE BELIEVE IN THE PARANORMAL? p. 53

One question to ask is Do most people even hear about the negative scientific evidence and controversies concerning paranormal activity? We doubt it. Instead, they are most likely to see eye-catching paranormal headlines in tabloid newspapers, interviews with self-proclaimed psychics on TV, or science-fiction TV programs or movies that make these phenomena seem real and credible.

Even if believers knew about the evidence, it might not have much effect because many *want to believe* in the paranormal and might rationalize the negative evidence away. The paranormal appeals to our sense of wonder about the unknown. Moreover, many people welcome the notion that psychics can help them discover their destinies or that channelers can help them communicate with loved ones who have died. And, ironically, the very institution—science—that is so skeptical of the paranormal may help promote people's belief in it because the dizzying pace of scientific discovery mistakenly reinforces the belief that almost anything is possible. At present, as Dutch physicist and Nobel Prize–winner Gerard 't Hooft (2000) notes, "The laws of physics, biology, and psychology point all to the most plausible explanation . . . paranormal phenomena are in the eye of the beholder."

Want to learn more about the controversies concerning psychic activity? The Committee for the Scientific Investigation of Claims of the Paranormal publishes *Skeptical Inquirer*. Another organization, The Skeptics Society, publishes *Skeptic*. These magazines may be available at your campus or public library or online. (You can find the web sites for these organizations at the Online Learning Center [OLC] for this textbook. After reaching the OLC, go to Chapter 2). ■

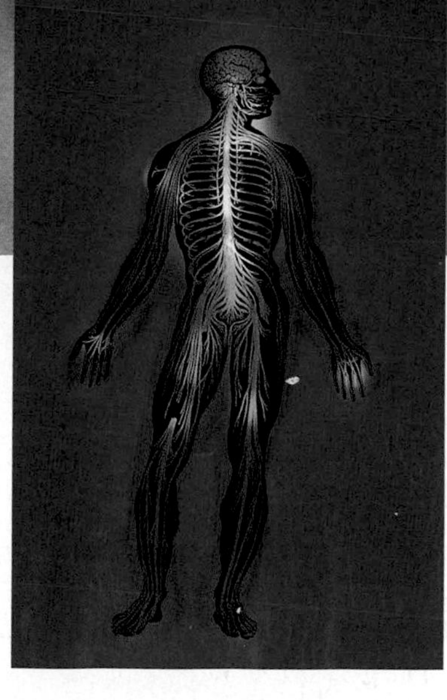

3

BIOLOGICAL FOUNDATIONS OF BEHAVIOR
Evolution, Genetics, and the Brain

CHAPTER OUTLINE

The brain is the last and grandest biological frontier, the most complex thing we have yet discovered in our universe. It contains hundreds of billions of cells interlinked through trillions of connections. The brain boggles the mind.

—James Watson

Identical twins Jim Springer and Jim Lewis met for the first time when they were 39 years old. They discovered each other through a landmark University of Minnesota study of twins who had been separated shortly after birth and raised by different adoptive parents. Although they had been raised in different families, the two Jims found that they had many things in common. Both had been married twice, and each had a son named James. Both men smoked Salem cigarettes and preferred Miller Lite beer. Both worked part-time as sheriffs, suffered from the same kind of headache symptoms when under stress, and bit their fingernails. Both twins were the only people in their neighborhoods to have built a circular bench around a tree in their front yard (Figure 3.1). When given a series of psychological tests, they were strikingly similar in their pattern of personality traits. (Tellegen et al., 1988)

FIGURE 3.1

Jim Springer and Jim Lewis are identical twins who were separated when 4 weeks old and raised in different families. When reunited in adulthood, they showed striking similarities in personality, interests, and behavior. They both favored poodles as pets and had built similar but unusual benches around trees in their yards.

■■■

The year was 1848. As the Vermont winter approached, a railroad construction crew hurried to complete its work on a new track. They could not know that they were about to witness one of the most celebrated incidents in the annals of neuroscience.

As a blasting crew prepared its charges, the dynamite accidentally exploded. A 13-pound spike more than 3 feet long was propelled through the face and head of Phineas Gage, a 25-year-old foreman. The spike entered through the left cheek, passed through the brain, and emerged through the top of the skull (Figure 3.2). Dr. J. M. Harlow, who treated Gage, described the incident:

> *The patient was thrown upon his back by the explosion, and gave a few convulsive motions of the extremities, but spoke in a few minutes. He . . . seemed perfectly conscious, but was becoming exhausted from the hemorrhage, . . . the blood pouring from the top of his head. . . . He bore his sufferings with firmness, and directed my attention to the hole in his cheek, saying, "the iron entered there and passed through my head." (1868, pp. 330–332)*

Miraculously, Gage survived. Or did he?

> *His physical health is good, and I am inclined to say that he has recovered. Has no pain in his head, but says it has a queer feeling that he is not able to describe. . . . His contractors, who regarded him as the most efficient and capable foreman in their employ previous to his injury, considered the change in his mind so marked that they could not give him his place again. The equilibrium or balance, so to speak, between his intellectual faculties and animal propensities, seems to have been destroyed. He is fitful, irreverent, indulging at times in the grossest profanity (which was not previously his custom), manifesting but little deference for his fellows, impatient of restraint or advice when it conflicts with his desires . . . devising many plans of future operations, which are no sooner arranged than they are abandoned in turn for others. . . . His mind is radically changed, so decidedly that his friends and acquaintances say that he is "no longer Gage." (pp. 339–340)*

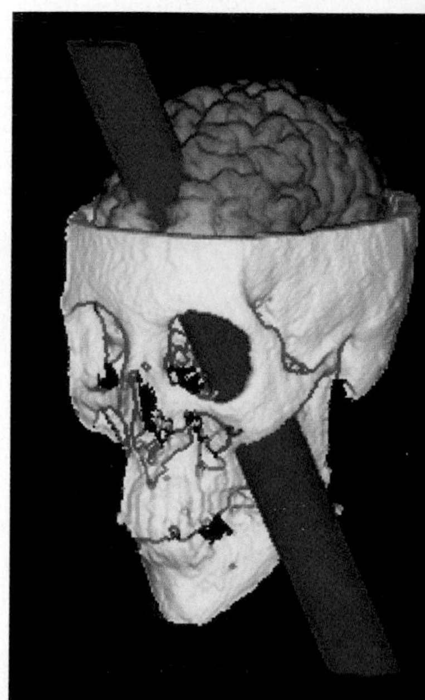

FIGURE 3.2

The brain damage suffered by Phineas Gage seemed to change him into a new person. The red image shows the path of the spike that shot through Gage's brain.

How can we explain the behavioral similarities in Jim Springer and Jim Lewis? The Minnesota researchers found that the adoptive families of the "Jim twins" differed in important ways. What the Jims did have in common, however, was their identical genes. Although their behavioral commonalities could be coincidental, the Minnesota researchers found that other identical-twin pairs separated early in life also showed striking similarities. When a pair of twin housewives from England met one another in Minneapolis, they found to their amazement that each was wearing seven rings, two bracelets on one wrist, and a watch and bracelet on the other. Another pair of men, one raised in Germany and the other in the Caribbean, shared a host of unusual behaviors, such as reading magazines from back to front, flushing toilets before using them, and dipping buttered toast in their coffee. Whether raised together or apart, the identical twins were far more similar in personality and intelligence test scores than were nontwins or fraternal twins raised in the same families (Tellegen et al., 1988). To psychologists, the connections between the twins' biological and behavioral similarities present a set of fascinating questions that may be answered by examining the biological foundations of behavior.

The tragic story of Phineas Gage poses different questions. Physical damage to Gage's brain changed his thinking and behavior so radically that he became, psychologically, a different person. Is our personal identity so thoroughly locked within our skull? Is who we are and what we do reducible to the electrochemical activities of the nervous system?

It has been said that each of us is (1) what all humans are; (2) what some other humans are; and (3) what no other human in the history of the world has been, is, or will be (Kluckhohn & Murray, 1953). In this chapter we explore the biological factors that underlie the behavioral commonalities and differences among humans. First, we explore the role of evolutionary forces. Some of what you are was forged millions of years before your birth as your human ancestors struggled to adapt to their ancient environments and survive. Second, we consider the role of the genes, passed on to you at conception. As we will see, genetic factors influence many of your psychological characteristics and behaviors. Finally, we enter the realm of neuroscience, where we focus on the brain and other physiological systems whose functions underlie your every thought, feeling, and behavior. In each instance, whether considering evolutionary, genetic, or neural functions, we will see that neither biological nor environmental factors act in isolation; rather, they interact with one another in complex ways.

EVOLUTION AND BEHAVIOR

In the misty forests and verdant grasslands of past eons, our early human ancestors faced many environmental challenges as they struggled to survive. If even one of your ancestors had not behaved adaptively enough to survive and reproduce, he or she would not have passed on his or her genes and you would not be here to contemplate your existence. In this sense, each of us is an evolutionary success story. As descendants of those successful forebears, we carry within us genes that contributed to their adaptive and reproductive success. The vast majority of genes we share in common with all other humans create the "human nature" that makes us like all other people. We enter the world with inborn biological mechanisms that enable and predispose us to behave, to feel, and even to think in certain ways.

▶ 1. Define evolution and explain how genetic variation and natural selection produce adaptations.

The field of *evolutionary psychology* seeks to understand how the behavioral abilities and tendencies of modern humans have evolved over the course of millions of years in response to environmental demands. No behavior by any organism can occur in the absence of **biologically based mechanisms** *that receive input from the environment, process the information, and respond to it* (Tooby & Cosmides, 1992). In humans, these inborn mechanisms allow us to, among other things, learn, remember, speak a language, perceive certain aspects of our environment at birth, respond with universal emotions, and bond with other humans. Evolutionary psychologists also believe that important aspects of social behavior, such as aggression, altruism, sex roles, protecting kin, and mate selection, are the products of evolved mechanisms. They are quick to point out that no behavior as such ever evolves; what evolves are genetically produced physical structures that interact with the demands of the environment to produce a behavior.

Cartoon by Don Wright, © 2001.

NOW SHOWING
PLANET OF THE HUMANS
THERE ARE SIMILARITIES— THE WAY THEY USE THEIR HANDS, THEIR PRIMITIVE PROBLEM-SOLVING SKILLS. REALLY GIVES YOU THE WILLIES, DOESN'T IT?

Evolution of Adaptive Mechanisms

Evolution *is a change over time in the frequency with which particular genes—and the characteristics they produce—occur within an interbreeding population.* As particular genes become more or less frequent in a population, so do the characteristics they influence. Some genetic variations arise in a population through *mutations,* random events and accidents in gene reproduction during the division of cells. If mutations occur in the cells that become sperm and egg cells, the altered genes will be passed on to offspring. Mutations help create variation within a population's physical characteristics. It is this variation that makes evolution possible.

Long before Charles Darwin published his theory of evolution in 1859, people knew that animals and plants could be changed over time by breeding members of a species that shared desired traits. Although Darwin knew nothing about genes, he knew that *something* must be passed on to the next generation through reproduction in order for evolution to occur. Darwin's landmark contribution was in specifying the process by which species change over time as they adapt to environmental demands.

Natural Selection

Just as plant and animal breeders "select" for certain characteristics, so, too, does nature. According to Darwin's principle of **natural selection,** *characteristics that increase the likelihood of survival and ability to reproduce within a particular environment will be more likely to be preserved in the population and therefore will become more common in the species over time.* As environmental changes produce new and different demands, some different characteristics may contribute to survival and the ability to pass on one's genes (Barrow, 2003). In this way, natural selection acts as a set of filters, allowing certain characteristics of survivors to become more common and those of nonsurvivors to become less common and, perhaps, even extinct over time. The filters also allow "neutral" variations that neither facilitate nor impede fitness to pass through and be preserved in a population. These neutral variations, sometimes called *evolutionary noise*, could conceivably become important in meeting some future environmental demand. For example, people differ in their ability to tolerate radiation (Vral et al., 2002). In today's world, these variations are of limited importance, but they could clearly affect survivability if a future nuclear war were to increase levels of radioactivity around the world. As those who could tolerate higher levels of radiation survived and those who could not perished, the genetic basis for radiation tolerance would become increasingly more common in the human species. Thus, for natural selection to work, there must be individual variation in a relevant species characteristic.

The products of natural selection are called adaptations. **Adaptations** *allow organisms to meet recurring environmental challenges to their survival, thereby increasing their reproductive ability*. In the final analysis, the name of the natural selection game is to pass on one's genes, either personally or through kin who share at least some of them. Some evolutionary psychologists believe this is why animals and humans may risk or even sacrifice their lives to protect their kin.

Let us apply these concepts to human evolution. We begin with the notion that an organism's biology determines its behavioral capabilities, and its behavior (including its mental abilities) determines whether or not it will survive. In this manner, successful human behavior evolved along with a changing body (Buss, 1995; Tooby & Cosmides, 1992).

One theory is that, when dwindling vegetation in some parts of the world forced apelike animals from the trees and required that they hunt for food on open, grassy plains, chances for survival were greater for those who were capable of *bipedal locomotion* (walking on two legs), thereby freeing the hands to use weapons that could kill at a distance (Lewin, 1998). By freeing the hands, bipedalism fostered the development and use of tools and weapons, and hunting in groups encouraged social organization. Social organization required the development of specialized social roles (such as "hunter and protector" in the male and "nurturer of children" in the female) that still exist in most cultures. It also favored the development of language, which enhanced social communication and the transmission of knowledge.

Tool use, bipedal locomotion, and social organization put new selection pressures on many parts of the body. These included the teeth, the hands, and the pelvis, all of which changed over time in response to the new dietary and behavioral demands. But the greatest pressure was placed on the brain structures involved in the abilities most critical to the emerging way of life: attention, memory, language, and thought. These mental abilities became important to survival in an environment that required the ability to learn quickly and to solve problems. In the evolutionary progression from *Australopithecus* (an early human ancestor who lived about 4 million years ago) through *Homo erectus* (1.6 million to 100,000 years ago) to the human subspecies Neandertal of 75,000 years ago, the brain tripled in size, and the most dramatic growth occurred in the parts of the brain that are the seat of the higher mental processes (Figure 3.3). Thus, evolved changes in

FIGURE 3.3

The human brain evolved over a period of several million years. The greatest growth occurred in those areas concerned with the higher mental processes, particularly attention, memory, thought, and language.

Australopithecus
(4 million years ago)

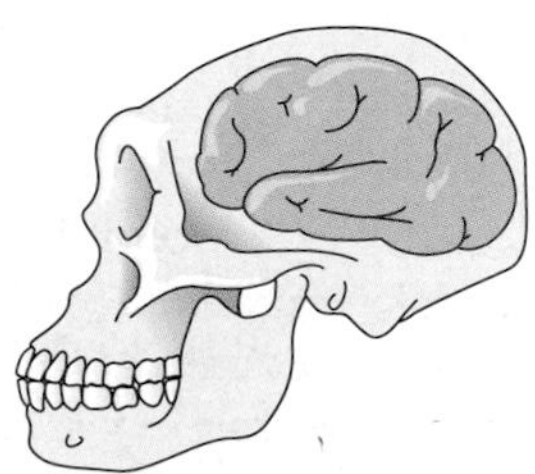

The brain capacity ranges from 450 to 650 cubic centimeters (cc).

Homo erectus
(1.6 million to 100,000 years ago)

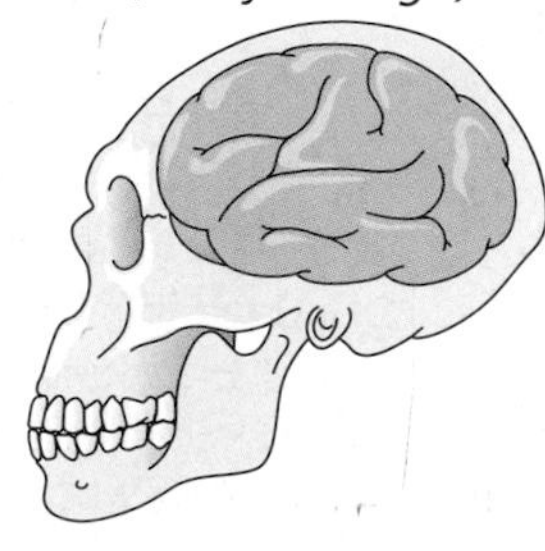

Further development of skull and jaw are evident and brain capacity is 900 cc.

Neandertal
(75,000 years ago)

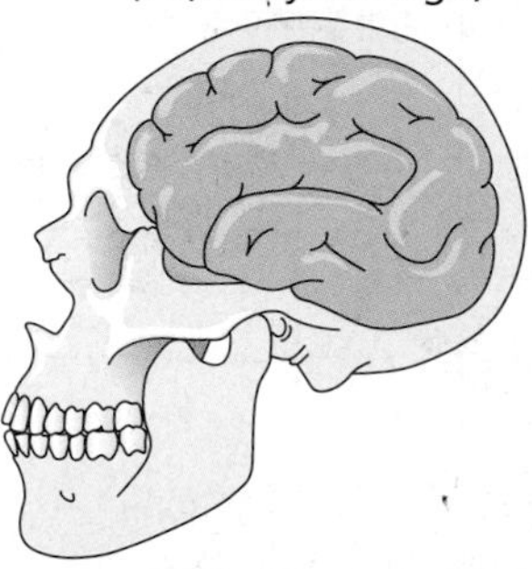

The human skull has now taken shape: the skull case has elongated to hold a complex brain of 1,450 cc.

Homo sapiens

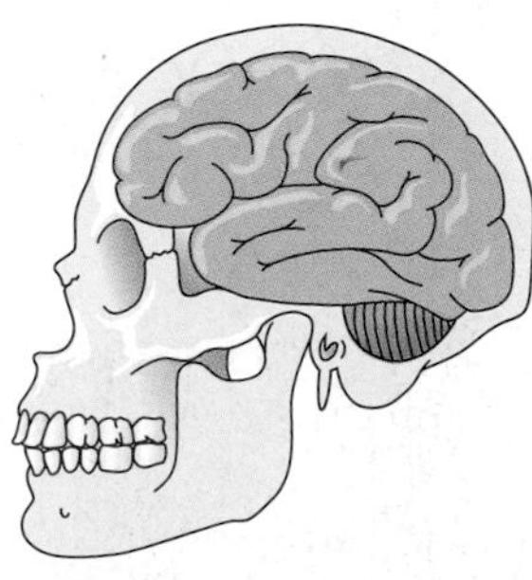

The deeply convoluted brain reflects growth in areas concerned with higher mental processes.

behavior seem to have contributed to the development of the brain, just as the growth of the brain contributed to evolving human behavior.

Surprisingly, perhaps, today's human brain does not differ much from the Stone Age brain of our ancient ancestors. In fact, Neanderthal had a slightly larger brain. Yet the fact that we perform mental activities that could not have been imagined in those ancient times tells us that human capabilities are not solely determined by the brain; cultural evolution is also important in the development of adaptations. From an evolutionary perspective, culture provides important environmental input to evolutionary mechanisms.

Some evolved biological mechanisms allow broad adaptations, such as the ability to learn a language, repeat behaviors that are rewarded and suppress those that are punished, reason logically, and imagine future events. Others are considered to be **domain-specific adaptations,** *designed to solve a particular problem*, such as selecting a suitable mate, choosing safe foods to eat, avoiding certain environmental hazards (snakes, cliff edges, spiders), detecting cheating and deception in others, and forming cooperative alliances with other people. Domain-specific mechanisms suggest that the human mind is not a general, all-purpose problem solver but rather a collection of specialized and somewhat independent *modules* that evolved to handle specific adaptive problems. As we shall see throughout the book, this modular approach to brain/mind functioning helps us understand many aspects of consciousness, problem solving, emotion, personality, and behavior.

? What Do You Think?

NATURAL SELECTION AND GENETIC DISEASES

If Darwin was right about natural selection, then why do we have so many harmful genetic disorders? Consider, for example, cystic fibrosis, a European-based hereditary disorder that clogs one's lungs with mucus and prevents digestion; or sickle cell anemia, which causes early deaths in many people of African descent. Can you reconcile the existence of such disorders with "survival of the fittest"? Think about it, then see page 107.

An Evolutionary Snapshot of Human Nature

▶ 2. Describe examples of human behavior that suggest innate evolved mechanisms. Differentiate between remote and proximate causal factors.

Evolutionary psychologists suggest that the essence of human nature is the adaptations that have evolved through natural selection to solve problems specific to the human environment. We now consider a sampling of common aspects of human behavior that will be discussed in greater detail throughout the book.

- Infants are born with an innate ability to acquire any language spoken in the world. The specific language(s) learned depends on which ones they are exposed to. Deaf children have a similar innate ability to acquire any sign language, and their language acquisition pattern parallels the learning of spoken language. Language is central to human thought and communication.
- Newborns are prewired to perceive specific stimuli. For example, they are more responsive to pictures of human faces than to pictures of the same facial features arranged in a random pattern (Fantz, 1961). They are also able to discriminate the odor of their mother's milk from that of other women (McFarlane, 1975). Both adaptations improve human bonding with caregivers.
- At one week of age, human infants show primitive mathematical skills, successfully discriminating between two and three objects. These abilities improve with age in the absence of any training. The brain seems designed to make "greater than" and "less than" judgments, which are clearly important in decision making (Geary, 1995).
- According to Robert Hogan (1983), establishing cooperative relationships with a group was critical to the human species' survival and reproductive success. Thus, humans seem to have a need to belong and strongly fear being ostracized from the group. Social anxiety (fear of social disapproval) may be an adaptive mechanism to protect against doing things that will prompt group rejection (Baumeister & Tice, 1990).
- As a species, humans tend to be altruistic and helpful to one another, especially to children and relatives. Research shows that altruism increases with degree of relatedness. People are also more ready to help young people than old ones (Burnstein et al., 1994). Evolutionary theorists suggest that helping family members and relatives increases the likelihood that they will be able to pass on the genes they share with you. Likewise, from a species perspective, younger people have more reproductive value than do older people.
- As we will see in Chapter 10, there is much evidence for a set of basic emotions that are universally recognized (Ekman, 1973).

FIGURE 3.4

The human smile seems to be a universal expression of positive emotion and is universally perceived that way. Evolutionary psychologists believe that expressions of basic emotions are hard-wired biological mechanisms that have adaptive value as methods of communication.

Smiling, for example, is a universal expression of happiness and goodwill that typically evokes positive reactions from others (Figure 3.4). Emotions are important means of social communication that evoke psychological mechansims in others (Ketellar, 1995).

- In virtually all cultures, males are more violent and more likely to kill others (particularly other males) than are females. Across many cultures, male-male killings outnumber female-female killings by about 30 to 1 (Daly & Wilson, 1988). Evolutionary researchers suggest that male-male violence is rooted in hunting, dominance hierarchies, and competition for mates, all of which enhance personal and reproductive survival.

Some Caveats Concerning Evolutionary Theory

Adaptations are forged over a long period of time—perhaps thousands of generations—and we cannot go back to prehistoric times and determine with certainty what the environmental demands were. For this reason evolutionary theorists are often forced to infer the forces to which our ancestors adapted, leading to after-the-fact speculation that is difficult to prove or disprove. A challenge for evolutionary theorists is to avoid the logical fallacy of circular reasoning:

"Why does behavioral tendency X exist?"

"Because of environmental demand Y."

"How do we know that demand Y existed?"

"Because otherwise behavior X would not have developed."

Evolutionary theorists have sometimes been accused of giving insufficient weight to cultural learning factors, and many debates about evolutionary explanations involve this issue. To an increasing degree, modern evolutionary theorists acknowledge the role of both *remote causes* (including past evolutionary pressures that may have prompted natural selection) and *proximate (near-term) causes*, such as cultural learning and the immediate environment, that influence current behavior. Figure 3.5 shows how remote and proximate biological and environmental factors interact with one another as determinants of behavior—from the distant evolutionary past to the present.

In thinking about behavior from an evolutionary point of view, it is important to avoid two fallacies. The first is that evolution is purposive, or "has a plan." There is, in fact, no "plan" in evolution; there is only adaptation to environmental demands and the natural selection process that results. Second, it makes no sense to conclude that because something in nature (such as male violence) is influenced by our genes, it is either unavoidable, "natural," or "right." In many cases, what we consider to be self-control or morality requires that we override our biological, or "natural," inclinations. Our ability to regulate our own behavior and to exercise moral control is often just as important to our survival (i.e., as adaptive) as are our biological tendencies.

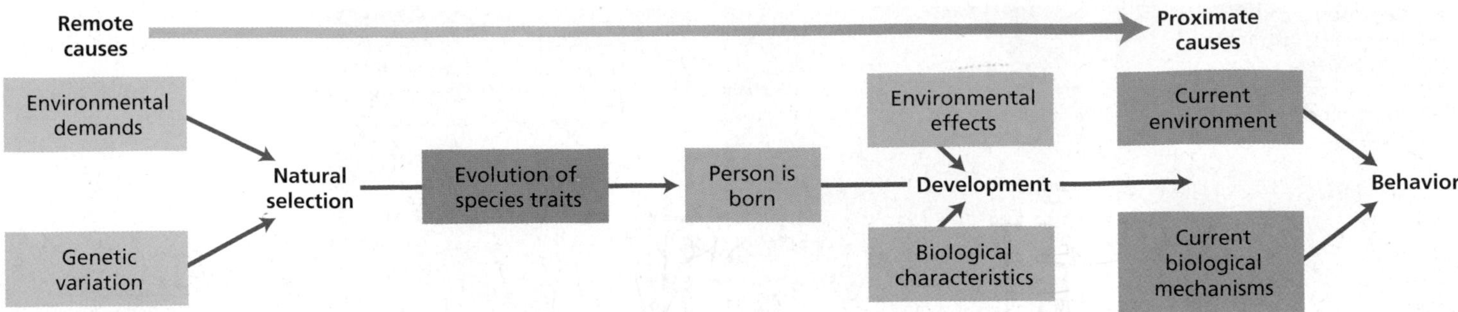

FIGURE 3.5

Biological and environmental factors interact and influence one another as both remote and proximate causes of behavior. From evolution to the immediate environment, we see the interaction of nature and nurture.

IN REVIEW

- *Evolutionary psychology focuses on biologically based mechanisms sculpted by evolutionary forces as solutions to the problems of adaptation faced by species. Some of these genetically based mechanisms are general (e.g., the ability to learn from the consequences of our behavior), but many are domain-specific, devoted to solving specific problems (e.g., mate selection).*
- *Evolution is a change over time in the frequency with which particular genes—and the characteristics they produce—occur within an interbreeding population. Evolution represents an interaction between biological and environmental factors in both its original and later influences on behavior.*
- *The cornerstone of Darwin's theory of evolution is the principle of natural selection, which posits that biologically based characteristics that contribute to survival and reproductive success increase in the population over time because those who lack the characteristics are less likely to pass on their genes.*
- *Critical thinking helps counter circular reasoning about evolutionary causes and effects. We should also recognize that harmful genetically-based behavior tendencies can be overridden by human decision and self-control.*

GENETIC INFLUENCES ON BEHAVIOR

Our physical development, including the development of the nervous system, is in large part directed by an elaborate genetic blueprint passed on to us by our parents. Since antiquity, humans have questioned how physical characteristics are passed on from parents to their offspring. The ancient Greek physician Hippocrates was one of the first to provide a semicorrect answer. Hippocrates suggested that semen contains not body parts but rather some sort of design for the formation of the offspring.

It was not until over 2,000 years later that the wisdom of Hippocrates' answer was confirmed by Gregor Mendel, an Austrian monk whose research with garden peas in the 1860s marked the beginning of modern genetic theory. Mendel showed that heredity involves the passing on of specific organic factors, not a simple blending of the parents' characteristics. These specific factors might produce visible characteristics in the offspring, or they might simply be carried for possible transmission to another generation. In any case, the offspring of one set of parents do not all inherit the same traits, as is evident in the differences we see among brothers and sisters.

▶ 3. Differentiate between genotype and phenotype. How do genes regulate biological structures and functions?

Early in the 20th century, geneticists made the important distinction between **genotype,** *the specific genetic makeup of the individual*, and **phenotype,** *the individual's observable characteristics*. A person's genotype is like the commands in a computer software program. Some of the directives are used on one occasion, some on another. Some are never used at all, either because they are contradicted by other genetic directives or because the environment never calls them forth. For example, geneticists discovered that chickens have retained the genetic code for teeth (Kollar & Fisher, 1980). Yet, because the code is prevented from being expressed phenotypically, there's not a chicken anywhere that can sink its teeth into a mailman. Genotype is present from conception, but phenotype can be affected both by other genes and by the environment.

Chromosomes and Genes

The union of two cells—the egg from the mother and the sperm from the father—is the beginning of a new individual. Like all other cells in the body except red blood cells, which have no nucleus, the egg

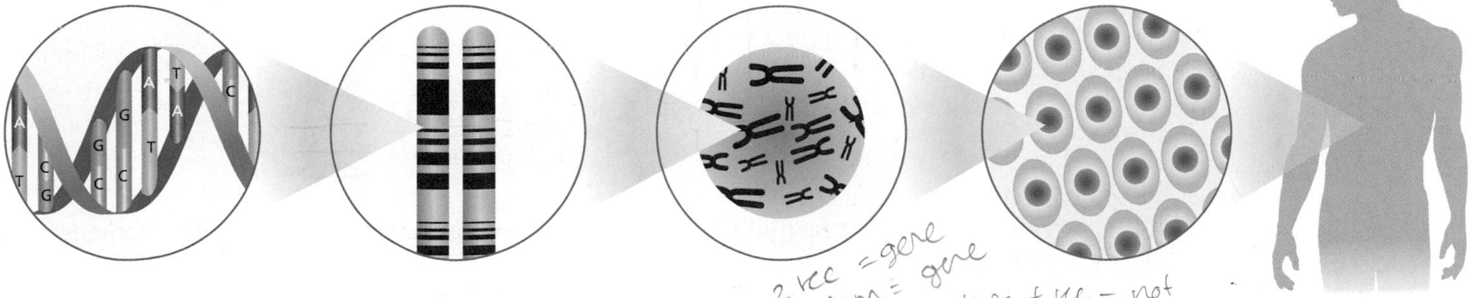

Each chromosome contains numerous **genes**, segments of DNA that contain instructions to make proteins—the building blocks of life.

One **chromosome** of every pair is from each parent.

Each nucleus contains 46 **chromosomes**, arranged in 23 pairs.

Each human cell (except red blood cells) contains a **nucleus.**

The human body contains 100 trillion **cells.**

FIGURE 3.6

The ladder of life. Chromosomes consist of two long, twisted strands of DNA, the chemical that carries genetic information. Every cell in the body carries within its nucleus 23 pairs of chromosomes, each containing numerous genes that regulate every aspect of cellular functioning.

and sperm carry within their nuclei the material of heredity in the form of rodlike units called *chromosomes*. A **chromosome** *is a double-stranded and tightly coiled molecule of deoxyribonucleic acid (DNA) whose strands coil around one another*. All of the information of heredity is encoded in the various combinations of four chemical bases—adenine, thymine, guanine, and cytosine—that occur throughout the chromosome. The specific arrangement of these ATGC bases on the chromosome creates the specific commands for every feature and function of your body. The ordering of 99.9 percent of these bases is exactly the same in all people.

The DNA portion of the chromosome carries the **genes,** *the biological units of heredity* (Figure 3.6). The average gene has about 3,000 ATGC bases, but sizes vary greatly; the largest has 2.4 million bases. Each gene carries the codes for manufacturing specific proteins somewhere in the body. These proteins can take an infinite variety of forms, and they underlie every bodily structure and chemical process. It is estimated that about half of all genes target brain structure and functions (Kolb & Whishaw, 2003). Every moment of every day, the strands of DNA silently transmit their detailed instructions for cellular functioning.

With one exception, every cell in the human body with a nucleus has 46 chromosomes. The exception is the *sex cell* (the egg or sperm), which has only 23. At conception, the 23 chromosomes from the egg combine with the 23 corresponding chromosomes from the sperm to form a new cell containing 46 chromosomes. Within each chromosome, the corresponding genes received from each parent occur in matched pairs.

Dominant, Recessive, and Polygenic Effects

▶ 4. Describe dominant, recessive, and polygenic influences on phenotype.

Genotype and phenotype are not identical because some genes are dominant and some are recessive. If a gene in the pair received from both the mother and father is *dominant*, the particular characteristic that it controls will be displayed. If, however, a gene received from one parent is *recessive*, the characteristic will not show up unless the partner gene inherited from the other parent is also recessive. In humans, for example, brown eyes are dominant over blue eyes. A child will have blue eyes only if both parents have contributed recessive genes for blue eyes. However, even if the blue-eyed trait remains hidden (as would occur if one parent has brown eyes), the recessive gene for blue eyes will be passed on to offspring by the brown-eyed child.

In a great many instances, *a number of gene pairs combine their influences to create a single phenotypic trait. This is known as* **polygenic transmission,** and it complicates the straightforward picture that would occur if all characteristics were determined by one pair of genes. It also magnifies the number of possible variations in a trait that can occur. It is estimated that the union of sperm and egg can result in about 70 trillion potential genotypes, accounting for the great diversity of characteristics that occurs even in siblings.

At present, our knowledge of phenotypes greatly exceeds our understanding of the underlying genotype, but that may soon change. In 1990, geneticists began the Human Genome Project, a coordinated effort to map the DNA, including all the genes of the human organism. The genetic structure in every one of the 23 chromosome pairs has now been mapped by methods that allow the investigators to literally disassemble the genes on each chromosome and study their specific sequence of substances (A,T,G, and C; see Figure 3.6).

The first results of the genome project provided a surprise: The genome consists of approximately 35,000 genes rather than the 100,000 previously estimated. That result told geneticists that gene interactions are even more complex than formerly believed and that it's highly unlikely that manipulating a single gene could solve a complex problem such as anorexia or schizophrenia. Even given this reduced number of genes, the 3.1 billion ATGC combinations in the entire human genome, if printed consecutively, would add about 150,000 pages to this book.

The "book of life" revealed by the Human Genome Project will soon give us greater knowledge of which specific genes or gene combinations are involved in normal and abnormal characteristics. The location and structure of more than 80 genes that contribute to hereditary diseases have already been identified through gene mapping (Human Genome Project, 2003). On another front, behavioral scientists are exploring the gene combinations that underlie behavior and, in some cases, are modifying those processes.

Behavior Genetics

Degree of relatedness to one another tells us how genetically similar people are. Recall that children get half of their genetic material from each parent. Thus the probability of sharing any particular gene with one of your parents is 50 percent, or .50. Brothers and sisters also have a .50 probability of sharing the same gene with one another, since they get their genetic material from the same parents. And what about a grandparent? Here, the probability of a shared gene is .25 because, for example, your maternal grandmother passed half of her genes on to your mother, who passed half of hers on to you. Thus the likelihood that you inherited one of your grandmother's genes is .50 × .50, or .25. The probability of sharing a gene is also .25 for half siblings, who share half their genes with the common biological parent but none with the other parent. If you have a first cousin, you share 12.5 of your genes with him or her. Theoretically, an adopted child has an entirely different genotype from those of his or her adoptive parents, and the same is true for unrelated people. These facts about genetic similarity give us a basis for studying the role of genetic factors in physical and behavioral characteristics.

▶ 5. Define heritability. How are heritability coefficients estimated?

Researchers in the field of **behavior genetics** *study how heredity and environment interact to influence psychological characteristics*. Whereas evolutionary psychologists are interested in the commonalities among people, behavior geneticists focus on the potential role of genetic factors in accounting for differences among people.

A **heritability coefficient** *estimates the extent to which the differences, or variation, in a specific characteristic within a group of people can be attributed to genetic factors*. Heritability estimates are most frequently computed by doubling the absolute difference between correlation coefficients derived from identical and fraternal twins. For example, if the correlation in IQ scores between many sets of identical twins is .85 and that between fraternal twins is .55, the difference of .30 between those correlations is multiplied by 2 to give us a heritability estimate of .60.

This heritability coefficient of .60 indicates that 60 percent of the amount of variation in people's IQ scores can be attributed to genetic differences among them. Note carefully that it does *not* mean that 60 percent of a person's intelligence is due to genetic factors and the rest to the environment. It is important to remember that heritability applies only to differences within groups (and estimates can vary, depending on the group), not to the contribution of genetic factors to any individual member of that group. Heritability estimates for various human characteristics are shown in Table 3.1.

TABLE 3.1 Heritability Estimates for Various Human Characteristics

Trait	Heritability Estimate
Height	.80
Weight	.60
Intelligence (IQ)	.50–.70
School achievement	.40
Personality	
Extraversion	.36
Conscientiousness	.28
Agreeableness	.28
Emotional stability	.31
Temperament	
Emotional reactivity	.40
Activity level	.25
Sociability	.25
Impulsivity	.45

SOURCES: Bouchard et al., 1990; Dunn & Plomin, 1990; Tellegen et al., 1988.

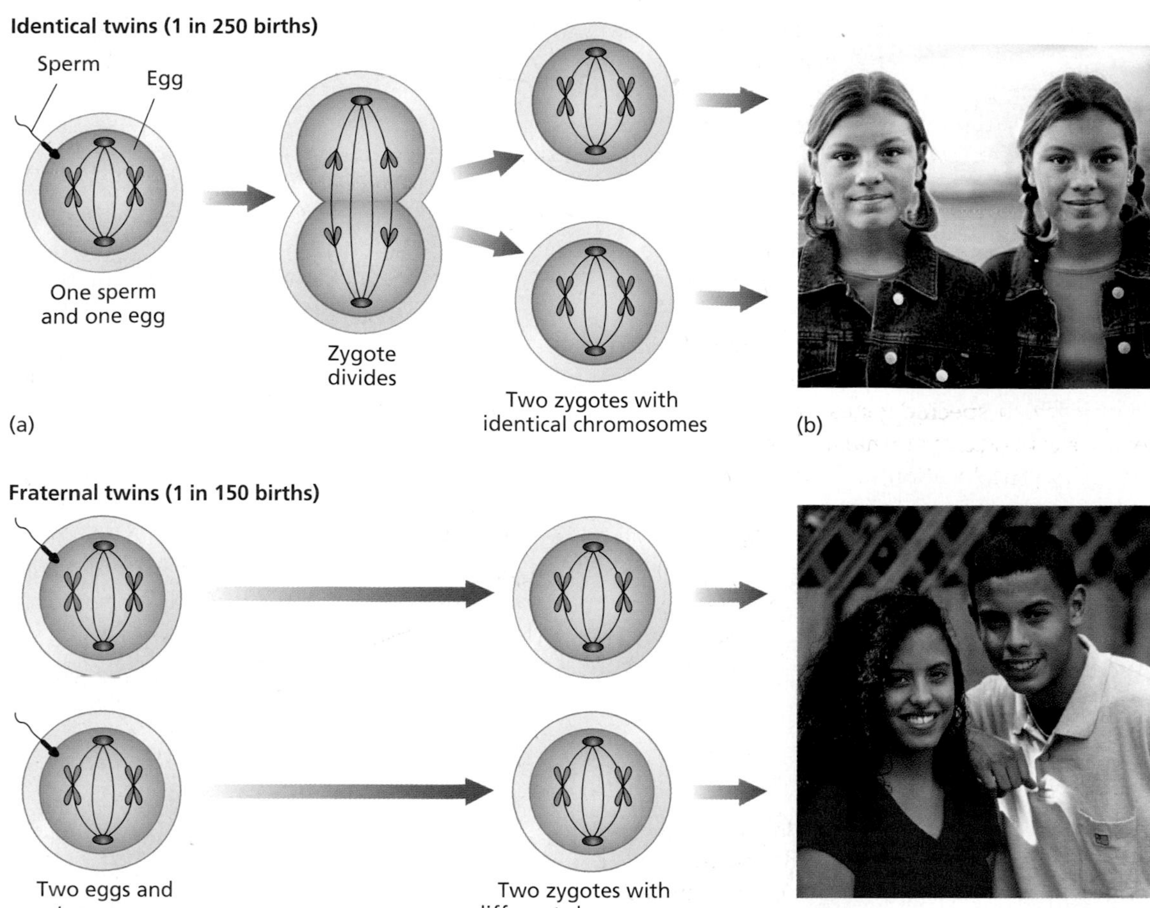

FIGURE 3.7

Identical (monozygotic) twins come from a single egg and sperm as a result of a division of the zygote. They have all of their genes in common. Fraternal (dizygotic) twins result from two eggs fertilized by two sperm. They share only half of their genes as a result.
SOURCE (a, c): Smith, 1998.

Knowing the level of genetic similarity among family members and kin provides a basis for estimating the relative contributions of heredity and environment to a physical or psychological characteristic (Plomin, 1997). If a characteristic has higher **concordance**, or *co-occurrence*, in people who are more closely related to one another, this points to a possible genetic contribution, particularly if the people have lived in different environments.

Adoption and Twin Studies

One research method based on the principle of concordance is the **adoption study**, *in which people who were adopted early in life are compared on some characteristic with both their biological parents, with whom they share genetic endowment, and with their adoptive parents, with whom they share no genes.* If adopted people are more similar to their biological parents than to their adoptive parents in a given trait, a genetic influence on that trait is suggested. If they're more similar to their adoptive parents, environmental factors are judged to be more important for that particular characteristic.

In one study of genetic factors in schizophrenia, Seymour Kety and coworkers (1978) identified adult adoptees who were diagnosed with the disorder later in life. They then examined the backgrounds of the biological and adoptive parents and relatives to determine the rate of schizophrenia in the two sets of families. The researchers found that 12 percent of biological family members had also been diagnosed with schizophrenia, compared with a concordance rate of only 3 percent of adoptive family members, suggesting a hereditary link.

Twin studies, *which compare trait similarities in identical and fraternal twins*, are one of the more powerful techniques used in behavior genetics. Because *monozygotic*, or identical, twins develop from the same fertilized egg, they are genetically identical (Figure 3.7). Approximately 1 in 250 births produces identical twins. *Dizygotic*, or fraternal, twins develop from two fertilized eggs, so they share 50 percent of their genetic endowment, like any other set of brothers and

▶ 6. How are adoption and twin studies used to estimate genetic and environmental determinants of behavior?

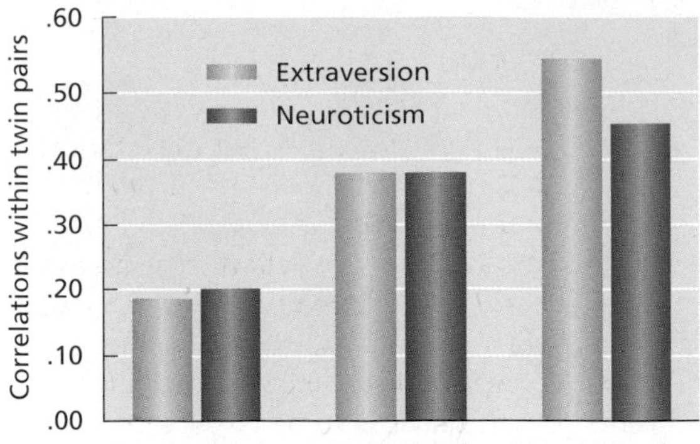

FIGURE 3.8

Degree of similarity on personality measures of extraversion and neuroticism among 24,000 pairs of twins who were reared together and apart.
SOURCE: Based on Loehlin, 1992.

sisters. Approximately 1 in 150 births produces fraternal twins.

Twins, like other siblings, are usually raised in the same familial environment. Thus we can compare concordance rates or behavioral similarity in samples of identical and fraternal twins, assuming that if the identical twins are far more similar to one another than are the fraternal twins in a specific characteristic, a genetic factor is likely to be involved. Of course, the fly in this ointment is the possibility that because identical twins are more similar to one another in appearance than fraternal twins are, they are treated more alike and therefore share a more similar environment. This environmental factor could partially account for greater behavioral similarity in identical twins.

▶ 7. Describe some of the gene-modification methods used to study causes of behavior.

To rule out this environmental explanation for greater psychological similarity in identical twins, behavior geneticists have adopted an even more elegant research method. Sometimes, as in the University of Minnesota study in which the Jim twins participated, researchers are able to find and compare sets of identical and fraternal twins who were separated very early in life and raised in *different* environments (Bouchard et al., 1990). By eliminating environmental similarity, this design permits a better basis for evaluating the respective contributions of genes and environment.

As the heritability data in Table 3.1 would suggest, many psychological characteristics, including intelligence, personality traits, and certain psychological disorders have a notable genetic contribution. Adoptive children are typically found to be more similar to their biological parents than to their adoptive parents on these measures, and identical twins tend to be more similar to one another than are fraternal twins, even if they were separated early in life and reared in different environments (Loehlin, 1992; Lykken et al., 1992; Plomin, 1997). Figure 3.8 shows the results of one such twin comparison. Three groups of twins—identical twins reared together, those reared apart, and fraternal twins reared together—completed personality tests of extraversion (sociability, liveliness, impulsiveness) and neuroticism (moodiness, anxiousness, and irritability). The higher correlation coefficients for the identical twins indicate that even when reared apart, they are more similar to one another in both extraversion and neuroticism than are the fraternal twins. On the other hand, the still greater similarity among the identical twins reared together suggests that environment also plays a role in the development of these traits (Loehlin, 1992). Other behavior genetics studies have also demonstrated that environmental factors interact with genetic endowment in important ways. In the chapters to follow, we will frequently revisit behavior genetics findings in relation to many aspects of development and behavior.

Genetic Engineering: The Edge of Creation

Until recently, genetics researchers had to be content with studying genetic phenomena occurring in nature. Aside from selectively breeding plants and animals for certain characteristics, or studying the effects of genetic mutations, they had no ability to influence genes directly. Today, however, technological advances and a greater body of knowledge have enabled scientists not only to map the human genome but also to duplicate and modify the structures of genes themselves (Aldridge, 1998).

In **recombinant DNA procedures,** *researchers use certain enzymes (proteins that create chemical reactions) to cut the long threadlike molecules of genetic DNA into pieces, combine it with DNA from another organism, and insert it into a host organism, such as a bacterium.* Inside the host, the new DNA combination continues to divide and produce many copies of itself. Researchers can also insert new genetic material into viruses that can infiltrate the brain and modify the genetic structure of *neurons,* or nerve cells, which we will discuss shortly. Recent gene-modification research by psychologists has focused on processes such as learning, memory, emotion, and motivation. One procedure done with animals (typically mice) is to alter a specific gene in a way that prevents it from carrying out its normal function. This is called a *knockout procedure* because that particular function of the gene is "knocked out," or eliminated. The effects on behavior are then observed. For example, psychologists can insert genetic material that will prevent neurons from responding to a particular neurotransmitter; they can then measure whether the animal's ability to learn or remember is subsequently affected. This can help psychologists determine the importance of particular transmitter substances in relation to the behaviors of interest (Thomas & Palmiter, 1997). Gene modification techniques may one day enable us to alter genes that contribute to psychological disorders, such as depression and schizophrenia.

At one time, geneticists thought that each gene encoded only a single protein. We now know that each gene can encode many proteins. In a new technology originally developed by Carl Pabo at the Massachusetts Institute of Technology, scientists are learning to turn gene commands on or off by engineering specific proteins known as *zinc fingers*. Zinc fingers occur naturally within the cell nucleus, where they "splice," or turn on or off, the production of a particular protein. For example, one gene called *bcl-x* can splice one way to cause cell death and another way to turn off programmed cell death.

Yale researchers have used virus technology to insert zinc fingers into cells and turn on the gene command that produces a protein that is essential for blood vessel growth. This technique holds great promise for cardiovascular therapy. By experimenting with zinc fingers, scientists have also discovered a protein that makes new fat cells. Turning off the gene that produces that protein could become a new gene therapy for obesity. There is also the hope of altering genes that contribute to positive or negative psychological outcomes. Of course, the development of these technologies rests on increased understanding of which genes produce which effects. In this way, basic research informs future application.

IN REVIEW

- *Hereditary potential is carried within the DNA portion of the 23 pairs of chromosomes in units called* genes, *whose commands trigger the production of proteins that control body structures and processes. Genotype (genetic structure) and phenotype (outward appearance) are not identical, in part because some genes are dominant while others are recessive. Many characteristics are polygenic in origin, influenced by the interactions of multiple genes.*
- *The field of behavior genetics studies the contributions of genetic and environmental factors to psychological traits and behaviors. Adoption and twin studies are the major research methods used in an attempt to disentangle hereditary and environmental factors. Especially useful is the study of identical and fraternal twins who were separated early in life and raised in different environments. As in the case of the Jim twins described at the beginning of the chapter, identical twins are quite similar on a host of intellectual and personality characteristics even when reared apart. Many psychological characteristics have appreciable genetic contributions.*
- *Genetic engineering allows scientists to duplicate and alter genetic material or, potentially, to repair dysfunctional genes. These procedures promise groundbreaking advances in treating diseases, but they also raise momentous ethical and moral issues.*

What Do You Think?

FROM GENE THERAPY TO DESIGNER BABIES

Genetic diagnostic and engineering procedures give humans potential control over the processes of heredity and evolution. But they also raise many ethical and moral issues. How and when should these techniques be used? To prevent genetic disorders? To propagate desirable human characteristics? To duplicate or clone exceptional people? What are the social and environmental consequences of using genetic engineering to greatly extend the healthy life span of people? Where do you stand on these issues, and why? Think about it, then turn to page 107.

The brain is a grapefruit-size mass of tissue that feels like jelly and has the gnarled appearance of a grayish walnut. One of the true marvels of nature, it has been termed "our three-pound universe" (Hooper & Teresi, 1986). To understand how the brain controls our experience and behavior, we must first understand how its individual cells function and how they communicate with one another.

FIGURE 3.9

Structural elements of a typical neuron. Stimulation received by the dendrites or soma (cell body) may trigger a nerve impulse, which travels down the axon to stimulate other neurons, muscles, or glands. Some axons have a fatty myelin sheath interrupted at intervals by the nodes of Ranvier. The myelin sheath helps increase the speed of nerve conduction.

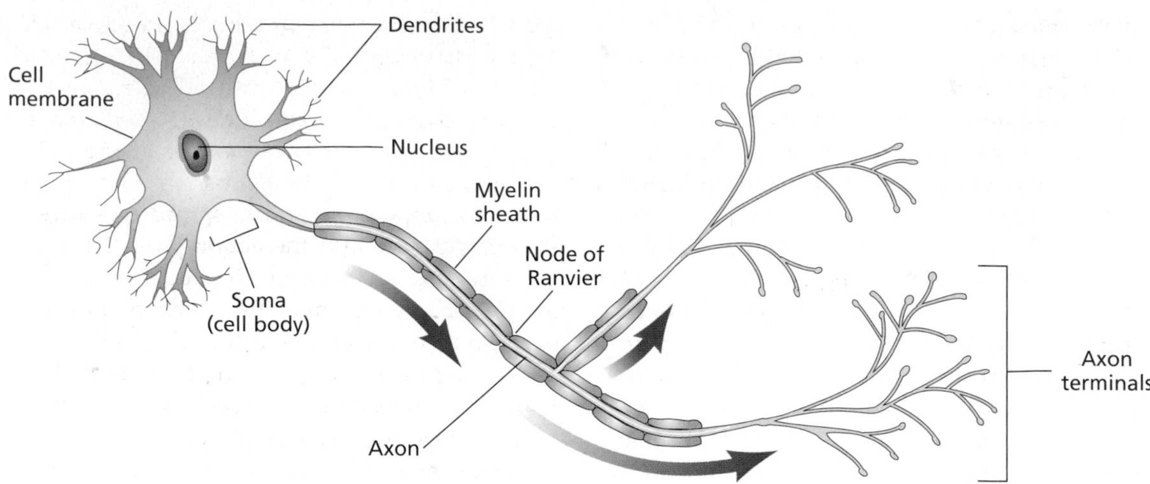

Neurons

Specialized cells called **neurons** *are the basic building blocks of the nervous system*. The estimated 100 billion nerve cells in your brain and spinal cord are linked together in circuits, not unlike the electrical circuits in a computer.

▶ 8. Name and describe the functions of the three main parts of the neuron. What do glial cells do?

Each neuron has three main parts: a cell body, dendrites, and an axon (Figure 3.9). The cell body, or *soma*, contains the biochemical structures needed to keep the neuron alive, and its nucleus carries the genetic information that determines how the cell develops and functions. Emerging from the cell body are branchlike fibers called **dendrites** (from the Greek word meaning "tree"), *specialized receiving units like antennae that collect messages from neighboring neurons and send them on to the cell body*. There, the incoming information is combined and processed. The many branches of the dendrites can receive input from 1,000 or more neighboring neurons. The surface of the cell body also has receptor areas that can be directly stimulated by other neurons. All parts of a neuron are covered by a protective membrane that controls the exchange of chemical substances between the inside and outside of the cell. These exchanges play a critical role in the electrical activities of nerve cells.

Extending from one side of the cell body is a single **axon**, *which conducts electrical impulses away from the cell body to other neurons, muscles, or glands*. The axon branches out at its end to form a number of *axon terminals*—as many as several hundred in some cases. Each axon terminal may connect with dendritic branches from numerous neurons, making it possible for a single neuron to pass messages to as many as 50,000 other neurons (Kolb & Whishaw, 2003). Given the structure of the dendrites and axons, it is easy to see how there can be trillions of interconnections in the brain, making it capable of performing the complex activities that are of interest to psychologists.

Neurons can vary greatly in size and shape; researchers using electron microscopes have viewed more than 200 different types of nerve cells (Nolte, 1998). A neuron with its cell body in your spinal cord may have an axon that extends several feet to one of your fingertips, whereas a neuron in your brain may be no more than a thousandth of an inch long. Regardless of their shape or size, neurons have been exquisitely sculpted by nature to perform their function of receiving, processing, and sending messages.

Neurons are supported in their functions by *glial cells* (from the Greek word meaning "glue"). Glial cells do not send or receive nerve impulses, but they surround neurons and hold them in place. The glial cells also manufacture nutrient chemicals that neurons need, as well as a fatty insulating substance called *myelin* that covers the axons of some neurons and helps speed nerve conduction (we will say more about myelin shortly).

Glial cells carry out important sanitizing functions as well, absorbing toxins and waste materials that, if allowed to remain in the neurons, might cause damage. During prenatal brain development, as new neurons are being formed through cell division, glial cells send out long fibers that guide newly divided neurons to their targeted places in the brain (Filogamo, 1998). Within the brain, glial cells outnumber neurons about 10 to 1.

The Electrical Activity of Neurons

Neurons do two important things. They generate electricity and they release chemicals that allow them to communicate with other neurons and with muscles and glands. Like other cells, neurons are surrounded by body fluids and separated from this liquid environment by a protective membrane.

This cell membrane is a bit like a selective sieve, allowing certain substances in the body fluid to pass through *ion channels* into the cell while refusing or limiting passage to other substances.

The chemical environment inside the neuron differs from its external environment in significant ways, and the process whereby a nerve impulse is created involves the exchange of electrically charged atoms called *ions*. In the salty fluid outside the neuron are positively charged sodium ions (Na^+) and negatively charged chloride ions (Cl^-). Inside the neuron are large negatively charged protein molecules (*anions*, or A^-) and positively charged potassium ions (K^+). The high concentration of sodium ions in the fluid outside the cell, together with the negatively charged protein ions inside, results in an uneven distribution of positive and negative ions. This uneven distribution of ions makes the interior of the cell negative compared to the outside (Figure 3.10 a). *This internal difference of around −70 millivolts (mV) is called the neuron's* **resting potential;** the neuron at rest is said to be in a state of *polarization*.

The Action Potential

All cells in the body have a resting potential. Neurons, however, have a unique property: Sudden and extreme changes can occur in the inside-outside voltage differential. In research that won them the 1963 Nobel Prize, neuroscientists Alan Hodgkin and Andrew Huxley found that if they stimulated the axon with a mild electrical stimulus, the interior voltage differential shifted instantaneously from −70 millivolts to +40 millivolts. *This electrical shift, which lasts about a millisecond (1/1,000 of a second), is called the* **action potential**, or *nerve impulse*.

What happens in the neuron to cause the action potential? Hodgkin and Huxley found that the key mechanism was the action of sodium and potassium ion channels in the cell membrane. In a resting state, the sodium channels are closed, so that the concentration of Na^+ ions is 10 times higher outside of the neuron than inside it. But when a neuron is stimulated sufficiently, the sodium channels open up. Attracted by the negatively charged protein ions inside, positively charged sodium ions flood into the axon, creating a reduction in the negative potential known as *depolarization* (Figure 3.10b). In an instant, the interior now becomes positive (by about +40 millivolts) in relation to the outside, creating the action potential. In a reflex action to restore the resting potential, the cell closes its sodium channels, and positively charged potassium ions flow out through their channels, restoring the negative resting potential (Figure 3.10c). Eventually, the excess sodium ions are pumped out of the neuron, and the escaped potassium ions are recovered. The resulting voltage changes are shown in Figure 3.10d.

▶ 9. What chemical actions create the neuron's resting potential? What chemical changes cause the action potential?

Once an action potential occurs at any point on the membrane, its effects spread to adjacent sodium channels and the action potential flows down the length of the axon. Immediately after an impulse passes a point along the axon, however, there is a recovery period as the K^+ ions flow out of the interior. During this **absolute refractory period,** *the membrane is not excitable and cannot discharge another impulse*. This places an upper limit on the rate at which nerve impulses can occur. In humans, the limit seems to be about 300 impulses per second (Kolb & Whishaw, 2003).

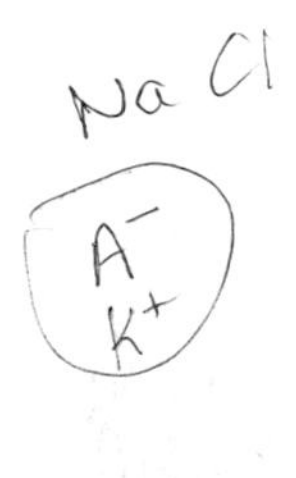

One other feature of the action potential is noteworthy. In accordance with the so-called **all-or-none law,** *action potentials occur at a uniform and maximum intensity, or they do not occur at all*. Like firing a gun, which requires that a certain amount of pressure be placed on the trigger, the negative potential inside the axon has to be lowered from −70 millivolts to about −50 millivolts (the *action potential threshold*) by the influx of sodium ions into the axon before the action potential will be triggered. *Changes in the negative resting potential that do not reach the −50 millivolt action potential threshold are called* **graded potentials.** Under certain circumstances, several of these graded potentials may add up to trigger an action potential.

For a neuron to function properly, sodium and potassium ions must enter and leave the membrane at just the right rate. Drugs that alter this transit system can decrease or prevent neural functioning. For example, local anesthetics such as Novocain and Xylocaine attach themselves to the sodium channels, stopping the flow of sodium ions into the neurons and thereby preventing action potentials in the affected area. General anesthetics such as ether and chloroform work in a different way, opening potassium channels so that potassium ions flow out as fast as sodium ions flow into the cell. This prevents most action potentials from occurring (Ray & Ksir, 2002).

▶ 10. What is the nature and importance of the myelin sheath? Which disorder results from damage to it?

Many axons that transmit information throughout the brain and spinal cord are covered by a tubelike **myelin sheath,** *a whitish, fatty insulation layer derived from glial cells during development*. The myelin sheath is interrupted at regular intervals by the *nodes of Ranvier,* where the myelin is either extremely thin or absent, so that myelinated axons look a bit like sausages placed end to end (see Figure 3.9). In axons lacking the myelin sheath, the action potential travels down the axon

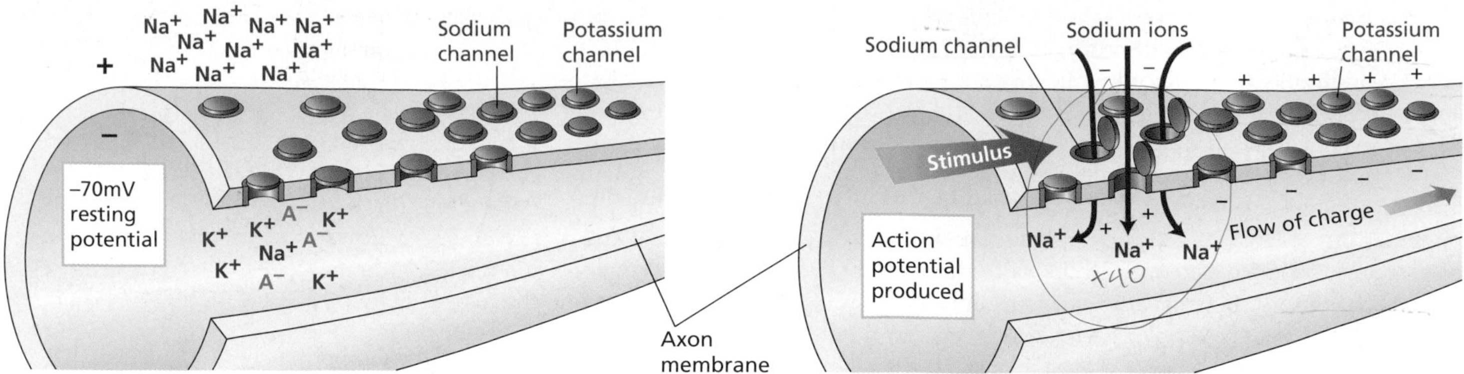

(a) The 10:1 concentration of sodium (Na^+) ions outside the neuron and the negative protein (A^-) ions inside contribute to a resting potential of –70mV.

(b) Sodium channels open and sodium ions flood into the axon. Note that the potassium channels are still closed.

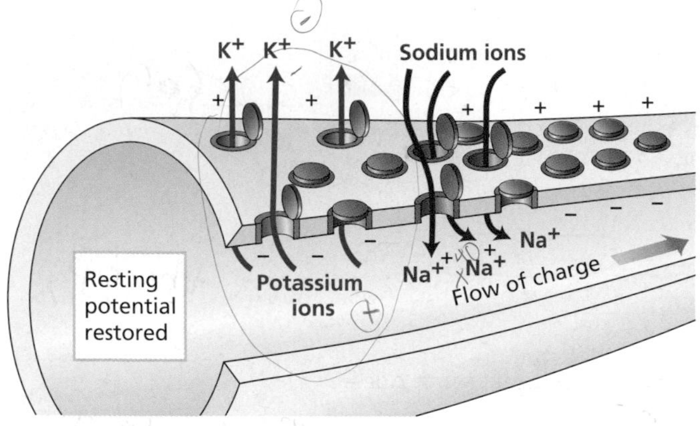

(c) Sodium channels that were open in (b) have now closed and potassium channels behind them are open, allowing potassium ions to exit and restoring the resting potential at that point. Sodium channels are opening at the next point.

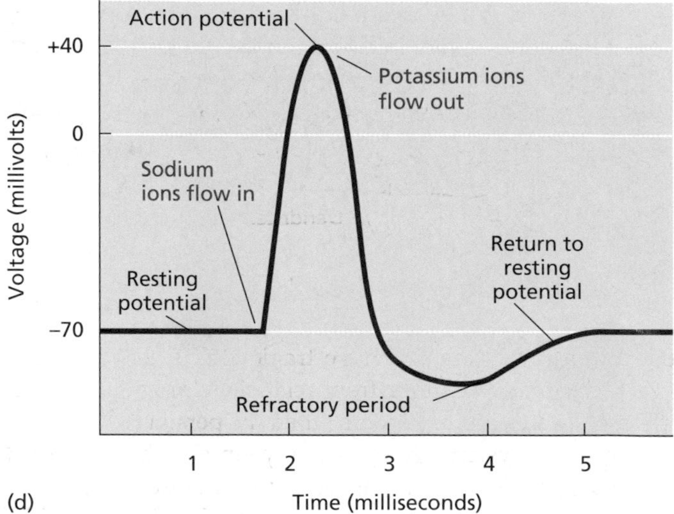

(d)

FIGURE 3.10

From resting potential to action potential. When a neuron is not being stimulated, a difference in electrical charge of about −70 millivolts (mV) exists between the interior and the surface of the neuron. (a) This resting potential is caused by the uneven distribution of positively and negatively charged ions, with a greater concentration of positively charged sodium ions kept outside the cell by closed sodium channels, and the presence of negatively charged protein (A^-) ions inside the cell. In addition, the action of sodium-potassium pumps helps maintain the negative interior by pumping out three sodium (Na^+) ions for every two positively charged potassium (K^+) ions pumped into the cell. (b) Sufficient stimulation of the neuron causes an action potential. Sodium channels open for an instant, and Na^+ ions flood into the axon, reversing the electrical potential from −70 mV to +40 mV. (c) Within a millisecond, the sodium channels close and many K^+ ions flow out of the cell through open potassium channels, helping to restore the interior negative potential. As adjacent sodium channels are opened and the sequence in (b) and (c) is repeated, the action potential moves down the length of the neuron. (d) Shown here are the changes in potential that would be recorded from a particular point on the axon. After a brief refractory period during which the neuron cannot be stimulated, another action potential can follow.

length in a point-to-point fashion like a burning fuse. But in myelinated axons, the flow of ions needed to create action potentials cannot occur through the insulating layer. However, the nodes of Ranvier are close enough to one another so that depolarization at one node can activate the next node, allowing electrical conduction to "jump" from node to node at high speeds.

The myelin sheath is most commonly found in the nervous systems of higher animals. In many neurons, the myelin sheath is not completely formed until some time after birth. The increased efficiency of neural transmission that results is partly responsible for the gains that infants exhibit in muscular coordination and psychological processes as they grow older (Kolb, 1989). Damage

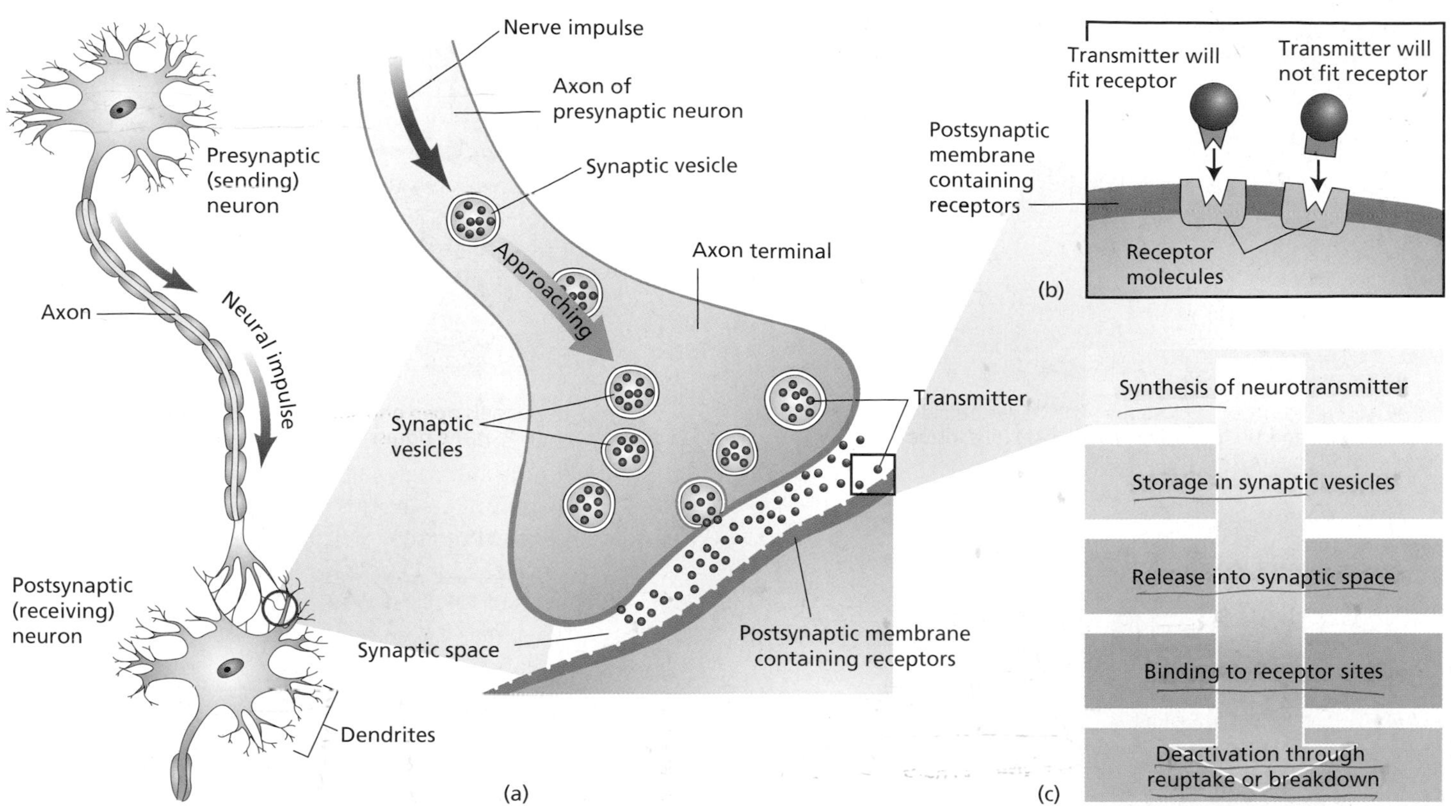

FIGURE 3.11

A synapse between two neurons. The action potential travels to the axon terminals, where it stimulates the release of transmitter molecules from the synaptic vesicles. (a) These molecules travel across the synaptic space and bind to specially keyed receptor sites on the cell body or dendrite of the postsynaptic neuron. (b) The lock-and key nature of neurotransmitters and receptor sites means that only transmitters that fit the receptor will influence membrane potentials. (c) Neurotransmitter activity moves from synthesis to deactivation. If the neurotransmitter has an excitatory effect on the neuron, the chemical reaction creates a graded or an action potential. If the neurotransmitter has an inhibitory effect, the negative potential inside the neuron increases and makes it more difficult to trigger an action potential.

to the myelin coating can have tragic effects, as seen in people who suffer from *multiple sclerosis*. This progressive disease occurs when the person's own immune system attacks the myelin sheath, disrupting the delicate timing of nerve impulses. The result is increasingly jerky and uncoordinated movements and, in the final stages, paralysis.

We've now seen how nerve impulses are generated. However, the activity of a single neuron means little unless it can communicate its message to other neurons. This is where the chemical activities of neurons come into play.

How Neurons Communicate: Synaptic Transmission

The nervous system operates as a giant communications network, and its action requires the transmission of nerve impulses from one neuron to another. Early in the history of brain research, scientists thought that the tip of the axon made physical contact with the dendrites or cell bodies of other neurons, passing electricity directly from one neuron to the next. With the advent of the electron microscope, however, researchers discovered a **synaptic space,** *a tiny gap between the axon terminal and the next neuron.* This discovery raised new and perplexing questions: If neurons do not physically touch the other neurons to which they send signals, how does communication occur? If the action potential does not cross the synapse, what does? What carries the message?

Neurotransmitters

We now know that in addition to generating electricity, neurons produce **neurotransmitters,** *chemical substances that carry messages across the synapse either to excite other neurons or to inhibit their firing.* This process of chemical communication involves five steps: synthesis, storage, release, binding, and deactivation. In the *synthesis* stage, the transmitter molecules are formed inside the neuron. The molecules are then *stored* in **synaptic vesicles,** *chambers within the axon terminals.* When an action potential comes down the axon, these vesicles move to the surface of the axon terminal and the molecules are *released* into the fluid-filled space between the axon of the *presynaptic* (sending) neuron and the membrane of the *postsynaptic* (receiving) neuron. The molecules cross the synaptic space and *bind* (attach themselves) to **receptor sites,** *large protein molecules embedded in the receiving neuron's cell membrane.* These receptor sites have a specially shaped surface that fits a specific transmitter molecule much like a lock accommodates a single key (Figure 3.11).

When a transmitter molecule binds to a receptor site, a chemical reaction occurs. This reaction can have two different effects on the receiving neuron. In some cases, the chemical reaction causes the postsynaptic neuron's sodium channels to open. As

▶ 11. Describe 5 important steps in neurotransmitter function. How do transmitters produce excitation and inhibition? How are they deactivated?

TABLE 3.2 Some Neurotransmitters and Their Effects

Neurotransmitter	Major Function	Disorders Associated With Malfunctioning
Acetylcholine (ACh)	Excitatory at synapses involved in muscular movement and memory	Undersupply produces memory loss in Alzheimer's disease; absence produces paralysis.
Norepinephrine	Excitatory and inhibitory functions at various sites; involved in neural circuits controlling learning, memory, wakefulness, and eating	Depression (undersupply)
Serotonin	Inhibitory or excitatory; involved in mood, sleep, eating, and arousal, and may be an important transmitter underlying pleasure and pain	Depression, sleeping, and eating disorders (undersupply)
Dopamine	Excitatory; involved in voluntary movement, emotional arousal, learning, memory, and experiencing pleasure or pain	Parkinson's disease and depression (undersupply); schizophrenia (oversupply)
GABA (gamma-aminobutyric acid)	Inhibitory transmitter in motor system	Destruction of GABA-producing neurons in Huntington's disease produces tremors and loss of motor control, as well as personality changes

▶ 12. Describe the roles played by acetylcholine and the consequences that occur when its functioning is disrupted.

sodium ions flood into the cell and depolarize it, they create either a graded potential or an action potential as just described. This is what *excitatory* neurotransmitters do. An *inhibitory* neurotransmitter will do the opposite. It may cause positive potassium ions to flow out of the neuron or negative chloride ions from the exterior to flow into it through chloride channels in the membrane, increasing the neuron's negative potential (perhaps from −70 to −75 millivolts) and pulling it further away from the −50 millivolt action potential threshold. This process of *hyperpolarization* will make it harder to fire the neuron. The action of an inhibitory neurotransmitter from one presynaptic neuron may prevent the postsynaptic neuron from firing an action potential even if it is receiving excitatory stimulation from other neurons at the same time. If the nervous system is to function properly, it must maintain an exceptionally finely-tuned balance between excitation and inhibition. We should note, however, that some neurotransmitters can have either excitatory or inhibitory effects, depending on which receptor sites they bind to.

Once a neurotransmitter molecule binds to its receptor, it continues to activate or inhibit the neuron until it is *deactivated*, or shut off. This occurs in two major ways (Fain, 1999). Some transmitter molecules are deactivated by other chemicals located in the synaptic space that break them down into their chemical components. In other instances, the deactivation mechanism is **reuptake,** *in which the transmitter molecules are taken back into the presynaptic axon terminal.* Once the receptor molecule is vacant, the postsynaptic neuron returns to its former resting state, awaiting the next chemical stimulation.

Specialized Transmitter Systems

Through the use of chemical transmitters, nature has found an ingenious way of dividing up the brain into systems that are uniquely sensitive to certain messages. There is only one kind of electricity, but there are many shapes that can be assumed by transmitter molecules. Because the various systems in the brain recognize only certain chemical messengers, they are immune to cross talk from other systems.

There clearly are many different neurotransmitter substances, some of which can coexist within the same neuron. A given neuron may use one transmitter at one synapse and a different one at another synapse. Moreover, different transmitters may be found within the same axon terminal or in the same synapse, adding another layer of complexity (Kolb & Whishaw, 2003). Each substance has a specific excitatory or inhibitory effect on certain neurons. Table 3.2 lists several of the more important neurotransmitters that have been linked to psychological phenomena.

Perhaps the best understood is **acetylcholine (ACh),** *a neurotransmitter involved in memory and in muscle activity.* Underproduction of ACh is an important factor in *Alzheimer's disease,* a degenerative brain disorder involving profound memory impairments that afflicts 5 to 10 percent of all people over 65 years of age (Ron & David, 1997). Reductions in ACh weaken or deactivate neural circuitry that stores memories. ACh is also an excitatory transmitter at the synapses where neurons activate muscle cells, helping to account for the severe motor impairments found in the later stages of Alzheimer's disease.

Drugs that block the action of ACh can prevent muscle activation and cause paralysis. One example occurs in *botulism,* a serious type of food poisoning that can result from improperly canned food. The toxin formed by the botulinum bacteria blocks the release of ACh from the axon terminal, resulting in a potentially fatal paralysis of the muscles, including those of the respiratory system. A mild form of the toxin, known as Botox, is used cosmetically to remove skin wrinkles by paralyzing the underlying muscles whose contraction causes them.

The opposite effect on ACh occurs with the bite of the black widow spider. The spider's venom triggers a torrent of ACh, resulting in violent muscle contractions, convulsions, and possible death. Some chemical agents, such as the deadly sarin gas released into the Tokyo subway system by terrorists in 1995, also raise havoc by allowing ACh to run wild in the nervous system. Sarin and similar nerve gas agents prevent the activity of an enzyme that normally degrades ACh at the synapse. The result is uncontrolled seizures and convulsions that can kill. Among antidotes issued to coalition troops during the Iraq War was a substance that inhibits nerve agents from preventing the action of the enzyme.

Most neurotransmitters have their excitatory or inhibitory effects only on specific neurons that have receptors for them. Others, called **neuromodulators,** *have a more widespread and generalized influence on synaptic transmission*. These substances circulate through the brain and either increase or decrease (i.e., modulate) the sensitivity of thousands, perhaps millions, of neurons to their specific transmitters. The best known neuromodulators are the *endorphins,* which travel through the brain's circulatory system and inhibit pain transmission while enhancing neural activity that produces pleasurable feelings. Other neuromodulators play important roles in functions such as eating, sleeping, and coping with stress.

Knowledge about neurotransmitter systems has many important applied implications. For one thing, it helps us understand the mechanisms that underlie the effects of **psychoactive drugs,** *chemicals that produce alterations in consciousness, emotion, and behavior*. The following *Applying Psychological Science* feature focuses on mechanisms of drug effects within the brain.

For more on neural functioning, see Interactive Segment 3.1.

▶ 13. How do agonist and antagonist functions underlie the neural and behavioral effects of psychoactive drugs?

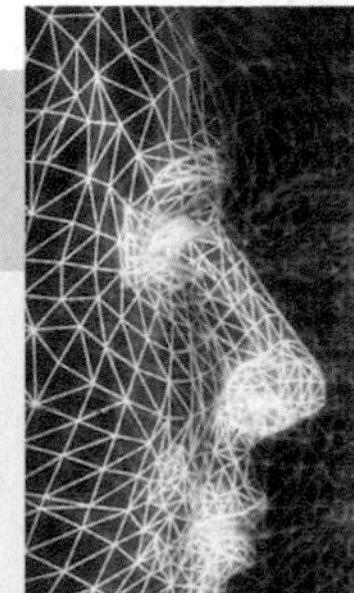

APPLYING PSYCHOLOGICAL SCIENCE

UNDERSTANDING HOW DRUGS AFFECT YOUR BRAIN

Drugs affect consciousness and behavior by influencing the activity of neurons. If you've had a soft drink or a cup of coffee, taken an aspirin or smoked a cigarette, you've ingested a drug. A recent survey of 55,000 students at 132 colleges in the United States revealed that in the past year, 47 percent had used tobacco; 84 percent, alcohol; 33.6 percent, marijuana; and 5 to 10 percent, cocaine, amphetamines, hallucinogenic drugs such as LSD, and designer drugs such as Ecstasy (Core Institute, 2002). Countless students ingest caffeine in coffee, chocolate, cocoa, and soft drinks. Perhaps you have wondered exactly how these drugs exert their diverse effects.

Most psychoactive drugs produce their effects by either increasing or decreasing the synthesis, storage, release, binding, or deactivation of neurotransmitters. An **agonist** *is a drug that increases the activity of a neurotransmitter.* Agonists may (1) enhance a neuron's ability to synthesize, store, or release neurotransmitters; (2) bind with and stimulate postsynaptic receptor sites; or (3) make it more difficult for neurotransmitters to be deactivated, such as by inhibiting reuptake.

An **antagonist** *is a drug that inhibits or decreases the action of a neurotransmitter.* An antagonist may (1) reduce a neuron's ability to synthesize, store, or release neurotransmitters; or (2) prevent a neurotransmitter from binding with the postsynaptic neuron by fitting into and blocking the receptor sites on the postsynaptic neuron.

With the distinction between agonist and antagonist functions in mind, let us consider how some commonly used drugs work within the brain. We will discuss drug effects on consciousness and behavior in greater detail in Chapter 5.

Alcohol is a depressant drug having both agonist and antagonist effects. As an agonist, it stimulates the activity of the inhibitory transmitter GABA, thereby depressing neural activity. As an antagonist, it decreases the activity of glutamate, an excitatory transmitter (Gonzalez & Jaworski, 1997). The double-barreled effect is a neural slowdown that inhibits normal brain functions of clear thinking, emotional control, and motor coordination. Sedative drugs, including barbiturates and tranquilizers, also increase GABA activity, and mixing them with alcohol intake can be a deadly combination when their depressant effects on neural activity are combined with those of alcohol.

Caffeine is a stimulant drug that increases the activity of neurons and other cells. It is an antagonist for the transmitter adenosine. Adenosine inhibits the release of excitatory transmitters. By reducing adenosine activity, caffeine helps produce higher rates of cellular activity and more available energy. Although caffeine is a stimulant, it is important to note that, contrary to popular belief, caffeine does *not* counteract the effects of alcohol

Continued

and sober people up. What your drunken friend needs is a ride home with a driver who is sober—not a cup of coffee.

Nicotine is an agonist for the excitatory transmitter acetylcholine. Its chemical structure is similar enough to ACh to allow it to fit into ACh binding sites and create action potentials. At other receptor sites, nicotine stimulates dopamine activity, which seems to be an important chemical mediator of energy and pleasure. This may help account for nicotine's powerful addictive properties. Researchers are working to develop medications that could wean people off cigarettes and other tobacco products by blocking or occupying the specific receptor sites that trigger dopamine release.

Amphetamines are stimulant drugs that boost arousal and mood by increasing the activity of the excitatory neurotransmitters dopamine and norepinephrine. They do so in two major ways. First, they cause presynaptic neurons to release greater amounts of these neurotransmitters. Second, they inhibit reuptake, allowing dopamine and norepinephrine to keep stimulating postsynaptic neurons (Diaz, 1997).

Cocaine produces excitation, a sense of increased muscular strength, and euphoria. Like amphetamines, cocaine increases the activity of norepinephrine and dopamine, but it does so in only one major way: It blocks their reuptake. Thus amphetamines and cocaine have different mechanisms of action on the dopamine and norepinephrine transmitter systems, but both drugs produce highly stimulating effects on mood, thinking, and behavior.

We should comment on two other drugs that, unfortunately, are also found on college campuses. Rohypnol (flunitrazepam, known as "roofies" or "rope") and GHB (gamma hydroxybutyrate, known as "easy lay") are so-called date-rape drugs. Partygoers sometimes add these drugs to punch and other drinks in hopes of lowering drinkers' inhibitions and facilitating noncensual sexual conquest. The drugs are powerful sedatives that suppress general neural activity by enhancing the action of the inhibitory transmitter GABA (Lobina et al., 1999). Rohypnol is about 10 times more potent than Valium. At high doses or when mixed with alcohol or other drugs, these substances may lead to respiratory depression, loss of consciousness, coma, and even death. Rohypnol also attacks neurotransmission in areas of the brain involved in memory, producing an amnesia effect that may prevent users from remembering the circumstances under which they ingested the drug or what happened to them afterwards. GHB, which makes its victim appear drunk and helpless, is now a restricted drug, and slipping it into someone's drink is a criminal act. The bottom line is that these drugs are good neither to give nor to receive (Figure 3.12). Increasingly, women are being advised against accepting an opened drink from a fellow reveler or leaving their own drink unattended at parties.

FIGURE 3.12

Brain activity is being altered in several ways in this scene. Nicotine from cigarette smoke is activating acetylcholine and dopamine neurons, increasing neural excitation. The alcohol is stimulating the activity of the inhibitory transmitter GABA and decreasing the activity of the excitatory transmitter glutamate, thus depressing brain functions. The possibility of the drink having been spiked with one of the powerful and potentially deadly "date-rape" sedative drugs could place this woman at great risk.

IN REVIEW

- *Each neuron has dendrites, which receive nerve impulses from other neurons; a cell body, which controls the vital processes of the cell; and an axon, which conducts nerve impulses to adjacent neurons, muscles, and glands.*
- *Neural transmission is an electrochemical process. The nerve impulse, or action potential, is a brief reversal in the electrical potential of the cell membrane from negative to positive as sodium ions from the surrounding fluid flow into the cell through sodium ion channels. The action potential obeys the all-or-none law, firing completely or not at all. The myelin sheath increases the speed of neural transmission.*
- *Passage of the impulse across the synapse is mediated by chemical transmitter substances. Neurons are selective in the neurotransmitters that can stimulate them. Some neurotransmitters excite neurons, whereas others inhibit firing of the postsynaptic neuron. The nervous system requires a delicate balance of excitation and inhibition of neurons. Agonists can mimic or increase the action of neurotransmitters, whereas antagonists prevent the effects of a transmitter from occurring.*

THE NERVOUS SYSTEM

The nervous system is the body's master control center. Three major types of neurons carry out the system's input, output, and integration functions. **Sensory neurons** *carry input messages from the sense organs to the spinal cord and brain.* **Motor neurons** *transmit output impulses from the brain and spinal cord to the body's muscles and organs.* Finally, there are neurons that link the input and output functions; these **interneurons**, which far outnumber sensory and motor neurons, *perform connective or associative functions within the nervous system.* For example, interneurons would allow us to succeed at playing "name that tune" by linking the sensory input from the song we're hearing with the memory of that song stored elsewhere in the brain. The activity of interneurons makes possible the complexity of our higher mental functions, emotions, and behavioral capabilities.

The nervous system can be broken down into several interrelated subsystems (Figure 3.13). The two major divisions are the **central nervous system**, *consisting of all the neurons that connect the central nervous system with the muscles, glands, and sensory receptors;* and the **peripheral nervous system,** *consisting of all the neurons in the brain and spinal cord.*

The Peripheral Nervous System

The peripheral nervous system contains all the neural structures that lie outside of the brain and spinal cord. Its specialized neurons help carry out the input and output functions that are necessary for us to sense what is going on inside and outside our bodies and to respond with our muscles and glands. The peripheral nervous system has two major divisions, the somatic nervous system and the autonomic nervous system.

▶ 14. What are the 3 major types of neurons in the nervous system? What are their functions?

▶ 15. Name the 2 divisions of the peripheral nervous system. How does the autonomic system maintain homeostasis?

The Somatic Nervous System

The **somatic nervous system** *consists of sensory neurons that are specialized to transmit messages from the eyes, ears, and other sensory receptors and motor neurons that send messages from the brain and spinal cord to the muscles that control our voluntary movements.* The axons of sensory neurons group together like many strands of a rope to form *sensory nerves,* and motor neuron axons combine to form *motor nerves.* (Inside the brain and spinal cord, nerves are called *tracts.*) As you read this page, sensory neurons located in your eyes are sending impulses to a complex network of specialized visual tracts that course through your brain. At the same time, motor neurons are stimulating the eye movements that allow you to scan the lines of type and turn the

FIGURE 3.13

Structural organization of the nervous system.

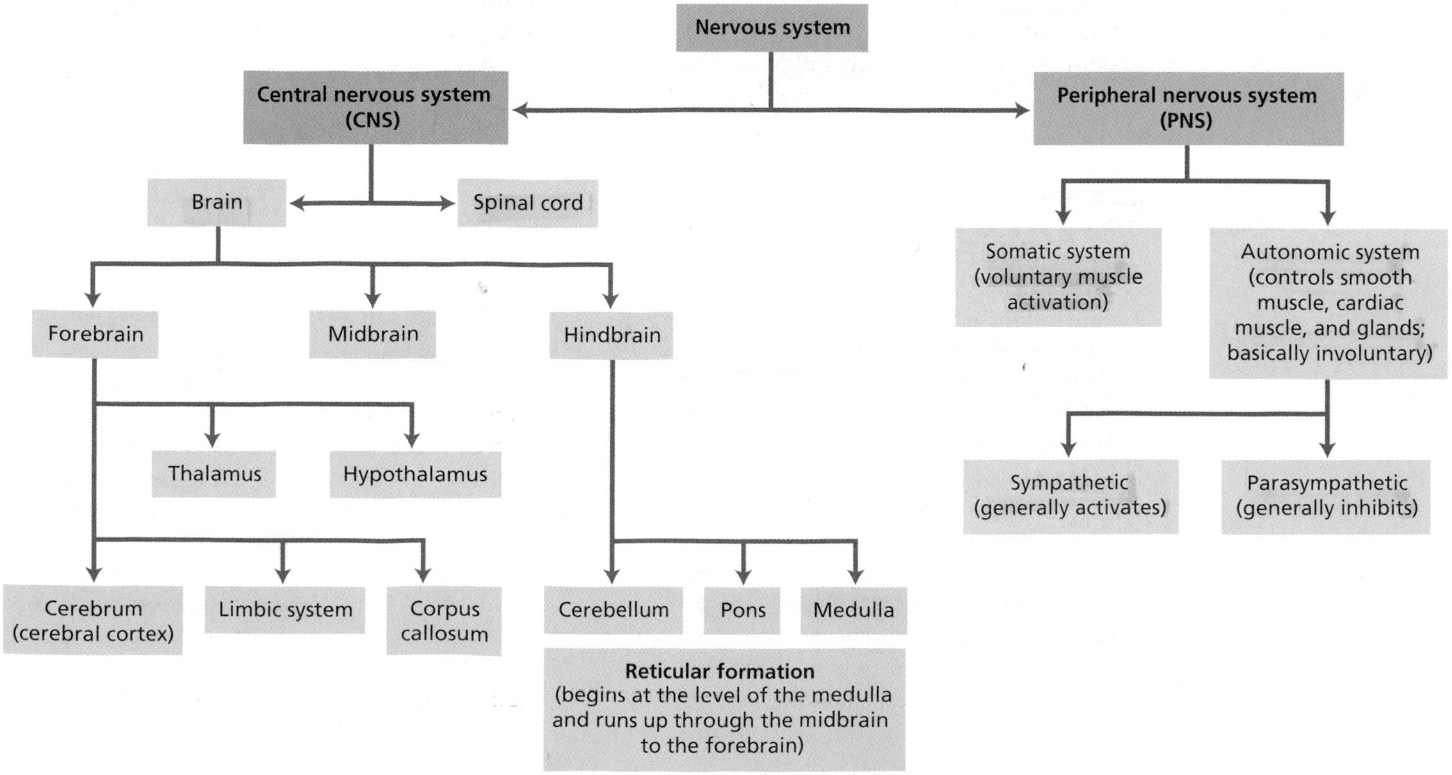

- Nervous system
  - Central nervous system (CNS)
    - Brain
      - Forebrain
        - Thalamus
        - Hypothalamus
        - Cerebrum (cerebral cortex)
        - Limbic system
        - Corpus callosum
      - Midbrain
      - Hindbrain
        - Cerebellum
        - Pons
        - Medulla
        - **Reticular formation** (begins at the level of the medulla and runs up through the midbrain to the forebrain)
    - Spinal cord
  - Peripheral nervous system (PNS)
    - Somatic system (voluntary muscle activation)
    - Autonomic system (controls smooth muscle, cardiac muscle, and glands; basically involuntary)
      - Sympathetic (generally activates)
      - Parasympathetic (generally inhibits)

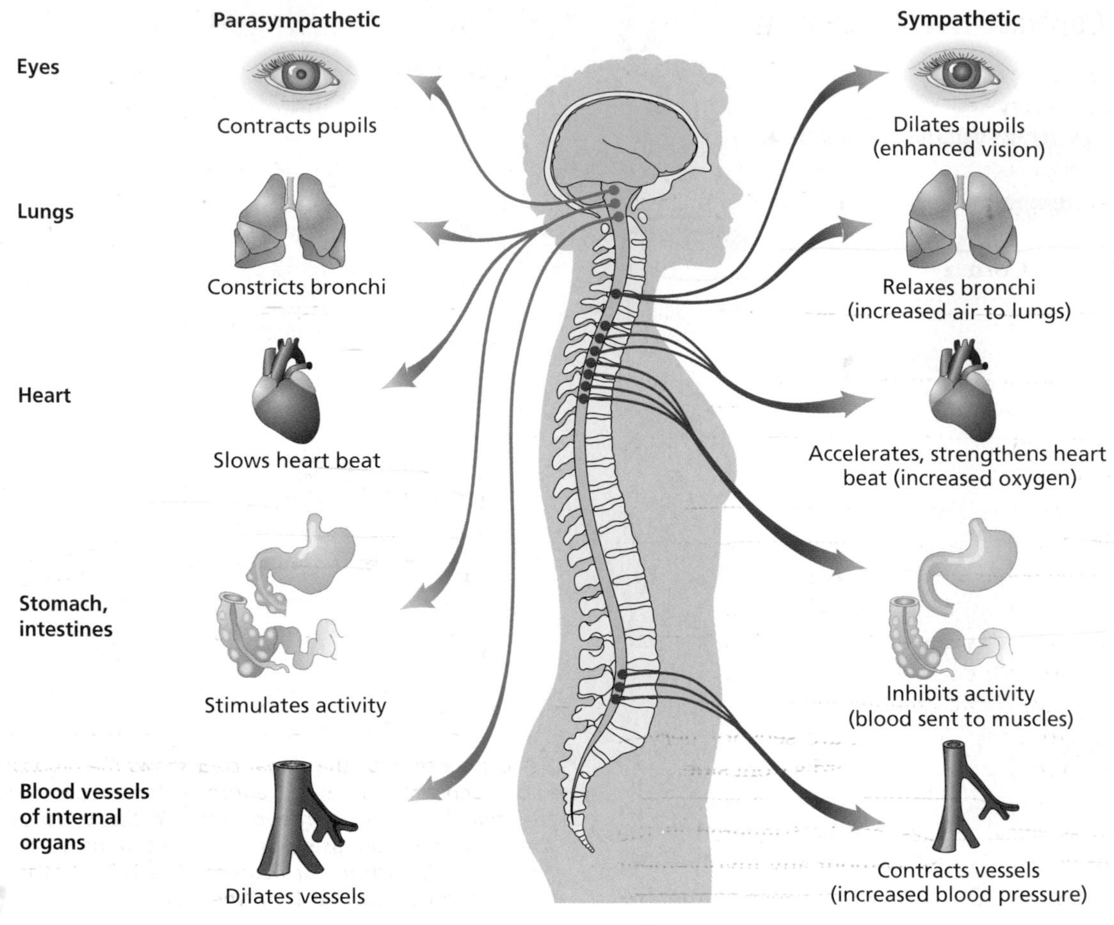

FIGURE 3.14

The sympathetic branch of the autonomic nervous system arouses the body and speeds up its vital processes. It tends to act in a nonspecific fashion, activating many processes at the same time. The parasympathetic division, which is more specific in its opposing actions, slows down body processes. The two divisions work in concert to maintain an equilibrium within the body.

pages. The somatic system thus allows you to sense and respond to your environment.

The Autonomic Nervous System

The body's internal environment is regulated largely through the activities of the **autonomic nervous system**, *which senses the body's internal functions and controls the glands and the smooth (involuntary) muscles that form the heart, the blood vessels, and the lining of the stomach and intestines.* The autonomic system is largely concerned with involuntary functions, such as respiration, circulation, and digestion; it is also involved in many aspects of motivation, emotional behavior, and stress responses. It consists of two subdivisions, the sympathetic nervous system and the parasympathetic nervous system (Figure 3.14). Typically, these two divisions affect the same organ or gland in opposing ways.

The **sympathetic nervous system** *has an activation, or arousal, function, and it tends to act as a total unit.* For example, when you encounter a stressful situation, your sympathetic nervous system helps you confront the stressor in several ways. It speeds your heart rate so that it can pump more blood to your muscles, dilates your pupils so that more light can enter the eye and improve your vision, slows down your digestive system so that blood can be transferred to the muscles, increases your rate of respiration so that your body can get more oxygen, and, in general, mobilizes your body. This is sometimes called the *fight-or-flight response*.

Compared with the sympathetic branch, which tends to act as a unit, the **parasympathetic nervous system** *is far more specific in its opposing actions, affecting one or a few organs at a time. In general, it slows down body processes and maintains a state of tranquility.* Thus your sympathetic system speeds up your heart rate; your parasympathetic system slows it down. By working together to maintain equilibrium in our internal organs, the two divisions can maintain *homeostasis*, a delicately balanced or constant internal state. In addition, sympathetic and parasympathetic activities sometimes coordinate to enable us to perform certain behaviors. For example, sexual function in the male involves penile erection (through parasympathetic dilation of the blood vessels) followed by ejaculation (a primarily sympathetic function; Masters et al., 1988).

The Central Nervous System

More than any other system in our body, the central nervous system distinguishes us from other creatures. This system contains the spinal cord—which connects most parts of the peripheral nervous system with the brain—and the brain itself.

The Spinal Cord

Most nerves enter and leave the central nervous system by way of the spinal cord, a structure that in a human adult is 16 to 18 inches long and about 1 inch in diameter. The *vertebrae* (bones of the spine) protect the spinal cord's neurons. When the spinal cord is viewed in cross section (Figure 3.15), its central portion resembles an H, or a butterfly. The H-shaped portion consists largely of gray-colored neuron cell bodies and their interconnections. Surrounding the gray matter are white-colored myelinated axons that connect various levels of the spinal cord with each other and with the higher centers of the brain. Entering the back side of the spinal cord along its length are sensory nerves. Motor nerves exit the spinal cord's front side.

Some simple stimulus-response sequences, known as *spinal reflexes*, can be triggered at the level of the spinal cord without any involvement of the brain. For example, if you touch something hot, sensory receptors in your skin trigger nerve impulses in sensory nerves that flash into your spinal cord and synapse inside with interneurons. The interneurons then excite motor neurons that send impulses to your hand so that it pulls away. Other interneurons simultaneously carry the "Hot!" message up the spinal cord to your brain, but it is a good thing that you don't have to wait for the brain to tell you what to do in such emergencies. Getting messages to and from the brain takes slightly longer, so the spinal cord reflex system significantly reduces reaction time and, in this case, potential tissue damage.

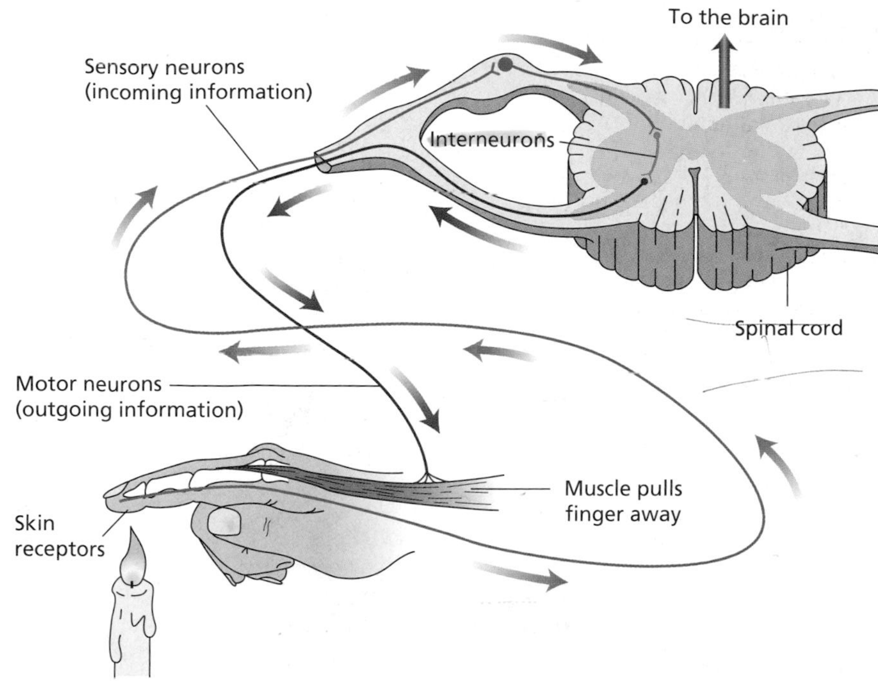

FIGURE 3.15

A cross section of the spinal cord shows the organization of sensory and motor neurons. Sensory and motor neurons enter and exit the spinal cord on both sides of the spinal column. Interneurons within the H-shaped spinal gray matter can serve a connective function, as shown here, but in many cases, sensory neurons can also synapse directly with motor neurons. At this level of the nervous system, reflex activity is possible without involving the brain.

The Brain

The three pounds of protein, fat, and fluid that you carry around inside your skull is the real "you." It is also the most complex structure in the known universe and the only one that can wonder about itself. As befits this biological marvel, your brain is the most active energy consumer of all your body organs. Although your brain accounts for only about 2 percent of your total body weight, it consumes about 25 percent of your body's oxygen and 70 percent of its glucose. Moreover, the brain never rests; its rate of energy metabolism is relatively constant day and night. In fact, when you dream, the brain's metabolic rate actually increases slightly (Hobson, 1996).

How can this rather nondescript blob of grayish tissue discover the principle of relativity, build the Hubble Space Telescope, and produce great works of art, music, and literature? Answering such questions requires the ability to study the brain and how it functions. To do so, neuroscientists use a diverse set of tools and procedures.

Unlocking the Secrets of the Brain

Because of scientific advances, more has been learned over the past three decades about the brain and its role in behavior than was known throughout all the preceding ages. Investigators now use a variety of methods to study the brain's structures and activities.

▶ 16. Describe four methods used to study brain-behavior relations.

Neuropsychological Tests Psychologists have developed a variety of *neuropsychological tests* to measure verbal and nonverbal behaviors that are used in clinical evaluations of people who may have suffered brain damage through accident or disease (Lezak, 1995). They are also important research tools. For example, Figure 3.16 shows a

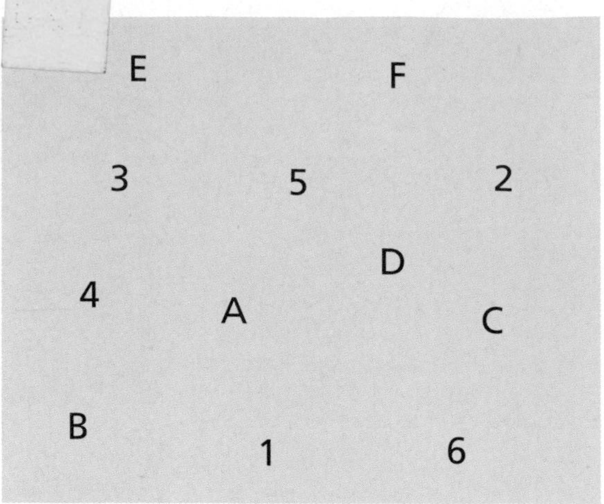

FIGURE 3.16

Psychologists use the Trail Making Test to assess brain functioning. It consists of a randomly scattered set of numbers and letters. On this timed test, the patient must connect the numbers and letters consecutively with a continuous line, or "trail" (i.e., A to 1 to B to 2 to C to 3, and so on). People with certain kinds of brain damage have trouble alternating between the numbers and letters because they cannot retain a plan in memory long enough, and poor performance on this test picks up such a deficit.

portion of a Trail Making Test, used to test memory and planning. Scores on the test give an indication of the type and severity of damage the person may have. Neuropsychological tests of this kind have provided much information about brain-behavior relations.

▶ 17. How are CAT scans, PET scans, and MRIs produced, and what kinds of information does each furnish?

Destruction and Stimulation Techniques Experimental studies are another useful method of learning about the brain. Researchers can produce brain damage (lesions) under carefully controlled conditions in which specific nervous tissue is destroyed with electricity, with cold or heat, or with chemicals. They can also surgically remove some portion of the brain and study the consequences. Most experiments of this kind are performed on animals, but humans can also be studied when accident or disease produces a specific lesion or when abnormal brain tissue must be surgically removed.

An alternative to destroying neurons is stimulating them, which typically produces opposite effects. A specific region of the brain can be stimulated by a mild electric current or by chemicals that excite neurons. Chemical stimulation involves inserting a tiny tube, or *cannula*, into a precise area of the brain so that chemicals, including neurotransmitters, can be delivered directly to the area to be studied and their effects on behavior studied. A specific region of the brain can also be stimulated by a mild electric current. Electrodes can be permanently implanted so that the region of interest can be stimulated repeatedly. Some electrodes are so tiny that they can stimulate individual neurons. In a recent electrical stimulation study, placement of electrodes on a specific region of the brain's outer surface above the right ear produced a surprising effect. The woman experienced herself as floating in the air above her body, as if she had departed from her body (Blanke et al., 2002). Neuroscientists wonder if the researchers may have accidentally discovered a neural basis for "near death" and other paranormal "out-of-body" experiences that have been reported by many people.

Electrical Recording Because electrodes can record brain activity as well as stimulate it, it is also possible to "eavesdrop" on the electrical "conversations" occurring within the brain. Neurons' electrical activity can be measured by inserting small electrodes in particular areas of the brain or even in individual neurons.

In addition to measuring individual "voices," scientists can tune in to "crowd noise." The **electroencephalograph (EEG)** *measures the activity of large groups of neurons through a series of large electrodes placed on the scalp* (Figure 3.17a, b). Although the EEG is a rather gross measure that taps the electrical activity of thousands of neurons in many parts of the brain, specific EEG patterns correspond to certain states of consciousness, such as wakefulness and sleep. Clinicians also use the EEG to detect abnormal electrical patterns that signal the presence of brain disorders.

Brain Imaging The newest tools of discovery are imaging techniques that permit neuroscientists to peer into the living brain (Figure 3.17c). The most important of these technological "windows" are CT scans, PET scans, and MRIs.

Developed in the 1970s, **computerized axial tomography (CT, or CAT) scans** *use X-ray technology to study brain structures* (Peyster, 2000). A highly focused beam of X rays takes pictures of narrow slices of the brain. A computer analyzes the X-rayed slices and creates pictures of the brain's interior from many different angles (Figure 3.17d). Pinpointing where deterioration or injuries have occurred helps clarify relations between brain damage and psychological functioning. CT scans are 100 times more sensitive than standard X-ray procedures, and the technological advance was so dramatic that its developers, Allan Cormack and Godfrey Hounsfield, were awarded the 1979 Nobel Prize for medicine.

Whereas CT scans provide pictures of brain structures, **positron emission tomography (PET) scans** *measure brain activity, including metabolism, blood flow, and neurotransmitter activity.* Glucose, a natural sugar, is the major nutrient of neurons. Thus when neurons are active, they consume more glucose. To prepare a patient for a PET scan, a radioactive (but harmless) form of glucose is injected into the bloodstream and travels to the brain, where it circulates in the blood supply. The PET scan measures the energy emitted by the radioactive substance, and the data are fed into a computer

(a)
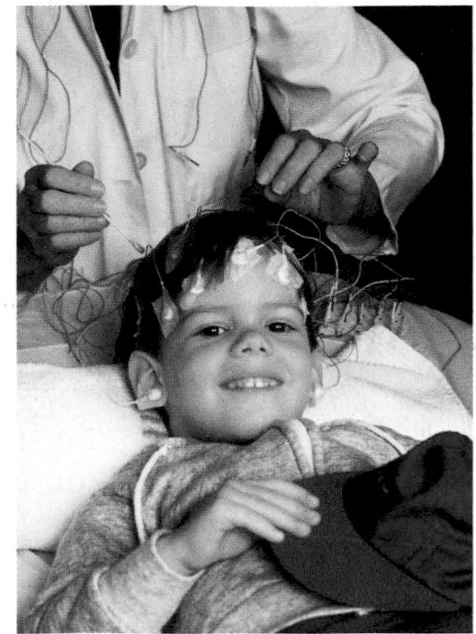

(b)

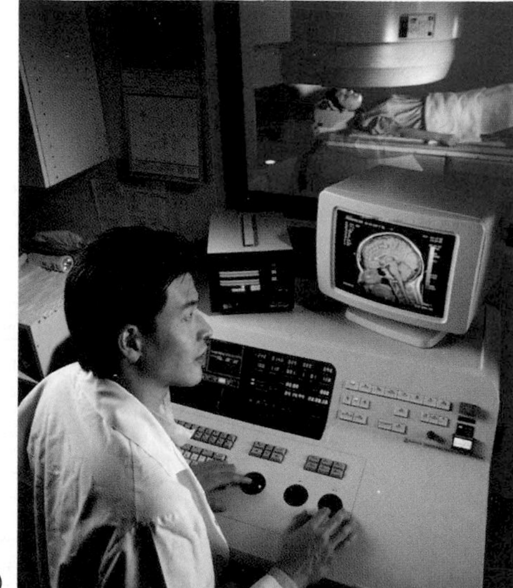
(c)

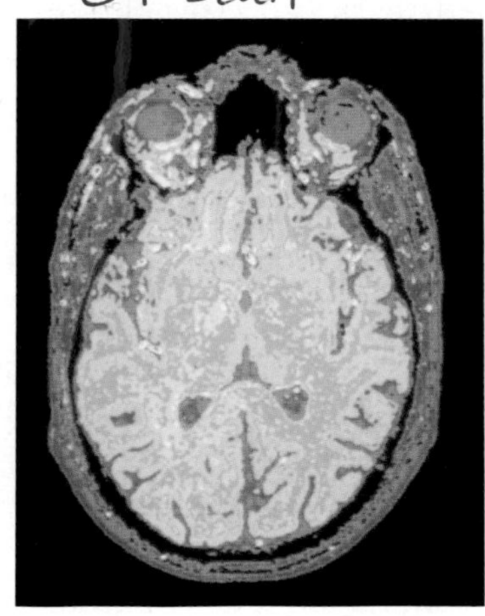
(d)

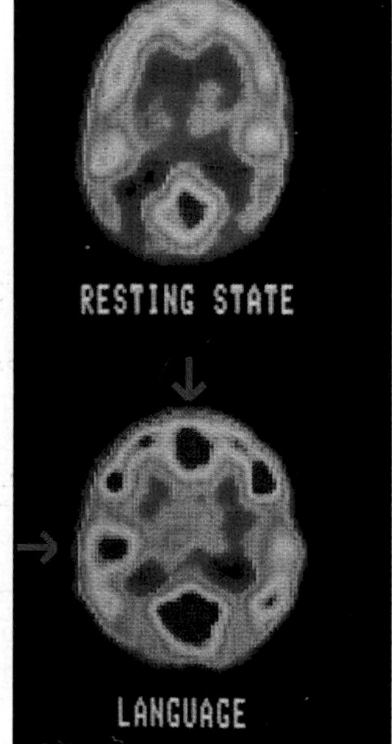

(e)

(f)

FIGURE 3.17

(a) An electroencephalograph (EEG) records the electrical activity of large groups of neurons in the brain through a series of electrodes attached to the scalp. (b) The results are recorded on an EEG readout. (c) Various brain scanning machines produce a number of different images. (d) CT scans use narrow beams of X rays to construct a composite picture of brain structures. (e) PET scans record the amount of radioactive substance that collects in various brain regions to assess brain activity. (f) MRI scanners produce vivid pictures of brain structures. Functional MRI procedures take images in rapid succession, showing neural activity as it occurs.

that uses the readings to produce a color picture of the brain on a display screen (Figure 3.17e). If the patient is performing a mental reasoning task, for example, a researcher can tell by the glucose-concentration pattern which parts of the brain are activated by the task (Raichle, 1994).

Magnetic resonance imaging (MRI) *combines features of CT and PET scans and can be used to study both brain structures and brain activity*. MRI can make out details one tenth the size of those detected by CT scans. MRI creates images based on how atoms in living tissue respond to a magnetic pulse delivered by the device. When the magnetic field is shut off, the magnetic energy absorbed by the atoms in the tissue emits a small electrical voltage that is picked up by detectors and relayed to a computer for analysis. In addition to providing color images of the tissue, MRI can also tell researchers which chemicals (such as neurotransmitters) are active in the tissue (Figure 3.17f).

The conventional MRI yields pictures taken several minutes apart. An important advance in MRI technology is **functional MRI (fMRI)**, *which can produce pictures of blood flow in the brain taken less than a second apart.* Researchers can now, quite literally, watch "live" presentations as different regions of the brain "light up" when participants are given various types of tasks to perform.

For a fascinating look at brain imaging methods, see Video Segment 3.1.

Advances in brain research represent an important frontier of psychology. Driven by its intense desire to "know thyself," the brain is beginning to yield its many secrets. Yet many important questions remain. This should not surprise us, for as one observer noted, "If the brain were so simple that we could understand it, we would be so simple that we couldn't" (Pugh, 1977).

IN REVIEW

- *The nervous system comprises the sensory neurons, motor neurons, and interneurons (associative neurons). Its two major divisions are the central nervous system, consisting of the brain and spinal cord, and the peripheral nervous system. The latter is divided into the somatic system, which is responsible for sensory and motor functions, and the autonomic nervous system, which directs the activity of the body's internal organs and glands.*
- *The autonomic nervous system consists of sympathetic and parasympathetic divisions. The sympathetic system has an arousal function and tends to act as a unit. The parasympathetic system slows down body processes and is more specific in its actions. Together, the two divisions maintain a state of homeostasis, or internal balance.*
- *The spinal cord contains sensory neurons and motor neurons. Interneurons inside the spinal cord serve a connective function between the two. Simple stimulus-response connections can occur as spinal reflexes.*
- *Neuropsychological tests, destruction and stimulation techniques, electrical recording, and brain imaging have facilitated discoveries about brain-behavior relations. Recently developed methods for producing computer-generated pictures of structures and processes within the living brain include the CT scan, PET scan, and MRI and fMRI.*

THE HIERARCHICAL BRAIN: STRUCTURES AND BEHAVIORAL FUNCTIONS

In an evolutionary sense, your brain is far older than you are, for it represents perhaps 500 million years of evolutionary development and fine tuning (Kaas, 2000). The human brain can be likened to a living archaeological site, with the more recently developed structures built atop structures from the distant evolutionary past. The structures at the brain's core govern the basic physiological functions, such as breathing and heart rate, that keep us alive. These we share with all other vertebrates. Built upon these basic structures are newer systems that involve progressively more complex functions—sensing, emoting, wanting, thinking, reasoning. Evolutionary theorists believe that as genetic variation and recombination sculpted these newer structures over time, natural selection favored their retention because animals who had them were more likely to survive in changing environments. The crowning feature of brain development is the *cerebral cortex*, the biological seat of Einstein's scientific genius, Mozart's creativity, Mother Teresa's compassion, and that which makes you a unique human being.

The major structures of the human brain, together with their psychological functions, are shown in Figure 3.18. The brain has traditionally been viewed as having three major subdivisions: the hindbrain; the midbrain, which lies above the hindbrain; and the forebrain.

The Hindbrain

The **hindbrain** *is the lowest and most primitive level of the brain.* As the spinal cord enters the brain, it enlarges to form the structures that compose the stalklike brain stem. Attached to the brain stem is the other major portion of the hindbrain, the cerebellum.

The Brain Stem: Life Support Systems

▶ 18. Which behavioral functions are controlled by the medulla, the pons, and the cerebellum? What occurs with damage to these structures?

The structures of the **brain stem** *support vital life functions.* Included are the medulla and the pons. The 1.5-inch-long medulla is the first structure above the spinal cord. Well developed at birth, the **medulla** *plays an important role in vital body functions such as heart rate and respiration.* Because of your medulla, these functions occur automatically. Damage to the medulla usually results in death or, at best, the need to be maintained on life support systems. Suppression of medulla activity

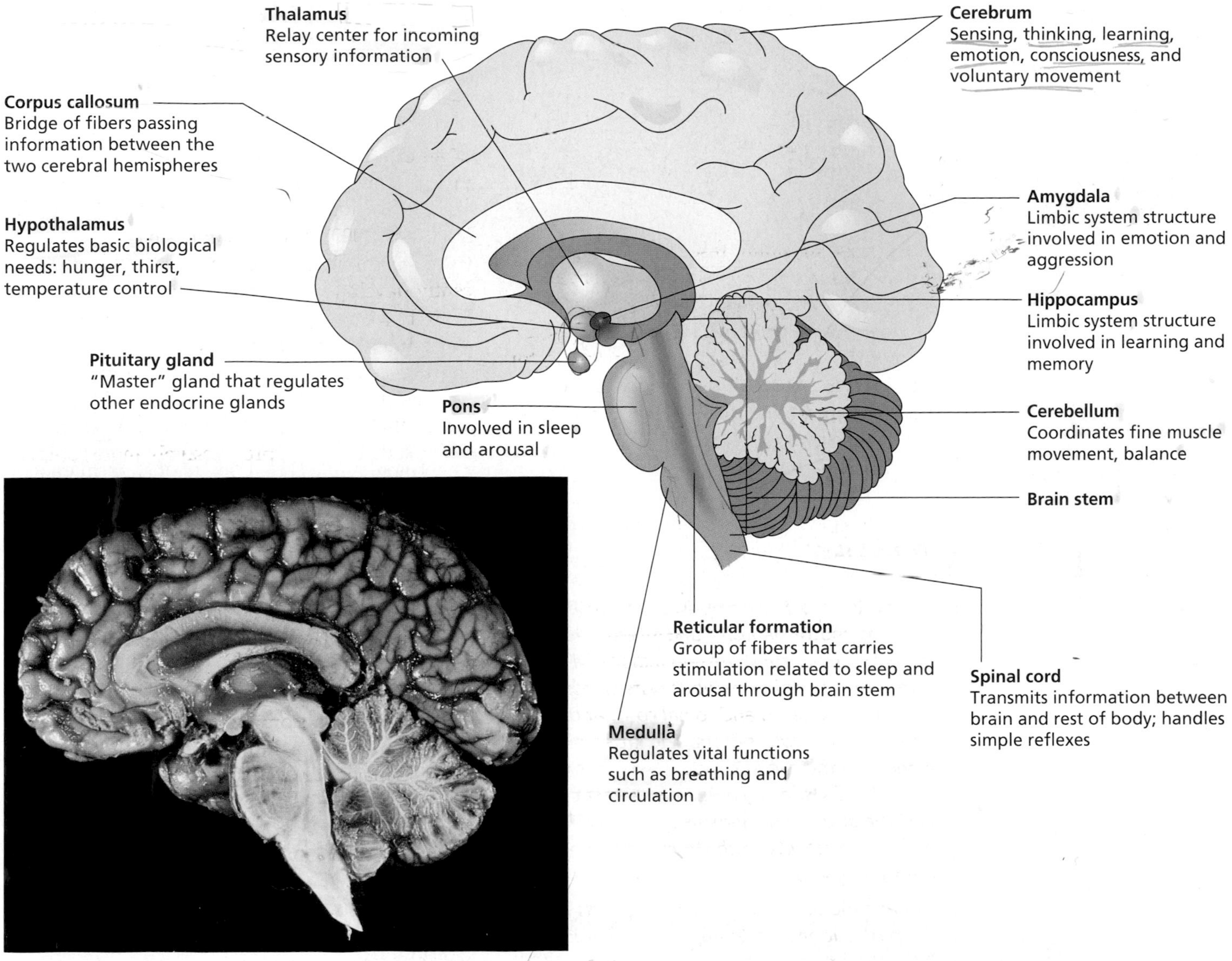

Thalamus
Relay center for incoming sensory information

Cerebrum
Sensing, thinking, learning, emotion, consciousness, and voluntary movement

Corpus callosum
Bridge of fibers passing information between the two cerebral hemispheres

Hypothalamus
Regulates basic biological needs: hunger, thirst, temperature control

Amygdala
Limbic system structure involved in emotion and aggression

Hippocampus
Limbic system structure involved in learning and memory

Pituitary gland
"Master" gland that regulates other endocrine glands

Pons
Involved in sleep and arousal

Cerebellum
Coordinates fine muscle movement, balance

Brain stem

Reticular formation
Group of fibers that carries stimulation related to sleep and arousal through brain stem

Spinal cord
Transmits information between brain and rest of body; handles simple reflexes

Medulla
Regulates vital functions such as breathing and circulation

FIGURE 3.18

This photograph shows a human brain sectioned at its midline. The drawing shows brain structures as they would appear if the left side of the brain were transparent, permitting a view to the midline.

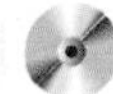
For more on the parts of the brain, see Interactive Segment 3.2.

can occur at high levels of alcohol intoxication, resulting in death by heart or respiratory failure (Blessing, 1997).

The medulla is also a two-way thoroughfare for all the sensory and motor nerve tracts coming up from the spinal cord and descending from the brain. Most of these tracts cross over within the medulla, so the left side of the brain receives sensory input from and exerts motor control over the right side of the body, and the right side of the brain serves the left side of the body. Why this crossover occurs is one of the unsolved mysteries of brain function.

The **pons** (meaning "bridge" in Latin) *lies just above the medulla, and it indeed serves as a bridge carrying nerve impulses between higher and lower levels of the nervous system*. The pons also has clusters of neurons that help regulate sleep. Like the medulla, the pons helps control vital functions, especially respiration, and damage to it can produce death.

The Cerebellum: Motor Coordination Center

Attached to the rear of the brain stem, the cerebellum ("little brain" in Latin) does indeed look like a miniature brain. Its wrinkled *cortex,* or covering, consists mainly of gray cell bodies *(gray matter).* The **cerebellum** *is concerned primarily with muscular movement coordination, but it also plays a role in learning and memory.*

Specific motor movements are initiated in higher brain centers, but their timing and coordination depend on the cerebellum (Thatch et al., 1992). The cerebellum regulates complex, rapidly changing movements that require precise timing,

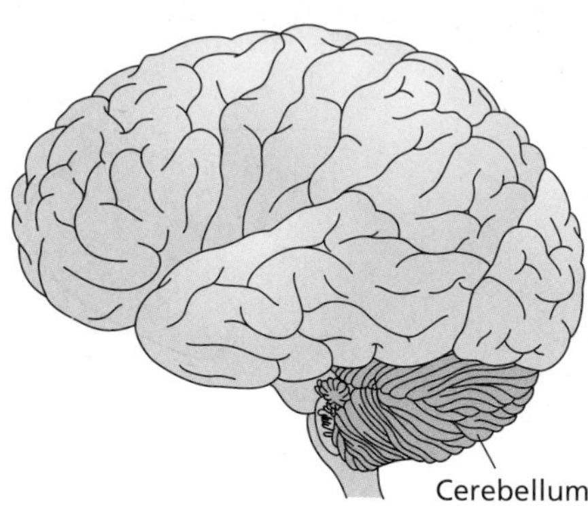

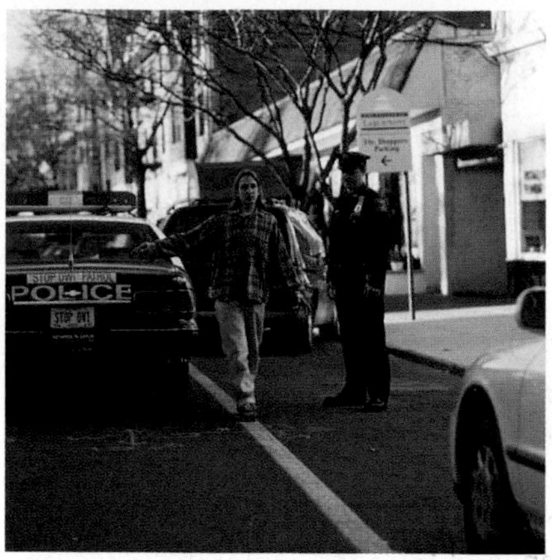

FIGURE 3.19

The cerebellum's movement-control functions are easily disrupted by alcohol, providing the neural basis for sobriety tests administered by police.

such as those of a ballet dancer or a competitive diver. Within the animal kingdom, cats have an especially well developed cerebellum, helping account for their graceful movement abilities (Altman & Bayer, 1996).

The motor-control functions of the cerebellum are easily disrupted by alcohol, producing the coordination difficulties that police look for in roadside sobriety tests. Intoxicated people may be unable to walk a straight line or touch their nose with their index finger (Figure 3.19). Physical damage to the cerebellum results in severe motor disturbances characterized by jerky, uncoordinated movements, as well as an inability to perform habitual movements such as walking.

The Midbrain

Lying just above the hindbrain, the **midbrain** *contains clusters of sensory and motor neurons.* The sensory portion of the midbrain contains important relay centers for the visual and auditory systems. Here, nerve impulses from the eyes and ears are organized and sent to forebrain structures involved in visual and auditory perception (Nolte, 1998). The midbrain also contains motor neurons that control eye movements.

The Reticular Formation: The Brain's Gatekeeper

▶ 19. Describe the roles played by the ascending and descending reticular formation. What occurs with damage to this structure?

▶ 20. Describe the structural characteristics and functions of the thalamus and the hypothalamus.

Buried within the midbrain is a finger-shaped structure that extends from the hindbrain up into the lower portions of the forebrain. This structure receives its name from its resemblance under a microscope to a *reticulum,* or net. The **reticular formation** *acts as a kind of sentry, both alerting higher centers of the brain that messages are coming and then either blocking those messages or allowing them to go forward.* The reticular formation has an ascending part, which sends input to higher regions of the brain to alert it, and a descending portion, through which higher brain centers can either admit or block out sensory input.

The reticular formation plays a central role in consciousness, sleep, and attention. Without reticular stimulation of higher brain regions, sensory messages do not register in conscious awareness even though the nerve impulses may reach the appropriate higher areas of the brain. It is as if the brain is not "awake" enough to notice them. In fact, some general anesthetics work by deactivating neurons of the ascending reticular formation so that sensory impulses that ordinarily would be experienced as pain never "register" in the sensory areas of the brain (Derogatis, 1986).

The reticular formation also affects sleep and wakefulness. In a classic series of experiments in the late 1940s, researchers discovered that electrical stimulation of different portions of the reticular formation can produce instant sleep in a wakeful cat and sudden wakefulness in a sleeping animal (Marshall & Magoun, 1997). Severe damage to the reticular formation can produce a permanent coma (Roland, 1997).

Attention is an active process in which only important or meaningful sensory inputs get through to our consciousness. Other inputs have to be toned down or completely blocked out or we'd be overwhelmed by stimulation. The descending reticular formation plays an important part in this process, serving as a kind of "gate" through which some inputs are admitted while others are blocked out by signals coming down from higher brain centers (Van Zomeren & Brouwer, 1994).

The Forebrain

The **forebrain** *is the brain's most advanced portion from an evolutionary standpoint.* Its major structure, the **cerebrum,** *consists of two large hemispheres, a left side and a right side,* that wrap around the brain stem as the two halves of a cut grapefruit might wrap around a large spoon. The outer portion of the forebrain has a thin covering, or *cortex.* Within are a number of important structures buried in the central regions of the hemispheres.

The Thalamus: The Brain's Sensory Switchboard

The thalamus is located above the midbrain. It resembles two small footballs, one within each cerebral hemisphere. The **thalamus** *has sometimes been likened to a switchboard that organizes input from* *sense organs and routes them to the appropriate areas of the brain.* The visual, auditory, and body senses (balance and equilibrium) all have major relay stations in the thalamus.

Because the thalamus plays such a key role in routing sensory information to higher brain regions, individuals with disrupted functioning in the thalamus often experience a highly confusing world. In research at the National Institute of Mental Health (NIMH) carried out by Nancy Andreason and her coworkers (1994), MRIs from 39 schizophrenic men were compared with those of 47 normal male volunteers. The brain images showed specific abnormalities in the thalamus of the schizophrenic brains. These findings suggest that the thalamus may have been sending garbled sensory information to the higher regions of the brain, creating the confusing sensory experiences and hallucinations reported by many patients.

The Hypothalamus: Motivation and Emotion

The hypothalamus (literally, "under the thalamus") consists of tiny groups of neuron cell bodies that lie at the base of the brain, above the roof of the mouth. The **hypothalamus** *plays a major role in many aspects of motivation and emotion, including sexual behavior, temperature regulation, sleeping, eating, drinking, and aggression.* Damage to the hypothalamus can disrupt all of these behaviors. For example, destruction of one area of a male's hypothalamus results in a complete loss of sex drive; damage to another portion produces an overwhelming urge to eat that results in extreme obesity.

The hypothalamus has important connections with the *endocrine system,* the body's collection of hormone-producing glands (discussed later in this chapter). Through its connection with the nearby pituitary gland (the master gland that exerts control over the other glands of the endocrine system), the hypothalamus directly controls many hormonal secretions that regulate sexual development and sexual behavior, metabolism, and reactions to stress.

The hypothalamus is also involved in our experiences of pleasure and displeasure. The discovery of this fact occurred quite by accident. In 1953, psychologist James Olds was conducting an experiment to study the effects of electrical stimulation in a rat's midbrain reticular formation. One of the electrodes missed the target and was mistakenly implanted in the hypothalamus. Olds noticed that whenever this rat was stimulated, it repeated whatever it had just done, as if it had been rewarded for that behavior. Olds then implanted electrodes in the hypothalamus of other animals and subjected them to a variety of learning situations. He found that they also learned and performed behaviors in order to receive what was clearly an electrical reward. Some of the rats pressed a pedal up to 5,000 times in an hour in order to receive their electrical reward until they dropped from exhaustion. Stimulation of other nearby areas produced just the opposite effect—a tendency to stop performing any behavior that was followed by stimulation, as if the animal had been punished. Olds and other researchers who replicated his work concluded that they had discovered what they called "reward and punishment areas" in the brain, some of which were in the hypothalamus. The "reward" areas are rich in neurons that release dopamine. Dopamine seems to be an important chemical mediator of pleasure (Kolb & Whishaw, 2003).

Humans who have had electrodes implanted in their brains to search for abnormal brain tissue have reported experiencing pleasure when these regions were electrically stimulated. One patient reportedly proposed marriage to the experimenter while being so stimulated (Heath, 1972). Thus a misplaced electrode led to a discovery that neural events occurring in the hypothalamus and adjacent areas have important roles in motivation.

The Limbic System: Memory, Emotion, and Goal-Directed Behavior

As we continue our journey up through the brain, we come to the limbic system, a set of structures lying deep within the cerebral hemispheres (Figure 3.20). The **limbic system** *helps coordinate behaviors needed to satisfy motivational and emotional urges that arise in the hypothalamus; it is also involved in memory.*

▶ 21. What roles do the hippocampus and amygdala play in psychological functions?

Two key structures in the limbic system are the hippocampus and the amygdala. The **hippocampus** *is involved in forming and retrieving memories.* Damage there can result in severe memory impairment for recent events (Isaacson, 2002). The **amygdala** (from the Greek word for "almond") *organizes motivational and emotional response patterns, particularly those linked to aggression and fear* (LeDoux, 1998). Electrically stimulating certain areas of the amygdala causes animals to snarl and assume aggressive postures (Figure 3.20b), whereas stimulation of other areas results in a fearful inability to respond aggressively, even in self-defense. For example, a normally aggressive

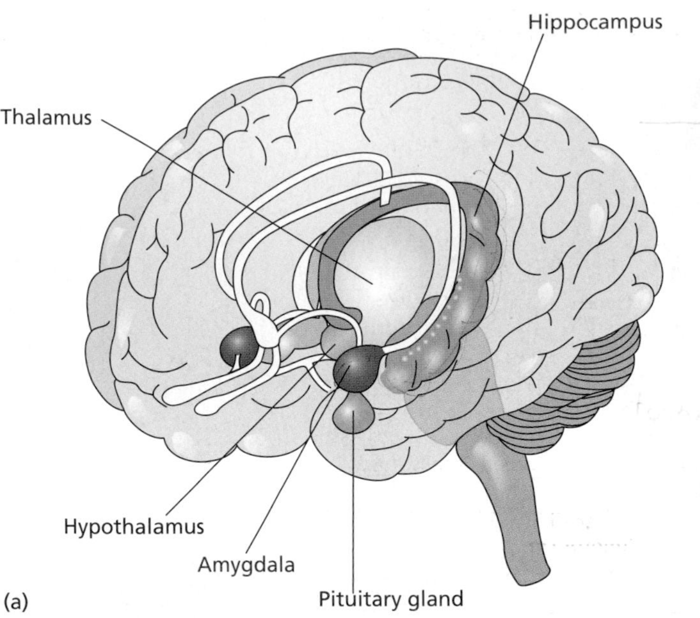

FIGURE 3.20

(a) The amygdala and hippocampus are major structures of the limbic system (indicated by red type). (b) Electrical stimulation of the amygdala, which organizes emotional responses, can evoke an immediate aggressive response.

and hungry cat will cower in fear from a tiny mouse placed in its cage. The amygdala is a key part of a larger control system for anger and fear that also involves other brain regions (Borod, 2000). It can also produce emotional responses without the higher centers of the brain "knowing" that we are emotionally aroused, providing a possible explanation for unconscious emotional responses (LeDoux, 1998).

Finally, like the hypothalamus, the limbic system contains reward and punishment areas that have important motivational functions. Certain drugs, such as cocaine and marijuana, seem to induce pleasure by stimulating limbic reward areas that use dopamine as their neurotransmitter (LeMoal, 1999).

▶ 22. Describe the locations of the four lobes of the brain and the organization of the sensory, motor, and association cortex.

The Cerebral Cortex: Crown of the Brain

The **cerebral cortex**, *a 1/4-inch-thick sheet of gray (unmyelinated) cells that form the outermost layer of the human brain,* is the crowning achievement of brain evolution. Fish and amphibians have no cerebral cortex, and the progression from more primitive to more advanced mammals is marked by a dramatic increase in the proportion of cortical tissue. In humans, the cortex constitutes fully 80 percent of brain tissue (Nolte, 1998).

The cerebral cortex is not essential for physical survival in the way that the brain stem structures are, but it is essential for human functioning. How much so is evident in this description of patients who, as a result of an accident during prenatal development, were born without a cerebral cortex:

> Some of these individuals may survive for years, in one case of mine for twenty years. From these cases, it appears that the human [lacking a cortex] sleeps and wakes; . . . reacts to hunger, loud sounds, and crude visual stimuli by movement of eyes, eyelids, and facial muscles; . . . may see and hear, . . . may be able to taste and smell, to reject the unpalatable and accept such food as it likes. . . . [They can] utter crude sounds, can cry and smile, showing displeasure when hungry and pleasure, in a babyish way, when being sung to; [they] may be able to perform spontaneously crude [limb] movements. (Cairns, 1952, p. 109)

Because the cortex is wrinkled and convoluted, like a wadded-up piece of paper, a great amount of cortical tissue is compressed into a relatively small space inside the skull. If we could remove the cortex and smooth it out, the tissue would cover an area roughly the size of a pillowcase. Perhaps 75 percent of the cortex's total surface area lies within its *fissures*, or canyonlike folds. Three of these fissures are important landmarks. One large fissure runs lengthwise across the top of the brain, dividing it into a right and a left hemisphere. Within each hemisphere, a *central fissure* divides the cerebrum into front and rear halves, and a third fissure runs from front to rear along the side of the brain. On the basis of these landmarks, neurologists have divided each hemisphere into four lobes: *frontal, parietal, occipital,* and *temporal.* A fist made with your right hand (with the side of your thumb facing

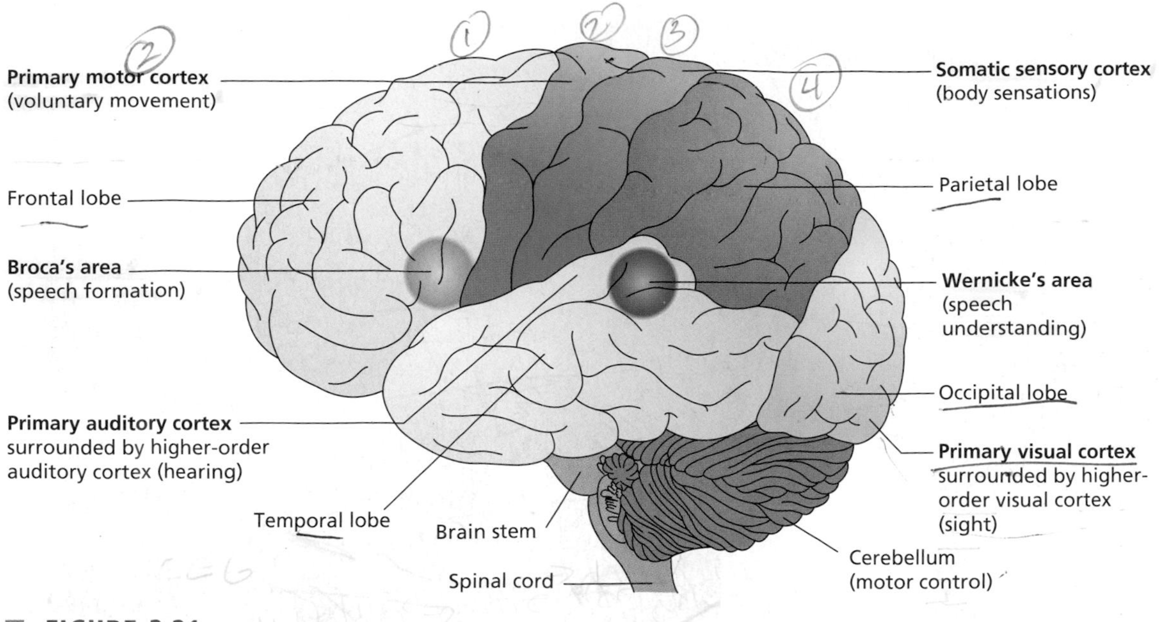

FIGURE 3.21

Division of the brain into frontal (beige/deep blue), parietal (purple/green), occipital, and temporal lobes, showing localization of sensory, motor, and some important language functions in the cortex. The remainder is primarily association cortex, consisting of interneurons involved in complex psychological functions, such as perception and reasoning.

you) can serve as a rough orientation to these lobes. The bend in your fingers represents the frontal lobe, your knuckles the parietal lobe, your wrist area the occipital lobe, and your thumb pointing forward the temporal lobe.

As shown in Figure 3.21, each of the four cerebral lobes is associated with particular sensory and motor functions, as well as with speech understanding and speech production. The large areas in Figure 3.21 that are not associated with sensory or motor functions (about three fourths of the cortex) make up the *association cortex*, involved in mental processes such as thought, memory, and perception. (We will discuss the association cortex in more detail shortly.)

The Motor Cortex The **motor cortex** *controls the 600 or more muscles involved in voluntary body movements.* It lies at the rear of the frontal lobe adjacent to the central fissure. Because the nerve tracts from the motor cortex cross over at the level of the medulla, each hemisphere governs movement on the opposite side of the body. Thus severe damage to the right motor cortex would produce paralysis in the left side of the body. The left side of Figure 3.22 shows the relative organization of function within the motor cortex. As you can see, specific body areas are represented in different parts of the motor cortex, and the amount of cortex devoted to each area depends on the complexity of the movements that are carried out by the body part. For example, the amount of cortical tissue devoted to your fingers is far greater than that devoted to your torso, even though your torso is much larger. If we electrically stimulate a particular point on the motor cortex, movements occur in the muscles governed by that part of the cortex.

The Sensory Cortex Specific areas of the cortex receive input from our sensory receptors. With the exception of taste and smell, at least one specific area in the cortex has been identified for each of the senses.

The **somatic sensory cortex** *receives sensory input that gives rise to our sensations of heat, touch, and cold and to our senses of balance and body movement (kinesthesis).* It lies in the parietal lobe just behind the motor cortex, separated from it by the central fissure that divides the frontal lobe from the parietal lobe. As in the case of the motor system, each side of the body sends sensory input to the opposite hemisphere. Like the motor area next to it, the somatic sensory area is basically organized in an upside-down fashion, with the feet being represented near the top of the brain. Likewise, the amount of cortex devoted to each body area is directly proportional to that region's sensory sensitivity. The organization of the sensory cortex is shown on the right side of Figure 3.22, as is the proportion of cortex devoted to each body area. As far as your sensory cortex is concerned, you

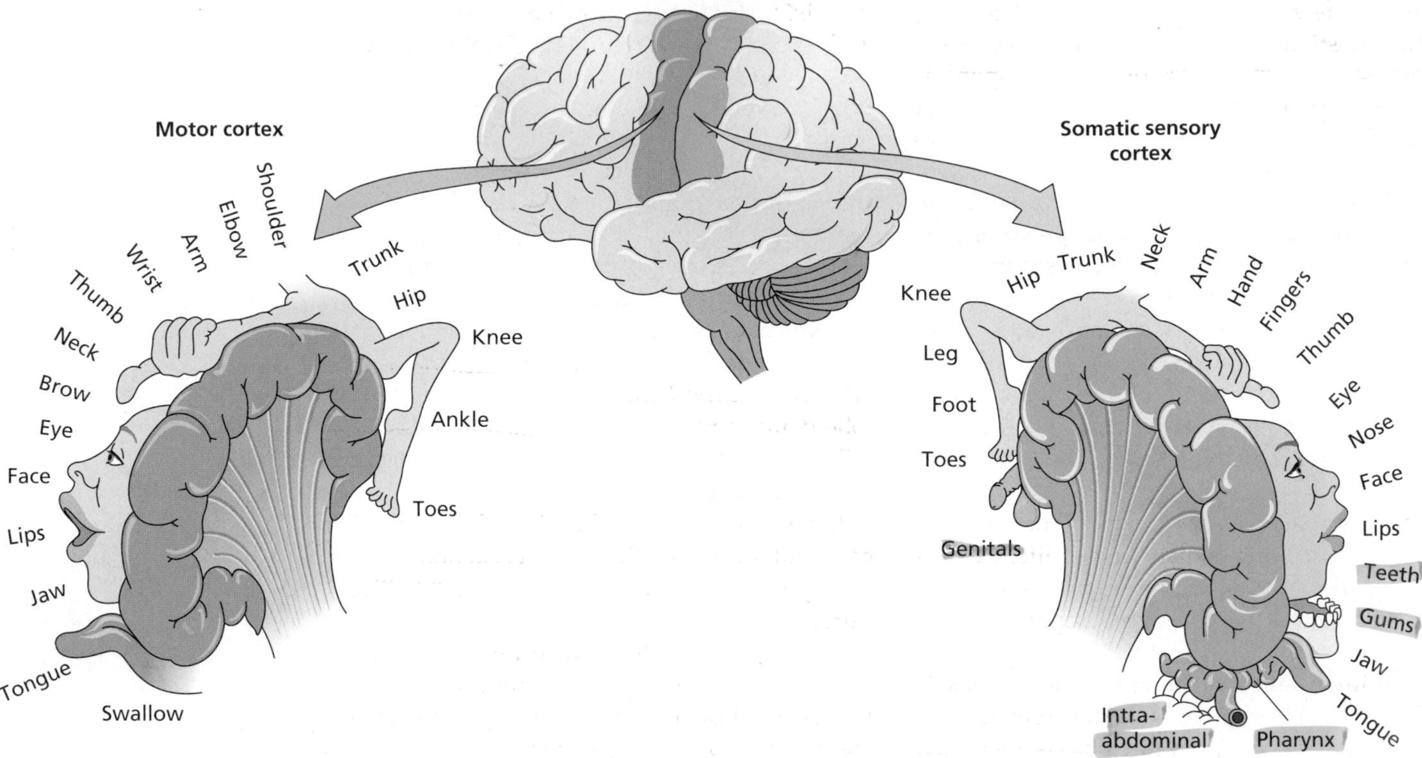

FIGURE 3.22

Both the motor cortex and the somatic sensory cortex are highly specialized so that every site is associated with a particular part of the body. The amount of cortex devoted to each body part is proportional to the sensitivity of that area's motor or sensory functions. Both the motor cortex and sensory cortex are arranged in an upside-down fashion and serve the opposite side of the body.

▶ 23. Where are Wernicke's and Broca's areas? How are they involved in speech?

are mainly fingers, lips, and tongue. Notice also that the organization of the sensory cortex is such that the body structures it serves lie side by side with those in the motor cortex, an arrangement that enhances sensory-motor interactions in the same body area.

The senses of hearing and sight are well represented in the cortex. As shown in Figure 3.21, the auditory area lies on the surface of the temporal lobe at the side of each hemisphere. Each ear sends messages to the auditory areas of both hemispheres, so the loss of one temporal lobe has little effect on hearing. The major sensory area for vision lies at the rear of the occipital lobe. Here messages from the visual receptors are analyzed, integrated, and translated into sight. As in the auditory system, each eye sends input to both hemispheres.

Within each sensory area, neurons respond to particular aspects of the sensory stimulus; they are tuned in to specific aspects of the environment. Thus certain cells in the visual cortex fire only when we look at a particular kind of stimulus, such as a vertical line or a corner (Hubel & Wiesel, 1979). In the auditory cortex, some neurons fire only in response to high tones, whereas others respond only to tones having some other specific frequency. Many of these single-cell responses are present at birth, suggesting that we are prewired to perceive many aspects of our sensory environment (Shair et al., 1991). Nonetheless, the sensory cortex, like other parts of the brain, is also sensitive to experience. For example, when people learn to read Braille, the area in the sensory cortex that receives input from the fingertips increases in size, making the person more sensitive to the tiny sets of raised dots (Pool, 1994).

Speech Comprehension and Production Two specific areas that govern the understanding and production of speech are also located in the cortex (see Figure 3.21). **Wernicke's area,** *in the temporal lobe, is involved in speech comprehension.* Damage to this cortical region leaves patients unable to understand written or spoken speech. **Broca's area,** *in the frontal lobe, is involved in the production of speech through its connections with the motor cortex region that controls the muscles used in speech.* Damage to this area leaves patients with the ability to comprehend speech but not to express themselves in words or sentences. These two speech areas normally work in concert when you are conversing with another person. They allow you to comprehend what the other person is saying and to express your own thoughts.

Association Cortex The **association cortex** *is involved in many important mental functions, including perception, language, and thought.* These areas are sometimes referred to as "silent areas" because electrically stimulating them does not give rise to either sensory experiences or motor responses. Damage to specific parts of the association cortex causes disruption or loss of functions such as speech, understanding, thinking, and problem solving. As we might expect, if the association cortex is involved in higher mental processes, the amount of association cortex increases dramatically as we move up the brain ladder from lower animals to human beings. It constitutes about 75 percent of the human cerebral cortex and accounts for people's superior cognitive abilities. One scientist has described our mass of association cortex as "evolution's missing link" (Skoyles, 1997). He suggests that its flexibility and learning capacity have allowed us to acquire new mental skills specific to our human way of life, such as reading and mathematics, far more quickly than could have occurred through natural selection alone.

The importance of the association cortex is demonstrated in people who suffer from *agnosia*, the inability to identify familiar objects. One such case is described by the neurologist Oliver Sacks (1985):

> Dr. P. [one of Sacks's patients] was a talented and accomplished musician whose behavior was quite normal except for one glaring exception: Although his vision was perfect, he often had difficulty recognizing familiar people and objects. Thus, he would chat with pieces of furniture and wonder why they did not reply, or pat the tops of fire hydrants, thinking they were children. One day, while visiting Sacks's office for an examination, Dr. P. looked for his hat as he was ready to depart. He suddenly reached out and grabbed his wife's head, trying to lift it. He had mistaken his wife for his hat! His wife smiled tolerantly; she had become accustomed to such actions on his part.

Dr. P. had suffered brain damage that left him unable to connect the information sent to the visual cortex with information stored in other cortical areas that concerned the nature of objects. The associative neurons responsible for linking the two types of information no longer served him.

The Frontal Lobes: The Human Difference Some neuroscientists suggest that the entire period of human evolutionary existence could well be termed the "age of the frontal lobe" (Krasnegor et al., 1997). This brain region hardly exists in mammals such as mice and rats. The frontal lobes compose about 3.5 percent of the cerebral cortex in the cat, 7 percent in the dog, and 17 percent in the chimpanzee. In a human, the frontal lobes constitute 29 percent of the cortex. The frontal lobes—the site of such human qualities as self-awareness, planning, initiative, and responsibility—are in some respects the most mysterious and least understood part of the brain.

Much of what we know about the frontal lobes comes from detailed studies of patients who have experienced brain damage. Frontal lobe damage results not so much in a loss of intellectual abilities as in an inability to plan and carry out a sequence of actions, even when patients can verbalize what they should do. This can result in an inability to correct actions that are clearly erroneous and self-defeating (Shallice & Burgess, 1991).

The frontal cortex is also involved in emotional experience. In people with normal brains, PET scans show increased activity in the frontal cortex when people are experiencing feelings of happiness, sadness, or disgust (Lane et al., 1997). In contrast, patients with frontal lobe damage often exhibit attitudes of apathy and lack of concern. They simply don't seem to care about anything.

A region of the frontal lobe has received increasing attention in recent years. The **prefrontal cortex**, *located just behind the forehead, is the seat of the so-called "executive functions."* Executive functions are mental abilities, such as goal setting, judgment, strategic planning, and impulse control, that allow people to direct their behavior in an adaptive fashion. Deficits in executive functions seem to underlie a number of problem behaviors. People with prefrontal cortex disorders seem oblivious to the future consequences of their actions and seem to be governed only by immediate consequences (Raine et al., 1997). As you may have guessed by now, Phineas Gage, the railroad foreman described in our chapter-opening case, suffered massive frontal lobe damage when the spike tore through his brain (see Figure 3.2). Thereafter he exhibited classic symptoms of disturbed executive functions, becoming behaviorally impulsive and losing his capacity for future planning.

A more ominous manifestation of prefrontal dysfunction—the capacity to kill—was recently discovered by researchers using PET-scan technology. We describe this landmark study in this chapter's *Research Close-Up*.

▶ 24. Describe the role of the frontal cortex in higher mental (including executive) functions.

RESEARCH CLOSE-UP

INSIDE THE BRAIN OF A KILLER

Introduction

What stops us from impulsively killing an irritating neighbor, a disloyal friend, or a total stranger wearing a coat we'd like to own? The answer may lie, at least in part, in our frontal lobes. Much of what makes you a "civilized" person—self-control, judgment, foresight, reasoning, delaying gratification—is regulated by the executive functions of your prefrontal cortex. As seen in the case of Phineas Gage, damage in this region of the brain can reduce those civilizing inhibitions.

Until recently, researchers could only infer that impulsively violent people without obvious brain damage had reduced prefrontal activity, for they could not look directly into the brain and see how it was functioning. That changed with the development of brain-imaging procedures, particularly the PET scan. In this study, Jacqueline Stoddard and her coworkers applied PET technology to examine brain functioning in a group of people who had committed savage acts of violence. They also examined the possible contribution of environmental factors in this violence-prone population.

Method

The researchers studied 41 individuals (39 men, 2 women) who had been tried for murder or manslaughter in the state of California. All had pleaded not guilty by reason of insanity or were judged mentally incompetent to stand trial. Each murderer was assigned a nonviolent control participant matched for age, sex, and ethnicity. A radioactive glucose substance was injected into the participants, and this nutrient traveled to the brain. PET scans were then taken to assess brain activity while the participants worked on a mental performance task that is known to require frontal lobe involvement.

To assess the potential role of environmental factors that might foster violent tendencies, the records of the murderers were independently reviewed by two raters for degree of psychosocial deprivation. Deprivation was defined as histories of physical or sexual abuse, severe family conflict, neglect, or being raised in a broken home. There was high agreement between the two raters, who knew nothing about the murderers' PET data.

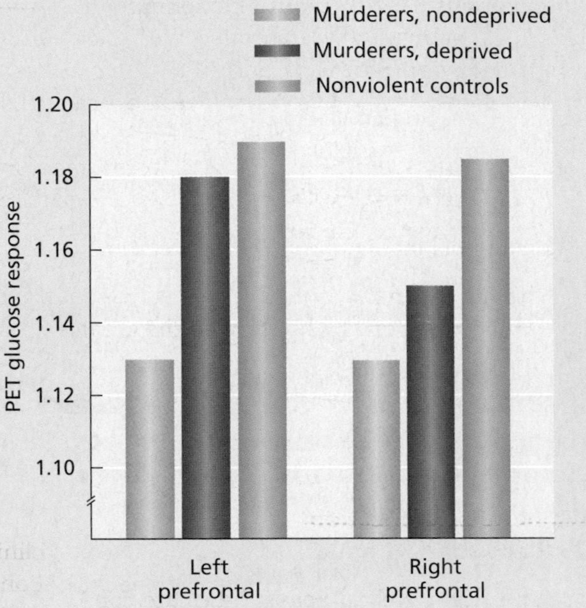

SOURCE: Jacqueline Stoddard, Adrian Raine, Susan Bihrle, and Monte Buchsbaum (1997). Prefrontal dysfunction in murderers lacking psychosocial deficits. In A. Raine, P. A. Brennan, D. P. Farrington, & S. A. Mednick (Eds.), *Biosocial bases of violence* (pp. 301–305). New York: Plenum.

FIGURE 3.23

Prefrontal activity measured by PET scans in murderers with no history of psychosocial deprivation, murderers with a history of psychosocial deprivation, and a nonviolent control group. Murderers with no history of deprivation showed notable prefrontal dysfunction.

SOURCE: Based on Stoddard et al., 1997.

Results

On the basis of the psychosocial history ratings, the murderers were divided into a deprived group, numbering 26, who clearly had grown up under adverse circumstances, and a second group of 12 whose histories showed no evidence of deprivation. (The other 3 murderers had only minor deprivation and were not included in the comparisons.) These groups were compared with the nonviolent controls in glucose metabolic rates, which measure the activity of neurons in the brain. The glucose recordings from the prefrontal areas of the left and right hemispheres are shown in Figure 3.23.

The murderers with no history of psychosocial deprivation differed significantly from their normal controls, the lower glucose readings indicating reduced activity in the prefrontal area. Although their prefrontal readings were also lower, the murderers with adverse environmental histories did not differ significantly from the nonviolent controls.

Discussion

This study illustrates the value of brain-imaging techniques for studying brain-behavior relations. Prior research using PET technology had suggested that violent individuals have reduced prefrontal activity (Raine et al., 1997). This study is a particularly important extension of earlier work because it took into account not only brain functioning but also environmental effects known to be associated with the development of violent behavior. Stoddard and her coworkers reasoned that both biological and environmental factors can prime people to become violent. In the absence of a prior social learning environment that would be expected to foster impulsive violence, a brain abnormality that affected the executive functions of the prefrontal cortex would be a likely biological suspect. In accord with the researchers' hypothesis, the murderers who did not have a history of adverse environmental experiences were the ones who showed the greatest prefrontal dysfunction.

Other questions remain to be answered, however. First, the 41 murderers were not only violent people, but they were also psychologically disturbed enough to plead not guilty by reason of insanity. Although these people are obviously an important and dangerous subset of murderers, the findings can be applied to differences only between disturbed murderers and nonviolent populations who are not psychologically disturbed. In this study, it would have been ideal to have a second control group that was nonviolent but psychologically disturbed so that we could be more assured that the group differences were related to violent tendencies and not simply to mental illness. Also needed to flesh out the links between brain and violence are future studies of prefrontal functioning in other populations who engage in impulsive, poorly planned violence, such as certain types of juvenile delinquents or violent children. However, no single study can address all of these questions, and this study is an excellent start in understanding the biological underpinnings of violence and how they might interact with environmental factors.

Hemispheric Lateralization: The Left and Right Brains

The left and right cerebral hemispheres are connected by a broad white band of myelinated nerve fibers. The **corpus callosum** (Figure 3.18) *is a neural bridge that acts as a major communication link between the two hemispheres and allows them to function as a single unit.* Despite the fact that they normally act in concert, however, there are important differences between the psychological functions that are represented in the two cerebral hemispheres. **Lateralization** *refers to the relatively greater localization of a function in one hemisphere or the other.*

Medical studies of patients who suffered various types of brain damage provided the first clues that certain complex psychological functions were lateralized on one side of the brain or the other. The deficits observed in people with damage to either the left or right hemisphere suggested that, for most people, verbal abilities and speech are localized in the left hemisphere, as are mathematical and logical abilities (Springer, 1997). When Broca's or Wernicke's speech areas in the left hemisphere are damaged, the result is **aphasia**, *the partial or total loss of the ability to communicate.* Depending on the location of the damage, the problem may lie in recognizing the meaning of words, in communicating verbally with others, or in both functions. We should note, however, that women are less likely to suffer aphasia when their left hemisphere is damaged, suggesting that language is not as strongly left-lateralized in women as it is in men (Rossell et al., 2002).

When the right hemisphere is damaged, the clinical picture is quite different. Language functions are not ordinarily affected, but the person has great difficulty in performing tasks that demand the ability to perceive spatial relations. A patient may have a hard time recognizing faces and may even forget a well-traveled route or, as in the case of Dr. P., mistake his wife for a hat (Sacks, 1985). It appears that mental imagery, musical and artistic abilities, and the ability to perceive and understand spatial relationships are primarily right-hemisphere functions (Ornstein, 1997).

▶ 25. What is hemispheric lateralization and what functions are localized in the left and right hemispheres?

The two hemispheres differ not only in the cognitive functions that reside there but also in their links with positive and negative emotions. EEG studies have shown that the right hemisphere is relatively more active when negative emotions such as sadness and anger are being experienced. Positive emotions such as joy and happiness are accompanied by relatively greater left-hemisphere activation (Marshall & Fox, 2000).

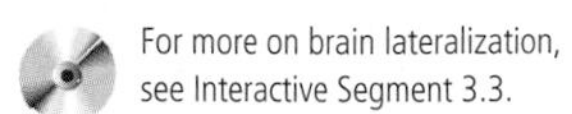
For more on brain lateralization, see Interactive Segment 3.3.

The Split Brain: Two Minds in One Body? Despite the lateralization of specific functions in the two cerebral hemispheres, the brain normally functions as a unified whole because the two hemispheres communicate with one another through the corpus callosum. But what would happen if this communication link between the two hemispheres were cut? Would we, in effect, produce two different and largely independent minds in the same person? A series of Nobel Prize–winning

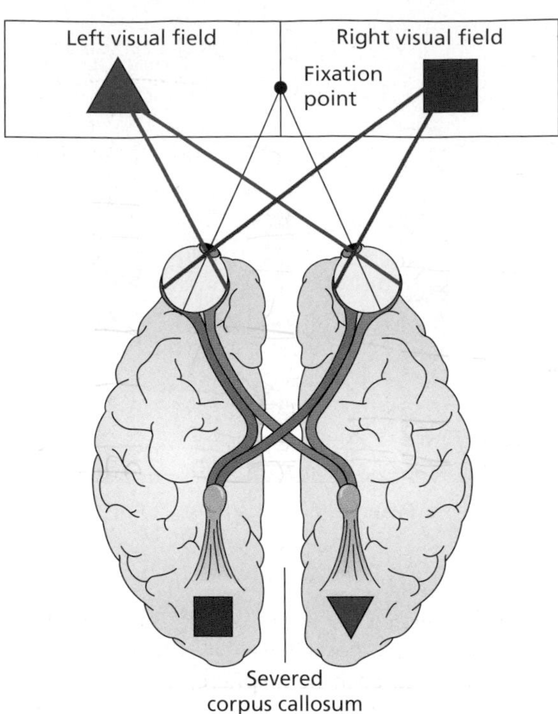

FIGURE 3.24

The visual system's anatomy makes studies of split-brain patients possible. Light waves from the right visual field fall on the left side of each eye's retina. The left visual field is projected on the right side of the retinas. Optic nerve fibers from the inner portion of the retina (toward the nose) cross over at the optic chiasma, whereas the fibers from the outer portion of the retina do not. As a result, the right side of the visual field projects to the visual cortex of the left hemisphere, whereas the left visual field projects to the right hemisphere. When the corpus callosum is cut, the two hemispheres no longer communicate with each other. By presenting stimuli to either side of the visual fixation point, researchers can control which hemisphere receives the information.

studies by Roger Sperry (1970) and his associates addressed this question.

Like many scientific advances, Sperry's discovery resulted from natural human misfortune. Some patients suffer from a form of epilepsy in which a seizure that begins as an uncontrolled electrical discharge of neurons on one side of the brain spreads to the other hemisphere. Years ago, neurosurgeons found that by cutting the nerve fibers of the corpus callosum, they could prevent the seizure from spreading to the other hemisphere. Moreover, the operation did not seem to disrupt other major psychological functions. Sperry's studies of patients who had had such operations involved some ingenious ways to test the functions of the two hemispheres after the corpus callosum was cut.

Split-brain research was made possible by the way in which our visual input to the brain is organized. To illustrate, extend your two hands straight out in front of you, separated by about one foot. Now focus on the point between them. You'll find that you can still see both hands in your peripheral vision and that you have a unified view of the scene. It therefore might surprise you to know that your left hand is being "seen" only by your right hemisphere and your right hand only by your left hemisphere. To see how this occurs, examine Figure 3.24, which shows that some of the fibers of the optic nerve from each eye cross over at the *optic chiasma* and travel to the opposite brain hemisphere. Fibers that transmit messages from the right side of the visual field project to the left hemisphere; fibers from the visual field's left side project to the right hemisphere. Despite this arrangement, we experience a unified visual world (as you did when you looked at your hands), rather than two half-worlds, because the hemispheres' visual areas are normally connected by the corpus callosum. When the corpus callosum is cut, however, visual input to one hemisphere can be restricted by projecting the stimulus to either the right side of the visual field, in which case the image goes only to the left hemisphere, or to the left side of the visual field, which sends it to the right hemisphere.

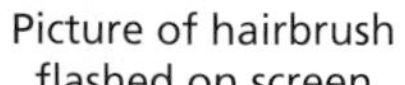
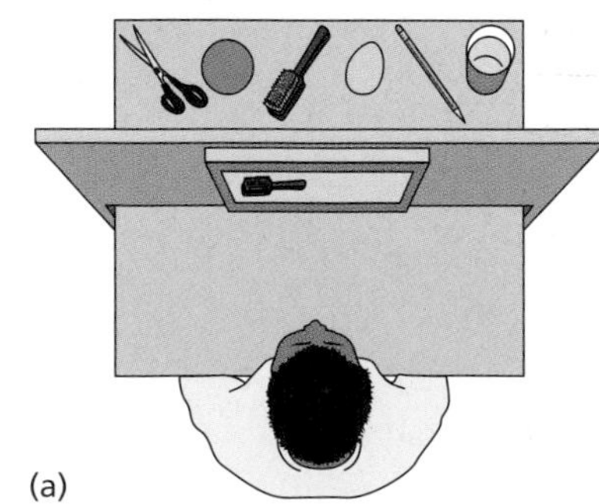

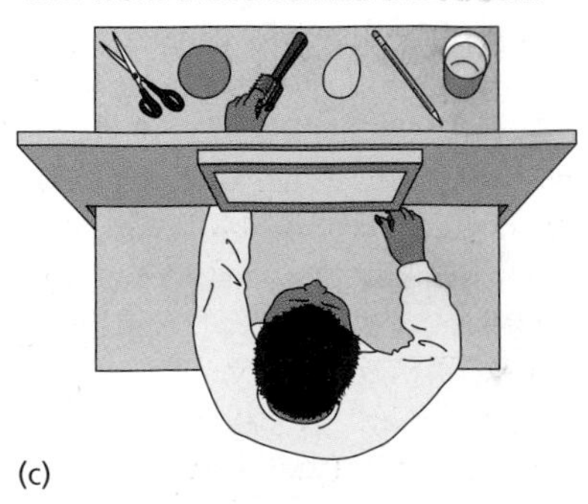

FIGURE 3.25

A split-brain patient focuses on the fixation point in the center of the screen. (a) A picture of a hairbrush is briefly projected to the left side of the visual field, thus sending the information to the right hemisphere. (b) The patient is asked to report verbally what she saw. She cannot name the object. (c) She is asked to select the object she saw and quickly finds it with her left hand. What would happen if the object were to be transferred to her right hand or if the word hairbrush *were to be projected to the right side of the visual field? In either case, the information would be sent to the language-rich left hemisphere, and she would be able to name the object.*

In Sperry's experiments, split-brain patients basically did what you did with your hands: They focused on a fixation point, a dot on the center of a screen, while slides containing visual stimuli (words, pictures, and so on) were flashed to the right or to the left side of the fixation point (Figure 3.25).

Sperry found that when words were flashed to the right side of the visual field, resulting in their being sent to the language-rich left hemisphere, patients could verbally describe what they had seen. They could also write what they had seen with their right hand (which is controlled by the left hemisphere). However, if words were flashed to the left side of the visual field and sent on to the right hemisphere, the patients could not describe what they had seen on the screen. This pattern of findings indicates that the right hemisphere does not have well-developed language abilities.

The inability to describe stimuli verbally did not mean, however, that the right hemisphere was incapable of recognizing them. If a picture of an object (e.g., a hairbrush) was flashed to the right hemisphere and the left hand (controlled by the right hemisphere) was allowed to feel different objects behind the screen, the person's hand would immediately select the brush. As long as the person continued to hold the brush in the left hand, sending sensory input about the object to the "nonverbal" right hemisphere, the person was unable to name it. However, if the brush was transferred to the right hand, the person could immediately name it. In other words, until the object was transferred to the right hand, the left hemisphere had no knowledge of what the right hemisphere was experiencing.

Later research showed the right hemisphere's definite superiority over the left in the recognition of patterns. In one study, three split-brain patients were presented with photographs of similar-looking faces projected in either the left or right visual fields. On each trial, they were asked to select the photo they had just seen from a set of 10 cards. On this task, the spatially oriented right hemisphere was far more accurate than the linguistic left hemisphere in correctly identifying the photos (Figure 3.26). Apparently, the faces were too similar to one another to be differentiated very easily by left-hemisphere verbal descriptions, but the spatial abilities of the right hemisphere could discriminate among them (Gazzaniga & Smylie, 1983).

Some psychologists have suggested that what we call the *conscious self* resides in the left hemisphere, because consciousness is based on our ability to verbalize about the past and present. Is the right hemisphere, then, an unconscious (nonverbal) mind? Yes, these psychologists answer, except when it communicates with the left hemisphere across the corpus callosum (Ornstein, 1997). But when the connections between the two hemispheres are cut, each hemisphere, in a sense, can have a "mind of its own," as this example shows:

> One split-brain patient learned to use Scrabble letters to communicate from his right hemisphere using his left hand. To test the dual-mind hypothesis, researchers asked the two hemispheres the same questions—and found that the answers often disagreed. For example, when asked what occupation he would prefer, the left hemisphere responded verbally, "a draftsman." But the right hemisphere used the Scrabble pieces to spell out, "race car driver." (LeDoux et al., 1977)

Keep in mind that in daily life, the split-brain patients could function adequately because they had learned to compensate for their disconnected hemispheres. For example, they could scan the visual environment so that input from both the left and right visual fields got into both hemispheres. The "split-mind" phenomena shown in the laboratory appeared because the patients were tested under experimental conditions that were specifically designed to isolate the functions of the two hemispheres. Nonetheless, the results of split-brain research are so dramatic that they have led some people (and even some scientists) to promote a conception of brain functions as being highly localized and restricted to one hemisphere or the other. Even today, we hear about education programs directed at developing the untapped potentials of the "right brain." Certainly, there is some degree of localization of brain functions, but a far more important principle is that in the normal brain, most functions involve many areas of the brain working together. The brain is an exquisitely integrated system, not a collection of isolated functions.

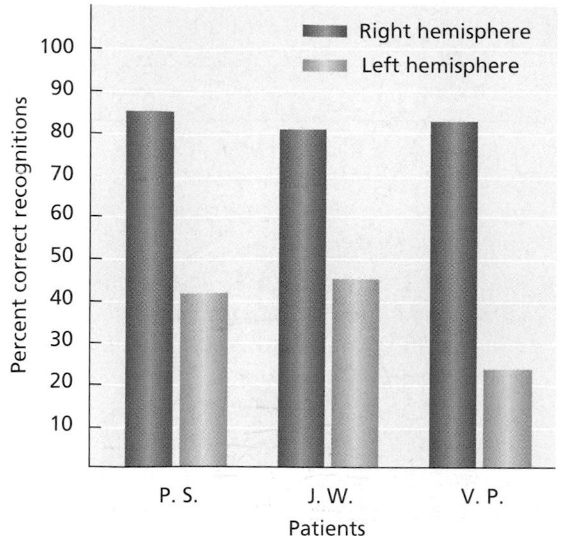

FIGURE 3.26

Facial-recognition accuracy by the left and right hemispheres of three split-brain patients, showing greater accuracy when information is flashed to the right hemisphere, which has stronger pattern-recognition abilities. SOURCE: Based on Gazzaniga & Smylie, 1983.

IN REVIEW

- *The brain consists of the hindbrain, the midbrain, and the forebrain, an organization that reflects the evolution of increasingly more complex brain structures related to behavioral capabilities.*
- *Major structures within the hindbrain include the medulla, which monitors and controls vital body functions; the pons, which contains important groups of sensory and motor neurons; and the cerebellum, which is concerned with motor coordination.*
- *The reticular formation, located in the midbrain, plays a vital role in consciousness, attention, and sleep. Activity of the ascending reticular formation excites higher areas of the brain and prepares them to respond to stimulation. The descending reticular formation acts as a gate, determining which stimuli get through to enter into consciousness.*
- *The forebrain consists of two cerebral hemispheres and a number of subcortical structures. The cerebral hemispheres are connected by the corpus callosum.*
- *The thalamus acts as a switchboard through which impulses originating in sense organs are routed to the appropriate sensory projection areas. The hypothalamus plays a major role in many aspects of motivational and emotional behavior. The limbic system seems to be involved in organizing the behaviors involved in motivation and emotion.*
- *The cerebral cortex is divided into frontal, parietal, occipital, and temporal lobes. Some areas of the cerebral cortex receive sensory input, some control motor functions, and others (the association cortex) are involved in higher mental processes in humans. The frontal lobes are particularly important in such executive functions as planning, voluntary behavior, and self-awareness. The case of Phineas Gage and the "Research Close-Up" study of violent murderers attest to the importance of the prefrontal area in behavioral self-control.*
- *Although the two cerebral hemispheres ordinarily work in coordination with one another, they appear to have different functions and abilities. Studies of split-brain patients who have had the corpus callosum cut indicate that the left hemisphere commands language and mathematical abilities, whereas the right hemisphere has well-developed spatial abilities but a generally limited ability to communicate through speech. Positive emotions are linked to relatively greater left-hemisphere activation and negative emotions to relatively greater right-hemisphere involvement. Despite hemispheric localization, however, most behaviors involve interactions between both hemispheres; the brain normally operates as a highly integrated system.*

Plasticity in the Brain: The Role of Experience and the Recovery of Function

For an amazing story of brain plasticity, see Video Segment 3.2.

Learn to walk, acquire speech, begin to read, fall in love, and your brain changes in a way that makes you a different person from who you were before. Learning and practicing a mental or physical skill may change the size or number of brain areas involved and alter the neural pathways used in the skill (Adams & Cox, 2002). This process of brain alteration begins in the womb and continues throughout life. It is governed in important ways by genetic factors but is also strongly influenced by the environment.

▶ 26. What is neural plasticity? How do age, environment, and behavior affect plasticity?

Neural plasticity *refers to the ability of neurons to change in structure and function* (Huttenlocher, 2002). Two aspects of neural plasticity—the effects of early experience on brain development and recovery from brain damage—are at the forefront of current research.

The Role of Early Experience Brain development is programmed by complex commands from our genes, but how these genetic commands express themselves can be powerfully affected by the environment in which we develop, including the environment we are exposed to in the womb (Filogamo, 1998). Consider the following research findings:

- For the fetus in the womb, exposure to high levels of alcohol ingested by the pregnant mother can disrupt brain development and produce the lifelong mental and behavioral damage seen in fetal alcohol syndrome. Drinking during the first weeks of pregnancy—sometimes before a woman is even aware that she's pregnant—is particularly risky in this regard (Streissguth et al., 1985).

- As discussed in Chapter 2, the brains of rat pups raised in a stimulating early environment weighed more and had larger neurons, more dendritic branches, and greater concentrations of acetylcholine, a neurotransmitter involved in motor control and in memory (Rosenzweig, 1984).
- As we also discussed in Chapter 2, prematurely born human infants who were caressed and massaged on a regular basis showed faster neurological development than did those given normal care and human contact (Field et al., 1986).
- MRI recordings revealed that experienced violinists and other string-instrument players who do elaborate movements on the strings with their left hands had a larger right-hemisphere somatosensory area devoted to these fingers than did nonmusicians. The corresponding left-hemisphere (right-hand) cortical areas of the musicians and nonmusicians did not differ. The earlier in life the musicians had started playing their instruments, the more cortical change had occurred (Elbert et al., 1995).
- Cultural factors may affect brain development as well. For example, the Chinese language uses complex pictorial images (rather than words) to represent objects or concepts. Because pictorial stimuli are processed in the right hemisphere, we might expect less left-hemisphere lateralization of language among speakers of Chinese than among people who speak English or other alphabet-based languages. There is evidence to support this hypothesis in the areas of reading and writing (Tzeng et al., 1979).

These and other findings show that in a sense, your brain goes through its own personal "evolutionary" process as it adapts to and is molded by your individual environment during the course of your life. Once again we can see why the nature-nurture debate described in Chapter 1 has given way to an appreciation for the many ways in which biology and experience continually interact.

The brain is clearly capable of greater plasticity early in life. In one study, researchers took neurons from the visual cortex of cats and then raised the neurons in a culture containing the nutrients needed for survival. They found that the neurons could survive and create new synapses with other neurons in the culture quite well if they were taken from kittens who were 2 to 4 weeks old, but not if they were obtained from older animals (Schoop et al., 1997).

Studies using the electron microscope help explain why such plasticity is possible early in life. The 1- to 2-year-old child has about 50 percent more brain synapses than mature adults do (Huttenlocher, 1979). This greater availability of synapses may help to explain why children can recover from brain damage more quickly and completely than adults. But, sadly, the days of synaptic riches don't last forever. Unused or weaker synapses deteriorate with age, so that the brain loses some of its plasticity (Huttenlocher, 2002). Moreover, cell death is programmed into every neuron by its genes, and what some neuroscientists refer to as the neuron's "suicide apparatus" is activated by a lack of stimulation from other neurons and by many other factors that are not yet known. As a result, adults actually have fewer synapses in the brain than do children, despite their more advanced cognitive and motor capabilities.

▶ 27. Describe the ways in which neural function can be restored following damage.

Healing the Nervous System When nerve tissue is destroyed or neurons die as part of the aging process, surviving neurons can restore functioning by modifying themselves either structurally or biochemically. They can alter their structure by sprouting enlarged networks of dendrites or by extending axons from surviving neurons to form new synapses (Shepherd, 1997). Surviving neurons may also make up for the loss by increasing the volume of neurotransmitters they release (Robinson, 1997). Moreover, research findings have disproved the long-standing assumption of brain scientists that dead neurons cannot be replaced in the mature brain (McMillan et al., 1999). In 1998, evidence for the birth of new cells *(neurogenesis)* in the human adult hippocampus appeared (Eriksson et al., 1998). Then, in what could be a landmark scientific discovery, psychologist Elizabeth Gould and her Princeton coworkers (1999) provided the first evidence of neurogenesis in the cerebral cortex of a primate. Using complex chemical and microscopic analysis techniques with adult macaque monkeys, Gould's team tracked newly developed neurons from their birthplace in subcortical tissue. The immature neurons migrated upward along myelinated nerve tracts into the association areas of the cerebral cortex, where they sprouted axons and extended them toward existing neurons. The researchers speculated that these new neurons may be involved in higher-order mental functions, such as complex learning and memory. However, some other scientists have been unable to replicate the findings of cortical neurogenesis, so the jury is still out (Rakic, 2002). Nonetheless, if similar results are found in humans, whose brain structures and functions are similar to those of other primates, new light could be shed on brain mechanisms of information storage and plasticity.

Until recently, scientists thought that once neurons die, they cannot be replaced. Now, that long-standing belief has been challenged. One revolutionary technique involves the transplantation into the brain of **neural stem cells,** *immature "uncommitted" cells that can mature into any type of neuron or glial cell needed by the brain*. These cells, found in both the developing and adult nervous system, can be put into a liquid medium and injected directly into the brain. Once in the brain, they can travel to any of its regions, especially developing or degenerating areas. There they can detect defective or genetically impaired cells and somehow convert themselves into healthy forms of the defective cells. To this point, most of the research has been done with animals.

Researchers at Harvard Medical School demonstrated the potential value of stem cell transplantation (Yandava et al., 1999). They worked with a strain of mice called *shiverers,* who have a genetic defect that prevents their glial cells from producing the insulating myelin sheath on axons. Within 3 weeks after birth, the animals begin to develop severe tremors similar to those seen in humans with multiple sclerosis, a disease produced by insufficient myelin. Using a neural stem cell culture grown from cells removed 13 years earlier from the brain of a newborn mouse, the researchers injected stem cells directly into the brains of randomly selected newborn shiverers. A control group did not receive the cells. In the injected rats, the stem cells apparently detected the defective gene and converted themselves into the myelin-producing cells. They then began to produce the missing myelin throughout the brain, and some of the mice developed myelin sheaths that could not be distinguished from those of normal mice. About 60 percent of the experimental group appeared to behave like normal mice, showing no signs of the motor disturbances that accompany insufficient myelinization. Others showed greatly reduced motor symptoms. All of the control animals exhibited shivering as they matured.

The fact that transplanted stem cells can apparently go anywhere in the brain and become any kind of cell suggests the possibility of revolutionary treatments for diseases involving widespread neural degeneration and dysfunction, such as Alzheimer's disease, multiple sclerosis, strokes, mental disorders, and genetically based birth defects, all of which have serious psychological consequences (Wernig & Brustle, 2002). Stem cells have also been successfully transplanted into the spinal cords of injured animals, where they have taken hold and organized themselves into neural networks (Tzeng, 1997). This success may herald an eventual ability to do what has never before been possible: repair the severed spinal cord. In one study, human stem cells transplanted into the brains of aged rats migrated to the hippocampus and cortex. Four weeks later, these rats showed improved performance in a water maze task, suggesting improved learning and memory ability (Qu et al., 2001). Much more research is needed, but, at long last, we may be on the threshold of being able to heal the damaged brain and restore lost psychological functions.

BENEATH THE SURFACE

DO WE REALLY USE ONLY TEN PERCENT OF OUR BRAIN CAPACITY?

How often have you heard the statement that we only use 10 percent of our brain capacity? Is there any truth to this notion?

Let's apply what we've learned in this chapter to critically evaluate that statement. One principle of critical thinking is that the best way to test an idea is to try to find evidence against it. The reason is that we can find something to support almost any statement, even if it's false. In contrast, one disconfirming piece of evidence tells us the statement is not true as is.

First, let's consider what we know about brain activity from PET and fMRI imaging studies. Do they show that only 10 percent of the brain is active at any time? Certainly not. Instead, the brain exhibits widespread activity even during sleep. Although certain functions may use only a small part of the brain at one time, any sufficiently complex set of activities or thought patterns involves many parts of the brain. For any given activity, such as eating, watching television, making love, or reading this book, you may use a few specific parts of your brain. Over the course of a whole day, however, just about all of the brain is used at one time or another. Thus, brain activity data fly in the face of the 10-percent truism.

Next, we might consider what we know about brain damage. Does the 10-percent principle mean that we would be just fine if 90 percent of our brain were removed? Hardly. It is well known that damage to a relatively small area of the brain, such as that caused by a stroke, may cause devastating disabilities. Yet the damage caused by these conditions is far less than what would occur if 90 percent of the brain were damaged. As a prominent neurologist once said, "If a surgeon tells you they're going to remove the 90 percent of the brain you don't need, run like hell."

We might also apply what we've learned about neural development, particularly the "use it or lose it" principle. The process of brain development involves pruning synapses that are not used, thereby fine-tuning brain functioning. Many studies have shown that if the input to a particular neural system is eliminated, then neurons in this system will not function properly. If we were really using only 10 percent of the brain, we could expect the other 90 percent to atrophy over time.

Where did the 10-percent idea come from in the first place? Perhaps it was inspired in part by the work of psychologist Karl Lashley in the 1920s and 1930s. Lashley removed large areas of the cerebral cortex in rats and found that these animals could still relearn specific tasks. This did not mean, however, that other functions were not severely affected. But psychics and other "human potential" marketeers found the idea intriguing and have kept it alive over the decades. After all, if we use only 10 percent of our brain, imagine the untapped psychic abilities that lie dormant, just waiting to be released using their methods. Psychics often attribute their special, if fraudulent, "gifts" to the release of neural potential that other people have not accessed.

This does not mean that we don't have untapped potentials; it's just that if realized, they would be represented in the form of new synapses within brain tissue that you're already using. A final reason why the myth persists is that it's been repeated so often over the years in the mass media that it's become a part of popular culture, an unquestioned "factoid" that's taken on a life of its own. However, there's no question that the 10-percent principle is a myth without scientific foundation.

IN REVIEW

- *Neural plasticity refers to the ability of neurons to change in structure and function. Environmental factors, particularly early in life, have notable effects on brain development. There are often critical periods during which environmental factors have their greatest (or only) effects on plasticity.*
- *A person's ability to recover from brain damage depends on several factors. Other things being equal, recovery is greatest early in life and declines with age.*
- *When neurons die, surviving neurons can alter their structure and functions to recover the ability to send and receive nerve impulses. Neurons can also increase the amount of neurotransmitters they release. Recent findings suggest that the brains of mature primates and humans are capable of producing new neurons (neurogenesis).*
- *Current advances in the treatment of neurological disorders include experiments on neuron regeneration and the injection of neural stem cells into the brain, where they find and replace diseased or dead neurons.*

THE NERVOUS SYSTEM INTERACTS WITH THE ENDOCRINE AND IMMUNE SYSTEMS

The nervous system interacts with two other communication systems within the body, namely, the endocrine and immune systems. These interactions have major influences on behavior and on psychological and physical well-being.

Interactions With the Endocrine System

▶ 28. How does the endocrine system differ from the nervous system? How do hormones affect development and behavior?

The **endocrine system** *consists of numerous hormone-secreting glands distributed throughout the body*. The locations of the endocrine glands within the human body and a list of their functions are presented in Figure 3.27.

Like the nervous system, the endocrine system's function is to convey information from one area of the body to another. Rather than using nerve impulses, however, the endocrine system conveys information in the form of **hormones,** *chemical messengers that are secreted from its glands into the bloodstream*. Just as neurons have receptors for certain neurotransmitters, cells in the body

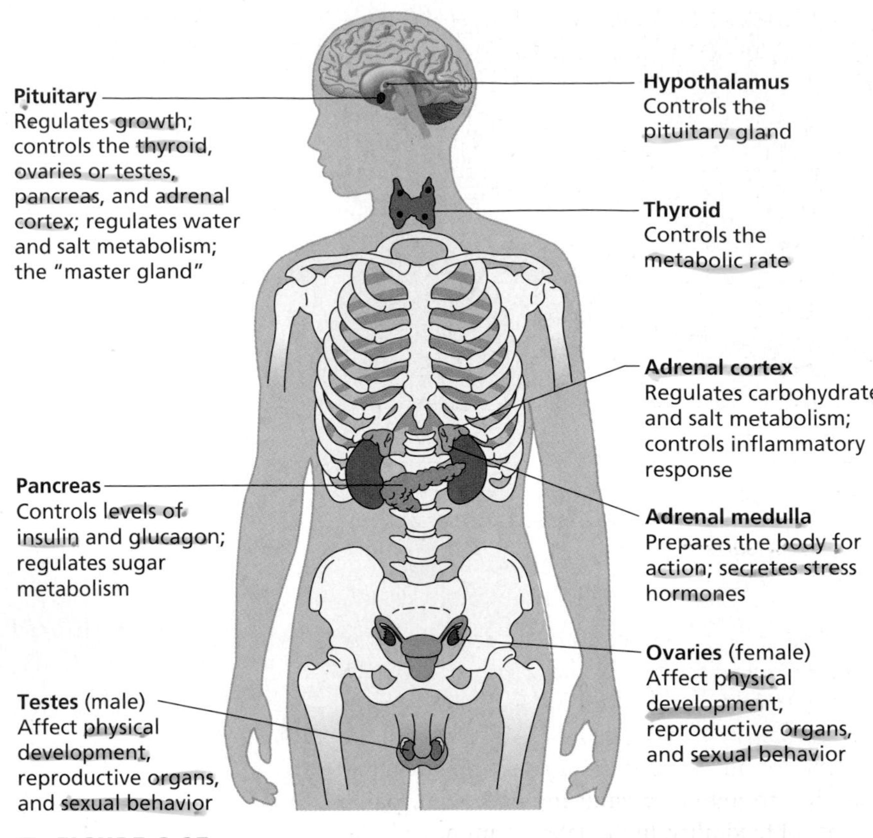

FIGURE 3.27

The glands that constitute the endocrine system and the effects of their hormones on bodily functions.

(including neurons) have receptor molecules that respond to specific hormones from the endocrine glands. Many of the hormones secreted by these glands affect psychological development and functioning.

Endocrine messages trigger responses in the brain, and mental processes within the brain can affect endocrine functioning. For example, negative thoughts about a stressful situation can quickly trigger the secretion of stress hormones within the body (Borod, 2000).

The nervous system transmits information rapidly, with the speed of nerve impulses. In contrast, the endocrine system is much slower because the delivery of its messages depends on the rate of blood flow. Nonetheless, hormones travel throughout the body in the bloodstream and can reach billions of individual cells. Thus when the brain has important information to transmit, it has the choice of sending it directly in the form of nerve impulses to a relatively small number of neurons or indirectly by means of hormones to a large number of cells. Often both communication networks are used, resulting in both immediate and prolonged stimulation.

Hormones begin to influence our development, capacities, and behavior long before we're born. In the third to fourth month of pregnancy, genetically programmed releases of sex hormones in the fetus determine the biological sex of the child, as well as differences in the structure and function of several parts of the nervous system, including the hypothalamus. One area of the hypothalamus affected in this manner continues to influence hormonal release in later life, such as the cyclic pattern of hormonal release during the female menstrual cycle.

Aside from reproductive structures and sexual behaviors, prenatal hormones affect a variety of other characteristics. Males tend to be more aggressive than females, and females live longer than men (Nelson & Luciana, 2001). Hormones also produce differences in brain structures in males and females. Females have greater density of neurons in language-relevant areas of the temporal lobe, which may contribute to the small overall superiority they manifest in verbal skills (Collins & Kimura, 1997). They also tend to have a relatively larger corpus callosum than males, which may help account for the fact that language functions are less localized in the left hemisphere in females (Rossell et al., 2002). These sex differences will be discussed in greater detail in Chapter 8.

Of special interest to psychologists are the **adrenal glands,** *twin structures perched atop the kidneys that serve, quite literally, as hormone factories, producing and secreting about 50 different hormones that regulate many metabolic processes within the brain and other parts of the body.* The neurotransmitter dopamine is one substance produced in the adrenals. Also produced there are several stress hormones. In an emergency, the adrenal glands are activated by the sympathetic branch of the autonomic nervous system. Stress hormones are then secreted into the bloodstream, mobilizing the body's emergency response system. Because hormones remain in the bloodstream for some time, the action of these adrenal hormones is especially important under conditions of prolonged stress. If not for the long-term influence of hormones, the autonomic nervous system would have to produce a constant barrage of nerve impulses to the organs involved in responding to stress.

Interactions Involving the Immune System

The nervous and endocrine systems interact not only with one another but also with the immune system. A normal, healthy immune system is a wonder of nature. At this moment, microscopic soldiers patrol every part of your body, including your brain. They are on a search-and-destroy mission, seeking out biological invaders that could disable or kill you. Programmed into this legion of tiny defenders is an innate ability to recognize which substances belong to the body and which are foreign and must be destroyed. Such recognition occurs because *foreign substances known as* **antigens** (meaning *anti*body *gen*erators) *trigger a biochemical response from the immune system.* Bacteria, viruses, abnormal cells, and many chemical molecules with antigenic properties start the wars that rage inside our bodies every moment of every day (Figure 3.28).

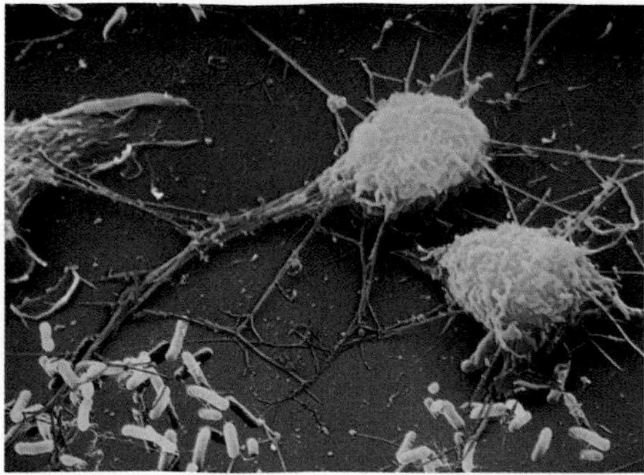

FIGURE 3.28

Immune system cells reach out to capture bacteria, shown here in yellow-green. Bacteria that are pulled to the surface of the cell will be engulfed and devoured.

The immune system has a remarkable memory. Once it has encountered one of the millions of different antigens that enter the body, it will recognize the antigen immediately in the future and produce the biochemical weapons, or *antibodies,* needed to destroy it (Nossal & Hall, 1995). This memory is the basis for developing vaccines to protect animals and people from some diseases; it is also the reason we normally catch diseases such as mumps and chicken pox only once in our lives. Unfortunately, though the memory may be perfect, our body's defenses may not be. Some bacteria and viruses evolve so rapidly that they can change just enough over time to slip past the sentinels in our immune system and give us this year's cold or flu.

Antigens can originate externally (a flu virus or a pollen) or internally (a cancerous tumor). Problems arise when the immune system has either an underactive or an overactive response (Figure 3.29). An *underactive* immune system response to external antigens is dramatically illustrated in acquired immune deficiency syndrome (AIDS). The human immunodeficiency virus (HIV) attacks immune cells and disables them. This leaves the body defenseless against virtually anything that can infect humans: bacteria, viruses of all kinds, fungi, and protozoa. Underreaction can also occur to an internal antigen. This is what occurs in cancer. Abnormal body cells are allowed to proliferate, resulting in the formation of tumors.

An *overactive* response to an external antigen presents problems in the form of an allergy. For example, in its violent reaction to an allergen, an asthmatic's immune system releases a torrent of histamine, a chemical that causes critical breathing muscles around the bronchial tubes to contract, leaving the asthmatic person wheezing and gasping for air.

Another type of overactive response, an **autoimmune reaction,** *results when the immune system mistakenly identifies part of the body as an enemy and attacks it.* For example, in rheumatoid arthritis, the immune system attacks connective tissue in the joints, causing inflammation, pain, and loss of flexibility. In diabetes, immune cells attack cells in the pancreas that produce the hormone insulin, which regulates one's blood sugar level. As a result, the diabetic person may experience an abnormally high blood sugar level that can damage other organs or a drop in blood sugar that can result in a coma.

The immune system, like the nervous system, thus has an exquisite capacity to receive, interpret, and respond to specific forms of stimulation. It senses, learns, remembers, and reacts; in other words, it behaves. Despite these similarities, research on the nervous and immune systems proceeded along independent paths for many years, with only a few visionaries suggesting that the two systems might be able to communicate and

▶ 29. What evidence exists that the nervous, endocrine, and immune systems communicate with and influence one another?

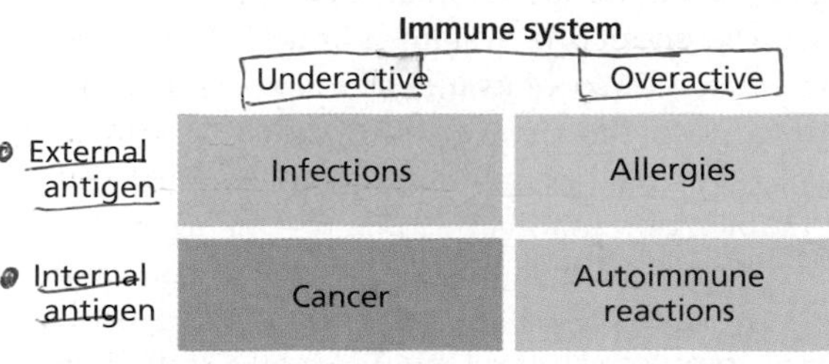

Immune system	Underactive	Overactive
External antigen	Infections	Allergies
Internal antigen	Cancer	Autoimmune reactions

FIGURE 3.29

Disorders of the immune system created by underactive or overactive responses to either internal or external antigens.

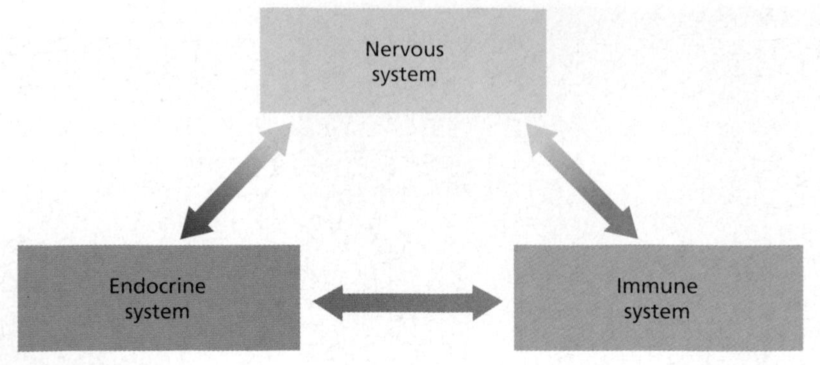

FIGURE 3.30

The nervous, endocrine, and immune systems are part of a complex communication system in which each can affect and be affected by the others. This fact accounts for many of the so-called body-mind interactions that are the focus of current interest in psychology.

influence each others' activities. They were right. We now know that the nervous, endocrine, and immune systems are all parts of a communication network that so completely underlies our every mental, emotional, and physical action that neuroscientist Candace Pert (1986), one of the pioneers in this area of research, has dubbed this network "bodymind."

Pieces of this communication puzzle began to fall into place with several key discoveries. The first was that selective electrical stimulation or destruction of certain areas of the hypothalamus and cerebral cortex resulted in almost instantaneous increases or decreases in immune system activity. Conversely, activation of the immune system by injecting antigens into the body resulted in increased electrical activity in several brain regions (Saphier, 1992). Clearly, the nervous and immune systems were communicating with and influencing one another.

Later research showed that the nervous and immune systems are chemically connected as well. Immune system cells contain receptors keyed to specific neurotransmitter substances, meaning that the action of immune cells can be directly influenced by chemical messengers from the brain (Maier & Watkins, 1999). An equally startling discovery was that immune cells can actually produce hormones and neurotransmitters, allowing them to directly influence the brain and the endocrine system's glands. The immune system is therefore not only a response system but also a giant sensory system. It responds to antigens by sending chemical messengers that affect neurotransmitter activity in the brain and the autonomic nervous system. The brain, in turn, responds with a cascade of chemical and neural signals to both the immune cells and to the endocrine glands and organs of the body (Felton & Maida, 2000). In sum, the brain, endocrine glands, and immune system form a complete communication loop, with each having sensory and motor functions and each influencing and being influenced by one another (Figure 3.30).

Inspired by these findings, many researchers began to study psychological influences on the immune system. Scientific investigations soon revealed a host of psychosocial factors that can increase or decrease immunity. For example, stress, depression, and pessimistic thinking reduce immune functioning, whereas stress management skills, an optimistic outlook, a sense of humor, and social support help preserve immunity (Kiecolt-Glaser et al., 2002). As Figure 3.31 indicates, immune functioning is now being studied at biological, psychological, and environmental levels of analysis. We will examine these findings, and their applied implications, in greater depth in Chapter 12.

IN REVIEW

- *The nervous, endocrine, and immune systems have extensive neural and chemical means of communication, and each is capable of affecting and being affected by the others.*
- *The endocrine system secretes hormones into the bloodstream. These chemical messengers affect many body processes, including the activities of the central and autonomic nervous systems. Because of the adrenal glands' relation to functions of the nervous system, they are of particular interest to psychologists. Hormonal effects in the womb may produce brain differences in males and females that influence sex differences in certain psychological functions.*
- *The immune system interacts extensively with the central and autonomic nervous systems and with the endocrine system. All of these systems can directly affect one another. As a behaving entity, it has the capacity to sense, interpret, and respond to specific forms of stimulation. Immune system disorders can occur because of either an underactive or an overactive immune system. Cancer and AIDS result from underactivity; allergic reactions and autoimmune conditions result from overactivity.*

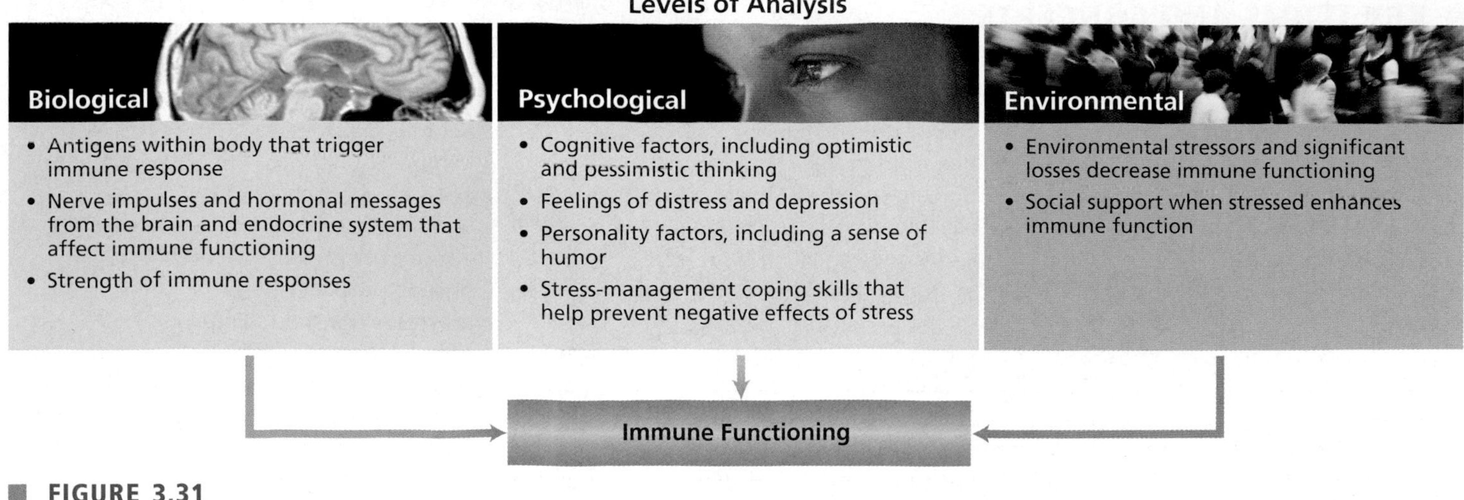

Levels of Analysis
Biological
• Antigens within body that trigger immune response
• Nerve impulses and hormonal messages from the brain and endocrine system that affect immune functioning
• Strength of immune responses
Psychological
• Cognitive factors, including optimistic and pessimistic thinking
• Feelings of distress and depression
• Personality factors, including a sense of humor
• Stress-management coping skills that help prevent negative effects of stress
Environmental
• Environmental stressors and significant losses decrease immune functioning
• Social support when stressed enhances immune function
Immune Functioning

FIGURE 3.31

Understanding Behavior: Levels of analysis in understanding immune functioning.

Some Final Reflections

We've considered three aspects of biological foundations of behavior. First, evolutionary forces have forged the development of innate biological mechanisms that underlie human capabilities and behavioral tendencies. Second, genetic factors help determine not only evolution-based adaptive mechanisms that we have in common with other humans, but also important mental, emotional, and behavioral aspects of our individual identities. Third, we've considered the biological structures and functions that compose the nervous, endocrine, and immune systems. In each instance, we've seen that biological and environmental factors affect one another and combine to influence development and behavior.

Reflecting on the many ways that biological and environmental factors interact at the evolutionary, genetic, and nervous system levels helps bring perspective to our understanding of behavior and its causes: It tempers the tendency of some people to believe that if a behavior is based on biological factors, it can't be changed. We've seen, to the contrary, that the environment can affect the manner in which a human characteristic expresses itself. Consider, for example, male identical twins: One is encouraged to cultivate his interest in the cello and devotes himself to that activity on a daily basis. The other begins to associate with a group of athletes, takes up weight lifting for a hobby, and gulps protein supplements. Despite their identical genotype, we can anticipate that at a phenotypic level, these twins will eventually differ quite dramatically in musical talent and physique. It is therefore a myth that if a trait is inherited, it will have identical effects in the various people who inherit it. Biological factors allow a range of effects, depending on the environment in which they function. Thus, cultural factors, learning experiences, interpersonal relations, and other environmental effects will combine with biological factors to influence behavior.

Discovering the nature and extent of biological and environmental influences for various behaviors is a major frontier in psychology. The manner in which the brain, mind, and world interact to cause behavior is the basis for psychology's use of the biological, psychological, and environmental levels of analysis that we feature throughout this book.

KEY TERMS AND CONCEPTS

Each term has been boldfaced and defined in the chapter on the page indicated in parentheses.

absolute refractory period (p. 75)
acetylcholine (ACh; p. 78)
action potential (p. 75)
adaptations (p. 65)
adoption studies (p. 71)
adrenal glands (p. 102)
agonist (p. 79)
all-or-none law (p. 75)
amygdala (p. 89)
antagonist (p. 79)
antigens (p. 103)
aphasia (p. 95)
association cortex (p. 92)
autoimmune reactions (p. 103)
autonomic nervous system (p. 82)
axon (p. 74)
behavior genetics (p. 70)
biologically based mechanisms (p. 64)
brain stem (p. 86)
Broca's area (p. 92)
central nervous system (p. 81)
cerebellum (p. 87)
cerebral cortex (p. 90)
cerebrum (p. 88)
chromosome (p. 69)
computerized axial tomography (CT or CAT) scan (p. 84)
concordance (p. 71)
corpus callosum (p. 95)
dendrites (p. 74)
domain-specific adaptations (p. 66)
electroencephalograph (EEG; p. 84)
endocrine system (p. 101)
evolution (p. 64)
forebrain (p. 88)
functional MRI (fMRI; p. 86)
genes (p. 69)
genotype (p. 68)
graded potentials (p. 75)
heritability coefficient (p. 70)
hindbrain (p. 86)
hippocampus (p. 89)
hormones (p. 101)
hypothalamus (p. 89)
interneurons (p. 81)
lateralization (p. 95)
limbic system (p. 89)
magnetic resonance imaging (MRI; p. 85)
medulla (p. 86)
midbrain (p. 88)
motor cortex (p. 91)
motor neurons (p. 81)
myelin sheath (p. 75)
natural selection (p. 64)
neural plasticity (p. 98)
neural stem cells (p. 100)
neuromodulators (p. 79)
neurons (p. 74)
neurotransmitters (p. 77)
parasympathetic nervous system (p. 82)
peripheral nervous system (p. 81)
phenotype (p. 68)
polygenic transmission (p. 69)
pons (p. 87)
positron emission tomography (PET) scan (p. 84)
prefrontal cortex (p. 93)
psychoactive drugs (p. 79)
receptor sites (p. 77)
recombinant DNA procedures (p. 72)
resting potential (p. 75)
reticular formation (p. 88)
reuptake (p. 78)
sensory neurons (p. 81)
somatic nervous system (p. 81)
somatic sensory cortex (p. 91)
sympathetic nervous system (p. 82)
synaptic space (p. 77)
synaptic vesicles (p. 77)
thalamus (p. 88)
twin studies (p. 71)
Wernicke's area (p. 92)

What Do You Think?

NATURAL SELECTION AND GENETIC DISEASES p. 66

Genetics research shows that, in most cases, there's not a one-to-one relation between a particular gene and a particular trait. Most traits involve the influence of many genes, and a given gene can contribute to many traits. Traits, therefore, come in packages, with some of the traits in the package being adaptive and others maladaptive. In fact, cystic fibrosis (CF) is one such example. CF is the most commonly inherited disorder among people of European descent. Why would such a damaging genetic trait survive in the gene pool? Geneticists have found that people with CF also have a trait that slows the release of salts into the intestine. Some scientists believe that this related trait might have helped save carriers from severe dehydration and death from the diarrheal diseases that killed 7 out of every 10 newborns in medieval Europe. Perhaps CF was preserved in the population because another part of the trait package made carriers more likely to survive and pass on their genes.

Let's consider sickle cell anemia. Many people of African descent suffer from this genetically caused blood disorder that lowers one's life expectancy. Why would a disorder that decreases survival be preserved in a population? The answer may be that, despite its negatives, the sickle cell gene has an important redeeming quality: It makes people more resistant to malaria, the most lethal disease in the African environment. Because it enhanced survival from malaria, the sickle trait can be seen as a product of natural selection. We see, therefore, that we should be careful not to oversimplify the concept of adaptation and assume that any trait that survives, whether physical or psychological, is of immediate benefit to the species. ■

FROM GENE THERAPY TO DESIGNER BABIES p. 73

Genetic engineering advances have raised a host of moral and ethical questions that are already topics of intense discussion and debate as we move toward their practical application. Consider one recent case. A woman suffers from a hereditary disorder that produces Alzheimer's disease at a very young age—usually in the 40s—because of a mutant gene. At age 33, she desperately wanted to have a child. Using a procedure called *preimplantation genetic diagnosis* (PGD), the eggs she produced were screened for the mutant gene. When some were found that were free of the mutant gene, those eggs were fertilized and implanted in her womb. She bore a daughter who is free of the genetic factor and soon repeated the procedure to have a second child.

Certainly it seems laudable to ensure that a child is not brought into the world with a dread disease. And certainly we should try to prevent the kind of tragedy that occurred when a Dutch sperm-bank donor, whose sperm fathered 18 children, was found to have a genetically caused degenerative brain disease that is likely to appear in half of the children. Doctors had to decide whether or not to inform the 18 families. After three years of debate, they decided to do so. Obviously, the news was heartbreaking to the parents.

Even in the case of the early-Alzheimer's mother, some bioethicists raise the practical issue of how long the woman will be able to care for her children before her dementia overtakes her. Beyond this, however, other issues loom about the application of such procedures. As a parent, would you use genetic screening or engineering to have a child of a specific sex, appearance, personality, or intellectual level? Is it possible that you would choose to abort a normal, healthy fetus shown by genetic testing to lack the desired characteristics? Producing so-called designer babies, by choosing from a catalogue of traits linked to genes that can be altered, is already a subject of intense debate and controversy. On the horizon looms the potential to produce duplicate humans through cloning. Cloning of human embryos to obtain stem cells for research purposes is currently allowed in England under highly controlled conditions. Will those conditions be applied elsewhere and relaxed over time? As you can see, there's no shortage of important issues in this field. ■

4

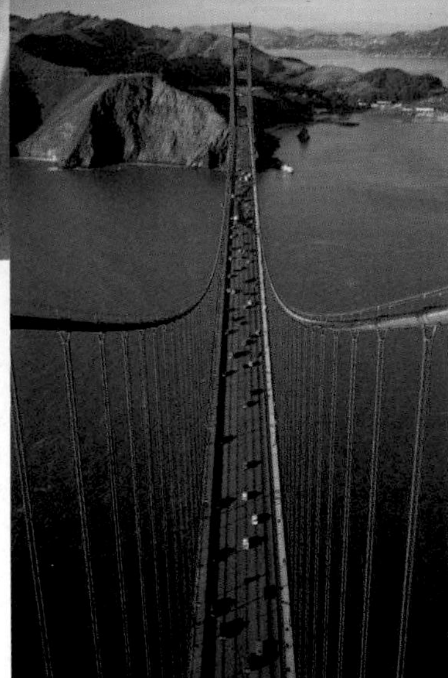

SENSATION AND PERCEPTION

CHAPTER OUTLINE

All our knowledge has its origins in our perceptions.

—Leonardo da Vinci

FIGURE 4.1

Helen Keller (left) "hears" her teacher Anne Sullivan by reading Sullivan's lips with her fingers. AP/Wide World Photos Helen Keller/Anne Sullivan.

> *Sometimes, it is true, a sense of isolation enfolds me like a cold mist as I sit alone and wait at life's shut gate. Beyond, there is light, and music, and sweet companionship; but I may not enter. Fate, silent, pitiless, bars the way. . . . Silence sits immense upon my soul. (Keller, 1955, p. 62)*

So wrote Helen Keller (Figure 4.1), deprived of both vision and hearing by an acute illness she suffered at the age of 19 months. For those of us who enjoy and take for granted the use of these senses, it is hard to imagine what it would be like to sink into a dark and silent universe, cut off from all sight and sound. Helen Keller was saved from this abyss by her teacher, Anne Sullivan, who tried day after day to communicate with her by tapping signs onto the little girl's palm. One day, Anne tapped water *onto Helen's palm as she placed the child's hand under the gushing spout of a pump.*

> *That living word awakened my soul, gave it light, hope, joy, set it free! That was because I saw everything with a strange new sight that had come to me. . . . It would have been difficult to find a happier child than I was. (p. 103)*

Helen Keller went on to write her celebrated book The Story of My Life *while an undergraduate at Radcliffe College. She became an inspiration and advocate for people with disabilities.*

■■■

Nature gives us a marvelous set of sensory contacts with our world. If our sense organs are not defective, we experience light waves as brightnesses and colors, air vibrations as sounds, chemical substances as odors or tastes, and so on. However, such is not the case for people with a rare condition called **synesthesia,** *which means, quite literally,* "mixing of the senses" *(Cytowic, 2002; Harrison & Baron-Cohen, 1997). Individuals with synesthesia may experience sounds as colors, or tastes as touch sensations of different shapes.*

Russian psychologist A. R. Luria (1968) studied a highly successful writer and musician whose life was a perpetual stream of mixed-up sensations. On one occasion, Luria asked him to report on his experiences while listening to electronically generated musical tones. To a medium-pitched tone, the man experienced a brown strip with red edges, together with a sweet and sour flavor. A very high-pitched tone evoked the following sensation: "It looks something like a fireworks tinged with a pink-red hue. The strip of color feels rough and unpleasant, and it has an ugly taste—rather like that of a briny pickle. . . . You could hurt your hand on this." Mixed sensations like these frequently occurred in the man's daily life, and they were sometimes disconcerting. On one occasion, the man asked an ice cream vendor what flavors she sold. "But she answered in such a tone that a whole pile of coals, of black cinders, came bursting out of her mouth, and I couldn't bring myself to buy any ice cream after she answered that way."

▶1. Describe the six stages in the sensory processing and perception of information. Differentiate between sensation and perception.

Sensory-impaired people like Helen Keller and those who experience synesthesia provide glimpses into different aspects of how we sense and understand our world. These processes, previewed in Figure 4.2, begin when specific types of stimuli activate specialized sensory receptors. Whether the stimulus is light, sound waves, a chemical molecule, or pressure, your sensory receptors must translate this information into the only language your nervous system understands: the language of nerve impulses. Once this translation occurs, specialized neurons break down and analyze the specific features of the stimuli. At the next stage, these numerous stimulus "pieces" are reconstructed into a neural representation that is then compared with previously stored information, such as our knowledge of how particular objects look, smell, or feel. This matching of a new stimulus with our internal storehouse of knowledge allows us to recognize the stimulus and give it meaning. We then consciously experience a *perception*.

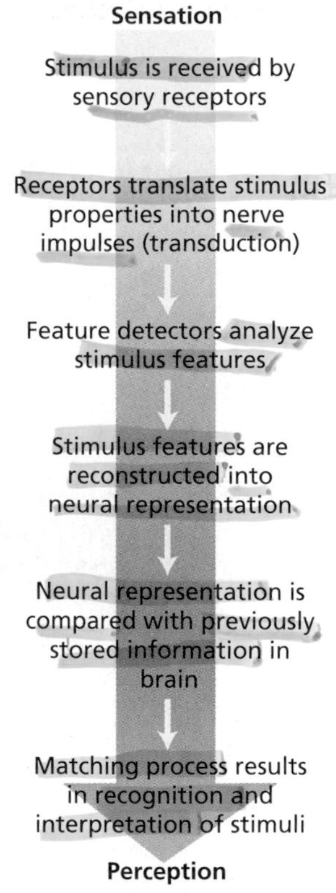

Helen Keller could not detect light waves or sound waves, the stimuli for sight and hearing. But, for her, the sense of touch helped make up for this deficit, giving her a substitute window to her world. In the mysterious condition of synesthesia, something goes wrong at the level of either feature detection or the recombining of the elements of a stimulus so that light waves might give rise to an experience of a sound or texture (Cytowic, 2002).

In some ways, sensation and perception blend together so completely that they are difficult to separate, for the stimulation we receive through our sense organs is instantaneously organized and transformed into the experiences that we refer to as perceptions. Nevertheless, psychologists do distinguish between them. **Sensation** *is the stimulus-detection process by which our sense organs respond to and translate environmental stimuli into nerve impulses that are sent to the brain.* **Perception**—*making "sense" of what our senses tell us—is the active process of organizing this stimulus input and giving it meaning* (Pashler & Yantis, 2002).

Because perception is an active and creative process, the same sensory input may be perceived in different ways at different times. For example, read the two sets of symbols in Figure 4.3. The middle symbols in both sets are exactly the same, and they sent identical input to your brain, but you probably perceived them differently. Your interpretation, or perception, of the characters was influenced by their *context*—that is, by the characters that preceded and followed them and by your learned expectation of what normally follows the letter *A* and the number *12*. This is a simple illustration of how perception takes us a step beyond sensation.

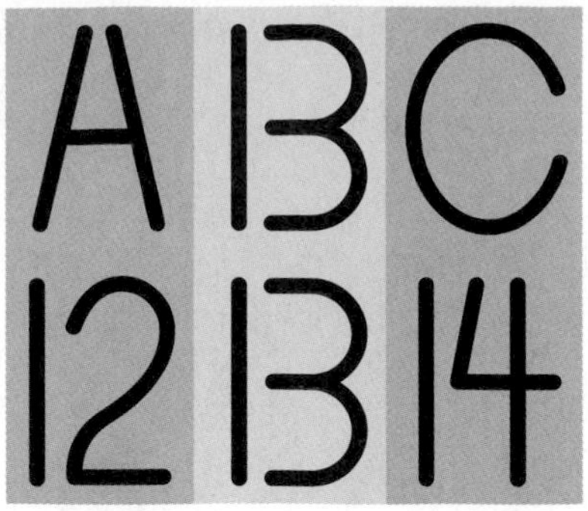

Sensation

Stimulus is received by sensory receptors

Receptors translate stimulus properties into nerve impulses (transduction)

Feature detectors analyze stimulus features

Stimulus features are reconstructed into neural representation

Neural representation is compared with previously stored information in brain

Matching process results in recognition and interpretation of stimuli

Perception

FIGURE 4.2

Sensory and perceptual processes proceed from the reception and translation of physical energies into nerve impulses. Then occurs the active process by which the brain receives the nerve impulses, organizes and confers meaning on them, and constructs a perceptual experience.

FIGURE 4.3

Quickly read these two lines of symbols out loud. Did your perception of the middle symbol in each line depend on the symbols that surrounded it?

SENSORY PROCESSES

Locked within the silent, dark recesses of your skull, your brain cannot "understand" light waves, sound waves, or the other forms of energy that make up the language of the environment. Contact with the outer world is possible only because certain neurons have developed into specialized sensory receptors that can transform these energy forms into the code language of nerve impulses.

As a starting point, we might ask: How many senses are there? Certainly there appear to be more than the five classical senses: vision, audition (hearing), touch, gustation (taste), and olfaction (smell). For example, there are senses that provide information about balance and body position. Also, the sense of touch can be subdivided into separate senses of pressure, pain, and temperature. Receptors deep within the brain monitor the chemical composition of our blood. The immune system also has sensory functions that allow it to detect foreign invaders and to receive stimulation from the brain.

Like those of other organisms, human sensory systems are designed to extract from the environment the information that we need to function and survive. Although our survival does not depend on having eyes like eagles or owls, noses like bloodhounds, or ears as sensitive as those of the worm-hunting robin, we do have specialized sensors that can detect many different kinds of stimuli with considerable sensitivity. The scientific area of **psychophysics,** *which studies relations between the physical characteristics of stimuli and sensory capabilities,* is concerned with two kinds of sensitivity. The first concerns the absolute limits of sensitivity. For example, what is the dimmest light, the softest sound, or the weakest salt solution that humans can detect? The second kind of sensitivity has to do with differences between stimuli. What is the smallest difference in brightness that we can detect? How much difference must there be in two tones before we can tell that they are not identical?

TABLE 4.1 Some Approximate Absolute Thresholds for Various Senses

Sensory Modality	Absolute Threshold
Vision	Candle flame seen at 30 miles on a clear, dark night
Hearing	Tick of a watch under quiet conditions at 20 feet
Taste	1 teaspoon of sugar in 2 gallons of water
Smell	1 drop of perfume diffused into the entire volume of a large apartment
Touch	Wing of a fly or bee falling on your cheek from a distance of 1 centimeter

SOURCE: Based on Galanter, 1962.

Stimulus Detection: The Absolute Threshold

How intense must a stimulus be before we can detect its presence? Researchers answer this question by systematically presenting stimuli of varying intensities and asking people whether they can detect them. Researchers designate the **absolute threshold** *as the lowest intensity at which a stimulus can be detected 50 percent of the time.* Thus the *lower* the absolute threshold, the *greater* the sensitivity. From studies of absolute thresholds, we can estimate the general limits of human sensitivity for the five major senses. Some examples are presented in Table 4.1. As you can see, many of our absolute thresholds are surprisingly low. Yet some other species have sensitivities that far surpass those of humans. For example, a female silkworm moth who is ready to mate needs to release only a billionth of an ounce of an attractant chemical molecule per second to attract every male silkworm moth within a radius of a mile.

Signal Detection Theory

Perhaps you can remember lying in bed as a child after seeing a horror movie, straining your ears to detect any unusual sound that might signal the presence of a monster in the house. Your vigilance may have caused you to detect faint and ominous sounds that would have probably gone unnoticed had you just watched a comedy or a romantic movie.

At one time scientists thought that, although some people have greater sensory acuity than others, each person has a more or less fixed level of sensitivity for each sense. But psychologists who study stimulus detection have found that an individual's apparent sensitivity can fluctuate quite a bit. The concept of a fixed absolute threshold is inaccurate because there is no single point on the intensity scale that separates nondetection from detection of a stimulus. There is instead a range of uncertainty, and people set their own **decision criterion,** *a standard of how certain they must be that a stimulus is present before they will say they detect it.* The decision criterion can also change from time to time, depending on such factors as fatigue, expectation (e.g., having watched a horror movie), and the potential significance of the stimulus. **Signal detection theory** *is concerned with the factors that influence sensory judgments.*

▶ 2. Define the absolute threshold from traditional and signal-detection perspectives.

In a typical signal detection experiment, participants are told that after a warning light appears, a barely perceptible tone may or may not be presented. Their task is to tell the experimenter whether or not they hear the tone. Under these conditions, there are four possible outcomes, as shown in Figure 4.4. When the tone is in fact

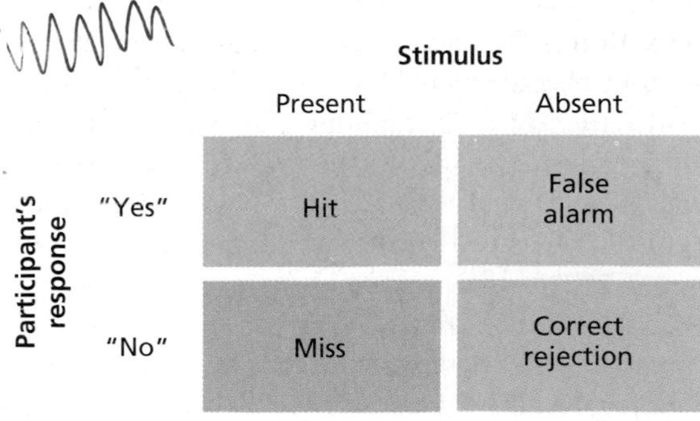

FIGURE 4.4

This matrix shows the four possible outcomes in a signal detection experiment in which participants decide whether or not a stimulus has been presented. The percentage of responses that fall within each category are affected by the characteristics of the participants and the nature of the situation.

presented, the participant may say "yes" (a hit) or "no" (a miss). When no tone is presented, the participant may also say "yes" (a false alarm) or "no" (a correct rejection).

At low stimulus intensities, both the participant's and the situation's characteristics influence the decision criterion (Methot & Huitema, 1998; Pitz & Sachs, 1984). Bold participants who frequently say "yes" have more hits, but they also have more false alarms than do conservative participants. Researchers can also influence participants to become bolder, or more conservative, by manipulating the rewards and costs for giving correct or incorrect responses. Increasing the rewards for hits or the costs for misses results in lower detection thresholds (more "yes" responses at low intensities). Thus a Navy radar operator may be more likely to notice a faint blip on her screen during a wartime mission, where a miss might have disastrous consequences, than during a peacetime voyage. Conversely, like physicians who will not perform a risky medical procedure without strong evidence to support their diagnosis, participants become more conservative in their "yes" responses as costs for false alarms are increased, resulting in higher detection thresholds (Irwin & McCarthy, 1998). Signal detection research shows us that perception is, in part, a decision.

Subliminal Stimuli: Can They Affect Behavior?

▶ 3. How do subliminal stimuli affect consumer behavior, attitudes, and self-improvement outcomes?

A **subliminal stimulus** *is one that is so weak or brief that although it is received by the senses, it cannot be perceived consciously.* There is little question that subliminal stimuli can register in the nervous system (Kihlstrom, 1999; MacLeod, 1998). But can such stimuli affect attitudes and behavior without our knowing it? The answer appears to be yes—to a limited extent.

In the late 1950s, James Vicary, a public relations executive, arranged to have subliminal messages flashed on a theater screen during a movie. The messages urged the audience to "drink Coca-Cola" and "eat popcorn." Vicary's claim that the subliminal messages increased popcorn sales by 50 percent and soft drink sales by 18 percent aroused a public furor. Consumers and scientists feared the possible abuse of subliminal messages to covertly influence the buying habits of consumers; they were concerned such messages might be used for "mind control" and "brainwashing" purposes. The National Association of Broadcasters reacted by outlawing subliminal messages on American television.

The outcries were, in large part, false alarms. Several attempts to reproduce Vicary's results under controlled conditions failed, and many other studies conducted in laboratory settings, on TV and radio, and in movie theaters indicated that there is little reason to be seriously concerned about significant or widespread control of consumer behavior through subliminal stimulation (Dixon, 1981; Drukin, 1998). Years later, Vicary admitted that his study was a hoax designed to revive his floundering advertising agency. Nonetheless, his false report stimulated a great deal of useful research on the power of subliminal stimuli to influence behavior. Where consumer behavior is concerned, the conclusion is that persuasive stimuli above the perceptual threshold are far more influential than subliminal attempts to sneak into our subconscious mind.

Although subliminal stimuli cannot control consumer behavior, can such stimuli affect more subtle phenomena, such as perceptions and attitudes? Research suggests that the answer is yes (Greenwald & Benaji, 1995). In one study, Jon Krosnick and his coworkers (1992) showed participants a series of nine different slides of the same person and then measured their attitudes toward the target person. For half of the participants, each photographic slide was immediately preceded by a subliminally presented unpleasant image (e.g., a face on fire). For the remaining participants, the preceding slides showed pleasant subliminal images, (e.g., smiling babies). Participants shown the associated unpleasant subliminal stimuli expressed negative attitudes toward the person, indicating a process of subconscious attitude conditioning, whereas those who saw the positive subliminal stimuli evaluated the person positively. Other research has shown that subliminal presentations of aggressively toned words cause people to judge ambiguous behaviors of others as more aggressive, and also increase their own tendency to behave aggressively (Todorov & Bargh, 2002). Although the original fears about brainwashing with subliminal stimuli may be unfounded, there is little doubt that subliminal stimuli can have subtle effects on attitudes, judgments, and behavior.

The Difference Threshold

Distinguishing between stimuli can sometimes be as important as detecting stimuli in the first place. When we try to match the colors of paints or clothing, very subtle differences can be quite important. Likewise, a slight variation in taste might signal that food is tainted or spoiled. Professional

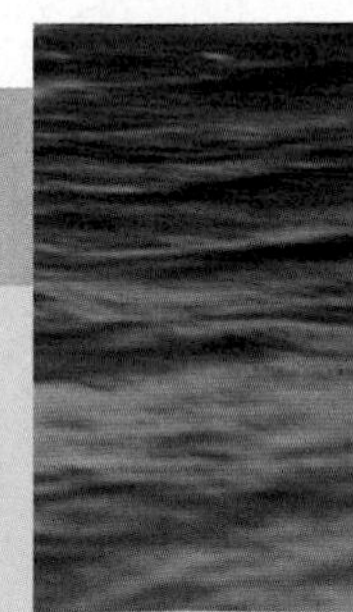

BENEATH THE SURFACE

ARE SUBLIMINAL SELF-HELP PRODUCTS EFFECTIVE?

You have probably seen advertisements for audiotapes or CDs that use subliminal messages to help people improve themselves. In fact, consumers spend millions of dollars on these products, which promise to help them lose weight, stop smoking, conquer fears, feel better about themselves, and achieve other self-improvement goals. How well do these tapes work?

Many people believe that such products were helpful to them. If so, why do these positive effects occur? Are they due to the programming of the subconscious mind to make the changes, or is it possible that the changes occur simply because people believe in the tapes? Can you think of a way to test these two possibilities?

Let's suppose you have a research group of people who want to change in one of two ways. Some want to improve their memory and others want to increase their self-esteem. You then pretest them on both a memory task and a psychological test measuring self-esteem so that you can determine later whether they've improved or not. You're now ready for your critical experiment.

You've purchased two commercial subliminal tapes: one for memory improvement, the other to increase self-esteem. Each person who came for memory improvement is given a tape labeled "memory improvement" and told to use it once a day for a month. What they don't know is that half of them have actually been given the self-esteem improvement tape. Similarly, the self-esteem seekers are each given a tape labeled "self-esteem improvement," but half of them have actually received the tape containing subliminal memory-improvement messages. This experimental design lets you control for participants' expectations. A month later you bring the people back and retest them on the memory and self-esteem measures. Theoretically, if change is being produced by the subliminal messages, people should improve only in the area addressed by the tape they actually heard. What do you expect to find?

Social psychologist Anthony Greenwald and coworkers (1991) conducted an experiment exactly like this. They found that people generally improved in both self-esteem and memory, regardless of which tape they heard. More significantly, self-esteem improvement was actually greater for those who listened to the memory-improvement tape, and those who listened to the self-esteem tape improved more in memory than they did in self-esteem. Thus, the power of an expectancy, or a placebo effect, explains the results better than does the power of subliminal programming of the unconscious mind. And the bottom line is that while subliminal products may appeal to some people as a relatively effortless way to change, they remain unproven scientifically, especially in comparison with other behavior-change methods. Personally, we have much greater faith in the effectiveness of the techniques presented in this book's "Applying Psychological Science" features, because they're backed up by scientific evidence.

wine tasters and piano tuners make their living by being able to make very subtle discriminations between stimuli.

The **difference threshold** *is defined as the smallest difference between two stimuli that people can perceive 50 percent of the time. The difference threshold is sometimes called the just noticeable difference (jnd).* German physiologist Ernst Weber discovered in the 1830s that there is some degree of lawfulness in the range of sensitivities within our sensory systems. **Weber's law** *states that the difference threshold, or jnd, is directly proportional to the magnitude of the stimulus with which the comparison is being made* and can be expressed as a *Weber fraction*. For example, the jnd value for weights is a Weber fraction of approximately 1/50 (Teghtsoonian, 1971). This means that if you lift a weight of 50 grams, a comparison weight must be at least 51 grams in order for you to be able to judge it as heavier. If the weight were 500 grams, a second weight must be at least 510 grams (i.e., 1/50 = 10g/500 g) for you to discriminate between them.

▶ 4. What is the difference threshold? What is Weber's law and why is it important?

Although Weber's law breaks down at extremely high and low intensities of stimulation, it holds up reasonably well within the most frequently encountered range, thereby providing a useful barometer of our abilities to discern differences in the various sensory modalities. Table 4.2 lists Weber fractions for the various senses. The smaller the fraction, the greater the sensitivity to differences. As highly visual creatures, humans show greater sensitivity in their visual sense than they do in, for example, their sense of

TABLE 4.2 Weber Fractions for Various Sensory Modalities

Sensory Modality	Weber Fraction
Audition (tonal pitch)	1/333
Vision (brightness, white light)	1/60
Kinesthesis (lifted weights)	1/50
Pain (heat produced)	1/30
Audition (loudness)	1/20
Touch (pressure applied to skin)	1/7
Smell (India rubber)	1/4
Taste (salt concentration)	1/3

SOURCE: Based on Teghtsoonian, 1971.

smell. Undoubtedly many creatures who depend on their sense of smell to track their prey would show quite a different order of sensitivity. Weber fractions also show that humans are highly sensitive to differences in the pitch of sounds, but far less sensitive to loudness differences.

Sensory Adaptation

From a survival perspective, it's important to know when important new developments are occurring. If you were relaxing outdoors, you would want to be aware of the whine of a mosquito approaching you. Because changes in our environment are usually most noteworthy, sensory systems are finely attuned to *changes* in stimulation (Rensink, 2002). Sensory neurons are engineered to respond to a constant stimulus by decreasing their activity, and *the diminishing sensitivity to an unchanging stimulus is called* **sensory adaptation.**

Adaptation (sometimes called *habituation*) is a part of everyday experience. After a while, monotonous background sounds are largely unheard. The feel of your wristwatch against your skin recedes from awareness. When you dive into a swimming pool, the water may feel cold at first because your body's temperature sensors respond to the change in temperature. Over time, however, you become used to the water temperature.

Adaptation occurs in all sensory modalities, including vision. Indeed, were it not for tiny involuntary eye movements that keep images moving about the retina, stationary objects would simply fade from sight if we stared at them. In an ingenious demonstration of this type of adaptation, R. M. Pritchard (1961) attached a tiny projector to a contact lens worn by the participant (Figure 4.5a). This procedure guaranteed that visual images presented through the projector would maintain a constant position on the retina, even when the eye moved. When a stabilized image was projected through the lens onto the retina, participants reported that the image appeared in its entirety for a time, then began to vanish and reappear as parts of the original stimulus (Figure 4.5b).

Although sensory adaptation may reduce our overall sensitivity, it is adaptive, for it frees our senses from the constant and the mundane, allowing them to pick up informative changes in the environment that could be important to our well-being or survival.

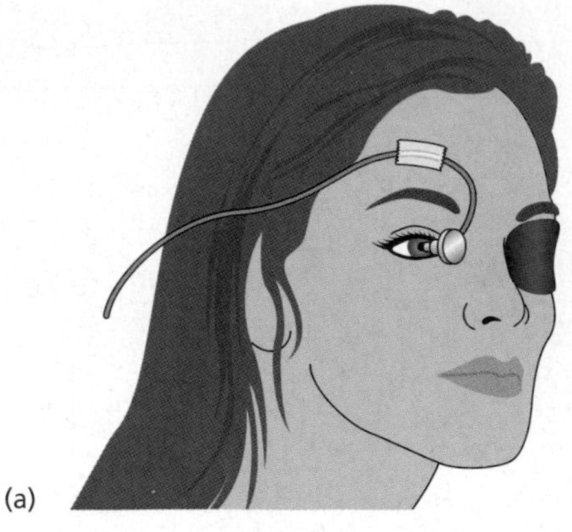

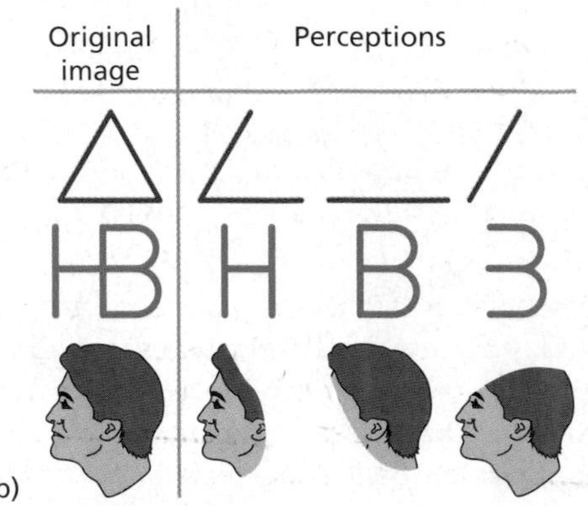

FIGURE 4.5

(a) To create a stabilized retinal image, a person wears a contact lens to which a tiny projector has been attached. Despite eye movements, images are cast on the same region of the retina. (b) Under these conditions, the stabilized image is clear at first, but then it begins to fade and reappear in meaningful segments as the receptors fatigue and recover.
SOURCE: Adapted from Pritchard, 1961.

IN REVIEW

- *Sensation refers to the activities by which our sense organs receive and transmit information, whereas perception involves the brain's processing and interpretation of the information.*
- *Psychophysics is the scientific study of how the physical properties of stimuli are related to sensory experiences. Sensory sensitivity is concerned in part with the limits of stimulus detectability (absolute threshold) and the ability to discriminate between stimuli (difference threshold). The absolute threshold is the intensity at which a stimulus is detected 50 percent of the time. Signal detection theory is concerned with factors that influence decisions about whether or not a stimulus is present.*
- *Research indicates that subliminal stimuli, which are not consciously perceived, can influence perceptions and behavior in subtle ways, but not strongly enough to justify concerns about the subconscious control of behavior through subliminal messages. The use of subliminal self-help materials sometimes results in positive behavior changes that may be a product of expectancy factors rather than the subliminal messages themselves.*
- *The difference threshold, or just noticeable difference (jnd), is the amount by which two stimuli must differ for them to be perceived as different 50 percent of the time. Studies of the jnd led to Weber's law, which states that the jnd is proportional to the intensity of the original stimulus and is constant within a given sense modality.*
- *Sensory systems are particularly responsive to changes in stimulation, and adaptation occurs in response to unchanging stimuli.*

THE SENSORY SYSTEMS

The particular stimuli to which different animals are sensitive vary considerably. The sensory equipment of any species is an adaptation to the environment in which it lives. Many species have senses that humans lack altogether.

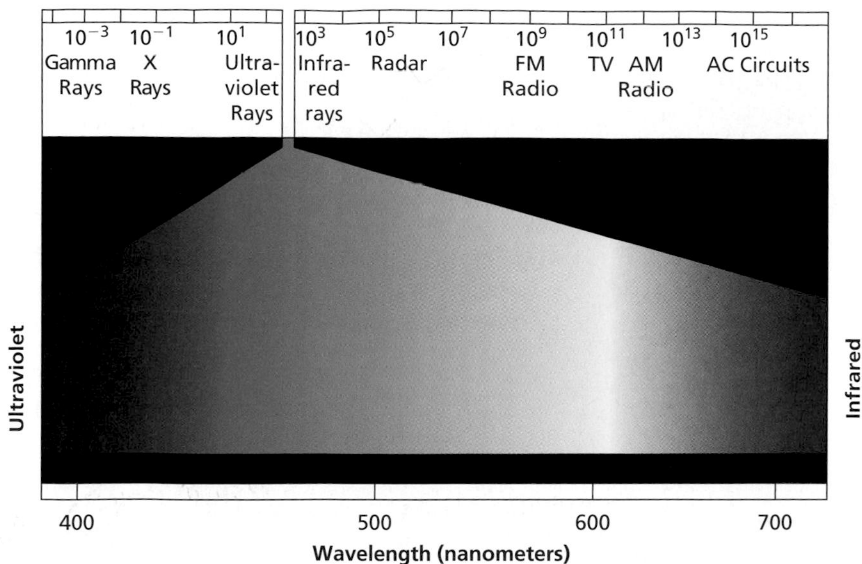

FIGURE 4.6

The full spectrum of electromagnetic radiation. Only the narrow band between 400 and 700 nanometers (nm) is visible to the human eye. One nanometer equals one 1,000,000,000th of a meter.

Carrier pigeons, for example, use the earth's magnetic field to find their destination on cloudy nights when they can't navigate by the stars. Sharks sense electric currents leaking through the skins of fish hiding in undersea crevices, and rattlesnakes find their prey by detecting infrared radiation given off by small rodents.

Whatever the source of stimulation, its energy must be converted into nerve impulses, the only language the nervous system understands. **Transduction** *is the process whereby the characteristics of a stimulus are converted into nerve impulses.* We now consider the range of stimuli to which humans and other mammals are attuned and the manner in which the various sense organs carry out the transduction process.

Vision

The normal stimulus for vision is electromagnetic energy, or light waves, which are measured in *nanometers (nm),* or one billionth of a meter. In addition to that tiny portion of light waves that humans can perceive, the electromagnetic spectrum encompasses X rays, television and radio signals, and infrared and ultraviolet rays (Figure 4.6). Bees are able to see ultraviolet light, and rattlesnakes can detect infrared energy. Our visual system is sensitive only to wavelengths extending from about 700 nm (red) down to about 400 nm (blue-violet). (You can remember the order of the spectrum, from higher wavelengths to lower ones, with the name ROY G. BIV—red, orange, yellow, green, blue, indigo, and violet.)

▶ 5. How does the lens affect visual acuity, and how does its dysfunction cause myopia and hyperopia?

The Human Eye

Light waves enter the eye through the *cornea,* a transparent protective structure at the front of the eye (Figure 4.7). Behind the cornea is the *pupil,* an adjustable opening that can dilate or constrict to control the amount of light that enters the eye. The pupil's size is controlled by muscles in the colored *iris* that surrounds the pupil. Low levels of illumination cause the pupil to dilate, letting more light into the eye to improve optical clarity; bright light makes the pupil constrict.

Behind the pupil is the **lens,** *an elastic structure that becomes thinner to focus on distant objects and thicker to focus on nearby objects.* Just as the lens of a camera focuses an image on a photosensitive material (film), so the lens of the eye focuses the visual image on the **retina,** *a multilayered light-sensitive tissue at the rear of the fluid-filled eyeball.* As seen in Figure 4.7, the lens reverses the

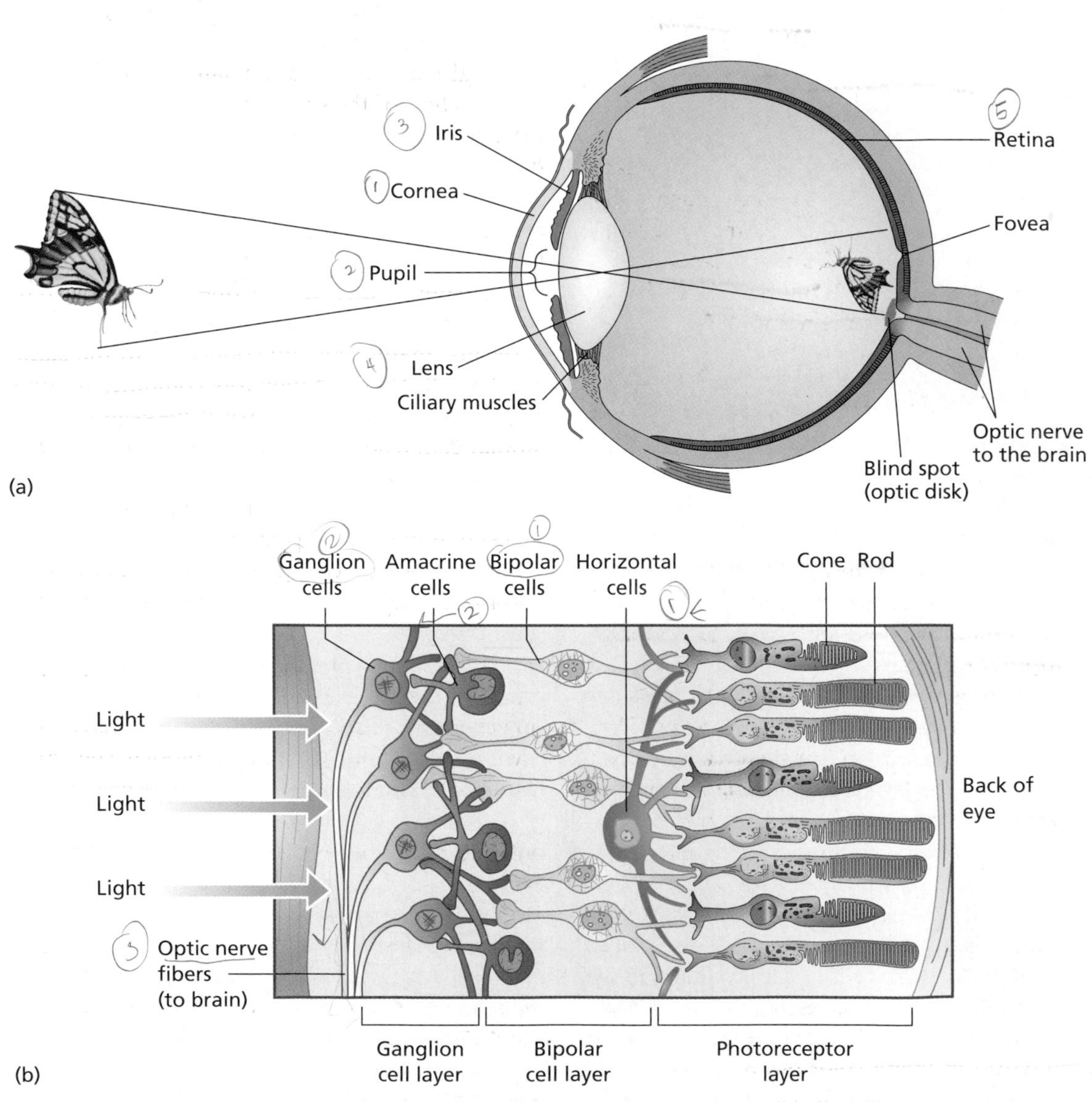

FIGURE 4.7

(a) This cross section shows the major parts of the human eye. The iris regulates the size of the pupil. The ciliary muscles regulate the shape of the lens. The image entering the eye is reversed by the lens and cast on the retina, which contains the photoreceptor cells. The optic disk, where the optic nerve exits the eye, has no receptors and produces a "blind spot" as demonstrated by Figure 4.8. (b) Photoreceptor connections in the retina. The rods and cones synapse with bipolar cells, which in turn synapse with ganglion cells, whose axons form the optic nerve. The horizontal and amacrine cells allow sideways integration of retinal activity across areas of the retina.

image from right to left and top to bottom when it is projected upon the retina, but the brain reverses the visual input into the image that we perceive.

The ability to see clearly depends on the lens's ability to focus the image directly onto the retina (Pedrotti & Pedrotti, 1997). If you have good vision for nearby objects but have difficulty seeing faraway objects, you probably suffer from *myopia* (nearsightedness). In nearsighted people, the lens focuses the visual image in front of the retina (or too near the lens), resulting in a blurred image for faraway objects. This condition generally occurs because the eyeball is longer (front to back) than normal. In contrast, some people have excellent distance vision but have difficulty seeing close-up objects clearly. *Hyperopia* (farsightedness) occurs when the lens does not thicken enough and the image is therefore focused on a point behind the retina (or too far from the lens). Eyeglasses and contact lenses are designed to correct for the natural lens's inability to focus the visual image directly onto the retina.

Photoreceptors: The Rods and Cones

The retina, a multilayered screen that lines the back surface of the eyeball and contains specialized sensory neurons, is actually an extension of the brain (Bullier, 2002). The retina contains two types of light-sensitive receptor cells, called *rods* and *cones* because of their shapes (Figure 4.7b). There are about 120 million rods and 6 million cones in the human eye.

The **rods**, *which function best in dim light, are primarily black-and-white brightness receptors.* They are about 500 times more sensitive to light than are the cones, but they do not give rise to color sensations. The retinas of some nocturnal creatures, such as owls, contain only rods, giving them exceptional vision in very dim light but no color vision (Dossenbach & Dossenbach, 1998). The **cones**, *which are color receptors, function best in bright illumination.* Some creatures that are active only during the day, such as pigeons and chipmunks, have only cones in their retinas, so they see the world in living color but have very poor night vision (Dossenbach & Dossenbach, 1998). Animals that are active during both day and night, as humans are, have a mixture of rods and cones. In humans, rods are found throughout the retina except in the **fovea**, *a small area in the center of the retina that contains only cones.* Cones decrease in concentration the farther away they are from the center of the retina, and the periphery of the retina contains mainly rods. Rods and cones send their messages to the brain via two additional layers of cells. The rods and cones have synaptic connections with *bipolar cells,* which, in turn, synapse with a layer of about 1 million *ganglion cells,* *whose axons are collected into a bundle to form the* **optic nerve.** Thus input from more than 126 million rods and cones is eventually funneled into only 1 million traffic lanes leading out of the retina toward higher visual centers. Figure 4.7b shows how the rods and cones are connected to the bipolar and ganglion cells. One interesting aspect of these connections is the fact that the rods and cones not only form the *rear layer of the retina,* but their light-sensitive ends actually point *away from* the direction of the entering light so that they receive only a fraction of the light energy that enters the eye.

The manner in which the rods and cones are connected to the bipolar cells accounts for both the greater importance of rods in dim light and our greater ability to see fine detail in bright illumination, when the cones are most active. Typically, many rods are connected to the same bipolar cell. They can therefore combine, or "funnel," their individual electrical messages to the bipolar cell, where the additive effect of the many signals may be enough to fire it. That is why we can more easily detect a faint stimulus, such as a dim star, if we look slightly to one side so that its image falls not on the fovea but on the peripheral portion of the retina, where the rods are packed most densely.

▶ 6. How are the rods and cones distributed in the retina, and how do they contribute to brightness perception, color vision, and visual acuity?

Like the rods, the cones that lie in the periphery of the retina share bipolar cells. In the fovea, however, the densely packed cones each have their own "private line" to a single bipolar cell. As a result, our **visual acuity**, *or ability to see fine detail,* is greatest when the visual image projects directly onto the fovea. Such focusing results in the firing of a large number of cones and their private-line bipolar cells. Some birds of prey, such as eagles and hawks, are blessed with not one, but two foveas in each eye, contributing to a visual acuity that allows them to see small prey on the ground as they soar thousands of feet above the earth (Tucker, 2000).

The optic nerve formed by the axons of the ganglion cells exits through the back of the eye not far from the fovea, producing a *blind spot* where there are no photoreceptors. You can demonstrate the existence of your blind spot by following the directions in Figure 4.8. Ordinarily, we are unaware of the blind spot because our perceptual system "fills in" the missing part of the visual field (Rolls & Deco, 2002).

FIGURE 4.8

Close your right eye and from a distance of about 12 inches, focus steadily on the X with your left eye as you slowly move the book toward your face. At some point the image of the dot will cross your optic disk (blind spot) and disappear. It will reappear after it crosses the blind spot. Note how the checkerboard remains wholly visible even though part of it falls on the blind spot. Your perceptual system "fills in" the missing information.

Visual Transduction: From Light to Nerve Impulses

▶ 7. What is transduction, and how does this process occur in the photoreceptors of the eye?

▶ 8. What is the physiological basis for dark adaptation and for the two components of the dark adaptation curve?

Rods and cones translate light waves into nerve impulses through the action of protein molecules called photopigments (Stryer, 1987; Wolken, 1995). *The absorption of light by the* **photopigments** *produces a chemical reaction that changes the rate of neurotransmitter release at the receptor's synapse with the bipolar cells.* The greater the change in transmitter release, the stronger the signal passed on to the bipolar cell and, in turn, to the ganglion cells whose axons form the optic nerve. If a stimulus triggers nerve responses at each of the three levels (rod or cone, bipolar cell, and ganglion cell), the message is instantaneously on its way to the visual relay station in the thalamus, and then on to the visual cortex of the brain.

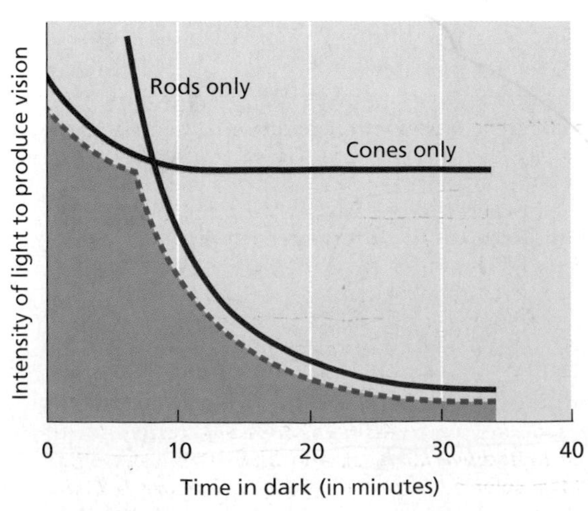

FIGURE 4.9

The course of dark adaptation is graphed over time. The curve has two parts, one for the cones and one for the rods. The cones adapt completely in about 10 minutes, whereas the rods continue to increase their sensitivity for another 20 minutes.

Brightness Vision and Dark Adaptation

As noted earlier, rods are far more sensitive than cones under conditions of low illumination. Nonetheless, the brightness sensitivity of both the rods and the cones depends in part on the wavelength of the light. Research has shown that rods have a much greater brightness sensitivity than cones throughout the color spectrum *except* at the red end, where rods are relatively insensitive. Cones are most sensitive to low illumination in the greenish yellow range of the spectrum. These findings have prompted many cities to change the color of their fire engines from the traditional red (to which rods are insensitive) to a yellowish green in order to increase the vehicles' visibility to both rods and cones in dim lighting.

Although the rods are by nature sensitive to low illumination, they are not always ready to fulfill their function. Perhaps you have had the embarrassing experience of entering a movie theater on a sunny day, groping around in the darkness, and finally sitting down in someone's lap. Although one can meet interesting people this way, most of us prefer to stand in the rear of the theater until our eyes adapt to the dimly lit interior.

Dark adaptation *is the progressive improvement in brightness sensitivity that occurs over time under conditions of low illumination.* After absorbing light, a photoreceptor is depleted of its pigment molecules for a period of time. If the eye has been exposed to conditions of high illumination, such as bright sunlight, a substantial amount of photopigment will be depleted. During dark adaptation, the photopigment molecules are regenerated and the receptor's sensitivity increases greatly.

Vision researchers have plotted the course of dark adaptation as people move from conditions of bright light into darkness (Carpenter & Robson, 1999). By focusing light flashes of varying wavelengths and brightness on the fovea, which contains only cones, or on the periphery of the retina, where rods reside, they discovered the two-part curve shown in Figure 4.9. The first part of the curve is due to dark adaptation of the cones. As you can see, the cones gradually become sensitive to fainter lights as time passes, but after about 5 to 10 minutes in the dark, their sensitivity has reached its maximum. The rods, whose photopigments regenerate more slowly, do not reach their maximum sensitivity for about half an hour. It is estimated that after complete adaptation, rods are able to detect light intensities 1/10,000 as great as those that could be detected before dark adaptation began (Stryer, 1987).

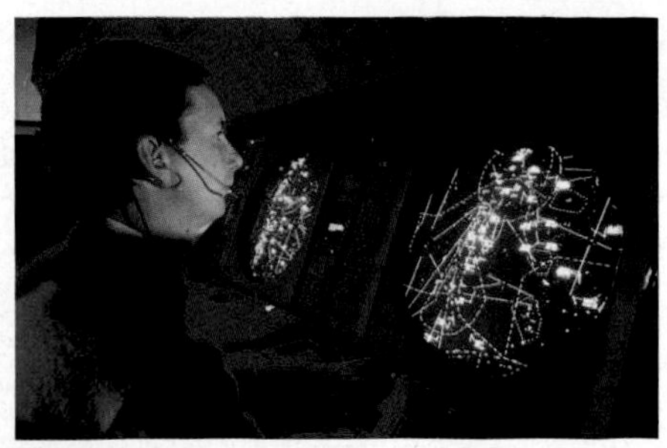

FIGURE 4.10

Working in red light keeps the rods in a state of dark adaptation. Because rods are quite insensitive to that wavelength, they retain high levels of photopigment and thus remain sensitive to low illumination.

During World War II, psychologists familiar with the process of dark adaptation provided a method for enhancing night vision in pilots who needed to take off on a moment's notice and see their targets under conditions of low illumination. Knowing that the rods are important in night vision and relatively insensitive to red wavelengths, they suggested that fighter pilots either wear goggles with red lenses or work in rooms lit only by red lights while waiting to be called for a mission. Because red light stimulates only the cones, the rods remain in a state of dark adaptation, ready for immediate service in the dark. That highly practical principle continues to be useful to this day (Figure 4.10).

Color Vision

▶ 9. Summarize the trichromatic, opponent-process, and dual-process theories of color vision. What evidence supports each theory?

We are blessed with a world rich in color. The majesty of a glowing sunset, the rich blues and greens of a tropical bay, the brilliant colors of fall foliage all produce visual delights. Human vision is finely attuned to color; our difference thresholds for light wavelengths are so small that we are able to distinguish an estimated 7.5 million hue variations (Backhaus et al., 1998). Historically, two different theories of color vision have tried to explain how this occurs.

The Trichromatic Theory Around 1800, it was discovered that any color in the visible spectrum can be produced by some combination of the wavelengths that correspond to the colors blue, green, and red in what is known as *additive color mixture* (Figure 4.11a). This fact was the basis of an important trichromatic (three-color) theory of color vision advanced by Thomas Young, an English physicist, and Hermann von Helmholtz, a German physiologist. According to the **Young-Helmholtz**

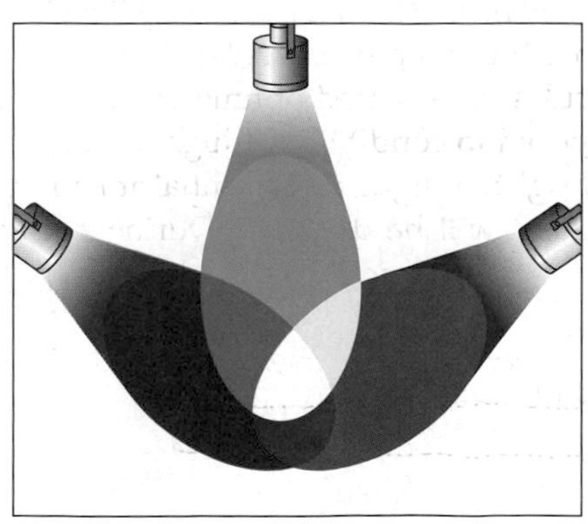

(a)

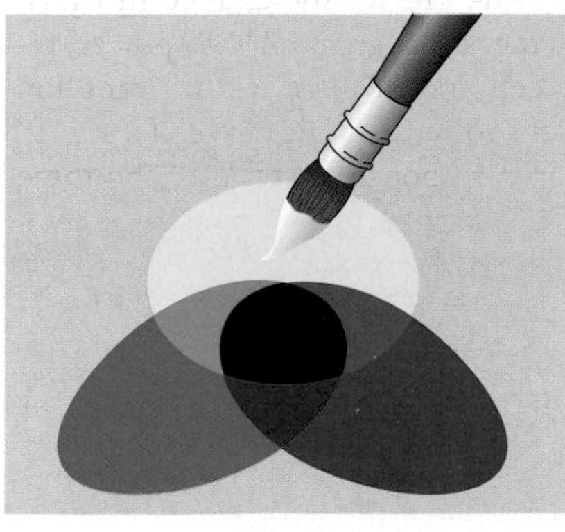

(b)

FIGURE 4.11

Additive color mixture and subtractive color mixture are different processes. (a) Additive color mixture. A beam of light of a specific wavelength directed onto a white surface is perceived as the color that corresponds to that wavelength on the visible spectrum. If beams of light that fall at certain points within the red, green, or blue color range are directed together onto the surface in the correct proportions, a combined, or additive, mixture of wavelengths will result and any color in the visible spectrum can be produced (including white at the point where all three colors intersect). The Young-Helmholtz trichromatic theory of color vision assumes that color perception results from the additive mixture of impulses from cones that are sensitive to red, blue, and green. (b) Subtractive color mixture. Mixing pigments or paints produces new colors by subtraction—that is, by removing (i.e., absorbing) other wavelengths. Paints absorb (subtract) colors different from themselves while reflecting their own color. For example, blue paint mainly absorbs wavelengths that correspond to non-blue hues. Mixing blue paint with yellow paint (which absorbs wavelengths other than yellow) will produce a subtractive mixture that emits wavelengths between yellow and blue (i.e., green). Theoretically, certain wavelengths of the three primary colors red, yellow (not green, as in additive mixture), and blue can produce the whole spectrum of colors by subtractive mixture. Thus in additive color mixture, the primary colors are red, blue and green; in subtractive color mixture, they are red, yellow, and blue.

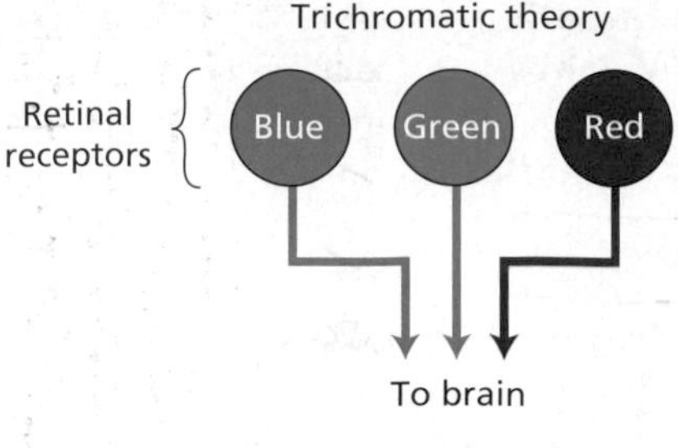

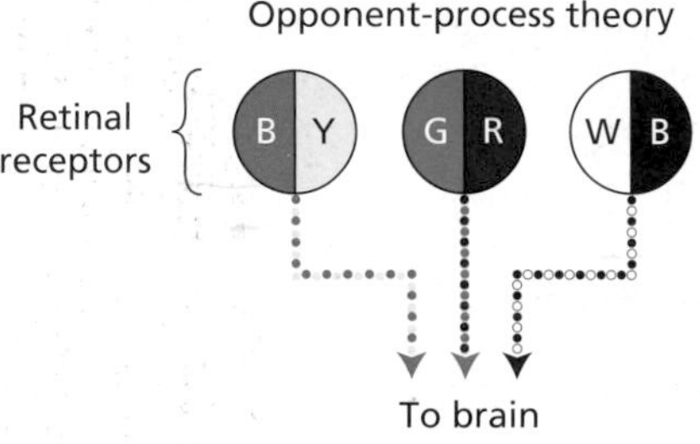

FIGURE 4.12

Two classic theories of color vision. The Young-Helmholtz trichromatic theory proposed three different receptors, one for blue, one for red, and one for green. The ratio of activity in the three types of cones in response to a stimulus yields our experience of color. Hering's opponent-process theory also assumed that there are three different receptors: one for red or green, one for blue or yellow, and one for black or white. Each of these receptors can function in two possible ways, depending on the wavelength of the stimulus. Again, the pattern of activity in the receptors yields our perception of the hue.

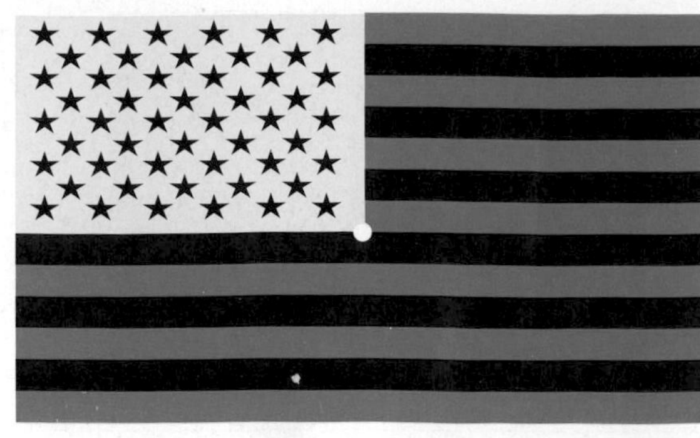

FIGURE 4.13

Negative-color afterimages demonstrate opponent processes occurring somewhere in the visual system. Stare steadily at the white dot in the center of the flag for about a minute, then shift your gaze to the gray dot in the blank space. The opponent colors should appear.

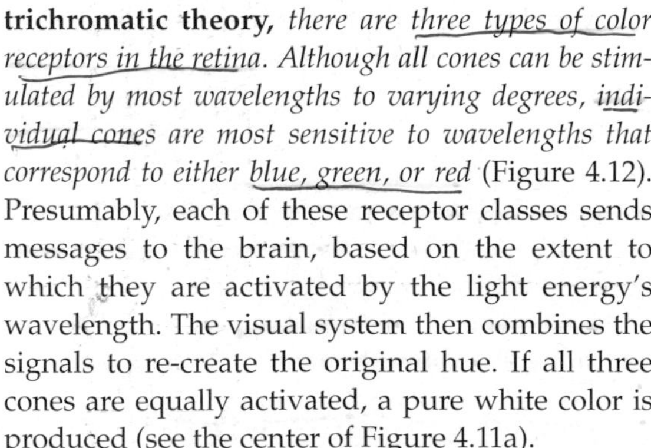

trichromatic theory, *there are three types of color receptors in the retina. Although all cones can be stimulated by most wavelengths to varying degrees, individual cones are most sensitive to wavelengths that correspond to either blue, green, or red* (Figure 4.12). Presumably, each of these receptor classes sends messages to the brain, based on the extent to which they are activated by the light energy's wavelength. The visual system then combines the signals to re-create the original hue. If all three cones are equally activated, a pure white color is produced (see the center of Figure 4.11a).

Although the Young-Helmholtz theory was consistent with the laws of additive color mixture, there are several facts that did not fit the theory. Take our perception of yellow, for example. According to the theory, yellow is produced by the activity of red and green receptors. Yet certain people with red-green color blindness, who are unable to perceive either color, are somehow able to experience yellow. A second phenomenon that posed problems for the trichromatic theory was the color *afterimage,* in which an image in a different color appears after a color stimulus has been viewed steadily and then withdrawn. To experience an afterimage, stare at the white dot in the top portion of Figure 4.13 for a full minute, then shift your gaze to the dot in the blank space. Trichromatic theory cannot account for what you'll see.

Opponent-Process Theory A second influential color theory, formulated by Ewald Hering in 1870, also assumed that there are three types of cones. **Hering's opponent-process theory** *proposed that each of the three cone types responds to two different wavelengths. One type responds to red or green, another to blue or yellow, and a third to black or white.* For example, a red-green cone responds with one chemical reaction to a green stimulus and with its other chemical reaction (opponent process) to a red stimulus (see Figure 4.12). You have experienced one of the phenomena that support the existence of opponent processes if you did the exercise in Figure 4.13. The color afterimage that you saw in the blank space contains the colors specified by opponent-process theory: The black portion of the flag appeared as white; the green as red; and the yellow as blue. According to opponent-process

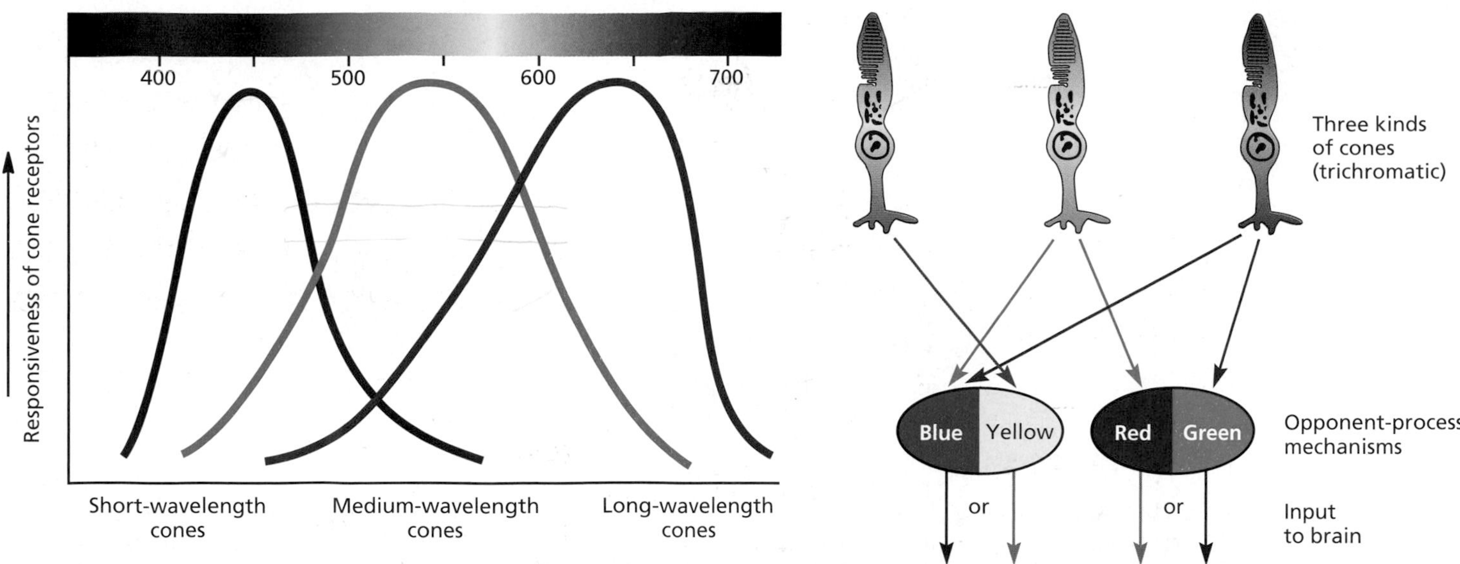

FIGURE 4.14

Color vision involves both trichromatic and opponent processes that occur at different places in the visual system. Consistent with trichromatic theory, three types of cones are maximally sensitive to short (blue), medium (green), and long (red) wavelengths, respectively. However, opponent processes occur further along in the visual system, as opponent cells in the retina, visual relay stations, and the visual cortex respond differentially to red versus green, blue versus yellow, and black versus white stimuli. Shown here are the inputs from the cones that produce the red-green and blue-yellow opponent processes.

theory, as you stared at the green, black, and yellow colors, the neural processes that register these colors became fatigued. Then when you cast your gaze on the white surface, which reflects all wavelengths, a "rebound" opponent reaction occurred as each receptor responded with its opposing red, white, or blue reactions.

Dual Processes in Color Transduction Which theory—the trichromatic theory or the opponent-process theory—is correct? Two centuries of research have yielded verifying evidence for each theory. Today's **dual-process theory** *combines the trichromatic and opponent-process theories to account for the color transduction process* (Knoblauch, 2002).

The trichromatic theorists Young and Helmholtz were right about the cones. The cones do indeed contain one of three different protein photopigments that are most sensitive to wavelengths roughly corresponding to the colors blue, red, and green (Abramov & Gordon, 1994). Different ratios of activity in the blue-, red-, and green-sensitive cones can produce a pattern of neural activity that corresponds to any hue in the spectrum (Backhaus et al., 1998). This process is similar to that which occurs on your TV screen, where color pictures (including white hues) are produced by activating combinations of tiny blue, red, and green dots in a process of additive color mixture.

Hering's opponent-process theory was also partly correct, but opponent processes do not occur at the level of the cones, as he maintained. When researchers began to use microelectrodes to record from single cells in the visual system, they discovered that ganglion cells in the retina, as well as neurons in visual relay stations and the visual cortex, respond in an opponent-process fashion by altering their rate of firing (Knoblauch, 2002). For example, if a red light is shone on the retina, an opponent-process ganglion cell may respond with a high rate of firing, but a green light will cause the same cell to fire at a very low rate. Other neurons respond in a similar opponent fashion to blue and yellow stimuli.

The red-green opponent processes are triggered directly by input from the red- or green-sensitive cones in the retina (Figure 4.14). The blue-yellow opponent process is a bit more complex. Activity of blue-sensitive cones directly stimulates the blue process further along in the visual system. And yellow? The yellow opponent process is triggered not by a yellow-sensitive cone, as Hering proposed, but rather by simultaneous input from the red- and green-sensitive cones (Abramov & Gordon, 1994).

Color-Deficient Vision People with normal color vision are referred to as *trichromats*. They are

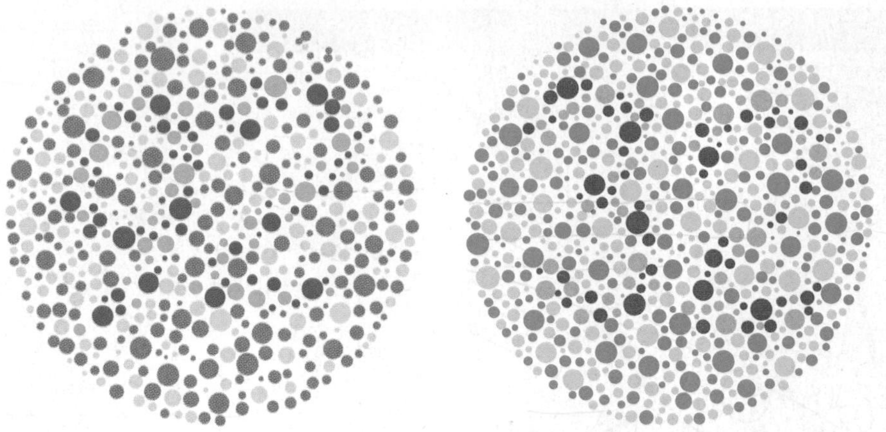

FIGURE 4.15

These dotted figures are used to test for color-deficient vision. The left one tests for blue-yellow color blindness, the right one for red-green color blindness. Because the dots in the picture are of equal brightness, color is the only available cue for perceiving the numbers in the chips.

sensitive to all three systems: red-green, blue-yellow, and black-white. However, about 7 percent of the male population and 1 percent of the female population have a deficiency in the red-green system, the blue-yellow system, or both. This deficiency is caused by an absence of hue-sensitive photopigment in certain cone types. A *dichromat* is a person who is color-blind in only one of the systems (red-green or blue-yellow). A *monochromat* is sensitive only to the black-white system and is totally color-blind. Most color-deficient people are dichromats and have their deficiency in the red-green system. Color blindness tests typically employ sets of colored dots such as those in Figure 4.15. Depending on the type of deficit, a color-blind person cannot discern the number embedded in one or the other circles.

Analysis and Reconstruction of Visual Scenes

Once the transformation of light energy to nerve impulses occurs, the process of combining the messages received from the photoreceptors into the perception of a visual scene begins. As you read this page, nerve impulses from countless neurons are being analyzed and the visual image that you perceive is being reconstructed. Moreover, you know what these black squiggles on the page mean. How does this occur?

▶ 10. What kinds of feature detectors exist in the visual system? What is parallel processing of sensory information?

Feature Detectors From the retina, the optic nerve sends nerve impulses to a visual relay station in the thalamus, the brain's sensory switchboard. From there, the input is routed to various parts of the cortex, particularly the *primary visual cortex* in the occipital lobe at the rear of the brain. Microelectrode studies have shown that there is a point-to-point correspondence between tiny regions of the retina and groups of neurons in the visual cortex. As you might expect, the fovea, where the one-to-one synapses of cones with bipolar cells produce high visual acuity, is represented by a disproportionately large area of the visual cortex. Somewhat more surprising is the fact that there is more than one cortical "map" of the retina; there are at least 10 duplicate mappings. Perhaps this is nature's insurance policy against damage to any one of them, or perhaps the duplicate maps are somehow involved in the integration of visual input (Bullier, 2002).

Groups of neurons within the primary visual cortex are organized to receive and integrate sensory nerve impulses originating in specific regions of the retina. Some of these cells, known as **feature detectors**, *fire selectively in response to visual stimuli that have specific characteristics* (Kanwisher, 1998). Discovery of these feature detectors won David Hubel and Torsten Wiesel of Harvard University the 1981 Nobel Prize. Using tiny electrodes to record the activity of individual cells of the visual cortex of animals (Figure 4.16), Hubel and Wiesel found that certain neurons fired most frequently when lines of certain orientations were presented. One neuron might fire most frequently when a horizontal line was presented; another neuron would fire most frequently to a line of a slightly different orientation; and so on "around the clock." For example, a letter *A* could be constructed from the response of feature detectors that responded to three different line orientations: /, \, and –.

The discovery of feature detectors revolutionized vision research. Since then, scientists have found cells that respond most strongly to bars, slits, and edges in certain positions. Within the

FIGURE 4.16

A partially anesthetized monkey views an image projected on the screen while an electrode embedded in its visual cortex records the activity of a single neuron. This research by Hubel and Wiesel led to the discovery of feature detectors, which analyze visual stimulus features such as contours and shapes, movement, and color.

cortex, this information is integrated and analyzed by successively more complex feature-detector systems to produce our perception of objects (Palmer, 2002). This process is illustrated by the illusion shown in Figure 4.17.

Other classes of feature detectors respond to color, to depth, or to movement (Livingstone & Hubel, 1994). These feature-detector "modules" subdivide a visual scene into its component dimensions and process them simultaneously. Thus, as a red, white, and green beach ball sails toward you, separate but overlapping modules within the brain are simultaneously analyzing its colors, shape, distance, and movement by engaging in *parallel processing* of the information and constructing a unified image of its properties (Tarr & Vuong, 2002).

Visual Association Processes The final stages in the process of constructing a visual representation occur when the information analyzed and recombined by the primary visual cortex is routed to other cortical regions known as *visual association cortex*. Here successively more complex features of the visual scene are combined and interpreted in light of our memories and knowledge. If all goes correctly, a process that began with nerve impulses from the rods and cones now ends with us recognizing the beach ball for what it is and catching it. Quite another conscious experience and response would probably occur if we interpreted the oncoming object as a water balloon.

For more on vision, see Animated Segment 4.1.

IN REVIEW

- *The senses may be classified in terms of the energy to which they respond. Through the process of transduction, these energy forms are transformed into the common language of nerve impulses.*
- *The normal stimulus for vision is electromagnetic energy, or light waves. Light-sensitive visual receptor cells are located in the retina. The rods are brightness receptors, and the less numerous cones are color receptors. Light energy striking the retina is converted into nerve impulses by chemical reactions in the photopigments of the rods and cones. Dark adaptation involves the gradual regeneration of photopigments that have been depleted by brighter illumination.*
- *Color vision is a two-stage process having both trichromatic and opponent-process components. The first stage involves the reactions of cones that are maximally sensitive to red, green, and blue wavelengths. In the second stage, color information from the cones is coded through an opponent-process mechanism further along in the visual system.*

- *Visual stimuli are analyzed by feature detectors in the primary visual cortex, and the stimulus elements are reconstructed and interpreted in light of input from the visual association cortex.*

FIGURE 4.17

Is the white triangle "real"? It appears to be because feature detectors that analyze the contours of the pie-shaped circles analyze the corners and the brain fills in the "missing" lines. The contours are illusory, but they appear real. See what happens to the triangle if you cover up one or two of the circles.

Audition

▶ 11. Describe the two physical characteristics of sound waves and their relation to auditory experience.

▶ 12. Describe how the middle and inner ear structures are involved in the auditory transduction process.

The stimuli for our sense of hearing are sound waves, a form of mechanical energy. What we call sound is actually pressure waves in air, water, or some other conducting medium. When a stereo's volume is high enough, you can actually see cloth speaker covers moving in and out. The resulting vibrations cause successive waves of compression and expansion among the air molecules surrounding the source of the sound. These sound waves have two characteristics: frequency and amplitude (Figure 4.18).

Frequency *is the number of sound waves, or cycles, per second*. The **hertz (Hz)** *is the technical measure of cycles per second; 1 Hz equals 1 cycle per second*. The sound waves' frequency is related to the pitch that we perceive; the higher the frequency (Hz), the higher the perceived pitch. Humans are capable of detecting sound frequencies from 20 Hz up to 20,000 Hz (about 12,000 Hz in older people). Most common sounds are in the lower frequencies. Among musical instruments, the piano can play the widest range of frequencies, from 27.5 Hz at the low end of the keyboard to 4,186 Hz at the high end. An operatic soprano's voice, in comparison, has a range of only about 250 Hz to 1,100 Hz (Aiello, 1994).

Amplitude *refers to the vertical size of the sound waves—that is, the amount of compression and expansion of the molecules in the conducting medium*. The sound wave's amplitude is the primary determinant of the sound's perceived loudness. Differences in amplitude are expressed as **decibels (dB)**, *a measure of the physical pressures that occur at the eardrum*. The absolute threshold for hearing is arbitrarily designated as 0 dB, and each increase of 10 dB represents a tenfold increase in loudness. Table 4.3 shows various sounds scaled in decibels.

Auditory Transduction: From Pressure Waves to Nerve Impulses

The transduction system of the ear is made up of tiny bones, membranes, and liquid-filled tubes designed to translate pressure waves into nerve impulses (Figure 4.19). Sound waves travel into an auditory canal leading to the *eardrum*, a movable membrane that vibrates in response to the sound waves. Beyond the eardrum is the *middle ear*, a cavity housing three tiny bones (the smallest in the body, in fact). The vibrating activity of these bones—the *hammer (malleus), anvil (incus),* and *stirrup (stapes)*—amplifies the sound waves more than 30 times. The first bone, the hammer, is attached firmly to the eardrum, and the stirrup is attached to another membrane, the *oval window*, which forms the boundary between the middle ear and the *inner ear*.

The inner ear contains the **cochlea,** *a coiled, snail-shaped tube about 3.5 centimeters (1.4 inches) in length that is filled with fluid* and contains the **basilar membrane,** *a sheet of tissue that runs its length*. Resting on the basilar membrane is the **organ of Corti,** *which contains thousands of tiny hair cells that are the actual sound receptors*. The tips of the hair cells are attached to another membrane, the *tectorial membrane*, that overhangs the

FIGURE 4.18

Sound waves are a form of mechanical energy. As the tuning fork vibrates, it produces successive waves of compression and expansion of air molecules. The number of compressions (cycles) per second is the sound's frequency, measured in hertz (Hz). The height of the wave above zero air pressure is the sound's amplitude. Frequency determines pitch; amplitude determines loudness, measured in decibels (dB).

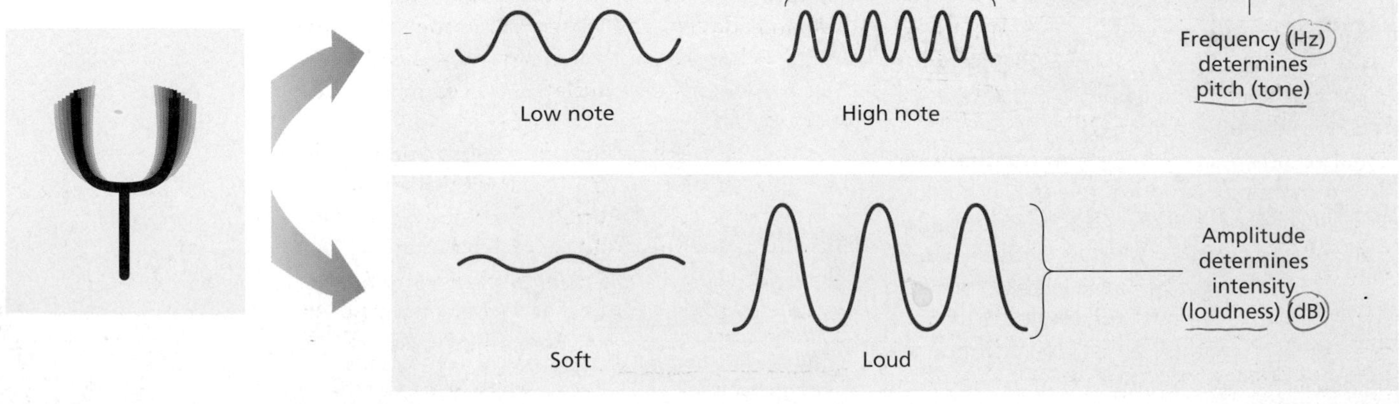

basilar membrane along the entire length of the cochlea. The hair cells synapse with the neurons of the *auditory nerve,* which in turn sends impulses via an auditory relay station in the thalamus to the temporal lobe's auditory cortex.

When sound waves strike the eardrum, pressure created at the oval window by the hammer, anvil, and stirrup of the middle ear sets the fluid inside the cochlea into motion. The fluid waves that result vibrate the basilar membrane and the tectorial membrane, causing a bending of the hair cells in the organ of Corti (Figure 4.19b). This bending of the hair cells triggers a release of neurotransmitter substance into the synaptic space between the hair cells and the neurons of the auditory nerve, resulting in nerve impulses that are sent to the brain. Within the auditory cortex are feature-detector neurons that respond to specific kinds of auditory input, much as occurs in the visual system (Goldstein, 2002).

TABLE 4.3 Decibel Scaling of Common Sounds

Level in Decibels (dB)	Common Sounds	Threshold Levels
140	50 hp siren at a distance of 100 feet; Jet fighter taking off at 80 feet from plane	Potential damage to auditory system
130	Boiler shop	
120	Air hammer at position of operator; Rock and roll band; Jet aircraft at 500 feet overhead	Human pain threshold
110	Trumpet automobile horn at 3 feet	
100	Crosscut saw at position of operator	
90	Inside subway car	Hearing damage with prolonged exposure
80	Train whistle at 500 feet	
70	Inside automobile in city	
60	Downtown city street (Chicago); Average traffic	
50	Restaurant; Business office	
40	Classroom; Church	
30	Hospital room Quiet bedroom	
20	Recording studio	Threshold of hearing (young men)
10		
0		Minimum threshold of hearing

NOTE: The decibel scale relates a physical quantity—sound intensity—to the human perception of that quantity—sound loudness. It is a logarithmic scale—that is, each increment of 10 dB represents a tenfold increase in loudness. The table indicates the decibel ranges of some common sounds as well as thresholds for hearing, hearing damage, and pain. Prolonged exposure at 150 dB causes death in laboratory rats.

Coding of Pitch and Loudness

The auditory system transforms the sensory qualities of loudness and pitch into the language of nerve impulses. In the case of loudness, high-amplitude sound waves cause the hair cells to bend more and release more neurotransmitter substance at the point where they synapse with auditory nerve cells, resulting in a higher rate of firing within the auditory nerve. Also, certain receptor neurons have higher thresholds than others, so that they will fire only when the hair cells bend considerably in response to an intense sound. Thus loudness is coded in terms of both the rate of firing in the axons of the auditory nerve and which specific hair cells are sending messages (Carney, 2002).

The coding of pitch also involves two different processes, one for frequencies below about 1,000 Hz (two octaves below the top of the piano keyboard) and another for higher frequencies. Historically, as in the case of color vision, two competing theories were advanced to account for pitch perception. According to the **frequency theory of pitch perception,** *nerve impulses sent to the brain match the frequency of the sound wave.* Thus a 30-Hz (cycles per second) sound wave from a piano should send 30 volleys of nerve impulses per second to the brain.

Unfortunately, frequency theory encounters a major problem. Because neurons are limited in their rate of firing, individual impulses or volleys of impulses fired by groups of neurons cannot produce high enough frequencies of firing to match sound wave frequencies above 1,000 Hz. How then do we perceive higher frequencies, such as a 4,000-Hz note from the same piano? Experiments conducted by Georg von Bekesy (1957) uncovered a second mechanism for coding pitch and earned him the 1961 Nobel Prize. Bekesy cut tiny holes in the cochleas of guinea pigs and human cadavers and observed through a microscope what happened inside the fluid-filled cochlea when he stimulated the eardrum with tones of varying frequencies. He found that high-frequency sounds produced an abrupt fluid wave that peaked close to the oval window, whereas lower-frequency vibrations produced a slower fluid wave that peaked farther down the cochlear canal (Figure 4.19c). Bekesy's observations supported a **place theory of pitch perception,** *suggesting that the specific point in the cochlea where the fluid wave peaks and most strongly bends the hair*

▶ 13. Describe the frequency and place theories of pitch perception. In what sense are both theories correct?

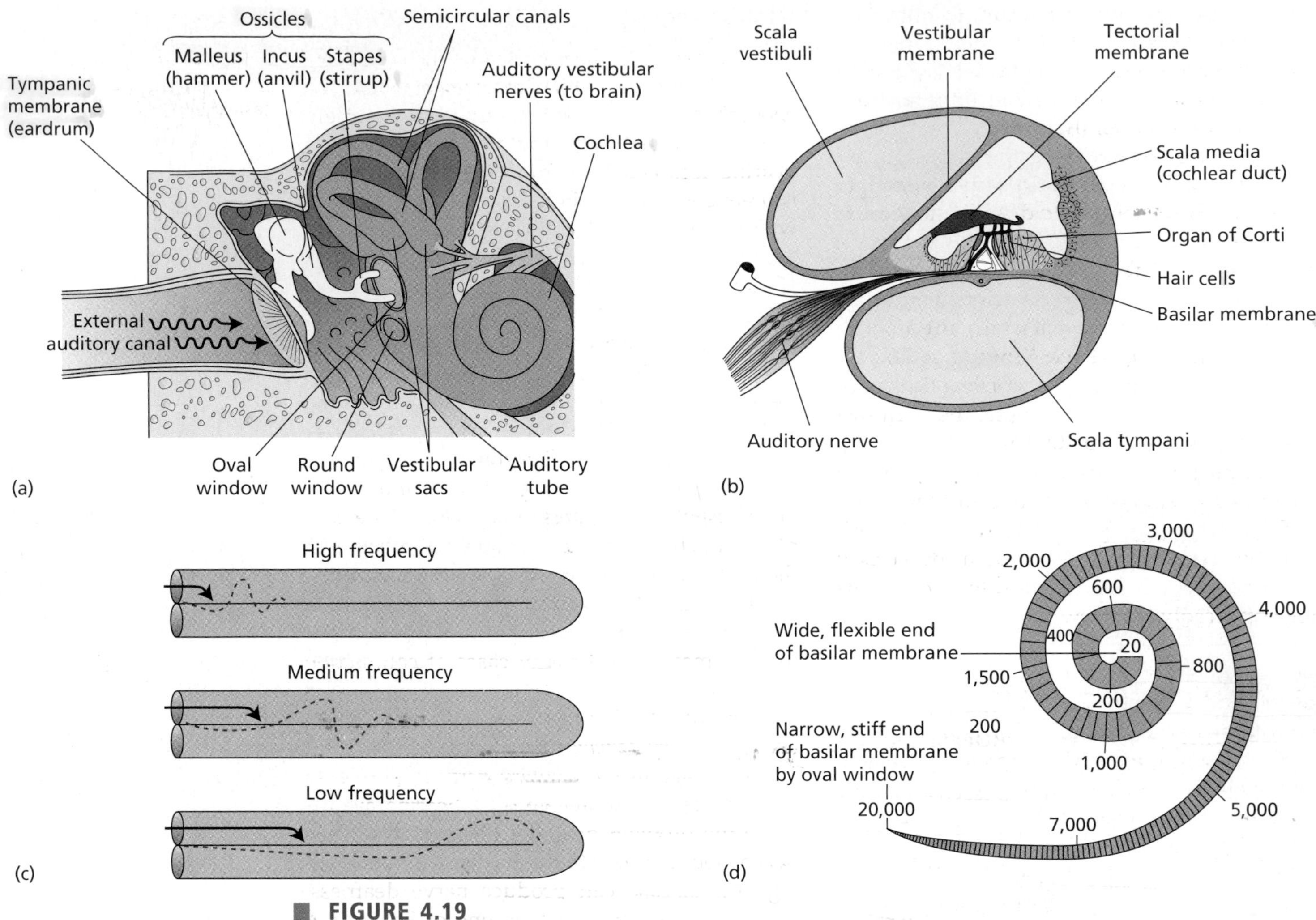

FIGURE 4.19

(a) A cross section of the ear shows the structures that transmit sound waves from the auditory canal to the cochlea. (b) In the cochlea, sound waves are translated into fluid waves that stimulate hair cells in the organ of Corti. The resulting nerve impulses reach the brain via the auditory nerve. The semicircular and vestibular sacs of the inner ear contain sense organs for equilibrium. (c) Fluid waves are created by different sound frequencies. (d) Varying frequencies maximally stimulate different areas of the basilar membrane. High-frequency waves peak quickly and stimulate the membrane close to the oval window.

cells serves as a frequency coding cue (Figure 4.19d). Researchers later found that, similar to the manner in which the retina is "mapped" onto the visual cortex, the auditory cortex has a tonal frequency "map" that corresponds to specific areas of the cochlea. By analyzing the specific location of the cochlea from which auditory nerve impulses are being received, the brain can code pitches like our 4,000-Hz piano note (Carney, 2002).

▶ 14. What sensory information is used by the brain in localizing sounds?

Thus, like trichromatic and opponent-process theories of color vision, which were once thought to contradict one another, frequency and place theories of pitch transduction both proved applicable in their own ways. At low frequencies, frequency theory holds true; at higher frequencies, place theory provides the mechanism for coding the pitch of a sound.

Sound Localization

Have you ever wondered why you have two ears, one located on each side of your head? As is usually the case in nature's designs, there is a good reason. Our very survival can depend on our ability to locate objects that emit sounds. The two ears play a crucial role in *sound localization*. The nervous system uses information concerning the time and intensity differences of sounds arriving at the two ears to locate the source of sounds in space (Luck & Vecera, 2002).

Sounds arrive first and loudest at the ear closest to the sound. When the source of the sound is directly in front of us, the sound wave reaches both ears at the same time and at the same intensity, so the source is perceived as being straight ahead. Our *binaural* (two-eared) ability to localize sounds is amazingly sensitive. For example, a sound 3 degrees to the right arrives at the right ear only 300 millionths of a second before it arrives at the left ear, and yet we can tell which direction the sound is coming from (Yin & Kuwada, 1984).

Other animals have even more exotic sound-localization systems. For example, the barn owl comes equipped with ears that are exquisitely tailored for pinpoint localization of its prey during night hunting. Its right ear is directed slightly upward, its left ear slightly downward. This allows it to localize sounds precisely in both the vertical and horizontal planes and thereby to zero in on its prey with deadly accuracy.

? What Do You Think?

NAVIGATING THE FOG: PROFESSOR MAYER'S TOPOPHONE

The device shown in Figure 4.20 is called a *topophone*. It was designed to help sailors locate sounds while navigating in thick fog. Based on what you've learned about the principles of sound localization, can you identify two features of this instrument that would assist sailors in detecting and locating sounds? Think about it, then see page 153.

FIGURE 4.20

The topophone, used in the late 1800s by sailors to increase their ability to locate sounds while navigating in thick fog, assisted in two ways. Can you identify the relevant principles?

Hearing Loss

▶ 15. What are the two kinds of deafness, and how can they be treated?

If you had to make the unwelcome choice of being blind or being deaf, which impairment would you choose? When asked this question, most of our students say that they would rather be deaf. Yet hearing loss can have more devastating social consequences than blindness does. Helen Keller, who was both blind and deaf, considered deafness to be more socially debilitating. She wrote, "Blindness cuts people off from things. Deafness cuts people off from people."

In the United States alone, more than 20 million people suffer from impaired hearing. Of these, 90 percent were born with normal hearing (Scheetz, 2002). They suffer from two major types of hearing loss. **Conduction deafness** *is caused by problems involving the mechanical system that transmits sound waves to the cochlea*. For example, a punctured eardrum or a loss of function in the tiny bones of the middle ear can reduce the ear's capacity to transmit vibrations. Use of a hearing aid, which amplifies the sounds entering the ear, may correct many cases of conduction deafness.

An entirely different matter is **nerve deafness,** *caused by damaged receptors within the inner ear or damage to the auditory nerve itself*. Nerve deafness cannot be helped by a hearing aid because the problem does not lie in the transmission of sound waves to the cochlea. Although aging and disease can produce nerve deafness, exposure to loud sounds is one of its leading causes. Repeated exposure to loud sounds of a particular frequency (as might be produced by a machine in a factory) can eventually cause the loss of hair cells at a particular point on the basilar membrane, thereby causing hearing loss for that frequency.

Extremely loud music can also take a serious toll on hearing (West & Evans, 1990). Figure 4.21 shows the devastating results of a guinea pig's exposure to a sound level approximating that of loud rock music heard through earphones. As Table 4.3 shows, even brief exposure to sounds exceeding 140 dB can cause irreversible damage to the receptors in the inner ear, as can more continuous sounds at lower decibel levels. In 1986, a rock concert by The Who reached 120 dB at a distance of 164 feet from the speakers. Although this earned The Who a place in the *Guinness Book of Records* for the all-time loudest concert, it inflicted severe and permanent damage to many in the audience. The Who's lead guitarist, Pete Townshend, eventually suffered severe hearing loss from prolonged noise exposure.

For more on hearing, see Animated Segment 4.2.

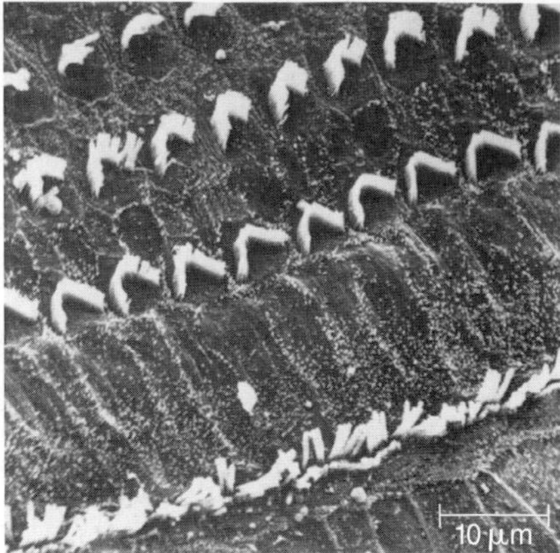

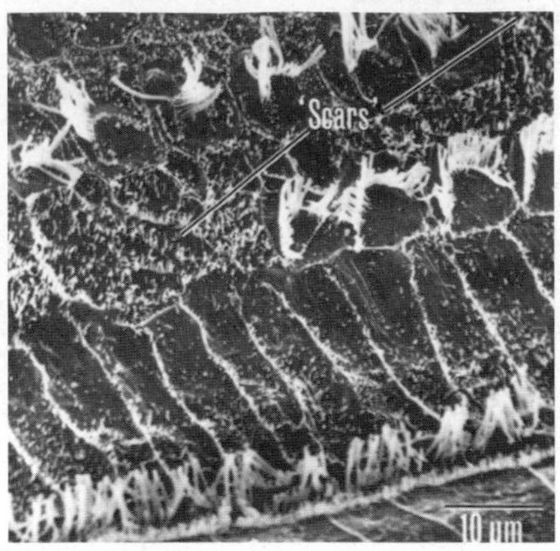

FIGURE 4.21

Exposure to loud sounds can destroy auditory receptors in the inner ear. These pictures, taken through an electron microscope, show the hair cells of a guinea pig before (left) and after (right) exposure to 24 hours of noise comparable to that of a loud rock concert. Micrographs by Robert E. Preston, courtesy of Professor J. E. Hawkins, Kresge Hearing Research Institute, University of Michigan.

▶ 16. Describe the stimuli and the receptors involved in gustation and olfaction.

Taste and Smell: The Chemical Senses

Gustation, *the sense of taste*, and **olfaction,** *the sense of smell*, are chemical senses; their receptors are sensitive to chemical molecules rather than to some form of energy. These senses are so intertwined that some scientists refer to a "common chemical sense" (B. Halpern, 2002). Enjoying a good meal usually depends on the simultaneous activity of taste and odor receptors, as becomes apparent when we have a stuffy nose and our food tastes bland. People who lose their sense of smell typically believe they have lost their sense of taste as well (Beauchamp & Bartoshuk, 1997).

FIGURE 4.22

The receptors for taste are specialized cells located in the tongue's taste buds. The tongue's 9,000 taste buds are grouped in different areas according to the taste sensation they produce. The center of the tongue is relatively insensitive to the chemical molecules that constitute gustatory stimuli.

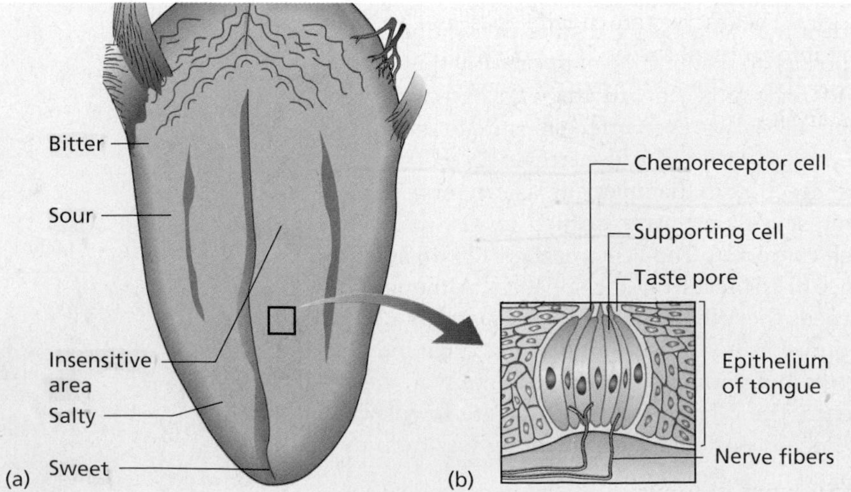

Gustation: The Sense of Taste

People who consider themselves gourmets are frequently surprised to learn that their sense of taste responds to only four qualities: sweet, sour, salty, and bitter. Every other taste experience combines these qualities and those of other senses, such as smell, temperature, and touch. For example, part of the "taste" of popcorn includes its complex texture, its crunchiness, and its odor. In addition to its chemical receptors, the tongue is richly endowed with tactile (touch) and temperature receptors.

Taste buds *are chemical receptors concentrated along the edges and back surface of the tongue.* Humans have about 9,000 taste buds, each one consisting of several receptor cells arranged like the segments of an orange (Figure 4.22). A small number of receptors are also found in the roof and back of the mouth, so that even people without a tongue can taste substances. Hairlike structures project from the top of each cell into the *taste pore,* an opening to the outside surface of the tongue. When a substance is taken into the mouth, it interacts with saliva to form a chemical solution that flows into the taste pore and stimulates the receptor cells. A "taste" results from complex patterns of neural activity produced by the four types of taste receptors (B. Halpern, 2002).

The sense of taste not only provides us with pleasure but also has adaptive significance in discriminating between nutrients and toxins (Scott, 1992). Our response to some taste qualities is innate. For example, newborn infants respond positively to sugar water placed on the tongue and negatively to bitter substances such as quinine (Davidson & Fox, 1988). Many poisonous substances in nature have bitter tastes, so this emotional response seems to be hard-wired into our physiology. In nature, sweet substances are more likely to occur in high-calorie (sugar-rich) foods. Unfortunately, many humans now live in an environment that is different from the food-scarce environment in which preferences for sweet substances evolved (Scott & Giza, 1993). As a result, people in affluent countries overconsume sweet foods that are good for us only in small quantities.

For more on taste, see Animated Segment 4.3.

Olfaction: The Sense of Smell

Humans are visually oriented creatures, but the sense of smell (olfaction) is of great importance for many species. Bloodhounds, for example, have poor eyesight but a highly developed olfactory sense that is about 2 million times more sensitive than ours (Thomas, 1974). A bloodhound can detect a person's scent in a footprint that is four days old, something no human could do. Yet people who are deprived of other senses often develop a highly sensitive olfactory sense. Helen Keller, though blind and deaf, exhibited a remarkable ability to smell her environment. With uncanny accuracy, she could tell when a storm was brewing by detecting subtle odor changes in the air. She could also identify people (even those who bathed regularly and did not wear perfumes or colognes) by their distinctive odors (Keller, 1955).

The receptors for smell are long cells that project through the lining of the upper part of the nasal cavity and into the mucous membrane. Humans have about 40 million olfactory receptors, dogs about 1 billion. Unfortunately, our ability to discriminate among different odors is not well understood. The most popular current theory is that olfactory receptors recognize diverse odors individually rather than by mixing the activity of a smaller number of basic receptors, as occurs in taste. Olfactory receptors have structures that resemble neurotransmitter binding sites on neurons. Any of the thousands of potential odor molecules can lock into sites that are tailored to fit them (Buck & Axel, 1991). The receptors that fire send their input to the **olfactory bulb,** *a forebrain structure immediately above the nasal cavity*. Each odorous chemical excites only a limited portion of the olfactory bulb, and odors are apparently coded in terms of the specific area of the olfactory bulb that is excited (Dalton, 2002).

The social and sexual behavior of animals is more strongly regulated by olfaction than is human behavior (Alcock, 2002). For example, many species use urine to mark their territories. We humans find other ways to mark our territories, such as erecting fences or spreading our belongings over the table we are using in the library. Nonetheless, like animals, we have special receptors in the nose that send impulses to a separate olfactory area in the brain that connects with brain structures involved in social and reproductive behavior. Some researchers believe that **pheromones,** *chemical signals found in natural body scents*, may affect human behavior in subtle ways (Beauchamp & Bartoshuk, 1997).

One interesting phenomenon known as **menstrual synchrony** *is the tendency of women who live together or are close friends to become more similar in their menstrual cycles*. Psychologist Martha McClintock (1971) tested 135 college women and found that during the course of an academic year, roommates moved from a mean of 8.5 days apart in their periods to 4.9 days apart. Another study of 51 women who worked together showed that close friends had menstrual onsets averaging 3.5 to 4.3 days apart, whereas those who were not close friends had onsets that averaged 8 to 9 days apart (Weller et al., 1999). Are pheromones responsible for synchrony? In experiments conducted at the Monell Chemical Senses Center in Philadelphia, 10 women with regular cycles were dabbed under the nose every few days with underarm secretions collected from other women. After 3 months, the participants' cycles began to coincide with the sweat donors' cycles. A control group of women who were dabbed with an alcohol solution rather than sweat showed no menstrual synchrony with a partner (Preti et al., 1986). In other studies, however, menstrual synchrony was not found for cohabitating lesbian couples or for Bedouin women who spent most of their time together, indicating that prolonged and very intensive contact may not be conducive to menstrual synchrony (Weller et al., 1999; Weller & Weller, 1997).

Do odors make us sexually attractive? The marketers of various "pheromone" perfumes tell us they do. And, if you have ever owned a dog or cat that went into heat, you can attest to the effects of such odors in animals. However, researchers have yet to find any solid evidence to back the claims of commercial products promising "instant sexual attraction." For humans, it appears that attributes such as a pleasant personality and good grooming are a better bet than artificially applied pheromones when it comes to finding a mate.

For more on olfaction, see Animated Segment 4.4.

The Skin and Body Senses

▶ 17. Describe the receptors and processing mechanisms for the skin and body senses.

The skin and body senses include the senses of touch, kinesthesis (muscle movement), and equilibrium. The last two are called *body senses* because they inform us of the body's position and movement. They tell us, for example, if we are running or standing still, lying down or sitting up.

The Tactile Senses

Touch is important to us in many ways. Sensitivity to extreme temperatures and to pain enables us to escape external danger and alerts us to disorders within our body. Tactile sensations are also a source of many of life's pleasures, including sexual orgasm. A lack of tactile contact with a caretaking adult retards physical, social, and emotional development (Harlow, 1958), whereas physically massaging newborn

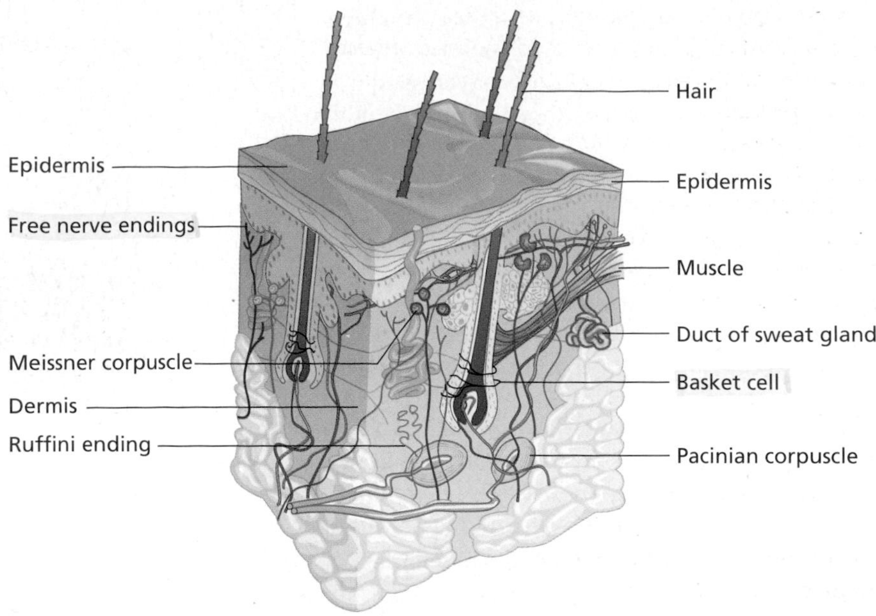

FIGURE 4.23

Various sensory receptors in the human skin and internal tissues allow us to sense touch and temperature. Basket cell receptors around hair follicles detect the bending of the hair in light touch, and the Meissner corpuscles detect light touch in hairless areas. Pacinian corpuscles and Ruffini endings provide deeper-touch sensations, and the free nerve endings respond to temperature and painful stimuli. SOURCE: Adapted from Smith, 1998.

babies enhances their development (Cigales et al., 1997; Field, 2000).

Humans are sensitive to at least four tactile sensations: pressure (touch), pain, warmth, and cold. These sensations are conveyed by receptors in the skin and in our internal organs. Mixtures of these four sensations form the basis for all other common skin sensations, such as itch.

Considering the importance of our skin senses, surprisingly little is known about how they work. The skin, a multilayered elastic structure that covers 2 square yards and weighs between 6 and 10 pounds, is the largest organ in our body. As shown in Figure 4.23, it contains a variety of receptor structures, but their role in specific sensations is less clear than for the other senses. Many sensations probably depend on specific patterns of activity in the various receptors (Goldstein, 2002). We do know that the primary receptors for pain and temperature are the *free nerve endings,* simple nerve cells beneath the skin's surface that resemble the bare branches of a tree in winter (Gracely et al., 2002). *Basket cell* fibers situated at the base of hair follicles are receptors for touch and light pressure (Heller & Schiff, 1991).

The brain can locate sensations because skin receptors send their messages to the point in the somatosensory cortex that corresponds to the area of the body where the receptor is located. As we saw in Chapter 3, the amount of cortex devoted to each area of the body is related to that part's sensitivity. Our fingers, lips, and tongue are well represented, accounting for their extreme sensitivity to stimulation.

Sometimes the brain "locates" sensations that cannot possibly be present. This occurs in the puzzling *phantom limb phenomenon,* in which amputees experience vivid sensations coming from the missing limb (Warga, 1987). Apparently an irritation of the nerves that used to originate in the limb fools the brain into interpreting the resulting nerve impulses as real sensations. Joel Katz and Ronald Melzack (1990) studied 68 amputees who insisted that they experienced pain from the amputated limb that was as vivid and real as any pain they had ever experienced. This pain was not merely a recollection of what pain used to feel like in the limb; it was actually experienced in the present. The phantom limb phenomenon can be quite maddening. Imagine having an intense itch that you never can scratch or an ache that you cannot rub. When amputees are fitted with prosthetic limbs and begin using them, phantom pain tends to disappear (Gracely et al., 2002).

For more on tactile information processing, see Video Segment 4.1.

FIGURE 4.24

World-renowned percussionist Evelyn Glennie became deaf many years ago. She now uses her tactile sense to detect distinct vibrations that correspond with individual tones. Though deaf, she is capable of perfect tonal discrimination.

The Body Senses

We would be totally unable to coordinate our body movements were it not for the sense of

kinesthesis, *which provides us with feedback about our muscles' and joints' positions and movements.* Kinesthetic receptors are nerve endings in the muscles, tendons, and joints. The information this sense gives us is the basis for making coordinated movements. Cooperating with kinesthesis is the **vestibular sense,** *the sense of body orientation or equilibrium* (Figure 4.25).

The vestibular receptors are located in the *vestibular apparatus* of the inner ear (see Figure 4.19). One part of the equilibrium system consists of three *semicircular canals,* which contain the receptors for head movement. Each canal lies in a different plane: left-right, backward-forward, or up-down. These canals are filled with fluid and lined with hairlike cells that function as receptors. When the head moves, the fluid in the appropriate canal shifts, stimulating the hair cells and sending messages to the brain. The semicircular canals respond only to acceleration and deceleration; when a constant speed is reached (no matter how high), the fluid and the hair cells return to their normal resting state. That's why airplane takeoffs and landings give a sense of movement, whereas cruising along at 500 miles per hour does not. Located at the base of the semicircular canals, the *vestibular sacs* also contain hair cells that respond to the position of the body and tell us whether we are upright or tilted at an angle. These structures form the second part of the body-sense system.

You have now learned a considerable amount about the principles underlying stimulus detection and transduction. As the following *Applying Psychological Science* section shows, these principles have not only informational value for understanding how our sensory systems operate, but also applied value in helping people with sensory impairments.

FIGURE 4.25

Kinesthesis and the vestibular sense are especially well developed in some people—and essential for performing feats like this one.

▶ 18. What sensory principles underlie sensory prosthetics for the blind and the hearing-impaired?

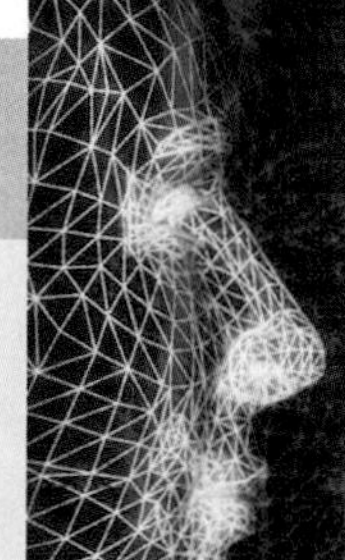

APPLYING PSYCHOLOGICAL SCIENCE

SENSORY PROSTHETICS: "EYES" FOR THE BLIND, "EARS" FOR THE HEARING IMPAIRED

Millions of people suffer from blindness and deafness, living in sightless or soundless worlds. A promising development that combines psychological research on the workings of the sensory systems with technical advances in bioengineering is the production of **sensory prosthetic devices** *that provide sensory input that can, to some extent, substitute for what cannot be supplied by the person's sensory receptors.* In considering these devices, we should remind ourselves that we don't see with the eyes, hear with the ears, or taste with the taste buds; we see, hear, and taste with our brain, and the nerve impulses sent from the retina or the organ of Corti or the taste buds are no different from those sent from anywhere else in the body. Sight or hearing is simply the brain's adaptation to the input it receives.

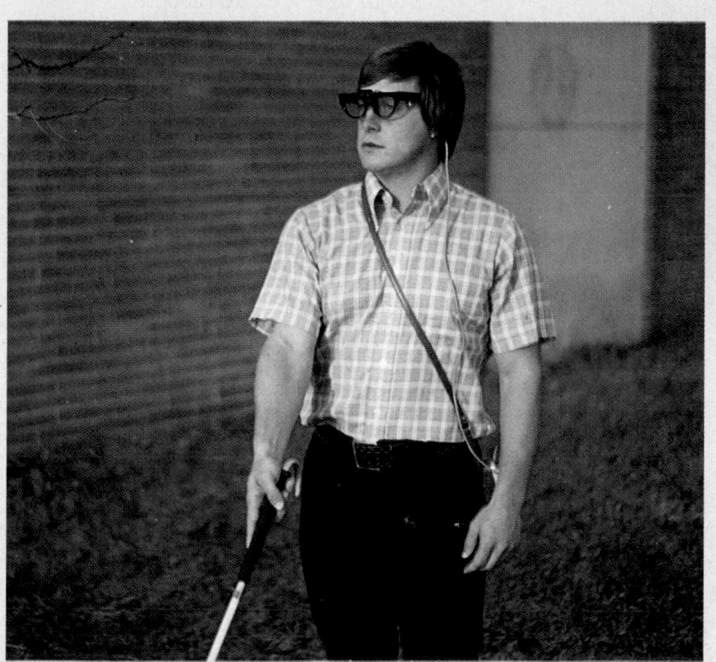

FIGURE 4.26

The Sonicguide allows a blind person to perceive the size, distance, movement, shape, and texture of objects through sound waves that represent the visual features of objects.

Seeing With the Ears

One device, known as a Sonicguide, provides new "eyes" through the ears, capitalizing on principles of auditory localization (Kay, 1982). The Sonicguide (Figure 4.26) works on the same principle as *echolocation*, the sensory tool used by bats to

Continued

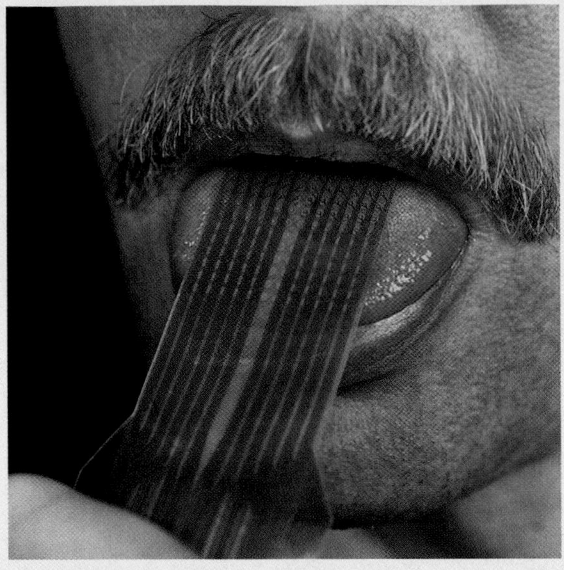

(a)

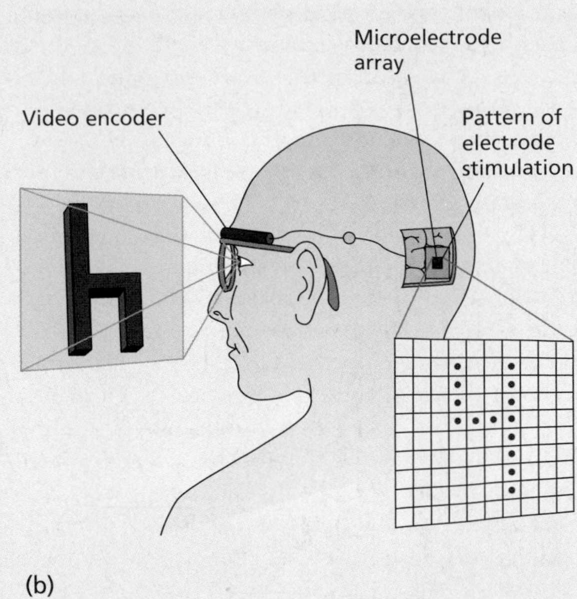

(b)

FIGURE 4.27

Two approaches to providing artificial vision for the blind. (a) Bach-y-Rita's device converts digitized stimuli from a camera to a matrix of electrical impulses to route spatial information through the tongue to the brain. (b) Tiny electrodes implanted into individual neurons in the visual cortex produce patterns of phosphenes that correspond to the visual scene observed through the video camera and encoder. Note how the cortical image is reversed as in normal visual input.

navigate in total darkness. The headset contains a transmitter that emits high-frequency sound waves beyond the range of human hearing. These waves bounce back from objects in the environment and are transformed by the Sonicguide into sounds that can be heard through earphones. Different sound qualities match specific features of external objects, and the wearer must learn to interpret the sonic messages. For example, the sound's pitch tells the person how far away the object is; a low pitch signals a nearby object and becomes higher as the distance to the object increases. The loudness of the sound tells how large the object is, and the clarity of the sound (ranging from a staticlike sound to a clear tone) signals the texture of the object, from very rough to very smooth. Finally, the sound localization principle described earlier tells the person where the object is located in the environment by means of differences in the time at which sounds arrive at the two ears.

In the first laboratory tests of the Sonicguide, psychologists Stuart Aitken and T. G. R. Bower (1982) used the apparatus with 6 blind babies who ranged in age from 5 to 16 months. Within hours or days, all of the babies using the Sonicguide could reach for objects, walk or crawl through doorways, and follow the movement of their hands and arms as they moved them about. Moreover, abilities such as reaching for objects, recognizing favorite toys, and reaching out to be picked up when mother (but not someone else) approached seemed to occur on the same developmental timetable as in sighted children. Aitken and Bower concluded that blind infants can extract the same information from sonic cues as sighted babies do from visual cues.

Older children and adults can learn to use the device, too, but not as easily as babies can. Older children trained with the device can easily find objects, such as water fountains and specific toys with which they want to play. They can thread their way through crowded school corridors and can even play hide-and-seek. The Sonicguide is now being used by visually impaired children in schools and other natural settings, as well as by adults (e.g., Hill et al., 1995).

The Seeing Tongue

Paul Bach-y-Rita, professor of rehabilitative medicine and biomedical engineering at the University of Wisconsin Medical School, has developed a tactile tongue-based, electrical input sensor as a substitute for visual input. The tongue seems an unlikely substitute for the eye, hidden as it is in the dark recess of the mouth. Yet in many ways it may be the second-best organ for providing detailed input, for it is densely packed with tactile receptors, thus allowing the transmission of high-resolution data. Moreover, its moist surface is a good conducting medium for electricity, meaning that minimum voltage is required to stimulate the receptors.

The researchers have built an experimental prototype of a device that eventually will be small enough to be invisibly attached directly to the teeth. The current stimulator, shown in Figure 4.27a, receives digital data from a camera and provides patterns of stimulation to the tongue through a 144-electrode array. The array can transmit shapes that correspond to the main features of the visual stimulus. Initial trials with blindfolded sighted and blind people show that with about 9 hours of training, users can "read" the letters of a Snellen eye chart with an acuity of 20/430, a modest but noteworthy beginning (Simpaio et al., 2001). With continued development, a miniature camera in an eyeglass will transmit wireless data to a more densely packed electrode array attached to a dental retainer. Bach-y-Rita believes the device also might have both military and civilian applications. For example, it could help soldiers locate objects in

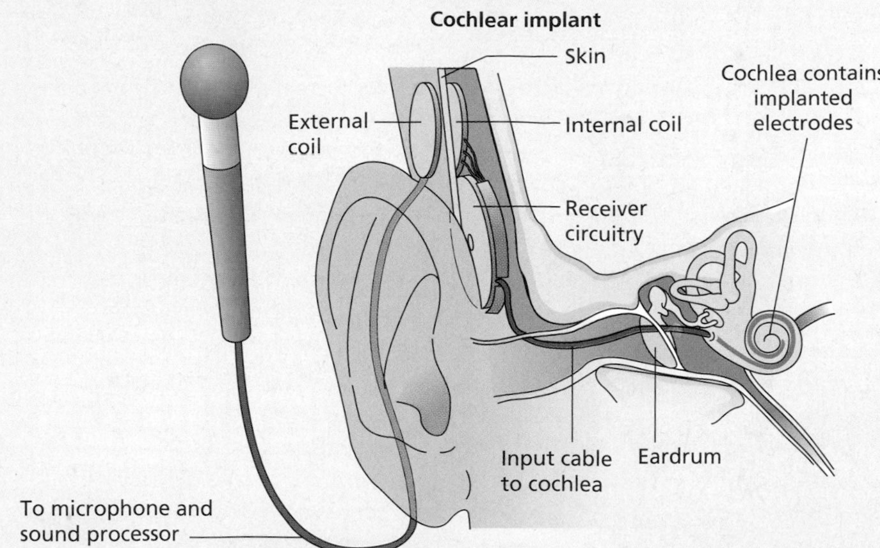

FIGURE 4.28

Cochlear implants provide direct stimulation of the auditory nerve in people whose hair cells are too damaged to respond to fluid waves in the cochlea. Sounds enter a microphone worn by the person and are sent to a processor that breaks the sound down into its principal frequencies and sends electrical signals to external and internal coils. The receiver circuitry stimulates electrodes implanted in cochlear areas associated with particular frequencies.

pitch-black environments, such as caves, where night-vision devices are useless; it could also aid firefighters as they search smoke-filled buildings for people to rescue.

Cortical Implants

A different approach to a visual prosthesis is being perfected at the University of Utah, where researchers have developed a device to stimulate the visual cortex directly (Normann et al., 1999). When cells in the visual cortex are stimulated electrically, discrete flashes of light called *phosphenes* are experienced by both sighted and blind people. Because sensory neurons in the visual cortex are arranged in a manner that corresponds to the organization of the retina, a specific pattern of stimulation applied to individual neurons in the cortex can form a phosphene pattern that conforms to the shapes of letters or objects. The detail or acuity of the pattern depends on the area of the visual cortex that is stimulated (the portion receiving input from the densely packed fovea produces greatest acuity) and on the number of stimulating electrodes in the array.

Building on this approach, researchers have developed the device shown in Figure 4.27b. The Utah Intracortical Electrode Array consists of a silicon strip containing thousands of tiny stimulating electrodes that penetrate directly into individual neurons in the visual cortex, where they can stimulate phosphene patterns. Eventually, a tiny television camera mounted in specially designed eyeglasses will provide visual information to a microcomputer that will analyze the scene and then send the appropriate patterns of electrical stimulation through the implanted electrodes to produce corresponding phosphene patterns in the visual cortex. The researchers have shown that sighted participants who wear darkened goggles that produce phosphenelike patterns of light flashes like those provided by cortical stimulation can quickly learn to navigate through complex environments and are able to read text at about two thirds their normal rate (Normann et al., 1996, 1999). Blind people who have had the stimulating electrodes implanted in their visual cortex have also been able to learn a kind of "cortical braille" for reading purposes. Although still experimental, a commercially available intracortical prosthetic device should be available in the near future.

Cochlear Implants

People with hearing impairments have also been assisted by the development of prosthetic devices. The *cochlear implant*, a device that can restore hearing in people suffering from nerve deafness, has helped many. Instead of amplifying sound like a conventional hearing aid (people with nerve deafness cannot be helped by mere sound amplification), the cochlear implant sorts out useful sounds and converts them into electrical impulses, bypassing the disabled hair cells in the cochlea and stimulating the auditory nerve directly (Figure 4.28). With a cochlear implant, patients can hear everyday sounds such as sirens, and many of them can understand speech (Meyer et al., 1998; Parkinson et al., 1998). But because sounds heard with currently developed implants tend to be muffled, patients who expect the device to restore normal hearing are invariably disappointed.

Sensory prosthetics illustrate the ways in which knowledge about sensory phenomena such as phosphenes, the organization of the visual cortex, sound localization, and the place theory of pitch perception can provide the information needed to take advantage of new technological advances. Yet, even with all our present ingenuity, prosthetic devices are not substitutes for our normal sensory systems, a fact that should increase our appreciation for what nature has given us.

IN REVIEW

- *Sound waves, the stimuli for audition, have two characteristics: frequency, measured in terms of cycles per second or hertz (Hz), and amplitude, measured in terms of decibels (dB). Frequency is related to pitch, amplitude to loudness. The receptors for hearing are hair cells in the organ of Corti of the inner ear.*
- *Loudness is coded in terms of the number and types of auditory nerve fibers that fire. Pitch is coded in two ways. Low-frequency tones are coded in terms of corresponding numbers of nerve impulses in individual receptors or by volleys of impulses from a number of receptors. Frequencies above 4,000 Hz are coded according to the region of the basilar membrane that is displaced most by the fluid wave in the cochlear canal.*
- *Hearing loss may result from conduction deafness, produced by problems involving the structures of the inner ear that transmit vibrations to the cochlea, or from nerve deafness, in which the receptors of the inner ear or the auditory nerve are damaged.*
- *The receptors for taste and smell respond to chemical molecules. Taste buds are responsive to four basic qualities: sweet, sour, salty, and bitter. The receptors for smell (olfaction) are long cells in the upper nasal cavity. Natural body odors produced by pheromones appear to account for a menstrual synchrony that sometimes occurs among women who are in frequent contact.*
- *The skin and body senses include touch, kinesthesis, and equilibrium. Receptors in the skin and body tissues are sensitive to touch, pain, warmth, and cold. Kinesthesis functions by means of nerve endings in the muscles, tendons, and joints. The sense organs for equilibrium are in the vestibular apparatus of the inner ear.*
- *Principles derived from the study of sensory processes have been applied in developing sensory prosthetics for the blind and the hearing impaired. Examples include the Sonicguide, a device that provides visual information through tactile stimulation of the tongue, direct electrical stimulation of the visual cortex, and cochlear implants.*

PERCEPTION: THE CREATION OF EXPERIENCE

▶ 19. Compare bottom-up and top-down processing of sensory information.

Sensory systems provide the raw materials from which experiences are formed. Our sense organs do not select what we will be aware of or how we will experience it; they merely transmit as much information as they can through our nervous system. Yet our experiences are not simply a one-to-one reflection of what is external to our senses. Different people may experience the same sensory information in radically different ways because perception is an active, creative process in which raw sensory data are organized and given meaning.

To create our perceptions, the brain carries out two different kinds of processing functions (Figure 4.29). In **bottom-up processing,** *the system takes in individual elements of the stimulus and then combines them into a unified perception*. Your visual system operates in a bottom-up fashion as you read. Its feature detectors analyze the elements in each letter of every word and then recombine them into your visual perception of the letters and words. In **top-down processing,** *sensory information is interpreted in light of existing knowledge, concepts, ideas, and expectations*. Top-down processing is occurring as you interpret the words and sentences constructed by the bottom-up process. Here you make use of higher-order knowledge, including what you have learned about the meaning of words and sentence construction. Indeed, a given sentence may convey a different personal

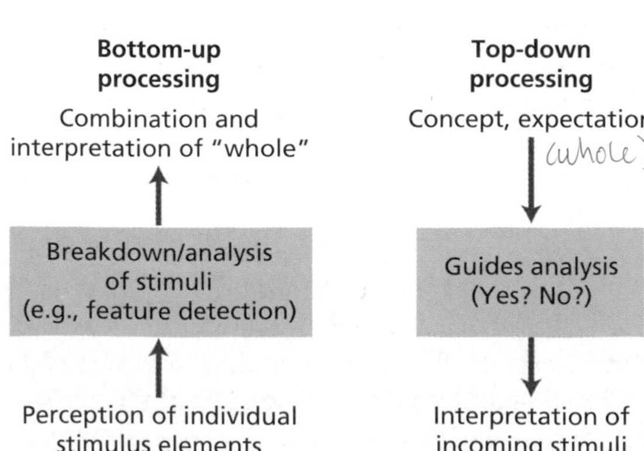

FIGURE 4.29

Bottom-up perceptual processing builds from an analysis of individual stimulus features to a unified perception. Top-down processing begins with a perceptual whole, such as an expectation or an image of an object, and then determines the degree of fit with the stimulus features.

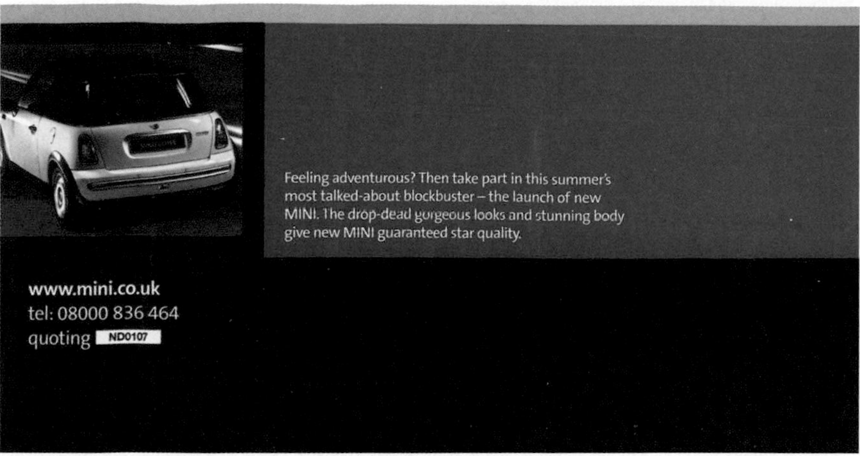

Feeling adventurous? Then take part in this summer's most talked-about blockbuster – the launch of new MINI. The drop-dead gorgeous looks and stunning body give new MINI guaranteed star quality.
www.mini.co.uk
tel: 08000 836 464
quoting ND0107

FIGURE 4.30

Marketing experts are adept at using attention-attracting stimulus characteristics in their advertisements. Personal characteristics are also important. What kinds of individuals do you suppose would be most attentive to these ads?

meaning to you than to another person if you relate its content to some unique personal experiences. Top-down processing accounts for many psychological influences on perception, such as the roles played by our motives, expectations, previous experiences, and cultural learning.

Perception Is Selective: The Role of Attention

As you read these words, 100 million sensory messages may be clamoring for your attention. Only a few of these messages register in awareness; the rest you perceive either dimly or not at all. But you can shift your attention to one of those unregistered stimuli at any time. (For example, how does the big toe of your right foot feel right now?) Attention, then, involves two processes of selection: (1) focusing on certain stimuli and (2) filtering out other incoming information (Luck & Vecera, 2002).

These processes have been studied experimentally through a technique called *shadowing*. Participants wear earphones and listen simultaneously to two messages, one sent through each earphone. They are asked to repeat (or "shadow") one of the messages word for word as they listen. Most participants can do this quite successfully, but only at the cost of not remembering what the other message was about. Shadowing experiments demonstrate that we cannot attend completely to more than one thing at a time. But we can shift our attention rapidly back and forth between the two messages, drawing on our general knowledge to fill in the gaps (Bonnel & Hafter, 1998; Sperling, 1984).

Environmental and Personal Factors in Attention

Attention is strongly affected by both the nature of the stimulus and by personal factors. Stimulus characteristics that attract our attention include intensity, novelty, movement, contrast, and repetition. Advertisers use these properties in their commercials and packaging (Figure 4.30). Internal factors, such as our motives and interests, act as powerful filters and influence which stimuli in our environment we will notice. For example, when we are hungry, we are especially sensitive to food-related cues. A botanist walking through a park is especially attentive to the plants; a landscape architect attends primarily to the layout of the park.

▶ 20. What two complementary processes occur in attention? What kinds of stimulus and personal factors influence attention?

People are especially attentive to stimuli that might represent a threat to their well-being, a tendency that would clearly have biological survival value (Izard, 1989; Oehman et al., 2001). A study by Christine and Ranald Hansen (1988) illustrates this tendency. They presented slides showing

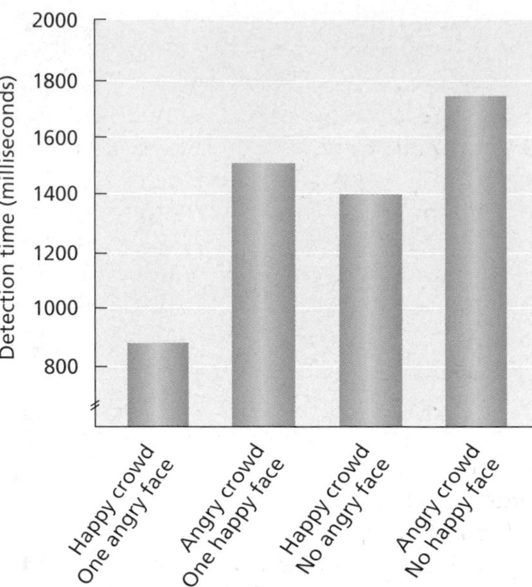

FIGURE 4.31

Perceptual vigilance to threatening stimuli is shown in the finding that people required less time to detect an angry face in a happy crowd than to detect a happy face in an angry crowd or to determine if there was any discrepant face in a happy or an angry crowd. SOURCE: Based on Hansen & Hansen, 1988.

groups of nine people. In half of the pictures, all of the people looked either angry or happy. In the other half, there was one discrepant face, either an angry face in a happy crowd or a happy face in an angry crowd. Participants were asked to judge as quickly as possible whether there was a discrepant face in the crowd, then press "yes" or "no" buttons attached to electrical timers. The dependent variable was the length of time required to make this judgment, measured in milliseconds (thousandths of a second).

The results, summarized in Figure 4.31, showed that participants were much faster at detecting a single angry face in an otherwise happy crowd than at finding a happy face in an angry crowd. It was as if the angry face, which the experimenters assumed to have threat value, "jumped out" of the crowd when the stimuli were scanned. Swedish psychologist Ulf Dimberg (1997) also believes that humans are biologically programmed to detect threatening faces, and he has shown via high-speed photography that emotional facial responses to such stimuli occur in observers within one third of a second. Attentional processes are thus based both on innate biological factors and on past experiences that make certain stimuli important or meaningful to us.

Advertisers are adept at using attention-attracting stimuli to call attention to their products. Sometimes, however, the process backfires, as in the following case.

> A famous model glides down a staircase, removing articles of clothing as she goes. Once inside the car being promoted in this British advertisement, she removes her panties and flings them out the window. The only problem with this wildly popular ad? An informal survey by a Welsh psychologist revealed that the visual image was so compelling that virtually no one remembered the brand of car being advertised. (Clay, 2002, p. 38)

Perceptions Have Organization and Structure

Have you ever stopped to wonder why we perceive the visual world as being composed of distinct objects? After all, the information sent by the retina reflects nothing but an array of varying intensities and frequencies of light energy. The light rays reflected from different parts of a single object have no more natural "belongingness" to one another than those coming from two different objects. Yet we perceive scenes as involving separate objects, such as trees, buildings, and people. These perceptions must be a product of an organization imposed by our nervous system (Tarr & Vuong, 2002). This top-down process of perceptual organization occurs so automatically that we take it for granted. But Dr. Richard, a prominent psychologist who suffered brain damage in an accident, no longer does.

> There was nothing wrong with his eyes, yet the input he received from them was not put together correctly. Dr. Richard reported that if he saw a person, he sometimes would perceive the separate parts of the person as not belonging together in a single body. But if all the parts moved in the same direction, Dr. Richard then saw them as one complete person. At other times, he would perceive people in crowds wearing the same color clothes as "going together" rather than as separate people. He also had difficulty putting sights and sounds together. Sometimes, the movement of the lips did not correspond to the sounds he heard, as if he were watching a badly dubbed foreign movie. Dr. Richard's experience of his environment was thus disjointed and fragmented. (Sacks, 1986, p. 76)

Another, more extreme example of perceptual organization gone awry is synesthesia, or "mixed senses," which we described at the beginning of this chapter. What, then, are the processes whereby sensory nonsense becomes perceptual sense?

Gestalt Principles of Perceptual Organization

▶ 21. Which Gestalt psychology principles and laws underlie perceptual organization?

Early in the 20th century, psychologists from the German school of Gestalt psychology set out to

FIGURE 4.32

As Gestalt psychologists emphasized, what we perceive (i.e., the name spelled out by the band) is more than simply the sum of its individual parts.

discover how we organize the separate parts of our perceptual field into a unified and meaningful whole. *Gestalt* is the German term for "pattern," "shape," or "form." Gestalt theorists were early champions of top-down processing, arguing that the wholes we perceive are often more than (and frequently different from) the sum of their parts. Thus your perception of the photo in Figure 4.32 is likely to be more than "people on the field."

The Gestalt theorists emphasized the importance of **figure-ground relations.** *We tend to organize stimuli into a central or foreground figure and a background.* In vision, the central figure is usually in front of or on top of what we perceive as background. It has a distinct shape and is more striking in our perceptions and memory than the background. We perceive borders or contours wherever there is a distinct change in the color or brightness of a visual scene, but we interpret these contours as part of the figure rather than background. Likewise, we tend to hear instrumental music as a melody (figure) surrounded by other chords or harmonies (ground).

Separating figure from ground can be challenging (Figure 4.33), yet our perceptual systems are usually equal to the task. Sometimes, however, what's figure and what's ground is not completely obvious, and the same stimulus can give rise to two different perceptions. Consider Figure 4.34, for example. If you examine it for a while, two alternating but equally plausible perceptions will emerge, one based on the inner portion and the other formed by the two outer portions. When the alternative perception (figure) occurs, what was previously the figure becomes the background.

In addition to figure-ground relations, the Gestalt psychologists were interested in how separate stimuli come to be perceived as parts of larger wholes. They suggested that *people group and interpret stimuli in accordance with four* **Gestalt laws of perceptual organization:** *similarity, proximity, closure, and continuity.* These organizing principles are illustrated in Figure 4.35.

What is your perception of Figure 4.35a? Do you perceive 16 unrelated dots, or do you view the stimulus as two triangles formed by different-sized dots? If you see triangles, your perception obeys the Gestalt *law of similarity,* which says that when parts of a configuration are perceived as similar, they will be perceived as belonging together. The *law of*

FIGURE 4.34

This reversible figure illustrates alternating figure-ground relations. It can be seen as a vase or as two people facing one another. Whichever percept exists at the moment is seen as figure against background.

FIGURE 4.33

Figure-ground relations are important in perceptual organization. Here the artist Bev Doolittle has created great similarity between figure and ground in this representation of natural camouflage, yet enough figural cues remain to permit most people to detect the horses. Pintos, Bev Doolittle, 1979. The Greenwich Workshop, Trumbull, CT.

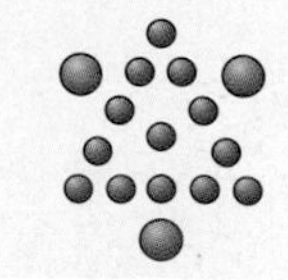

(a) Similarity

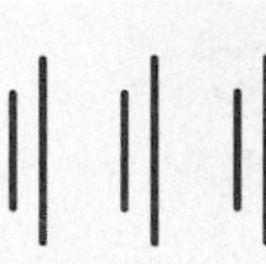

(b) Proximity

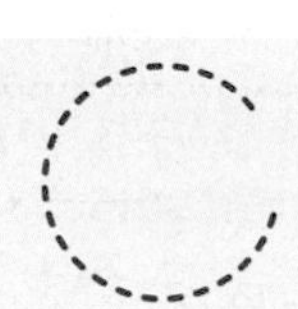

(c) Closure

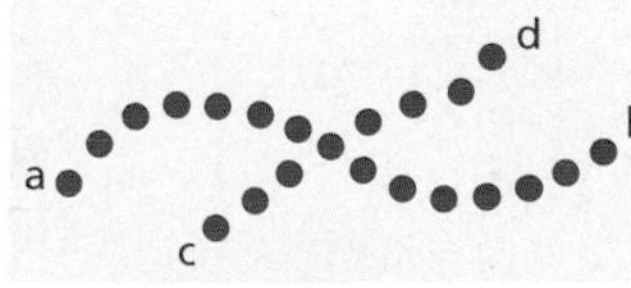

(d) Continuity

FIGURE 4.35

Among the Gestalt principles for perceptual organization are the laws of (a) similarity, (b) proximity, (c) closure, and (d) continuity. Each principle causes us to organize stimuli into wholes that are greater than the sums of their parts.

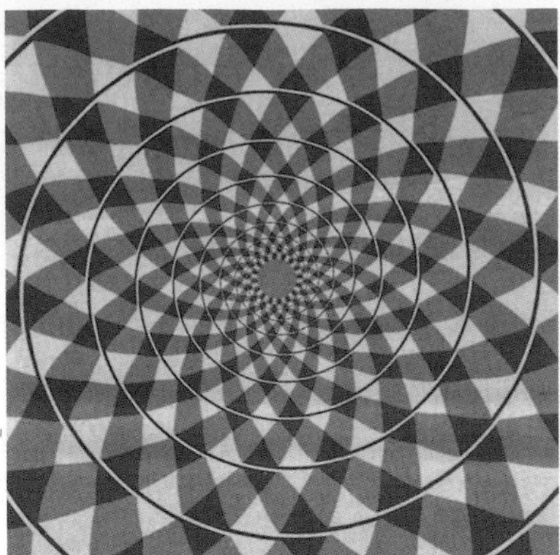

FIGURE 4.36

Fraser's spiral illustrates the Gestalt law of continuity. If you follow any part of the "spiral" with your finger, you will find that it is not a spiral at all but a series of concentric circles. The "spiral" is created by your nervous system because that perception is more consistent with continuity of the individual elements.

proximity says that elements that are near each other are likely to be perceived as part of the same configuration. Thus most people perceive Figure 4.35b as three sets of two lines rather than as six separate lines. Illustrated in Figure 4.35c is the *law of closure,* which states that people tend to close the open edges of a figure or fill in gaps in an incomplete figure, so that their identification of the form (in this case, a circle) is more complete than what is actually there. Finally, the *law of continuity* holds that people link individual elements together so they form a continuous line or pattern that makes sense. Thus Figure 4.35d is far more likely to be seen as combining components *ab* and *cd* rather than *ad* and *cb,* which have poor continuity. Or consider Fraser's spiral, shown in Figure 4.36, which is not really a spiral at all! (To demonstrate, trace one of the circles with a pencil.) We perceive the concentric circles as a spiral because, to our nervous system, a spiral gives better continuity between individual elements than does a set of circles. The spiral is created by us, not by the stimulus.

Perception Involves Hypothesis Testing

▶ 22. What roles do perceptual schemas and perceptual sets play in our sensory interpretations?

"Recognizing" a stimulus implies that we have a **perceptual schema**—*a mental representation or image*—to compare it with. Our schemas contain the critical features of objects, events, and other perceptual phenomena (Wade & Swanston, 1991). They allow us to classify and identify sensory input in a top-down fashion.

Imagine, for example, that a person approaches you and calls out your name. Who is this person? If the stimuli match your inner representation of your best friend's appearance and voice closely enough, you identify the person as your friend (McAdams & Drake, 2002). Many political cartoonists have an uncanny ability to capture the most noteworthy facial features of famous people, so that we can easily recognize the person represented by even the simplest line sketch.

Perception is, in this sense, an attempt to make sense of stimulus input, to search for the best interpretation of sensory information we can arrive at based on our knowledge and experience. Likening the process to the scientific process described in Chapter 2, Richard L. Gregory (1966) suggested that each of our perceptions is essentially a hypothesis about the nature of the object or, more generally, the meaning of the sensory information. The perceptual system actively searches its gigantic library of internal schemas for the interpretation that best fits the sensory data.

An example of how effortlessly our perceptual systems build up descriptions or hypotheses that best fit the available evidence is found in the comic strips created by Gustave Verbeek in the early 1900s. The Sunday *New York Herald* told Verbeek that his comic strip had to be restricted to 6 panels. Verbeek wanted 12 panels, so he ingeniously created 12-panel cartoons in only 6 panels by drawing pictures like that shown in Figure 4.37a. The reader viewed the first 6 panels, then turned the newspaper upside down to read the last 6 and finish the story. Try this yourself on the panel shown in the figure, and you will find that a bird story becomes a fish story! The point is that you do not simply see an upside-down bird, even though the physical stimuli remain exactly the same. You see an entirely different picture because the new stimulus closely matches another of your perceptual schemas.

In some instances, sensory information fits two different internal representations, and there is not enough information to permanently rule out one of them in favor of the other. For example, examine the Necker cube, shown in Figure 4.37b. If you stare at the cube for a while, you will find that it changes before your very eyes as your nervous system "tries out" a new perceptual hypothesis.

Perception Is Influenced by Expectations: Perceptual Sets

On July 3, 1988, the warship USS *Vincennes* was engaged in a pitched battle with several speedy Iranian gunboats. Suddenly, the *Vincennes*'s advanced

(a)

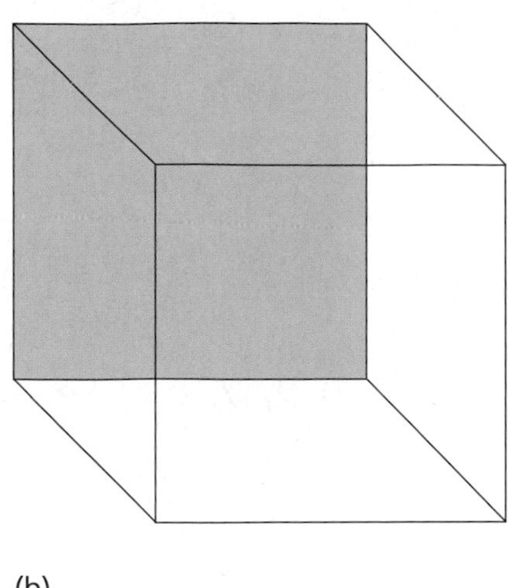

(b)

FIGURE 4.37

Two examples of how the same stimulus can give rise to different perceptions are found in (a) the comic strips of Gustave Verbeek and (b) the Necker cube. To produce the first reversal, turn the page upside down. The "bird story" becomes a "fish story." Next, stare at the cube. The front of the cube will suddenly become the back, and it also will appear that the cube is being viewed from a different angle.

radar system detected an aircraft taking off from a military-civilian airfield in Iran and heading straight toward the American vessel. Radar operators identified the plane as an Iranian F-14 fighter, known to carry lethal missiles used earlier in a damaging attack on another U.S. warship. Repeated requests to the plane to identify itself yielded no response. The plane was now only 10 miles from the ship and, according to the crewmen watching on radar, descending toward the *Vincennes* on an attack course. As a final warning evoked no response, the *Vincennes*'s captain gave the command to fire on the plane. Two surface-to-air missiles streaked into the sky. Moments later, all that remained of the plane was a shower of flaming debris.

The jubilation and relief of the *Vincennes*'s crew was short-lived. Soon the awful truth was known. The plane they had shot down was not an attacking F-14 warplane. Instead, it was a commercial airliner carrying 290 passengers, all of whom died when the aircraft was destroyed. Moreover, videotape recordings of the electronic information used by the crew to identify the plane and its flight pattern showed conclusively that the aircraft was not an F-14 and that it had actually been climbing rather than descending toward the ship.

How could such a tragic error have been made by a well-trained and experienced crew with access to the world's most sophisticated radar equipment? At a congressional hearing on the incident, several prominent perception researchers reconstructed the psychological environment that could have caused the radar operators' eyes to "lie."

Clearly, the situation was stressful and dangerous. The *Vincennes* was already under attack by Iranian gunboats, and other attacks could be expected. It was easy for the radar operators, observing a plane taking off from a military field and heading toward the ship, to interpret this as a prelude to an air attack. The *Vincennes*'s crew was determined to avoid the fate of the other American warship, producing a high level of vigilance to any stimuli that suggested an impending attack. Fear and expectation thus created a psychological context within which the sensory input from the computer system was interpreted in a top-down fashion. The perception that the aircraft was a warplane and that it was descending toward the ship fit the crew's expectations and fears, and it became the "reality" that they experienced. They had a **perceptual set**—*a readiness to perceive stimuli in a particular way.* Sometimes believing is seeing.

Stimuli Are Recognizable Under Changing Conditions: Perceptual Constancies

▶ 23. What factors account for shape, brightness, and size constancy in vision?

When a door swings open, it casts a different image on our retina, but we still perceive it as the door. Our perceptual hypothesis remains the same. Were it not for **perceptual constancies** *that allow us to recognize familiar stimuli under varying conditions*, we would have to literally rediscover what something is each time it appeared under different conditions. Thus you can recognize a tune even if it is played in a different octave, as long as the relations among its notes are maintained. You can detect the flavor of a particular spice even when it occurs in foods having very different tastes.

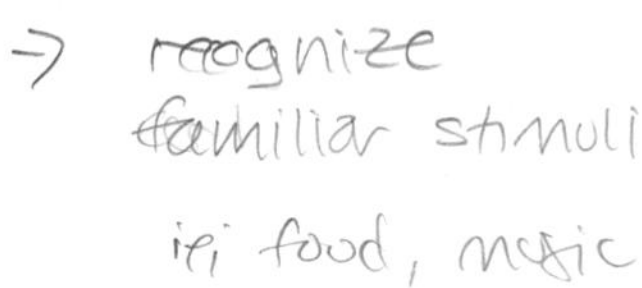

FIGURE 4.38

Size constancy based on distance cues causes us to perceive the person in the background as being of normal size. When the same stimulus is seen in the absence of distance cues, size constancy breaks down.

In vision, several constancies are important. *Shape constancy* allows us to recognize people and other objects from many different angles, as in the case of the swinging door. Perhaps you have had the experience of sitting up front and off to one side of the screen in a crowded movie theater. At first, the picture probably looked distorted, but after a while your visual system corrected for the distortion and objects on the screen looked normal again.

Because of *brightness constancy,* the relative brightness of objects remains the same under different conditions of illumination, such as full sunlight and shade. Brightness constancy occurs because the ratio of light intensity between an object and its surroundings is usually constant. The actual brightness of the light that illuminates the objects does not matter, as long as the same light intensity illuminates both an object and its surroundings.

When we take off in an airplane, we know that the cars on the highway below are not shrinking and becoming the size of ants. *Size constancy* is the perception that the size of objects remains relatively constant even though images on our retina change in size with variations in distance. Thus a man who is judged to be 6 feet tall when standing 5 feet away is not perceived to be 3 feet tall at a distance of 10 feet, even though the size of his image on the retina is reduced to half its original size (Figure 4.38).

What Do You Think?

WHY DOES THAT RISING MOON LOOK SO BIG?

Just before bedding down for the night on a backpacking trip, a friend of ours poked his head outside of his tent and gasped to his wife, "Look at the moon! Just look at that moon!" Indeed, a bright red full moon had just come over the horizon, and it was so enormous that it dwarfed the mammoth peaks surrounding them. The couple gazed at it in wonder for a few minutes and then retired into their tent. Later that night, they looked outside again and were puzzled to see a rather small, ordinary full moon approaching the zenith.

You too may have exclaimed over the size of a rising moon, only to notice later that the moon, well above the horizon, seemed to have shrunk. What can explain this phenomenon? Think about it, then see page 153.

IN REVIEW

- *Perception involves both bottom-up processing, in which individual stimulus fragments are combined into a perception, and top-down processing, in which existing knowledge and perceptual schemas are applied to interpret stimuli.*
- *Attention is an active process in which we focus on certain stimuli while blocking out other stimuli. We cannot attend completely to more than one thing at a time, but we are capable of rapid attentional shifts. Attentional processes are affected by the nature of the stimulus and by personal factors such as motives and interests. The perceptual system appears to be especially vigilant to stimuli that denote threat or danger.*
- *The Gestalt psychologists identified a number of principles of perceptual organization, including figure-ground relations and the laws of similarity, proximity, closure, and continuity. R. L. Gregory suggested that perception is essentially a hypothesis about what a stimulus is, based on previous experience and the nature of the stimulus.*
- *Perceptual sets involve a readiness to perceive stimuli in certain ways, based on our expectations, assumptions, motivations, and current emotional state.*
- *Perceptual constancies allow us to recognize familiar stimuli under changing conditions. In the visual realm, there are three constancies: shape, brightness, and size.*

PERCEPTION OF DEPTH, DISTANCE, AND MOVEMENT

▶ 24. Describe the major monocular and binocular depth/distance cues, as well as the bases for movement perception.

The ability to adapt to a spatial world requires that we make fine distinctions involving distances and the movement of objects within the environment. Humans are capable of great precision in making such judgments. Consider, for example, the perceptual task faced by a baseball batter (Figure 4.39). A fast ball thrown by the pitcher at 90 miles per hour (mph) from 60 feet will reach the batter who is trying to hit it in about 42/100 of a second. A curve ball thrown at 80 mph will reach the hitting zone in 47/100 of a second, a difference of only 5/100 of a second, but a world of difference for timing and hitting the pitch. Within the first 6 to 8 feet of a ball's flight from the pitcher's hand (an interval of about 25/1,000 of a second), the batter must correctly judge the speed, spin, and location of the pitch. If any of the judgments are wrong, the hitter will probably be unable to hit a fair ball, for the ball will be in the bat's "contact zone" only 2/1,000 of a second (Adair, 1990). The perceptual demands of such a task are imposing indeed—as are the salaries earned by those who can perform this task consistently. How does the visual perception system make such judgments?

Depth and Distance Perception

One of the more intriguing aspects of visual perception is our ability to perceive depth. The retina receives information in only two dimensions (length and width), but the brain translates these cues into three-dimensional perceptions. It does this by using both **monocular depth cues,** *which require only one eye,* and **binocular depth cues,** *which require both eyes.*

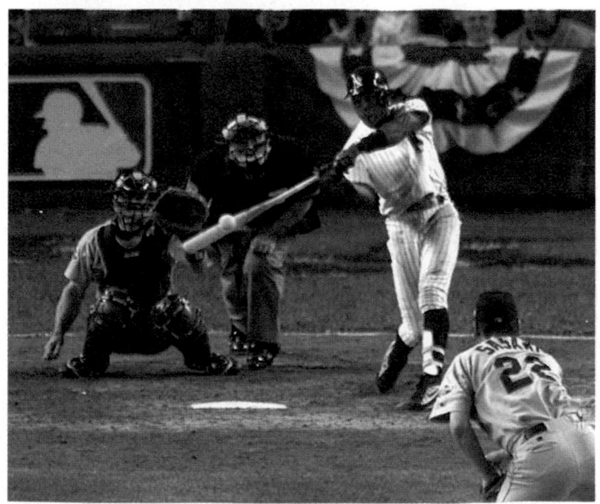

FIGURE 4.39

The demands faced by a batter in judging the speed, distance, and movements of a pitched baseball within thousandths of a second underscore the capabilities of the visual perceptual system.

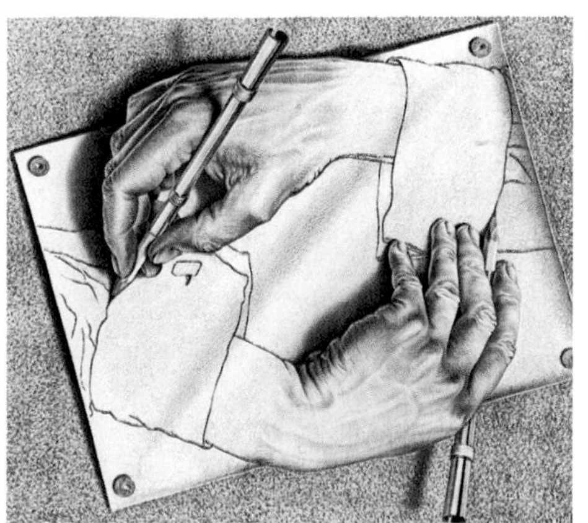

FIGURE 4.40

Patterns of light and shadow can serve as monocular depth cues, as shown in Drawing Hands *by M. C. Escher.*

Monocular Depth Cues

Judging the relative distances of objects is one important key to perceiving depth. When artists paint on a flat canvas, they depend on a variety of monocular cues to create perceptions of depth in their pictures. One such cue is patterns of *light and shadow.* The 20th-century artist M. C. Escher skillfully used light and shadow to create the three-dimensional effect shown in Figure 4.40. The depth effect is as powerful if you close one eye as it is when you use both.

Another cue, *linear perspective,* refers to the perception that parallel lines converge, or angle toward one another, as they recede into the distance. Thus if you look down railroad tracks, they appear to angle toward one another with increased distance, and we use this as a depth cue. The same occurs with the edges of a highway or the sides of an elevator shaft. *Interposition,* in which objects closer to us may cut off part of our view of more distant objects, provides another cue for distance and depth.

An object's *height in the horizontal plane* provides another source of information. For example, a ship 5 miles offshore appears in a higher plane and closer to the horizon than does one that is only 1 mile from shore. *Texture* is a fifth cue, because the texture or grain of an object appears

FIGURE 4.41

The School of Athens, *by Raphael Sanzio, illustrates seven monocular depth cues. (1) Linear perspective is produced by the converging lines of the corridor in the background, which angle toward one another. (2) The arches and the people in the background are smaller than those in front (relative size). (3) The back of the floor is in a higher horizontal plane than the foreground. (4, 5) The objects in the background are less detailed than the closer ones (texture and clarity). (6) Light and shadow are used to create depth. (7) The arches and people in the front of the painting cut off parts of the corridor behind them (interposition).*

finer as distance increases. Likewise, *clarity* can be an important cue for judging distance; we can see nearby hills more clearly than ones that are far away, especially on hazy days.

Relative size is yet another basis for distance judgments. If we see two objects that we know to be of similar size, then the one that looks smaller will be judged to be farther away. For example, this cue may figure prominently in the moon illusion.

None of these monocular cues involve movement of the object(s). A final monocular cue is *motion parallax,* which tells us that if we are moving, nearby objects appear to move faster in the opposite direction than do faraway ones. Like the other monocular cues, motion provides us with information that we can use to make judgments about distance and therefore about depth.

The artist Raphael Sanzio was a master at using monocular depth and distance cues. *The School of Athens,* shown in Figure 4.41, illustrates all of the monocular cues just described, with the exception of motion parallax.

Binocular Depth Cues

The most dramatic perceptions of depth arise with binocular depth cues, which require the use of both eyes. For an interesting binocular effect, hold your two index fingers about 6 inches in front of your eyes with their tips about 1 inch apart. Focus on your fingers first, then focus beyond them across the room. The two different views will produce the image of a third finger between the other two. This "third finger" will disappear if you close either eye.

Most of us are familiar with the delightful depth experiences provided by View Master slides and 3-D movies watched through special glasses. These devices make use of the principle of **binocular disparity,** *in which each eye sees a slightly different image*. Within the brain, the visual input from the two eyes is analyzed by feature detectors that are attuned to depth (Howard, 2002; Livingstone & Hubel, 1994). Some of the feature detectors respond only to stimuli that are either in front of or behind the point on which we are fixing our gaze. The responses of these depth-sensitive neurons are integrated to produce our perception of depth (Goldstein, 2002).

A second binocular distance cue, **convergence,** *is produced by feedback from the muscles that turn your eyes inward to view a near object*. You can experience this cue by holding a finger about 1 foot in front of your face, then moving it slowly toward you. Messages sent to your brain by the eye muscles provide it with a depth cue.

Perception of Movement

The perception of movement is a complex process, requiring the brain to integrate information from several different senses. Try this demonstration: Hold your pen in front of your face. Now, while holding your head still, move the pen back and forth. You will perceive the pen moving. Now hold the pen still and move your head back and forth at the same rate of speed. In both cases, the image of the pen moved across your retina in about the same way. But when you moved your head, your brain took into account input from your kinesthetic and vestibular systems and "concluded" that you were moving but the pen was not.

The primary cue for perceiving motion is the movement of the stimulus across the retina (Sekuler et al., 2002). Under optimal conditions, a retinal image need move only about one fifth the diameter of a single cone for us to detect

FIGURE 4.42

Moving pictures produce stroboscopic movement by projecting a series of still photographs at a rate of 24 per second.

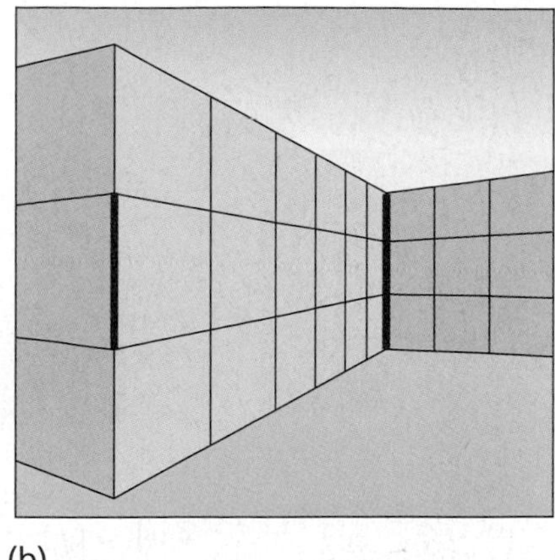

(a) (b)

FIGURE 4.43

The Ponzo illusion. Which lines in (a) and (b) are longer? Measure them and see. The distance cues provided by the converging railroad tracks and staggered walls affect size perception and disrupt size constancy. SOURCE: Smith, 1998.

movement (Nakayama & Tyler, 1981). The relative movement of an object against a structured background is also a movement cue (Gibson, 1979). For example, if you fixate on a bird in flight, the relative motion of the bird against its background is a strong cue for perceived speed of movement.

The illusion of smooth motion can be produced if we arrange for the sequential appearance of two or more stimuli. Gestalt psychologist Max Wertheimer (1912) demonstrated this in his studies of **stroboscopic movement,** *illusory movement produced when a light is briefly flashed in darkness and then, a few milliseconds later, another light is flashed nearby*. If the timing is just right, the first light seems to move from one place to the other in a manner indistinguishable from real movement.

Stroboscopic movement (termed the "phi phenomenon" by Wertheimer) has been used commercially in numerous ways. For example, think of the strings of successively illuminated lights on theater marquees that seem to move endlessly around the border or that spell out messages in a "moving" script. Stroboscopic movement is also the principle behind motion pictures, which consist of a series of still photographs, or frames, that are projected on a screen in rapid succession with dark intervals in between (Figure 4.42). The rate at which the frames are projected is critical to our perception of smooth movement. Early movies, such as the silent films of the 1920s, projected the stills at only 16 frames per second, and the movements appeared fast and jerky. Today the usual speed is 24 frames per second, which more perfectly produces an illusion of smooth movement. Television presents at 30 images per second.

For more on the phi phenomenon, see Interactive Segment 4.1.

ILLUSIONS: FALSE PERCEPTUAL HYPOTHESES

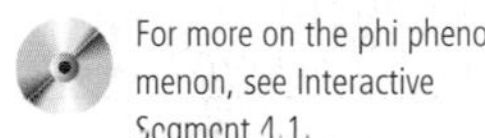

▶ 25. What is an illusion? How are constancies and context involved in visual illusions?

Our analysis of perceptual schemas, hypotheses, sets, and constancies allows us to understand some interesting perceptual experiences known as *illusions*. **Illusions** *are compelling but incorrect perceptions*. Such perceptions can be understood as erroneous perceptual hypotheses about the nature of the stimulus. Illusions are not only intriguing and sometimes delightful visual experiences, but they also provide important information about how our perceptual processes work under normal conditions.

Ironically, most visual illusions can be attributed to perceptual constancies that ordinarily help us perceive more accurately (Frisby, 1980). For example, size constancy results in part from our ability to use distance cues to judge the size of objects. But, as we saw in the discussion of the moon illusion, distance cues can sometimes fool us. In the *Ponzo illusion,* shown in Figure 4.43a, the depth cues of linear perspective (the tracks converging) and height in the horizontal plane provide distance cues that make the upper bar appear farther away than the lower bar. Because it seems farther away, the perceptual system concludes that the bar in the background must be larger than the bar in the foreground, despite the fact that the two

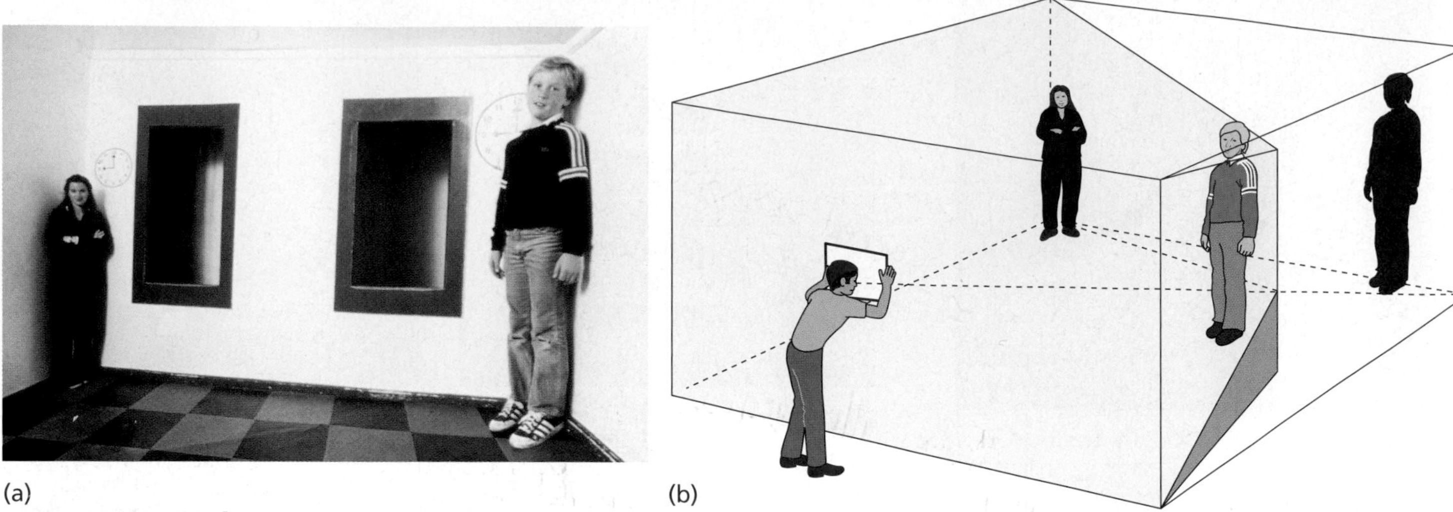

FIGURE 4.44

(a) The Ames Room produces a striking size perception because it is designed to appear rectangular. (b) The room, however, is actually trapezoidal in shape, and the figure on the left is actually much farther away from the viewer than the one on the right and thus appears smaller. We perceive the boy as if he were the blue figure.

bars cast retinal images of the same size. The same occurs in the vertical arrangement seen in Figure 4.43b.

Distance cues can be manipulated to create other size illusions. One occurs in a room constructed by Adelbert Ames. Viewed through a peephole with one eye, the scene presents a startling size reversal (Figure 4.44a). Our perceptual system assumes that the room has a normal rectangular shape because, in fact, most rooms do. Monocular depth cues do not allow us to see that, in reality, the left corner of the room is twice as far away as the right corner (Figure 4.44b). As a result, size constancy breaks down, and we base our judgment of size on the sizes of the retinal images cast by the two people.

The study of perceptual constancies shows that our perceptual hypotheses are strongly influenced by the *context*, or surroundings, in which a stimulus occurs. Figure 4.45 shows some examples of how context can produce illusory perceptions.

Some of the most intriguing perceptual distortions are produced when monocular depth cues are manipulated to produce a figure or scene whose individual parts make sense but whose overall organization is "impossible" in terms of our existing perceptual schemas. Figure 4.46 shows three impossible figures. In each case, our brain extracts information about depth from the individual features of the objects, but when this information is put together and matched with our

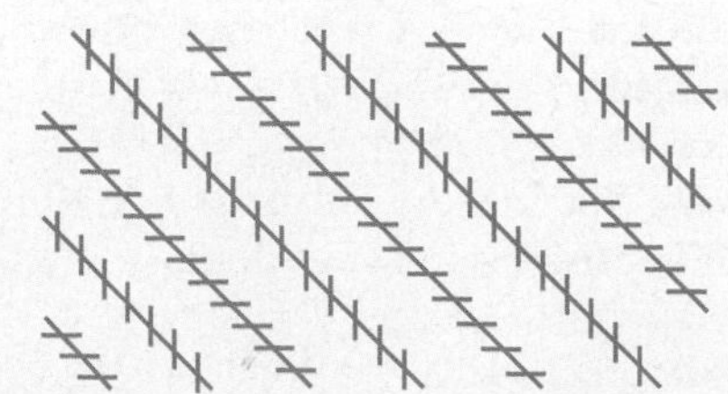

The long lines are actually parallel, but the small lines make them appear crooked.

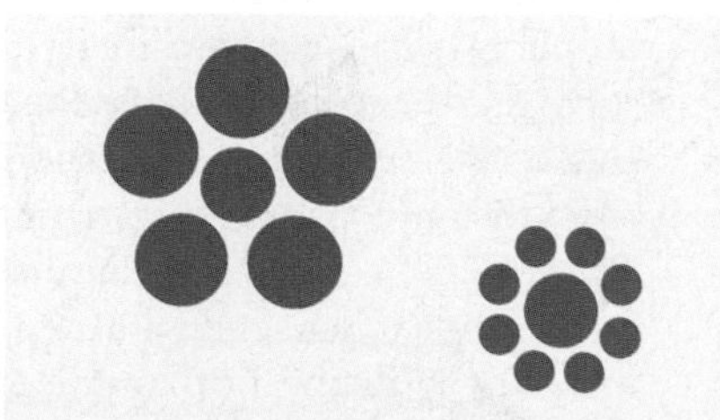

Which inner circle is larger? Check and see.

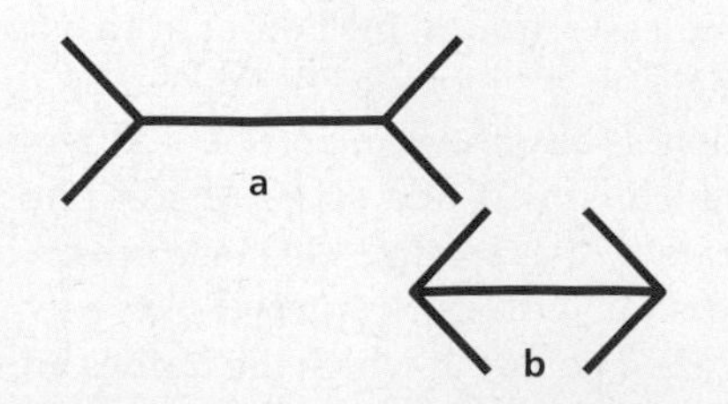

The Müller-Lyer illusion. Which line, a or b, is longer? Compare them with a ruler.

FIGURE 4.45

Context-produced geometric illusions.

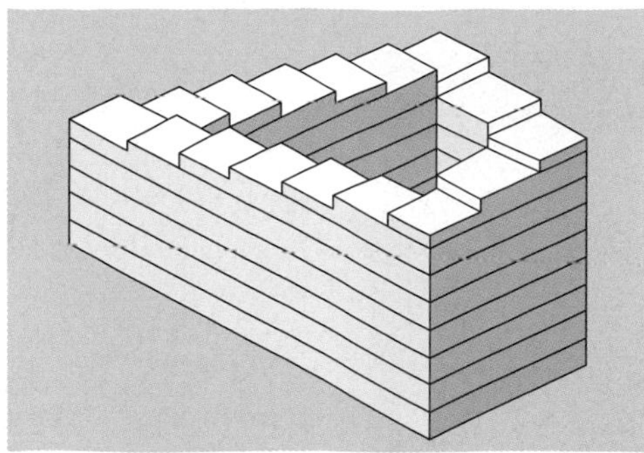

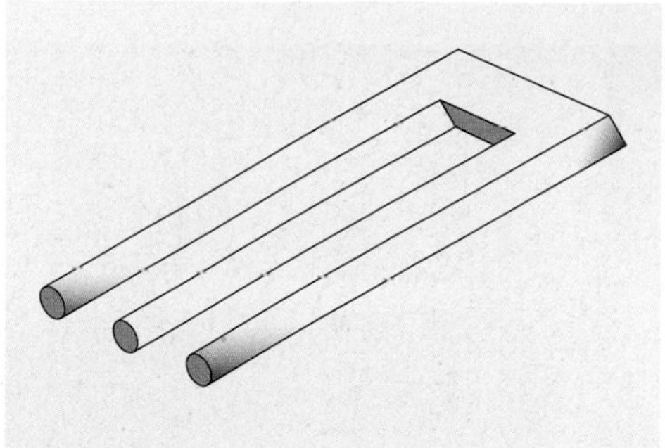

FIGURE 4.46

Monocular depth cues are cleverly manipulated to produce an impossible triangle, a never-ending staircase, and the "devil's tuning fork."

existing schemas, the percept that results simply doesn't make sense. The "devil's tuning fork," for example, could not exist in our universe. It is a two-dimensional image containing paradoxical depth cues. Your brain, however, automatically interprets it as a three-dimensional object and matches it with its internal schema of a fork—a bad fit indeed. The never-ending staircase provides another compelling example of an impossible scene that seems perfectly reasonable when we focus only on its individual elements.

Illusions are not only personally and scientifically interesting, but they can have important real-life implications. Our *Research Close-up* describes one scientist's search for an illusion having life-and-death implications.

What Do You Think?

EXPLAIN THIS STRIKING ILLUSION

We'd like you to experience a truly interesting illusion. To do so, all you need is a piece of fairly heavy paper and a little patience.

Fold the piece of paper down the middle and set it on a table with one of the open ends facing you like an open tent. Close one eye and, from slightly above the object, stare at a point midway along the top fold of the paper. At first, the object looks like a tent, but after a while, the paper will suddenly "stand up" and look like a corner viewed from the inside. When this happens, gently move your head back and forth while continuing to view with one eye. The movement will produce a striking perception. Can you explain what you now see? For a discussion of this illusion, see page 153.

RESEARCH CLOSE-UP

STALKING A DEADLY ILLUSION

Introduction

When the Boeing Company introduced the 727 jet airliner in the mid-1960s, it was the latest word in aviation technology. The plane performed well in test flights, but four fatal crashes soon after it was placed in service raised fears that there might be some fatal flaw in its design.

The first accident occurred as a 727 made its approach to Chicago over Lake Michigan on a clear night. The plane plunged into the lake 19 miles offshore. About a month later, another 727 glided in over the Ohio River to land in Cincinnati. Unaccountably, it struck the ground about 12 feet below the runway elevation and burst into flames. The third accident occurred as an aircraft approached Salt Lake City over dark land. The lights of the city twinkled in the distance, but the plane made too rapid a descent and crashed short of the runway. Months later, a Japanese airliner approached Tokyo at night. The flight ended tragically as the plane, its landing gear not yet lowered, struck the waters of Tokyo Bay 6 miles from the runway.

Analysis of these four accidents, as well as others, suggested a common pattern. All occurred at night under clear weather conditions, so the pilots were operating under visual

Continued

SOURCE: Conrad L. Kraft (1978). A psychophysical contribution to air safety: Simulator studies of illusions in night visual approaches. In H. L. Pick, Jr., H. W. Leibowitz, J. E. Singer, A. Steinschneider, & H. W. Stevenson (Eds.), *Psychology: From research to practice.* New York: Plenum.

FIGURE 4.47

Conrad L. Kraft, a Boeing psychologist, created an apparatus to study how visual cues can affect the simulated landings of airline pilots. Pilots approached Nightertown in a simulated cockpit. The computer-controlled city could be tilted to reproduce the illusion thought to be responsible for several fatal air crashes. Based on Kraft, 1978.

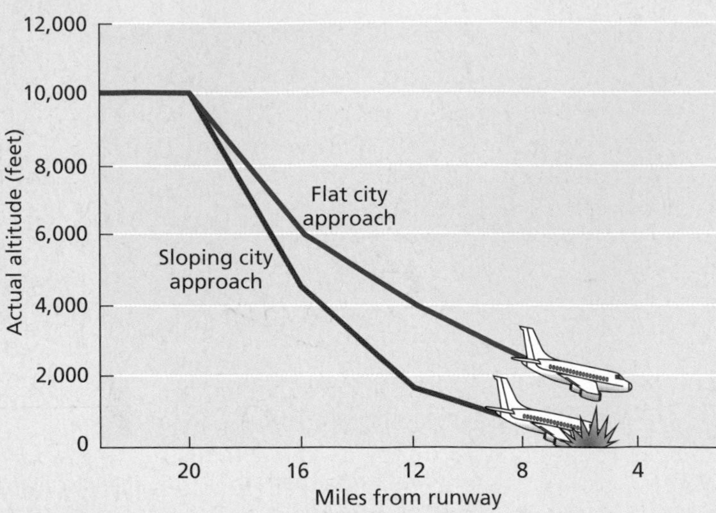

FIGURE 4.48

The illusion caused by upward-sloping city lights caused even highly experienced pilots to overestimate their altitude, and 11 of the 12 flight instructors "crashed" short of the runway. When the lights were flat, all the pilots made perfect approaches. SOURCE: Based on Kraft, 1978.

flight rules rather than performing instrument landings. In each instance, the plane was approaching city lights over dark areas of water or land. In all cases, the lights in the background sloped upward to varying degrees. Finally, all of the planes crashed short of the runway. These observations led a Boeing psychologist, Conrad L. Kraft, to suspect that the cause of the crashes might be pilot error based on some sort of visual illusion.

Method

To test this possibility, Boeing engineers constructed an apparatus to simulate night landings (Figure 4.47). It consisted of a cockpit and a miniature lighted "city" named Nightertown. The city moved toward the cockpit on computer-controlled rollers, and it could be tilted to simulate various terrain slopes. The pilot could control simulated air speed and rate of climb and descent, and the Nightertown scene was controlled by the pilot's responses just as a true visual scene would be.

The participants were 12 experienced Boeing flight instructors who made virtual reality "landings" at Nightertown under systematically varied conditions created by the computerized simulator. All of their landings were visual landings so as to be able to test whether a visual illusion was occurring. Every aspect of their approach and the manner in which they controlled the aircraft were measured precisely.

Results

The landings made by the flight instructors were nearly flawless until Kraft duplicated the conditions of the fatal crashes by having the pilots approach an upward-sloping distant city over a dark area. When this occurred, the pilots were unable to detect the upward slope, assumed that the background city was flat, and consistently overestimated their approach altitude. On a normal landing, the preferred altitude at 4.5 miles from the runway is about 1,240 feet. As Figure 4.48 shows, the pilots approached at about this altitude when the simulated city was in a flat position. But when it was sloped upward, 11 of the 12 experienced pilot instructors "crashed" about 4.5 miles short of the runway.

Critical Discussion

This study shows the value of being able to study behavior under highly controlled conditions and with precise measurements. By simulating the conditions under which the fatal crashes had occurred, Kraft identified the visual illusion that was the source of pilot error. He showed that the perceptual hypotheses of the flight instructors, like those of the pilots involved in the real crashes, were tragically incorrect. It would have been ironic if one of the finest jetliners ever built had been removed from service because of presumed mechanical defects while other aircraft remained aloft and at risk for tragedy.

Kraft's research not only saved the 727 from months—or perhaps years—of needless mechanical analysis but, more important, it also identified a potentially deadly illusion and the precise conditions under which it occurred. On the basis of Kraft's findings, Boeing recommended that pilots attend carefully to their instruments when landing at night, even under perfect weather conditions. Today, commercial airline pilots are required to make instrument landings not only at night but also during the day.

IN REVIEW

- *Monocular cues to judge distance include linear perspective, relative size, height in the horizontal plane, texture, and clarity. These distance cues also help us judge depth. Depth perception also occurs through the monocular cues of light and shadow patterns, interposition, and motion parallax.*
- *Binocular disparity occurs as slightly different images are viewed by each eye and acted on by feature detectors for depth. Convergence of the eyes provides a second binocular cue.*
- *The basis for perception of movement is absolute movement of a stimulus across the retina or relative movement of an object in relation to its background. Stroboscopic movement is illusory.*
- *Illusions are erroneous perceptions. They may be regarded as incorrect perceptual hypotheses. Perceptual constancies help produce many illusions, including the moon illusion and a variety of other context-produced illusions.*

FIGURE 4.49

Eleanor Gibson and Richard Walk constructed this "visual cliff" with a glass-covered drop-off to determine whether crawling infants and newborn animals can perceive depth. Even when coaxed by their mothers, infants refuse to venture onto the glass over the cliff. Newborn animals also avoid the cliff.

EXPERIENCE, CRITICAL PERIODS, AND PERCEPTUAL DEVELOPMENT

Development of sensory and perceptual systems results from the interplay of biological and experiential factors. Genes program biological development, but this development is also influenced by environmental experiences. For example, if you were to be blinded in an accident and later learned to read braille, the area of the somatosensory cortex that is devoted to the fingertips would enlarge over time as it "borrowed" other neurons to increase its sensitivity (Pool, 1994). By the time they are old enough to crawl, children placed on a "visual cliff" formed by a glass-covered table that suddenly drops off beneath the glass will not ordinarily venture "over the edge" (Figure 4.49). This aversion may result from the interaction of innate depth perception abilities and previous experience (Gibson & Walk, 1960).

What might a lifetime of experience in a limited environment do to perceptual abilities that seem innate? Sometimes, conditions under which people live create "natural experiments" that help provide answers. For example, the Ba Mbuti pygmies, who live in the rain forests of Central Africa, spend their lives in a closed-in green world of densely packed trees without open spaces. The anthropologist C. M. Turnbull (1961) once brought a man named Kenge out of the forest to the edge of a vast plain. A herd of buffalo grazed in the distance. To Turnbull's surprise, Kenge remarked that he had never seen insects of that kind. When told that they were buffalo, not insects, Kenge was deeply offended and felt that Turnbull was insulting his intelligence. To prove his point, Turnbull drove Kenge in his jeep toward the animals. Kenge's stared in amazement as the "insects" grew into buffalo before his eyes. To explain his perceptual experience to himself, he concluded that witchcraft was being used to fool him. Kenge's misperception occurred as a failure in size constancy. Having lived in an environment without open spaces, he had no experience in judging the size of objects at great distances.

As noted earlier, when light passes through the lens of the eye, the image projected on the retina is reversed, so that right is left and up is down. What would happen if you were to wear a special set of glasses that undid this natural reversal of the visual image and created a world like that in Figure 4.50? In 1896, perception researcher George Stratton did just that, possibly becoming the first human ever to have a right-side-up image on his retina while standing upright. Reversing how nature and a lifetime of experience had fashioned his perceptual system disoriented Stratton at first. The ground and his feet were now up, and he had to put on his hat from the bottom

FIGURE 4.50

Inverted vision would create a world that looks like this. How would you make your way around in this upside-down environment where right is left and left is right? Adaptation to such a world is possible, but challenging.

▶ 26. What evidence shows that cultural factors can influence perceptual interpretations, constancies, and susceptibility to illusions?

up. He had to reach to his left to touch something he saw on his right. Stratton suffered from nausea and couldn't eat or get around for several days. Gradually, however, he adapted to his inverted world, and by the end of 8 days, he was able to successfully reach for objects and walk around. Years later, people who wore inverting lenses for longer periods of time did the same. Some were able to ski down mountain slopes or ride motorcycles while wearing the lenses, even though their visual world remained upside down and never became normal for them. When they removed the inverting lenses, they had some initial problems but soon readapted to the normal visual world (Dolezal, 1982).

Cross-Cultural Research on Perception

As far as we know, humans come into the world with the same perceptual abilities regardless of where they are born. From that point on, however, the culture they grow up in helps determine the kinds of perceptual learning experiences people have. Cross-cultural research can help identify which aspects of perception occur in all people, regardless of their culture, as well as perceptual differences that result from cultural experiences (Deregowski & Kinnear, 1997). Athough there are far more perceptual similarities than differences among the peoples of the world, the differences that do exist show us that perception can indeed be influenced by experience.

Consider the perception of a picture that depends on both the nature of the picture and characteristics of the perceiver. In Figure 4.51a, what is the object above the woman's head? Most North Americans and Europeans instantly identify it as a window. They also tend to see the family sitting inside a dwelling. But when the same picture was shown to East Africans, nearly all perceived the

(a)

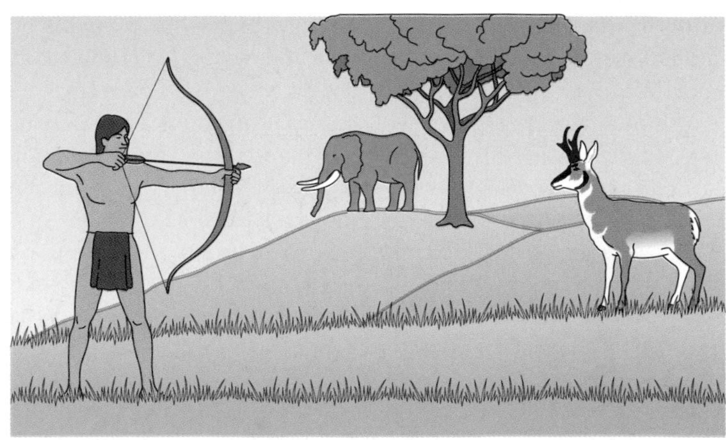

(b)

FIGURE 4.51

(a) What is the object above the woman's head? East Africans had a far different answer than did North Americans. (b) Cultural differences also occurred when people were asked which animal the archer was about to shoot. Sources: (a) Adapted from Gregory & Gombrich, 1973; (b) adapted from Hudson, 1960.

object as a basket or box that the woman is balancing on her head. To them, the family is sitting outside under a tree (Gregory & Gombrich, 1973). These interpretations are more consistent with their own cultural experiences.

In our earlier discussion of monocular depth cues, we used paintings such as the one in Figure 4.41 to illustrate monocular depth perception. In Western culture, we have constant exposure to two-dimensional pictures that our perceptual system effortlessly turns into three-dimensional perceptions. Do people who grow up in cultures where they are not exposed to pictures have the same perceptions? When presented with the picture in Figure 4.51b and asked which animal the hunter was about to shoot, tribal African people answered that he was about to kill the "baby elephant." They did not use the monocular cues that cause Westerners to perceive the man as hunting the antelope and to view the elephant as an adult animal in the distance (Hudson, 1960).

Illusions occur when one of our common perceptual hypotheses is in error. Earlier, we showed you the Müller-Lyer illusion (see Figure 4.44), in which a line appears longer when the V-shaped lines at its ends radiate outward rather than inward. Westerners are very susceptible to this illusion. They have learned that, in their "carpentered" environment, which has many corners and square shapes, inward-facing lines occur when corners are closer, outward-facing lines when they are farther away (Figure 4.52). But when people from other cultures who live in more rounded environments are shown the Müller-Lyer stimuli, they are more likely to correctly perceive the lines as equal in length (Segall et al., 1966). They do not fall prey to a perceptual hypothesis that normally is correct in an environment like ours that is filled with sharp corners but wrong when applied to the lines in the Müller-Lyer illusion (Deregowski & Kinnear, 1997).

Cultural learning affects perceptions in other modalities as well. Our perceptions of tastes, odors, and textures are strongly influenced by our cultural experiences. A taste that might produce nausea in one culture may be considered delicious in another. The taste and gritty texture experienced when chewing a large raw insect or the rubbery texture of a fish eye may appeal far less to you than it would to a person from a culture in which that food is a staple.

Critical Periods: The Role of Early Experience

▶ 27. How do studies of restricted stimulation and restored vision illustrate the role of critical periods in perceptual development?

The examples in the preceding section suggest that experience is essential for the development of perceptual abilities. For some aspects of perception, there are also **critical periods** *during which certain kinds of experiences must occur if perceptual abilities and the brain mechanisms that underlie them are to develop normally*. If the critical period passes without the experience occurring, it is too late to undo the deficit that results.

Earlier we saw that the visual cortex has feature detectors composed of neurons that respond only to lines at particular angles. What would happen if newborn animals grew up in a world in which they saw some angles but not others? In a classic experiment, British researchers Colin Blakemore and Grahame Cooper (1970) created such a world for newborn kittens. The animals were raised in the dark except for a 5-hour period each day during which they were placed in round chambers that had either vertical or horizonal stripes on the walls. Figure 4.53a shows one of the kittens in a vertically striped chamber. A special

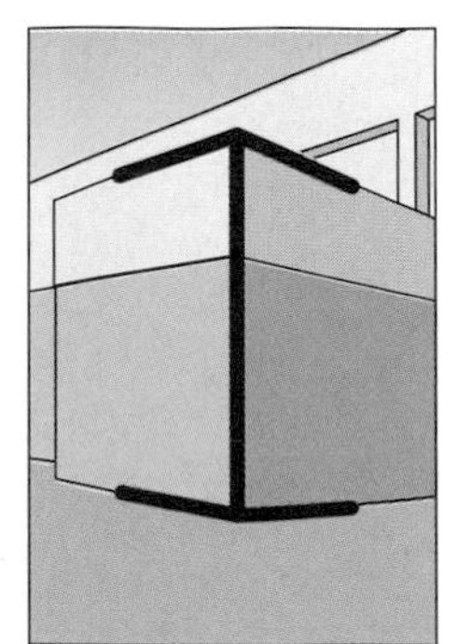

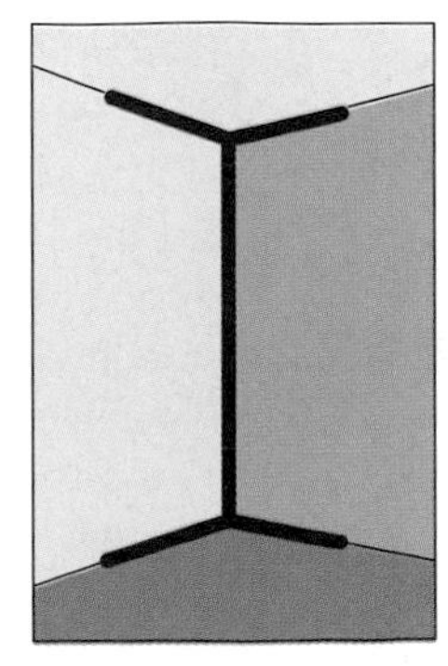

FIGURE 4.52

Perceptual experiences within our "carpentered" environment make us susceptible to the Müller-Lyer illusion (see Figure 4.45), which appears here in vertical form. Again, the vertical lines are the same length.

(a)

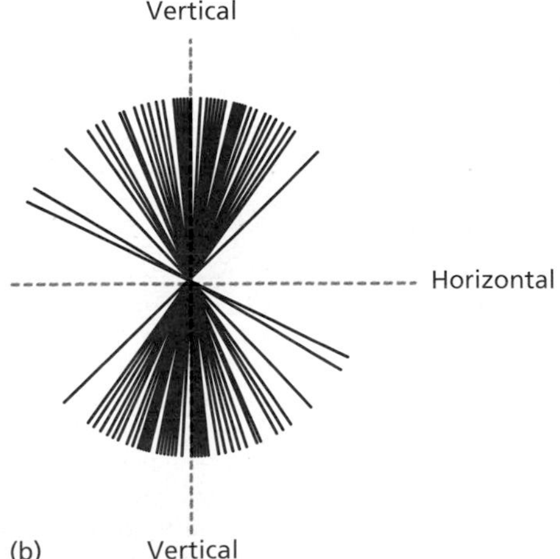

(b)

FIGURE 4.53

Kittens raised in a vertically striped chamber (a) lacked cortical cells that fired in response to horizontal stimuli. The perceptual gaps are easily seen in (b), which shows the orientation angles that resulted in evoked potentials from feature detectors. SOURCE: Adapted from Blakemore & Cooper, 1970.

collar prevented the kittens from seeing their own bodies while they were in the chamber, guaranteeing that they saw nothing but stripes.

When the kittens were 5 months old, Blakemore and Cooper presented them with bars of light at differing angles and used microelectrodes to test the electrical responses of individual feature-detector cells in their visual cortex. The results for the kittens raised in the vertically striped environment are shown in Figure 4.53b. As you can see, the kittens had no cells that fired in response to horizontal stimuli, resulting in visual impairments. They also acted as if they could not see a pencil when it was held in a horizontal position and moved up and down in front of them. However, as soon as the pencil was rotated to a vertical position, the animals began to follow it with their eyes as it was moved back and forth.

As you might expect, the animals raised in the horizontally striped environment showed the opposite effect. They had no feature detectors for vertical stimuli and did not seem to see them. Thus the cortical neurons of both groups of kittens developed in accordance with the stimulus features of their environments.

Some perceptual abilities are influenced more than others by restricted stimulation. In other research, monkeys, chimpanzees, and kittens were raised in an environment devoid of shapes. The animals distinguished differences in size, brightness, and color almost as well as normally reared animals do, but, for the rest of their lives they performed poorly on more complex tasks, such as distinguishing different types of objects and geometric shapes (Riesen, 1965).

Restored Sensory Capacity

Suppose it had been possible to restore Helen Keller's vision when she reached adulthood. What would she have seen? Could she have perceived visually the things that she had learned to identify through her other senses?

Unfortunately, it was not possible to provide Helen Keller with the miracle of restored vision. However, scientists have studied the experiences of other visually impaired people who acquired the ability to see later in life. For example, people born with cataracts grow up in a visual world without form. The clouded lenses of their eyes permit them to perceive light but not patterns or shapes. One such person was Virgil, who had been almost totally blind since childhood. He read braille, enjoyed listening to sports on the radio and conversing with other people, and had adjusted quite well to his disability. At the urging of his fiancée, Virgil agreed to undergo surgery to remove his thick cataracts. The day after the surgery, his bandages were removed. Neurologist Oliver Sacks (1999) recounts what happened next.

> There was light, there was color, all mixed up, meaningless, a blur. Then out of the blur came a voice that said, "Well?" Then, and only then . . . did he finally realize that this chaos of light and shadow was a face—and, indeed, the face of his surgeon. . . . His retina and optic nerve were active, transmitting impulses, but his brain could make no sense of them.

Virgil was never able to adjust to his new visual world. He had to touch objects in order to identify them. He had to be led through his own house and would quickly become disoriented if he deviated from his path. Eventually, Virgil lost his sight once again. This time, however, he regarded his blindness as a gift, a release from a sighted world that was bewildering to him.

Virgil's experiences are characteristic of people who have their vision restored later in life. A German physician, Marius von Senden (1960), compiled data on patients born with cataracts who were tested soon after their cataracts were surgically removed in adulthood. These people were immediately able to perceive figure-ground relations, to scan objects visually, and to follow moving targets with their eyes, indicating that such abilities are innate. However, they could not visually identify objects, such as eating utensils, that they were familiar with through touch; nor were they able to distinguish simple geometric figures without counting the corners or tracing the figures with their fingers.

After several weeks of training, the patients were able to identify simple objects by sight, but their perceptual constancies were very poor. Often they were unable to recognize the same shape in another color, even though they could discriminate between colors. Years later, some patients could identify only a few of the faces of people they knew well. Many also had great difficulty judging distances. Apparently, no amount of subsequent experience could make up for their lack of visual experience during the critical period of childhood.

All of these lines of evidence—cross-cultural perceptual differences, animal studies involving visual deprivation, and observations of congenitally impaired people whose vision has been restored—suggest that biological and experiential factors interact in complex ways. Some of our perceptual abilities are at least partially present at birth, but experience plays an important role in

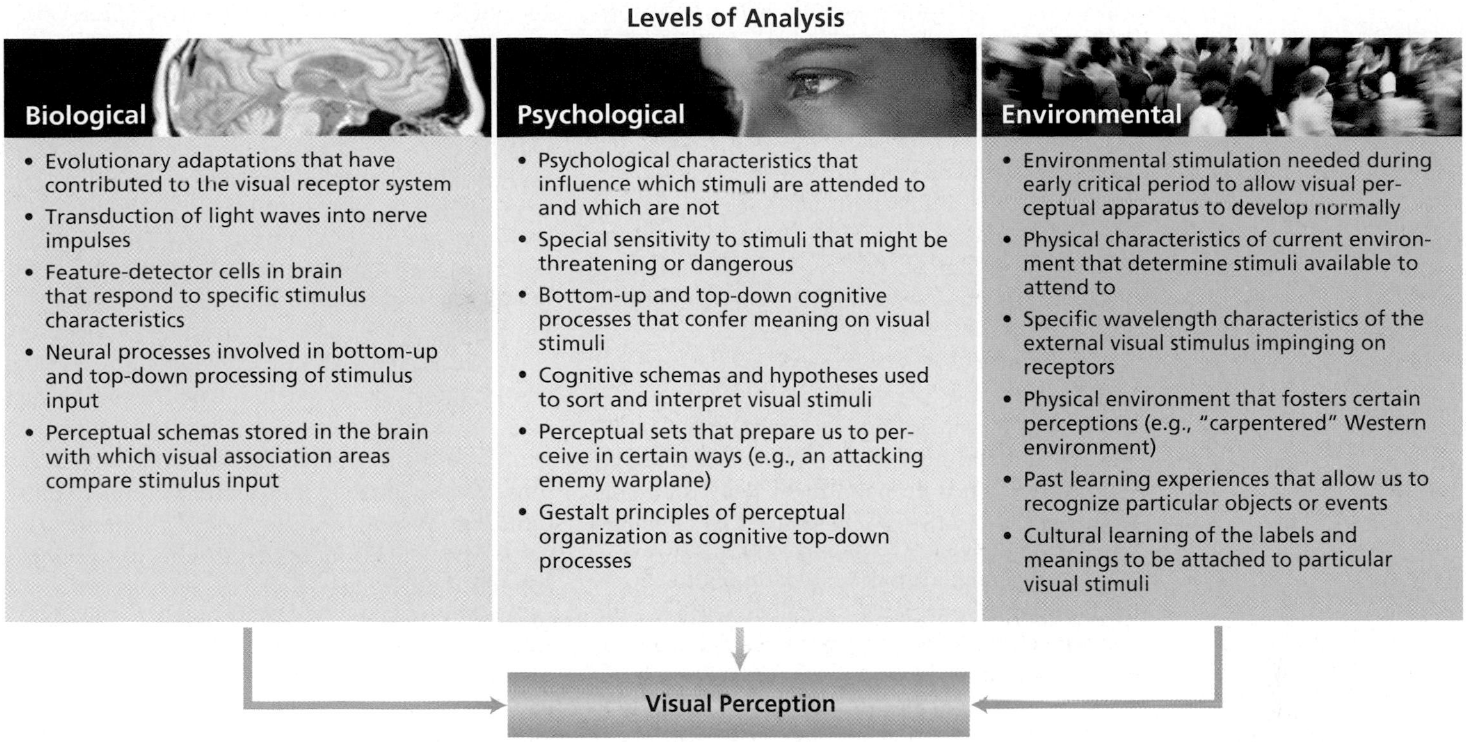

Levels of Analysis

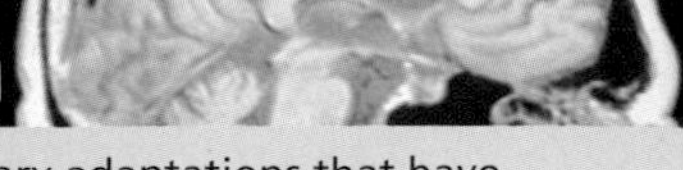

Biological

- Evolutionary adaptations that have contributed to the visual receptor system
- Transduction of light waves into nerve impulses
- Feature-detector cells in brain that respond to specific stimulus characteristics
- Neural processes involved in bottom-up and top-down processing of stimulus input
- Perceptual schemas stored in the brain with which visual association areas compare stimulus input

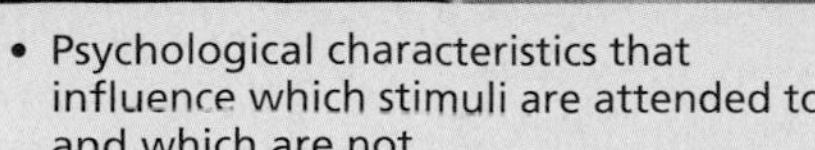

Psychological

- Psychological characteristics that influence which stimuli are attended to and which are not
- Special sensitivity to stimuli that might be threatening or dangerous
- Bottom-up and top-down cognitive processes that confer meaning on visual stimuli
- Cognitive schemas and hypotheses used to sort and interpret visual stimuli
- Perceptual sets that prepare us to perceive in certain ways (e.g., an attacking enemy warplane)
- Gestalt principles of perceptual organization as cognitive top-down processes

Environmental

- Environmental stimulation needed during early critical period to allow visual perceptual apparatus to develop normally
- Physical characteristics of current environment that determine stimuli available to attend to
- Specific wavelength characteristics of the external visual stimulus impinging on receptors
- Physical environment that fosters certain perceptions (e.g., "carpentered" Western environment)
- Past learning experiences that allow us to recognize particular objects or events
- Cultural learning of the labels and meanings to be attached to particular visual stimuli

Visual Perception

FIGURE 4.54

Understanding Behavior: Biological, psychological, and environmental factors in visual perception.

their normal development. How innate and experiential factors interact promises to be a continued focus of perception research. Thus perception is very much a biopsychological process whose mysteries are best explored by examining them from biological, psychological, and environmental levels of analysis (see Figure 4.54)

IN REVIEW

- *Perceptual development involves both physical maturation and learning. Some perceptual abilities are innate or develop shortly after birth, whereas others require particular experiences early in life in order to develop.*
- *Cultural factors can influence certain aspects of perception, including picture perception and susceptibility to illusions. However, many aspects of perception seem constant across cultures.*
- *Visual deprivation studies, manipulation of visual input, and studies of restored vision have shown that the normal biological development of the perceptual system depends on certain sensory experiences at early periods of development.*

Some Final Reflections

Suppose someone were to be born cut off not only from sight and sound, as Helen Keller was, but from all internal and external sensory stimulation. What would that person's conscious life be like? With the brain deprived of all sensory input from world and body, what mental processes could exist? What knowledge could accrue? What memories could form? Would the brain itself atrophy as it was deprived of the sensory input needed for neuronal development and synaptic network formation?

As far as we know, such a scenario has never occurred. However, imagining such a condition does bring home the vital role our sensory and perceptual systems play in being a functioning organism. Leonardo da Vinci was indeed correct when he proclaimed, "All knowledge has its origin in our perceptions." Nature has given us specialized sensors that allow the brain to convert the many kinds of energy into the common language of nerve impulses through the process of transduction. In this chapter, you've learned how light and sound energy, pressure and temperature, chemical molecules, muscle movements, and other kinds of stimulation are detected, processed, and sent to the brain as nerve impulses. Once there, however, the miracles of perception occur as attentional factors, bottom-up and top-down processing, and other brain processes "put together" our perceptual experiences. Attentional factors make our perceptions selective; without them we would be totally overwhelmed by the continuous input we receive from every sense. As the Gestalt psychologists established, principles of perceptual organization are built into our nervous system and are present almost from birth. Thus, an intricate mosaic of biological, environmental, and psychological processes occurs every moment of our conscious life.

These processes are sculpted in part by the adaptive demands of human living. We have different sensory capabilities than a mole does, but we'd be in real trouble if we suddenly had to live a mole's existence in that animal's environment. As we've seen in the case of perceptual development, our marvelous innate mechanisms are not enough to ensure that the sensory and perceptual apparatus develops as it should. We also need specific kinds of environmental input at developmentally important periods early in life. On a broader level, cultural learning experiences and the specific environments humans grow up in help determine how they perceive their world. Perceptions (including illusions) that occur universally within some cultures do not occur in others. Thus, nature and nurture combine in important ways to ensure our adaptive success in interacting with our world.

Sensation and perception are the basis for our existence as sentient, conscious creatures. In the next chapter, we explore in greater detail the varieties of consciousness. As we do so, reflect back occasionally on what you've learned in this chapter and ask yourself what sensory and perceptual building blocks underlie such phenomena as sleep and wakefulness, drug- and hypnotically produced alterations in conscious experience, and other aspects of our conscious life.

KEY TERMS AND CONCEPTS

Each term has been boldfaced and defined in the chapter on the page indicated in parentheses.

absolute threshold (p. 111)
amplitude (p. 124)
basilar membrane (p. 124)
binocular depth cues (p. 141)
binocular disparity (p. 142)
bottom-up processing (p. 134)
cochlea (p. 124)
conduction deafness (p. 127)
cones (p. 117)
convergence (p. 142)
critical periods (p. 149)
dark adaptation (p. 118)
decibel (dB; p. 124)
decision criterion (p. 111)
difference threshold (p. 113)
dual-process theory (p. 121)
feature detectors (p. 123)
figure-ground relations (p. 137)
fovea (p. 117)
frequency (p. 124)
frequency theory of pitch perception (p. 125)
Gestalt laws of perceptual organization (p. 137)
gustation (p. 128)
Hering's opponent-process theory (p. 120)
hertz (Hz; p. 124)
illusion (p. 143)
kinesthesis (p. 131)
lens (p. 116)
menstrual synchrony (p. 129)
monocular depth cues (p. 141)
nerve deafness (p. 127)
olfaction (p. 128)
olfactory bulb (p. 129)
optic nerve (p. 117)
organ of Corti (p. 124)
perception (p. 110)
perceptual constancies (p. 139)
perceptual schema (p. 138)
perceptual set (p. 139)
pheromones (p. 129)
photopigments (p. 118)
place theory of pitch perception (p. 125)
psychophysics (p. 110)
retina (p. 116)
rods (p. 117)
sensation (p. 110)
sensory adaptation (p. 114)
sensory prosthetic devices (p. 131)
signal detection theory (p. 111)
stroboscopic movement (p. 143)
subliminal stimulus (p. 112)
synesthesia (p. 109)
taste buds (p. 128)
top-down processing (p. 134)
transduction (p. 115)
vestibular sense (p. 131)
visual acuity (p. 117)
Weber's law (p. 113)
Young-Helmholtz trichromatic theory (p. 119)

What Do You Think?

NAVIGATING IN THE FOG: PROFESSOR MAYER'S TOPOPHONE p. 127

The device shown in Figure 4.20 made use of two principles of sound localization. First, because the two ear receptors were much larger than human ears, they could capture more sound waves and funnel them to the sailor's ears. Second, the wide spacing between the two receptors increased the time difference between the sound's arrival at the two human ears, thus increasing directional sensitivity. ■

WHY DOES THAT RISING MOON LOOK SO BIG? p. 140

To begin with, let's emphasize the obvious: The moon is *not* actually larger when it's on the horizon. Photographs show that the size of the image cast on the retina is exactly the same in both cases. So what psychologists call the *moon illusion* must be created by our perceptual system. Though not completely understood, the illusion seems to be a false perception caused by cues that ordinarily contribute to maintaining size constancy. The chief suspect is apparent distance, which figures importantly in our size judgments. One theory holds that the moon looks bigger as it's rising over the horizon because we use objects in our field of vision, such as trees, buildings, and landscape features to estimate its distance. Experiments have shown that objects look farther away when viewed through "filled" spaces than they do when viewed through "empty" spaces (such as the sky overhead). Filled space can make objects look as much as 2.5 to 4 times farther away. According to the theory, the perceptual system basically says, "If the size of the retinal image is the same but it's farther away, then it must be bigger."

This explanation can't be the whole story, however, because some people perceive the moon on the horizon as being *closer*, rather than farther away. If something the same size seems closer, it will look larger even though it isn't. It may be that there are individual differences in the size judgment processes that cause the illusion, so that no single explanation applies to everybody. ■

EXPLAIN THIS STRIKING ILLUSION p. 145

To analyze your experience, it is important to understand that both the "tent" and the "corner" cast identical images on your retina. After perceiving the tent for a while, your brain shifted to the second perceptual hypothesis, as it did in response to the Necker cube shown in Figure 4.37. When the object looked like a tent, all the depth information was consistent with that perception. But when you began to see it as a corner and then moved your head slowly back and forth, the object seemed to twist and turn as if it were made of rubber. This occurred because when you moved, the image of the near point of the fold moved across your retina faster than the image of the far point. This is the normal pattern of stimulation for points at different depths and is known as *motion parallax*. Thus, when you were seeing a tent, the monocular cue of motion parallax was consistent with the shape of the object. But when the object was later seen as standing upright, all the points along the fold appeared to be the same distance away, yet they were moving at different rates of speed! The only way your brain could maintain its "corner" perception in the face of the motion parallax cues was to see the object as twisting and turning. Again, as in other illusions, forcing all of the sensory data to fit the perceptual hypothesis produced an unusual experience. ■

5

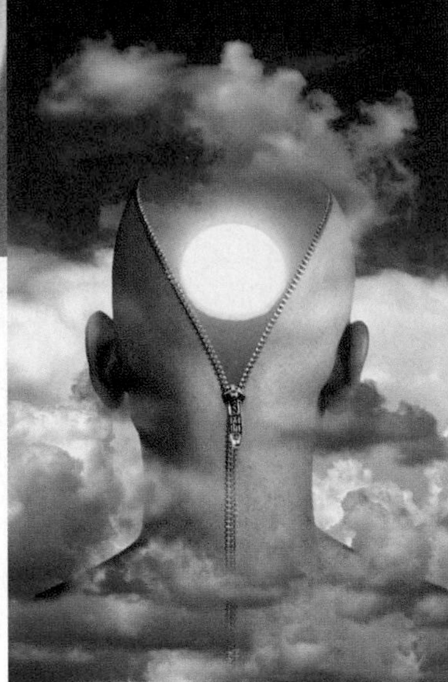

STATES OF CONSCIOUSNESS

CHAPTER OUTLINE

Our normal waking consciousness is but one special type of consciousness, whilst all about it, parted from it by the filmiest of screens, there lie potential forms of consciousness entirely different.

—William James

One autumn afternoon in 1943, Swiss chemist Albert Hofmann became unable to concentrate and noticed that his laboratory assistants were changing shape. He went home to bed and experienced vivid dreams with intense colors. Back at the laboratory the next day, Hofmann concluded that a chemical he synthesized had been absorbed through his skin. Curious, he put a tiny bit on his tongue and soon felt like he was splitting into two people. Hofmann's alarmed assistants took him home, where his strange experiences continued:

> *Everything in the room spun around and the familiar objects and pieces of furniture assumed grotesque, mostly threatening forms. . . . The neighbor woman who brought me milk . . . was no longer Mrs. R., but rather a malevolent insidious witch with a colored mask. Even worse . . . were the alterations that I perceived in myself, in my inner being. . . . A demon had invaded me and had taken possession of my body, mind and soul. (Hofmann, 1980, p. 58)*

So it was that Albert Hofmann accidentally discovered the striking and potentially disturbing alterations in consciousness that can be produced by a dose of lysergic acid diethylamide (LSD) no larger than the tip of a pin.

■■■

Three unrelated people, whom we'll call Sondra, Jason, and Ellen, sought treatment for an unusual problem that had begun in their early to mid-20s: eating while asleep. Now in their 40s, they would rise from bed several times each night and sleepwalk to the kitchen. Sondra would

> *consume cat food or salt sandwiches, buttered cigarettes and odd concoctions prepared in a blender. . . . She frequently binged on large quantities of peanut butter, butter, salt and sugar. . . . Once she awakened while struggling to open a bottle of ammonia cleaning fluid, which she was prepared to drink on account of being thirsty. (Schenck et al., 1991, p. 430)*

During sleepwalking episodes Jason and Ellen also would consume odd foods (such as raw bacon), and sometimes Jason would converse coherently with his wife. But, upon awakening, neither Jason nor Ellen would remember their experiences. Containers, packages, and other strewn evidence of fully or half-eaten food, however, made it clear that something was wrong.

After being evaluated by sleep disorder specialists, Sondra was successfully treated with ongoing medication and Jason was referred back to his primary physician. Neither drugs nor psychotherapy ended Ellen's sleepeating, so a new plan was tried: locking the kitchen door before turning in, putting the key in a hard-to-retrieve location, and placing crackers and a pitcher of water by the bed. Usually, when Ellen awakens in the morning, the crackers and water are gone, and she has no memory of having consumed them (Whyte & Kavey, 1990).

Hofmann's drug-induced experiences and Sondra, Jason, and Ellen's sleepeating involve clear departures from the normal state of active, waking human consciousness. Yet these events contain features that are not as far removed from our daily existence as we might think. All of us drift through changing states of consciousness. While asleep, we may experience vivid images that rival Hofmann's hallucinations, and our dreams may be as emotionally charged as his drug-induced perceptions.

We also experience divisions of awareness—divisions in which we have no conscious memory of behaviors that seem to occur automatically. Few of us eat while asleep, but consider this: Why don't you fall out of bed at night? You are not consciously aware of major postural shifts when you are sound asleep, yet a part of you somehow knows where the edge of the bed is. Similarly, have you ever spaced out while driving, because you were deeply engrossed in thought? Suddenly you snap out of it, with no memory of the miles you've just driven. While you were consciously focused inward, some part of you kept track of the road and controlled your responses at the wheel.

▶ 1. Describe basic characteristics of consciousness. How are states of consciousness measured?

Philosopher David Chalmers (1995) notes that consciousness "is at once the most familiar thing in the world and the most mysterious." Its mysteries span normal waking states to sleep and dreams, drug-induced experiences, and beyond (Figure 5.1). When psychology was founded in the late 1800s, its "Great Project" was to unravel the puzzles of consciousness (Natsoulas, 1999). This interest waned during behaviorism's mid-20th century dominance, but resurgence of the cognitive and biological perspectives has led us to rethink long-standing conceptions about the mind.

THE PUZZLE OF CONSCIOUSNESS

What is consciousness, and how does it arise? In psychology, **consciousness** *is often defined as our moment-to-moment awareness of ourselves and our environment.* Among its characteristics, consciousness is

- *subjective and private.* Other people cannot directly know what reality is for you, nor can you enter directly into their experience.
- *dynamic (ever changing).* We drift in and out of various states throughout each day. Moreover, though the stimuli of which we are aware constantly change, we typically experience consciousness as a continuously

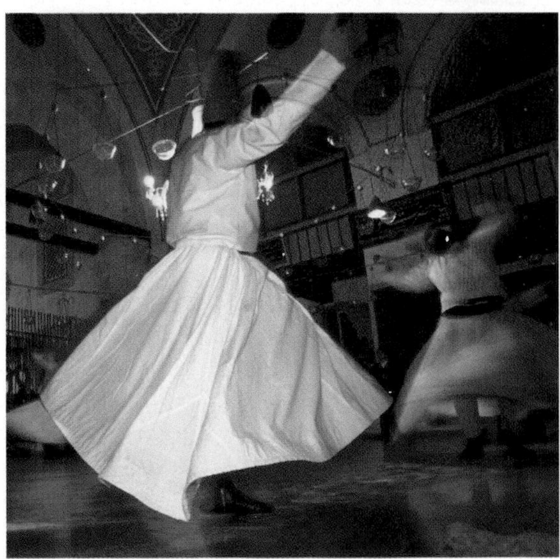

FIGURE 5.1

(left) During a religious ceremony in Istanbul, Turkey, whirling dervishes, members of a Sufi order, perform a spinning dance—a prayer in motion—that induces an altered state of consciousness. The extended right palm, facing upward, is believed to receive the power of God, which then passes through the body, leaves through the downward facing left palm, and enters the earth. (right) For Buddhists, meditation produces an inner peace that facilitates insight and the search for enlightenment. They believe that meditation (and, in some Buddhist schools, rhythmic chanting) opens the path to different dimensions of consciousness and reality.

FIGURE 5.2

Gordon Gallup (1970) exposed 4 chimps to a mirror. By Day 3 they used it to inspect hard-to-see parts of their own bodies and began making odd faces at themselves in the mirror. To further test whether the chimps knew the mirror image was their own reflection, Gordon anesthetized them and put a red mark on their faces. Later, with no mirror, the chimps rarely touched the red mark. But upon seeing it when a mirror was introduced, they touched the red spot almost 30 times in 30 minutes, suggesting that the chimps had some self-awareness. Using a similar test in which a red mark was placed on the tip of infants' noses, researchers found that infants begin to recognize themselves in a mirror around 18 months of age.

flowing "stream" of mental activity, rather than as disjointed perceptions and thoughts (James, 1890/1950).

- *self-reflective and central to our sense of self.* The mind is aware of its own consciousness. Thus no matter what your awareness is focused on—a lovely sunset or an itch on your back—you can reflect on the fact that *you* are the one who is conscious of it.

Finally, consciousness is *intimately connected with the process of selective attention*, discussed in Chapter 4. William James noted that "the mind is at every stage a theatre of simultaneous possibilities. Consciousness consists in . . . the selection of some, and the suppression of the rest by the . . . agency of Attention" (1879, p. 13). Selective attention focuses conscious awareness on some stimuli to the exclusion of others. If the mind is a "theatre" of mental activity, then consciousness reflects whatever is illuminated at the moment—the "bright spot on the stage"—and selective attention is the "spotlight" or mechanism behind it (Baars, 1997).

Measuring States of Consciousness

Scientists who study consciousness must operationally define private inner states in terms of measurable responses. *Self-reports*, in which people describe their inner experiences, offer the most direct insight into a person's subjective experiences, but they are not always verifiable. Hofmann's description of his LSD-induced thoughts and hallucinations represents a self-report, as would your responses to a questionnaire about your current mood state.

Physiological measures establish the correspondence between bodily processes and mental states. For example, EEG recordings of brain activity help identify lighter versus deeper stages of sleep during the night. Physiological measures are objective but cannot tell us what a person is experiencing subjectively. *Behavioral measures* record, among other things, performance on special tasks, such as the *rouge test* (Figure 5.2). Behavioral measures are objective, but they still require us to infer the person's state of mind.

Levels of Consciousness

▶ 2. Contrast psychodynamic versus cognitive views of the mind, and controlled versus automatic processing.

A century ago Sigmund Freud (1900/1953) proposed that the human mind consists of three levels of awareness. The *conscious* mind contains thoughts and perceptions of which we are currently aware. *Preconscious* mental events are outside current awareness but can easily be recalled under certain conditions. For instance, you may not have thought about a friend for years, but when someone mentions your friend's name, you become aware of pleasant memories. *Unconscious events* cannot be brought into conscious awareness under ordinary circumstances. Some unconscious content—such as unacceptable sexual and aggressive urges, traumatic memories, and threatening emotional conflicts—is kept out of conscious awareness because it would arouse anxiety, guilt, or other negative emotions.

Behaviorists roundly criticized Freud's theory. After all, they sought to explain behavior without invoking conscious mental processes, much less unconscious ones. Cognitive psychologists and many contemporary psychodynamic psychologists also take issue with specific aspects of Freud's theory. As psychodynamic psychologist Drew Westen (1998) notes, "Many aspects of Freudian theory are indeed out of date, and they should be. Freud died in 1939, and he has been slow to undertake further revisions" (p. 333).

On a broad level, however, research supports Freud's general premise: Nonconscious processes influence behavior (Todorov & Bargh, 2002). Studies of *placebo effects* (see Chapter 2), *split-brain patients* (see Chapter 3), *subliminal perception* (see Chapter 4), and phenomena discussed in upcoming chapters all indicate that mental processes can affect our behavior without conscious awareness.

The Cognitive Unconscious

Cognitive psychologists reject the notion of an unconscious mind driven by instinctive urges and repressed conflicts. Rather, they view conscious and unconscious mental life as complementary forms of information processing that work in harmony (Reisberg, 1997). To illustrate, consider how we perform everyday tasks.

Many activities, such as planning a vacation or studying, involve **controlled (effortful) processing**, *the conscious use of attention and effort*. Other activities involve **automatic processing** *and can be performed with little or no conscious awareness or effort*. Automatic processing occurs most often when we carry out routine actions or well-learned tasks, particularly under constant or familiar circumstances (Ouellette & Wood, 1998). The cases of Sondra, Jason, and Mark—and some of the bizarre foods that they ate—illustrate how the behavior of sleepwalkers often is automated and not monitored consciously. In everyday life, learning to write, drive, shoot a basketball through a hoop, and play a musical instrument all involve controlled processing; you have to pay a lot of attention to what you are doing as you learn. With practice, though, performance becomes more automatic and certain brain areas involved in conscious thought become less active (Jansma et al., 2001). Through years of practice, athletes and musicians program themselves to execute highly complex skills with a minimum of conscious thought.

Automatic processing, however, has a key disadvantage because it can reduce our chances of finding new ways to approach problems (Langer, 1989). Controlled processing requires effort and is therefore slower than automatic processing, but it is more flexible and open to change. Still, automatic processing offers speed and economy of effort, and many well learned behaviors seem performed best when our mind is on autopilot, with controlled processing taking a backseat. The famous baseball player Yogi Berra captured this idea in his classic statement, "You can't think and hit at the same time." At tasks ranging from golf putting to playing video games, experiments suggest that too much self-focused thinking can hurt task performance and cause people to "choke" under pressure (Beilcock & Carr, 2001).

Automatic processing also facilitates **divided attention,** *the capacity to attend to and perform more than one activity at the same time*. We can talk while we walk, type as we read, munch popcorn while watching a movie, and so on. Yet divided attention has limits and is more difficult when two tasks require similar mental resources. For example, we cannot fully attend to separate messages delivered simultaneously through two earphones.

Although divided attention is wonderfully adaptive most of the time, it can have serious negative consequences in certain situations. For example, having a phone conversation—even with a hands-free phone—impairs the ability to simultaneously perform other tasks that require careful monitoring and attention (Strayer & Johnston, 2001). Some studies have found that collision rates triple or quadruple when people talk on cell phones while driving; they are more likely to speed, drive on the wrong side of the road, run off the road, hit fixed objects, and overturn their cars (Redelmeier & Tibshirani, 1997). Driving-simulator and actual on-road experiments also indicate that using a cell phone slows drivers' reaction times to traffic hazards (Lamble et al., 1999).

The Emotional Unconscious

Modern psychodynamic psychologists emphasize that beyond nonconscious information processing, emotional and motivational processes also operate unconsciously and influence behavior (Westen, 1998). At times, these hidden processes can cause us to feel and act in ways that mystify us. Consider the case of a 47-year-old amnesia patient who could not remember new

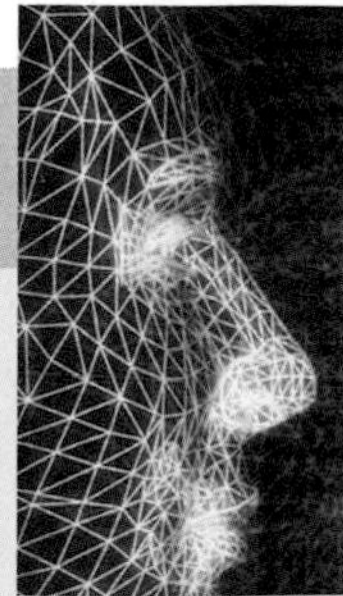

APPLYING PSYCHOLOGICAL SCIENCE

OUTSMARTING JET LAG, NIGHT-WORK DISRUPTIONS, AND WINTER DEPRESSION

Circadian research provides important insights on the nature of consciousness. It also offers several treatments for circadian disruptions affecting millions of people.

Controlling Exposure to Light

Reducing Jet Lag

When you fly east across time zones, your body's internal clock falls behind the time at your destination. Exposure to outdoor light in the morning—and avoiding light late in the day—moves the circadian clock forward and helps it catch up to local time. (Think of morning light as jump-starting your circadian clock at a time when you would be asleep back home.) Flying west, your body clock moves ahead of local time. So to reduce jet lag, you want to delay your circadian cycle by avoiding bright light in the morning and exposing yourself to light in the afternoon or early evening. These are general rules, but the specific timing and length of exposure to light depend on the number of time zones crossed (Houpt et al., 1996). For jet travelers, spending time outside (even on cloudy days) is the easiest way to get the needed exposure to light.

Adjusting to Night Work

Many night employees work indoors, where the artificial light is too weak to shift their circadian rhythms toward a night-day schedule. Circadian adjustment can be increased by keeping the bedroom dark and quiet to foster daytime sleep, and by maintaining a schedule of daytime sleep even during days off (Boulos, 1998). Because getting daytime sleep can be difficult for a number of reasons, day sleepers are advised to install light-blocking window shades, unplug the phone, post a "do not disturb" sign, use earplugs, and select a bedroom as far away as possible from the waking activities of roommates or family members.

Treating SAD

Many experts believe that *phototherapy*, which involves properly timed exposure to specially prescribed bright artificial lights, is the best treatment for SAD and milder "winter blues" (Leppämäki et al., 2002). Several hours of daily phototherapy, especially in the early morning, can shift circadian rhythms by as much as 2 to 3 hours per day (Terman et al., 2001). In *dawn simulation,* artificial lights gradually intensify to normal light levels over the course of 1 to 2 hours in the early morning, which helps reset the circadian clock to an earlier time. The fact that phototherapy effectively treats SAD is the strongest evidence that SAD is triggered by winter's lack of sunlight rather than by its colder temperatures (Figure 5.9).

FIGURE 5.9

For many people, the depression from SAD can be reduced by daily exposure to bright fluorescent lights.

Melatonin Treatment: Uses and Cautions

The hormone melatonin is a key player in the brain's circadian clock. Melatonin also exists in pill or capsule form; it is a prescription drug in some countries and is unavailable to the public in others. In the United States it is a nonprescription dietary supplement. Depending on when it is taken, oral melatonin can shift some circadian cycles forward or backward by as much as 30 to 60 minutes per day of use. Melatonin treatment has been used with some success to decrease jet lag, help employees adapt to night-shift work, and alleviate SAD (Arendt et al., 1997).

But there is reason for caution, as tablet doses are often 3 to 5 milligrams, producing melatonin levels in the blood that are over 10 times the normal concentration (Sack et al., 1997). In contrast, doses of 0.1 to 0.5 milligrams produce blood concentrations more typical of normal levels and are often sufficient to produce circadian shifts. Melatonin use is supervised when it is used in research, but individuals who self-administer it may do themselves more harm than good. Taking melatonin at the wrong time can backfire and make circadian adjustments more difficult. Daytime use may decrease alertness (Graw et al., 2001). Some experts are also concerned that millions of people

Continued

are using melatonin tablets as a nightly sleeping aid, even though possible side effects of long-term use have not been adequately studied.

Regulating Activity Schedules

Some studies suggest that properly timed physical exercise can help shift the circadian clock (Mistlberger et al., 2000). For example, compared to merely staying up later than normal, exercising at the time when you would normally go to bed may help push back your circadian clock, as you would want to do when flying from east to west (Baehr, 2001). To reduce jet lag, you can also begin synchronizing your biological clock to the new time zone in advance. To do so, adjust your sleep and eating schedules by 30 minutes to 1 hour per day, starting several days before you leave. Schedule management can also apply to night-shift work. For workers on rotating shifts, circadian disruptions can be reduced significantly by a *forward-rotating shift schedule*—moving from day to evening to night shift—rather than a schedule that rotates backward from day to night to evening shift (Knauth, 1996). The forward schedule takes advantage of our free-running circadian rhythms. When work shifts change, it is easier to extend the waking day than to compress it.

▶ 6. Describe ways to minimize circadian disruptions involved in jet lag, night shiftwork, and SAD.

IN REVIEW

- *Circadian rhythms are 24-hour biological cycles that help regulate many bodily processes and influence our alertness and readiness for sleep. The suprachiasmatic nuclei (SCN) are the brain's master circadian clock.*
- *Our free-running circadian rhythm is roughly 24.2 hours, but environmental factors such as the day-night cycle help reset our daily clocks to a 24-hour schedule.*
- *Circadian rhythms influence our tendency to be either a morning person or a night person, but cultural factors may also play a role.*
- *In general, our alertness is lowest in the early morning hours between 12 A.M. and 6 A.M. Job performance errors, major industrial accidents, and fatal and nonfatal auto accidents peak during these hours.*
- *Jet lag, night-shift work, and seasonal affective disorder (SAD) involve environmental disruptions of circadian rhythms. Treatments for circadian disruptions include controlling one's exposure to light, taking oral melatonin, and regulating one's daily activity schedule.*

SLEEP AND DREAMING

Sweet, refreshing, mysterious sleep. We spend about one third of our lives in this altered state, relinquishing conscious control of our thoughts and actions, entering a world of dreams, and remembering so little of it upon awakening. Yet sleep, like other behaviors, can be studied scientifically at biological, psychological, and environmental levels.

▶ 7. What brain wave patterns distinguish the stages of sleep? Describe the characteristics of REM sleep.

Stages of Sleep

Circadian rhythms promote a readiness for sleep by decreasing alertness, but they do not regulate sleep directly. Instead, roughly every 90 minutes while asleep, we cycle through different stages in which brain activity and other physiological responses change in a generally predictable way (Kleitman, 1963; Dement, 1974).

As Figure 5.10 shows, sleep research is often carried out in specially equipped laboratories where sleepers' physiological responses are recorded. EEG recordings of your brain's electrical activity would show a pattern of **beta waves** *when you are awake and alert*. Beta waves have a high frequency (of about 15 to 30 cycles per second, or cps) but a low amplitude, or height (Figure 5.11). As you close your eyes, *feeling relaxed and drowsy, your brain waves slow down and* **alpha waves** *occur at about 8 to 12 cps.*

Stage 1 Through Stage 4

As sleep begins, your brain-wave pattern becomes more irregular, and slower *theta waves* (3.5 to 7.5 cps) increase. You are now in *stage 1*, a form of light sleep from which you can easily be awakened. You'll probably spend just a few minutes in stage 1, during which time some people experience dreams, vivid images, and sudden body jerks. As sleep becomes deeper, *sleep spindles*—periodic 1- to 2-second bursts of rapid brain-wave activity (12 to 15 cps)—begin to appear. Sleep spindles indicate that you are now in *stage 2*

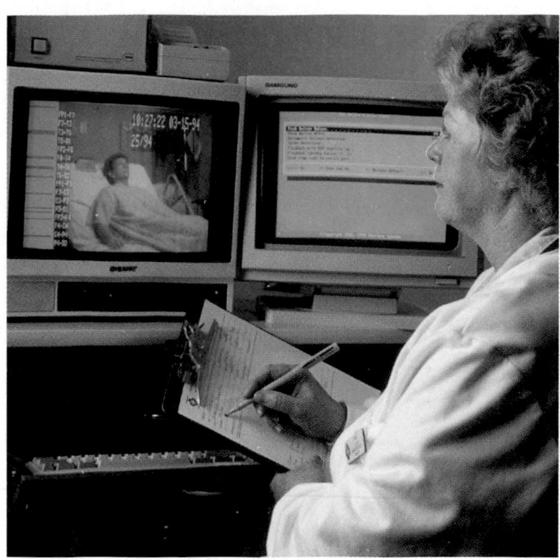

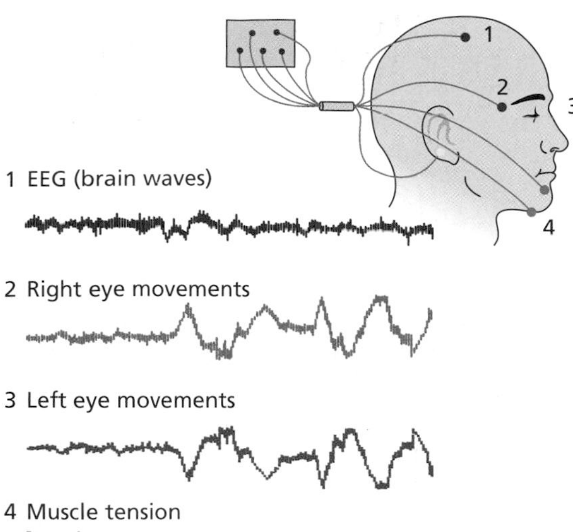

FIGURE 5.10

In a modern sleep laboratory, people sleep while their physiological responses are monitored. Electrodes attached to the scalp record the person's EEG brain-wave patterns. Electrodes attached beside the eyes record eye movements during sleep. Electrodes attached to the jaw record muscle tension. A neutral electrode is attached to the ear.

(see Figure 5.11). Your muscles are more relaxed, breathing and heart rate are slower, dreams may occur, and you are harder to awaken.

Sleep deepens as you move into *stage 3*, marked by the regular appearance of *very slow (0.5 to 2 cps) and large* **delta waves.** As time passes, they occur more often, and when delta waves dominate the EEG pattern, you have reached *stage 4*. Together, *stage 3 and stage 4 are often referred to as* **slow-wave sleep.** Your body is relaxed, activity in various parts of your brain has decreased, you are hard to awaken, and you may have dreams. After 20 to 30 minutes of stage-4 sleep, your EEG pattern changes as you go back through stages 3 and 2, spending a little time in each. Overall, within 60 to 90 minutes of going to sleep, you have completed a cycle of stages: 1-2-3-4-3-2. At this point, a remarkably different sleep stage ensues.

REM Sleep

In 1953, Eugene Aserinsky and Nathaniel Kleitman of the University of Chicago struck scientific gold when they identified a unique sleep stage called **REM sleep,** *characterized by rapid eye movements (REM), high arousal, and frequent dreaming*. They found that every half minute or so during REM sleep, bursts of muscular activity caused sleepers' eyeballs to vigorously move back and forth beneath their closed eyelids. Moreover, sleepers awakened from REM periods—including people who swore they "never had dreams"—almost always reported a dream. At last, scientists could examine dreaming more closely. Wait for REM, awaken the sleeper, and catch a dream.

During REM sleep, physiological arousal may increase to daytime levels. The heart rate quickens, breathing becomes more rapid and irregular, and brain-wave activity resembles that of active wakefulness. Regardless of dream content (most dreams are not sexual), men have penile erections and women experience vaginal lubrication. The brain also sends signals making it more difficult for voluntary muscles to contract. As a result, muscles in the arms, legs, and torso lose tone

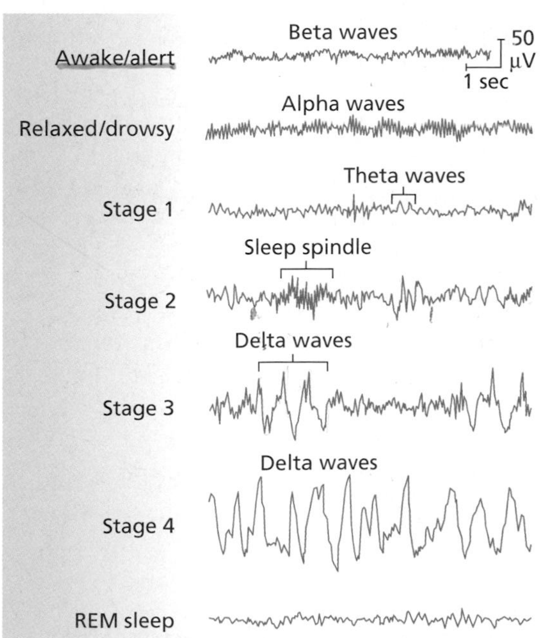

FIGURE 5.11

Changing patterns of brain-wave activity help define the various stages of sleep. Note that brain waves become slower and larger as sleep deepens and that the general pattern of REM sleep is similar to that of stage 1. Source: Based on Hauri, 1982.

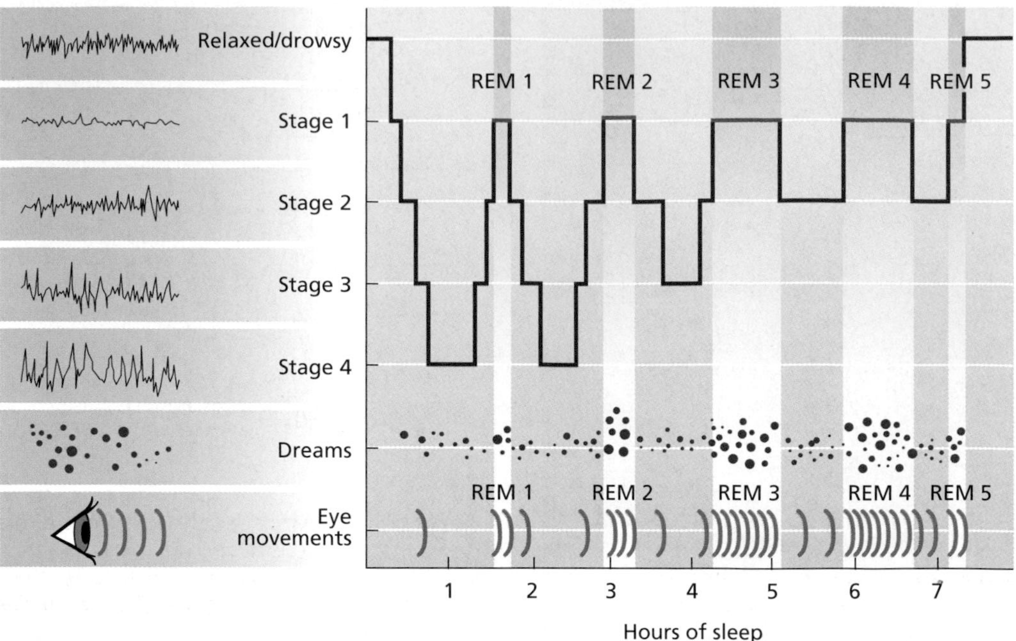

FIGURE 5.12

This graph shows a record of a night's sleep. The REM stages are shown in blue. People typically average four to five REM periods during the night, and these tend to become longer as the night wears on.

and become relaxed. These muscles may twitch, but in effect you are "paralyzed," unable to move. This state is called *REM sleep paralysis*, and because of it REM sleep is sometimes called *paradoxical sleep:* Your body is highly aroused, yet it looks like you are sleeping peacefully because there is so little movement.

Although each cycle through the sleep stages takes an average of about 90 minutes, Figure 5.12 shows that as the hours pass, stage 4 and stage 3 drop out and REM periods become longer.

For more on sleep stages, see Interactive Segment 5.1.

Getting a Night's Sleep: From Brain to Culture

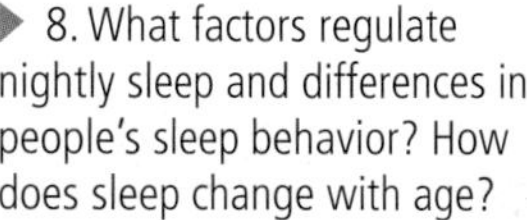

▶ 8. What factors regulate nightly sleep and differences in people's sleep behavior? How does sleep change with age?

The brain steers our passage through sleep, but it has no single "sleep center." Different aspects of sleep, such as falling asleep, REM sleep, and slow-wave sleep are controlled by the interaction of various brain mechanisms. Moreover, falling asleep is not just a matter of "turning off" brain systems that keep us awake. There are separate systems that "turn on" and actively promote sleep.

Certain areas at the base of the forebrain (called the *basal forebrain*) and within the brain stem are particularly important in regulating our falling asleep. Different brain stem areas—including where the reticular formation passes through the pons (called the *pontine reticular formation*)—play a key role in regulating REM sleep (Hobson et al., 2000). This region contains neurons that periodically activate other brain systems, each of which controls a different aspect of REM sleep, such as eye movement, muscular paralysis, and genital arousal.

Brain images taken during REM sleep also reveal intense activity in limbic system structures, such as the amygdala, that regulate emotions—a pattern that may reflect the emotional nature of many REM-sleep dreams (Figure 5.13). The motor cortex is active, but its signals for movement are blocked and don't reach our limbs, and association areas near the primary visual cortex are active, which may reflect the processing of visual dream images. At the same time, there seems to be decreased activity in certain regions of the prefrontal cortex involved in high-level mental functions, such as planning and logical analysis. This, say some researchers, indicates that our sleeping mind does not monitor and organize its mental activity as carefully as our awake mind does, enabling dreams to be illogical and bizarre (Hobson et al., 2000).

Environmental factors, such as changes in season, also affect sleep. In fall and winter, most people sleep about 15 to 60 minutes longer per night (Campbell, 1993). Shift work, stress at work and school, and nighttime noise can decrease sleep quality (Bronzaft et al., 1998).

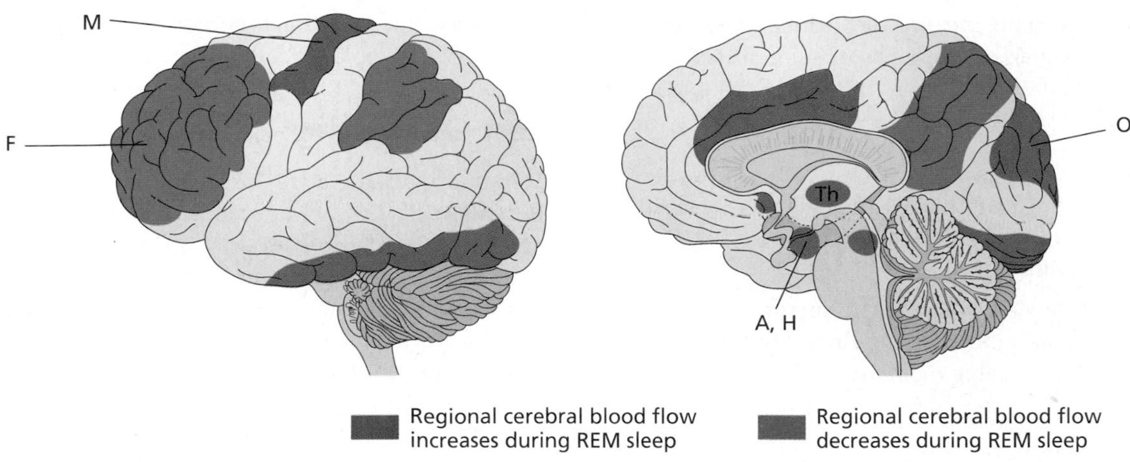

FIGURE 5.13

The REM-sleep brain. As compared to the waking brain, during REM sleep several brain regions display markedly increased (maroon) or decreased (blue) activity. Note the decreased activation in certain prefrontal lobe regions (area F) and increased activity in parts of the amygdala and hypothalamus (areas A, H), thalamus (area Th), and primary motor cortex (M), as well as association areas near the primary visual cortex in the occipital lobe (area O). SOURCE: S. Schwartz and P. Maquet, 2002.

FIGURE 5.15

The percentage of sleep time in REM and non-REM (NREM) sleep changes with age. Average daily sleep time decreases over the life span, and most of the decrease in NREM sleep is due to decreasing delta sleep (stages 3 and 4). REM sleep decreases throughout childhood and then is relatively stable through adulthood. SOURCE: Adapted from Roffwarg, H. P., Muzio, J. N., & Dement, W. C. (1966). Ontogenic development of human dream-sleep cycle. *Science, 152*, 604, figure 1. Copyright © 1966 American Association for the Advancement of Science. Reprinted with permission.

Cultural norms influence several sleep-related behaviors. Do you sleep on a cushioned bed? In some cultures people sleep on floors or hard wood beds or suspended in hammocks (Figure 5.14). *Co-sleeping*, in which children sleep with their parents in the same bed or room, is not common in the United States, as children's sleeping alone is seen as a way to foster independence (and maintain parents' privacy). But in most cultures, co-sleeping is the norm (Ball et al., 2000). In Japan's collectivistic culture, in which interdependence is highly valued, children traditionally slept in their parents' room until they were adolescents, even when separate sleeping space was available (Caudill & Plath, 1966).

How Much Do We Sleep?

The question seems simple enough, as does the answer for many of us: Not enough! In reality, though, the issue is complex. First, Figure 5.15 reveals that there are substantial differences in

FIGURE 5.14

In warmer regions of the Americas, the use of hammocks for sleeping has been common among various indigenous peoples for centuries. This photo shows a Mayan family in the Yucatan, Mexico.

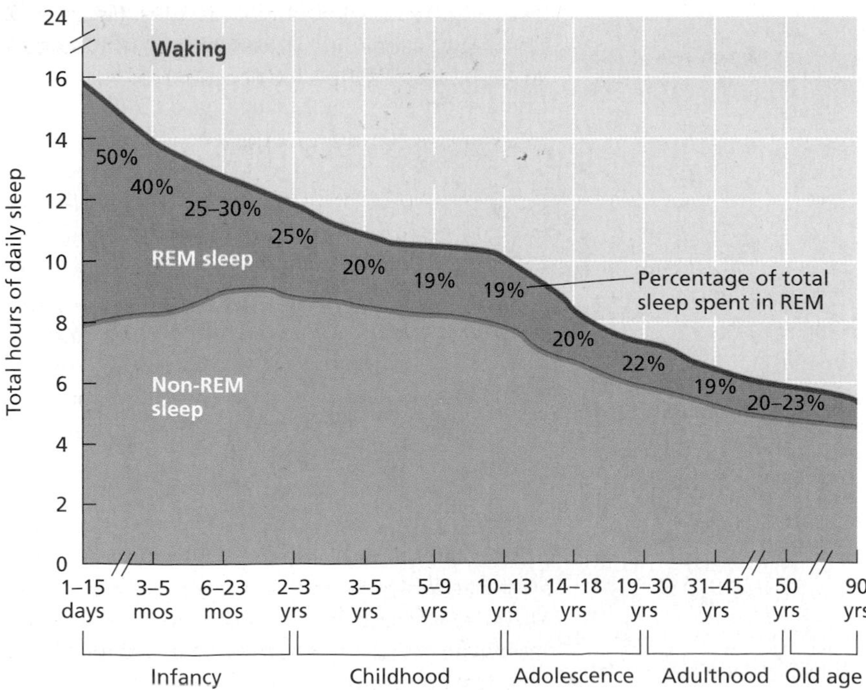

how much people sleep at various ages. Newborn infants average 16 hours of sleep a day, and almost half of their sleep time is in REM. But as we age, three important changes occur:

▶ 9. How do different types of sleep deprivation affect mood and behavior?

- We sleep less. On average, 19- to 30-year-olds average slightly less than 8 hours of sleep a night, and elderly adults average just under 6 hours.
- REM sleep decreases dramatically during infancy and early childhood but remains relatively stable thereafter.
- Time spent in stages 3 and 4 declines. By late adulthood we get relatively little slow-wave sleep.

Second, there are individual differences within each age range. Based on various surveys, Wilse Webb (1992) of the University of Florida estimates that two thirds of young adults sleep between 6.5 and 8.5 hours a night. About 1 percent sleep more than 10 hours a night and 1 percent less than 5.

Sleep surveys describe how much sleep people believe they get, not how much they need. Still, it appears that the old adage, "everyone needs 8 hours of sleep a night," is not true (Monk et al., 2001). Indeed, laboratory studies confirm that a few people function well on very little sleep. Researchers in London examined a healthy, energetic 70-year-old woman who claimed to sleep less than 1 hour a night (Meddis et al., 1973). Over five consecutive nights at the sleep lab, she averaged 67 minutes of sleep a night and showed no ill effects. During another observation period, she stayed awake for 56 hours and recovered by sleeping only 99 minutes the next night. Such extreme short-sleepers, however, are rare.

What accounts for differences in how much we sleep? Part of the answer appears to reside in our genes. Surveys of almost 7,000 pairs of twins in Finland and of almost 4,000 Australian twin pairs reveal that identical twins have more similar sleep length, bedtimes, and sleep patterns than do fraternal twins (Heath et al., 1990). Using selective breeding, researchers have developed some genetic strains of mice that are long- versus short-sleepers, other strains that spend more or less time in REM, and still others that spend more or less time in slow-wave sleep (Xu et al., 2001).

The twin studies indicate that differences in sleep length and sleep patterns are also affected by nongenetic factors. Working day versus night jobs, having low-key versus high-pressure lifestyles, and sleeping in quiet versus noisy environments are among the many factors contributing to the variability in people's sleep.

Sleep Deprivation

Sleep deprivation is a way of life for many college students, and they are not alone. Among American adults, 37 percent report they are so sleepy that it intereferes with their daily activities a few days a month or more (National Sleep Foundation, 2002). June Pilcher and Allen Huffcutt (1996) meta-analyzed 19 studies in which participants underwent either *short-term total sleep deprivation* (up to 45 hours without sleep), *long-term total sleep deprivation* (more than 45 hours without sleep), or *partial deprivation* (being allowed to sleep no more than 5 hours a night for one or more consecutive nights). The researchers measured participants' self-reported mood (e.g., irritability, disorientation) and responses on mental tasks (e.g., logical reasoning, word memory) and physical tasks (e.g., manual dexterity, treadmill walking).

What would you predict? Would all types of deprivation affect behavior, and which behaviors would be affected the most? In fact, all three types of sleep deprivation impaired functioning. The average sleep-deprived person functioned only as well as someone in the bottom 9 percent of non-deprived participants. Overall, mood suffered most, followed by cognitive and then physical performance, although sleep loss significantly impaired *all three* behaviors. On some cognitive tasks, the performance impairments after a night of sleep deprivation are similar to those found in people who have consumed several alcoholic drinks (Williamson et al., 2001).

What about students who pull all-nighters or drastically cut back their sleep, claiming they still perform as well as ever? June Pilcher & Amy Walters (1997) found that college students deprived of one night's sleep performed more poorly on a critical-thinking task than students allowed to sleep—yet they incorrectly perceived that they had performed better. The authors concluded that students underestimate the negative effects of sleep loss on performance.

Most total sleep deprivation studies with humans last less than 5 days, but 17-year-old Randy Gardner set a world record (since broken) of staying awake for 11 days as his project for a 1964 high school science fair in San Diego. Grateful sleep researchers received permission to study him (Gulevich et al., 1966). Contrary to a popular myth that Randy suffered few negative effects, at times during the first few days he became irritable, forgetful, nauseated, and intensely tired. By

Day 5 he had periods of disorientation, distorted thinking, and mild hallucinations. Over the last 4 days he developed finger tremors and slurred speech. Still, in his final day without sleep he beat sleep researcher William Dement 100 consecutive times at a pinball-type game. When Randy finally went to bed, he slept almost 15 hours the first night and returned to his normal amount of sleep within a week. In general, it takes several nights to recover from extended total sleep deprivation, and we do not "make up" all the sleep time that we have lost.

Why Do We Sleep?

Given that we spend almost a third of our lives sleeping, it must serve an important purpose. According to the **restoration model,** *sleep recharges our run-down bodies and allows us to recover from physical and mental fatigue* (Hess, 1965). Sleep deprivation and night-shift work studies strongly support this view, indicating that we need sleep to function at our emotional, mental, and physical best.

If the restoration model is correct, activities that increase daily wear on the body should increase sleep. Evidence is mildly supportive. A study of 18- to 26-year-old ultramarathon runners found that they slept much longer and spent a greater percentage of time in slow-wave sleep on the two nights following their 57-mile run (Shapiro et al., 1981). For the rest of us mere mortals, a meta-analysis of 38 studies found that we tend to sleep longer by only about 10 minutes on days we have exercised (Youngstedt et al., 1997).

What is it that "gets restored" in our bodies while we sleep? Are vital chemicals depleted during the day and replenished at night? Does waking activity produce toxins that are purged during sleep? We don't have precise answers, but many researchers believe that a cellular waste product called *adenosine* may play a role (Mendelson, 2000). Like a car's exhaust emissions, adenosine is produced as cells consume fuel. As adenosine accumulates, it inhibits brain circuits responsible for keeping us awake, thereby signaling the body to slow down because too much cellular fuel has been burned. Adenosine levels decrease as we sleep. Interestingly, caffeine has a molecular structure similar to adenosine's. It fits into adenosine receptor sites but doesn't stimulate them. This blocks the action of adenosine and prevents it from signaling the brain to "slow down," thereby increasing alertness.

Evolutionary/Circadian Sleep Models *emphasize that sleep's main purpose is to increase a species' chances of survival in relation to its environmental demands* (Webb, 1974). Our prehistoric ancestors had little to gain, and much to lose, by being active at night. Hunting, food gathering, and traveling were accomplished more easily and safely during daylight. Leaving the protection of one's shelter at night would have served little purpose other than to become dinner for night-time predators.

Over the course of evolution, each species developed a circadian sleep-wake pattern that was adaptive in terms of its status as predator or prey, its food requirements, and its methods of defense from attack. For small prey animals such as mice and squirrels, which reside in burrows or trees safely away from predators, spending a lot of time asleep is adaptive. For large prey animals such as horses, deer, and zebras, which sleep in relatively exposed environments and whose safety from predators depends on running away, spending a lot of time asleep would be hazardous (Figure 5.16). Sleep may also have evolved as a mechanism for conserving energy. Our body's overall metabolic rate during sleep is about 10 to 25 percent slower than during waking rest (McGinty, 1993). The restoration and evolutionary theories highlight complementary functions of sleep, and both contribute to a two-factor model of why we sleep (Webb, 1994).

▶ 10. Explain the restoration, evolutionary/circadian, and memory consolidation models of sleep.

Do specific sleep stages have special functions? To answer this question, imagine volunteering for a sleep deprivation study in which we will awaken you only when you enter REM sleep; you will be undisturbed through the other sleep stages. In this situation, two things will happen (beyond any unpleasant looks you may give us). First, on successive nights, we will have to awaken you more often, because your brain will be fighting back to get REM sleep (Figure 5.17a). Second, when the study ends, for the first few nights you probably will experience a *REM-rebound effect,* a tendency to increase the amount of REM sleep after being deprived of it (Figure 5.17b). REM-rebound occurs in rats as well as humans (Rechtschaffen et al., 1999).

This suggests that the body needs REM sleep (similar effects are found for slow-wave sleep). But for what purpose? Many theorists believe that the high level of brain activity in REM sleep enhances **memory consolidation,** *the strengthening of neural circuits involved in remembering important information or experiences that we encountered during the day* (Winson, 1990). There have been many experiments on this topic, including brain-imaging studies, but in a nutshell, the evidence is mixed and controversial (Vertes & Eastman, 2000). For

FIGURE 5.16

Average daily hours of sleep for various species.

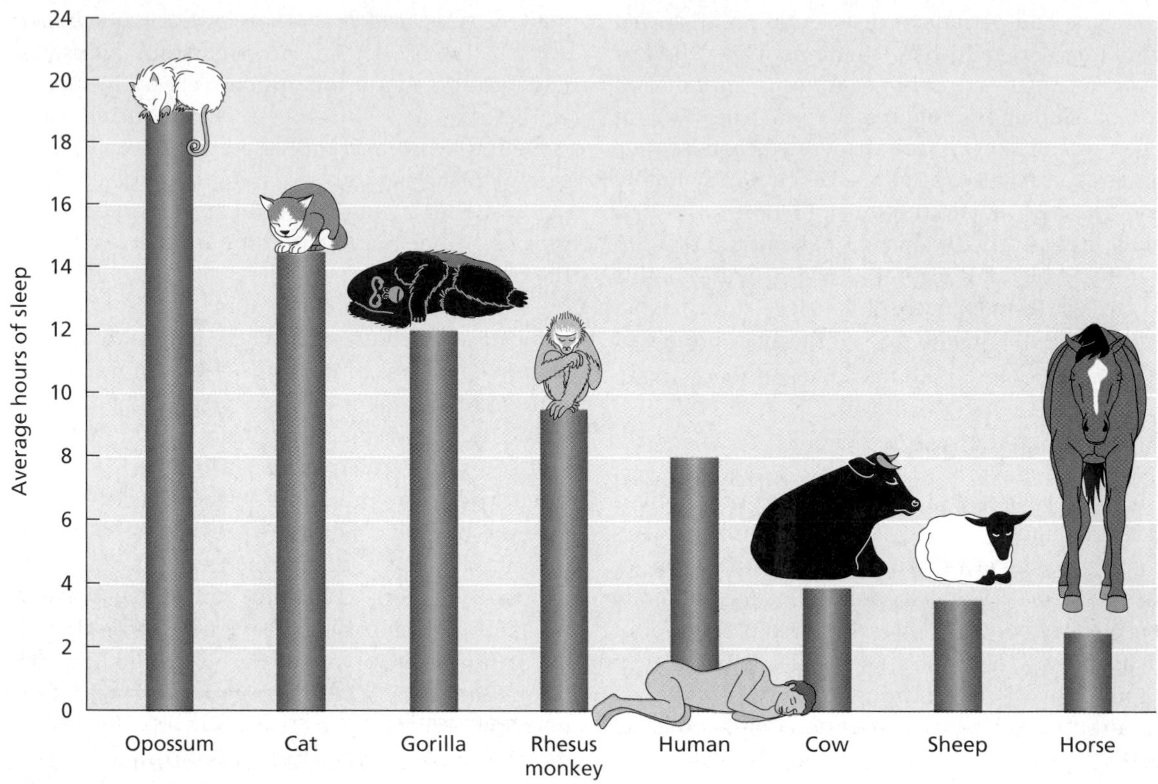

example, the consolidation hypothesis is contradicted by the fact that, although many antidepressant drugs greatly suppress or nearly eliminate REM sleep, patients taking these drugs for long periods of time do not show impaired abilities to remember new information or experiences.

In contrast to the memory consolidation view, some researchers argue that the function of REM sleep is purely biological. The periodic high activation of REM sleep keeps the brain healthy during sleep and offsets the periods of low brain arousal during restful slow-wave sleep (Vertes & Eastman, 2000). At present, the unique functions of REM and other sleep stages are still being debated.

Sleep Disorders

▶ 11. Describe the symptoms, causes, and treatment of major sleep disorders.

As the sleepeating cases of Sondra, Jason, and Ellen illustrate, the processes that regulate sleep are complex and can go wrong in many ways. Almost 75 percent of American adults feel that they have some type of sleep problem (National Sleep Foundation, 2002).

Insomnia

True or False: Someone who falls asleep easily can still have insomnia. The statement is true because **insomnia** *refers to chronic difficulty in falling asleep, staying asleep, or experiencing restful sleep.* If you occasionally have trouble getting a good night's

FIGURE 5.17

(a) In REM-sleep deprivation studies, participants start to go into REM periods more times with each passing night, as the brain tries to get REM sleep. (b) After REM deprivation ends, the sleeper spends more time than usual in REM sleep for a few nights. This is the REM-rebound effect. Source: Adapted from Agnew et al., 1967.

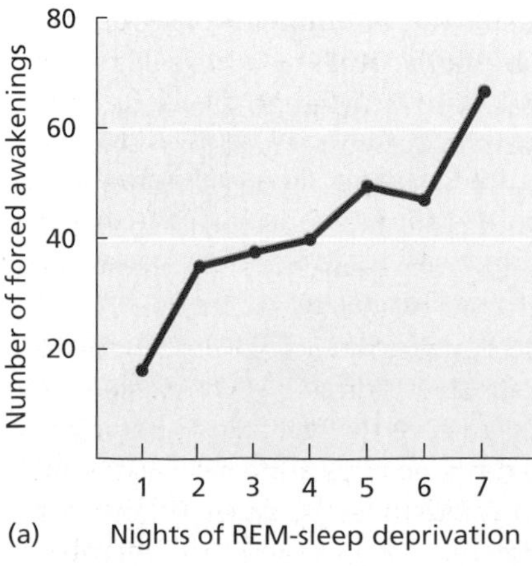

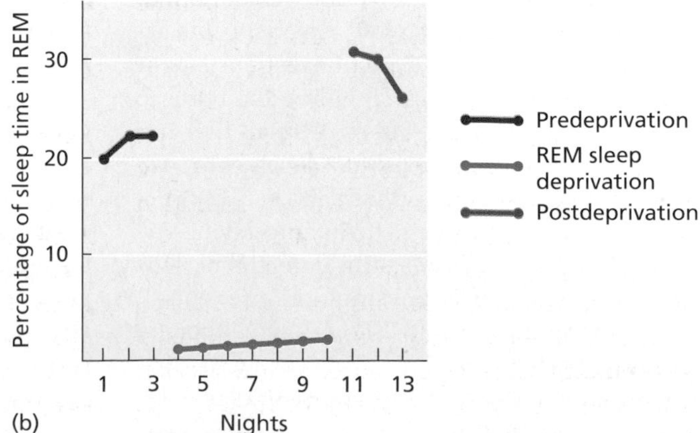

sleep, don't worry. Almost everyone does. People with true insomnia have frequent and persistent sleep troubles.

Insomnia is the most common sleep disorder, experienced by 10 to 40 percent of the population of various countries (Janson et al., 2001). Many people with insomnia overestimate how much sleep they lose and how long it takes them to fall asleep. To some, 20 minutes of lying awake may seem like an hour. Some people display *pseudoinsomnia;* these patients complain of insomnia but sleep normally when examined in the laboratory (McCall & Edinger, 1992).

Some people are genetically predisposed toward insomnia. Moreover, medical conditions, mental disorders such as anxiety and depression, and many drugs can disrupt sleep, as can general worrying, stress at home and work, poor lifestyle habits, and circadian disruptions such as jet lag and night-shift work.

Psychologists have pioneered many nondrug treatments to reduce insomnia and improve sleep quality. One treatment, called *stimulus control,* involves conditioning your body to associate stimuli in your sleep environment (such as your bed) with sleep, rather than with waking activities and sleeplessness (Bootzin, 2002). For example, if you are having sleep difficulties, do not study, watch TV, or snack in your bedroom. Use your bed only for sleeping. If you cannot fall asleep within 10 minutes, get up and leave the bedroom. Do something relaxing until you feel sleepy, then return to bed. Table 5.2 contains more guidelines from sleep experts for reducing insomnia and achieving better sleep.

TABLE 5.2 How to Improve the Quality of Your Sleep.

Sleep experts recommend a variety of procedures to reduce insomnia and improve the general quality of sleep.

- Maintain a regular sleep-wake pattern to establish a stable circadian rhythm.
- Get the amount of sleep you need during the week, and avoid sleeping in on weekends, as doing so will disrupt your sleep rhythm. Even if you sleep poorly or not at all on one night, try to maintain your regular schedule the next.
- If you have trouble falling asleep at night, avoid napping if possible. Evening naps should be especially avoided because they will make you less sleepy when you go to bed.
- Do not eat a lot before going to sleep. If you must eat something, have a light snack, preferably one that contains L-tryptophan. L-tryptophan is an amino acid that helps the brain produce serotonin, and it can have a sedating effect. It is found in milk and other dairy foods.
- Avoid stimulants. This includes not just tobacco products and coffee but also soft drinks and chocolate (sorry), both of which contain caffeine. It can take the body 4 to 5 hours to reduce the amount of caffeine in the bloodstream by 50 percent.
- Avoid alcohol and sleeping pills. As a depressant, alcohol may make it easier to go to sleep, but it disrupts the sleep cycle and interferes with REM sleep. Sleeping pills also impair REM sleep, and their constant use can lead to dependence and insomnia.
- Try to go to bed in a relaxed state. Muscle-relaxation techniques and meditation can reduce tension, remove worrisome thoughts, and help induce sleep.
- Avoid physical exercise before bedtime because it is too stimulating. If you are unable to fall asleep, do not use exercise to try and wear yourself out.
- As noted in the text, if you are having sleep difficulties, avoid performing nonsleep activities in your bedroom.

SOURCES: Bootzin, 2002; King et al., 2001.

Narcolepsy

About 1 out of every 1,000 people suffers not from an inability to sleep, but from an inability to stay awake (Mignot, 1998). **Narcolepsy** *involves extreme daytime sleepiness and sudden, uncontrollable sleep attacks* that may last from less than a minute to an hour. No matter how much they rest at night, individuals with narcolepsy may experience sleep attacks at any time.

When a sleep attacks occurs, they may go right into a REM stage. People with narcolepsy also may experience attacks of *cataplexy,* a sudden loss of muscle tone often triggered by laughter, excitement, and other strong emotions. In severe cases, the knees buckle and the person collapses, conscious but unable to move for a few seconds to a few minutes. Cataplexy is an abnormal version of the normal muscular paralysis that takes place during nighttime REM sleep, and some experts view narcolepsy as a disorder in which REM sleep intrudes into waking consciousness.

Narcolepsy can be devastating. People with narcolepsy (1) are often misdiagnosed by medical doctors as having a mental disorder rather than a sleep disorder, (2) may be mistakenly viewed as lazy at work, (3) report a lowered quality of life, and (4) are more prone to accidents (Kryger et al., 2002).

What causes narcolepsy? Some people may be genetically predisposed toward developing this disorder. Narcolepsy can be selectively bred in dogs (Figure 5.18), and in humans, if one identical twin has narcolepsy, the other twin has a 30 percent chance of developing it (Mignot, 1998). Research also shows that people with narcolepsy who also have cataplexy lack certain types of *hypocretins* (also know as *orexins*), brain chemicals normally produced in the hypothalamus that appear to play a role in regulating wakefulness. In animals this hypocretin deficiency appears to be genetically based, but the cause in humans is not yet clear. At present there is no cure for narcolepsy, but stimulant drugs and daytime naps often reduce daytime sleepiness, and antidepressant drugs (which suppress REM sleep) can decrease attacks of cataplexy.

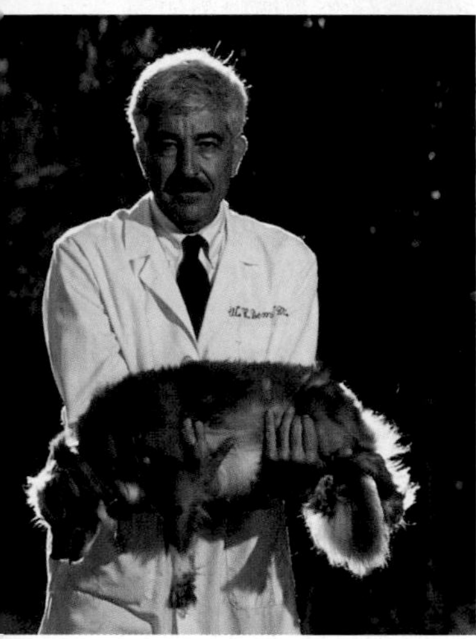

FIGURE 5.18

This dog lapses suddenly from alert wakefulness into a limp sleep while being held by sleep researcher William Dement. Narcolepsy occurs naturally in some dogs. Using selective breeding, researchers at Stanford's Sleep Disorders Center have established a colony of narcoleptic canines.

REM-Sleep Behavior Disorder

Kaku Kimura and his colleagues in Japan (1997) reported the case of a 72-year-old woman who, during a night in a sleep laboratory, repeatedly talked, sang, and waved her hands during REM sleep. One singing episode lasted 3 minutes. She was experiencing **REM-sleep behavior disorder (RBD),** *in which the loss of muscle tone that causes normal REM sleep paralysis is absent.* If awakened, RBD patients often report dream content that matches their behavior, as if they were acting out their dreams. Carlos Schenck, one of the researchers who first identified this disorder, describes how the consequences of RBD can be severe:

> A 67-year-old man . . . was awakened one night by his wife's yelling as he was choking her. He was dreaming of breaking the neck of a deer he had just knocked down. (Schenck et al., 1989, p. 1169)

RBD sleepers may kick violently, throw punches, or get out of bed and move about wildly, leaving the bedroom in shambles. Many RBD patients have injured themselves while sleeping or have injured their sleeping partners. Some research suggests that brain abnormalities may interfere with signals from the brain stem that normally inhibit movement during REM sleep, but in many cases the causes of RBD are unknown (Zambelis et al., 2002).

Sleepwalking

Unlike RBD, sleepwalking typically occurs during a stage-3 or stage-4 period of slow-wave sleep (Guilleminault et al., 2001). People who sleepwalk often have blank stares, are unresponsive to other people, may talk or mumble, and seem vaguely conscious of the environment as they navigate around furniture, go to the bathroom, or find something to eat. The pattern, however, is variable; recall that Jason, while eating during his sleepwalking episodes, could have intelligible conversations with his wife. People who sleepwalk often return to bed and awaken in the morning with no memory of the event.

About 10 to 30 percent of children sleepwalk at least once, but less than 5 percent of adults do. If you did not sleepwalk as a child, the odds are less than 1 percent that you will do so as an adult (Hublin et al., 1997). While sleepwalking, people can injure themselves accidentally, such as by falling down stairs or wandering out of their home.

A tendency to sleepwalk may be inherited, and daytime stress, alcohol, and certain illnesses and medications also increase sleepwalking (Hublin et al., 2001). Various treatments may be used, including psychotherapy, hypnosis, medication, and routinely awakening children before the time they typically sleepwalk (Frank et al., 1997). But for children, the most common "treatment" is simply to wait for the child to outgrow it while creating a safe home environment so that she or he will not get injured. Contrary to common belief, awakening people who sleepwalk is not harmful, although they may be confused for a few minutes.

Nightmares and Night Terrors

Nightmares are "bad" dreams and virtually everyone has them. Like all dreams, they occur more often during REM sleep. Arousal during nightmares is similar to levels experienced during pleasant dreams.

Night terrors *are frightening dreams that arouse the sleeper to a near-panic state.* They are more intense than nightmares. The terrified sleeper may suddenly sit up and seem to awaken, letting out a blood-curdling scream. The person might thrash about in bed or flee the room, as if trying to escape from something, and come morning have no memory of the episode. If brought to full consciousness during an episode—which is hard to do—the person may report a sense of having been choked, crushed, or attacked (Fisher et al., 1974).

Unlike nightmares, night terrors are most common during slow-wave sleep (stages 3 and 4) and involve greatly elevated physiological arousal; the heart rate may double or triple. Up to 6 percent of children, but only 1 to 2 percent of adults, experience night terrors (Ohayon et al., 1999). In most childhood cases, treatment is simply to wait for the night terrors to diminish with age.

Sleep Apnea

People with **sleep apnea** *repeatedly stop and restart breathing during sleep.* Stoppages usually last 20 to 40 seconds but can continue for 1 to 2 minutes. In severe cases they occur 400 to 500 times a night. Sleep apnea is most commonly caused by an obstruction in the upper airways, such as sagging tissue as muscles lose tone during sleep. The chest and abdomen keep moving, but no air gets through to the lungs. Finally, reflexes kick in and the person gasps or produces a loud, startling snore, followed by a several-second awakening. The person typically falls asleep again without remembering having been awake.

About 1 to 5 percent of people have some form of sleep apnea, and the obstructive type is most common among overweight, middle-aged males (Ip et al., 1998). Surgery may be performed to remove the obstruction blocking the airways, and sleep apnea sometimes is treated by having the sleeper wear a mask that continuously pumps air to keep the air passages open (Sage et al., 2001). Sleep apnea stresses the heart and contributes to hypertension and daytime fatigue. It is often the partner of a person with sleep apnea—repeatedly awakened by the gasps, loud snores, and jerking body movements—who encourages the person to seek treatment.

The Nature of Dreams

Dreams play a key role in the religious and social fabric of many traditional cultures, such as the Timiar (Senoi) of Malaysia (Greenleaf, 1973). To the Timiar, dreams provide a link to the spirit world and can represent omens of good or bad fortune. Dream interpretation, particularly when performed by shamans, is valued in Timiar culture. Although Western societies attach less importance to dreams than do many cultures, dreams remain a source of endless curiosity in everyday life (Figure 5.19).

FIGURE 5.19

The Wizard of Oz, *one of the most famous movies, focuses almost entirely on the dream sequence of a girl named Dorothy. Her dream includes witches, an army of flying monkeys, and, of course, the Scarecrow, Cowardly Lion, and Tin Man—who talk and act like humans. Are most of our dreams this bizarre?*

When Do We Dream?

Mental activity occurs throughout the sleep cycle. Some of our students say they experience vivid images soon after going to bed and ask if this is unusual. It isn't. When Jason Rowley and his colleagues (1998) awakened college students merely 45 seconds after sleep onset, about 25 percent of the students reported that they had been experiencing visual hallucinations (visual images that seemed real). As this *hypnagogic state*—the transitional state from wakefulness through early stage-2 sleep—continued, mental activity became less "thoughtlike" and more "dreamlike." By 5 minutes after sleep onset, visual hallucinations were reported after 40 percent of awakenings.

Throughout the night we dream most often during REM sleep, when activity in many brain areas is highest. Awaken a REM sleeper and you have about an 80 to 85 percent chance of catching a dream. In contrast, people awakened from non-REM (NREM) sleep report dreams about 15 to 50 percent of the time. Also, our REM dreams are more likely to be vivid, bizarre, and storylike than NREM dreams. Some researchers attribute this to the fact that REM dreams typically are longer, allowing more time for vivid content to unfold (Domhoff, 1999). But like the proverbial chicken and the egg, other researchers argue that it is the greater richness of REM dreams that causes them to be longer (Hobson et al., 2000).

Despite these REM-NREM differences, don't believe the fallacy (often reinforced by the popular media) that dreaming only happens during REM sleep. Figure 5.20 shows an analysis of 1,576 reports collected from 16 college students awakened from various sleep stages (Fosse et al., 2001). During REM sleep, hallucinations were more

▶ 12. When do dreams occur and what are common characteristics of dream content? How can science explain "psychic" dreams?

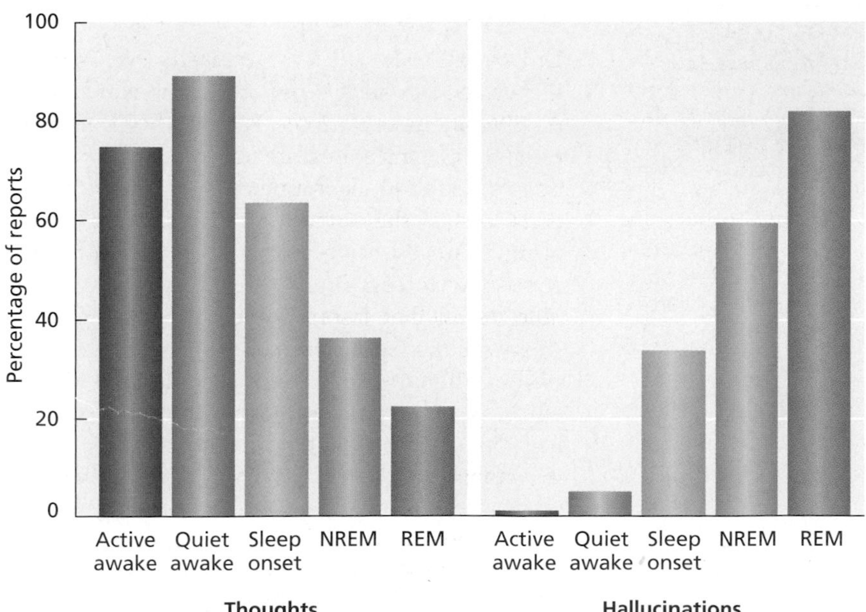

FIGURE 5.20

This graph shows the percentage of verbal reports that reflected thoughts and visual hallucinations recorded during active and quiet wakefulness and when awakened during sleep onset, REM sleep, and NREM sleep. Source: Adapted from Fosse et al., 2001.

common and nondreamlike thoughts were less common than during NREM sleep, but even during NREM sleep, hallucinations occurred often. Hallucinatory images, of course, may only be part of what makes mental activity feel like a dream (the sense of a storyline often is another). Still, by some estimates, about 25 percent of the vivid dreams we have each night actually occur during NREM periods (Solms, 2002).

What Do We Dream About?

Much of our knowledge about dream content derives from 35 years of research using a coding system developed by Calvin Hall and Robert Van de Castle (1966). Analyzing 1,000 dream reports (mostly from college students), they found that although some dreams certainly are bizarre, overall dreams are not nearly as strange as they are stereotyped to be. Most take place in familiar settings and often involve people we know.

Given the stereotype of "blissful dreaming," it may surprise you that most dreams contain negative content. In their research, Hall and Van de Castle (1966) found that 80 percent of dream reports involved negative emotions, almost half contained aggressive acts, and a third involved some type of misfortune. They also found that women dreamt almost equally about male and female characters, whereas about two thirds of men's dream characters were male. Although the reason for this gender difference is not clear, a similar pattern has been found across several cultures and among teenagers and preadolescents.

Our cultural background, life experiences, and current concerns can shape dream content (Domhoff, 2001). Pregnant women, for example, have dreams with many pregnancy themes, and Palestinian children living in violent regions of the Gaza Strip dream about persecution and aggression more often than do their peers living in nonviolent areas (Punamäki & Joustie, 1998). In the weeks following the September 11, 2001, terrorist attacks, a study of 1,000 residents of Manhattan found that 1 in 10 experienced distressing dreams about the attacks (Galea et al., 2002). Overall, it appears that up to half of our dreams contain some content reflecting our recent experiences (Harlow & Roll, 1992).

BENEATH THE SURFACE

WHEN DREAMS COME TRUE

"Last summer, I had a dream that my sister was hurt in an accident. A week later, she was seriously injured in a bicycle crash! Why does this happen? Are some dreams psychic?"

Have you ever had a dream that came true? Many of our students say they have, and they often ask us whether this has some special meaning. As critical thinkers, let's consider a few issues. First, what are we being asked to believe? Two things really: one, that a dream foretold the future, and two, that this signifies something special or psychic.

Second, what's the evidence? Well, the evidence is that a dream supposedly came true. So let's think about this. Did the dream really come true? In the example above, what type of accident did the dream involve? A car, train, plane, boat, home, sports, or work accident? If it wasn't a bicycle accident, then the dream really didn't come true. Perhaps you think we're being too picky. After all, the dream was "close"—the main theme was that the sister was injured. Well, suppose you picked a number from 1 to 1,000, we bet you $500 that we could guess it, and we guessed 625. You actually picked 638, but we said, "Our prediction came true. We were very close." Would you agree and pay us $500? If not, then why set a sloppy standard for accuracy when it comes to deciding whether a dream comes true? Nonetheless, for the sake of argument let's assume that the dream did involve a bicycle accident and came true a week later.

Third, what is the most plausible explanation? Given all the dreams that we recall, some of them are bound to come true simply by sheer coincidence—if you consider how many dreams you have had that did *not* come true, you will realize this. By some estimates we have dozens of dreams nightly, most of which we forget; but let's suppose we remember one dream every two nights. Between the ages of 15 and 75 we'll have almost 11,000 opportunities for a remembered dream to come true the same day, 77,000 opportunities for a remembered dream to come true within a week, and so on. Thus, a good number of our dreams *should* come true simply by coincidence. Collectively, if you consider that hundreds of millions of people may recall a dream each day, the odds are that someone, somewhere, by sheer coincidence, will have had a recent dream come true. This

Continued

is especially true given that ongoing events or issues in our lives can influence the content of our dreams.

In short, we don't need to resort to mystical phenomena to explain why some dreams come true. Rather, we need only consider the likelihood that certain events will occur periodically by chance and coincidence alone. Unfortunately, research shows that most of us badly underestimate how often coincidences actually occur (Matthews & Blackmore, 1995). For example, suppose you have 23 randomly chosen students in a class. Given that there are 365 days in a year, what is the probability that at least 2 students will have the same birthday? Ready for the answer? There is a 50 percent chance that a "birthday coincidence" will happen (Paulos, 1988). Are you surprised that the odds are so high? (If you're curious, go to your web browser, type in *birthday coincidence*, and you'll get plenty of web sites that will explain why the odds are so high.)

Why Do We Dream?

▶ 13. Contrast the psychoanalytic, activation-synthesis, and cognitive dream theories.

Questions about the purpose and meaning of dreams have intrigued humankind for ages. Let's examine a few viewpoints.

Freud's Psychoanalytic Theory Sigmund Freud (1900/1953) believed that the main purpose of dreaming is **wish fulfillment,** *the gratification of our unconscious desires and needs*. These desires include sexual and aggressive urges that are too unacceptable to be consciously acknowledged and fulfilled in real life. Freud distinguished between a dream's *manifest content*—the "surface" story that the dreamer reports—and its *latent content*, which is its disguised psychological meaning. Thus a dream about being with a stranger on a train that goes through a tunnel (manifest content) might represent a hidden desire for sexual intercourse with a "forbidden" partner (latent content). *Dream work* was Freud's term for the process by which the dream's latent content is transformed into the manifest content. This occurs through symbols (e.g., train = penis; tunnel = vagina) and by creating individual dream characters who combine the features of several people in real life. In this way, unconscious needs can be fulfilled, and because they are disguised within the dream, the sleeper does not become anxious and can sleep peacefully.

Although dreams often reflect ongoing emotional concerns, many researchers reject the specific postulates of Freud's theory. They find little evidence that dreams have disguised meaning or that their general purpose is to satisfy forbidden, unconscious needs and conflicts (Domhoff, 1999; Fisher & Greenberg, 1996). Critics of dream analysis say that it is highly subjective; the same dream can be interpreted differently to fit the particular analyst's point of view.

For insights into Freud's *The Interpretation of Dreams*, see Video Segment 5.1.

Activation-Synthesis Theory Is it possible that dreams serve no special purpose? In 1977, J. Allan Hobson and Robert McCarley proposed a physiological theory of dreaming. When we are awake, neural circuits in our brain are activated by sensory input—sights, sounds, tastes, and so on. The cerebral cortex interprets these patterns of neural activation, producing meaningful perceptions. According to the **activation-synthesis theory,** *dreams do not serve any particular function—they are merely a by-product of REM neural activity*. During REM sleep the brain stem bombards our higher brain centers with random neural activity (the *activation* component). Because we are asleep, this neural activity does not match any external sensory events, but our cerebral cortex continues to perform its job of interpretation. It does this by creating a dream—a perception—that provides the best fit to the particular pattern of neural activation that exists at any particular moment (the *synthesis* component). This process helps explain the bizarreness of many dreams, as the brain is trying to make sense out of random neural activity. Our memories and experiences can influence the stories that our brain develops, and therefore dream content may reflect themes pertaining to our lives. In this limited sense, dreams can have meaning (McCarley, 1998).

Critics of the activation-synthesis theory claim that it overestimates the bizarreness of dreams, pays too little attention to NREM dreaming, and overemphasizes the role of the brain stem in initiating dreaming (Domhoff, 1999; Solms, 2002). Nevertheless, this theory revolutionized dream research by calling attention to a physiological basis for dreaming, and it remains a dominant dream theory (Hobson et al., 2000).

Cognitive Approaches According to **problem-solving dream models,** *because dreams are not constrained by reality they can help us find creative solutions to our problems and ongoing concerns* (Cartwright et al., 1977). Self-help books and numerous web sites promote this idea, and history offers some intriguing examples of inventors, scientists, and authors who allegedly came upon creative ideas or solutions to problems in a dream (Figure 5.21). But

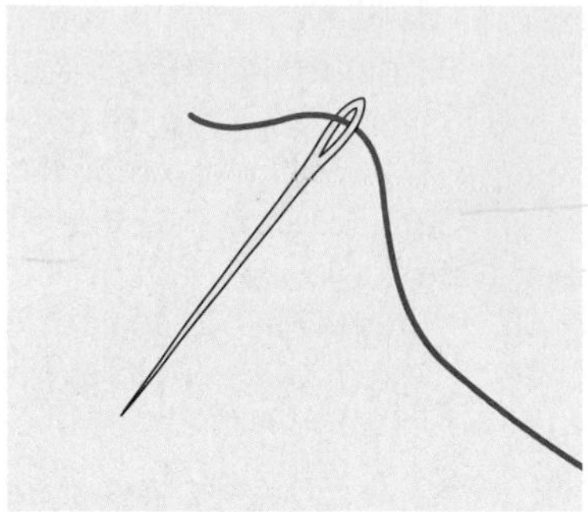
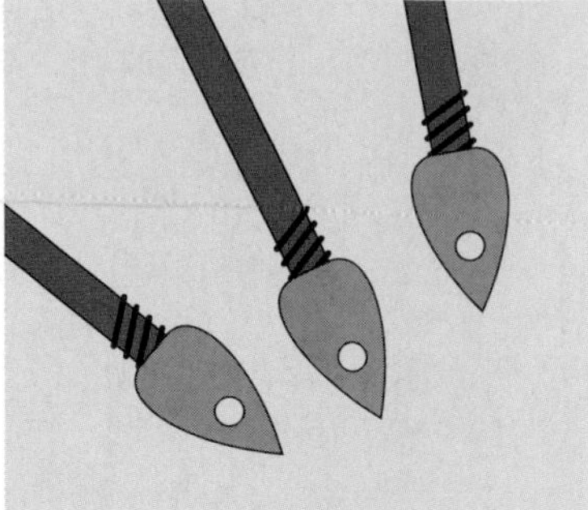
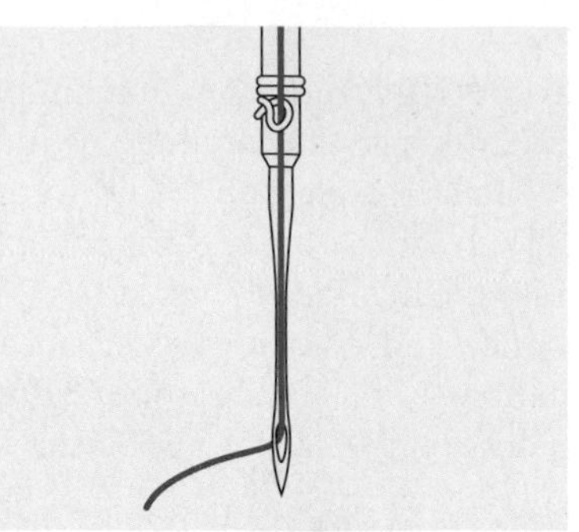

Hand-held needle   Howe's dream   Sewing machine needle

FIGURE 5.21

In 1846, American inventor Elias Howe patented a sewing machine that could sew 250 stitches per minute. He had struggled unsuccessfully for years to figure out how to get a machine to stitch using a needle with the threading hole in the back (blunt) end—as in a traditional hand-held needle. Allegedly, one night he had a dream that he was being pursued by spear-throwing tribesmen. In the dream he saw that each spearhead had a hole in it. When Howe woke up, he recognized that for a sewing machine to work, the threading hole needed to be at the front (sharp) end of the needle, as it had been on the spears.

critics note that just because a problem shows up in a dream, this does not mean that the dream involved an attempt to solve it. Moreover, we may think consciously about our dreams after awakening and obtain important new insights; in this sense dreams may indeed help us work through ongoing concerns. However, this is not the same as solving problems *while* dreaming (Squier & Domhoff, 1998).

Cognitive-process dream theories *focus on the process of how we dream* (Foulkes, 1982). Based on the modular model of consciousness, these theories propose that dreaming and waking thought are produced by the same mental systems in the brain. Consider that when 3- and 4-year-old children are awakened from REM sleep, they rarely report dreams, whereas 8- and 9-year-olds display some features of adult dreaming (Foulkes, 1982). Why should this be? According to David Foulkes (1999), it is because dreaming requires imagery skills and other cognitive abilities that young children have not yet developed sufficiently in waking life. As children's mental abilities mature with age, so does their ability to dream.

▶ 14. What functions do daydreams serve? How are they different from, and similar to, nighttime dreams?

Research indicates more similarity between dreaming and waking mental processes than was traditionally believed (Domhoff, 2001). Consider that one reason many dreams appear bizarre is because their content shifts rapidly. "I was dreaming about an exam and all of a sudden, the next thing I knew, I was in Hawaii on the beach." (Don't we wish!) Yet if you reflect on the contents of your waking thoughts—your stream of consciousness—you will realize they also shift suddenly. About half of REM dream reports involve rapid content shifts, but when people are awake and placed in the same environmental conditions as sleepers (a dark, quiet room), about 90 percent of their reports involve rapid content shifts (Antrobus, 1991). Thus rapid shifting of attention is a process common to dreaming and waking mental activity.

Toward Integration Although there is no agreed-upon model of why, or even of how, we dream, theorists are developing models that integrate several perspectives. In general, these models are consistent with the notion of modular consciousness that we discussed earlier. That is, dreaming involves an integration of perceptual, emotional, motivational, and cognitive processes. For example, *neurocognitive models* (such as the activation-synthesis model) bridge the biological and cognitive perspectives by attempting to explain how various aspects of dreaming correspond to the physiological changes that occur during sleep (Hobson et al., 2000; Solms, 2002).

Daydreams and Waking Fantasies

Our dreams and fantasy lives are not restricted to the nocturnal realm. Daydreams are a significant part of waking consciousness, providing stimulation during periods of boredom and letting us experience a range of emotions (Hartmann et al., 2001). In *The Secret Life of Walter Mitty,* author James Thurber portrayed the main character as a person who transformed his humdrum existence into an exhilarating fantasy world of adventure and personal fulfillment. Like the fictional Mitty, people who have a **fantasy-prone personality** *often live in a vivid, rich fantasy world that they control.* They comprise about 2 to 4 percent of the population, and most are female. In one study, about three quarters of fantasy-prone people were able to achieve sexual orgasm merely by fantasizing about sexual activity,

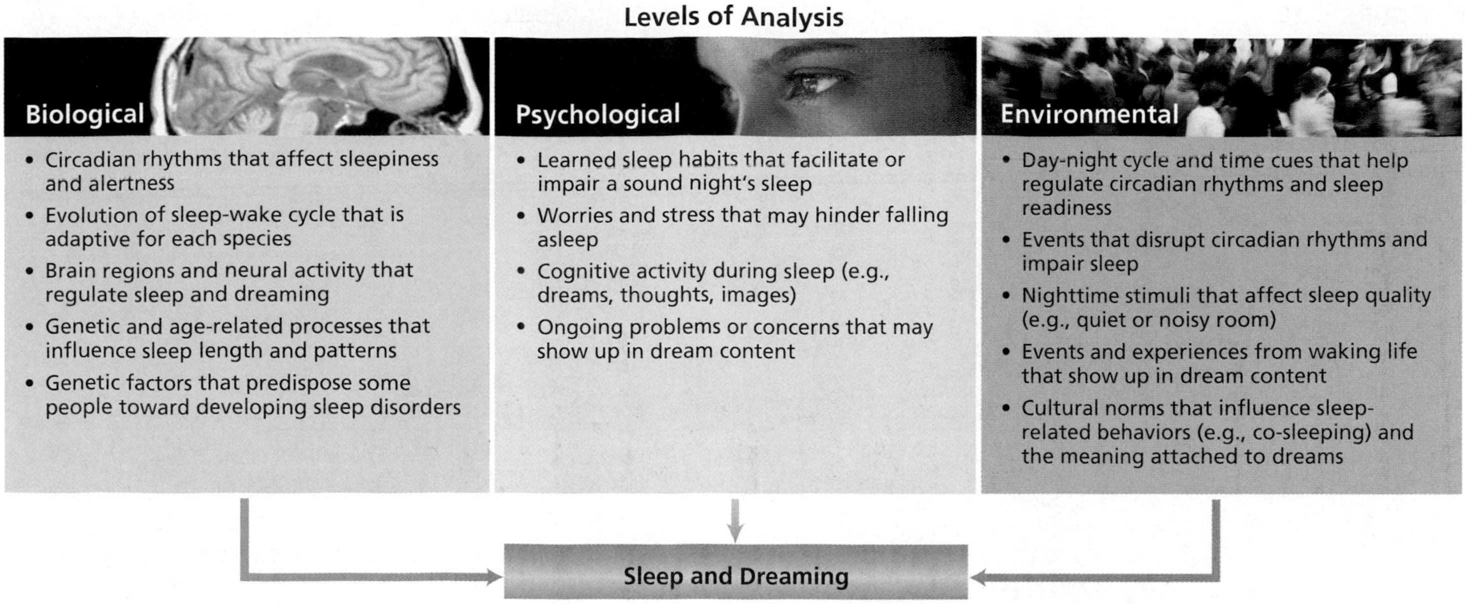

Levels of Analysis

Biological	Psychological	Environmental
• Circadian rhythms that affect sleepiness and alertness • Evolution of sleep-wake cycle that is adaptive for each species • Brain regions and neural activity that regulate sleep and dreaming • Genetic and age-related processes that influence sleep length and patterns • Genetic factors that predispose some people toward developing sleep disorders	• Learned sleep habits that facilitate or impair a sound night's sleep • Worries and stress that may hinder falling asleep • Cognitive activity during sleep (e.g., dreams, thoughts, images) • Ongoing problems or concerns that may show up in dream content	• Day-night cycle and time cues that help regulate circadian rhythms and sleep readiness • Events that disrupt circadian rhythms and impair sleep • Nighttime stimuli that affect sleep quality (e.g., quiet or noisy room) • Events and experiences from waking life that show up in dream content • Cultural norms that influence sleep-related behaviors (e.g., co-sleeping) and the meaning attached to dreams

Sleep and Dreaming

FIGURE 5.22

Understanding Behavior: Sleep and dreaming.

and all could experience fantasies "as real as real" in each of the five senses (Wilson & Barber, 1982).

Daydreams typically involve greater visual imagery than other forms of waking mental activity but tend to be less vivid, emotional, and bizarre than nighttime dreams (Kunzendorf et al., 1997). Their content often reflects personal concerns. There also is a surprising degree of similarity in the themes of daydreams and nighttime dreams, suggesting once again that nocturnal dreams may be an extension of daytime mental activity, sometimes reflecting current concerns in the person's life (Beck, 2002). Figure 5.22 summarizes some of biological, psychological, and environmental factors that contribute to our understanding of sleep and dreaming.

IN REVIEW

- *Sleep has five main stages. Stages 1 and 2 are lighter sleep, and stages 3 and 4 are deeper, slow-wave sleep. High physiological arousal and periods of rapid eye movements characterize the fifth stage, REM sleep.*
- *Several brain regions regulate sleep, and the amount we sleep changes as we age. Genetic, psychological, and environmental factors affect our sleep duration and quality.*
- *Sleep deprivation negatively affects mood, mental performance, and physical performance. The restoration model proposes that we sleep to recover from accumulated physical and mental fatigue. Evolutionary/circadian models state that each species evolved a waking-sleeping cycle that maximized its chance of survival.*
- *Insomnia is the most common sleep disorder, but less common disorders such as narcolepsy, REM-sleep behavior disorder, and sleep apnea can have extremely serious consequences. Sleepwalking typically occurs during slow-wave sleep, whereas nightmares most often occur during REM sleep. Night terrors create a near-panic state of arousal and typically occur in slow-wave sleep.*
- *Dreams occur throughout sleep but are most common during REM periods. Unpleasant dreams are common. Our cultural background, current concerns, and recent events influence what we dream about.*
- *Freud proposed that dreams fulfill unconscious wishes that show up in disguised form within our dreams. Activation-synthesis theory regards dreaming as the brain's attempt to fit a story to random neural activity. Cognitive-process dream theories emphasize that dreaming and waking thought are produced by the same mental systems.*
- *Daydreams and nocturnal dreams often share similar themes. People with fantasy-prone personalities have especially vivid daydreams.*

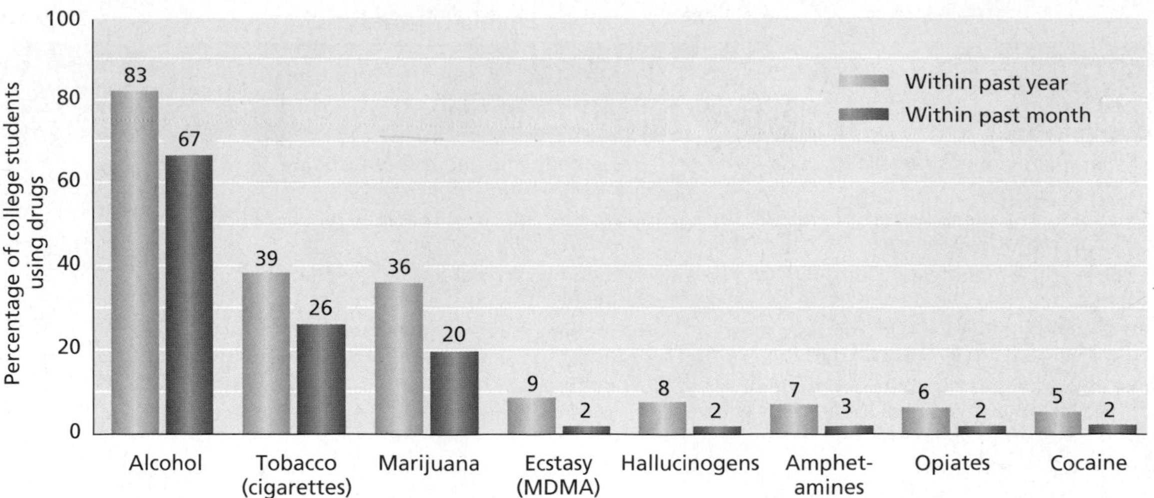

FIGURE 5.23

Nonmedical drug use among 19- to 22-year-old American college students. These data are based on a nationally representative survey of 1,340 students.
Source: Johnston et al., 2002.

DRUG-INDUCED STATES

Like sleep and dreaming, drug-induced states have mystified humans for ages. Three thousand years ago, the Aztecs considered hallucinogenic mushrooms to be a sacred substance for communicating with the spirit world. Today drugs are a cornerstone of medical practice and, as Figure 5.23 shows, a pervasive part of social life. They alter consciousness by modifying brain chemistry, but drug effects are also influenced by psychological, environmental, and cultural factors (Stewart, 2002).

Drugs and the Brain

▶ 15. Describe several ways in which agonist and antagonist drugs influence synaptic transmission.

Like any cell, a neuron is essentially a fragile bag of chemicals, and it takes a delicate chemical balancing act for neurons to function properly. Drugs work their way into the bloodstream and are carried throughout the brain by an extensive network of small blood vessels called *capillaries*. These capillaries contain a **blood-brain barrier,** *a special lining of tightly packed cells that lets vital nutrients pass through so neurons can function*. The blood-brain barrier screens out many foreign substances, but some, including various drugs, can pass through. Once inside, they alter consciousness by facilitating or inhibiting synaptic transmission (Julien, 2001).

How Drugs Facilitate Synaptic Transmission

Recall from Chapter 3 that synaptic transmission involves several basic steps. First, neurotransmitters are synthesized inside the presynaptic (sending) neuron and stored in vesicles. Next, neurotransmitters are released into the synapse, where they bind with and stimulate receptor sites on the postsynaptic (receiving) neuron. Finally, neurotransmitter molecules are deactivated by enzymes or by reuptake.

An **agonist** *is a drug that increases the activity of a neurotransmitter*. Figure 5.24 shows that agonists may

- enhance a neuron's ability to synthesize, store, or release neurotransmitters;
- bind with and stimulate postsynaptic receptor sites (or make it easier for neurotransmitters to stimulate these sites); and
- make it more difficult for neurotransmitters to be deactivated, such as by inhibiting reuptake.

Consider two examples: opiates and amphetamines. *Opiates* (such as morphine and codeine) are effective pain relievers. Recall that the brain contains its own chemicals, endorphins, which play a major role in pain relief. Opiates have a molecular structure similar to that of endorphins. They bind to and activate receptor sites that receive endorphins. To draw an analogy, think of trying to open a lock with a key. Normally an endorphin molecule acts as the key, but due to its similar shape, an opiate molecule can fit into the lock and open it.

Amphetamines boost arousal and mood by causing neurons to release greater amounts of dopamine and norepinephrine and by inhibiting reuptake. During reuptake, neurotransmitters in the synapse are absorbed back into presynaptic neurons through special channels. As shown in Figure 5.24c, amphetamine molecules block this process. Therefore, dopamine and norepinephrine remain in the synapse longer and keep stimulating postsynaptic neurons.

Agonistic drugs

(a) **Synthesis, storage, release**

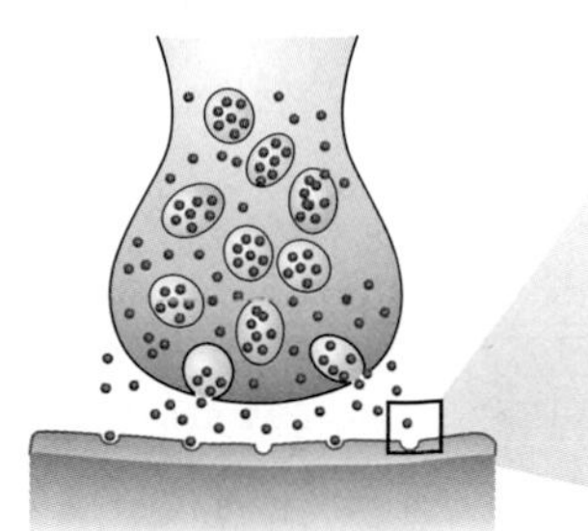

Drug causes neuron to synthesize more transmitter molecules, store them more safely, or release them.

(b) **Binding**

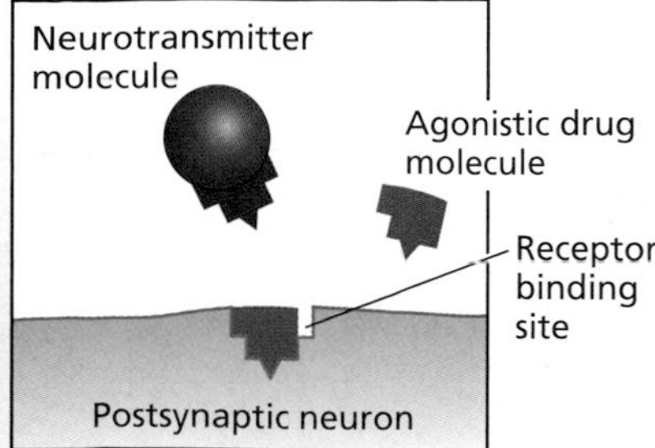

Drug and neurotransmitter have similar structure. Drug binds with receptor site and activates it.

(c) **Reuptake**

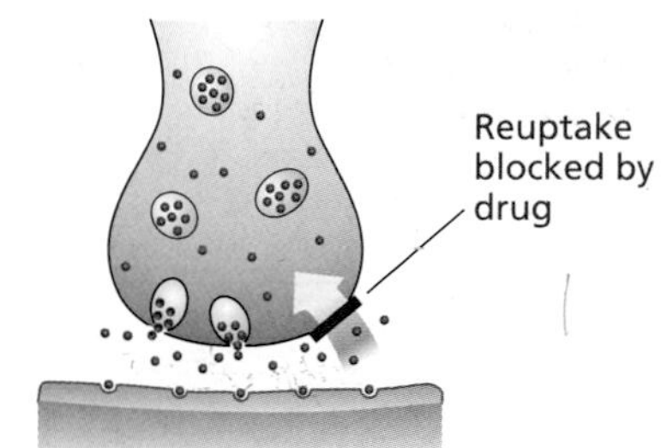

Drug blocks reuptake. More transmitter molecules remain in synapse, available to activate receptor sites.

Antagonistic drugs

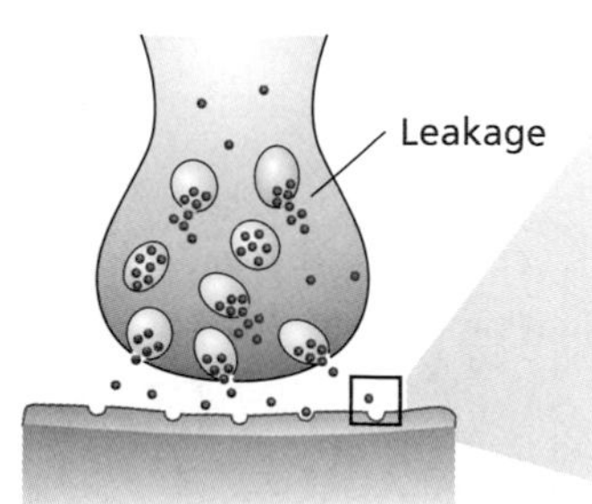

Drug impairs neuron's ability to synthesize, store, or release transmitter. Molecules may leak and degrade prematurely.

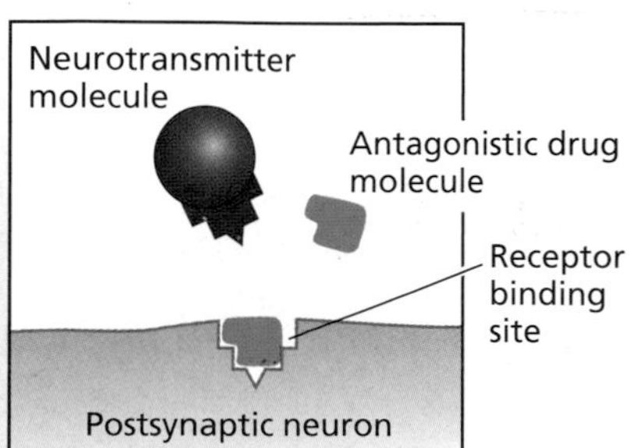

Drug binds with receptor site but is not similar enough to transmitter to activate site. Blocks transmitter from activating site.

FIGURE 5.24

(a) Agonists cause neurons to synthesize more neurotransmitter molecules, store them more safely, or release them. In contrast, antagonists impair neurons' ability to synthesize, store, or release neurotransmitters. (b) The agonist and neurotransmitter have similar molecular structures. The drug binds with the receptor site and activates it. In contrast, the antagonist binds with the receptor site but is not structurally similar enough to the neurotransmitter to activate the site. This prevents the real neurotransmitter from binding with and activating the site. (c) The agonist blocks the reuptake of the neurotransmitter into the presynaptic neuron. More neurotransmitter molecules remain in the synapse, available to activate the postsynaptic neuron.

How Drugs Inhibit Synaptic Transmission

An **antagonist** *is a drug that inhibits or decreases the action of a neurotransmitter*. As Figure 5.24 shows, an antagonist may

- reduce a neuron's ability to synthesize, store, or release neurotransmitters; or
- prevent a neurotransmitter from binding with the postsynaptic neuron, such as by fitting into and blocking the receptor sites on the postsynaptic neuron.

Consider the action of drugs (called *antipsychotics*) used to treat *schizophrenia*, a severe psychological disorder whose symptoms may include hallucinations (e.g., hearing voices) and delusions (clearly false beliefs, such as believing you are Joan of Arc). These symptoms are often associated with overactivity of the dopamine system. To bring dopamine activity down to more normal levels, pharmaceutical companies have developed drugs with a molecular structure similar to dopamine, but not too similar. Returning to the lock-and-key analogy, imagine finding a key that fits into a lock but won't turn. The key's shape is close enough to the real key to get in but not to open the lock. Similarly, antipsychotic drugs fit into dopamine receptor sites, but not well enough to stimulate them. While they occupy the sites, dopamine released by presynaptic neurons is blocked and cannot get in, and the schizophrenic symptoms usually decrease.

16. How are tolerance, compensatory responses, withdrawal, and dependence related? How does learning affect tolerance?

Tolerance and Withdrawal

When a drug is used repeatedly, the intensity of effects produced by the same dosage level may decrease over time. This *decreasing responsivity to a drug is called* **tolerance.** As it develops, the person must take increasingly larger doses to achieve the same physical and psychological effects. Tolerance stems from the body's attempt to maintain a state of optimal physiological balance, called *homeostasis*. If a drug changes bodily functioning in a certain way, say by increasing heart rate, the brain will try to adjust for this imbalance by producing **compensatory responses**, *which are reactions opposite to that of the drug* (e.g., reactions that decrease heart rate). In effect, compensatory responses represent the body's way of fighting the invasion of drugs.

What happens when drug tolerance develops and the person suddenly stops using the drug? The body's compensatory responses may continue and, no longer balanced out by the drug's effects, the person can experience strong reactions opposite to those produced by the drug. *This occurrence of compensatory responses after discontinued drug use is known as* **withdrawal.** For example, in the absence of alcohol's sedating and relaxing effects, a chronic drinker may experience anxiety and hypertension.

Learning, Drug Tolerance, and Overdose

Tolerance for various drugs depends partly on the familiarity of the drug setting. Figure 5.25 illustrates how environmental stimuli associated with repeated drug use begin to elicit compensatory responses through a learning process called *classical conditioning*. As drug use continues, the physical setting triggers progressively stronger compensatory responses, increasing the user's tolerance. This helps explain why drug addicts often experience increased cravings when they enter a setting associated with drug use; it also explains why recovering alcoholics are advised to stay out of bars. The environmental stimuli trigger compensatory responses that, without drugs to mask their effect, cause the user to feel withdrawal symptoms (Duncan et al., 2000).

There is a hidden danger in this process, particularly for experienced drug users. Compensatory responses serve a protective function by physiologically countering part of the drug's effects. If a user takes his or her usual high dose in a familiar environment, the body's compensatory responses are at full strength—a combination of compensatory reactions to the drug itself and also to the familiar, conditioned environmental stimuli. But in an *unfamiliar* environment, the conditioned compensatory responses are weaker, and the drug has a stronger physiological net effect than usual (Siegel et al., 2000).

Shepard Siegel (1984) interviewed people addicted to heroin who experienced near-fatal overdoses. He found that in most cases they had not taken a dose larger than their customary one. However, in 70 percent of the cases they had injected themselves in unfamiliar environments. Siegel concluded that the addicts were not protected by their usual compensatory responses, resulting in an "overdose" reaction.

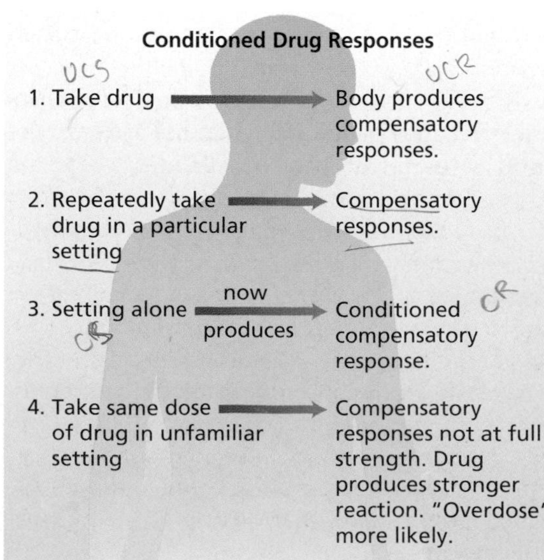

Conditioned Drug Responses
1. Take drug
Body produces compensatory responses.
2. Repeatedly take drug in a particular setting
Compensatory responses.
3. Setting alone
now
produces
Conditioned compensatory response.
4. Take same dose of drug in unfamiliar setting
Compensatory responses not at full strength. Drug produces stronger reaction. "Overdose" more likely.

FIGURE 5.25

Environmental stimuli that are repeatedly paired with the use of a drug can trigger compensatory responses on their own.

Drug Addiction and Dependence

Drug addiction, which is formally called **substance dependence,** *represents a maladaptive pattern of substance use that causes a person significant distress or substantially impairs that person's life.* Substance dependence is diagnosed as occurring with *physiological dependence* if drug tolerance or withdrawal symptoms have developed. You probably have heard the term *psychological dependence* used to describe situations in which people strongly crave a drug because of its pleasurable effects, even if they are not physiologically dependent. However, this is not a diagnostic term, and some drug experts feel it is misleading (Díaz, 1997). Cravings for a drug do have a physical basis, though, because they are rooted in patterns of brain activity (Bonson et al., 2002).

Several misconceptions surround the issue of substance dependence. For example, many people mistakenly believe that if a drug does not produce tolerance or withdrawal, you cannot become dependent on it. In reality, neither tolerance nor withdrawal is needed for a diagnosis of substance dependence (Nathan, 1997).

The popular media image of a shaking alcoholic desperately searching for a drink or a "heroin junkie" looking for a "fix" reinforces another misconception, namely that the motivation to avoid or end withdrawal symptoms is the primary cause of addiction. Such physiological dependence contributes powerfully to drug dependence, but consider these points:

- People become highly dependent on some drugs, such as cocaine, that produce only mild withdrawal in many users (Kampmann et al., 2002). The pleasurable effects of these drugs—often produced by boosting dopamine activity—play a major role in drug dependence.
- Many drug users who quit and make it through withdrawal eventually start using again, even though they are no longer physiologically dependent.
- Drug dependence is influenced by factors beyond a drug's chemical effects, including genetic predispositions, personality traits, religious beliefs, family and peer influences, and cultural norms.

Depressants

Depressants *decrease nervous system activity*. In moderate doses, they reduce feelings of tension and anxiety and produce a state of relaxed euphoria. In extremely high doses, depressants can slow down vital life processes to the point of death.

Alcohol

Alcohol is the most widely used recreational drug in many cultures. A national survey of American college students found that 67 percent had consumed alcohol within the previous month, with 41 percent bingeing (five or more drinks at one time) within the previous two weeks (Johnston et al., 2002). Tolerance develops gradually and can lead to physiological dependence.

Alcohol dampens down the nervous system by increasing the activity of GABA, the brain's main *inhibitory* neurotransmitter, and by decreasing the activity of glutamate, a major *excitatory* neurotransmitter (Anton, 2001). Why, then, do many people report getting a "high" from alcohol and initially seem livelier? The answer is that the neural slowdown depresses the action of inhibitory control centers in the cerebral cortex, so the person literally becomes less inhibited and feels euphoric. At higher doses, the brain's control centers become increasingly disrupted, thinking and physical coordination become disorganized, and fatigue and psychological depression may occur (Table 5.3). Thus alcohol's subjective effects seem to have an initial "upper" phase from the release of inhibitions, followed by a "downer" phase as brain centers become increasingly depressed, but *both* phases result from alcohol's action as a nervous system depressant (Marlatt, 1987).

TABLE 5.3 Behavioral Effects of Alcohol

BAL	Hours to Leave Body	Behavioral Effects
.03	1	Decreased alertness, impaired reaction time in some people
.05	2	Decreased alertness, impaired judgment and reaction time, good feeling, release of inhibitions
.10	4	Severely impaired reaction time, motor function, and judgment; lack of caution
.15	10	Gross intoxication, worsening impairments
.25	?	Extreme sensory and motor impairment, staggering
.30	?	Stuporous but conscious, cannot comprehend immediate environment
.40	?	Lethal in over 50 percent of cases

▶ 17. How do depressants affect the brain? How does alcohol intoxication affect decisions about drinking and driving?

The *blood-alcohol level (BAL)* is a measure of alcohol concentration in the body. Elevated BAL is linked to many risky and harmful behaviors. About 40 percent of American and Canadian traffic accident deaths involve alcohol (National Highway Traffic Safety Administration, 2002). As the BAL increases, reaction time, eye-hand coordination, and decision making are impaired (Figure 5.26).

Why do intoxicated people often act in risky ways that they wouldn't when sober? It is not simply a matter of lowered inhibitions; alcohol also produces what Claude Steele and Robert Josephs (1990) call **alcohol myopia,** *a "shortsightedness" in thinking caused by the inability to pay attention to as much information as sober people.* People who drink start to focus only on those aspects of the situation (called *cues*) that stand out. As a result, in the absence of strong cautionary cues (such as immediate warnings) to inhibit risky behavior, they don't think about the long-term consequences of their actions as carefully as when they are sober. Our *Research Close-Up* illustrates this effect.

For a story of overcoming alcohol addiction, see Video Segment 5.2.

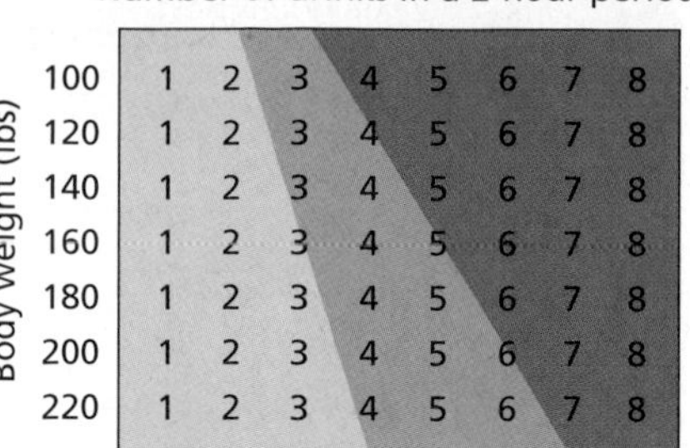

Caution: some impairment BAL up to .05

Definite impairment: legally drunk in some areas BAL .05 to .09

Marked impairment: legally drunk in all areas BAL .10 or more

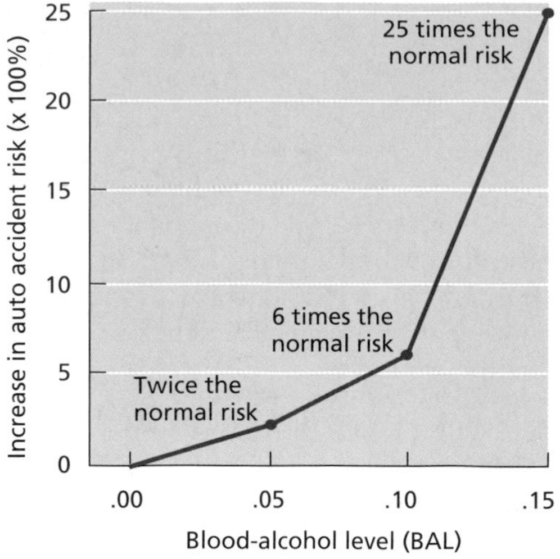

FIGURE 5.26

Relation between blood-alcohol level and risk of having an auto accident. At .08 to 0.10, the legal definition of intoxication in most American states and Canadian provinces, the risk is 5 to 6 times greater than at 0.00, and the risk climbs to 25 times higher at a BAL of 0.15. SOURCE: Based on National Safety Council, 1992.

RESEARCH CLOSE-UP

DRINKING AND DRIVING: DECISION MAKING IN ALTERED STATES

Background

Most people have negative attitudes about drunk driving and say they would not do it. They realize that the cons (e.g., risk of accident, injury, death, and police arrest) far outweigh the pros (e.g., not having to ask someone for a lift). Why, then, do so many people decide to drive after becoming intoxicated?

Based on alcohol myopia principles, Tara MacDonald and her colleagues reasoned that when intoxicated people decide whether to drive, they may focus on the pros or the cons but do not have the attentional capacity to focus on both. If a circumstance that favors driving (a "facilitating cue") is called to the intoxicated person's attention (e.g., "It's only a short distance"), she or he will latch on to it and fail to consider the cons. But in general situations that do not contain facilitating cues, intoxicated people's feelings about driving should remain as negative as when they were sober.

The authors made two predictions. First, intoxicated and sober people will have equally negative *general attitudes and intentions* toward drinking and driving. Second, intoxicated people will have less negative attitudes and greater intentions to drive than sober people in situations that contain a facilitating cue.

Method

Laboratory Experiment

Fifty-seven male introductory psychology students, all regular drinkers who owned cars, participated. They were randomly assigned to either the sober condition, in which they received no alcohol, or the alcohol condition, in which they received three alcoholic drinks within an hour (the average BAL was .074 percent, just below the .08 percent legal driving limit in Ontario, Canada).

Participants then completed a "drinking-and-driving" questionnaire. Some items asked about *general* attitudes and intentions (e.g., "I will drink and drive the next time that I am out at a party or bar with friends"). Other items contained a *facilitating cue*, a special circumstance that suggested a possible

SOURCE: Tara K. MacDonald, Mark P. Zanna, and Geoffrey T. Fong (1995). Decision making in altered states: Effects of alcohol on attitudes toward drinking and driving. *Journal of Personality and Social Psychology, 68*, 973–985.

reason for drinking and driving (" If I only had a short distance to drive home . . . / If my friends tried to persuade me to drink and drive . . . I would drive while intoxicated"). Participants rated each item on a 9-point scale (1 = strongly disagree; 9 = strongly agree).

Party/Bar Diary Study

Fifty-one male and female college students recorded a telephone diary while at a party or bar where they were going to drink alcohol. Some were randomly assigned to record the diary when they first arrived; others, just before they left. To record the diary, participants opened up a packet containing the same drinking-and-driving questionnaire described above, called a number on the packet, and recorded their responses on the researchers' answering machine. Based on participants' descriptions of how much alcohol they had consumed, the researchers estimated their BAL and identified two groups: sober participants (average BAL = .01) and intoxicated participants (average BAL = .11).

Results

The findings from both studies supported the predictions. Sober participants and intoxicated participants both expressed negative general attitudes about drinking and driving, and indicated they would not drive when intoxicated. But, as Figure 5.27 shows, when the questions presented a special circumstance, intoxicated participants expressed more favorable attitudes and a greater intention to drive than sober participants.

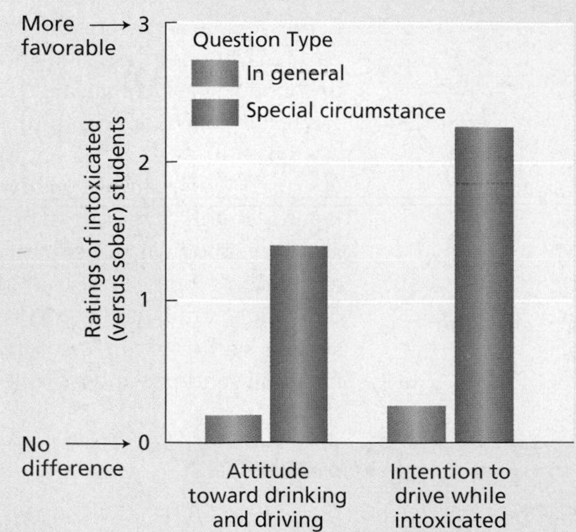

FIGURE 5.27

When general attitudes and intentions toward drinking and driving are measured, intoxicated and sober participants have similarly negative reactions. But when questioned about situations involving special circumstances (facilitating cues), intoxicated participants have less negative attitudes and intentions about drinking and driving than do sober participants. SOURCE: MacDonald et al., 1995.

Discussion

This study nicely illustrates how a person's physiological state (sober versus intoxicated) and an environmental factor (general situation versus special circumstance) interact to influence psychological functioning (attitudes and decision making). However, let's think critically about the results. Was it really narrowed attention—leading to a failure to consider negative consequences—that caused the results? The authors anticipated two alternative explanations. First, perhaps people who drink do not realize how intoxicated they are. Second, perhaps intoxicated people overestimate their driving ability, a belief called *drunken invincibility.* The authors tested and ruled out these explanations. Intoxicated participants believed they were *more* intoxicated than they actually were and also estimated that they would drive *more poorly* than the average person.

Is it possible that the findings were caused by participants' expectations about alcohol rather than its chemical effects? The authors conducted a placebo control experiment in which some participants were convincingly misled to believe they were intoxicated. Results showed that the alcohol myopia effect occurred only for participants who truly had consumed alcohol. It was not caused by participants' expectations.

What practical value do these findings have? The researchers suggest that a sign saying "Drinking and Driving Kills," or a large photograph of a police officer administering a breathalyzer test, be made highly visible near the exit of a bar. Alcohol myopia should cause intoxicated people to narrow their focus of attention to these *inhibiting cues*, causing them to rethink any decision to drink and drive. In subsequent research, MacDonald and coworkers (2000) found that making strong inhibiting cues salient did indeed lead intoxicated people to behave more cautiously.

Barbiturates and Tranquilizers

Physicians frequently prescribe barbiturates ("sleeping pills") and tranquilizers (antianxiety drugs, such as Valium) as sedatives and relaxants. Like alcohol, most of these drugs depress the nervous system by increasing the activity of the inhibitory neurotransmitter GABA (Nishino et al., 2001).

Mild doses are effective as sleeping pills but are highly addictive. As tolerance builds, addicted people may take up to 50 sleeping pills a day. At high doses, barbiturates trigger initial excitation, followed by slurred speech, loss of coordination, depression, and memory impairment. Overdoses, particularly when taken with alcohol, may cause unconsciousness, coma, and even death. Death also can result from sudden withdrawal after heavy use.

Barbiturates and tranquilizers are widely overused. For example, many people mistakenly regard Valium as harmless, but it is not. Tolerance and physiological dependence can occur. Users often don't recognize that they have become dependent until they try to stop and experience serious withdrawal symptoms, such as anxiety, insomnia, and possibly seizures.

Stimulants

▶ 18. How do amphetamines, cocaine, and Ecstasy affect the brain? Why can use lead to a "crash?"

Stimulants *increase neural firing and arouse the nervous system.* They increase blood pressure, respiration, heart rate, and overall alertness. While they can elevate mood to the point of euphoria, they also can heighten irritability.

Amphetamines

Amphetamines—popularly known as "speed," "uppers," and "bennies"—are powerful stimulants. They are prescribed to reduce appetite and fatigue, to decrease the need for sleep, and sometimes to reduce depression. Unfortunately, they are widely overused to boost energy and mood (Anthony et al., 1997).

Amphetamines increase dopamine and norepinephrine activity. Tolerance develops, and users may crave their pleasurable effects. Eventually, many heavy users start injecting large quantities, producing a sudden surge of energy and rush of intense pleasure. With frequent injections, they may remain awake continuously for as long as a week, their bodily systems racing at breakneck speed. Injecting amphetamines greatly increases blood pressure and can lead to heart failure and cerebral hemorrhage (stroke); repeated high doses may cause brain damage (Diaz, 1997).

Recall that in schizophrenia, hallucinations and delusions are associated with excess dopamine activity. Imagine what happens when the brain's dopamine activity is artificially increased well beyond normal levels by continuous, heavy amphetamine use. It can cause *schizophrenia-like hallucinations and paranoid delusions, a reaction called* **amphetamine psychosis** (Lynn, 1971). There is an inevitable "crash" when heavy users stop taking the drug. They may sleep for 1 to 2 days, waking up depressed, exhausted, and irritable. This crash occurs because the neurons' norepinephrine and dopamine supplies have become depleted. Amphetamines tax the body heavily, and those addicted have a short life expectancy.

Cocaine

Cocaine is a powder derived from the coca plant, which grows mainly in western South America. Usually inhaled or injected, it produces excitation, a sense of increased muscular strength, and euphoria. Cocaine increases the activity of norepinephrine and dopamine by blocking their reuptake.

At various times in history, cocaine has been hailed as a wonder drug and branded as a menace. It was once widely used as a local anesthetic in eye, nose, and throat surgery. Novocain, a synthetic form of cocaine, is still used in dentistry as an anesthetic. Due to its stimulating effects, cocaine found its way into potions and tonics sold to the public to enhance health and emotional well-being. In 1885, John Pemberton mixed cocaine with the kola nut and syrup and developed a soda fountain drink that has become one of the icons of American beverages (Figure 5.28).

In large doses, cocaine can produce fever, vomiting, convulsions, hallucinations, and paranoid delusions (Boutros et al., 2002). A severe depressive crash may occur after a cocaine high, particularly with repeated doses. Tolerance develops to many of cocaine's effects, and chronic use has been associated with an increased risk of cognitive impairments and brain damage (Franklin et al., 2002). *Crack* is a chemically converted form of cocaine that can be smoked, and its effects are faster, more intense, and more dangerous. Overdoses of crack cocaine can cause sudden death from cardiorespiratory arrest (Ruttenber et al., 1997).

Ecstasy (MDMA)

Ecstasy, also known as *MDMA* (methylenedioxy-methamphetamine), is artificially synthesized by altering the molecular structure of amphetamine. This produces a new chemical structure that partly resembles both *methamphetamine* (a stimulant) and *mescaline* (a hallucinogen). Ecstasy is sometimes classified as a hallucinogen even though its hallucinogenic effects are relatively mild (Ray & Ksir, 2001). Ecstasy produces feelings of pleasure, elation, empathy, and warmth. It affects several neurotransmitters, including dopamine, but primarily alters serotonin functioning by interfering with reuptake and by causing neurons to release more serotonin (Parrott, 2001). The short-term overabundance of serotonin boosts one's mood but may also cause hyperactivity and agitation. After the drug wears off, users often feel sluggish and depressed—a rebound effect due to serotonin

FIGURE 5.28

(a) When Coca-Cola was first produced, there was a clear reason why it relieved fatigue: It contained cocaine. (b) Before it was made illegal, cocaine was found in a variety of medicinal products.

depletion. They also may have to take increasingly stronger doses to overcome the tolerance to Ecstasy.

Ecstasy is frequently called a "rave drug" because it is used at nightclubs and "rave" parties. In experiments with laboratory rats, Ecstasy has produced long-lasting damage to the axon terminals of neurons that release serotonin (Mechan et al., 2002). Human studies of habitual Ecstasy users increasingly suggest a similar possibility (Figure 5.29), but it is not clear whether such damage is permanent. Ironically, in the long run Ecstasy may produce consequences that are anything but pleasurable. Some findings suggest that along with poorer memory and other cognitive impairments, continued Ecstasy use is associated with sleep difficulties and a diminished capacity to enjoy sexual pleasure (Parrott, 2001).

Opiates

Opium is a product of the opium poppy, a plant grown in hot, dry climates. *Opium and drugs derived from it, such as morphine, codeine, and heroin, are called* **opiates.** Opiates have two major effects. First, they provide pain relief. Second, they cause mood changes, which may include intense euphoria. Opiates bind to and stimulate receptors normally activated by endorphins, thereby producing pain relief. Opiates also increase dopamine activity, which may be one reason they induce euphoria (Bardo, 1998).

In medical use, opiates are the most effective agents known for relieving intense pain. Heroin was developed in 1889 by the Bayer company (which today produces aspirin). Although it was initially believed to be a nonaddictive painkiller, tolerance develops rapidly, and like other opiates it is highly addictive. In the 1920s, it was made illegal in the United States.

▶ 19. Describe the major effects and dangers of opiates, hallucinogens, and marijuana.

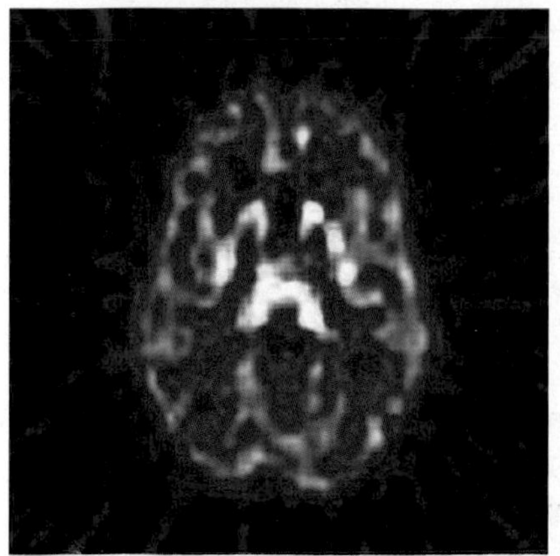

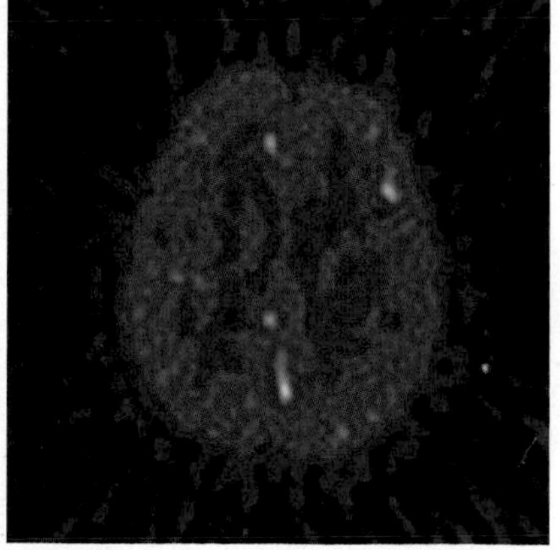

FIGURE 5.29

The left PET-scan image shows the brain of a person who never used Ecstasy. The right image shows the brain of a person who used Ecstasy 70 times or more over a period of at least 1.5 years but who stopped using the drug for several weeks before these images were taken. Areas of lighter color indicate a higher density of special proteins (called transporters*) necessary for normal serotonin reuptake. The darker image of the brain on the right suggests that there is damage to the serotonin reuptake system.* SOURCE: McCann et al., 1998.

Experienced heroin users feel an intense "rush" within several minutes of an injection. For a time, they feel peaceful and nonaggressive, as if they were "on top of the world." Heroin users, however, often pay a high price for these transient pleasures. High doses can greatly reduce breathing and may lead to coma. Overdoses can cause death (Julien, 2001). As a former addict describes, withdrawal symptoms are traumatic:

> Your joints move involuntarily. That's where the phrase "kick the habit" comes from. You jerk and twitch and you just can't control it. You throw up. You can't control your bowels either and this goes on for four or five days afterwards. You can't sleep and you cough up blood, because . . . you can't eat and that's all there is to cough up.

Hallucinogens

Hallucinogens *are powerful mind-altering drugs that produce hallucinations*. Many are derived from natural sources; mescaline, for example, comes from the peyote cactus, and psilocybin from mushrooms. Natural hallucinogens have been considered sacred in many tribal cultures because of their ability to produce "unearthly" states of consciousness and contact with spiritual forces (Figure 5.30). Other hallucinogens, such as LSD ("acid") and phencyclidine ("angel dust") are synthetic.

Hallucinogens distort or intensify sensory experience and can blur the boundaries between reality and fantasy. Users may speak of seeing sounds and hearing colors, of having mystical experiences and insights, and of feeling exhilarated. They may also have violent outbursts, experience paranoia and panic, and have flashbacks after the "trip" has ended. The mental effects of hallucinogens are always unpredictable, even if they are taken repeatedly. This unpredictability constitutes their greatest danger.

FIGURE 5.30

In some cultures, potent hallucinogenic drugs are thought to have spiritual powers. Under the influence of peyote, this modern Indian shaman prepares to conduct a religious ceremony.

As our opening story about Albert Hofmann illustrated, LSD is a powerful hallucinogen. It causes a flooding of excitation in the nervous system. A dose of pure LSD no larger than the tip of a pin can affect a user for 8 to 16 hours. Tolerance develops rapidly but decreases quickly. Part of the LSD molecule has a shape similar to serotonin, and it increases the activity of serotonin and dopamine at certain receptor sites (Nichols & Sanders-Bush, 2002). However, scientists still do not know precisely how LSD produces its effects.

Marijuana

Marijuana, a product of the hemp plant (*Cannabis sativa*), is the most widely used illegal drug in the United States (Office of Applied Studies, 2002). Some experts classify it as a hallucinogen, others as a sedative, and some feel it belongs in its own category (Diaz, 1997).

THC (tetrahydrocannabinol) *is marijuana's major active ingredient*, and it binds to receptors on neurons throughout the brain. You might wonder, as scientists have, why the brain would have specific receptor sites for a foreign substance such as marijuana? The answer is that the brain produces its own THC-like substances called *cannabinoids* (Devane et al., 1992). With chronic use, THC may increase GABA activity, which slows down neural activity and produces relaxing effects (Diaz, 1997). THC also increases dopamine activity, which may account for some of its pleasurable subjective effects (Maldonado & Rodriguez de Fonseca, 2002). Attempts to legalize marijuana use for medical purposes have stirred up waves of political controversy (Figure 5.31).

Certain misconceptions exist about marijuana. One is that chronic use causes people to become unmotivated and apathetic toward everything, a condition called *amotivational syndrome*. Another misconception is that marijuana causes people to start using more dangerous drugs. Neither statement is supported by good scientific evidence (Diaz, 1997; Rao, 2001). A third misconception, however, is that using marijuana has no significant dangers. In fact, marijuana smoke contains more cancer-causing substances than does tobacco smoke. At high doses, users may experience negative changes in mood, sensory distortions, and feelings of panic and anxiety. While users are "high," marijuana can impair their reaction time, thinking, memory, learning, and driving skills (Ramaekers et al., 2000).

Repeated marijuana use produces tolerance. At typical doses, some chronic users may experience mild withdrawal symptoms, such as restlessness. But people who use it at chronically high

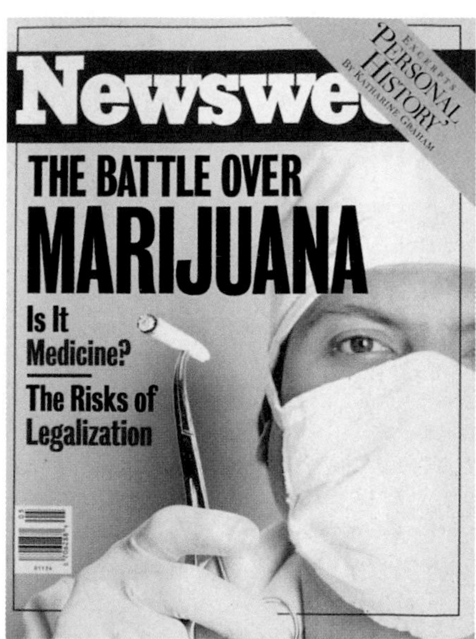

FIGURE 5.31

Marijuana is an illegal drug in the United States at the federal level. However, in some jurisdictions voters have legalized marijuana use for certain medical purposes, such as helping patients with cancer reduce some of the negative side effects (e.g., nausea) of chemotherapy. The medical legalization of marijuana is hotly debated.

doses and suddenly stop may experience nausea and vomiting, sleep disruptions, and irritability. About 5 to 10 percent of people who use marijuana develop dependence (Coffey et al., 2002).

From Genes to Culture: Determinants of Drug Effects

▶ 20. Explain how drug reactions depend on biological, psychological, and environmental factors.

Table 5.4 summarizes some typical drug effects, but a user's reaction depends on more than the drug's chemical structure. Other biological, psychological, and environmental factors can influence the drug experience.

At the biological level, animal research indicates that genetic factors influence sensitivity and tolerance to drugs' effects (Boehm et al., 2002). This has been examined most extensively with a lcohol. Rats and mice can be genetically bred to inherit a strong preference for drinking alcohol instead of water. Even in their first exposure to alcohol, these rats show greater tolerance than normal rats.

In human research on alcoholism, three types of correlational evidence are intriguing. First, identical twins have a higher concordance rate for alcoholism than do fraternal twins (Heath et al., 1997). Second, scientists have identified a particular gene that is found more often among alcoholics and their children than among nonalcoholics and

TABLE 5.4 Effects of Some Major Drugs

Class	Typical Effects	Risks of High Doses and/or Chronic Use
Depressants		
Alcohol	Relaxation, lowered inhibition, impaired physical and psychological functioning	Disorientation, unconsciousness, possible death at extreme doses
Barbiturates/Tranquilizers	Reduced tension, impaired reflexes and motor functioning, drowsiness	Shallow breathing, clammy skin, weak and rapid pulse, coma, possible death
Stimulants		
Amphetamines, Cocaine, Ecstasy	Increased alertness, pulse, and blood pressure; elevated mood; suppressed appetite; agitation; sleeplessness	Hallucinations, paranoid delusions, convulsions, long-term cognitive impairments, brain damage, possible death
Opiates		
Opium, Morphine, Heroin	Euphoria, pain relief, drowsiness, impaired motor and psychological functioning	Shallow breathing, convulsions, coma, possible death
Hallucinogens		
LSD, Mescaline, Psilocybin	Hallucinations and visions, distorted time perception, loss of contact with reality, nausea	Psychotic reactions (delusions, paranoia), panic, possible death
Marijuana	Mild euphoria, relaxation, enhanced sensory experiences, increased appetite, impaired memory and reaction time	Fatigue, anxiety, disorientation, sensory distortions, possible psychotic reactions, exposure to carcinogens

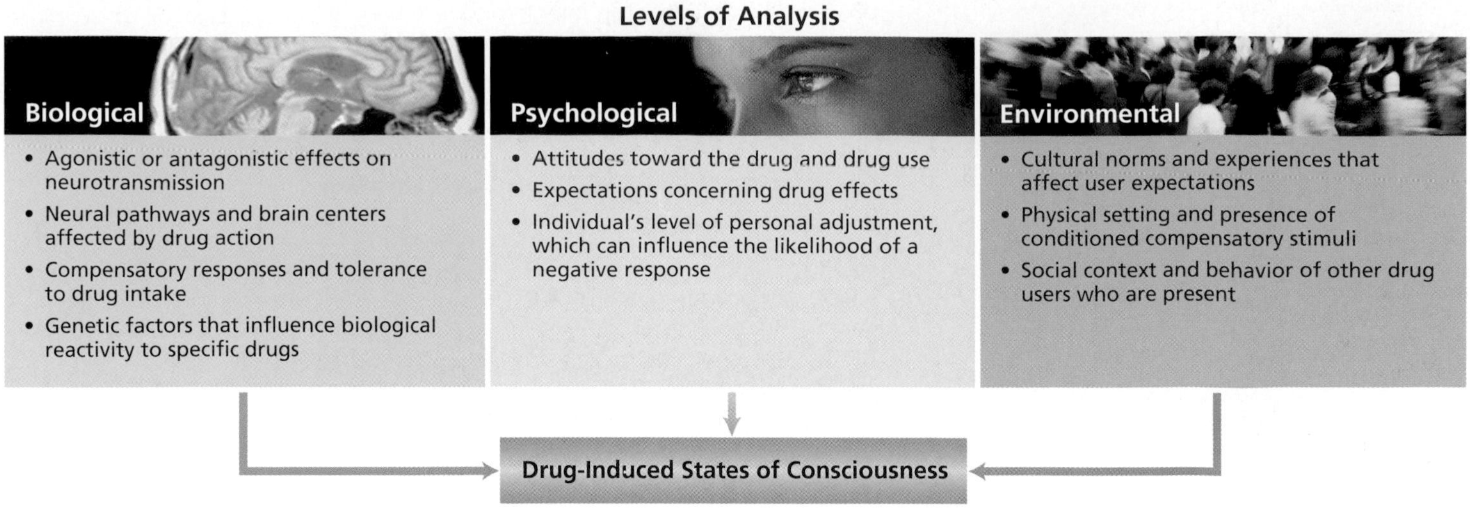

Levels of Analysis

Biological	Psychological	Environmental
• Agonistic or antagonistic effects on neurotransmission • Neural pathways and brain centers affected by drug action • Compensatory responses and tolerance to drug intake • Genetic factors that influence biological reactivity to specific drugs	• Attitudes toward the drug and drug use • Expectations concerning drug effects • Individual's level of personal adjustment, which can influence the likelihood of a negative response	• Cultural norms and experiences that affect user expectations • Physical setting and presence of conditioned compensatory stimuli • Social context and behavior of other drug users who are present

Drug-Induced States of Consciousness

FIGURE 5.32

Understanding Behavior: Factors influencing drug effects.

their offspring (Noble, 1998). No one is proposing that this gene causes alcoholism. Rather, it may influence how the brain responds to alcohol.

Third, people who grow up with alcoholic versus nonalcoholic parents respond differently to drinking alcohol under laboratory conditions. Adults who had alcoholic parents typically display faster hormonal and psychological reactions as blood-alcohol levels rise, but these responses drop off more quickly as blood-alcohol levels decrease (Newlin & Thomson, 1997). Compared with other people, they must drink more alcohol over the course of a few hours to maintain their feeling of intoxication. Overall, many scientists find compelling evidence for a genetic role in determining responsiveness to alcohol (Li, 2000).

At the environmental level, the physical and social setting in which a drug is taken can strongly influence a user's reactions. As noted earlier, compensatory physiological responses to a drug can become associated with, and ultimately triggered by, environmental stimuli in the drug setting. The behavior of other people who are sharing the drug experience provides important cues for how to respond, and a hostile environment may increase the chances of a "bad trip" with drugs such as LSD (Palfai & Jankiewicz, 1991).

Cultural learning also affects how people respond to a drug (Bloomfield et al., 2002). In many Western cultures, increased aggressiveness and sexual promiscuity are commonly associated with drunken excess. In contrast, members of the Camba culture of Bolivia customarily drink large quantities of a 178-proof beverage, remaining cordial and nonaggressive between episodes of passing out. In the 1700s, Tahitians introduced to alcohol by European sailors reacted at first with pleasant relaxation when intoxicated, but after witnessing the violent aggressiveness exhibited by drunken sailors, they too began behaving aggressively (MacAndrew & Edgerton, 1969).

Cultural factors also affect drug consumption. Traditionally, members of the Navajo tribe do not consider drinking any amount of alcohol to be normal, whereas drinking wine or beer is central to social life and cultural identity in some European countries and other parts of the world (Tanaka-Matsumi & Draguns, 1997). In some cultures, hallucinogenic drugs are feared and even outlawed, whereas in others they are used in medicinal or religious contexts to provide new types of awareness and seek advice from spirits. In many countries, drug use varies across ethnic groups. For example, Asian, Black, and Hispanic Americans are less likely to have ever used an "illicit" drug (e.g., illegal drugs, inhalants, prescription drugs used nonmedically) than are White Americans (Office of Applied Studies, 2002).

Finally, at the psychological level, people's beliefs and expectancies also can influence drug reactions (George et al., 2000). Experiments show that people may behave as if drunk if they simply think they have consumed alcohol but actually have not. If a person's fellow drinkers are happy and gregarious, he or she may feel it's expected to respond the same way. Personality factors also influence drug reactions and usage. People who have difficulty adjusting to life's demands or whose contact with reality is marginal may be particularly vulnerable to severe and negative drug reactions and to drug addiction (Ray & Ksir, 2001). Figure 5.32 illustrates some of the biological, environmental, and psychological factors that may determine drug experiences.

IN REVIEW

- *Drugs alter consciousness by modifying neurotransmitter activity. Agonists increase the activity of a neurotransmitter, whereas antagonists decrease it.*
- *Tolerance develops when the body produces compensatory responses to counteract a drug's effects. When drug use is stopped, compensatory responses continue and produce withdrawal symptoms.*
- *Substance dependence represents a maladaptive pattern of substance use that causes a person significant distress or substantially impairs that person's life. It can occur with or without physiological dependence.*
- *Depressants decrease neural activity. The subjective "high" and liveliness often associated with low alcohol doses occurs because alcohol depresses the activity of inhibitory brain centers and because many drinkers expect that alcohol will make them feel lively.*
- *Amphetamines and cocaine are stimulants that increase arousal and boost one's mood by enhancing dopamine and norepinephrine activity, whereas Ecstasy primarily increases serotonin activity. A depressive "crash" can occur after the drug wears off, and repeated use may produce serious negative psychological effects and bodily damage.*
- *Opiates increase endorphin activity, producing pain relief and mood changes that may include euphoria. Opiates are important in medicine but are highly addictive.*
- *Hallucinogens, such as LSD, powerfully distort sensory experience and can blur the line between reality and fantasy.*
- *THC, the main active ingredient in marijuana, produces relaxation and a sense of well-being at low doses, but it can cause anxiety and sensory distortions at higher doses. Marijuana can impair thinking and reflexes.*
- *A drug's effect depends on its chemical actions, the physical and social setting, cultural norms, and learning, as well as the user's genetic predispositions, expectations, and personality.*

HYPNOSIS

In 18th-century Vienna, physician Anton Mesmer gained fame for using magnetized objects to cure patients. He claimed that illness was caused by blockages of an invisible bodily fluid and that his technique of *animal magnetism* (later named *mesmerism* in his honor) would restore the fluid's normal flow. A scientific commission discredited mesmerism, but its use continued. Decades later, Scottish surgeon James Braid investigated the fact that mesmerized patients often went into a trance in which they seemed oblivious to their surroundings (Figure 5.33). Braid concluded that mesmerism was a state of "nervous sleep" produced by concentrated attention, and he renamed it *hypnosis*, after Hypnos, the Greek god of sleep.

The Scientific Study of Hypnosis

Hypnosis *is a state of heightened suggestibility in which some people are able to experience imagined situations as if they were real.* Hypnosis draws great interest because many therapists use it in treating mental disorders. In the United States, about 25 percent of psychology Ph.D. programs offer a course in hypnosis (Walling et al., 1998). Basic scientists, exploring whether hypnosis is a unique state of altered consciousness, put its claims to rigorous test.

Hypnotic induction is the process by which one person (a researcher or hypnotist) leads another person (the subject) into hypnosis. A hypnotist

FIGURE 5.33

An 18th-century "animal magnetizer" places his patients into a trance.

TABLE 5.5 Sample Test Items From the Stanford Hypnotic Susceptibility Scale, Form C

Item	Suggested Behavior	Criterion for Passing
Lowering arm	Right arm is held out; subject is told arm will become heavy and drop	Arm is lowered by 6 inches in 10 seconds
Moving hands apart	With hands extended and close together, subject is asked to imagine a force pushing them apart	Hands are 6 or more inches apart in 10 seconds
Mosquito hallucination	It is suggested that a mosquito is buzzing nearby and lands on subject	Any grimace or acknowledgment of mosquito
Posthypnotic amnesia	Subject is awakened and asked to recall suggestions after being told under hypnosis that he or she will not remember the suggestions	Three or fewer items recalled before subject is told, "Now you can remember everything."

SOURCE: Based on Weitzenhoffer & Hilgard, 1962.

FIGURE 5.34

The human-plank demonstration, a favorite of stage hypnotists, seems to demonstrate the power of the hypnotic trance. Are you convinced?

▶ 21. Evaluate claims that hypnosis can produce involuntary behavior, amazing feats, pain relief, and altered memory.

may invite the subject to sit down, relax, and gaze at an object on the wall; then, in a quiet voice, the hypnotist may suggest that the subject's eyes are becoming heavy and tired. The goal is to relax the subject and increase her or his concentration. Contrary to popular belief, people cannot be hypnotized against their will. Even when people want to be hypnotized, they differ in how susceptible (i.e., responsive) they are to hypnotic suggestions. **Hypnotic susceptibility scales** *contain a standard series of pass-fail suggestions that are read to a subject after a hypnotic induction* (Table 5.5). The subject's score is based on the number of passes. About 10 percent of subjects are completely nonresponsive, 10 percent pass all or nearly all of the items, and the rest fall in between (Hilgard, 1977). Hypnotic susceptibility is a stable characteristic. In one study, Stanford students differed by no more than 1 point on a 12-item scale when retested 25 years later (Piccione et al., 1989).

Hypnotic Behaviors and Experiences

It is widely claimed that hypnotized people experience substantial alterations in psychological functioning and behavior. Let's examine some of these claims.

Involuntary Control and Behaving Against One's Will

Hypnotized people *subjectively experience* their actions to be involuntary (Kirsch, 2001). For example, look at the second test item in Table 5.5. To hypnotized subjects, it really does feel like their hands are being pushed apart by some mysterious force, rather than by any conscious control of bodily movements.

If behavior seems involuntary under hypnosis, then can a hypnotist make people perform acts that are harmful to themselves or others? Martin Orne and Frederick Evans (1965) found that hypnotized subjects could be induced to dip their hands briefly in a foaming solution they were told was acid and then to throw the "acid" in another person's face. This might appear to be a striking example of the power of hypnosis to get people to act against their will. However, Orne and Evans tested a control group of subjects who were asked to simply pretend that they were hypnotized. These subjects were just as likely as hypnotized subjects to put their hands in the "acid" and throw it at someone.

In Chapter 15 you will learn about experiments in which researchers induced hundreds of "normal" adults to keep giving what they believed were extremely painful electric shocks to an innocent man with a heart condition who begged them to stop (Milgram, 1974). Not a single one of these participants was hypnotized; they were simply following the researcher's orders. Hypnosis does not involve any unique power to get people to behave against their will (Kirsch & Braffman, 2001). An authority figure in a legitimate context can induce people to commit highly "out of character" and dangerous acts, whether they are hypnotized or not.

Amazing Feats

Have you seen or heard about stage hypnotists who get an audience member to perform an amazing physical feat, such as the "human plank" (Figure 5.34)? A subject, usually male, is hypnotized and lies outstretched between two chairs. He is told that his body is rigid and then, amazingly, another person successfully stands on the subject's leg and chest.

Similarly, hypnosis can have striking physiological effects. Consider a classic experiment involving 13 people who were strongly allergic to the toxic leaves of a certain tree (Ikemi & Nakagawa, 1962). Five of them were hypnotized, blindfolded, and told that a leaf from a harmless tree to which they were not allergic was touching one of their arms. In fact, the leaf really was toxic, but 4 out of the 5 hypnotized people had no allergic reaction. Next, the other arm of each hypnotized person was rubbed with a leaf from a harmless tree, but he or she was falsely told that the leaf

was toxic. All 5 people responded to the harmless leaf with allergic reactions.

Should we, however, attribute the human-plank feat and the unusual responses of the allergic people to unique powers of hypnosis? Here is where a healthy dose of critical thinking is important.

What Do You Think?

HYPNOSIS AND AMAZING FEATS

In the case of the human plank and in the allergy experiment, what additional evidence do you need to determine whether these amazing feats and responses really are caused by hypnosis? How could you gather this evidence? Think about it, then see page 196.

Pain Tolerance

Scottish surgeon James Esdaile performed more than 300 major operations in the mid-1800s using hypnosis as the sole anesthetic (Figure 5.35). Experiments confirm that hypnosis often increases pain tolerance and that this is not due to a placebo effect (Montgomery et al., 2000). For patients who experience chronic pain, hypnosis can produce relief that lasts for months or even years (Barber, 1998). Brain-imaging research reveals that hypnosis modifies neural activity in brain areas that process painful stimuli, but this research also shows that nonhypnotic psychological techniques, such as mental imagery and performing distracting cognitive tasks, also alter neural functioning and reduce pain (Petrovic & Ingvar, 2002).

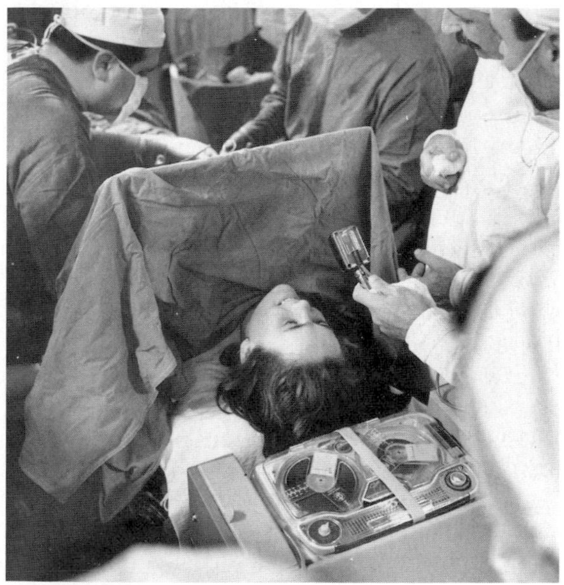

FIGURE 5.35

This patient is having her appendix removed with hypnosis as the sole anesthetic. Her verbal reports that she feels no pain are being tape-recorded.

We do not know exactly how hypnosis produces its pain-killing effects. It may influence the release of endorphins, decrease patients' fear and anxiety about pain, distract patients from their pain, or somehow help them separate the pain from conscious experience (Barber, 1998).

Hypnotic Amnesia

You may have seen TV shows or movies in which hypnotized people are given a suggestion that they will not remember something, either during the session itself (*hypnotic amnesia*) or after coming out of hypnosis (*posthypnotic amnesia*). A reversal cue also is given, such as a phrase ("You will now remember everything") that ends the amnesia once the person hears it. Is this Hollywood fiction?

In one interesting case, a math teacher was given a hypnotic suggestion that he would be unable to recall the number 6 during the session. The teacher mistakenly interpreted the suggestion as including *post* hypnotic amnesia. Can you imagine someone trying to teach math while being unable to recall the number 6? Indeed, it proved difficult until the hypnotist reversed the amnesia suggestion at a later session.

More extensive research indicates that about 25 percent of hypnotized college students can be led to experience amnesia (Kirsch, 2001). Although researchers agree that hypnotic and posthypnotic amnesia occur, they debate the causes. Some feel it results from voluntary attempts to avoid thinking about certain information, and others believe it is caused by an altered state of consciousness or weakening of normal memory systems (Kihlstrom, 1998; Spanos, 1986).

Hypnosis, Memory Enhancement, and Eyewitness Testimony

In contrast to producing forgetting, can hypnosis enhance memory? Law enforcement agencies sometimes use hypnosis to aid the memory of eyewitnesses to crimes. In a famous 1977 case in California, a bus carrying 26 children and its driver disappeared without a trace. The victims, buried underground in an abandoned trailer truck by three kidnappers, were later found

▶ 22. Contrast dissociation and social-cognitive theories of hypnosis. What does research on the hypnotized brain reveal?

alive. After the rescue, a police expert hypnotized the bus driver and asked him to recall the ordeal. The driver formed a vivid image of the kidnapper's white van and could "read" all but one digit on the van's license plate. This information allowed the police to track down the kidnappers.

Despite occasional success stories like this one, controlled experiments find that hypnosis does not reliably improve memory. In some experiments, participants watch videotapes of simulated bank robberies or other crimes and are then questioned—while hypnotized or not—by police investigators or criminal lawyers. Hypnotized people display better recall than nonhypnotized people in some studies, but no better recall in others (Lynn et al., 2001). And in still other experiments, hypnotized participants perform more poorly than nonhypnotized controls; they recall more information, but much of that "extra recall" is inaccurate (Burgess & Kirsch, 1999).

Another concern is that some "memories" recalled under hypnosis are actually *pseudomemories*, false memories *created* during the hypnosis session by statements or leading suggestions made by the examiner. In one study, Australian college students watched a brief videotape in which an unmasked man with a pistol entered a bank from the left door, robbed the bank, but didn't swear (Sheehan et al., 1992). Students were then randomly assigned and either hypnotized (experimental group) or not hypnotized (control group). Hypnotized students were told that their subconscious mind had recorded details of the robbery that their conscious mind had forgotten. Next, the researchers intentionally described the robbery inaccurately, stating that the robber had worn a mask, entered from the right, and swore. Students were then brought out of hypnosis and both they and the nonhypnotized participants were introduced to a new experimenter who asked them to describe the robbery.

The nonhypnotized control group displayed highly accurate recall, but hypnotized students identified as having "high suggestibility" typically misreported one or sometimes two of the three key events. Equally disturbing was the fact that they were highly confident that their false memories were accurate.

Many courts have banned or limited testimony obtained under hypnosis. The increased suggestibility of hypnotized people makes them particularly susceptible to memory distortion caused by leading questions asked by the examiner, and they may honestly come to believe "facts" that never really occurred (Scoboria et al., 2002). Similarly, if a therapist uses hypnosis to help patients recall "long-forgotten" memories of sexual abuse, what shall we conclude? Are the horrible memories real, or are they pseudomemories created during therapy (Loftus, 2000)? We explore this issue further in Chapter 7.

Theories of Hypnosis

Hypnos may have been the Greek god of sleep, but studies of brain physiology reveal that hypnosis definitely is *not* sleep. What, then, is hypnosis, and how does it produce its effects?

Dissociation Theories

Several influential researchers propose **dissociation theories** *that view hypnosis as an altered state involving a division (dissociation) of consciousness* (Bowers, 1992; Kihlstrom, 1985). For example, Ernest Hilgard of Stanford University (1977, 1991) proposed that hypnosis creates a *division of awareness* in which the person simultaneously experiences two streams of consciousness that are cut off from one another. One stream responds to the hypnotist's suggestions, while the second stream—the part of consciousness that monitors behavior—remains in the background but is aware of everything that goes on. Metaphorically, Hilgard refers to this second "part" of consciousness as the *hidden observer.*

Suppose a hypnotized subject is given a suggestion that she will not feel pain. Her arm is lowered into a tub of ice-cold water for 45 seconds and every few seconds she reports the amount of pain. In contrast to nonhypnotized subjects, who find this experience moderately painful, she probably will report feeling little pain. But suppose the procedure is done differently. Before lowering the subject's arm, the hypnotist says, "Perhaps there is another part of you that is more aware than your hypnotized part. If so, would that part of you report the amount of pain." In this case, the subject's other stream of consciousness, the hidden observer, will report a higher level of pain (Figure 5.36).

For Hilgard, this dissociation explained why behaviors that occur under hypnosis seem involuntary or automatic. Given the suggestion that "your arm will start to feel lighter and will begin to rise," the subject intentionally raises his or her arm, but only the hidden observer is aware of this. The main stream of consciousness that responds to the command is blocked from this awareness and thus perceives that the arm is rising all by itself.

Social-Cognitive Theories

To other theorists, hypnosis does not represent a special state of dissociated consciousness (Kirsch, 2001; Spanos, 1991). Instead, **social-cognitive theories** *propose that hypnotic experiences result from expectations of people who are motivated to take on the role of being hypnotized.* Most people believe that hypnosis involves a trancelike state and responsiveness to suggestions. People highly motivated to conform to this role develop a perceptual set—a readiness to respond to the hypnotist's suggestions and to perceive hypnotic experiences as real and involuntary.

In a classic study, Martin Orne (1959) of the University of Pennsylvania illustrated the importance of expectations about hypnosis. During a classroom demonstration, college students were told that hypnotized people frequently exhibit spontaneous stiffening of the muscles in the dominant hand. (Actually, this rarely occurs.) An accomplice of the lecturer pretended to be hypnotized and, sure enough, he "spontaneously" exhibited hand stiffness. When students who had seen the demonstration were later hypnotized, 55 percent of them exhibited stiffening of the hand without any suggestion from the hypnotist. Control group participants saw a demonstration that did not mention or display hand stiffening. Not one of these students exhibited hand stiffening when they were hypnotized.

Does social-cognitive theory imply that hypnotized people are faking or playacting? Not at all. Role theorists emphasize that when people immerse themselves in the hypnotic role, their responses are completely real and may indeed represent altered experiences (Kirsch, 2001). Recall from the chapter on perception that perceptual sets strongly influence how the brain organizes sensory information. Often we literally see what we expect to see. According to social-cognitive theory, many effects of hypnosis represent an extension of this principle. The hypnotized subject whose arm "automatically" rises in response to a suggestion genuinely perceives the behavior to be involuntary because this is what the subject expects, and because attention is focused externally on the hypnotist and hypnotic suggestion.

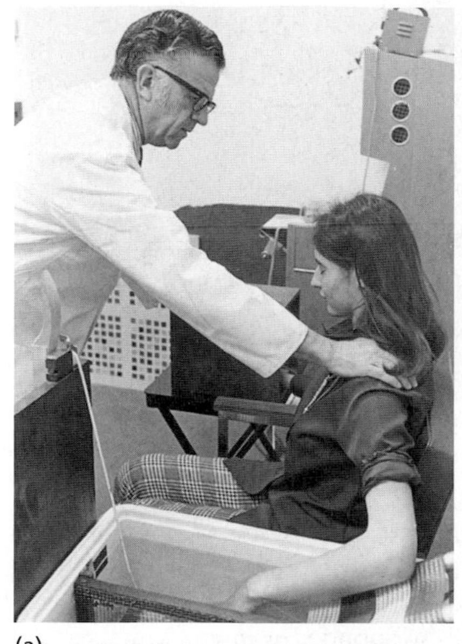
(a)

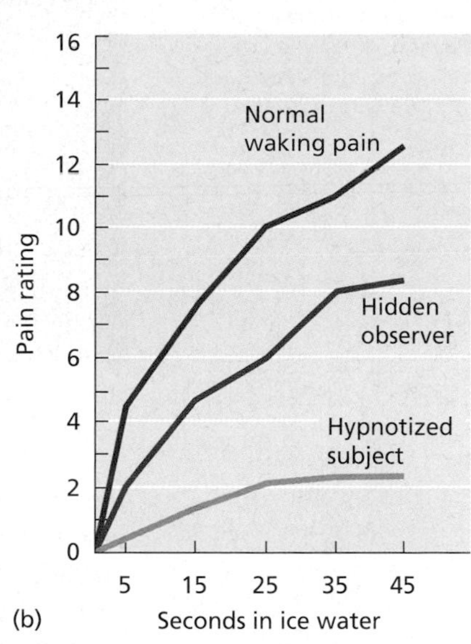

(b)

FIGURE 5.36

(a) This hypnotized woman's hand is immersed in painfully cold ice water. Placing his hand on her shoulder, Ernest Hilgard contacts her dissociated hidden observer. (b) This graph shows pain intensity ratings given by a woman when she is not hypnotized, by the woman under hypnosis, and by her hidden observer in the same hypnotic state. The hidden observer reports more pain than the hypnotized woman but less than the woman when she is not hypnotized. Source: Based on Hilgard, 1977.

The Hypnotized Brain

Can peering inside the brain help us resolve the debate about the nature of hypnosis? To find out, take a look at the colored drawing and the gray-scale drawing in Figure 5.37. Now, do two simple tasks:

1. Look at the colored drawing again, form a mental image of it, and try to drain the color out of it. In other words, try to visualize it as if it were a gray-scale figure.
2. Next, look at the gray-scale drawing, form a mental picture of it, and try to add color to it. In other words, visualize it as if it were a colored figure.

Psychologist Stephen Kosslyn and coworkers (2000) identified 8 people who scored high in hypnotic susceptibility and who reported they could successfully drain away or add color to their mental images of such drawings. Subjects then performed these tasks (in varying order) while inside a PET scanner. On some trials they were hypnotized, and on other trials they were not hypnotized.

The PET scans revealed that whether subjects were hypnotized or not, an area in the right hemisphere that processes information about color was more active when subjects visualized

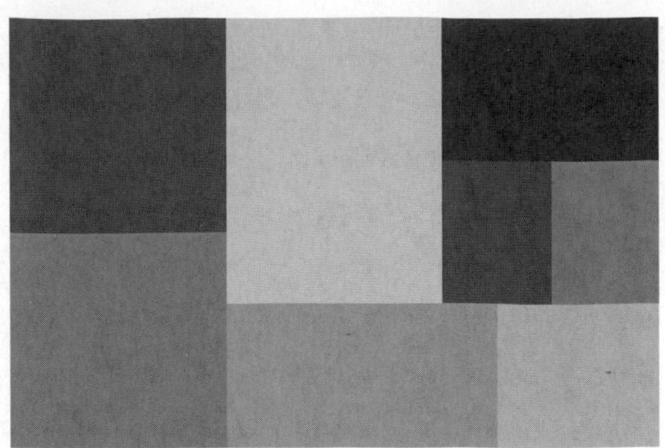

FIGURE 5.37

Color and gray-scale drawings similar to the ones used by Kosslyn and his colleagues (2000).

the gray drawing as having color (Task 2) than when they visualized the color drawing as gray (Task 1). In other words, this right-hemisphere region actually responded to mental images involving color, and subjects didn't need to be hypnotized for this brain activity to occur. In the left hemisphere, however, visualizing the gray drawing as having color increased brain activation in one particular region only when the subjects were hypnotized. As the researchers noted, "The right hemisphere appeared to respond to imagery per se, whereas the left required the additional boost provided by hypnosis" (Kosslyn et al., 2000, p. 1283).

The results of brain-imaging studies like this one converge with other physiological findings in leading to an important conclusion: Hypnotized people are not simply "faking it" or playacting but rather are indeed experiencing an altered state of brain activation that matches their verbal reports (Raz & Shapiro, 2002). In this study, when hypnotized subjects mentally added color to the drawing and drained color from it, their brain activity changed in ways beyond those brought about by mental imagery in a nonhypnotized state. Likewise, other brain-imaging studies reveal that giving hypnotized subjects pain-reducing suggestions not only decreases their subjective report of pain but also decreases activity in several brain regions that process pain signals (Petrovic & Ingvar, 2002). But do these findings indicate that hypnosis is an altered state of dissociation?

Social-cognitive theorists would argue that these findings do not resolve the issue (Kirsch, 2001). They note that hypnotic experiences are indeed subjectively real, and the fact that brain activity patterns under hypnosis differ from those of simple mental imagery does not contradict their position that people's expectations are what lead them to become hypnotized in the first place. In sum, cognitive neuroscience is providing us with fascinating new windows through which to view the hypnotized brain, but it will take more research before the basic nature of hypnosis is resolved.

I'm Intoxicated, No Matter What You Say!

To close our discussion of hypnosis and altered states, consider the behavior of a college student in the *Research Close-Up* experiment on drinking and driving. (Nobody was hypnotized in this study.) This student consumed three nonalcoholic drinks, but through taste and smell cues, he was convincingly led to believe that they were alcoholic. Prior to taking a Breathalyzer test, he estimated his blood-alcohol level to be .07, just below the .08 legal driving limit where he lived. He felt intoxicated, and when told the drinks were nonalcoholic, he argued that there had to be a mistake. When shown his true Breathalyzer result of .000, he claimed it was rigged and refused to drive home until the effects of his "drinks" wore off (MacDonald et al., 1995).

This example, along with topics previously covered (e.g., voodoo spells, placebo effects, alcohol expectation effects on sexual arousal), suggests that we have a remarkable capacity to alter our own state of consciousness without being aware that we ourselves are responsible for causing the change. The popular belief about hypnosis is that a hypnotist places the subject under a mysterious spell or into a trance, but as the dissociation and social-cognitive camps agree, this is a myth (Kirsch, 2001; Raz & Shapiro, 2002). Rather, more like a guide on a wilderness hike, the hypnotist may point the way, but the subject is doing the actual mental work and ultimately altering her or his own state of consciousness.

IN REVIEW

- *Hypnosis involves an increased receptiveness to suggestions. Hypnotic susceptibility scales measure people's responsiveness to hypnosis.*
- *Hypnotized people subjectively experience their actions as involuntary, but hypnosis has no unique power to make people behave against their will. In experiments, hypnotized and nonhypnotized people are equally likely to show striking physiological reactions and perform "amazing" physical feats. Hypnosis increases pain tolerance, as do other psychological techniques.*
- *Some people can be led to experience hypnotic and posthypnotic amnesia. The use of hypnosis to improve memory is controversial. Hypnosis increases the danger that people will develop distorted memories about events in response to leading questions asked by a hypnotist or examiner.*
- *Dissociation theories view hypnosis as an altered state of divided consciousness, whereas social-cognitive theories state that hypnotic experiences occur because people have strong beliefs and expectations about hypnosis and are highly motivated to enter a hypnotized "role."*
- *Brain-imaging studies reveal that hypnotized people display changes in neural activity consistent with their subjectively reported experiences. This and other physiological evidence support the view that hypnosis involves an altered state of consciousness, but whether it is a dissociated state and the extent to which people's beliefs and expectations bring about this state are still unclear.*

KEY TERMS AND CONCEPTS

Each term has been boldfaced and defined in the chapter on the page indicated in parentheses.

What Do You Think?

EARLY BIRDS, CLIMATE, AND CULTURE p. 161

As a critical thinker, it's important to keep in mind that correlation does not establish causation. This is a correlational study, not an experiment. The major variables (climate of country, students' degree of morningness) were not manipulated, they were only measured. The association between climate and morningness suggests the possibility of a causal relation, but we must consider other possible explanations.

First, why might climate affect morningness? The researchers (who were from India, Spain, the United Kingdom, and the United States) hypothesized that to avoid performing daily activities during the hottest part of the day, people who live in warmer climates would adapt to a pattern of rising early in the morning, a finding consistent with a prior study that revealed strong tendencies toward morningness among Brazilians (Benedito-Silva et al., 1989).

Second, as the authors note, these results could be due to factors other than climate. The Netherlands, the United Kingdom, and the United States share a northern European heritage, and perhaps some aspect of this common background predisposes people toward less morningness. Yet, say the authors, India's cultural traditions are distinct from those of Spain and Colombia, so it's difficult to apply the "common cultural heritage" argument to explain the greater morningness found among students from these countries. If not cultural heritage, perhaps the greater industrialization and use of air-conditioned environments in the Netherlands, the United Kingdom, and the United States to avoid summer heat reduce the necessity for residents to adapt circadian cycles to local climatic conditions. Strip away the air-conditioning from homes, workplaces, food markets, shopping centers, and cars, buses, and trains, and it would be interesting to see whether people would gradually shift toward greater morningness in hot weather. Aware of the limitations of the study, the authors suggest that climate may be just one of several factors that contribute to cross-cultural differences in morningness. ■

HYPNOSIS AND AMAZING FEATS p. 191

No matter the claim, as critical thinkers, it's always important to think about the concept of control groups. Thus, you should keep this question in mind: What would have happened anyway, even without this special treatment, intervention, or condition? Applied to hypnosis, the key question is whether people can exhibit these same amazing feats when they are not hypnotized. When a stage hypnotist gets someone to perform the human plank, the audience indeed attributes this feat to the hypnotic trance. What the audience doesn't know is that an average man suspended in this manner can support 300 pounds on his chest with little discomfort and no need of a hypnotic trance. Indeed, Figure 5.34 shows The Amazing Kreskin, a professional performer and self-proclaimed "mentalist," standing on someone who is *not* hypnotized.

As for the allergy experiment, the findings are impressive, but we must ask whether allergic people might show the same reactions if they were not hypnotized. For this reason, the researchers properly designed their experiment to measure the responses of 8 nonhypnotized control participants (Ikemi & Nakagawa, 1962). When blindfolded and exposed to a toxic leaf but misled to believe that it was harmless, 7 out of the 8 nonhypnotized people did not show an allergic response. Conversely, when their arm was rubbed with a harmless leaf but they were falsely told it was toxic, all 8 had an allergic reaction. In short, the nonhypnotized people responded the same way as the hypnotized subjects.

Other research shows that under hypnosis, vision in nearsighted people can be improved, warts can be cured, and stomach acidity can be increased. However, well-controlled studies show that nonhypnotized subjects can exhibit these same responses (Spanos & Chaves, 1988). As we have already seen when discussing placebo effects and other mind-body interactions, people's beliefs and expectations can produce real physiological effects. ■

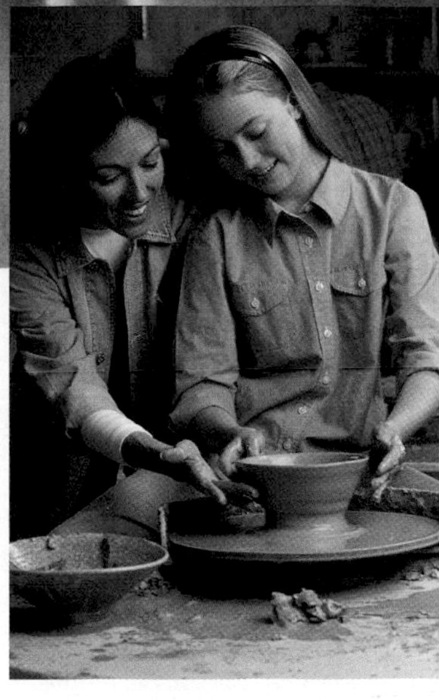

6

LEARNING AND ADAPTATION
The Role of Experience

CHAPTER OUTLINE

A man who carries a cat by the tail learns something he can learn in no other way.

—Mark Twain

Thanks to six sessions of psychotherapy, Carol's life is normal again. She is now free from the intense fear of something most of us take for granted: riding in a car. Carol was severely injured in a car crash and hospitalized for months. A year later, she described to a therapist how the fear began when her husband came to take her home from the hospital.

> *As we walked toward the new car he had bought, I began to feel uneasy. I felt nervous all the way home. It started to get worse after that. I found myself avoiding riding in the car, and couldn't drive it at all. I stopped visiting friends and tried to get them to come to our house. . . . After a while, even the sight of a car started to make me nervous. . . . You know, this is the first time I've left the house in about four months.*

To help Carol, the therapist used a highly successful procedure based, in part, on century-old principles of learning discovered in laboratory investigations of salivating dogs.

■■■

O*utside a Las Vegas casino, a woman volunteers her time soliciting donations for a local charity. Though hot and tired, she remains upbeat and thanks each person who drops money in her collection can. Inside, exhausted and down to his last dollar, a man has been playing the slot machines for 36 hours. A casino guard mutters to a cocktail waitress, "I'll never understand what keeps these guys going."*

■■■

A *judge in New York City prohibited two teenage brothers from watching professional wrestling on television because they were becoming too violent. The boys vigorously practiced body slams and choke-holds, repeatedly injuring one another. Their frightened mother reported that her 13-year-old son tried to apply a "sleeper-hold" on her as she was cooking in the kitchen. Fortunately, she broke free before losing consciousness. The judge told the mother that either she had to prohibit the boys from watching wrestling or he would have the family's TV set removed and might place the boys in foster homes (*Sporting News, *August 19, 1985).*

▶ 1. What is learning? Contrast the behavioral and ethological approaches.

Although vastly different, the behaviors in these examples share an important characteristic: They are all learned. Our genetic endowment creates the potential for these behaviors to occur, but we are not biologically programmed to fear cars, solicit donations, play slot machines, or wrestle people by applying sleeper-holds.

Reflect for a moment on how much of your behavior is learned: telling time, getting dressed, driving, reading, using money, playing sports, and so on. Beyond such skills, learning affects our emotional reactions, perceptions, and physiological responses. Through experience, we learn to think, act, and feel in ways that contribute richly to our individual identity.

Learning *is a process by which experience produces a relatively enduring change in an organism's behavior or capabilities.* The term *capabilities* highlights a distinction made by many theorists: "knowing how" versus "doing." For example, experience may provide us with immediate knowledge (e.g., the boys *learned how* to apply a choke-hold when they watched a wrestling match on TV), but in science we must measure learning by actual changes in *performance* (e.g., later that day they began applying choke-holds to each other).

ADAPTING TO THE ENVIRONMENT

We encounter changing environments from the moment we are born, each with its unique challenges. Some challenges, such as acquiring food and shelter, affect survival. Others, such as deciding where to go on a date, do not. But no matter what the challenge, learning makes it possible for us to adapt to it. In fact, we can view learning as a process of *personal adaptation* to the circumstances of our lives.

How Do We Learn? The Search for Mechanisms

For a long time, the study of learning proceeded along two largely separate paths, guided by two different perspectives on behavior: *behaviorism* and *ethology* (Bolles & Beecher, 1988). Within psychology, behaviorists focused on how organisms learn, examining the *processes* by which experience influences behavior. Behaviorists assumed that there are laws of learning that apply to virtually all organisms. For example, each species they studied—whether birds, reptiles, rats, monkeys, or humans—responded in predictable ways to patterns of reward or punishment.

Behaviorists treated the organism as a *tabula rasa*, or "blank tablet," on which learning experiences were inscribed. Most of their research was conducted with nonhuman species in controlled laboratory settings. Behaviorists explained learning solely in terms of directly observable events and avoided speculating about an organism's unobservable "mental state." The learning principles they discovered are the main focus of this chapter.

Why Do We Learn? The Search for Functions

While behaviorism flourished in America, a specialty area called *ethology* arose in Europe within the discipline of biology (Lorenz, 1937; Tinbergen, 1951). Ethology focused on animal behavior in the natural environment. Ethologists viewed the organism as anything but a blank tablet, arguing that because of evolution, every species comes into the world biologically prepared to act in certain ways. They focused on the *functions* of behavior, particularly its **adaptive significance:** *how a behavior influences an organism's chances of survival and reproduction in its natural environment.*

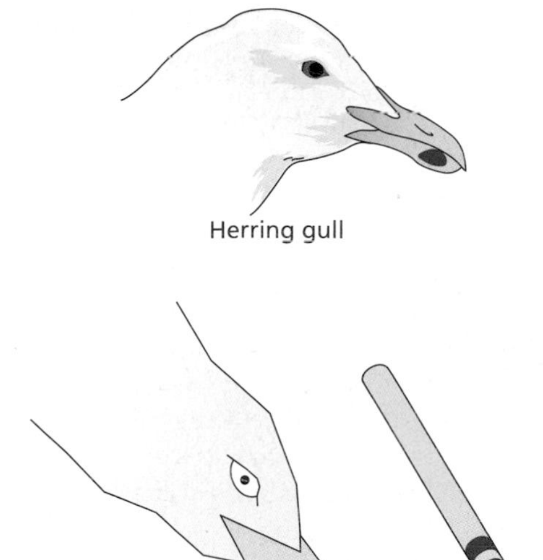

FIGURE 6.1

A herring gull hatchling will peck most frequently at objects that are long and have red markings, even if they are inanimate models or do not look like an adult gull. This fixed action pattern is present from birth and does not require learning. The stimuli that trigger a fixed action pattern are called releaser stimuli. SOURCE: Adapted from Hailman, 1969.

Consider how newly hatched herring gulls beg for food by pecking at a red mark on their parents' bills. Parents respond by regurgitating food, which the chicks ingest. Seeing the red mark and long shape of the parent's bill automatically triggers the chicks' pecking. This behavior is so strongly prewired that chicks will peck just as much at long inanimate models or objects with red dots or stripes (Figure 6.1). Ethologists call this instinctive behavior a **fixed action pattern,** *an unlearned response automatically triggered by a particular stimulus.*

As ethology grew, two things became clear. First, some fixed action patterns could be modified by experience. Unlike herring gull hatchlings, older chicks have learned what an adult gull looks like and will not peck at inanimate objects unless they resemble the head of an adult (Hailman, 1967). Second, in many cases what appeared to be "instinctive" behavior actually involved learning. Ethologists noted striking differences among species, not so much in how they learned but in what they learned in order to survive.

Consider the indigo bunting, a beautiful songbird that migrates every spring from Central America to eastern North America. It flies during the night, navigating by flying toward the North Star, which, by virtue of being directly over the North Pole, is the only star in the Northern Hemisphere that maintains a fixed compass position as the earth rotates on its axis. In autumn, the bunting migrates south at night by flying away from the North Star. Were the bird to navigate by any other star, it would fly increasingly off course because all other stars move across the night sky.

Navigating by the North Star would seem to be a fixed action pattern, as if birds instinctively know where north is. To test this idea, Stephen Emlen (1975) raised indigo buntings in a planetarium with either a true sky (with the North Star as the stationary star) or a false sky (in which a star in a different portion of the sky was the only one that remained stationary). In the fall, the birds became restless in their cages because it was time to migrate. As expected, the buntings raised with a true sky moved away from the North Star. But the other group moved away from the false stationary star, indicating that environmental changes could modify the bunting's navigational behavior. Emlen concluded that the bunting is genetically prewired to navigate by a fixed star, but it has to learn through observation and experience which specific star is stationary.

Learning, Evolution, and Culture

▶ 2. Discuss the relation of evolution and culture to learning. Describe habituation and its adaptive significance.

The separate paths of behaviorism and ethology have increasingly converged (Papini, 2002), reminding us that the environment shapes behavior in two fundamental ways: through *personal adaptation* and through *species adaptation*. Our personal adaptation to life's circumstances occurs through the laws of learning that the behaviorists examined, and it results from our interactions with immediate and past environments. When you drive or go out on a date, your behavior is influenced by the immediate environment (e.g., traffic, your date's smiles) and by capabilities you acquired through past experiences (e.g., driving skills, social skills).

The environment also influences species adaptation. Over the course of evolution, environmental conditions faced by each species help shape its biology. This does not occur directly. Learning, for example, does not modify an organism's genes, and therefore learned behaviors cannot pass genetically from one generation to the next. But through natural selection, genetically based characteristics that enhance a species' ability to adapt to the environment—and thus to survive and reproduce—are more likely to be passed on to the next generation. Eventually, as physical features (e.g., the red mark on the adult gull's beak) and behavioral tendencies (e.g., the chick's pecking the mark) influenced by those genes become more common, they become a part of a species' very nature.

Theorists propose that as the human brain evolved, it acquired adaptive capacities that enhanced our ability to learn and solve problems (Cosmides & Tooby, 2002). In essence, we have become prewired to learn. Of course, so have other species. Because all species face some common adaptive challenges, we might expect some similarity in their library of learning mechanisms. Every environment is full of events, and each organism must learn

- which events are, or are not, important to its survival and well-being;
- which stimuli signal that an important event is about to occur; and
- whether its responses will produce positive or negative consequences.

As we will see, each learning process examined in this chapter helps us respond to one or more of these adaptive challenges.

Just as evolution shapes the underlying processes by which we learn, culture shapes much of what we learn. Cultural norms and socialization influence skills that we acquire, our patterns of social behavior, our beliefs and preferences, our very sense of identity, and even the fundamental way our brain organizes its perceptions (Figure 6.2). That culture influences who each of us becomes should not be surprising, given that learning represents adaptation to the environment and culture is the human-made part of our environment (Herskovits, 1948). Yet the basic learning mechanisms that foster this adaptation are found across countless species. Consider, for example, a learning process known as *habituation*.

Habituation

Imagine that you are a participant in an experiment. You're sitting alone in a quiet laboratory when suddenly (as part of the experiment) a loud sound startles you. Your body jerks slightly, you become aroused, and you look toward the source of the sound. Over time, as you hear it again and again, your startle response diminishes until eventually you ignore the sound.

Habituation *is a decrease in the strength of response to a repeated stimulus*. It may be the simplest form of learning and occurs across species ranging from humans to dragonflies to sea snails. Touch the skin of a sea snail in a certain location, and it will

FIGURE 6.2

People in each culture learn specific behaviors in order to adapt to their environment. Even the same general skill may take on different forms depending on unique environmental demands. The skill that most urbanized people have learned to acquire food—navigating around a supermarket—would have little adaptive value in some other cultures.

reflexively contract its gill. With repeated touches, this response habituates. Habituation serves a key adaptive function. If an organism responded to every stimulus in its environment, it would rapidly become overwhelmed and exhausted. By learning not to respond to uneventful familiar stimuli, organisms conserve energy and can attend to other stimuli that are important (Eisenstein et al., 2001). As Figure 6.3 explains, habituation also plays an important role in enabling scientists to study behavior.

"March 5, 1984: After several months, I now feel that these strange little rodents have finally accepted me as one of their own."

FIGURE 6.3

Before collecting data, scientists often allow the people or animals that they are studying to habituate to their presence.

IN REVIEW

- *Learning is a process by which experience produces a relatively enduring change in an organism's behavior or capabilities. Learning is measured by changes in performance.*
- *Learning involves adapting to the environment. Historically, behaviorists focused on the processes by which organisms learn, and ethologists focused on the adaptive significance of learning.*
- *The environment influences adaption in two major ways: personal adaptation, which occurs through the laws of learning that the behaviorists examined, and species adaptation, which occurs through natural selection pressures that guide evolution.*
- *Habituation is a decrease in the strength of a response to a repeated stimulus. It may be the simplest form of learning and allows organisms to attend to other stimuli that are more important.*

(a)

(b)

FIGURE 6.4

(a) Ivan Pavlov (the man with the white beard) is shown here with colleagues and one of his canine subjects. (b) In his early research, Pavlov measured salivation using a simple device similar to the one shown here. In later research, a collection tube was inserted directly into the salivary gland.

CLASSICAL CONDITIONING: ASSOCIATING ONE STIMULUS WITH ANOTHER

Life is full of interesting associations. Do you ever hear songs on the radio or find yourself in places that instantly make you feel good because they're connected to special times you've had? When you smell the aroma of popcorn or freshly baked cookies, does your mouth water or your stomach growl? These examples illustrate a learning process called **classical conditioning,** *in which an organism learns to associate two stimuli* (e.g., a song and a pleasant event), *such that one stimulus* (the song) *comes to elicit a response* (feeling happy) *that originally was elicited only by the other stimulus* (the pleasurable event).

Like habituation, classical conditioning is a basic form of learning that occurs across numerous species (Antonov et al., 2001). Its discovery dates back to the late 1800s and an odd twist of fate.

Pavlov's Pioneering Research

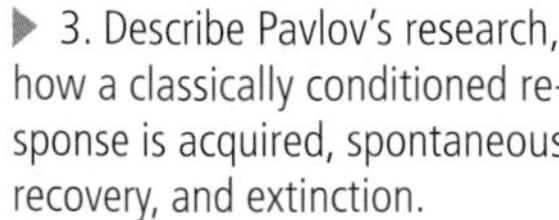

▶ 3. Describe Pavlov's research, how a classically conditioned response is acquired, spontaneous recovery, and extinction.

In the 1860s, Ivan Pavlov was studying theology in a Russian seminary when his plans to join the priesthood unexpectedly changed. A new government policy allowed the translation of Western scientific publications into Russian. Pavlov read Darwin's theory of evolution and other works, which sparked a strong interest in the sciences (Windholz, 1997). Pavlov became a renowned physiologist, conducting research on digestion in dogs that won him the Nobel Prize in 1904.

To study digestion, Pavlov presented food to dogs and measured their natural salivary response (Figure 6.4). But, as often occurs in science, Pavlov made an accidental but important discovery through astute observation. He noticed that with repeated testing, the dogs began to salivate before the food was presented, such as when they heard the footsteps of the approaching experimenter.

Further study confirmed Pavlov's observation. Dogs have a natural reflex to salivate to food but not to tones. Yet when a tone or other stimulus that ordinarily did not cause salivation was presented just before food powder was squirted into a dog's mouth, the sound of the tone alone soon made the dog salivate. Pavlov's (1923/1928) research team rigorously studied this process of learning by association, which came to be called *classical*, or *Pavlovian, conditioning*. Many psychologists regard Pavlov's discovery as "among the most important in the history of psychology" (Dewsbury, 1997). But why all the fuss about dogs salivating to tones?

This question raises a widely misunderstood point about basic scientific research: It is the *underlying principle*—not the specific findings—that is paramount. Here is a basic learning process that performs a key adaptive function: Classical conditioning alerts organisms to stimuli that signal the impending arrival of an important event. And, Pavlov noted, if salivation could be conditioned, so might other bodily processes, including those affecting susceptibility to disease and mental disorders.

Basic Principles

What factors influence the acquisition and persistence of conditioned responses? Let's examine some basic principles of conditioning.

Acquisition

Acquisition refers to the period during which a response is being learned. Suppose we wish to condition a dog to salivate to a tone. Sounding the tone initially may cause the dog to perk up its ears but not to salivate. At this time, the tone is a *neutral stimulus* because it does not elicit salivation (Figure 6.5). If, however, we place food in the dog's mouth, the dog will salivate. This salivation response to food is *reflexive*—it's what dogs do by nature. Because no learning is required for food to produce salivation, the food is an **unconditioned stimulus (UCS):** *a stimulus that elicits a reflexive or innate response (the UCR) without prior learning.* Salivation is an **unconditioned response (UCR):** *a reflexive or innate response that is elicited by a stimulus (the UCS) without prior learning.*

Next the tone and the food are paired—each pairing is called a *learning trial*—and the dog salivates. After several learning trials, if the tone is presented by itself, the dog salivates even though there is no food. The tone has now become a **conditioned stimulus (CS)**, *a stimulus that, through association with a UCS, comes to elicit a conditioned response similar to the original UCR.* Because the dog is now salivating to the tone, salivation has become a **conditioned response (CR)**, *a response elicited by a conditioned stimulus.* Notice that we have two terms for salivation: UCR and CR. When the dog salivates to food, this UCR is a natural, unlearned (unconditioned) reflex. But when it salivates to a tone, this CR represents a learned (conditioned) response.

During acquisition, a CS typically must be paired multiple times with a UCS to establish a strong CR (Figure 6.6). Pavlov also found that a tone became a CS more rapidly when it was followed by greater amounts of food. Indeed, when the UCS is intense and aversive—such as an electric shock or a traumatic event—conditioning may require only one CS-UCS pairing (Richard et al.,

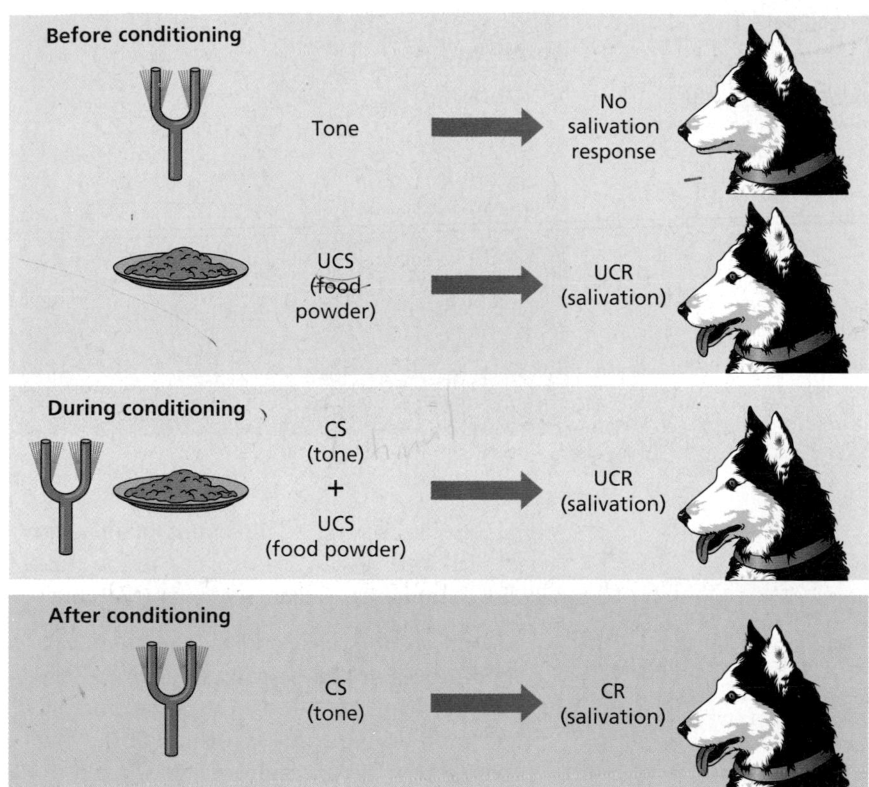

FIGURE 6.5

In classical conditioning, after a neutral stimulus such as a tone is repeatedly associated with food (unconditioned stimulus), the tone becomes a conditioned stimulus capable of eliciting a salivation response (conditioned response).

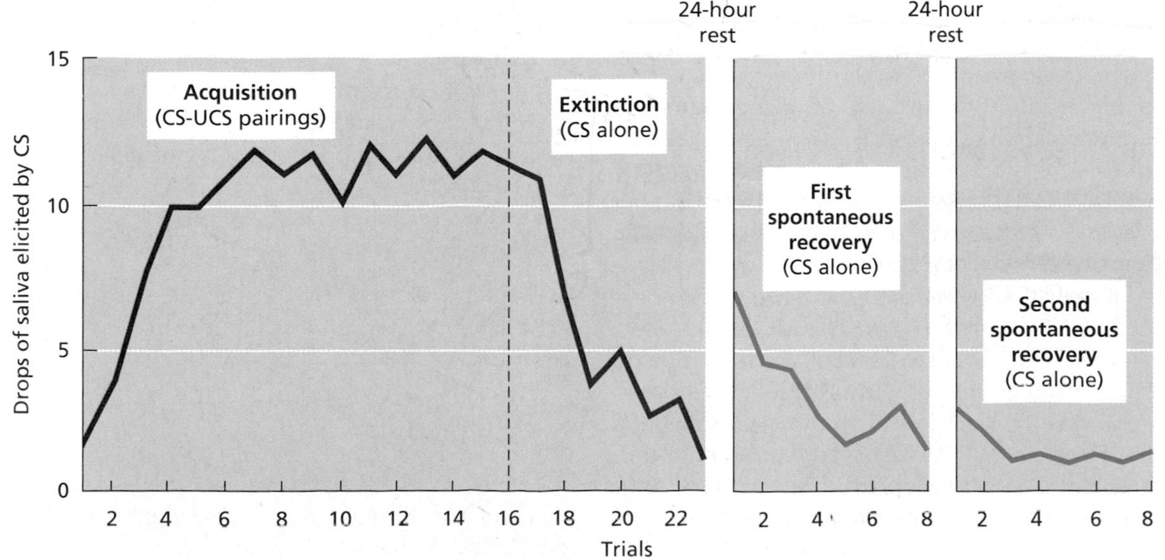

FIGURE 6.6

The strength of the CR (salivation) increases during the acquisition phase as the CS (tone) and the UCS (food) are paired on each trial. During the extinction phase, only the CS is presented, and the strength of the CR decreases and finally disappears. After a rest period following extinction, presentation of the CS elicits a weaker CR (spontaneous recovery) that extinguishes more quickly than before.

FIGURE 6.7

It is likely that Carol's phobia of cars was acquired through classical conditioning.

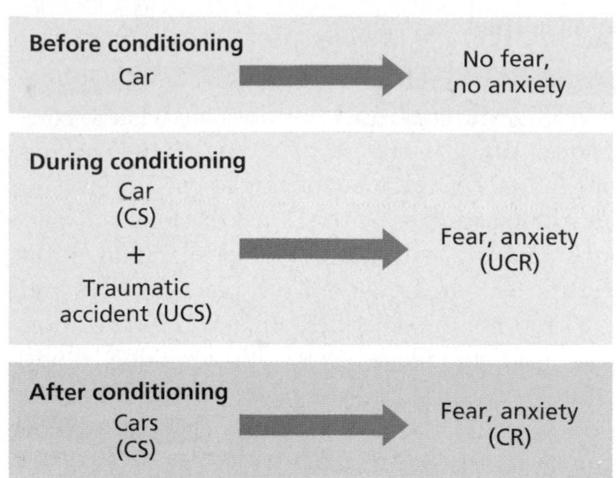

2000). Carol's car phobia illustrates this *one-trial (single-trial) learning*. As she explains to the therapist, her automobile accident was very traumatic:

> My car went out of control. It crashed into a light pole, rolled over, and began to burn. I . . . couldn't get out . . . I'm sorry, doctor, but even thinking about it is horrible. I had a broken pelvis and third-degree burns over half my body.

In Carol's example, a stimulus (riding in or seeing a car) became a CS after only one pairing with an intense UCS (an extremely painful crash). Fear was the UCR, and it became a CR triggered by the sight of cars (Figure 6.7).

The sequence and time interval of the CS-UCS pairing also affect conditioning. Learning usually occurs most quickly with *forward short-delay pairing:* The CS (tone) appears first and is still present when the UCS (food) appears. In *forward trace pairing*, the tone would come on and off, and afterward the food would be presented. In forward pairing, it is often optimal for the CS to appear no more than 2 or 3 seconds before the UCS (Klein & Mowrer, 1989). Forward pairing has adaptive value because the CS signals the impending arrival of the UCS. Typically, presenting the CS and UCS at the same time *(simultaneous pairing)* produces less rapid conditioning, and learning is slowest when the CS is presented after the UCS *(backward pairing)*.

Once a CR has become established, it may persist for a long time. In one study, hospitalized Navy veterans who had seen combat aboard ships in World War II showed strong physiological responses to the sound of a "call-to-battle-stations" gong, even though 15 years had passed since this stimulus had been associated with danger. Hospitalized Army veterans who had not served on ships were much less emotionally responsive to this stimulus (Edwards, 1962). Similarly, after her horrible accident, Carol's fear of cars persisted for months despite the fact that she was in no further crashes.

To summarize, classical conditioning usually is strongest when (1) there are repeated CS-UCS pairings, (2) the UCS is more intense, (3) the sequence involves forward pairing, and (4) the time interval between the CS and UCS is short.

Extinction and Spontaneous Recovery

If the function of classical conditioning is to help organisms adapt to their environment, there must be a way of eliminating the CR when it is no longer appropriate. Fortunately there is. **Extinction** *is a process in which the CS is presented repeatedly in the absence of the UCS, causing the CR to weaken and eventually disappear*. Each presentation of the CS without the UCS is called an *extinction trial*. When Pavlov repeatedly presented the tone without the food, the dogs eventually stopped salivating to the tone (see Figure 6.6). Occasional re-pairings of the CS (e.g., tone) and the UCS (e.g., food) usually are required to maintain a CR.

Perhaps it seems inconsistent to you that Pavlov's dogs would eventually stop salivating to the tone if food no longer was presented with it, whereas Carol's phobia of cars persisted for months even though she was not in any additional crashes. How can we explain this?

What Do You Think?

WHY DID CAROL'S CAR PHOBIA PERSIST?

Reread the definition of extinction carefully. In Carol's case, identify the CS, UCS, and CR. Can you explain why her fear of cars did not extinguish on its own? Think about it, then see page 237.

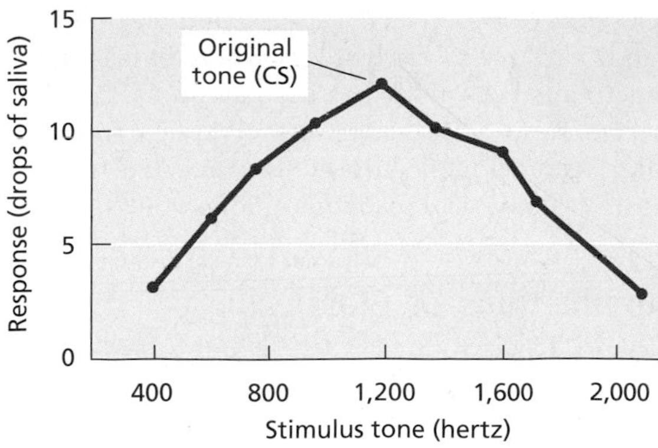

FIGURE 6.8

A stimulus generalization curve. An animal will salivate most strongly to the CS that was originally paired with the UCS. Progressively weaker conditioned responses occur as stimuli become less similar to the CS, as seen here with tones of lower or higher frequencies (pitch).

Even when a CR extinguishes, this does not mean that all traces of it are erased. Suppose we condition a dog to salivate to a tone. Then we repeatedly present the tone without food, and the dog eventually stops salivating to the tone. Later, if we present the tone alone, the dog may salivate once again. This is called **spontaneous recovery,** *the reappearance of a previously extinguished CR after a rest period and without new learning trials.* As Figure 6.6 shows, the spontaneously recovered CR usually is weaker than the initial CR and extinguishes more rapidly in the absence of the UCS.

Generalization and Discrimination

Thus far we have explained Carol's car phobia as a case of one-trial conditioning in which being in a car was paired with a traumatic experience. But why would Carol fear other cars when it was her old car—now long gone—that was in the accident?

Pavlov found that once a CR is acquired, the organism often responds not only to the original CS but also to stimuli that are similar to it. The greater the stimulus similarity, the greater the chance that a CR will occur. A dog that salivates to a medium-pitched tone is more likely to salivate to a new tone slightly different in pitch than to a very low- or high-pitched tone. Learning theorists call this **stimulus generalization:** *stimuli similar to the initial CS elicit a CR* (Figure 6.8).

Stimulus generalization serves critical adaptive functions. An animal that ignores the sound of rustling bushes and then is attacked by a hidden predator will (assuming it survives) become alarmed by the sound of a rustling bush in the future. If stimulus generalization did not occur, then the next time the animal heard rustling it would become alarmed only if the sound was identical to the rustling that preceded the earlier attack. This would be of little value to the animal's survival. Through stimulus generalization, however, the animal develops an alarm response to a range of rustling sounds. Some will be false alarms, but safe is better than sorry.

Unfortunately, maladaptive responses can occur when generalization spreads too far. The car involved in Carol's crash was gone, but after leaving the hospital her fear immediately generalized to the new car her husband bought. Over time, stimulus generalization continued, though the fear was weaker:

> CAROL: After a while, even the sight of a car started to make me nervous.
>
> THERAPIST: As nervous as riding in one?
>
> CAROL: No, but still nervous. It's so stupid. I'd even turn off the TV during scenes involving car crashes.

To prevent stimulus generalization from running amok, organisms must be able to discriminate (i.e., detect) differences among stimuli. An animal that becomes alarmed at every sound it hears would exhaust itself from stress. It must learn to distinguish irrelevant sounds from those that may signal danger. In classical conditioning, **discrimination** *is demonstrated when a CR* (such as an alarm reaction) *occurs to one stimulus* (a sound) *but not to others.* Carol's fear of cars was widespread, but it did not occur when she saw bicycles, trains, or airplanes.

As another example, when my mother was a girl a large dog bit her several times. From that painful moment on, she was extremely afraid of dogs. Many years later, when my brother wanted a dog, my mother would have none of it. But he pleaded endlessly. How could our family satisfy my brother's wish yet not trigger my mother's fear? The solution was to get a dog as dissimilar as possible to the large dog that bit her, in hopes that my mother's fear would display stimulus discrimination. So we adopted a tiny Chihuahua puppy—and the plan was half-successful. My mother was not afraid and adored the dog. Alas, my brother's fondness for big dogs failed to generalize to Chihuahuas, and he was repeatedly observed muttering, "yippity oversized rat."

▶ 4. Explain stimulus generalization, discrimination, higher-order conditioning, and their adaptive significance.

Higher-Order Conditioning

Imagine that we have exposed a dog to repeated tone-food pairings and the tone is now a well-established CS that elicits a strong salivation

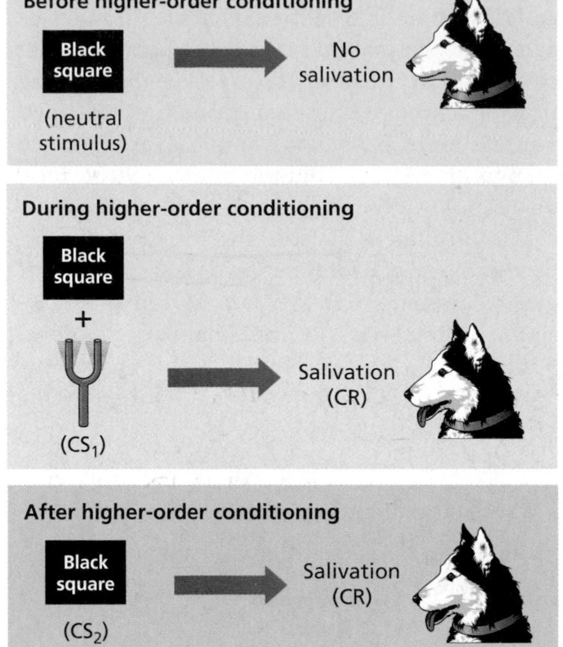

FIGURE 6.9

Once a tone has become a conditioned stimulus that triggers salivation, we can now use it to condition a salivation response to a new neutral stimulus: a black square. The tone is the CS_1. The black square becomes the CS_2.

▶ 5. How is classical conditioning relevant to fear acquisition and treatment, attraction and aversion, and health?

response. Next, suppose that we present a neutral stimulus, such as a black square, and the dog does not salivate. Now, we present the black square just prior to sounding the tone but do not present any food. After repeated square-tone pairings, the square will become a CS and elicit salivation by itself (Figure 6.9). This process, discovered by Pavlov, is called **higher-order conditioning:** *A neutral stimulus becomes a CS after being paired with an already established CS.* Typically, a higher-order CS produces a CR that is weaker and extinguishes more rapidly than the original CR: The dog will salivate less to the black square than to the tone, and its response to the square will extinguish sooner.

Higher-order conditioning greatly expands the influence of conditioned stimuli and can affect what we come to value, fear, like or dislike (Gerwitz & Davis, 2000). For example, political candidates try to get us to like them by associating themselves with patriotic symbols, cuddly babies, admired athletes and civic leaders, and other conditioned stimuli that already trigger positive emotional reactions among voters.

FIGURE 6.10

John Watson and Rosalie Rayner examine how Little Albert reacts to a furry mask.

Applications of Classical Conditioning

Pavlov's belief that salivation was merely the tip of the classical conditioning iceberg has proven correct. Conditioning principles discovered in laboratory research—much of it with nonhuman species—help us understand diverse human behaviors and problems.

Acquiring and Overcoming Fear

Pavlov's discoveries enabled early American behaviorists to challenge Freud's psychoanalytic view of the causes of anxiety disorders, such as phobias. To explain Carol's car phobia, no Freudian assumptions about hidden unconscious conflicts or repressed traumas are needed. Instead, the behaviorist view is that cars have become a fear-triggering CS due to one-trial pairing with the UCS (crash) and subsequent stimulus generalization.

Does this explanation seem reasonable? It may, but it suffers from a serious limitation: Almost any explanation can seem plausible when it is provided after some event occurs. Behaviorists John B. Watson and Rosalie Rayner (1920) set out to obtain stronger evidence that fear could be conditioned. They studied an 11-month-old infant named Albert. One day, as Little Albert played in a hospital room, Watson and Rayner showed him a white rat. Albert displayed no sign of fear. Later, knowing that Albert was afraid of loud noises, they hit a steel bar with a hammer, making a loud noise as they showed Albert the rat. The noise scared Albert and made him cry. After several rat-noise pairings, the sight of the white rat alone made Albert cry.

To examine stimulus discrimination and generalization, Watson and Rayner exposed Albert to other test stimuli several days later. Albert displayed no fear when shown colored blocks, but furry white or gray objects, such as a rabbit and a bearded Santa Claus mask, made him cry (Figure 6.10). By the time Albert's mother took him from the hospital, he had not been exposed to any treatment designed to extinguish his fear. Unfortunately, we do not know what became of Albert after that.

TABLE 6.1 Using Exposure Training to Reduce Fear

This table lists 10 of the 17 steps Mary Cover Jones used to eliminate Peter's fear of rabbits.

Step	Peter's Progress
1.	Rabbit anywhere in room triggers fear.
2.	Rabbit 12 feet away tolerated.
4.	Rabbit 3 feet away tolerated.
5.	Rabbit close in cage tolerated.
6.	Rabbit free in room tolerated.
8.	Rabbit touched when free in room.
10.	Rabbit allowed on tray of high chair.
12.	Holds rabbit on lap.
16.	Fondles rabbit affectionately.
17.	Lets rabbit nibble his fingers.

SOURCE: Adapted from Jones, 1924.

Two other sources of evidence suggest that at least some fears are conditioned. First, laboratory experiments convincingly show that animals become afraid of neutral stimuli that are paired with electric shock (Ayres, 1998). Second, in humans, behavioral treatments partially based on classical conditioning principles are among the most effective psychotherapies for phobias (Wolpe & Plaud, 1997). The key assumption is that if phobias are learned, they can be unlearned.

In 1924, psychologist Mary Cover Jones successfully treated a boy named Peter who had a strong fear of rabbits. Jones, who acknowledged Watson and Rayner's work, gradually extinguished Peter's fear using the procedure shown in Table 6.1. Her approach was a forerunner of current behavior therapies, discussed in Chapter 14. Collectively, they are called **exposure therapies,** *in which a patient is exposed to a stimulus (CS) that arouses an anxiety response (such as fear) without the presence of the UCS, allowing extinction to occur.* In reality, the origin of a patient's phobia is often unknown, and psychologists debate whether all phobias are learned. But, even in such cases, exposure treatments are effective.

Mental imagery, real-life situations, or both can be used to present the phobic stimulus. In one approach, called *systematic desensitization,* the patient learns muscle-relaxation techniques and then is gradually exposed to the fear-provoking stimulus (Wolpe, 1958). Another approach, sometimes called *flooding,* immediately exposes the person to the phobic stimulus (Nesbitt, 1973). In Carol's case, her therapist extinguished the car phobia in six sessions of flooding. He asked her to imagine vivid scenes in which she drove in freeway traffic and traveled at high speeds on narrow mountain roads. As Carol's initially strong anxiety decreased, she was able to sit in her car and eventually drive it. Exposure therapies are highly effective and represent one of behaviorism's important applied legacies (Barlow et al., 2002).

What Do You Think?

WAS THE "LITTLE ALBERT" STUDY ETHICAL?

Review boards to oversee research ethics did not exist in the 1920s. Would you have approved Watson and Rayner's request to conduct the Little Albert study? Why or why not? Think about it, then see page 237.

Attraction and Aversion

Much of what attracts and pleasurably arouses us is influenced by classical conditioning. Consider sexual arousal. The comment, "It really turns me on when you wear that," reflects how a garment or scent of a partner's cologne can become a conditioned stimulus for arousal. Research has shown that pairing a neutral odor with pleasing physical massage increases people's attraction to that odor. Research has also revealed that people, fish, birds, and rats become more sexually aroused to originally neutral stimuli after those stimuli have been paired with a naturally arousing UCS (Domjan, 2000b).

Classical conditioning also can decrease our arousal and attraction to stimuli. This principle is used in **aversion therapy,** *which attempts to condition an aversion (a repulsion) to a stimulus that triggers unwanted behavior by pairing it with a noxious UCS.* To treat pedophiles (child molesters), a therapist may pair pictures of children with strong electric shock, and to reduce an alcoholic's attraction to alcohol, the patient may be given a drug that induces severe nausea when alcohol is consumed (Nathan, 1985). Aversion therapies yield mixed results, often producing short-term changes that extinguish over time.

Conditioned attraction and aversion also influence our attitudes (Walther, 2002). By repeatedly pairing a CS with pleasant or unpleasant stimuli, we may develop a favorable or unfavorable attitude toward that CS. Advertising executives are keenly aware of classical conditioning's power. They carefully link products to

FIGURE 6.11

Advertisers attempt to classically condition favorable consumer attitudes to products by associating the products with other positive stimuli, such as physically attractive models.

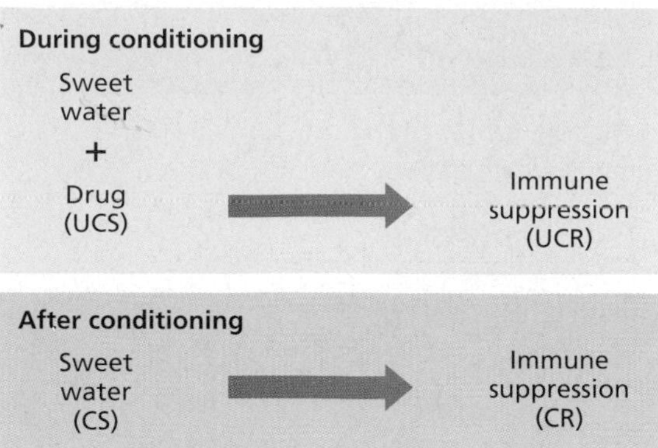

FIGURE 6.12

After being paired with an immune-suppressant drug, sweet water becomes a CS that triggers a reduced immune response.

cute animals, attractive and famous people, humor, "fuzzy-warm" family images, and, most of all, to pleasurable interactions with the opposite sex (Figure 6.11). Marketing experiments show that the products become conditioned stimuli that elicit favorable consumer attitudes (Till & Priluck, 2000).

Sickness and Health

Classical conditioning often can account for the appearance of physical symptoms that do not seem to have a medical cause. Consider the case of an asthma patient who experienced wheezing attacks whenever she saw goldfish. To confirm this, doctors showed her a live goldfish in a bowl: "Under our eyes she developed a severe asthmatic attack with loud wheezing. . . . During the next experiment the goldfish was replaced by a plastic toy fish which was easily recognized as such . . . but a fierce attack resulted" (Dekker and Groen, 1956, p. 62). For the asthma patient, goldfish appear to be conditioned stimuli that trigger wheezing attacks, and her response to the plastic fish indicates stimulus generalization. Experiments with allergy patients and animals suggest how this might happen. By consistently pairing a neutral stimulus (e.g., a distinct odor) with a substance that naturally triggers an allergic reaction, the odor can become a CS that elicits a similar allergic response (Irie et al., 2001).

Our bodies actually can learn to respond in ways that either promote or harm our health. Consider how chemotherapy and radiation therapy save countless lives in the fight against cancer but often cause nausea and vomiting after treatment sessions. Many cancer patients eventually develop **anticipatory nausea and vomiting (ANV);** *they become nauseated and may vomit anywhere from minutes to hours before a treatment session.*

ANV is a classically conditioned response (Tyc et al., 1997). Initially neutral stimuli, such as hypodermic needles or the hospital room, become associated with the treatment (the UCS) and then act as conditioned stimuli that trigger nausea and vomiting (the conditioned responses). Stimulus generalization often occurs, so that the mere sight of the hospital may trigger nausea. Fortunately, like conditioned fear, psychological treatments can help patients unlearn the ANV response (Edser, 2002). The patient may first be taught how to physically relax, and then the conditioned stimuli that trigger ANV are paired with relaxation and pleasant mental imagery.

As psychologist Robert Ader (2001; Ader & Cohen, 1975) discovered decades ago, even the immune system can be classically conditioned, affecting susceptibility to disease and fatal illness. As Figure 6.12 shows, when rats drink sweetened water (a neutral stimulus) that is paired with injections of a drug (the UCS) that suppresses immune activity (the UCR), the sweetened water becomes a CS that suppresses immune activity. Conversely, conditioning can also increase immune functioning (DeMoranville et al., 2000). German researchers gave sweet sherbet to experimental group volunteers, along with an injection of epinephrine (i.e., adrenaline), which increases the activity of immune system cells that attack tumors. Compared with control groups, people receiving the sherbet-epinephrine pairings subsequently reacted to the sherbet alone with a stronger immune response (Buske-Kirschbaum et al., 1992, 1994).

Can classical conditioning help fight disease? One experiment involved mice suffering from a normally fatal illness that caused their immune systems to attack their own bodies (Ader & Cohen, 1982). By classically conditioning a sweet taste (CS) to trigger immune suppression (CR), the researchers reduced the mice's mortality rate. Later, this procedure was used with an 11-year-old-girl who had a similar life-threatening disease in which her immune system was overactive. Cod liver oil (a distinct taste!) was paired with an immune suppressant drug. Then, over the next 12 months, she was given 6 treatments with the immune suppressant drug interspersed with 6 treatments using only cod liver oil (rather than the normal 12 drug treatments). The patient improved and was still doing well after a 5-year follow-up (Olness & Ader, 1992).

For more on classical conditioning, see Interactive Segment 6.1

IN REVIEW

- *Classical conditioning involves pairing a neutral stimulus with an unconditioned stimulus (UCS) that elicits an unconditioned response (UCR). Through repeated pairing, the neutral stimulus becomes a conditioned stimulus (CS) that evokes a conditioned response (CR) similar to the original UCR.*
- *The acquisition phase involves pairing the CS with the UCS. Extinction, the disappearance of the CR, occurs when the CS is presented repeatedly in the absence of the UCS. Sometimes spontaneous recovery occurs after a rest period, and the CS will temporarily evoke a response even after extinction has taken place.*
- *Stimulus generalization occurs when a CR is evoked by a stimulus similar to the original CS. Discrimination occurs when a CR occurs to one stimulus but not another.*
- *In higher-order conditioning, once a stimulus (e.g., a tone) becomes a CS, it can be used in place of the original UCS (food) to condition other neutral stimuli.*
- *A wide range of bodily and psychological responses can be classically conditioned, including fears, sexual attraction, and positive and negative attitudes. Techniques based on classical conditioning are highly successful in treating fears and phobias.*
- *Cancer patients may develop anticipatory nausea and vomiting (ANV) to stimuli that are paired with their chemotherapy. ANV is a classically conditioned response. Classical conditioning also can increase or decrease immune system responses.*

OPERANT CONDITIONING: LEARNING THROUGH CONSEQUENCES

▶ 6. Describe how Thorndike and Skinner pioneered the study of operant conditioning.

For all its power to affect our emotions, attitudes, physiology, and health, classical conditioning cannot explain how a dog learns to sit on command. Nor can it account for how we learn to drive cars, use computers, or make friends. Unlike salivating to a tone, these are not *elicited responses* automatically triggered by some stimulus. Rather, they are *emitted (voluntary) responses*, and they are learned in a different way.

Thorndike's Law of Effect

While Pavlov was studying classical conditioning, American psychology student Edward L. Thorndike (1898) was exploring how animals learn to solve problems. He built a special cage, called a *puzzle box*, that could be opened from the inside by pulling a string or stepping on a lever (Figure 6.13). Thorndike placed a hungry animal, such as a cat, inside the box. Food was put outside, and to get it the animal had to learn how to open the box. The cat scratched and pushed the bars, paced, and tried to dig through the floor. By chance, it eventually stepped on the lever, opening the door. Performance slowly improved with repeated trials, and over time the cat learned to press the lever soon after the door was shut.

Because performance improved slowly, Thorndike concluded that the animals did not attain "insight" into the solution. Rather, with trial and error, they gradually eliminated responses that failed to open the door and became more likely to perform the actions that worked. Thorndike (1911) called this process *instrumental learning* because an organism's behavior is instrumental in bringing about certain outcomes. He also proposed the **law of effect,** *which states that, in a given situation, a response followed by a "satisfying" consequence will become more likely to occur and a response followed by an "unsatisfying" consequence will become less likely to occur*. The law of effect became the foundation for the school of behaviorism.

Skinner's Analysis of Operant Conditioning

▶ 7. Contrast operant and classical conditioning. Why are antecedent stimuli important in operant conditioning?

Harvard psychologist B. F. Skinner, who built on and expanded Thorndike's work, was America's leading proponent of behaviorism throughout most of the 20th century. Skinner coined the term

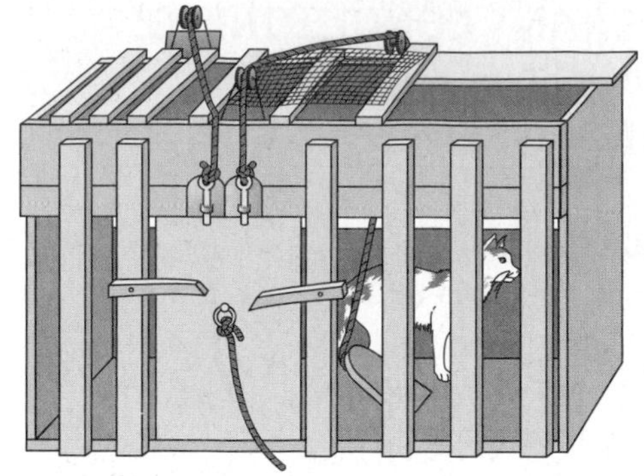

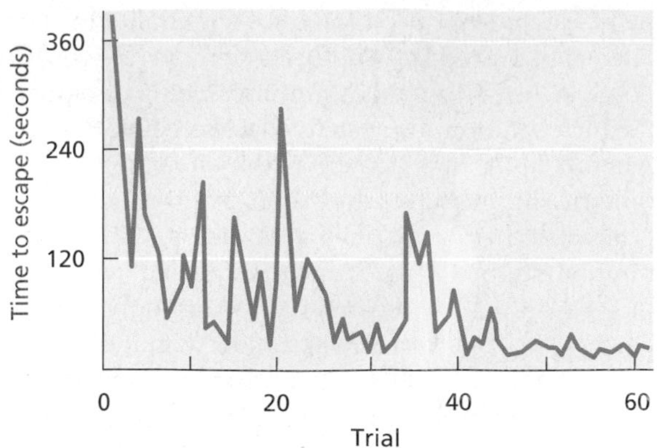

FIGURE 6.13

Through trial and error, cats eventually learned to open Thorndike's puzzle boxes in order to obtain food. SOURCE: Based on Thorndike, 1898, 1911.

operant behavior, meaning that an organism *operates* on its environment in some way.

Operant conditioning *is a type of learning in which behavior is influenced by the consequences that follow it* (Skinner, 1938, 1953). Skinner designed what has come to be known as a **Skinner box,** *a special chamber used to study operant conditioning experimentally*. A lever on one wall is positioned above a small cup. When the lever is depressed, a food pellet automatically drops into the cup. As shown in Figure 6.14, a hungry rat is put into the chamber and, as it moves about, it accidentally presses the lever. A food pellet clinks into the cup, and the rat eats it. We record the rat's behavior on a cumulative recorder, which shows that the rat presses the bar more frequently over time.

Skinner identified several types of consequences. For now, we focus on two: reinforcement and punishment. With **reinforcement,** *a response is strengthened by an outcome that follows it*. Typically, *strengthened* is operationally defined as an increase in the frequency of a response. The outcome (a stimulus or event) that increases the frequency of a response is a called a *reinforcer*. Food pellets are reinforcers because they increase the rat's frequency of lever pressing. Once a response becomes established, reinforcers maintain it: The rat keeps pressing the lever because it continues to receive food.

In contrast to reinforcement, **punishment** *occurs when a response is* weakened *by outcomes that follow it*. Take our lever-pressing rat. Suppose we change things so that pressing the lever delivers a brief electric shock rather than food. If lever-pressing decreases (which it will), then the electric shock represents a *punisher:* a consequence that weakens the behavior. Notice that reinforcers and punishers are defined in terms of their observable effects on behavior. If the food doesn't increase lever pressing, then it is not a reinforcer for this rat at this time.

Following Darwin's notion of natural selection, which applies to species adaptation, Skinner

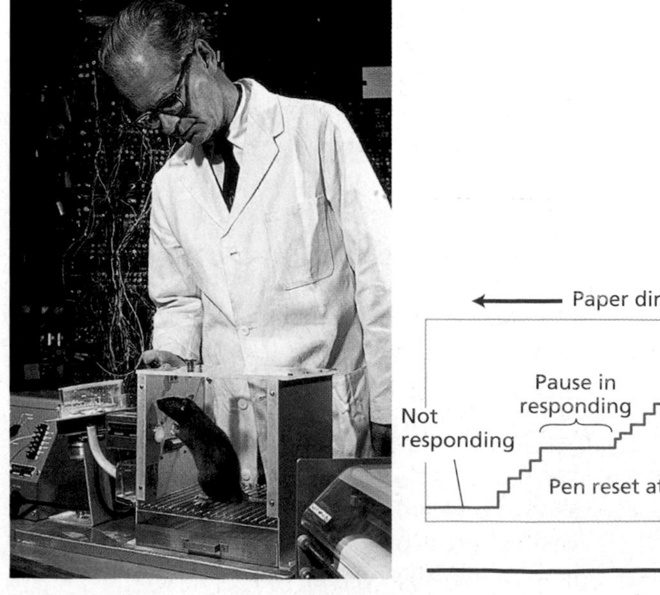

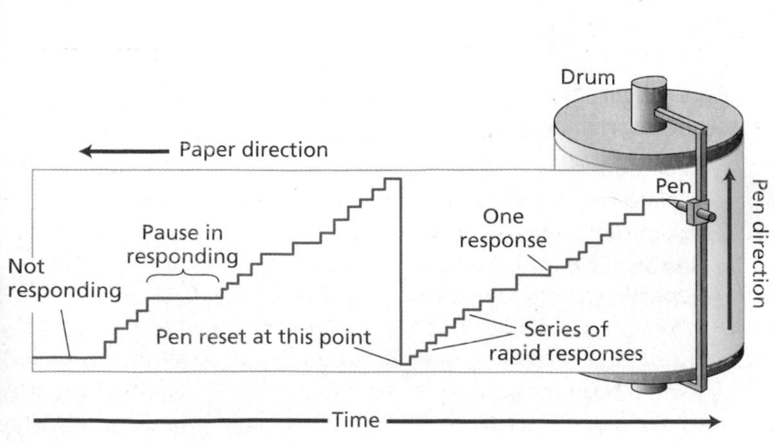

FIGURE 6.14

With B. F. Skinner watching, a rat raises up and presses a lever in a Skinner box (an operant experimental chamber). This turns on a light inside the chamber (notice the lever just below and to the right of the light). A food reinforcer is automatically delivered by the apparatus to the left of the box, and the rat's performance is displayed on a cumulative recorder.

viewed operant conditioning as a type of "natural selection" that facilitates an organism's personal adaptation to the environment. Through operant conditioning, organisms generally learn to increase behaviors that are followed by favorable consequences and reduce behaviors that are followed by unfavorable consequences, a pattern consistent with Thorndike's law of effect.

Skinner's analysis of operant behavior involves three kinds of events that form a *three-part contingency:* (A) *antecedents,* which are stimuli that are present before a behavior occurs; (B) *behaviors* that the organism emits; and (C) *consequences* that follow the behaviors. Thus,

> IF antecedent stimuli are present (IF I say, "Sit!")
>
> AND behavior is emitted (AND my dog Jessie sits),
>
> THEN consequences will occur (THEN I give Jessie a treat).

The relation between the behavior and the consequence is called a *contingency.* After I say, "Sit!" the consequence of receiving food is contingent on Jessie's response of sitting.

As we explore operant conditioning more closely, keep in mind two key differences between classical and operant conditioning:

- In classical conditioning the organism learns an *association between two stimuli*—the CS and UCS (e.g., a tone and food)—that occurs *before* the behavior (e.g., salivation). In operant conditioning, the organism learns an *association between a behavior and its consequences.* Behavior changes because of events that occur *after* it.
- Classical conditioning focuses on *elicited* behaviors: The conditioned response is triggered involuntarily, almost like a reflex, by a stimulus that precedes it. Operant conditioning focuses on *emitted* behaviors: In a given situation, the organism generates responses (e.g., pressing a lever) that are under its physical control.

Also realize that, although classical and operant conditioning are different processes, many learning situations involve both. Have you ever had a teacher who squeaked chalk when writing on a blackboard? One of your authors had a high school teacher who was a pro at this. Soon the mere sight of him raising the chalk to the board became a CS that automatically triggered a CR of shivers up the spine. It also was a signal for the students to put their fingers in their ears (an operant response), which was reinforced by the consequence of reducing the squeaking sound. Thus one stimulus (raising the chalk) can have classical as well as operant functions.

Antecedent Conditions: Identifying When to Respond

In operant conditioning, the antecedent may be a general situation or a specific stimulus. Let's return to our lever-pressing rat. At present, simply being in the Skinner box is the antecedent condition. In this situation, the rat will press the lever. Suppose we place a light on the wall above the lever. When the light is on, pressing the lever dispenses food, but when the light is off, no food is given. The rat will soon learn to press the lever only when the light is on. The light becomes a **discriminative stimulus,** *a signal that a particular response will now produce certain consequences.* Discriminative stimuli set the occasion for operant responses. The sight of the teacher raising chalk to the blackboard was—in operant conditioning terms—a discriminative stimulus signaling it was time for the students to put their fingers in their ears.

Discriminative stimuli guide much of our everyday behavior. If you are hungry, food on your plate is a discriminative stimulus to start eating. Classroom bells, the words people speak to us, and the sight of a friend's face are all discriminative stimuli that set the occasion for us to make certain responses.

Consequences: Determining How to Respond

▶ 8. Explain and illustrate positive and negative reinforcement, operant extinction, aversive punishment, and response cost.

Behavior is governed by its consequences. Two major types of reinforcement strengthen responses, and two major types of punishment weaken them. Operant behavior also is weakened by extinction. Figure 6.15 shows these processes.

Positive Reinforcement

Positive reinforcement *occurs when a response is strengthened by the subsequent presentation of a stimulus.* A rat receives food pellets when it presses a lever and eventually begins to press the lever more often. A new employee, praised by her boss for completing a small project quickly, begins to complete more of her projects on time. The stimulus that follows and strengthens the response is called a *positive reinforcer.* Food, drink, comforting physical contact, attention, praise, and money are common positive reinforcers. In

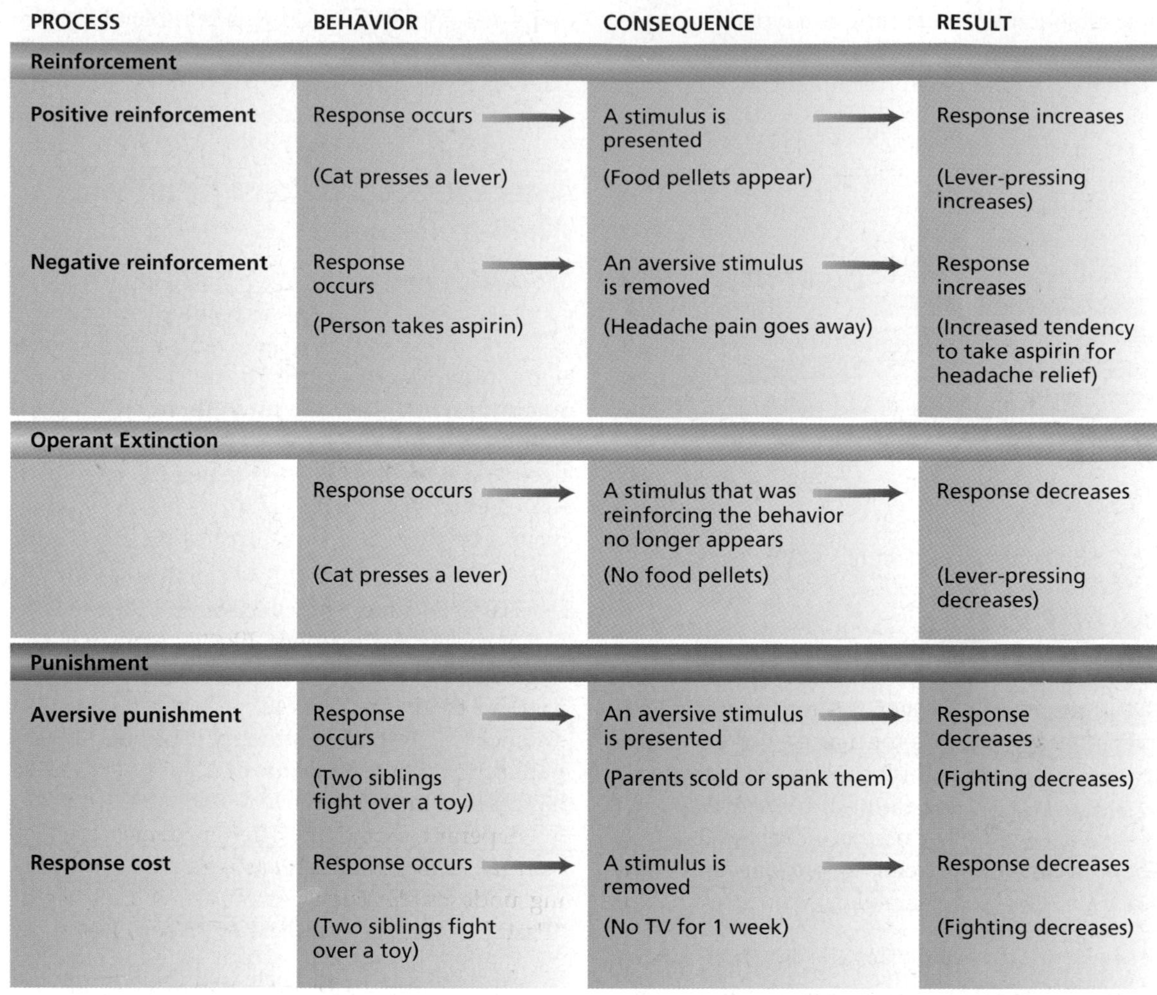

PROCESS	BEHAVIOR	CONSEQUENCE	RESULT
Reinforcement			
Positive reinforcement	Response occurs → (Cat presses a lever)	A stimulus is presented → (Food pellets appear)	Response increases (Lever-pressing increases)
Negative reinforcement	Response occurs → (Person takes aspirin)	An aversive stimulus is removed → (Headache pain goes away)	Response increases (Increased tendency to take aspirin for headache relief)
Operant Extinction			
	Response occurs → (Cat presses a lever)	A stimulus that was reinforcing the behavior no longer appears → (No food pellets)	Response decreases (Lever-pressing decreases)
Punishment			
Aversive punishment	Response occurs → (Two siblings fight over a toy)	An aversive stimulus is presented → (Parents scold or spank them)	Response decreases (Fighting decreases)
Response cost	Response occurs → (Two siblings fight over a toy)	A stimulus is removed → (No TV for 1 week)	Response decreases (Fighting decreases)

FIGURE 6.15 *Five major operant processes.*

our chapter-opening vignette, the volunteer's behavior of soliciting money for charity is positively reinforced by each donation, by the praise of fellow workers at the charity, and by her feeling of pride in helping people.

The term *reward* is often misused as a synonym for the term *positive reinforcer*. Behaviorists prefer the term *positive reinforcer* because it focuses on how consequences affect behavior. In many instances "rewards" do not function as positive reinforcers. Parents may give a child a reward (such as a new toy) for cleaning her room, but if the child does not clean her room in the future, then the toy was not a positive reinforcer for that behavior.

Primary and Secondary Reinforcers Psychologists distinguish between two broad types of positive reinforcers: **Primary reinforcers** *are stimuli, such as food and water, that an organism naturally finds reinforcing because they satisfy biological needs.* **Secondary (or conditioned) reinforcers** *are stimuli that acquire reinforcing properties through their association with primary reinforcers.* Money is a conditioned reinforcer. In similar fashion, chimpanzees will learn to value and work for (and even hoard) tokens, a secondary reinforcer that they can place into a vending machine to obtain raisins. Secondary reinforcers, including praise, performance feedback, and grades, are crucial in everyday life (Figure 6.16).

Secondary reinforcers illustrate how behavior often depends on both classical and operant conditioning. Consider dog training. Correct responses, such as sitting on command, initially are operantly reinforced with food. But just before delivering food, the trainer enthusiastically says, "Good Dog!" At first the phrase "Good Dog!" is just meaningless sounds to the dog. But by repeatedly pairing "Good Dog!" with food each time the dog sits, "Good Dog!" becomes a classically conditioned stimulus that elicits excitement (salivation, tail wagging). Now the trainer can use the phrase "Good Dog!" as a secondary reinforcer, instead of always having to carry and provide food.

Negative Reinforcement

B. F. Skinner noted that when a response "pays off," it is more likely to occur in the future. In everyday life, our behaviors pay off not only when they lead to the presentation of praise, attention, money, and so on, but also when they enable us to get rid of or avoid something we find aversive. We learn to take aspirin to relieve a headache, to open an umbrella when it starts raining to stop getting wet, to wear sunscreen outdoors to avoid damaging our skin, and to buckle up our seat belt to avoid or turn off an annoying warning buzzer. This process is called **negative reinforcement:** *A response is strengthened by the subsequent removal (or avoidance) of a stimulus* (see Figure 6.15). The aversive stimulus that is removed (the headache, the rain falling on us, the threat of sunburn, the buzzer) is called a *negative reinforcer* (Hill, 1963).

Do not confuse negative reinforcement with punishment. Punishment weakens a response. Reinforcement—whether positive or negative—strengthens a response (or maintains it once it has reached full strength). When it comes to the terms *positive reinforcement* and *negative reinforcement*, the prefixes *positive* and *negative* do not mean "good" or "bad." Rather they refer to procedures: *positive* refers to presenting a stimulus; *negative* refers to removing a stimulus.

Negative reinforcement plays a key role in helping us learn to escape from and avoid aversive situations. While showering, have you ever heard someone flush a toilet, only to have your shower water turn scalding hot? Your response of backing away is negatively reinforced—strengthened—by the escape from (i.e., removal of) the scalding water. Soon the mere sound of the flush becomes a signal—a discriminative stimulus—for you to back away. You successfully avoid the scalding water, which negatively reinforces your response of backing away as soon as you hear the flush.

Operant Extinction

Operant **extinction** *is the weakening and eventual disappearance of a response because it is no longer reinforced.* When previously reinforced behaviors no longer pay off, we are likely to abandon and replace them with more successful ones. If pressing a lever no longer results in food pellets, the rat will eventually stop making this response.

The degree to which nonreinforced responses persist is called *resistance to extinction*. Nonreinforced responses may stop quickly (low resistance), or they may keep occurring hundreds or thousands of times (high resistance). People who solicit charitable donations, like the woman in Las Vegas, do not stop just because 100 passersby in a row fail to give money. As we examine later, resistance to extinction is strongly influenced by the pattern of reinforcement that has previously maintained the behavior.

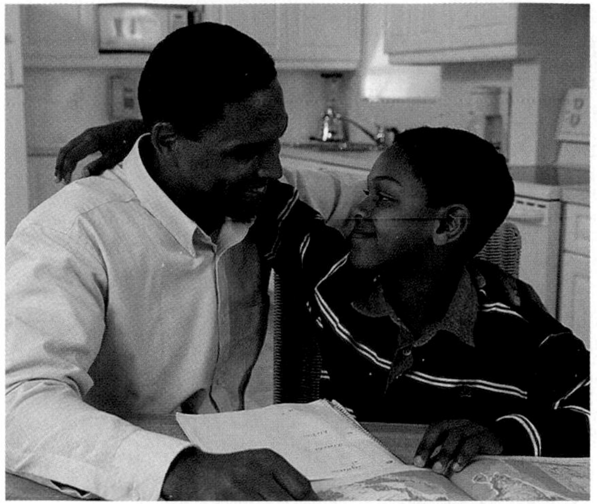

FIGURE 6.16

Attention and praise can be powerful secondary reinforcers. Comforting physical contact, some research suggests, may be a primary reinforcer.

Operant extinction often provides a good alternative to punishment as a method for reducing undesirable behaviors. Consider the case of "Pascal the Rascal" (O'Leary & Wilson, 1987):

> Mrs. Adams sought help at a child guidance clinic because her 4-year-old son, Pascal, delighted in misbehaving. She had tried to reason with him. Then she resorted to yelling. When that failed, Mrs. Adams began spanking Pascal. Even that did not work.

The intended punishments failed because they actually reinforced Pascal with what he wanted most: attention. The psychologist told Mrs. Adams that as difficult as it might be at times, she needed to ignore Pascal when he misbehaved, thereby depriving him of attention. Mrs. Adams was also told to reinforce Pascal's desirable behaviors by paying attention to him when he acted accordingly. Soon thereafter, Pascal was no longer a rascal.

Aversive Punishment

Like reinforcement, punishment comes in two forms. One involves actively *applying* aversive stimuli, such as painful slaps, electric shock, and verbal reprimands. This is called **aversive punishment** (also called **punishment by application):** *A response is weakened by the subsequent presentation of a stimulus.* Spanking and scolding a child for misbehaving are obvious examples, but so is a child's touching

▶ 9. Discuss the corporal punishment debate and some limitations of punishment and reinforcement.

a hot stovetop burner. The pain delivered by the burner makes it less likely that the child will touch it in the future. Aversive punishment often is subtle. A high school student wears a new blouse, and her friends halfheartedly say "Uh-huh, nice," but their facial expressions show dislike. The student ends up putting the blouse at the back of her closet.

Aversive punishment can produce rapid results, an important consideration when it is necessary to stop a particularly dangerous behavior, such as an animal or person attacking someone. Although aversive punishment often works, the use of spanking and other forms of physical punishment for disciplinary purposes is controversial. Let's explore this issue.

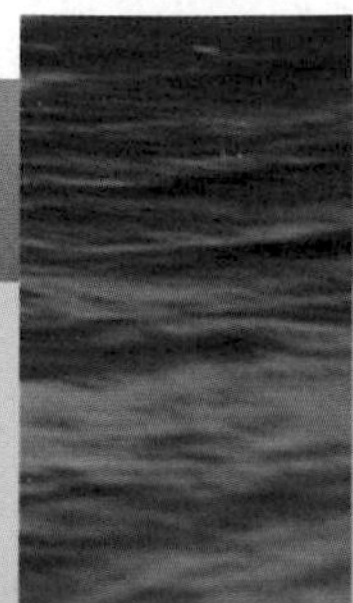

BENEATH THE SURFACE

SPARE THE ROD, SPOIL THE CHILD?

As a child, were you spanked for misbehaving? And, as someone who may one day become a parent or may already be one, do you believe that there are times when parents should spank their children? If you grew up in the United States, odds are high that your answer to both questions is yes. In one national survey of American parents, 94 percent reported that by the time their children reached the age of 4, they had spanked them (Straus & Stewart, 1999). Yet your answers would likely be different if you grew up in Sweden, which banned corporal (i.e, physical) punishment of children in 1979. Ten other countries, including Austria, Denmark, and Norway have since passed similar bans.

The Corporal Punishment Debate

Should parents physically punish children's misbehavior? Newspapers, magazines, and TV shows frequently raise this issue, so let's probe beneath the surface.

What's the claim? Conventional wisdom says that sparing the rod spoils the child. What's the evidence? Psychologist Elizabeth Gershoff (2002a) of Columbia University recently meta-analyzed 88 studies on parental use of corporal punishment, involving about 36,000 participants (Figure 6.17). Five of these studies examined whether corporal punishment was effective in temporarily suppressing children's misbehavior. Overall the answer was yes, but Gershoff cautioned that this result was inconsistent because it was found in only 3 of the studies.

In contrast, the other major outcomes that Gershoff studied consistently showed unfavorable associations with child corporal punishment. These outcomes, based almost entirely on correlational studies, included

- decreased quality of the parent-child relationship;
- poorer internalization of moral standards during childhood;

FIGURE 6.17

Psychology in the public eye. Radio, TV, and print media brought Dr. Elizabeth Gershoff's review of corporal punishment research to national attention.

- increased aggressive behavior during childhood and, later, during adulthood;
- increased deliquent and antisocial behavior (e.g., truancy, stealing) during childhood and adulthood;
- poorer mental health during childhood and adulthood;
- increased childhood risk of physical abuse; and
- increased risk, upon becoming an adult, of physically abusing one's own children or spouse.

Gershoff (2002a) emphasizes that these findings "do not imply that all children who experience corporal punishment turn out to be aggressive or delinquent. . . . Corporal punishment may make certain behaviors more likely but clearly not inevitable" (p. 551). Remember, most people who are spanked do not grow up to be violent or antisocial adults.

What are the alternative explanations? As critical thinkers, how should we interpret these findings? Recall that correlation does not prove causation. To see why, let's examine the association between corporal punishment and child aggression. Before reading further, can you identify three possible causal explanations for this correlation? (If you have trouble, refer back to Figure 2.11 on page 43).

One possibility is that corporal punishment causes children to behave more aggressively. Many psychologists have expressed this concern because physical punishment amounts to control by aggression and may send a message to the child that aggression is appropriate and effective. Moreover, laboratory experiments indicate that children learn aggressive behaviors by watching aggressive adult models (Bandura, 1965).

We also must consider the bidirectionality problem. Perhaps children who are more aggressive cause their parents to be more physically punitive. In other words, greater misbehavior may lead to greater punishment. And finally, we must consider the third-variable problem. Perhaps another factor—an inherited tendency or an aspect of the environment—causes children to behave more aggressively and also causes parents to punish more aggressively (i.e., physically), making it seem like aggression and corporal punishment are directly related when in fact they are not.

Some child psychologists criticized Gershoff's meta-analysis because it included studies in which parents used strong physical punishment, such as spanking with objects, which might be considered abusive (Baumrind et al., 2002). Gershoff's (2002b) reply: Almost 30 percent of American parents spank with objects, and although some of us might consider this to be harsh, it is common but not abusive unless it causes physical injury or harm, and thus it needed to be included.

What additional evidence would be helpful? After child corporal punishment was banned in Sweden, did new generations of children grow up to become poorly socialized teenagers? Examining national statistics from 1975 through 1996, Joan Durrant (2000) found post-ban declines in teenage rates of theft, rape, narcotics trafficking, use of alcohol and other drugs, and suicide. Durrant points out that these results are likely influenced by many factors—economic, social, and otherwise—so we cannot conclude that banning corporal punishment caused these changes. Yet, whatever the cause, the direction of the findings runs counter to "spare the rod, spoil the child." As Durrant notes, "Swedish youth have not become more unruly, undersocialized, or self-destructive following the . . . ban. In fact, most measures demonstrated a substantial improvement in youth well-being" (p. 451).

What should we conclude? The study of Swedish youth and Gershoff's meta-analysis converge on the same point: Causality is unclear, but the direction of the association runs counter to common folklore. Based on current evidence, it appears that using the rod—rather than sparing it—may be associated with poorer child development outcomes. Some psychologists cite evidence that mild to moderate spanking has its place, such as a backup technique when other types of discipline fail with young children who have behavior problems. But, even so, they acknowledge, "The issue that was and remains controversial is whether mild to moderate disciplinary spanking . . . has been shown to be *harmful*" (Baumrind et al., 2002, p. 581; italics added).

Would You Ban Corporal Punishment?

Decisions about banning child corporal punishment involve more than scientific evidence. University of Texas psychologist George Holden (2002) notes, "Parents' belief in their entitlement to use corporal punishment is deeply embedded in American history, beliefs about the privacy of the family and personal freedoms, and attitudes about children and how to rear them" (p. 594). Indeed, in almost half of the states (23) in the United States, even schoolteachers are allowed to discipline misbehaving children physically (Gershoff, 2002b). After examining the preceding evidence, what are your thoughts about the appropriateness of spanking? Are your feelings different now from what they were before you read this section?

Response Cost

A parent we know recently told us, "Just because you don't spank doesn't mean you have to let your kids have their own way all the time. You can still set limits, have structure and discipline in the family." Indeed, groundings, loss of privileges, and monetary fines represent another approach to modifying behavior. They take away something that an individual finds satisfying. In **response cost** (also called **punishment by removal**), *a response is weakened by the subsequent removal of a stimulus* (i.e., "that'll cost you"). A child who misbehaves, perhaps by starting a fight with another child, may be punished with a *time-out,* in which he or she has to sit quietly (possibly in isolation) for a period of time; this temporarily removes opportunities to play, watch TV, or participate in other enjoyable activities. Response cost, of course, is not limited to disciplining children or teenagers, as any automobile driver who has paid a fine for speeding knows (that'll really

FIGURE 6.18

In ice hockey, misbehavior can earn a time-out in the penalty box.

▶ 10. How do immediate, delayed, and reciprocal consequences affect learning?

cost you). And even adults can receive a time-out (Figure 6.18).

Many psychologists and therapists who counsel parents on modifying children's behavior favor using time-out as a punishment technique (Baumrind et al., 2002). When parents use response cost to punish children's behavior, the withheld reinforcer should be some prized object or activity rather than love. Withholding love and rejecting the child can damage the child's self-concept (Brown, 1998). The same principle applies, of course, to using aversive punishment: Communicate dislike for the behavior, not for the child.

As disciplinary techniques, aversive punishment and response cost have limitations. They suppress behavior, but do not cause an organism to forget how to make the response. Because they tell us what not to do but don't necessarily help us learn what to do, it is important to use positive reinforcement to strengthen desirable alternative responses directly. Finally, punishment of any type may arouse negative emotions, such as fear and anger, that can produce dislike and avoidance of the person delivering the punishment.

B. F. Skinner (1953) believed that punishing behavior was not an effective way to produce long-term change; instead, he advocated the use of reinforcement. Yet learning theory and research indicate that, under the proper conditions, punishment can promote enduring changes in behavior (Domjan, 2000a). As psychologist George Holden (2002) notes, "To be effective, it must occur after every transgression, be immediate, be intense at least for the first transgression, and not be signaled by a discriminative stimulus," (p. 591) such as a threat or warning. Unfortunately, as Holden also notes, "These conditions represent a tall order for parents; in fact, it is likely parents are destined to fail on all four counts." For example, parents cannot always be present when children transgress.

Reinforcing desired responses and operantly extinguishing misbehavior often provide good alternatives to punishment (recall the case of Pascal the Rascal). But these approaches also have limits. Reinforced behaviors may extinguish or fail to generalize (as when children act politely when parents are present but not when parents are absent), and attempts to operantly extinguish misbehavior may fail. Thus, in practice, many psychologists believe that punishment must remain a disciplinary option.

Immediate, Delayed, and Reciprocal Consequences

In general, reinforcement or punishment that occurs immediately after a behavior has a stronger effect than when it is delayed. Training animals typically requires immediate reinforcement so that they associate the correct response—rather than some subsequent behavior—with the satisfying outcome.

Because humans have the ability to imagine future consequences, our behavior often is less rigidly controlled by the timing of consequences than that of other species. Still, the power of immediate reinforcement helps explain why many people continue to engage in behaviors with maladaptive long-term consequences. Chronic drug users, for example, usually find it difficult to stop because the immediate reinforcing consequences of the drug override the delayed benefits of not using the drug (e.g., being healthier, living longer, saving money). With many drugs, such as cocaine, use is positively reinforced by feelings of pleasure that seem to result from enhanced dopamine activity (Martin et al., 2001). Powerful negative reinforcers also play a role. Chronic cigarette smokers experience increased tension as the nicotine level in their blood drops after their last cigarette. When they smoke again, the tension is reduced. Thus smoking is negatively reinforced by the removal of unpleasant tension. The typical chronic smoker inhales about 60,000 cigarette puffs a year (Parrott, 1999), which adds up to a lot of negative reinforcement.

Finally, realize that, in everyday life, learning frequently is a reciprocal process—a two-way street involving a sequence of responses between organisms. Whether it's friends hanging out, a woman walking a dog, or a tiger chasing a gazelle, each response by one organism may reinforce, punish, help extinguish, or classically condition the other organism's behavior.

Consider a father and child shopping at the market. The child asks Dad to buy candy, the father refuses, and the child screams and won't stop. Soon the father can't stand it, buys the candy, and the child's tantrum ends. A week later this scene repeats, but the father gives in as soon as the tantrum starts. The next time the child asks for candy, the father just says, "OK." Using the concepts of reinforcement and punishment, how would you analyze these events?

The father's initial refusal is followed by the presentation of an aversive stimulus (the tantrum). This punishes the father's response, and after two tantrums he no longer refuses the request. When the father eventually gives in, this removes the aversive stimulus (the tantrum), which negatively reinforces (strengthens) the father's response. Thus, the father's response of refusing to buy candy is weakened by punishment, and the response of giving in is strengthened by negative reinforcement. Just as important, the child has learned that throwing a tantrum pays off. The tantrum was positively reinforced by the consequence of buying candy.

Shaping and Chaining: Taking One Step at a Time

Mark is a 4-year-old who attends preschool. He doesn't play much with other children, rarely engages in physical activity, and during outdoor recess spends most of his time sitting in the sandbox. His teachers and parents would like him to be more active, so how can we use operant conditioning to change Mark's behavior?

First, let's set a specific goal: getting Mark to play on the monkey bars. Second, let's select a positive reinforcer: attention. Now, all we need to do is reinforce Mark with attention when he plays on the monkey bars. The problem is, we'll be waiting a long time because Mark rarely displays this behavior.

Fortunately, Skinner discovered a powerful process for overcoming this problem. We begin by reinforcing Mark with attention every time he stands up in the sandbox. This is the first approximation toward our final goal. Once this response is established, we reinforce him only if he stands up and walks from the sandbox toward the monkey bars. This is the second approximation. Then we reinforce him only when he stands next to the bars, and finally only when he is on the bars and moving. This process, known as **shaping** (also called the *method of successive approximations*), *involves reinforcing successive approximations toward a final response.* Using a shaping procedure similar to the one just described, researchers took little time to get Mark playing on monkey bars (Johnston et al., 1966).

Even when behaviors might reasonably be learned through trial and error—such as the rat learning to press a lever for food—shaping can speed up the process. By reinforcing successive approximations—such as standing near the lever, raising a front paw, touching the lever, and finally depressing the lever—acquisition time is drastically reduced.

Another procedure, **chaining,** *is used to develop a sequence (chain) of responses by reinforcing each response with the opportunity to perform the next response.* For example, suppose that a rat has learned to press a lever when a light is on to receive food. Next we place a bell nearby. By accident, the rat eventually bumps into and rings the bell, which turns on the light. Seeing the light, the rat runs to and presses the lever. Over time, the rat will learn to ring the bell because this response is reinforced by the light turning on, which provides the opportunity to press the lever for food. As in this example, chaining usually begins with the final response in the sequence and works backward toward the first response (Catania, 1998). Figure 6.19 shows another example.

From a behavioral viewpoint, the behaviors that we and other species display in everyday life often develop through shaping and chaining. Recall the father who initially refused his child's request for candy, then gave in after a lengthy tantrum, then gave in as soon as a tantrum started, and finally just said "OK" to the request. In essence, his response of agreeing immediately was shaped. Instructors who teach musical, athletic, and academic skills often shape their students' performance by starting with a basic, simplified response and reinforcing progressively closer approximations to the response that is ultimately desired.

▶ 11. Explain how behaviors develop through shaping and chaining. Describe operant generalization and discrimination.

Generalization and Discrimination

As in classical conditioning, operant responses may generalize to similar antecedent situations. A dog taught by its owner to "Sit" will likely start sitting when other people give the command. A young child who touches a hot stovetop burner learns to avoid touching not only that burner but other hot burners as well. Thus in **operant generalization,** *an operant response occurs to a new antecedent stimulus or situation that is similar to the original one.*

Through experience, we also learn to discriminate between antecedent conditions. Children learn to raid the cookie jar only when the parents are not in the kitchen. We learn to board buses and

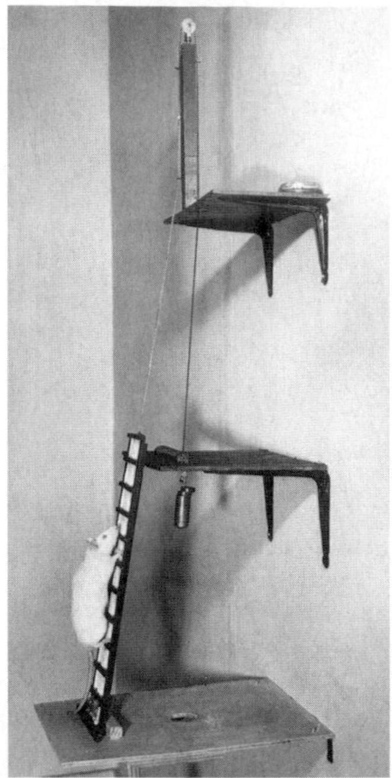
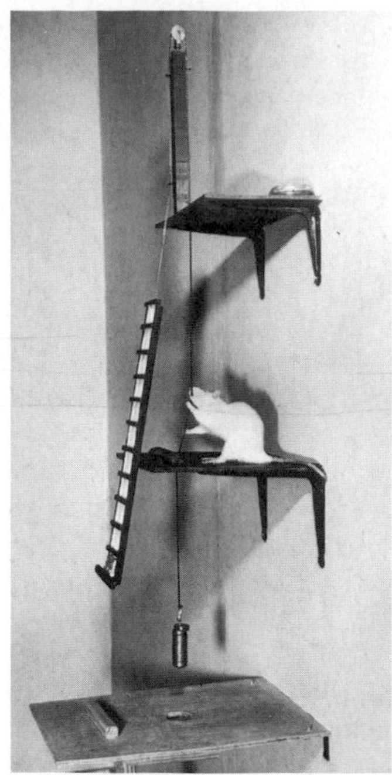
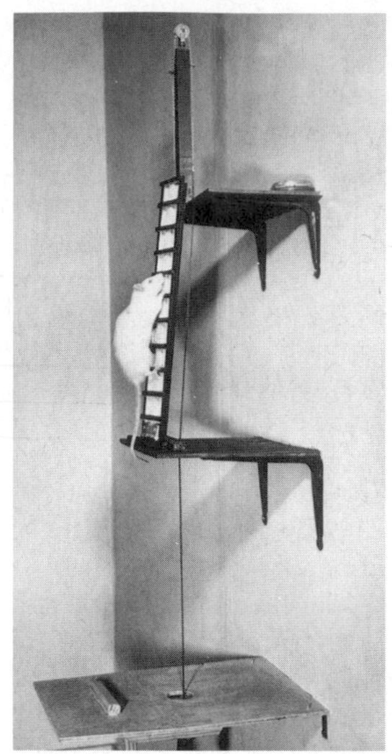

FIGURE 6.19

Through chaining, this rat has learned to climb a ladder to reach a string, pull on the string to raise the ladder, and then climb the ladder again to reach food at the top. Typically, you begin this training with the last step in the chain. Then, working backward, each prior step in the chain is reinforced by the opportunity to perform the next step.

▶ 12. Describe and illustrate schedules of reinforcement. How do they affect performance, learning rates, and extinction?

trains marked by specific symbols (79: Express) and avoid otherwise identical vehicles with different symbols (78: Local). **Operant discrimination** *means that an operant response will occur to one antecedent stimulus but not to another*. As already discussed, these antecedent stimuli—parent's presence or absence, bus markings—are discriminative stimuli. *When discriminative stimuli influence a behavior, that behavior is said to be under* **stimulus control.** For example, the sight of a police car exerts stimulus control over most people's driving behavior.

The concept of operant discrimination gives science a powerful tool for examining the perceptual and cognitive abilities of human infants and nonhuman species (Berg & Boswell, 1998; Lashley, 1930). We can't ask infants and animals to tell us if they can distinguish between different colors, sounds, shapes, faces, and so on. But, by using a procedure called *operant discrimination training*, we can teach an organism that making a response (e.g., pressing a lever) when a discriminative stimulus is present (e.g., a red light is on) produces food or some other positive consequence. Now all we have to do is change the color of the light and not reinforce any response when that light is on. If the organism learns to respond to one color and not the other, we infer that it can discriminate between them.

Schedules of Reinforcement

In daily life, reinforcement comes in different patterns and frequencies. These patterns, called *schedules of reinforcement*, have strong and predictable effects on learning, extinction, and performance (Ferster & Skinner, 1957). The most basic distinction is between continuous and partial reinforcement. With **continuous reinforcement,** *every response of a particular type is reinforced*. Every press of the lever results in food pellets. Every $1.25 deposit in the soda machine results in a can of cool, bubbly drink. With **partial reinforcement** (also called **intermittent reinforcement**), *only some responses are reinforced*.

Partial reinforcement schedules can be categorized along two important dimensions. The first is ratio versus interval schedules. On *ratio schedules*, a certain percentage of responses are reinforced. For example, we might decide to reinforce only 50 percent of the rat's lever presses with food. The key factor is that ratio schedules are based on the number of correct responses: more responses, more reinforcement.

On *interval schedules*, a certain amount of time must elapse between reinforcements, regardless of how many correct responses might occur during that interval. We might reinforce lever pressing only once per minute, whether the rat presses the lever 5, 10, or 60 times. The key factor is that interval schedules are based on the passage of time.

The second dimension is fixed versus variable schedules. On a *fixed schedule*, reinforcement always occurs after a fixed number of responses or after a fixed time interval. On a *variable schedule*, the required number of responses or the time interval varies at random around an average. Combining these two dimensions creates four types of reinforcement schedules (Figure 6.20).

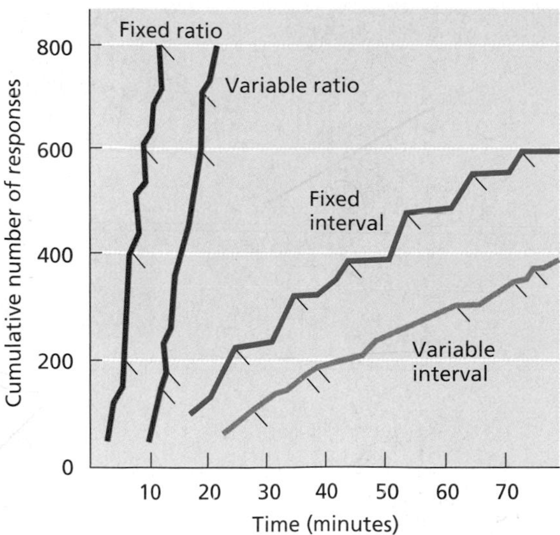

FIGURE 6.20

Each type of positive reinforcement schedule produces a typical cumulative response curve. The hatch marks indicate the delivery of a reinforcer. Ratio schedules produce a high rate of responding, as shown in the steep slopes of the curves. Variable schedules produce a steadier rate of responding. Notice the prominent scalloped pattern in the fixed-interval schedule; the organism learns to stop responding until the time interval for the next reinforcement approaches.

Fixed-Ratio Schedule

On a **fixed-ratio (FR) schedule,** *reinforcement is given after a fixed number of responses*. For example, FR-3 means that reinforcement occurs after every 3rd response, regardless of how long it takes for those responses to occur.

If we told you that you would receive $1 every 3 times you pressed a lever, would you work hard? Skinner found that fixed-ratio schedules produce high rates of responding. That is one reason why some businesses prefer paying employees' wages based on a set number of items produced. If the ratio is gradually increased over time, many responses can be obtained with relatively few reinforcements. Pigeons in a Skinner box have been known to wear down their beaks pecking a disc on an FR-20,000 schedule (one reinforcer per 20,000 responses).

FR schedules have a second characteristic effect. As shown in Figure 6.20, the organism may pause briefly after each reinforcement, perhaps because the next response (or responses) is never reinforced.

Variable-Ratio Schedule

On a **variable-ratio (VR) schedule,** *reinforcement is given after a variable number of correct responses, all centered around an average*. A VR-3 schedule means that, *on average,* 3 responses are required for reinforcement. For example, for the first 12 responses, reinforcement might occur after responses 2, 3, 6, and 11.

VR schedules, like FR schedules, produce a high rate of responding. But because reinforcement is less predictable (the next response *might* be reinforced), there often is less pausing after reinforcement and a steadier rate of responding, as shown in Figure 6.20. VR schedules also are highly resistant to extinction because the organism learns that long periods of no payoff will eventually be followed by reinforcement.

Gambling activities are maintained by VR schedules (Figure 6.21). For example, the slot-machine gambler in our opening vignette plays a slot machine programmed to pay off an average of every 20 pulls (VR-20). After 8 pulls, he receives a 10-coin jackpot. After 2 more attempts, he hits a 15-coin jackpot. But then, after 30 more attempts—nothing. He's frustrated but still "hooked" by the VR schedule. That next attempt just might be the one that pays off, so he plays again . . . and again.

FIGURE 6.21

Gambling is reinforced on a variable-ratio schedule. The ratio component means that the frequency of reinforcement is based on the amount of performance. On average, you will receive more payoffs when you play 100 times than when you play only 10 times. The variable component is not knowing when the next jackpot might occur.

Fixed-Interval Schedule

On a **fixed-interval (FI) schedule,** *the first correct response that occurs after a fixed time interval is reinforced*. Suppose a rat is pressing a lever on an FI-3 (3-minute) schedule. After a lever press is reinforced, for the next 3 minutes it makes no difference how many more times the rat responds. There will be no further reinforcement. Once these 3 minutes elapse, the next lever-press is reinforced. The FI schedule's characteristic response pattern is shown in Figure 6.20. Notice the pronounced *scalloping* after each reinforcement. Responding slows after reinforcement and then becomes increasingly frequent as the time for the next reinforcement draws near (Hill, 1963).

In college, many instructors give exams at equal (or nearly equal) intervals, perhaps one exam every 3 or 4 weeks. Does your study behavior resemble the scalloped pattern shown in Figure 6.20, reflecting little studying immediately following

FIGURE 6.22

As some of us know all too well, procrastination can lead to a heavy burden of cramming before an assignment is due. This pattern often results when assignments and tests occur on a fixed-interval schedule. © Zits Partnership. Reprinted with Special Permission of King Features Syndicate.

each exam and cramming just before the next one? This uneven performance rate is typical of FI schedules (Figure 6.22).

Variable-Interval Schedule

On a **variable-interval (VI) schedule,** *reinforcement is given for the first response that occurs after a variable time interval.* A VI-3 schedule means that, *on average,* there is a 3-minute interval between opportunities to obtain reinforcement. Sometimes, responses a few seconds apart may be reinforced; at other times the interval may be many minutes. As Figure 6.20 shows, because the availability of reinforcement is less predictable than on an FI schedule, the VI schedule produces a steadier response rate.

▶ 13. Describe and illustrate escape and avoidance conditioning. Explain the two-factor theory of avoidance learning.

Pop quizzes represent a VI schedule. A course might average a quiz every week, but their unpredictable timing will likely produce a steadier approach to studying than regularly scheduled quizzes. Random drug testing of athletes and roadside speed traps also reflect VI schedules. They reinforce desired behaviors (staying drug-free, driving within the speed limit) by appearing at unpredictable intervals. Of course, they also punish undesired behaviors with suspensions and fines!

Reinforcement Schedules, Learning, and Extinction

Continuous reinforcement has an important advantage over partial reinforcement: It produces more rapid learning because the association between a behavior and its consequences is easier to perceive. However, it also has a disadvantage: Continuously reinforced responses extinguish more rapidly, because the shift to no reinforcement is sudden and easier to perceive.

Partial reinforcement produces behavior that is learned more slowly but is more resistant to extinction. Especially when reinforcement has been unpredictable in the past, it takes longer to learn that it is gone forever. People do not continue to drop coins into a soda machine that doesn't deliver, because vending machines are supposed to operate on a continuous schedule. But it would take many pulls on a slot machine to recognize that it had stopped paying off completely. To sum up, the best way to promote fast learning and high resistance to extinction is to begin reinforcing a desired behavior on a continuous schedule until the behavior is well established and then shift to a partial (preferably variable) schedule that is gradually made more demanding.

Escape and Avoidance Conditioning

Behavior often involves escaping from or avoiding aversive situations. Escape occurs when we take medications to relieve pain or put on more clothes when we are cold. Avoidance occurs when we put on sunscreen to prevent sunburn or obey traffic laws to avoid tickets. You can probably think of many more examples.

In **escape conditioning,** *the organism learns a response to terminate an aversive stimulus.* Escape behaviors are acquired and maintained through negative reinforcement. If you're cold, putting on a sweater is negatively reinforced by the desirable consequence that you no longer shiver. Taking a pain reliever is negatively reinforced by the reduction of pain. In **avoidance conditioning,** *the organism learns a response to avoid an aversive stimulus.* We learn to dress warmly to avoid feeling cold in the first place.

Escape and avoidance conditioning can be demonstrated experimentally (Candido et al., 2002; Solomon & Wynne, 1953). For example, researchers may place an animal in a *shuttlebox,* a rectangular chamber divided into two compartments and connected by a doorway (Figure 6.23). The floor is a grid through which electric shock can be delivered to either compartment. When the

FIGURE 6.23

Researchers use the shuttlebox to study escape and avoidance learning.

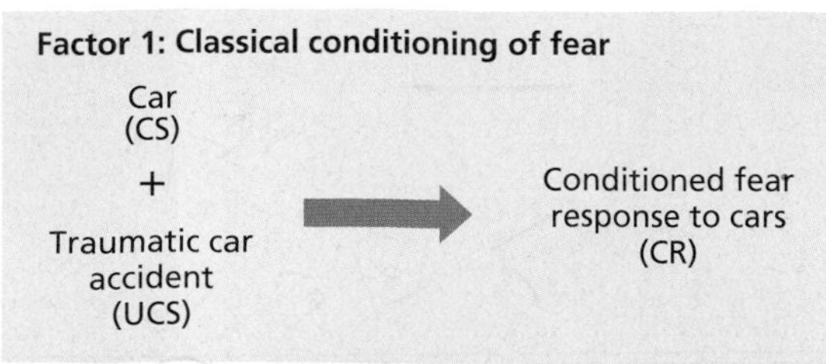

FIGURE 6.24

The two-factor theory of avoidance learning would account for Carol's car phobia in terms of two sets of learning processes: classical conditioning of a fear response and the negative reinforcement of avoidance of cars through fear reduction.

animal receives a shock in its compartment, it attempts to escape. Eventually, it runs through the door and into the other compartment. When shock is delivered to that compartment, the animal can escape by running back to the original side. Running through the door removes the shock, which negatively reinforces this escape behavior. Over a few trials, the animal learns to escape as soon as the shock is administered.

To study avoidance conditioning experimentally, researchers introduce a discriminative stimulus—a warning signal such as a light—that precedes the shock by a few seconds. After a few trials, the animal learns that the light signals impending shock. It runs to the other compartment as soon as it sees the light and thereby avoids being shocked.

Once this avoidance response is learned, it often is hard to extinguish, even though the animal no longer experiences any shock after the light is turned on. We saw the same situation with Carol's car phobia. She continued to avoid cars even though the intense pain from her accident was no longer experienced. What makes avoidance so resistant to extinction?

According to one model, the **two-factor theory of avoidance learning,** *both classical and operant conditioning are involved in avoidance learning* (Mowrer, 1947; Rescorla & Solomon, 1967). For our rat, the warning light is initially a neutral stimulus paired with shock (UCS). Through classical conditioning, the light becomes a CS that elicits fear. Now operant conditioning takes over. Fleeing from the light is negatively reinforced by the termination of fear. This strengthens and maintains the avoidance response. Now if we permanently turn off the shock, the avoidance response prevents extinction from taking place. Seeing the light come on, the animal will not hang around long enough to learn that the shock no longer occurs.

In similar fashion, Carol's fear of cars was classically conditioned. The mere sight of a car (like the light for the rat) elicits fear and she flees, thereby avoiding riding in or driving the car. This avoidance is negatively reinforced by fear reduction, so it remains strong (Figure 6.24). Extinction is difficult because Carol doesn't give herself the opportunity to be in the car without experiencing physical pain and trauma. This is why exposure therapies for phobias are so effective. By preventing avoidance responses, they provide the key ingredient for extinction: exposure to the CS in the absence of the UCS.

The two-factor theory helps us understand how many avoidance behaviors develop (Baron & Perone, 2001). However, it has trouble explaining some aspects of avoidance, such as why people and other animals develop phobic avoidance to some stimuli (e.g., snakes) much more easily than to others (e.g., flowers). As we shall explore shortly, other factors—such as our biological predispositions—also regulate our avoidance responses.

Applications of Operant Conditioning

In his best-selling books *Walden Two* (1948) and *Beyond Freedom and Dignity* (1971), Skinner set forth his utopian vision of how a "technology of behavior" based on positive reinforcement could put an end to war, deteriorating education, and other social problems. To his critics, Skinner's ideas conjured up images of people manipulated like rats, of a "Big Brother" government controlling its citizens. But Skinner's point was that social influence is a natural part of human existence. Parents and children influence each other, as do employees and employers, teachers and students, friends, and romantic partners. In Skinner's and other behaviorists' view, individual and societal problems are created by the all-too-common *haphazard* use of reinforcement and overreliance on punishment (Catania, 2001).

FIGURE 6.25

(left) A trainer uses a laser to point out an object for the monkey to pick up. (right) Because of injuries suffered in an accident, this woman cannot move her arms or legs. The monkey has been operantly trained to assist her with basic chores, such as eating.

▶ 14. How have operant principles been applied to education, the workplace, animal training, and solving problem behaviors?

Education and the Workplace

Walk into your local computer store and you likely will find shelves of educational software, teaching everything from math to foreign languages. The effectiveness of such computerized instruction rests on two key principles championed by Skinner: *immediate performance feedback* and *self-paced learning.*

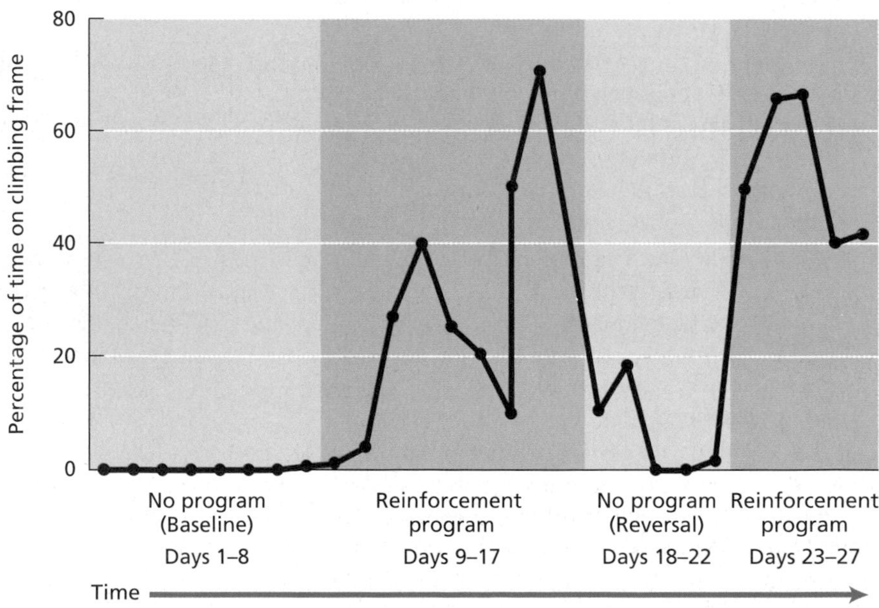

FIGURE 6.26

Mark, a 4-year-old, was observed for 8 days (baseline) under natural circumstances. He spent virtually no time on the climbing frame (monkey bars). During Days 9 to 17, he was reinforced with attention for climbing on the frame, and his behavior changed. During Days 18 to 22, the program was withdrawn (reversal), and his climbing decreased. It increased again on Days 23 to 27, when reinforcement was reintroduced. This pattern provides reasonable evidence that the reinforcement caused his behavior to change. Ultimately, the researchers shifted to a partial reinforcement schedule and reinforced him for climbing on other equipment. Mark remained physically active.
SOURCE: Adapted from Johnston et. al., 1966.

Skinner was deeply concerned about the inefficiency of traditional instructional methods (1968, 1989). Decades ago, long before the advent of personal computers, he developed mechanical teaching machines. Each machine presented material, quizzed the student, and provided immediate feedback. Students who did not learn the material the first time could repeat steps; those who did could advance to the next set of information. Today personal computers are helping Skinner's vision become an educational reality. Computer-assisted instruction (CAI) also is found in business, industry, and the military (Parchman et al., 2000).

Skinner's work also heightened societal attention to the broad issue of motivation and reinforcing desired behavior. A key behaviorist assumption is that poor performance should not be attributed to laziness or a bad attitude. Instead, we should assume that the environment is not providing the proper consequences to reinforce the desired behaviors. Many corporations invest heavily in training programs designed to enhance managers' effectiveness in reinforcing desired worker behaviors. Incentive systems—from stock options to bonuses for meeting performance goals—are now common in business and professional sports. **Token economies,** *in which desirable behaviors are quickly reinforced with "tokens"* (e.g., points, gold stars) *that are later turned in for tangible rewards* (e.g., prizes, recreation time), have been used to enhance academic and job performance. In one study, a token economy reduced the number of work injuries among open-pit mine workers (Fox et al., 1987). Miners received stamp awards for making safety suggestions and avoiding injuries, and they lost stamps for unsafe behaviors. Stamps were later traded in for tangible reinforcers. The program cost money, but far less than the cost of worker absenteeism due to accidents.

Specialized Animal Training

Through shaping and chaining, animals can learn to perform some truly remarkable behaviors. Some are trained to be TV, movie, or circus performers, whereas others learn to assist people who are blind or have other disabilities (Figure 6.25). Police dogs assist officers on routine patrol, and other dogs learn to use their sense of smell to help locate hidden bombs, illegal drugs, and missing persons. The U.S. Navy trains sea lions to dive and retrieve sunken test weapons, and dolphins learn to patrol waters around nuclear submarine bases and search for underwater intruders (Morrison, 1988). Operantly trained dolphins also patrolled the waters around some U.S. ships during the Vietnam and Persian Gulf Wars.

Modifying Problem Behaviors

Research on operant conditioning gave rise to a field called **applied behavior analysis,** *which combines a behavioral approach with the scientific method to solve individual and societal problems* (Kazdin, 1975). Essentially, applied behavior analysts design and implement a program to change behavior and measure its effectiveness objectively by gathering data before and after the program is in place (Figure 6.26). The actual procedures (e.g., reinforcement, shaping) that are used to change behavior are collectively known as *behavior modification*.

Applied behavior analysis has reduced an incredible range of behavior problems, from chronic hair pulling to drivers' failure to use seat belts (Byrd et al., 2002). It has improved students' academic performance and social skills, enhanced elite athletes' performance, increased employee productivity, reduced worker injuries and accidents, and increased energy conservation (Staats et al., 2000).

Operant conditioning demonstrates the environment's power in shaping behavior. But this does not mean we are at its mercy. The following *Applying Psychological Science* describes how you can use your knowledge of learning principles to gain greater control over your own behavior.

▶ 15. Describe five main steps in a behavioral self-regulation program.

For more on operant conditioning, see Interactive Segment 6.3.

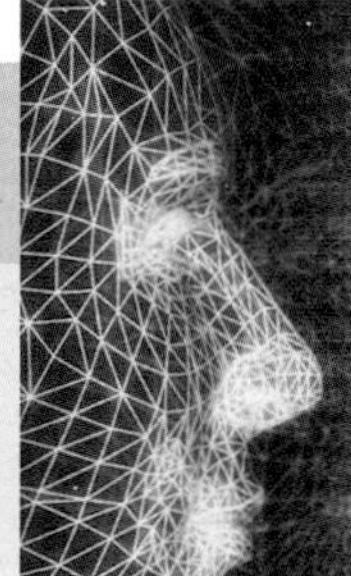

APPLYING PSYCHOLOGICAL SCIENCE

USING OPERANT PRINCIPLES TO MODIFY YOUR BEHAVIOR

People often blame the inability to overcome bad habits or maladaptive behaviors on vague concepts such as poor willpower and lack of self-control. Behaviorists prefer the more optimistic assumption that we can acquire *self-regulation*, which means using learning principles to change our behavior (Kanfer & Goldstein, 1991). This approach has helped people overcome addictions, lose excess weight, reduce their risk of heart disease, and improve their lives in many other ways. Let's examine how a college student could use self-regulation principles to increase the amount and effectiveness of studying.

Step 1: Specify the Problem

The first step in a self-regulation program is to pinpoint the behaviors you want to change (Watson & Tharp, 1997). This may be more challenging than it sounds, because we often use vague words to describe our problems. One of our students described her study problem by saying, "I'm just not motivated to study hard." With a little help, she redefined her problem in more specific behavioral terms as follows: "Between 7 P.M. and 10 P.M. I don't spend enough time at my desk reading and outlining my textbook."

Whenever possible, design your program to positively reinforce desirable behaviors (i.e., studying) rather than punish undesirable ones (i.e., not studying). Therefore we define this student's *target behavior* (the specific goal) as follows: "Four nights a week, between 7 and 10 P.M., spend 2½ hours studying."

Step 2: Collect Baseline Data

The next step is to collect *baseline (preintervention) data* on your behavior. Baseline data provide information about how frequently the target behavior currently occurs. Without it, you have no way of measuring how much you change after starting your program. The most effective approach is to plot data on a graph. Figure 6.27 shows data collected by one of our students.

Continued

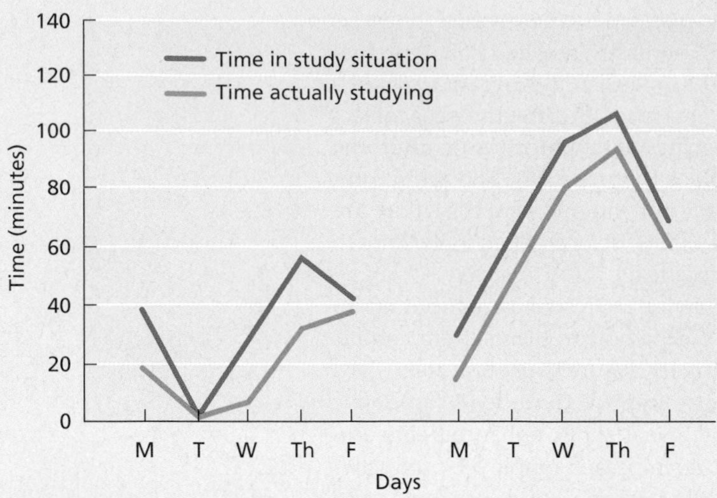

FIGURE 6.27

This student graphed the amount of time he spent in the study environment and the time actually spent studying. Study time increased when he began to self-reinforce study behavior in the second week.

Step 3: Identify Antecedents and Consequences

While you collect baseline data, try to identify *antecedent* factors that disrupt study behavior, such as friends calling or stopping by (Watson & Tharp, 1997). Also focus on the *consequences* of your behavior. Does studying produce outcomes that are satisfying?

Step 4: Develop a Plan to Modify the Antecedents and Consequences

Once you have identified key antecedents and consequences, you are in position to modify either or both.

Altering the Antecedents

You can modify the environment so that different stimuli control your behavior. To increase studying, select a specific place where you do nothing but study. If your attention wanders, get up and leave the study area. Your objective is to condition yourself to study in response to the stimuli present in the study area. B. F. Skinner used this technique throughout his own career: He did all of his writing at a particular desk and did nothing else there.

Altering the Consequences

Consequences determine whether behavior is repeated. Fortunately, we have the power to arrange many of our own consequences. Self-administered *positive reinforcement* should be the cornerstone of most programs. Find an effective reinforcer that you can control, and make it available only if you engage in the desired behavior. Almost any activity or object you enjoy can serve as a reinforcer, but it must be potent enough to maintain the desired behavior. Awarding yourself a penny for each hour of study time is unlikely to modify your behavior, whereas a 30-minute credit toward a recreational activity might be very effective. After selecting a reinforcer, decide how to use it. Draw up and sign a contract with yourself. The contract should precisely state

- how often or how long you must perform the target behavior (or refrain from performing it if the goal is to reduce an undesirable behavior) and
- the kind and amount of reinforcement you will receive for specific achievements.

Use Reinforcers Effectively

Immediately reinforce the target behavior whenever possible. If your reinforcer cannot be available immediately, use tokens that can later be converted into a reinforcer. One student who wanted to increase her study time awarded herself 1 point per 15 minutes of study time. Points were redeemed for rewards that varied in their reinforcement value. For example, 1 point was worth 15 minutes of TV viewing, but 15 points earned the right to "do anything I want to, all day." Behavior analysists have used token economies successfully with workers, children, patients in mental hospitals, prison inmates, and other groups (Swain & McLaughlin, 1998). If it works for them, it can work for you.

Use Shaping

If you collect good baseline data, you will know the level at which you currently perform your target behavior. Begin at this level or slightly beyond it and move *slowly* toward your final goal, reinforcing yourself at each step. For example, begin by reinforcing yourself for each 10-minute increase in study time. If you have trouble, reduce the size of your steps. Attaining each small goal along the way can be reinforcing and provides motivation to continue (Locke & Latham, 2002). The goal is to bring about gradual change while enjoying plenty of reinforcers, as well as the satisfaction that comes from increasing self-mastery. *The way you arrange reinforcement contingencies is the most critical determinant of whether your goal will be achieved.*

Step 5: Implement the Program and Keep Measuring Behavior

Most people experience occasional setbacks or plateaus where progress seems to stop. If this happens repeatedly, it is not a sign of weak willpower but rather a need to modify the program. Yes, self-regulation programs can fail, but failure calls for resourcefulness rather than despair. If need be, change the terms of your contract, but always operate under a specific contract. Keep recording and graphing the target behavior. This is the only way to identify your progress accurately.

This five-step process is one of several behavioral approaches to gaining greater control of our lives. Psychologists continue to design and test methods to increase self-regulation, adding new meaning to the phrase "Power to the people."

IN REVIEW

- *Thorndike's law of effect states that responses followed by satisfying consequences will be strengthened, whereas those followed by unsatisfying consequences will be weakened.*
- *Skinner analyzed operant conditioning in terms of relations between antecedents, behaviors, and consequences. Discriminative stimuli are antecedents that signal the likely consequences of particular behaviors in a given situation.*
- *Reinforcement occurs when a response is strengthened by an outcome (a reinforcer) that follows it. With positive reinforcement, a response is strengthened by the presentation of a stimulus that follows it. With negative reinforcement, a response is strengthened by the removal of an aversive stimulus.*
- *Operant extinction is the weakening and eventual disappearance of a response because it no longer is reinforced.*
- *Punishment occurs when a behavior is weakened by an outcome (a punisher) that follows it. With aversive punishment, the behavior becomes weaker when it is followed by the presentation of an aversive stimulus. With response cost, the behavior becomes weaker when it is followed by the removal of a stimulus.*
- *The use of corporal punishment with children is controversial and is correlated with several negative outcomes for children's development. However, the cause-effect relation between corporal punishment and negative outcomes is unclear.*
- *Shaping, which uses the method of successive approximations, involves the reinforcement of behaviors that increasingly resemble the final desired behavior.*
- *Operant generalization occurs when behavior changes in one situation due to reinforcement or punishment, and the new response then carries over to similar situations. In contrast, operant discrimination occurs when an operant response is made to one discriminative stimulus but not to another.*
- *On a continuous reinforcement schedule, every response is reinforced. Partial reinforcement may occur on a ratio schedule, in which a certain percentage of responses are reinforced, or on an interval schedule, in which a certain amount of time must pass before a response gets reinforced. In general, ratio schedules produce higher rates of performance than interval schedules.*
- *On a fixed-ratio schedule, reinforcement occurs after a fixed number of correct responses; on a fixed-interval schedule, it occurs after a fixed time interval. On variable schedules, the required number of responses or interval of time varies around some average.*
- *Learning occurs most rapidly under continuous reinforcement, but partial schedules produce behaviors that are more resistant to extinction.*
- *Escape conditioning and avoidance conditioning result from negative reinforcement. According to the two-factor theory, fear is created through classical conditioning. This fear motivates escape and avoidance, which are then negatively reinforced by fear reduction.*
- *Operant conditioning principles can enhance human performance in educational and work settings, reduce a wide array of behavior problems, and help people self-regulate their behavior. Animals can be operantly trained to perform many specialized tasks.*

OBSERVATIONAL LEARNING: WHEN OTHERS SHOW THE WAY

How did you learn to write, dance, and drive a car, or even to spread peanut butter and jelly across a piece of bread rather than piling it up in the center? Reinforcement certainly was involved, but so was **observational learning,** *the learning that occurs by observing the behavior of a model.* Teachers, parents, and coaches often help us learn by intentionally modeling skills, but observational learning extends beyond such contexts. We also learn fears, prejudices, likes and dislikes, and social behaviors by watching others (Hendy & Raudenbush, 2000).

▶ 16. What is the adaptive significance of observational learning? Describe four steps in the modeling process.

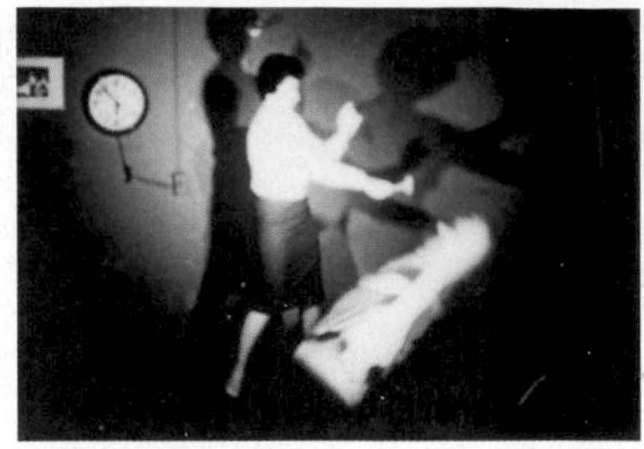

FIGURE 6.28

In Bandura's (1965) experiment, most children who watched an aggressive model attack a Bobo doll later imitated that behavior. These photos show only one of several specific actions that the children spontaneously imitated.

Through observation we may learn desirable responses, or, like the two boys in our opening vignette who overzealously emulated their TV wrestling heroes, we may acquire undesirable behaviors. When parents who swear in front of their children complain to one another, "Where did our kids learn that damn language?" the answer should be self-explanatory.

Observational learning can be highly adaptive. By observing others, an organism can learn which events are important, which stimuli signal that such events are about to occur, and which responses are likely to produce positive or negative consequences. For example, hens may learn which hens they can reasonably pick a fight with and which ones they should avoid by observing the hens that emerge as the victors and losers in battles (Hogue et al., 1996). And monkeys may learn adaptive fears—such as a fear of snakes—by observing other monkeys react with fear (Öhman & Mineka, 2001).

Our capacity to learn by observation, which is also called *modeling*, far outstrips that of other creatures. It saves us enormous time and effort and helps us bypass the potentially time-consuming and dangerous process of trial and error. We would not want each new generation of brain surgeons or airline pilots to learn their craft only through trial and error.

The Modeling Process

Psychologist Albert Bandura (1977), who helped pioneer the study of observational learning, views modeling as a four-step process involving *attention, retention, reproduction,* and *motivation.* First, we must pay attention to the model's behavior. Second, we must retain that information in memory so that it can be recalled when needed. Third, we must be physically capable of reproducing the model's behavior or something similar to it. And fourth, we must be motivated to display the behavior.

The fourth step, motivation, highlights the important distinction between learning and performance. Recall that we defined learning as a change in an organism's behavior or capabilities based on experience. Research on modeling demonstrates that knowledge and the capability to perform a behavior may be acquired at one time but not displayed until a later time. Bandura (1965) demonstrated this point in a classic experiment. Children watched a film in which a model acted aggressively toward a "Bobo doll" (an inflatable plastic clown), punching, kicking, and hitting it with a mallet. One group saw the model rewarded with praise and candy, a second group saw the model reprimanded for aggression, and a third group saw no consequences for the model. After the film, each child was placed in a room with various toys, including a Bobo doll (Figure 6.28).

Children who saw the model punished performed fewer aggressive actions toward the Bobo than did children in the other two groups. Does this mean that the first group failed to learn how to respond aggressively? To find out, the experimenter later offered the children attractive prizes if they could do what the model had done. All of the children quickly reproduced the model's aggressive responses.

Bandura's research helped stir a societal controversy that was brewing in the 1960s and continues to this day: What effect does viewing aggressive models on TV or in movies have on our attitudes and behavior? We discuss this issue more fully in Chapter 15. In brief, research strongly suggests that viewing media violence has the following effects (Eron, 2000; Smith & Donnerstein, 1998):

- It decreases viewers' concerns about the suffering of victims.
- It habituates us (reduces our sensitivity) to the sight of violence.
- It provides aggressive models that increase viewers' tendency to act aggressively.

If watching media violence can enhance our tendency to aggress, might watching prosocial models (models who do good deeds) increase our tendency to help others? We examine this question in the following *Research Close-Up*.

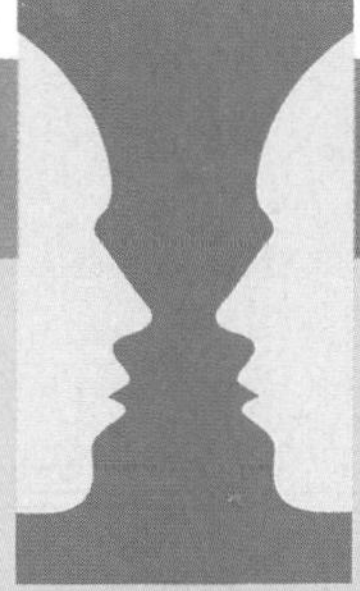

RESEARCH CLOSE-UP

LESSONS FROM LASSIE: CAN WATCHING TV INCREASE HELPING BEHAVIOR?

Background

Joyce Sprafkin and her colleagues conducted one of the earliest experiments to investigate whether children behave more helpfully after watching prosocial models on TV. The authors also examined whether a specific act of helping had to be modeled *during* the TV program to enhance children's prosocial behavior, or whether merely watching a popular prosocial "action hero" (the dog Lassie) would produce the same effect. Children's prosocial behavior was measured in a specific situation, in which a decision to help meant reducing their own chances to obtain a very attractive prize.

Method

With their parents' permission, 15 girls and 15 boys were randomly selected from several first-grade classes at a suburban school on New York's Long Island. Each child watched a half-hour TV program to pass the time while a special game "was being set up in another room." Children were randomly assigned to one of three TV programs (the independent variable). In the experimental condition ("prosocial Lassie"), children watched a *Lassie* episode in which a puppy fell into a mine shaft and Lassie ran to get her young master and lead him back to the mine, where he risked his life to save the puppy. In one control condition ("neutral Lassie"), children watched a *Lassie* episode that did not involve a human helping a dog. In a second control condition, children watched a *Brady Bunch* episode portraying positive family interactions (but no dogs). *Lassie* and *The Brady Bunch* were both popular shows at the time.

A second experimenter, blind to each child's TV condition, led each child to a "Point Game" room containing prizes that ranged in size and attractiveness. Nicer prizes cost more points, earned by pressing a button that lit a bulb as fast as possible. Points were automatically recorded and displayed, so the child could watch them accrue. Before leaving the child to play alone, the experimenter said,

> I'm in charge of a dog kennel . . . a place that we keep puppies until a home can be found for them. I had to leave the puppies alone so that I could come here today, but I know whether the dogs are safe or not by listening through these earphones . . . connected to the kennel. When I don't hear any noises . . . I know the dogs are O.K. . . . but if I hear them barking, I know . . . that they are in trouble and need help. If I hear barking, I press this button [a "Help Button"] which signals my helper. . . . He goes over . . . to make sure nothing bad happened to the dogs.

The children were asked to wear the headphones while playing the Point Game and press the Help Button if the puppies barked. The experimenter reminded each child that nicer prizes cost more points, that the goal was to get as many points as possible, and that, if the dogs barked, the child would have to decide what to do, because it was impossible to play the Point Game and signal for help at the same time.

The experimenter left, turned on a tape recorder that fed sound into the earphones, and played the same tape for each child. It began with 30 seconds of silence, followed by 120 seconds of escalating barking. Two dependent variables were recorded: the number of times each child pressed the Help Button during the barking and the speed with which they intervened once the barking began.

Results

During the 120-second barking period, children in the prosocial Lassie, neutral Lassie, and Brady Bunch conditions spent 77 percent, 43 percent, and 31 percent of their time pressing the Help Button, respectively. Children's gender did not influence the results. In addition to pressing the Help Button more, the prosocial Lassie children were faster to respond. On average, they began helping 25 seconds after the barking began, compared to 36 seconds and 55 seconds for the other groups.

Discussion

This study examined a socially important question under controlled conditions. However, before we can accept the authors' conclusion that the prosocial behavior modeled in *Lassie* was the likely cause of why children helped more, we must ask whether other factors could have caused these findings. In other words, did the experiment have high internal validity?

The experimenters did many things to reduce alternative explanations. The children were randomly assigned to the TV conditions and treated as similarly as possible except for the show they viewed. To minimize the potential for experimenter bias, the researcher who interacted with the children during the Point Game and measured their behavior did not know (was blind to) which TV program each child had watched.

Continued

SOURCE: Joyce N. Sprafkin, Robert M. Liebert, and Rita Wicks Poulous (1975). Effects of a prosocial televised example on children's helping. *Journal of Experimental Child Psychology, 20*, 119–126.

Using two control groups was also a positive feature, but the authors did not specify whether the neutral Lassie episode also involved a puppy (one that didn't have to be rescued). If it didn't, can you see why this might be a problem? Is it possible that simply seeing a cute puppy on TV increased children's empathy for the barking puppies in the "kennel" and that this is why they helped more? If we knew the neutral program had a puppy, this concern would be eliminated.

Finally, there is the question of external validity. Do the results generalize to other settings, especially real-world ones? The answer appears to be yes. A survey of nearly 200 studies examining the effects of prosocial TV within and outside the laboratory indicates that such programs positively affect children's behavior (Hearold, 1986). The implication for TV programming seems clear: Lassie, come home.

▶ 17. How did researchers examine whether watching TV increases children's prosocial behavior? What did they find?

IN REVIEW

- *Observational learning, or modeling, is learning that occurs by observing the behavior of a model.*
- *Bandura proposes that modeling involves four steps: attention, retention, reproduction, and motivation. Knowledge of how to perform a behavior may be learned at one point in time, but the behavior may not be displayed until the proper incentives are present.*
- *Experiments indicate that children can learn aggressive behaviors by watching aggressive models. Studies also suggest that watching aggressive models on TV and in movies can enhance the viewer's tendency to aggress.*
- *Watching a model engage in prosocial behavior can increase a viewer's tendency to help others.*

CROSSROADS OF LEARNING

The discovery of laws of learning represents one of the greatest contributions of psychological science, and behaviorists built the foundation on which our knowledge of learning principles rests. Other psychologists, viewing behavior from biological and cognitive perspectives, also have contributed to our understanding of learning.

Evolution and Preparedness

▶ 18. How does research on learned taste aversions and fear conditioning support the concept of biological preparedness?

Behaviorists never suggested that a rat could learn to fly, but for decades they assumed that they could condition virtually any behavior an organism was physically capable of performing. Yet evidence mounted that "conditioned" animals did not always respond as they were supposed to. The behaviorist assumption was wrong because it ignored a key principle discussed at the outset of this chapter: Behavior is influenced by an organism's evolutionary history, and this places biological constraints on learning.

Martin Seligman's (1970) concept of "preparedness" captures this idea. **Preparedness** *means that through evolution, animals are biologically predisposed (prewired) to learn some associations more easily than others.* In general, behaviors related to a species' survival are learned more easily than behaviors contrary to an organism's natural tendencies. Let's consider some examples.

Constraints on Classical Conditioning: Learned Taste Aversions

Imagine eating or drinking something, then becoming sick to your stomach and throwing up. Perhaps it is a case of the flu, or it could be food poisoning. Cancer patients may become ill after a session of chemotherapy or radiation therapy. When a food is associated with nausea or vomiting, that particular food can become a CS that triggers a **conditioned taste aversion,** *a conditioned response in which the taste (and sometimes the sight and smell) of the food now disgusts and repulses us* (Garcia et al., 1985). The very thought of it may even make us feel queasy, and we learn to avoid it. During pregnancy many women experience nausea and vomiting, and they may develop aversions to foods associated with these symptoms (Bayley et al., 2002). Cancer patients may develop aversions to foods they eat before treatment, even though they know that the food did not cause their post-treatment stomach upset. Like other conditioned responses, the aversion develops involuntarily.

Psychologist John Garcia pioneered numerous taste aversion experiments that challenged two basic assumptions of classical conditioning. First, behaviorists had assumed that the CS-UCS time interval had to be relatively short: usually a few seconds. Garcia showed that animals learned taste aversions even though the food (CS) was consumed up to several hours—or even a day—before they became ill (in this case, the UCS).

Second, in a classic experiment, Garcia illustrated how biological preparedness influences learned aversions (Garcia & Koelling, 1966). Whenever rats licked a drinking tube, they were simultaneously exposed to three neutral stimuli: sweet-tasting water, a bright light, and a buzzer (Figure 6.29). In one condition, half the rats were exposed to X rays upon drinking the water, which later made them ill (UCS). Would the rats develop an aversion to all three neutral stimuli? No, they avoided the sweet water but not the light or buzzer. Why did only the sweet taste become a CS? Because rats are biologically primed to form taste-illness associations, which means that in nature they most easily identify poisonous or "bad" food by its taste (or smell). In nature, sounds and lights don't make rats sick.

When rats in a second condition licked the tube, the light, buzzer, and sweet taste were all paired with an electric shock. Would the rats learn to fear all three neutral stimuli? No, they avoided the light and buzzer but kept drinking the sweet water. This also makes adaptive sense. In nature, sights and sounds—but not how food and drink taste—signal fear-provoking situations (e.g., a cat about to pounce).

The same adaptive principle applies to humans. A hunter-gatherer who becomes ill after eating an unfamiliar food might develop an aversion to that food but not to clan members who were present at the time. Likewise, when a food makes us violently sick, we may develop an aversion to it but not to the friends we ate with. Further, seeing the food again may repulse us but not make us afraid.

Psychologists have applied their knowledge about conditioned aversions to save animals' lives. To prevent coyotes from killing ranchers' sheep, Carl Gustavson and his colleagues (1974) laced pieces of meat with lithium chloride, a nausea-inducing drug. They wrapped the meat in sheep hide and left it out for coyotes to eat. The coyotes ate it, became ill, and developed an aversion to the meat, thereby becoming less likely to kill sheep. This saved the lives of sheep—and also of the coyotes, which otherwise would have been shot by the ranchers. Figure 6.30 illustrates an intriguing example of nature's own "wildlife management" based on learned taste aversions.

Applying taste aversion principles to children with cancer, Darla Broberg and Ilene Bernstein (1987) gave young patients an unusual-tasting candy before their chemotherapy treatments. As hypothesized, the candy served as a scapegoat for the children's conditioned taste aversions, protecting them from developing aversions to their normal foods. Thus the candy—rather than their normal food—became the aversive CS.

Stage 1: All Rats
When rats touch the drinking tube, sweet water is delivered and a light and buzzer turn on.

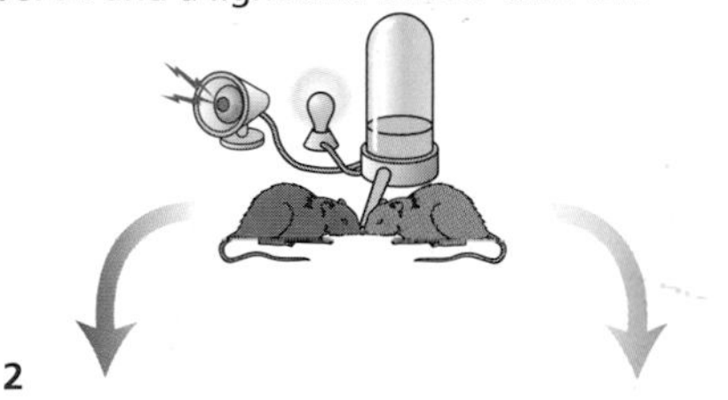

Stage 2

Illness condition

Group 1 rats get nauseating X rays when they drink.

Fear condition

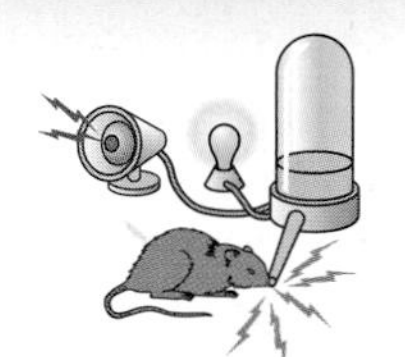

Group 2 rats get electric shocks when they drink.

Stage 3

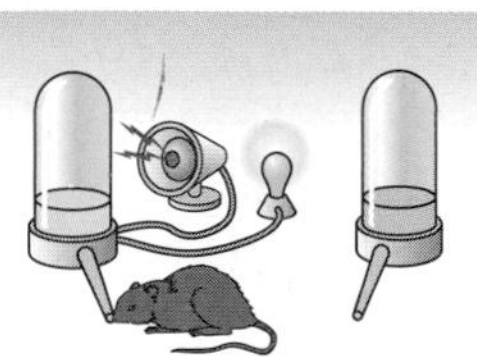

Group 1 rats avoid the sweet water and prefer the plain water with the light and buzzer.

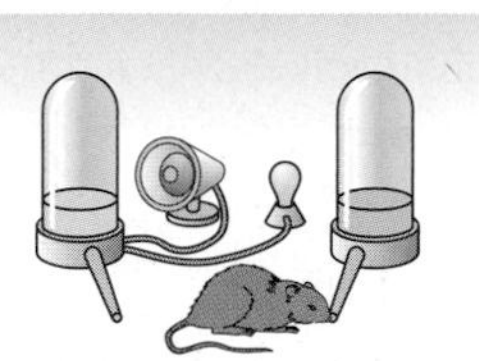

Group 2 rats still drink the sweet water, but avoid the plain water with the light and buzzer.

FIGURE 6.29

Biological preparedness in classical conditioning. This figure illustrates the design and main results of Garcia and Koelling's (1966) aversion experiment.

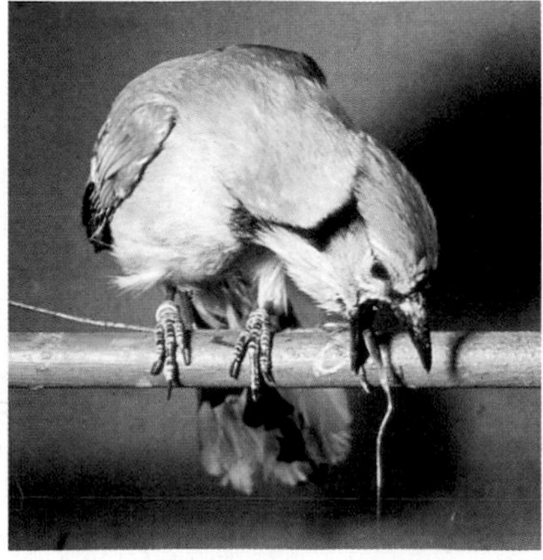

FIGURE 6.30

This blue jay has never eaten a monarch butterfly before, but doesn't pass up an easy meal. Soon, toxins in the butterfly cause food poisoning. The jay feels discomfort, vomits, and develops a conditioned aversion triggered by the sight of the monarch's brightly patterned wings. From now on, it will leave monarchs alone. Photos courtesy of Lincoln P. Brower.

Are We Biologically Prepared to Fear Certain Things?

Seligman (1971) proposes that, like other animals, humans are biologically prepared to acquire certain fears more readily than others. Case studies of phobic patients support this idea. British therapist Isaac Marks (1977) tells of a 4-year-old girl who saw a snake while walking through a park. She found the snake interesting and didn't fear it. Soon after seeing the snake, she returned to the family car and accidentally smashed her hand when the car door closed. She developed a lifelong phobia not of car doors or automobiles, but of snakes!

Experiments by Arne Öhman and his Swedish research team provide evidence of preparedness (Öhman & Soares, 1998). These researchers paired various neutral stimuli with electric shock (the unconditioned stimulus), and measured participants' physiological responses when those stimuli were subsequently presented alone. People who received shocks each time pictures of snakes, spiders, or angry faces were flashed on a screen quickly acquired conditioned fear responses to these stimuli, even when the pictures were displayed too briefly to be consciously perceived. But participants who received shocks while looking at slides of flowers, houses, berries, or happy faces displayed much weaker fear conditioning.

Humans develop phobias to many stimuli, but most often we fear things that seem to have greater evolutionary significance: snakes, spiders, other potentially dangerous animals, and dangerous places. Is this the result of evolution-based preparedness, or might it be due to learning experiences within our own lifetime? Through cultural transmission of knowledge, perhaps we come to expect that some stimuli can be dangerous, making us cognitively rather than biologically prepared to acquire certain fears. The role of multiple factors in human fear conditioning continues to be examined, but one thing is clear: As with taste aversions, fear can be conditioned much more easily to some stimuli than others (Öhman & Mineka, 2001).

Constraints on Operant Conditioning: Animals That "Won't Shape Up"

▶ 19. How does instinctive drift illustrate preparedness and why is it important? How are the brain and learning related?

Two of B. F. Skinner's students, Keller Breland and Marian Breland, became renowned animal trainers. They used shaping and chaining to train thousands of animals for circuses, advertising agencies, TV, and the movies. Training was usually successful, but not always. Sometimes the animals simply refused to behave according to the "laws" of operant conditioning (Breland & Breland, 1961, 1966).

On one occasion, the Brelands tried to train a chicken to play baseball. A small ball would roll toward home plate, and the chicken would pull a chain to swing a small metal bat. If the ball was hit, a bell would ring and the chicken was supposed to run to first base to get its food. The Brelands easily trained the chicken to pull the chain that swung the bat and to run to first base when it heard the bell. But when the ball was introduced into the game, utter chaos ensued. Whenever the chicken hit the ball, instead of running to first base to collect its food reinforcement, it chased the ball all over the playing field, pecking furiously at it and flapping its wings. Try as they might, the Brelands could not extinguish these behaviors. End of training and end of the chicken's baseball career. This and other similar cases suggest that in operant conditioning (as in classical conditioning), organisms are biologically prepared to learn some types of associations more readily than others.

The Brelands also found that once a particular stimulus came to represent food, animals began to act as if it were food. The chicken pecked at the ball as if it were something to eat. In another example, raccoons kept rubbing tokens given to them as reinforcers as if they were "washing" real food. The raccoons had successfully performed the conditioned response of dropping a token in a box several times, but their "washing" behavior was so deeply rooted in their evolutionary history that it simply overrode the conditioning procedure. The Brelands called this **instinctive drift,** *the tendency for a conditioned response to "drift back" toward instinctive behavior.*

Research provides other evidence of instinctive drift. It is relatively easy to train a pigeon to peck a novel object (such as a disc on a wall) for food reinforcers, because pigeons come into the world biologically primed to peck for food. Training a pigeon to peck an object to escape from electric shock is more difficult, because in their natural environment pigeons do not escape from danger by pecking. They fly away. As another example, wild rats trained to press a lever for food will often drift back to instinctive behaviors and instead scratch and bite the lever (Powell & Curley, 1976).

Instinctive drift also has practical importance. People who adopt wild animals as pets, or who train them for circuses, face some personal risk no matter how hard they try to domesticate these animals. An acquaintance of ours once rescued a cuddly baby raccoon and raised it lovingly for nearly a year, at which time the raccoon unexpectedly reverted to its more instinctive, aggressive behavior. Our friend, now known as "Three Fingers," returned his pet to the wild.

The Adaptive Brain

No single part of the brain controls learning. Rather, our ability to learn and adapt to the environment depends on a network of brain structures and circuits. The hypothalamus and neural pathways involving dopamine play a key role in regulating our ability to experience reward (Olds, 1958; Rolls, 2000). Humans report pleasure when specific areas of the hypothalamus are electrically stimulated, and rats will repeatedly press a lever to receive a similar electrical reinforcer. The cerebellum plays an important role in acquiring classically conditioned movements, such as conditioned eyeblink responses, whereas the amygdala is centrally involved in acquiring conditioned fears (Schafe & LeDoux, 2002). We'll examine how the brain underlies learning more closely in Chapter 7.

Biology affects learning, but learning experiences also influence brain functioning (Wachs, 2000). As we discussed in Chapter 2, young animals who are exposed to enriched environments—with toys and greater opportunities to learn—develop heavier brains with more dendrites and synapses and greater concentrations of various neurotransmitters (Rosenzweig, 1984). In turn, this increased brain development enables animals to perform better on subsequent learning tasks (Meaney et al., 1991).

In humans, exposure to stimulating environments during late adulthood seems to slow declines in brain functioning, as measured by better performance on intellectual and perceptual tasks (Schaie, 1998). In a sense, then, every day you are alive your brain adapts and continues its own "personal evolution"; its neural networks and patterns of activity are affected not only by your genetic endowment but, as Figure 6.31 shows, by your learning experiences as well.

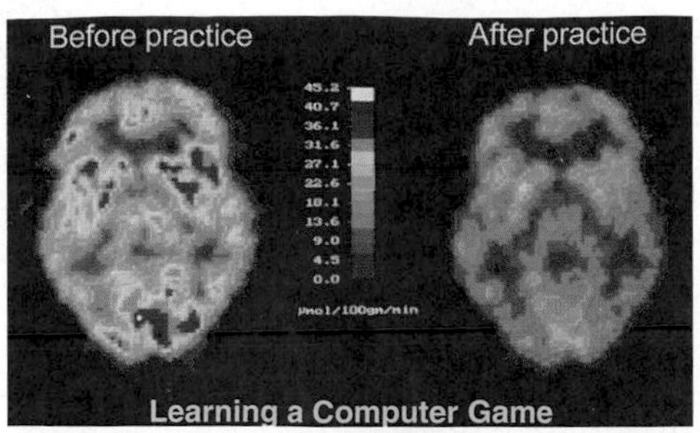

FIGURE 6.31

While learning a computer game, the brain of a novice player is highly active and uses a lot of energy, as indicated by the large yellow and red areas in the left PET scan. As the right scan shows, energy consumption decreases with experience.

Cognition and Learning

Early behaviorists believed that learning involves the relatively automatic formation of bonds between stimuli and responses. In classical conditioning, the CS elicits the CR (e.g., tone-salivation). In operant conditioning, a discriminative stimulus leads to an emitted response (e.g., a light comes on, a hungry rat presses the lever to obtain food). This behaviorist orientation came to be known as *S-R (stimulus-response) psychology*. Behaviorists opposed explanations of learning that went beyond observable stimuli and responses. They did not deny that people had thoughts and feelings but argued that behavior could be explained without referring to such mentalistic concepts (Skinner, 1953, 1990).

Behaviorism guided much learning research from the early 1900s through the 1960s, and it remains influential today (Leslie, 2002). But even in psychology's early days, some learning theorists argued that in between stimulus (S) and response (R) there was something else: the organism's (O) cognitive representation of the world. This came to be known as the *S-O-R*, or *cognitive, model of learning*. Today the cognitive perspective represents an important force in learning theory.

Insight and Cognitive Maps

▶ 20. Discuss how research on insight and cognitive maps challenged behaviorist views of learning.

In the 1920s, German psychologist Wolfgang Köhler (1925) challenged Thorndike's behaviorist assumption that animals learn to perform tasks only by trial and error. Köhler exposed chimpanzees to novel learning tasks and concluded that they were able to learn by **insight,** *the sudden perception of a useful relationship that helps to solve a problem*. Figure 6.32 shows how one of his apes solved the problem of how to retrieve bananas that were dangling beyond reach. Köhler emphasized that the apes often spent time staring at the bananas and available tools, as if they were contemplating the problem, after which the solution suddenly appeared.

Behaviorists argued that "insight" actually represents the combining of previously learned responses (Epstein et al., 1984). Imagine a pigeon placed inside a chamber where a miniature model of a banana dangles from the ceiling, out of reach. A small box sits in the corner of the chamber. Similar to Köhler's apes, the pigeon looks around, goes

FIGURE 6.32

Sultan seems to study the hanging bananas that are out reach. After looking around, Sultan suddenly grabs some crates, stacks them, and obtains the tasty reward.

to the box, moves it under the banana by pushing it with its beak, then stands on the box and pecks the banana. Without knowing the pigeon's behavioral history (just as we don't know the entire behavioral history of Köhler's apes), we might conclude that this is a novel behavior reflecting remarkable insight. But instead, the pigeon has simply combined several independent behaviors (e.g., pushing a box, stepping onto a box) that researchers had operantly conditioned using reinforcement. Although this example provides fuel for the debate about insight that continues to this day, Köhler's work nevertheless helped place the cognitive learning viewpoint on the map.

Another cognitive pioneer, learning theorist Edward Tolman of the University of California, Berkeley, studied spatial learning in rats. Look at the maze in Figure 6.33a. A rat runs to an open circular table, continues across, and follows the only path available to a goal box containing food. After 12 trials, the rat easily negotiates the maze. Next, the maze is changed. The rat runs its usual route and reaches a dead-end (Figure 6.33b). What will the rat do?

Tolman found that rats returned to the table, briefly explored most of the 18 new paths for just a few inches, and then chose one. By far, the largest number—36 percent—chose the 4th path to the right of their original route, which took them to about 4 inches in front of where the goal box had been. In short, the rats behaved as you would, given your advantage of seeing the maps in Figure 6.33.

Tolman (1948) argued that reinforcement theory could not explain this behavior but that he could: The rats had developed a **cognitive map,** *a mental representation of the spatial layout*. The concept of cognitive maps supported Tolman's belief that

FIGURE 6.33

(a) Rats first learned to run the simple maze. (b) When the maze was switched, many rats chose the fourth path to the right of the original route. Tolman proposed that the rats had developed a cognitive map of the maze. Source: Adapted from Tolman, 1948.

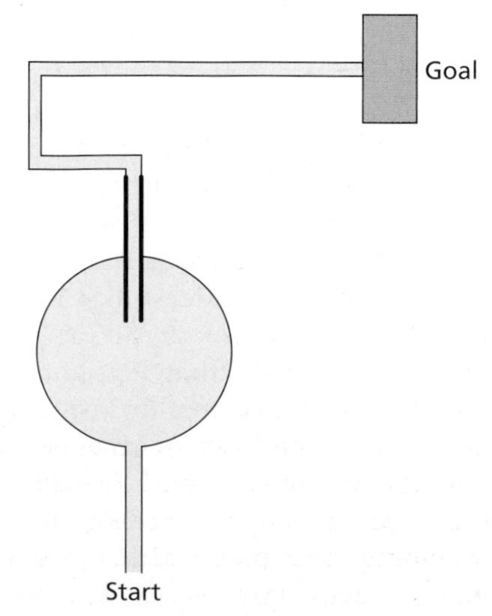

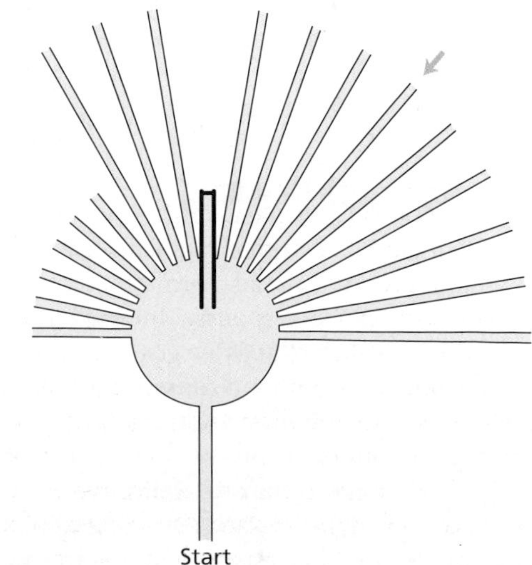

learning does not merely "stamp in" stimulus-response connections. Rather, learning provides knowledge, and based on their knowledge, organisms develop an expectancy, a cognitive representation, of "what leads to what."

Behaviorists disagreed with Tolman's interpretations and developed noncognitive models to explain how organisms learn their way around (Hull, 1943). As with insight, the debate over cognitive maps continues but, most important, Tolman's concept of expectancy remains a cornerstone of today's cognitive approaches to both classical and operant conditioning.

Cognition in Classical Conditioning

Early American behaviorists believed that classical conditioning created a direct reflexlike connection between the CS (e.g., tone) and CR (e.g., salivation). Interestingly, Pavlov held a different view, proposing that a neural bond is formed between the CS and the UCS. Thus, for Pavlov's dogs, the tone triggered an association with food, which then triggered the reflexive salivation response.

Cognitive learning theorists also believe that classical conditioning forms a CS-UCS link. In cognitive terminology, the link is an expectancy that the CS will be followed by the UCS (Hollis, 1997). This *expectancy model* states that the most important factor in classical conditioning is not how often the CS and the UCS are paired, but how well the CS predicts (i.e., signals) the appearance of the UCS (Rescorla & Wagner, 1972).

Robert Rescorla (1968) of Yale University demonstrated this principle in an experiment on fear conditioning. Rats in one condition received electric shocks (UCS), and each shock was preceded by a tone. As usual, the tone soon became a CS that elicited a fear response when presented alone. In a second condition, rats received the same number of tone-shock pairings as the first group, but they also received as many shocks that were not preceded by the tone. Would the tone become a CS for fear? According to traditional learning theory, the answer should be yes, because the number of tone-shock pairings was the same as in the first group. But the expectancy model predicts no, because the tone does not reliably predict when the shock will occur. The results supported Rescorla's hypothesis: The tone did not elicit a fear response for the second group.

CS-UCS inconsistency also explains why we don't become conditioned to all the neutral stimuli that are present just before a UCS appears. For example, when Pavlov's dogs were presented with tone-food pairings, there was light in the room. Why didn't the dogs learn to salivate whenever they saw light? The key is that when the room was lit, the dogs often were *not* receiving food. From a cognitive viewpoint, these neutral stimuli do not consistently predict the arrival of the UCS, dramatically reducing the chance that they will become a CS. This is highly adaptive; if it were not the case, you and I (along with Pavlov's dogs) would be twitching, salivating, blinking, and exhibiting all sorts of embarrassing reflexive responses to so many stimuli that it would be difficult to function.

Other evidence supports this cognitive model over a simple CS-UCS pairing model. For example, recall that forward pairing (CS followed by UCS) typically produces the strongest learning, simultaneous pairing produces weaker learning, and backward pairing (UCS followed by CS) produces the weakest or no learning. This makes sense based on the expectancy model. In forward tone-food pairing, the tone predicts the imminent arrival of the food; it is a signal that something meaningful is about to happen. With simultaneous pairing, the tone has less value as a signal because the food arrives at the same time. And in backward pairing, the tone has no predictive value because the food has already arrived.

▶ 21. Describe the role of cognition in classical and operant conditioning. How did Tolman illustrate latent learning?

Learning theorists continue to test other models of classical conditioning, but the expectancy model has been highly influential (Siegel & Allan, 1996). Those who adhere to the S-O-R model believe there is good evidence that cognition plays a role in classical conditioning.

Cognition in Operant Conditioning

Cognitive theorists believe that mental processes also play a key role in operant conditioning. Let's examine three issues.

The Role of Awareness To demonstrate operant conditioning to an introductory psychology class, an instructor sent one student out of the room and instructed another student in how to shape the response of flicking a light switch on and off, using small chocolate candies as the reinforcer. When the naive student returned, he was given a piece of chocolate first for looking at the wall that held the light switch, then for approaching the wall, and so on. After 25 minutes of shaping, he was happily flicking the switch and chomping one piece of chocolate after another.

FIGURE 6.34

Perception versus reality. Cartoon by H. Mazzeo and P. Ganler, 1951. Reprinted with permission of Jester of Columbia.

"Boy, have I got this guy conditioned! Every time I press the bar down, he drops in a piece of food."

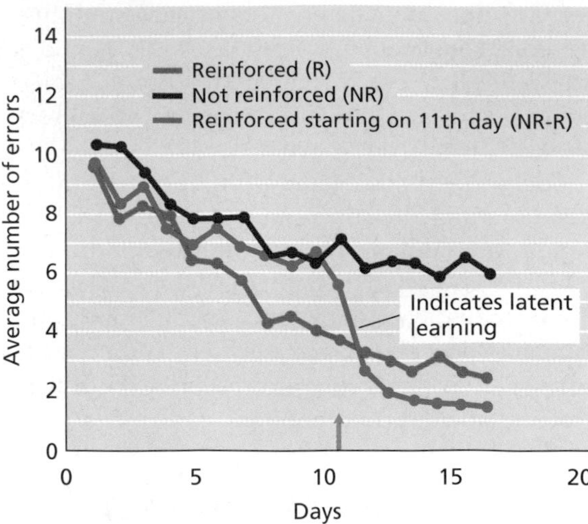

FIGURE 6.35

Tolman's demonstration of latent learning. Rats had one trial in the maze per day. Group R was reinforced with food every time they reached the end of the maze. Group NR received no reinforcement in the maze at any time. The critical group (NR-R) had food reward introduced on the 11th day. Their immediate performance improvement suggested that they had learned the maze prior to the introduction of reinforcement. SOURCE: Tolman & Honzik, 1930.

At this point, another student asked if she could serve as experimenter. A new participant left the room while the class decided that he should be shaped to erase the blackboard. When the student returned to the classroom, the new experimenter said, "Jeff, if you'll erase the blackboard immediately, I'll give you this whole bag of candy." This time, it took all of 5 seconds to produce the desired behavior.

Cognitive theorists emphasize that organisms develop an *awareness,* or *expectancy,* of the relations between their responses and probable consequences. From this viewpoint, whether through shaping or verbal communication, the operant responses of flicking the light switch and erasing the blackboard came about and were then maintained by the expectation that a delicious consequence would follow. Similarly, suppose you are in an experiment and your task is to make up a sentence and tell it to me. As you speak, I say "good" or "mmm-hmm" every time your sentence contains a noun that refers to humans (e.g., *boy, woman, people*). We go through this process for 10 sentences, and I measure whether your usage of human nouns changes. In the actual experiment, only those participants who received praise *and* who became aware of the reinforcement contingency increased their usage of human nouns (Spielberger & DeNike, 1966). Those who received praise but remained unaware of why it was given performed no differently than a control group receiving no praise.

From a cognitive perspective, the concept of awareness implies that the best predictor of behavior is the perceived contingency, not the actual one (Figure 6.34). In many instances the two are identical, but sometimes people perceive contingencies that do not actually exist. One common example is *superstitious behavior.* In cognitive terms, the organism misperceives that a specific behavior produces favorable consequences or helps avoid bad ones. Humans often engage in superstitious behaviors to gain a sense of control over environmental events (Keinan, 2002). One frequent traveler we know insists on eating ice cream prior to taking any trip on a train (even for early morning departures) because this will guarantee a safe journey. This superstitious behavior, of course, has been reinforced each time by a safe arrival.

Latent Learning Tolman's research illustrated in Figure 6.33 suggested that rats developed cognitive maps when they were reinforced with food for running a maze. Tolman also believed that cognitive maps could be learned without reinforcement, posing an even greater challenge to the behaviorist viewpoint. In one experiment, three groups of rats learned the correct path through a complex maze (Tolman & Honzik, 1930). Rats in the first group found food each time they reached the goal box. Rats in the second group found the goal box empty each time they reached it. Rats in

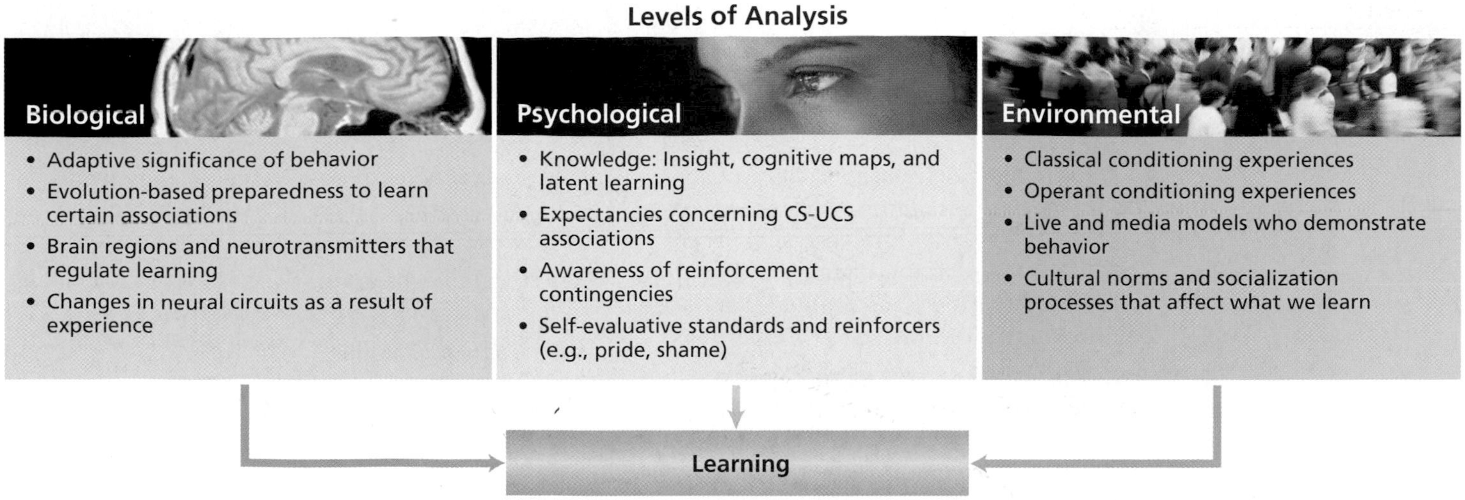

Levels of Analysis

Biological	Psychological	Environmental
• Adaptive significance of behavior • Evolution-based preparedness to learn certain associations • Brain regions and neurotransmitters that regulate learning • Changes in neural circuits as a result of experience	• Knowledge: Insight, cognitive maps, and latent learning • Expectancies concerning CS-UCS associations • Awareness of reinforcement contingencies • Self-evaluative standards and reinforcers (e.g., pride, shame)	• Classical conditioning experiences • Operant conditioning experiences • Live and media models who demonstrate behavior • Cultural norms and socialization processes that affect what we learn

Learning

FIGURE 6.36

Understanding Behavior: Factors involved in learning.

the third group found no food at the end of the maze for the first 10 days but did find food in the goal box starting on the 11th day.

The results are shown in Figure 6.35, and the key finding is this: On Day 11, the rats in the third group discovered food in the goal box for the first time. By the very next day, they were performing just as well as the first group, which had been reinforced all along. What could explain this significant, sudden performance improvement? According to Tolman, during Days 1 to 10, rats in the third group were learning the spatial layout of the maze as they wandered about. They were not being reinforced by food, but they gained knowledge and developed their cognitive maps. This learning remained *latent* (hidden) until the rats discovered a good reason on Day 11 to get to the goal box quickly, and then it immediately was manifested in performance the next day. Tolman's experiments support the concept of **latent learning,** *which refers to learning that occurs but is not demonstrated until later, when there is an incentive to perform* (Blodgett, 1929). If you recall Bandura's (1965) experiments in which children watched aggressive models get punished but imitated the models' behavior later when offered prizes, you will realize that these findings also illustrate latent learning: We may learn how to do something (gain knowledge) at one time but not display that knowledge outwardly (performance) until some future time.

Self-Evaluations as Reinforcers and Punishers Students called him "Holy Hubert," and he visited our college campus for over 10 years. His fire-and-brimstone exhortations to repent and avoid damnation often evoked amused smiles, loud insults, and ridicule. One could hardly imagine less positive consequences for an evangelist. One day, we asked Hubert why he continued to preach when students' responses were so negative. He answered, "I don't care what they say. When I know I'm doing the Lord's work, I feel so good that they could hang me for all I care."

Hubert's persistence in the face of adversity illustrates that external reinforcement and punishment are not the only consequences controlling behavior. If they were, how could we account for the actions of people who resist temptation even when they know they won't be discovered or punished? We often feel pride for doing something even if others do not know or approve of our deeds. In this sense, virtue is indeed its own reward. We may also disapprove of ourselves for failing to live up to our own standards. These *cognitive self-evaluations* represent important internal reinforcers and punishers (Scott & Cervone, 2002). Think back to the chapter-opening vignette of the woman who solicits charitable donations, and consider that her strong belief that she is doing something valuable may be all the positive reinforcement she needs.

In closing, you have seen that environmental, psychological, and biological factors play key roles in learning. Figure 6.36 summarizes many of the factors discussed in the chapter. As you study the learning concepts we've covered, try to apply them to your own behavior. Think about the roles that classical conditioning, operant conditioning, and observational learning play in developing and maintaining important behaviors in your life.

▶ 22. Summarize how biological, psychological, and environmental factors influence learning.

IN REVIEW

- *An organism's evolutionary history prepares it to learn certain associations more easily than others. The concept of biological preparedness illustrates that there are biological constraints on learning. For example, organisms show faster classical conditioning to conditioned stimuli that have evolutionary significance.*
- *It is difficult to operantly condition animals to perform behaviors that are contrary to their evolved natural tendencies. Instinctive drift occurs when such conditioned behaviors are abandoned in favor of a more natural response.*
- *Various brain regions, circuits, and chemicals regulate learning. Environmental experiences affect brain development and functioning, which in turn influence our future ability to learn.*
- *Köhler's early research on animal insight and Tolman's pioneering research on cognitive maps suggested that cognitive factors play a role in learning. Tolman emphasized that learning is based on knowledge and an expectation of "what leads to what."*
- *Cognitive interpretations of classical conditioning propose that what is learned is an expectancy that the CS will be followed by the UCS.*
- *Cognitive learning theorists view operant conditioning as the development of an expectancy that certain behaviors will produce certain consequences under certain conditions. Tolman's research on latent learning indicates that "knowledge" and "performance" are conceptually distinct and that learning can occur without reinforcement.*
- *In humans, cognitive self-evaluations (e.g., pride and shame) can function as reinforcers and punishers.*

KEY TERMS AND CONCEPTS

Each term has been boldfaced and defined in the chapter on the page indicated in parentheses.

What Do You Think?

WHY DID CAROL'S CAR PHOBIA PERSIST? p. 204

As often happens to people who have phobias, Carol may have been saddled with her phobia for life had she not sought therapy. We can't know for sure why Carol's anxiety reaction failed to extinguish, but a strong possibility is that she was not exposed to sufficient extinction trials. The key to extinction is the presentation of the CS (a car) without the UCS (events of the crash). If Carol avoided cars after her accident, then there was little opportunity for the CS to occur without the UCS. This is the unfortunate irony of phobias: People avoid the stimulus they fear, thereby depriving themselves of extinction trials. Thus, *the key ingredient to extinction is not the mere passage of time but repeated presentation of the CS without the UCS*. Without exposure to the CS, the CR will be difficult to extinguish.

Applying this same principle to the Navy veterans who heard the battle gong, can you explain why they automatically showed a strong alarm reaction 15 years after the war's end? Think about it before reading the next sentence. Again, we can't know for sure, but once the combat ended, the sailors likely had insufficient opportunities to experience extinction trials. In other words, the way to extinguish their fear would be to sound the battle gong (CS) repeatedly without the associated danger of manning battle stations and preparing for combat (UCS). ■

WAS THE "LITTLE ALBERT" STUDY ETHICAL? p. 207

In forming your ethical judgment, did you consider the various ethical criteria discussed in Chapter 2 (see pp. 55–56)? With those modern criteria in mind, let's examine some ethical issues and imagine that we are reviewing this research proposal in the early 1900s.

(1) *If you initially thought that you would not approve a study like this, then consider the following:*

- Suppose the experimenters promise to obtain informed consent from the infant's parents and keep everyone's identity confidential.
- Although the infant will experience some short-term stress, consider the enormous potential scientific and practical benefits of this study. If we can indeed classically condition phobias in humans, this may revolutionize thinking about how phobias develop and could lead to faster, less expensive, and more effective phobia treatments. These treatments, based on learning theory, could benefit countless people who suffer from phobias.
- Suppose that after the study the experimenters promise to use procedures based on learning theory to extinguish the infant's phobia, so that he will not suffer any negative long-term consequences.

Under these conditions and with these issues in mind, would you now approve the study?

(2) *If your initial judgment (or new judgment) is that you would approve this study, then consider the following:*

- Would it be ethical to proceed with the study if the parents did not give informed consent?
- Based on learning theory, isn't there a risk that the phobia will generalize to other stimuli? Consider the short-term and long-term psychological risks associated with this possibility if the infant's phobia persists.
- If a phobia is successfully conditioned, what about the treatment to eliminate it? What steps are in place to guarantee that the infant will receive this treatment? Has the treatment been scientifically tested with humans? What is the failure rate? If there already is good evidence that the treatment is effective, then why conduct this study?

Applying today's ethical standards to this "proposed" study, we believe it clearly would be rejected. Even with informed consent and a secure system in place to guarantee that an infant would receive treatment afterward, the risks would be considered too high. At the time of the actual experiment, there would have been insufficient evidence to clearly support the effectiveness of the extinction treatment with humans. An alternative, ethical research approach would be to study whether learning-based treatments are effective with patients who already have phobias. ■

7

MEMORY

CHAPTER OUTLINE

The charm, one might say the genius of memory, is that it is choosy, chancy, and temperamental.

—Elizabeth Bowen

Some people are famous for their extraordinary remembering; others, for their extraordinary forgetting. Consider Rajan Mahadevan, who at age 5 sauntered outside one day while his parents entertained about 40 to 50 guests at a party. Rajan studied the guests' parked cars, returned to the party, and then recited all the license plate numbers from memory, matching each to the proper guest in the order they had parked. While in college, Rajan set a world record by flawlessly recalling the first 31,811 digits of π (pi). He averaged 3.5 digits per second!

Rajan left India to attend graduate school at Kansas State University, where a team of psychologists (at Rajan's request) studied his memory abilities. They describe another of his remarkable feats. Suppose you have a sheet of paper containing the first 5,000 digits of pi, arranged in 500 blocks of 10 digits. Pick any block, start reading the first few digits, and, before you can finish, Rajan will recite the remaining digits from memory (Thompson et al., 1993). How does he do it? "Rajan said . . . that being asked to describe how he learned numbers was like being asked to describe how he rode a bicycle. He knew how to do both tasks, but he found it difficult to describe either process" (p. 13).

In most other ways, however, Rajan's memory is ordinary. Indeed, he uses a grocery list to help him remember what to buy at the market, and, as he notes, "Unless I put my glasses, wallet and keys together near the door before I leave to start my day, I will surely forget them" (Harris, 2002).

■■■

You are about to meet H. M., who at age 27 had most of his hippocampus and surrounding brain tissue surgically removed to reduce his severe epileptic seizures. The operation succeeded, but it unexpectedly left H. M. with **amnesia, or memory loss**.

When you first meet H. M. he might appear normal, for he is bright and has retained good language and social skills. He can discuss his childhood, teens, and early 20s, for those memories are intact. Indeed, for the most part, H. M.'s amnesia did not rob him of his past. Rather, as of age 27, it robbed him of his future.

H. M. lost the ability to form new memories that he can consciously recall. Typically, once an experience or fact leaves his immediate train of thought, he cannot remember it. Spend the day with H. M., depart and return minutes later, and he will not recall having met you. He reads magazines over and over as if he has never seen them before. A favorite uncle has died, but H. M. cannot remember. Thus every time H. M. asks how his uncle is, he experiences shock and grief as though it were the first time he learned of his uncle's death.

H. M.'s surgery took place in 1953, and researchers have studied him for over 40 years (Xu & Corkin, 2001). No matter how many years pass, H. M.'s memory for events contains little after 1953. Even his sense of identity is frozen in time. H. M. recalls himself looking like a young man and cannot remember the aging image of himself that he sees in the mirror. H. M. describes what his existence is like: "Every day is alone in itself. . . . You see, at this moment, everything looks clear to me, but what happened just before? It's like waking from a dream. I just don't remember" (Milner, 1970, p. 37).

Memory *refers to the processes that allow us to record, store, and later retrieve experiences and information.* Memory adds richness and context to our lives, but even more fundamentally, it allows us to learn from experience and thus adapt to changing environments. From an evolutionary standpoint, without the capacity to remember we would not have survived as a species.

As the cases of Rajan and H. M. illustrate, memory is complex. How did Rajan remember over 30,000 digits of pi? Why is it, as Figure 7.1 shows, that H. M. can remember how to perform new tasks yet swear each time he encounters these tasks that he has never even seen them before? In this chapter we explore the fascinating nature of memory.

REMEMBERING: MEMORY AS INFORMATION PROCESSING

▶ 1. What is memory and how is it likened to an information-processing system?

Psychological research on memory has a rich tradition, dating back to late 19th-century Europe. By the 1960s, computer advancements and the cognitive revolution in psychology led to a new metaphor that continues to guide memory research: the mind as a processing system that encodes, stores, and retrieves information. **Encoding** *refers to getting information into the system by translating it into a neural code that your brain processes.* This is a little like what happens when you type on a computer keyboard, as your keystrokes are translated into an electrical code that the computer can understand and process. **Storage** *involves retaining information over time.* Once in the system, information must be filed away and saved, as happens when a computer stores information temporarily in RAM (remote access memory) and more permanently on a hard drive. Finally, **retrieval** *refers to processes that access stored information.* On a computer, retrieval occurs when you give a software command (e.g., "Open File") that transfers information from the hard drive back to RAM and the screen, where you can scroll through it. Keep in mind, however, that this analogy between human and computer is crude. For one thing, people routinely forget and distort information and sometimes "remember" events that never occurred (Loftus, 2003; Pickrell et al. 2003). Human memory is highly dynamic, and its complexity cannot be fully captured by any existing information-processing model.

Encoding, storage, and retrieval represent what our memory system does with information. Before exploring these processes more fully, let's examine some basic components of memory.

FIGURE 7.1

(a) On this complex task, participants trace a pattern while looking at its mirror image, which also shows their hand moving in the direction opposite to its actual movement. (b) H. M.'s performance on this task rapidly improved over time—he made fewer and fewer errors—indicating that he had retained a memory of how to perform the task*. Yet each time he performed it, he stated that he had never seen the task before and had to have the instructions explained again.* SOURCE: Adapted from Milner, 1965.

(a)

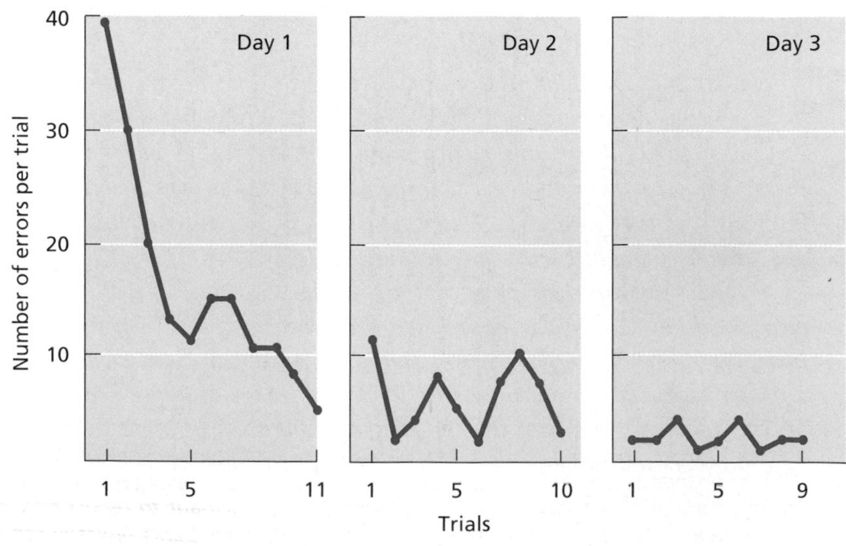

(b)

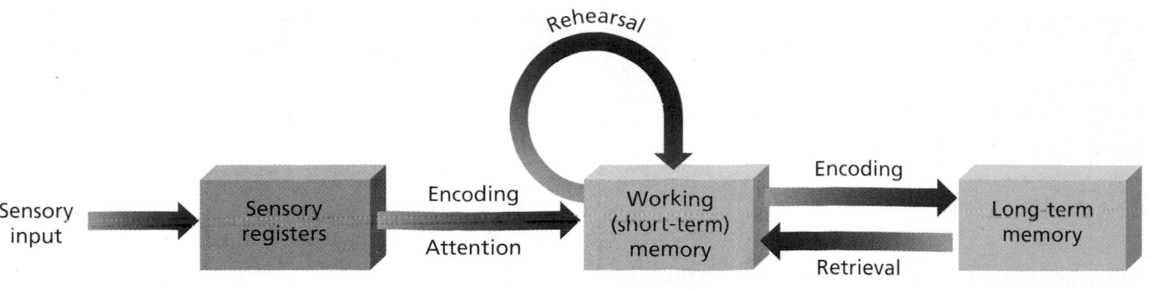

FIGURE 7.2

In this model, memory has three major components: (1) sensory registers, which detect and briefly hold incoming sensory information; (2) working (short-term) memory, which processes certain information received from the sensory registers and information retrieved from long-term memory; and (3) long-term memory, which stores information for longer periods of time. SOURCE: Adapted from Atkinson & Shiffrin, 1968.

A Three-Stage Model

The model in Figure 7.2, developed by Richard Atkinson and Richard Shiffrin (1968) and subsequently modified, depicts memory as having three major components: sensory memory, working (short-term) memory, and long-term memory. Other memory models have been proposed, but this three-stage framework has been the most influential.

Sensory Memory

Sensory memory *briefly holds incoming sensory information.* It comprises different subsystems, called *sensory registers,* which are the initial information processors. Our visual sensory register is called the *iconic store,* and in 1960 George Sperling conducted a classic experiment to assess how long it holds information. On one task, Sperling arranged 12 letters in three rows and four columns, like those in Figure 7.3. He flashed the array on a screen for 1/20 of a second, after which participants immediately recalled as many letters as they could. Typically, they were able to recall only 3 to 5 letters.

Why was recall so poor? Did participants have too little time to scan all the letters, or had they seen the whole array, only to have their iconic memory fade before they could report all the letters? To find out, Sperling conducted another experimental condition. This time, just as the letters were flashed off, participants heard either a high-, medium-, or low-pitched tone, which signaled them to report either the top, middle, or bottom row of letters.

▶ 2. Describe sensory memory. How long does information remain in iconic memory and how did Sperling determine this?

In this case, participants often could report all 4 letters in whichever row was signaled. Because they did not know which row would be signaled ahead of time, this implies that their iconic memory had stored an image of the whole array, and they now had time to "read" their iconic image of any one line before it rapidly disappeared. If this logic is correct, then participants should do poorly if the signaling tone is delayed. Indeed,

Fixation

Display (1/20 sec.) plus tone

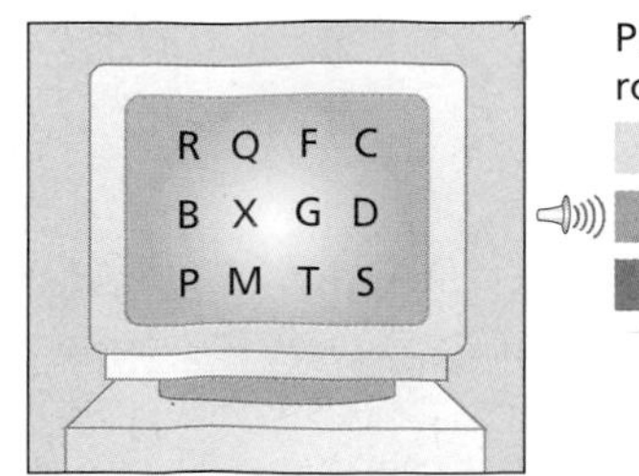

Report

FIGURE 7.3

After a participant fixates on a screen, a matrix of letters is flashed for 1/20 of a second. In one condition, participants do not hear any tone and must immediately report as many letters as they can. In another condition, a high-, medium-, or low-pitched tone signals the participant to report either the top, middle, or bottom row. If the tone occurs just as the letters are flashed off, participants typically can report three or all four letters, no matter which row is signaled.

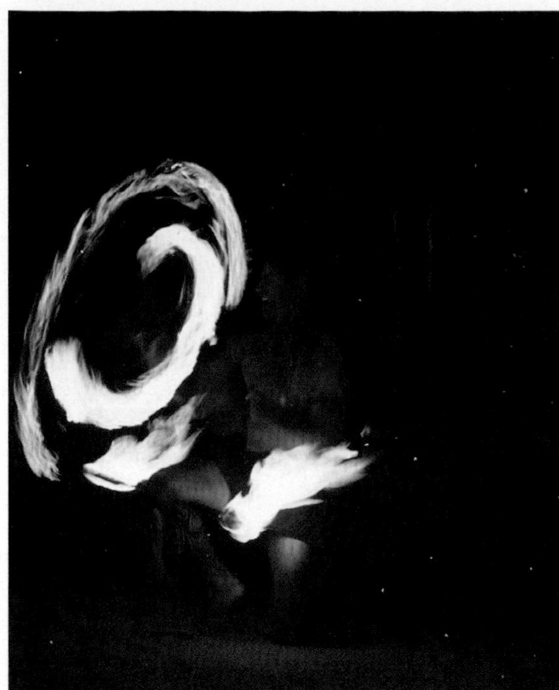

FIGURE 7.4

The arc of light that you see traced by a fiery baton, or the lingering flash that you see after observing a lightning bolt, results from the brief duration of information in iconic memory. Due to a slow camera shutter speed, this photo captures more arcs of light than you could actually see: Because your iconic memory stores complete information for only a fraction of a second, the image would quickly vanish.

with just a 1-second delay, performance was no better than without the tone. As Figure 7.4 illustrates, it is difficult, perhaps impossible, to retain complete information in purely visual form for more than a fraction of a second. In contrast, our auditory sensory register, called the *echoic store,* can hold information about the precise details of a sound for several seconds (Winkler et al., 2002).

For more on iconic memory, see Interactive Segment 7.1.

Short-Term/Working Memory

▶ 3. Discuss short-term memory and its limits. Contrast the concept of short-term memory with the working memory model.

Most information in sensory memory rapidly fades away. But, through selective attention, some information enters **short-term memory,** *a memory store that temporarily holds a limited amount of information.*

Memory Codes Once information leaves sensory memory, it must be represented by some type of code if it is to be retained in short-term memory. For example, the words that someone just spoke to you ("I like your new haircut") must somehow become represented in your mind. **Memory codes** *are mental representations of some type of information or stimulus,* and they can take various forms. We may try to form mental images (*visual codes*), code something by sound (*phonological codes*), or focus on the meaning of a stimulus (*semantic codes*). For physical actions, such as learning sports or playing musical instruments, we code patterns of movement (*motor codes*).

Realize that the form of a memory code often does not correspond to the form of the original stimulus. For example, as you read these words (visual stimuli) you are probably not storing images of the way the letters look. Rather, you are likely forming phonological codes (as you say the words silently to yourself) and semantic codes that represent their meaning (as you think about the material). Thus when people are presented with lists of words or letters and asked to recall them immediately, they often make phonetic errors. They might mistakenly recall a *V* as a *B* because of the similarity in how the letters sound (Conrad, 1964).

Capacity and Duration Short-term memory can hold only a limited amount of information at a time, as you may have observed if you've tried to memorize two or three different phone numbers at the same time. Depending on the stimulus, such as a series of unrelated numbers or letters, most people can hold no more than five to nine meaningful items in short-term memory, leading George Miller (1956) to set the capacity limit at "the magical number seven, plus or minus two." To demonstrate this, try administering the digit-span test in Table 7.1 to some people you know.

TABLE 7.1 Digit-Span Test

Directions: Starting with the top sequence, read these numbers at a steady rate of one per second. Immediately after saying the last number in each series, signal the person to recall the numbers in order. Most people can recall a maximum sequence of 5 to 9 digits.
8 3 5 2
4 3 9 3 1
7 1 4 9 3 7
5 4 6 9 2 3 6
1 5 2 4 8 5 8 4
9 3 2 6 5 8 2 1 4
6 8 1 3 1 9 4 7 3 5
4 2 4 6 9 5 2 1 7 4 3
3 7 9 8 4 6 1 7 2 4 9 5

(a)

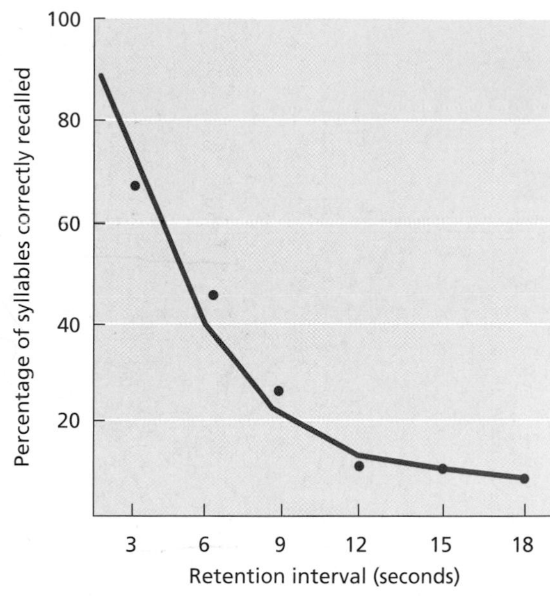

(b)

FIGURE 7.5

(a) When you meet someone in a social situation, you can help yourself remember his or her name by repeating it. (b) Participants who were prevented from rehearsing three-letter syllables in working memory showed almost no recall of the letters within 18 seconds, illustrating the rapid forgetting of information in short-term memory.
SOURCE: Based on Peterson & Peterson, 1959.

If short-term memory capacity is so limited, how can we remember and understand sentences as we read? For a partial answer to this, read the following line of letters below (about one per second); then cover it up and write down as many letters as you can remember, in the order presented.

B I R C D E R Y K A E U Q S A S A W T I

Did you have trouble? Now let's reverse the letters and repeat the task. Here are the 20 letters: "It was a squeaky red crib." No doubt, you find this task much easier. The limit on short-term storage capacity concerns the number of meaningful *units* that can be recalled, and the 20 letters have been combined into 6 meaningful units (words). *Combining individual items into larger units of meaning is called* **chunking,** and it can greatly aid recall.

Short-term memory is limited in duration as well as capacity. Have you ever been introduced to someone and then, moments later, realized that you've forgotten her or his name? Without rehearsal, information in working memory generally has a "shelf life" of up to 20 seconds (Figure 7.5; Peterson & Peterson, 1959). However, by rehearsing information—such as when you look up a telephone number and keep saying it to yourself while waiting to use a phone—we can extend its duration in short-term memory.

Putting Short-Term Memory to Work The original three-stage model viewed short-term memory primarily as a temporary holding station along the route from sensory to long-term memory. Information that remained in short-term memory long enough presumably was transferred into more permanent storage. Cognitive scientists now reject this view as too passive. Instead, they view short-term memory as **working memory**—*a limited-capacity system that temporarily stores and processes information* (Baddeley, 2002). In other words, *working memory* is a "mental workspace" that not only stores information but also actively manipulates it and supports other cognitive functions such as problem solving and planning. To illustrate, add the numbers 87 and 36 in your head. To enable you to solve this problem, your working memory must store the numbers, call up information from long-term memory on how to add, keep track of the interim steps (7 + 6 = 13, carry the 1), and coordinate all of these mental processes.

According to one influential model, working memory has several components (Baddeley & Hitch, 1974, 2000). For example, we temporarily store and process some information in an auditory component called the *phonological loop*, as occurs when you repeat to yourself the name of someone you have just met. Another component, the *visuo-spatial sketchpad*, temporarily stores and manipulates mental images and spatial information, as when forming a mental map of the route to the home of a new friend. In addition, a control process called the *central executive* directs the action. It decides how much attention to allocate to mental imagery and auditory rehearsal, calls up information from long-term memory, and integrates the

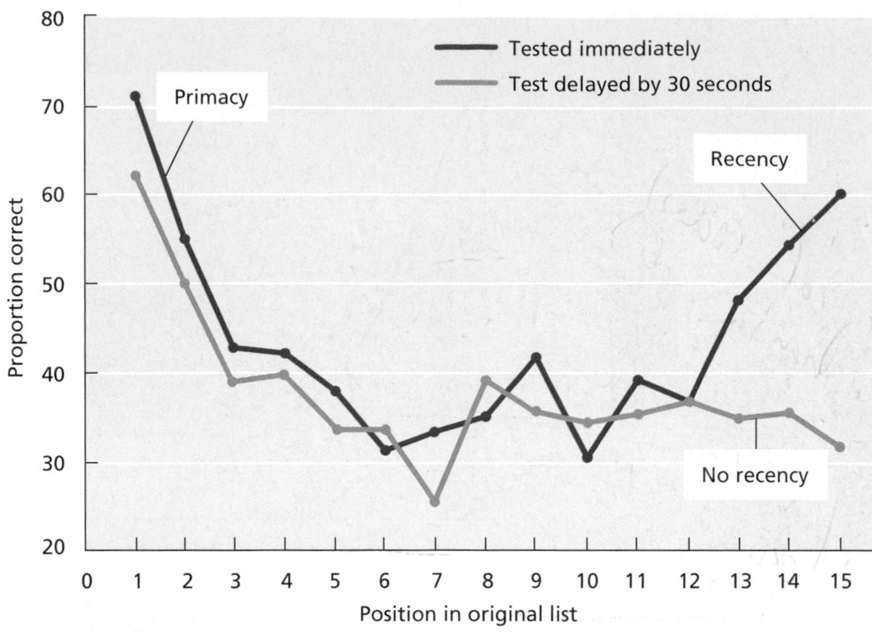

FIGURE 7.6

Immediate recall of word lists produces a serial position curve, where primacy and recency effects are both evident. However, even a delay of 15 to 30 seconds in recall (during which rehearsal is prevented) eliminates the recency effect, indicating that the later items in the word list have disappeared from short-term memory.
SOURCE: Adapted from Glanzer & Cunitz, 1966.

For more on working memory, see Interactive Segment 7.2.

input. Psychologists are also exploring other components of working memory (Baddeley, 2002).

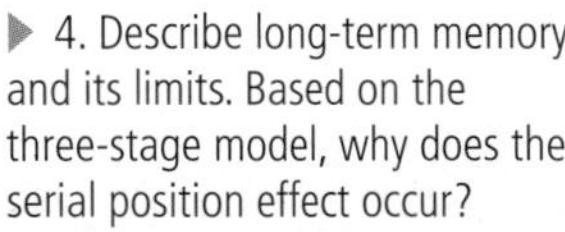

Long-Term Memory

▶ 4. Describe long-term memory and its limits. Based on the three-stage model, why does the serial position effect occur?

Long-term memory *is our vast library of more durable stored memories.* Perhaps there have been times in your life, such as periods of intensive study during final exams, when you have felt as if "the library is full," with no room for storing so much as one more new fact inside your brain. Yet as far as we know, long-term storage capacity essentially is unlimited, and once formed, a long-term memory can endure for up to a lifetime.

Are short-term and long-term memory really distinct? Case studies of amnesia victims like H. M. suggest so. If you told H. M. your name or some fact, he could remember it briefly but could not form a long-term memory of it. Experiments in which people with normal memory learn lists of words also support this distinction. Suppose that we present you with a series of 15 unrelated words, one word at a time. Immediately after seeing or hearing the last word, you are to recall as many words as you can, in any order you wish. As Figure 7.6 illustrates, most experiments find that words at the end and beginning of the list are the easiest to recall. This U-shaped pattern is called the **serial position effect,** *meaning that the ability to recall an item is influenced by the item's position in a series.* The serial position effect has two components: a *primacy effect*, reflecting the superior recall of the earliest items, and a *recency effect*, representing the superior recall of the most recent items.

What causes the primacy effect? According to the three-stage model, as the first few words enter short-term memory, we can quickly rehearse them and transfer them into longer-term memory. However, as the list gets longer, short-term memory rapidly fills up and there are too many words to keep repeating before the next word arrives. Therefore, beyond the first few words, it is harder to rehearse the items and they are less likely to get transferred into long-term memory. If this hypothesis is correct, then the primacy effect should decrease if we can prevent people from rehearsing the early words, say by presenting the list at a faster rate. Indeed, this is what happens (Glanzer, 1972).

As for the recency effect, the last few words still linger in short-term memory and have the benefit of not being bumped out by new information. Thus if we try to recall the list immediately, all we have to do is "read out" the last words from short-term memory before they decay (i.e., fade away). In sum, according to the three-stage model, the primacy effect is due to the transfer of early words into long-term memory, whereas the recency effect is due to the continued presence of information in short-term memory.

If this explanation is correct, then we should be able to wipe out the recency effect—but not the primacy effect—by eliminating the last words from short-term memory. This happens when the recall test is delayed, even for as little as 15 to 30 seconds, *and* you are prevented from rehearsing the last words. To prevent rehearsal, we might briefly ask you to count a series of numbers immediately after presenting the last word (Glanzer & Cunitz, 1966; Postman & Phillips, 1965). Now by the time you try to recall the last words, they will have faded from short-term memory or been bumped out by the arithmetic task (6 . . . 7 . . . 8 . . . 9 . . .). Figure 7.6 shows that under delayed conditions, the recency effect disappears while the primacy effect remains.

Having examined some basic components of memory, let us now explore more fully how information is encoded, stored, and retrieved.

Encoding: Entering Information

The holdings of your long-term memory, like those of a library, must be organized if they are to be available when you wish to retrieve them. The more effectively we encode material into long-term memory, the greater the likelihood of retrieving it (Figure 7.7).

Effortful and Automatic Processing

Think of the parade of information that you have to remember every day: names, meeting times, and mountains of schoolwork. Remembering it all involves *effortful processing,* encoding that is initiated intentionally and requires conscious attention (Hasher & Zacks, 1979). When you rehearse information, make lists, and take notes, you are engaging in effortful processing.

In contrast, have you ever been unable to answer an exam question and thought, "I should be able to answer this! I can even picture the diagram on the upper corner of the page!" In this case, you have apparently transferred incidental information about the diagram's location on the page (which you were not trying to learn) into your long-term memory through *automatic processing,* encoding that occurs without intention and requires minimal attention. Information about the frequency, spatial location, and sequence of events is often encoded automatically (Jimenez & Mendez, 2001).

"The matters about which I'm being questioned, Your Honor, are all things I should have included in my long-term memory but which I mistakenly inserted in my short-term memory."

FIGURE 7.7

Ineffective encoding can have practical as well as theoretical significance.

▶ 5. Contrast effortful and automatic processing and discuss the levels of processing model.

Levels of Processing: When Deeper Is Better

Imagine that you are participating in a laboratory experiment and are about to be shown a list of words, one at a time. Each word will be followed by a question, and all you have to do is answer "yes" or "no." Here are three examples:

1. POTATO "Is the word in capital letters?"
2. HORSE "Does the word rhyme with course?"
3. TABLE "Does the word fit in the sentence, 'The man peeled the ________'?"

Each question requires effort but differs from the others in an important way. Question 1 requires superficial *structural encoding,* as you only have to notice how the word looks. Question 2 requires a little more effort. You must engage in *phonological* (also called *phonemic) encoding* by sounding out the word to yourself and then judging whether it matches the sound of another word. Question 3 requires *semantic encoding* because you must pay attention to what the word means.

In this experiment, every word you will be shown will be followed by a question that requires either structural, phonological, or semantic encoding. Unexpectedly, you will then be given a memory test in which you will be shown a list of words and asked to identify which words were presented earlier. Which group of words will you recognize most easily? Those processed structurally, phonologically, or semantically?

According to the concept of **levels of processing,** *the more deeply we process information, the better we will remember it* (Craik & Lockhart, 1972). Thus you should best remember those words that you processed semantically. Semantic encoding involves the deepest processing because it requires us to focus on the meaning of information. Merely perceiving the structural properties of the words (e.g., uppercase versus lowercase) involves shallow processing, and phonemically encoding words is intermediate. Figure 7.8a shows that the semantically encoded words were best remembered (Craik & Tulving, 1975). Moreover, as Figure 7.8b shows, deeper processing of words produces greater neural activity in several areas of the cerebral cortex (Walla et al., 2001).

Exposure and Rehearsal

Years ago one of our students sought advice after failing an exam. He said that he had been to all the lectures and read each chapter three times. Yet not a word in his textbook had been underlined or highlighted. When asked whether he took notes as he read the text or paused to reflect on the information, he said no. Instead, he read and reread each chapter quickly, much like a novel, and assumed that the information would somehow sink in.

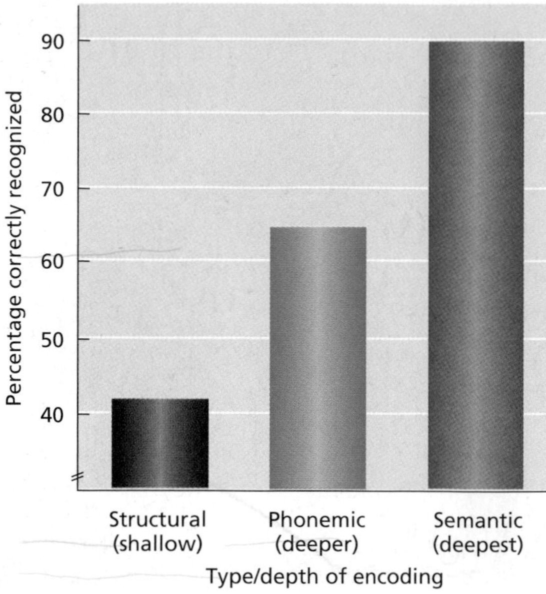

(a)

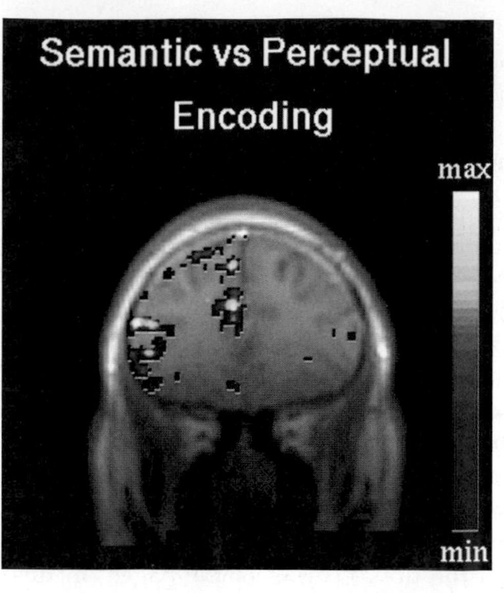

(b)

FIGURE 7.8

(a) Depth of processing facilitates memory. Participants were shown words and asked questions that required (1) superficial structural processing, (2) somewhat deeper phonemic processing, or (3) deeper semantic processing of each word. Depth of processing increased later recognition of the words in a larger list. SOURCE: Based on Craik & Tulving, 1975. *(b) Four of the participants in this experiment performed shallow perceptual (i.e., structural) encoding and deep (semantic) encoding tasks while undergoing functional magnetic resonance imaging (fMRI). Activity in a section of their prefrontal cortex was imaged every 1.5 seconds, yielding 224 images per participant. The results, shown here for one participant, revealed that semantic encoding was accompanied by greater neural activity in specific regions of the left prefrontal cortex.* Photo courtesy of John Gabrieli.

Unfortunately, mere exposure to a stimulus without focusing on it represents shallow processing. To demonstrate this for yourself, try drawing from memory a picture of the smallest-denomination coin in your country (e.g., a U.S. penny), accurately locating all the markings. Few people can do this. Even thousands of shallow exposures to a stimulus do not guarantee long-term retention.

▶ 6. Contrast maintenance and elaborative rehearsal. Describe ways to use organization and imagery to enhance encoding.

Rehearsal is a step beyond mere exposure; when we rehearse information, we are thinking about it. But not all rehearsal is created equal. Have you ever seen a play and been amazed at the way professional actors flawlessly recall volumes of material in front of live audiences? You may picture the actors reading the script and saying the words over and over, day after day, until they've memorized their lines. This approach, called **maintenance rehearsal,** *involves simple, rote repetition,* and some students rely on it to learn their course material.

Maintenance rehearsal keeps information active in short-term memory, as when someone tells you a phone number and you repeat it to yourself as you place the call. It can also help transfer information into long-term memory (Wixted, 1991). However, rote memorization usually is not an optimal method for bringing about long-term transfer.

What, then, is the best way to bring material—such as an actor's script or information in a textbook—into long-term memory? It may surprise you to know that professional actors begin not by memorizing but by studying the script in great depth, trying to get into the mindset of their characters (Figure 7.9). Based on detailed research, psychologists Tony and Helga Noice (2002a) note that actors, "before they gave any thought to memorization, stressed the notion of understanding the ideas behind the utterances, and the reasons the characters used those words to express those ideas." The techniques actors use are examples of **elaborative rehearsal,** *which involves focusing on the meaning of information or expanding (i.e., elaborating) on it in some way.*

If your study habits include (1) organizing and trying to understand the material rather than just memorizing it, (2) thinking about how it applies to your own life, and (3) relating it to concepts or examples you already know, then you are using elaboration. According to Craik and

Lockhart (1972), elaborative rehearsal involves deeper processing than maintenance rehearsal, and experiments show that it is more effective in transferring information into long-term memory (Benjamin & Bjork, 2000).

Organization and Imagery

J. C. is an awe-inspiring restaurant waiter. Perhaps you would like a filet mignon, medium-rare, a baked potato, and Thousand Island dressing on your salad? Whatever you order, it represents only one of over 500 options (7 entrees × 5 serving temperatures × 3 side dishes × 5 salad dressings) available at the restaurant where J. C. works. Yet you and 20 or so of your best friends can place your selections with J. C., and he will remember them perfectly without writing them down.

Psychologists K. Anders Ericsson and Peter Polson (1988), who studied J. C., found that he invented an organizational scheme to aid his memory. He divided customers' orders into four categories (entree, temperature, side dish, dressing) and then used a different system to encode the orders in each category. For example, he encoded dressings by their initial letter, so orders of Thousand Island, oil and vinegar, blue cheese, and oil and vinegar would become *TOBO*. Organizational schemes are an excellent way to enhance memory. They can enhance the meaningfulness of information and also serve as cues that help trigger our memory, just as the word *TOBO* jogs J. C.'s memory of the four orders of salad.

Hierarchies and Chunking Organizing material in a *hierarchy* takes advantage of the principle that memory is enhanced by associations between concepts (Bower et al., 1969). A logical hierarchy enhances our *understanding* of how individual items are related; as we proceed from top to bottom, each category serves as a cue that triggers our memory for the items below it. Because hierarchies have a visual organization, imagery can be used as a supplemental memory code. The hierarchy in Figure 7.10, for example, may help you remember some concepts about encoding.

As we discussed earlier, chunking refers to combining individual items into a larger unit of meaning. To refresh your memory, read the line of letters below to yourself (about one per second) and try to recall as many as you can, in the same sequence.

I R S Y M C A I B M K G B F B I

If you recalled 5 to 9 letters in order, you did well. Now let's reorganize these 16 letters into

FIGURE 7.9

Professional stage actors use elaborative rehearsal extensively to learn their roles and numerous lines. They employ many of the memory techniques discussed in the Applying Psychological Science *feature on page 276.*

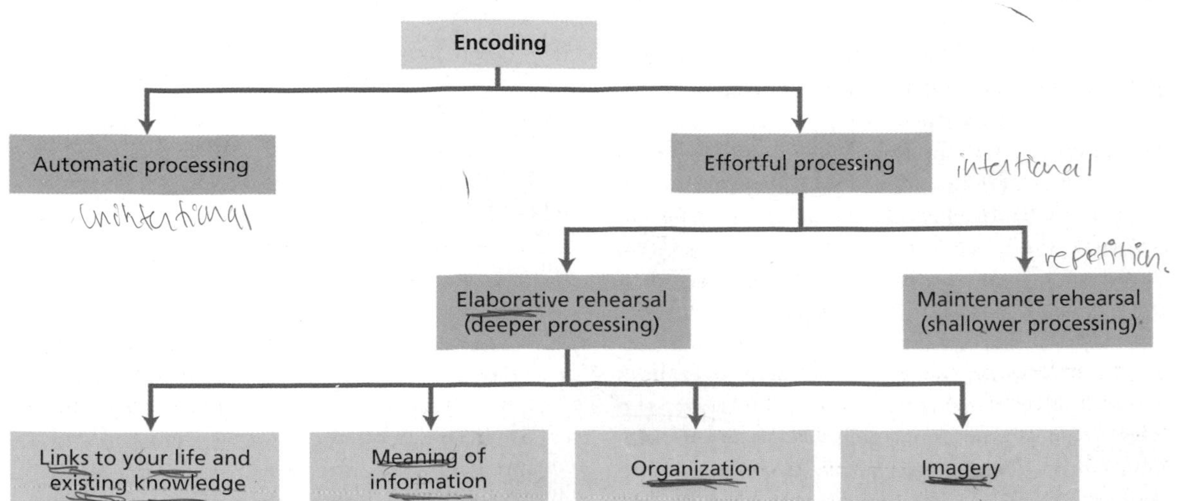

FIGURE 7.10

Placing information into a meaningful hierarchy enhances encoding and memory. This hierarchy could be developed further by adding a fifth level of boxes under "Organization" labeled Hierarchies, Chunking, Acronyms, *and* Rhymes. *A box labeled* Method of Loci *could be added under "Imagery," although it also organizes information.*

For more on chunking in memory, see Interactive Segment 7.3.

5 larger, more meaningful chunks: IRS, YMCA, IBM, KGB, and FBI. These chunks are easier to rehearse, keep active in working memory, and transfer into long-term memory. When learning a new telephone number (e.g., 123-456-7890), you probably encode it in chunks.

Visual Imagery How many windows are there in your home? What did your bedroom look like during your high school years? To answer these questions, you might try to construct a series of mental images in your working memory, based on information that you draw out of long-term memory.

Allan Paivio (1969) proposes that information is stored in long-term memory in two forms: verbal codes and visual codes. According to his **dual coding theory,** *encoding information using both verbal and visual codes enhances memory*, because the odds improve that at least one of the codes will be available later to support recall. Dual coding, however, is harder to use with some types of stimuli than others. Try to construct a mental image of (1) a fire truck and (2) a lightbulb. Now construct an image of (1) jealousy and (2) knowledge. You probably found the second task more difficult, because those words represent abstract concepts rather than concrete objects (Paivio et al., 2000).

Memory improvement books often recommend using imagery to dual-code information, and research supports this approach. The ancient Greeks developed the **method of loci** (*loci* is Latin for "places"), *a memory aid that associates information with mental images of physical locations.* To use this well-known technique, imagine a physical environment with a sequence of distinct landmarks, such as the rooms in a house or places on your campus. Next, to remember a list of items, take an imaginary stroll through this environment and form an image linking each place with an item. It may be challenging to use this imagery technique to learn abstract concepts, but here's one example: To remember the three major components of working memory, you might imagine walking into the president's office at your college (*central executive*), then watching a band rehearsal in your gym (*phonological loop*), and visiting an art class (*visuospatial sketchpad*). Many studies support the method of loci's effectiveness (Wang & Thomas, 2000).

▶ 7. How do schemas affect encoding? What role do schemas and mnemonic devices play in expertise and exceptional memory?

Other Mnemonic Devices The term *mnemonics* (nee-MON-iks) refers to the art of improving memory, and a **mnemonic device** *is a memory aid.* Mnemonic devices reorganize information into more meaningful units and provide extra cues to help retrieve information from long-term memory. Hierarchies, chunking, visual imagery, and the method of loci are mnemonic devices. So are *acronyms*, which combine one or more letters (usually the first letter) from each piece of information you wish to remember. For example, many students learn the acronyms HOMES and ROY G. BIV to help remember the names of the five Great Lakes of North America (Huron, Ontario, Michigan, Erie, Superior) and the hues in the visible spectrum (the colors of the rainbow: red, orange, yellow, green, blue, indigo, violet).

Even putting information in a rhyme may help you remember it. Some of our own students use this technique. Advertisers also employ this principle when they include rhyming phrases or jingles in their messages. In one experiment, college students and other adults listened to a 10-minute radio program into which researchers had inserted an advertisement for a fictitious mouth rinse (Cavoloss). The advertisement either contained a rhyme ("Toss the floss, use Cavoloss") or presented the same information without a rhyme. Tested 1 week later, participants exposed to the rhyme remembered more product information and showed better brand name recall (Smith & Phillips, 2001).

How Prior Knowledge Shapes Encoding

Can you recall the paragraph you just read word for word? Typically, when we read, listen to someone speak, or experience some event, we do not precisely encode every word, sentence, or moment. Rather, we usually encode the gist—the general theme (e.g., "rhymes can enhance memory")—of that information or event.

Schemas: Our Mental Organizers The themes that we extract from events and encode into memory are often organized around schemas. A **schema** (plural: *schemas,* or *schemata*) *is a "mental framework"—an organized pattern of thought—about some aspect of the world* (Bartlett, 1932; Koriat et al., 2000). For example, the concepts "dog," "shopping," and "love" serve as schemas that help you organize your world. To see more clearly what a schema is and how it can influence the way we encode material in memory, read the following paragraph.

> The procedure is actually quite simple. First you arrange things into different groups. Of course, one pile may be sufficient depending on how much there is to do. If you have to go somewhere else due to lack of facilities, that is the next step; otherwise you are pretty

> well set. It is important not to overdo things. That is, it is better to do too few things at once than too many. In the short run this might not seem important, but complications can easily arise. A mistake can be expensive as well. . . . After the procedure is completed, one arranges the materials into different groups again. Then they can be put into their appropriate places. Eventually they will be used once more, and the whole cycle will have to be repeated. However, that is part of life. (Bransford & Johnson, 1972, p. 722)

Asked to recall the details of the preceding paragraph, you would probably have trouble. However, suppose we tell you that the paragraph is about a common activity: washing clothes. Now if you read the paragraph again, you will find that the abstract and seemingly unrelated details suddenly make sense. Your schema—your mental framework for "washing clothes"—helps you organize and interpret these details and thus remember more of them.

Schemas and Expert Knowledge When people who have never learned to read music look at a musical score, they see an uninterpretable mass of information. In contrast, musicians see organized patterns that they can easily encode. In music as in other fields, from computer programming to rock climbing, acquiring *expert knowledge* can be viewed as a process of developing schemas—mental frameworks—that help encode information into meaningful patterns (Boschker et al., 2002).

William Chase and Herbert Simon (1973) demonstrated the relation between expertise, schemas, and encoding in an intriguing study. Three chess players—an expert ("master"), an intermediate player, and a beginner—were allowed 5 seconds to look at a chessboard containing about 25 pieces. Then they looked away and, on an empty board, attempted to reconstruct the placement of the pieces from memory. This was repeated over several trials, each with a different arrangement of pieces. On some trials, the chess pieces were arranged in *meaningful positions* that actually might occur in game situations. With only a 5-second glance, the expert typically recalled 16 pieces, the intermediate player 8, and the novice only 4. What may surprise you is that when the pieces were in *random positions*, there was no difference in recall between the three players. They each did poorly, accurately recalling only 2 or 3 pieces.

How would you explain these results? We have to reject the conclusion that the expert had better overall memory than the other players, because he performed no better than they did with the random arrangements. But the concepts of schemas and chunking do explain the findings (Gobet & Simon, 2000). When the chess pieces were arranged in meaningful positions, the expert could apply well-developed schemas to recognize patterns and group pieces together. For example, he would treat as a unit all pieces that were positioned to attack the king. The intermediate player and especially the novice, who did not have well-developed chess schemas, could not construct the chunks and had to try to memorize the position of each piece. However, when the pieces were not in positions that would occur in a real game, they were no more meaningful to the expert than to the other players. When that happened, the expert lost the advantage of schemas and had to approach the task on a piece-by-piece basis just as the other players did. Similarly, football coaches show much better recall than novices do after looking at diagrams of football plays (patterns of X's and O's), but only when the plays are logical (Figure 7.11).

You may not be an advanced chess player or coach, but you have years of experience about how various aspects of the world work. As the clothes-washing example illustrates, your own "expert schemas" influence what you encode and remember.

Encoding and Exceptional Memory

After witnessing an impressive memory feat—a waiter's remembering 20 dinner orders without writing them down or Rajan Mahadevan's recalling 31,811 digits of pi—it's tempting to assume that the person has an innate, so-called photographic memory. But K. Anders Ericsson and William Chase (1982) argue that such exceptional memory is a highly learned skill that can be explained by three basic principles: (1) prior knowledge and extensive practice, (2) meaningful associations, and (3) efficient storage and retrieval structures.

They tested their hypothesis by examining whether S. F., a college student with average memory skills, could develop exceptional memory (Ericsson et al., 1980). S. F. practiced digit-span tasks for 1 hour a day, 3 to 5 days a week, for 20 months. If he correctly recalled a string of digits (one digit was presented per second), the next string was increased by a digit. After an error, the next sequence was decreased by a digit. S. F.'s digit-span performance improved steadily, and after 190 hours of practice, he could listen to a string of 80 digits and recall them perfectly.

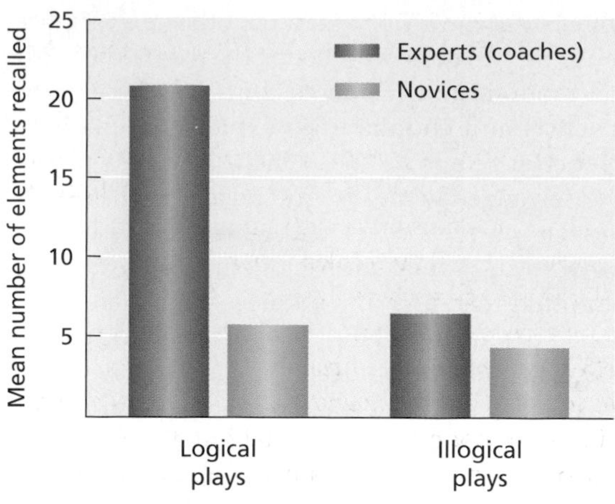

FIGURE 7.11

Diagrams of football plays were shown to football coaches (experts) and to people who had played football but were not coaches (novices). Given 5 seconds to see each play, coaches displayed excellent memory—but only when the plays were logical. Their well-developed football schemas were of little use when the patterns of Xs and Os were illogical. These findings are similar to those obtained when expert and novice chess players tried to reproduce meaningful and random arrangements of chess pieces. SOURCE: Based on Garland & Barry, 1991.

How did S. F. do it? On his own, he learned to use chunking, associations, and hierarchical organization to rapidly transfer digits into long-term memory. S. F. was an experienced runner, and he grouped digits into chunks that he associated with running times, ages, or dates. Thus 3492 became become "3 minutes and 49.2 seconds, near world-record time for running a mile"; 893 became "89.3 years old, a very old person"; and 1944 became "near the end of World War II." As digit strings became longer, S. F. used hierarchical organization to arrange individual chunks into larger groups.

A **mnemonist (**or **memorist)** *is a person who displays extraordinary memory skills.* Studies reveal that like S. F., mnemonists take advantage of basic memory principles. They often chunk information into larger units and combine smaller chunks into larger ones. Many elaborate on the material by associating chunks with other information, as S. F. did when he linked chunks to running times, ages, and dates. Many mnemonists create visual images or stories to help them encode information; they may also combine several techniques.

How, then, did Rajan learn 31,811 digits of pi? Rajan said that he did not have a photographic memory, and Richard Thompson and coworkers (1993), who studied Rajan intensively, agreed. Instead, they found that Rajan used chunking; the mathematical tables of pi that he studied grouped digits in chunks of 10, so Rajan did the same. But, surprisingly, Rajan did not associate the chunks with meaningful material. Rather, beyond basic chunking, Rajan relied primarily on the brute force of rote memorization and extensive practice. How much practice? Thompson and coworkers estimated that it took Rajan over a year to learn the digits of pi.

Realize that just because rote memorization can transfer information into long-term memory doesn't mean that it's the best way. Mnemonists (including the person who broke Rajan's record by recalling 40,000 digits of pi) often use elaborative rehearsal to achieve their amazing feats. More important, rote memorization is better suited to learning a string of numbers than to learning material that has meaning. When Rajan applied his rote strategy to memory tasks that involved meaningful stimuli (e.g., written stories, complex visual figures), he performed more poorly or no better than college students in a control group.

Should we accept the conclusion that exceptional memory is a learned skill? After thousands of hours of practice using effective encoding techniques, could the average person really remember 30,000 to 40,000 digits of pi? Thompson and coworkers (1993) believe that in memory, as in sports and music, endless skilled practice will not enable most people to rise to the top unless they also have the requisite ability. Yet Ericsson and coworkers (1993) disagree, arguing that "many characteristics once believed to reflect innate talent are actually the result of intense practice" (p. 363). This debate extends to cases of *savants*, people with mental disabilities who display exceptional memory for particular tasks. Some savants can reproduce complex musical pieces or highly detailed drawings after hearing or seeing them only once, but researchers disagree as to whether this reflects natural ability or a highly practiced skill (Winner, 2000).

For more on mnemonic strategies in memory, see Video Segment 7.1.

What Do You Think?

WOULD PERFECT MEMORY BE A GIFT OR A CURSE?

If you could have a perfect memory, would you want it? What might be the drawbacks? Think about it, then see page 278.

Storage: Retaining Information

Think for a moment about the incredible wealth of information that you can recall at a moment's notice. With little effort, you can probably remember the name of the capital of Russia, how to multiply 10 times 25, the flavor of your favorite ice cream, and how you spent your most recent vacation. This ability to rapidly access diverse facts, concepts, and experiences has influenced many cognitive models of how information is stored and organized in memory.

Memory as a Network

We noted that memory is enhanced by elaborative rehearsal, which involves forming associations between new information and other items already in memory. The general principle that memory involves associations goes to the heart of the *network* approach.

Associative Networks One group of theories proposes that memory can be represented as an **associative network,** *a massive network of associated ideas and concepts* (Collins & Loftus, 1975). Figure 7.12 shows what a tiny portion of such a network might be like. In this network, each concept or unit of information—"fire engine," "red," and so on—is represented by a *node* somewhat akin to each knot in a huge fishing net. The lines in this network represent associations between concepts, with shorter lines indicating stronger associations. For simplicity, Figure 7.12 shows only a few connections extending from each node, but there could be hundreds or more. Notice that items within the same category—types of flowers, types of fruits, colors, and so on—generally have the strongest associations and therefore tend to be clustered closer together. In essence, an associative network is a type of schema; it is a mental framework that represents how we have organized information and how we understand the world (Roediger & McDermott, 2000).

Alan Collins and Elizabeth Loftus (1975) theorize that when people think about a concept, such as "fire engine," there is a *spreading activation* of related concepts throughout the network. For example, when you think about a "fire engine" related concepts such as "truck," "fire," and "red" should be partially activated as well. The term **priming** *refers to the activation of one concept (or one unit of information) by another*. Thus "fire engine" primes the node for "red," making it more likely that our memory for this color will be accessed (Chwilla & Kolk, 2002).

The notion that memory stores information in an associative network also provides one possible explanation for why hints and mnemonic devices help stimulate our recall (Reisberg, 1997). For example, when you hear "Name the colors of the rainbow," the nodes for "color" and "rainbow" jointly activate the node for "ROY G. BIV," which in turn primes your recall for "red," "orange," and so forth.

▶ 8. Contrast associative network and neural network models of memory, and explain priming.

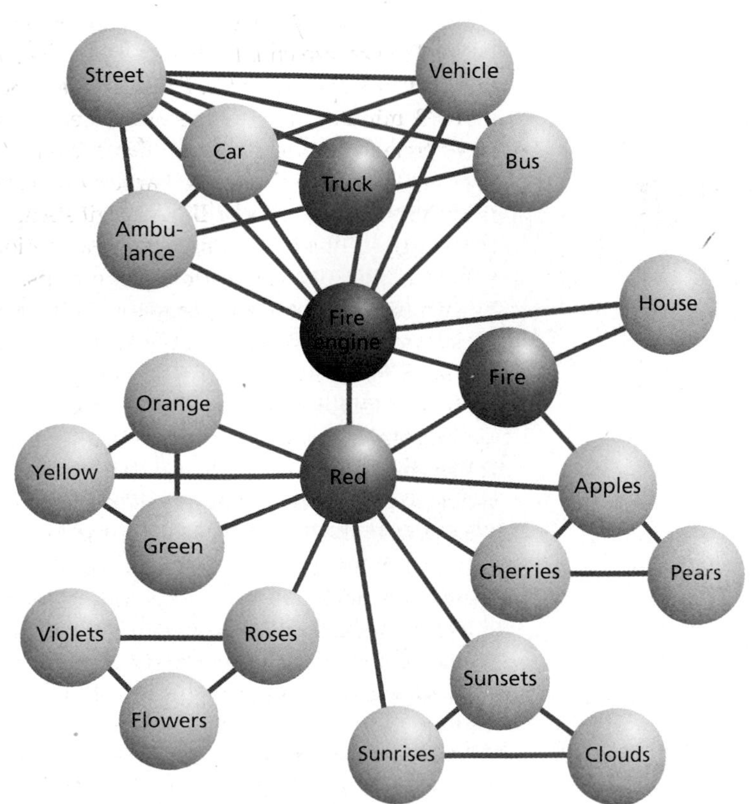

FIGURE 7.12

A network of concepts in semantic memory. The lines in the semantic network represent associations between concepts, with shorter lines indicating stronger associations. SOURCE: Adapted from Collins & Loftus, 1975.

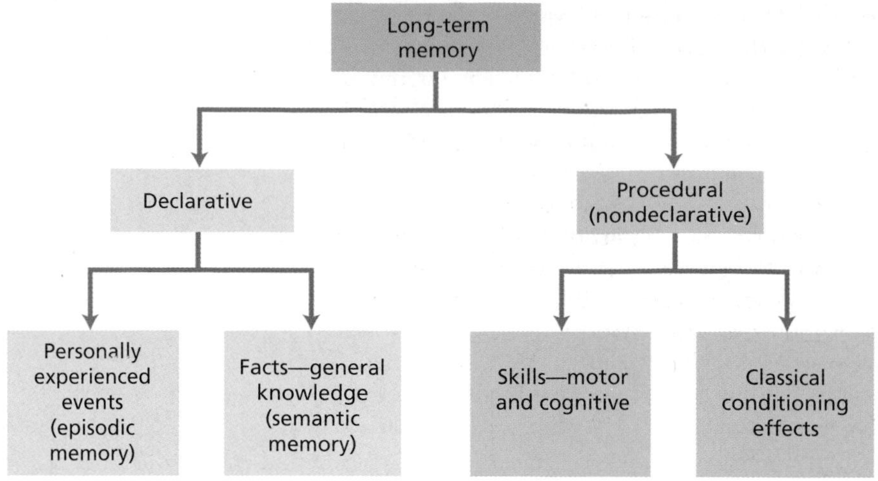

FIGURE 7.13

Some theorists propose that we have separate but interacting declarative and procedural memory systems. Episodic and semantic memories are declarative; their contents can be verbalized. Procedural memory is nondeclarative; its contents cannot readily be verbalized.

▶ 9. Contrast and illustrate declarative versus procedural memory and explicit versus implicit memory.

Neural Networks The neural network approach also can explain why spreading activation and priming occur, but it does so using a different model of memory (Chappell & Humphreys, 1994). A neural network has nodes that are linked to each other, but these nodes are physical in nature and do not contain individual units of information. There is no single node for "red," no single node for "fire engine," and so on. Instead, each node is more like a small information-processing unit. As an analogy, some proponents would say, think of each neuron in your brain as a node. A neuron processes inputs and sends outputs to other neurons, but as far as we know, the concepts of "red" and "fire engine," or your mental image of an elephant, are not stored within any single neuron.

Where, then, is a concept such as "red" stored? In **neural network models,** *each item in memory is represented by a particular pattern or set of nodes that becomes activated simultaneously.* When node 4 is activated simultaneously (i.e., in parallel) with nodes 9 and 42, the concept "red" comes to mind. But when node 4 is simultaneously activated with nodes 75 and 901, another concept enters our thoughts. As we look across the entire neural network, various nodes distributed throughout the brain fire in parallel at each instant and spread their activation to other nodes. In this manner, certain nodes prime other nodes, concepts and information are retrieved from memory, and thoughts arise. For this reason, neural network models are often called *parallel distributed processing models,* and scientists in many fields have become increasingly interested in them in recent years (Tryon, 2002).

Types of Long-Term Memory

Think back for a moment to the nature of H. M.'s amnesia. Since his brain operation, H. M. has been unable to consciously recall new facts or personal experiences once they leave his short-term memory. Each time he meets you he will believe it is the first time. Yet with practice, H. M. has learned new tasks even though he will never remember having seen them before (Milner, 1965).

Based on research with amnesia patients, brain-imaging studies, and animal experiments, many scientists believe that we possess several long-term memory systems that interact with one another (Nyberg et al., 2002; Tulving, 2002). This view is consistent with the concept, described in Chapter 5, that the mind involves distinct yet interrelated modules.

Declarative and Procedural Memory **Declarative memory** *involves factual knowledge,* and includes two subcategories (Figure 7.13). **Episodic memory** *is our store of knowledge concerning personal experiences:* when, where, and what happened in the *episodes* of our lives. Your recollections of childhood friends, how you spent last summer, and what you ate this morning represent episodic memories. **Semantic memory** *represents general factual knowledge about the world and language,* including memory for words and concepts. You know that Mount Everest is the world's tallest peak and that $e = mc^2$. Episodic and semantic memories are called *declarative* because to demonstrate our knowledge, we typically have to "declare it": We tell other people what we know.

H. M.'s brain damage severely impaired both components of his declarative memory. Not only was he unable to remember new personal experiences, he also could not remember new general facts. For example, H. M. retained good memory for words that he had learned growing up (Kensinger et al., 2001). Yet no matter how many times he was told their definition, he could not remember the meaning of new words (e.g., *xerox, biodegradable*) that entered the English language in the years after his operation. In contrast, some brain-injured children with amnesia cannot remember their daily personal experiences but can indeed form memories for general factual knowledge, enabling them to learn language and attend mainstream schools (Vargha-Khadem et al., 1997).

Procedural (nondeclarative) memory *is reflected in skills and actions* (Gupta & Cohen, 2002). One component of procedural memory consists of skills that are expressed by doing things in particular situations, such as typing, riding a bicycle, or playing a musical instrument. Classically conditioned responses also reflect procedural memory. After a tone was repeatedly paired with a puff of air blown toward H. M.'s eye, he began to blink involuntarily to the tone alone (Woodruff-Pak, 1993). Although H. M. could not consciously remember undergoing this procedure (i.e., he did not form a declarative memory), his brain stored a memory for the tone–air puff association, and thus he blinked when subsequently exposed to the tone alone (i.e., he formed a procedural memory).

Explicit and Implicit Memory Many researchers distinguish between explicit and implicit memory (Schacter & Badgaiyan, 2001). **Explicit memory** *involves conscious or intentional memory retrieval, as when you consciously recognize or recall something. Recognition* requires us to decide whether a stimulus is familiar, as when an eyewitness is asked to pick out a suspect from a police lineup or when students take multiple-choice tests. In recognition tasks, the "target stimuli" (possible suspects or answers) are provided to you. *Recall* involves spontaneous memory retrieval, in the sense that you must retrieve the target stimuli or information on your own. This occurs when you are briefly shown a list of words and then asked to recall them. With *cued recall,* hints are given to stimulate memory. If you cannot recall the word *hat* from the list, we might say, "It rhymes with 'bat.'" As a student, you are no doubt familiar with test items that involve recall or cued recall, such as essay, short-answer, and fill-in-the-blank questions.

Implicit memory *occurs when memory influences our behavior without conscious awareness.* H. M. was able to remember how to perform the mirror-tracing task, although he had no conscious awareness of having learned it. His memory for the task (in this case, procedural memory) was implicit. In Chapter 5 we encountered another amnesia patient, whose hand Edouard Claparède (1911) intentionally pricked with a pin during a handshake. Shortly thereafter she could not consciously recall this incident, but despite her amnesia, she showed implicit memory of their encounter by withdrawing her hand when Claparède offered to shake it again.

In less dramatic ways, each of us demonstrates memory without conscious awareness. Riding a bicycle, driving, or performing any well-learned skill provides a common example. Bicycling to class, you may be consciously thinking about an upcoming exam while your implicit, procedural memory enables you to keep pedaling and maintain your balance.

Consider another example of implicit memory. Suppose that as part of an experiment you read a list of words (one word per second) that includes *kitchen, moon,* and *defend.* Days, weeks, or even a year later, you participate in another, seemingly unrelated, study. The experimenter rapidly shows you many word stems, some of which might be *KIT—, MO—,* and *DE—,* and asks you to complete each stem to form a word. You are not aware that this is a memory test, but compared with people not given the original list of words, you will be more likely to complete the stems with words on the original list (e.g., *MOon,* rather than *MOther* or *MOney*). This represents one of many types of *priming tasks:* The word stems (*KIT, MO, DE*) have activated, or "primed," your stored mental representations of the original complete words. This suggests that information from the original list is still in your memory and is implicitly influencing your behavior even though you may have no explicit, conscious recall of the original words (Schacter, 1992).

Retrieval: Accessing Information

▶ 10. How do retrieval cues assist memory? What is the benefit of having multiple, self-generated, and distinctive cues?

Storing information is useless without the ability to retrieve it. Imagine having to search for a specific title in a library where the books have been shelved without catalog (i.e., call) numbers. In contrast, if we have a catalog number and the book is shelved correctly, we can easily find it.

A retrieval cue—like a library catalog number—*is any stimulus, whether internal or external, that stimulates the activation of information stored in long-term memory.* If I ask you, "Have you seen Sonia today?" the word Sonia is intended to serve as a retrieval cue. Likewise, seeing a yearbook picture of a high school classmate can act as a retrieval cue that triggers memories of that person. Priming is another example of how a retrieval cue ("fire engine," "MO—") can trigger associated elements ("red," "MOon") in memory, presumably via a process of spreading activation (Chwilla & Kolk, 2002).

The Value of Multiple Cues

Experiments by Timo Mäntylä (1986) vividly show the value of having multiple retrieval cues. In one,

Swedish college students were presented with a list of 504 words. Some students were asked to think of and write down one association for each word, while others produced three associations per word. To illustrate, what three words come to your mind when I say "banana"? Perhaps you might think of "peel," "fruit," and "ice cream."

The students had no idea that their memory would be tested, and after finishing the association task they were given an unexpected recall test for 252 of the original words. For some words, students were first shown the one or three associations they had just generated. As a control, for other words they were first shown one or three associations another participant had generated. Then they tried to recall the original word.

The results were remarkable. When the associations (i.e., retrieval cues) were self-generated, students shown one cue recalled 61 percent of the words and those shown three cues recalled 91 percent. In contrast, when students were shown cues that someone else had generated, recall with one cue dropped to 11 percent and with three cues to 55 percent. Further, when given another surprise recall test 1 week later on the remaining 252 words, students still remembered 65 percent of the words when they were first provided with three self-generated retrieval cues—far better than any other condition.

Across many experiments, Mäntylä consistently found that having multiple, self-generated retrieval cues maximized recall. Why might this be? On the encoding side, generating our own associations involves deeper, more elaborative processing than does being presented with associations generated by someone else. Similarly, generating three associations involves deeper processing than thinking of only one. On the retrieval side, these self-generated associations become cues that have personal meaning. And with multiple cues, if one fails, another may activate the memory. The implication for studying academic material is clear. Think about the material you are studying, and draw one or (preferably) more links to ideas, knowledge, or experiences that have meaning for you.

The Value of Distinctiveness

To demonstrate a simple point, here is a brief self-test. A list of words appears below. Say each word to yourself (one per second); then when you see the word *WRITE*, look away and write down as many words as you can recall, in any order. Here's the list:

> *sparrow, eagle, nest, owl, feather, goose, crow, tomato, rooster, fly, robin, parrot, chirp, hawk, pigeon, WRITE.*

If you are like most of our own students, you probably recalled *tomato* even though it appeared in the middle of the list. In this list, *tomato* is distinctive. It's a food, and thus it stands out from the crowd (or at least, from the flock). It catches our attention. In general, distinctive stimuli are better remembered than nondistinctive ones (Ghetti et al., 2002).

In school, when all the material "starts looking alike," you can make it more distinctive by associating it with other information that is personally meaningful to you. According to Mäntylä (1986), this is one reason why students who generated their own three-word associations remembered almost all of the original 504 words. The associations formed a distinctive set of cues.

Distinctive events stand a greater chance of etching long-term memories that seem vivid and clear. In one study, college students listed their three clearest memories (Rubin & Kozin, 1984). Distinctive events such as weddings, romantic encounters, births and deaths, vacations, and accidents were among the most frequently recalled. In another study, college students watched a videotape of a guest lecturer who engaged in some distinctive, atypical behaviors (e.g., ate potato chips, burped) and some typical ones (e.g., sat down, took off jacket). A week later, students were given a list of behaviors and asked to identify which ones had taken place during that lecture. Half of the listed items actually appeared in the videotape, and half did not (e.g., zipped up pants, erased board). Students correctly identified about 80 percent of the behaviors that had occurred, but they were more likely to report being able to "mentally relive"—to have a clear image of—the distinctive events (Neuschatz et al., 2002).

Of course, just because a memory seems vivid or we are confident of it doesn't guarantee its accuracy. Students falsely "recognized" 45 percent of the typical behaviors and 25 percent of the distinctive behaviors that actually had never occurred. In most cases, they felt sure that the behavior had taken place, although they said they couldn't consciously remember it. But, for a third of these false recognitions, students said they had a clear memory of a nonexistent event.

Do similar errors occur when we retrieve memories of even more distinctive, dramatic real-world events—events that we can "remember like it was yesterday"? Let's take a look *Beneath the Surface*.

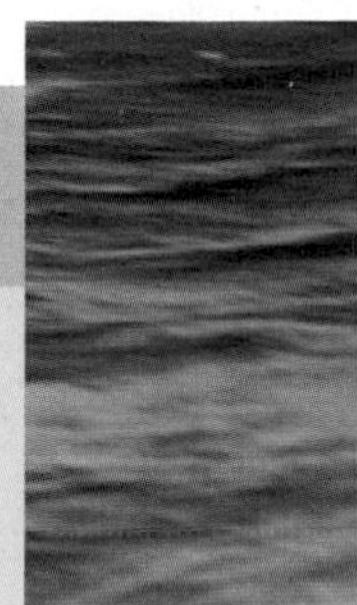

Beneath the Surface

DO WE REALLY "REMEMBER IT LIKE IT WAS YESTERDAY"?

Can you picture the tragic moment on September 11, 2001, when you first heard or saw that jetliners had crashed into the World Trade Center and the Pentagon (Figure 7.14)? Do you recall what you were doing when you learned that Princess Diana had been killed in a car crash? Your authors, like others of our generation, can vividly recall the moment over 40 years ago when we heard that President John F. Kennedy had been assassinated.

Flashbulb memories *are recollections that seem so vivid, so clear, that we can picture them as if they were a snapshot of a moment in time.* They are most likely to occur for distinctive, positive or negative, events that evoke strong emotional reactions and that are repeatedly recalled in conversations with other people (Brown & Kulik, 1977).

Flashbulb Memories: Fogging Up the Picture?

Because flashbulb memories seem vivid and are easily recalled, we often feel confident of their accuracy. But are they accurate? In 1986, the space shuttle Challenger exploded shortly after takeoff, killing all on board. It was a horrific event, replayed on TV worldwide, and the American public was shocked. The next day, Ulric Neisser and Nicole Harsch (1993) asked college students to describe how they learned of the disaster, where they were, who they were with, and so on. Reinterviewed 3 years later, about half of the students remembered some details correctly but recalled other details inaccurately. One fourth of the students completely misremembered all the major details and were astonished at how inaccurate their memories were after reading their original descriptions.

For a captivated public that followed the 1995 O. J. Simpson murder trial, the jury's verdict of "not guilty" seemed to be an unforgettable moment. Was it? Three days later researchers asked college undergraduates how, when, with whom, and where they had learned of the verdict (Schmolck et al., 2000). Students reported whether they agreed with the verdict and how emotional they felt about it. When some students' memory was retested 15 months later, only 10 percent made major mistakes in recalling the event. Over time, however, the flashbulb seemed to fade. Among other students retested 32 months after

FIGURE 7.14

A flashbulb memory is a recollection that seems so vivid and clear that we can picture it as if it were a snapshot of a moment in time.

Continued

the verdict, 43 percent misremembered major details. Here's how one student's memory changed:

> [3 days after the verdict] I was in the Commuter Lounge at Revelle [College] and saw it on TV . . . more and more people came into the room. We kept having to turn up the volume, but it was kind of cool.
>
> [32 months after the verdict] I first heard it while I was watching TV. At home in my living room. My sister and father were with me . . . eating and watching. (p. 41)

Memory accuracy was not related to whether students had originally agreed or disagreed with the verdict; instead, those who reported a stronger emotional reaction in 1995 displayed better memory 32 months later.

Confidence and Memory Accuracy

If people are highly confident in their memory, is it likely to be accurate? Three years after the O. J. Simpson verdict, almost all the students who had accurate memories displayed high confidence. But one of the most striking findings was that among students with grossly inaccurate recall, 61 percent also were highly confident of their memories.

In the 7th week after the 9/11 terrorist attacks, psychologist Kathy Pezdek (2002) asked 569 students attending college in New York City (Manhattan), Southern California, and Hawaii to complete a memory questionnaire. One item asked, "On September 11, did you see the videotape on television of the first plane striking the first tower." Overall, 73 percent of the students said yes. Yet this was impossible, because the videotape of the first plane crashing was not broadcast until after September 11. Moreover, students who incorrectly responded yes were more confident in their memory than the students who correctly said no! Similarly, after Princess Diana died, a study in England found that 44 percent of participants said that they had seen a videotape on the TV news showing the crash take place. No such tape was ever shown; in fact, it is highly doubtful that such a tape even exists, yet they were as confident in their memory as participants who said they never saw such a tape (Ost et al., 2002).

Memory researchers have studied the relation between confidence and accuracy with children and adults, inside and outside the laboratory, and for many types of events. Overall, confidence and accuracy are weakly related (Busey et al., 2000). People accurately recall many events—even after years pass— and typically are very confident when they do. But people often swear by inaccurate memories too. Even for a distinctive event, a memory can feel "like it just happened yesterday" when, in truth, it's foggy.

▶ 11. Are flashbulb memories always accurate? Describe evidence. Are confidence and memory accuracy related?

▶ 12. Describe and illustrate encoding specificity, context- and state-dependent memory, and mood-congruent recall.

Context, State, and Mood Effects on Memory

Our ability to retrieve a memory is influenced not only by the nature of the original stimulus (such as its distinctiveness) but also by aspects of the situation and person. Years ago, two Swedish researchers reported the case of a young woman who was raped while out for a jog (Christianson & Nilsson, 1989). When found by a passerby, she was in shock and could not remember the assault. Over the next 3 months the police took her back to the crime scene several times. Although she could not recall the rape, she became emotionally aroused, suggesting implicit memory of the event. While jogging one day shortly thereafter, she consciously recalled the rape.

Why did her memory return? One possibility is based on the **encoding specificity principle,** *which states that memory is enhanced when conditions present during retrieval match those that were present during encoding* (Tulving & Thomson, 1973). When stimuli associated with an event become encoded as part of the memory, they may later serve as retrieval cues.

Context-Dependent Memory: Returning to the Scene Applying the encoding specificity principle to *external* cues leads us to **context-dependent memory:** *It typically is easier to remember something in the same environment in which it was originally encoded.* Thus, if you return to your elementary school or old neighborhood, sights and sounds may trigger memories of teachers, classmates, and friends. As with the Swedish jogger, police detectives may take an eyewitness or crime victim back to the crime scene, hoping to stimulate the person's memory.

In a classic experiment, Duncan Godden and Alan Baddeley (1975) asked scuba divers to learn some lists of words underwater and some on dry land. As Figure 7.15 shows, when the divers were later retested in both environments, lists learned underwater were recalled better underwater and those learned on land were better recalled while on land. Many other studies, spanning diverse environmental contexts, have replicated this finding (Smith and Vela, 2001).

Consider how to your life as a student the concept of context-dependent memory might be relevant. In one experiment, when randomly assigned college students studied material in either a quiet or noisy room, they later displayed better memory on short-answer and multiple-choice

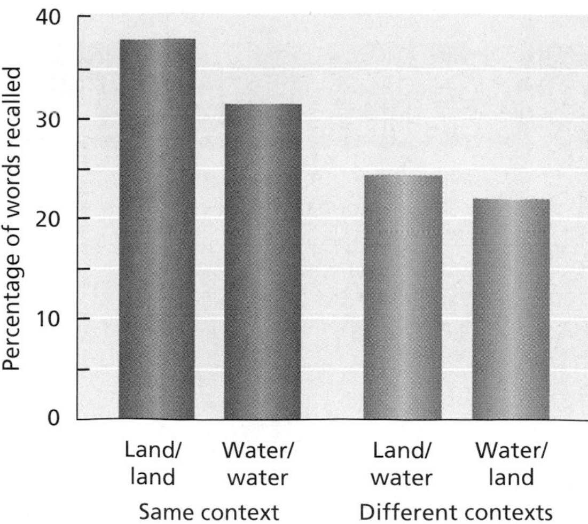

FIGURE 7.15

Context-dependent memory. Scuba divers who learned lists of words while underwater later recalled them best while underwater, whereas words they learned on land were best recalled on land. Recall was poorer when the learning and testing environments were mismatched. SOURCE: Adapted from Godden & Baddeley, 1975.

questions when tested in a similar (quiet or noisy) environment (Grant et al., 1998). Thus, if you take exams in quiet environments, try to study in a quiet environment.

State-Dependent Memory: Arousal, Drugs, and Mood Moving from external to internal cues, the concept of **state-dependent memory** *proposes that our ability to retrieve information is greater when our internal state at the time of retrieval matches our original state during learning*. The Swedish jogger who was raped consciously remembered her assault for the first time while jogging. In her case, both context-dependent cues (similar environment) and state-dependent cues (arousal while jogging) may have stimulated her memory.

Diverse experiments support this effect. Many students at the campus gym read course materials while exercising on a bicycle, treadmill, or stair-climber machine. Christopher Miles and Elinor Hardman (1998) found that material learned while we are aroused during aerobic exercise is later recalled more effectively if we are once again aerobically aroused, rather than at rest. Conversely, material learned at rest is better recalled at rest.

Many drugs produce physiological effects that directly impair memory, but state-dependent memory also explains why events experienced in a drug state may be difficult to recall later while in a drug-free state (Figure 7.16). Experiments examining alcohol, marijuana, amphetamines, and other drugs have often found that information recall is poorer when there is a mismatch between the person's states during learning and testing (Carter & Cassady, 1998). This *does not* mean, by the way, that drugs improve memory relative to not taking drugs during initial learning.

Does state-dependent memory extend to mood states? Is material learned while in a happy mood or a sad mood better recalled when we are in that mood again? Inconsistent findings suggest that such *mood-dependent memory* is not a reliable phenomenon. Instead, there is more consistent evidence of **mood-congruent recall:** *We tend to recall information or events that are congruent with our current mood* (Fiedler et al., 2001). When happy we are more likely to remember positive events, and when sad we tend to remember negative events. This perpetuates our mood and may be one factor

FIGURE 7.16

State-dependent memory. In the film City Lights, *a drunken millionaire befriends and spends the evening partying with Charlie Chaplin after Chaplin saves his life. The next day, in a sober state, the millionaire doesn't remember Chaplin and considers him an unwanted pest. After getting drunk again, he remembers Chaplin and treats him like a good buddy.*

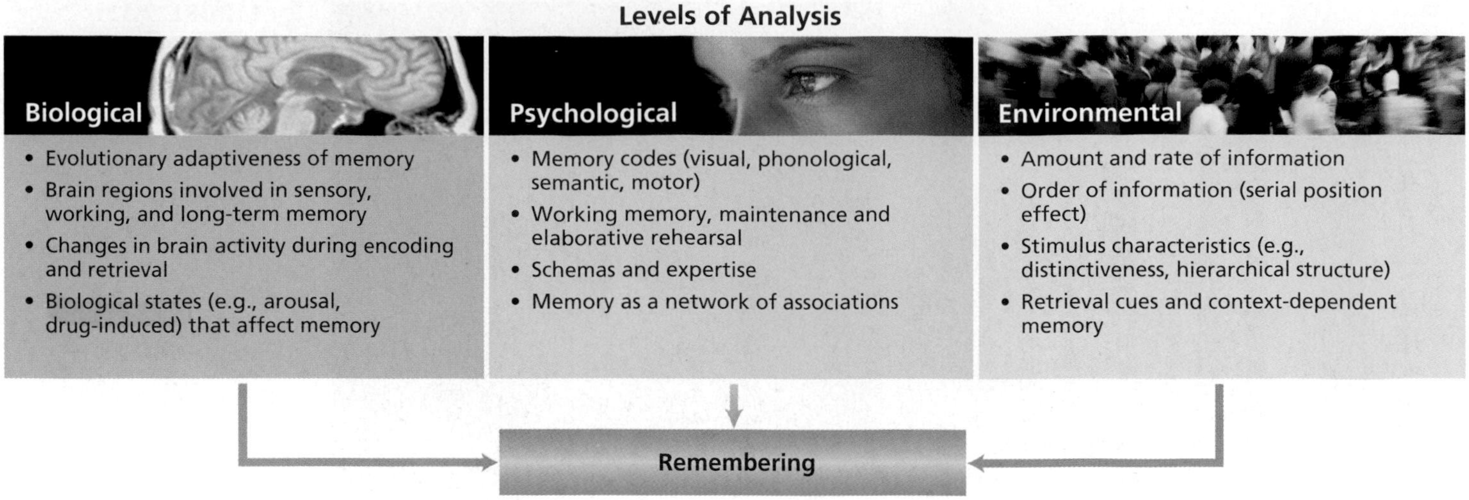

Levels of Analysis

Biological	Psychological	Environmental
• Evolutionary adaptiveness of memory • Brain regions involved in sensory, working, and long-term memory • Changes in brain activity during encoding and retrieval • Biological states (e.g., arousal, drug-induced) that affect memory	• Memory codes (visual, phonological, semantic, motor) • Working memory, maintenance and elaborative rehearsal • Schemas and expertise • Memory as a network of associations	• Amount and rate of information • Order of information (serial position effect) • Stimulus characteristics (e.g., distinctiveness, hierarchical structure) • Retrieval cues and context-dependent memory

Remembering

FIGURE 7.17

Understanding Behavior: Factors that enable us to remember.

that maintains depression once people have entered a depressed state (Pyszczynski et al., 1991).

Thus far we have focused on how information is remembered, and Figure 7.17 summarizes some of the factors involved. We'll have more to say about the brain's role later, but first, in the next two sections we examine why we forget and why we sometimes remember events that never occurred.

IN REVIEW

- *Memory involves three main processes (encoding, storage, and retrieval) and three main components (sensory memory, short-term/ working memory, and long-term memory).*
- *Sensory memory briefly holds incoming sensory information. Some information reaches working memory and long-term memory, where it is mentally represented by phonological, visual, semantic, or motor codes.*
- *Short-term/working memory actively processes information and supports other cognitive functions. It has auditory, visuospatial, and executive (coordinating) components. Long-term memory stores enormous amounts of information for up to a lifetime. Studies of amnesia patients and research on the serial position effect support the distinction between short- and long-term memory.*
- *Effortful processing involves intentional encoding and conscious attention. Automatic processing occurs without intention and requires minimal effort.*
- *Deep processing enhances memory. Elaborative rehearsal provides deeper processing than maintenance rehearsal. Hierarchies, chunking, dual-coding by adding visual imagery, and other mnemonic devices facilitate deeper encoding.*
- *Schemas are mental frameworks that shape how we encode information. As we become experts in any given field, we develop schemas that allow us to encode information into memory more efficiently.*
- *People who display exceptional memory take advantage of sound memory principles and mnemonic devices. Researchers disagree as to whether exceptional memory also requires special, innate talent.*
- *Associative network models view long-term memory as a network of associated nodes, with each node representing a concept or unit of information. Neural network models propose that each piece of information in memory is represented not by a single node but by multiple nodes distributed*

throughout the brain. Each memory is represented by a unique pattern of simultaneously activated nodes.

- *Declarative long-term memories involve factual knowledge and include episodic memories (knowledge concerning personal experiences) and semantic memories (facts about the world and language). In contrast, procedural memory is reflected in skills and actions. Explicit memory involves conscious or intentional memory retrieval, whereas implicit memory occurs when memory influences our behavior without conscious awareness.*
- *Retrieval cues activate information stored in long-term memory. Memory retrieval is more likely to occur when we have multiple cues, self-generated cues, and distinctive cues.*
- *We experience flashbulb memories as vivid and clear "snapshots" of an event and are confident of their accuracy. However, over time many flashbulb memories become inaccurate. Overall, memory accuracy and memory confidence are only weakly related.*
- *The encoding specificity principle states that memory is enhanced when cues present during retrieval match those that were present during encoding. Typically it is easier to remember a stimulus when we are in the same environment (context-dependent memory) or same internal state (state-dependent memory) as when the stimulus was originally encoded. One exception is mood states, where we tend to recall information or events that are congruent with our current mood.*

FORGETTING

Some very bright people are legendary for their memory failures. The eminent French writer Voltaire began a passionate letter, "My Dear Hortense," and ended it, "Farewell, my dear Adele." The splendid absentmindedness of English nobleman Canon Sawyer once led him, while welcoming a visitor at the railroad station, to board the departing train and disappear (Bryan, 1986). Indeed, how we forget is as interesting a scientific question as how we remember.

The Course of Forgetting

▶ 13. Describe Ebbinghaus's research, its value, and its limitations.

German psychologist Hermann Ebbinghaus (1885/1964) pioneered the study of forgetting by testing only one person—himself (Figure 7.18). He created over 2,000 *nonsense syllables,* meaningless letter combinations (e.g., *biv, zaj, xew*), to study memory with minimal influence from prior learning, as would happen if he used actual words. In one study, Ebbinghaus spent over 14,000 practice repetitions trying to memorize 420 lists of nonsense syllables.

Ebbinghaus typically measured memory by using a method called *relearning* and computing a savings percentage. For example, if it initially took him 20 trials to learn a list but only half as many trials to relearn it a week later, then the savings percentage was 50 percent. In one series of studies, he retested his memory at various time intervals after mastering several lists of nonsense syllables. As Figure 7.19a shows, forgetting occurred rapidly at first and slowed noticeably thereafter.

FIGURE 7.18

Hermann Ebbinghaus was a pioneering memory researcher.

Perhaps you are dismayed by this finding, which suggests that we quickly forget most of what we learn. Ebbinghaus, however, studied so many lists of nonsense syllables that his ability to distinguish among them undoubtedly suffered. If you learned just one or a few lists of syllables, the general shape of your forgetting curve might

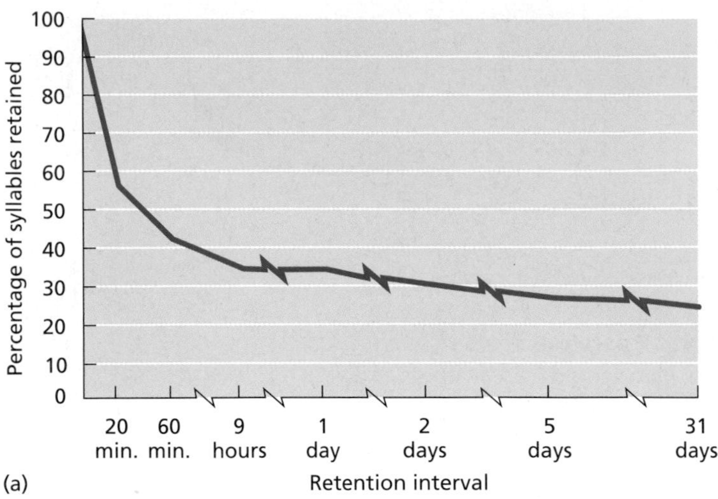

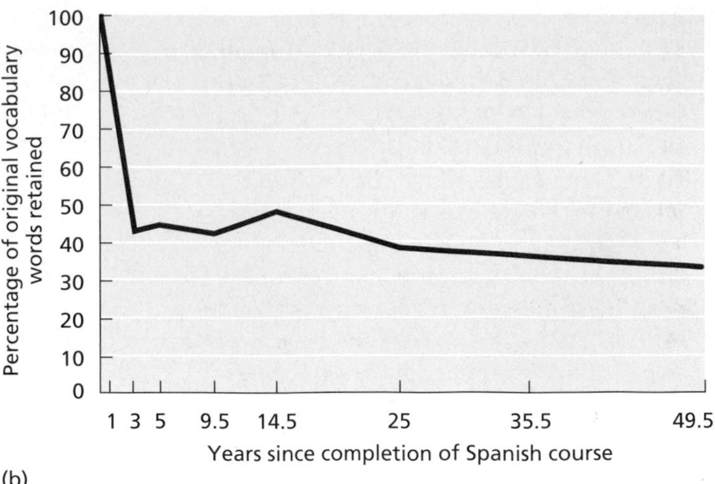

FIGURE 7.19

(a) Hermann Ebbinghaus's forgetting curve shows a rapid loss of memory for nonsense syllables at first and then a more gradual decline. The rapid decline is probably due to the meaningless nature of the nonsense syllables. (b) The forgetting of vocabulary from high school Spanish language classes follows a similar curve, except that the time frame is in years, not days. SOURCES: Based on (a) Ebbinghaus, 1885/1964, and (b) Bahrick, 1984.

resemble Ebbinghaus's over the first 24 hours, but the amount you forgot would likely be much less. Moreover, when material is meaningful (unlike nonsense syllables), we are likely to retain more of it over a longer time.

Consider the forgetting curve shown in Figure 7.19b, based on a study examining the vocabulary retention of people who had studied Spanish in school anywhere from 3 to 50 years earlier and then rarely used it (Bahrick, 1984). Once again, forgetting occurred more rapidly at first and then more slowly as time passed. Notice, however, that the Spanish-retention study employed a time frame of years rather than hours and days as in Ebbinghaus's studies.

Why Do We Forget?

▶ 14. Explain why we forget based on concepts of encoding failure, decay, and interference. What causes TOT experiences?

Given that some memories last a lifetime, why do we forget so much? Researchers have proposed several explanations for normal memory loss, emphasizing difficulties in encoding, storage, and retrieval.

Encoding Failure

Many memory failures result not from forgetting information that we once knew well but from failing to encode the information into long-term memory in the first place. Perhaps you had the radio on this morning while showering or eating breakfast, but do you remember every song or news story you heard? Chances are you can recall only the songs or stories that you found particularly interesting. This is because much of what we sense simply is not processed deeply enough to commit to memory.

We noted earlier that few people can draw a penny (or other coin) from memory, with accurate detail. Even when the task is made easier by requiring only recognition, as in Figure 7.20, most people cannot identify the correct coin (Nickerson & Adams, 1979). Can you? The details of a coin's appearance are not meaningful to most of us, and we may not even notice them, no matter how often we see coins in our daily lives.

At other times, we may notice information but fail to encode it deeply because we turn our attention to something else. Brad Bushman and Angelica Bonacci (2002) randomly assigned 328 adults to watch either a sexually explicit, violent, or neutral TV program. Nine commercial advertisements (e.g., for snacks, cereal, laundry detergent) appeared during each program. Immediately afterward and again a day later, the researchers tested viewers' memory for the ads. When analyzing their findings, Bushman and Bonnaci adjusted for the fact that some of the TV programs were more interesting and arousing than others. Even so, at both time periods, viewers who watched the sexually explicit and violent programs remembered the fewest number of ads (Figure 7.21). Several factors might account for this, and, as the researchers proposed, one of them is encoding failure: All the viewers clearly saw the ads, but those watching the sexually explicit and violent programs likely were the most preoccupied with thoughts about the content of the shows.

Decay of the Memory Trace

Information in sensory memory and short-term memory decays quickly with the passage of time. But what happens after a long-term memory is formed? One early explanation for forgetting was **decay theory,** *which proposed that with time and disuse the long-term physical memory trace in the nervous system fades away*. Decay theory soon fell into disfavor because scientists could not identify what physical memory traces were, where they were located, or how physical decay could be measured. In recent decades, however, scientists have begun to unravel some of the ways that neural circuits change when a long-term memory is formed. This research has sparked new interest in examining how these changes might decay over time (Villarreal et al., 2002).

Unfortunately, decay theory's prediction—that the longer the time interval of disuse between learning and recall, the less should be recalled—is problematic. As measured by cued recall and recognition tests, some professional actors display perfect memory for words they had last spoken on stage 2 years earlier—this despite the fact that they had moved on to different acting roles and had learned new scripts (Noice & Noice, 2002b). Moreover, when research participants learn a list of words or a set of visual patterns and are retested at two different times, they sometimes recall material during the second testing that they could not remember during the first. This phenomenon, called *reminiscence,* seems inconsistent with the concept that a memory trace decays over time (Greene, 1992). In sum, scientists still debate the validity of decay theory.

Interference

According to *interference theory,* we forget information because other items in long-term memory impair our ability to retrieve it (Postman & Underwood, 1973). Figure 7.22 illustrates two major types of interference. **Proactive interference** *occurs when material learned in the past interferes with recall of newer material*. Suppose that Alison changes residences, acquires a new phone number, and memorizes it. That night she sees a friend who asks for her new number. When Alison tries to recall it, she can remember only two or three digits, and instead keeps remembering the digits of her old phone number. Memory of her old

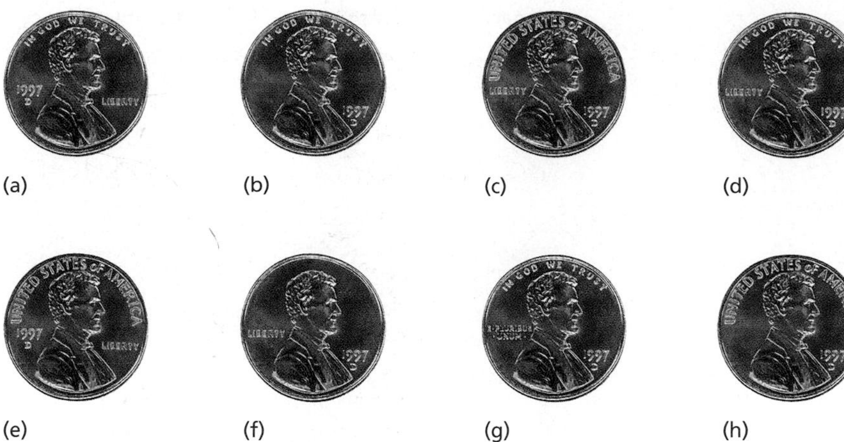

FIGURE 7.20

Which of the coins pictured here corresponds to a real penny? Most people have difficulty choosing the correct one because they have never bothered to encode all of the features of a real penny. If you want to try your skill at picking it out, don't read the next sentence yet. The correct penny is "d," the fourth one. SOURCE: Adapted from Nickerson & Adams, 1979.

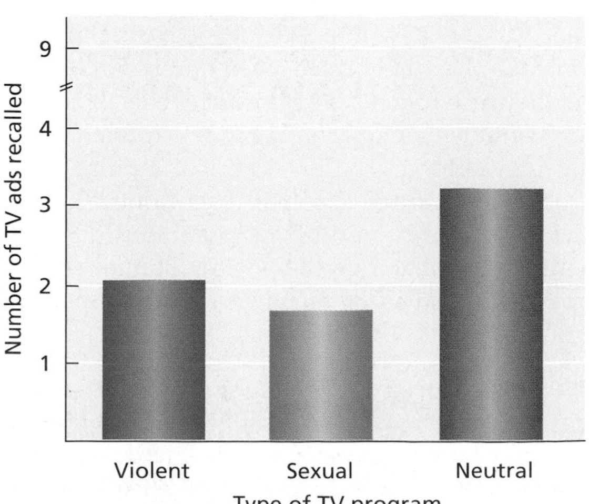

FIGURE 7.21

In one study, TV viewers who watched programs with violent or sexual content recalled fewer commercials than viewers who watched a neutral program. SOURCE: Based on Bushman & Bonacci, 2002.

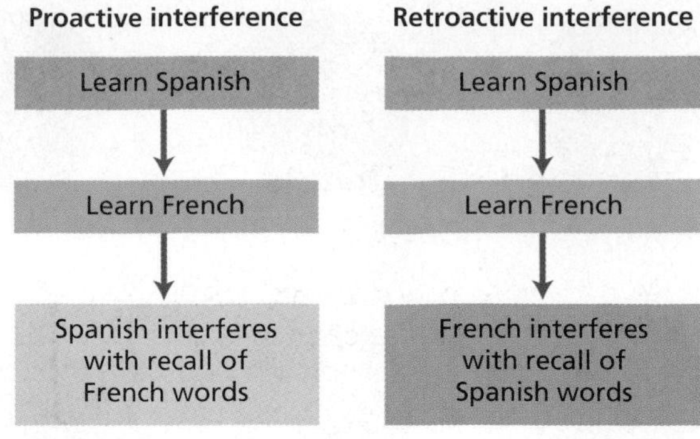

FIGURE 7.22

Interference is a major cause of forgetting. With proactive interference, older memories interfere with the retrieval of newer ones. With retroactive interference, newer memories interfere with the retrieval of older ones.

▶ 15. Why is motivated forgetting a controversial concept? Describe types of amnesia and the nature of prospective memory.

phone number is interfering with her ability to retrieve the new one.

Retroactive interference *occurs when newly acquired information interferes with the ability to recall information learned at an earlier time* (Tulving & Psotka, 1971). Suppose Alison has now had her new phone number for several months and recalls it perfectly each time. If we ask her, "What was your old phone number?" Alison may have trouble remembering it, perhaps mixing up the digits with her new number. In general, the more similar two sets of information are, the more likely it is that interference will occur. Alison (or you) would probably experience little interference in recalling highly dissimilar material, such as her new phone number and French vocabulary.

Some researchers believe that interference is caused by competition among retrieval cues (Anderson & Neely, 1996). When different memories become associated with similar or identical retrieval cues, confusion can result and accessing a cue may call up the wrong memory. Retrieval failure also can occur because we have too few retrieval cues or the cues may be too weak.

Almost all of us have experienced a retrieval problem called the **tip-of-the-tongue (TOT) state,** *in which we cannot recall something but feel that we are on the verge of remembering it*. The title of the radio quiz show "Wait, Wait—Don't Tell Me!" plays on this phenomenon. When Bennett Schwartz (2002) asked 56 college students to record a diary for 4 weeks, he found that they averaged just over one TOT experience per week. Most often, TOT states were triggered by the inability to remember the name of an acquaintance, famous person, or object. Students usually felt emotionally aroused while wrapped up in a TOT state and were relieved when the answer arrived. Sooner or later, it usually did. The answer often "popped into the mind" spontaneously, but in many cases students had to consult a book or another person.

What Do You Think?

IS IT REALLY ON THE TIP OF YOUR TONGUE?

Suppose you're having a TOT experience. Should we always assume that it's a retrieval problem? What else might explain your inability to come up with the answer? Think about it, then see page 278.

Motivated Forgetting

Psychodynamic and other psychologists propose that, at times, people are consciously or unconsciously motivated to forget. During therapy sessions, Sigmund Freud often observed that his patients remembered traumatic or anxiety-arousing events that had long seemed forgotten. For example, one of his patients suddenly remembered with great shame that while standing beside her sister's coffin she had thought, "Now my brother-in-law is free to marry me." Freud concluded that the thought had been so shocking and anxiety arousing that the woman had *repressed* it—pushed it down into her unconscious mind—there to remain until it was uncovered years later during psychoanalysis. **Repression** *is a motivational process that protects us by blocking the conscious recall of anxiety-arousing memories.*

The concept of repression is highly controversial. Some evidence supports it, and other evidence does not (Karon, 2002). People certainly do forget unpleasant events—even traumatic ones—yet they also forget very pleasant events. If a person cannot remember a negative experience, is this due to repression or to normal information-processing failures (Epstein & Bottoms, 2002)? Overall, it has been difficult to demonstrate experimentally that a special process akin to repression is the cause of memory loss for anxiety-arousing events (Holmes, 1990). We will return to this topic shortly.

Amnesia

The most dramatic instances of forgetting occur in amnesia, which takes several forms. **Retrograde**

amnesia *represents memory loss for events that took place sometime in life before the onset of amnesia*. For example, H. M. suffered mild memory loss for events in his life that had occurred during the year or two *before* he had his operation. Football players experience retrograde amnesia when they are "knocked out" in a concussion, regain consciousness, and cannot remember the events just before being hit.

Anterograde amnesia *refers to memory loss for events that occur after the initial onset of amnesia*. H. M.'s brain operation, and particularly the removal of much of his hippocampus, produced severe anterograde amnesia and robbed him of the ability to consciously remember new experiences and facts. In a similar fashion, the woman whose hand was pinpricked by Claparède during a handshake also experienced anterograde amnesia; moments later she could not consciously remember the episode. Unlike H. M.'s anterograde amnesia, hers was caused by *Korsakoff's syndrome*, which can result from chronic alcoholism and may also cause severe retrograde amnesia.

Alzheimer's disease, the most common form of senile dementia that affects millions of elderly adults, produces severe retrograde and anterograde amnesia. This memory loss may be due to a decline in the function of several neurotransmitter systems, especially the acetylcholine system (Ballard, 2002). Acetylcholine plays a key role in synaptic transmission in several brain areas involved in memory.

Finally, there is one type of amnesia that almost all of us encounter: an inability to remember personal experiences from the first few years of our lives. Even though infants and preschoolers can form long-term memories of events in their lives (Peterson & Whalen, 2001), as adults we typically are unable to recall these events consciously. *This memory loss for early experiences is called* **infantile amnesia** (also known as *childhood amnesia*). Our memories of childhood typically do not include events that occurred before the age of 3 or 4, although some adults can partially recall major events (e.g., the birth of a sibling, hospitalization, or a death in the family) that happened before the age of 2 (Eacott & Crawley, 1998).

What causes infantile amnesia? One hypothesis is that brain regions that encode long-term episodic memories are still immature in the first years after birth. Another is that we do not encode our earliest experiences deeply and fail to form rich retrieval cues for them. Additionally, because infants lack a clear self-concept, they do not have a personal frame of reference around which to organize rich memories (Harley & Reese, 1999).

Forgetting to Do Things: Prospective Memory

Have you ever forgotten to mail a letter, turn off the oven, keep an appointment, or purchase something at the market? In contrast to *retrospective memory*, which refers to memory for past events, **prospective memory** *concerns remembering to perform an activity in the future*. That people forget to do things as often as they do is interesting, because prospective memories typically involve little content. Often we need only recall that we must perform some event-based task ("Remember, on your way out, mail the letter") or time-based task ("Remember, take your medication at 4 P.M."). Successful prospective memory, however, draws on other cognitive abilities, such as planning and allocating attention while performing other tasks (Kliegel et al., 2002).

Are people with better retrospective memory less likely to be forgetful on prospective memory tasks? In one experiment, researchers assessed participants' retrospective memory ability by having them recall lists of words (Wilkins & Baddeley, 1978). Next, participants performed a prospective simulated pill-taking task by carrying around a small box with a button. Four times a day at a specified time they had to remember to press the button, which time-stamped their response. Overall, participants who performed better on the word-recall task did not display better memory on the simulated pill-taking task.

During adulthood, do we become increasingly absentminded about remembering to do things, as a common stereotype suggests? Numerous laboratory experiments support this view (Vogels et al., 2002). Typically, participants perform a task that requires their ongoing attention while trying to remember to signal the experimenter at certain time intervals or whenever specific events take place. Older adults generally display poorer prospective memory, especially when signaling is time-based. However, when prospective memory is tested outside the laboratory using tasks such as simulated pill-taking, healthy adults in their 60s to 80s often perform as well as or better than adults in their 20s (Rendell & Thomson, 1999). Perhaps older adults are more motivated to remember in such situations, or they rely more on habit and setting up a standard routine (Anderson & Craik, 2000). In sum, prospective memory—like other areas of memory—is far from simple.

IN REVIEW

- *Forgetting tends to be most rapid relatively soon after initial learning, but the time frame and degree of forgetting can vary widely depending on many factors.*
- *Due to encoding failure, we often cannot recall information because we never entered it into long-term memory in the first place.*
- *Decay theory proposes that physical memory traces in long-term memory deteriorate with disuse over time, but evidence of reminiscence contradicts this view.*
- *Proactive interference occurs when material learned in the past interferes with recall of newer material. Retroactive interference occurs when newly acquired information interferes with the ability to recall information learned at an earlier time.*
- *Psychodynamic theorists propose that we may forget anxiety-arousing material through repression, an unconscious process of motivated forgetting.*
- *Retrograde amnesia represents memory loss for events that occurred prior to the onset of amnesia. Anterograde amnesia refers to memory loss for events that occur after the initial onset of amnesia. Infantile amnesia is our inability to remember personal experiences from the first few years of our lives.*
- *Whereas retrospective memory refers to memory for past events, prospective memory refers to our ability to remember to perform some activity in the future.*

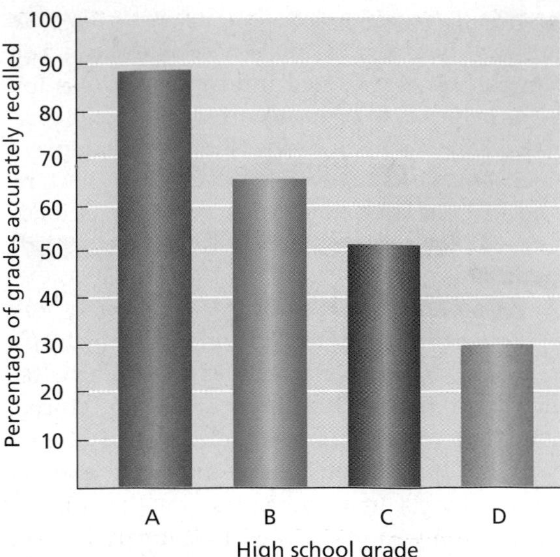

FIGURE 7.23

The lower the grade, the less likely students were to accurately recall it. Note also that when students incorrectly recalled a grade, they almost always overestimated how well they did. SOURCE: Adapted from Bahrick et al., 1996.

MEMORY AS A CONSTRUCTIVE PROCESS

▶ 16. Discuss examples of memory construction and explain how schemas influence this process.

Retrieving information from long-term memory is not like viewing a videotaped replay. Our memories of things past often are incomplete or sketchy. In such situations, we may literally *construct* (or, as some say, *reconstruct*) a memory by piecing together bits of stored information in a way that intuitively makes sense and seems real and accurate. As our earlier discussion of flashbulb memories illustrated, at times we may be highly confident of memories that in fact are partly, or completely, inaccurate.

Memory construction can be amusing at times, and a tendency to recall the world through slightly rosy glasses can even help us feel good about ourselves. For example, when college students in one study recalled their high school grades, the worse the grade was, the less often students remembered it accurately. Students correctly recalled almost all of their As, but only a third of their Ds (Figure 7.23). Most important, errors were positively biased; students usually misremembered their Bs as having been As, their Cs as Bs, and their Ds as Cs (Bahrick et al., 1996). As we will see, however, memory construction also can have serious personal and societal consequences.

Memory Distortion and Schemas

Decades ago, Sir Frederick Bartlett (1932) asked residents of Cambridge, England, to read stories and then retell them days or months later. One story, a Pacific Northwest Indian tale called "The War of the Ghosts," describes two young men who go down to a river to hunt seals. While there, warriors in canoes come up the river, and one of the young men agrees to join them for a raid on a

(a)

(b)

FIGURE 7.24

Boundary extension. (a) What you see. (b) What you remember. Helene Intraub and her colleagues (1996) have found that when people briefly look at close-up pictures, such as this one of a teddy bear, and then draw the pictures from memory, they unknowingly convert the image into a "wide-angle" scene in which the size of the main object (e.g., the teddy bear) shrinks. This effect is less likely to occur if the original picture already is a wide-angle scene. SOURCE: Images courtesy of Helene Intraub.

town. During the raid, the man discovers that his companions are ghosts, and later he dies a mysterious death.

Bartlett's participants, however, were 20th-century residents of England, not 18th-century Native Americans. When they retold the story, they partly reconstructed it in a way that made sense to them. For example, 20 hours after reading "The War of the Ghosts," one participant shortened the story by almost half, described the hero as fishing rather than as hunting seals, substituted the word *boat* for *canoe,* and said that the enemy—not his companions—were ghosts. Bartlett found that the longer the time interval between the reading and retelling of the story, the more the story changed to fit English culture.

Bartlett, who coined the term *schema,* believed that people have generalized ideas (schemas) about how events happen and that they use these ideas to organize and construct their memories. As we described earlier, schemas often enhance memory by helping us organize and understand information (recall the clothes-washing description). The price, however, is that schemas may distort our memories by leading us to encode or retrieve information in ways that "make sense" and fit in with our preexisting assumptions about the world.

Quite literally, memory construction extends to how we visualize the world (Intraub, 2002). As Figure 7.24 illustrates, when college students in one study looked at photographs that had a main object within a scene and then drew what they saw from memory, they consistently displayed *boundary extension:* remembering the scene as more expansive—as being "wider-angle"—than it really was (Intraub et al., 1996). In real life, objects usually occur against an expansive background, creating a schema for how we expect scenes to look. Thus when we remember close-up images, our schemas lead us to "see beyond the edge" and retrieve a broader scene than the one we saw.

Advertisers often exploit people's tendency to elaborate and change their memories, thereby skirting laws against false advertising. Consider the following commercial for the mouthwash Listerine.

> "Wouldn't it be great," asks the mother, "if you could make him coldproof? Well, you can't. Nothing can do that. [Boy sneezes.] But there is something you can do that may help. Have him gargle with Listerine antiseptic. Listerine can't promise to keep him cold-free, but it may help him fight off colds. During the cold-catching season, have him gargle twice a day with full-strength Listerine. Watch his diet, see he gets plenty of sleep, and there's a good chance he'll have fewer colds, milder colds, this year." (Anderson, 1980, p. 203)

This commercial, with the product's name changed to *Gargoil,* was used in a memory experiment (Harris, 1977). When participants were asked to recall the commercial, they agreed with the statement "Gargoil antiseptic helps prevent colds," although the commercial did not say that. (It said, "Gargoil *may* help.") Participants elaborated on what the ad said when they constructed their memories. Undoubtedly, this is what the advertisers hoped for. The *Research Close-Up* on the next page offers some insight into how schemas can affect memory and lead us to remember things that never happened.

▶ 17. How did the *Research Close-Up* studies investigate false memories? What might have caused the false memories?

Misinformation Effects and Eyewitness Testimony

If memories are constructed, then information that occurs *after* an event may shape that construction process. This **misinformation effect,** *the*

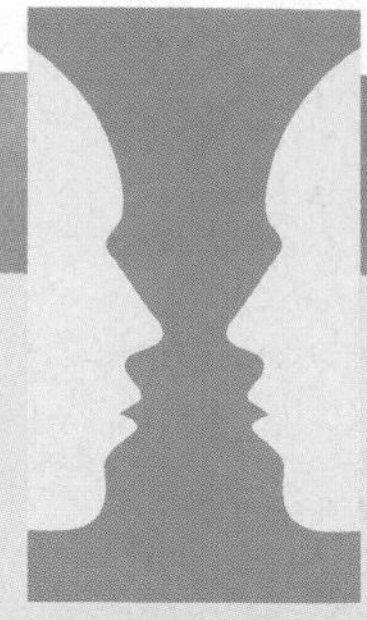

RESEARCH CLOSE-UP

MEMORY ILLUSIONS: REMEMBERING THINGS THAT NEVER OCCURRED

Study 1: College Students

Background

In this famous experiment, Henry Roediger III and Kathleen McDermott examined how often false memories occurred while people performed a simple laboratory task: remembering lists of words. They also investigated whether false memory rates depend on how memory is measured (i.e., recall versus recognition) and whether people experience false memories as being vivid and clear.

Method

Building on previous research (Deese, 1959), the researchers created 24 lists of 15 words. Each list contained words that, to varying degrees, were associated with a central organizing word. To illustrate, look at the following list:

sour, candy, sugar, bitter, good, taste, tooth, nice, honey, soda, chocolate, heart, cake, tart, pie

The word *sweet* doesn't occur in the list, yet it is associated with these items. The central word (*sweet*) is called a *critical lure*.

Thirty-six college students each listened to 16 of the 24 lists. For 8 lists, students' recall was measured as soon as each list ended. For 8 other lists, recall was not measured. After finishing all 16 lists, students performed a recognition task. They were given a sheet of paper with 96 words, half of which actually had been on the lists. The other words were critical lures and filler items from the final 8 lists not read to each student. Students identified whether each word had been on the lists they heard. If they selected a word, they also reported whether they had a vivid memory of having heard it or, instead, were sure that they had heard it but lacked a vivid memory.

Results

Students correctly recalled 62 percent of the real words but falsely recalled almost as many (55 percent) of the critical lures. For the 8 lists where students performed only a recognition task, they correctly identified words 62 percent of the time but falsely identified even more of the critical lures (72 percent). Furthermore, in just over half of the cases where students falsely recognized a critical lure, they reported having a vivid memory of it.

Discussion

Although critical lures were never presented, students falsely recalled them half the time and falsely recognized them almost three quarters of the time. Moreover, students often reported having a clear memory of the nonexistent critical lure. Many researchers have replicated this finding.

What causes these false memories? Roediger and McDermott (1995, 2000) argue that hearing the words activates an associative network—a schema—for the critical lure. For some people, the words (*sour*, *candy*, *sugar*, etc.) may consciously trigger a thought of "sweet." For others, spreading activation from the words unconsciously primes the concept of "sweet." (Look back at Figure 7.12. If you heard the words *roses*, *fire*, *cherries*, *orange*, *apple*, they would prime the word *red*). Whether consciously or unconsciously, the critical lure is activated. This creates a problem during retrieval, because people may misinterpret the source of activation and thus falsely remember the lure as being on the list (Figure 7.25a).

In your view, are these findings relevant to everyday memory in the real world? Critics emphasize that the research context—college students learning word lists—may have little relevance to situations involving memory for important events. Yet Roediger and McDermott argue that this research context makes the findings more impressive. Participants knew it was a memory test and knew that inaccurate memories would be spotted. Further, memory was tested soon after hearing each list, and "we used college students—professional memorizers—as subjects." If people can be highly confident of their false memories in this straightforward situation, the researchers ask, then what might happen in real-world contexts where conditions for remembering events are more complex and not as optimal?

Study 2: People Reporting Abduction by Aliens

Background

Is there a relation between false memories on the word-list task in Study 1 and false memories for significant events in real life? To examine this question, Susan Clancy and coworkers recruited three groups of participants through newspaper advertisements: a control group of 13 people who said they had never been abducted by aliens, 9 people who were sure

SOURCES: Henry L. Roediger III and Kathleen McDermott (1995). Creating false memories: Remembering words not presented in lists. *Journal of Experimental Psychology: Learning, Memory, and Cognition, 21*, 803–814; Susan A. Clancy, Richard J. McNally, Daniel L. Schacter, Mark F. Lenzeweger, and Roger K. Pitman (2002). Memory distortion in people reporting abduction by aliens. *Journal of Abnormal Psychology, 111*, 455–461.

FIGURE 7.25

(a) After listening to a list of related words, people often remember hearing a critical lure ("sweet") that was never presented. (b) The degree of false recognition of critical lures among three groups of participants. SOURCE: Based on Clancy et al., 2002.

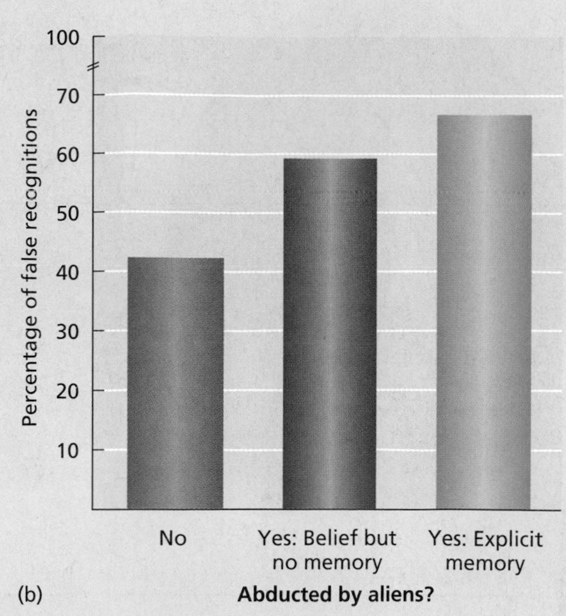

they had been abducted by aliens but who had no explicit memory of it, and 11 people who said that, for a time, they had forgotten that they had been abducted but then had a clear memory of the abduction gradually return to them. Why study people claiming to be alien abductees? Because, say the researchers, these individuals are reporting a major traumatic event that in reality we can assume is unlikely to have occurred.

Method and Results

Participants listened to word lists of varying lengths, based on the lists used in Study 1. The three groups did not differ in how accurately they recalled and recognized words that actually had been on the lists. However, the two abductee groups falsely recalled and falsely recognized more critical lures than the control group, and those with explicit memories of abduction made the most recognition errors (Figure 7.25b).

Discussion

The authors note that, assuming the alien abductions were unlikely to have occurred, the findings indicate a relation between how prone people are to display false memories both inside and outside the laboratory. They also speculate that both types of false memories may share a common basis: a confusion over the source of the memory. In the lab, spreading activation caused by the word lists is mistakenly attributed to a false source: the presence of a critical lure that actually was not on the list. A similar type of confusion could occur, for example, when "an individual might watch a movie about alien abductions as a child and then—years later—come to believe that the events in the movie actually occurred because he or she has forgotten the actual source of the memory."

distortion of a memory by misleading postevent information, has frequently been investigated in relation to mistaken eyewitness testimony. In one celebrated case, Father Bernard Pagano, a Roman Catholic priest, was positively identified by seven eyewitnesses as the perpetrator of a series of armed robberies in the Wilmington, Delaware, area. He was saved from almost certain conviction when the true robber, dubbed the "gentleman bandit" because of his politeness and concern for the victims, confessed to the crimes. You can see in Figure 7.26 that there was little physical resemblance between the two men.

Two pieces of information may have affected the witnesses' memory. First, the gentlemanly and concerned manner of the robber is consistent with the schema many people have of priests. Second, before presenting pictures of suspects to the

▶ 18. Describe the misinformation effect, why it occurs, and how it affects memory accuracy in children and adults.

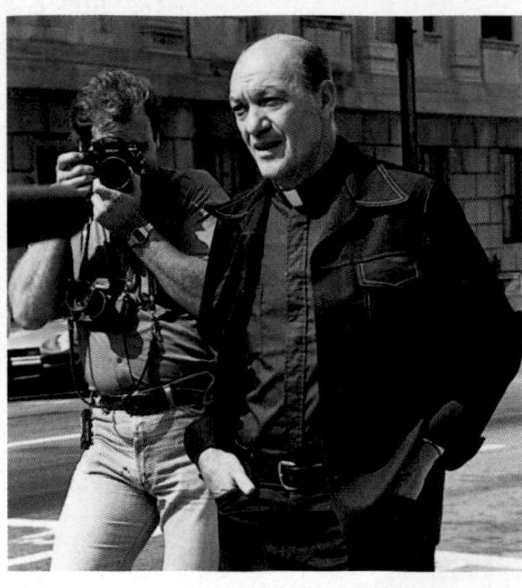

FIGURE 7.26

Seven eyewitnesses to armed robberies committed by Ronald Clouser (left) mistakenly identified Father Bernard Pagano (right) as the robber, probably as a result of information from police that influenced their memory reconstructions.

eyewitnesses, the police let it be known that the suspect might be a priest. Because Father Pagano was the only suspect wearing a clerical collar, the witnesses' memories may have been strongly affected by this information (Tversky & Tuchin, 1989).

Even one or two words can produce a powerful misinformation effect while questioning an eyewitness. Imagine that after you witness a two-car crash, a police officer takes your statement and simply asks you, "About how fast were the cars going when they *contacted* each other?" In one experiment, college students viewed brief films of car accidents and then judged how fast the cars were going. As Figure 7.27 shows, the judged speed increased by about 33 percent when the word *contacted* was changed to *hit, bumped, collided with, or smashed into* (Loftus & Palmer, 1974).

Misinformation effects also occur because of **source confusion** (also called *source monitoring error*), *our tendency to recall something or recognize it as familiar but to forget where we encountered it.* Suppose an eyewitness to a crime looks through a series of mug shots and reports that none of the individuals is the perpetrator. Several days later, the eyewitness is brought back to view a live lineup and is asked to identify the person who committed the crime. In reality, none of the people in the lineup did, but one suspect was pictured in a mug shot that the eyewitness had seen days earlier. "That's the person," says the eyewitness. Source confusion occurred because the eyewitness recognized that the individual's face was familiar but failed to remember that this familiarity stemmed from the mug shot. Instead, the witness mistakenly assumed that he or she saw the familiar-looking suspect committing the crime.

In an experimental analog to this situation, 29 percent of participants who witnessed a staged event and later viewed mug shots misidentified *innocent* suspects as having been involved in the event because of source confusion (Brown et al., 1977). Source confusion also occurs when people witness an event (e.g., a video of a home burglary) and then are exposed to misleading statements about it (e.g., that a bare-handed, unarmed burglar wore gloves and had a gun). They may eventually forget that the source of the misinformation was a question or statement made by someone else and come to believe it was part of what they saw while witnessing the event (Mitchell & Zaragoza, 2001).

Does postevent information permanently alter a witness's original memory so that the original memory can never again be retrieved? Researchers debate the answer, but all agree that eyewitness reports can be influenced by postevent information. Results like these have raised concerns about the reliability of eyewitness testimony not only from adults but also from children in cases of alleged physical and sexual abuse.

For more on the dilemma of eyewitness testimony, see Video Segment 7.2.

FIGURE 7.27

College students' memory of how fast two cars were moving just before an accident varied significantly depending on how the question was phrased.

How fast were the two cars going when they ________ each other?

Words	Perceived speed
smashed into	41 mph
collided with	39 mph
bumped into	38 mph
hit	34 mph
contacted	31 mph

The Child as Eyewitness

In cases of alleged child sexual abuse, there is often no conclusive corroborating medical evidence and the child is usually the only witness (Bruck et al., 1998). If the charges are true, the thought of failing to convict the abuser and returning the child to an abusive environment is frightening. Conversely, if the charges are false, the consequences of convicting an innocent person are equally distressing.

Accuracy and Suggestibility

As with adults, a single instance of suggestive questioning can distort some children's memory, but suggestive questioning most often leads to false memories when it is repeated. Young children are typically more susceptible to misleading suggestions than older children (Ceci et al., 2000).

In one experiment by Michelle Leichtman and Stephen Ceci (1995), 3- to 6-year-old children were told about a man named Sam Stone. Over several weeks, some children were repeatedly told stories that portrayed Sam as clumsy. Later Sam visited their classroom, was introduced, and behaved innocuously. The next day, the children were shown a ripped book and soiled teddy bear, things for which Sam was not responsible. Over the next 10 weeks they were interviewed several times, and some were asked suggestive questions about Sam (e.g., "When Sam Stone tore the book, did he do it on purpose or was he being silly?"). Two weeks later a new interviewer asked all the children to describe Sam's visit to the classroom.

Children who heard suggestive information about Sam—whether before, after, or especially before *and* after Sam's appearance—made more false reports about Sam's behavior than a control group that never heard suggestive information. One child stated that after soaking the teddy bear in the bath, Sam smeared it with a crayon. These findings are troubling, because during many sexual abuse investigations, the child initially denies being abused, but then after repeated suggestive questioning during therapy or police interviewing, the child acknowledges the abuse (Bruck et al., 1998). Was the child understandably reluctant to open up at first, or did suggestive questions produce a false allegation?

How well do children remember traumatic events? Elaine Burgwyn-Bailes and coworkers (2001) interviewed 3- to 7-year-olds a few days, 6 weeks, and 1 year after the children underwent emergency plastic surgery for facial lacerations. At each time period, children accurately remembered most of the details of their operation, but they also mistakenly agreed with about 15 percent of leading questions ("Did the doctor's helper use any needles?") and suggestive questions ("The lady took off your watch, didn't she?") about events that never occurred. Compared to older children, younger children remembered fewer true details and agreed more often to leading and suggestive questions.

True Versus False Reports: Can Professionals Tell Them Apart?

Can professionals reliably distinguish between children's accurate and false reports? The answer appears to be no, at least when false reports are caused by repeated, suggestive questioning. Mental-health and social workers, prosecutors, and judges shown videotapes of children's reports in the Sam Stone experiment often rated false reports as highly credible, perhaps because many children who make them are not intentionally lying. Rather, the children believe that their memory is accurate. After suggestive questioning, children are as confident of their false memories as they are of their accurate ones (Roebers, 2002).

What should society do? Like adults, young children accurately remember a lot, but they also misremember and are susceptible to repeated suggestive questioning. Thanks to psychological research, law enforcement, mental-health, and legal professionals are now paying more attention to how children's admissions of abuse are elicited, and training programs are helping practitioners minimize suggestive interviewing techniques (Sternberg et al., 2002). The goal is not to discredit children's allegations of abuse. To the contrary, the hope is that by minimizing the risk of false allegations, nonsuggestive interviewing will elicit allegations judged as even more compelling, thereby helping to ensure that justice is done.

The "Recovered Memory" Controversy

▶ 19. Discuss the recovered memory controversy, the two key issues involved, and relevant evidence.

In 1997, a woman from Illinois settled a lawsuit against two psychiatrists and their hospital for $10.6 million. She alleged that her psychiatrists used hypnosis, drugs, and other treatments that led her to develop false memories of having been a high priestess in a sexually abusive satanic cult (APA Monitor, December 1997, p. 9). Yet only years

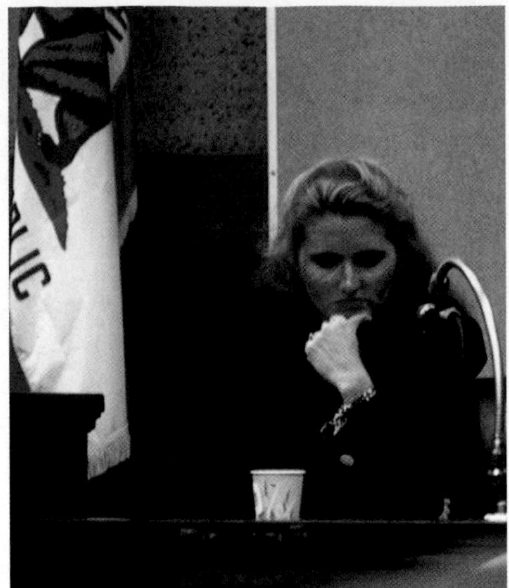

FIGURE 7.28

In a famous 1990 repressed-memory case, George Franklin was convicted of murdering Susan Nason, an 8-year-old girl killed in 1969. Franklin's 28-year-old daughter Eileen (shown here), who had been Susan's childhood friend, provided the key evidence. During therapy Eileen recovered memories of her father sexually assaulting and killing Susan. A judge overturned the conviction after learning that Eileen's memories had been recovered under hypnosis. All of the details about the case that Eileen recalled had been published in the newspapers, creating the possibility of source confusion in her memory. Eileen also had other recovered memories that were proven to be untrue, such as those of her father killing two other girls.

earlier, there had been a wave of cases in which adults—usually in the course of psychotherapy—began to remember long-forgotten childhood sexual abuse and sued their parents, other family members, and former teachers for the alleged trauma (Figure 7.28).

The scientific controversy over the validity of "recovered memories" of childhood trauma can be broken down into two issues. First, when a recovered memory of sexual abuse occurs, is it accurate? Second, if the abuse really happened, what caused the memory to be forgotten for so long—repression, or some other psychological process?

Let's briefly examine the second issue. Many scientists and therapists question Freud's concept of repression. Repression implies a special psychological mechanism that actively pushes traumatic memories into the unconscious mind, and we have already noted that researchers have had difficulty demonstrating it experimentally. Recovered memories of childhood sexual abuse or other traumas cannot be taken as automatic evidence of repression. Memory loss may have occurred because of ordinary sources of forgetting or because the victim intentionally avoided thinking about the abuse or reinterpreted the trauma to make it less upsetting (Epstein & Bottoms, 2002). But beyond these factors, other researchers and many therapists believe that repression is a valid concept (Karon, 2002). This controversy will not be resolved soon.

What about the more basic question? Can someone forget childhood sexual abuse, by whatever psychological mechanism, and then recover that memory as an adult? Indeed, full or partial memory loss for a traumatic event has been reported among survivors of natural disasters, children who witnessed the violent death of a parent, victims of rape, combat veterans, and victims of sexual and physical abuse (Arrigo & Pezdek, 1997; Epstein & Bottoms, 2002). Moreover, laboratory experiments indicate that a mentally shocking event (e.g., viewing a sudden, violent film scene) can produce retrograde amnesia for information presented just before the shocking event occurred (Loftus & Burns, 1982).

Some victims of documented child sexual abuse do not recall their trauma when they are adults, and accurate memories of the abuse can indeed return after many years of posttrauma forgetting (Kluft, 1999; Williams, 1995). Yet memory loss after psychological trauma is usually far shorter, with memory returning over weeks, months, or perhaps a few years. In many cases of trauma, the victim's primary problem is not memory loss but rather an *inability* to forget, which may involve involuntary nightmares or flashbacks (Berntsen, 2001).

Experiments indicate that college students may develop false memories of personal childhood events that never happened—being hospitalized overnight for a high fever, accidentally spilling a bowl of punch on the parents of the bride at a wedding reception, being rescued by an elderly lady while lost and crying in a shopping mall—after being exposed to suggestive questioning or merely by repeatedly imagining that the event took place (Hyman et al., 1995). Obviously, these events do not approximate the magnitude of experiencing sexual abuse, and for ethical reasons experimenters do not test whether false memories of sexual abuse can be implanted. Nevertheless, say many researchers and clinicians, add these findings to everything science has taught us about forgetting, constructive memory, and the "fogging up" of even flashbulb memories,

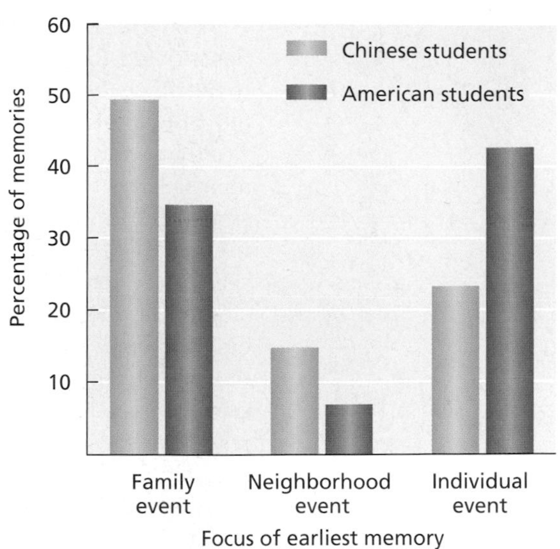

FIGURE 7.29

What is your earliest memory? In this study, Chinese students recalled events that, overall, were more family and neighborhood oriented than events recalled by American students. How else might our cultural upbringing and worldview influence memory? SOURCE: Based on Wang, 2002.

and the conclusion is that we should not take the accuracy of recovered memories at face value (Pickrell et al., 2003). They are especially concerned that in "recovered-memory therapy," therapists repeatedly suggest the possibility of abuse to people who are already emotionally vulnerable.

The message from science is not that all claims of recovered traumatic memories should be dismissed. Rather, it is to urge caution in unconditionally accepting those memories, particularly in cases where suggestive techniques are used to recover the memories (Brandon et al., 1998). Some day it may be possible scientifically to separate true memories from false ones. Researchers have begun to examine whether some types of true versus false memories are associated with different patterns of brain activity, and true memories often are described in greater detail than false ones. But at present, these findings cannot be used to determine reliably whether any individual memory is true or false (Pickrell et al., 2003).

Culture and Memory Construction

Culture and memory have a reciprocal relation. On the one hand, whether through modeling, print or electronic media, or oral traditions, cultural survival depends on transmitting knowledge and customs from one generation to the next. Without our capacity to remember events and information, culture simply could not exist (and neither could we, as a species).

At the same time, culture influences memory. Our cultural upbringing shapes the schemas—the mental frameworks—that we acquire and use to perceive ourselves and the world. For example, as we discussed in Chapter 1, most people living in northern Europe and North America learn to view the world through a relatively *individualistic* lens in which self-identity is based primarily on one's own attributes and achievements. People living in many Asian, African, and South American cultures tend to see the world through a more *collectivistic* framework in which personal identity is defined largely by the ties that bind one to the extended family and other social groups. Thus it stands to reason that if cultural socialization influences our schemas, and our schemas in turn influence how we encode and also reconstruct events, then people from different cultures may recall the events of their lives in somewhat distinct ways.

Let's consider an example: our earliest memories. In one study, Qi Wang (2001) asked over 200 college students from Harvard University and Beijing University to describe their earliest memories (Figure 7.29). He predicted and found that the Americans were more likely than their Chinese counterparts to recall events that focused on individual experiences and feelings, autonomy, and self-determination (e.g., "I was sorting baseball cards when I dropped them. As I reached down to get them, I knocked over a jug of iced tea."). In contrast, Chinese students were more likely than American students to recall memories that involved family or neighborhood activities and to mention other people (e.g., "Dad taught me ancient poems. It was always when he was washing vegetables that he would explain a poem to me.")

▶ 20. Illustrate how culture influences memory construction.

Wang also found that American college students dated their earliest personal memory back to the time when they were, on average, 3 ½ years old. Students in China, however, reported memories that on average dated to the time they were almost 4 years old. Several studies have obtained similar findings. Although the reason isn't clear, in part it may relate to American students' greater tendency to report earliest memories of single, distinctive events that involved greater emotionality, whereas Chinese students were more likely than Americans to report more routine events that involved collective activity. Other researchers also have found cross-cultural differences in age of earliest memories. When Shelley MacDonald and coworkers (2000) studied New Zealand European, New Zealand Asian, New Zealand Maori, and Chinese adults, they found that Maori adults—whose traditional culture strongly values the past—recalled the earliest personal memories.

IN REVIEW

- *Our schemas may cause us to remember events not as they actually occurred but in ways that fit with our preexisting concepts about the world.*
- *At times we may recall information that never occurred. Schemas, spreading activation, and priming are some of the reasons why this occurs.*
- *Misinformation effects occur when our memory is distorted by misleading postevent information, and they often occur because of source confusion—our tendency to recall something or recognize it as familiar but to forget where we encountered it.*
- *Like adults, children experience misinformation effects. Vulnerability is greatest among younger children and when suggestive questions are asked repeatedly. Experts cannot reliably tell when children are reporting accurate versus sincerely believed false memories.*
- *Psychologists debate whether recovered memories of child abuse are accurate and whether they are forgotten through repression or other psychological processes. Concern about the possibility of false memory has led many experts to urge caution in unconditionally accepting the validity of recovered memories.*

MEMORY AND THE BRAIN

Where in your brain are memories located? How were they formed? The quest for answers has taken some remarkable twists. Psychologist Karl Lashley spent decades searching for the *engram*—the physical trace that presumably was stored in the brain when a memory was formed. Lashley (1950) trained animals to perform tasks, such as running mazes, and later removed or damaged (lesioned) specific regions of their cortex to see if they would forget how to perform the task. No matter what small area was lesioned, memories remained intact. Lashley never found the engram and concluded that a memory is stored throughout the brain.

In contrast, while performing brain surgery on patients who were under local anesthesia and fully conscious, Wilder Penfield (Penfield & Percot, 1963) seemed to trigger memories when electrically stimulating specific sites on the patients' cerebral cortex. One patient reported seeing the office in which she had worked a long time ago. Unfortunately, such instances were rare and probably involved inaccurate, reconstructed information, such as images of being in places where the patients had never been (Loftus & Loftus, 1980).

Perhaps most striking was James McConnell's (1962) discovery of "memory transfer." He classically conditioned flatworms to a light that was paired with electric shock, eventually causing the worms to contract to the light alone. Next he chopped them up and fed the RNA (ribonucleic acid) from their cells to untrained worms. Amazingly, the untrained worms showed some conditioning to the light, suggesting that RNA might be a memory molecule that stores experiences. Some scientists replicated these findings, but others were unable to, and McConnell eventually gave up on the idea (Rilling, 1996). Yet, despite the inevitable dead ends, scientists have learned a great deal about memory processes in the brain.

Where Are Memories Located?

▶ 21. Describe brain structures involved in memory and how changes in neural circuitry may underlie memory formation.

To answer this question, scientists map the "geography" of memory. In *human lesion studies,* they examine memory loss caused by damage (e.g., from disease, accidents) to different brain regions. In *nonhuman animal lesion experiments,* researchers damage a specific part of the brain and observe how this affects memory. Finally, *brain-imaging studies* examine the healthy brain as participants perform various memory tasks. These lines of research increasingly reveal that memory involves

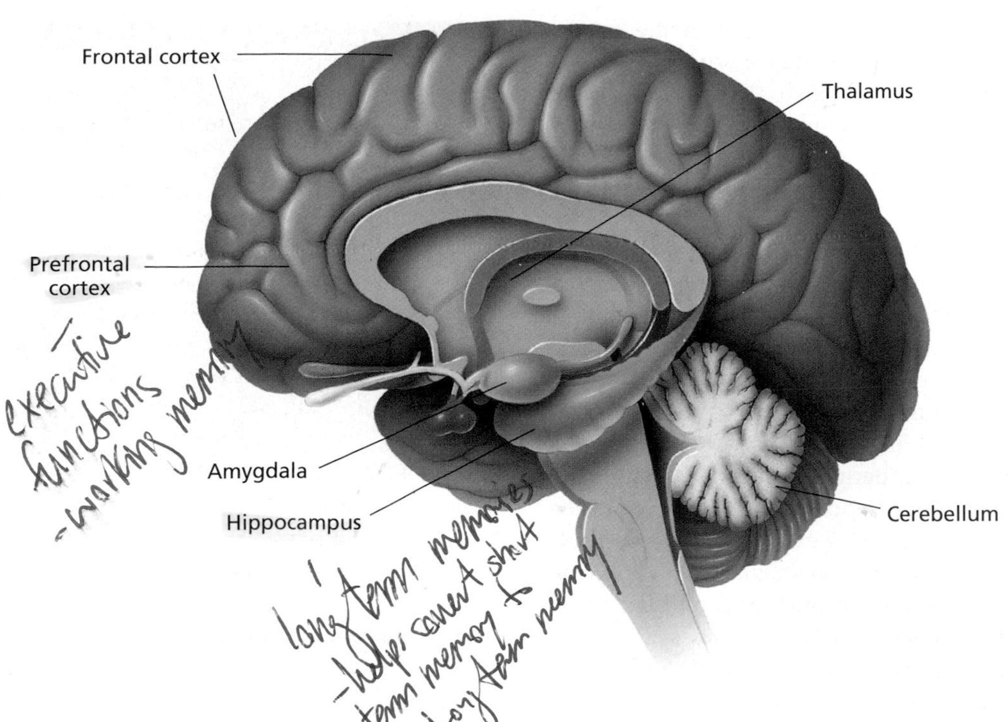

FIGURE 7.30

Many areas of the brain, such as the regions shown here, play key roles in memory.

many interacting brain regions (Nyberg et al., 2002). Figure 7.30 shows a few of these regions.

Sensory memory depends on our visual, auditory, and other sensory systems to detect stimulus information (e.g., the sounds of "Hi, my name is Carlos"), transform it into neural codes, and send it to the brain, where sensory areas of the cerebral cortex initially process it. As working memory becomes involved in different types of tasks—remembering a person's name and face or learning and rehearsing a concept in your textbook—a network of cortical areas located across different lobes of the brain becomes more active. Within this network, the frontal lobes—especially the prefrontal cortex—play a key role (Nyberg et al., 2002). They seem to be particularly important in supporting executive functions, such as allocating attention to the other components of working memory. The frontal lobes generally become more active during tasks that place greater demands on working memory (Gabrieli et al., 1996).

Where are long-term memories formed and stored? Once again, multiple brain areas are involved, but the hippocampus and its adjacent areas appear to play an important role in encoding certain types of long-term memories (Rolls, 2000). Like H. M., many patients with extensive hippocampal damage retain the use of their short-term memory but cannot form new, explicit long-term declarative memories—memories for new personal experiences and facts. For example, one patient could recall the names of presidents elected before his brain injury occurred but not the names of presidents elected after his injury (Squire, 1987). The hippocampus does not seem to be the site where long-term declarative memories are permanently stored, which is why H. M. retained his long-term memories acquired earlier in life. Rather, it helps to gradually convert short-term memories into permanent ones.

According to one view, the diverse components of an experience—where something happened, what the scene or people looked like, sounds we heard, the meaning of events or information, and so on—are processed initially in different regions of the cortex and then gradually "bound" together in the hippocampus (Squire & Zola-Morgan, 1991). *This hypothetical and gradual "binding" process is called* **memory consolidation.** Once a memory for a personal experience is consolidated, its various components appear to be stored across wide areas of the cortex, although we retrieve and reintegrate these components as a "unified memory." Semantic memories (factual information) also appear to be stored across wide-ranging areas of the brain. As John Gabrieli (1998) notes, "knowledge in any domain [e.g., for pictures or words] . . . is distributed over a specific, but extensive, neural network that often extends over several lobes" (p. 94). Several brain regions, including portions of the prefrontal cortex and hippocampus, appear to be involved in consciously retrieving declarative memories (LePage et al., 1998; Tulving, 2002).

Although we have focused on the frontal lobes and hippocampus, memory formation also depends on other brain areas. For example, damage to the thalamus can produce severe amnesia, although we are not sure why this happens. In one famous case, a young U.S. Air Force technician named N. A. was injured in a freak accident (Squire, 1987). While his roommate was practicing thrusts with a miniature fencing foil, N. A. suddenly turned around in his seat and was stabbed through the right nostril, piercing his brain and damaging a portion of his thalamus. The damage permanently limited his ability to form new declarative memories. In many cases, thalamic damage also can cause permanent retrograde amnesia.

The amygdala appears to encode emotionally arousing aspects of events (Rodrigues et al., 2002). In laboratory experiments, most people remember emotionally arousing stimuli (e.g., film clips, slides) better than neutral ones. But damage to the amygdala would eliminate much of this "memory advantage" from arousing stimuli (LaBar & Phelps, 1998).

Finally, along with other parts of the brain, the cerebellum plays an important role in forming procedural memories. This helps to explain why H. M., whose cerebellum was not damaged by the operation, showed improved performance at various hand-eye coordination tasks (e.g., mirror-tracing) even though he was unable to consciously remember having performed the tasks.

Richard Thompson (1985) and coworkers have examined another type of procedural memory. Studying rabbits, they repeatedly paired a tone (CS) with a puff of air to the eyes (UCS), and soon the tone alone caused the rabbits to blink. As the rabbits learned this conditioned response, electrical recordings revealed increased electrical activity in the cerebellum. Later Thompson found that removing a tiny portion of the cerebellum completely abolished the memory for the *conditioned* eyeblink but did not affect the rabbits' general (unconditioned) eyeblink response. Similarly, eyeblink conditioning fails to work with human patients who have damaged a cerebellum (Green & Woodruff, 2000).

How Are Memories Formed?

How does the nervous system form a memory? The answer appears to lie in chemical and physical changes that take place in the brain's neural circuitry.

Eric Kandel (2001) and his coworkers have studied a marine snail, *Aplysia californica,* for over 25 years—work for which Kandel received a Nobel Prize in 2000. *Aplysia* is no mental giant, but it can learn, form memories, and has only about 20,000 neurons (compared with our 100 billion) that are larger and easier to study than ours (Figure 7.31). For example, *Aplysia* retracts its gill slightly in self-defense when a breathing organ atop the gill is gently squirted with water. But if a squirt is paired with electric shock to its tail, *Aplysia* covers up its gill with a protective flap of skin. After repeated pairings, *Aplysia* acquires a classically conditioned response and will cover its gills with the protective flap when the water is squirted alone. In other words, *Aplysia* forms a simple procedural memory.

FIGURE 7.31

The marine snail Aplysia californica.

Kandel and his coworkers have traced the formation of this procedural memory to a series of biochemical events that occur between and within various sensory neurons and motor neurons. How long these events last seems to be one key in determining whether short-term memories become long-term ones. If a single shock is paired with the squirt of water, certain chemical reactions "shut off" after a brief period and no permanent memory is formed. But with repeated pairings, these chemical reactions persist and a long-term memory forms. Days later, a squirt of water will still trigger a conditioned response.

During the conditioning procedure, various sensory neurons become densely packed with neurotransmitter release points, and postsynaptic motor neurons (which cause the protective flap to retract) develop more receptor sites. These structural changes result in a greater ease of synaptic transmission that may be the basis for memory consolidation (Abel & Kandel, 1998).

A different line of research, involving rats and other species with more complex nervous systems,

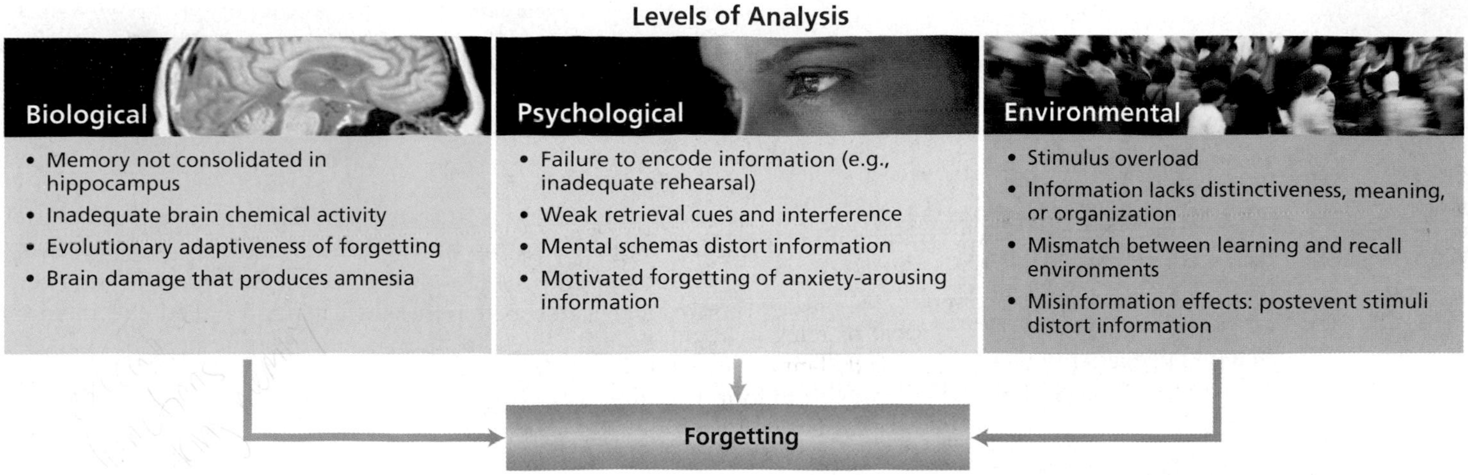

Levels of Analysis

Biological	Psychological	Environmental
• Memory not consolidated in hippocampus • Inadequate brain chemical activity • Evolutionary adaptiveness of forgetting • Brain damage that produces amnesia	• Failure to encode information (e.g., inadequate rehearsal) • Weak retrieval cues and interference • Mental schemas distort information • Motivated forgetting of anxiety-arousing information	• Stimulus overload • Information lacks distinctiveness, meaning, or organization • Mismatch between learning and recall environments • Misinformation effects: postevent stimuli distort information

Forgetting

FIGURE 7.32

Understanding Behavior: Some factors that contribute to forgetting.

supports this hypothesis. Here, researchers try to mimic (albeit very crudely) a process of long-term memory formation by stimulating specific neural pathways with rapid bursts of electricity (say, 100 impulses per second for several seconds). They find that once this rapid stimulation ends, the neural pathway becomes stronger—synaptic connections are activated more easily—for days or even weeks (Martinez et al., 1998). *This enduring increase in synaptic strength is called* **long-term potentiation (LTP).** LTP has been studied most extensively in regions of the hippocampus where neurons send and receive glutamate, the most abundant neurotransmitter in the brain.

For LTP to occur, certain biochemical events must take place inside and between these neurons. Administering drugs that inhibit these events will block LTP. Moreover, mice can be genetically bred to be deficient in certain proteins required for LTP. These mice not only have impaired long-term potentiation but also display memory deficits on a variety of learning tasks (Rotenberg et al., 2000).

How, then, does LTP occur? At least in some cases, it appears that when neural pathways are sufficiently stimulated, the postsynaptic neurons alter their structure so that they become more responsive to glutamate. For example, postsynaptic neurons may change the shape of some receptor sites, or they may increase the number of receptor sites by developing additional tiny branches (spines) on their dendrites. This means that in the future, presynaptic neurons will not need to release as much glutamate in order to stimulate postsynaptic neurons to fire. In sum, the formation of a long-term memory seems to involve long-lasting changes in synaptic efficiency that result from new or enhanced connections between presynaptic and postsynaptic neurons (Kandel, 2001).

In closing, we hope that this chapter has piqued your interest in understanding why we remember, forget, and sometimes misremember. Figure 7.32 summarizes some factors involved in forgetting and memory distortion. We also hope that the chapter has applied value for you. Following the *In Review* summary, our *Applying Psychological Science* feature summarizes some ways to enhance your own memory and academic learning.

IN REVIEW

- *Memory involves numerous interacting brain regions. Sensory memory depends on input from our sensory systems and sensory areas of the cortex that initially process this information.*
- *Working memory involves a network of brain regions. The frontal lobes play a key role in performing the executive functions of working memory.*
- *The hippocampus helps consolidate long-term declarative memories. The cerebral cortex stores declarative memories across distributed sites.*
- *The amygdala encodes emotionally arousing aspects of events, and the cerebellum helps form procedural memories. Damage to the thalamus can produce severe amnesia.*
- *Research with sea snails and studies of long-term potentiation in other species indicate that as memories form, complex chemical and structural changes occur in neurons that enhance synaptic efficiency.*

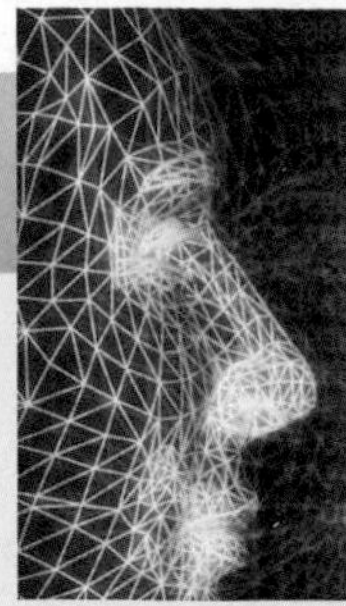

APPLYING PSYCHOLOGICAL SCIENCE

IMPROVING MEMORY AND ACADEMIC LEARNING

There are no magical or effortless ways to enhance memory, but psychological research offers many principles that you can put to your advantage. Memory enhancement strategies fall into three broad categories:

- *external aids,* such as shopping lists, notes, and appointment calendars;
- *general memory strategies,* such as organizing and rehearsing information; and
- *formal mnemonic techniques,* such as acronyms, the method of loci, and other systems that take training to be used effectively.

Memory researchers strongly recommend using external aids and general strategies to enhance memory (Park et al., 1990). Of course, during "closed-book" college exams, external aids may land you in the Dean's office! The following principles can enhance memory.

Use Elaborative Rehearsal to Process Information Deeply

Elaborative rehearsal—focusing on the meaning of information—enhances deep processing and memory (Benjamin & Bjork, 2000). Put simply, *if you are trying to commit information to memory, make sure that you understand what it means.* You may think we're daffy for stating such an obvious point, but many students try to learn material by rote memorization rather than by making an effort to understand it. Students who find material confusing sometimes try to bypass their confusion with rote memorization—an approach that often fails—whereas they should be seeking assistance to have the material explained. The learning objectives and practice tests that appear in the Online Learning Center (OLC) can help you process the course material more deeply by helping you focus on and think about key points.

Link New Information to Examples and Items Already in Memory

Once you understand the material, process it more deeply by associating it with information you already know. This creates memory "hooks" onto which you can hang new information. Because you already have many memorable life experiences, *make new information personally meaningful* by relating it to your life.

Pay attention to examples, even if they are unrelated to your own experiences. In one study, participants read a 32-paragraph essay about a fictitious African nation. Each paragraph presented a topic sentence stating a main theme along with zero, one, two, or three examples illustrating that theme. The greater the number of examples, the better the participants recalled the themes (Palmere et al., 1983).

Organize Information

Organizing information keeps you actively thinking about the material and makes it more meaningful. Before reading a chapter, look at its outline or headings to determine how the material is logically developed. When studying, take notes from a chapter and use outlining to organize the information. This hierarchical structure forces you to arrange main ideas above subordinate ones and becomes an additional retrieval cue that facilitates recall (Bower et al., 1969).

Use Imagery

As dual coding theory predicts, images provide a splendid additional "cognitive hook" on which to hang and retrieve information (Paivio et al., 2000). Instead of writing down customers' orders, some restaurant waiters and waitresses form images, such as visualizing a man who has ordered a margarita turning light green. As one waitress remarked, "After a while, customers start looking like drinks" (Bennett, 1983, p. 165). Be creative. For example, to help you remember that flashbulb memories often are less accurate than people think, imagine a camera flashbulb with a big red X through it.

Overlearn the Material

Overlearning *refers to continued rehearsal past the point of initial learning, and it significantly improves performance on memory tasks* (Driskell et al., 1992). Moreover, much of this memory boost persists for a long time after overlearning ends. In short, just as elite athletes keep practicing their already honed skills and professional actors continue to rehearse scripts they already know, keep studying material after you have first learned it (Noice & Noice, 2002a).

Distribute Learning Over Time and Test Yourself

You have finished the readings and organized your notes for an upcoming test. Now it's time to study and review. Are you better off with *massed practice,* a marathon session of highly concentrated learning, or with *distributed practice,* several shorter sessions spread out over a few days? Research indicates that you will retain more information with distributed practice, and that periodically testing yourself on the material before an exam can further enhance learning (Cull, 2000). Distributed practice can reduce fatigue and anxiety, both of which impair learning. Testing yourself ahead of time (e.g., using practice items, if available, or questions such as those in the margin of this textbook) helps you to further rehearse the material and to identify content that you don't understand.

Minimize Interference

Distributed practice is effective because rest periods between study sessions reduce interference from competing material. However, when you need to study for several exams on the same or consecutive days, there really are few rest periods. There is no simple solution to this problem. Suppose you have a psychology exam on Thursday and a sociology exam on Friday. Try to arrange several sessions of distributed practice for each exam over the preceding week. On Wednesday, limit your studying to psychology if possible. Once your psychology exam is over, return your attention to studying sociology. This way, the final study period for each course will occur as close as possible to test time and minimize interference from other cognitive activities.

Studying before you go to sleep may enhance retention by temporarily minimizing interference, but if you are carrying a typical college course load, you will likely have to contend with interference much of the time. This is why overlearning is so important, and why you are advised to study the material beyond the point where you feel you have learned it.

▶ 22. Identify practical principles for enhancing memory.

KEY TERMS AND CONCEPTS

Each term has been boldfaced and defined in the chapter on the page indicated in parentheses.

What Do You Think?

WOULD PERFECT MEMORY BE A GIFT OR A CURSE? p. 251

No doubt, perfect memory would have advantages, but were you able to think of any liabilities? Russian newspaper reporter S. V. Shereshevski—arguably the most famous mnemonist in history—had a remarkable capacity to remember numbers, poems in foreign languages, complex mathematical formulas, nonsense syllables, and sounds. Psychologist Aleksandr Luria (1968), who studied "S." for decades, describes how S. was tyrannized by his seeming inability to forget meaningless information. Almost any stimulus might unleash a flood of trivial memories that dominated S.'s consciousness and made it difficult for him to concentrate or think abstractly.

S.'s experience may have been atypical, but perfect memory could indeed clutter up our thinking with trivial information. Moreover, perfect memory would deprive us of one of life's blessings: the ability to forget unpleasant experiences from our past. As illustrated in this chapter, *imperfect* memory allows us to view our past through slightly rosy glasses (Bahrick et al., 1996).

Would a perfect memory help you perform better on exams? On test questions calling only for definitions, formulas, or facts, probably so. But on questions asking you to apply concepts, synthesize ideas, analyze issues, and so forth, perfect memory might be of little benefit unless you also understood the material. In his graduate school classes,

> Rajan had a tendency to try to commit the reading assignments to memory and reproduce them on tests. The strategy . . . is counterproductive in graduate courses where students are asked to apply their knowledge and understanding to new situations. . . . When taking tests, Rajan would write furiously . . . in hopes that the correct answer was somewhere in his response. . . . As he progressed in our graduate program, he tended to rely less on the strategy of memorizing everything and more on trying to understand and organize the information. (Thompson et al.,1993, p. 15)

Rajan's extraordinary memory for numbers did not extend to reading or visual tasks, but even if yours did, it still might tempt you to focus too heavily on sheer memorization and cause you to neglect paying attention to the meaning of the material. In sum, although imperfect memory can be frustrating and cause important problems (as when eyewitnesses identify the wrong suspect), we should also appreciate how our memory system is balanced between the adaptiveness of remembering and the benefits of forgetting.

(By the way, in case you're curious, the current record for recalling pi is 42,195 digits. In 1999, Sim Pohann of Malaysia recalled 67,053 digits but, alas, he made 15 errors. To put this feat in perspective, imagine the next 12 pages of this textbook filled up with nothing but numbers!) ■

IS IT REALLY ON THE TIP OF YOUR TONGUE? p. 262

Please try to answer the following questions:

- What is the name of the only kind of living reptile that flies?
- What is the name of the only type of cat native to Australia?
- What is the name of the planet Mercury's moon?

Did you feel like the answer to any of these questions was on the tip of your tongue? If you didn't, that's OK. We just want to illustrate some of the questions that Bennett Schwartz (1998) asked college students in a clever TOT study.

Schwartz asked students 100 questions, but 20 of them—like the ones above—were unanswerable (e.g., Mercury has no moon). If there was no correct answer, then students could not have a true retrieval problem, because there was no stored information to retrieve. Yet nearly one fifth of the time, students felt that the answer was on the tip of their tongue when they were contemplating these questions. Schwartz obtained similar findings in another experiment.

Schwartz calls these experiences "illusory TOT states": People feel that the answer is on the tip of their tongue when it can't possibly be. Illusory TOT states raise complex issues about the nature of memory, but for the moment, let's just focus on a simple point. Sometimes, when we feel that an answer is on the tip of our tongue, the cause may not be an inability to retrieve information stored in long-term memory, but rather it may be that the information never got stored in the first place. In other words, whether due to encoding failure (we've encountered the information but didn't process it adequately) or some other reason, we really may not know the answer, although we think we do. This may help explain why we never resolve some of our TOT states and often turn to other people or reference books to help find an answer.

If you're curious, try reading the three questions above to several friends (give them time to think about each question). Don't expect to trigger a lot of illusory TOT states, but even eliciting one or two would provide an interesting demonstration. Afterward, be sure to let them know that the questions are unanswerable (so they won't keep thinking about them!) and explain the purpose of the exercise. ■

8

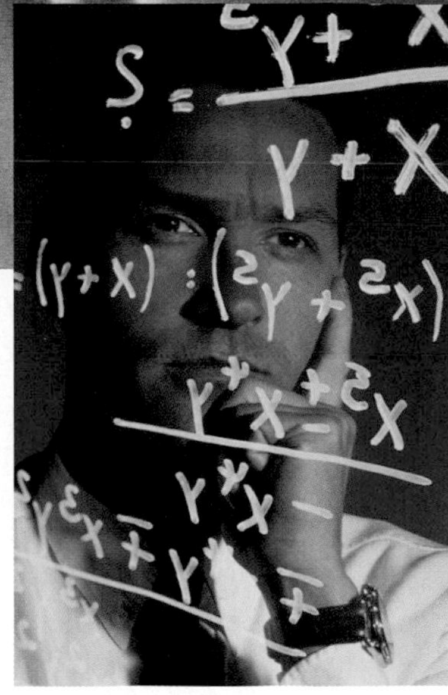

LANGUAGE, THINKING, AND INTELLIGENT BEHAVIOR

CHAPTER OUTLINE

"A moment's insight is sometimes worth a life's experience."

—Oliver Wendell Holmes

For the crew and passengers of United Airlines Flight 118, the skies over Hawaii were about to become the scene of a terrifying test of human resourcefulness, with survival at stake. On a routine flight 20,000 feet above the Pacific Ocean, the unthinkable happened. With an explosive popping of rivets and a shriek of tearing metal, part of the surface at the front of the plane suddenly ripped away from the rest of the aircraft, leaving the flight deck and forward passenger compartments exposed to the air. Inside, terrified passengers and flight attendants quite literally hung on for dear life as gale-force winds swirled through the cabin and the plane threatened to spin out of control.

The sudden change in the aerodynamics of the plane meant that it could not be flown normally. The captain, an experienced pilot, needed to develop a mental model of the plane in its altered form to keep it from plunging into the ocean. Thanks to his flight experience and his knowledge of the principles under which the aircraft normally responded to its controls, the captain quickly recognized what needed to be done, formulated a plan for doing it, and then executed the appropriate actions. Unable to communicate with one another verbally because of the noise from the engines and the roar of the wind, the captain and the first officer used hand signals to coordinate their activities. Through perfect teamwork, they landed the aircraft safely at an auxiliary airfield (Figure 8.1), a feat labeled by one aeronautical engineer as "astonishing."

FIGURE 8.1

The successful landing of United Airlines Flight 118 was a tribute to the power of human reasoning, language, and problem solving.

Incidents like this one illustrate the power of human reasoning, communication, and problem solving—cognitive skills that underlie adaptive behavior. Yet as we shall see, the basic mental operations and communication procedures the aviators used to deal with this life-and-death challenge were really no different from many of the reasoning, problem-solving, and linguistic activities that we engage in each day.

Although human beings are physically puny and relatively defenseless in comparison with some other species, we dominate our world because we think better and communicate more effectively than other animals do. Humans have remarkable abilities to create "mental representations" of the world and to manipulate them in the forms of language, thinking, reasoning, and problem solving (Simon, 1990). **Mental representations** *take a variety of forms, including images, ideas, concepts, and principles.* At this very moment, through the printed words you are reading, mental representations are being transferred from our minds to yours. Indeed, the process of education is all about transferring ideas and skills from one mind to another.

Much of our thinking involves the use of language, and intelligent behavior is a product of thinking. Thus language, thinking, and intelligent behavior are intimately connected with one another. These advanced cognitive processes build upon the large store of knowledge that resides in memory and upon our ability to learn, yet they also enable us to go beyond what we have previously learned to create novel mental products.

LANGUAGE

According to anthropologists who have studied the skulls of prehistoric humans, the brain probably achieved its present form some 50,000 years ago (Churchland, 2002; Pilbeam, 1984). Yet it took another 35,000 years before lifelike paintings began to appear on cave walls and another 12,000 years after that before humans developed a way to store knowledge outside the brain in the form of writing (Kottak, 2000). These time lags tell us that human thought and behavior depend on more than the physical structure of the brain; although the structure of the brain may not have evolved much over the past 50,000 years, human cognitive skills clearly have.

Language, which has at various times been called "the jewel in the crown of cognition" (Pinker, 2000) and "the human essence" (Chomsky, 1972), may be the most important of our cognitive skills. Evolutionary theorists believe that language evolved as humans gathered to form larger social units. The ability to form cooperative social systems, develop social customs, communicate thoughts to others, create divisions of labor, and pass on knowledge and wisdom were made easier by the development of language (Bjorklund & Pellegrini, 2002). Given the enormous adaptive value of language for the emerging human way of life, it is not surprising that the human brain developed an inborn capacity to acquire any of the thousands of languages that are spoken throughout the world (Figure 8.2).

S. Harris
"GOT IDEA. TALK BETTER. COMBINE WORDS. MAKE SENTENCES."

FIGURE 8.2

According to many theorists, the development of language was a major milestone in the human evolutionary process.
© 2004 by Sidney Harris.

The Nature and Structure of Language

Language *consists of a system of symbols and rules for combining these symbols in ways that can generate an infinite number of possible messages or meanings.* This definition encompasses three critical properties that are essential to any language.

First, language is *symbolic.* It uses sounds, written signs, or gestures to refer to objects, events, ideas, and feelings. Language allows communicators to form and then transfer mental representations to the mind of another person. Thus you can tell another person about your house, what you did last week, your plans after graduation, and how you feel. The linguistic feature of **displacement** *refers to the fact that past, future, and imaginary events and objects that are not physically present can be symbolically represented and communicated through the medium of language.* Language thus helps free us from being restricted to the present.

Second, language has a *rule-governed structure.* Specific rules dictate how symbols can be combined to create meaningful communication units. Thus if we ask you whether or not *zpflrovc* is an English word, you will almost certainly say that it is not. Why? Because it violates rules of the English language; *z* is not to be followed by *pf,* and five consonants cannot be combined. Likewise, you would not consider the string of words *Bananas have sale for I no* an appropriate English sentence. You may not be able to verbalize the formal rules of English that are violated in these examples, but you know them implicitly because they are part of the language you speak. Although language evolves, with new words appearing regularly, new words and new phrases always conform to the basic rules of that language.

▶ 1. Identify the three properties common to human language. Differentiate between surface structure and deep structure.

Third, language is *generative.* This means that its symbols can be combined to generate an infinite number of messages that have novel meaning. Thus you can create and understand a sentence like "Who put the nightingale under my strudel?" even though you are unlikely to have heard anything like it before. Indeed, in reading that sentence, you may have formed a mental representation (most likely an image) of that unlikely scene, illustrating the concept of displacement.

Surface Structure and Deep Structure

Psycholinguists, who study the psychological properties of language and the underlying mechanisms that produce it, describe language as having both a surface structure and a deep structure. The **surface structure** *consists of the way symbols are combined within a given language.* The rules for such combination are called the **syntax** (*rules of grammar*) of a language. Thus the "banana" sentence just discussed violates English grammatic rules.

Deep structure *refers to the underlying meaning of the combined symbols. The rules for connecting the*

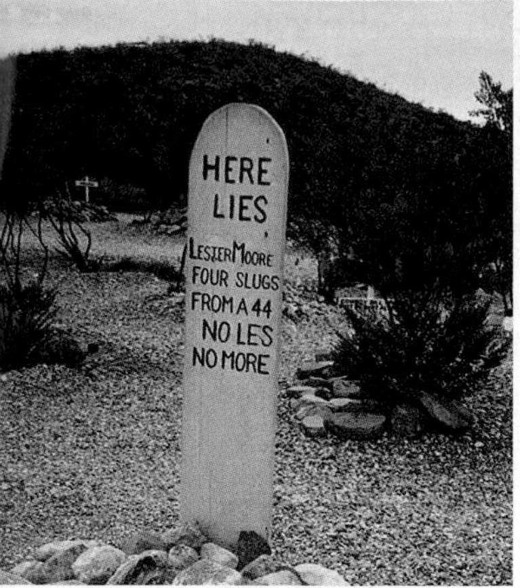

FIGURE 8.3

This grave marker in Boothill Graveyard illustrates an interesting relation between surface structure and deep structure.

symbols to what they represent are known as **semantics.** To distinguish surface structure from deep structure, consider the following sentences (the first taken from an actual high school essay):

- The toy boat floated across the pond, exactly as a bowling ball wouldn't.
- In contrast to what a bowling ball would do, the toy boat floated across the pond.
- The police must stop drinking after midnight.

The first two sentences have different surface structures, but they share the same deep structure; they have different syntax but similar semantic meaning. Either way, the little boat stayed afloat. The third sentence is an ambiguous one that can be interpreted as having two different deep structures, one relating to the enforcement of liquor laws by the police, the other to the personal conduct of police officers.

The rules for surface structure and deep structure are both stored in long-term semantic memory. However, when we recall something, we are likely to retrieve deep structure (meaning) rather than the specific words. That's why you can often recall the meaning of what someone said or wrote without being able to reconstruct the exact words they used.

When we read or when someone speaks to us, understanding requires that we move from surface structure to the meaning level of deep structure. In contrast, expressing our thoughts to others involves transforming deep structure (the meaning we want to communicate) into a surface structure that others can understand. Eloquent speakers and writers have the ability to convert their deep-structure meanings into pleasing surface-structure expressions.

? *What Do You Think?*

DISCERNING SURFACE AND DEEP STRUCTURES OF LANGUAGE

Figure 8.3 shows a grave marker in the Boothill Graveyard in Tombstone, Arizona, where many notorious outlaws and gunfighters were buried. Analyze the marker carefully in relation to what you have learned about surface structure and deep structure. Think about it, then see page 324.

Language From the Bottom Up

▶ 2. What are phonemes and morphemes? Where do they fit in the hierarchy of language?

Human language has a hierarchical structure, and its most elementary building block is the phoneme. **Phonemes** *are the smallest units of sound that are recognized as separate in a given language.* Phonemes have no inherent meaning, but they alter meaning when combined with other elements. For example, the *d* phoneme creates a different meaning from the *l* phoneme when it precedes *og* (i.e., *dog* versus *log*). Linguists have identified about 100 phonemes that humans can produce, including the clicking sounds used in some African languages, but no language uses all of these sounds. The world's languages vary considerably in phonemes, some employing as few as 15 and others more than 80. English uses about 40 phonemes, consisting of the various vowel and consonant sounds, as well as certain letter combinations such as *th* and *sh*. Thus the sounds *h*, *a*, and *t* can be combined to form the three-phoneme word *hat*.

At the next level of the hierarchy, phonemes are combined into **morphemes,** *the smallest units of meaning in a language.* Morphemes consist of a single syllable. Thus *hat*, *sick*, and *ball* are all morphemes, as are prefixes and suffixes such as *pre-*, *un-*, *-ed*, and *-ous*. The suffix *-ous* is formed from two phonemes, *uh* and *s*. In every language, rules of syntax determine how phonemes can be combined into morphemes. English's 40 phonemes can be combined into more than 100,000 morphemes.

Morphemes, in turn, are the stuff of which words are formed. English morphemes can be combined into nearly 500,000 words, words into countless phrases, and phrases into an infinite number of sentences. Thus from the humble phoneme to the elegant sentence, we have a five-step language hierarchy (Figure 8.4). Beyond this basic hierarchy lies the sixth and most comprehensive level, that of **discourse,** *in which sentences are combined into paragraphs, articles, books, conversations, and so forth.*

Acquiring a Language

Language acquisition is one of the most striking events in human cognitive development. It represents the joint influences of biology (nature) and environment (nurture). Many language experts believe that humans are born linguists, inheriting a biological readiness to recognize and eventually produce the sounds and structure of whatever language they are exposed to through a process of social learning (Chomsky, 1965; Pinker 1994).

Biological Foundations

Several facts suggest a biological basis for language acquisition. First, human children, despite

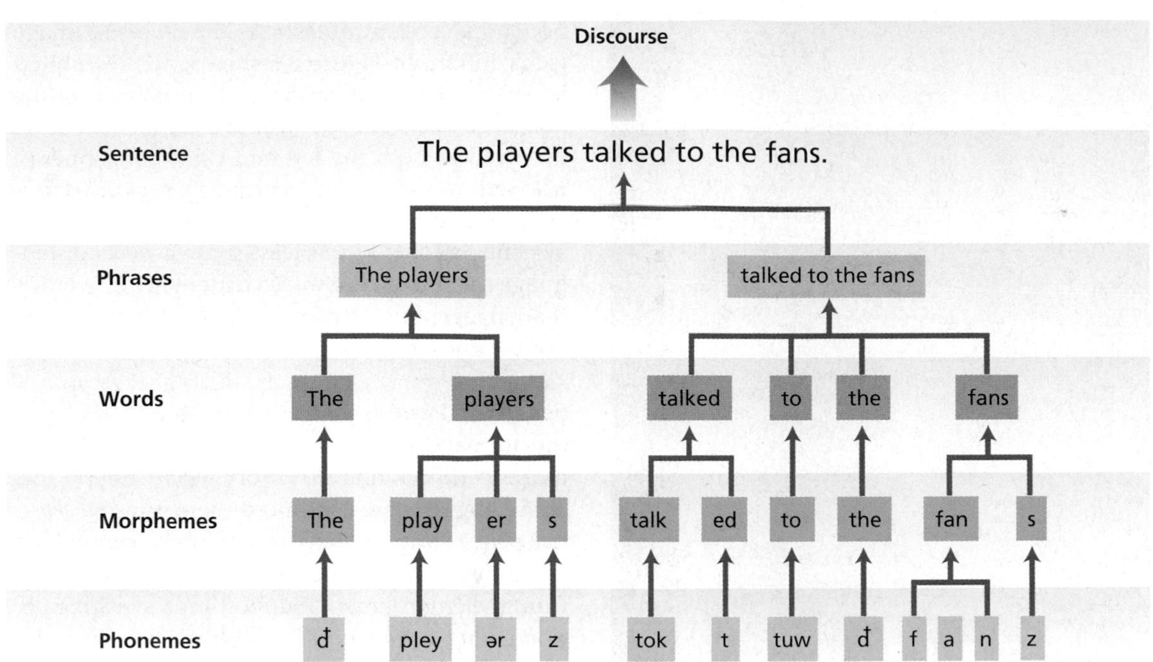

FIGURE 8.4

Human language is structured hierarchically, with phonemes being the most basic unit. The row of phonemes contains symbols used by linguists to denote particular sounds.

their limited thinking skills, begin to master language early in life without any formal instruction. Moreover, despite their differences at the phoneme level, all adult languages throughout the world—including sign languages for the deaf that developed independently in different parts of the world—seem to have common underlying structural characteristics (Anderson & Lightfoot, 1999). Language acquisition thus represents the unfolding of a biologically primed process within a social learning environment (Aitchison, 1998; Chomsky, 1987).

Whether born in Toledo, Taiwan, or Tanzania, young infants vocalize the entire range of phonemes found in the world's languages. At about 6 months of age, however, they begin to make only those sounds that are specific to their native tongue and abandon those of other languages. For example, Japanese children lose the ability to distinguish between the *r* and *l* sounds because their language does not make this phonetic distinction, but children exposed to English continue to discriminate these sounds from an early age. Likewise, Japanese-speaking children learn the syntactic rule to put the object before the verb ("Ichiro the ball hit"), whereas English-speaking children learn the syntactic rule that the verb comes before the object ("Ichiro hit the ball"). The linguist Noam Chomsky (1987) proposed that humans are born with a **language acquisition device (LAD),** *an innate biological mechanism that contains the general grammatical rules (which he terms "universal grammar") common to all languages.* Among the principles inherent in LAD are that languages contain such things as noun phrases and verb phrases that are arranged in particular ways, such as subjects, predicates, and adjectives. Chomsky likened LAD to a huge electrical panel with banks of linguistic switches that are thrown as children hear the words and syntax of their native language. For example, for a child learning to speak English, the "switch" that indicates whether to insert a pronoun before a verb (as in "*I* want") is set to "yes." But in Spanish, the same switch is set to "no," for the applicable verb (in this case, *deseo*) already includes the first person singular and inserting a pronoun is not necessary. In this manner, universal grammar becomes calibrated to the grammar and syntax of one's native tongue.

▶ 3. Describe how biological, maturational, and social learning factors are involved in language acquisition. What sex difference exists in language functions within the brain?

Sex Differences Language functions are distributed in diverse areas of the brain, but the regions shown in Figure 8.5 are especially significant. As discussed in Chapter 3, Broca's area, located in the left hemisphere's frontal lobe, is involved in speech production (lower right brain scan). Wernicke's area, in the rear portion of the temporal lobe, is involved in speech comprehension (upper left scan). People with damage in one or both areas suffer from *aphasia*, a disruption in speech comprehension and/or production. The visual area is also involved in recognizing written words.

Years ago, scientists noted that men who suffer left hemisphere strokes are more likely than women to show severe aphasic symptoms. In female stroke

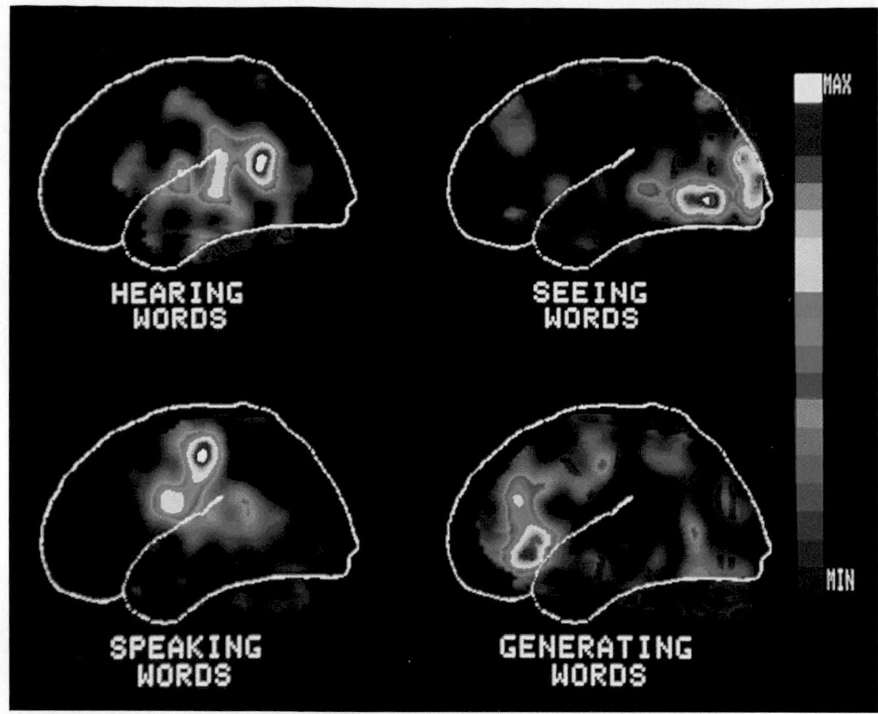

FIGURE 8.5

Different brain areas are involved in various aspects of language. Regions of white, red, and yellow show the greatest activity. Broca's area, located in the frontal lobe below the motor cortex, is important in speech production (generating words). Wernicke's area, in the temporal lobe, is important in speech comprehension (hearing words). Damage to these areas can produce aphasia, a disruption in speech comprehension and/or production.

victims with left hemisphere damage, language functions are more likely to be spared, suggesting that more of their language function is shared with the right hemisphere.

Recent brain imaging research by Susan Rossell and coworkers (2002) supports this hypothesis. In their study, men and women engaged in a language task in which words and nonwords were presented on each side of a computer screen. Participants had to identify which was the real word as quickly as possible by pressing one of two computer keys. Functional MRIs (fMRIs) were recorded during the task and during a nonlanguage control task. As the reversed image (see caption) in Figure 8.6 shows, men exhibited left-hemisphere activation (red areas) during the language task, whereas women's brain activation occurred in both the left and right hemispheres. Maximum activation occurred in regions corresponding to Broca's and Wernicke's areas. Neural systems involved in at least some aspects of language seem to be organized differently in women than in men, but the reasons for the differences are not yet known (Gleason & Ely, 2002).

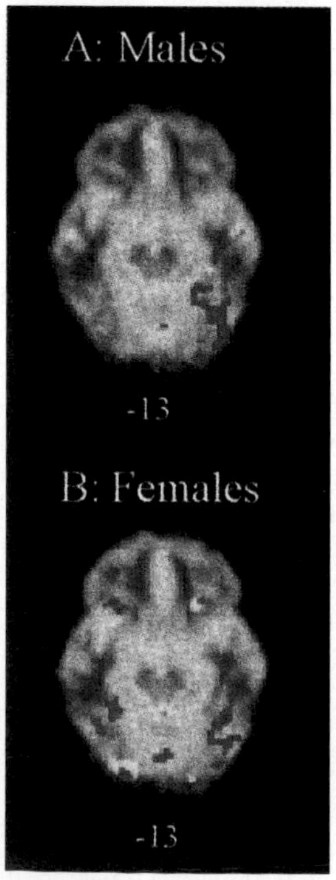

FIGURE 8.6

Sex differences in brain activation during a language task as shown by fMRI. Activation is shown in the red areas. The image is reversed, as if taken from below the brain, so that the activation in males is actually in the left hemisphere. Females' activation patterns are distributed in corresponding areas of both hemispheres, indicating less lateralization of language functions. The yellow activation patterns occurred in response to a nonlanguage control task.
SOURCE: Rossell et al., 2002.

Sensitive Periods In Chapter 4 we saw how the normal development of perceptual abilities requires certain kinds of sensory input early in life. Some linguists are convinced there is also a *sensitive period* from infancy to puberty during which the brain is most responsive to language input from the environment. Support for a sensitive period comes from studies of children who lived by themselves in the wild or who were isolated from human contact by deranged parents. One such child, found when she was 6 years old, immediately received language training and seemed to develop normal language abilities (Brown, 1958). In contrast, language-deprived children who were found when they were past puberty seemed unable to acquire normal language skills despite extensive training (Clarke & Clarke, 2000; Curtiss, 1977).

The importance of early language exposure applies to any language, not just spoken language. Because sign languages share the deep structure characteristics of spoken languages, deaf children who learn sign language before puberty develop normal linguistic and cognitive abilities even though they never hear a spoken word (Marschark & Mayer, 1998). In contrast, deaf people who are not exposed to sign language before age 12 show a distinct language-learning deficit even at age 30 (Meier, 1991).

Social Learning Processes

Given the required biological foundation, social learning plays a central role in acquiring a language (Kramsch, 2003). Early on, mothers and fathers attract their children's attention and maintain their interest by conversing with them in what has been termed *motherese,* a high-pitched intonation that seems to be used all over the world (Fernald et al., 1989). Parents also teach their children words by pointing out objects and naming them, by reading aloud to them, and by responding to the never-ending question, "What dat?" (Figure 8.7).

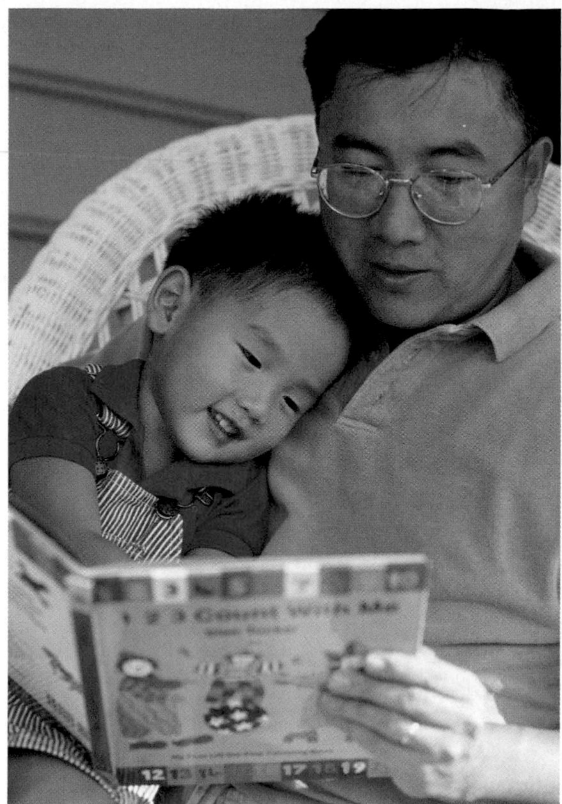

FIGURE 8.7

Language development depends not only on the brain's biological programming device but also on exposure to one's language. Childhood is an important sensitive period for such exposure.

TABLE 8.1 Course of Normal Language Development in Children

Age	Speech Characteristics
1–3 months	Infant can distinguish speech from nonspeech sounds and prefers speech sounds (phonemes). Undifferentiated crying gives way to cooing when happy.
4–6 months	Babbling sounds begin to occur. These contain sounds from virtually every language. Child vocalizes in response to verbalizations of others.
7–11 months	Babbling sounds narrow to include only the phonemes heard in the languages spoken by others in the environment. Child moves tongue with vocalizations ("lalling"). Child discriminates between some words without understanding their meaning and begins to imitate word sounds heard from others.
12 months	First recognizable words typically spoken as one-word utterances to name familiar people and objects (e.g., *da-da* or *block*).
12–18 months	Child increases knowledge of word meanings and begins to use single words to express whole phrases or requests (e.g., *out* to express a desire to get out of the crib); primarily uses nouns.
18–24 months	Vocabulary expands to between 50 and 100 words. First rudimentary sentences appear, usually consisting of two words (e.g., *more milk*) with little or no use of articles (*the*, *a*), conjunctions (*and*), or auxiliary verbs (*can*, *will*). This condensed, or telegraphic, speech is characteristic of first sentences throughout the world.
2–4 years	Vocabulary expands rapidly at the rate of several hundred words every 6 months. Two-word sentences give way to longer sentences that, though often grammatically incorrect, exhibit basic language syntax. Child begins to express concepts with words and to use language to describe imaginary objects and ideas. Sentences become more correct syntactically.
4–5 years	Child has learned the basic grammatical rules for combining nouns, adjectives, articles, conjunctions, and verbs into meaningful sentences.

The behaviorist B. F. Skinner (1957) developed an operant conditioning explanation for language acquisition. His basic premise was that children's language development is strongly governed by adults' positive reinforcement of appropriate language and nonreinforcement or correction of inappropriate verbalizations. However, most modern psycholinguists doubt that operant learning principles alone can account for language development. For one thing, children learn too much too fast. By 30 months of age, they already have learned several hundred words. By age 6, children are learning an average of more than 15 words per day, and their vocabularies have grown to between 8,000 and 14,000 words (Carey, 1977; Smith, 1926). Moreover, observational studies have shown that parents do *not* typically correct their children's grammar as language skills are developing. Rather, parents' corrections focus primarily on the "truth value" (or deep structure) of what the child is trying to communicate. Thus they are less likely to correct a young child who says, "I have two foots," than they are to correct one who says, "I have four feet," even though the latter statement is grammatically correct (Brown, 1973). As this point also shows, much of children's language is very different from that of their parents, and thus it can't be explained simply as an imitative process. Nonetheless, social learning is a crucial contributor to language acquisition, and the interplay between biological and environmental factors is a given for most modern theorists. Psychologist Jerome Bruner (1983) proposed that *the social environment provides a* **language acquisition support system (LASS)** *that facilitates the learning of a language.* One could say that when LAD and LASS interact in a mutually supportive fashion, normal language development occurs.

As biological factors (including the maturation of speech production mechanisms) and experiential factors combine their influences, language acquisition proceeds according to a developmental timetable that is common to all cultures. As shown in Table 8.1, children progress from reflexive crying

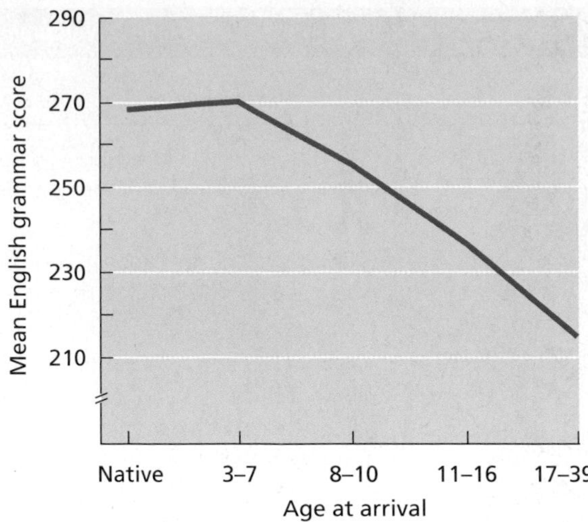

FIGURE 8.8

A sensitive period also exists for second-language learning. These data show the relation between age at arrival in the United States by Korean and Chinese individuals and their scores on a 276-item test of English grammar administered 5 years after their arrival, compared with scores of native speakers of English. After about age 7, the older the immigrants were when they began learning English, the lower their level of mastery. SOURCE: Based on Johnson & Newport, 1989.

at birth through stages of cooing, babbling, and one-word utterances. By 2 years of age, children are uttering sentences called *telegraphic speech* that at first consist of a noun and a verb (e.g., "Want cookie"), with nonessential words left out as in a telegraph message. Soon, additional words may be added (e.g., "Daddy go car"). From that point on, speech development accelerates as vocabulary increases and sentences become more grammatically correct. In the short span of 5 years, an initially nonverbal creature has come to understand and produce a complex language.

Bilingualism: Learning a Second Language

▶ 4. How does bilingualism influence thinking? What factors influence the learning of a second language?

For those of us laboring to learn a second language (or to gain full mastery of our native language), there are models to inspire us. M. D. Berlitz, inventor of the system for teaching languages that bears his name, spoke 58 of them. Sir John Bowring, once the British governor of Hong Kong, could speak 100 languages and read 100 more. And some sort of record must be held by Benjamin Schulze (1699–1760), who could recite the Lord's Prayer in 215 languages (Bryan, 1986).

A second language is learned best and spoken most fluently when it is acquired during the sensitive period of childhood (White, 2003). As shown in Figure 8.8, for example, Korean and Chinese immigrants to the United States who learned English early in life mastered that grammar about as well as native-born Americans. For immigrants older than about age 7, however, mastery of English grammar became progressively more difficult (Johnson & Newport, 1989).

Studies in Switzerland, South Africa, Israel, and Canada show that bilingualism is associated with greater thinking flexibility and higher performance on intelligence tests. However, such effects are not likely to appear until both languages are well learned (Lambert et al., 1993). Non-English-speaking immigrant children perform best in bilingual educational settings in which they are taught in both their native language and in English. Compared with similar children who are placed in English-only classrooms and left to struggle, those in bilingual classes drop out of school less frequently, develop higher self-esteem, and exhibit better academic performance and English fluency (Thomas & Collier, 1997).

Is learning a second language equivalent to learning one's native language, and is the second language represented in the same part of the brain as the native language? Again, the answer may depend on how early in life the new language is acquired and how well it is learned. At the University of Milan, Daniela Perani and her coworkers (1998) used PET scans to measure cortical activation patterns in the brains of English-speaking Italians as they listened to stories read aloud in Italian and in English. People who were highly proficient in English and who had learned this second language before the age of 10 showed representation of the two languages in the same cortical areas. The two languages had, in a sense, become one, accounting for the fluent participants' ability to use the languages interchangeably. In contrast, less-fluent Italians who had learned English later in life showed brain activity in different areas than those activated by stories in Italian when they listened to stories in English, indicating different patterns of language processing. Such people also had greater difficulty in switching rapidly back and forth from one language to the other. For them, the two languages were neither biologically nor psychologically equivalent.

Can Animals Acquire Human Language?

▶ 5. What evidence exists that animals can acquire language? What evidence is cited by those who disagree?

Noam Chomsky referred to language as the "human essence." Yet nonhuman species also communicate in diverse ways. Many use special calls to warn of predators and to attract mates (Alcock, 2002). In some species, communication

"Although humans make sounds with their mouths and occasionally look at each other, there is no solid evidence that they actually communicate with each other."

FIGURE 8.9

Human scientists have been debating the existence and use of language in dolphins and other animals. Could the opposite also be occurring? © 2004 by Sidney Harris.

shows interesting parallels to human language (Figure 8.9). Just as humans have different languages, each songbird species has its own songs. Remarkably, some songbirds also have "local dialects," as humans do (Catchpole & Rowell, 1993). Thus, experts can tell whether a male white-crowned sparrow lives in certain areas north, south, or east of San Francisco by how it sings. And just as humans have a sensitive period in childhood for language acquisition, some songbirds do not sing normally in adulthood unless they hear the songs of their species while growing up (Marler, 1970).

Research with apes provides the most controversial challenge to the long-held assumption that only humans are capable of language. At first, investigators tried to teach chimpanzees to speak verbally, but chimps lack a vocal system that would permit humanlike speech. A breakthrough came in 1966 when Allen Gardner and Beatrice Gardner (1969) took advantage of chimps' hand and finger dexterity and began teaching American Sign Language to a 10-month-old chimp named Washoe. They raised Washoe at home and treated her like a human child. By age 5, Washoe had learned 160 signs. More important, at times she combined signs (e.g., "more fruit," "you tickle Washoe") in novel ways. For example, when a researcher showed Washoe a baby doll inside a cup and signed, "What that?" Washoe signed back, "Baby in my drink." Other researchers also had success. A gorilla named Koko learned over 600 signs (Bonvillian & Patterson, 1997), and a chimp named Lana was taught to communicate via visual symbols on a specially designed keyboard (Rumbaugh, 1990).

At Columbia University, behaviorist Herbert Terrace (1979) taught sign language to a chimp he named Nim Chimpsky—a play on the name of linguist Noam Chomsky. But after years of work and videotape analysis of Nim's "conversations," Terrace concluded that when Nim combined symbols into longer sequences, he was either imitating his trainer's previous signs or "running on" with his hands until he got what he wanted. Moreover, Nim spontaneously signed only when he wanted something, which is not how humans use language. Terrace concluded that Nim had not learned language.

Not surprisingly, some ape-language researchers disputed Terrace's conclusions. They agreed that although apes mainly signed to request things, other types of communications also occurred. For example, Chantek, an orangutan who had been taught a symbol for "dirty" in regard to feces and urine, spontaneously began applying the symbol to spilled food, soiled objects, and toilets (Miles et al., 1996). At Central Washington University, Roger Fouts and Deborah Fouts continued working with Washoe and other chimps raised like human children. They intentionally refrained from signing in front of Loulis, Washoe's adopted son, and found that Loulis acquired over 50 signs by observing other chimps communicate (Fouts et al., 1989). By using remote video cameras, Deborah Fouts (1994) also discovered that the chimps signed with each other even when humans were not present. Moreover, chimp-to-chimp signing occurred across various contexts, such as when they were playing, feeding, and fighting (Cianelli and Fouts, 1998).

Sue Savage-Rumbaugh of Georgia State University has worked extensively with a chimp named Kanzi (Figure 8.10). At age 1 1/2, Kanzi spontaneously showed an interest in using plastic geometric symbols that were associated with words. By age 4, with only informal training during social interactions, Kanzi had learned more than 80 symbols and produced a number of two- and three-word communications. Kanzi typically combined gestures and symbols that he pointed to on a laminated board or typed on a specially designed keyboard. For example, Kanzi created the combinations "Person chase Kanzi," "Kanzi chase person," and "Person chase person" to designate who should chase whom during play. Kanzi also responded readily to spoken English commands.

Savage-Rumbaugh and her coworkers (1993) also tested Kanzi's ability to understand unfamiliar spoken sentences under controlled conditions. For example, when told, "Give the doggie a shot,"

FIGURE 8.10

(a) Using complex symbols, a chimpanzee communicates with his trainer, psychologist Sue Savage-Rumbaugh. (b) This graph shows the rate of Kanzi's symbol acquisition over 17 months of informal training.
SOURCE: Adapted from Savage-Rumbaugh et al., 1986.

(a)

80
70
60
50
40
30
20
10
0
Number of words acquired
30 32 34 36 38 40 42 44 46
Age (in months)

(b)

Kanzi picked up a toy dog, grabbed a toy hypodermic needle, and gave the dog a shot. Kanzi also appeared to understand syntax. Given slightly different requests, such as "Make the [toy] snake bite the [toy] doggie," and "Make the doggie bite the snake," Kanzi responded appropriately. For comparison, one of the researcher's daughters, Alia, was tested under the same conditions between the ages of 2 and 2 1/2. Kanzi correctly responded to 74 percent of the novel requests and Alia to 65 percent. In short, Kanzi was comprehending speech at the level of a human toddler.

What, then, should we conclude about apes' language abilities? Recall that language is (1) symbolic, (2) structured, and (3) generative. Evidence is strongest for the first criterion. Apes clearly are capable of communicating with symbols and hand signs, and they can learn a small vocabulary of several hundred words. Whether the apes perceive the symbols and signs as words in the sense that humans do is still debated. As for structure and generativity, the evidence remains mixed and highly controversial. Both sides can point to examples of how apes are sensitive to—or disregard—syntax. Even proponents would agree, however, that whatever linguistic abilities apes acquire are quite modest, similar at best to those of a very young child. Although the issue of animal language is still being debated, the scientific work should remind us to appreciate something that we tend to take for granted, namely the seemingly natural ease with which humans acquire language.

Linguistic Influences on Thinking

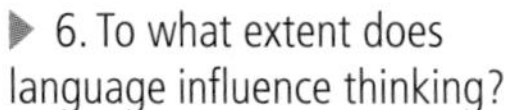

▶ 6. To what extent does language influence thinking?

Although many political leaders prove on a daily basis that a well-developed larynx bears little relation to the capacity for sound thinking, a relation between language and thinking has long been assumed. The linguist Benjamin Lee Whorf (1956) took an extreme position on this matter, contending in his **linguistic relativity hypothesis** *that language not only influences, but also determines, what we are capable of thinking.*

In the hindsight provided by nearly a half century of research, Whorf's position clearly was overstated. For example, if the linguistic relativity hypothesis were correct, then people whose cultures have only a few words for colors should have greater difficulty in perceiving the spectrum of colors than do people whose languages have many color words. To test this proposition, Eleanor Rosch (1973) studied the Dani of New Guinea, who have only two color words in their language, one for bright warm colors, the other for cool dark ones. She found that, contrary to what strict linguistic determinism would suggest, the Dani could discriminate among and remember a wide assortment of hues in much the same manner as can speakers of the English language, which contains many color names.

Today most linguists do not agree with Whorf that language *determines* how we think. They would say instead that language can *influence* how we think, how efficiently we can categorize our experiences, and perhaps how much detail we attend to in our daily experience (Hunt & Agnoli, 1991). Language can also color our perceptions, the decisions we make, and the conclusions we draw (Figure 8.11). Consider, for example, the ability of sexist language to evoke gender stereotypes. In one study, college students read one of the following statements about psychology:

> "The psychologist believes in the dignity and worth of the individual human being. He is committed to increasing man's understanding of himself and others."

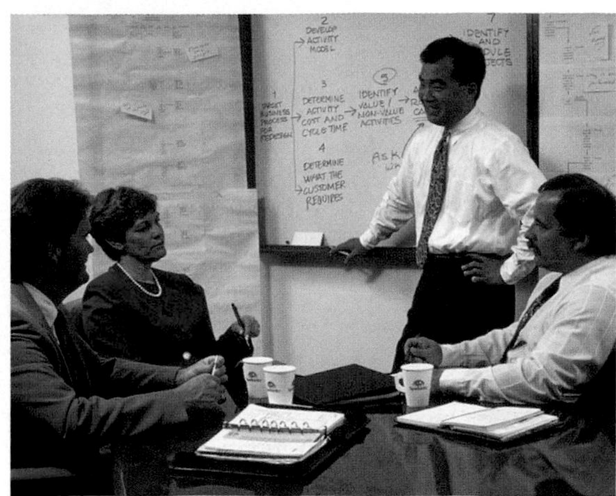

FIGURE 8.11

Sexist language influences our perceptions, our decisions, and the conclusions we draw. Which of these people would you assume is the supervisor of the others?

> "Psychologists believe in the dignity and worth of the individual human being. They are committed to increasing people's understanding of themselves and others."

The students then were asked to rate the attractiveness of a career in psychology for men and women. Those who had read the first statement rated psychology as a less attractive profession for women than did the students who read the second statement, written in gender-neutral language (Briere & Lanktree, 1983). Apparently, the first statement implied that psychology is a male profession (when, actually, the majority of psychology doctorates awarded over the past decade went to women). In such ways, language can help create and maintain stereotypes.

Language not only influences how we think but also may influence how well we think in certain domains. For example, English-speaking children consistently score lower than children from Asian countries in mathematical skills such as counting, addition, and subtraction (Geary, 1995). One reason may be the words and symbols the languages use to represent numbers. Asian languages make it far easier to learn the base-10 number system, particularly the numbers between 10 and 100. For example, in Chinese, the number 11 is "ten one," 13 is "ten three," and 46 is "four ten six." In contrast, English speakers struggle with such words as *eleven, twelve,* and *thirteen,* which bear little conceptual relation to a base-10 mode of thinking. Regardless of their counting proficiency, American and British children fail to grasp the base-10 system by age 5, whereas many Chinese children do, enabling them to do addition and subtraction with greater ease (Miller & Stigler, 1987). In this manner, the English language appears to hamper the development of skills in using numbers, whereas Asian languages facilitate the development of mathematical skills.

Thinking may be considered the internal language of the mind, but it actually includes several mental activities. One mode of thought takes the form of verbal sentences that we seem to say or hear in our minds. This is called **propositional thought** *because it expresses a proposition, or statement.* Another thought mode, **imaginal thought,** *consists of images that we can "see," "hear," or "feel" in our mind.* A third mode, **motoric thought,** *relates to mental representations of motor movements,* such as throwing an object. All three modes of thinking enter into our abilities to reason, solve problems, and engage in many forms of intelligent behavior. Let's examine propositional thought.

Concepts and Propositions

▶ 7. What are concepts, and how do they enter into propositions? How are prototypes involved in concept formation?

Much of our thinking occurs in the form of **propositions,** *statements that express facts.* "College students are intelligent people" is a proposition. All propositions consist of concepts combined in a particular way. Typically, one concept is a *subject* and another is a *predicate* (Figure 8.12). **Concepts** *are basic units of semantic memory—mental categories into which we place objects, activities, abstractions (such as "liberal" and "conservative"), and events that have essential features in common.* Every psychological term you are learning in this course is a concept. Concepts can be acquired through explicit instruction or through our own observations of similarities and differences among various objects and events.

Many concepts are difficult to define explicitly. For example, you are quite familiar with the

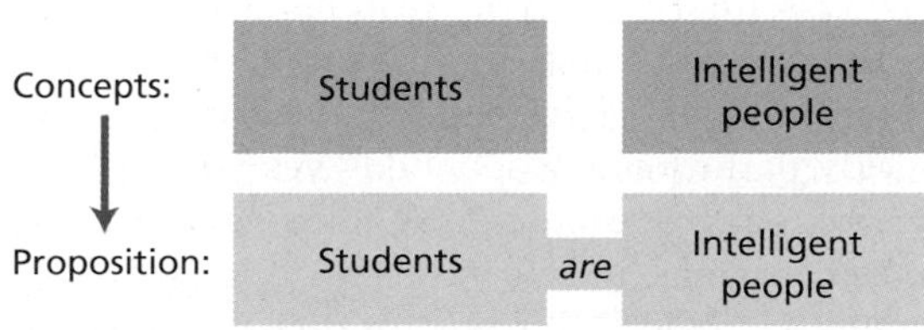

FIGURE 8.12

Concepts are the building blocks of thinking and reasoning. They can be combined into propositions to create both simple and complex thoughts, and the propositions can serve as the basis for reasoning and discourse.

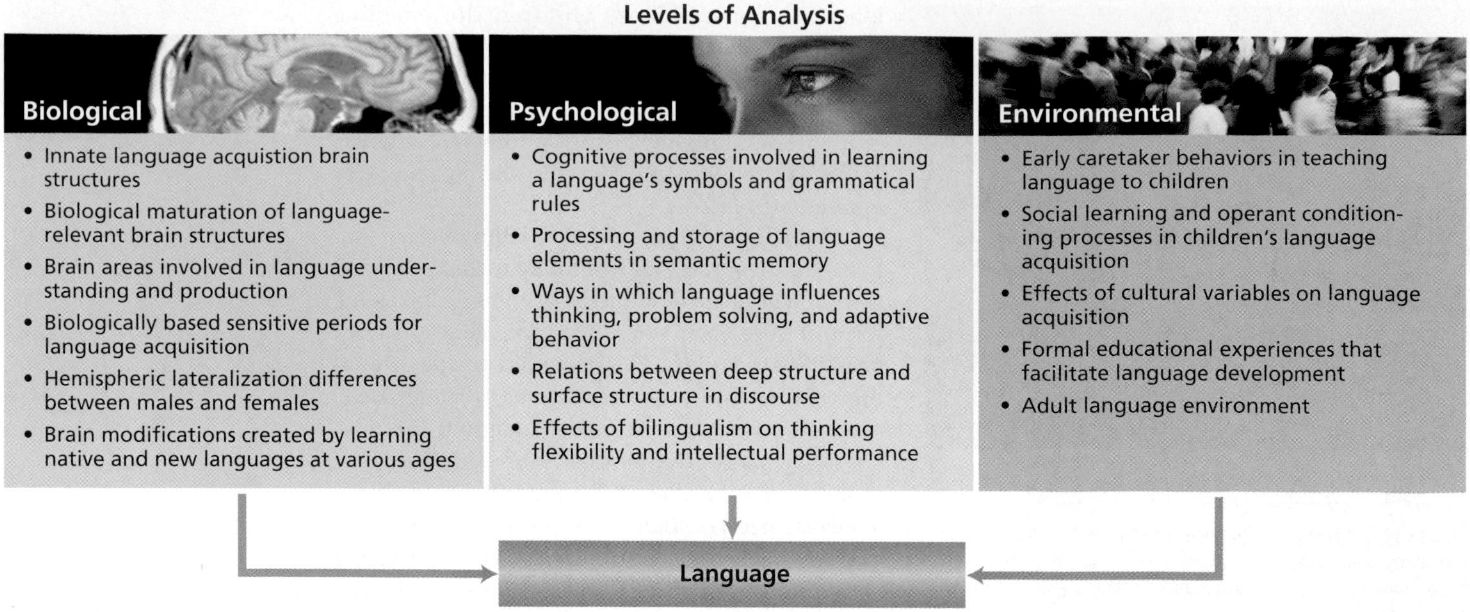

Levels of Analysis

Biological	Psychological	Environmental
• Innate language acquistion brain structures • Biological maturation of language-relevant brain structures • Brain areas involved in language understanding and production • Biologically based sensitive periods for language acquisition • Hemispheric lateralization differences between males and females • Brain modifications created by learning native and new languages at various ages	• Cognitive processes involved in learning a language's symbols and grammatical rules • Processing and storage of language elements in semantic memory • Ways in which language influences thinking, problem solving, and adaptive behavior • Relations between deep structure and surface structure in discourse • Effects of bilingualism on thinking flexibility and intellectual performance	• Early caretaker behaviors in teaching language to children • Social learning and operant conditioning processes in children's language acquisition • Effects of cultural variables on language acquisition • Formal educational experiences that facilitate language development • Adult language environment

Language

FIGURE 8.13

Understanding Behavior: Language analyzed at biological, psychological, and environmental levels of analysis.

concept "vegetable," yet you might have difficulty coming up with an explicit definition of what a vegetable is. However, you can quickly think of a good example of a vegetable, such as broccoli or a carrot. According to Eleanor Rosch (1977), many concepts are defined by **prototypes**—*the most typical and familiar members of a category, or class.* Rosch suggests that we often decide which category something belongs to by its degree of resemblance to the prototype.

Consider the following questions:

- Is an eagle a bird?
- Is a penguin a bird?
- Is a bat a bird?

According to the prototype view, you should have come to a quicker decision on the first question than on the last two. Why? Because an eagle fits most people's "bird" prototype better than does a penguin (which is a bird, though it lacks some essential prototypic features, such as the ability to fly) or a bat (which is not a bird, even though it flies). Experiments measuring how quickly participants responded "yes" or "no" to the preceding questions have found that it does indeed take most people longer to decide whether penguins or bats are birds (Rips, 1997).

The use of prototypes is perhaps the most elementary method of forming concepts. It requires that we note similarities *only* among objects. Thus children's early concepts are based on prototypes of the objects and people they encounter personally. They then decide if new objects are similar enough to the prototype to be a "Mommy," a "cookie," a "doggie," and so on (Smith & Zarate, 1992). Because prototypes may differ as a result of personal experience, there is considerable room for arbitrariness and individual differences in prototypic concepts. Thus one person's "terrorist" can be another person's "freedom fighter."

How we state propositions can influence how we try to solve a problem, reason through to a decision, or make a judgment (Anderson, 1991). For example, in one study college students who were told that a cancer treatment had a 50 percent success rate judged the treatment to be significantly more effective and expressed a greater willingness to have it administered to a family member than did participants who were told that it had a 50 percent failure rate (Kahneman & Tversky, 1979). Representing outcomes in terms of positives or negatives has this effect because people tend to assign greater costs to negative outcomes (such as losing $100) than they assign value to an equivalent positive outcome (finding $100). The proposition that "there is a 50 percent chance of failure" evokes thoughts about the patient's dying and causes the "50-50" treatment to appear more risky (Slovic et al., 1988). Thus differences in how we verbally represent choices and goals can make a difference in our perceptions and decisions.

Language is the foundation of many human behaviors and capabilities. As a central topic of psychological research, it is being studied at the biological, psychological, and environmental levels of analysis (Figure 8.13).

IN REVIEW

- *Human language is symbolic, structured, and generative. The surface structure of a language refers to how symbols are combined; the deep structure refers to the underlying meaning of the symbols. Language elements are hierarchically arranged from the phoneme to morphemes and on to words, phrases, and sentences. Discourse involves higher-level combinations of sentences.*
- *In infancy, babies emit all the phonemes that exist in all the languages of the world. At about 6 months of age, babbling sounds narrow to include only the sounds spoken by others in the environment. By ages 4 to 5, most children have learned the basic grammatical rules for combining words into meaningful sentences.*
- *Language development seems to depend heavily on innate mechanisms that permit the learning and production of language, provided that the child is exposed to an appropriate linguistic environment during a sensitive period that extends from early childhood to puberty.*
- *When both languages are well learned, bilingualism has been shown to have positive influences on cognitive performance. A second language is most easily mastered and fluently spoken if it is learned during the sensitive period of childhood.*
- *Animals can communicate. At best, apes are capable of learning, combining, and communicating symbols at a level similar to that of a young child. Skeptics question, however, whether they can learn syntax and generate novel ideas.*
- *Language influences what and how effectively people think. Expansion of vocabulary allows people to encode and process information in more sophisticated ways.*
- *Concepts are mental categories, or classes, that share certain characteristics. Many concepts are based on prototypes, the most typical and familiar members of a class. How much something resembles the prototype determines whether the concept is applied to it. Propositional thought involves the use of concepts in the form of statements having subjects and predicates.*

REASONING AND PROBLEM SOLVING

What is intelligent thinking? Certainly one aspect is the ability to reason and think logically. Such thinking helps us acquire knowledge, make sound decisions, and solve problems. Reasoning helps us avoid the hazards and time-consuming efforts of trial and error, in which we try out one solution after another until one works. Most of the time, people solve problems by developing solutions in their minds before applying them in the external world. For example, if you decide to build a bookcase, you are unlikely to nail or screw boards together at random in the hope that the finished product will serve your purposes. Instead, you will develop mental representations to guide your efforts, such as a visual image of the finished product and general principles for its successful construction (e.g., "build from the bottom up").

Reasoning

▶ 8. Distinguish between deductive reasoning and inductive reasoning. How do irrelevant information and belief bias affect reasoning?

Two types of reasoning underlie many of our attempts to make decisions and solve problems (Figure 8.14). In **deductive reasoning,** *we reason from the "top down," that is, from general principles to a conclusion about a specific case.* When people reason deductively, they begin with a set of *premises* (propositions assumed to be true) and determine what the premises imply about a specific situation. Deductive reasoning is the basis of formal mathematics and logic. Logicians regard it as the strongest and most valid form of reasoning because the conclusion *cannot be false* if the premises (factual statements) are true. More formally, the underlying deductive principle may be stated:

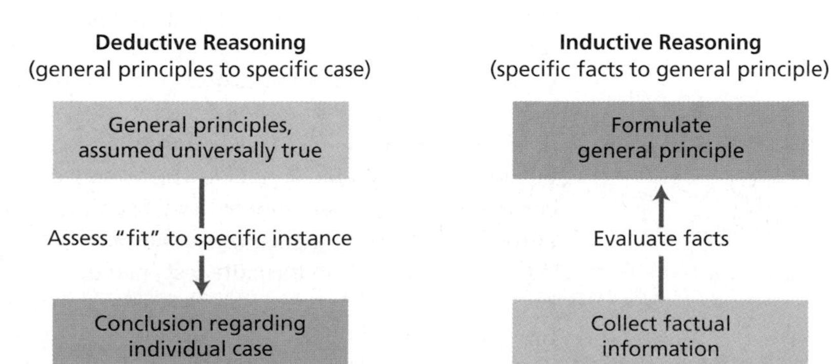

FIGURE 8.14

A comparison of deductive and inductive reasoning.

Given the general proposition "if X then Y," if X occurs, then you can infer Y. Thus, to use a classic deductive argument, or *syllogism,*

> *If* all humans are mortal (first premise), and
> *if* Socrates is a human (second premise),
> *then* Socrates must be mortal (conclusion).

In **inductive reasoning,** *we reason in a "bottom-up" fashion, starting with specific facts and trying to develop a general principle.* Scientists use induction when they discover general principles, or laws, as a result of observing a number of specific instances of a phenomenon. After Ivan Pavlov observed repeatedly that the dogs in his laboratory began to salivate when approached by the experimenter who fed them, he began to think in terms of a general principle that eventually became the foundation of classical conditioning (repeated CS-UCS pairings produce a CR). A college student who experiences repeated negative consequences when she gets drunk may eventually conclude that binge drinking is a high-risk behavior to be avoided.

An important difference between deductive and inductive reasoning lies in the certainty of the results. Deductive conclusions are certain to be true *if* the premises are true, but inductive reasoning leads to likelihood rather than certainty. Even if we reason inductively in a flawless manner, the possibility of error always remains because some new observation may disprove our conclusion. Thus you may observe that every person named Jordan you have ever met had blue eyes, but it would obviously be inaccurate to reason that, therefore, all people named Jordan have blue eyes.

In daily life and in science, inductive and deductive reasoning may be used at different points in problem solving and decision making. For example, psychologists often make informal observations (e.g., hearing about people like Kitty Genovese who do not receive help when many bystanders are present). These specific observations may prompt them to construct an initial explanation (e.g., diffusion of responsibility) for the observed phenomenon. This is inductive reasoning, so the explanation could be wrong even if it is consistent with all the known facts. Therefore scientists move to a deductive process in which they design experiments to formally test specific *if-then* hypotheses, moving now from a general explanatory principle to a specific observation (the experiment's results). If the results of these experimental tests do *not* support their hypotheses, they conclude that their explanation or theory cannot be correct and needs to be revised or discarded.

Stumbling Blocks in Reasoning

The ability to reason effectively is a key factor in critical thinking, in making sound decisions, and in solving problems. Unfortunately, several factors may prevent us from selecting the information needed to draw sound conclusions.

Distraction by Irrelevant Information Distinguishing relevant from irrelevant information can be challenging. Consider the following problem. As you solve it, analyze the mental steps you take, and do not read on until you have decided on an answer.

> Your drawer contains 19 black socks and 13 blue socks. Without turning on the light, how many socks do you have to pull out of the drawer to have a matching pair?

As you solved the problem, what information entered into your reasoning? Did you take into account the fact that there were 19 black socks and 13 blue ones? If so, you're like many of Robert Sternberg's (1988) Yale University students who did the same thing, thereby making the problem much more difficult than it should be. In this case, all that matters is how many *colors* of socks there are. It wouldn't matter if there were 1,000 socks of each color; once you have selected any 3 of them, you are bound to have at least 2 of the same color. People often fail to solve problems because they simply don't focus on the *relevant* information. Instead, they take into account irrelevant information that leads them astray.

Belief Bias **Belief bias** *is the tendency to abandon logical rules in favor of our own personal beliefs.* To illustrate, let us consider an experiment in which college students were asked to judge whether conclusions followed logically from syllogisms like the following:

> All things that are smoked are good for one's health.
>
> Cigarettes are smoked.
>
> Therefore cigarettes are good for one's health.

What do you think? Is the logic correct?

Actually, it is. If we accept (for the moment) that the premises are true, then the conclusion *does* follow logically from the premises. Yet students frequently claimed that the conclusion was not *logically correct* because they disagreed with the first premise that all things smoked are good for one's health. In this case, their beliefs about the harmful effects of smoking got in the way of their logic. When the same syllogism was presented with a nonsense word such as *ramadians* substituted for *cigarettes*, the errors in logic were markedly reduced (Markowitz & Nantel, 1989). Incidentally, we agree that the conclusion that cigarettes are good for one's health is factually false. However, it is false because the first premise is false, not because the logic is faulty. Unfortunately, many people confuse factual correctness with logical correctness. The two are not at all the same.

Steps in Problem Solving

Humans have an unmatched ability to solve problems and adapt to the challenges of their world. Such problem solving proceeds through four stages (Figure 8.15). How well we carry out each of these stages determines our success in solving the problem.

Understanding, or Framing, the Problem

Most of us have had the experience of feeling totally frustrated in our attempts to solve a problem. We may even think that the problem is unsolvable. Then someone suggests a new way of looking at the problem, and the solution suddenly becomes obvious. How we mentally represent, or *frame*, a problem can make a huge difference. Consider the following problem (illustrated in Figure 8.16):

> Train A leaves Baltimore for its 50-mile trip to Washington, D.C., at a constant speed of 25 mph. At the same time, train B leaves Washington, bound for Baltimore at the same speed of 25 mph. A crow that happened on a methamphetamine lab and sampled its product leaves Baltimore at the same time as train A, flying above the tracks toward Washington at a speed of 60 mph. When the crow encounters train B, it turns and flies back to train A, then instantly reverses its direction and flies back to train B. The supercharged bird continues this sequence until trains A and B meet midway between Baltimore and Washington. Try to solve this problem before reading on: What is the total distance the bird will have traveled in its excursions between trains A and B?

Many people approach the problem as a distance problem, which is quite natural because the question is stated in terms of distance. They try to compute how far the bird will fly during each segment of its flight between trains A and B, sometimes filling up several pages with increasingly frenzied computations in the process. But suppose you approach the problem by asking not how far the bird will fly but *how long* it will take the trains to meet. The crow will have flown the same period of time at 60 mph. Now that you have reframed it as a time problem, the problem becomes much easier to solve. (You can check your solution against the answer given on page 323.)

As you can see, our initial understanding of a problem is a key step toward a successful solution. If we frame a problem poorly, we can easily be led into a maze of blind alleys and ineffective solutions. If we frame it optimally, we at least have a chance to generate an effective solution. A knack for framing problems in effective ways that differ from conventional expectations has been called "outside-the-box thinking"; it is a prized ability in many workplace environments as well as in academic work.

Generating Potential Solutions

Once we have interpreted the problem, we can begin to formulate potential solutions or explanations. Ideally, we might proceed in the following fashion:

1. Determine which procedures and explanations will be considered.
2. Determine which solutions are consistent with the evidence that has so far been observed. Rule out any solutions that do not fit the evidence.

Testing the Solutions

Consider the possible solutions that remain. If the solution requires you to choose between specific explanations, ask if there is any test that should

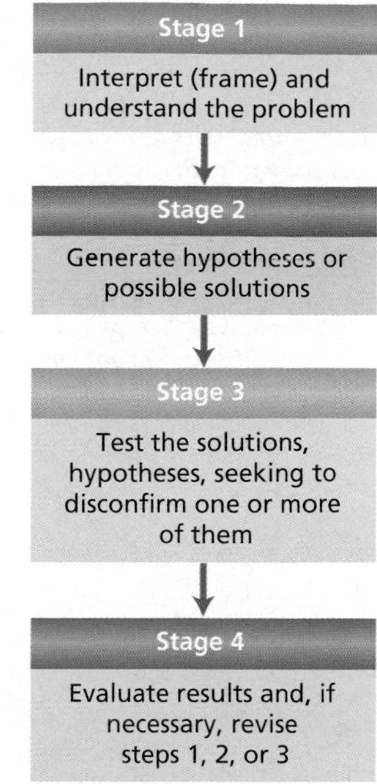

FIGURE 8.15

The stages of problem solving.

▶ 9. Summarize the four major stages of problem solving. What is the importance of problem framing and mental sets?

FIGURE 8.16

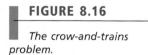

The crow-and-trains problem.

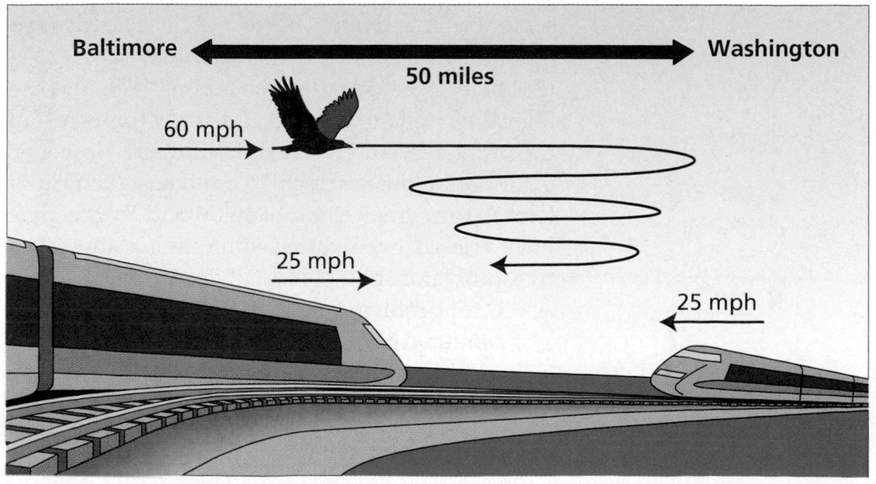

FIGURE 8.17

Luchins's water jugs problems. Using containers A, B, and C with the capacities shown in the table, how would you measure out the volumes indicated in the right column? You may discover a general problem-solving schema that fits all seven problems.

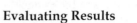

Problem	Given jugs of these sizes *A*	*B*	*C*	Measure out this much water
1	21	127	3	100
2	14	46	5	22
3	18	43	10	5
4	7	42	6	23
5	20	57	4	29
6	23	49	3	20
7	15	39	3	18

give one result if one explanation is true and another result if a different explanation is true. If so, evaluate the explanations again in light of the evidence from that test. In essence, this is what scientists do when they design experiments.

▶ 10. What are problem-solving schemas? How do they relate to expertise and to the strengths and weaknesses of human memory?

Mental Sets Let us consider a common difficulty that can arise in the process of discovering and applying solutions to problems. Consider problem 1 in Figure 8.17:

> Suppose you have a 21-cup jug, a 127-cup jug, and a 3-cup jug. Drawing and discarding as much water as you like, how will you measure out exactly 100 cups of water?

Problem 1 is followed by six additional problems in Figure 8.17. Try to solve all of them in order, and write your calculations for each one before reading on. Does a common solution emerge? If so, can you specify what it is?

As you worked the problems, you probably discovered that they are all solvable by the same formula, namely $B - A - (2 \times C)$ = desired amount. In problem 1, for example, $127 - 21 - (2 \times 3) = 100$. If you discovered this, it gave you a logical formula that you could apply to the rest of the problems. And it worked, didn't it? However, by applying the successful formula used on problems 1 through 5 to problems 6 and 7, you may have missed even easier solutions for these last two problems, namely $A - C$ for problem 6 and $A + C$ for problem 7.

Abraham Luchins (1942) developed the water jugs problems to demonstrate the manner in which a **mental set**—*the tendency to stick to solutions that have worked in the past*—can result in less effective problem solving. Luchins found that most people who worked on problems 6 and 7 were blinded by the mental set they had developed by working the first five problems. In contrast, people who had not worked on problems 1 through 5 almost always applied the simple solutions to problems 6 and 7. Studies of mental set show how easy it is to become rigidly fixated on one particular approach that has been successful in the past.

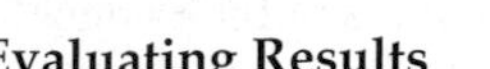
For more on mental sets, see Interactive Segment 8.1.

Evaluating Results

The final stage of problem solving is to evaluate the solutions. As we saw in the water jugs problems, even solutions that prove successful may not be the easiest or the best. Thus after solving a problem, we should ask ourselves, "Would there have been an easier or more effective way to accomplish the same objective?" This can lead to the development of additional problem-solving principles that may be applicable to future problems.

Problem-Solving Schemas

In solving problems, people often learn to employ shortcut methods that apply to specific situations (Rips, 1997). **Problem-solving schemas** *can be likened to mental blueprints or step-by-step scripts for selecting information and solving specialized classes of problems.* We have all learned a great many of them, from schemas for cooking dinner to schemas for studying and mastering academic course content (Figure 8.18). Once we master

FIGURE 8.18

Experienced snowboarders learn schemas for various types of snow, and the discriminations made possible by these schemas can affect planning and decision making. This boarder might approach a slope covered with "powder" differently than one covered with "corn" because of their different effects on the board and potentially on the boarder's physical well-being.

them, we seem to know what to do without having to engage in step-by-step formal problem-solving procedures.

The Nature of Expertise

Schemas help explain what it means to be an expert. Masters and grand masters in chess can glance at a chessboard and quickly plan strategies and make adjustments in the heat of competition. The world's best players can store in memory as many as 50,000 board configurations, together with the locations of each of the individual pieces (Chase & Simon, 1973). For years, world chess champion Gary Kasparov's sophisticated schemas enabled him to regularly defeat chess-playing computers that used logical rules, even those capable of logically analyzing up to 100,000 moves per second. It took Deep Blue, a 1.4-ton behemoth capable of calculating at a rate of 200 million positions and 200,000 moves per second, to finally defeat the schemas within Kasparov's 3-pound brain (Figure 8.19).

Expert athletic coaches, surgeons, military leaders, and political consultants all rely on the schemas they have developed from experience. Training world-class athletes, performing medical operations, planning military strategies, and running political campaigns are very different activities. Nevertheless, researchers have found a common factor underlying expertise: Experts have developed a great many schemas to guide problem solving in their field, and they are much better than novices at recognizing when each schema should be applied (Bedard & Chi, 1992). Applying the correct mental blueprint provides a proven route to solving a problem quickly and effectively.

Consider what this difference in schema application means in terms of what we know about human memory. As we learned in Chapter 7, human long-term memory is impressive, and that is where schemas reside. Because they rely on learned schemas, experts depend on their spacious long-term memory. They can quickly analyze a problem deductively, select the retrieval cues needed to pull the appropriate schema from memory, and apply the schema to solve the problem at hand (Horn & Masunaga, 2000). In contrast, novices who haven't yet learned specialized schemas must use general problem-solving methods that force them to solve problems in working memory, on the space-limited "blackboard of the mind" (Newell & Simon, 1972). In so doing, they tax their working memory—the weakest link in the human mind.

FIGURE 8.19

Chess master Garry Kasparov has developed chess schemas that make him a worthy opponent for even the most sophisticated computers, including IBM's Deep Blue.

The development of expertise is accompanied by alterations in brain functioning that increase processing efficiency. This occurs even in animals. Thus, as macaque monkeys in one study became experts in categorizing objects, recordings from individual feature-detector neurons in the brain revealed quicker and stronger activity in the specific neurons that responded to the stimulus features of importance in categorizing the stimuli (Sigala & Logothetis, 2002). These feature detectors were referred to as "expert neurons" (Hasegawa & Myashita, 2002).

Algorithms and Heuristics

▶ 11. Distinguish between an algorithm and a heuristic. Describe the means-ends and subgoal analysis heuristics.

Algorithms and heuristics are two important strategies for problem solving. **Algorithms** *are formulas or procedures that automatically generate correct solutions*. Mathematical and chemical formulas are algorithms; if you use them correctly, you will always get the correct answer. Consider another example of an algorithm. If the letters of a word are scrambled in random order to produce an anagram like *teralbay*, we can identify the word using a process in which we rearrange the letters in all possible combinations. As this example illustrates, using algorithms can at times be very time-consuming. In this case, the eight letters can be rearranged in 40,320 different ways, and applying the algorithm might significantly delay your college graduation. You might therefore decide to use some more general rule-of-thumb strategy, such as trying out only consonants in the first and last positions, because you know that more words begin and end in consonants than begin and end in vowels. When we adopt rule-of-thumb approaches like this, we are using heuristics.

Heuristics *are general problem-solving strategies that we apply to certain classes of situations*. Means-ends analysis is one example of a heuristic (Newell & Simon, 1972). In **means-ends analysis,**

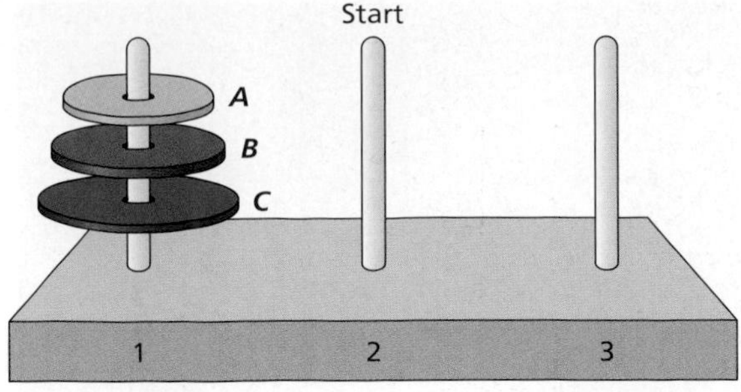

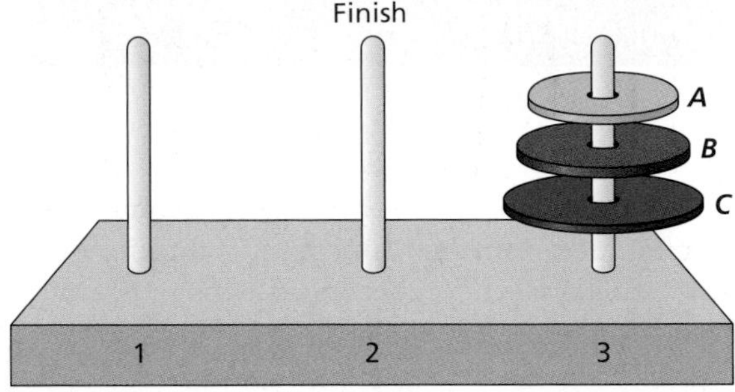

FIGURE 8.20

The tower-of-Hanoi problem. The object is to move the rings one at a time from peg 1 to peg 3 in no more than seven moves. Only the top ring on a peg can be moved, and a larger ring can never be placed on top of a smaller one. (The answer appears on page 323).

we identify differences between the present situation and the desired state, or goal, and then make changes that will reduce these differences. Assume, for example, that you have a 30-page paper due at the end of the term and have not begun working on it yet. The present situation is no pages written; the desired end state is a 30-page paper. What, specifically, needs to be done to reduce that discrepancy, and how are you going to do it?

You would be foolish to decide, "There are 30 days until the paper is due, so all I have to do is write 1 page a day." This approach is likely to result in a 30-page paper but is unlikely to result in one that will earn a passing grade. Instead, you would be wise to use another heuristic known as **subgoal analysis,** *in which we formulate subgoals, or intermediate steps, toward a solution.* In this case, your expertise as a student will likely lead you to break down the task of writing a paper into subgoals, such as (1) choosing a topic, (2) doing library and Internet research on the topic to get the facts you need, (3) organizing the facts within a general outline of the paper, (4) writing a first draft or specific sections of the paper, (5) reorganizing and refining the first draft, and so on. In so doing, a huge task becomes a series of smaller and more manageable tasks, each with a subgoal that leads you toward the ultimate goal of a quality 30-page paper.

The value of setting subgoals can be seen in the tower-of-Hanoi problem, depicted in Figure 8.20. The ultimate goal for this problem is to move all three rings on peg 1 to peg 3 using no more than seven moves. There are, however, two restrictions. First, only the top ring on a peg can be moved. Second, a larger ring must never be placed above a smaller ring. Can you solve this challenging problem?

Breaking this task into subgoals helps us solve the problem. The first subgoal is to get ring C to the bottom of peg 3. The second subgoal is to get ring B over to peg 3. With these two subgoals accomplished, the final subgoal of getting ring A to peg 3 is quite easy. The solution requires planning (hypothesis formation), checking, and revising hypotheses. The correct seven-step sequence of moves appears on page 323.

Heuristics enter not only into problem-solving strategies but also into judgments and decisions. As we shall see, they can also contribute to errors in judgment.

Uncertainty, Heuristics, and Decision Making

Few decisions in everyday life can be made with the absolute certainty that comes from applying some mathematical formula or other algorithm. Typically, the best we can hope for is a decision that has a high probability of a positive outcome. Because we seldom know what the exact probabilities are (for example, how likely it is that the stock market will be up or down when you need your money at a specific time in the future, or how probable it is that a new dating relationship will become permanent), we tend to apply certain heuristics to form judgments of likelihood.

In daily life, we routinely make decisions about what other people are like. Suppose, for example, you are given the following description of a young woman:

> Linda is 31 years old, single, outspoken, and very bright. She majored in philosophy. As a student, she was deeply concerned with issues of discrimination and social justice, and she also participated in antinuclear demonstrations.

Now rate the likelihood that each of the following hypotheses is true. Use 1 to indicate the most likely statement, 8 to indicate the least likely statement, and any number between 2 and 7 to indicate the likelihood of the second most likely statement.

_______ Hypothesis A: Linda is active in the feminist movement.

_______ Hypothesis B: Linda is a bank teller.

_______ Hypothesis C: Linda is active in the feminist movement and is a bank teller.

This problem was used in a series of experiments conducted by cognitive psychologists Daniel Kahneman and Amos Tversky (1982) to study the role of heuristics in judgment and decision making. They showed that certain heuristics underlie much of our inductive decision making (drawing conclusions from facts) and that their misuse results in many of our thinking errors. Let us examine how that occurs.

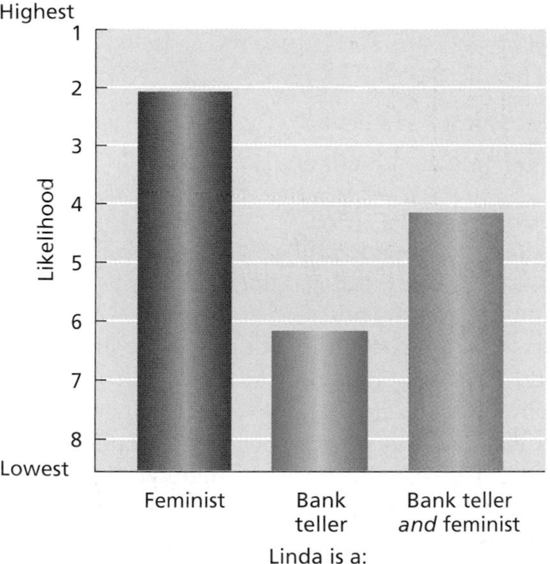

FIGURE 8.21

Mean likelihood judgments made by subjects on the basis of the description of Linda on page 296.
SOURCE: Based on Tversky & Kahneman, 1982.

The Representativeness Heuristic "What does it look (or seem) like?" This is probably the first task faced by our perceptual system when it processes incoming stimuli. Earlier, we discussed the importance of prototypes in concept formation. We use the **representativeness heuristic** *to infer how closely something or someone fits our prototype for a particular concept, or class, and therefore how likely it is to be a member of that class.* In essence, we are asking, "How likely is it that this [person, object, event] *represents* that class?" In this case, does Linda seem like a feminist? This is a perfectly logical question to ask ourselves. Sometimes, however, our use of representativeness can cause us to make decisions that fly in the face of logic.

For example, what was your order of likelihood judgments concerning Linda? Figure 8.21 shows the mean likelihood estimates that college students attached to each statement (a low number indicating greater likelihood). First of all, there is a clear tendency to favor hypothesis A (Linda is a feminist). This is not surprising; the description does make her sound like a feminist. However, the significant finding is that hypothesis C (Linda is a feminist bank teller) was favored over hypothesis B (Linda is a bank teller). But this cannot possibly be correct. Why not? Because everyone who is both a feminist and a bank teller is also *simply* a bank teller. Furthermore, there are many bank tellers who are not feminists, and Linda could be one of them. Stated differently, any person is more likely to be simply a bank teller than to be a bank teller *and* a feminist—or for that matter, a bank teller and anything else. People who say that hypothesis C is more likely than hypothesis B (and about 85 percent of people given this problem do so) violate the logical principle that the combination of two events cannot be more likely than either event alone.

▶ 12. Define the representativeness and availability heuristics and indicate how they can distort probability judgments.

Tversky and Kahneman believe that the reason people make this sort of error is that they confuse representativeness with probability. Linda represents our prototype for a feminist bank teller better than she fits our prototype for a bank teller. Therefore, we erroneously think the former is more likely than the latter. Notice how this argument fits with the ideas about memory discussed in Chapter 7. The description of Linda as "outspoken" and "concerned with issues of discrimination and social justice" serves a *priming* function, activating the elements in memory that are associated with the concept of "feminist," so it is hard to think of Linda without thinking of a feminist. On the other hand, there is nothing in Linda's description that would activate the concept of "bank teller." Thus if Linda is to be a bank teller at all, we think she must be a feminist bank teller.

The Availability Heuristic Another heuristic that can sometimes lead us astray is the **availability heuristic,** *which causes us to base judgments and decisions on the availability of information in memory.* We tend to remember events that are most important and significant to us. Usually that principle serves us well, keeping important information at the forefront in our memories, ready to be applied. But if something easily comes to mind, we may exaggerate the likelihood that it could occur. For example, consider each of the following pairs and choose the more likely cause of death:

- murder or suicide?
- botulism or lightning?
- asthma or tornadoes?

When Paul Slovic and coworkers (1988) asked people to make this judgment, 80 percent chose murder over suicide as the more likely cause of death, 63 percent chose botulism over lightning, and 43 percent thought tornadoes took a greater toll of human life than asthma does. In actuality, public health statistics show that people are 25 percent less likely to be murdered than to kill themselves, that lightning kills 53 times more people than botulism does, and that death by asthma is 21 times more likely than death as a result of a tornado. Yet which of the alternatives are more highly and dramatically publicized when they do occur and thus are more likely to come to mind?

A recent memorable event can increase people's belief that they could suffer a similar fate. After the terrorist hijackings of September 11, 2001, airline bookings and tourism declined dramatically within the United States for a significant period. Demand for office space in landmark high-rise buildings also declined, and many businesses sought space in less conspicuous suburban settings. Similarly, in the summer of 1975, when Steven Spielberg's movie *Jaws* burned into people's memories graphic images of a great white shark devouring swimmers at a New England seaside town, beach attendance all over the country decreased. In fact, *Jaws* was blamed for a drop in tourism on the New England coast so dramatic that in the summer of 1976 many beachfront resorts nearly went bankrupt. The images available in memory—even though the movie was clearly fiction—increased people's perceived likelihood that they, too, could become shark bait.

Thus at times the representativeness and availability heuristics can lead us astray by distorting our estimates of how likely an event really is. In other words, they can blind us to the *base rates*, or actual frequencies at which things occur. In general, it's always best to find out what the actual probabilities are and make judgments on that basis. That's the strategy that allows insurance companies to flourish.

▶ 13. What is the value of disconfirming evidence? How does overconfidence contribute to confirmation bias?

Confirmation Bias and Overconfidence

Sometimes one of the most challenging tasks is obtaining new evidence to test our hypothesis or solution. What's the best type of evidence you can have?

Here is a principle that may seem puzzling to you: The best thing we can do to test our ideas is to seek evidence that will *disconfirm* them, rather than look for evidence that supports them. Why? Because the most informative piece of evidence we can obtain is one that rules out a hypothesis or causes us to change our ideas. Disconfirming evidence proves conclusively that our idea *cannot* be true in its current form. In contrast, confirming evidence only supports our idea. It doesn't prove it with certainty, for it is possible that some future observation will disconfirm it or that another explanation fits the facts even better. Especially in the area of causal beliefs, you can be absolutely sure when you're wrong about something, but you can't be absolutely sure when you're right because there might be a better explanation or an impending observation that calls your belief into question.

Following this disconfirmation principle is easier said than done, because people are often unwilling to challenge their cherished beliefs. Instead, they are prone to fall into a trap called **confirmation bias,** *tending to look for evidence that will confirm what they currently believe rather than looking for evidence that could disconfirm their beliefs.* Many studies have shown that if people have strong beliefs about something, they are very selective in the kinds of information they expose themselves to. They seek out like-minded people, mass media sources, and Internet sites. Likewise, when people are given the choice of what kinds of feedback they would like to have about themselves, they have a strong tendency to seek out and recall feedback from others that confirms their beliefs about themselves. They tend to avoid and "forget" evidence that disconfirms these self-beliefs (Swann et al., 1992). The fact that people find it difficult or even upsetting to test and challenge their ideas, particularly those to which they are strongly committed, can be a major obstacle to getting the evidence needed to make a correct decision.

Confirmation bias often contributes to a distorted sense of how correct our opinions and beliefs are. **Overconfidence,** *the tendency to overestimate one's correctness in factual knowledge, beliefs, and decisions,* is another reason people do not challenge their beliefs. This tendency, like confirmation bias, is widespread. In one study, college students were asked at the beginning of the academic year to make predictions about how likely it was (from 0 percent to 100 percent) that they would experience any of a long list of personal events, such as dropping a course, breaking up with a romantic partner, or joining a fraternity or sorority. They also indicated how confident they were in their probability estimates (i.e., how likely it was that they would be correct). At the end of the following semester and at the end of the academic year, they indicated which events had in fact occurred. As shown in Figure 8.22, confidence exceeded accuracy overall, and the difference between the two was equally great when the students were originally 100 percent confident in their predictions (Vallone et al., 1990). Similar overconfidence effects have been found in studies involving investment professionals, military strategists, weather forecasters, and other populations. It apparently stems from people's need to see themselves as knowledgeable and competent (Blanton et al., 2001).

Overconfidence and confirmation bias can be potent adversaries in our search for correct predictions and decisions. When we're confident in the correctness of our views and reluctant to seek evidence that could prove them wrong, we can easily be blinded to the truth.

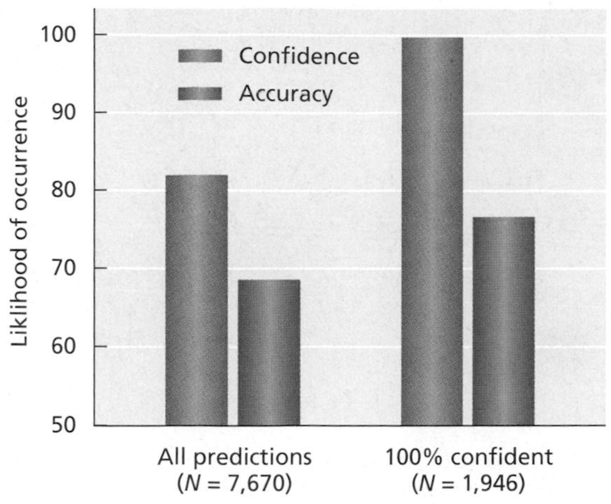

FIGURE 8.22

The phenomenon of overconfidence is illustrated in the discrepancy between the accuracy with which students predicted that specific events would occur to them during the coming academic year and the degree of confidence that they had in their predictions. Overall, accuracy was considerably lower than confidence level, even for those events for which the students expressed complete certainty. SOURCE: Based on Vallone et al., 1990.

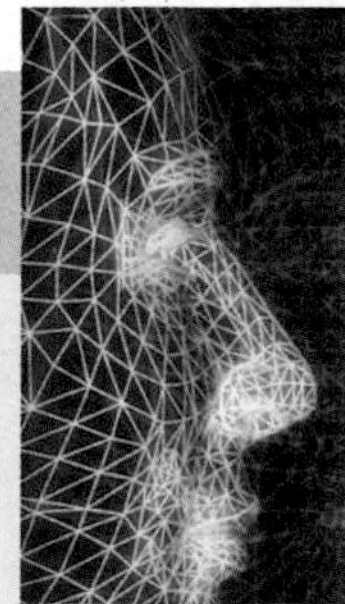

APPLYING PSYCHOLOGICAL SCIENCE

GUIDELINES FOR CREATIVE PROBLEM SOLVING

Creativity *is the ability to produce something that is both new and valuable.* The product may be virtually anything, from a creative painting to a novel approach to solving a problem. In this case, we will be concerned with creative problem solving.

Research on reasoning offers insights into how effective and creative problem solvers think and how they approach problems. In some ways, as experts so often demonstrate, there is no substitute for experience, for it teaches us heuristics and problem-solving schemas that can be very useful. Yet one of the marks of creativity is the ability to break out of conventional schemas when the occasion demands it and to engage in **divergent thinking,** *the generation of novel ideas that depart from the norm* (Guilford, 1959). In part, this means being able to apply concepts or propositions from one domain to another unrelated domain in a manner that produces a new insight (Chi, 1997). It also means refusing to be constrained by traditional approaches to a problem. Creative people are, in this respect, intellectual rebels. The constraints created by the tried-and-true can be difficult to overcome. Consider, for example, the nine-dot problem in Figure 8.23. The task is this: Without lifting your pencil from the paper, draw no more than four straight lines that will pass through all nine dots.

Many people have difficulty solving this problem. Did you? If so, it is probably because you imposed a traditional but unnecessary constraint on yourself and tried to stay within the boundary formed by the dots. But nothing in the statement of the problem forced you to do so. To solve the problem, you have to think "outside the box."

Creative problem solvers are often able to ask themselves questions like the following to stimulate divergent thinking (Simonton, 1999):

Continued

FIGURE 8.23

The nine-dot problem. Without lifting your pencil from the paper, draw no more than four straight lines that will pass through all nine dots. (The answer appears on page 323).

FIGURE 8.24

The candlestick problem. Using these objects, find a way to mount the candle on a wall so it functions like a lamp. (The answer appears on page 323).

- What would work instead?
- Are there new ways to use this? How else could it be used if I modified it in some way? By adding, subtracting, or rearranging parts, or by modifying the sequence in which things are done, could I make it more useful?
- Do the elements remind me of anything else? What else is like this?

Use some of these questions in the problem illustrated in Figure 8.24. How could you use these objects to mount a candle on the wall and light it so that you could study for your next exam if the power went out. Solving the problem requires using some of the objects in unconventional ways. Many people, however, are prevented from doing so because of **functional fixedness,** *the tendency to be so fixed in their perception of the proper function of an object or procedure that they are blinded to new ways of using it.*

Sometimes creative solutions to problems seemingly appear out of the blue, suddenly popping into our mind in a flash of insight after we have temporarily given up and put the problem aside. **Incubation** *is the name given to this phenomenon; it is as if the problem is "incubating" and being worked on at a subconscious level* (Cattell, 1971). Sometimes the best approach when we are stymied by a problem is to put it aside for a while and gain a bit of psychological distance from it. Perhaps this causes mental sets and other biases to dissipate somewhat, allowing a new idea to emerge (Anderson, 1985). In addition, as time passes, new internal or external stimuli may activate a different perspective on the problem, aiding its solution (Bastik, 1982).

As you can see, creative problem solving involves many of the principles discussed earlier in the chapter. We see the operation of means-ends reasoning, the testing of hypotheses, and the need to overcome biases that may cause us to overestimate or underestimate the likelihood of certain outcomes. Here are some other general problem-solving guidelines:

1. When you encounter a new problem you haven't solved before, ask yourself if it is similar to other problems you've solved. Maybe the schema for solving a problem with similar features can be modified to solve this one. Take advantage of the storehouse of knowledge in long-term memory.
2. Make a true effort to test your ideas. Try to find evidence that would disconfirm your ideas, not evidence that confirms what you already believe. For example, if you are asked to accept statement X as true, see if you can imagine situations in which X would be false. Beware of the human tendency toward confirmation bias.
3. Be careful not to confuse representativeness with probability. The odds are overwhelming that the bird in that tree that is a little big for a sparrow but looks to be exactly the right size for the rare Patagonian warbler is probably . . . a big sparrow, because there are so many more sparrows (even oversized ones) than Patagonian warblers.
4. Make use of the means-ends problem-solving heuristic. Ask yourself what you are trying to accomplish, what the present state of affairs is, and what means you have for reducing the discrepancy.
5. Don't be afraid to use pencil and paper. Orderly notes and schematics can substitute for our rather limited working memory and allow us to have more information at hand to work with.

IN REVIEW

- *In deductive reasoning, we reason from general principles to a conclusion about a specific case. Inductive reasoning, in contrast, involves reasoning from a set of specific facts or observations to a general principle. Deduction is the strongest and most valid form of reasoning, because the conclusion cannot be false if the premises are true. Inductive reasoning cannot yield certainty.*
- *Unsuccessful deductive reasoning can result from (1) failure to select the appropriate information; (2) failure to apply the appropriate deductive reasoning rules, particularly in novel situations; and (3) belief bias, the tendency to abandon logical rules in favor of personal beliefs.*
- *Problem solving proceeds through a number of steps: (1) understanding the nature of the problem, (2) establishing initial hypotheses or potential solutions, (3) testing the solutions against existing evidence to rule out hypotheses that do not apply, and (4) evaluating results.*
- *Problem-solving schemas are shortcut methods for solving specialized classes of problems. They are stored in long-term memory and can help overcome the limitations of working memory. Expertise results from acquiring a range of successful problem-solving schemas through training and practical experience, as well as knowing when to apply them.*
- *Algorithms are formulas or procedures that guarantee correct solutions. Heuristics are general strategies that may or may not provide correct solutions. Means-ends analysis is one commonly used heuristic. The representativeness heuristic is the tendency to judge evidence according to whether it is consistent with an existing concept or schema. The availability heuristic is the tendency to base conclusions and probability judgments on what is readily available in memory. Humans exhibit confirmation bias, a tendency to look for facts to support hypotheses rather than to disprove them; and they suffer from overconfidence, a tendency to overestimate their knowledge, beliefs, and decisions.*
- *In some situations, divergent thinking is needed for generating novel ideas or variations on ideas. Functional fixedness can blind us to new ways of using an object or procedure, thereby interfering with creative problem solving. In some cases, a period of incubation permits problem solving to proceed on a subconscious level while giving the problem solver psychological distance from the problem.*

▶ 14. What is our working definition of intelligence?

▶ 15. How did Galton and Binet differ in their approaches to measuring mental abilities?

INTELLIGENCE

We have considered general principles of human thinking, reasoning, and problem solving, yet it is readily apparent that people differ widely in how effectively they think and behave. Is it true that some people are generally more "intelligent" than others? If so, can we measure these differences and use the measures to predict success and failure in real-life settings? What is the nature of intelligence, and what factors account for the differences we observe in people's cognitive, emotional, and behavioral skills? These and related questions have inspired more than a century of scientific research, and attempts to answer them have influenced our culture enormously. Even today, there are disagreements concerning the nature of intelligence. In our discussion, we use the following definition, which accommodates most viewpoints: **Intelligence** *is the ability to acquire knowledge, to think and reason effectively, and to deal adaptively with the environment.*

Intelligence in Historical Perspective

Historically, two scientists with different agendas played seminal roles in the study and measurement of mental skills (Figure 8.25). The contributions of Sir Francis Galton and Alfred Binet set the stage for later attempts to measure intelligence and discover its causes.

Sir Francis Galton: Quantifying Mental Ability

Sir Francis Galton was a cousin of Charles Darwin and was strongly influenced by Darwin's theory

FIGURE 8.25

Sir Francis Galton (top) and Alfred Binet (bottom) pioneered the study and measurement of intelligence.

TABLE 8.2 Sample Problems From the Stanford-Binet Intelligence Test That Should Be Answered Correctly at Particular Ages

Age 3—Child should be able to:	Point to objects that serve various functions such as "goes on your feet." Name pictures of objects such as *chair, flag.* Repeat a list of 2 words or digits such as *car, dog.*
Age 4—Child should be able to:	Discriminate visual forms such as squares, circles, and triangles. Define words such as *ball* and *bat.* Repeat 10-word sentences. Count up to 4 objects. Solve problems such as "In daytime it is light; at night it is . . ."
Age 6—Child should be able to:	State the differences between similar items such as *bird* and *dog.* Count up to 9 blocks. Solve analogies such as "An inch is short; a mile is . . ."
Age 9—Child should be able to:	Solve verbal problems such as "Tell me a number that rhymes with tree." Solve simple arithmetic problems such as "If I buy 4 cents' worth of candy and give the storekeeper 10 cents, how much money will I get back?" Repeat 4 digits in reverse order.
Age 12—Child should be able to:	Define words such as *muzzle.* Repeat 5 digits in reverse order. Solve verbal absurdities such as "Bill's feet are so big he has to pull his trousers over his head. What is foolish about that?"

SOURCE: Terman & Merrill, 1972.

of evolution. In his book *Hereditary Genius* (1869), Galton showed through the study of family trees that eminence and genius seemed to occur across generations within certain families. These studies convinced him that such people had "inherited mental constitutions" that made them more fit for thinking than their less successful counterparts. Exhibiting his own belief bias, Galton dismissed the fact that the more successful people he studied almost invariably came from privileged environments.

Galton then attempted to demonstrate a biological basis for eminence by showing that people who were more socially and occupationally successful would also perform better on a variety of laboratory tasks thought to measure the "efficiency of the nervous system." He developed measures of reaction speed, hand strength, and sensory acuity. He even measured the size of people's skulls, believing that skull size reflected brain size and hence intelligence. However, Galton's approach to mental skills measurement fell into disfavor because his measures of nervous system efficiency proved unrelated to socially relevant measures of mental ability, such as academic and occupational success. Nonetheless, Galton's work created an interest in the measurement of mental abilities, setting the stage for the pioneering work of Alfred Binet.

Alfred Binet's Mental Tests

The modern intelligence testing movement began at the turn of the 20th century when the French psychologist Alfred Binet was commissioned by France's ministry of public education to develop the test that was to become the forerunner of all modern intelligence tests. Unlike Galton (with whom he had trained), Binet was interested in solving a practical problem rather than supporting a theory. Certain children seemed unable to benefit from normal public schooling. Educators wanted an objective way to identify these children as early as possible so that some form of special education could be arranged for them.

In developing his tests, Binet made two assumptions about intelligence. The first was that mental abilities develop with age. The second was that the rate at which people gain mental competence is a characteristic of the person and is fairly constant over time. If this is true, then a child who is less competent than expected at age 5 should also be lagging at age 10.

To develop a measure of mental skills, Binet asked experienced teachers what sorts of problems children could solve at ages 3, 4, 5, and so on, up through the school years. He then used their answers to develop a "standardized interview" in which an adult examiner posed a series of questions to a child to determine whether the child was performing at the correct mental level for his or her age (Table 8.2). The result of the testing was a score called the *mental age.* For instance, if a child of 8 could solve problems at the level of the average 10-year-old, the child would be said to have a mental age of 10. For the French school system, the practical implication was that educational attainment could be enhanced if placement in school were based at least in part on the child's mental age. An 8-year-old child with a mental age of 6 could hardly be expected to cope with the academic demands of a normal classroom for 8-year-olds.

The concept of mental age was subsequently expanded by the German psychologist William Stern to provide a relative score—a common yardstick of intellectual attainment—for people of different chronological ages. Stern's **intelligence quotient (IQ)** *was the ratio of mental age to Chronological age, multiplied by 100, i.e., IQ = (Mental age/Chronological age) × 100.* Thus a child who was performing at exactly his or her age level would have an IQ of 100. In our previous example, the child with a mental age of 10 and a chronological age of 8 would have an IQ of (10/8) × 100 = 125. A 16-year-old with a mental age of 20 would also have an IQ of 125, so the two would be comparable in intelligence even though their ages differed.

Today's tests no longer use the concept of mental age. Although the concept of mental age works pretty well for children, many of the skills measured by intelligence tests are learned by about age 16 through normal life experiences and schooling, so that Stern's quotient is less useful for adults. Moreover, some intellectual skills show an actual decline at advanced ages, yet if we applied Stern's definition of IQ to a 20-year-old who performed at the typical level of an 80-year-old, we would have to say that the 20-year-old's IQ was 400! To deal with these problems, today's intelligence tests provide an "IQ" score that is not a quotient at all but rather is based on a person's performance relative to the scores of a large sample of other people the same age, with a score of 100 corresponding to the average performance of that sample.

The Stanford-Binet and Wechsler Scales

Lewis Terman, a professor at Stanford University, revised Binet's test for use in the United States, translating it into English and rewriting some of its items to improve their relevance to American culture. Terman's revised test became known as the *Stanford-Binet*. By the mid-1920s, it had been widely accepted in North America. The Stanford-Binet contained mostly verbal items, and it yielded a single IQ score.

Somewhat later, a major competitor to the Stanford-Binet emerged in the form of the *Wechsler scales*. Psychologist David Wechsler believed that the Stanford-Binet relied too much on verbal skills. He thought that intelligence should be measured as a group of distinct but related verbal and nonverbal abilities. He therefore developed intelligence tests for adults and for children that measured a range of intellectual skills. In 1939, the Wechsler Adult Intelligence Scale (WAIS) appeared, followed by the Wechsler Intelligence Scale for Children (WISC) in 1955 and the Wechsler Preschool and Primary Scale of Intelligence (WPPSI) in 1967. The Wechsler scales have undergone several revisions. Following Wechsler's lead, the Stanford-Binet has also been revised to measure a wider range of mental abilities. Today, however, the Wechsler tests (WAIS-III and WISC-III) are the most popular individually administered intelligence tests in the United States (Groth-Marnat, 1999).

The Wechsler scales consist of a series of subtests that fall into two classes: verbal and performance (Figure 8.26). A psychologist can therefore plot a profile of the scores on each of the subtests to assess a person's pattern of intellectual strengths and weaknesses. The test yields three summary scores: a *Verbal IQ* based on the sum of the verbal subtests; a *Performance IQ* based on the performance subtests; and a *Full-Scale IQ* based on all of the subtests. For some purposes, it is useful to examine differences between the Verbal IQ and the Performance IQ. For example, individuals from an impoverished environment with little formal schooling might score higher on the performance subtests than on the verbal subtests, suggesting that their overall IQ might be an underestimate of their intellectual potential. Sometimes, too, various types of brain damage are reflected in large discrepancies between certain subtest scores (Goldstein, 2000).

▶ 16. Why do today's intelligence tests no longer use the mental age concept? How is IQ now defined?

Group Tests of Aptitude and Achievement

Intelligence tests like the Stanford-Binet and the Wechsler scales are administered to an individual by a trained tester. They typically take as long as 2 hours to administer and are therefore impractical for large-scale screening purposes. In contrast, tests such as the Lorge-Thorndike Intelligence Test and the Otis-Lennon School Ability Test can be used to obtain IQ scores from groups of people at the same time. Many school districts use these tests routinely; you may very well have taken one of these during your earlier school years.

▶ 17. What was Wechsler's concept of intelligence? How do the Wechsler scales reflect this concept?

Other group tests do not provide IQ scores but instead measure specific mental skills. These include the Scholastic Assessment Test (SAT), widely used to select college applicants in the United States; the Graduate Record Examination (GRE), used to select applicants for postgraduate study; the Medical College Admission Test (MCAT); the Law School Aptitude Test (LSAT); and the Armed Services Vocational Aptitude Battery (ASVAB), used to screen recruits for the U.S. Armed Services.

▶ 18. Differentiate between aptitude and achievement tests in relation to the measurement of intelligence.

Using written tests for selection purposes highlights an issue that Binet faced and that continues to plague test developers today. Should we test a person's abstract "aptitude for learning," or

Wechsler Adult Intelligence Scale (WAIS-III)

Subtest	Description	Example
Verbal scales		
Information	Taps general range of knowledge	On what continent is Italy?
Comprehension	Tests understanding of social conventions and ability to evaluate past experience	Why are children required to go to school?
Arithmetic	Tests arithmetic reasoning through verbal problems	How many hours will it take to drive 120 miles at 40 miles per hour?
Similarities	Asks in what way certain objects or concepts are similar; measures abstract thinking	How are a computer and a typewriter alike?
Digit span	Tests attention and rote memory by orally presenting series of digits to be repeated forward or backward	Repeat the following numbers backward: 7 3 5 1 6 8
Vocabulary	Tests ability to define increasingly difficult words	What does "formidable" mean?
Performance scales		
Digit symbol	Tests speed of learning through timed coding tasks in which numbers must be associated with drawings of various shapes	Shown: 1 2 3 4 ○ □ △ ◇ Fill in appropriate symbol: 1 4 3 2 __ __ __ __
Picture completion	Tests visual alertness and visual memory through presentation of an incompletely drawn figure; the missing part must be discovered and named	What is missing in this picture? 
Block design	Tests ability to perceive and analyze patterns by presenting designs that must be copied with blocks	Assemble blocks to match this design: 
Picture arrangement	Tests understanding of social situations through a series of comic-strip-type pictures that must be arranged in the right sequence to tell a story	Put the pictures in the correct order: 1 2 3 
Object assembly	Tests ability to deal with part/whole relationships by presenting puzzle pieces that must be assembled to form a complete object	Assemble the pieces into a complete object: 

FIGURE 8.26

Sample items resembling those found on the subtests of the Wechsler Adult Intelligence Scale (WAIS-III).

should we test what a person already knows? Consider an example. In selecting applicants for college, we could either give students an **achievement test** *designed to find out how much they have learned so far in their lives,* or we could present them with an **aptitude test** *containing novel puzzle-like problems that presumably go beyond prior learning and are thought to measure the applicant's potential for future learning and performance.*

The argument for achievement testing is that it is usually a good predictor of future performance in a similar situation–if a student learned a lot of academic material in high school (and therefore scored well on the test), he or she is likely to also learn a lot in college. The argument against achievement testing is that it assumes that everyone has had the same opportunity to learn the material being tested. In college selection, for example, a given applicant's test score could depend on whether that person went to a good school rather than on his or her ability to learn in college.

The argument for aptitude testing is that it is "fairer," since aptitude tests are supposed to depend less on prior knowledge than on a person's ability to react to the problems presented on the test. The argument against aptitude testing is that it is difficult to construct a test that is independent of prior learning. Further, such a test may require an ability to deal with puzzles that is not relevant to success in situations other than the test itself.

In fact, most intelligence tests measure a combination of aptitude and achievement, reflecting both native ability and previous learning. This has raised major scientific and social issues concerning the meaning of test scores and the use fulness of the measures for describing mental competence and predicting performance in nontest situations.

Scientific Standards for Psychological Tests

A **psychological test** *is a method for measuring individual differences related to some psychological concept, or construct, based on a sample of relevant behavior in a scientifically designed and controlled situation.* In the case of intelligence testing, intelligence is the *construct* and scores obtained on the test are its *operational definition.* To design a test, we need to decide which specific behaviors serve as indicators or reflections of intellectual abilities. Then we need to devise test items that allow us to assess individual differences in those behaviors. We will, of course, need evidence that our sample of items (a sample, because we can't ask every conceivable question) actually measures the abilities we are assessing. As in designing an experiment (see Chapter 2), we will want to collect a *sample of relevant behavior* under standardized conditions, attempting to control for other factors that could influence responses to the items. To understand how psychologists meet these requirements, we must examine three key measurement concepts: reliability, validity, and standardization.

TABLE 8.3 Types of Reliability and Validity in Psychological Testing

Types of Reliability	Meaning and Critical Questions
Test-retest reliability	Are scores on the measure stable over time?
Internal consistency	Do all of the items on the measure seem to be measuring the same thing, as indicated by high correlations among them?
Interjudge reliability	Do different raters or scorers agree on their scoring or observations?
Types of Validity	
Construct validity	To what extent is the test actually measuring the construct of interest (e.g., intelligence)?
Content validity	Do the questions or test items relate to all aspects of the construct being measured?
Predictive validity	Do scores on the test predict some present or future behavior or outcome assumed to be affected by the construct being measured?

Reliability

Reliability *refers to consistency of measurement.* As shown in Table 8.3, consistency can take several forms when applied to psychological tests. One of the most important is consistency over time. If you step on your bathroom scale five times in a row, you should expect it to register the same weight each time unless you have a very unusual metabolism. Likewise, if we assume that intelligence is a relatively stable trait (and virtually all psychologists do), then scores on our measure should be stable, or consistent, over time. Where psychological tests are concerned, this type of measurement stability over time is defined as **test-retest reliability,** *which is assessed by administering the measure to the same group of participants on two (or more) separate occasions and correlating the two (or more) sets of scores.*

After about age 7, scores on intelligence tests show considerable stability, even over many years (Gregory, 1998). Over a short interval (2 to 12 weeks), the test-retest correlation of adult IQs on the WAIS is .96, or nearly perfect (Tulsky et al., 2003). Correlations between IQs at age 9 and age 40 are in the .70 to .80 range (McCall, 1977), indicating a high degree of stability. Thus, *relative to her age group,* a person who achieves an above-average IQ at age 9 is very likely to also be above the average for 40-year-olds when she reaches that age. Even during middle childhood, when children's cognitive skills are developing rapidly, IQs are quite stable, with test-retest coefficients around .90 (Canivez & Watkins, 1998).

Another form of reliability, **internal consistency,** *has to do with consistency of measurement within the test itself.* For example, if a Wechsler subtest is internally consistent, all of its items are measuring the same thing, as evidenced by high correlations among the items. As desired, the items within the Wechsler subtests all correlate substantially with one another (Gregory, 1998).

▶ 19. Define reliability, validity, and standardization. Which forms do each of these test characteristics take?

Finally, **interjudge reliability** *refers to consistency of measurement when different people observe the same event or score the same test.* Ideally, two psychologists who independently score the same test will assign exactly the same scores. To attain high interjudge reliability, the scoring instructions must be so explicit that trained professionals will use the scoring system in the same way.

Validity

As a general concept, **validity** *refers to how well a test actually measures what it is designed to measure.* As in the case of reliability, there are several types of validity (see Table 8.3).

As noted earlier, intelligence is a concept, or mental construct. **Construct validity** *exists when a* *test successfully measures the psychological construct it is designed to measure, as indicated by relations between test scores and other behaviors that it should be related to.* If an intelligence test had perfect construct validity, individual differences in IQs would be due to differences in intelligence and nothing else. In reality, this ideal is never attained, for other factors such as motivation and educational background also influence test scores.

Two other kinds of validity contribute to construct validity. **Content validity** *refers to whether the items on a test measure all the knowledge or skills that are assumed to compose the construct of interest.* For example, if we want the arithmetic subtest of the WAIS-III to measure general mathematical reasoning skills, we would not want to have only addition problems; we would want the items to sample other relevant mathematical abilities as well, such as subtraction, division, and fractions.

If an intelligence test is valid, the IQ it yields should allow us to predict other behaviors that are assumed to be influenced by intelligence, such as school grades or job performance. These outcome measures are called *criterion measures.* **Predictive validity** *is defined by how highly test scores correlate with, or can predict, criterion measures.* Thus we could determine how well students' IQ scores predict current or future college grades.

Intelligence tests were originally developed to predict academic and other forms of achievement. How well do they do so? Correlations of IQ with school grades are in the .60 range for high school students and in the .30 to .50 range for college students (Aiken, 1996). In general, then, people who score well on the tests tend to do well academically. Likewise, the college entrance examination you took while in high school is designed to predict the criterion of grades in college. In fact, SAT scores do predict college grades, with correlations slightly below .50 (Willingham et al., 1990). This correlation, which is about the same magnitude as the correlation between people's height and weight, is high enough to justify using the tests for screening purposes but low enough to suggest the use of other predictors (such as high school grades) in combination with SAT scores.

Intelligence test scores also predict military and job performance, yielding correlations of .20 to .50 with various measures of job performance across different occupations (Hartigan & Wigdor, 1989; Hunter & Hunter, 1984). Generally, intelligence tests are better at predicting academic success—which requires the kinds of cognitive skills they measure—than success on a job, which may require other skills as well. However, they are far from perfect predictors in any achievement domain. In many performance settings, including college, a certain level of intellectual ability is needed to survive, but, for people who have that requisite level, other factors, such as motivation and work habits, may assume greater importance.

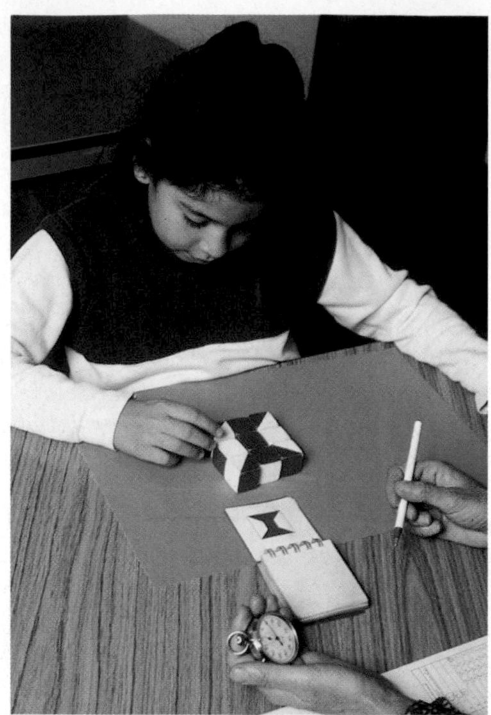

FIGURE 8.27

A psychologist administers the Wechsler Intelligence Scale for Children (WISC-III) using explicit instructions and procedures in order to create a standard testing environment.

Standardization and Norms

The third measurement requirement, **standardization,** *has two facets: controlled testing procedures and the development of norms.* Test instructions and procedures create a well-controlled, or standardized, environment for administering the intelligence test so that other uncontrolled factors will not influence scores. Tests like the Stanford-Binet and Wechsler scales have very detailed instructions that must be closely adhered to, even to the point of reading the instructions and items to the person being tested (Figure 8.27).

The second facet of standardization is especially important in providing a meaningful IQ score. It involves the collection of **norms,** *test scores derived from a large sample that represents particular age segments of the population.* These normative scores provide a basis for interpreting a given individual's score, just as the distribution of scores in a course exam allows you to determine how well you did relative to your classmates.

When norms are collected for mental skills (and for many other human characteristics), the scores usually form *a bell-shaped curve known as a* **normal distribution,** with most scores clustering around the center of the curve. On intelligence tests, the center of the distribution for each age group from childhood to late adulthood is assigned an IQ score of 100. Because the normal distribution has known statistical properties, we can specify what percentage of the population will score higher than a given score. Thus, as Figure 8.28 shows, an IQ score of 100 cuts the distribution in half, with an equal percentage of the population scoring above and below this midpoint. The farther we move from this average score of 100 in either direction, the fewer people attain the higher or lower scores. The figure also shows the percentage of people who score above certain IQ levels. On modern intelligence tests, this method of assigning an IQ score has replaced the original formula of mental age divided by chronological age.

The relative nature of the IQ allows its meaning to be preserved even if performance changes within the population. A notable discovery by New Zealand researcher James Flynn (1987, 1998) suggests that much of the world's population is scoring progressively higher on intelligence tests. This "rising curve" phenomenon has produced IQ increases of 28 points in the United States since 1910 and a similar increase in Britain since 1942. Whether this increase is due to better nutrition, richer learning environments, or some unknown factor is unclear at this time (Neisser et al., 1998). What is clear, however, is that the intelligence score distribution has to be recalibrated upward if the average IQ is to remain at 100, the traditional midpoint of the intelligence range.

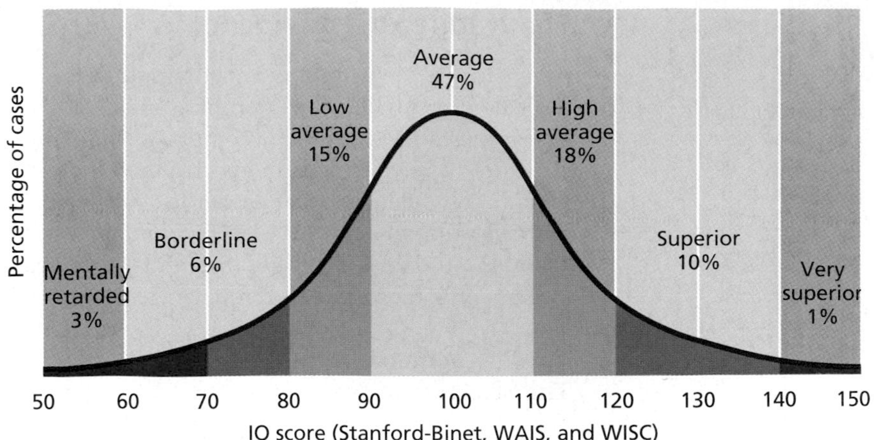

FIGURE 8.28

When administered to large groups of people, intelligence tests yield a normal distribution, or bell curve, of IQ scores that has known statistical properties. The mean of the distribution is set at 100. It is possible to specify for any given score which percentage of the standardization group achieved higher or lower scores. Common descriptive labels are shown relative to the bell-shaped distribution. The range of scores from 90 to 110 is labeled average and includes nearly half of the population.

IN REVIEW

- *Intelligence is a construct that refers to the ability to acquire knowledge, to think and reason effectively, and to deal adaptively with the environment.*
- *The IQ is a relative measure that indicates where a person falls within the normal distribution of IQ scores derived in the process of standardization. The concept of mental age introduced by Binet is no longer used.*
- *The Wechsler scales, separately developed for adults, children, and preschoolers, are the most widely used individual intelligence tests. They consist of a series of verbal and performance subtests that yield separate Verbal and Performance IQs, as well as a Full-Scale IQ.*
- *An aptitude test is designed to measure potential for future learning and performance, whereas an achievement test is designed to measure what one has already learned. In practice, most intelligence tests measure both aptitude and achievement.*
- *Among the standards that are required for a psychological test are reliability (or consistency) of measurement, validity (the extent to which it relates to its underlying construct and predicts relevant behaviors), and standardization (which involves both standard items and procedures for obtaining scores and the development of norms). IQ is a better predictor of academic success than of job success, which often requires abilities that are not measured by the tests.*

The Nature of Intelligence

▶ 20. What kinds of evidence supported the *g* factor and specific mental abilities concepts of intelligence?

Psychologists have used two major approaches in the study of intelligence (Sternberg et al., 2003). The *psychometric approach* attempts to map the structure of intellect and to specify the kinds of mental competencies that underlie test performance. A second approach, the *cognitive processes approach,* studies the specific thought processes that underlie those mental competencies.

The Psychometric Approach: The Structure of Intellect

Psychometrics *is the statistical study of psychological tests.* Thus standardization, reliability, and validity are all psychometric concepts. The psychometric approach to intelligence tries to identify and measure the abilities that underlie individual differences in performance. In essence, the psychometric approach to intelligence tries to produce a measurement-based map of the mind.

One of the major tools used by psychometric researchers is **factor analysis,** *which analyzes patterns of correlations between test scores to discover clusters of measures that correlate highly with one another but not with measures in other clusters.* When such clusters, or factors, are found, the investigator tries to decide what common underlying ability accounts for the high correlations. For example, if we were to find that four different tests were highly correlated with one another and that the tests all required people to solve mathematical problems, we might conclude that the underlying factor was "mathematical reasoning ability." If another cluster of correlated tests all required the ability to define and use words, we might conclude that the underlying intellectual factor was "verbal ability." (A more detailed discussion of factor analysis appears in the Statistics Appendix following chapter 15.)

Psychometric theorists disagree on the nature of intelligence. Some believe that intelligence is a single global mental capability that cuts across all of what we would call thinking. At the other extreme are those who regard intelligence not as a unitary trait but as a set of specific abilities to do different types of thinking.

The* g *Factor: Intelligence as General Mental Capacity The psychometric argument for intelligence as a general ability was first advanced by the British psychologist Charles Spearman (1923), who observed that school grades in different subjects, such as English and mathematics, were almost always positively correlated but that the correlations were not perfect. Spearman found the same to be true for different types of Binet intelligence test items, such as vocabulary questions, arithmetic reasoning problems, and the ability to construct puzzles.

Faced with this pattern of results, Spearman concluded that intellectual performance is determined partly by *general intelligence* (usually indicated by the symbol *g*), and partly by whatever special abilities might be required to perform that particular task. Spearman contended that since the general factor—the *g* factor—cut across virtually all tasks, it constituted the foundation of intelligence. For instance, Spearman would argue that your performance in a mathematics course would depend mainly on your general intelligence but also on your specific ability to learn mathematics. Today many theorists continue to believe that the *g* factor is the core of what we call intelligence (Jensen, 1998).

Intelligence as Specific Mental Abilities Spearman's conclusion concerning the *g* factor was soon challenged by L. L. Thurstone of the University of Chicago. Where Spearman had been impressed by the fact that scores on different mental tasks are correlated, Thurstone was impressed by the fact that the correlations are far from perfect. Thurstone concluded that human mental performance depends not on a general factor but rather on seven distinct abilities, which he called *primary mental abilities* (Table 8.4). Contesting Spearman's position, Thurstone maintained that performance on any mental task is influenced more by the specific abilities relevant to that task than by any underlying *g* factor. Following Thurstone's lead, other investigators claimed to have found even more factors. One prominent theorist maintained that there are more than 100 distinct

TABLE 8.4 Thurstone's Primary Mental Abilities

Ability Name	Description
S—Space	Reasoning about visual scenes
V—Verbal comprehension	Understanding verbal statements
W—Word fluency	Producing verbal statements
N—Number facility	Dealing with numbers
P—Perceptual speed	Recognizing visual patterns
M—Rote memory	Memorization
R—Reasoning	Dealing with novel problems

SOURCE: Thurstone, L. L. (1938). *Primary Mental Abilities.* Reprinted by permission of the University of Chicago Press.

and measurable mental abilities (Guilford, 1967). Other theorists agree concerning the complexity of intelligence (e.g., Stankov, 2003).

Despite the lack of agreement as to whether intelligence is best conceived of as a single *g* ability that is applicable in many settings or as a set of specialized abilities, a clear distinction seems to exist between the ability to deal with verbal information and the ability to solve visuospatial problems, such as the one shown in Figure 8.29. Mathematical reasoning is more strongly related to visual-spatial ability than it is to verbal ability (Hunt, 1997).

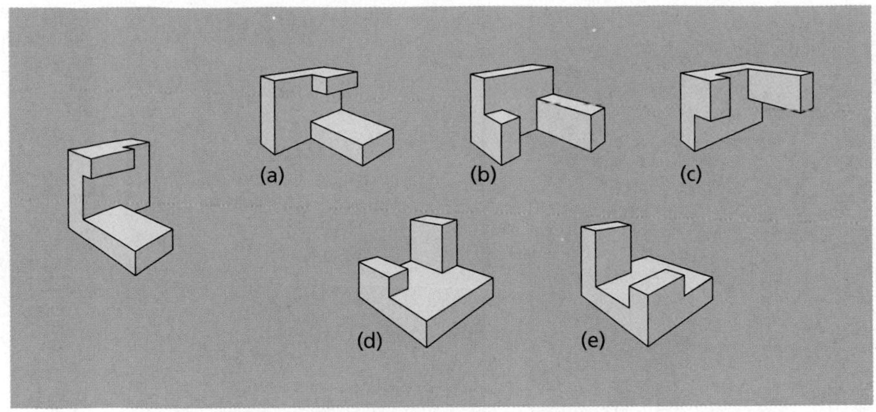

FIGURE 8.29

Visuo-spatial skills are assessed with problems like this one. Which of the five objects on the right is the same as the object on the left? (The answer appears on page 323).

What Do You Think?

IS INTELLIGENCE FIXED OR MALLEABLE?

Consider at this point one aspect of your personal conception of intelligence. Do you view intelligence to be relatively fixed and unchanging or to be quite changeable? How might your position influence your view of your (and others') potential and your approach to achievement situations? Think about it, then see page 324.

Crystallized and Fluid Intelligence Current knowledge about the nature of mental abilities suggests a position intermediate between Spearman's general intelligence and Thurstone's separate factors of the mind (Hunt, 1997). This position, originally developed by Raymond Cattell (1971) and subsequently extended by John Horn (1985), breaks down Spearman's general intelligence into two correlated (around .50) but distinct subtypes (Figure 8.30). **Crystallized intelligence** *is the ability to apply previously acquired knowledge to current problems.* It involves knowing facts and concepts and applying this knowledge. Vocabulary and information tests are good measures of crystallized intelligence. Crystallized intelligence, which is the basis for expertise, depends on the ability to retrieve previously learned information and problem-solving schemas from long-term memory (Horn & Masunaga, 2000; Hunt, 1997).

Cattell and Horn's second general factor is **fluid intelligence,** *defined as the ability to deal with novel problem-solving situations for which personal experience does not provide a solution.* It involves inductive reasoning and creative problem-solving skills like those discussed earlier in the chapter. The tower-of-Hanoi and nine-dot problems you worked on earlier in the chapter are fluid intelligence tasks. Fluid intelligence requires the abilities to reason abstractly, think logically, and manage information in working (short-term) memory so that new problems can be solved on the "blackboard of the mind" (Hunt, 1997). Thus long-term memory contributes strongly to crystallized intelligence and working memory to fluid intelligence.

Cattell and Horn argue that over our life span, we progress from using fluid intelligence to depending more on crystallized intelligence. Early in life, we encounter many problems for the first time, so we need fluid intelligence to figure out solutions. As experience makes us more knowledgeable, we have less need to approach each situation as a new problem. Instead, we simply call up appropriate information and schemas from long-term memory, thereby utilizing our crystallized intelligence. This is the essence of *wisdom*

▶ 21. Differentiate between crystallized and fluid intelligence and indicate their relation to aging and types of memory.

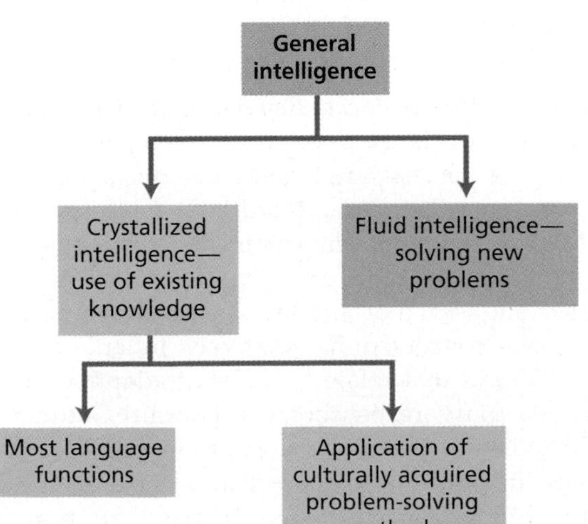

FIGURE 8.30

Cattell and Horn made an important distinction between crystallized and fluid intelligence. Crystallized intelligence is based more strongly on previous learning and experience, whereas fluid intelligence is a more creative type of intelligence.

FIGURE 8.31

According to Howard Gardner, these people are exhibiting specific forms of intelligence that are not measured on traditional intelligence tests.

(Kunzman & Baltes, 2003). Because long-term memory remains strong even as we age, performance on tests of crystallized intelligence improves during adulthood and remains stable well into late adulthood. In contrast, performance on tests of fluid intelligence begins to decline as people enter late adulthood (Schaie, 1998). Thus the issue of whether intelligence declines in old age depends on whether you are talking about crystallized or fluid intelligence (Cattell, 1998). The fact that age affects the two forms of intelligence differently is additional evidence that they represent different classes of mental abilities (Weinert & Hany, 2003).

▶ 22. What kinds of abilities are included in Gardner's multiple intelligences and in emotional intelligence?

Multiple Intelligences: Beyond Mental Competencies All the conceptions of intelligence discussed so far view intelligence in terms of *mental* competence. Yet if we regard intelligence as the ability to adapt to environmental demands, a broader conception emerges. Some psychologists suggest that intelligence may be more broadly conceived as relatively independent *intelligences* that relate to different adaptive demands. Harvard psychologist Howard Gardner (2003) is one of the strongest proponents of this view. Inspired by his observations of how specific human abilities were affected by brain damage, Gardner advanced a theory of multiple intelligences. The number of intelligences has varied as Gardner's work has progressed; he currently defines eight distinct varieties of adaptive abilities (Gardner, 2000):

1. *linguistic intelligence,* the ability to use language well, as writers do;
2. *logical-mathematical intelligence,* the ability to reason mathematically and logically;
3. *visuospatial intelligence,* the ability to solve spatial problems (such as the one in Figure 8.29) or to succeed in a field such as architecture;
4. *musical intelligence,* the ability to perceive pitch and rhythm and to understand and produce music;
5. *bodily-kinesthetic intelligence,* the ability to control body movements and skillfully manipulate objects, as demonstrated by a highly skilled dancer, athlete, or surgeon;
6. *interpersonal intelligence,* the ability to understand and relate well to others;
7. *intrapersonal intelligence,* the ability to understand oneself; and
8. *naturalistic intelligence,* the ability to detect and understand phenomena in the natural world, as a zoologist or meteorologist might.

Gardner's first three intelligences are measured by existing intelligence tests, but the others are not. Indeed, some of Gardner's critics insist that these other abilities are not really part of the traditional concept of intelligence. However, Gardner replies that the form of intelligence that is most highly valued within a given culture depends on the adaptive requirements of that culture. In Gardner's view, the abilities exhibited by Albert Einstein, Tiger Woods, and a "street-smart" gang leader exemplify different forms of intelligence that are highly adaptive within their respective environments (Figure 8.31). Gardner further suggests that these different classes of abilities require the functioning of separate but interacting modules in the brain. Gardner's approach, though provocative, remains controversial because it goes far beyond traditional conceptions of intelligence as mental skills.

Emotional Intelligence Another form of adaptive ability lies within the emotional realm. **Emotional intelligence** *involves the abilities to read others' emotions accurately, to respond to them appropriately, to motivate oneself, to be aware of one's own emotions, and to regulate and control one's own emotional responses* (Mayer & Salovey, 1997). Emotional intelligence combines elements of Gardner's interpersonal and intrapersonal intelligences.

Proponents of emotional intelligence point to the important adaptive advantages of emotional skills in meeting the challenges of daily life. Emotionally intelligent people, they suggest, form stronger emotional bonds with others; enjoy greater success in careers, marriage, and childrearing; modulate their own emotions so as to avoid strong depression, anger, or anxiety; and work more effectively toward long-term goals by being able to control impulses for immediate gratification. In the end, those high in emotional intelligence may enjoy more success in life than do others who surpass them in mental intelligence (Salovey & Pizzaro, 2003). Table 8.5 shows sample items from one self-report measure of emotional intelligence.

Critics of noncognitive forms of intelligence are concerned that the concept of intelligence is being stretched too far from its original focus on mental ability (e.g., Cooper, 1998). Proponents respond that if we regard intelligence as adaptive abilities, we ought not limit ourselves to the purely cognitive realms of human ability. This debate promises to continue long into the future.

For more on nonverbal language, see Interactive Segment 8.2.

TABLE 8.5 Sample Items From a Test of Emotional Intelligence

I am aware of the nonverbal messages I send to others.
I help other people feel better when they're down.
I have control over my emotions.
I easily recognize my emotions as I experience them.
I motivate myself by imagining a good outcome to tasks I take on.
I know why my emotions change.

NOTE: Items are answered on a 5-point scale ranging from 1, *strongly disagree*, to 5, *strongly agree*.
SOURCE: Schutte et al., 1998.

Cognitive Process Approaches: The Nature of Intelligent Thinking

Psychometric theories of intelligence are statistically sophisticated ways of describing *how* people differ from one another. What psychometric theories don't explain is *why* people vary in these ways. **Cognitive process theories** *explore the specific information-processing and cognitive processes that underlie intellectual ability*. Recall that this was the logic behind Galton's early attempts to relate thinking ability to speed of reaction and sensory acuity.

▶ 23. What three classes of psychological processes and forms of intelligence are found in Sternberg's triarchic theory?

Sternberg's Triarchic Theory Robert Sternberg (1988) is a leading proponent of the cognitive processes approach to intelligence. His **triarchic theory of intelligence** *addresses both the psychological processes involved in intelligent behavior and the diverse forms that intelligence can take.* Sternberg's theory divides the cognitive processes that underlie intelligent behavior into three specific components (Figure 8.32).

Metacomponents are the higher-order processes used to plan and regulate task performance. They include the problem-solving skills discussed earlier in the chapter: identifying problems, formulating hypotheses and strategies, testing them logically, and evaluating performance feedback. Sternberg believes that metacomponents are the fundamental sources of individual differences in fluid intelligence. He finds that intelligent people spend more time framing problems and developing strategies than do less intelligent people, who have a tendency to plunge right in without sufficient forethought.

The second-level components, *performance components*, are the actual mental processes used to perform the task. They include perceptual processing, retrieving appropriate memories and schemas from long-term memory, and making

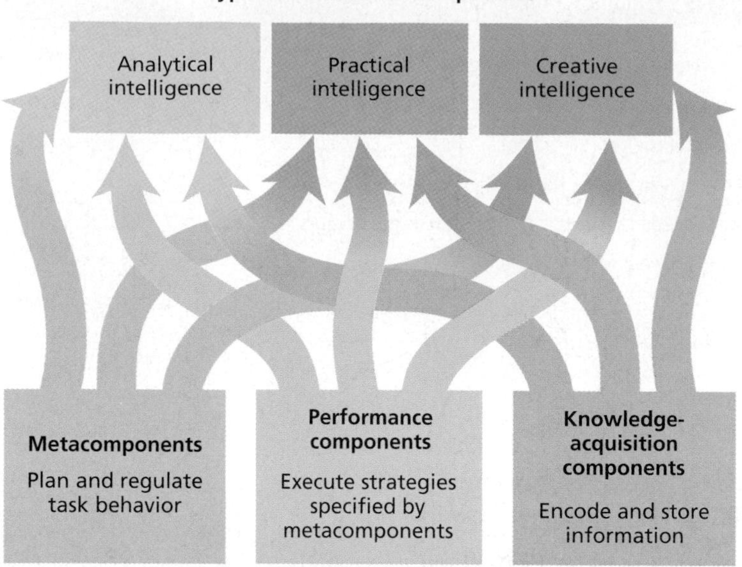

FIGURE 8.32

Sternberg's triarchic theory of intelligence includes three different types of intelligence and three classes of cognitive processes that underlie each type of intelligence.

responses. The third-level components are *knowledge acquisition components,* which allow us to learn from our experiences, store information in memory, and combine new insights with previously acquired information. These abilities underlie individual differences in crystallized intelligence. Thus Sternberg's theory addresses the processes that underlie the distinction made by Cattell and Horn between fluid and crystallized intelligences.

▶ 24. What evidence exists that neural efficiency and brain size underlie high intelligence?

Sternberg's theory, like Gardner's, proposes multiple intelligences. He suggests that environmental demands may call for three different classes of adaptive problem solving and that people differ in their intellectual strengths in these areas:

1. *Analytical intelligence* involves the kinds of academically oriented problem-solving skills assessed by traditional intelligence tests.
2. *Practical intelligence* refers to the skills needed to cope with everyday demands and to manage oneself and other people effectively. Emotional intelligence would fall within this category.
3. *Creative intelligence* comprises the mental skills needed to deal adaptively with novel problems.

Sternberg has shown that these forms of intelligence, while having a modest underlying *g* factor, are distinct from one another. Consider, for example, the relation between academic and practical skills. In one study, Kenyan adolescents were given one set of tests measuring traditional academic knowledge and another set measuring their knowledge of natural herbal medicines used to treat illnesses, a kind of knowledge viewed by villagers as important to their survival. The results indicated that the practical intelligence measure of herbal knowledge was unrelated to (and sometimes negatively correlated with) the academic measures (Sternberg et al., 2001).

Sternberg believes that educational programs should teach all three classes of skills, not just analytical-academic skills. In studies with elementary school children, he and his colleagues have shown that a curriculum that also teaches practical and creative skills results in greater mastery of course material than does a traditional analytic memory-based approach to learning course content (Sternberg et al., 1998). As Sternberg's work illustrates, cognitive science is leading us in a new direction in which the focus is on understanding and enhancing the mental processes that underlie intelligent behavior.

▶ ***Galton Resurrected: Intelligence and Neural Efficiency*** The scientific study of intelligence began in part with Sir Francis Galton's attempts to develop measures of nervous system efficiency that might underlie mental skills. As noted earlier, these attempts fell into disfavor because scores on his measures were unrelated to one another and to external criteria of success. As tools for directly measuring brain functions become more sophisticated, however, Galton's legacy lives on in current attempts to relate IQ to brain functioning (Posthuma et al., 2001). For example, one line of evidence comes from studies of brain metabolism. PET scans of people's brains taken while they engage in problem-solving tasks have shown lower levels of glucose consumption in people of high intelligence than in those of average or low intelligence, suggesting that intelligent brains work more efficiently and expend less energy (Haier et al., 1993). Whether these findings herald a new way of measuring intelligence is an unanswered question. The proof of this pudding will be in the ability of such measures to predict external achievement and performance criteria, as traditional intelligence tests do.

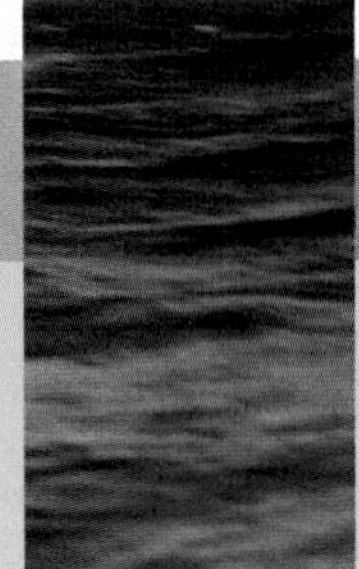

Beneath the Surface

BRAIN SIZE AND INTELLIGENCE: IS BIGGER BETTER?

The brain is clearly the locus of intellectual activities. As noted in Chapter 3, evolutionary evidence indicates a progressive increase in brain size as humanoid species evolved over the ages. Particularly evident is growth in the parts of the brain involved in higher mental functions, especially the cerebral cortex and frontal lobes (Kolb & Whishaw, 2002). Not suprisingly, therefore, scientists have entertained the hypothesis that within a given species, individual differences in brain size might be related to intellectual competency.

One intriguing way of testing this hypothesis might be to study the brains of dead geniuses to see if they differ from the brains of less brilliant people and, if so, how. Consider, for example, Albert Einstein's brain. After Albert Einstein's death in 1955, a Missouri physician removed and preserved his brain. The brain has undergone several analyses by neuroscientists over the years. Based on your knowledge of brain functions, what differences would you expect to find?

Perhaps Einstein's brain should be larger than average, at least in the areas related to his notable abilities. The examinations have shown that Einstein's brain was not larger than average overall; it was actually smaller than average in some regions. But it was indeed bigger in some ways. His parietal lobes were densely packed with both neurons and glial cells (which produce nutrients for neurons and support them). As a result, his parietal lobes were about 15 percent wider than normal. So densely was this brain area packed that some major fissures were no longer visible. Significantly, this area of the brain is involved in mathematical thinking and visual-spatial functions—precisely the kinds of abilities that seemed to underlie his creative genius (Witelson et al., 1999).

These findings are intriguing, but are you ready to conclude that the larger your brain is, the more intelligent you're likely to be? If so, consider these points: Women and men have virtually identical mean IQs, but women's brains are smaller on average (Ankney, 1992). Other research, beginning with Galton's, indicates that brain size is pretty much unrelated to intelligence. It's not how large your brain is but how efficiently it functions, and it is the efficiency question that drives today's research. Indeed, we can be thankful that brain size does not determine intelligence, for Neandertals, ancient humans hardly known for their intellectual brilliance, had slightly larger brains than we do (Kolb & Whishaw, 2002).

IN REVIEW

- *The psychometric approach to intelligence attempts to map the structure of intellect and establish how many different classes of mental ability underlie test performance. A newer approach, the cognitive processes approach, focuses on the specific thought processes that underlie mental competencies.*
- *Spearman believed that intelligence is determined both by specific cognitive abilities and by a general intelligence* (g) *factor that constitutes the core of intelligence. Thurstone disagreed, viewing intelligence as a set of specific abilities. Thurstone's position is best supported by observed distinctions between verbal and visual-spatial abilities.*
- *Cattell and Horn have differentiated between crystallized intelligence, the ability to apply previously learned knowledge to current problems, and fluid intelligence, the ability to deal with novel problem-solving situations for which personal experience does not provide a solution. They argue that over our life span, we show a progressive shift from using fluid intelligence to using crystallized intelligence as we attain wisdom.*
- *Gardner and Sternberg maintain that there are distinct forms of intelligence beyond the traditional concept. Emotional intelligence refers to people's ability to read and respond appropriately to others' emotions, to motivate themselves, and to be aware of and in control of their emotions.*
- *Cognitive process theories of intelligence have focused on the elementary information-processing abilities that contribute to intelligence. Sternberg's triarchic theory of intelligence includes a components subtheory that addresses the specific cognitive processes that underlie intelligent behavior. Recent physiological evidence suggests that the brains of intelligent people may function more efficiently.*

TABLE 8.6 Correlations in Intelligence Among People Who Differ in Genetic Similarity and Who Live Together or Apart

Relationship	Percentage of Shared Genes	Correlation of IQ Scores
Identical twins reared together	100	.86
Identical twins reared apart	100	.75
Nonidentical twins reared together	50	.57
Siblings reared together	50	.45
Siblings reared apart	50	.21
Biological parent–offspring reared by parent	50	.36
Biological parent–offspring not reared by parent	50	.20
Cousins	25	.25
Adopted child-adoptive parent	0	.19
Adopted children reared together	0	.02

SOURCES: Based on Bouchard & McGue, 1981; Bouchard et al., 1990; Scarr, 1992.

Heredity, Environment, and Intelligence

▶ 25. What evidence supports a genetic contribution to intelligence, and how much IQ group variation is accounted for?

To what extent are differences in intelligence due to genetic factors, and to what extent does environment determine such differences? This seemingly simple question has long been a source of controversy and, at times, bitter debate.

▶ 26. How does the concept of reaction range illustrate the interaction between heredity and environment?

Let's first examine the genetic argument. Suppose that intelligence is totally determined by genes. (No psychologist today would maintain that it is, but examining the extreme view can be instructive.) In that case, any two individuals with exactly the same genes would have identical test scores, so the correlation between the test scores of identical (monozygotic) twins would be +1.00. Nonidentical brothers and sisters (including fraternal twins, who result from two fertilized eggs) share only half their genes. Therefore the correlation between the test scores of fraternal twins and other siblings should be substantially lower. Extending the argument, the correlation between a parent's test scores and his or her children's scores should be about the same as that between siblings, because a child inherits only half of his or her genes from each parent.

What do the actual data look like? Table 8.6 summarizes the results from many studies. As you can see, the correlations between the test scores of identical twins are substantially higher than any other correlations. Identical twins separated early in life and reared apart are of special interest because they have identical genes but experienced different environments. The correlation for identical twins raised apart is nearly as high as that for identical twins reared together, and higher than that for nonidentical twins raised together (Bouchard et al., 1990). Moreover, as Table 8.6 shows, IQs of adopted children correlate as highly with their biological parents' IQ as with the IQs of the adoptive parents who reared them. The pattern is quite clear: The more genes people have in common, the more similar they tend to be in IQ. This is very strong evidence that genes play a significant role in intelligence (Petrill, 2003).

Notice, however, that the figure for identical twins raised together is higher than the figure for identical twins raised apart. The same is true for other types of siblings raised together and raised apart. This rules out an entirely genetic explanation. Although one's genotype seems to be an important factor in determining intelligence test scores, it probably accounts for only 50 to 70 percent of the IQ variation between people in the United States (Bouchard et al., 1990; Plomin, 1997). Thus environment, too, contributes significantly to intelligence. Obviously, then, the question with which this section began is too simplistic. The real question should be, "How do heredity and environment *interact* to affect intelligence?"

For more on the study of twins, see Video Segment 8.1.

Biological Reaction Range, Environment, and Intelligence

The concept of reaction range contributes to our understanding of genetic-environmental interactions. The **reaction range** *for a genetically influenced trait is the range of possibilities—the upper and lower limits—that the genetic code allows.* Thus, to say that intelligence is genetically influenced does not mean that intelligence is fixed at birth. Instead, it means that an individual inherits a range for potential intelligence that has upper and lower limits. Environmental effects will then determine where the person falls within these genetically determined boundaries. Each of us has a range of intellectual potential that is jointly influenced by two factors: our genetic inheritance and the opportunities our environment provides for acquiring intellectual skills. Although there is evidence for a genetic basis for the *g* factor (Plomin & Craig, 2002), there clearly is not a single "intelligence gene." The diverse abilities measured by intelligence tests are undoubtedly influenced by large numbers of interacting genes, and different combinations seem to underlie specific abilities (Luciano et al., 2001).

At present, genetic reaction ranges cannot be measured directly, and we do not know if their sizes differ from one person to another. But studies of IQ gains associated with environmental enrichment and adoption programs suggest that the ranges could be as large as 15 to 20 points on the IQ scale (Dunn & Plomin, 1990). If this is indeed the case, then the influence of environmental factors on intelligence would be highly significant.

Some practical implications of the reaction range concept are illustrated in Figure 8.33. First, consider persons B and H. They have identical reaction ranges, but B develops in a very deprived environment and H in an enriched environment with many cultural and educational advantages. Person H is able to realize her innate potential and has an IQ that is 20 points higher than person B's. Now compare persons C and I. Person C actually has greater intellectual potential than person I, but ends up with a lower IQ as a result of living in an environment that does not allow that potential to develop. Finally, note person G, who was born with high genetic endowment and reared in an enriched environment. His IQ of 110 is lower than we would expect, suggesting that he did not take advantage of either his biological capacity or his environmental advantages. This serves to reminds us that intellectual growth depends not only on genetic endowment and environmental advantage but also on interests, motivation, and other personal characteristics that affect how much we "apply ourselves," or take advantage of our gifts and opportunities.

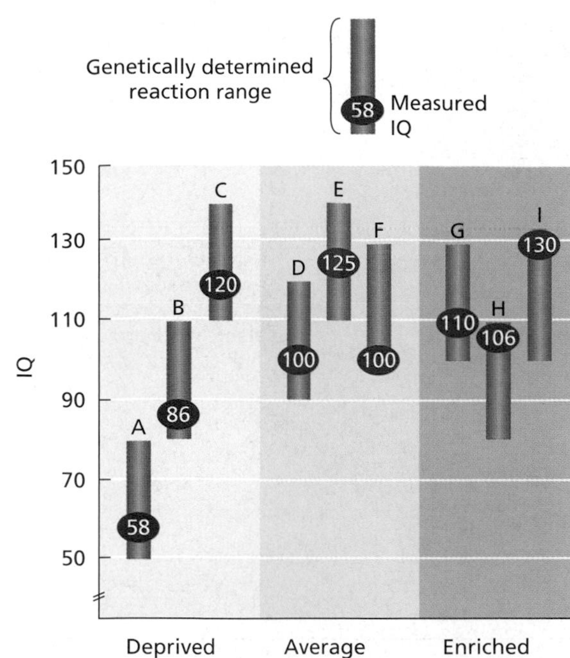

FIGURE 8.33

Reaction ranges, environment, and intelligence. Genetic endowment is believed to create a reaction range within which environment exerts its effects. Enriched environments are expected to allow a person's intelligence to develop to the upper region of his or her reaction range, whereas deprived environments may limit intelligence to the lower portion of the range. The reaction range may cover as much as 15 to 20 points on the IQ scale.

Cultural and Group Differences in Intelligence

> We know that you highly esteem the kind of learning taught in those colleges. . . . But you, who are wise, must know that different nations have different conceptions of things: and you will not therefore take it amiss, if our ideas of this kind of education happen not to be the same with yours. We have had some experience of it; several of our young people were formerly brought up at the colleges of the Northern provinces; they were instructed in all your sciences; but, when they came back to us, they were bad runners, ignorant of every means of living in the woods, unable to bear either cold or hunger, knew neither how to build a cabin, take a deer, nor kill an enemy, spoke our language imperfectly, were therefore neither fit for hunters, warriors, nor counselors; they were totally good for nothing. . . . We are, however not the less obligated by your kind offer, though we decline accepting it; and to show our grateful sense of it, if the gentlemen of Virginia will send us a dozen of their sons, we will take care of their education, instruct them in all we know, and make men of them. (A Native American leader quoted in Benjamin Franklin, *Remarks Concerning the Savage of North America* [1784])

This response to a well-intentioned offer by colonists to provide Native American children with access to White educational opportunities reminds us that if we view intelligence as adaptive behavior, people in other cultures may have entirely different conceptions of which behaviors are intelligent. This should serve to remind us that intelligence is a cultural construction, based on the adaptive demands that confront a culture and the behaviors that are required to cope with those demands. Consider, for example, what the items on an intelligence test constructed within that traditional Native American culture might be like. Undoubtedly, they would bear little resemblance to test items on a Wechsler scale.

▶ 27. What explanations have been offered for group differences in IQ between ethnic groups?

Ethnic Group Differences Some of the most contentious debates in psychology have concerned the existence and meaning of ethnic and racial group differences in intelligence. Discussions of

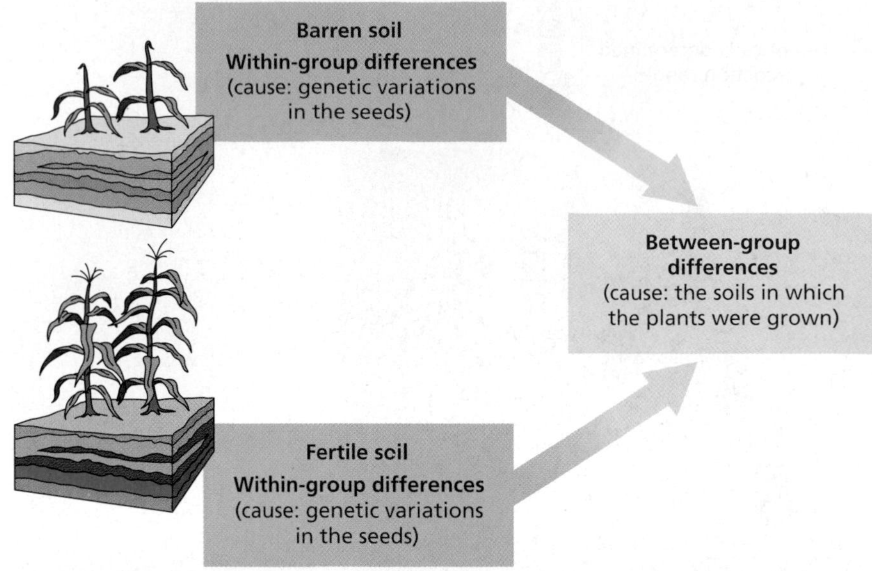

FIGURE 8.34

The interaction of heredity and environment is shown in this agricultural analogy. Seeds planted in a fertile field will yield plants, on average, larger than those planted in poor soil. This between-groups variability is attributable to environment. Within each field, however, plants will also differ in size as a result of genetic factors. Applied to intelligence, this analogy indicates how between-group differences could result from environmental factors despite the fact that intelligence has a strong genetic component.

intellectual differences between ethnic groups and between men and women touch on deeply held notions of social equality. Because the questions under scrutiny are complex and the evidence does not warrant any simple conclusion, the debate is unlikely to be resolved any time soon.

Where ethnic groups are concerned, everyone agrees on certain facts. Today there are consistent differences in the average intelligence test scores of members of different racial and national groups. National comparisons indicate that Japanese children have the highest mean IQ in the world (Hunt, 1995). Their mean score of 111 places 77 percent of Japanese children above the mean scores of U.S. and European children. Within the United States, significant ethnic differences also exist. Asian Americans test somewhat above White American norms, especially on tests related to visual-spatial and mathematical reasoning. Hispanics who have become U.S.-acculturated score at about the same level as White Americans. African Americans score, on average, about 12 to 15 IQ points below the White American average (Jencks et al., 1998). This, of course, does not mean that all White Americans and Hispanic Americans test lower than Asian Americans or that all African Americans test lower than the other ethnic groups. There is great overlap among group IQ distributions, and in all groups, some individuals score at the highest levels. Nonetheless, the average group differences are large enough to have practical consequences, such as ethnic differences in academic achievement. The unanswered question is: Where do these differences come from? Much work is currently underway to separate science from myth (Fish, 2002).

Keep in mind that these group differences apply to test scores, which are the standard operational definition of the construct we call "intelligence." Some have expressed concerns that these tests underestimate the mental competence of minority group members because the tests are based on Euro-American White culture and therefore are culturally biased. But defenders of the tests point out that racial differences appear throughout intelligence tests, not just on those items that would, at face value, appear to be culturally biased (Jensen, 1980, 1998). They also point out that intelligence test scores predict the performance of minority group members as accurately as they predict White performance (Barrett & Depinet, 1991; Hartigan & Wigdor, 1989). For example, even though African Americans as a group score lower than White Americans, the tests predict academic and occupational performance with equal (if somewhat modest) accuracy for both racial groups, indicating that they are measuring relevant mental skills (Hunt, 1995).

The next dispute about racial differences is a rather different one. The nature-nurture discussion tentatively accepts the differences in measures of mental abilities as being real and then asks why they exist. Consider the differences between White Americans and African Americans. On the nurture side, there is no question that a higher proportion of White American than African American children are raised and schooled in enriched environments that optimize the development of cognitive skills. However, social changes over the past 25 years have provided African Americans with greater access to educational and vocational opportunities and have coincided with an increase in African American IQs that has reduced the IQ difference between African Americans and White Americans (Barnett & Camilli, 2002). These shrinking ethnic differences also extend to reading and mathematics achievement tests in grades 1 through 12, as well as to scores on the SAT (Block, 2002). People who are impressed by this decreasing test gap tend to attribute racial differences to environmental differences that could be changed, ranging from nutritional factors to educational opportunities (Grigorenko, 2003; Nisbett, 1998).

Consider, for example, the results of one intervention program for impoverished African

American children in North Carolina (Landesman & Ramey, 1989). The children were exposed to an intensive early-education program that began when they were 6 months old and lasted until they entered kindergarten. At age 15, these children had higher IQs and higher scores on standardized tests of reading and mathematics than did a control group of similar children. The study also showed, however, that such interventions need to start early in life to counteract an intellectually impoverished home environment, for children exposed to the program once they entered school did not show these gains. In another study, Meredith Phillips and coworkers (1998) analyzed a wide range of family environment factors in relation to intellectual differences between 5- and 6-year-old African American and White children. They concluded that family environment factors alone could account for about two thirds of the test score gap. Figure 8.34 provides an agricultural analogue of how environmental factors can produce group differences even for a genetically influenced variable.

The key role played by the cultural environment also may be illustrated by a historical example involving a different minority group. Early in the 20th century, the average Italian American child had an IQ of 87, about the same as the average score of African Americans today. Henry Goddard (1917), a leading hereditarian researcher of the time, concluded that 79 percent of Italian American immigrants were "feebleminded," posed a danger to the U.S. gene pool, and should not be allowed to immigrate to the United States. Today, the average Italian American student obtains an above-average IQ (Ceci, 1996). Obviously, genetic changes could not produce a result of this size over such a short time. Cultural assimilation and educational and economic opportunity seem much more reasonable explanations for this pronounced increase in test scores.

Another factor worth noting is a tendency, even among some scientists, to overemphasize genetic differences between groups. Indeed, where measured directly, gene differences tend to be greater *within* any given racial group than they are between racial groups (Block, 2002). For example, both African Americans and White Americans exhibit greater genetic variation among themselves than that which exists between the average African American and the average White American.

Sex Differences in Cognitive Abilities Men and women differ in physical attributes and reproductive function. They also differ in their performance on certain types of intellectual tasks. The gender differences lie not in levels of general intelligence but rather in the patterns of cognitive skills that men and women exhibit. Men, on average, tend to outperform women slightly on certain spatial tasks, such as the ones shown in Figure 8.35. Men are more accurate in target-directed skills, such as throwing and catching objects, and they tend to perform slightly better on tests of mathematical reasoning. Women, on average, perform better on tests of perceptual speed, verbal fluency, mathematical calculation, and on precise manual tasks requiring fine motor coordination (Collins & Kimura, 1997). Although relatively small, these ability differences have been reported quite consistently by researchers (Halpern, 2000; Hampson & Kimura, 1992). Keep in mind, however, that men and women also vary considerably among themselves in all of these skills, and the performance distributions of males and females overlap considerably.

Psychologists have proposed explanations for these gender differences, citing both biological and environmental factors. The environmental explanations typically focus on the socialization experiences that males and females have as they grow up, especially the kinds of sex-typed

▶ 28. What sex differences exist in cognitive skills? What biological and environmental factors might be involved?

Problem-solving tasks favoring women

Women tend to perform better than men on tests of perceptual speed, in which people must rapidly identify matching items—for example, pairing the house on the far left with its twin.

On some tests of ideational fluency, for example those in which people must list objects that are the same color, and on tests of verbal fluency, for example those in which participants must list words that begin with the same letter, women also outperform men.

L _ _ _ _ | Limp, Livery, Love, Laser, Liquid, Low, Like, Lag, Live, Lug, Light, Lift, Liver, Lime, Leg, Load, Lap, Lucid . . .

Problem-solving tasks favoring men

Men tend to perform better than women on certain spatial tasks. They do well on tests that involve mentally rotating an object or manipulating it in some fashion such as choosing which of the 3 objects at the right is the same as the one on the left.

Men also are more accurate than women in target-directed motor skills, such as guiding or intercepting projectiles.

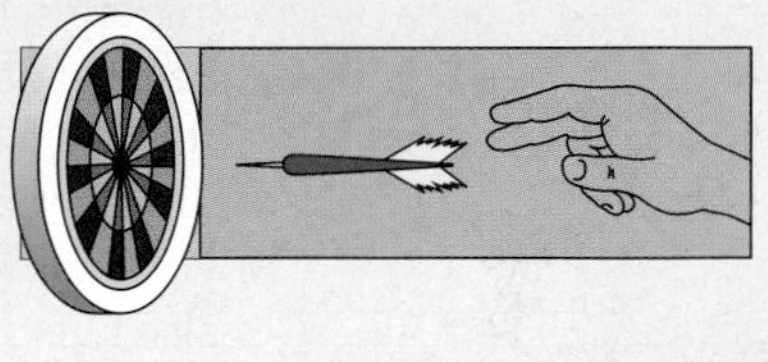

FIGURE 8.35

Among the most consistent gender differences in cognitive abilities reported in the scientific literature are skills involved in tasks like these. Adapted from Kimura, 1992.

▶ 29. How can teachers' expectations and stereotype threat influence academic performance?

activities that boys and girls are steered into (Crawford & Chaffin, 1997). Prior to the early 1980s, for example, boys were far more likely than girls to play sports that involve throwing and catching balls, which might help account for their general superiority in this ability. Evolutionary theorists have also weighed in on the differences, suggesting that sex role specialization developed in ancestral environments. Men's roles, such as navigating and hunting, favored the development of the visual-spatial abilities that show up in sex-difference research. Women's roles, such as child-rearing and tool-making activities, favored the development of verbal and manual precision abilities (Joseph, 2000).

Biological explanations have increasingly focused on the effects of hormones on the developing brain (Halpern & Tan, 2001). These influences begin during a critical period shortly after conception, when the sex hormones establish sexual differentiation. The hormonal effects go far beyond reproductive characteristics, however. They also alter brain organization and appear to extend to a variety of behavioral differences between men and women, including aggression and problem-solving approaches (Nelson & Luciana, 2001). Hormonal factors also influence performance later in life, as fluctuations in women's hormonal levels during the menstrual cycle are related to fluctuations in task performance. When women have high levels of the female hormone estrogen, they perform better on some of the "feminine" ability measures while showing declines in performance on some of the "male" ones (Kimura, 1992; Moody, 1997).

Beliefs, Expectations, and Cognitive Performance

Cognitive abilities are not the only mental determinants of how well people perform on intellectual and academic measures. Beliefs are also very important. Our beliefs about others' capabilities can affect how we respond to them. For example, many studies have shown that if teachers are told that a particular child has hidden potential (or, alternatively, has intellectual limitations), they increase or decrease the amount of attention and effort expended on that child, thereby influencing the child's development of cognitive skills (Rosenthal, 1985).

Even more important at times are our own self-beliefs, which tell us who we are and what we can and cannot do. Can self-beliefs and widely held social beliefs about groups we identify with affect our performance on cognitive tasks? An important line of research, described in the following *Research Close-Up*, suggests that stereotypes about the capabilities of minorities and women may indeed affect their performance.

RESEARCH CLOSE-UP

STEREOTYPE THREAT AND COGNITIVE PERFORMANCE

Background

Our self-concept is based on numerous experiences that convey to us who we are, how valued we are, and what we are capable of achieving in our lives. Some of this information comes from observing the consequences of our own behavior. But our self-concept can also be influenced by our membership in racial and gender groups. If certain stereotypes are widely associated with these groups, we may incorporate them into our self-concept. Once accepted, these self-beliefs may push us to behave in a way that is consistent with our self-concept. But even if not incorporated into the self, group members can experience **stereotype threat** *if they believe that certain behaviors on their part would confirm a negative stereotype in the minds of others.* Claude Steele believes that stereotype threat evokes anxiety and undermines performance. To test this hypothesis, Steele and his coworkers assessed the academic performance effects of evoking two widely held stereotypes: (1) that African Americans have less intellectual ability than do White Americans, and (2) that women have less mathematical ability than men do.

SOURCE: Claude M. Steele (1997). A threat in the air: How stereotypes shape intellectual identity and performance. *American Psychologist, 52,* 613–629.

Method

Two studies were conducted with students at Stanford University (Spencer et al., 1999; Steele & Aronson, 1995). In the first, men and women who were good in math were given a difficult mathematics exam whose items were taken from the advanced mathematics test of the Graduate Record Examination (GRE). Participants were randomly assigned to one of two experimental conditions designed to either activate the stereotype or not. Participants in the stereotype-relevant condition were told that the test generally showed sex differences (expected to activate the stereotype of women as being inferior to men in math). In the other condition, the students were told that scores on the test showed no sex differences. The dependent variable was the students' scores on the math problems.

In the second study, African American and White American students were tested on the most difficult items from the GRE verbal test. Again, there were two experimental conditions, this time varying the racial relevance of the test. In one condition, the students were told that the test was a measure of intelligence (expected to activate the stereotype of African Americans as being less intelligent than White Americans). In the other condition, the students were told that the items were part of a laboratory task that was unrelated to general intellectual ability.

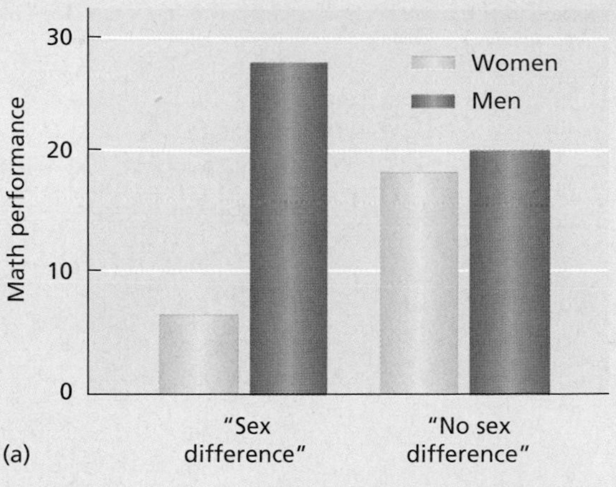

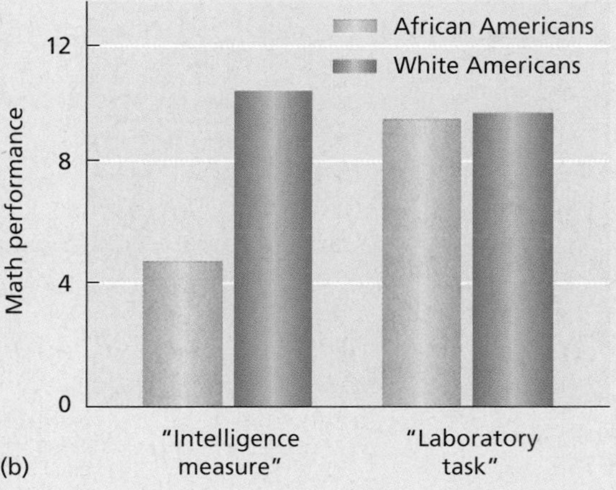

FIGURE 8.36

Effects of stereotype threat on cognitive performance. (a) The activation of the stereotype that women do less well than males in math was associated with poorer performance by women and enhanced performance by men, compared with the control condition, where men and women performed at the same level. (b) Reference to racial differences on the task resulted in reduced performance by African American students. SOURCE: Steele, 1997.

Results

The results of the two experiments, shown in Figure 8.36, were strikingly similar. In the first (Figure 8.36a), women and men performed at an equivalent level on the math problems when they were told there were no sex differences on the test. However, the picture changed dramatically when the task was made relevant to the gender stereotype. Women's performance dropped, and men's performance increased, producing a marked performance difference between the two sexes. In Figure 8.36b, we see a similar pattern of results when the racial stereotype was made relevant to the task. African American students performed more poorly than White American students when it was implied that test performance was influenced by intelligence, but there were no racial differences in performance when students were told that the task was not affected by level of mental ability.

Discussion

This research dramatically illustrates how stereotype-based aspects of the self-concept can affect behavior, in this case, cognitive performance. Steele (1997) believes that in the stereotype-relevant conditions, the threat of doing poorly on the test and being branded as a "math-deficient woman" or an "intellectually inferior African American" aroused anxiety that lowered performance.

The results have broad societal implications and might help explain the fact that, over the course of their academic careers, women exhibit less inclination to pursue mathematics, even though, on average, they are slightly superior to men in mathematical calculation skills (Kimura, 1992; Lee, 1998). Later research has shown that the more strongly women are identified with their female sex role, the more susceptible they are to stereotype threat (Schmader, 2002). Perhaps stereotype threat also helps account for the fact that African American children become progressively less identified with and invested in academics as they progress through school and that many drop out altogether (Major et al., 1998). In both cases, the sex and racial ability differences are slight to nonexistent when children first enter school. What happens thereafter as females and minorities confront, and perhaps internalize, the stereotypes about their mental abilities may be an important environmental determinant of their performance.

TABLE 8.7 Adaptive Capabilities of Cognitively Challenged People Over the Life Span

Category	Percentage of Retarded Population	Characteristics from Birth to Adulthood: Birth Through Age 5	Age 6 Through Age 20	Age 21 and Older
Mild: 50–70 IQ	85	Often not noticed as delayed by casual observer but is slower to walk, feed him- or herself, and talk than most children.	Can acquire practical skills and master reading and arithmetic to a third- to sixth-grade level with special education. Can be guided toward social conformity.	Can usually achieve adequate social, vocational, and self-maintenance skills. May need occasional guidance and support when under unusual social or economic stress.
Moderate: 35–50 IQ	10	Noticeable delays in motor development, especially in speech. Responds to training in various self-help activities.	Can learn simple communication, elementary health and safety habits, and simple manual skills. Does not progress in functional reading or arithmetic.	Can perform simple tasks under sheltered conditions, participate in simple recreation, and travel alone in familiar places. Usually incapable of self-maintenance.
Severe: 20–35 IQ	4	Marked delay in motor development. Little or no communication skill. May respond to training in elementary self-help, such as self-feeding.	Usually walks, barring specific disability. Has some understanding of speech and some response. Can profit from systematic habit training.	Can conform to daily routines and repetitive activities. Needs continuing direction and supervision in protective environment.
Profound: below 20 IQ	1	Gross disability. Minimal capacity for functioning in sensorimotor areas. Needs nursing care.	Obvious delays in all areas of development. Shows basic emotional responses. May respond to skillful training in use of legs, hands, and jaws. Needs close supervision.	May walk, need nursing care, have primitive speech. Usually benefits from regular physical activity. Incapable of self-maintenance.

Extremes of Intelligence

Because of the many genetic and environmental influences on intelligence, there are individuals at both ends of the intelligence distribution who have unusual mental abilities. At the low end are those labeled "mentally retarded" or "cognitively disabled"; at the upper end are the "intellectually gifted."

The Cognitively Disabled

Approximately 3 to 5 percent of the U.S. population, or about 10 million people, are classified as mentally retarded, or cognitively disabled. The American Psychiatric Association has devised a four-level system that classifies cognitive disability as mild, moderate, severe, or profound on the basis of IQ scores. Table 8.7 describes these classifications. As you can see, the vast majority are mildly disabled, obtaining IQs between about 50 and 70. Most members of this largest group, given appropriate social and educational support, are capable of functioning adequately in mainstream society, holding jobs and raising families. Progressively greater environmental support is needed as we move toward the profoundly disabled range, where institutional care is usually required.

Mildly disabled children can attend school, but they have difficulties with tasks requiring reading, writing, memory, and mathematical computation. Many of their difficulties result from poorly developed problem-solving strategies. They often have difficulties in the executive functions discussed in Chapter 3: reasoning, planning, and evaluating feedback from their efforts (Molfese & Molfese, 2002).

Cognitive disability has a variety of causes, some genetic, some due to other biological factors, and some due to environmental causes. Genetic abnormalities account for about 28 percent of all mental retardation cases (Winnepenninckx et al., 2003). More than 100 different genetic causes of retardation have been identified. For example, *Down syndrome* (formerly called *mongolism*), which is characterized by mild to severe mental retardation, is caused by an abnormal division of the 21st chromosome pair. Retardation can also be caused by accidents at birth, such as severe deprivation of oxygen (anoxia); and by diseases experienced by the mother during pregnancy, such as rubella or syphilis. Likewise, drugs and alcohol taken by the mother—especially in the first weeks of pregnancy when a woman is often unaware she is pregnant—can cause neural damage and mental retardation. Despite this range of potential causes, in a significant majority (75 to 80 percent) of cases, no clear biological cause can be found. Experts theorize that that these cases may be due to undetectable brain damage, extreme environmental deprivation, or a combination of the two.

In the United States, federal law requires that cognitively disabled children, who were formerly segregated into special education classes, be given individualized instruction in the "least restrictive environment." This has resulted in the practice of *mainstreaming*, or *inclusion programs*, which allows many cognitively challenged children to attend school in regular classrooms and experience a more normal peer environment (Figure 8.37).

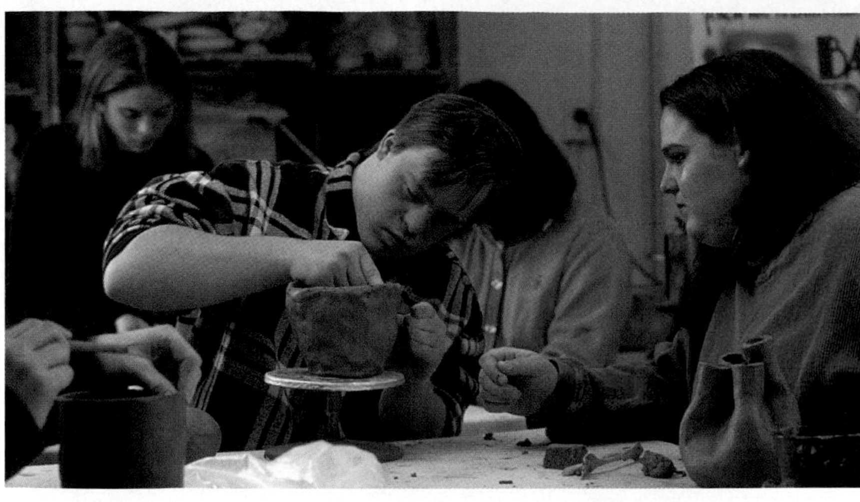

FIGURE 8.37

Increasingly, children of low intelligence have been included in normal classrooms rather than being confined to special education programs.

The Intellectually Gifted

At the other end of the intelligence bell curve are the intellectually gifted, whose IQs over 135 place them in the top 1 percent of the population. Their high IQs do not mean that they are good at everything. As we might expect from the theories of multiple intelligences, many are enormously talented in one area of mental competence but quite average in other domains. Even with IQs over 150, large discrepancies are often found between verbal and spatial-mathematical skills (Achter et al., 1996). Thus a mathematical prodigy who figures out rules of algebra on her own at age 3 may have relatively undistinguished verbal skills.

What distinguishes the thought processes of the gifted? Some theorists believe that gifted children think in the same way as average children but simply do it much more efficiently (Jackson & Butterfield, 1986). Others disagree. When they see a child capable of memorizing an entire musical score after hearing it once, they conclude that this ability is based on a different quality of thinking that involves great intuition and a passion for the specific domain in which the child excels (Winner, 2000).

Like children at the low end of the competence continuum, intellectually gifted children often need special educational opportunities. They may become bored in regular classrooms and even drop out of school if they are not sufficiently challenged (Fetterman, 1988). Yet many school systems have deemphasized programs for the gifted in the same spirit of egalitarianism that underlies inclusion programs for the cognitively challenged. Increasingly, parents of gifted children are enrolling their children in special camps and extracurricular programs to provide the needed intellectual stimulation and exposure to peer groups with common interests and abilities (Winner, 2000).

Giftedness and Adjustment Like the cognitively disabled, the gifted are often the victims of stereotypes. Some characterize them as "geeks" and "nerds" who are eccentric and socially maladjusted. As is the case with many stereotypes, there is a grain of truth here. A review of the scientific literature on giftedness by Ellen Winner (2000) revealed that nearly a fourth of children with truly exceptional IQs (in the 180 range) have social and psychological problems, about twice the rate found in nongifted children. Such children often have different interest patterns and find it difficult to find like-minded peers to relate to, resulting in solitude and loneliness. The research also revealed, however, that the vast majority of these highly intelligent children show adequate adjustment, providing evidence against any stereotype that would be applied to gifted children in general.

▶ 30. How does intellectual giftedness relate to personal adjustment?

Consider a project begun in the 1920s by Lewis Terman, the psychologist who developed the Stanford-Binet test. Terman identified 1,528 California children who had a mean IQ of 150 and began an extensive study of them that has continued for over 70 years. Terman and the researchers who inherited the project found the "Termites," as they were called, to be above average not only in intelligence but also in height, weight, strength, physical health, emotional adjustment, and social maturity. They continued to exhibit high levels of adjustment throughout their adolescent and adult years. By midlife, the 1,528 Termites had authored 92 books, 2,200 scientific articles, and 235 patents. Their marriages tended to be happy and successful, and they seemed well adjusted psychologically (Sears, 1977). Nonetheless, some of the Termites underachieved and experienced social and psychological problems. These tended to come from lower

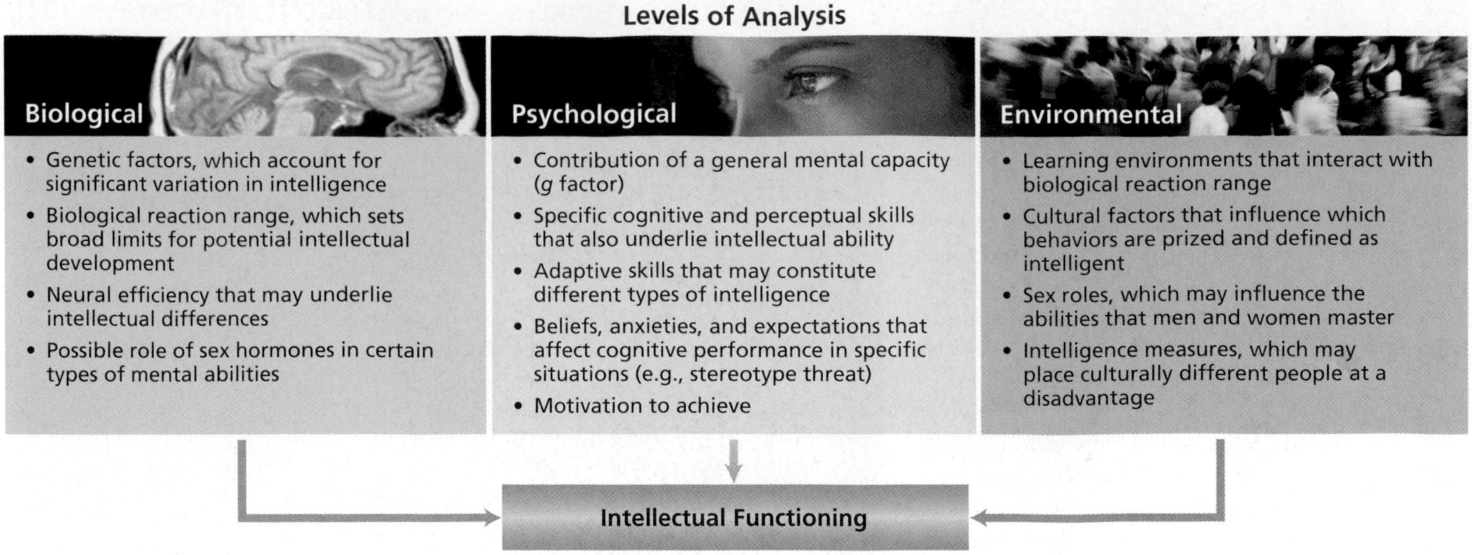

Levels of Analysis

Biological	Psychological	Environmental
• Genetic factors, which account for significant variation in intelligence • Biological reaction range, which sets broad limits for potential intellectual development • Neural efficiency that may underlie intellectual differences • Possible role of sex hormones in certain types of mental abilities	• Contribution of a general mental capacity (*g* factor) • Specific cognitive and perceptual skills that also underlie intellectual ability • Adaptive skills that may constitute different types of intelligence • Beliefs, anxieties, and expectations that affect cognitive performance in specific situations (e.g., stereotype threat) • Motivation to achieve	• Learning environments that interact with biological reaction range • Cultural factors that influence which behaviors are prized and defined as intelligent • Sex roles, which may influence the abilities that men and women master • Intelligence measures, which may place culturally different people at a disadvantage

Intellectual Functioning

FIGURE 8.38

Understanding Behavior: Factors that influence intellectual performance.

socioeconomic backgrounds and to have parents who did not emphasize success or convey success expectations. The results were lowered motivation to achieve and a lack of confidence that they could accomplish their goals.

Findings such as these have led to a broadening of the concept of giftedness beyond simply having a high IQ. Many theorists also include high levels of motivation to develop one's gifts, exceptional interest in the domain, and the ability to capitalize on whatever one is exceptionally good at (Renzulli, 1986). These nonintellectual factors support the development of the person's giftedness.

We began this chapter with an incident that demonstrated an uncommon level of expertise and mental resourcefulness that saved an airliner from almost certain destruction. Over the past three chapters, we have seen how humans learn, how they remember what they've learned, and how they use their minds to adapt to environmental demands. Language, thinking, and intelligent behavior are intimately connected with one another and with the processes of learning and memory. As we have also seen, intelligent behavior has many causal factors. Some of these factors are summarized in Figure 8.38.

IN REVIEW

- *Intelligence is determined by interacting hereditary and environmental factors. Heredity establishes a reaction range with upper and lower limits for intellectual potential. Environment affects the point within that range that will be reached.*
- *Cultural and ethnic differences in intelligence exist (though they may be narrowing), but the relative contributions of genetic and environmental factors are still in question. Evidence exists for both genetic and environmental determinants.*
- *Although the differences are not large, men tend as a group to score higher than women on certain spatial and mathematical reasoning tasks. Women perform slightly better than men on tests of perceptual speed, verbal fluency, mathematical calculation, and fine motor coordination. Both environmental and biological bases of such differences have been suggested. Stereotype threat is one potential psychological factor for both sex-based and racial performance differences.*
- *Cognitive disability can be caused by a number of factors. Biological causes are identified in only about 25 percent of cases. Cognitive disability can range from mild to profound. The vast majority of disabled individuals are able to function in the mainstream of society, given appropriate support.*
- *People with exceptionally high IQs have a higher frequency of social and psychological problems than do people of normal intelligence, but most adjust adequately. Lewis Terman's longitudinal study of gifted children indicated that these individuals, as a group, tended to be well adjusted and to have happy and productive adulthoods. Other personality, motivational, and environmental factors—combined with their high intelligence—also contributed to their success.*

Answers to Problems in Text

Figure 8.16 Baltimore and Washington are 50 miles apart. The trains are traveling at the same speed (25 mph). Hence, they will meet at the halfway point, which is 25 miles, after one hour of travel time. Since the crow is flying at 60 mph, it will have flown a total of 60 miles when the trains meet.

Figure 8.20 Sequence of moves: **A** to **3**, **B** to **2**, **A** to **2**, **C** to **3**, **A** to **1**, **B** to **3**, **A** to **3**.

Figure 8.23 Here are two solutions to the nine-dot problem. Both require you to think "outside the box."

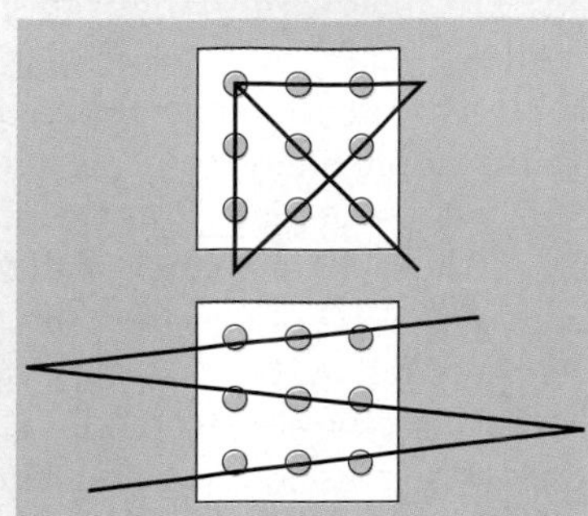

Figure 8.24 Solution to the candlestick problem.

Figure 8.29 Object **b** is identical.

KEY TERMS AND CONCEPTS

Each term has been boldfaced and defined in the chapter on the page indicated in parentheses.

achievement test (p. 304)
algorithms (p. 295)
aptitude test (p. 304)
availability heuristic (p. 297)
belief bias (p. 292)
cognitive process theories (p. 311)
concept (p. 289)
confirmation bias (p. 298)
construct validity (p. 305)
content validity (p. 306)
creativity (p. 299)
crystallized intelligence (p. 309)
deductive reasoning (p. 291)
deep structure (p. 281)
discourse (p. 282)
displacement (p. 281)
divergent thinking (p. 299)
emotional intelligence (p. 311)
factor analysis (p. 308)
fluid intelligence (p. 309)
functional fixedness (p. 300)
heuristics (p. 295)
imaginal thought (p. 289)
incubation (p. 300)
inductive reasoning (p. 292)
intelligence (p. 301)
intelligence quotient (IQ; p. 303)
interjudge reliability (p. 305)
internal consistency (p. 305)
language (p. 281)
language acquisition device (LAD; p. 283)
language acquisition support system (LASS; p. 285)
linguistic relativity hypothesis (p. 288)
means-ends analysis (p. 295)
mental representations (p. 280)
mental set (p. 294)
morpheme (p. 282)
motoric thought (p. 289)
normal distribution (p. 307)
norms (p. 306)
overconfidence (p. 298)
phoneme (p. 282)
predictive validity (p. 306)
problem-solving schemas (p. 294)
proposition (p. 289)
propositional thought (p. 289)
prototype (p. 290)
psychological test (p. 305)
psychometrics (p. 308)
reaction range (p. 314)
reliability (p. 305)
representativeness heuristic (p. 297)
semantics (p. 282)
standardization (p. 306)
stereotype threat (p. 318)
subgoal analysis (p. 296)
surface structure (p. 281)
syntax (p. 281)
test-retest reliability (p. 305)
triarchic theory of intelligence (p. 311)
validity (p. 305)

What Do You Think?

DISCERNING SURFACE AND DEEP STRUCTURES OF LANGUAGE p. 282

The final words on the grave marker ("No Les No More") have a single surface structure but two possible deep structures (with a generous allowance for spelling). It could either refer to the number of bullets that resulted in Mr. Moore's demise or to Lester's existential status. In this sense, it is like the sentence, "The police must stop drinking after midnight," which also contains two different deep structures.

Most ambiguous sentences achieve their status by evoking two possible deep structures. Sometimes taking such sentences literally might yield humorous results. For example, in a restaurant washroom you might see a sign, "Employees must wash hands." Should you therefore go back into the restaurant to find an employee who will wash your hands? Reportedly, there is a sign at the top of the escalator leading to the London subway that reads, "Dogs Must Be Carried." If you took that one literally, you might not use the escalator unless you had a dog in your possession. These examples may strike you as a bit silly, but they illustrate how the existence of ambiguity in language highlights the need to make a distinction between surface and deep structure and to understand how we translate one into the other in sending or receiving messages. ■

IS INTELLIGENCE FIXED OR MALLEABLE? p. 309

Research has shown that people differ in their "lay theories" of intelligence. For example, do you see intelligence as a relatively fixed quality of intellectual competence, or do you see it as being malleable or changeable? According to Carol Dweck (1991), *entity theorists* believe that personal characteristics, including intelligence, are largely fixed and unchangeable, whereas *incremental theorists* believe that people are capable of significant change, including increases in mental skills. Consider where you stand on this distinction: Are you more an entity theorist or an incremental theorist?

Now consider the implications of these two conceptions—fixed versus malleable—on the kinds of achievement orientations people might have. Would they differ in how long and hard they kept trying if they were having trouble succeeding at something? Dweck's research has shown that people who see intelligence as unchangeable (entity theorists) are more likely to decide quickly whether they can succeed in a particular situation. If they think the demands exceed their abilities, they tend to give up. Likewise, their ability self-perceptions are more strongly affected by recent success or failure because they view achievement outcomes as indicative of a stable ability. In a sense, they're only as good as their last success, and their self-concept can be easily shaken by a significant failure. Incremental theorists, on the other hand, view themselves as capable of positive change and are more likely to attribute negative achievement outcomes to insufficient effort or skills, both of which can potentially be remedied. They are therefore more likely to persist in their achievement efforts in the face of setbacks.

Here are some other questions to consider, based on what you've already learned about entity theorists: Would they tend to emphasize relatively more the contributions of genetic or environmental factors in intelligence? How supportive would they be of early education programs for disadvantaged children? If you thoughtfully consider these questions, we think you'll agree that your (and other people's) conceptions of intelligence can make a difference in how you perceive, think, and behave. ■

9

MOTIVATION AND EMOTION

CHAPTER OUTLINE

One can never consent to creep when one feels an impulse to soar.

—Helen Keller

Sampson Davis, Rameck Hunt, and George Jenkins became best friends in high school. They graduated from college and medical school together, established careers as physicians and a dentist, created an educational foundation that sponsors programs for poor inner-city families, and wrote a best-selling book of their experiences to inspire others to achieve. Without doubt, theirs is a record of accomplishment that anyone would be proud of—a record, they note, that beat the odds.

Davis, Hunt, and Jenkins came from broken homes with absentee or drug-addicted fathers. Crime, violence, drugs, and the specter of death pervaded the streets of their impoverished communities in and around Newark, New Jersey—a place, says Hunt, "where the neighborhood either makes you or breaks you." By age 18, Davis and Hunt ran afoul of the law and spent time in juvenile detention.

Throughout his teens, however, Jenkins had cherished the dream of becoming a dentist. In their senior year of high school, Jenkins persuaded Davis and Hunt to form a pact: attend a special prefreshman remedial program at Seton Hall University, strive academically, and become doctors. For years to come, they studied together, supported each other, and inspired one another. At times the obstacles seemed insurmountable, but the pact kept them going. As Davis notes: "When you've failed repeatedly and think you're done, that last try—the one that requires every ounce of will and strength you have—is often the one to pull you through." (Davis et al., 2002, p. 211)

■ ■ ■

Sara, a former high school valedictorian, gained 15 pounds during her first year of college thanks to late-night pizza-and-beer parties. She dieted and returned to her normal weight of 115 pounds. Proud of her success, Sara (just over 5 feet tall) continued dieting and lost 25 more pounds. Her menstrual period stopped, but she was so afraid of gaining weight that she could not bring herself to eat normally. Finally, weighing a mere 80 pounds, she was hospitalized and began psychotherapy.

Lisa also gained weight during her freshman year and felt like a "big fat failure." Then she began to eat lightly during the day but binge at night on pizza and cookies. After bingeing she waited for the laxatives to kick in—the 50 laxatives she usually took, along with 10 diet pills, each morning with breakfast. After a laxative-consuming friend suffered a heart attack at age 20, Lisa became scared. Worried about her own eating patterns, Lisa sought professional help (Hubbard et al., 1999).

▶ 1. How are motivation and emotion related? Describe various psychological perspectives on motivation.

Motivation and emotion, two central concepts in psychology, are closely linked. We often experience emotions when our motives and goals are gratified, threatened, or thwarted. Davis, Hunt, and Jenkins worked hard to become doctors and felt tremendous pride when they succeeded. Sara also took pride in her success at losing weight. Conversely, emotions can motivate us to act. Lisa's fear upon seeing a friend nearly die from bingeing and purging prompted her to seek treatment. As we will now explore, our motives and emotions stem from a confluence of biological, psychological, and environmental factors.

MOTIVATION

The term *motivation* often triggers images of people who, like Davis, Hunt, and Jenkins, strive to attain success. But to psychologists, motivational issues are broader. What motivates people to eat, have sex, and affiliate? What motivated Sara's self-starvation?

Perspectives on Motivation

Motivation *is a process that influences the direction, persistence, and vigor of goal-directed behavior*. Psychology's diverse theoretical perspectives view motivation through different lenses.

Evolution, Instincts, and Genes

Darwin's theory of evolution inspired early psychological views that instincts motivate much of our behavior. An **instinct** (also called a *fixed action pattern*) *is an inherited characteristic, common to all members of a species, that automatically produces a particular response when the organism is exposed to a particular stimulus*. By the 1920s, researchers had proposed thousands of human instincts (Atkinson, 1964).

Human instinct theories faded because little evidence supported them and they often relied on circular reasoning: Why are people greedy? Because greed is an instinct. How do we know that greed is an instinct? Because people are greedy. As we have seen in earlier discussions of scientific thinking, circular reasoning explains nothing.

Scientists now study genetic contributions to motivation more productively. In *gene knockout experiments*, they disable specific genes and then examine the resulting effects on motivation. Researchers conduct twin and adoption studies to examine how strongly heredity accounts for differences among people in many aspects of motivated behavior, such as the tendencies to be outgoing or to behave antisocially. Modern evolutionary psychologists also propose that many human motives have evolutionary underpinnings expressed through the actions of genes (Palmer & Palmer, 2002).

Homeostasis and Drives

Your body's biological systems are delicately balanced to ensure survival. For example, when you are hot, your body automatically tries to cool itself by perspiring. When you are cold, your body generates warmth by shivering. In 1932, Walter Cannon proposed the concept of **homeostasis,** *a state of internal physiological equilibrium that the body strives to maintain.*

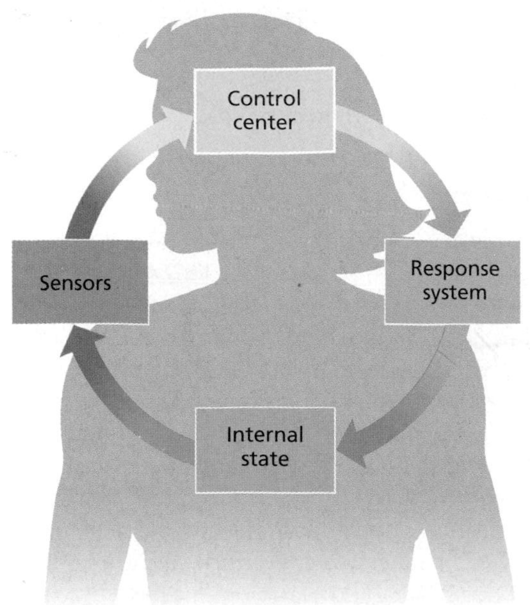

FIGURE 9.1

Your body's internal environment is regulated by homeostatic mechanisms. Sensors detect bodily changes and send this information to a control center, which regulates a response system that restores bodily equilibrium.

Maintaining homeostasis requires a sensory mechanism for detecting changes in the internal environment, a response system that can restore equilibrium, and a control center that receives information from the sensors and activates the response system (Figure 9.1). The control center functions somewhat like the thermostat in a furnace or air-conditioning unit. Once the thermostat is set at a fixed temperature, or *set point*, sensors detect temperature changes in either direction. The control unit responds by turning on the furnace or air conditioner until the sensor indicates that the set point has been restored, and then turns it off.

According to Clark Hull's (1943) influential *drive theory of motivation*, physiological disruptions to homeostasis produce **drives**, *states of internal tension that motivate an organism to behave in ways that reduce this tension.* Drives such as hunger and thirst arise from tissue deficits (e.g., lack of food and water) and push an organism into action. Hull, a learning theorist, proposed that reducing drives is the ultimate goal of motivated behavior.

Homeostatic models are applied to many aspects of motivation, such as the regulation of hunger and thirst (Woods & Seeley, 2002). But drive concepts are less influential than in the past.

For one thing, we often behave in ways that seem to increase rather than reduce states of arousal, as when we skip meals in order to diet or flock to tension-generating horror movies.

Incentives and Expectancies

Whereas drives are viewed as internal factors that "push" an organism into action, **incentives** *represent environmental stimuli that "pull" an organism toward a goal.* To a student, a good grade can be an incentive for studying, just as food can be an incentive for someone who is hungry (i.e., someone motivated by the hunger drive).

Why is it, however, that people often respond differently to the same incentive? Consider James, Lenora, and Harrison, students in a calculus class who have similar math aptitude. James studies hard, but Lenora and Harrison put forth little effort. According to one cognitive approach, called **expectancy × value theory,** *goal-directed behavior is jointly determined by the strength of the person's expectation that particular behaviors will lead to a goal and by the incentive value the individual places on that goal* (Brehm & Self, 1989).

These two factors are multiplied, producing the following equation: Motivation = expectancy × incentive value. James works hard because he believes (expectancy) that the more he studies, the greater the probability is of getting an A (incentive), and he values an A highly. Lenora also believes that studying hard will lead to an A, but an A holds little value for her in this course. In contrast, Harrison values an A but believes that studying hard is unlikely to produce a high grade.

Cognitive theorists also distinguish between **extrinsic motivation,** *performing an activity to obtain an external reward or avoid punishment,* and **intrinsic motivation,** *performing an activity for its own sake*—because you find it enjoyable or challenging. In terms of incentives, a student who studies hard solely to get a good grade is demonstrating extrinsic motivation.

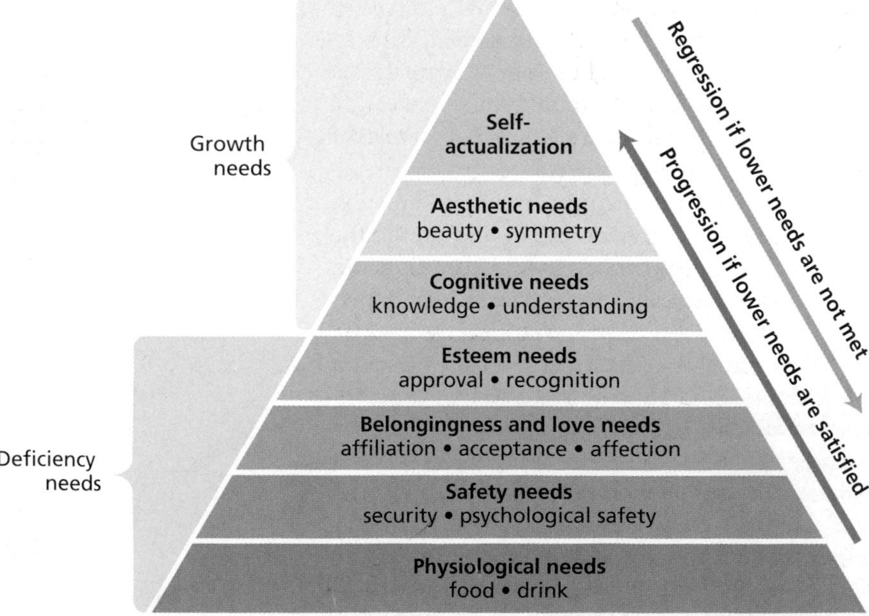

FIGURE 9.2

Maslow proposed that needs are arranged in a hierarchy. After meeting our more basic needs, we experience need progression *and focus on needs at the next higher level. If a need at a lower level is no longer satisfied, we experience* need regression *and focus once again on meeting that lower-level need.*

Psychodynamic and Humanistic Views

The psychodynamic and humanistic perspectives view motivation within a broader context of personality development. Freud (1923) proposed that energy from unconscious motives—especially sexual and aggressive instincts—is often disguised and expressed through socially acceptable behaviors. Thus hidden aggressive impulses may fuel one's motivation to be a trial attorney or an athlete.

Research offers little support for Freud's "dual-instinct" model, but his work stimulated other psychodynamic theories that highlight motives such as people's desires for self-esteem and social belonging (Kohut, 1977). Modern psychodynamic theorists continue to emphasize that, along with conscious mental processes, unconscious motives guide how we act and feel (Westen, 1998). Cognitive psychologists hold a different (i. e., information-processing) view of the unconscious mind, but their research—along with studies of human social behavior—indicates that, indeed, people are not always aware of the factors that motivate them to act as they do (Chartrand & Bargh, 2002).

Abraham Maslow, a humanistic theorist, proposed a broad motivational model (1954). He believed that psychology's other perspectives ignored a key human motive: our striving for personal growth. He proposed the concept of a *need hierarchy,* a progression containing *deficiency needs* (needs concerned with physical and social survival) at the bottom and uniquely human *growth needs* at the top (Figure 9.2). After our basic physiological needs are satisfied, we focus on our need for safety and security. Once that is met, we then attend to needs at the next higher level, and so on. If situations change and lower-level needs are no longer met, we refocus our attention on them until they are satisfied. To Maslow, **self-actualization,** *which represents the need to fulfill our potential,* is the ultimate human motive.

What Do You Think?

IS MASLOW'S NEED HIERARCHY VALID?

Does the concept of a need hierarchy make sense to you? How do you feel about the ordering of needs in Maslow's hierarchy? Think about it, then see page 372.

IN REVIEW

- *Motivation is a process that influences the direction, vigor, and persistence of behavior. On several fronts, scientists are actively exploring how heredity influences motivation.*
- *Homeostatic models view motivation as an attempt to maintain equilibrium in bodily systems. Drive theories propose that tissue deficits create drives, such as hunger, that "push" an organism from within to reduce that deficit and restore homeostasis.*
- *Incentive theories emphasize environmental factors that "pull" people toward a goal. Expectancy × value theory explains why the same incentive may motivate some people but not others.*
- *Psychodynamic theories emphasize that unconscious motives guide much of our behavior. Humanist Abraham Maslow proposed that needs exist in a hierarchy, from basic biological needs to the ultimate need for self-actualization.*

Hunger and Weight Regulation

As we have seen in the previous section, psychology's diverse perspectives underscore the complexity of studying motivation. Let's now turn to one of our most basic motives: hunger. If you could give up all food forever and satisfy your nutritional needs with a daily pill, would you? Eating is a necessity, but for many people it also is one of life's delicious pleasures. Numerous biological, psychological, and environmental factors regulate our food intake.

The Physiology of Hunger

Eating and digestion supply the body with the fuel it needs to function and survive. **Metabolism** *is the body's rate of energy (or caloric) utilization*, and several physiological mechanisms keep your body in energy homeostasis by regulating how much you eat. For example, some physiological signals induce hunger and prompt eating, whereas others stop food intake by producing **satiety** (*the state in which, due to eating, we no longer feel hungry*).

However, it is not the case—as many people believe—that hunger and eating simply occur when we begin to "run low on energy" and that we feel full when immediate energy supplies are restored (Assanand et al., 1998). Your body monitors its energy supplies, but this information interacts with other factors (e.g., the amount and variety of food) to regulate food intake. Thus hunger and satiety are not necessarily linked to immediate energy needs (Woods & Seeley, 2002). Moreover, homeostatic mechanisms are designed to *prevent* us from running low on energy in the first place. In evolutionary terms, an organism that did not eat until its energy supply started to become low (in any absolute sense) would be at a serious survival disadvantage.

Finally, many researchers believe that there is a **set point**, *a biologically determined standard around which body weight (or, more accurately, fat mass) is regulated* (Powley & Keesey, 1970). This view holds that if we overeat or eat too little, homeostatic mechanisms alter our energy utilization and hunger so as to return us close to our original weight. Other researchers argue that set point theory has limitations. They propose that as we overeat or undereat, homeostatic mechanisms make it harder to keep gaining or losing weight but do not necessarily return us to our original weight. Over time, we may "settle in" at a new weight. Stated differently, in this view "biology does not determine a fixed body weight, but rather a range or zone of body weight" (Levitsky, 2002, p. 147).

Signals That Start and Terminate a Meal Do the muscular contractions ("hunger pangs") of an empty stomach produce hunger? In an early experiment, A. L. Washburn swallowed a balloon. When it reached his stomach, the balloon was inflated and hooked up to an amplifying device to record his stomach contractions (Figure 9.3). Washburn then pressed a key every time he felt hungry. The results: Washburn's stomach contractions did indeed correspond with his feelings of hunger (Cannon & Washburn, 1912). But did they *cause* the experience of hunger?

Subsequent research found that hunger does not depend on an empty or twitching stomach, or any stomach at all! Animals display hunger and satiety even if all nerves from their stomach to their brain are cut, and people who have had their stomach surgically removed for medical reasons

▶ 2. What physiological factors help regulate hunger, satiety, general appetite, and weight?

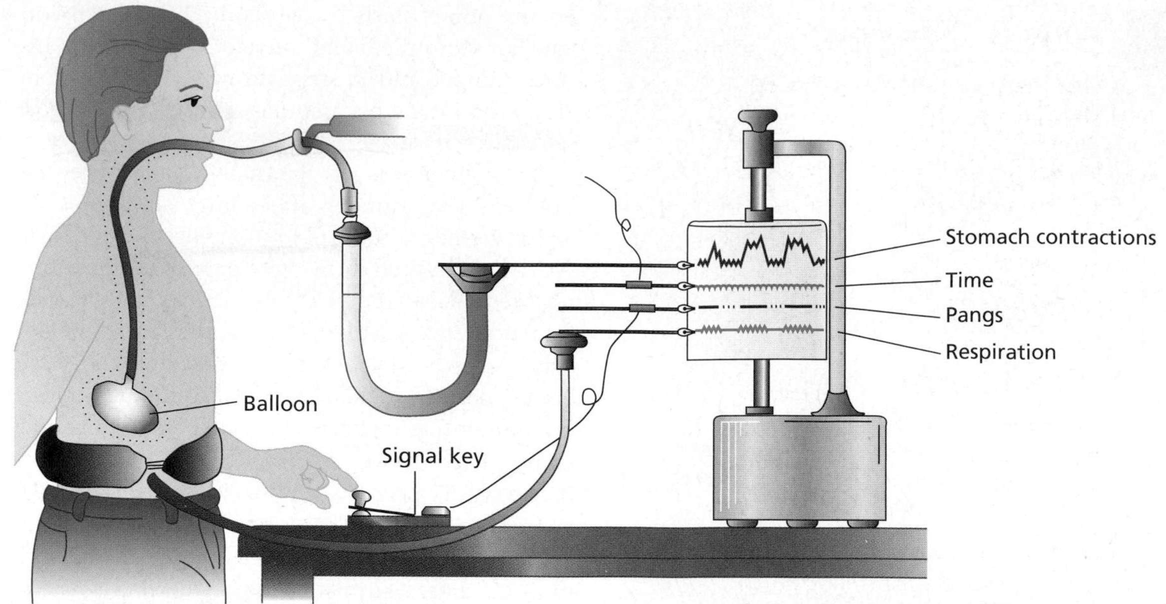

FIGURE 9.3

A. L. Washburn swallowed a balloon and inflated it in his stomach. A machine recorded stomach contractions by amplifying changes in the pressure on the balloon, and Washburn pressed a telegraph key every time he felt a hunger pang. Hunger pangs occurred when the stomach contracted. SOURCE: Based on Cannon and Washburn, 1912.

continue to feel hungry and satiated (Brown & Wallace, 1980). Thus other signals must help trigger hunger.

When you eat, digestive enzymes break food down into key nutrients, such as **glucose**, *a simple sugar that is the body's (and especially the brain's) major source of immediately usable fuel*. After a meal, some glucose is transported into cells to provide energy, but a large portion is transferred into your liver and fat cells, where it is converted into other nutrients and stored for later use. Sensors in the hypothalamus and liver monitor blood glucose concentrations. When blood glucose levels decrease slightly, the liver responds by converting stored nutrients back into glucose, causing blood glucose levels to rise. Changes in the supply of glucose available to cells contain information that helps the brain regulate hunger (Campfield, 1997).

As you eat, several bodily signals cause you to end your meal. Stomach and intestinal distention are satiety signals (French & Cecil, 2001). The walls of these organs stretch as food fills them up, sending nerve signals to the brain. This does not mean, however, that your stomach has to be full for you to feel satiated. As we just noted, patients who have had their stomachs removed continue to experience satiety; this is due not only to intestinal distention but also to chemical signals. For example, **cholecystokinin (CCK)**—*a peptide (a type of hormone) that helps produce satiety*—and other peptides are released into the bloodstream by the small intestine as food arrives from the stomach. These peptides travel to the brain and stimulate receptors in several regions that decrease food intake (Degen et al., 2001).

Signals That Regulate General Appetite and Weight **Leptin** *is a hormone secreted by fat cells*. It enters the bloodstream and reaches the brain, where it decreases appetite and increases energy expenditure.

Leptin is a long-term "background" signal. It does not make us feel full like CCK and other short-term satiety signals that respond directly to food intake during a meal. Instead, one way leptin may influence appetite is by increasing the potency of these other signals (Woods & Seeley, 2002). Thus as we gain fat and secrete more leptin, we may tend to eat less because mealtime satiety factors make us feel full sooner. As we lose fat and secrete less leptin, it may take a greater accumulation of satiety signals and thus more food to make us feel full. In essence, lower leptin levels may tell the brain, "There isn't enough fat tissue, so it's time to eat more." Leptin levels, however, seem to fall more quickly when we lose fat (thus increasing appetite) than they rise when we gain fat. Some researchers suggest that this imbalance served a key adaptive function over the course of evolution; it tilted our ancestral scales in favor of maintaining an adequate fat mass when food was plentiful so that the odds of survival would be increased during times when food was scarce (Jéquier, 2002).

Evidence for leptin's important role grew out of research with genetically obese mice (Zhang et al., 1994). A gene called the *ob* gene (*ob* = obesity) normally directs fat cells to produce leptin, but mice with an *ob* gene mutation lack leptin. As they gain weight, the brain does not receive this "curb your appetite" signal, and the mice overeat and

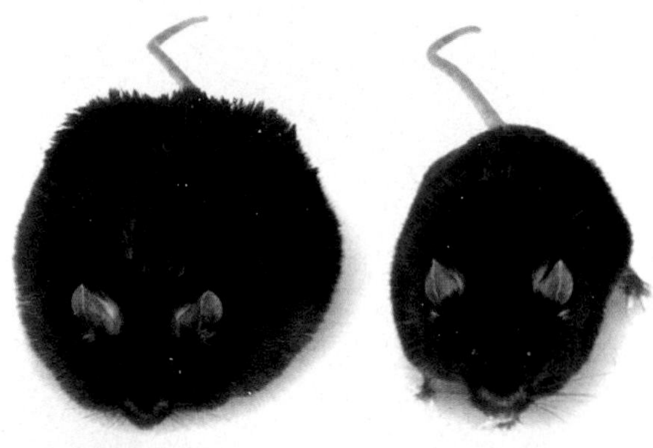

FIGURE 9.4

The mouse on the left has an ob gene mutation. Its fat cells fail to produce leptin, and it becomes obese. Leptin injections help these mice return to normal weight.

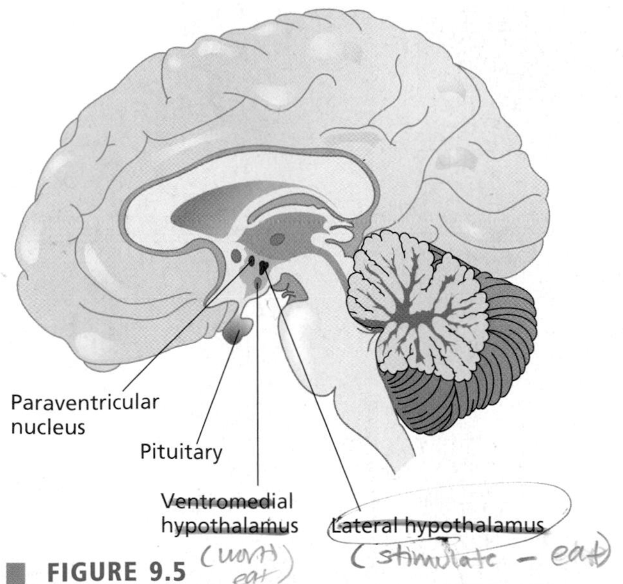

FIGURE 9.5

Various structures within the hypothalamus play a role in regulating hunger, thirst, sexual arousal, and body temperature. The lateral hypothalamus (LH), ventromedial hypothalamus (VMH), and paraventricular nucleus (PVN) are involved in hunger regulation.

become obese (Figure 9.4). Daily leptin injections reduce their appetite, and the mice become thinner. Another strain of obese mice produces ample leptin, but because of a mutation in a different gene (the *db* gene), their brain receptors are insensitive to leptin (Chen et al., 1996). The "curb your appetite" signal is there, but because they can't detect it they become obese. Even injecting these mice with additional leptin does not reduce their food intake and weight.

Are these specific *ob* and *db* gene mutations a major source of human obesity? Probably not, for these genetic conditions seem to be rare among humans. However, when these gene mutations do occur, they are associated with extreme obesity, suggesting the importance of normal leptin functioning in human weight regulation. Might leptin injections be the "magic bullet" that helps most obese people lose weight? Unfortunately, probably not, because obese people already have ample leptin in their blood due to their fat mass, but their brain may be "resistant" to that information (Ravussin & Gautier, 1999).

Brain Mechanisms Many brain regions from the primitive brain stem to the lofty cerebral cortex—help regulate hunger and eating (Berthoud, 2002). But is there a master control center? Early experiments pointed to two regions in the hypothalamus. Areas near the side, called the *lateral hypothalamus (LH)*, seemed to be a "hunger-on" center (Figure 9.5). Electrically stimulating a rat's LH would cause it to start eating, and lesioning (damaging or destroying) the LH would cause it to refuse to eat, even to the point of starvation (Anand & Brobeck, 1951).

In contrast, structures in the lower-middle area, called the *ventromedial hypothalamus (VMH)*, seemed to be a "hunger-off" center. Electrically stimulating the VMH caused even a hungry rat to stop eating, whereas lesioning the VMH produced gluttons—like the rat shown in Figure 1.3 on page 6—that ate frequently and doubled or tripled their body weight.

As scientists explored further, they learned that although the LH and VMH play a role in hunger regulation, they are not really hunger-on and hunger-off centers. For example, rats with LH damage stop eating and lose weight in part because they develop trouble swallowing and digesting, and they become generally unresponsive to external stimuli, not just to food. Moreover, axons from many brain areas funnel into the hypothalamus and then fan out again upon leaving it. Cutting these nerve tracts anywhere along their path—not just within the hypothalamus—duplicates some of the effects of the LH and VMH lesions (Schwartz, 1984).

Researchers are examining how specific neural circuits within the hypothalamus regulate food intake. Many pathways involve the **paraventricular nucleus (PVN)**, *a cluster of neurons packed with receptor sites for various transmitters that stimulate or reduce appetite*. The PVN appears to integrate several short-term and long-term signals that influence metabolic and digestive processes (Berthoud, 2002). One such signal, a chemical

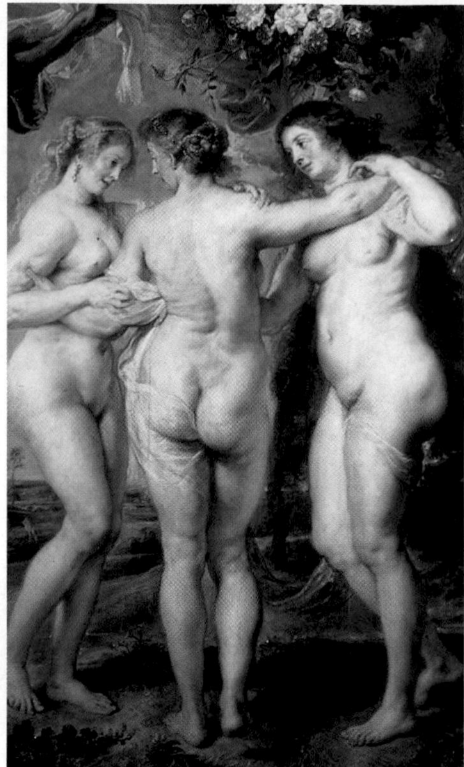

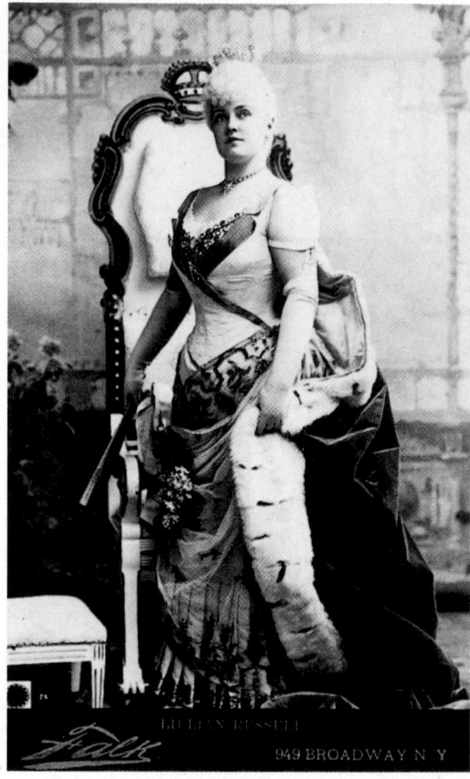

FIGURE 9.6

Throughout much of Western history, a full-bodied woman's figure was esteemed. This is illustrated by (left) Peter Paul Rubens's 17th-century painting, The Three Graces, *and by (center) actress Lillian Russell, who represented the American ideal of feminine beauty a century ago. In recent decades, the norm of "thin = attractive" has evolved, as illustrated (right) by this contemporary swimsuit model.*

transmitter called *neuropeptide Y,* is a powerful appetite stimulant. Rats in one experiment quickly became obese when they received injections of neuropeptide Y into their PVN for 10 days. Their food intake doubled, and their body weight increased sixfold (Stanley et al., 1986).

Psychological Aspects of Hunger

▶ 3. Describe how psychological, environmental, and cultural factors influence hunger and eating.

Eating is positively reinforced by the good taste of food and negatively reinforced by hunger reduction. We develop an expectation that eating will be pleasurable, and this becomes an important motivator to seek and consume food. Indeed, even the mere thought of food can trigger hunger.

Our memory of when and how much we last ate also affects food consumption. Consider amnesia patients who forget that they have eaten within a minute or two after finishing a meal. Paul Rozin and his colleagues (1998) presented two amnesia patients with multiple lunches on various days. The patients fully or partially ate the second meal (presented 10 to 30 minutes after the initial lunch) and partially ate a third meal shortly thereafter. In contrast, patients without amnesia rejected all of the additional lunches.

Attitudes, habits, and psychological needs also regulate food intake. Have you ever felt stuffed during a meal, yet finished it and even had dessert? Beliefs such as "don't leave food on your plate" and conditioned habits ("autopilot snacking" while watching TV) may lead us to eat even when we do not feel hungry. Conversely, countless dieters intentionally restrict their food intake even though they *are* hungry.

Especially for women, such food restriction often stems from social pressures to conform to cultural standards of beauty (Figure 9.6). Studies of *Playboy* magazine centerfolds, Miss America contestants, and fashion models indicate a clear trend toward a thinner and increasingly unrealistic ideal female body shape from the 1950s into the 1990s (Owen & Laurel-Seller, 2000). Given the deluge of "thin = attractive" mass media messages in many parts of the globe, it's no wonder national surveys have revealed that

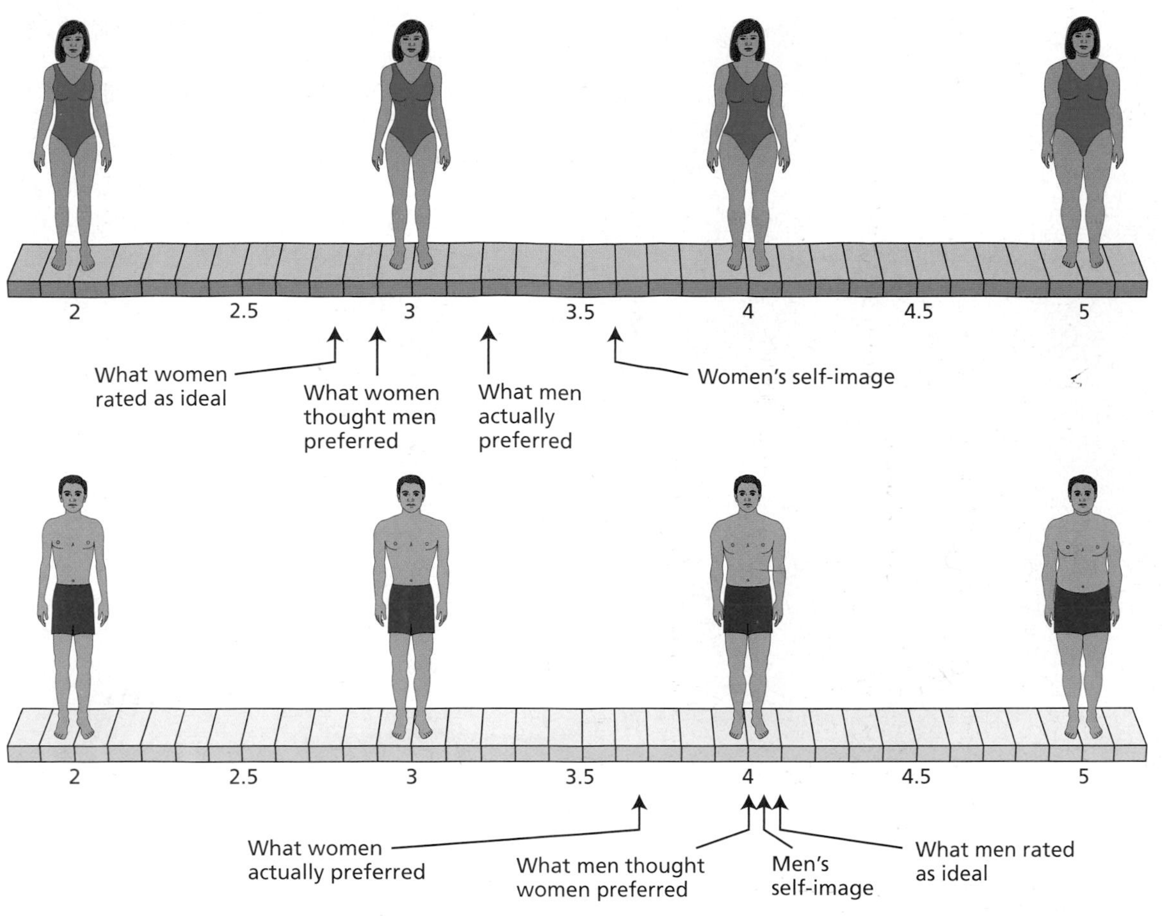

FIGURE 9.7

College women overestimated how thin they needed to be to conform to men's preferences and viewed their body shape as heavier than ideal. Men overestimated how bulky they needed to be to conform to women's preferences but viewed their body shape as close to ideal. SOURCE: Based on Fallon & Rozin, 1985.

- although most young Australian women are of average, healthy weight, only a fifth are happy with their weight (Kenardy et al., 2001);
- among 12- to 19-year-old female Chinese students, 80 percent are concerned about their weight and feel fat at least some of the time (Huon et al., 2002); and
- compared to male American high school students, female students are less likely to be overweight but much more likely to diet and think of themselves as overweight (Centers for Disease Control and Prevention [CDC], 2002).

Indeed, relative to men, women became increasingly dissatisfied with their body image throughout the last half of the 20th century (Feingold & Mazzella, 1998).

A classic study by April Fallon and Paul Rozin (1985) suggests an additional reason why this is so. College women overestimated how thin they needed to be to conform to men's preferences, whereas men overestimated how bulky they should be to conform to women's preferences (Figure 9.7). Women also perceived their body shape as heavier than ideal, whereas men viewed their body shape as close to ideal. As Fallon and Rozin noted, "Overall, men's perceptions serve to keep them satisfied with their figures, whereas women's perceptions place pressure on them to lose weight" (1985, p. 102). Whether African American, Hispanic American, or Caucasian American, men seem more likely to have these ego-protective perceptions about their body shape than do women (Demarest & Allen, 2000).

For more on perception of body shape, see Interactive Segment 9.1.

Environmental and Cultural Factors

Food availability is the most obvious environmental regulator of eating. For millions of people who live in poverty or famine-ravaged regions, food scarcity limits consumption. In contrast, abundant high-fat food in many countries contributes to a high rate of obesity (Wadden et al., 2002).

Food taste and variety also regulate eating. Good-tasting food increases food consumption, but during a meal and from meal to meal we can become tired of eating the same thing, causing us to terminate a meal more quickly (Rolls et al., 1981). In contrast, food variety increases consumption, which you may have observed when you eat at a buffet.

FIGURE 9.8

Cultural upbringing strongly affects food preferences. Would you like to eat these insect-topped appetizers? Not interested? Perhaps you would prefer some other insects, reptiles, camel eyes, or dog—all delicacies in other cultures.

Through classical conditioning, we learn to associate the smell and sight of food with its taste, and these food cues can trigger hunger. Eating may be the last thing on your mind until your nose detects the sensuous aroma wafting from a bakery or popcorn machine. Rats who have recently eaten and do not appear to be hungry (e.g., they ignore available food) will eat again when presented with classically conditioned sounds and lights that they have learned to associate with food (Weingarten, 1983). Similarly, does the musical jingle of the neighborhood ice cream truck tweak your hunger?

Many other environmental stimuli affect food intake. For example, we typically eat more when dining with other people than when we eat alone (deCastro, 2002). Cultural norms influence when, how, and what we eat. In Mediterranean countries such as Spain and Greece, people often begin dinner in the late evening (say, around 9 P.M.), by which time most North Americans have finished supper. And although we like variety, we usually feel most comfortable selecting familiar foods and often have difficulty overcoming our squeamish thoughts about unfamiliar dishes (Figure 9.8). Figure 9.9 summarizes several factors that help regulate hunger and eating.

▶ 4. Describe biological and environmental factors in obesity and how their interaction affects obesity among the Pima.

Obesity

The heaviest known man and woman in recorded history, both Americans, weighed 1,400 and 1,200 pounds, respectively (*Guinness Book,* 2000). Few people approach such extreme weight, but as measured by their *body mass index* (BMI), which takes height and weight into account, a staggering 25 to 30 percent of American adults are obese and another 30 to 35 percent are overweight (Flegal et al., 2002). From Canada to the Palestinian West Bank, adult obesity rates of 20 to 50 percent have been reported in many studies (Abdul-Rahim et al., 2003).

Obesity places people at greater risk not only for some medical problems but also for being the target of stereotypes and prejudice (Teachman et al., 2003). Obesity is often blamed on a lack of willpower, a dysfunctional way of coping with stress, heightened sensitivity to external food cues (e.g., to the sight and aroma of food), and emotional disturbances. Research, however, does not consistently find such psychological differences between obese and nonobese people (Faith et al., 2002; Leon & Roth, 1977).

Genes and Environment Do you know people who seem to gain weight easily and others who seem to be able to eat as much as they want without adding pounds? Heredity influences one's basal metabolic rate and the tendency to store energy as either fat or lean tissue. Indeed, identical twins raised apart are about as similar in body mass as identical twins reared together. Overall, genetic factors appear to account for about 40 to 70 percent of the variation in BMI among women and among men (Maes et al., 1997).

Over 200 genes have been identified as possible contributors to human obesity (Comuzzie & Allison, 1998). However, although heredity affects our susceptibility to obesity, so does the environment. Genes have not changed much in recent decades, but obesity rates have increased significantly. According to some experts, the culprits are

- an abundance of inexpensive, tasty foods that are high in fat and/or carbohydrates;
- a cultural emphasis on getting the best value, which contributes to supersizing menu items; and
- technological advances that decrease the need for daily physical activity (Wadden et al., 2002).

The Pima Indians of Arizona provide a striking example of how genes and environment interact to produce obesity. The Pimas are genetically predisposed to obesity and diabetes, but both conditions were rare among tribe members before the

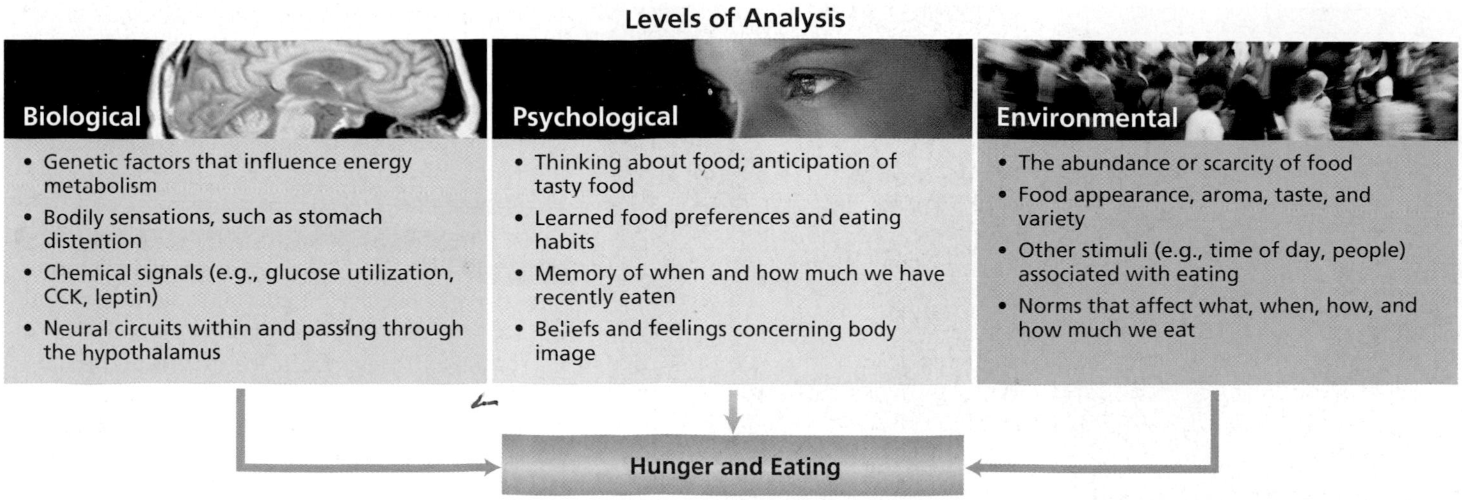

Levels of Analysis

Biological
- Genetic factors that influence energy metabolism
- Bodily sensations, such as stomach distention
- Chemical signals (e.g., glucose utilization, CCK, leptin)
- Neural circuits within and passing through the hypothalamus

Psychological
- Thinking about food; anticipation of tasty food
- Learned food preferences and eating habits
- Memory of when and how much we have recently eaten
- Beliefs and feelings concerning body image

Environmental
- The abundance or scarcity of food
- Food appearance, aroma, taste, and variety
- Other stimuli (e.g., time of day, people) associated with eating
- Norms that affect what, when, how, and how much we eat

Hunger and Eating

FIGURE 9.9

Understanding Behavior: Factors that regulate hunger and eating.

20th century. Their native diet and physically active lifestyle prevented their genetic predisposition from expressing itself. But particularly among Pimas born after World War II, obesity rates increased dramatically as they adopted a Westernized diet and sedentary lifestyle. Today Pimas living in Arizona have one of the highest rates of obesity (and diabetes) in the world. In contrast, Pimas living in northwest Mexico eat a more traditional diet and perform more physical labor, and their obesity rate is much lower than that of their Arizonan counterparts (Esparza et al., 2000).

Dieting and Weight Loss Unfortunately for millions of overweight people, being fat primes people to stay fat, in part by altering body chemistry and energy expenditure (Logue, 1991). For example, obese people generally have higher levels of *insulin* (a hormone secreted by the pancreas that helps convert glucose into fat) than do people of normal weight. Substantial weight gain also makes it harder to exercise vigorously, and dieting slows basal metabolism because the body responds to food deprivation with decreased energy expenditure.

Does this mean that diets are doomed to fail? The common adage that "95 percent of people who lose weight regain it within a few years" evolved from just one study decades ago. According to Albert Stunkard, one of the researchers, 100 obesity patients were "just given a diet and sent on their way. That was state of the art in 1959" (Fritsch, 1999). In truth, we do not have good long-term estimates of weight-loss success rates, partly because we rarely hear from people who succeed (or fail) on their own without going to clinics or treatment programs.

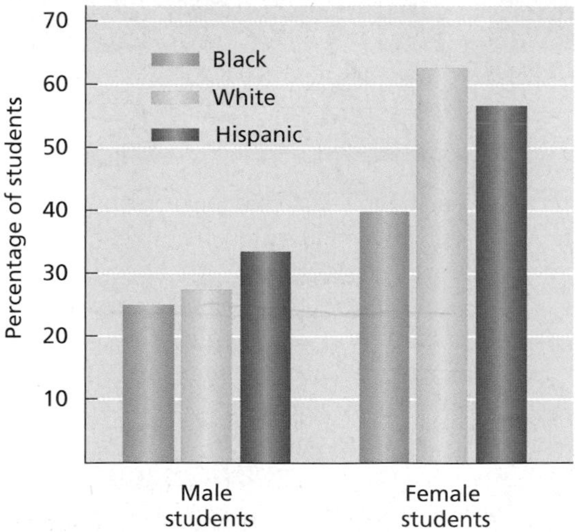

FIGURE 9.10

Whether Hispanic, Black, or White, female high school students are less likely than male students to be overweight or obese, but as this graph shows they are more likely to be "dieting to lose weight." Especially among female students, Hispanics and Whites are most likely to diet. SOURCE: Based on CDC, 2002.

We do know that about one third of Americans report that they are trying to lose weight, although not all are necessarily the ones who need to lose it. As Figure 9.10 shows, there are significant sex and ethnic differences in dieting that emerge even in adolescence (CDC, 2002). Health concerns motivate some dieters, but psychological concerns and social pressures to be thin are the primary motivators for many others. Especially among women, what begins as a diet may unfortunately evolve into a health-threatening eating disorder.

FIGURE 9.11

Anorexia nervosa is a potentially life-threatening disorder in which people starve themselves to be thin. This anorexic woman returned to normal weight after therapy.

▶ 5. What are the major symptoms, health consequences, and causes of anorexia and bulimia?

Eating Disorders: Anorexia and Bulimia

Sara and Lisa, the college freshmen described at the beginning of the chapter, suffered from eating disorders. Victims of **anorexia nervosa,** like Sara, *have an intense fear of being fat and severely restrict their food intake to the point of self-starvation* (Figure 9.11). Despite looking emaciated and weighing less than 85 percent of what would be expected for their age and height, anorexics continue to view themselves as fat. Anorexia causes menstruation to stop, produces bone loss, stresses the heart, and increases the risk of death (Neumäker, 2000).

People like Lisa who suffer from **bulimia nervosa** *are also afraid of becoming fat, and they binge-eat and then purge the food,* usually by inducing vomiting or using laxatives. Bulimics often consume 2,000 to 4,000 calories during binges, and in some cases may consume 20,000 calories per day (Geracioti et al., 1995). Although most bulimics are of normal body weight, repeated purging can produce severe physical consequences, including gastric problems and badly eroded teeth.

About 90 percent of anorexics and bulimics are women. Some surveys indicate that up to 10 percent of college women exhibit symptoms of bulimia, although its general prevalence among North American women is 1 to 3 percent—compared with 0.5 percent for anorexia (Becker et al., 1999).

For a personal story of bulimia nervosa, see Video Segment 9.1

Causes of Anorexia and Bulimia What motivates such abnormal eating patterns? The answer seems to lie in a combination of environmental, psychological, and biological factors. Anorexia and bulimia are more common in industrialized cultures where thinness is equated with beauty. However, cultural norms alone cannot account for eating disorders, because only a small percentage of women within a particular culture are anorexic or bulimic.

Personality factors are another piece of the puzzle. Anorexics often are perfectionists—high achievers like Sara (a high school valedictorian) who strive to live up to lofty self-standards, including strict ideals of an acceptably thin body (Tyrka et al., 2002). For anorexics, losing weight becomes a battle for success and control: "It's me versus food, and I'm going to win." Their perfectionism and need for control may partly stem from their upbringing. Anorexics often describe their parents as disapproving and as setting abnormally high achievement standards. For some anorexic children and teens, food refusal may be reinforced by the distress they cause their parents to feel. In essence, self-starvation becomes a way to punish parents and gain some control (Chan & Ma, 2002). As one young anorexic teen said in a therapy session,

> It was, like, a power thing. I was like, look mom, I don't have to eat. I can piss you off. . . . That's the last thing your parents want is for you to die. . . . You can get back at anybody. And I guess . . . I need to find a way to forgive her . . . because . . . I'm killing myself. ("Dying to be Thin," 2000)

A different pattern emerges for bulimics, who tend to be depressed and anxious, exhibit low impulse control, and seem to lack a stable sense of personal identity (Strober & Humphrey, 1987). Bulimics' food cravings are often triggered by stress and negative mood, and bingeing temporarily reduces their negative emotional state (Waters et al., 2001). But guilt, self-contempt, and anxiety follow the binge, and purging may be a means of reducing these negative feelings.

On the biological side, genetic factors appear to predispose some people toward eating disorders. Concordance rates for eating disorders are higher among identical twins than fraternal twins and higher among first-degree relatives (parents and siblings) than second- or third-degree relatives (Kortegaard et al., 2001). Researchers are now searching for specific genes and combinations of genes that contribute to eating disorders.

Anorexics and bulimics also exhibit abnormal activity of serotonin, leptin, and other body chemicals (Kaye et al., 2002). Some researchers believe that neurotransmitter and hormonal imbalances help cause eating disorders. Others propose that such chemical changes initially are a *response* to abnormal eating patterns, but that once started they *perpetuate* eating and digestive irregularities (Walsh & Devlin, 1998). Other bodily changes also help perpetuate eating disorders. For example, stomach acids expelled into the mouth during vomiting cause bulimics to lose taste sensitivity, making the normally unpleasant taste of vomit more tolerable (Rodin et al., 1990).

Treating eating disorders is difficult and may take years, but with professional help, about half of anorexics and bulimics fully recover (Becker et al., 1999). Others are able to eat more normally but maintain their preoccupation with food and weight.

IN REVIEW

- *Physiological processes attempt to keep the body in energy homeostasis. Changes in the supply of glucose available to cells provide one signal that helps initiate hunger. During meals, hormones such as CCK are released into the bloodstream and help signal the brain to stop eating. Fat cells release leptin, which acts as a long-term signal that helps regulate appetite. The hypothalamus plays an important role in hunger regulation.*
- *The expected good taste of food motivates eating, and the thought of food can trigger hunger. Our memory, habits, and psychological needs affect our food intake.*
- *The availability, taste, and variety of food powerfully regulate eating. Through classical conditioning, neutral stimuli can acquire the capacity to trigger hunger. Cultural norms affect our food preferences and eating habits.*
- *Heredity and the environment affect our susceptibility to becoming obese.*
- *Anorexia and bulimia occur more often in cultures that value thinness and are associated with somewhat different psychological profiles. Heredity predisposes some people toward developing these eating disorders.*

Sexual Motivation

Why do people have sex? If you're thinking, "Isn't it obvious?" let's take a look. Sex often is described as a biological "reproductive motive," yet people usually do not have sex to conceive children. A drive to reproduce does not explain why people masturbate or why couples in their 70s and 80s have sex. Pleasure, then, must be the key. Evolution shaped our physiology so that sex feels good; periodically, having sex for pleasure also leads to childbirth, through which our genes are passed on. But consider this:

- In a study asking adolescents why they have sex, both genders cited peer pressure more often than sexual gratification (Stark, 1989).
- In the 1920s, British sex researcher Helena Wright found that most women she surveyed viewed sex as an unenjoyable marital duty (Kelly, 2001).
- About 10 percent of American men and 20 percent of women report that sex is not pleasurable (Laumann et al., 1994).

In reality, people engage in sex to reproduce, obtain and give sensual pleasure, express love, foster intimacy, fulfill one's "duty," conform to peer pressure, and for a host of other reasons.

Sexual Behavior: Patterns and Changes

▶ 6. How have patterns of sexual behavior changed in recent decades?

Because most people don't care to let researchers into their bedrooms, scientists typically learn about people's sexual activities by conducting surveys. Alfred Kinsey and his colleagues (1948, 1953) conducted the first large-scale American sex surveys in the late 1930s, and many others have been conducted since then. One of the most thorough surveys, based on a nationally representative sample, found that about 70 percent of 18- to 59-year-old Americans have sex with a partner at least a few times per month (Figure 9.12; Laumann et al., 1994). In general, single adults who cohabit (are not married but live with a sexual partner) are the most sexually active, followed by married adults. Single adults who do not cohabit are the least active.

By their first year in American high school, 41 percent of male students and 29 percent of female students say they have had sexual intercourse (CDC, 2002). Among unmarried American females in the early 1960s, 27 percent of 19-year-olds had engaged in sexual intercourse. In 1995, the corresponding figure was 72 percent (CDC, 1997). Changing social norms and a tendency to delay marriage have contributed to this rise in premarital sex. Premarital intercourse also became more common in a number of foreign countries during the last half of the 20th century. Findings over the past few years, however, suggest that this trend has leveled off and may be

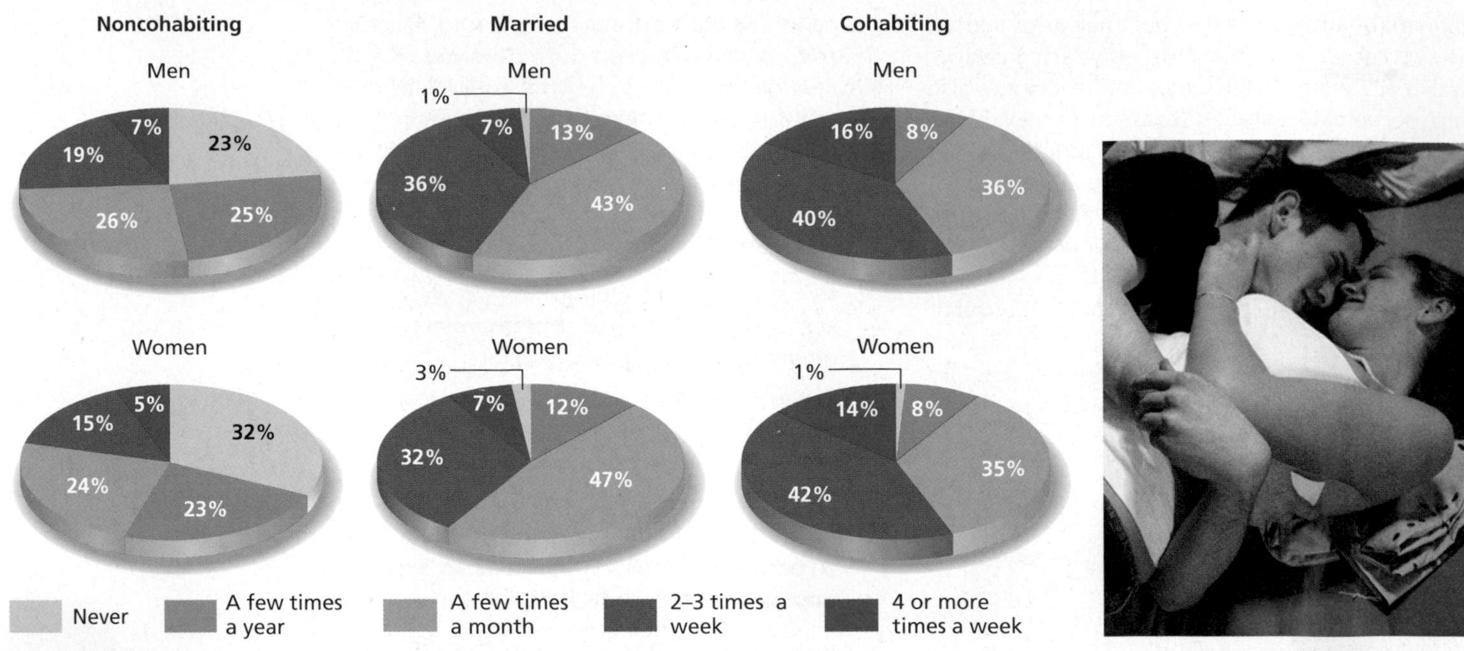

FIGURE 9.12

Frequency of sex over the past 12 months by gender and marital status, based on a nationally representative sample of 18- to 59-year-old Americans. SOURCE: Adapted from Michael et al., 1994.

reversing (Figure 9.13; CDC, 2002). This could be a response to an increased cultural emphasis on the depth of relationships and to the crisis concerning AIDS and other sexually transmitted diseases.

The Physiology of Sex

▶ 7. Describe the sexual response cycle. How do hormones influence sex characteristics and sexual behavior?

In 1953, William Masters and Virginia Johnson began a landmark study in which they examined the sexual responses of 694 men and women under laboratory conditions. In total, they physiologically monitored about 10,000 sexual episodes.

The Sexual Response Cycle Masters and Johnson (1966) concluded that most people, when sexually aroused, go through a four-stage **sexual response cycle** *of excitement, plateau, orgasm, and resolution* (Figure 9.14). During the *excitement phase,* arousal builds rapidly. Blood flow increases to arteries in and around the genital organs, nipples, and women's breasts, where it pools and causes these body areas to swell. The penis and clitoris begin to become erect, the vagina becomes lubricated, and muscle tension increases throughout the body. In the *plateau phase,* arousal continues to build until there is enough muscle tension to trigger orgasm.

During the *orgasm phase* in males, rhythmic contractions of internal organs and muscle tissue surrounding the urethra project semen out of the penis. In females, orgasm involves rhythmic contractions of the outer third of the vagina, surrounding muscles, and the uterus. In males, orgasm is ordinarily followed by a *resolution phase,* during which physiological arousal decreases rapidly and the genital organs return to their normal condition. During the resolution phase, males enter a *refractory period,* during which they are temporarily incapable of another orgasm. Females may have two or more successive orgasms before the onset of the resolution phase, but Masters and Johnson reported that most women experience only one. Of course, people may experience orgasm on some occasions but not others, and orgasm is not the only goal of all human sexual activity.

Hormonal Influences As with hunger, the hypothalamus plays a key role in sexual motivation. It controls the pituitary gland, which regulates the secretion of hormones called *gonadotropins* into the bloodstream. In turn, these hormones affect the rate at which the *gonads* (testes in the male and ovaries in the female) secrete *androgens,* the so-called "masculine" sex hormones such as *testosterone,* and *estrogens,* the so-called "feminine" sex hormones such as *estradiol.* Realize that despite these labels, both men and women produce androgens and estrogens.

Sex hormones have *organizational effects* that direct the development of male and female sex characteristics (Byer et al., 2002). In the womb, male and female embryos form a primitive gonad that has the potential to develop into either testes or ovaries. If genetically male, the embryo forms testes about

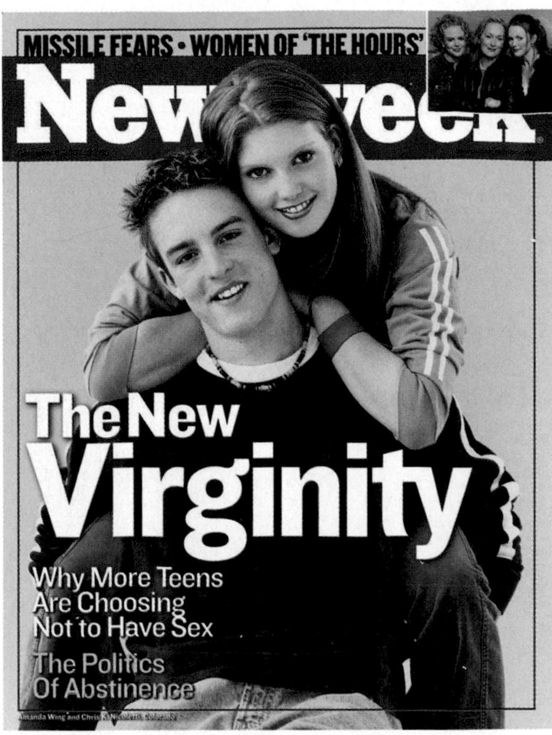

FIGURE 9.13

Surveys from the past few years have found that the trend toward increasing premarital intercourse among American teens has leveled off and begun to decline slightly.

8 weeks after conception. Then, as the testes release sex hormones during a key period of prenatal development, there typically is sufficient androgen activity to produce a male pattern of genital, reproductive, brain, and other organ development. Years later, as part of this pattern, the hypothalamus stimulates an increased release of sex hormones from the testes when the male reaches puberty. In contrast, a genetically female embryo does not form testes, and in the absence of sufficient androgen activity during this prenatal period, a female pattern of development ensues. As part of this pattern, at puberty the hypothalamus stimulates the release of sex hormones from the ovaries on a cyclical basis that regulates the female menstrual cycle.

Sex hormones also have *activational effects* that stimulate sexual desire and behavior. In nonhuman animals, mature males have a relatively constant secretion of sex hormones, and their readiness for sex is largely governed by the presence of environmental stimuli (e.g., a receptive female). In contrast, hormonal secretions in female animals follow an *estrus cycle*, and they are sexually receptive only during periods of high estrogen secretion (i.e., when they are "in heat").

Sex hormones also influence human sexual desire. The natural hormonal surge of puberty increases sexual motivation, as would an artificial boost from receiving doses of testosterone (Tuiten et al., 2000). But in humans, normal short-term hormonal fluctuations have relatively little effect on sexual arousability (Morrell et al., 1984). Desire does not go up and down like a yo-yo as blood levels of sex hormones change, and women may experience high sexual desire at any time during their menstrual cycle. Moreover, in men and women, androgens—rather than estrogens—appear to have the primary influence on sexual desire (Hyde & DeLamater, 2003).

The Psychology of Sex

▶ 8. Discuss how psychological, cultural, and environmental factors influence sexual behavior.

Sexual arousal involves more than physiological responses. It typically begins with desire and a

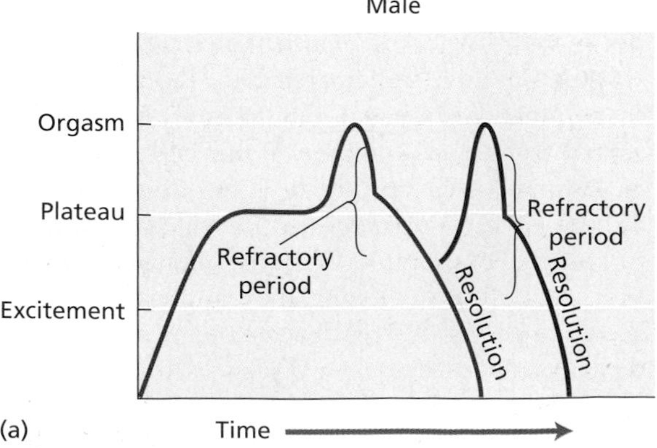

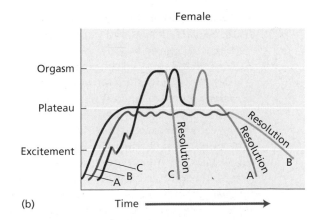

FIGURE 9.14

Masters and Johnson discovered a four-stage pattern of sexual response. (a) In males, there is a refractory period after orgasm, during which no further response is possible. (b) In females, pattern A represents one or more orgasms followed by resolution, pattern B shows a plateau stage with no orgasm, and pattern C shows an orgasm with no preceding plateau stage. Source: Based on Masters & Johnson, 1966.

FIGURE 9.15

Habits of dress that many people take for granted in some societies, such as wearing tank tops, short-sleeve shirts, and shorts, are unacceptable in other cultures because they would be considered sexually provocative.

sexual stimulus that is perceived positively (Walen & Roth, 1987). Such stimuli can even be imaginary.

Sexual fantasy is an important component of many people's lives, although studies in Europe, South America, and North America indicate that men sexually fantasize more often than women (Martinez & Raul, 2000). Among American adults, for example, about half of men and a fifth of women fantasize about sex at least once a day (Laumann et al., 1994). Fantasy nicely illustrates how mental processes can affect physiological functioning. Indeed, sexual fantasies alone may trigger genital erection and orgasm in some people and are often used to enhance arousal during masturbation.

Psychological factors can not only trigger sexual arousal but also inhibit it. A person may be engaged in sexual activity and then become turned off by something a partner does. About 1 in 3 American women and 1 in 6 men report that they simply lack an interest in sex (Laumann et al., 1994). Other people desire sex but have difficulty becoming or staying aroused. Stress, fatigue, and anger at one's partner can lead to temporary arousal problems. **Sexual dysfunction** *refers to chronic, impaired sexual functioning that distresses a person*. It may result from injuries, diseases, and drug effects, but some causes are psychological. Arousal difficulties also may stem from performance anxiety or may be a psychological consequence of sexual assault or childhood sexual abuse (Rumstein & Hunsley, 2001).

Cultural and Environmental Influences

Anyone who doubts culture's power to shape human behavior need only examine sexual customs around the globe. During sex, most Westerners probably do not poke a finger into their partner's ear, as do Trukese women of Micronesia, or bite off and then spit out hairs from their partner's eyebrow, as do South American Apinaye women (Hyde & DeLamater, 2003). You may find these practices unusual, but consider how some sexual techniques common in our culture—such as kissing—seem to members of other cultures: "There are a few societies . . . in which kissing is unknown. For example, when the Thonga of Africa first saw Europeans kissing, they laughed and said, 'Look at them; they eat each other's saliva and dirt'" (Hyde & DeLamater, 2003, pp. 10–11).

More important, the psychological meaning of sex itself depends on cultural contexts. Some societies and religions forbid premarital sex and may also prohibit public dress and behavior that arouses sexual desire (Figure 9.15). Many people who view themselves as very religious believe it is important to bring their sexual practices into harmony with their religious beliefs, which may condone sex only within marriage (Janus & Janus, 1993).

In contrast, some societies openly encourage premarital sex. Among Marquesan Islanders of eastern Polynesia, families sleep together in one room, and children have ample opportunity to observe sexual activity. When boys and girls reach adolescence, a middle-aged adult of the opposite sex instructs them in sexual techniques and has intercourse with them. Having other sexual partners prior to marriage is considered normal (Frayser, 1985). Clearly, what is regarded as proper, moral, and desirable varies enormously across cultures.

The environment affects sexuality not only through cultural experiences but also by providing sexually arousing stimuli. A lover's caress can trigger sexual desire in an instant. So too can watching a partner undress, which ranks second only to vaginal intercourse as the sexual activity that most American men and women find appealing (Laumann et al., 1994). Indeed, just listening to an erotic description of sex from a romance novel can increase women's and men's sexual arousal, as Julia Heiman (1977) found in a study of college students.

Pornography and Sexual Violence

By today's standards, romance novels are a tame form of erotica. Pornography is a multibillion dollar industry, and most of its consumers are men, raising the question of whether pornography affects men's sexual attitudes and fosters sexual violence toward women. Twenty percent of 15- to 44-year-old American women report having been victims of forced sexual intercourse, and contrary to a common belief, most rapes are *not* committed by strangers (CDC, 1997). Before reading further, look at Table 9.1 and make a prediction about each statement.

Many pornographic materials model *rape myths,* themes that men are entitled to sex and that women enjoy being coerced into sex. According to *social learning theory,* people learn through observation. Thus men who view such materials should become more likely to aggress sexually toward women. In contrast, Freud and other psychoanalysts advocated a *catharsis principle,* which states that as inborn aggressive and sexual impulses build up, actions that release this tension provide a catharsis that temporarily returns us to a more balanced physiological state. In this view, pornography—especially materials containing aggressive content—should provide a safe outlet for releasing sexual and aggressive tensions and decrease sexually aggressive behavior toward women.

TABLE 9.1 Is Each of the Following Statements True or False?

Compared to men in general, convicted sex offenders

- report being exposed to pornography at a younger age
- report being exposed to more pornography
- are more physiologically aroused by depictions of nonviolent sex
- are more physiologically aroused by depictions of violent sex
- report being likelier to masturbate or engage in consensual or coercive sex after viewing pornography

In the real world, then, is exposure to pornography related to higher or lower rates of sexual aggression? Correlational studies do not clearly support either the social learning or catharsis predictions. Some countries with high rates of rape have little pornography, whereas others have a great deal. Conversely, in some countries pornography is widely available but rates of rape are low (Bauserman, 1996). Similarly, sex offenders do not differ from other men in amount or earliest age of exposure to pornography, and they are actually *less* aroused by nonviolent pornography. Yet they are more aroused by violent pornography and are also more likely to act sexually after viewing violent or even nonviolent pornography (Allen et al., 1995, 2000).

▶ 9. Evaluate the social learning and catharsis viewpoints regarding the effects of watching violent pornography.

Controlled experiments paint a clearer causal picture. In some, male college students are randomly assigned to view material whose content is either neutral (i.e., nonsexual), sexually explicit but nonviolent (e.g. a couple having consensual sex), or sexually aggressive (e.g., a rape-myth depiction showing a woman who initially resists sexual assault but then becomes a willing participant). Later, the students interact with another person (a female or male accomplice of the experimenter), who makes errors on a learning task. Participants must "punish" the person with electric shock for each error, but they may freely choose the shock intensity and thus aggress by giving stronger shocks. (The confederate does not really receive any shock.)

The strongest experimental effects emerge when participants view violent pornography (Malamuth et al., 2000). At least temporarily, this increases men's tendency to aggress toward women but not toward other men. However, certain types of people, such as those who report the greatest attraction to sexual violence, are most strongly affected by viewing it. In addition to its

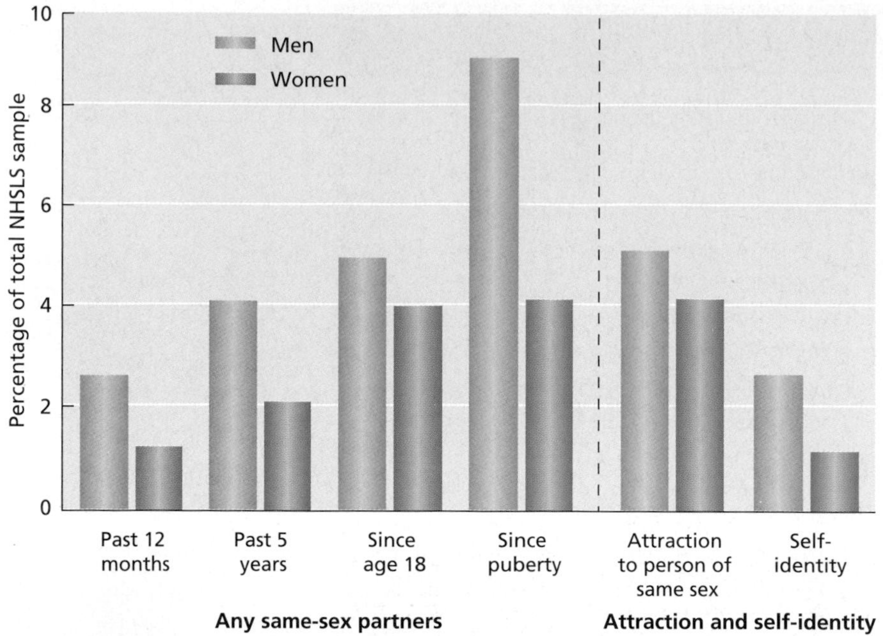

FIGURE 9.16

More men and women report same-sex attraction and same-sex activity than view themselves as homosexual or bisexual. SOURCE: Adapted from Michael et al., 1994.

connection with aggression, pornography also promotes a belief that sex is impersonal and decreases viewers' satisfaction with their own sexual partners (Donnerstein & Malamuth, 1997).

Should pornography be banned? This is a moral and political question that goes beyond what science can answer. Like everyone else, researchers have personal values, and some take a strong stand on this issue. Fortunately, research shows that providing men with realistic information about sexual assault can lead them to reject rape myths (Linz & Donnerstein, 1989). Strong messages against coercive sexual practices may promote attitudes that help reduce sexual crimes against women.

Sexual Orientation

▶ 10. Describe three dimensions of sexual orientation. Discuss research on the determinants of sexual orientation.

Sexual orientation *refers to one's emotional and erotic preference for partners of a particular sex.* Determining one's sexual orientation seems simple: Heterosexuals prefer opposite-sex partners, homosexuals prefer same-sex partners, and bisexuals are sexually attracted to members of both sexes. So how would you classify the sexual orientation of these two 25-year-olds?

- Susan feels sexually attracted to men and women, but she has had sex only with men and thinks of herself as heterosexual.
- Larry has had sex with other men twice since puberty, yet he isn't attracted to men and views himself as heterosexual.

Prevalence of Different Sexual Orientations Some researchers view sexual orientation as a single dimension ranging from "exclusively heterosexual" to "exclusively homosexual," with "equally heterosexual and homosexual" at the midpoint. But others argue that sexual orientation has three dimensions: *self-identity, sexual attraction,* and *actual sexual behavior* (Kelly, 2001).

Figure 9.16 shows that about 2 to 3 percent of American men and 1 percent of American women identify themselves as homosexual or bisexual, but higher percentages report same-sex attraction and at least one same-sex sexual experience (Laumann et al., 1994). Overall, 10 percent of men and 9 percent of women answer affirmatively to at least one of the items in Figure 9.16. Rates of same-sex sexual activity seem to be slightly lower in England and France and slightly higher in Australia (Dunne et al., 2000; Johnson et al., 1992).

Determinants of Sexual Orientation Theories about the origins of sexual orientation abound. An early and unsupported biological view proposed that homosexual and heterosexual males differ in their adult levels of sex hormones. Other early theories hypothesized that male homosexuality develops when boys grow up with a weak ineffectual father and identify with a domineering mother, or that being sexually seduced by an adult homosexual causes children to divert their sex drive toward members of their own sex.

All of these theories have taken a scientific beating. In one study, Alan Bell and coworkers (1981) interviewed nearly 1,000 homosexual and over 500 heterosexual men and women from the San Francisco area. They searched extensively for childhood or adolescent experiences that might predict adult sexual orientation, but only one consistent pattern emerged. Even in childhood, homosexual men and women felt that they were somehow different from their same-sex peers and were more likely to engage in *gender-nonconforming behaviors*. Similarly, compared with heterosexual women, homosexual women in Brazil, Peru, the Philippines, and the United States were about twice as likely during childhood to be considered tomboys and be interested in boys' clothes and toys (Whitam & Mathy, 1991). Study after study has obtained similar results (Cohen, 2002).

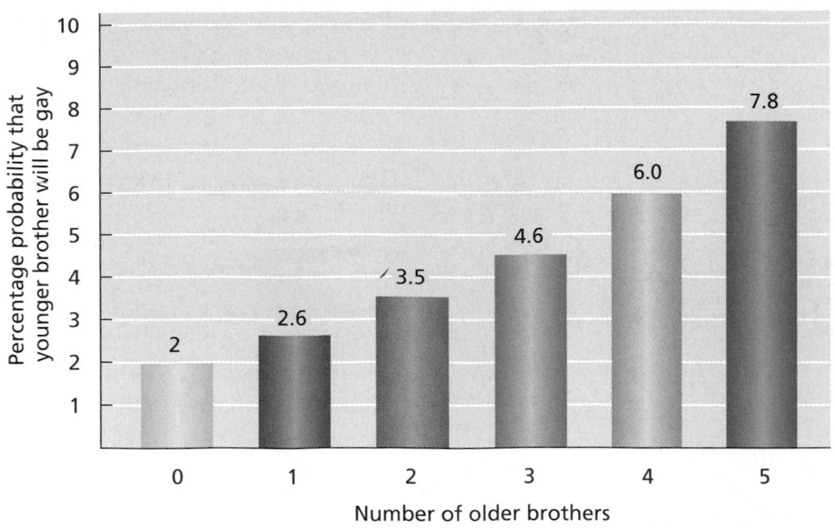

FIGURE 9.17

The fraternal birth order effect. The presence of each older brother increases by about one third the relative probability that a later-born male child will be gay. Thus if there is a 2-percent probability that a man with no older brothers is gay, then the probabililty for a man with one older brother is about 2.6 to 2.7 percent, roughly a one-third relative increase. SOURCE: Adapted from Blanchard and Bogaert, 1996.

Still, why do such patterns arise? Highly publicized studies appeared in the early 1990s reporting anatomical differences in the brains of heterosexual versus homosexual men and identifying a genetic marker shared by some homosexual men. Subsequent research, however, has not consistently replicated these findings (Lasco et al., 2002). Nonetheless, there is growing evidence that heredity influences human sexual orientation. In one study, among gay men who had a brother, the concordance rates for sexual orientation (i.e., the brother was gay also) were 52 percent among identical twins, 22 percent among fraternal twins, and 11 percent among adoptive brothers (Bailey & Pillard, 1991). A later study of lesbian women yielded similar results (Bailey et al., 1993). Thus the closer the genetic relatedness, the higher the concordance rates for sexual orientation (Kirk et al., 2000).

According to another theory, the brain develops a neural pattern that predisposes an individual to prefer either female or male sex partners, depending on whether prenatal sex hormone activity follows a masculine or feminine path (Ellis & Ames, 1987). Experimentally altering animals' prenatal exposure to sex hormones can influence their sexual orientation. Moreover, in rare cases among humans, some genetically male fetuses are insensitive to their own androgen secretions and some female fetuses experience an atypical buildup of androgens. Studies of these individuals suggest a relation between prenatal sex hormone exposure and adulthood sexual orientation (Williams et al., 2000). Of course, the human research is correlational and must be interpreted cautiously. For example, male fetuses who have androgen insensitivity develop the external anatomy of females and are typically raised as girls; socialization could account for their sexual orientation.

What about environmental influences? Even among identical twins, when one is homosexual, often the other is heterosexual. Thus a biological predisposition and socialization experiences may combine to determine sexual orientation. At present, scientists simply do not know what all the factors are. It is also possible, argues Daryl Bem (1996, 2001), that heredity affects sexual orientation only indirectly, by influencing children's basic personality style. He proposes that different personality styles then steer children toward gender-conforming or gender-nonconforming activities, causing them to feel similar to or different from same-sex peers. Ultimately, this affects their attraction to same-sex and opposite-sex peers. Bem's theory has mixed support and needs further testing (Bailey et al., 2000; Peplau et al., 1998).

Finally, there may be multiple paths toward developing a sexual orientation, and the paths for men and women may differ. Consider the intriguing finding shown in Figure 9.17: The greater the number of older brothers (but not older sisters) a newborn boy has, the greater the probability that he will develop a homosexual orientation. In contrast, a woman's sexual orientation is not related to the number of older sisters or brothers in the family. Ray Blanchard (2001), the leading researcher of this *fraternal birth order effect*, has found it in 14 studies, involving over 7,000 total participants.

What Do You Think?

FRATERNAL BIRTH ORDER AND MALE HOMOSEXUALITY

Why might having older brothers increase the odds that a later-born male will have a homosexual orientation? Think about possible explanations, then see page 372.

IN REVIEW

- *The past half century has witnessed changing patterns of sexual activity, such as an increase in premarital sex, that now appears to have leveled off.*
- *During sexual intercourse, people often experience a four-stage physiological response pattern consisting of excitement, plateau, orgasm, and resolution.*
- *Sex hormones have organizational effects that guide prenatal organ development along either a male or female pattern. Sex hormones also have activational effects that influence sexual desire.*
- *Sexual fantasy can trigger arousal, whereas psychological difficulties can interfere with sexual arousal. Cultural norms help determine the sexual practices and beliefs that are considered proper.*
- *Environmental stimuli affect sexual desire. Viewing sexual violence reinforces men's belief in rape myths and generally increases men's aggression toward women, at least temporarily.*
- *Sexual orientation involves dimensions of self-identity, sexual attraction, and actual sexual behavior. Scientists still do not know conclusively what determines an individual's sexual orientation.*

The Desire to Affiliate

▶ 11. Discuss evolutionary and psychological views of affiliation and factors that influence the desire to affiliate.

What makes your life most meaningful? To many people, close relationships are one key. The three doctors Sampson Davis, Rameck Hunt, and George Jenkins surely agree. Their deep friendship and mutual support sustained them through arduous years of college and medical school. Abraham Maslow (1954) viewed belongingness as a basic psychological need, and considerable research indicates that, indeed, "the need to belong is a powerful, fundamental, and extremely pervasive motivation" (Baumeister & Leary, 1995, p. 497).

Why Do We Affiliate?

Humans are social beings who affiliate in many ways (Figure 9.18). Some theorists propose that, over the course of evolution, individuals whose biological makeup predisposed them to affiliate were more likely to survive and reproduce than those who were reclusive. By affording greater access to sexual mates, more protection from predators, an efficient division of labor, and the passing of knowledge across generations, a socially oriented lifestyle had considerable adaptive value (Kottak, 2000).

Craig Hill (1987) suggests that we affiliate for four basic psychological reasons:

- to obtain positive stimulation,
- to receive emotional support,
- to gain attention, and
- to permit social comparison.

Social comparison *involves comparing our beliefs, feelings, and behaviors with those of other people.* This helps us determine whether our responses are "normal" and enables us to judge the level of our cognitive and physical abilities (Festinger, 1954).

People differ in how strongly they desire to affiliate. In one study, college students who scored high on a personality test of *need for affiliation* made more friends during the semester than students who scored low (Byrne & Greendlinger, 1989). In another study, high school students wore beepers over a 1-week period. They were signaled approximately every 2 hours, and recorded their thoughts and activities. Participants with a high need for affiliation were more likely than their peers to report that they were thinking about friends and wishing that they could be with people (Wong & Csikszentmihalyi, 1991).

Even people with strong affiliation needs, however, usually desire some time alone. Conversely, people with lower affiliation needs still seek periodic social contact. Some theorists, therefore, view affiliation needs within a homeostatic model (O'Connor & Rosenblood, 1996). They propose that each of us has our own optimal range of social contact. After periods when contact exceeds that range, we compensate by temporarily seeking more solitude. After periods when social contact falls below the optimal range, we increase our

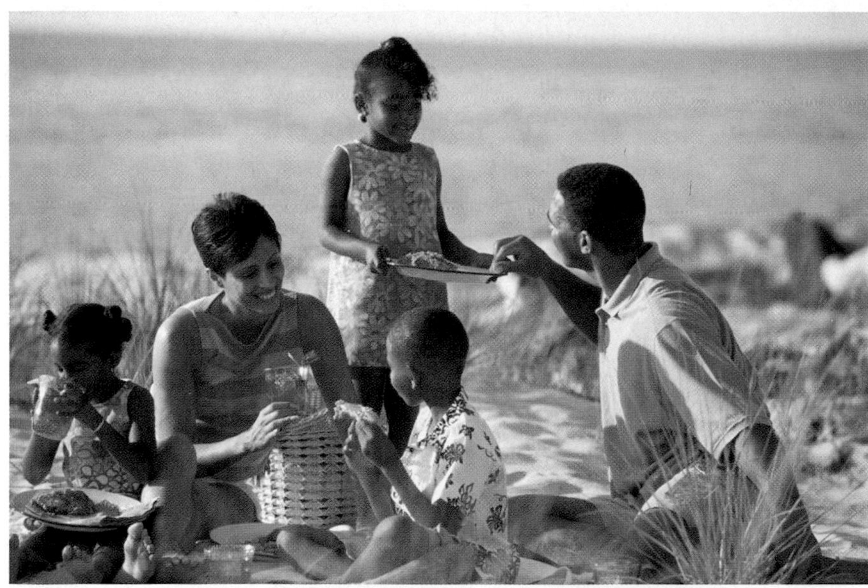

FIGURE 9.18

Affiliation brings us companionship, intimacy, love, support, and also basic social contact. To satisfy these desires we form friendships, interact with family members, join groups, converse with strangers, and flock together in crowds.

effort to be with others. Although some human and animal findings are consistent with this model, it needs much more testing.

Many studies have shown, however, that situational factors influence our tendency to affiliate. For example, fear-inducing situations increase our desire to be with others. During emergencies, as in the aftermath of earthquakes, floods, and hurricanes, many people find themselves bonding with strangers. When afraid, we may prefer to be with others who face the same situation we do, which helps us gauge the normalcy of our reactions (Schachter, 1959).

When possible, we seem to desire most strongly to be with others who have already been through the same or similar situations (Kulik & Mahler, 2000). Doing so can provide us with information about what to expect. In one study, hospital patients awaiting open-heart surgery expressed a stronger desire to have a roommate who already had been through surgery than a preoperative roommate like themselves. In a later study, when patients were actually assigned postoperative rather than preoperative roommates, they became less anxious and later recovered from surgery more quickly (Kulik et al., 1996).

Seeking a Mate

One of the most important and intimate ways that humans affiliate is by seeking a mate. Marriage seems to be universal across the globe, but people also seek mates in other types of relationships (Buss & Schmitt, 1993). Much research has found, however, that on average women and men display different mating strategies and preferences. Compared with women, men typically show more interest in short-term mating, prefer a greater number of short-term sexual mates, have more permissive sexual attitudes, and have more sexual partners over their lifetime (Schmitt et al., 2001).

But how strong are these male-female differences? In part the answer depends on how you examine the issue. Consider the following question: Over the next 30 years, how many sexual partners would you ideally like to have? In one study, men reported desiring an average of about 16 sexual partners, whereas women on average reported desiring about 4 (Buss & Schmitt, 1993). No matter what time period was specified—6 months, 1 year, 5 years, and so on—on average, men reported wanting a greater number of sexual mates.

But in some circumstances averages can be deceiving, as a study of 266 college undergraduates reveals (Pedersen et al., 2002). When asked about how many sexual partners they desired over the next 30 years, on average men said almost 8 and women said almost 3. Now take a look at Figure 9.19. You can see that almost half of the men and two thirds of the women wished to have only 1 partner. Overall, men's and women's patterns of preferences are far more similar than dissimilar. Also, you can see why the mathematical averages differ by so much: A few men desired between 30 and 99 partners, whereas almost no women did. Such extreme responses from a few people can inflate the mathematical average, causing it to portray an inaccurate picture. Of course, even ignoring the extreme cases, Figure 9.19 still reveals that the desire for more than 1 sexual partner is more common among men. But unlike some popular stereotypes that portray men and women as

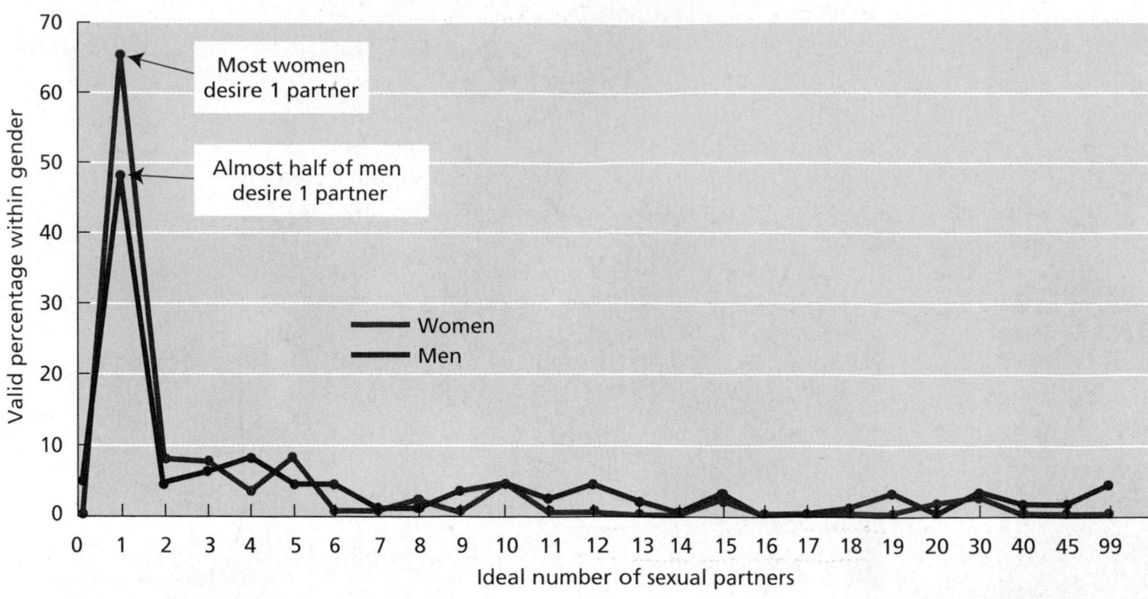

FIGURE 9.19

Different planets or adjacent neighborhoods? From this graph, would you conclude that men and women are mostly similar or mostly different in the number of sexual partners they ideally would like to have over the next 30 years? Source: Adapted with permission from Pedersen et al., 2002.

coming from different planets, these findings suggest that they come from adjacent neighborhoods.

What Do Men and Women Desire in a Long-Term Partner?

▶ 12. Contrast sexual strategies and social structure explanations for mate preferences. Describe cross-cultural evidence.

What about the commitment that most men and women make at some point in their lives to a long-term mate? What qualities do women and men seek in such a mate? Once again, we see sex differences. Men typically prefer women somewhat younger than themselves, whereas women prefer somewhat older men. In terms of personal qualities, Table 9.2 shows the overall results of a worldwide study of mate preferences in 37 cultures (Buss et al., 1990). Men and women again show considerable overall agreement, but some differences emerge. Men place greater value on a potential mate's being physically attractive and possessing good domestic skills, whereas women place greater value on a potential mate's earning potential, status, and ambitiousness. The question is, why?

According to an evolutionary viewpoint called **sexual strategies theory** (and a related model called *parental investment theory*), *mating strategies and preferences reflect inherited tendencies, shaped over the ages in response to different types of adaptive problems that men and women faced* (Buss & Schmitt, 1993; Trivers, 1972). In evolutionary terms, our most successful ancestors were those who survived and passed down the greatest numbers of their genes to future generations. According to this viewpoint, men who had sex with more partners increased the likelihood of fathering more children. Men also may have used a woman's youth and

TABLE 9.2 What Do You Look for in a Mate?

Women and men rated each characteristic on a 4 point scale. From top to bottom, the following numbers represent the order (rank) of most highly rated to least highly rated items for Buss's worldwide sample. How would you rate their importance?

Characteristic Desired in a Mate	Rated by Women	Rated by Men
Mutual attraction/love	1	1
Dependable character	2	2
Emotional stability/maturity	3	3
Pleasing disposition	4	4
Education/intelligence	5	6
Sociability	6	7
Good health	7	5
Desire for home/children	8	8
Ambitious	9	11
Refinement	10	9
Similar education	11	14
Good financial prospect	12	13
Good looks	13	10
Social status	14	15
Good cook/housekeeper	15	12
Similar religion	16	17
Similar politics	17	18
Chastity	18	16

Source: Based on Buss et al., 1990.

attractive, healthy appearance as signs that she was fertile and had many years left to bear children (Buss, 1989).

In contrast, ancestral women had little to gain and much to lose by mating with many men. The gender with a greater investment (costs) in producing offspring will be more selective in choosing a mate. In humans and other mammals, females typically make a greater investment than males. Females carry the fetus, incur health risks, and nourish the newborn. Engaging in short-term sexual relationships with multiple males creates uncertainty about which one is the father, thereby decreasing a male's willingness to commit resources to helping the mother raise the child. Thus women maximized their reproductive success by being selective and choosing mates who were willing and able to commit time, energy, and other resources (e.g., food, shelter, protection) to the family. Through natural selection, according to evolutionary psychologists, the differing qualities that maximized men's and women's reproductive success eventually became part of their biological nature.

Many scientists challenge this evolutionary explanation for human mating patterns and other social behaviors. Adaptive behavior patterns may have been passed from parents to children not through genes but through learning. In addition, **social structure theory** *proposes that men and women display different mating preferences because society directs them into different social roles* (Eagly & Wood, 1999). Despite the shift over the past several decades toward greater gender equality, women today in general still have less power, lower wages, and less access to resources than men do. In two-income marriages, women are more likely to be the partner who switches to part-time work or becomes a full-time homemaker after childbirth. Thus society's division of labor still tends to socialize men into the "breadwinner" role and women into the "homemaker" role.

It makes sense, then, for women to seek men who will be successful wage earners and for men to seek women who can have children and fulfill the domestic worker role. An older male–younger female age gap is favorable because older men are likely to be further along in earning power and younger women more economically dependent, and this conforms to cultural expectations of marital roles. This division-of-labor hypothesis does not directly address why men emphasize a mate's physical attractiveness more than women do, but Alice Eagly and Wendy Wood (1999) speculate that attractiveness is viewed as part of what women "exchange" in return for a male's earning capacity.

We now have two competing explanations for sex differences in mating behavior: the evolutionary approach and the social structure view. Which view is more valid? Our *Research Close-Up* looks at one attempt to answer this question.

RESEARCH CLOSE-UP

SEX DIFFERENCES IN THE IDEAL MATE: EVOLUTION OR SOCIAL ROLES?

Background

How can we possibly test the hypothesis that over the ages, evolution has shaped the psyche of men and women to be inherently different? Evolutionary psychologist David Buss proposes that as a start, we can examine whether gender differences in mating preferences are consistent across cultures. If they are, this would be consistent with the view that men and women follow universal, biologically based mating strategies that transcend culture. Based on principles of evolutionary psychology, Buss hypothesized that *across cultures*

- men will prefer to marry younger women, because such women have greater reproductive capacity;
- men will value a potential mate's attractiveness more than women will, because men use attractiveness as a sign of health and fertility; and
- women will place greater value than men on a potential mate's earning potential, because this provides survival advantages for the woman and her offspring.

Method

A team of 50 scientists administered questionnaires to women and men from 37 cultures around the globe. Although random sampling could not be used, the sample of 10,047 participants was ethnically, religiously, and socioeconomically diverse. Participants reported the ideal ages at which they and a spouse would marry, rank-ordered (from "most desirable" to "least

Continued

desirable") a list of 13 qualities that a potential mate might have, and rated the importance of 18 mate qualities on a second list (see Table 9.2).

Results

In every culture, men desired to marry younger women. Overall, they believed that the ideal ages for men and women to marry were 27.5 and 24.8 years, respectively. Similarly, women preferred older men, reporting on average an ideal marriage age of 28.8 for husbands and 25.4 for wives. In every culture, men valued having a physically attractive mate more than women did, and in 36 of 37 cultures, women attached more importance than men did to a mate's earning potential.

Evolutionary and Social Roles Interpretations

David Buss concluded that the findings strongly supported the predictions of evolutionary theory. Subsequently, Alice Eagly and Wendy Wood analyzed Buss's data further in order to test the following predictions derived from their social structure theory:

- Men place greater value than women on a mate's having good domestic skills, because this is consistent with culturally defined gender roles.
- If economic and power inequalities cause men and women to attach different values to a mate's age, earning potential, and domestic skills, then these gender differences should be smaller in cultures where there is less inequality between men and women.

The characteristic "good cook/housekeeper" produced large overall gender differences, with men valuing it more highly. Eagly and Wood then used the United Nations Gender Empowerment Measure to assess the degree of gender equality in each culture. This measure reflects women's percentage share of administrative, managerial, professional, and technical jobs; seats in parliament; and earned income relative to men.

As predicted by the social structure model, in cultures with greater gender equality men showed less of a preference for younger women, women displayed less of a preference for older men, and the gender gap decreased in mate preferences for a "good cook/housekeeper" and "good financial prospect." Recall that this division-of-labor model does not directly address why men value physical attractiveness more than women; indeed, that gender difference was *not* smaller in cultures with greater gender equality.

Discussion

Buss found remarkably consistent sex differences in worldwide mate preferences. He interprets this cross-cultural consistency as evidence that men and women follow universal, biologically based mating strategies. Yet the fact that behavior is consistent across cultures does not, by itself, demonstrate *why* those patterns occur (Wood & Eagly, 2000). Eagly and Wood found that a common social condition across cultures, gender inequality, accounts for some—but not all—of the sex differences in mating preferences.

In science, such controversy stimulates opposing camps to find more sophisticated ways to test their hypotheses. Ultimately, everyone's goal is to arrive at the most plausible explanation for behavior. This is why scientists make their data available to one another, regardless of the possibility that their peers may use the data to bolster an opposing point of view.

Although men and women differ in some of their mating preferences and strategies, the similar overall order of mate preferences shown in Table 9.2 indicates that we are talking once again about shades of the same color, not different colors. In fact, Buss and coworkers (1990) found that "there may be more similarity between men and women from the same culture than between men and men or women and women from different cultures" (p. 17).

The sexual strategies and social structure theories are not the only ones to address mate preferences. Indeed, not all evolutionary theorists agree with the sexual strategies model. For example, Cindy Hazan and Lisa Diamond (2000) argue that evolution has shaped the human psyche toward seeking **attachment,** *a deep bond between two individuals.* In their view, the same biological prewiring that predisposes infants to bond with a caregiver also steers adults toward becoming attached to a mate. As they note,

> The (over)emphasis on sex differences has distracted us from the reality that men and women are basically similar in what they seek in a mate, the processes by which they become attached to a mate, and the benefits that accrue to them as a result of being in a stable pair bond. (2000, p. 194)

Sources: David M. Buss (1989). Sex differences in human mate preferences: Evolutionary hypotheses tested in 37 cultures. *Behavioral and Brain Sciences, 12,* 1–49; Alice Eagly and Wendy Wood (1999). The origins of sex differences in human behavior: Evolved dispositions versus social roles. *American Psychologist, 54,* 408–423.

IN REVIEW

- *Humans seek to affiliate in many ways. Affiliation has adaptive advantages and allows people to obtain positive stimulation, receive emotional support, gain attention, and engage in social comparison.*
- *People differ in how strongly they need to affiliate, and some theorists view affiliative behavior as governed by homeostatic principles.*
- *Situations that induce fear often increase people's tendency to affiliate. When afraid, people often seek the company of others who have been through or are currently experiencing the same or a similar situation.*
- *Some reliable sex differences occur in people's mating strategies and preferences, such as men's tendency to seek younger women and women's tendency to seek older men.*
- *Evolutionary theorists propose that these sex differences in mate preferences reflect inherited biological tendencies, whereas social structure theorists argue that these differences result from sex-role socialization and gender inequities in economic opportunities.*

Achievement and Work Motivation

In striving to become doctors, Sampson Davis, Rameck Hunt, and George Jenkins exemplified the desire to achieve. As a college student, you are keenly aware of society's emphasis on achievement, and you know that whether in school, sports, music, or other fields, some people seek out and thrive on challenges, whereas others do not. In the 1950s, David McClelland, John Atkinson, and their coworkers (1953) began to explore individual differences in **need for achievement,** *a personality characteristic representing the desire to accomplish tasks and attain standards of excellence.*

Motive for Success and Fear of Failure

McClelland and Atkinson proposed that achievement behavior can stem from a positively oriented *motive for success* and a negatively oriented motivation to avoid failure, more commonly called *fear of failure.* They measured the motive for success with a psychological test that asked participants to interpret a series of pictures (Figure 9.20). Fear of failure was measured by psychological tests that asked people to report how much anxiety they experienced in achievement situations.

People who have a strong motive for success seek the "thrill of victory," whereas those motivated by fear of failure seek to avoid the "agony of defeat." Common sense suggests that a strong motive for success combined with a strong fear of failure might lead a person to perform better than someone who is motivated only by a desire for success. But this is not so. The anxiety associated with fear of failure impairs performance. In sports, this is the athlete who chokes under pressure (Smith, 1996).

People with high overall achievement motivation (called *high-need achievers*) have a strong motive for success and a weak fear of failure. *Low-need achievers* display the opposite pattern. McClelland and Atkinson found that high-need achievers persist longer after encountering difficulty than do low-need achievers, but in general they don't outperform low-need achievers when conditions are relaxed and tasks are easy. However, when tasks are challenging or the importance of doing well is stressed, high-need achievers outshine low-need achievers (McClelland, 1989). In general, high-need achievers are most likely to strive hard for success when

- they perceive themselves as personally responsible for the outcome;
- they perceive some risk of not succeeding; and
- there is an opportunity to receive performance feedback (Koestner & McClelland, 1990).

When given a choice of performing a task that is very easy (a high probability of success), moderately difficult (a 40 to 60 percent probability of success), or very difficult (a low probability of success), which do you predict that high-need achievers will choose? Contrary to what you might expect, they prefer intermediate risks to extremely high or low risks because the outcome—success versus failure—*is most uncertain* (Atkinson & Birch, 1978). In contrast, low-need achievers are more likely to choose tasks that are easy (where success is almost assured) or very difficult (where success is not expected).

To understand this pattern, realize that it is the individual's *perception* of outcome uncertainty that counts. For most of us, the probability of successfully climbing Mt. Everest is virtually zero. But to highly trained mountaineers, the task is neither impossible nor easy. Decades ago, sociologist and mountain climber Dick Emerson (1966)

FIGURE 9.20

Pictures like this have been used to elicit stories that are scored for the motive to succeed. Which of the following two stories, written by different people, reflects a stronger motive to succeed? (1) This young man is sitting in school, but he is dreaming about the day when he will become a doctor. He will study and work harder than anyone else. He goes on to become one of the top medical researchers in the world. (2) The boy is daydreaming about how much he hates being in school. He would like to run away from home and just take it easy on a tropical island. However, he is doomed to be in the rat race the rest of his life.

▶ 13. How do the motives and task behaviors of high- versus low-need achievers differ? How does need for achievement develop?

joined a Mt. Everest expedition. As he predicted, the team members' communications with one another throughout the long climb struck a balance between optimistic and pessimistic comments about the chances of reaching their goal. This kept the climbers' perceived chance of success-failure close to 50-50 and maintained maximum motivation.

Family, Culture, and Achievement Needs

How does achievement motivation develop? Providing a cognitively stimulating home environment fosters children's intrinsic motivation to perform academic tasks (Gottfried et al., 1998). And when parents or other key caregivers encourage and reward achievement but do not punish failure, they foster a strong motive for success (Koestner & McClelland, 1990). Conversely, fear of failure seems to develop when caregivers take successful achievement for granted but punish failure, thereby teaching the child to dread the possibility of failing (Weiner, 1992).

Cultural norms also shape achievement motivation. Individualistic cultures, such as those in North America and much of Europe, tend to stress personal achievement. In cultures that nurture collectivism, such as those in China and Japan, achievement motivation more strongly reflects a desire to fit into the family and social group, meet its expectations, and work for its goals (Markus & Kitayama, 1991). Chinese high school students, for example, typically care more about meeting their parents' expectations for academic success than do American students (Chen & Lan, 1998).

At the same time, the human desire to achieve transcends culture and can manifest itself in intriguing ways. Throughout history, some people have left their homelands to seek adventure or better lives elsewhere. Might achievement motivation relate to the desire to emigrate? To answer this question, researchers measured the achievement motivation of college students in Albania, the Czech Republic, and Slovenia, and also asked students where they would like to live for most of their adult lives. In each sample, students who expressed a desire to emigrate had higher average achievement motivation scores than students who said they wanted to remain in their homeland (Boneva et al., 1998).

Achievement Goals

▶ 14. Identify three types of achievement goals and how they relate to achievement motivation and behavior.

Another way to understand achievement motivation is to examine the goals that people seek to attain in task situations. Think for a moment about a class you currently are taking. On a scale of 1 ("not at all true of me") to 7 ("very true of me"), rate these statements:

1. I want to learn as much as possible from this class.
2. I am motivated by the thought of outperforming my peers in this class.
3. I just want to avoid doing poorly in this class.

These statements represent three different achievement goals (Elliot & Church, 1997). **Mastery goals** (statement 1) *focus on the desire to master a task and learn new knowledge or skills*. In essence, mastery goals reflect intrinsic motivation. **Performance-approach goals** (statement 2) *reflect a competitive orientation that focuses on being judged favorably relative to other people*, whereas **performance-avoidance goals** (statement 3) *center on avoiding negative judgments*. In general, high-need achievers tend to adopt mastery and performance-approach goals. Low-need achievers, however, tend not to focus on mastery and instead display performance-approach and performance-avoidance goals (Elliot et al., 1999).

Do college students' achievement goals for a particular class, measured a couple of weeks after classes begin, help predict their psychological responses to upcoming exams and to that course? Do goals predict course grades? Overall, performance-avoidance goals are associated with perceiving exams as anxiety-provoking threats, to reporting at the end of the term that the course was a little less interesting and enjoyable, and to slightly poorer course grades (Harackiewicz et al., 2002; McGregor & Elliot, 2002).

In contrast, mastery goals predict the tendency to perceive exams as a positive challenge and rate the course as more interesting and enjoyable, even though mastery goals are unrelated to course grades. Performance-approach goals, however, predict grades but not final interest or enjoyment. When it comes to exams, they are weakly associated with feelings of both challenge and threat. Given this pattern of findings, some researchers believe that students who adopt both mastery and performance-approach goals display the optimal pattern of motivation for college courses (Harackiewicz et al., 2002).

Motivation in the Workplace

The workplace is one of life's most important achievement arenas, and people typically desire careers that are motivating and satisfying. Motivation also is vital to organizations. To succeed, an organization needs workers who are motivated to join it, remain in it, and perform their jobs well.

Why Do People Work? The earliest psychological theory of work motivation held that employees are motivated almost entirely by money (Taylor, 1911). This may characterize some workers, but opportunities for mastery, social recognition, growth, and satisfying interpersonal relationships are key motivators for many employees (Stajkovic & Luthans, 2001).

Cultural factors also influence work motivation (Figure 9.21). In collectivistic Japan, business organizations have traditionally adopted a concept of *Kaizen* (continuous improvement), encouraging workers to develop skills and increase productivity (Elsey & Fujiwara, 2000). Such companies assume responsibility for their employees' welfare, promote them gradually, and are willing to retain them for life. As the company becomes integral to the workers' identity, they are strongly motivated by loyalty to their managers and to the organization.

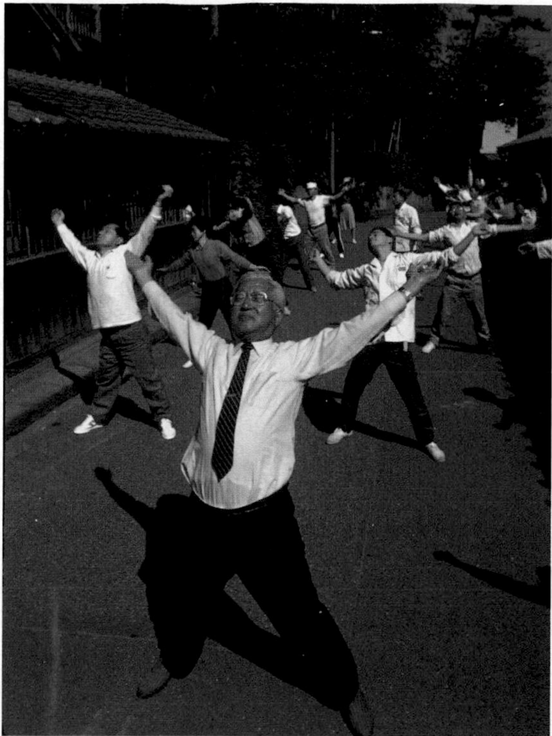

FIGURE 9.21

In Japan, achievement motivation traditionally manifests itself as a desire to conform to the expectations of the social group and to contribute to the attainment of group goals. Demanding but caring managers and leaders are highly effective because they foster a sense of obligation that causes employees to work hard.

▶ 15. Describe how job enrichment, incentive programs, and goal-setting programs enhance work motivation.

Enhancing Work Motivation Industrial/organizational (I/O) psychologists have designed many programs to enhance employee motivation and performance. Partly reflecting Maslow's humanistic theory, **job enrichment** *attempts to increase motivation by making jobs more fulfilling and providing workers with opportunities for growth.* Jobs typically are most fulfilling when they involve task variety (requiring many talents) and important tasks, when a "whole" product is completed from beginning to end, when they allow the worker some freedom to determine work procedures, and when they provide performance feedback (Hackman and Lawler, 1971).

For example, at a truck assembly plant owned by Volvo in Sweden, performance production teams of 5 to 12 workers replaced assembly lines. Team members decided how to distribute tasks, managed their own quality control, and could vary their work provided they met production standards. As a result, performance increased, absenteeism decreased, and workers were less likely to quit their jobs (Wexley & Yukl, 1977). Other studies have found that workers who perform enriched jobs procrastinate less and display greater loyalty to their company (Niehoff et al., 2001).

Employee **incentive programs** *rest on the learning theory principle that performance will increase when reinforcement is contingent on productivity.* When Union National Bank began paying workers based on the number of customers served and new accounts opened, employees' pay and the bank's profits increased (Aamodt, 1991). Another employer reduced tardiness and absenteeism among industrial workers in an unusual way. Every day, each worker who arrived on time was dealt a card from a poker deck; those who were late did not receive a card. At the end of the week, the worker with the best five-card poker hand won a $20 prize (Pedalino & Gamboa, 1974).

Incentives, however, don't have to be monetary. The Emery Air Freight Corporation used praise and recognition to reinforce desired employee behaviors, and a garment factory used a recognition program to reduce absenteeism by 29 to 52 percent for each 3-month period over the course of a year (Markham et al., 2002).

Consistent with the expectancy × value model, **goal-setting programs** *rest on the premise that motivation increases when people consciously pursue goals that they value and expect they can reach.* In dozens of studies, businesses have used goal setting to improve worker output, reduce absenteeism and theft, cut operating costs, and enhance employee satisfaction (Locke & Latham, 2002). In Chapter 11, you will learn more about principles of effective goal setting and how to apply them to your life.

IN REVIEW

- *High-need achievers have a strong motive for success and relatively low fear of failure. They tend to seek moderately difficult tasks that are challenging but attainable. Low-need achievers are more likely to choose easy tasks where success is assured or very difficult tasks where success is not expected.*
- *Child-rearing and cultural factors influence our expression of achievement motivation.*
- *Mastery, performance-approach, and performance-avoidance goals are three basic achievement goals. Mastery goals are associated with viewing achievement tasks as a positive challenge, whereas performance-avoidance goals are linked to viewing such tasks as threatening. Of the three goals, performance-approach goals are most strongly linked to eventual course grades for college students.*
- *For many workers, opportunities for accomplishment and growth are stronger motivators than money.*
- *Job enrichment programs increase employee motivation by making work tasks more personally fulfilling. Incentive programs make reinforcers contingent on desirable performance, and goal-setting programs are most effective when they provide feedback about goal progress and set specific, attainable goals that workers view as important.*

"C'mon, c'mon—it's either one or the other."

FIGURE 9.22

An unfortunate avoidance-avoidance conflict.

Motivational Conflict

▶ 16. Explain and illustrate three types of motivational conflict.

Motivational goals sometimes conflict with one another. Our desires to achieve success and to have fun may clash, for example, when we must choose between studying for an exam and attending a party. When something attracts us, we tend to approach it; when something repels us, we tend to avoid it. Different combinations of these tendencies can produce three basic types of conflict.

Approach-approach conflict *occurs when we face two attractive alternatives and selecting one means losing the other.* Conflict is greatest when both alternatives, such as a choice between two desirable careers, are equally attractive. In contrast, **avoidance-avoidance conflict** *occurs when we must choose between two undesirable alternatives* (Figure 9.22). Do I study boring material for an exam, or do I skip studying and fail?

Approach-avoidance conflict *involves being attracted to and repelled by the same goal.* A college senior thinking of changing majors is attracted to job opportunities in the new major but is repelled by the prospect of a fifth year of classes. A squirrel being offered food by a person on a park bench is motivated by hunger to approach and by fear to keep its distance.

Approach and avoidance tendencies grow stronger as we get nearer to a desired goal (Miller, 1944). Usually, the avoidance tendency increases in strength faster than the approach tendency (Figure 9.23). Thus at first we may be attracted to a goal and only slightly repelled by its drawbacks, but as we get closer to it the negative aspects become dominant. We may stop, retreat, approach again, and continue to vacillate in a state of conflict. However, the general strength of approach and avoidance tendencies differs across people; some individuals are more attuned to positive stimuli and the possibility of obtaining desired outcomes, whereas others are more sensitive to actual and anticipated negative outcomes (Elliot & Thrash, 2002).

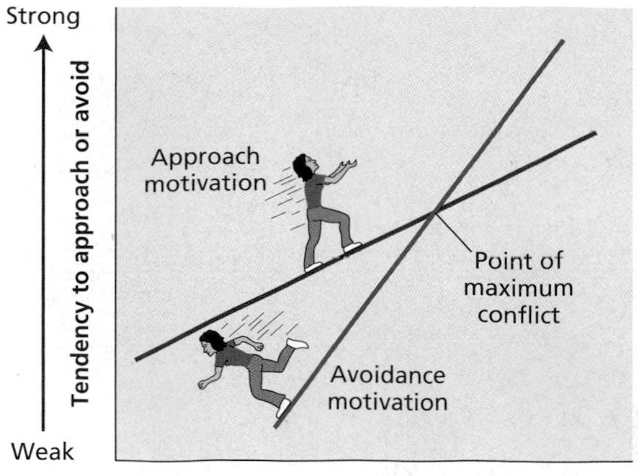

FIGURE 9.23

Approach-avoidance conflict. According to Neal Miller (1944), the tendency to approach and the tendency to avoid grow stronger as one moves closer to the goal. However, the tendency to avoid increases faster than the tendency to approach. Maximum conflict is experienced where the two gradients cross, because at this point the opposing motives are equal in strength.

IN REVIEW

- *Motivational goals may conflict with one another. Approach-approach conflict occurs when a person has to select between two attractive alternatives, whereas avoidance-avoidance conflict involves choosing between two undesirable alternatives.*
- *Approach-avoidance conflict occurs when we are attracted to and repelled by the same goal.*

EMOTION

Life without emotion would be bland and empty. Our experiences of love, anger, joy, fear, and other emotions energize and add color to our lives. **Emotions** *are feeling (or affect) states that involve a pattern of cognitive, physiological, and behavioral reactions to events.* Emotion theorist Richard Lazarus (2001) believed that motivation and emotions are always linked, because we react emotionally only when our motives and goals are gratified, threatened, or frustrated (Figure 9.24).

▶ 17. In what ways are negative and positive emotions adaptive?

Emotions have important adaptive functions. Some emotions, such as fear and alarm, are part of an emergency arousal system that increases our chances of survival, as when we fight or flee when confronted by threat or danger. But positive emotions such as interest, joy, excitement, contentment, and love also have important adaptive functions. They help us form intimate relationships and broaden our thinking and behavior so that we explore, consider new ideas, try out new ways to achieve goals, play, and savor what we have (Fredrickson, 1998).

Emotions are also an important form of social communication. By providing clues about our internal states and intentions, emotions influence how other people behave toward us (Isaacs, 1998). Consider, for example, the effects of a baby's crying on adults, who generally respond with caretaking responses that have obvious survival value for the infant. Adults' expressions of sadness and distress also evoke concern, empathy, and helping behavior from others.

Positive emotional expressions also pay off. A smiling infant is likely to increase parents' feelings of affection and caring, thereby increasing the likelihood that the child's biological and emotional needs will be satisfied. Happy adults also tend to attract others and to have richer and more supportive relationships (Diener & Seligman, 2002).

The Nature of Emotions

▶ 18. Describe the 4 major components of emotion and how they influence one another.

Our emotional states share four common features:

1. Emotions are triggered by *external* or *internal eliciting stimuli.*
2. Emotional responses result from our interpretations or *appraisals* of these stimuli, which give the situation its perceived meaning and significance.
3. Our *bodies respond physiologically* to our appraisal. We may become physically aroused or "stirred up," as when we feel fear, joy, or anger; or we may experience decreased arousal, as when we feel contentment or depression.
4. Emotions include *behavior tendencies*. Some are *expressive behaviors* (e.g., smiling with joy, crying). Others are *instrumental behaviors,* ways of doing something about the stimulus that evoked the emotion (e.g., studying for an anxiety-arousing test, fighting back in self-defense).

Figure 9.25 illustrates the general relations among these four emotional components. For

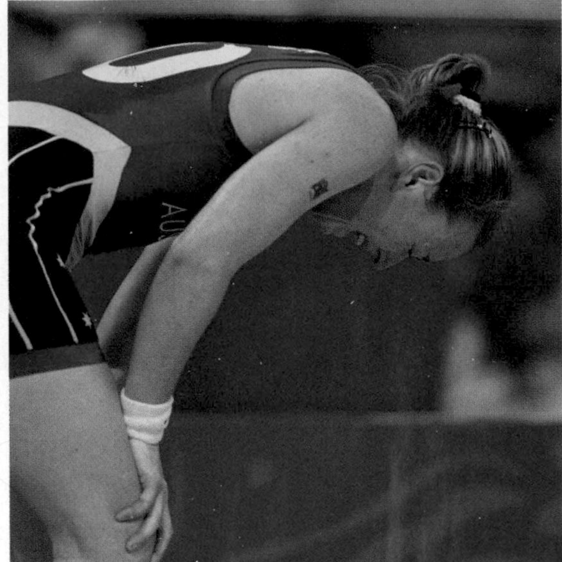

FIGURE 9.24

The intimate relations between motivation and emotion are seen in the strong emotional responses that occur when important goals are either attained or lost.

example, an insulting remark from another person (eliciting stimulus) may evoke a cognitive appraisal that we have been unfairly demeaned, an increase in physiological arousal, a clenching of jaw and fists (expressive behavior), and a verbal attack on the other person (instrumental behavior). As the two-way arrows indicate, these emotional components can influence one another. Thus emotion is a dynamic, ongoing *process,* and any of its four elements can change rapidly in the course of an emotional episode.

Eliciting Stimuli

Emotions do not occur in a vacuum. They are responses to situations, people, objects, or events. We become angry *at* something or someone; fearful or proud *of* something; in love *with* someone. Moreover, the **eliciting stimuli** *that trigger cognitive appraisals and emotional responses* are not always external; they can be internal stimuli, such as a mental image of an upcoming vacation that makes us feel happy or a memory of an unpleasant encounter that arouses anger in us.

Innate biological factors help determine which stimuli have the greatest potential to arouse emotions. Newborn infants come equipped with the capacity to respond emotionally with either interest or distress to events in their environment (Galati & Lavelli, 1997). Adults, too, may be biologically primed to experience emotions in response to certain stimuli that have evolutionary significance. As we saw in Chapter 6, this may

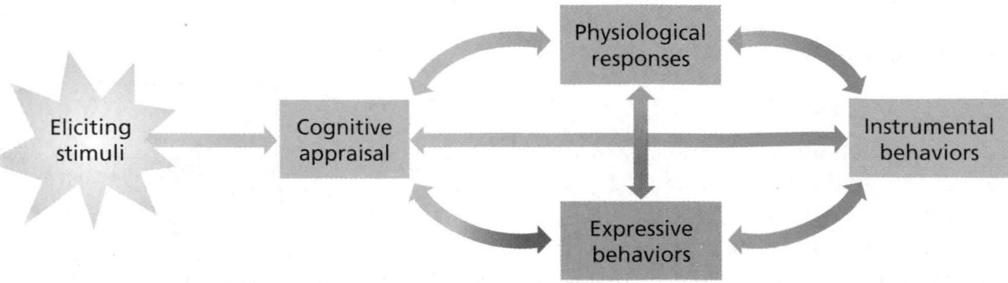

FIGURE 9.25

Components of emotion, showing relations between eliciting stimuli, cognitive appraisal processes, physiological arousal, expressive behaviors, and instrumental behaviors. Note the reciprocal (two-way) causal relations that are thought to exist among the appraisal, physiological arousal, and expressive behavior components. Appraisal influences arousal and expressive behaviors, and the latter affect ongoing appraisals.

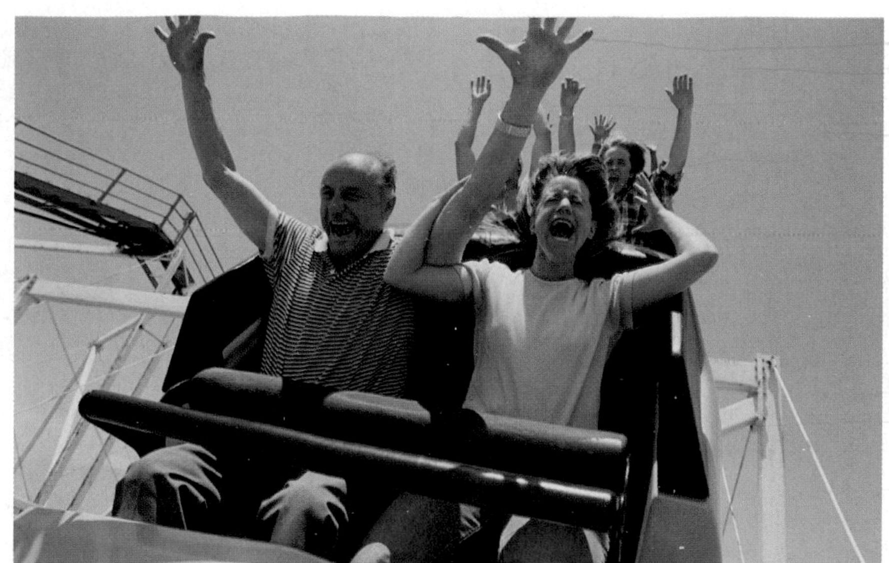

FIGURE 9.26

Differences in appraisal can trigger entirely different emotional reactions, as in this instance. What kinds of appraisals are likely occurring in these two people?

help explain why the majority of human phobias involve "primal" stimuli such as heights, water, sharks, snakes, or spiders, rather than modern threats such as guns, electrical transformers, and automobiles (Öhman, 2000).

Learning also influences our emotions. Previous experiences can turn certain people or situations into eliciting stimuli. The mere sight of one's lover can evoke feelings of passion; the sight of a disliked person can trigger instantaneous revulsion that seems almost reflexive in nature. On the broadest level, cultures have different standards for defining the good, the bad, and the ugly that affect how we appraise and respond to stimuli. Physical features that provoke sexual arousal and feelings of infatuation in one culture, such as ornamental facial scars or a bone through the nose, may elicit feelings of disgust in another.

The Cognitive Component

Cognitions (thoughts, images, memories, interpretations) are involved in virtually every aspect of emotion. Mental processes can evoke emotional responses. They are part of our inner experience of the emotion, and they influence how we express our emotions and act on them. A situation may evoke pleasure or distress, depending on how we appraise it. For example, a sexual advance may elicit anger, fear, or disgust instead of pleasure if it is unwanted or deemed inappropriate. **Cognitive appraisals** *are the interpretations and meanings that we attach to sensory stimuli.*

Often we are not consciously aware of the appraisals that underlie emotional responses. Some appraisals seem to involve little more than an almost automatic interpretation of sensory input (Cacioppo & Gardner, 1999). Indeed, our habitual ways of thinking can run off in a subconscious shorthand with little or no awareness on our part (Bargh, 1997). We often fail to appreciate how arbitrarily we interpret "the way things are."

The idea that emotional reactions are triggered by cognitive appraisals rather than external situations helps account for the fact that different people (or even the same person at different times) can have different emotional reactions to the same object, situation, or person (Figure 9.26). Statements like "I have a new attitude toward her now" or "I've decided what's really important in life" reflect changes in appraisals of certain situations or people.

Culture and Appraisal Cultural learning influences our thinking. Researchers have asked people in various countries to recall events that triggered certain emotions and to answer questions about how they appraised or interpreted the situations. In one study conducted in 27 different countries, people exhibited strong cross-cultural similarities in the types of appraisals that evoked joy, fear, anger, sadness, disgust, shame, and guilt (Wallbott & Scherer, 1988). Whenever any of these emotions occured, similar appraisals were involved, regardless of the culture.

Despite these cross-cultural commonalities in appraisal, particular situations can evoke different appraisals and emotional reactions, depending on one's culture. Consider, for example, the circumstance of "being alone." Tahitians often appraise being alone as an opportunity for bad spirits to bother a person, and fear is the most common emotional response. In the close-knit Utku Inuit, an Eskimo culture, being alone signifies social rejection and isolation, triggering sadness and loneliness. In Western cultures, being alone may at times represent a welcome respite from the frantic pace of daily life, evoking contentment and happiness (Mesquita et al., 1997). Thus, where appraisals are concerned, there seem to be certain universals but also some degree of cultural diversity in the more subtle aspects of interpreting situations.

IN REVIEW

- *An emotion is a positive or negative feeling (or affective) state consisting of a pattern of cognitive, physiological, and behavioral reactions to events that have relevance to important goals or motives. Emotions further our well-being in several ways: by rousing us to action, by helping us communicate with others, and by eliciting empathy and help.*
- *The primary components of emotion are the eliciting stimuli, cognitive appraisals, physiological arousal, and expressive and instrumental behaviors. Although innate factors can affect the eliciting properties of certain stimuli, learning can also play an important role in determining the arousal properties of stimuli.*
- *The cognitive component of emotional experience involves the evaluative and personal appraisal of the eliciting stimuli. The ability of thoughts to elicit emotional arousal has been demonstrated clinically and in experimental research. Cross-cultural research indicates considerable agreement across cultures in the appraisals that evoke basic emotions but also some degree of variation in more complex appraisals.*

The Physiological Component

When our feelings are stirred up, one of the first things we notice is bodily changes. Many parts of the body are involved in emotional arousal, but certain brain regions, the autonomic nervous system, and the endocrine system play especially significant roles.

▶ 19. According to LeDoux, which brain structures allow emotional responses to occur at two levels of mental processing?

Brain Structures and Neurotransmitters Emotions involve important interactions between several brain areas, including the limbic system and cerebral cortex (LeDoux, 2000). If animals are electrically stimulated in specific areas of the limbic system, they will growl at and attack anything that approaches. Destroying the same sites produces an absence of aggression, even if the animal is provoked or attacked. Other limbic areas show the opposite pattern: lack of emotion when they are stimulated and unrestrained emotion when they are removed.

The cerebral cortex has many connections with the hypothalamus, amygdala, and other limbic system structures. Cognitive appraisal processes surely involve the cortex, where the mechanisms for language and complex thought reside. Moreover, the ability to regulate emotion depends heavily on the executive functions of the prefrontal cortex, which lies immediately behind the forehead (LeDoux & Phelps, 2000).

Groundbreaking research by psychologist Joseph LeDoux (2000) has revealed that when the thalamus (the brain's sensory switchboard) receives input from the senses, it can send messages along two independent neural pathways, one traveling up to the cortex and the other going directly to the nearby amygdala (Figure 9.27). This enables the amygdala to receive direct input from the senses and generate emotional reactions before the cerebral cortex has had time to fully interpret what is causing the reaction. LeDoux suggests that this primitive mechanism (which is the only emotional mechanism in species like birds and reptiles) has survival value because it enables the organism to react with great speed before the cerebral cortex responds with a more carefully processed cognitive interpretation of the situation. This may be what occurs when a hiker sees what looks like a snake and jumps out of the way, only to realize an instant later that the object is actually a piece of rope.

The amygdala also seems to function as an early-warning system for threatening social stimuli. In one study, participants were asked to rate photos of people on how trustworthy they appeared to be. When the photos were presented later, brain scans using fMRI showed a burst of activity in the amygdala when people viewed those faces they had rated as untrustworthy, but participants showed no such response to faces they judged earlier as trustworthy (Winston et al., 2002). Another fMRI study showed that the amygdala also reacts to stimuli that evoke strong positive emotions (Hamann & Mao, 2002).

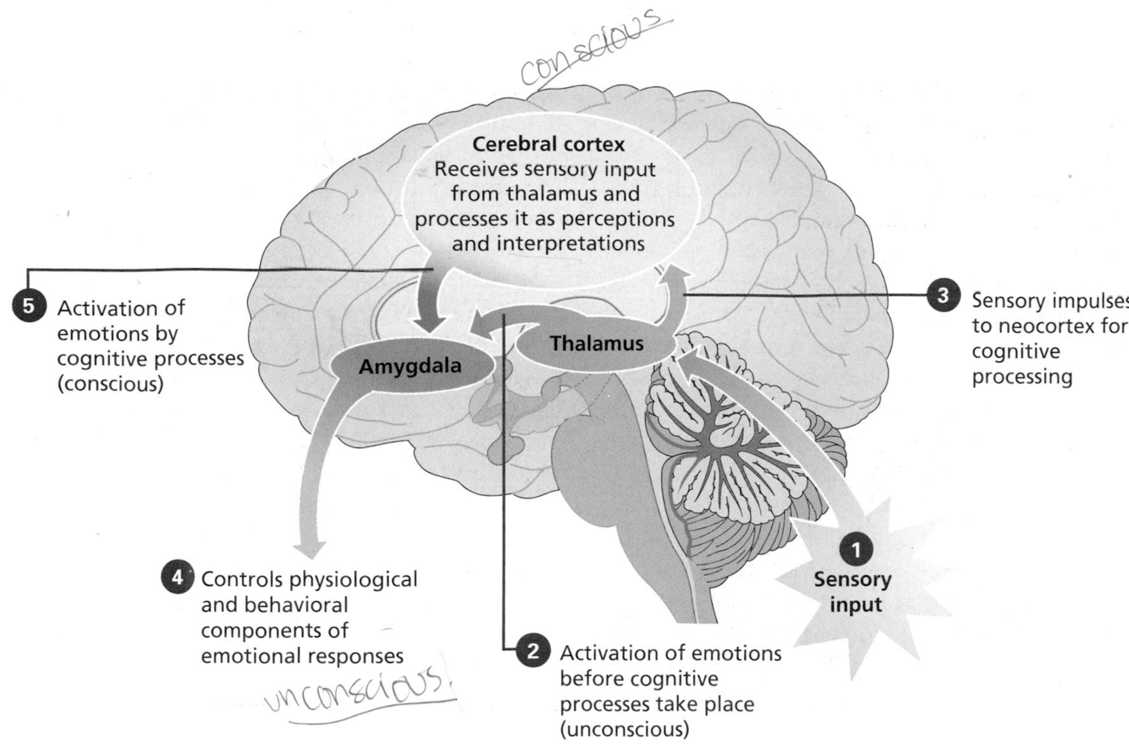

FIGURE 9.27

Parallel neural processes may produce conscious and unconscious emotional responses at about the same time. LeDoux's research suggests that sensory input to the thalamus can be routed directly to the amygdala in the limbic system, producing an "unconscious" emotional response before cognitive responses evoked by the other pathway to the cortex can occur.

The existence of a dual system for emotional processing may help explain some puzzling aspects of our emotional lives. For example, most of us have had the experience of suddenly feeling a strong emotion without understanding why. LeDoux (2000) suggests that not all emotional responses register at the level of the cortex. He also suggests that people can have two simultaneous but different emotional reactions to the same event, a conscious one occurring as a result of cortical activity and an unconscious one triggered by the amygdala. This might help explain instances in which people are puzzled by behavioral reactions that seem to be at odds with the emotion they are consciously experiencing: "I don't know why I came across as being angry. I felt very warm and friendly." Some psychodynamic theorists are hailing these discoveries as support for the existence of unconscious emotional processes (Westen, 1998). Indeed, there is now little doubt that important aspects of emotional life can occur outside of conscious awareness (Bargh & Chartrand, 1999).

Neuroscientist Candace Pert (1997) argues that because all of the neural structures involved in emotion operate biochemically, it is the ebb and flow of various neurotransmitter substances that activate the emotional programs residing in the brain. For example, dopamine activity appears to underlie some pleasurable emotions, whereas serotonin and norepinephrine play a role in anger and in fear (Depue & Collins, 1999). When the final story of the brain and emotion can at last be told, it will undoubtedly involve complex interactions between brain chemicals and neural structures.

Hemispheric Activation and Emotion Decades ago in Italy, psychiatrists tried treating clinically depressed patients with electroshock treatments to either the right or the left hemisphere. The electric current temporarily disrupted activity in the targeted hemisphere. With the left hemisphere knocked out (forcing the right hemisphere to take charge), patients had what physicians termed a "catastrophic" reaction, wailing and crying until the shock effects wore off. But when they applied shock to the right hemisphere, allowing the left hemisphere to dominate, the patients reacted much differently; they seemed unconcerned, happy, and sometimes even euphoric. Researchers noted a similar pattern of emotions in patients in whom one hemisphere had been damaged by lesions or strokes (Gainotti, 1972).

▶ 20. What evidence exists that positive and negative emotions involve different patterns of brain activation?

These findings suggest that left-hemisphere activation may underlie certain positive emotions and right-hemisphere functioning negative ones (Sutton, 2002). To test this proposition, Richard Davidson and Nathan Fox (1988) obtained EEG measures of frontal lobe activity as people experienced positive and negative emotions. They found that when people felt positive emotions by recalling pleasurable experiences or watching a happy film, the left hemisphere was relatively more active than the right. But when sadness or other negative emotions were evoked by memories or watching disgusting films, the right hemisphere became relatively more active. Moreover, this hemispheric pattern seems to be innate. Infants as young as 3 to 4 days old showed a similar pattern of hemispheric activation: left-hemisphere activation when given a sweet sucrose solution, which infants like, and right-hemisphere dominance in response to a citric acid solution, which apparently disgusts them.

Davidson and Fox also found individual differences in typical, or *resting*, hemispheric activation when they recorded people's EEG responses under emotionally neutral conditions. These resting differences predicted the tendency to experience positive or negative emotions. For example, human infants with resting right-hemisphere dominance were more likely to become upset and cry if their mothers later left the room than were those with resting left-hemisphere dominance. In adults, a higher resting level of right-hemisphere EEG activity may be a risk factor for the later development of adult depressive disorders (Tomarken & Keener, 1998).

▶ 21. Are autonomic measures of "lie detection" scientifically defensible? What factors influence their validity?

Autonomic and Hormonal Processes You are afraid. Your heart starts to beat faster. Your body draws blood from your stomach to your muscles, and digestion slows to a crawl. You breathe harder and faster to get more energy-sustaining oxygen. Your blood sugar level increases, producing more nutrients for your muscles. The pupils of your eyes dilate, admitting more light to increase your visual acuity. Your skin perspires to keep you cool and to flush out waste products created by extra exertion. Your muscles tense, ready for action.

Some theorists call this state of arousal the *fight-or-flight response*. It is produced by the sympathetic branch of the autonomic nervous system and by hormones from the endocrine system. The sympathetic nervous system produces arousal within a few seconds by directly stimulating the organs and muscles of the body. Meanwhile, the endocrine system pumps epinephrine, cortisol, and other stress hormones into the bloodstream. These hormones produce physiological effects like those triggered by the sympathetic nervous system, but their effects are longer lasting and can keep the body aroused for a considerable length of time.

Do different emotions produce different patterns of arousal? Only subtle autonomic differences occur among basic emotions as different as anger and fear (Cacioppo et al., 2000). Moreover, people differ from one another in their patterns of general arousal, so that we don't all show the same pattern of bodily arousal even when we're experiencing the same emotion. For example, when afraid, some of us might show marked changes in heart rate or blood pressure but only minor changes in muscle tension and respiration. Others would show different patterns.

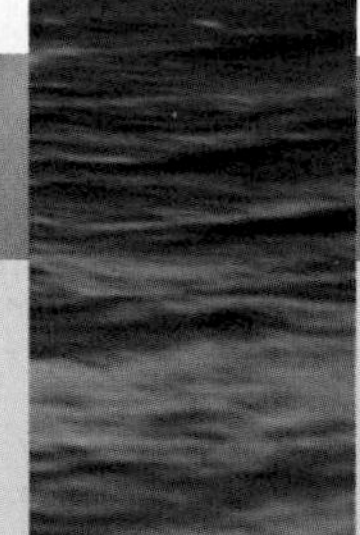

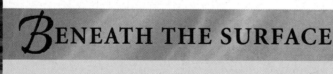

BENEATH THE SURFACE

THE LIE DETECTOR CONTROVERSY

Given what you have learned so far about the physiology of emotion, do you think emotional arousal can tell us whether someone is telling the truth or lying? A scientific instrument known as a **polygraph** (Figure 9.28) *measures physiological responses, such as respiration, heart rate, and skin conductance (which increases in the presence of emotion due to sweat gland activity)*. Because we have less control over physiological responses than over numerous other behaviors, many people regard the polygraph as a nearly infallible means of establishing whether someone is telling the truth. However, this approach to detecting "lying" by increases in emotional arousal is highly controversial (Kleiner, 2002).

Figure 9.28 shows a portion of a polygraph record. Polygraph examiners compare physiological responses to critical questions (e.g., "Were you present at the Jesse James National Bank when it was robbed the night of August 4, 2003?") with responses to control questions ("Have you ever lived in U-Turn, Montana?"). In this case, note the changes that occurred on the autonomic measures after an emotionally loaded question was asked (point A to point B in Figure 9.28).

The issue, however, is whether this emotional response means that the person was lying. Herein lies one major problem with polygraph tests. Innocent people may appear guilty when doubt,

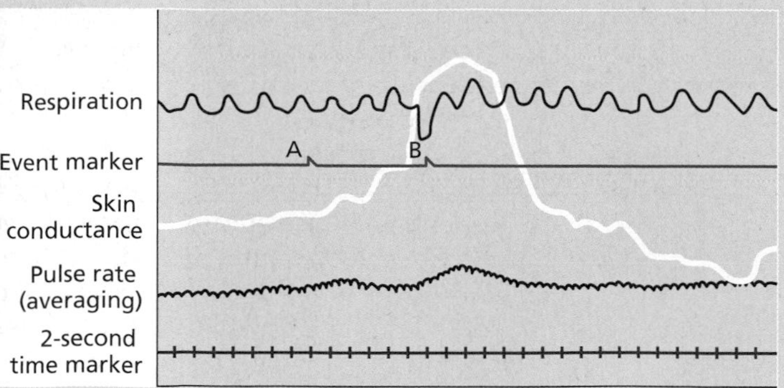

FIGURE 9.28

The polygraph records physiological changes that are part of emotional responses. Between points A and B, an emotionally loaded question was asked. Within 2 seconds, the effects of the question were visible in the subject's respiration, skin conductance, and pulse rate. Does this mean he was lying?

fear, or lack of confidence increases their autonomic activity. Even a thought like, "What if my answer makes me look guilty, even though I'm not?" in response to a critical question could send the polygraph pens into spasms that might suggest a lie. As David Lykken, a leading critic of the lie detector, has noted, "polygraph pens do no special dance when we are lying" (1981, p. 10).

Not only can innocent people appear guilty, but guilty people can also learn to beat the polygraph. For example, by biting their tongue, curling their toes, or contracting their anal sphincter when control questions are asked, people can produce an arousal response to those questions that looks similar to the arousal that occurs when they actually lie on critical questions. William Casey, former director of the U.S. Central Intelligence Agency, used to delight in his ability to fool the lie detector (Carlson & Hatfield, 1992). Fred Fay, a prison convict who had been falsely convicted of murder partly on the basis of a polygraph test, also became an expert at defeating polygraph tests (too late, unfortunately, for his acquittal). On one occasion, Fay coached 27 fellow inmates who were scheduled for polygraph tests. All of the inmates told Fay they were guilty of the relevant crimes. Yet after only 20 minutes of instruction, 23 of the 27 inmates managed to beat the polygraph (Lykken, 1981). Such results sharply contradict the notion of an infallible lie detector.

Misgivings about the validity of polygraph tests are supported by studies in which experienced polygraph examiners were given the polygraph records of suspects known to be either innocent or guilty on the basis of other evidence. The experts were asked to judge the guilt or innocence of the suspects. They usually did quite well in identifying the guilty, attaining accuracy rates of 80 to 98 percent (Honts & Perry, 1992). However, they were less accurate in identifying the innocent, judging as many as 55 percent of the truly innocent suspects to be guilty in some studies (Kleinmuntz & Szucko, 1984; Lykken, 1984). These error rates call into question the adage that an innocent person has nothing to fear from a polygraph test.

Largely because of an unacceptably high likelihood that an innocent person might be judged guilty, the American Psychological Association has supported legal challenges to polygraph testing. Congressional testimony by psychologists strongly influenced passage of the Employee Polygraph Protection Act of 1988, which prohibits most nongovernmental polygraph testing. Moreover, polygraph results alone cannot be used to convict people of crimes in most jurisdictions (Daniels, 2002). Nonetheless, the federal government continues to use polygraph tests in internal criminal investigations and in national security screening, despite the weight of research evidence against their validity for these purposes (Kleiner, 2002).

The Behavioral Component

Although we can never directly experience another person's feelings, we can often infer that someone is angry, sad, fearful, or happy on the basis of **expressive behaviors,** *the person's observable emotional displays*. Indeed, others' emotional displays can even evoke similar responses in us, a process known as *empathy*. While watching a movie, have you ever experienced the same emotion as the central character? Professional actors sometimes become so immersed in the expressive behaviors of a character they are portraying that the boundaries between self and role begin to fade, as Kirk Douglas reported when he played Vincent Van Gogh, the painter who on one occasion cut off an ear and offered it to a prostitute.

> I was close to getting lost in the character of Van Gogh. . . . I felt myself going over the line, into the skin of Van Gogh. . . . Sometimes I had to stop myself from reaching my hand up and touching my ear to find out if it was actually there. It was a frightening experience. That way lies madness. . . . I could never play him again. (Lehmann-Haupt, 1988, p. 10)

▶ 22. How do evolutionary and cultural factors influence emotionally expressive behavior?

FIGURE 9.29

Similarities among species in the expression of certain basic emotions convinced Darwin and other theorists that some expressive behaviors have an evolutionary origin.

Evolution and Emotional Expression Where do emotional expressions come from? In his classic work *The Expression of Emotions in Man and Animals* (1872/1965), Charles Darwin argued that emotional displays are products of evolution that developed because they contributed to species survival. Darwin emphasized the basic similarity of emotional expression among animals and humans. For example, both wolves and humans bare their teeth when they are angry (Figure 9.29). As Darwin explained it, this behavior makes the animal look more ferocious and thus decreases its chances of being attacked and perhaps killed in a fight. Darwin did not maintain that all forms of emotional expression are innate, but he believed that many of them are.

Like Darwin, modern evolutionary theorists stress the adaptive value of emotional expression (Izard, 1989; Plutchik, 1994). They believe that a set of **fundamental emotional patterns,** *or innate emotional reactions*, are wired into the nervous system (Ekman, 1999a). Their research shows that certain emotional expressions (e.g., rage and terror) are similar across all cultures, suggesting a universal biological basis for them. The fundamental emotional patterns proposed by three leading evolutionary theorists are shown in Table 9.3.

TABLE 9.3 Fundamental or Primary Innate Emotions Proposed by Three Leading Evolutionary Theorists

Carroll Izard	Silvan Tomkins	Robert Plutchik
Anger	Anger	Anger
Fear	Fear	Fear
Joy	Joy	Enjoyment
Disgust	Disgust	Disgust
Interest	Interest	Anticipation
Surprise	Surprise	Surprise
Contempt	Contempt	
Shame	Shame	
	Sadness	Sadness
	Distress	
Guilt		
		Acceptance

SOURCES: Based on Izard, 1982; Tomkins, 1991; and Plutchik, 1994.

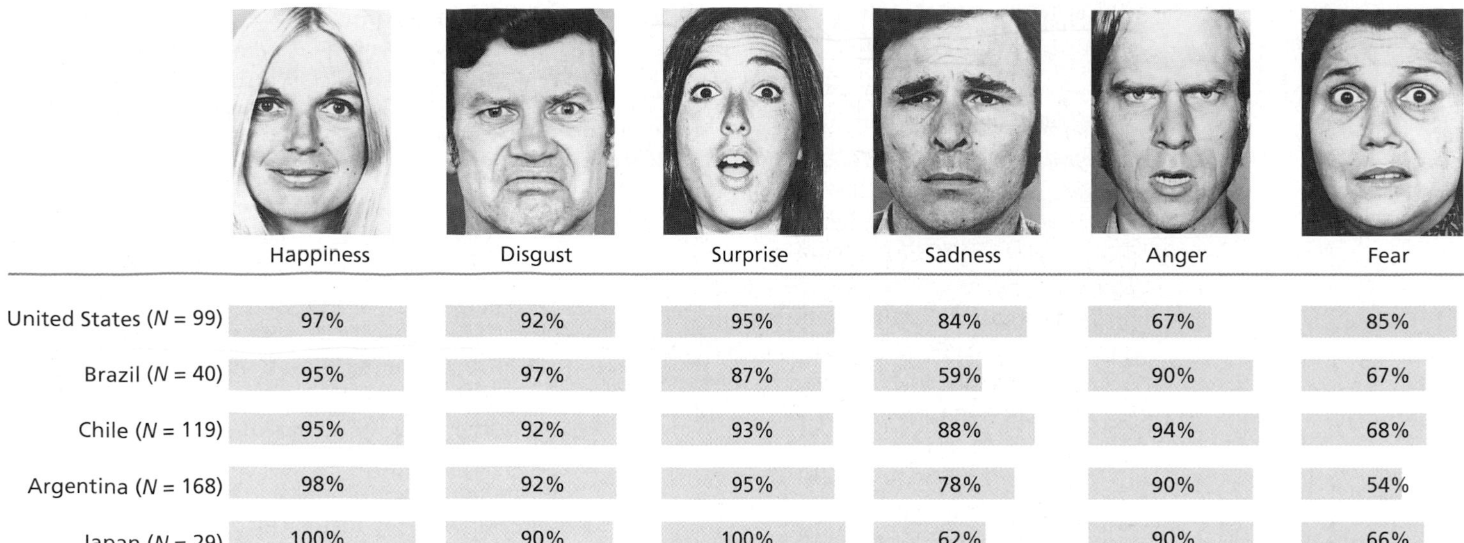

	Happiness	Disgust	Surprise	Sadness	Anger	Fear
United States (*N* = 99)	97%	92%	95%	84%	67%	85%
Brazil (*N* = 40)	95%	97%	87%	59%	90%	67%
Chile (*N* = 119)	95%	92%	93%	88%	94%	68%
Argentina (*N* = 168)	98%	92%	95%	78%	90%	54%
Japan (*N* = 29)	100%	90%	100%	62%	90%	66%

FIGURE 9.30

Percent of people in samples from five different cultures who judged each face as expressing the emotions listed below the pictures. SOURCE: Ekman, 1973.

Other emotions are based on some combination of these innate emotions. The evolutionary view does *not* assume that all emotional expressions are innate, nor does it deny that innate emotional expressions can be modified or inhibited as a result of social learning.

Facial Expression of Emotion Most of us are fairly confident in our ability to read the emotions of others. Although many parts of the body can communicate feelings, we tend to concentrate on what the face tells us. Most other species have relatively few facial muscles, so their facial expressions are limited. Only monkeys, apes, and humans have the well-developed facial muscles needed to produce a large number of expressions.

The development of sophisticated measuring procedures, such as Paul Ekman and Wallace Friesen's (1987) Facial Action Coding System (FACS), permitted the precise study of facial expressions. FACS requires a trained observer to dissect an observed expression in terms of all the muscular actions that produced it. It takes about 100 minutes to score each minute of observed facial expression.

Although facial expressions can be valuable cues for judging emotion, even people within the same culture may learn to express the same emotions differently. For example, some people can appear very calm when they are angry or fearful, whereas others express even mild forms of those same emotions in a highly expressive manner. Fortunately, we usually know something about the situation to which people are reacting, and this often helps us judge their emotions. If a woman is crying, is she weeping because of sadness or because of happiness? A background showing her being declared the winner of a lottery will result in a different emotional judgment than one showing her standing at a graveside. People's accuracy and agreement in labeling emotions from pictures are considerably higher when the pictures reveal situational cues (Keltner & Ekman, 2000).

Across many different cultures, women have proven to be more accurate judges of emotional expressions than men (Zuckerman et al., 1976). Perhaps the ability to read emotions accurately has greater adaptive significance for women, whose traditional role within many cultures has been to care for others and attend to their needs (Buss, 1991). This ability may also result from cultural encouragement for women to be sensitive to others' emotions and to express their feelings openly (Taylor et al., 2000). However, it is worth nothing that men who work in professions that emphasize these skills (such as psychotherapy, drama, and art) are as accurate as women are in judging others' emotional expressions (Rosenthal et al., 1974).

What of Darwin's claim that certain facial expressions universally indicate specific emotions? Do people in different cultures agree on the emotions being expressed in facial photographs? Figure 9.30 shows the results of one study. You can see that there is generally high agreement on these photos of basic emotions, but also some cultural variations. Other researchers have found levels of agreement ranging from 40 to 70 percent across a variety of

For more on the language of facial expressions, see Video Segment 9.2.

cultures, well above chance but still far from perfect (Russell, 1994).

Cultural Display Rules **Cultural display rules** *dictate when and how particular emotions are to be expressed* (Yrizarry et al., 2001). Certain gestures, body postures, and physical movements can convey vastly different meanings in different cultures. For example, using the American upright thumb gesture while hitchhiking in certain regions of Greece could result in decidedly negative consequences, such as tire tracks on one's body. In those regions, an upright thumb is the equivalent of a raised middle finger in the United States (Morris et al., 1979). In most cultures, spitting on someone is a sign of contempt. Yet in the traditions of the Masai tribe of East Africa, being spat on is considered a great compliment, particularly if the person doing the spitting is a member of the opposite sex (Wierzbicka, 1986). One can only imagine what a Masai singles bar might be like.

An experiment by Paul Ekman, Wallace Friesen, and Phoebe Ellsworth (1972) nicely illustrates cultural commonalities and differences in emotional expression. Japanese and American students viewed a gory, stressful film in private. Unbeknownst to them, their facial expressions were being videotaped by a hidden camera.

FACS codings of the facial displays that occurred while watching the film showed no differences between the Japanese and American students; they expressed their negative emotions of disgust and anxiety in the same way and with similar intensity. Afterward, the students were individually interviewed by a person of their ethnic group concerning their reactions to the film. Their facial expressions were also coded during the interview. Now, however, major ethnic differences appeared. The Japanese masked their earlier feelings of anxiety and disgust and presented a happy face throughout the interview. In contrast, the Americans' negative facial expressions closely mirrored those photographed while they watched the stressful movie. Based on such findings, many emotion theorists conclude that innate biological factors and cultural display rules *combine* to shape emotional expression across different cultures.

▶ 23. How do level of arousal and task complexity interact to affect task performance?

Instrumental Behaviors Emotional responses are often "calls to action," requiring a response to the situation that aroused the emotion. A highly anxious student must find some way to cope with an impending test. A mother angered by her child's behavior must find a nondestructive way to get her point across. A person in love searches for ways to evoke affection from his or her partner. These are **instrumental behaviors,** *directed at achieving some emotion-relevant goal.*

People often assume that high emotional arousal enhances task performance, as when athletes try to "psych themselves up" for competition. Yet as students who have experienced extreme anxiety during exams could testify, high emotional arousal can also interfere with performance. In many situations, the relation between emotional arousal and performance seems to take the shape of an upside-down, or inverted, *U.* As physiological arousal increases up to some optimal level, performance improves. But beyond that optimal level, further increases in arousal impair performance. It is thus possible to be either too "flat" or too "high" to perform well.

The relation between arousal and performance depends not only on arousal level but also on how complicated the task is and how much precision it requires (Yerkes & Dodson, 1908). Generally speaking, the more complex the task, the lower the optimal arousal level. Thus even a moderate level of arousal can disrupt performance on a highly complex mental or motor task.

Figure 9.31 illustrates this principle and also shows that performance drops off less at high levels of arousal for the simple task than for the others. In fact, even extreme arousal can enhance performance of very simple motor tasks, such as running or lifting something. This may account for seemingly "superhuman" feats we hear about occasionally. When a 110-pound New Hampshire woman was asked how she had managed to lift up a 4,000-pound van that had rolled on top of her trapped husband, she answered, "I don't know how I did it. It didn't feel that heavy. I think it was the adrenaline." (*Newsweek,* March 11, 2002, p. 19)

In contrast, high emotionality can interfere with performance on complex mental and physical tasks. People may underachieve on intelligence tests if they are too anxious, and muscle tension can interfere with the skillful execution of complex physical movements (Landers & Arent, 2001). For example, the sport of golf requires precise and complex movements, so the optimal level of arousal is relatively low. Champion golfers such as Tiger Woods often exhibit peak performance in high-pressure competition because they can control their level of arousal and keep it within the optimal range, while their opponents choke under the pressure.

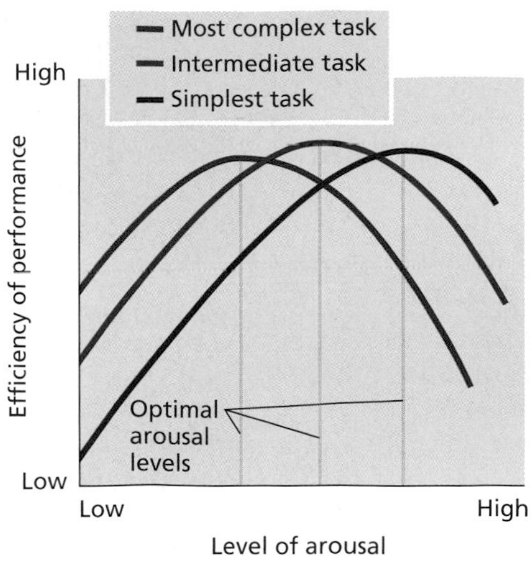

FIGURE 9.31

The relation between arousal and performance takes the form of an inverted U, with performance declining above and below an optimal arousal level. However, the more complex a task is, the lower is the optimal level of arousal for performing it. For which of the tasks on the right should the optimal arousal level be lower?

IN REVIEW

- *Our physiological responses in emotion are produced by the hypothalamus, the limbic system, the cortex, and by the autonomic and endocrine systems. There appear to be two systems for emotional behavior, one involving conscious processing by the cortex, the other unconscious processing by the amygdala.*
- *Negative emotions seem to reflect greater relative activation of the right hemisphere, whereas positive emotions are related to relatively greater activation in the left hemisphere.*
- *The validity of the polygraph as a "lie detector" has been questioned largely because of the difficulty of establishing the meaning of physiological responses.*
- *The behavioral component of emotion includes expressive and instrumental behaviors. Different parts of the face are important in the expression of various emotions. The accuracy of people's interpretation of these expressions is enhanced when situational cues are also available. Evolutionary theorists propose that certain fundamental emotional patterns are innate but agree that cultural learning can influence emotional expression.*
- *There is an optimal level of arousal for the performance of any task. This optimal level varies with the complexity of the task; complex tasks have lower optimal levels.*

Theories of Emotion

Where do emotional experiences come from? For more than 100 years, scientists have explored this question. Several classic theories have guided their efforts.

▶ 24. Evaluate scientific evidence that supports the James-Lange and Cannon-Bard theories.

The James-Lange Somatic Theory

In 1890, the eminent psychologist William James ignited a controversy when he wrote:

> Common sense says . . . we meet a bear, are frightened, and run; we are insulted by a rival, are angry, and strike. The hypothesis here to be defended says that this order of sequence is incorrect . . . and that the more rational statement is that we feel sorry *because* we cry, angry *because* we strike, afraid *because* we tremble. (James, 1890/1950, p. 451 [italics added])

At about the same time, Danish psychologist Carl Lange reached a similar conclusion. According to the **James-Lange theory,** *our bodily reactions determine the subjective emotion we experience.* We

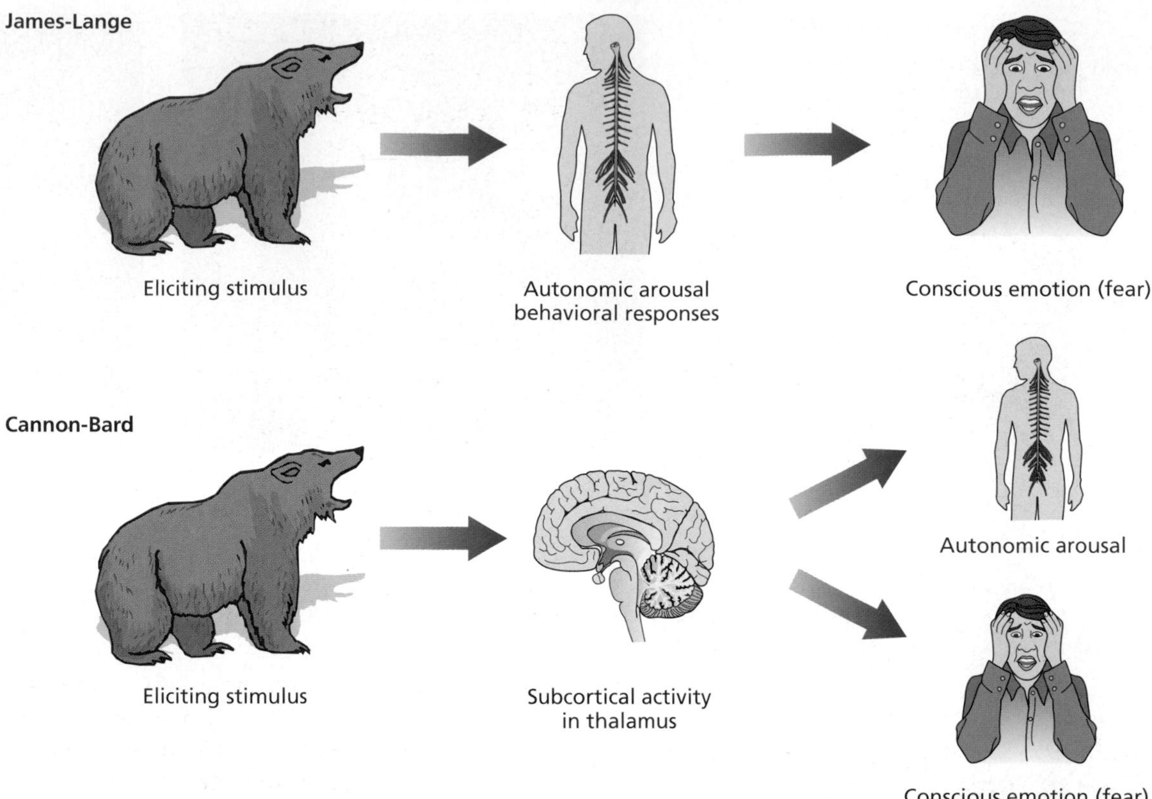

FIGURE 9.32

Two early theories of emotion continue to influence current-day theorizing. The James-Lange theory holds that the experience of emotion is caused by somatic feedback and physiological arousal. According to the Cannon-Bard theory, the thalamus receives sensory input and simultaneously stimulates physiological responses and cognitive awareness.

know we are afraid or in love because our body's reactions tell us so. Today, this theory lives on as the *somatic theory of emotion* (Papanicolaou, 1989).

The Cannon-Bard Theory

It wasn't long before the James-Lange theory was challenged. In 1927, physiologist Walter Cannon fired back. He pointed out that people's bodies do *not* respond instantaneously to an emotional stimulus; several seconds may pass before signs of physiological arousal appear. Yet people typically experience the emotion immediately. This would be impossible according to the James-Lange theory. Cannon and his colleague L. L. Bard concluded that cognition must be involved as well.

The **Cannon-Bard theory** *proposed that the subjective experience of emotion and physiological arousal do not cause one another but instead are independent responses to an emotion-arousing situation.* When we encounter such a situation, sensory information is sent to the brain's thalamus, which simultaneously sends messages to the cerebral cortex and to the body's internal organs. The message to the cortex produces the experience of emotion, and the message to the internal organs produces physiological arousal. Figure 9.32 compares the James-Lange and Cannon-Bard theories.

The Role of Autonomic Feedback

The James-Lange and Cannon-Bard theories raised intriguing questions about how the various aspects of an emotional experience interact with one another. The theories differ on one crucial point. According to the James-Lange theory, feedback from the body's reactions to a situation tells the brain that we are experiencing an emotion. Without such bodily feedback, there would be no emotional response. In contrast, the Cannon-Bard theory maintains that emotional experiences result from signals sent directly from the thalamus to the cortex, not from bodily feedback. Is there any way to test whether bodily feedback is necessary?

In fact, there is. What if organisms were deprived of sensory feedback from their internal organs? Would they be devoid of emotional reactions? To answer this question, Cannon (1929) carried out experiments with animals in which he severed the nerves that provide feedback from the internal organs to the brain. He found that even after such surgery, the animals exhibited emotional responses, lending support to his theory that direct sensory messages to the brain are the emotional triggers. In like manner, people whose spinal cords have been severed in accidents and

(a) 

(b) 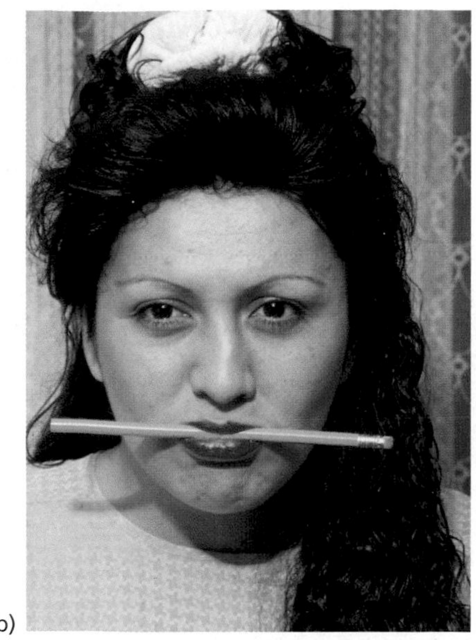

(c) 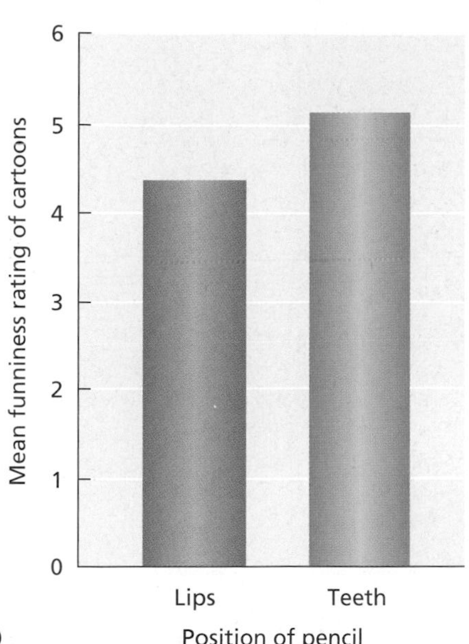

FIGURE 9.33

Holding a pencil in one's teeth (a), which activates the muscles used in smiling, evokes more pleasant feelings than holding the pencil in one's lips (b), which activates muscles associated with negative emotions. This finding (c) provides support for the facial feedback hypothesis. SOURCE: Based on Strack et al., 1988.

who receive no sensory feedback from body areas below the injury continue to feel intense emotions—sometimes more intense than those they experienced before their injury. Moreover, people with upper and lower spinal cord injuries, who differ in the amount of bodily feedback they receive, do not differ in the intensity of their emotions (Chwalisz et al., 1988).

These results appear to cast doubt on the claim that arousal feedback from the body is absolutely necessary for people to experience intense emotions. But let's take this issue one step further.

The Role of Expressive Behaviors

Arousal feedback is not the only kind of bodily feedback considered important by the James-Lange somatic theory. Facial muscles involved in emotional displays also feed messages to the brain, and these muscles are active even in patients with spinal injuries who receive no sensory input from below the neck. According to the **facial feedback hypothesis,** *feedback from the facial muscles to the brain plays a key role in determining the nature and intensity of emotions that we experience,* as the James-Lange theory would suggest (Adelmann & Zajonc, 1989).

According to the theory, sensory input is first routed to the subcortical areas of the brain that control facial movements. These centers immediately send signals that activate the facial muscles. Sensory feedback from movement of facial muscles is then routed to the cerebral cortex, which produces our conscious experience of the emotion. To return to James's example of the bear, the facial feedback hypothesis says that we are frightened when the bear approaches partly because an automatic expression of terror appears on our face and sends signals from our facial muscles to the cortex, where the subjective feelings of fear are produced.

In support of the facial feedback hypothesis, research shows that feedback from facial muscle patterns can arouse specific emotional reactions (Soussignan, 2002). In one study, Fritz Strack and coworkers (1988) found that when participants held pens in their teeth, activating muscles used in smiling (Figure 9.33a), they rated themselves as feeling more pleasant than when they held the pens with their lips, activating the muscles involved in frowning (Figure 9.33b). Participants also rated cartoons as funnier while holding pens in their teeth and activating the "happy muscles" than while holding pens with their lips (Figure 9.33c). In another study, researchers compared the subjective experiences of people who pronounced different sounds, such as *eee* and *ooh.* Saying the *eee* sound, which activates muscles used in smiling, was associated with more pleasant feelings than saying the *ooh* sound, which activates muscles involved in negative facial expressions (Zajonc et al., 1989). Perhaps portrait photographers should ask us to say *cheese* not only when they take our picture but also later, when they show us photo proofs that not even our mothers could love.

Cognitive-Affective Theories

▸ 25. According to the theories of Lazarus and Schachter, how do appraisal and arousal interact to influence emotions?

Nowhere are mind-body interactions more obvious than in the emotions, where thinking and feeling are intimately connected. *Cognitive-affective theories* examine how cognitions and physiological

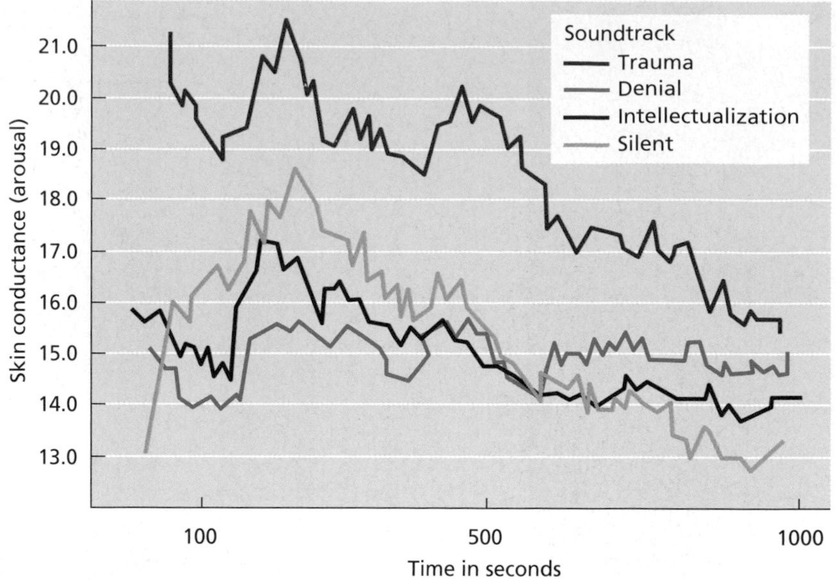

FIGURE 9.34

Appraisal influences arousal. Participants who viewed a film showing a painful tribal rite in vivid detail exhibited different levels of physiological arousal, depending on the sound track that accompanied the film. SOURCE: Speisman et al., 1964.

responses interact. Historically, Richard Lazarus and Stanley Schachter have been major figures in this approach.

Lazarus (2001) argued that all emotional responses require some sort of appraisal, whether we are aware of that appraisal or not. Schachter was intrigued with the factors that determine our emotional perceptions. According to Schachter's **two-factor theory of emotion**, *the intensity of physiological arousal tells us how strongly we are feeling something, but situational cues give us the information we need in order to label the arousal and tell ourselves what we are feeling*—fear, anger, love, or some other emotion (Schachter, 1966).

If appraisal and arousal affect one another in the ways these theories suggest, then by manipulating appraisals we should be able to influence physiological arousal. Moreover, if we can manipulate arousal, we should be able to influence cognitive appraisals of the situation. Let's examine some research that tests these propositions.

Manipulating Appraisal to Influence Arousal In one classic study, Lazarus and coworkers showed college students an anthropology film that contained vivid footage of a puberty rite in which the penises of aboriginal boys are cut with a jagged flint knife. The researchers tried to influence the participants' appraisals by experimentally varying the film's sound track (Speisman et al., 1964).

Four different sound tracks were used: A "trauma" sound track emphasized the pain suffered by the boys, the danger of infection, the jaggedness of the flint knife, and other unpleasant aspects of the operation. A "denial" sound track did just the opposite; it denied that the operation was excessively painful or traumatic and emphasized that the boys looked forward to entering adulthood by undergoing the rite and demonstrating their bravery. An "intellectualization" sound track, also designed to produce a less negative appraisal, ignored the emotional elements of the scenes and focused on the traditions and history of the tribe. In a "silent" control condition, the film was shown without any sound track at all.

Physiological arousal was measured through electrodes attached to the participants' palms, recording skin conductance due to sweat gland activity. As shown in Figure 9.34, the sound tracks produced markedly different levels of arousal in response to the same visual stimuli. The trauma sound track resulted in the highest arousal, and the silent condition turned out to be more arousing than either the denial or intellectualization condition, presumably because it left people free to make their own negative appraisals. It seems the denial and intellectualization sound tracks made the subjects' appraisals more benign, resulting in lower levels of arousal. This study, as well as many others, indicate that what we tell ourselves about external situations influences the level of arousal that we experience.

Manipulating Arousal to Influence Appraisal Is the reverse also true? Can arousal affect our appraisal of situations by giving us feedback about how our bodies are responding or by making us search for situational reasons for the arousal? To study this possibility, we'd have to influence arousal directly in some way, such as with drugs that either increase or decrease arousal. But it would have to be done in a way that left people unaware that their arousal was being caused by the drug. They'd have to believe that their arousal was being caused solely by the external situation they were appraising.

In a key experiment, Schachter and Ladd Wheeler (1962) directly manipulated participants' arousal by injecting them with either epinephrine to increase arousal, a tranquilizer drug to decrease arousal, or a placebo control substance. To hide the fact that participants were being given drugs that would affect their arousal, the researchers told them that they were being injected with a vitamin to study its effects on visual perception and that the vitamin would have no side effects. While presumably waiting for the vitamin to take effect, the participants were shown a short movie "to provide continuous black-and-white stimulation to the eyes." The movie was a comedy featuring a slapstick chase scene.

Schachter and Wheeler hypothesized that if the level of emotional arousal influences appraisals, then the viewers aroused by epinephrine should find the film funnier than the placebo control subjects. Having been told that the vitamin had no side effects, these viewers were likely to attribute their increased arousal to the slapstick comedy in the film. The researchers also reasoned that those given the tranquilizer should not find the film as funny because the drug would reduce their level of arousal.

While they watched the movie, participants were observed through a one-way mirror by raters who were unaware of which viewers had received which injections. The raters recorded how frequently the participants smiled, grinned, laughed, threw up their hands, slapped their legs, or doubled over with laughter. As Figure 9.35 shows, the results supported the hypothesis that level of arousal would influence viewers' appraisal of the film. The aroused viewers in the epinephrine group found the film funnier than the tranquilized viewers did, and the placebo control group was in the middle. It appears that as long as one's arousal is attributed to the external situation, arousal cues can affect appraisal.

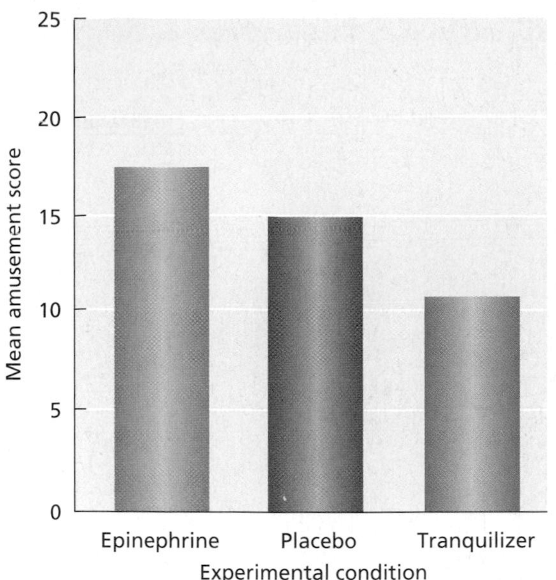

FIGURE 9.35

Arousal influences appraisal. Participants were injected with either epinephrine, a tranquilizer, or a placebo to affect arousal and then were shown a humorous film. The amount of amusement they displayed varied with their state of arousal. SOURCE: Based on Schachter & Wheeler, 1962.

Positive Psychology and the Pursuit of Happiness

For many years, researchers focused primarily on negative emotions such as anxiety, depression, and anger. More recently, however, attention has turned to the positive emotions. The **positive psychology movement** *addresses questions relating to happiness, well-being, and human potential* (Aspinwell & Staudinger, 2003). What is the good life? What makes people feel happy and fulfilled? How can we nurture what is best within ourselves to create a life of virtue and strength? What constitutes optimal living? (Seligman, 2002).

Among psychological researchers, there currently is growing interest in the topic of happiness, or its more technical term *subjective well-being.* **Subjective well-being (SWB)** *includes people's emotional responses and their degree of satisfaction with various aspects of their life* (Diener & Seligman, 2002). SWB is typically assessed by self-report ratings of contentment, happiness, and satisfaction. Before reading on, please see Table 9.4, p. 368.

How happy are people in general? Ed and Carol Diener (1996) reviewed findings from nearly 1,000 representative samples in 43 Westernized and developing nations. Across all countries, the mean rating of personal happiness on the 0-to-10 scale was 6.33, indicating mild happiness. Only in two economically poor nations, India and the Dominican Republic, did average SWB fall into the unhappy range of the scale. In the United States, all ethnic groups scored well above the neutral point on the happiness scale (Andrews, 1991). Nonetheless, as Table 9.5 shows, countries differed in their levels of subjective well-being.

On the second scale in Table 9.4, college students on average reported being happy 65 percent of the time, neutral 15 percent, and unhappy 20 percent of the time (Larsen & Diener, 1985). Thus it appears that across many populations, people report living lives that are more happy than unhappy.

Who's happier, men or women? Research shows that the sexes are about equal in global happiness, but there is an important qualifier: Women on average experience *both* positive and negative emotions more intensely than men do (Wood et al., 1989). The more extreme emotional responses of women balance out, resulting in an average level of happiness similar to that produced by men's less extreme highs and lows.

What Makes People Happy?

▶ 26. What factors predict and fail to predict happiness?

To answer this question, some researchers have examined the *resources* that might contribute to happiness, such as attractiveness, intelligence,

TABLE 9.4 How Happy Are You?

Here are two measures of subjective well-being. Answer the following questions, then see the text to compare yourself with others.

First, how would you rate your own general life satisfaction on the following scale?

0	1	2	3	4	5	6	7	8	9	10
Most unhappy										*Most happy*

Next, answer the following questions:

What percentage of the time are you happy? ________

What percentage of the time are you neutral? ________

What percentage of the time are you unhappy? ________

(Make sure your percentages add up to 100.)

wealth, and health. Others have studied internal *psychological processes* that underlie our experiences of happiness.

Is health required for happiness? Not necessarily. On average, individuals with severe and disabling medical conditions such as paralyses do report lower levels of life satisfaction than nondisabled people, yet about two thirds of the disabled rate their lives as somewhat or very satisfying (Mehnert et al., 1990).

If you had more money, you'd be happier, correct? Well, perhaps not. Although people in affluent countries are happier on average than people who live in abject poverty, such countries differ in many ways besides wealth (e.g., in terms of social and political turmoil) that could also affect SWB. When wealth and SWB are correlated within the same country, whether the country is poor or affluent, wealth is only weakly related to happiness (Diener et al., 1999). Even extreme changes in wealth, such as a big inheritance or winning a lottery, have only a temporary positive impact on SWB (Brickman et al., 1978). Thus where health and wealth are concerned, not having enough of the resource may create unhappiness because important basic needs can't be met, but once an adequate level is attained, further increases seem to do little to promote lasting happiness.

How about being wise? Overall, intelligence bears little relation to happiness (Seligman, 2002). Educational level does have a weak positive relation to SWB, probably because it helps people avoid poverty and compete for satisfying jobs. Unemployment is one of the strongest predictors of life dissatisfaction, and an adequate educational level can help people avoid this fate (Clark, 1998).

If being healthy, wealthy, and wise won't guarantee happiness, perhaps intimate relation-

TABLE 9.5 Subjective Well-Being Scores of Various Countries

Country	Happiness Ranking
Iceland	1
Sweden	2
Australia	3
Canada	4
United States	5
Norway	6
Britain	7
Ireland	8
Singapore	9
Philippines	10
Cuba	11
Israel	12
Mexico	13
France	14
Puerto Rico	15
Thailand	16
Jordan	17
Greece	18
Kenya	19
India	20
Dominican Republic	21

NOTE: Most nations (India and the Dominican Republic being exceptions) score in the positive range of the 10-point SWB scale.
SOURCE: Based on Diener et al., 1995.

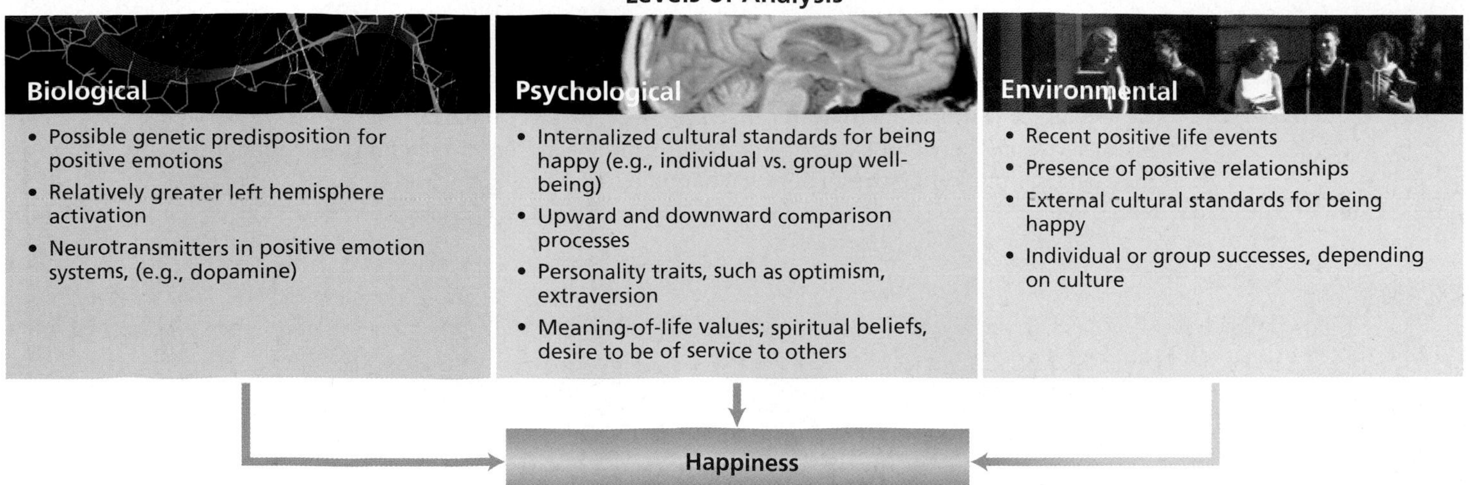

Levels of Analysis
Biological
Psychological
Environmental
• Possible genetic predisposition for positive emotions
• Relatively greater left hemisphere activation
• Neurotransmitters in positive emotion systems, (e.g., dopamine)
• Internalized cultural standards for being happy (e.g., individual vs. group well-being)
• Upward and downward comparison processes
• Personality traits, such as optimism, extraversion
• Meaning-of-life values; spiritual beliefs, desire to be of service to others
• Recent positive life events
• Presence of positive relationships
• External cultural standards for being happy
• Individual or group successes, depending on culture
Happiness

FIGURE 9.36

Understanding Behavior: Causal factors in happiness.

ships will. Here, researchers consistently find that happy people have more satisfying social relationships (Diener & Seligman, 2002). Additionally, married men and women are significantly happier on average than are single and divorced people. Still, the meaning of these correlational results is not clear. Do social relationships promote greater life satisfaction, or are happier, better-adjusted people more able to establish and sustain good social relationships and stable marriages? Or is there some third variable, such as a personality factor like being more extraverted (i.e., more outgoing), that promotes both happiness and the ability to develop satisfying social relations?

Having a sense of meaning in life also is correlated with happiness. Many people report that their spiritual or religious beliefs contribute to a sense of meaning, and some—though not all—studies find a positive correlation between religiosity and happiness (Diener et al., 1999; Diener & Seligman, 2002). Giving of oneself, such as helping others as a volunteer, contributes to a sense of meaning and life satisfaction (Snyder et al., 2000). But again, causality is difficult to infer. Does a greater sense of meaning promote happiness? Does happiness lead people to feel that their life is more meaningful? Or does some third factor cause both?

Overall, personal resources and external circumstances account for only about 15 to 20 percent of the variability among people in happiness ratings (Argyle, 1999). Perhaps psychological processes, rather than resources, are the keys to happiness. For example, research reveals that feelings of life satisfaction are based on how we compare ourselves and our circumstances with other people and their circumstances and with past conditions we have experienced (Bruunk & Gibbons, 1997). When we engage in **downward comparison,** *seeing ourselves as better off than the standard for comparison,* we experience increased satisfaction. In contrast, **upward comparison,** *when we view ourselves as worse off than the standard of comparison,* produces dissatisfaction. In one study, researchers asked college students to keep a written record of every time they compared their appearance, grades, abilities, possessions, or personality with someone else's over a 2-week period. At the same time, they recorded their current mood. Downward comparisons with less-fortunate or less-talented people were consistently associated with positive moods, and upward comparisons were associated with negative emotional reactions (Wheeler & Miyake, 1992). Thus depending on what or whom you compare yourself with, you can be an eagle among starlings or a moth among butterflies.

Personality factors clearly predispose some people to be happier than others. Individuals who are sociable, optimistic, altruistic, curious, and open to new experiences report higher levels of happiness and are rated by others as happier than are those who have the opposite traits (Larsen & Buss, 2002).

Biological factors may predispose some people to be happier than others. A study of 2,310 identical and fraternal twins revealed that the identical twins were far more similar in SWB, regardless of their life circumstances (Lykken & Tellegen, 1996). Perhaps genetic factors contribute in some way to the individual differences in right- and left-hemisphere activation discussed earlier, or maybe they influence neurotransmitter systems that underlie positive and negative emotions (Hamer & Copeland, 1998).

One's culture may also influence the factors that contribute to happiness. Eunkook Suh and coworkers (1998) found that in the individualistic "me" societies of North America and Europe, satisfaction in individual successes that people can attribute to their own skill and effort contributes to happiness. In contrast, in collectivistic cultures of Southeast Asia, the well-being of the group seems to be a more important factor in personal happiness than one's own emotional life, and people derive more pleasure from accomplishments achieved as part of a group effort (Kitayama et al., 2000).

Happiness thus turns out to be a rather complex phenomenon having biological, psychological, and environmental determinants. Figure 9.36 provides a levels-of-analysis summary of these factors.

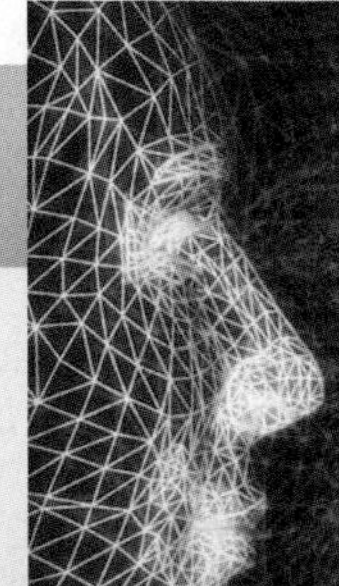

APPLYING PSYCHOLOGICAL SCIENCE

BEING HAPPY: GUIDELINES FROM PSYCHOLOGICAL RESEARCH

As research has accumulated on factors that relate to happiness, psychologists have been able to offer advice based on data rather than intuition (Seligman, 2002). Most psychologists believe that happiness, like a good marriage, is something that one must work at (Seligman & Peterson, 2004). Here, then, are some suggestions that may help you maintain and enhance personal happiness.

- *Spend time with other people and work to develop close relationships.* Research consistently suggests that good relationships provide the strongest basis for life satisfaction. Even if you tend to be introverted, form at least a few close relationships and nurture them. Make time for social interactions.
- *Look for ways to be helpful to others and reach out to the less fortunate.* Try to make a positive difference in the lives of others. Doing so will increase your sense of self-worth, add meaning to your life, and deepen relationships with those whose lives you touch. It will also help put your own problems in perspective and direct your energies away from self-absorption. There's a lot to be said for the proposition that we receive by giving.
- *Seek meaning and challenge in work.* Enjoying one's work is a prime ingredient of happiness. If you feel stuck doing something that provides little gratification, be it your job or your major, consider looking for something more satisfying. Everyone has to make a living, but many people spend their lives doing things they don't derive satisfaction or meaning from—hardly a recipe for a happy life. Even if you love your work, strive for balance between work and personal pursuits. People on their death beds rarely, if ever, express the wish that they had spent more time at the office.
- *Set meaningful personal goals for yourself and make progress toward them.* Whether in work, school, or relationships, engaging in goal-directed activity and seeing yourself moving toward your goals will provide a basis for life satisfaction and foster feelings of being in greater control of your life. Many people find that spiritual development (religiously based or not) confers meaning in their life.
- *Make time for enjoyable activities.* One of the benefits of time management skills is the ability to schedule everyday activities that provide pleasure around school, work, and other obligations. Make time for a hobby, reading, and recreational activities.
- *Nurture physical well-being.* Many studies show that even moderate physical exercise contributes to emotional well-being (Morgan, 1997). Such activities provide a temporary respite from life stressors. When done in a social context, they add the benefits of social interaction as well. People who exercise, get sufficient sleep, and practice good dietary habits tend to be more stress resistant and satisfied with themselves and their lives (Taylor, 2003).
- *Be open to new experiences.* Some of our most pleasurable experiences can occur when we try new things. It's easy to fall into a same-old, same-old rut, so whether it's traveling, developing a new hobby, or taking a college course on a new subject, be open to doing something you haven't done before.
- *Cultivate optimism and count your blessings.* As we've seen, cognitive appraisals influence emotions, and an upbeat, optimistic approach to life is linked with subjective well-being. Try to look on the positive side of things, to see demanding events as challenges and opportunities rather than threats. Learn to appreciate and be grateful for even the mundane, average day in which nothing bad happens to you. There is a Buddhist saying: Happiness is a day without a toothache. All of us are gifted in ways that we may take for granted. Perhaps we should focus more often on these typically ignored aspects of good fortune.

IN REVIEW

- *There are several theories of emotion. The James-Lange theory maintains that we first become aroused and then judge what we are feeling. The Cannon-Bard theory proposes that arousal and cognition are independent and simultaneously triggered by the thalamus. Lazarus's cognitive appraisal theory states that appraisals trigger emotional arousal, while according to Schachter's two-factor theory of emotion, arousal tells us how strongly we are feeling while cognitions derived from situational cues help us label the specific emotion.*
- *As the James-Lange theory maintained, expressive behaviors may trigger other aspects of emotions. The facial feedback hypothesis states that feedback from facial muscle patterns associated with innate emotional displays influences cognitive and physiological processes.*
- *There is a two-way relation between the cognitive and physiological components. It is possible to manipulate appraisals and thereby influence level of arousal, but arousal changes can also influence appraisal of the eliciting stimuli.*
- *In most countries, the average person is mildly happy. Psychological processes, such as downward comparison and a sense of personal meaning, are more consistently related to subjective well-being than are resources such as wealth, physical attractiveness, and high intelligence. Cultural differences may exist in the bases for happiness.*

A Concluding Thought

As you have seen in this chapter, motivation and emotion lie at the crossroads of cognition, physiology, and behavior. The diversity of human motives, factors that influence their development and strength, and methods for satisfying them help account for important differences both within and across cultures.

Emotion plays a central role in many aspects of normal and abnormal behavior. Emotion also illustrates the many fascinating interfaces between evolutionary processes and social learning. It's little wonder, then, that the study of emotion is a major thrust in contemporary psychological research. We still have much to learn about the basic mechanisms that underlie our emotional experiences and about what we can do to self-regulate them in order to amplify the pleasurable emotions and dampen those that create distress.

KEY TERMS AND CONCEPTS

Each term has been boldfaced and defined in the chapter on the page indicated in parentheses.

anorexia nervosa (p. 336)
approach-approach conflict (p. 352)
approach-avoidance conflict (p. 352)
attachment (p. 348)
avoidance-avoidance conflict (p. 352)
bulimia nervosa (p. 336)
Cannon-Bard theory (p. 364)
cholecystokinin (CCK; p. 330)
cognitive appraisal (p. 355)
cultural display rules (p. 362)
downward comparison (p. 369)
drive (p. 327)
eliciting stimuli (p. 354)
emotion (p. 353)
expectancy × value theory (p. 328)
expressive behaviors (p. 359)
extrinsic motivation (p. 328)
facial feedback hypothesis (p. 365)
fundamental emotional patterns (p. 360)
glucose (p. 330)
goal-setting program (p. 351)
homeostasis (p. 327)
incentive program (p. 351)
incentive (p. 328)
instinct (p. 327)
instrumental behaviors (p. 362)
intrinsic motivation (p. 328)
James-Lange theory (p. 363)
job enrichment (p. 351)
leptin (p. 330)
mastery goals (p. 350)
metabolism (p. 329)
motivation (p. 327)
need for achievement (p. 349)
paraventricular nucleus (PVN; p. 331)
performance-approach goals (p. 350)
performance-avoidance goals (p. 350)
polygraph (p. 358)
positive psychology movement (p. 367)
self-actualization (p. 328)
set point (p. 329)
sexual dysfunction (p. 340)
sexual orientation (p. 342)
sexual response cycle (p. 338)
sexual strategies theory (p. 346)
social comparison (p. 344)
social structure theory (p. 347)
subjective well-being (SWB; p. 367)
two-factor theory of emotion (p. 366)
upward comparison (p. 369)

What Do You Think?

IS MASLOW'S NEED HIERARCHY VALID? p. 329

More than most psychological theories of motivation, Maslow's model appropriately emphasizes that diverse motives influence human behavior. The concepts of need progression and need regression seem to make intuitive sense. Motives do become stronger and weaker as circumstances change, and it seems logical that when people are starving, finding food becomes more important than contemplating beauty and truth.

Critics, however, have long questioned the validity of the need hierarchy and have argued that the concept of "self-actualization" is vague and hard to measure (Heylighen, 1992). The ordering of needs seems arbitrary, and the concepts of need progression and regression cannot account for important aspects of motivated behavior. How does the hierarchy explain why prisoners of war endure torture rather than betray their comrades? Why millions of women choose to live in constant hunger to be thin? Why political protestors go on hunger strikes or risk their physical safety to defend principles they believe in? Does a need for knowledge and understanding really become prominent only after needs for social belonging and self-esteem are met? Throughout evolution, was seeking esteem and recognition more important and adaptive to our ancestors than acquiring knowledge to help them survive?

Finally, rather than viewing the journey toward self-actualization as a relatively independent striving to maximize one's potential, some modern humanists view the entire process as more relationship-oriented (Hanley and Abell, 2002). In their view, healthy social relationships not only satisfy deficiency needs for belonging and esteem but also are important for achieving and expressing self-actualization.

Despite these drawbacks, by calling attention to the human desire for growth and incorporating diverse motives, the intuitive appeal of Maslow's model has influenced thinking in fields such as philosophy, education, and business (Zinovieva, 2001). ■

FRATERNAL BIRTH ORDER AND MALE HOMOSEXUALITY p. 344

Blanchard (2001) estimates that the presence of each older brother increases by about one third the *relative probability* that a later-born male child will be gay. For example, if there is a 2-percent probability that a man with no older brothers is gay, then the probability for a man with one older brother is about 2.6 to 2.7 percent, roughly a one-third relative increase. As Blanchard (2001) notes, "the probability that a couple's son will be gay rises from 2 to 6 percent for their fifth son. That is a threefold increase. However, 94 percent of fifth sons will still be heterosexual" (p. 108).

So why does this effect occur? Perhaps you thought of one of these explanations: First, it may be that the greater the number of older brothers, the greater the possibility (however small) of having an incestuous sexual encounter with an older male while growing up. However, as Blanchard (2001) notes, evidence does not suggest that such incestuous experiences are linked to adulthood sexual orientation. Second, perhaps if an older brother has a homosexual orientation, awareness of this might influence a younger brother's sexual orientation. A study of gay men with gay brothers, however, found that most were aware of their own homosexual feelings before they became aware of their brother's homosexual orientation (Dawood et al., 2000).

Blanchard (2001) and his coworkers propose a biological explanation, called the *maternal immune hypothesis*. During pregnancy, male (but not female) fetuses contain substances that, as a group, are called *H-Y antigen*. H-Y antigen helps guide the fetal brain toward a male-typical pattern. Sometimes, H-Y antigen passes from the fetus to the mother's bloodstream, in which case it is a foreign substance to the mother. Thus, the mother's immune system responds by producing antibodies (proteins) to combat the H-Y antigen.

In turn, these antibodies pass from the mother to the fetus and reach the fetal brain. "When that happens, these antibodies partly prevent the fetal brain from developing in the male-typical pattern, so that the individual will later be attracted to men rather than women. The probability—or strength—of maternal immunization increases with each male fetus" (Blanchard, 2001, p. 110). Thus a mother with sons is more likely to carry and pass on these antibodies to any new male fetus, altering H-Y antigen's role in guiding fetal brain development toward a male-typical pattern. Blanchard estimates that for about one quarter of gay men, the development of their sexual orientation proceeded along this path. Of course, like other current theories, the maternal immune hypothesis needs much more testing. ■

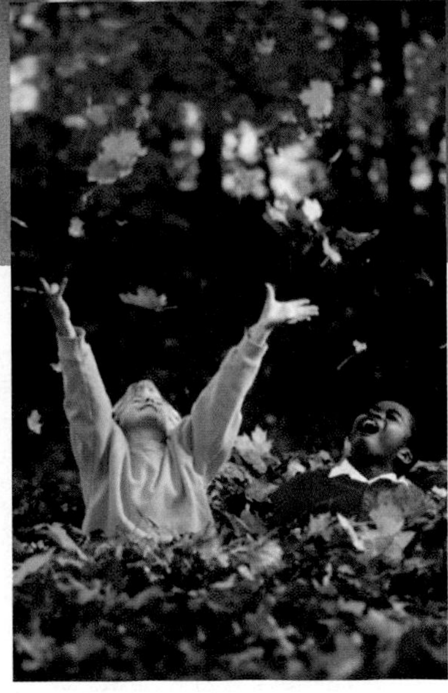

10

DEVELOPMENT OVER THE LIFE SPAN

CHAPTER OUTLINE

There are only two lasting bequests we can hope to give our children. One of these is roots; the other, wings.

—Hodding Carter

"Interesting lecture," said Ramona, as she left her anthropology class. "I never realized that families could be structured in so many different ways. Imagine growing up in a household with not just your parents but also your grandparents, great-grandparents, and other relatives. What was that cultural group called?" "I don't remember their name," said Katja, "but they were herders living in Mongolia."

"You know," said Enrique, "It got me thinking about my own family. Mom and Dad divorced when I was 4, so I grew up with a single mom. She worked two jobs, so Grandma really raised me. She was great . . . very warm and loving, and mentally sharp as a tack. I was 14 when Mom remarried. It took me a while to warm up to him, but my stepdad is really good to me and my mom."

"My parents worked full time," added Ramona, "so I was in day care until I started school. It was cool. I got to play with other kids all the time." "My dad," said Katja, "is a consultant, so he travels a lot and works crazy hours. But my mom stayed at home when I was little, so I always had a parent around—and a mischievous older brother!"

"I wonder," said Enrique, "if we become parents some day, what our families will be like?" "Don't know," said Ramona, "but we all had people who cared for us, and no matter what, I want that for my kids. Imagine growing up alone, like Victor." "Who's Victor?" asked Enrique. "You remember," answered Ramona, "we learned about him in psych class . . . the Wild Boy."

■■■

In 1799, three hunters discovered a remarkable child living in the forests of Aveyron, France. Most likely abandoned at a young age, he grew up isolated from human contact, foraging for food and surviving naked in the wild. About 12 years old, he easily climbed trees, ate nuts and roots, scratched and bit people who interfered with him, and made few sounds. He could walk upright yet ran quickly on all fours. Some regarded him as half-human, half-beast, and they called him the "Wild Boy of Aveyron" (Itard, 1894/1962).

Several medical experts concluded that the boy was incurably "mentally deficient," but others disagreed, noting that it took intelligence to survive in the wild. They argued that special education and care would enable the child to flower into a normal, civilized adult. In Paris, the boy was placed under the care of a prominent young physician, Jean-Marc Itard, who named him Victor and diligently supervised his training (Figure 10.1).

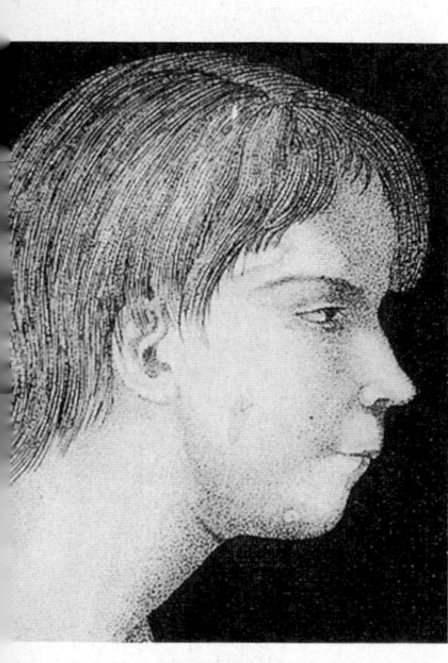

FIGURE 10.1

Victor, the "Wild Boy of Aveyron."

At first, Victor was unresponsive to stimuli that most people find aversive. Unfazed, he would stick his hand into boiling kitchen water to grab food or eagerly roll around half-naked on the cold winter ground. Eventually he learned to sense temperature differences, dress himself, and perform other self-care behaviors. Victor's emotional responses, which at first fluctuated without reason, began to fit the situation: He laughed in playful situations, shed tears over someone's death, and displayed some signs of affection toward Itard. Victor learned to read and write some words, communicate basic needs, and perform simple tasks.

Although Victor changed in important ways, as he grew older his progress slowed considerably. He never learned to speak, and after 5 years of education his cognitive, emotional, and social development remained limited. Pessimism over further progress grew, and Itard's "project" ended. Victor was moved to a nearby home, where a woman cared for him for the rest of his life.

In the early 1800s, people expected Victor's case to resolve an intense debate about the role of "nature versus nurture" in shaping who we are. But it raised more questions than it answered. Was Victor a normal, inherently noble infant who became irreparably harmed by his childhood isolation, or was he born "mentally deficient"?

Modern research tells us that some children exposed to extreme adversity are highly resilient and thrive later in life (Ryff & Singer, 2003). We cannot pinpoint why Victor failed to recover, but his famous case begs a fundamental question: Just how does the miracle of human development unfold, and what conditions are required for normal growth? To this search for the basics of normal development, modern society adds a chorus of issues—day care, divorce, stepfamilies, and so on—that reflect the increasingly complex world into which you, Ramona, Katja, and Enrique were born.

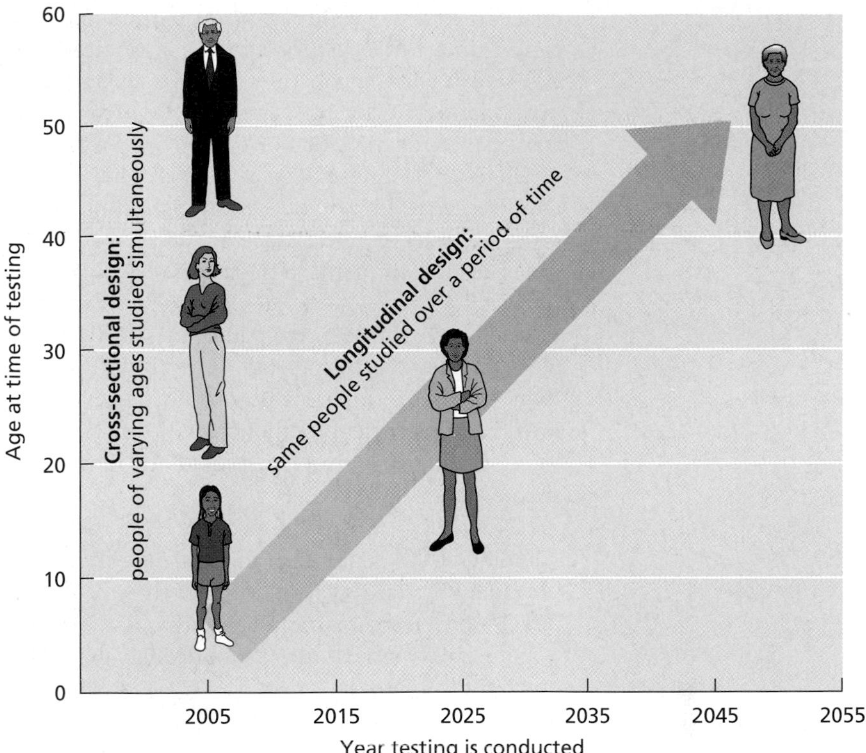

FIGURE 10.2

Using a cross-sectional design we would test different age groups in the year 2005 and compare their performance. Using a longitudinal design, we would test individuals of one age group and then retest them every 10 years until age 60. Using a sequential design, we would test 10- through 60-year-olds in the year 2005 and then retest them every 10 years until the youngest cohort reached age 60. Suppose that in 2005, 60-year-olds perform worse than younger adults and that as the 10- through 50-year-olds age, their performance declines by age 60. We are now more confident that this decline, replicated over different age cohorts, represents a true effect of aging.

MAJOR ISSUES AND METHODS

Developmental psychology examines biological, physical, psychological, and behavioral changes that occur as we age. Four broad issues guide much developmental research.

- *Nature and nurture.* To what extent is our development the product of heredity (nature) and the product of environment (nurture)? How do nature and nurture interact?
- *Critical and sensitive periods.* Are some experiences especially important at particular ages? A **critical period** *is an age range during which certain experiences must occur for development to proceed normally or along a certain path.* A **sensitive period** *is an optimal age range for certain experiences, but if those experiences occur at another time, normal development will still be possible.*
- *Continuity versus discontinuity.* Is development continuous and gradual, as when a sapling slowly grows into a tree? Or is it discontinuous, progressing through qualitatively distinct *stages*, as when a creeping caterpillar emerges from its cocoon as a soaring butterfly?
- *Stability versus change.* Do our characteristics remain consistent as we age?

Psychologists often use special research designs to investigate developmental questions (Figure 10.2). Suppose we wish to study how intellectual abilities change from age 10 to age 60. Using a **cross-sectional design** *we would compare people of different ages at the same point in time.* Thus in the next month we could administer intellectual tasks to 10-, 20-, 30-, 40-, 50-, and 60-year-olds. We would test each person only once and compare how well the different age groups performed. The cross-sectional design is widely used because data from many age groups can be collected relatively quickly, but a key drawback is that the different age groups, called *cohorts,* grew up in different historical periods. Thus if 60-year-olds have poorer intellectual abilities than 20-year-olds, we need to ask whether this is due to aging or possibly to broad environmental differences (e.g., poorer nutrition or medical care) between growing up in the 1940s versus the 1980s.

▶ 1. Describe four major issues and three special research designs often encountered in developmental research.

To avoid this problem, a **longitudinal design** *repeatedly tests the same cohort as it grows older.* We could test a sample of 10-year-olds this month and then retest them every 10 years, up to age 60, thus

▶ 2. Describe the stages of prenatal development, how sex is determined, and the effects of various teratogens.

ensuring that everyone is exposed to the same historical time frame. Unfortunately, a longitudinal design can be time-consuming, and as years pass, our sample may shrink as people move, drop out of the study, or die. Further, suppose we find that intelligence declines at age 60. Is this really due to aging or to developmental experiences unique to our particular cohort? Researchers can answer this question by using a **sequential design** *that combines the cross-sectional and longitudinal approaches*. For example, we could test 10- through 60-year-olds now, retest them every 10 years, and then examine whether the various cohorts followed a similar developmental pattern. This design is the most comprehensive but also the most time-consuming and costly.

Now let's turn to the process of human development. We begin with the *prenatal period*, approximately 266 days during which each of us developed from a single-cell organism barely larger than a pinhead into a wondrously complex newborn human.

IN REVIEW

- *Developmental psychology studies the process of aging. Questions about the influence of nature and nuture, the existence of critical and sensitive periods, continuity versus discontinuity, and stability versus change have played a major role in guiding much developmental research.*
- *Cross-sectional designs compare people of different age groups at a single point in time. A longitudinal design repeatedly tests the same age group as it grows older. A sequential design tests several groups at one point in time and then again when they are older.*

PRENATAL DEVELOPMENT

Prenatal development consists of three stages (Figure 10.3). The *germinal stage* comprises approximately the first 2 weeks of development, beginning when a sperm fertilizes a female egg *(ovum). This fertilized egg is called a* **zygote,** and through repeated cell division it becomes a mass of cells that attaches to the mother's uterus about 10 to 14 days after conception.

The *embryonic stage* is next. The cell mass, now called an **embryo,** *develops from the end of week 2 through week 8 after conception.* Two life-support structures, the placenta and umbilical cord, develop at the start of this stage. Located on the uterine wall, the *placenta* contains membranes that allow nutrients to pass from the mother's blood to the umbilical cord. In turn, the *umbilical cord* contains blood vessels that carry these nutrients and oxygen to the embryo and transport waste products back from the embryo to the mother. Supplied with nutrients, embryonic cells rapidly divide and become specialized. Bodily organs and systems begin to form, and by week 8 the heart of the inch-long embryo is beating, the brain is forming, and facial features such as eyes can be recognized.

Finally, during the *fetal stage*, the **fetus** *develops from week 9 after conception until birth.* Muscles become stronger, and other bodily systems continue to develop. At about 24 weeks the eyes open, and by 27 weeks (or several weeks younger, with top medical care) the fetus attains the *age of viability,* meaning it is likely to survive outside the womb in case of premature birth (Subramanian et al., 2002).

Genetics and Sex Determination

Throughout history, many women have been blamed for failing to give birth to a male heir. Ironically, any father who foolishly feels a need to "lay

FIGURE 10.3

These remarkable photos show (a) the moment of conception, as one of many sperm cells fertilizes the ovum, (b) the embryo at 6 to 7 weeks, and (c) the fetus at 3 months of age.

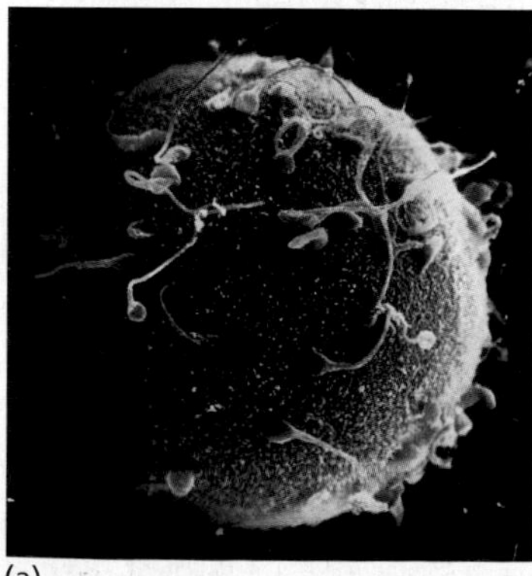
(a)

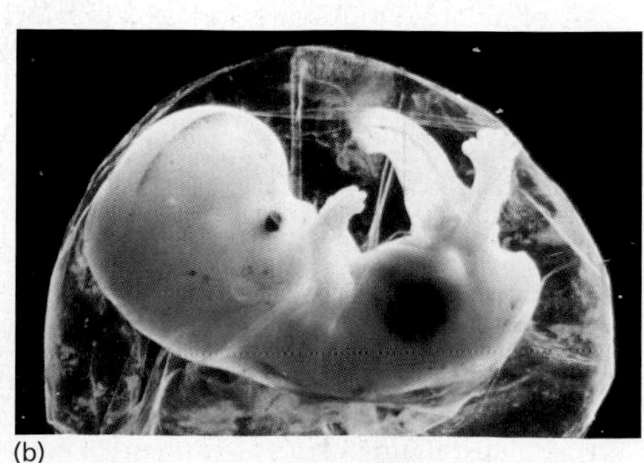
(b)

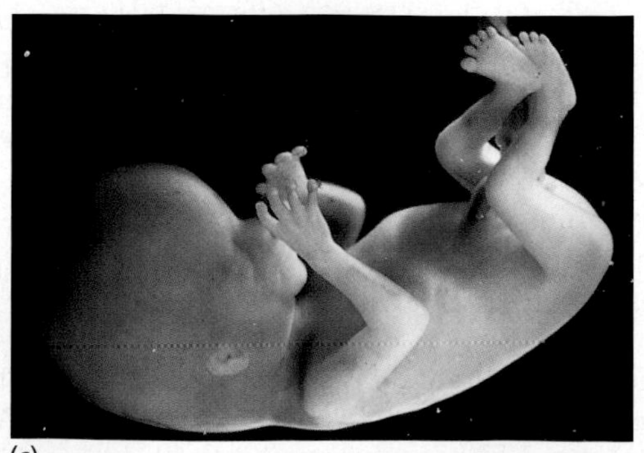
(c)

blame" should look in the mirror, for it is his genetic contribution that determines the sex of a baby. A female's egg cells and a male's sperm cells each have 23 chromosomes. At conception, an egg and sperm unite to form the zygote, which now contains the full set of 23 *pairs* found in other human cells. The 23rd pair of chromosomes determines the baby's sex. A genetic female's 23rd pair contains two X chromosomes (XX), so called because of their shape (Figure 10.4). Because women carry only X chromosomes, the 23rd chromosome in the egg is always an X. A genetic male's 23rd pair contains an X and a Y chromosome (XY). Thus, the 23rd chromosome in the sperm is an X in about half of the cases and a Y in the other half. The Y chromosome contains a specific gene, the *TDF gene*, that triggers male sexual development. The union of an egg with a sperm cell having a Y chromosome results in an XY combination and therefore a boy. A sperm containing an X chromosome produces an XX combination and therefore a baby girl.

How does the Y chromosome determine male sex characteristics? At roughly 6 to 8 weeks after conception, the TDF gene initiates the development of testes. In fact, the term *TDF* stands for "testis-determining factor." Once formed, the testes secrete sex hormones called *androgens* that continue to direct a male pattern of organ development. If the TDF gene is not present, as happens with an XX combination in the 23rd pair, testes do not form and—in the absence of sufficient androgen activity during this prenatal critical period—an inherent female pattern of organ development ensues.

Environmental Influences

Our genetic blueprint sets forth a path of prenatal development, but nature and nurture become intertwined even before we are born. **Teratogens** *are external agents that cause abnormal prenatal development.* The placenta prevents many dangerous substances from reaching the embryo and fetus, but some harmful chemicals and diseases can pass through. Stress hormones can cross the placenta, and prolonged maternal stress is associated with increased risk of premature birth (Austin & Leader, 2000). If the mother contracts *rubella* (German measles)—especially when the embryo's eyes, ears, heart, and central nervous system are beginning to form early in pregnancy—it can cause blindness, deafness, heart defects, and mental retardation, in the infant (Murdoch, 1984).

Sexually transmitted diseases can pass from mother to fetus and produce brain damage, blindness, and deafness depending on the disease. Among pregnant women with untreated syphilis, about 25 percent of fetuses are born dead. Similarly, without medical treatment during pregnancy, about 25 percent of fetuses born to mothers with the human immunodeficiency virus (HIV) that causes AIDS also are infected (Meleski & Damato, 2003).

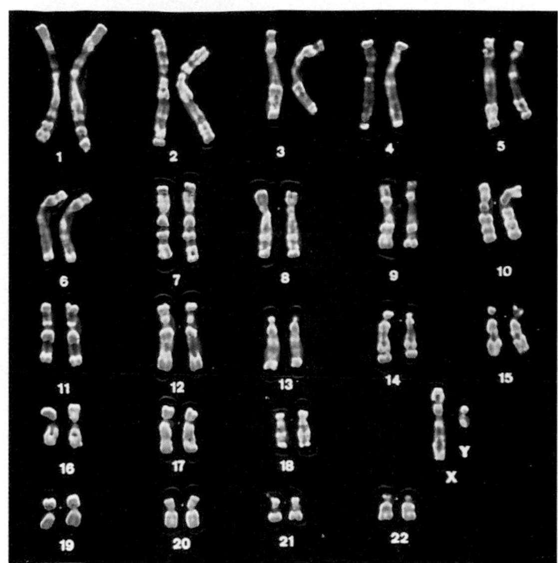

FIGURE 10.4

Most human cells contain 23 pairs of chromosomes. Each pair consists of one chromosome from each parent. The 23rd pair determines a person's sex. In males, the 23rd pair, which is shown in the lower right area of the photo, consists of an X chromosome and a Y chromosome. In females, the 23rd pair contains two X chromosomes.

Mercury, lead, radiation, and many other environmental toxins can produce birth defects, as can many drugs. **Fetal alcohol syndrome (FAS)** *is a severe group of abnormalities that results from prenatal exposure to alcohol* (Streissguth, 1977, 2001). FAS children have facial abnormalities and small, malformed brains (Figure 10.5). Psychological symptoms include mental retardation, attentional and perceptual deficits, irritability, and impulsivity. Other children exposed to alcohol in the womb may display only some or milder forms of these deficits.

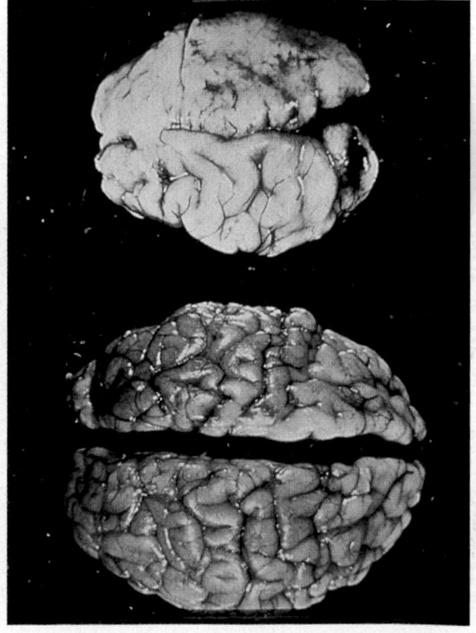

FIGURE 10.5

Children who suffer from fetal alcohol syndrome (FAS) not only look different but also have brains that are underdeveloped and smaller than those of normal children.

FAS is a major cause of mental retardation in Western countries, and the threshold level of alcohol exposure needed to produce FAS has not been determined. About one third to one half of infants born to alcoholic mothers have FAS, but even "social drinking" or an episode of binge drinking can increase the risk of prenatal damage and long-term cognitive impairment (Larroque & Kaminski, 1998). Because no amount of prenatal alcohol exposure has been confirmed to be absolutely safe, pregnant women and those trying to become pregnant are best advised to completely avoid drinking alcohol.

Nicotine is also a teratogen; maternal smoking increases the risk of miscarriage, premature birth, and low birth weight (Ernst et al., 2001). Due to secondhand smoke, regular tobacco use by fathers also has been linked to low infant birth weight and increased risk of respiratory infections (Wakefield et al., 1998). Babies of pregnant mothers who regularly use heroin or cocaine are often born addicted and experience withdrawal symptoms after birth. Their cognitive functioning and ability to regulate their arousal and attention may also be impaired (Mayes et al., 1998).

IN REVIEW

- *Prenatal development involves the germinal, embryonic, and fetal stages.*
- *The 23rd chromosome in a mother's egg cell is always an X chromosome. If the 23rd chromosome in the father's sperm cell is an X, the child will be genetically female (XX); if it is a Y, the child will be genetically male (XY).*
- *Maternal stress, illness, drug use, and environmental toxins can cause abnormal prenatal development.*

INFANCY AND CHILDHOOD

Studying infancy poses unique challenges. During research, infants may start to fuss, cry, soil their diapers, or simply fall asleep! Because infants cannot describe their experiences, psychologists must find clever ways to take advantage of responses that infants can make, such as sucking and moving their eyes, to draw inferences about their capabilities and preferences.

The Amazing Newborn

After emerging from the comfort of the mother's womb, does a newborn's world become a "buzzing, blooming confusion," as pioneering psychologist William James (1890/1950) proposed? Contrary to a long-held view of newborns as helpless and passive, research reveals that newborns are surprisingly sophisticated information processors.

▶ 3. Describe the newborn's sensory capabilities, perceptual preferences, reflexes, and ability to learn.

Sensory Capabilities and Perceptual Preferences

Newborns' visual systems are immature. Their eye movements are not well coordinated and they are very nearsighted (Dobson & Teller, 1978). Still, infants scan their environment, and although objects look blurry to them, they can perceive some forms only a few days after birth. Newborns can reasonably see objects about 1 foot away, the typical distance between their eyes and their mothers' eyes while nursing. As Figure 10.6 shows, visual acuity improves with age.

Infants also display visual preferences, which Robert Fantz (1961) studied using the *preferential looking procedure*. He placed infants on their backs, showed them two or more stimuli at the same time, and filmed their eyes to record how long

FIGURE 10.6

Seeing through an infant's eyes. These three images approximate the visual acuity of an infant at (a) 1 month, (b) 3 months, and (c) 12 months of age.

(a)
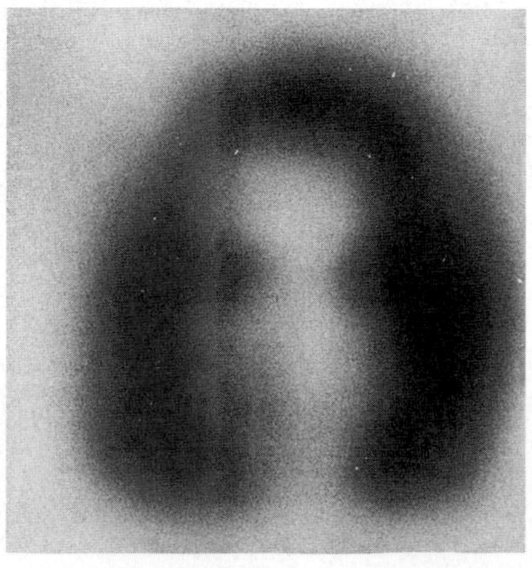
(b)
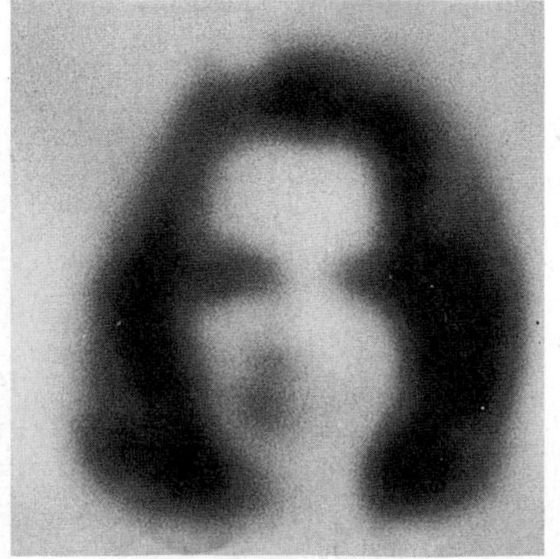
(c)

they looked at each stimulus. Infants preferred complex patterns—such as realistic or scrambled drawings of a human face—to simpler patterns and solid colors (Figure 10.7). Within just hours after birth, newborns are able to distinguish the familiar face of their mother from that of a female stranger, and they prefer to gaze at the mother's face (Bushnell, 2001).

Just as you would make different facial expressions after tasting sweet, sour, or bitter substances, newborns' facial responses tell us that they have a reasonably well developed sense of taste. Newborns also respond to touch, sense changes in temperature and body position, and distinguish different odors. If exposed to pads taken from inside the bras of several nursing mothers, week-old infants will orient toward the scent of their own mother's pad (Porter & Winberg, 1999). Newborns can hear fairly well. They prefer human voices to other sounds and high-pitched tones (more typical of a mother's voice) to low-pitched sounds, and they can distinguish their mother's voice from that of a female stranger (DeRegnier et al., 2002). As Figure 10.8 describes, newborns seem to prefer sounds that become familiar to them during their last weeks of fetal development, during which time they can hear sounds transmitted through the womb (DeCasper & Spence, 1986). Thus, in a rudimentary sense, simple forms of learning can occur inside the womb.

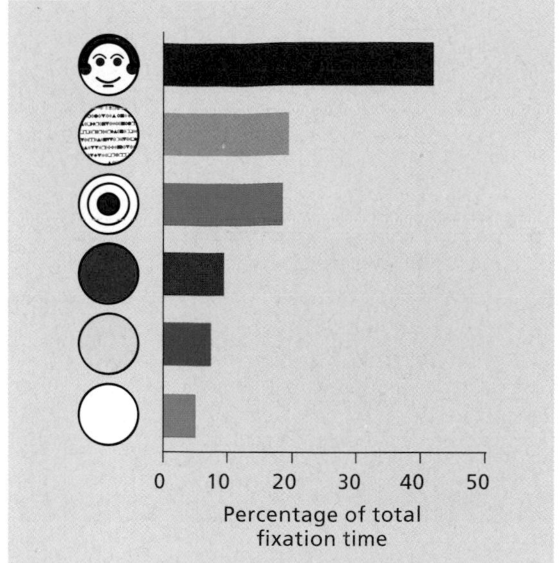

FIGURE 10.7

Whether 2 days old or, as shown here, 2 to 3 months old, infants preferred to look at complex patterns more than simple patterns or solid colors. SOURCE: Based on Fantz, 1961.

Reflexes and Learning

Neonates are equipped with many **reflexes,** *automatic, inborn behaviors that occur in response to specific stimuli.* Some, including breathing, have obvious adaptive significance. Stroke a baby's cheek, and it will turn its head toward the direction it was touched and open its mouth—the *rooting reflex.* When something is placed in the infant's mouth, it will suck on it—the *sucking reflex.* Together, these reflexes increase the infant's

FIGURE 10.8

Can the fetus learn? (left) Twice a day during their last 6 weeks of pregnancy, mothers read out loud the same passage from Dr. Seuss's The Cat in the Hat. *(right) Two or 3 days after birth, newborns were able to turn on a recording of their mother reading either the* Cat in the Hat *rhyme or an unfamiliar rhyme by sucking on a sensor-equipped nipple at different rates. Compared with infants in a control condition, these newborns more often altered their sucking rate in whichever direction (faster or slower) selected the familiar rhyme.* SOURCE: DeCasper & Spence, 1986.

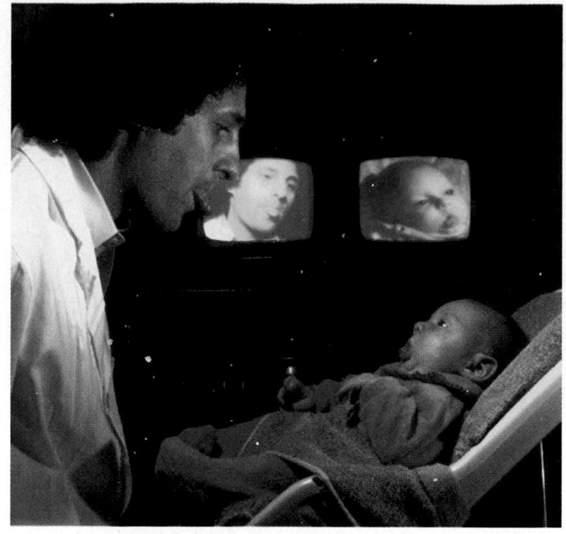

FIGURE 10.9

Young infants have been found to reproduce tongue protrusion after watching an adult model. Here researcher Andrew Meltzoff models the behavior and records an infant's response.

▶ 4. Explain how nature and nurture jointly influence infants' physical growth and motor development.

ability to feed. In general, healthy reflexes indicate normal neurological maturity at birth.

Newborns learn in several ways. They habituate to routine, repetitive, nonthreatening stimuli and can acquire classically conditioned responses. For example, after a tone (CS) is repeatedly paired with a gentle puff of air to the eye (UCS), infants as young as 10 days will develop a conditioned eyeblink response to the tone alone (Lipsitt, 1990). Through operant conditioning, newborns learn that they can "make things happen." Thus a 3-day-old in fant can learn to suck a plastic nipple with a certain pattern of bursts to activate a tape recorder playing his or her mother's voice (Moon & Fifer, 1990).

What about observational learning? As Figure 10.9 shows, research suggests that within weeks or possibly days after birth, some newborns can reproduce a simple facial expression made by an adult model (Meltzoff & Moore, 1977). This, says psychologist Andrew Meltzoff (2002), provides evidence of a biologically based capacity for imitation. Meltzoff also finds that by 9 months of age, infants who watch a model act in a novel way (e.g., pushing a button in a box to trigger a sound) can reproduce that action from memory a day later. In sum, a consistent pattern emerges. Infants appear to be born prewired with an array of mechanisms that help them respond to caretakers and learn other important information.

Physical Development

Thanks to **maturation,** *the genetically programmed biological process that governs our growth,* our bodies and movement (motor) skills develop rapidly during infancy and childhood. On average, by our 1st birthday body weight triples and height increases by 50 percent. As Figure 10.10 shows, infants vary in the age at which they acquire particular skills, but the sequence in which skills appear is typically the same across children.

Physical and motor development follow several biological principles. The **cephalocaudal principle** *reflects the tendency for development to proceed in a head-to-foot direction.* Thus the head of

FIGURE 10.10

Infant motor development occurs in an orderly sequence, but the age at which abilities emerge varies across children. The left end of each bar represents the age by which 25 percent of children exhibit the skill; the right end represents the age by which 90 percent have mastered it.

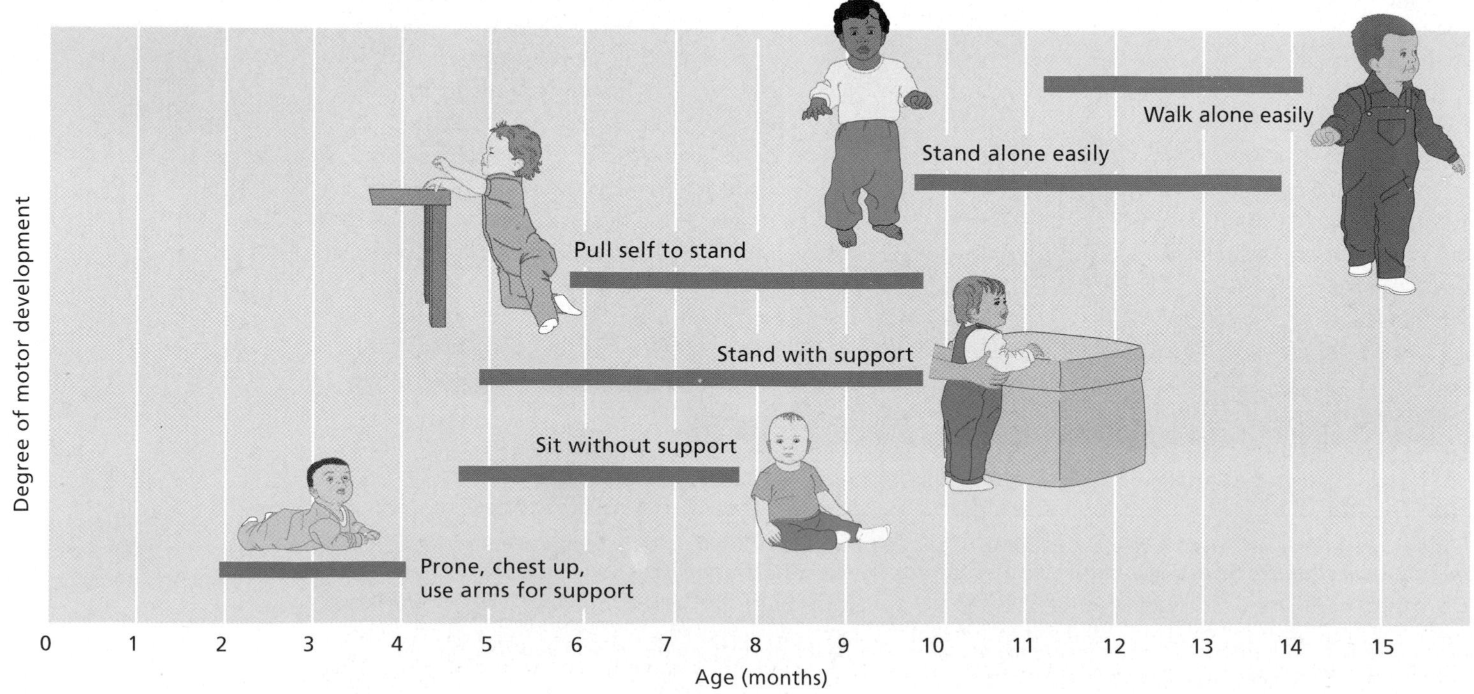

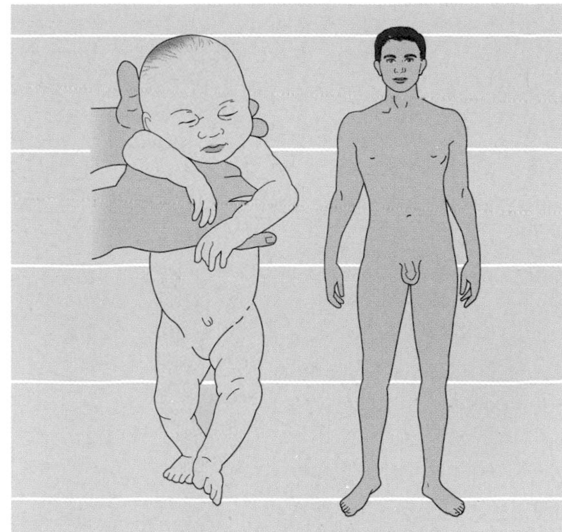

FIGURE 10.11

The cephalocaudal principle. Compared with adults, a newborn's head is disproportionately large relative to rest of the body, reflecting the tendency for development to proceed in a head-to-foot direction. In a fetus, the head represents an even greater proportion of the body (see Figure 10.3).

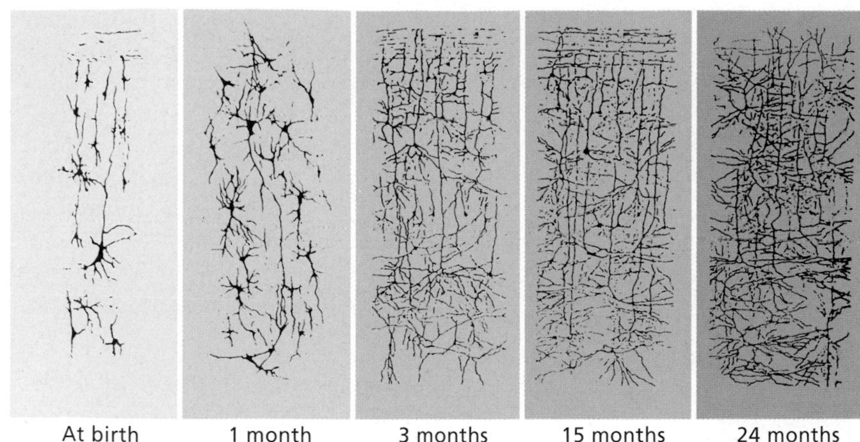

FIGURE 10.12

Increases in the density of neural networks during early development are apparent in these drawings of tissue from the human cerebral cortex. SOURCE: Reprinted by permission of Harvard University Press from *The postnatal development of the human cerebral cortex, Vols. I-VIII.* by Jesse LeRoy Conel. Copyright © 1939, 1975 by the President and Fellows of Harvard College.

a fetus or infant is disproportionately large because physical growth concentrates on the head and proceeds toward the lower part of the body (Figure 10.11). The **proximodistal principle** *states that development begins along the innermost parts of the body and continues toward the outermost parts.* Thus a fetus's arms develop before hands and fingers, and at birth infants can control their shoulders but not their arm or hand muscles.

No organ develops more dramatically than the brain (Kolb, 1989). At birth, the newborn's brain is far from mature and has reached only about 25 percent of its eventual adult weight. By age 6 months, however, the brain reaches 50 percent of its adult weight. As Figure 10.12 shows, neural networks that form the basis for cognitive and motor skills develop rapidly. The first brain areas to mature fully lie deep within the brain and regulate basic survival functions such as heartbeat and breathing. The last areas to mature include the frontal cortex, which is vital to our highest-level cognitive functions.

Rapid brain growth during infancy and early childhood slows in later childhood (Sowell et al., 2001). Yet, although 5-year-olds' brains have reached almost 90 percent of their adult size, brain maturation continues. New synapses form, association areas of the cortex mature, and the cerebral hemispheres become more highly specialized.

Environmental and Cultural Influences

Although guided by genetics, physical development is also influenced by experience. Diet is an obvious example. Chronic, severe malnutrition not only stunts general growth and brain development but also is a major source of infant death worldwide (Pelletier & Frongillo, 2003).

Researchers find that babies thrive in an enriched environment—one in which the infant has the opportunity to interact with others and to manipulate suitable toys and other objects (Needham et al., 2002). As we discussed in Chapter 2, rat pups raised in an enriched environment develop heavier brains, larger neurons, more synaptic connections, and greater amounts of brain neurotransmitters that enhance learning (Rosenzweig & Bennett, 1996).

Physical touch, too, affects growth in infancy. Deprived of normal physical contact with their mothers, even properly nourished newborn rats show stunted development, whereas vigorously stroking the rats with a brush helps restore normal physical growth (Kuhn & Schanberg, 1998). Similarly, premature and full-term human infants who are regularly massaged gain weight more rapidly and show faster neurological development (Field, 2000).

Experience also can influence basic motor skill development. For example, infants of the South American Ache tribe typically do not begin to walk until they are almost 2, about a year later than the average Western infant (Kaplan & Dove, 1987). The Ache people roam the dense rain

FIGURE 10.13

At the Parker Ranch in Hawaii, this 2-year-old is learning to ride a horse and use a lasso.

forests of eastern Paraguay, foraging for food and making temporary camp in different sites. For safety, mothers keep their children in direct physical contact almost constantly until the age of 3, providing them little opportunity to move about. Experience also affects various types of complex movement skills that toddlers and children acquire (Figure 10.13).

Our discussion of physical growth reinforces three points that apply across the realm of human development:

- *Biology sets limits on environmental influences.* For example, no infant can be toilet-trained before the nerve fibers that help regulate bladder control have biologically matured.
- *Environmental influences can be powerful.* Nurturing environments foster physical and psychological growth, and impoverished environments can stunt growth.
- *Biological and environmental factors interact.* Enriched environments enhance brain development. In turn, brain development facilitates our ability to learn and benefit from environmental experiences.

Cognitive Development

What are the thought processes of a child like, and how do they change with age? Swiss psychologist Jean Piaget (1926, 1977) spent over 50 years exploring these questions, and his ideas influence developmental research to this day.

Piaget's Stage Model

▶ 5. Discuss Piaget's concepts of assimilation and accommodation, his four-stage model, and cross-cultural findings.

Early in his career, Piaget worked for French psychologist Alfred Binet, a pioneer of intelligence testing. Piaget became intrigued by the errors children made on test questions, with children of the same age often making similar mistakes. The key to understanding how children think, Piaget believed, was not whether they got the right answers but *how* they arrived at their answers.

Piaget carefully observed children and listened to their reasoning as they tried to solve problems. He proposed that children's thinking changes *qualitatively* with age and that it differs from the way adults think. Piaget believed that cognitive development results from an interaction of the brain's biological maturation and personal experiences. He viewed children as natural-born "scientists" who actively explore and seek to understand their world.

To achieve this understanding, the brain builds **schemas** (or *schemata*), *which are organized patterns of thought and action*. Think of a schema as an internal framework that guides our interaction with the world. For example, infants are born with a sucking reflex that provides a primitive framework—a schema—for interacting with physical objects. To the infant, the world is meant to be sucked. In a sense, sucking is a basic way in which the infant "knows" the world. Similarly, when a child says "doggie" to describe the family pet, this word reflects an underlying schema—a concept or framework—that the child is using to understand this particular experience.

Cognitive development occurs as we acquire new schemas and as our existing schemas become more complex. According to Piaget, two key processes are involved. **Assimilation** *is the process by which new experiences are incorporated into existing schemas*. For example, when a young infant encounters a new object—a small plastic toy, a blanket, a doll—she will try to suck it. She tries to "fit" this new experience into a schema that she already has: Objects are suckable. Similarly, a child who sees a skunk for the first time may exclaim, "kitty!" After all, the skunk is about the size of a cat, is furry, and has four legs and a tail, so the child tries to make sense of this new experience by applying his familiar schema: "kitty."

Accommodation *is the process by which new experiences cause existing schemas to change*. As the infant tries to suck different objects, she will eventually encounter ones that are too big to go into her mouth or that taste bad. Similarly, the child who calls a skunk a "kitty" may discover with olfactory dismay that this "kitty" exhibits some distinctive behaviors not found in cats. This imbalance, or *disequilibrium*, between existing schemas and new experiences ultimately forces those schemas to change. Thus the infant's "suckability" schema will become more complex: Some objects are suckable, some are not. The child's "kitty" schema also will change, and he will begin to develop new schemas for "doggie," "horsie," and so on. This may not seem earth-shaking to us, but to infants it is a fundamental change in their understanding of the world. Every time a schema is modified, it helps create a better balance, or *equilibrium*, between the environment and the child's understanding of it.

Cognitive growth thus involves a give-and-take between trying to understand new experiences in terms of what we already know (assimilation) and having to modify our thinking when new experiences don't fit into our current schemas (accommodation). As Table 10.1 shows, Piaget charted four major stages of cognitive growth.

Sensorimotor Stage From birth to about age 2, infants in the **sensorimotor stage** *understand their world primarily through sensory experiences and physical (motor) interactions with objects.* Reflexes are infants' earliest schemas, but as sensory and motor capabilities increase, babies begin to explore their surroundings. Eventually, they realize that they can "make things happen." They bang spoons, take objects apart, and find amazing ways to get themselves into trouble.

For young infants, said Piaget, "out of sight" literally means "out of mind." If you hide 3-month-old Cindy's favorite toy from view, she will not search for it, as if the toy no longer exists (Figure 10.14). But around age 8 months, Cindy will search for and retrieve the hidden toy. She now grasps the concept of **object permanence,** *the understanding that an object continues to exist even when it no longer can be seen.* This developmental milestone frees the child from having to rely on immediate sensory experience.

Infants begin to acquire language after age 1, and toward the end of the sensorimotor period they increasingly use words to represent objects, needs, and actions. Thus in the space of 2 years, infants have grown into planful thinkers who can form simple concepts, solve some problems mentally, and communicate their thoughts to others.

TABLE 10.1 Piaget's Stages of Cogitive Development

Stage	Age (Years)	Major Characteristics
Sensorimotor	Birth to 2	• Infant understands world through sensory and motor experiences • Achieves object permanence • Exhibits emergence of symbolic thought
Preoperational	2 to 7	• Child uses symbolic thinking in the form of words and images to represent objects and experiences • Symbolic thinking enables child to engage in pretend play • Thinking displays egocentrism, irreversibility, and centration
Concrete operational	7 to 12	• Child can think logically about concrete events • Grasps concepts of conservation and serial ordering
Formal operational	12 on	• Adolescent can think more logically, abstractly, and flexibly • Can form hypotheses and systematically test them

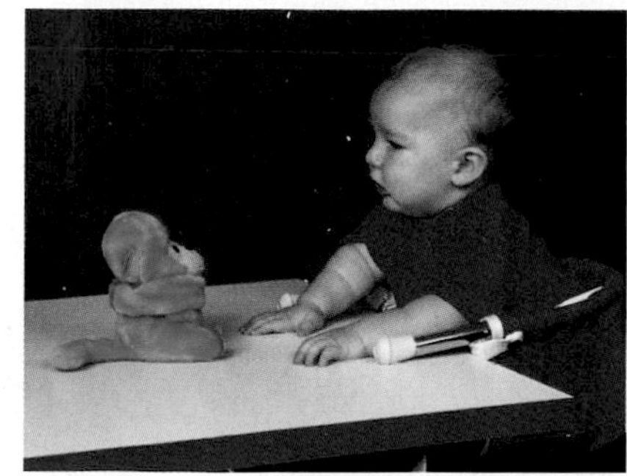

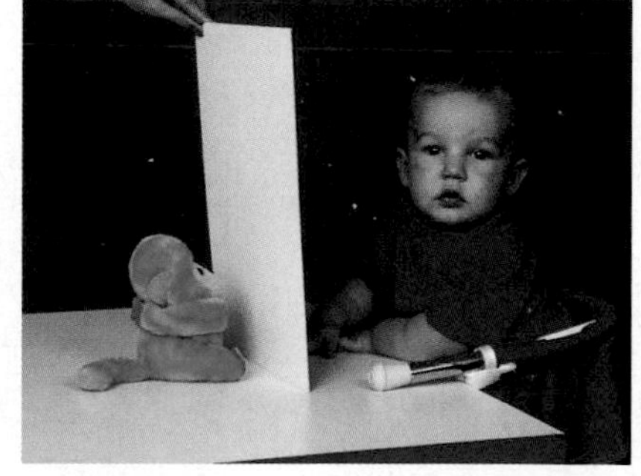

FIGURE 10.14

During the early sensorimotor period, a baby will reach for a visible toy (left) but not for one that has been hidden from view while the infant watches (right). According to Piaget, the child lacks the concept of object permanence; when something is out of sight, it ceases to exist.

Preoperational Stage At about age 2, children enter a **preoperational stage,** *in which they represent the world symbolically through words and mental images but do not yet understand basic mental operations or rules.* Rapid language development helps children label objects and represent simple concepts, such as that two objects can be the "same" or "different." Children can think about the past ("yesterday") and future ("soon") and can better anticipate the consequences of their actions. Symbolic thinking enables them to engage in make-believe, or *pretend play.*

Despite these advances, children's cognitive abilities have important limitations. The preoperational child does not understand **conservation,** *the principle that basic properties of objects, such as their volume, mass, or quantity, stay the same (are "conserved") even though their outward appearance may change* (Figure 10.15). For example, 4-year-olds often say that the taller beaker in Figure 10.15c has more liquid than the shorter one. Whereas you understand that the liquid can be poured back into the short beaker to return to the original, equal state of affairs, the child's thinking displays *irreversibility:* It is difficult for them to reverse an action mentally. You also pay attention to height and width, recognizing that the liquid is "taller" because the beaker is narrower. But the child exhibits *centration,* focusing (centering) on only one aspect of the situation. Usually, this is the most striking feature, such as the height of the liquid.

Preoperational children often display *animism,* attributing lifelike qualities to physical objects and natural events. When it rains, "the sky is crying," and stars twinkle at night "because they're winking at you." Their thinking also reflects **egocentrism,** *difficulty in viewing the world from someone else's perspective.* By *egocentrism* Piaget did not mean "selfishness" but rather

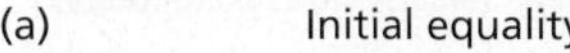

(a) Initial equality

(b) Transformation

(c) Which glass has more juice?

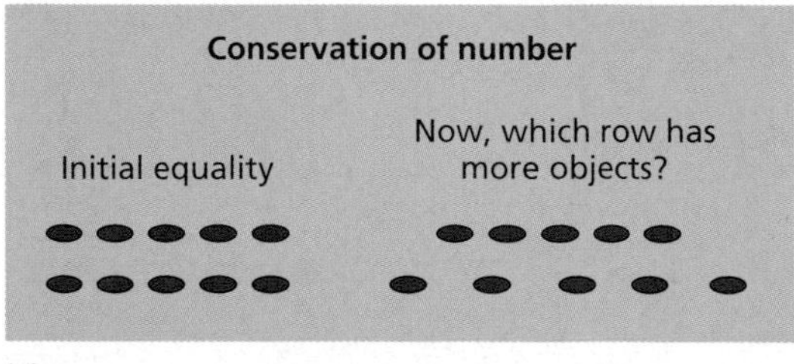

(d)

Conservation of mass

Initial equality

Now, which piece has more clay?

(e)

FIGURE 10.15

(a, b, c) Conservation of volume. *At the end of this sequence (from left to right), when the preoperational child is asked which beaker contains more liquid, he points to the taller one. (d)* Conservation of number. *Two rows with an equal number of objects are aligned. After one row is spread out, preoperational children will say that it has more objects than the other row. (e)* Conservation of mass. *Preoperational children watch as one of two identically sized clay balls is rolled into a new shape. They typically will say that it now has more clay.*

that children at this stage believe that other people perceive things in the same way they do (Figure 10.16).

Concrete Operational Stage From about ages 7 to 12, said Piaget, children in the **concrete operational stage** *can perform basic mental operations concerning problems that involve tangible (i.e., "concrete") objects and situations.* They now grasp the concept of reversibility, display less centration, and easily solve conservation problems that baffled them as preschoolers.

Unlike younger children, concrete operational children also can form mental representations of a series of actions. For example, a concrete operational child could draw a map showing the route to get to school. A preoperational child might be able to lead you to school but would have difficulty representing the route symbolically.

When concrete operational children confront problems that are hypothetical or require abstract reasoning, however, they often have difficulty or show rigid types of thinking. To demonstrate this, ask a few 9-year-olds, "If you could have a third eye, where on your body would you put it? Draw a picture." Then ask them to explain their reason. David Shaffer (1989) reports that 9-year-olds typically draw a face with a row of three eyes across it. Their thinking is concrete, bound by the reality that eyes appear on the face, and their justifications often are unsophisticated (e.g., "so I could see you better"). Many find the task silly because "Nobody has three eyes" (Shaffer, 1989, p. 324).

Formal Operational Stage Piaget's model ends with the **formal operational stage,** *in which individuals are able to think logically and systematically about both concrete and abstract problems, form hypotheses, and test them in a thoughtful way.* Formal thinking begins around ages 11 to 12 and increases through adolescence (Ward & Overton, 1990).

Children entering this stage begin to think more flexibly when tackling hypothetical problems, such as brainteasers, and typically enjoy

FIGURE 10.16

Piaget used the three-mountain problem to illustrate the egocentrism of young children. Suppose that a preoperational child named Ted is looking at the mountains just as you are. Another child, Beth, is standing at the opposite (far) side of the table. Ted is asked what Beth sees. Because Ted is able to see the road he will mistakenly say that Beth also can see it, indicating that he has failed to recognize Beth's perspective as different from his own.

the challenge. Shaffer (1989) reports that 11 1/2- to 12-year-olds provide more creative answers and better justifications to the "third-eye problem" than do 9-year-old concrete thinkers. One child placed the eye on the palm of his hands so that he could use it to "see around corners." Another placed it on top of his head, so that he could "revolve the eye to look in all directions." Formal operational children enjoy these hypothetical tasks and often beg for more.

Stages, Ages, and Culture

Tests of Piaget's theory conducted around the world have yielded several general findings. First, it appears that *the general cognitive abilities associated with Piaget's four stages occur in the same order across cultures* (Berry et al., 1992). For example, children understand object permanence before symbolic thinking blooms. Formal operational thinking may not be as common as Piaget believed, but when it occurs it is mastered after concrete reasoning develops.

Second, *children acquire many cognitive skills at an earlier age than Piaget believed* (Aguiar & Baillargeon, 2002). As Figure 10.17 shows, even 3 1/2- to 4 1/2-month-olds display a basic grasp of objective permanence when they are tested on special tasks that do not require them to physically search for a hidden object.

Third, *cognitive development within each stage seems to proceed inconsistently.* A child may perform at the preoperational level on most tasks yet solve some tasks at a concrete operational level (Siegler, 1986). This problem goes to the heart of the continuity-discontinuity debate. If development proceeds in discontinuous stages, then a child at a given stage should not show large inconsistencies in solving conceptually similar tasks.

Fourth, *culture influences cognitive development.* Piaget's Western perspective equated cognitive development with scientific-logical thinking, but as David Matsumoto and Philip Hull (1994, p. 105) note, "Many cultures . . . consider cognitive development to be more relational, involving the thinking skills and processes to engage in successful interpersonal contexts."

In Africa's Ivory Coast, for example, the Baoulé people most strongly value a type of "social intelligence" that reflects the skills to get along with others and to be respectful, helpful, and responsible (Dasen et al., 1985). Moreover, compared with Westerners, people from developing countries or tribal societies often appear to show a large "age delay" or achieve less success in solving Piaget's concrete and formal operational tasks. But these differences shrink or disappear when culturally appropriate tasks are chosen or when children receive special training or formal schooling (Jahoda, 1983).

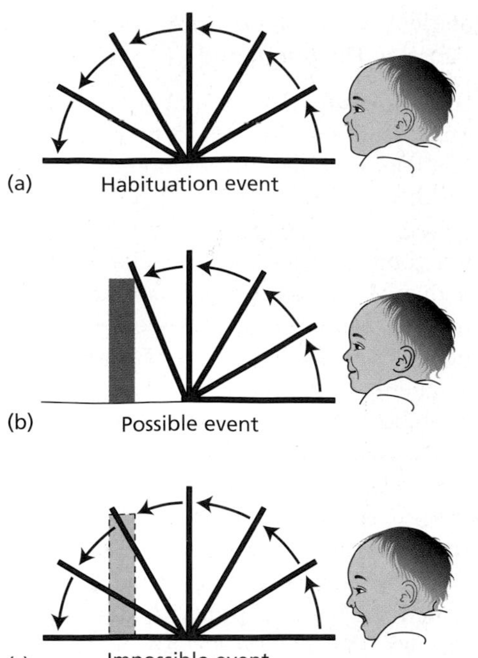

FIGURE 10.17

(a) Habituation. *Researcher Renée Baillargeon repeatedly exposes young infants to a screen that slowly rotates 180 degrees. Eventually, they habituate and become bored. Then the infants watch as a box is placed in the screen's path.* (b) Possible event. *The screen rotates, conceals the infant's view of the box, and then stops as the box blocks it.* (c) Impossible event. *The screen rotates, conceals the view of the box, and continues a full 180 degrees because the box is secretly removed. Infants stare longer at the impossible than at the possible event, as if they are surprised that the box did not stop the screen. This can only happen, reasons Baillargeon, if the infants understand that the box continues to exist even when concealed from view (i.e., object permanence).* SOURCE: Adapted from Baillargeon, 1987.

Fifth, and most broadly, *cognitive development is more complex and variable than Piaget proposed* (Larivée et al., 2000). Although all children progress from simpler to more sophisticated thinking, they don't necessarily follow the same developmental path.

So what are we to conclude? Newer research challenges many of Piaget's ideas, but he revolutionized thinking about children's cognitive development, and his work guides many researchers, called *neo-Piagetians,* who have modified aspects of his theory to account for the issues discussed above.

Vygotsky: The Social Context of Cognitive Development

▶ 6. Explain how Vygotsky's approach, information-processing models, and theory of mind research challenge Piaget's views.

Piaget acknowledged that social factors influence children's thinking, but he focused mainly on children's independent exploration of the physical world. In contrast, Russian psychologist Lev Vygotsky (1935/1978) highlighted how the sociocultural context of cognitive development interacts with the brain's biological maturation.

To illustrate, suppose that 5-year-olds Joshua and Juanita have similar scores on cognitive tests and that neither child can solve Piaget's conservation problems. However, with guidance from a parent, teacher, or older sibling, Juanita gets it and can now solve these problems. Joshua, even with assistance, just doesn't understand. Were these two children really at the same cognitive level to begin with? Vygotsky says no, introducing a concept called the **zone of proximal development:** *the difference between what a child can do independently and what the child can do with assistance from adults or more advanced peers.*

Why is the zone of proximal development important? For one thing, it helps us recognize "those functions that have not yet matured but are in the process of maturation" (Vygotsky, 1935/1978, p. 86). In other words, it gives us an idea of what children may soon be able to do on their own. Second, this concept emphasizes that we can help "move" a child's cognitive development forward within limits (the "zone") dictated by the child's biological maturation. For example, when parents work with a child on scientific tasks, they may push the child's understanding further along by using age-appropriate but cognitively demanding speech (e.g., introducing scientific concepts and terms) than by using only simpler speech (Tenenbaum & Leaper, 2003).

Katja, one of the students in our opening vignette, grew up with an older brother. Having older siblings around the house may stimulate a younger child's cognitive development, as long as the child is biologically ready for the input. In one study of 2- to 6-year-old English and Japanese children, those over age 3 who grew up with older brothers and sisters performed better on a cognitive task than children who grew up alone or with younger brothers and sisters (Ruffman et al., 1998). However, children under age 3 performed poorly on the task regardless of how many older or younger siblings they had. The task was simply beyond their current cognitive capacity.

FIGURE 10.18

Stimuli used by Vurpillot to assess visual inspection through filmed eye movements. Preschoolers fail to scan the pictures systematically, which often leads them to claim that the two houses are identical. SOURCE: Adapted from Vurpillot, 1968.

Information-Processing Approaches

In contrast to Piaget's stage approach, many researchers view cognitive development as a continuous, gradual process in which the same set of information-processing abilities become more efficient over time. For example, perhaps young children fail to solve conservation problems because they don't search for key information or are unable to hold enough pieces of information in memory simultaneously (Siegler, 1996).

Consider children's *information-search strategies.* Look at the two houses in Figure 10.18. Are they identical? This task is easy for you but not for young children. Elaine Vurpillot (1968) recorded the eye movements of 3- to 10-year-olds during tasks like this one. Older children methodically scanned the houses, but preschoolers often failed to compare each window in the house on the left to the corresponding window in the house on the right. In short, preschoolers were less able to search systematically for relevant details.

Information-processing speed also improves during childhood, as Robert Kail's (1991) review of 72 studies shows in Figure 10.19 Notice that processing speed improves continuously and that the relatively rapid rate of change between ages 8 and about 12 slows during adolescence.

Memory capabilities improve significantly during childhood, and in part this may stem from faster information-processing speed as children age (Kail, 2002). Older children are also more likely than younger children to use strategies to improve memory. In one study, when given lists of words or numbers to remember, preschoolers rarely used rehearsal spontaneously, whereas 8- to 10-year-olds could often be heard rehearsing words or numbers under their breath (Flavell, 1970).

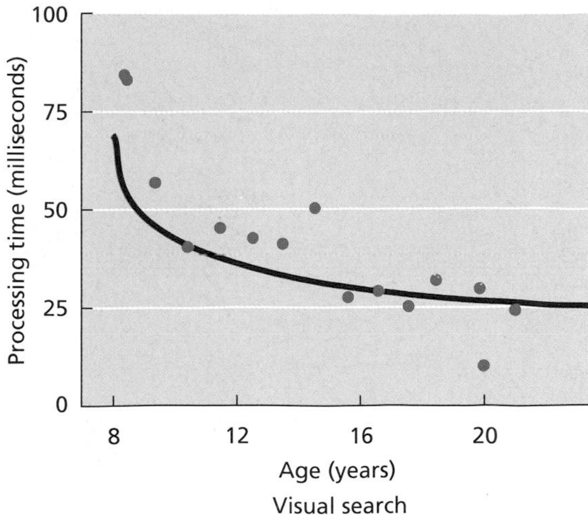

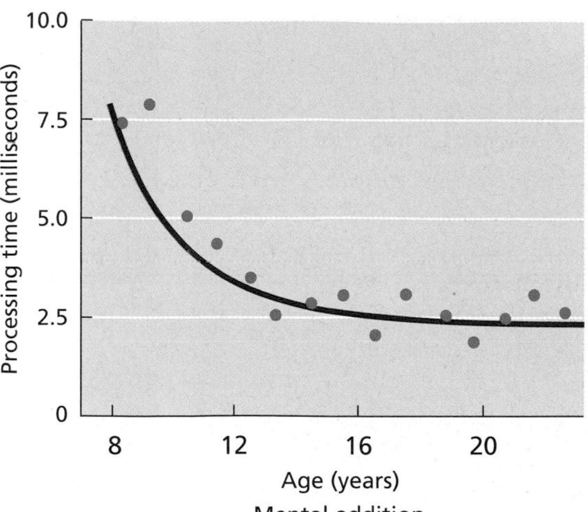

FIGURE 10.19

These two graphs show how information-processing speed for visual search and mental addition tasks becomes faster with age. The relatively rapid rate of change between ages 8 and about 12 slows during adolescence. A similar nonlinear pattern also occurs on name retrieval, mental rotation, and other cognitive tasks. SOURCE: Adapted from Kail, 1991.

Metacognition refers to an awareness of one's own cognitive processes. Compared to younger children, for example, older children better judge how well they understand material for a test. In turn, this helps them decide whether they need to study more or ask for help.

The *discontinuity (qualitative stages) versus continuity* debate is far from resolved, and some psychologists propose that development involves both processes. For example, Susan Gathercole (1998) suggests that memory capabilities change qualitatively (i.e., new abilities emerge) between infancy and age 7, but then undergo only gradual quantitative improvements through adolescence. Robbie Case (1987; Case et al., 2001) offers another integrative view, proposing that gradual increases in information-processing capabilities within stages enable children to move qualitatively from one stage of cognitive development to the next.

Theory of Mind: Children's Understanding of Mental States

The term **theory of mind** *refers to a person's beliefs about the "mind" and ability to understand other people's mental states.* Piaget believed that children younger than 6 or 7, have trouble recognizing what other people are thinking. Indeed, this is what Piaget's concept of egocentrism is all about: not being able to understand how someone else is perceiving a situation. But consider the following story:

> Angela puts a candy bar inside a green box on the table, and then she goes away. Then her mother takes the candy bar out of the box and puts it inside a red bag on the bed. Angela doesn't see her mother do this. Later, Angela comes back and wants to get her candy because she is hungry. Where will Angela look for her candy bar?

On problems like this, most 2- and 3-year-olds indicate that Angela will look in the red bag, as if she had the same knowledge that they have. Piaget would not have been surprised. But many 4-year-olds say she will choose the green box, recognizing that Angela does not have the information they do. Thus at some level, they comprehend that Angela's mental state—her "mind"—is different from theirs (Ruffman et al., 1998). Studies of young children from African tribal societies, Canada, China, Japan, the United Kingdom, and the United States yield similar findings (Vinden, 2002).

Lying and deception also provide evidence of theory of mind. They imply an ability to recognize that one person can have information that another does not and therefore that we can influence what other people think by withholding the truth. Researchers find that most 3-year-olds are capable of trying to deceive someone else and recognize the difference between providing someone with false information in the form of a lie and providing false information due to an innocent mistake (Carlson et al., 1998). Overall, it appears that children begin to understand some aspects of other people's thinking by age 3 to 4, well before Piaget proposed they could (Ritblatt, 2000).

Social-Emotional and Personality Development

Children grow not only physically and mentally but also emotionally and socially. They form attachments and relationships, and each child

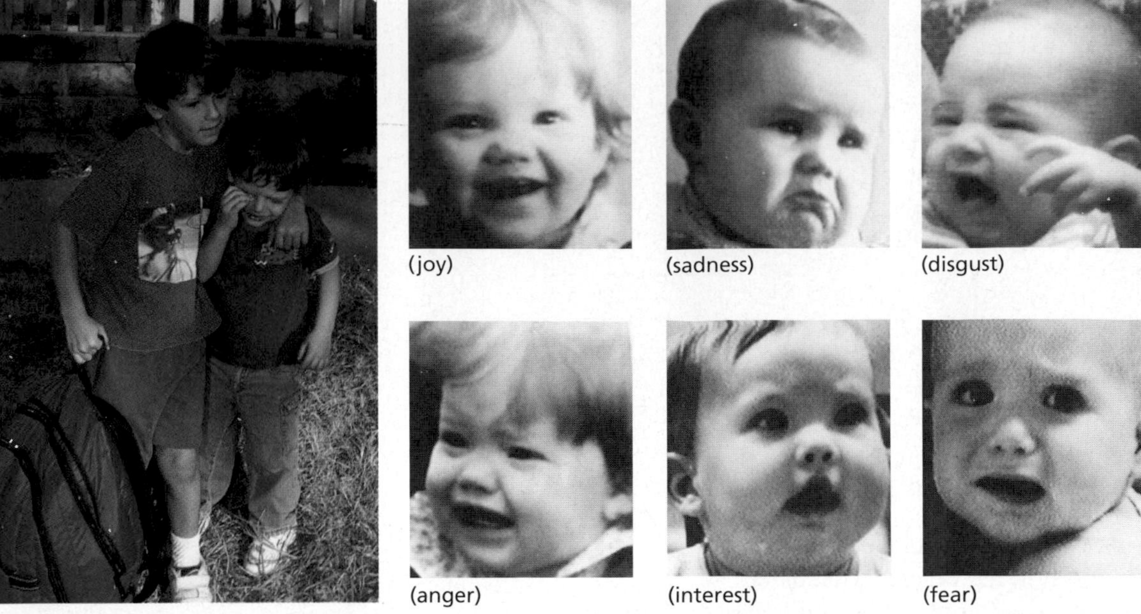

FIGURE 10.20

(left) Emotional responses communicate our internal states, and they can influence how others respond to us, providing us with the aid and comfort we need. (right) Young infants display a variety of basic emotions.

displays a unique personality—a distinctive yet somewhat consistent pattern of thinking, feeling, and behaving.

Early Emotions and Emotion Regulation

▶ 7. Discuss children's emotional development, including emotional expressiveness, emotion regulation, and temperament.

Emotional responses communicate our inner states to other people and influence how others respond to us (Figure 10.20). Although infants can't describe their feelings, Figure 10.20 illustrates that their facial expressions, vocalizations, and other behaviors provide a window into their increasingly diverse emotional life (Izard, 1982). If you've heard a newborn cry (and cry and cry) or watched a newborn's face after it has been fed, then you know that they can experience distress and contentment. By focusing their gaze and staring at objects and people, they also express interest. Around the world, over approximately the first 6 months of their lives, infants begin to express joy and surprise ("peekaboo . . . I see you!"), and distress becomes differentiated into the separate emotions of disgust, anger, fear, and sadness (Lewis, 2000).

Around 18 months of age, infants begin to develop a sense of self, as illustrated by their ability to recognize themselves in a mirror. This growing self-awareness sets the stage for envy, embarrassment, and empathy to emerge (Lewis, 2000). After age 2, as toddlers learn about performance standards and rules that they are supposed to follow, they begin to display pride and shame. Around the same age, and even a little earlier, they also display guilt—as evidenced by avoiding eye contact, shrugging their shoulders, and exhibiting certain facial expressions. In one study, 18- to 24-month-olds looked guilty and tried to fix a doll when they thought they had broken it (Kochanska et al., 1995).

Just as emotional reactions become more diverse and complex with age, so does **emotion regulation:** *the processes by which we evaluate and modify our emotional reactions*. Young infants may suck their thumb or pacifier, turn their head away from something unpleasant, or cling to a caretaker to soothe themselves. To reduce distress, toddlers may seek out a caretaker, cling to a doll or teddy bear, fling unpleasant objects away, and learn to smile, pout, or throw a tantrum to get what they want. Once they acquire language, they can reduce distress by talking to themselves. For example, a 2 1/2-year-old we know, separated from her parents for the first time (while they took a cruise-ship vacation), repeatedly calmed herself for 10 days by saying, "mommy and dada on the boat."

As children age, their emotional expressiveness and ability to regulate their emotions become part of their overall "emotional competence," which in turn influences their social behavior and how well their peers and other people like them (Denham et al., 2003). Children who frequently display sadness or who can't control their anger are less likely to be popular, and emotional competence remains important for well-being as children develop (Eisenberg et al., 2002). Moreover, as these examples illustrate, children's emotional development is linked to their cognitive and social development. And as you will now see, it also is interwined with their personality development

and the process of bonding to caretakers. Although influenced by socialization (e.g., parents and peers can reinforce children for some emotional responses but not others), heredity also contributes to children's basic emotional-behavioral style.

Temperament

From the moment of birth, infants differ from one another in **temperament,** *a biologically based general style of reacting emotionally and behaviorally to the environment.* Some infants are calm and happy, others are irritable and fussy. Some are outgoing and active, others shy and inactive. Indeed, within any age group—children, adolescents, or adults—people differ in temperament (McCrae & Costa, 1990; Shiner, 1998).

In a pioneering study, Alexander Thomas and Stella Chess (1977) had parents describe their babies' behavior. They found that most infants could be classified into three groups. "Easy infants" had regular sleeping and feeding patterns, were playful, and accepted new situations and frustration with little fuss. "Difficult infants" were irritable, had irregular eating and sleeping patterns, and reacted negatively to new situations and frustration. "Slow-to-warm-up infants" were the least active, had mildly negative responses to new situations, but slowly adapted over time. Over the next 10 years, children who had been difficult infants were most likely to have subsequent emotional and behavior problems.

This study attracted admiration and criticism. Other researchers identified different categories and measured infants' temperament not only by ratings from parents but also by observing the infants. This follow-up research indicated that temperament is only weakly to moderately stable during infancy (Carnicero et al., 2000). Some infants maintain a consistent temperament throughout their first 2 years of life, while others change.

Consider shyness, which forms part of a more general temperament style called *behavioral inhibition.* Inhibited infants are quiet and timid; they cry and withdraw when exposed to unfamiliar people, places, objects, and sounds. Uninhibited infants are more sociable, verbal, and spontaneous. Jerome Kagan and coworkers (Kagan et al., 1988) found that about 20 to 25 percent of infants displayed this inhibited pattern, which remained moderately stable during infancy. They also studied these infants until age 7 1/2. For the vast majority—those who were only mildly to moderately inhibited or uninhibited between the ages of 1 and 2 years—their temperament in infancy did not predict how shy or outgoing they would be as children. But for infants who were *extremely* uninhibited or inhibited (the top 15 percent of each group), the findings were different. Highly uninhibited infants tended to become sociable and talkative 7-year-olds, whereas extremely inhibited infants developed into quiet, cautious, and socially avoidant 7-year-olds, suggesting that for older infants who are highly inhibited or uninhibited, temperament may indeed predict childhood shyness and sociability (Kagan, 1989).

What Do You Think?

SHY CHILD, SHY ADULT?

We have just seen that very shy or very outgoing infants tend to retain these traits into early childhood. Do you think this relation holds true later in the life span—does the very shy or outgoing child grow into a shy or outgoing adult? In general, does childhood temperament predict patterns of adult behavior? Think about it, then see page 417.

Erikson's Psychosocial Theory

▶ 8. Describe Erikson's psychosocial theory, imprinting, Harlow's attachment research, and attachment in humans.

Psychoanalytic psychologist Erik Erikson (1968) believed that personality develops through confronting a series of eight major **psychosocial stages,** *each of which involves a different "crisis" (i.e., conflict) over how we view ourselves in relation to other people and the world* (Table 10.2). Each crisis is

TABLE 10.2 Erikson's Psychosocial Stages

Age (Approximate Years)	Major Psychosocial Crisis
Infancy (first year)	Basic trust vs. basic mistrust
Toddlerhood (1–2)	Autonomy vs. shame and doubt
Early childhood (3–5)	Initiative vs. guilt
Middle childhood (6–12)	Industry vs. inferiority
Adolescence (12–20)	Identity vs. role confusion
Early adulthood (20–40)	Intimacy vs. isolation
Middle adulthood (40–65)	Generativity vs. stagnation
Late adulthood (65+)	Integrity vs. despair

FIGURE 10.21

(top) When they were hatchlings, Canadian wildlife sculptor Bill Lishman imprinted these Canada geese to the sight of his ultralight airplane. Although they have now matured, the ultralight still represents "mother" to the geese, and they follow it in flight. (left) In humans, infant-caretaker attachment is more complex and forms over a much longer period.

present throughout life but takes on special importance during a particular age period. Four of these crises occur in infancy and childhood:

1. *Basic trust versus basic mistrust.* During the first year of life we depend totally on our parents or other caretakers. Whether we develop a basic trust or basic mistrust of the world depends on how adequately our needs are met and how much love and attention we receive.
2. *Autonomy versus shame and doubt.* During the next 2 years, children become ready to separate themselves from their parents and exercise their individuality. If parents unduly restrict children or make harsh demands during toilet training, children develop shame and doubt about their abilities and later lack the courage to be independent.
3. *Initiative versus guilt.* From age 3 through age 5, children display great curiosity about the world. If they are allowed freedom to explore and receive answers to their questions, they develop a sense of initiative. If they are held back or punished, they develop guilt about their desires and suppress their curiosity.
4. *Industry versus inferiority.* From age 6 until puberty, the child's life expands into school and peer activities. Children who experience pride and encouragement in mastering tasks develop *industry*—a striving to achieve. Repeated failure and lack of praise for trying leads to a sense of inferiority.

Although critics argue that Erikson's model lacks detail and question its "stage" approach, the model successfully captures several major issues that developing children confront. As Erikson proposed and as some research supports, successfully resolving each crisis helps prepare us to meet the next (Kahn et al., 1985; McAdams & de St. Aubin, 1998). Because each stage of life creates new opportunities, possibilities for change are ever present. Yet like the early chapters of a novel, themes that emerge in childhood help set the stage for the unfolding story of our lives.

Attachment

Imagine a single-file procession of ducklings following you around campus and everywhere you go, as if you were their mother. For this to happen, we need only isolate the ducklings after they hatch and then expose them to you at a certain time. If they later encounter their real parents, the ducklings will ignore them and continue to follow you. If the only moving object the ducklings see for their first 24 hours is a model duck or ball, they will faithfully follow that object as they grow up (Hess, 1959).

German ethologist Konrad Lorenz (1937) called this behavior **imprinting,** *a sudden, biologically primed form of attachment* (Figure 10.21). It occurs in some species of birds, including ducks, chickens, and geese, and in a few mammals, such as shrews. Imprinting illustrates the concept of critical periods. In mallard ducklings, for example, the strongest imprinting takes place within 1 day after hatching, and by 2 1/2 days the capacity to imprint is lost (Hess, 1959). Thus, depending on the species, offspring must be exposed to parents within hours or days after entering the world to attach to them.

Attachment *refers to the strong emotional bond that develops between children and their primary caregivers* (Figure 10.21). The students Ramona, Katja, and Enrique, although growing up in families with different structures, all felt a bond with one or more caregivers. Human infants do not automatically imprint on a caregiver, and there is not an immediate postbirth critical period during which contact is required for infant-caregiver bonding. Instead, the first few years of life seem to be a sensitive period when we can most easily form a secure bond with caregivers that enhances our adjustment later in life (Sroufe, 2002). Although it may be more difficult, strong first attachments to caregivers can still form later in childhood.

The Attachment Process For decades, people assumed that infant-caregiver bonding resulted primarily from the mother's role in satisfying the infant's need for nourishment. Harry Harlow (1958) tested this notion by separating infant rhesus monkeys from their biological mothers shortly after birth. Each infant was raised in a cage with two artificial "surrogate" mothers. One was a bare-wire cylinder with a feeding bottle attached to its "chest." The other was a wire cylinder covered with soft terry cloth without a feeding bottle (Figure 10.22).

Faced with this choice, the infant monkeys became attached to the cloth mother. When exposed to frightening situations, the infants ran to the terry cloth figure and clung tightly to it. They even maintained contact with the cloth mother while feeding from the wire mother's bottle. Thus Harlow showed that *contact comfort*—body contact with a comforting object—is more important in fostering attachment than the provision of nourishment.

Around this time, other researchers studied human attachment in African, European, and North American societies. Based on this work, British psychoanalyst John Bowlby (1969) proposed that attachment in infancy develops in three phases:

1. *Indiscriminate attachment behavior.* Newborns cry, vocalize, and smile, and they emit these behaviors toward everyone. In turn, these behaviors evoke caregiving from adults.
2. *Discriminate attachment behavior.* Around 3 months of age, infants direct their attachment behaviors more toward familiar, regular caregivers than toward strangers.
3. *Specific attachment behavior.* By 7 or 8 months of age, infants develop their first meaningful attachment to specific caregivers. Infants smile more at these caregivers, hold out their arms to be picked up by them, and want to be in their presence. The caregiver becomes a secure base from which the infant can crawl about and explore the environment.

As an infant's attachment becomes more focused, two types of anxiety occur. **Stranger anxiety,** *distress over contact with unfamiliar people,* often emerges around age 6 or 7 months and ends by age 18 months. When approached by, touched, or handed over to a stranger, the infant becomes afraid, cries, and reaches for the caregiver. **Separation anxiety,** *distress over being separated from a primary caregiver,* typically begins a little later, peaks around age 12 to 16 months, and disappears between 2 and 3 years of age. Here the infant becomes anxious and cries when the caregiver is out of sight. Both forms of anxiety show a similar pattern across many cultures (Figure 10.23).

These responses, which coincide with infants' increasing cognitive abilities, may be adaptive reactions shaped through evolution (Bowlby, 1973). Newborns don't have well-formed schemas that enable them to distinguish strangers from nonstrangers, but as these schemas develop, stranger anxiety emerges. At an age when infants master crawling and then learn to walk, fear of strangers and of separation may help prevent them from wandering beyond the sight of caretakers, especially in unfamiliar situations.

FIGURE 10.22

Infant monkeys, reared with a cloth-covered and a bare-wire surrogate from birth, preferred to remain in contact with the cloth "mother" even though the wire "mother" satisfied nutritional needs. SOURCE: From Harlow, 1958.

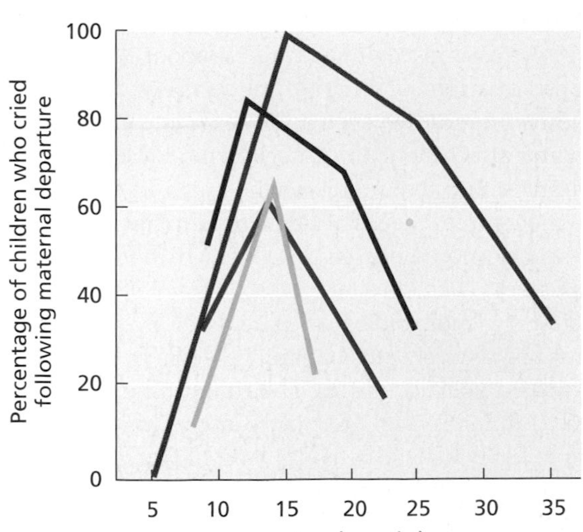

FIGURE 10.23

The rise and fall of separation anxiety in infancy shows a similar pattern across cultures. SOURCE: Based on Kagan et al., 1978.

Around age 3 to 4, as children's cognitive and verbal skills grow, they develop a better understanding of their attachment relationships. According to Bowlby (1969), a stage of *goal-corrected partnership* emerges, in which children and caregivers can describe their wishes and feelings to each other, and their relationship can be maintained whether they are together or apart.

▶ 9. Describe types of attachment, how they are measured, and how attachment deprivation affects development.

Types of Attachment Infants develop different types of attachments with their caretakers. Psychologist Mary Ainsworth and coworkers (1978) developed the **strange situation,** *a standardized procedure for examining infant attachment*. The infant, typically a 12- to 18-month-old, first plays with toys in the mother's presence. Then a stranger enters the room and interacts with the child. Soon the mother leaves the child with the stranger. Later the stranger leaves, and the child is alone. Finally, the mother returns. The infant's behavior is observed throughout this procedure.

In the mother's presence, "securely attached" infants explore the playroom and react positively to strangers (Ainsworth et al., 1978). They are distressed when the mother leaves and happily greet her when she returns. In contrast, there are two types of "insecurely attached" infants. "Anxious-resistant" infants are fearful when the mother is present, demand her attention, and are distressed when she leaves. They are not soothed when she returns and may angrily resist her attempts at contact. Anxious-avoidant infants show few signs of attachment, seldom cry when the mother leaves, and don't seek contact when she returns.

Across most cultures studied, about one half to three quarters of infants are securely attached. Numerous studies, such as one examining mother-infant attachment in American and Colombian families, find that mothers who are more sensitive to their babies' needs at home tend to have infants who are more securely attached in the "strange situation" (Posada et al., 2002). Moreover, whether raised by their biological parents or by adoptive parents, securely attached infants seem to be better adjusted socially during childhood (Stams et al., 2002). Infants who are not securely attached are more likely to have behavioral problems or seek attention in the classroom (Ainsworth, 1989). This lends credence to Erikson's view that establishing a stable, trusting relationship with a caregiver is an important component of early social development.

For more on secure attachment, see Interactive Segment 10.2.

Attachment Deprivation

If infants and young children are deprived of a stable attachment with a caregiver, how do they fare in the long run? Harry Harlow studied this issue under controlled conditions. After rearing "isolate" monkeys either alone or with artificial surrogate mothers, Harlow returned them to the monkey colony at 6 months of age. Exposed to other monkeys, the isolates were indifferent, terrified, or aggressive. When they became adults, these monkeys could not copulate normally. Some female isolates were artificially inseminated, and the researchers found that as parents they were highly abusive toward their firstborns (Harlow & Suomi, 1970). The conclusion: Being raised without a secure attachment to a real, interactive caregiver produced long-term social impairment.

What of isolate human children? Victor, the Wild Boy of Aveyron, was severely impaired after his isolation and showed only limited recovery after intensive remedial training. But was it a lack of human contact that severely stunted Victor's development, or was it brain damage, possibly present from birth? And if severe isolation was the cause, are its negative effects impossible to reverse?

In the 1960s, twin boys in Czechoslovakia were forced by their father and stepmother to live in extreme isolation beginning at 18 months of age. The twins were discovered at age 7, emotionally and socially retarded, with the cognitive development of a 3-year-old and speech skills of a 2-year-old. Jarmila Koluchova (1972, 1991) studied the boys for over 20 years and found that they went on to become happy, sociable, and firmly attached to their foster family. Their IQs increased to normal levels, and they became well-adjusted adolescents and young adults.

Why the difference? In case studies such as these, we can only speculate. Unlike Victor, the twins had each other's company, but in other cases even "lone" isolate children have recovered. Perhaps most important, the twins' isolation ended—and their rehabilitation began—at a younger age, when the brain's neural plasticity is greater. They were 7, whereas Victor was about 12.

Even when orphaned children are raised with little attention in substandard institutions, those adopted during their first year or two typically become attached to their new caregivers. But what about children adopted at an older age? Barbara Tizard and Jill Hodges (1978) studied children raised in stimulating, high-quality orphanages. The nurses were attentive, but the staff turnover was so high that the children had no opportunity to form a stable bond with any caretaker. Yet those adopted between ages 2 and 8 years typically formed healthy attachments with their adopted parents, though in adolescence many had difficulty forming peer relationships because they were viewed as needing "too much attention" (Hodges & Tizard, 1989). Although being adopted at a later age increases the risk of adjustment problems during the teen years, the vast majority of adopted children—especially those raised in two-parent families—are normally adjusted and differ little from children raised by their biological parents (Miller et al., 2000).

In sum, it appears that infancy is a sensitive, though not critical, period during which an initial attachment to caregivers forms most easily and facilitates subsequent development. Prolonged attachment deprivation creates developmental risks, but when deprived children are placed into a nurturing environment at a young enough age, most become attached to their caretakers and grow into well-adjusted adults.

For more on attachment, see Interactive Segment 10.3, titled "Learning to Solve Problems."

The Day-Care Controversy

When you were a young child, did someone other than a parent care for you during the day? Of the three students we described at the beginning of this chapter, only one—Katja—had a stay-at-home parent. Perhaps, like Enrique, a grandparent or other relative helped care for you or, like Ramona, you were in a day-care center (Figure 10.24). Indeed, over half of American preschoolers are regularly cared for during the day by someone other than a parent, and most who enter day care do so before age 1 (Brooks-Gunn et al., 2002). High-quality day care provides a stimulating environment with well-trained caretakers, few children per caretaker, and low staff turnover, whereas poor day care does not. But in either case, many parents worry about how day care will affect their child's development. Thirty years of research—mostly in North America, Sweden, and other European countries—suggests some interesting conclusions.

- *Attachment.* Overall, as measured by the strange-situation procedure, high-quality day care does not seem to disrupt infants' or very young children's attachment to their parents, even when they attend for many hours a week (National Institute of Child Health and Human Development [NICHD], 2001b). Poor-quality day care has impaired attachment in some studies but not others. When several negative factors combine—the day care is poor, the child spends many hours there, and parents are not sensitive to the child at home—the risk of insecure attachment increases (NICHD, 2001b; Sagi et al., 2002).
- *Social skills.* When researchers observed them at age 3, children with more experience in day-care settings where other children are present and those whose caregivers are responsive and sensitive, tend to display better social skills when interacting with peers at day care. But day-care experience does not seem to carry over, positively or negatively, to playing with friends outside of day care (NICHD, 2001a).
- *Longer-term effects.* Infants and preschoolers from low-income families who receive high-quality day care tend to be better adjusted socially and perform better in elementary school than their peers who either receive poor-quality day care or do not attend day care (Scarr, 1998). For infants and preschoolers from middle- and upper-income homes, their day-care experience—regardless of quality—seems to have little carryover effect to their elementary school years. The quality of their family relationship, rather than whether they are in day care, is the better predictor of social adjustment and academic performance in school.

Concerns about disrupted parent-child relations also surface when parents divorce. Recall that Enrique experienced his parent's divorce when he was 4 years old. Our *Applying Psychological Science* feature examines this societally important issue.

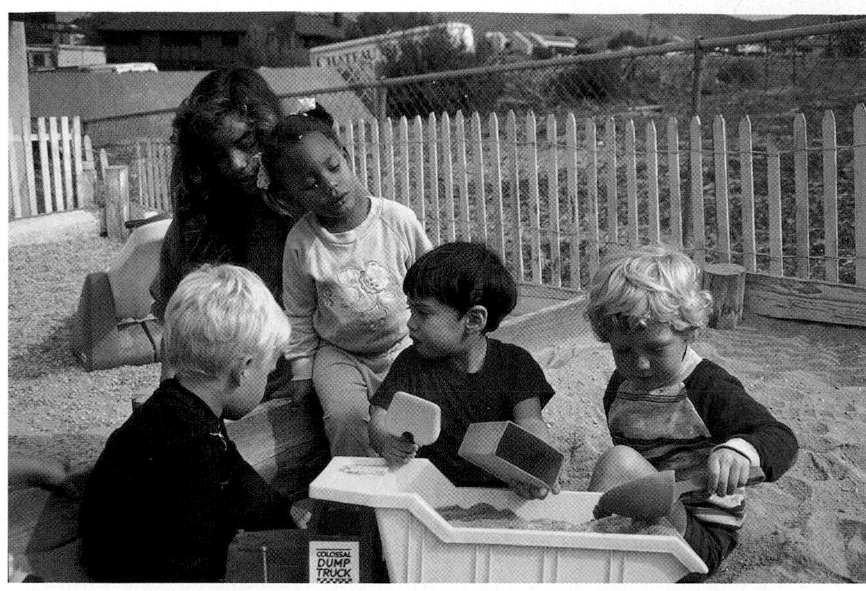

FIGURE 10.24

Over half of American preschoolers are cared for during the day by someone other than a parent.

▶ 10. How do day care, divorce, and remarriage affect children's development?

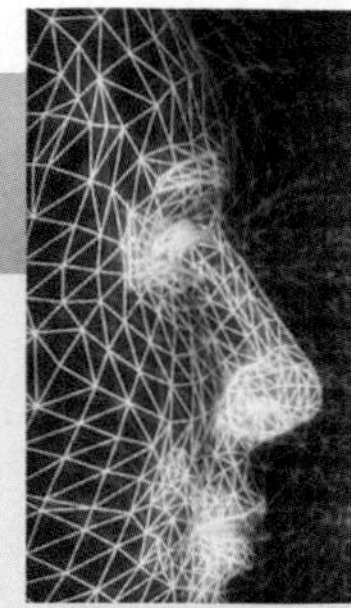

APPLYING PSYCHOLOGICAL SCIENCE

UNDERSTANDING HOW DIVORCE AND REMARRIAGE AFFECT CHILDREN

Divorce is more common in many countries than it was half a century ago, and it creates a stressful life transition for parents and their children. Because most divorced parents remarry, they and their children also experience a second major transition: becoming part of a stepfamily. In the United States, about half of children from divorced families have to adjust to a stepfamily within only 4 years after their parents' divorce.

Decades ago, there was little scientific information on children of divorce and remarriage, but research now provides us with a better understanding of how these major events affect children. With this knowledge, local governments in over 35 American states now require soon-to-be-divorced parents to take special classes that focus on helping children cope with divorce.

How Does Divorce Affect Children?

Many children report that parental divorce is one of the most painful experiences of their lives. In the short term, they may experience anxiety, fear, anger, confusion, and depression; regress to immature forms of behavior; and develop behavior problems at school.

In the long term, children of divorce remain at greater risk for a variety of difficulties, including academic problems, troubled relationships with family members and peers, low self-esteem, and depression (Reifman et al., 2001). When they become adolescents, children of divorced parents are more likely to disengage themselves from their family (or stepfamily), spending as little time at home as possible. They also are more likely to drop out of school, be unemployed, use drugs, have sex at an earlier age, and become unmarried teen parents. In adulthood, they display poorer problem-solving skills during marital interactions, experience more marital conflict, and have a higher divorce rate (Teachman, 2002).

Most of these problems, however, are interrelated; they tend to cluster together into an overall pattern of "maladjustment." Leading divorce researcher E. Mavis Hetherington and coworkers (1998) estimate that about 20 to 25 percent of children in divorced families, versus 10 percent of children in nondivorced families, experience this cluster of problems. This is a significantly elevated risk for maladjustment, but still, most children of divorced parents do not experience these long-term effects. Rather they grow up to be normally adjusted adults. Moreover, it appears that children's age at the time of divorce is only weakly related to how well they ultimately cope (Hetherington et al., 1998).

Should We Stay Together "For the Sake of the Child"?

Many parents considering divorce wonder whether they should stay together for the child's sake. The answer depends on the amount of conflict present in the marriage. Reviewing 92 studies, Paul Amato and Bruce Keith (1991) found that children living with married but contentious parents had poorer school achievement, lower self-esteem, and more behavior problems than children from divorced families and children from intact families with low parental conflict. When divorce ends a highly conflicted marriage, children's psychological adjustment typically benefits in the long run. But many unhappy marriages do not involve extensive conflict, and in those cases divorce usually puts children at greater risk for maladjustment (Booth & Amato, 2001).

How Can Divorced Parents Help Their Children?

The major factor affecting a child's adjustment to divorce is the quality of life within the postdivorce family, and it often takes a few years for divorced parents and children to redevelop stable family relationships. The period during and after divorce can intensify parents' anger and conflicts. By fighting over their children or trying to enlist them in loyalty battles, parents can damage their children's well-being. In contrast, cooperative and amicable parental behaviors can cushion the negative effects of divorce during this rocky transition (Hetherington & Stanley-Hagan, 2002). By remaining emotionally close to the children, the parent who does not have custody (usually the father) can help them adjust to living with the custodial parent (Marsiglio et al., 2000). For children, the lasting problems of divorce often lie in a disruption of parenting that follows marital breakdown, in lingering conflicts between parents, in economic hardships that parents—especially mothers—often experience after divorce, and in other factors that impair parents' ability to stabilize their own lives.

How Do Children Respond to Remarriage and Stepfamilies?

Loving stepfamilies in which children develop close relationships with their new stepparent and stepsiblings are to be admired, because it is more difficult to make a stepfamily function well than a nondivorced family. When one or both spouses bring children from a previous marriage with them, the odds of remarriage ending in divorce may increase by as much as 50 percent (Tzeng & Mare, 1995).

Forming a stepfamily requires new adaptations, temporarily disrupts children's relationships with the remarried custodial parent, and typically increases children's short-term problem behaviors (Hetherington & Stanley-Hagan, 2002). It can take several years for parents and children to adjust to their new roles within the stepfamily. In general, young adolescents seem to have the most difficulty coping with the transition into a stepfamily.

In remarriages, children may be hostile and reject the stepparent, especially when the stepparent attempts to be a strong disciplinarian. Research suggests that children usually adjust better to living in a stepfamily when discipline is handled in the following way. First, the custodial parent is warm but firm and has primary responsibility for discipline. Second, the stepparent is warm toward the child but supports the custodial parent's authority (Bray & Berger, 1993).

Styles of Parenting

Beyond divorce and remarriage, how do different child-rearing practices affect children's development in general? After studying how parents interacted with their preschool children, Diana Baumrind (1967) identified two key dimensions of parental behavior. The first is *warmth versus hostility*. Warm parents communicate love and caring for the child and respond with sensitivity to the child's feelings. Hostile parents express rejection and behave as if they do not care about the child. The second dimension is *restrictiveness versus permissiveness*. Parents differ in the extent to which they make and enforce rules, place demands on children, and discipline children. As Figure 10.25 shows, combining these dimensions yields four parenting styles that are associated with different patterns of child development (Ainsworth, 1989; Baumrind, 1991; Linver et al., 2002).

Authoritative parents *are controlling but warm*. They establish clear rules, consistently enforce them, and reward children's compliance with warmth and affection. They communicate high expectations, caring, and support. This style is associated with the most positive childhood outcomes. Children with authoritative parents tend to have higher self-esteem, are higher achievers in school, have fewer conduct problems, and are more considerate of others.

▶ 11. Identify parenting styles and their associated child outcomes. How do parenting and children's heredity interact?

	Warmth/acceptance	Hostility/rejection
Restrictive	**Authoritative** Demanding, but caring; good child-parent communication	**Authoritarian** Assertion of parental power without warmth
Permissive	**Indulgent** Warm toward child, but lax in setting limits	**Neglecting** Indifferent and uninvolved with child

FIGURE 10.25

Combining two basic dimensions of parental behavior (warmth-hostility and restrictiveness-permissiveness) yields four different styles of child rearing. SOURCE: Adapted from Maccoby & Martin, 1983.

Authoritarian parents *also exert control but do so within a cold, unresponsive, or rejecting relationship*. Their children tend to have lower self-esteem, be less popular with peers, and perform more poorly in school than children with authoritative parents.

Indulgent parents *have warm, caring relationships with their children but do not provide the guidance and discipline that help children learn responsibility and concern for others*. Their children tend to be more immature and self-centered.

Neglectful parents *provide neither warmth nor rules nor guidance*. Their children are most likely to be insecurely attached, to have low achievement motivation and disturbed peer relationships, and to be impulsive and aggressive. Neglectful parenting is associated with the most negative developmental outcomes.

Do these findings extend to adolescence? Laurence Steinberg and coworkers (1994) studied several thousand high school students in California and Wisconsin. Consistent with earlier research, they found that authoritative parenting generally was associated with the most positive developmental outcomes among adolescents and that neglectful parenting was associated with the poorest outcomes. Many of the findings held true across African American, Asian American, Caucasian American, and Hispanic American students (Lamborn et al., 1991).

Parenting-Heredity Interactions

Keep in mind that parent-child influences are bidirectional, illustrating once again the interaction of biology and environment in shaping behavior. For example, children whose biologically based temperament is irritable, hostile, and difficult tend to elicit harsher and less warm parenting behaviors, which in turn can further promote the child's difficult behavior. Also realize that parents do not mold their children's personality and behavior like lumps of clay. Parenting makes a difference, but the way children "turn out" also depends on their heredity, peer influences, other experiences, and interactions among these factors (Collins et al., 2000).

Consider two examples of how the family environment and heredity interact. In one study, biologically at-risk children (i.e., those with schizophrenic biological parents) who were placed into good adoptive homes were no more likely to develop various mental disorders in adulthood than adopted children who were not at biological risk (Tienari et al., 1994). But when the adoptive family environment was dysfunctional, the at-risk children later developed significantly more disorders than the children who were not at risk.

Now consider antisocial behavior. Children of a highly antisocial parent (i.e., a parent with high aggression, irritability, and a history of illegal activities) are at increased genetic risk for displaying antisocial behavior (e.g., lying, fighting, having a hot temper). This genetic risk is present, of course, even if the highly antisocial parent (usually the father) is completely absent from the home and the child is raised by the other parent. However, as Sara Jaffee and coworkers (2003) recently found in a study examining families with "high-antisocial" and "low-antisocial" fathers, when high-antisocial fathers lived at home and were involved in caretaking, this further increased children's antisocial behavior and their risk of developing a conduct disorder (Figure 10.26). In contrast, children with low-antisocial fathers tended to display, on average, less antisocial behavior when the father lived at home and was involved in caretaking. Jaffee and coworkers concluded that children of high-antisocial fathers who were involved in caretaking "received a 'double whammy' of genetic and environmental risk for conduct problems" (p. 109).

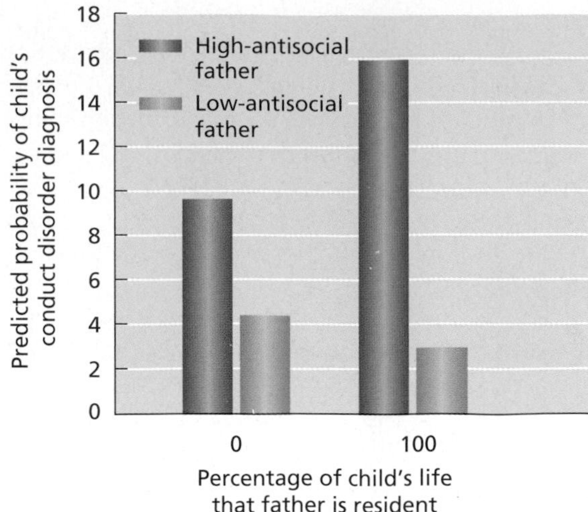

FIGURE 10.26

In this study, among children who had a "high-antisocial" father, the risk of developing a conduct disorder (e.g., aggression toward people and animals, property destruction, deceit, or theft) increased if the father lived at home with the mother and child. If the father was "low-antisocial," living at home slightly reduced the risk of developing a conduct disorder. Source: Adapted from Jaffee et al., 2003.

Gender Identity and Socialization

▶ 12. How does socialization influence children's beliefs about gender?

Parenting also influences children's development in other ways, such as helping children develop a **gender identity,** *a sense of "femaleness" or "maleness" that becomes a central aspect of one's personal identity*. Most children develop a basic gender identity between the ages of 2 and 3 and can label themselves (and others) as being either a boy or a girl, but their understanding of gender is still fragile. Just as young children often report that a cat wearing a dog mask has suddenly become a dog, they may believe that a boy wearing a dress is a girl and that a girl can grow up to become a man. **Gender constancy,** *which is the understanding that being male or female is a permanent part of a person*, develops around age 6 to 7 (Szkrybalo & Ruble, 1999).

As gender identity develops, children also acquire *sex-role stereotypes,* which are beliefs about the characteristics and behaviors that are appropriate for boys and girls to possess. Every group, including family and cultural groups, has norms that set standards for expected and accepted gender behavior. Parents, siblings, friends, the mass media, and other socializing agents convey these norms to us as we grow up. Ultimately, as we internalize these norms, they become part of our identity (Valsiner & Lawrence, 1997).

Sex-typing *involves treating others differently based on whether they are female or male*. From infancy onward, girls and boys are viewed and treated differently (Figure 10.27). Fathers use more physical and verbal prohibition with their 12-month-old sons than with their daughters, and they steer their sons away from activities that are considered stereotypically feminine (Snow et al., 1983). Even when their sons and daughters display equal interest and aptitude in science, fathers and mothers are more likely to believe that sons have the greater interest and will find science easier (Tenenbaum & Leaper, 2003). Indeed, as Figure 10.28 shows, when parents interact with their 1- to 8-year-olds at science exhibits in a children's museum, they are much more likely to explain the exhibits to their sons than to their daughters—even though the children rarely ask for such explanations (Crowley et al., 2001).

Sex-role stereotypes are also transmitted through observational learning and operant conditioning. Children observe parents, other adults, peers, and television and movie characters, and often attempt to emulate what they see (Bandura, 1965). In ways obvious and subtle, others approve of us and reinforce our behavior when we meet their expectations and disapprove of us when we don't. In turn, this influences the way children think about gender. Some children as young as 2 to 3 years of age display sex-role stereotypes in their ability to identify objects, such as hammers and brooms, as "belonging with" one gender or the other (Fagot et al., 1992). By age 7 or 8, stereotyped thinking is firmly in place; children believe that boys and girls possess different personality traits and should hold different occupations as adults (Miller & Budd, 1999).

As children enter junior high school, they often display more flexible thinking about gender. Some come to believe that traditionally masculine and feminine traits can be blended within a single person—what is called an *androgynous gender identity*—as when a person is both assertive and compassionate. During junior high and high school, some adolescents maintain this view, but overall, gender stereotypes seem to become a little more rigid at this age, so that by early adulthood most people continue to adhere to relatively traditional beliefs (Alfieri et al., 1996).

For a self-test on gender roles and characteristics, see Interactive Segment 10.4.

Moral Development

All societies have norms of moral conduct, and a major goal of socialization is to help children recognize right from wrong and become moral adults. How does children's moral thinking change as they grow older?

Moral Thinking

Drawing upon Piaget's cognitive stage model, Lawrence Kohlberg (1963, 1984) developed an influential theory of moral reasoning. He presented children, adolescents, and adults with hypothetical moral dilemmas such as the following:

> Heinz's wife was dying from cancer. There was a rare drug that might save her, but the druggist who made the drug for $200 would not sell it for less than $2,000. Heinz tried hard, but he could only raise $1,000. The druggist refused to give Heinz the drug for that price even though Heinz promised to pay the rest later. So Heinz broke into the store to steal the drug. What do you think? Should Heinz have stolen the drug? Why or why not?

Kohlberg was interested not in whether people agreed or disagreed with Heinz's behavior but rather in the *reasons for their judgment.* He analyzed responses to various moral dilemmas and identified three main levels of moral reasoning, with two substages within each level (Table 10.3).

Preconventional moral reasoning *is based on anticipated punishments or rewards.* Consider reasons given for stealing the drug. In stage 1,

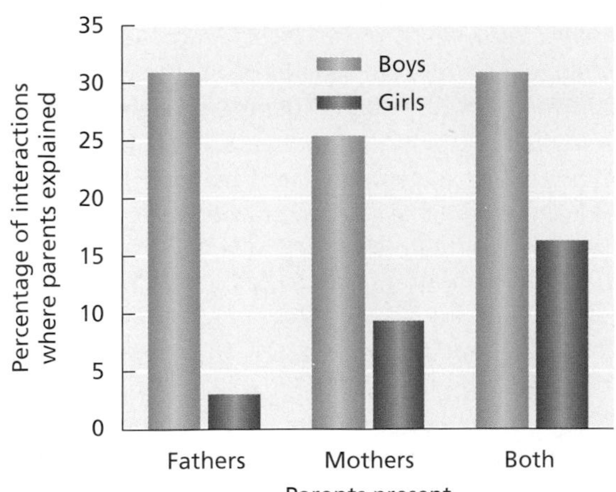

FIGURE 10.28

Fathers and mothers provided more explanations to their 1- to 8-year-old sons than to their daughters while engaged with science exhibits at a children's museum. Similar results were obtained regardless of the children's age. Source: Adapted from Crowley et al., 2001.

FIGURE 10.27

In subtle and not so subtle ways, cultures socialize most female and male children in gender-stereotypic ways.

13. Describe Kohlberg's model of moral thinking and factors that influence the development of moral behavior.

TABLE 10.3 Kohlberg's Stages of Moral Reasoning

Level of Moral Reasoning	Basis for Judging What Is Moral
Level 1: Preconventional Morality	**Actual or anticipated punishments or rewards, rather than internalized values**
Stage 1: Punishment-obedience orientation	Obeying rules and avoiding punishment
Stage 2: Instrumental-hedonistic orientation	Self-interest and gaining rewards
Level 2: Conventional Morality	**Conformity to the expectations of social groups; person adopts other people's values**
Stage 3: Good-child orientation	Gaining approval and maintaining good relationships with others
Stage 4: Law-and-order orientation	Doing one's duty, showing respect for authority, and maintaining social order
Level 3: Postconventional Morality	**Moral principles that have been internalized as part of one's belief and value system**
Stage 5: Social-contract orientation	General principles agreed upon by society that foster community welfare and individual rights; recognition that society can decide to modify laws that lose their social utility
Stage 6: Universal ethical principles	Abstract ethical principles based on justice and equality; following one's conscience

SOURCE: Adapted from Kohlberg, 1984.

children focus on punishment: "Heinz should steal the drug because if he lets his wife die he'll get into trouble." In stage 2, morality is judged by anticipated rewards and doing what is in the person's own interest: "Heinz should steal the drug because that way he'll still have his wife with him."

Conventional moral reasoning *is based on conformity to social expectations, laws, and duties.* In stage 3, conformity stems from the desire to gain people's approval: "People will think that Heinz is bad if he doesn't steal the drug to save his wife." In stage 4, children believe that laws and duties must be obeyed simply because rules are meant to be followed. Thus: "Heinz should steal the drug because it's his duty to take care of his wife."

Postconventional moral reasoning *is based on well thought out, general moral principles.* Stage 5 involves recognizing the importance of societal laws but also taking individual rights into account: "Stealing breaks the law, but what Heinz did was reasonable because he saved a life." In stage 6, morality is based on abstract, ethical principles of justice that are viewed as universal: "Saving life comes before financial gain, even if the person is a stranger."

Kohlberg believed that progress in moral reasoning depends on cognitive maturation and the opportunity to confront moral issues, particularly when such issues can be discussed with someone who is at a higher stage of development.

Culture, Gender, and Moral Reasoning

From North, Central, and South America to Africa, Asia, Europe, and India, studies of moral reasoning indicate that, overall:

- from childhood through adolescence, moral reasoning changes from preconventional to conventional levels;
- in adolescence and even in adulthood, postconventional reasoning is relatively uncommon; and
- a person's moral judgments do not always reflect the same level or stage within levels (Eckensberger & Zimba, 1997).

Research also finds that postconventional reasoning occurs more often among people from Westernized countries than among people from developing countries. Critics, however, claim that Kohlberg's theory has a Western cultural bias. Fairness and justice are Kohlberg's postconventional ideals, but in many cultures the highest moral values focus on principles that do not fit easily into Kohlberg's model, such as respect for all animal life, collective harmony, and respect for the elderly (Iwasa, 2001). Thus when people from other cultures provide answers to

Kohlberg's dilemmas that invoke such concepts, their level of reasoning may be scored as lower than it actually is.

Carol Gilligan (1982) argues that Kohlberg's emphasis on "justice" also reflects a male bias. She claims that highly moral women place greater value than men do on caring and responsibility for others' welfare. Overall, however, evidence of gender bias is mixed, and most cross-cultural studies find that women and men display similar levels of moral reasoning (Eckensberger & Zimba, 1997). Women use justice reasoning when the situation calls for it, and men use reasoning based on caring and relationships when appropriate. Nevertheless, Gilligan's analysis reinforces the key point that high-level moral reasoning can be based on values other than "justice" (Gump et al., 2000).

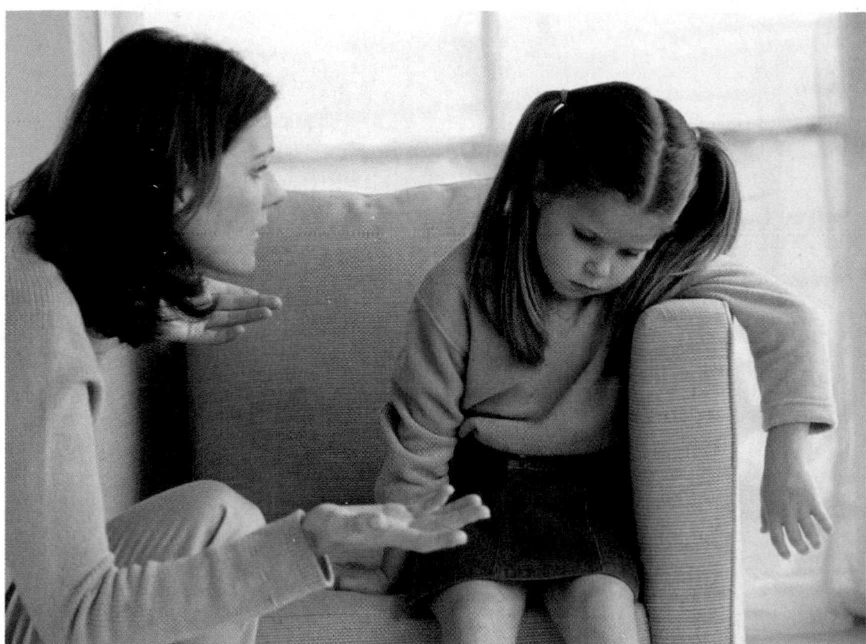

FIGURE 10.29

By firmly but not harshly signaling that this child's behavior was wrong and by explaining why it was wrong, a parent can help a child internalize moral values. The fact that the child experiences a negative emotion may be important to the internalization process.

Moral Behavior and Conscience

In addition to studying children's ability to reason about moral problems, psychologists also study how children develop the ability to act morally. B. F. Skinner (1971) proposed that we learn which behaviors and values are "good" and "bad" through their association with reinforcement and punishment. Other researchers propose that for children to conform to standards of moral behavior in their particular culture, they must come to understand that there are indeed moral rules, be able to control their impulses to engage in forbidden behavior, and experience some negative emotion when they violate these rules (Figure 10.29).

By the age of 2, children come to understand that there are rules for behavior, and their emotional expressions (such as when they believe that they have broken a doll) suggest that they experience guilt when they break a known rule. Although children's ability to stop themselves from engaging in forbidden behavior develops slowly over time, even toddlers can stop themselves from engaging in forbidden activities (Kochanska et al., 1997). This internal regulatory mechanism, often referred to as *conscience,* tends to restrain individuals from acting in destructive or antisocial ways when they are not being monitored by parents or other adults (Kochanska & Murray, 2000).

Sigmund Freud (1935) believed that children develop a moral conscience by identifying with their parents. Few developmentalists believe in Freud's theory of how identification occurs (which we will discuss in Chapter 11), but they widely acknowledge that internalizing societal values—as transmitted by parents or other caretakers—forms the basis of a moral conscience.

Children are most likely to internalize parents' values when they have a positive relationship with them, when parents establish clear rules and provide explanations that facilitate children's awareness of parental values, and when discipline is firm but not harsh (Laible & Thompson, 2000). Coercive discipline may raise children's arousal to the point where they may not be able to discern their parents' values and instead focus on their own upset feelings (Hoffman, 1994).

Children's temperament also enters into the picture. Fearful, inhibited children tend to internalize parental values more easily and at an earlier age than less fearful children, particularly when their parents provide gentle discipline (Fowles & Kochanska, 2000). For relatively fearless, uninhibited children, however, whether discipline is gentle or harsh is less important than having a secure attachment with warm, responsive parents. A secure attachment, rather than fear of punishment, appears to motivate fearless children to internalize their parent's standards. In sum, the development of moral behavior is linked not only to children's moral thinking but also to their emotional development, attachment, and temperament.

IN REVIEW

- *Although nearsighted, newborns can distinguish between different visual patterns, sounds, odors, and tastes. They display perceptual preferences, can learn through classical and operant conditioning, and have a primitive capacity for imitation.*
- *The cephalocaudal principle reflects the tendency for development to proceed in a head-to-foot direction. The proximodistal principle states that development begins along the innermost parts of the body and continues toward the outermost parts.*
- *According to Piaget, cognitive development depends on processes of assimilation and accommodation and occurs in four stages: sensorimotor, preoperational, concrete operational, and formal operational.*
- *Although the general cognitive abilities associated with Piaget's four stages occur in the same order across cultures, cognitive development is more complex and variable than Piaget believed. Vygotsky emphasized the sociocultural context of cognitive development. Each child has a zone of proximal development, reflecting the difference between what a child can do independently and what the child can do with assistance from others.*
- *Information-processing capacities improve with age. Older children search for information more systematically, process it more quickly, and display better memory.*
- *Children display more types and greater complexity of emotions as they age. The strategies that they use to regulate their emotions also become more varied.*
- *Temperament reflects a biologically based pattern of reacting emotionally and behaviorally to the environment. Extreme temperamental styles in infancy and childhood can predict some aspects of functioning years later.*
- *Erikson believed that personality development proceeds through eight major psychosocial stages. Each stage involves a major crisis, and the way we resolve it influences our ability to meet the challenges of the next stage.*
- *Infant-caretaker attachment develops in three phases, and infants experience periods of stranger and separation anxiety. Secure attachment is associated with better developmental outcomes than is insecure attachment. For most children, day care does not disrupt attachment. Divorce typically disrupts children's short-term psychological adjustment; for some, it is associated with a long-term pattern of maladjustment.*
- *Parenting styles vary along dimensions of warmth-hostility and restrictiveness-permissiveness. The children of authoritative parents generally display the best developmental outcomes. Gender identity begins to form early in childhood, and socialization influences children's acquisition of sex-role stereotypes.*
- *Kohlberg proposed that moral reasoning proceeds through preconventional, conventional, and postconventional levels. The development of moral behavior is linked to children's cognitive, emotional, and social development.*

ADOLESCENCE

> We call it Sunrise Dance. It's the biggest ceremony of the White Mountain Apache—when a girl passes from childhood to womanhood. . . . On Friday evening Godmother dressed me . . . Saturday is like an endurance test. Men begin prayer chants at dawn. Godmother tells me to dance. . . . When the time comes for running, I go fast around a sacred cane. . . . Next, my father pours candies and corn kernels over me to protect me from famine. My Godfather directs my dancing on Sunday. . . . Godfather paints me. . . . On Monday there is more visiting and blessing. (Quintero, 1980, pp. 262–271)

In some cultures, ceremonies like the Sunrise Dance represent *rites of passage* that mark a

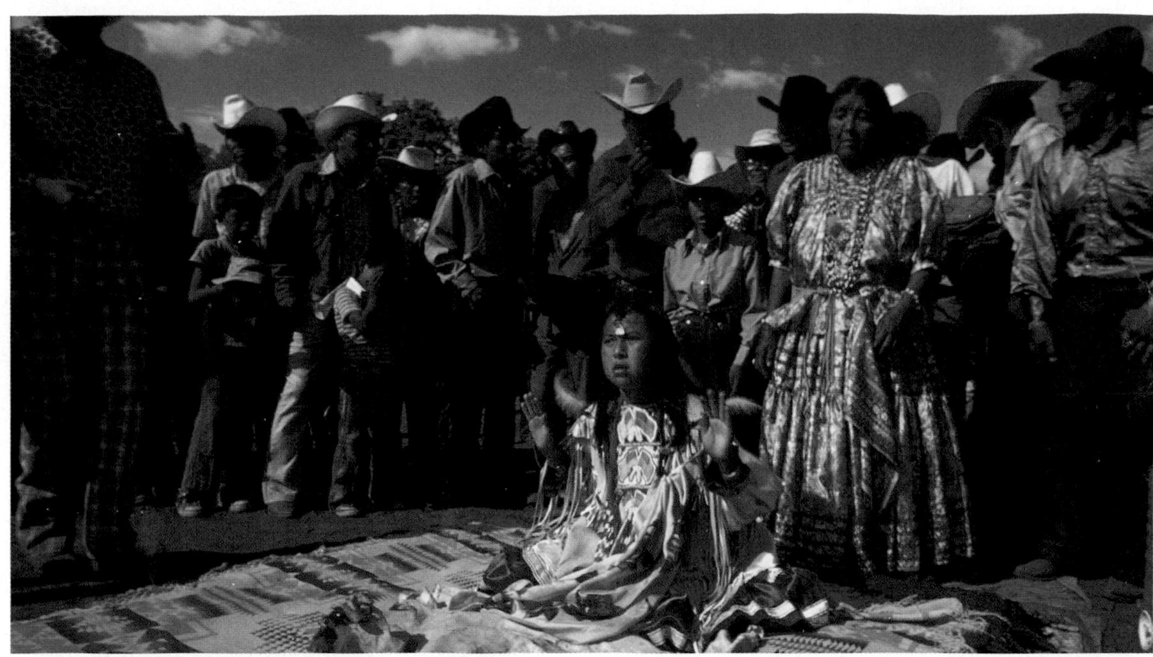

FIGURE 10.30

A White Mountain Apache girl participates in the Sunrise Dance, a four-day ceremony that initiates her into womanhood.

transition from childhood into adulthood status (Figure 10.30). But what of *adolescence,* the well-known period between childhood and adulthood? Alice Schlegel and Herbert Barry (1991) found that among almost 200 nonindustrial societies worldwide, nearly all recognize some type of transition period between childhood and adulthood. Yet in many societies this period is brief and is not marked by a special term analogous to *adolescence.*

As we know it, the lengthy period called *adolescence* is largely an invention of 18th- to 20th-century Western culture (Valsiner & Lawrence, 1997). In preindustrial times, biological maturity was a major criterion for adult status. In many cultures, for example, girls were expected to marry once they became capable of bearing children. But as the Industrial Revolution brought new technology and a need for more schooling, recognition of adult status was delayed and the long transition period of adolescence evolved.

Physical Development

Adolescence begins at **puberty,** *a period of rapid maturation in which the person becomes capable of sexual reproduction.* Compared to infancy and early childhood, overall brain growth slows dramatically from late childhood to adolescence (Sowell et al., 2001). However, when the brain's hypothalamus signals the pituitary gland to increase its hormonal secretions, marked bodily changes occur. Pituitary hormones stimulate other glands, speeding up maturation of the *primary sex characteristics* (the sex organs involved in reproduction). Hormonal changes also produce *secondary sex characteristics* (nonreproductive physical features, such as breasts in girls and facial hair in boys).

The pubertal landmark in girls is *menarche,* the first menstrual flow. For boys, it is the production of sperm and the first ejaculation. In North America and Europe, these events occur most often around age 12 or 13 for girls and 14 for boys, but variations occur across cultures. In parts of New Guinea, for example, 50 percent of girls have their first menstrual period after they turn 17 (Roche, 1979).

The physical changes of puberty have psychological consequences. For one thing, hormones that steer puberty also can affect mood and behavior. Reactions to puberty are also influenced by whether it occurs early or late. Overall, early maturation tends to be associated with more positive outcomes for boys than for girls. Early-maturing boys acquire physical strength and size, facilitating their success in athletics and other physical activities that contribute to a male's popularity and positive body image (Sigelman & Shaffer, 1991). In contrast, although some early-maturing girls welcome their mature appearance, the weight gain that comes with adolescence results in a negative body image for others (Striegel-Moore et al., 2001). Early-maturing girls are more likely than girls who mature later to feel self-conscious about their bodies, which

▶ 14. Describe psychological consequences of puberty and cognitive changes that occur during adolescence.

FIGURE 10.31

(a) When adolescents attain formal operational thought, they can use deductive reasoning to solve scientific problems systematically. (b) The materials for the pendulum problem used by Inhelder and Piaget include an adjustable string and a set of weights. The problem is to determine what factors influence how long it takes the pendulum to move through its arc. String length is the only relevant factor: The shorter the string, the less time it takes the pendulum to swing back and forth. SOURCE: Adapted from Inhelder & Piaget, 1958.

(a)

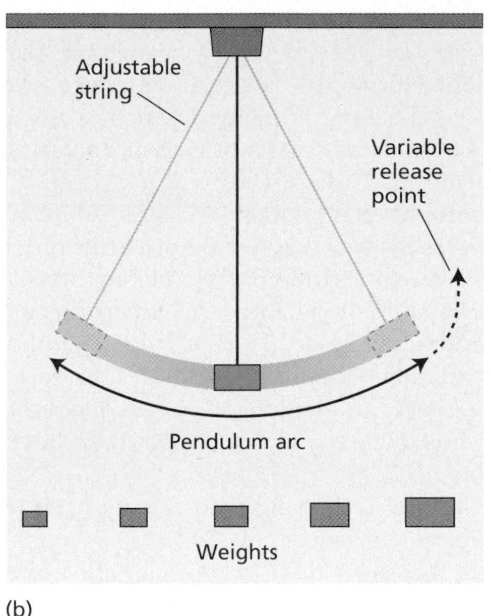

(b)

may lead to the development of eating disorders, problems in school, and psychological distress (Ge et al., 1996).

Cognitive Development

Cognitive changes during adolescence can be as dramatic as physical ones. Many teenagers acquire a new maturity that enables them to reason abstractly and reflect more deeply on their own and others' thoughts.

Abstract Reasoning Abilities

Recall Piaget's (1926, 1970) belief that the final stage of cognitive development, formal operational thinking, is attained during adolescence. Adolescents can more easily contemplate abstract and hypothetical issues, ranging from scientific problems to questions about social justice and the meaning of life (Figure 10.31a). They reason more flexibly than concrete thinkers and use both the deductive and inductive problem-solving methods described in Chapter 8.

Consider the pendulum problem in Figure 10.31b. Which variable(s)—length of string, weight of object, how hard it is pushed, and release point (height in the arc)—influence(s) how quickly the pendulum oscillates? This problem is best solved by forming and testing an organized set of deductive hypotheses (e.g., "*If* string length is a factor, *then* the swing time with a short versus long string should differ"). Concrete operational children find this task difficult (Inhelder & Piaget, 1958). For example, when they adjust the string length they often adjust the weight as well, making it impossible to draw a conclusion about either variable. In contrast, adolescents think more systematically and manipulate one variable at a time while holding the others constant.

The capacity for abstract reasoning increases substantially during adolescence (Chapell & Overton, 1998). Still, task performance depends partially on exposure to scientific-abstract tasks through schooling or direct experience. Moreover, even with schooling, many teens (and adults) struggle at formal operational tasks.

For more on formal operational thought, see Interactive Segment 10.1.

Social Thinking

Does Figure 10.32 strike a familiar chord? Teenagers can spend a lot of time thinking about themselves and their social circumstances. Such thinking, argues David Elkind (1967), often reflects **adolescent egocentrism,** *a self-absorbed and distorted view of one's uniqueness and importance*. Elkind proposes that adolescent egocentrism has two main parts. First, adolescents often overestimate the uniqueness of their feelings and experiences, which Elkind calls the *personal fable*. Examples would be, "My parents can't possibly understand how I really feel" and "Nobody's ever felt love as deeply as ours." Second, many adolescents feel that they are always "on stage" and that "everybody's going to notice" how they look and what they do. Elkind calls this oversensitivity to social evaluation the *imaginary audience*.

ZITS By Jerry Scott and Jim Borgman

FIGURE 10.32

According to David Elkind (1967), this type of thinking reflects adolescent egocentrism. © Zits Partnership. Reprinted with Special Permission of King Features Syndicate.

Adolescents who think more egocentrically are somewhat more likely to engage in risky behaviors, due perhaps in part to a sense of invulnerability (Greene et al., 2000). At the same time, it's not clear that this self-consciousness truly reflects a thinking bias or is restricted to teens. Some theorists view teens' greater self-reflection as a natural outgrowth of the search for individuality and independence, and they suggest that young adults, overall, can be just as self-absorbed as adolescents (Frankenberger, 2000; Vartanian, 2000).

Social-Emotional and Personality Development

G. Stanley Hall (1904), the first psychologist to study adolescence, viewed it as a time of "storm and stress." Indeed, as they cross the bridge between childhood and adulthood, adolescents may grapple with many difficult issues. Yet, although some experience adolescence as a period of conflict, others find it to be a positive period of life. Thus, Jeffrey Arnett proposes a modified view of storm and stress (1999, p. 317), noting that "not all adolescents experience storm and stress, but storm and stress is more likely during adolescence than at other ages."

The Search for Identity

"Who am I?" "What do I believe in?" Erik Erikson (1968) proposed that such questions reflect the pivotal crisis of adolescent personality development: *identity versus role confusion* (see Table 10.2, p. 389). Erikson believed that an adolescent's "identity crisis" (a term he coined) can be resolved positively, leading to a stable sense of identity, or it can end negatively, leading to confusion over one's identity and values.

Building upon Erikson's work, James Marcia (1966, 1994) studied adolescents' and young adults' search for identity. Marcia classified the "identity status" of each person as follows:

- *Identity diffusion.* These teens and adults had not yet gone through an identity crisis. They seemed unconcerned or even cynical about identity issues and were not committed to a coherent set of values.
- *Foreclosure.* These individuals had not yet gone through an identity crisis either but for a different reason: They committed to an identity and set of values before experiencing a crisis. For example, some automatically adopted peer group or parental values without giving these values much thought.
- *Moratorium:* These people wanted to establish a clear identity, were currently experiencing a crisis, but had not yet resolved it.
- *Identity achievement:* These individuals had gone through an identity crisis, successfully resolved it, and emerged with a coherent set of values.

Marcia found that most young adolescents are in identity diffusion or foreclosure; they have not experienced an identity crisis. But during the teen years, people typically begin to think more deeply about who they are, or they reconsider values they have adopted prematurely. This often leads to an identity crisis, and over half successfully resolve it by young adulthood.

▶ 15. Discuss adolescents' search for identity and the general nature of their relationships with parents and peers.

Identity, of course, is not a simple concept, and our sense of identity has multiple components (Camilleri & Malewska-Peyre, 1997). These include (1) our gender, ethnicity, and other attributes by which we define ourselves as members

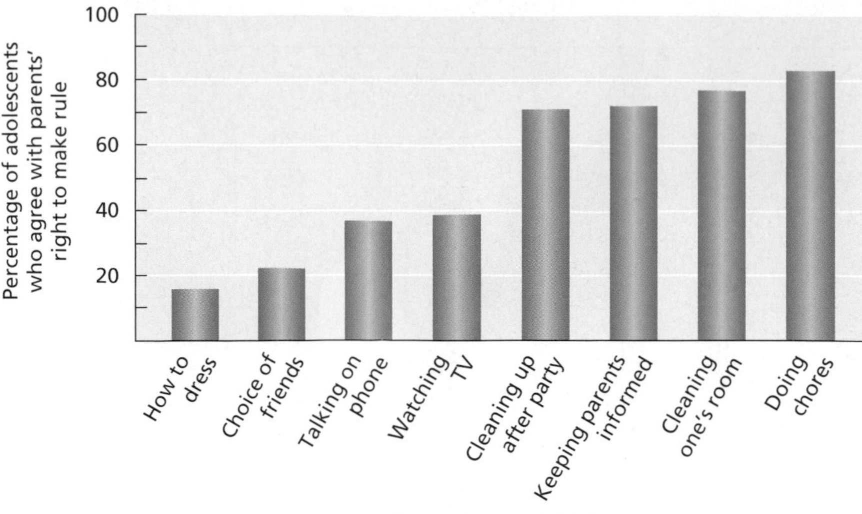

FIGURE 10.33

Using a questionnaire developed by Judy Smetana (1988), Andrew Fuligni found that the percentage of teenagers who agree that their parents have the right to make the rules depends on the particular issue. SOURCE: Based on Fuligni, 1998.

of social groups ("daughter," "student," "athlete"); (2) how we view our personal characteristics ("shy," "friendly"); and (3) our goals and values pertaining to areas we view as important, such as family and peer relations, career, and so forth. Typically, we achieve a stable identity regarding some components before others. And even after an identity crisis has been resolved, changing situations may trigger new crises and cause us to reevaluate prior goals and values.

Culture plays a key role in identity formation, one that goes beyond the simple idea that we view ourselves as belonging to certain cultural groups. Our cultural upbringing influences the very way we view concepts such as "self" and "identity." Having grown up in an individualistic culture, my sense of identity assumes that I am an autonomous individual with clear boundaries separating me from other people. But in collectivistic cultures, the concept of "self" is traditionally based more strongly on the interdependence and connectedness between people (Kagitçibasi, 1997). Thus the question "Who am I?" is more likely to be answered in ways that reflect a person's relationships with family members, friends, and others.

Relationships With Parents

When it comes to teenagers' relationships with parents, is "storm and stress" the rule or the exception? In a national survey conducted during the socially turbulent 1970s, 56 percent of American teens reported getting along "very well" with their parents and 41 percent reported getting along "fairly well" (Gallup Organization, 1988). More recent studies of American, Chinese, Dutch, and other families also suggest that storm and stress is less prevalent than commonly assumed (Chen et al., 1998). Even when conflict is moderately frequent, its intensity is usually mild.

Consider a study by Andrew Fuligni (1998) involving 1,341 female and male American students in 6th, 8th, and 10th grades. They came from immigrant and native-born families of Mexican, Chinese, Filipino, and European ancestry. Fuligni found that among all four ethnic groups,

- adolescents agreed with their parents' right to "make the rules" more strongly on some issues than others (Figure 10.33); and
- older adolescents felt it was less appropriate for parents to make the rules.

So what about actual conflicts with parents? Fuligni found that overall,

- there was somewhat more conflict with mothers than fathers; but
- regardless of adolescents' gender, ethnic group, or age, conflict was low with *both* mothers and fathers.

Of course, some parents and teenagers do struggle a lot, and parent-teen conflict is correlated with other signs of distress. Chuansheng Chen and coworkers (1998) studied 7th- and 8th-graders from America, Taiwan, and China. Among the 600 participants, parent-teen conflict was generally low in each cultural group, but young teens who reported more conflict had higher levels of school misconduct (e.g., cheating, skipping school) and more antisocial behavior (e.g., getting into fistfights, damaging property). Teens who report having more conflict with parents also experience greater hopelessness, lower self-esteem, and less life satisfaction (Shek, 1998). Recalling the principle that correlation does not equal causation, we must consider that although parent-teen conflict may be a cause of teens' psychological problems, it also is likely to be caused *by* such problems.

Peer Relationships

Peer relationships increase in importance during adolescence. From Alabama to the Arctic, teens like to spend time hanging out with friends.

According to some studies, adolescents spend more time with peers than doing almost anything else and tend to identify more with peers than with adults. But this pattern may be stronger in North America than in Europe or Asia, where people of all ages, teens included, generally place a relatively strong emphasis on family relationships (Chen et al., 1998).

Adolescent friendships are typically more intimate than those at previous ages and involve a greater sharing of problems. Perhaps one reason intimacy increases is that in choosing friends, adolescents (like older adults) tend to select peers who are similar to themselves (Iervolino et al., 2002). In turn, peer relationships facilitate the process of separating from parents and establishing one's own identity.

Peers can strongly influence a teenager's values and behaviors, and for some adolescents peer pressure increases the risk of misconduct, such as skipping school, damaging property, or disobeying parental rules. Fortunately, peer pressure *against* misconduct typically has an even stronger effect, and closeness to parents is an added buffer that helps many teenagers resist peer pressure to do misdeeds (Chen et al., 1998). Despite increased peer influence on dress, hairstyles, and attitudes toward other people, parental influence remains high on issues of politics, religion, morality, and career decisions (Bachman et al., 1987). In these and other important areas, the so-called "generation gap" is narrower than we might assume.

Given the many life changes that occur during adolescence, how do children fare emotionally as they make the transition into and through the teenage years? Our *Research Close-Up* takes a look at this question.

▶ 16. How do emotions change during the teenage years? Why is this important?

RESEARCH CLOSE-UP

THE UPS AND DOWNS OF ADOLESCENCE: DOES EMOTION CHANGE DURING THE TEEN YEARS?

Background

How happy were you in late childhood? As a teenager progressing through high school, did you generally become more or less happy? The question of "stability versus change" is a central developmental issue, and this study by Reed Larson and coworkers used a powerful method to examine whether boys' and girls' typical daily emotions changed during the teenage years.

Method

At Time 1, participants were 328 randomly selected 5th- through 8th-graders (ages 10 to 14) from working- and middle-class suburban families living near Chicago. Students carried electronic pagers and paper booklets with them for 1 week, and the time of year that each student did this was randomly determined. From morning through evening, each student was beeped at a random time once during each 2-hour period. The students rated how happy or unhappy, cheerful or irritable, and friendly or angry they felt at that moment, using a +3 to −3 scale (with 0 = neutral) for each emotion. At the end of the week, students completed psychological tests that measured their general self-esteem and level of depression and the number of major stressful events they had experienced over the last 6 months.

At Time 2 (4 years later), this procedure was repeated. The participants were now 9th- through 12th-graders (ages 13 to 18), and 220 were still living in the area and able to complete the study.

Results

On average, students' emotions became less positive with age, with this downward trend leveling off in later adolescence (Figure 10.34). Girls of all ages generally reported slightly more positive emotions than boys, but both sexes showed a similar downward trend between early and late adolescence.

Although emotions became less positive overall, students' average ratings remained on the positive side of the scale. Comparing students' emotions at Time 1 versus Time 2 revealed that as they became older,

SOURCE: Reed W. Larson, Giovanni Moneta, Maryse H. Richards, and Suzanne Wilson (2002). Continuity, stability, and change in daily emotional experience across adolescence. *Child Development, 73,* 1151–1165.

Continued

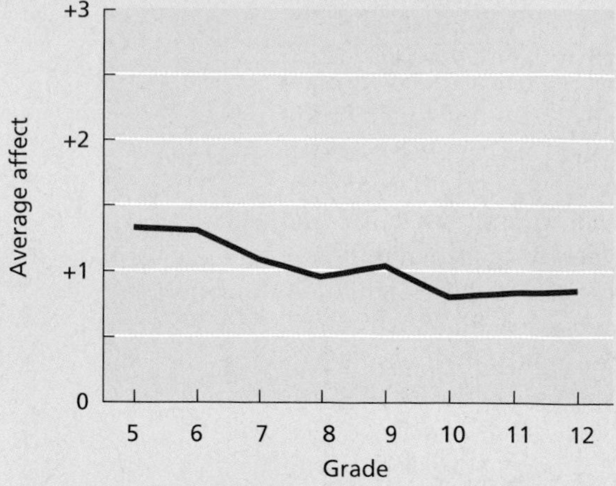

FIGURE 10.34

In this graph, the "0" (zero) point on the y-axis represents a neutral level of overall emotion. In general, students' emotions become less positive during early to middle adolescence and then level off in later adolescence. Source: Adapted from Larson et al., 2002.

- 34 percent showed a major downward change (more negative emotion), and 16 percent showed a major upward change (more positive emotion); and
- the remaining half of students showed a smaller amount of change in emotion, although once again, downward changes were twice as common as upward changes.

Finally, at both Time 1 and Time 2, students who reported less positive emotions tended to have lower self-esteem, higher depression scores, and a greater frequency of major stressful events over the preceding 6 months.

Discussion

Girls' and boys' daily emotional experience became less positive as they moved into and through early adolescence, with changes leveling off and emotion becoming more stable during late adolescence. These findings fit the modified storm-and-stress view of adolescence. Although emotions became less positive overall during the teen years, the typical amount of change was not great. One half of the teens studied showed a relatively small change in their general day-to-day emotionality, and one sixth even shifted substantially toward greater happiness. Still, we must remember that one third of the students reported substantially more negative emotion as they aged, and negative emotionality was related to more stressful life events, lower self-esteem, and greater depression.

Because emotions became more stable in later adolescence, a downward emotional shift during the early teen years may be especially significant. As the researchers note, "This suggests that individuals' baseline emotional states may be less easily changed after they pass early adolescence [and that] future efforts . . . need to focus on what factors account for the largest downturns in early adolescence and what can be done to avert them" (p. 1162). Perhaps averting emotional downturns early would help alleviate a growing problem of teen depression: The largest increase in the incidence of clinical depression occurs between 15 and 19 years of age (Hankin et al., 1998).

Finally, this study nicely illustrates a sequential research design. It combined a cross-sectional component (at each time period, four school grades were studied) with a longitudinal component (each participant was tested twice, 4 years apart). This allowed the researchers to compare different age groups with one another and to examine changes over time for each student. Moreover, rather than relying on students' memory by using general questions (e.g., "How happy or unhappy were you over the past week?"), the beeper procedure provided a powerful way to gather immediate, real-time ratings of students' emotions.

IN REVIEW

- *Puberty marks the onset of adolescence. Generally, early maturation is a more positive experience for boys than it is for girls.*
- *Abstract thinking abilities increase during adolescence, but adolescents may show egocentrism in their social thinking.*
- *The search for identity is a key task of adolescence. With age, teens who have not yet experienced an identity crisis become more likely to do so, and most resolve it successfully.*
- *During adolescence, peer relationships become more important. Most teens maintain good relationships with their parents.*
- *Overall, girls' and boys' daily emotional experience becomes less positive as they move into and through early adolescence, with changes leveling off and emotion becoming more stable during late adolescence.*

FIGURE 10.35

Jeanne Louise Calment of Arles, France, was born in 1875 and died in 1997 at the age of 122. Although other individuals have claimed to live this long or beyond, Calment's life is the longest that has been verified.

ADULTHOOD

It was a grand birthday party. Jeanne Louise Calment was born in France 10 years after the American Civil War, and as a girl she met Vincent Van Gogh in her father's shop. By age 60, she had lived through a world war and the invention of the radio, telephone, motion picture, automobile, and airplane. Still to come was another world war, television, space flight, computers, the Internet, and riding a bicycle until age 100. Yes, her 120th birthday was grand indeed. When a reporter asked how her future looked, Jeanne replied with a wry sense of humor, "Very brief" (Figure 10.35).

Older adults are the fastest-growing segment of the population in many countries. By 2025, almost 1 in 5 Americans will be over 65 years of age (Bureau of the Census, 2002). Here, we examine some of the physical, cognitive, and social changes that occur during young adulthood (roughly 20 to 40 years of age), middle adulthood (40 to 65), and late adulthood (65 and older).

Physical Development

▶ 17. Describe how physical and cognitive abilities change throughout adulthood.

Young adults are at the peak of their physical, sexual, and perceptual functioning. The legs, arms, and other body parts typically reach maximum muscle strength at age 25 to 30. Vision, hearing, reaction time, and coordination peak in the early to mid-20s (Hayslip & Panek, 1989). Yet although many physical capacities decline in the mid-30s, the changes aren't noticeable until years later.

After age 40, muscles become weaker and less flexible, particularly in people with sedentary habits. *Basal metabolism*, the rate at which the resting body converts food into energy, also slows, resulting in a tendency to gain weight. Middle age is also the time when many people find their visual acuity declining, especially for close viewing. Women's fertility, which begins to decrease in early adulthood, now drops dramatically as the ovaries produce less estrogen; this process culminates in *menopause*, the cessation of menstruation, which occurs on average around age 50. Male fertility often persists throughout the life span, although it tends to decline after middle age.

Despite these declines, many middle-aged adults remain in excellent health and are vigorously active. From climbing mountains to running marathons, they may achieve physical goals well

FIGURE 10.36

Many older adults maintain a physically active lifestyle. (left) Astronaut John Glenn made a space flight at age 77. (right) Thousands of older athletes compete in local, state, and national Senior Games.

beyond those attained by many younger adults. By late adulthood, physical changes become more pronounced. By age 70, bones become more brittle and hardened ligaments make movements stiffer and slower (Weg, 1983). At age 90, the brain of a healthy adult has lost 5 to 10 percent of its early adult weight, due to a normal loss of neurons that occurs as we grow older (Whitbourne, 1985). But with regular exercise and good nutrition and barring major disease, many adults maintain physical vigor and an active lifestyle well into old age (Figure 10.36).

Cognitive Development

Many people assume that cognitive functioning declines throughout middle and late adulthood. Research shows that this is true in some ways but not others (Baltes & Staudinger, 2000; Craik and Salthouse, 2000). For example, perceptual speed (reaction time) declines steadily after the mid-30s. Thus it takes older adults longer to visually identify and evaluate stimuli. Memory for new factual information also declines during adulthood. Compared with younger adults, older adults find it harder to remember new series of numbers, names and faces of unfamiliar people, map directions, and directions for using new prescription drugs. Certain types of verbal memory, however, show less decline with aging. Thus the ability to repeat just-heard sentences decreases more slowly than the ability to repeat single, unrelated words. Healthy elderly adults also do well in recalling personal events and recognizing familiar stimuli from long ago, such as the faces of high school classmates.

Intellectual Changes

How do intellectual abilities change in adulthood? The conclusion from early research seemed clear: After 30, adults are "over the hill." When IQ scores of different age groups were compared in cross-sectional studies, a noticeable decline began between ages 30 and 40 (Doppelt & Wallace, 1955).

Researchers made a breakthrough by examining separate intellectual abilities rather than overall IQ. They studied *fluid intelligence,* which reflects the ability to perform mental operations (e.g., abstract and logical reasoning, solving spatial problems), and *crystallized intelligence,* which reflects the accumulation of verbal skills and factual knowledge (Horn & Cattell, 1966). Cross-sectional research typically found that fluid intelligence began to decline steadily in young adulthood, whereas crystallized intelligence peaked during middle adulthood and then began to decline in late adulthood (Figure 10.37a).

Was this early decline in fluid abilities really a function of aging or instead the result of different experiences encountered by the various age generations? The older adults may have had less exposure to scientific problem solving in school or jobs that required less use of abstract intellectual skills. Such factors could have artificially depressed their scores.

To answer this question, K. Warner Schaie of Pennsylvania State University and coworkers (Schaie, 1994, 1998) began a study in 1956 that has now involved several thousand adults. This study uses a sequential design incorporating longitudinal and cross-sectional components. The longitudinal data do not support an early decline in either fluid or crystallized intelligence. Rather, most abilities are relatively stable throughout young and middle adulthood, and do not reliably decline until late adulthood (Figure 10.37b). But both the cross-sectional and longitudinal data, along with findings from other studies, indicate that fluid intellectual abilities typically begin to decline at an earlier age than crystallized intelligence (McArdle et al., 2002).

Use It or Lose It?

In our chapter-opening vignette, Enrique described his grandmother as "mentally sharp as a

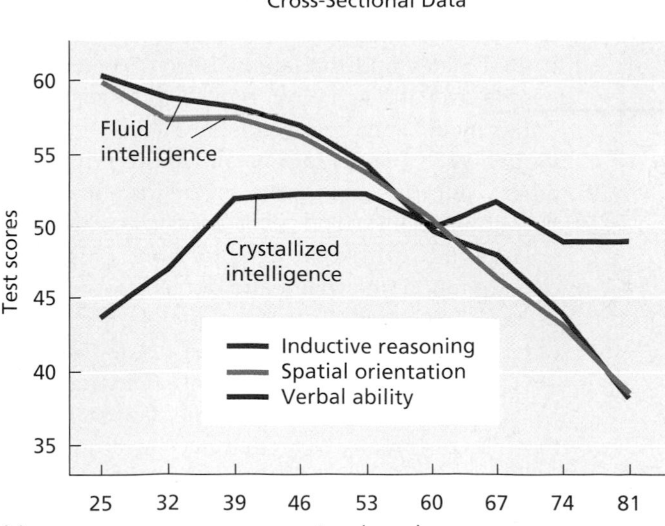

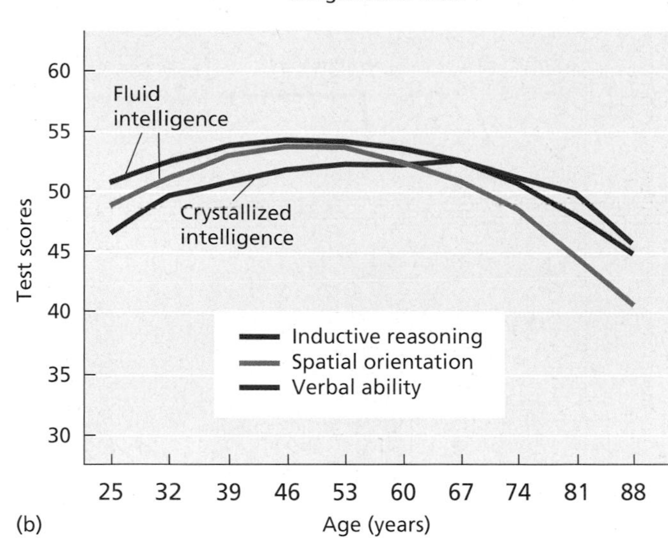

FIGURE 10.37

(a) Cross-sectional data indicate that fluid abilities (reasoning and spatial task performance) begin to decline in young adulthood, whereas crystallized intelligence (verbal ability) begins to decline in late adulthood. (b) However, longitudinal data from the same study indicate that both *fluid and crystallized intelligence remain fairly stable through young and middle adulthood and do not decline significantly until late adulthood. The longitudinal and cross-sectional data are consistent in showing that crystallized abilities decline at a later age than fluid abilities.* SOURCE: Adapted from Schaie, 1994.

tack." But as she and all of us age, is the declining trajectory painted in Figure 10.37b inevitable? Schaie notes that the average intellectual decline in old age shown in Figure 10.37b is a bit deceiving, disproportionately influenced by a minority of older participants who declined markedly. For each intellectual ability, he found that between 67 and 74 years of age about 70 percent of participants *maintained* their level of functioning and that 65 percent maintained it between ages 74 and 81.

Age-related intellectual declines are partly due to poorer perceptual speed, memory, vision, and hearing. Thus we find a bigger intellectual decline during old age when test questions call for quick responses (i.e., timed tests) than when they involve unlimited or ample time (untimed tests). This decrease in intellectual speed shows up in various real-world tasks, such as learning to use a computer. But although 75- to 89-year-olds may take longer to acquire computer skills than their 60- to 74-year-old counterparts, the key is that many retain the intellectual capacity to learn (Echt et al., 1998).

Can we predict who will maintain intellectual functioning the longest? According to Schaie (1994), it appears to be people who have above-average education, engage in cognitively stimulating jobs and personal activities, (e.g., reading, travel), marry a spouse with greater intellectual abilities than their own, and maintain a higher level of perceptual processing speed. Even more striking, Schaie and his coworkers have found that 65- to 95-year-old adults' spatial and reasoning abilities can be improved by teaching them strategies for performing such tasks (Saczynski et al., 2002; Willis & Schaie, 1986). For many adults who had previously shown intellectual declines in these areas, the training restored their performance to the level it had been 14 years earlier, and these gains often persisted for years.

As in the case of physical fitness, the moral for intellectual fitness appears to be "use it or lose it." In fact, regular physical exercise and perceptual-motor activities—even playing video games that that require fast reaction times—may help preserve 70- and 80-year olds' cognitive abilities (Goldstein et al., 1997).

At the same time, as Figure 10.38 shows, it's important not to sugarcoat the fact that the risk of cognitive impairment increases significantly

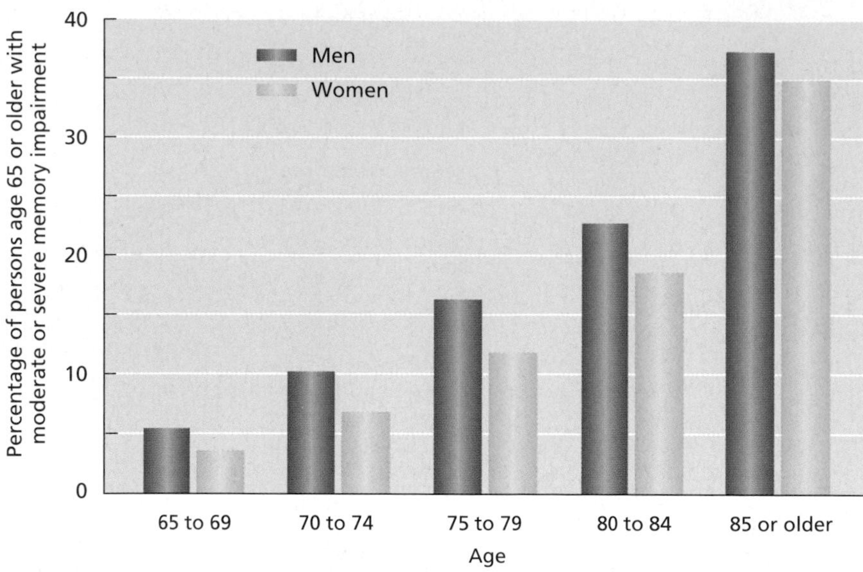

FIGURE 10.38

Participants in this nationally representative sample of Americans are read a list of 20 words and asked to recall as many as they can. Most healthy adults will be able to recall between 5 and 9 words. This graph shows that the percentage of people who recall 4 or fewer words increases steadily during late adulthood.
SOURCE: Federal Interagency Forum on Aging-Related Statistics, 2000.

throughout late adulthood. In-depth neuropsychological studies in Finland, Germany, and the United States find that about 23 to 27 percent of people over the age of 65 have a mild cognitive impairment, with age trends similar to those in Figure 10.38 (Unverzagt et al., 2001). With age, other adults develop a more severe form of cognitive impairment called *senile dementia*, which we will discuss further in Chapter 13. Combining cases of mild impairment and dementia, some experts estimate that 45 percent of people age 85 and older, compared to 79 percent of 65- to 74-year-olds, remain "cognitively normal" (Unverzagt et al., 2001). Surely, these are not pleasant statistics, but they also make clear that even well into old age, cognitive impairment is not inevitable. Moreover, even when some mental abilities decrease with age, common sense tells us that people can accumulate knowledge that leads to greater wisdom. Do we really become older but wiser? Let's take a look "Beneath the Surface."

For a glimpse into the cognitive functioning of a 100-year-old man, see Video Segment 10.1.

▶ 18. Identify aspects of wisdom and discuss whether science supports the adage "older but wiser."

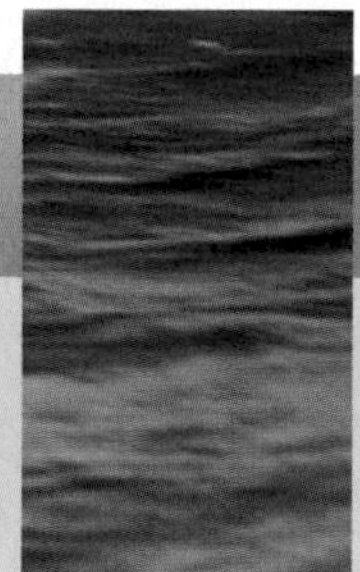

BENEATH THE SURFACE

OLDER BUT WISER?

Anthropologist Peter Collings (2001) notes that, as in many cultures, the Inuit living in the Arctic of western Canada accord their elders special status and great respect (Figure 10.39). Young and old Inuit alike regard wisdom as a key component of aging successfully, and it largely reflects "the individual's function as a repository of cultural knowledge and his or her involvement in community life by interacting with younger people and talking to them, teaching them about 'traditional' cultural values" (p. 146).

How would you define a "wise" person, and do you believe that as we age we become "older but wiser"?

What Is Wisdom?

After analyzing cultural, historical, philosophical, and psychological views of wisdom, German psychologists Paul Baltes and Ursula Staudinger (2000) concluded that wisdom includes the following components:

- rich factual knowledge about life (e.g., about human nature and social relationships);
- rich procedural knowledge about life (e.g., strategies for making decisions, handling conflict, giving advice);
- an understanding of life-span contexts (e.g., family, friends, work; past, present, future);
- an awareness that values and priorities differ across people and societies; and
- an ability to recognize and manage uncertainty (e.g., "the future cannot be fully known").

True wisdom, say Baltes and Staudinger, is hard to achieve, for it combines extraordinary scope with "a truly superior level of knowledge, judgment, and advice . . . used for the good or well-being of oneself and that of others" (2000, p. 123).

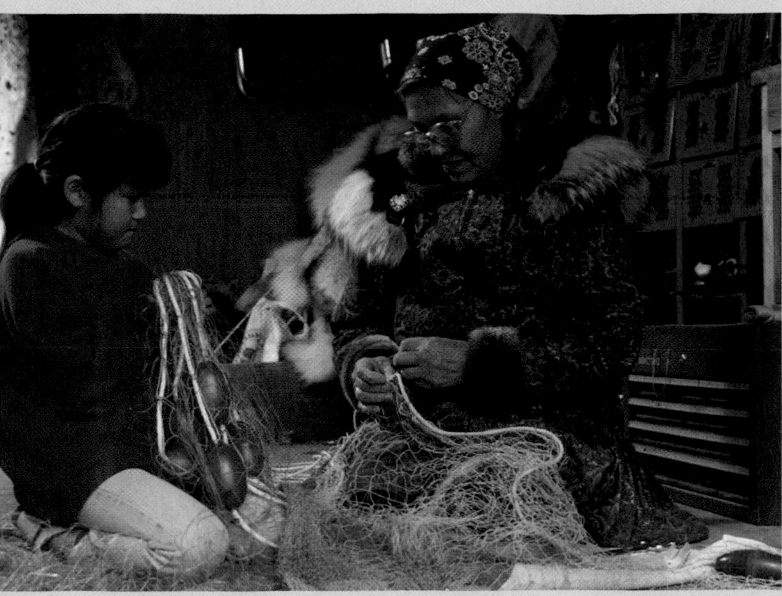

FIGURE 10.39

Among the Inuit of the Canadian Arctic, wisdom is regarded as a key component of successful aging.

Aging and Wisdom

Does age bring greater wisdom? To find out, Baltes, Staudinger, and other researchers present participants of different ages with various life problems (e.g., a 15-year-old girl wants to get married right away; an adult realizes that she hasn't achieved major goals) and ask them what the hypothetical person should do. Experts blind to the participants' ages then score their solutions, using the five criteria of wisdom described above.

What do they find? Older teens give wiser solutions than younger teens, younger adults give still wiser solutions, and older adults—on average—show no greater or lesser wisdom. Indeed, wisdom seems to rise steadily from age 13 to 25 and then remain relatively stable through age 75 (Baltes & Staudinger, 2000; Pasupathi et al., 2001). Beyond that, wisdom may decline, but the researchers were able to study relatively few people older than 75.

Let's turn, however, to a different type of task. Read the story below, then answer the question that follows.

> A burglar who has just robbed a shop is making his getaway. As he is running home, a policeman on his beat sees him drop his glove. He doesn't know the man is a burglar, he just wants to tell him he dropped his glove. But when the policeman shouts out to the burglar, "Hey, you! Stop!" the burglar turns round, sees the policeman, and gives himself up. *Question:* Why did the burglar do that? (Happé et al., 1998, p. 362)

Did you find this task easy? A good answer would be that the burglar mistakenly assumed that the officer knew he had robbed the shop and didn't realize that the officer was only trying to return the dropped glove. This task measures how well you understand "what someone else is thinking" based on their behavior. This type of social wisdom comes into play when we need to infer what people must have been thinking to have acted as they did or need to predict how others will behave based on what is "going on in their head." Francesca Happé and coworkers (1998) found that on such tasks, younger adults (average age 21 years) generally gave good responses, but on average older adults (average age 73 years) displayed superior social reasoning. Several other researchers also have found superior performance among older adults on various reasoning tasks.

As a critical thinker, you should recognize that all of the studies just mentioned are cross-sectional; that is, they compare people from different age groups. Asking whether 75-year-olds are wiser than 25-year-olds is not quite the same as asking whether the same young adults become wiser as they age. Only longitudinal and sequential studies can answer that question.

At present, then, research suggests that "older but wiser" may apply only up to a point, beyond which "older but at least as wise" is more appropriate. Of course, these are averages. Some older adults—even into their 80s—display greater wisdom than many young adults. To stereotype elderly adults as "wise," however, is just as inappropriate as to stereotype them as "senile." Erik Erikson (Erikson et al., 1986) emphasized that old age brings with it only the *potential* for wisdom, and as the Inuit acknowledge, not everyone ages successfully.

Social-Emotional and Personality Development

Adults display a great diversity of life paths. As Bernice Neugarten notes, "If you look at people's lives, they're like the spreading of a fan. The longer they live, the greater the differences between them" (Neugarten & Hall, 1980, p. 78). Yet all adults confront biological realities of aging, and most are also influenced by a **social clock,** *a set of cultural norms concerning the optimal age range for work, marriage, parenthood, and other life experiences.*

Stages and Critical Events

▶ 19. According to Erikson, what are three major developmental challenges of adulthood?

Many researchers view adult social development as a progression through age-related stages (Levinson, 1990). According to Erik Erikson (1959/1980; see

FIGURE 10.40

These children, from a family of herders in the Republic of Mongolia, are living in an extended family unit that includes parents, grandparents, great-grandparents, and other relatives. In the United States, in 2001, 69 percent of children lived with two parents, and 36 percent lived in a single-parent household (Bureau of the Census, 2002).

▶ 20. Describe research findings on family structure, cohabitation and divorce, and the course of marital satisfaction.

Table 10.2, p. 389), *intimacy versus isolation* is the major developmental challenge of young adulthood (ages 20 to 40). Intimacy is the ability to open oneself to another person and to form close relationships. This is the period of adulthood when many people form close adult friendships, fall in love, and marry.

Middle adulthood (ages 40 to 65) brings with it the issue of *generativity versus stagnation.* Through their careers, raising children, or involvement in other activities, people achieve generativity by doing things for others and making the world a better place. Certainly, many young adults make such contributions, but generativity typically becomes a more central issue later in adulthood (Strough et al., 1996).

Late adulthood (age 65 and older) accentuates the final crisis, *integrity versus despair.* Older adults review their life and evaluate its meaning. If the major crises of earlier stages have been successfully resolved, the person experiences integrity: a sense of completeness and fulfillment. Older adults who have not achieved positive outcomes at earlier stages may experience despair, regretting that they had not lived their lives in a more fulfilling way.

Consistent with Erikson's model, many goals increase in importance as people age, and successfully resolving certain life tasks contributes to mastering others (McAdams & de St. Aubin, 1998). But critics caution that we should avoid viewing early, middle, and late adulthood as strict "stages" in which one life task takes over while others fade away. Although older adults are more concerned about generativity and integrity than are younger adults, they remain highly concerned about intimacy (Sheldon & Kasser, 2001).

Another way to view adult social development is through the major life events that people experience. Sigmund Freud (1935) once defined psychological adjustment as "the ability to love and work," and many key life events revolve around these two themes.

Marriage and Family

Ramona, Enrique, and Katja are presently 20 years old and single. Like most people around the world, they will probably marry or form some other type of family union at some point in their lives, although as they learned in their anthropology lecture, family structures can vary both across and within different cultures (Figure 10.40).

Enrique wondered what his future family would be like, and while we can't say for sure, we do know that the "average" family in America and some other countries has changed in several ways over the past generation. Our three students belong to the tail end of so-called "Generation X." Their own parents were "Baby Boomers," born a few years after the end of World War II. As Figure 10.41 shows, compared to the families that Baby Boomers grew up in, members of Generation X are more likely to have experienced parental divorce, had two working parents, a smaller number of siblings, and yet maintained a similar level of closeness to their parents (Bengtson, 2001).

Like their parents, today's adults typically expect much from marriage, including satisfaction of social, emotional, and sexual needs. Many couples realize these goals, but a high divorce rate—not just in the United States but also in many foreign countries—indicates that marital happiness is by no means automatic. Successful marriages are characterized by emotional closeness, positive communication and problem solving, agreement on basic values and expectations, and a willingness to accept and support changes in the partner (Gottman & Levenson, 1992).

Some couples in committed relationships *cohabit*—that is, live together without being married. In 1960, the ratio of married to cohabiting households in the United States was about 95:1.

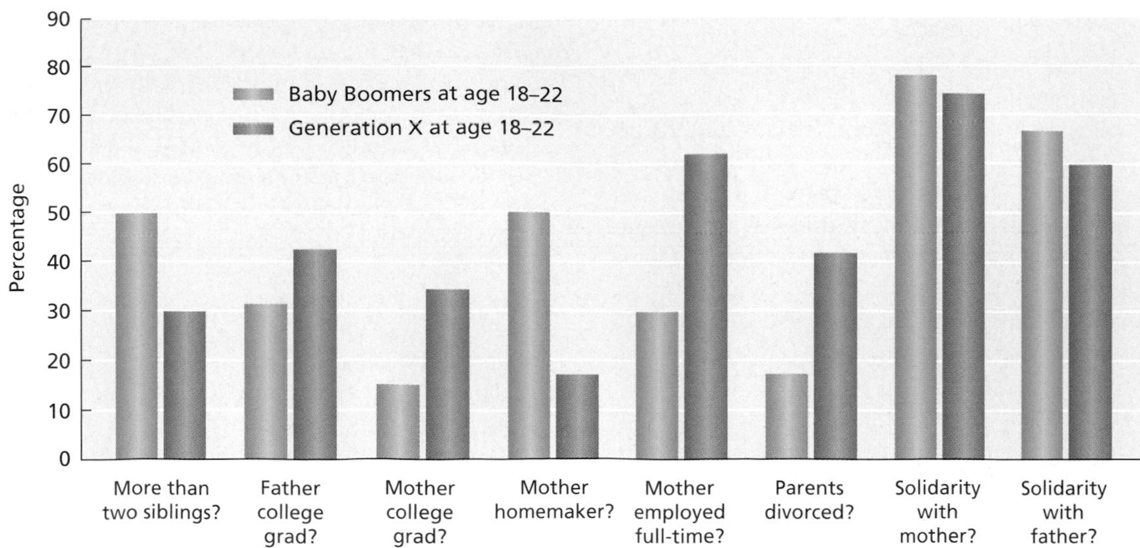

FIGURE 10.41

Baby Boomers were surveyed when they were 18 to 22 years old and asked to identify various characteristics of the families in which they had grown up. A generation later, when the Baby Boomers' children (Generation X) had turned 18 to 22 years old, they answered the same survey questions as their parents had.
SOURCE: Bengtson, 2001.

By 2000, that ratio had shrunk to 10:1, representing almost 5.5 million cohabiting households (Bureau of the Census, 2003). Some couples cohabit as a permanent alternative to marriage, but many do so as a "trial marriage" to determine if they are compatible before tying the knot. In Sweden, premarital cohabitation appears to be the norm (Duvander, 1999).

What Do You Think?

COHABITATION AS A "TRIAL MARRIAGE"

What would you predict? Do couples who live together before getting married have a lower, higher, or similar rate of divorce compared to couples who do not live together before they get married? Why? Think about it, then see page 417.

Marital Satisfaction, Parenthood, and the Empty Nest On average, marital satisfaction declines over the first few years after the knot is tied (Kurdek, 1999). This does not mean, however, that most couples are unhappy. They are still satisfied, just less so than they were. In a sense, the honeymoon is over.

The birth of a first baby dramatically alters the way couples spend their time. For many couples, marital satisfaction decreases in the year or two after their first child is born (Cowan & Cowan, 2000). Compared with husbands, wives are more likely to leave their outside job, spend more time parenting, and feel that their spouse is not helping enough. Disagreements over the division of labor and parenting are a major contributor to the drop in marital satisfaction (Frisco & Williams, 2003).

Over a broader age period, cross-sectional studies suggest a U-shaped relation between marital satisfaction and progression through major life events. The percentage of couples reporting that they are "very satisfied" in their marriage typically is highest before or just as the first child is born, drops during child-rearing years, and increases after all the children have left home (Orbuch et al., 1996; Rollins & Feldman, 1970). Although some longitudinal research does not find this late-adulthood rebound in marital satisfaction, overall these findings challenge a myth about the so-called "empty nest." Contrary to this popular stereotype, most middle-aged couples do not become significantly depressed or suffer a crisis when their children leave home (Chiriboga, 1989). Couples maintain meaningful relationships with their children but have more time to spend with each other and pursue leisure activities.

Despite the stresses that accompany marriage and parenthood, studies around the globe find that married people experience greater subjective well-being than unmarried adults (Diener et al., 2000). They tend to be happier, live longer, and have lower rates of depression and chronic illness. Although raising children is demanding, parents often report that having children is one of best things that has ever happened in their lives. Newlyweds can use the knowledge that many married couples experience a drop in marital satisfaction over time to help themselves establish more realistic expectations and to take a more active role in maintaining a satisfying relationship.

▶ 21. Identify common stages of establishing a career and describe sex differences in career paths.

▶ 22. Evaluate the concept of midlife crisis and the view that dying people experience a sequence of psychological stages.

Establishing a Career

In the adult world, one of the first questions a new acquaintance typically asks is, "What do you do?" A child might answer, "About what?" but adults know the question is short for, "What do you do for a living?" A career helps us earn a living and defines part of our identity. Work provides an outlet for achievement, gives us structure, and is a significant source of social interactions. Having satisfying relationships at work is especially important in collectivistic countries (Hui et al., 1995).

According to Donald Super (1957), a pioneer in the field of vocational psychology, from childhood through our mid-20s we first enter a *growth stage* of career interests, in which we form initial impressions about the types of jobs we like or dislike, followed by a more earnest *exploration stage,* in which we form tentative ideas about a preferred career and pursue the necessary education or training.

From the mid-20s to mid-40s, people often enter an *establishment phase,* during which they begin to make their mark. Initially, they may experience some job instability. After college, for example, many people are likely to change careers at least once (Holland, 1985). Eventually, careers tend to become more stable, and people enter a *maintenance stage* that continues into late adulthood. Finally, during the *decline stage,* people's investment in work tends to decrease, and they eventually retire.

Although this general model is useful, people's career paths vary quite a bit, and this is especially true for women. Joy Schneer and Frieda Reitman (1995, 1997) found, for example, that, among college students who obtained an M.B.A. (Master of Business Administration) degree and then pursued managerial careers, women were more likely than men to experience work gaps by mid-career. Such work gaps tended to retard professional advancement and salary level.

Overall, compared to their parents' generation at the same age, today's young women hold higher career aspirations than those of their mothers and fathers (Bengtson, 2001). Still, family responsibilities, which fall disproportionately on women even when married partners have similar job status, are a major cause of work gaps for women (Hinze, 2000). About 75 percent of employed women become pregnant during their working years, and over half of those return to work within a year (Muchinsky, 2000). Career gaps also occur when adults must temporarily leave the workforce to care for their elderly parents. As in raising children, women disproportionately fill this elder-care role. Not surprisingly, married women often experience greater *interrole conflict* than married men as they try to juggle the demands of career and family (Berry, 1998). But as children grow up and leave home, this conflict decreases. After raising a family, many women enter the workforce for the first time, reinvigorate an earlier career, or return to college to prepare for a new one.

Midlife Crisis: Fact or Fiction?

Popular wisdom holds that along the developmental path of career and family, people hit a massive pothole called the *midlife crisis.* Is it a reality? Daniel Levinson and his coworkers (1978, 1986) studied 85 men and women longitudinally and found that many experienced a turbulent midlife transition between the ages of 40 and 45. They began to focus on their mortality and realize that some of their life's dreams pertaining to career, family, and relationships would not come true.

Critics note that Levinson's sample was small and nonrepresentative. In fact, there is considerable evidence that the notion of a full-blown, turmoil-filled midlife crisis is largely a myth. Research conducted around the world shows that happiness and life satisfaction generally do not decrease throughout adulthod (Diener et al., 1999). In one study of adolescents and people in young, middle, and late adulthood from eight Western European countries, about 80 percent of each age group reported they were "satisfied" or "very satisfied" with their lives (Ingelhart & Rabier, 1986). Moreover, people in their 40s *do not* have higher rates of divorce, suicide, depression, feelings of meaninglessness, or emotional instability than younger or older adults (McCrae & Costa, 1990).

In sum, middle-aged adults surely experience important conflicts, disappointments, and worries—and some indeed experience major crises—but so do people of all ages (Wethington, 2000a). As Erikson emphasized, there are major goals to achieve, crises to resolve, and rewards to experience in every phase of life.

Retirement and the "Golden Years"

Retirement is an important milestone. Some adults view it as a reminder that they are growing older, but many look forward to leisure and other opportunities they were unable to pursue during their careers. Most retired people do not become more anxious, depressed, or lonely due to retirement, although those who have strong work values are most apt to miss their jobs (Hardy & Quadagno, 1995).

Levels of Analysis

Biological	Psychological	Environmental
• Sex determination and genetic contribution to temperament • Brain maturation underlying cognitive growth in childhood • Pubertal changes, including early and late maturation • Biologically based physical and cognitive changes in adulthood	• Changes in schemas, information-processing, and intellectual capacities • Secure or insecure attachment to caregiver; peer relations • Development of gender-identity and sex-role stereotypes • Personality formation and resolution of psychosocial stages	• Teratogens that affect prenatal development • Parenting styles and childhood socialization experiences • Major life events (marriage, parenthood, career) • Exercise and lifestyle norms that affect biological functions at all ages

Life-Span Development

FIGURE 10.42

Understanding Behavior: Factors that influence life-span development.

The decision to retire or keep working typically involves many factors, such as feelings about the job, leisure interests, one's physical health, and family relationships. Family income, leisure time, and family roles change with retirement, and married couples often experience increased marital stress after a spouse retires, especially if the other spouse is still working. Over time, however, they typically adjust to their new circumstances and marital quality is enhanced (Moen et al., 2001).

Some people, of course, do not have the luxury to choose their work status. They may be forced into retirement, or feel compelled to keep working for economic reasons, and these circumstances can have a significant impact on well-being. Whether in their 50s or 70s, adults who are working or retired because this is what *they* prefer report higher life satisfaction and better physical and mental health than adults who are involuntarily working or retired (Shultz et al., 1998).

Death and Dying

Part of being human is the fact that we are mortal. Like other aspects of life-span development summarized in Figure 10.42, death can be viewed at several levels. It is an inevitable biological process, but one with important psychological and environmental components.

In her pioneering work on dying, Elisabeth Kübler-Ross (1969) found that terminally ill patients often experienced five stages as they coped with impending death. *Denial* typically came first, as the person refused to accept that the illness was terminal. Next, denial often gave way to *anger* and then to *bargaining,* such as "Lord, please let me live long enough to see my grandchild." *Depression* ushered in the fourth stage, as patients began to grieve. Finally, many experienced *acceptance* and a resigned sense of peacefulness.

It is essential to keep in mind that these stages do not represent a "normal" or "correct" way to face death and that terminally ill patients' reactions may not typify those of people facing death under other circumstances (Doka, 1995). Indeed, even among terminally ill patients, some move back and forth between stages, do not experience all the stages, or look forward to death (Schulz &

FIGURE 10.43

Many cultures honor a person's death with a ceremony that involves family, friends, and the wider community. In some cultures, this traditionally is a somber occasion; in others, it is more joyous celebration.

Aderman, 1980). Nevertheless, Kübler-Ross's work spurred interest in understanding and helping people cope with death.

As Figure 10.43 illustrates, beliefs and customs concerning death vary across cultures and among individuals (Werth et al., 2002). To some, death means the complete end of one's existence. Others believe in reincarnation or an afterlife. Death also means different things to people of different ages (Cicirelli, 1998). Older adults typically have lost more friends and loved ones and have thought more about their own eventual death than have younger people. As one 80-year-old put it, "More of the people I know are in heaven now than on earth."

Understandably, the elderly are more accepting of their own death than any other age group. In the midst of a fatal heart attack, an 81-year-old man reassuringly told his family, "It's my time. It's been a good life." We should all wish for this blessing of a fulfilled life's journey.

IN REVIEW

- *Young adults are at the peak of their physical capabilities. Information-processing speed slows after reaching one's 30s, but many intellectual abilities do not begin to decline reliably until late adulthood. Wisdom appears to increase steadily from early adolescence through the mid-20s and then level off through the mid-70s.*
- *Erikson proposed that intimacy versus isolation, generativity versus stagnation, and integrity versus despair are the main crises of early, middle, and late adulthood.*
- *For many couples, marital satisfaction tends to decline in the years following the birth of children, but increases later in adulthood.*
- *Work serves important psychological and social functions. Overall, women experience more career gaps, and their career paths are more variable than men's. Most adults do not experience a full-blown midlife crisis. Similarly, most retired people do not become more anxious, depressed, or lonely due to retirement.*
- *Many terminally ill patients experience similar psychological reactions as they cope with their impending death, but beliefs and feelings about death vary with culture and age, and there is no "normal" way to approach death.*

KEY TERMS AND CONCEPTS

Each term has been boldfaced and defined in the chapter on the page indicated in parentheses.

What Do You Think?

SHY CHILD, SHY ADULT? p. 389

To answer this question, psychologists must patiently conduct longitudinal research, measuring people's temperament in childhood and then examining whether it correlates with people's traits or behaviors in adulthood. For example, studies find that in America and Sweden, shy, behaviorally inhibited 8- to 12-year-old boys are more likely than nonshy peers to delay marriage and fatherhood when they grow up, possibly reflecting their reluctance to enter new social relationships (Caspi et al., 1988; Kerr et al., 1996). Shy American girls are more likely as adults to quit work after marriage and become homemakers, whereas shy Swedish girls are less likely to complete college than nonshy girls.

Other childhood traits also are associated with adulthood outcomes. Longitudinal studies in Finland find that children who are more aggressive at age 8 are more likely to experience long-term unemployment 20 to 30 years later; and that 8-year-olds with a highly agreeable (e.g., compliant and self-controlled) or disagreeable temperament are, respectively, more likely to become generally pleasant or unpleasant adults (Kokko & Pulkkinen, 2000).

But what about temperament in early childhood? Denise Newman and coworkers (1997) measured the temperament of 961 New Zealanders at age 3, based on a 90-minute observation of each child. At age 21, participants were studied again. Compared with 3-years-olds with a "well-adjusted temperament," those who were "undercontrolled" (i.e., irritable, impulsive, inattentive) reported more antisocial behavior in adulthood and greater conflict in family and romantic relationships, and they were more likely to have been fired from a job. Other adults rated them as being less reliable. In contrast, children with an "inhibited temperament" (i.e., socially shy and fearful) reported having less overall companionship in adulthood, and other adults rated them as less affiliative.

What shall we conclude? Most young children are well adjusted or display only mild to moderately strong temperamental traits. Within this group, differences in childhood temperament predicted only weakly how they will function as adults. But for the remaining children, their strong temperamental traits can provide a better insight into adulthood functioning. Still, predicting how any individual child will turn out as an adult is difficult. Many factors influence development, and, even during childhood, strong temperaments often mellow (Pfeifer et al., 2002). Finally, temperament usually predicts overall *patterns* of adult functioning better than any single adult behavior. But as Newman and coworkers (1997) note, it is remarkable that a mere 90-minute observation of children at age 3 can modestly predict different patterns of adjustment 18 years later. ■

COHABITATION AS A "TRIAL MARRIAGE" p. 413

Scientists began to examine the relation between cohabitation and divorce rates in the 1980s. Since then, large national surveys in several countries, including Canada, Germany, Sweden, and the United States, have found that premarital cohabitation is associated with a *higher* risk of subsequent divorce (Hall & Zhao, 1995; Heaton, 2002). Conducting experiments to find out why this relation exists would, of course, be impractical, not to mention unethical. We cannot randomly assign engaged couples, for example, to cohabitation and no-cohabitation conditions and then try to explore factors that increase or decrease their divorce rate!

Many researchers feel that the cohabitation-divorce relation does not reflect cause and effect. Rather, couples who choose to cohabit before marriage appear to differ psychologically from couples who don't cohabit first. They tend to be less religious and report less commitment to marriage as an institution, and more of these couples are ambivalent about whether to marry. Taken together, these preexisting factors would increase the risk of divorce even if these couples had not cohabited before tying the knot. When researchers focus their analyses on cohabiting couples who start out with a strong orientation toward marriage, the risk of divorce is no higher and the quality of marital relations is no poorer than among couples who did not cohabit prior to marriage (Bruederl et al., 1997). Still, research does *not* support the view that, overall, cohabitation reduces the risk of subsequent divorce. ■

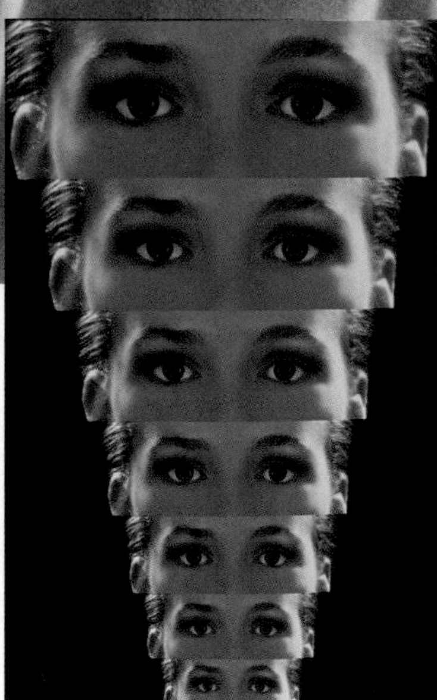

PERSONALITY

CHAPTER OUTLINE

Much of our lives is spent in trying to understand others and in wishing others understood us better than they do.

—Gordon Allport

On a hot summer evening in 1966, a University of Texas student wrote the following letter:

> *I don't really understand myself these days. I am supposed to be an average, reasonable, and intelligent young man. However, lately (I can't recall when it started) I have been the victim of many unusual and irrational thoughts. These thoughts constantly recur, and it requires a tremendous mental effort to concentrate on useful and progressive tasks. In March when my parents made a physical break I noticed a great deal of stress. I consulted a Dr. Cochrum at the University Health Center and asked him to recommend someone that I could consult with about some psychiatric disorders I felt I had. I talked with a doctor once for about two hours and tried to convey to him my fears that I felt overcome by overwhelming violent impulses. After one session I never saw the doctor again, and since then I have been fighting my mental turmoil alone, and seemingly to no avail. After my death I wish that an autopsy would be performed on me to see if there is any visible physical disorder. I have had some tremendous headaches in the past and have consumed two large bottles of Excedrin in the past three months. (Lavergne, 1997, p. 8)*

Later that night Charles Whitman killed his wife and mother, both of whom were lovingly supportive of him. The next morning he carried a high-powered hunting rifle to the top of a 307-foot tower on the busy University of Texas campus in Austin and opened fire on all those passing by below. Within 90 horrifying minutes, he killed 16 people and wounded 30 others before he himself was killed by police.

On the surface, Charles Whitman (Figure 11.1) seemed as solid and upstanding as the University of Texas tower from which he rained death on unsuspecting strangers. He came from a wealthy, prominent Florida family and was an outstanding student, an accomplished pianist, one of the youngest Eagle Scouts in state history, and a former U.S. Marine who had been awarded a Good Conduct Medal and the Marine Corps Expeditionary Medal. He married the woman of his dreams, and the two were seen as an ideal couple. Whitman became a University of Texas student when he was selected by the Marines for a prestigious engineering scholarship. In his spare time, he served as a scoutmaster in Austin.

What could have caused this exemplary citizen to commit such extraordinary acts of violence? On December 18, 2001, the Austin History Center opened its records on Charles Whitman to public scrutiny. These records provide important insights into the complexities of Whitman's personality and the turmoil that existed within him. Although the Whitman incident occurred decades ago, it is sadly reminiscent of more recent acts of violence in schools, communities, and workplaces across the United States. In this chapter, we will consider the factors that triggered Whitman's violence through the lenses of the major personality perspectives. Doing so can help us paint a more complete portrait of Whitman and may further our understanding not only of him but also of others who commit acts of violence and terrorism.

(a)

(b)

FIGURE 11.1

(a) Charles Whitman with his wife, whom he later murdered. Few thought this exemplary citizen capable of the heinous acts of violence he committed. (b) The University of Texas tower from which Whitman opened fire on the campus below.

▶ 1. Which observations give rise to the concept of personality? Cite three characteristics of "personality behaviors."

WHAT IS PERSONALITY?

The concept of personality arises from the fascinating spectrum of human individuality. We observe that people differ meaningfully in the ways they customarily think, feel, and act. These distinctive behavior patterns help define one's identity as a person. As one group of theorists noted, each of us is in certain respects like *all other* people, like *some other* people, and like *no other* person who has lived in the past or will exist in the future (Kluckhohn & Murray, 1953).

The concept of personality also rests on the observation that a given person seems to behave somewhat consistently over time and across different situations. From this perceived consistency comes the notion of *personality traits* that characterize individuals' customary ways of responding to their world. Although only modest consistency is found from childhood personality to adult personality, consistency becomes greater as we enter adulthood (Caspi & Roberts, 1999). Nonetheless, even in adulthood, a capacity for meaningful personality change remains (Lewis, 1999; Roberts et al., 2002). Combining these notions of individuality and consistency, we can define **personality** *as the distinctive and relatively enduring ways of thinking, feeling, and acting that characterize a person's responses to life situations.*

The thoughts, feelings, and actions that are seen as reflecting an individual's personality typically have three characteristics. First, they are seen as *behavioral components of identity* that distinguish that person from other people. Second, the behaviors are viewed as being caused primarily by *internal rather than environmental factors*. Third, the person's behaviors seem to have *organization and structure;* they seem to fit together in a meaningful fashion, suggesting an inner personality that guides and directs behavior (Figure 11.2).

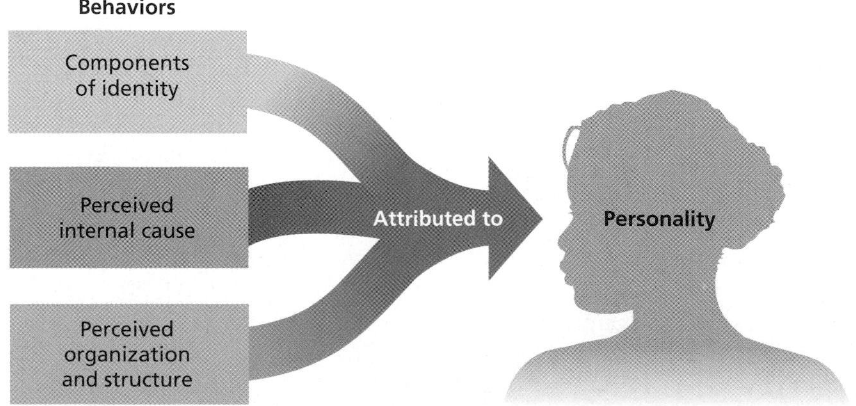

FIGURE 11.2

Perceived characteristics of behaviors that are seen as reflecting an individual's personality.

More than any other topic in psychology, the study of personality has been guided by the psychodynamic, humanistic, biological, behavioral, cognitive, and sociocultural perspectives. These perspectives provide different conceptions of what personality is and how it functions. As one pair of observers noted,

> It seems hard to believe that all the theorists are talking about the same creature, who is now angelic and now depraved, now a black-box robot shaped by reinforcers and now a shaper of its own destiny, now devious . . . and now hardheadedly oriented to solid reality. (Stone & Church, 1968, p. 4)

Yet this very diversity of viewpoints arises from the fact that the theorists have their own personalities that influence how they perceive and understand themselves and their world. No doubt, you will find some of their theories more in accord with your own life views than you will find others.

For personality psychologists, the subjective "truth" of a theory is less important than its *usefulness*. As discussed in Chapter 2, a scientific theory is useful to the extent that it (1) provides a comprehensive framework within which known facts can be incorporated, (2) allows us to predict future events with some precision, and (3) stimulates the discovery of new knowledge. We will evaluate each of the theories we describe in terms of these scientific standards.

▶ 2. What three standards determine the scientific usefulness of a personality theory?

THE TRAIT PERSPECTIVE: MAPPING THE STRUCTURE OF PERSONALITY

Personality traits *are relatively stable cognitive, emotional, and behavioral characteristics of people that help establish their individual identities and distinguish them from others.* Theorists approach trait concepts in two ways. Some regard them as descriptive summaries of people's attributes, whereas others see them not only as descriptive summaries but also internal causes that explain why people behave in their distinctive ways (Larsen & Buss, 2002). A good starting point for the study of personality is an examination of this influential perspective in current personality science. The goals of trait theorists are to describe the basic classes of behavior that define personality, to devise ways of measuring individual differences in personality traits, and to use these measures to understand and predict a person's behavior.

The starting point for the trait researcher is identifying the behaviors that define a particular trait. But here we have an embarrassment of riches. Years ago, the trait theorist Gordon Allport went through the English dictionary and painstakingly recorded all of the words that could be used to describe personal traits. The result: a gigantic list of 17,953 words (Allport & Odbert, 1936). Obviously, it would be impractical if not impossible to describe people in terms of where they fall on roughly 18,000 dimensions. The trait theorist's goal is to condense all of these behavioral descriptors into a manageable number of basic traits that can capture personal individuality.

Factor Analytic Approaches

Psychologists have taken two major approaches to define what Allport (1937) called "the building blocks of personality." One approach is to propose traits (e.g., "dominance," "friendliness," "self-esteem") on the basis of words or concepts from everyday discourse or from concepts in existing personality theories. A more systematic approach uses the statistical tool of **factor analysis** *to identify clusters of specific behaviors that are correlated with one another so highly that they can be viewed as reflecting a basic dimension, or trait, on which people vary.* For example, you might find that most people who are socially reserved also avoid parties, like quiet activities, and enjoy being alone. At the other end of the spectrum are people who are very talkative and sociable, like parties and excitement, dislike solitary activities such as reading, and constantly seek out new acquaintances. These behavioral patterns define a general factor, or dimension, that we might label *introversion-extraversion* (or simply *extraversion*). At one end of the dimension are highly introverted behaviors, and at the other end are highly extraverted behaviors (Figure 11.3). Presumably, each of us could be placed at some point along this dimension in terms of our customary behavior patterns. In fact, as we will see, factor analytic studies have shown introversion-extraversion to be a major dimension of personality.

▶ 3. In which two ways are trait concepts used by personality psychologists?

Cattell's Sixteen Personality Factors

If you were asked to describe and compare every person you know, how many different traits would it take to do the job? This is where trait theorists begin to part company. Because factor

FIGURE 11.3

Factor analysis allows researchers to reduce many behaviors to a smaller number of basic dimensions, or factors. A factor comprises behaviors that are highly correlated with one another and are therefore assumed to have common psychological meaning. Here we see the kinds of behaviors that might fall on the two ends of an introversion-extraversion factor. The two groups of behaviors are negatively correlated with one another.

Introversion
- Retiring
- Reserved
- Likes solitary activities
- Does not attend parties

Dimension (factor)

Extraversion
- Outgoing and talkative
- Wants many friends
- Enjoys parties
- Dislikes solitary activities
- Dominates social situations

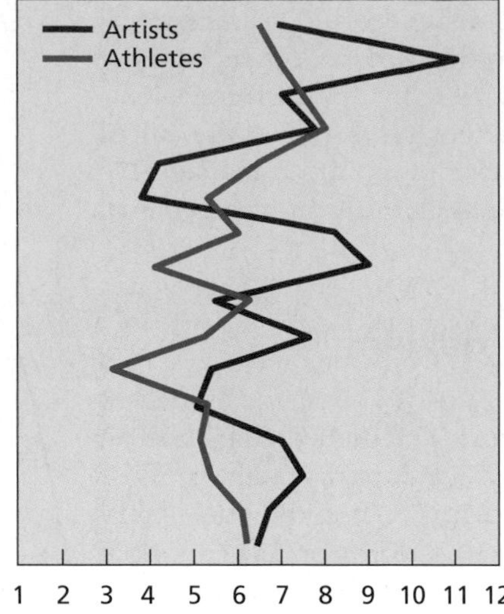

FIGURE 11.4

Raymond B. Cattell identified 16 basic personality traits through factor analysis. Here, we see personality profiles (mean scores) for Olympic athletes and creative artists on the 16PF, the test developed by Cattell to measure the traits. SOURCE: Based on Cattell, 1965.

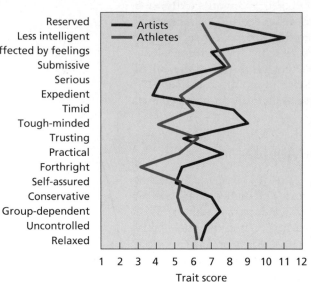

analysis can be used and interpreted in different ways, trait theorists have cut up the personality pie into smaller or larger pieces. For example, the pioneering trait theorist Raymond B. Cattell (1965) asked thousands of participants to rate themselves on numerous behavioral characteristics; he also obtained ratings from people who knew the participants well. When he subjected this mass of data to factor analysis, he identified 16 basic behavior clusters, or factors (Figure 11.4). Using this information, Cattell developed a widely used personality test called the *16 Personality Factor Questionnaire (16PF)* to measure individual differences on each of the dimensions and provide a comprehensive personality description. He was able to develop personality profiles not only for individuals but also for groups of people. For example, Figure 11.4 compares average scores obtained by creative artists and Olympic athletes.

The Five Factor Model

▶ 4. Describe and compare two models of personality derived from factor analysis.

Other trait researchers believe that Cattell's 16 dimensions are more than we need. Their factor analytic studies suggest that five "higher-order" factors, each including several of Cattell's more specific factors, are all that we need to capture the basic structure of personality (McCrae & Costa, 2003). These theorists also propose that these "Big Five" factors may be universal to the human species, for the same five factors have been found consistently in trait ratings within diverse North American, Asian, Hispanic, and European cultures (John & Srivastava, 1999; Trull & Geary, 1997).

TABLE 11.1 The Big Five Personality Factors and Their Lower-Order Traits

Big Five Factors	Lower-Order Traits
Openness	Artistically sensitive vs. artistically insensitive Intellectual vs. unreflective, narrow Polished, refined vs. crude, boorish Imaginative vs. simple, direct
Conscientiousness	Fussy, tidy vs. careless Responsible vs. undependable Scrupulous vs. unscrupulous Persevering vs. quitting, fickle
Extraversion	Talkative vs. silent Frank, open vs. secretive Adventurous vs. cautious Sociable vs. reclusive
Agreeableness	Good-natured vs. irritable Not jealous vs. jealous Mild, gentle vs. headstrong Cooperative vs. negativistic
Neuroticism	Poised vs. nervous, tense Calm vs. anxious Composed vs. excitable Emotionally stable vs. moody, unstable

The Big Five factors are shown in Table 11.1. (The acronym OCEAN—for Openness, Conscientiousness, Extraversion, Agreeableness, and Neuroticism—may help you remember them.) Proponents of the *Five Factor Model* believe that when a person is placed at a specific point on each of these five dimensions by means of a psychological test, behavior ratings, or direct observations of behavior, the essence of his or her personality has been captured (McCrae & Costa, 2003).

What do you think about that conclusion? Your reaction may be one of skepticism, since it seems that there *must* be more to individuality than can be captured by only five dimensions. However, we should remember that, as discussed in Chapter 4, the incredible number of colors that the human visual system can distinguish is based on the activity patterns of only *three* types of cones. Thus the many variations that can occur from the blending of five personality dimensions could account for enormous variation in personality patterns.

Trait theorists not only try to describe the basic structure of personality but also attempt to predict real-life behavior on the basis of a person's traits. Even if a few general traits such as the Big Five seem adequate to describe important features of personality, it is entirely possible that a larger number of specific traits such as Cattell's would capture nuances of behavior within particular situations and would therefore be better for predictive purposes. Measures of the global Big Five factors seldom correlate above .20 to .30 with real-life behavioral outcomes (e.g., Paunonen, 2003). In recognition of this fact, the Big Five model now includes six subcategories, or *facets*, under each of the five major factors, and the personality test used to measure the Big Five (the *NEO Personality Inventory*, or *NEO-PI*) now provides scores on each of these facets as well as on the corresponding major factor. For example, scores are obtained not only for the main factor of Extraversion, but also for facets such as Activity and Positive Emotions. These more specific dimensions permit sharper behavioral predictions (McCrae & Costa, 2003). Nonetheless, the ability of even these more specific traits to predict behavior across varying situations is rather limited (Cervone, 1999).

For more on assessing a personality trait, see Interactive Segment 11.1.

Stability of Personality Over Time

Because traits are viewed as enduring behavioral predispositions, they should show some degree of stability over time. Yet they should not be unchangeable. As we might expect, the research literature shows evidence for both stability and change (Caspi & Roberts, 1999; Helson et al., 2002). Some personality dimensions tend to be more stable than others. On the one hand, introversion-extraversion, as well as temperamental traits such as emotionality and activity level, tend to be quite stable from childhood into adulthood and across the adult years (Eysenck, 1990; Zuckerman, 1991). Self-esteem also shows strong stability (Trzesniewski et al., 2003). On the other hand, both cross-sectional and longitudinal studies indicate that, among the Big Five, Neuroticism, Openness, and Extraversion exhibit average declines from the late teens to the early 30s, whereas Agreeableness and Conscientiousness tend to increase (Costa & McCrae, 2002). Likewise, individuals can show developmental changes in many aspects of personality given influential life experiences, including involvement in counseling and psychotherapy.

Certain habits of thought may also be fairly stable. One is our tendency to think optimistically or pessimistically. Melanie Burns and Martin Seligman (1991) coded diaries and letters that elderly people had written approximately 50 years earlier for the tendency to respond either optimistically or pessimistically to life events. The elderly people also completed a personality test that measured their current optimistic-pessimistic tendencies. Although little consistency over time was shown for dealing optimistically or pessimistically with positive events, Burns and Seligman found a stable tendency to respond with optimism or pessimism to negative life events. The authors suggested that the tendency to be pessimistic might constitute an enduring risk factor for depression, low achievement, and physical illness, and they are presently studying such linkages. Table 11.2 contains items from the *Life Orientation Test* (Scheier & Carver, 1985), used by personality researchers to measure the disposition to be optimistic or pessimistic.

▶ 5. How stable are personality traits across time and situations? What factors decrease consistency across situations?

BENEATH THE SURFACE

ARE WE REALLY BEHAVIORALLY CONSISTENT ACROSS SITUATIONS?

As noted at the beginning of the chapter, one of the reasons we have a concept of personality is because we view people as behaving consistently across situations. Is that assumption of consistency warranted by the data? When Walter Mischel reviewed the evidence in 1969, he found more evidence for inconsistency than for consistency. Even on a trait so central as honesty, people can show considerable behavioral variability across situations. In a classic study done 60 years earlier, Hugh Hartshorne and Mark May (1928) tested the honesty of thousands of children. The children were given opportunities to lie, steal, and cheat in a number of different settings: at home, in school, at a party, and in an athletic contest. The rather surprising finding was that "lying, cheating and stealing as measured by the test situations in this study are only very loosely related. . . . Most children will deceive in certain

Continued

situations but not in others" (p. 411). More than a half century later, Mischel (1984) reported similar findings for college students on the trait of conscientiousness. A student might be highly conscientious in one situation (e.g., coming to work on time) without being conscientious in another (e.g., turning in class assignments on time). Many other studies revealed similar behavioral inconsistency across situations. To some, this called the very concept of personality into question. They reasoned that if behavior is so inconsistent, maybe only the situation is important and we don't need an internal concept called "personality" to account for behavior. This conclusion triggered a lively debate that continued for nearly two decades. The controversy required many psychologists to critically evaluate their own belief that personality is consistent. Before you continue reading, can you think of some ways to reconcile the concept of personality with evidence of (sometimes extreme) inconsistency?

Factors That Reduce Situational Consistency

The consistency issue has been a knotty one. Because behavior always results from a person's interacting with a situation, we could argue that it would be foolish to expect people to behave in the same manner from situation to situation. Let's consider some of the insights that have arisen from the consistency debate.

Three factors make it difficult to predict on the basis of personality traits how people will behave in particular situations. First, personality traits interact with other traits, as well as with characteristics of different situations. This melding accounts for the incredible richness we see in personality, but it also poses a challenge to psychologists who want to predict behavior. When two or more traits, such as honesty, dominance, and agreeableness influence a behavior in a particular situation, our ability to predict on the basis of only one of the traits is bound to be quite limited (Ahadi & Diener, 1989).

Second, the degree of consistency across situations is influenced by how important a given trait is for the person. A person for whom honesty is a cornerstone of the self-concept may show considerable stability in honest behaviors across situations because her or his feelings of self-worth may be linked to living up to moral standards regardless of the circumstances (Kenrick & Funder, 1988).

Third, people differ in their tendency to tailor their behavior to what is called for by the situation. This personality trait is called *self-monitoring* (Table 11.3). People who are high in **self-monitoring** *are very attentive to situational cues and adapt their behavior to what they think would be most appropriate.* Extreme self-monitors resemble "behavioral chameleons" who act very differently in various situations. Low self-monitors, on the other hand, tend to act primarily in terms of their internal beliefs and attitudes rather than the demands of the situation. The saying "What you see is what you get" applies well to low self-monitors, and such people show greater consistency across situations than do high self-monitors (Snyder, 1987).

According to some trait theorists, the stability and distinctiveness that we see in personality does not come from the fact that we behave the same way in every situation. Rather, people exhibit different *average* amounts of extraversion, emotional stability, agreeableness, honesty, and other traits

TABLE 11.2 Sample Items From a Trait Measure of Optimism-Pessimism*

1. In uncertain times, I usually expect the best.
2. Overall, I expect more good things to happen to me than bad.
3. If something can go wrong for me, it will.
4. I rarely count on good things happening to me.

*Items on the Life Orientation Test are answered on a 5-point scale ranging from "strongly disagree" to "strongly agree."

SOURCE: Adapted from Scheier et al., 1994.

TABLE 11.3 Sample Items From the Self-Monitoring Scale*

1. In different situations and with different people, I often act like very different persons.
2. I am not always the person I appear to be.
3. I have trouble changing my behavior to suit different people and different situations.
4. I would not change my opinion (or the way I do things) in order to please someone or win their favor.

*Items 1 and 2 are keyed "true" and items 3 and 4 "false" for self-monitoring.

SOURCE: Based on Snyder, 1987.

across many different situations (Epstein, 1983; Kenrick & Funder, 1988). Nonetheless, if they wish to understand more about these interactions between personality traits, situations, and behavior, personality researchers need to define the relevant characteristics of both the person and the situation (Shoda & Mischel, 2000).

Evaluating the Trait Approach

Despite differences of opinion concerning the nature and number of basic personality dimensions, trait theorists have made an important contribution by focusing attention on the value of identifying, classifying, and measuring stable, enduring personality dispositions. Several challenges confront trait theorists, however. If we are to capture the true complexities of personality, we must pay more attention to how traits combine with one another to affect various behaviors (Ahadi & Diener, 1989; Smith et al., 1990). All too often, researchers try to make specific predictions on the basis of a single measured personality trait without taking into account other personality factors that might also influence the behavior in question. This approach sells short the complexity of personality.

In evaluating the trait perspective, we must remember the distinction between description and explanation. To say that someone is outgoing and fun-loving *because* she is high in extraversion is merely to describe the behavior with a trait name, not to explain the inner disposition and how it operates. Traditionally, the trait perspective has been more concerned with describing the structure of personality, measuring individual differences in personality traits, and predicting behavior than with understanding the psychological processes that underlie the traits. For example, a shortcoming of the Five Factor Model is its lack of explanatory power; it tells us nothing about the causal factors that produce extraverted, neurotic, or agreeable people's experiences and actions (Cervone, 1999).

What can the trait perspective tell us about Charles Whitman? Personality psychologists with a trait orientation would be interested in where he falls on a number of relevant personality dimensions. On the Big Five, he likely would have scored high on Extraversion and Agreeableness (with some notable exceptions in Agreeableness when frustrated), inconsistent on Conscientiousness, and high on Neuroticism. If Whitman had been given a battery of personality tests shortly before the incident, would he have emerged with a profile showing a low level of self-esteem, poor stress-management skills, high hostility, and poor impulse control? How would his scores have changed from the period when he was functioning well in adolescence to the period after he was in the Marines? Unfortunately, we will never be able to answer these questions because, to our knowledge, Whitman never took a personality test. It's quite possible that had Whitman been tested in the days preceding his murderous acts, his test results might have served to warn professionals about his potential for violent behavior.

IN REVIEW

- *The concept of personality arises from observations of individual differences and consistencies in behavior. Personality refers to the distinctive and relatively enduring ways of thinking, feeling, and acting that characterize a person's responses to life situations. Behaviors attributed to personality are viewed as establishing an individual's personal identity, having an internal cause, and having a meaningful organization and structure.*
- *Personality theories differ considerably in their conceptions of what personality is and how it functions. Scientifically useful personality theories organize existing knowledge, allow prediction of future events, and stimulate the discovery of new knowledge.*
- *Trait theorists try to identify and measure the basic dimensions of personality. Factor analysis identifies clusters of behavior that are highly correlated with one another and thus constitute a dimension along which people may vary. Theorists disagree on the number of traits needed to describe personality adequately. Cattell suggested 16 basic traits; other theorists insist that 5 (or even fewer) may be adequate. Prediction studies indicate that a larger number of more specific traits may be superior for predicting behavior in specific situations.*
- *Traits have not proved to be highly consistent across situations, and they also vary in stability over time. Individuals differ in their self-monitoring tendencies, and this variable influences the amount of cross-situational consistency they exhibit in social situations. Traits produce inconsistency by interacting not only with situations but also with one another.*

FIGURE 11.5

According to Hans Eysenck (a), various combinations of two major dimensions of personality—Introversion-Extraversion and Stability-Instability—combine to form more specific traits. (b) Source: Eysenck, 1967.

(a)

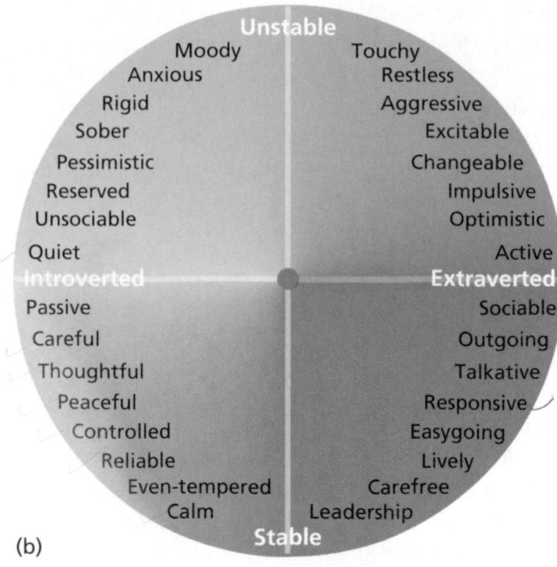

(b)

BIOLOGICAL FOUNDATIONS OF PERSONALITY

Both nature and nurture influence the development of personality traits, but their contributions differ according to the trait in question (Plomin & Caspi, 1999). Biological explanations for personality differences focus on three levels. Some researchers search for differences in the functioning of the nervous system (Pickering & Gray, 1999). Others seek the genetic bases for trait inheritance (Plomin, 1997). A third group of theorists apply evolutionary principles to explain why these traits exist in the human species (e.g., Buss, 1999).

Personality and the Nervous System

One logical place to look for biological underpinnings of personality is in individual differences in brain functioning. Two examples are Hans Eysenck's research and theorizing on extraversion and stability and more recent work on generalized approach and avoidance dispositions.

▶ 6. What biological factors underlie (1) Eysenck's extraversion and stability and (2) incentive/threat reactivity?

Eysenck's Extraversion-Stability Model

We've now seen that among trait theorists, there are "splitters," such as Cattell, who posit a large number of basic traits, and "lumpers," such as the Big Five theorists, who favor a smaller number. Hans J. Eysenck (1916–1997), one of Britain's leading psychologists, was the ultimate lumper. He maintained that normal personality can be understood in terms of only *two* basic dimensions. These dimensions of Introversion-Extraversion and Stability-Instability (sometimes called Neuroticism) blend together to form all of the more specific traits. Eysenck's two "supertraits" are comparable to the Big Five traits of Extraversion and Neuroticism. Eysenck (Figure 11.5a) believed that normal personality is captured quite well within this two-dimensional model.

Eysenck's Extraversion-Stability model is shown in Figure 11.5b. Note that the two basic dimensions intersect at right angles, meaning that they are statistically independent, or uncorrelated. The secondary traits shown in the circle reflect varying combinations or "mixtures" of the two primary dimensions. Thus we can see that the emotionally stable extravert is a carefree, lively person who tends to be well adjusted and to seek out leadership roles. In contrast, unstable (neurotic) extraverts tend to be touchy, aggressive, and restless. The stable introvert is calm, reliable, and even-tempered, but the unstable introvert tends to be rigid, anxious, and moody. Different combinations of the two basic personality dimensions can thus produce very diverse personality patterns.

Eysenck (1967) was one of the first modern theorists to suggest a biological basis for major personality traits. He linked Introversion-Extraversion and Stability-Instability to differences in individuals' normal patterns of arousal within the brain. He started with the notion that there is an optimal, or preferred, level of biological arousal in the brain. Eysenck believed that extreme introverts are chronically *overaroused;* their brains are too electrically active, so they try to minimize stimulation and reduce arousal to get down to their optimal arousal level, or "comfort zone." In contrast, the brains of extreme extraverts are chronically *underaroused*, so they need powerful or frequent stimulation to achieve an optimal level of cortical arousal and excitation. The extravert thus seeks social contact and physical arousal, likes parties, takes chances, is assertive, and suffers boredom easily.

Whereas Introversion-Extraversion reflects a person's customary level of arousal, Stability-Instability represents the suddenness with which shifts in arousal occur. Unstable people have hair-trigger nervous systems that show large and sudden shifts in arousal, whereas stable people show smaller and more gradual shifts (Pickering & Gray, 1999). Eysenck also called this stability dimension *Neuroticism* because he found that people with extremely unstable nervous systems are more likely to experience emotional problems that require clinical attention.

Eysenck proposed that the arousal patterns that underlie Introversion-Extraversion and Stability-Instability have genetic bases. A growing body of evidence from twin studies supports his view. Identical twins are much more alike on these traits than are fraternal twins, and about half of the variance among people can be attributed to hereditary factors (Loehlin et al., 1988; Plomin, 1997). Eysenck believed that although personality is strongly influenced by life experiences, the ways people respond to those experiences may be at least partly programmed by biological factors.

TABLE 11.4 Sample Items From a Measure of Incentive and Threat Reactivity

Incentive Reactivity

When I see an opportunity for something I like, I get excited right away.

When I want something, I usually go all-out to get it.

When I get something I want, I feel excited and energized.

When I am doing well at something, I love to keep at it.

I go out of my way to get things I want.

Threat Reactivity

If I think something unpleasant is going to happen, I usually get pretty worked up.

I worry about making mistakes.

Criticism or scolding hurts me quite a bit.

I have very few fears, compared with my friends.*

I feel pretty worried or upset when I think or know someone is angry at me.

NOTE: Respondents indicate the extent to which they agree with the statements. *Scored in "disagree" direction.

SOURCE: Adapted from Carver & White, 1994.

Individual Differences in Tendencies to Pursue Pleasure or Avoid Pain

In recent years, new findings have established biological linkages between Eysenck's factors and emotional and motivational factors that relate to basic tendencies to seek pleasure or avoid pain (Elliot & Thrash, 2002; Lucas & Diener, 2001). Individual differences in the relative strengths of these two tendencies are related to biological functions.

The Extraversion dimension seems to reflect pleasure seeking (sometimes called *incentive reactivity*), whereas the Instability (Neuroticism) dimension relates more to pain avoidance (or *threat reactivity*). Thus one student may work very hard in school in order to pursue a positive goal of academic success, whereas another may strive academically in order to avoid the pain of failure. One person may be extraverted and friendly in order to achieve the goal of forming friendships, whereas another may behave in that fashion in order to avoid disapproval and rejection. Incentive reactivity predicts greater striving for positive emotions, whereas threat reactivity involves greater potential to experience negative emotions (Sutton, 2002).

Recent research indicates that people who differ in these approach and avoidance orientations show different brain activation patterns. In one set of studies, participants were chosen on the basis of their response to a personality scale designed to measure these approach and avoidant orientations (Table 11.4). Electrical recordings of brain activity revealed that individuals oriented toward positive incentives (rewarding consequences) showed greater relative left-hemisphere activity, whereas threat-reactive people showed greater activation of the right hemisphere. These brain reactions seemed quite stable over time, indicating a trait-like biological characteristic (Heller et al., 2002; Sutton, 2002). You may recall that this left-hemisphere/positive emotion–right-hemisphere/negative emotion activation pattern is the same one discussed in Chapter 9.

Neurotransmitter systems, particularly those that use norepinephrine and serotonin, are also involved in incentive reactivity and threat reactivity. Norepinephrine is an important activator of reward areas in the brain. According to one theory, pleasure seekers have relatively low levels of norepinephrine, causing them to act in ways that produce more reward. In contrast, pain avoiders have low serotonin levels, making them more sensitive to unpleasant stimuli or to cues that have been associated with punishment in the past (Cloninger, 1987). This may account for the fact that incentive-reactive people change their behavior more in response to positive reinforcement, whereas threat-reactive individuals are more responsive to punishment (Carver et al., 1999).

Behavior Genetics and Personality

▶ 7. What do twin studies reveal about the roles of heredity and environment in personality development?

Twin studies are particularly informative for studying the role of genetic factors because they compare the degree of personality resemblance between monozygotic twins, who have identical genetic makeup, and dizygotic twins, who do not (Rowe, 1999). On a great many psychological characteristics, identical twins are more similar to one another than fraternal twins, suggesting a role for genetics. However, the issue is clouded by the possibility that identical twins may also have more similar environments than fraternal twins because others are inclined to treat them more similarly.

The ideal solution to this problem would be to compare personality traits in identical and fraternal twins who were raised together and those who were raised apart. If the identical twins who were reared in different families were as similar as those reared together, a more powerful argument could be made for the role of genetic factors. Moreover, this research design would allow us to divide the total variation among individuals on each personality trait into three components: (1) variation attributable to genetic factors; (2) variation due to a shared family environment in those raised together; and (3) variation attributable to other factors, including unique individual life experiences. The relative influence of these sources of variation can be estimated by comparing personality test correlations in four groups of twins. The following *Research Close-Up* describes a classic study that was especially informative about the respective roles of genetics and environment.

RESEARCH CLOSE-UP

GENETICS, EXPERIENCE, AND PERSONALITY DEVELOPMENT

Background

The comedian Rodney Dangerfield tells of the day his son came home from kindergarten looking very troubled. When asked why he seemed so depressed, the little boy replied that they had learned a new saying in school that day: "Like father, like son."

Have you ever been told that you share a personality trait with a parent or relative? Perhaps you wondered where the presumed similarity originated. Could it possibly have been genetically inherited? This study may provide a tentative answer to that question.

Comparisons of identical and fraternal twins has been a staple in the field of behavior genetics. So has the adoption study, in which adopted children are compared with both their biological and adoptive parents on characteristics of interest to see who they resemble more. The Minnesota twins study introduced an important advance by doing a worldwide search for identical and fraternal twin pairs who had been separated from one another early in life and reared in different environments. The Minnesota study thus combines the strengths of both approaches, allowing the researchers to test not only the effects of genetic similarity but also to separate out the effects of being reared in the same or in different families.

Method

The sample consisted of 217 pairs of monozygotic twins who had been reared together, 44 monozygotic pairs reared apart, 114 dizygotic pairs reared together, and 27 dizygotic pairs reared apart. For those reared apart, the median age at separation was 2.4 months, and the median time they had been apart at the time of testing was 33.8 years. Each twin completed the *Multidimensional Personality Questionnaire*, which measures 14 personality traits (Table 11.5).

Results

Correlations among twin pairs on the scales of the personality inventory were computed for each of the four groups of twins

SOURCE: Auke Tellegen, David T. Lykken, Thomas J. Bouchard, Kimberly L. Wilcox, Nancy L. Segal, and Stephen Rich (1988). Personality similarity in twins reared apart and together. *Journal of Personality and Social Psychology, 54,* 1031–1039.

Table 11.5 Estimates of the Percentages of Group Variance in 14 Personality Traits Attributable to Genetic and Environmental Factors

Trait	Genetic	Familial Environment	Unique Environment
Well-being	.48	.13	.39
Social potency	.54	.10	.36
Achievement	.39	.11	.50
Social closeness	.40	.19	.41
Stress reaction	.53	.00	.47
Alienation	.45	.11	.54
Aggression	.44	.00	.56
Control	.44	.00	.56
Harm avoidance	.55	.00	.45
Traditionalism	.45	.12	.43
Absorption	.50	.03	.47
Positive emotionality	.40	.22	.38
Negative emotionality	.55	.02	.43
Constraint	.58	.00	.42

NOTE: The variance estimates are based on a comparison of the degree of personality similarity in identical and fraternal twins who were reared together or apart.

SOURCE: Adapted from Tellegen et al., 1988.

(identicals reared together or apart; fraternals reared together or apart). By comparing the correlations, the researchers were able to divide the variation in personality test scores into three components. The first was personality similarity attributable to degree of genetic similarity (50 percent versus 100 percent common genes). The second was similarity attributable to being reared in the same family versus being raised in different families. The remaining variation in test scores could only be due to unique experiences and to imperfections in the measurement of the personality variables (assumed to be relatively minor).

The estimates of variance accounted for by the genetic and environmental factors are shown in Table 11.5. Overall, the identical twins were far more similar in personality than were the fraternal twins. This difference indicates a substantial genetic contribution to the personality scores, as shown in the second column of Table 11.5. As you can see, genetic factors accounted for 39 to 58 percent of the variation among people in personality trait scores. In contrast, the degree of trait similarity among identical and fraternal twins was about the same whether the twin pairs were reared together or apart, indicating that general features of the family environment, such as its emotional climate and degree of affluence, accounted for little variance in the traits.

Discussion

Genetic factors contributed substantially to differences on most of the personality traits measured in this study. On average, genetic factors accounted for about half of the variation in personality scores. The big surprise was that, contrary to what many personality psychologists have long assumed, differences in family environment had little influence on personality differences. It mattered little whether the twins were reared together or in different families.

This does not mean, however, that experience is not important. Rather than the family environment, it was individuals' *unique* environmental experiences, such as their school experiences and interactions with peers, that accounted for considerable personality variance. Even within the same family, individual children can have quite different experiences while growing up, including different relationships with other family members and differing experiences outside the home. Apparently, these unique experiences are the critical environmental factor.

This study illustrates the usefulness of the behavior genetics approach to personality development. It provides strong evidence that genetic factors contribute to individual differences in a wide range of personality traits. Of equal significance, the comparisons of twins reared together and apart challenged the long-held belief that family environment exerts a major effect on personality development. The critical environmental influences on personality appear to be the unique experiences that children have within the family as they strive to create their own identities, cultivate their abilities, and forge their unique life paths. Environment matters greatly in the development of personality, and the shared family environment, while apparently exerting little impact on personality traits, does influence some characteristics, such as religious beliefs, attitudes, political viewpoints, and certain health behaviors. In this study, the traits of "social closeness" and "positive emotionality" did show a small family influence. Clearly, however, more work is needed to identify the unique contributions of shared and nonshared environmental influences.

Although genetic factors are clearly important contributors to personality, researchers have had little success in identifying the specific genes involved. Most experts doubt that any particular trait will be linked to a single gene. Instead, a large number of interacting genes are likely involved. Until these interactions are discovered, the specific mechanisms of genetic influence remain a mystery.

Evolutionary Approaches to Personality

▶ 8. How does evolutionary theory account for personality similarities and differences?

Behavior genetics researchers attempt to understand how biological factors contribute to differences between individuals on personality traits. An approach called **evolutionary personality theory** *looks for the origin of personality traits in the adaptive demands of our species' evolutionary history.* It asks the basic question, "Where did the traits come from in the first place?"

Consider the Big Five personality factors. Why should these traits be found so consistently in the languages and behaviors of cultures around the world? According to David Buss, an evolutionary personality theorist, they exist in humans because they have helped us achieve two overriding goals: physical survival and reproductive success (Buss, 1999). Traits such as Extraversion and emotional stability were helpful in attaining positions of dominance and mate selection. Conscientiousness and Agreeableness are important in group survival, as well as in reproduction and the care of children. Finally, because Openness to experience may be the basis for problem solving and creative activities that could affect the ultimate survival of the species, there has always been a need for intelligent and creative people. Thus evolutionary theorists regard the behaviors underlying the Big Five as sculpted by natural selection pressures until they ultimately became part of human nature.

The Big Five may also reflect the ways in which we are biologically prepared to think about and discriminate among people. Lewis Goldberg (1981) suggests that over the course of evolution, people have had to ask five basic questions when interacting with another person, questions that have survival and reproductive implications:

1. Is Person X active and dominant or passive and submissive? Can I dominate X, or will I have to submit to X?
2. Is X agreeable and friendly or hostile and uncooperative?
3. Can I count on X? Is X conscientious and dependable?
4. Is X sane (stable, rational, predictable) or crazy (unstable, unpredictable, possibly dangerous)?
5. How smart is X, and how quickly can X learn and adapt?

Not surprisingly, according to Goldberg, these questions relate directly to the Big Five trait factors. He believes that this is the reason factor analyses of trait ratings reveal Big Five consistency across very diverse cultures.

Goldberg's analysis shows how an evolutionary approach can be applied to understanding human nature (i.e., the traits humans have in common). Evolutionary theorists account for individual differences in those personality traits by focusing on gene-environment interactions. Evolutionary development may provide humans with species-typical behavior patterns, but environmental inputs influence how they are manifested. For example, dominance may be the behavior pattern encouraged by innate mechanisms in males, but an individual male who has many early experiences of being subdued or dominated may develop a submissive personality. For evolutionists who assume that the innate female behavior pattern is submissiveness, an individual female who has the resources of high intelligence and physical strength may be quite willing and able to behave in a competitive and dominant fashion.

Evaluating the Biological Approach

Biological research, spurred by technical advances in measuring nervous system activity and in evaluating genetic influences, is forging new frontiers in personality science. As we learn more about how biological functions are affected by developmental experiences and how they interact with situational factors, new insights about personality development will be achieved.

Can the biological perspective offer clues to Charles Whitman's behavior? In Whitman's letter, we find references to "tremendous headaches" for which he had been medicating himself and a request that an autopsy be done after his death to see if a "visible physical disorder" existed. In fact, a postmortem examination of his brain detected a fast-growing tumor in the hypothalamus, an area that includes some of the aggression circuitry in the brain (Raine et al., 2000). Medical authorities evaluating Whitman's case differed on the importance of the tumor. If the tumor played a role in his violent acts, it seems unlikely that it was the primary causal factor. However, it could have been a predisposing factor that lowered his inhibitions against violent behavior.

Another possibility arises from information that Whitman's father had a penchant for violent behavior and frequently beat his wife and children. Thus a second potential biological factor could be the genes Whitman inherited from his father. Aggression can have a genetic basis (Wasserman &

Wachbroit, 2001), and it is possible that a genetic predisposition interacted with environmental factors to increase the potential for violent behavior.

IN REVIEW

- *Biological perspectives on personality traits focus on differences in the nervous system, the contribution of genetic factors, and the possible role of evolution in the development of universal human traits and ways of perceiving behavior.*
- *Eysenck suggested that normal personality differences can be accounted for by variations on the dimensions of Introversion-Extraversion and Stability-Instability, both of which are assumed to have a biological basis. In Eysenck's theory, Introversion-Extraversion reflects a person's customary level of arousal, whereas Stability-Instability represents the suddenness with which shifts in arousal occur.*
- *Another biologically based model focuses on differences in incentive reactivity and threat reactivity, which reflect broad orientations to approach positive incentives or to avoid negative ones.*
- *Studies comparing identical and fraternal twins reared together and apart indicate that genetic factors may account for as much as half of the variance in personality test scores, with individual experiences accounting for most of the remainder. Evolutionary theories of personality attribute some personality dispositions to genetically controlled mechanisms based on natural selection.*

THE PSYCHODYNAMIC PERSPECTIVE

Psychodynamic theorists look for the causes of behavior in a dynamic interplay of inner forces that often conflict with one another. They also focus on unconscious determinants of behavior. Sigmund Freud's psychoanalytic theory was the first and most influential of these theories, and his ideas continue to influence Western thought today.

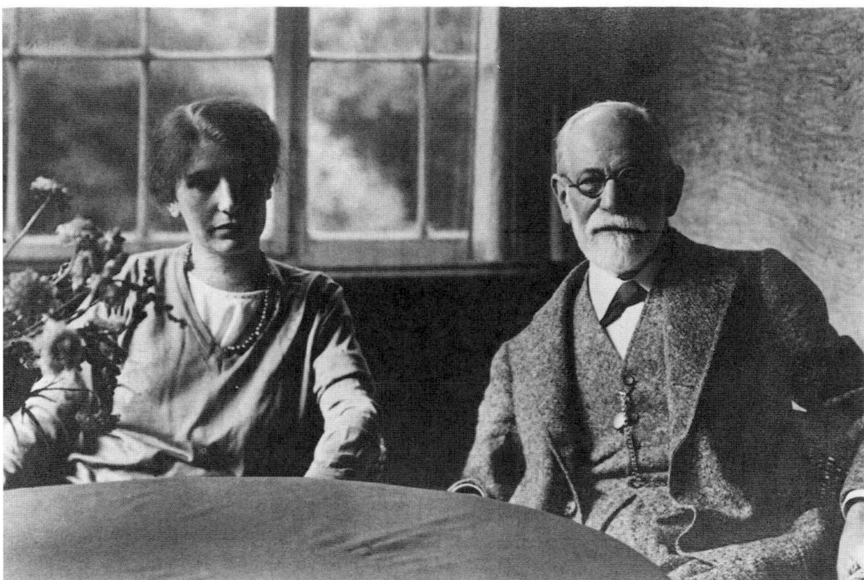

FIGURE 11.6

Sigmund Freud is shown here with his daughter Anna, who herself became an influential psychoanalytic theorist.

Freud's Psychoanalytic Theory

Freud (1856–1939) spent most of his life in Vienna, where he attended medical school with the intention of becoming a medical researcher (Figure 11.6). He was particularly interested in brain functioning. A pivotal event in his life occurred when he was awarded a fellowship to study in Paris with the famous French neurologist Jean Charcot. Charcot was treating patients who suffered from a disorder called *conversion hysteria*, in which physical symptoms such as paralysis and blindness appear suddenly and with no apparent physical cause. Freud's experiences in treating these patients convinced him that their symptoms were related to painful memories and feelings that seemed to have been *repressed*, or pushed out of awareness. When his patients were able to reexperience these traumatic memories and unacceptable feelings, which were often sexual or aggressive in nature, their physical symptoms often disappeared or improved markedly.

These observations convinced Freud that an unconscious part of the mind exerts great influence on behavior. He began to experiment with various techniques to unearth the buried contents of the unconscious mind, including hypnosis, *free association* (saying whatever comes to mind, no matter how trivial or embarrassing), and dream analysis. In an attempt to relieve painful bouts of depression that he was experiencing, Freud also conducted an extensive self-analysis based on his own dreams.

In 1900 Freud published *The Interpretation of Dreams*. The book sold only 600 copies in the first six years after its publication, but his revolutionary ideas began to attract followers. His theory also evoked scathing criticism from a Victorian society that was not ready to regard the human being as a seething cauldron of sexual and aggressive impulses. In the words of one commentator,

> It is a shattering experience for anyone seriously committed to the Western tradition of morality and rationality to take a steadfast, unflinching look at what Freud has to say. It is humiliating to be compelled to admit the grossly seamy side of so many grand ideals. . . . To experience Freud is to partake a second time of the forbidden fruit. (Brown, 1959, p. xi)

▶ 9. Describe Freud's structures of personality, their operating principles, and how they interact with one another.

Freud based his theory on careful clinical observation and constantly sought to expand it. Over time, psychoanalysis became (a) a theory of personality, (b) an approach to studying the mind, and (c) a method for treating psychological disorders.

Psychic Energy and Mental Events

Inspired by the hydraulic models of 19th-century physics, which emphasized exchanges and releases of physical energy, Freud considered personality to be an energy system, somewhat like the steam engines of his day. According to Freud, instinctual drives generate *psychic energy*, which powers the mind and constantly presses for either direct or indirect release. For example, a buildup of energy from sexual drives might be discharged directly in the form of sexual activity or indirectly through such diverse behaviors as sexual fantasies, farming, or painting.

Mental events may be conscious, preconscious, or unconscious. The *conscious mind* consists of mental events that we are presently aware of. The *preconscious mind* contains memories, feelings, thoughts, and images that we are unaware of at the moment but that can be recalled. A friend's telephone number or memories of your 16th birthday are likely to reside in the preconscious mind.

Because we can be aware of their contents, we are likely to see the conscious and preconscious areas of the mind as the most prominent ones. But Freud believed that these areas are dwarfed in both size and importance by the *unconscious mind*, a dynamic realm of wishes, feelings, and impulses that lies beyond our awareness. Only when impulses from the unconscious are discharged in one way or another, such as in dreams, slips of the tongue, or some disguised behavior, does the unconscious reveal itself. Sometimes this can have unfortunate consequences. In the throes of passion, a young man proclaimed his love for his fiancée by gasping, "I love you, Marcia." The only problem was that his fiancée's name was Amy. Marcia was a former girlfriend. Freud would probably have concluded (as did Amy) that the slip of the tongue was a sign that erotic feelings for Marcia, which the man vehemently denied, were still bubbling within his subconscious mind. Psychoanalysts believe that such verbal slips are holes in our armor of conscious control and expressions of our true feelings.

The Structure of Personality

Freud divided personality into three separate but interacting structures: id, ego, and superego. The **id** *is the innermost core of the personality, the only structure present at birth, and the source of all psychic energy*. It exists totally within the unconscious mind (Figure 11.7). Freud described the id as "a chaos, a cauldron of seething excitations" (Freud, 1900/1965, p. 73). The id has no direct contact with reality and functions in a totally irrational manner. Operating according to the **pleasure principle,** *it seeks immediate gratification or release, regardless of rational considerations and environmental realities*. Its dictum: "Want . . . take!"

The id cannot directly satisfy itself by obtaining what it needs from the environment because it has no contact with the outer world. In the course of development, a new structure therefore develops. The **ego** *has direct contact with reality and functions primarily at a conscious level*. It operates according to the **reality principle,** *testing reality to decide when and under what conditions the id can safely discharge its impulses and satisfy its needs*. For example, the ego would seek sexual gratification within a consenting relationship rather than allowing the pleasure principle to dictate an impulsive sexual assault on the first person who happened by.

The last personality structure to develop is the **superego,** *the moral arm of the personality*. Developing by the age of 4 or 5, the superego contains the traditional values and ideals of family and society. These ideals are internalized by the child through identification with his or her parents, who also use reinforcement and punishment to teach the child what is "right," what is "wrong," and how the child "should" be. With the development of the superego, self-control is substituted for external control.

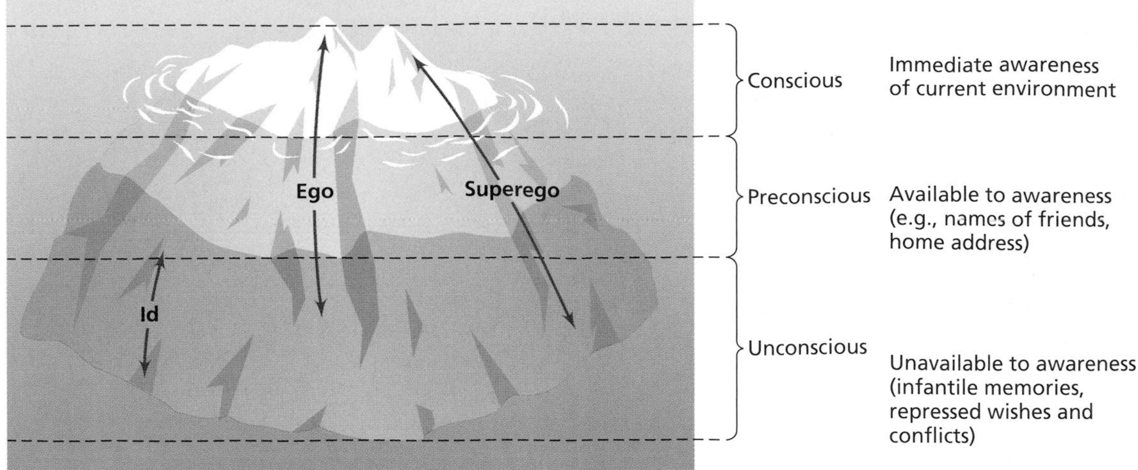

FIGURE 11.7

Freud's own representation of his three-part conception of personality shows the relation of the id, ego, and superego to the conscious, preconscious, and unconscious areas of the mind. Note how relatively small the conscious portion of the mind is compared with the unconscious. SOURCE: Adapted from Smith, 1998.

Like the ego, the superego strives to control the instincts of the id, particularly the sexual and aggressive impulses that are condemned by society. In a sense, the id says, "I want!" and the superego replies, "Don't you dare! That would be evil!" Whereas the ego simply tries to postpone instinctual gratification until conditions are safe and appropriate, the superego, in its blind quest for perfection, tries to block gratification permanently. For the superego, moralistic goals take precedence over realistic ones, regardless of the potential cost to the individual. Thus the superego might cause a person to experience intense guilt over sexual activity even within marriage because it has internalized the idea that sex is "dirty."

With the development of the superego, the ego is squarely in the eye of a psychic storm. It must achieve compromises between the demands of the id, the constraints of the superego, and the demands of reality. This balancing act has earned the ego the title, "executive of the personality."

For more on Freudian structures of the mind, see Video Segment 11.1.

Conflict, Anxiety, and Defense

The dynamics of personality involve a never-ending struggle between instincts and drives in the id striving for release and counterforces generated by the ego and superego to contain them. Observable behavior often represents compromises between motives, needs, impulses, and defenses. When the ego confronts impulses that threaten to get out of control or is faced with dangers from the environment, anxiety results. Like physical pain, anxiety serves as a danger signal and motivates the ego to deal with the problem at hand. In many instances, the anxiety can be reduced through realistic coping behaviors, as when a person who is extremely angry at someone works out the problem through rational discussion instead of a murderous assault. However, when realistic strategies are ineffective in reducing anxiety, the ego may resort to **defense mechanisms,** *unconscious mental operations that deny or distort reality.* Some of the defense mechanisms permit the release of impulses from the id in disguised forms that will not conflict with forces in the external world or with the prohibitions of the superego. The major defense mechanisms are described in Table 11.6.

Psychoanalysts believe that repression is the primary means by which the ego keeps the lid on the id. In **repression,** *the ego uses some of its energy to prevent anxiety-arousing memories, feelings, and impulses from entering consciousness.* Repressed thoughts and wishes remain in the unconscious, striving for release, but they may be expressed indirectly, as in slips of the tongue or in dreams. Through the defense mechanism of **sublimation,** *taboo impulses may even be channeled into socially desirable and admirable behaviors, completely masking the sinister underlying impulses.* For example, hostile impulses may find expression in tracking down criminals or being a successful trial lawyer. Although Freud described several defense mechanisms, his primary interest was in repression. His daughter

▶ 10. What roles do (1) conflict and defense, and (2) psychosexual development play in Freud's theory?

TABLE 11.6 Psychoanalytic Ego Defense Mechanisms

Defense Mechanism	Description	Example
Repression	An active defensive process pushes anxiety-arousing impulses or memories into the unconscious mind.	A person who was sexually abused in childhood develops amnesia for the event.
Denial	A person refuses to acknowledge anxiety-arousing aspects of the environment. The denial may involve either the emotions connected with the event or the event itself.	A man who is told he has terminal cancer refuses to consider the possibility that he will not recover.
Displacement	An unacceptable or dangerous impulse is repressed, then directed at a safer substitute target.	A man who is harassed by his boss experiences no anger at work but then goes home and abuses his wife and children.
Intellectualization	The emotion connected with an upsetting event is repressed, and the situation is dealt with as an intellectually interesting event.	A person who has been rejected in an important relationship talks in a highly rational manner about the "interesting unpredictability of love relationships."
Projection	An unacceptable impulse is repressed, then attributed to (projected onto) other people.	A woman with strong repressed desires to have an affair continually accuses her husband of being unfaithful to her.
Rationalization	A person constructs a false but plausible explanation or excuse for an anxiety-arousing behavior or event that has already occurred.	A student caught cheating on an exam justifies the act by pointing out that the professor's tests are unfair and, besides, everybody else was cheating, too.
Reaction formation	An anxiety-arousing impulse is repressed, and its psychic energy finds release in an exaggerated expression of the opposite behavior.	A mother who harbors feelings of resentment toward her child represses them and becomes overprotective of the child.
Sublimation	A repressed impulse is released in the form of a socially acceptable or even admired behavior.	A man with strong hostile impulses becomes an investigative reporter who ruins political careers with his stories.

Anna Freud, also a psychoanalyst, extended his ideas and described many of the defense mechanisms shown in Table 11.6.

Defense mechanisms operate unconsciously, so people are usually unaware that they are using self-deception to ward off anxiety. Almost everyone uses defense mechanisms at times, but maladjusted people use them excessively in place of more realistic approaches to dealing with problems.

Psychosexual Development

Freud's clinical experiences convinced him that adult personality traits are powerfully influenced by experiences in the first years of life. He proposed that children pass through a series of **psychosexual stages** *during which the id's pleasure-seeking tendencies are focused on specific pleasure-sensitive areas of the body called erogenous zones*. Potential deprivations or overindulgences can arise during any of these stages, resulting in **fixation,** *a state of arrested psychosexual development in which instincts are focused on a particular psychic theme*. **Regression,** *a psychological retreat to an earlier psychosexual stage*, can occur in the face of stressful demands that exceed one's coping capabilities.

The first of these stages is the *oral stage*, which occurs during infancy. Infants gain primary satisfaction from taking in food and from sucking on a breast, a thumb, or some other object. Freud proposed that either excessive gratification or frustration of oral needs can result in fixation on oral themes of self-indulgence or dependency as an adult.

In the second and third years of life, children enter the *anal stage* and pleasure becomes focused on the process of elimination. During toilet training, the child is faced with society's first attempt to control a biological urge. According to Freud, harsh toilet training can produce compulsions, overemphasis on cleanliness, obsessive concerns with orderliness, and insistence on rigid rules and rituals. In contrast, Freud speculated that extremely lax toilet training results in a messy, negative, and dominant adult personality.

The most controversial of Freud's stages is the *phallic stage*, which begins at 4 to 5 years of age. This is the time when children begin to derive pleasure from their sexual organs. Freud believed that during this stage of early sexual awakenings, the male child experiences erotic feelings toward his mother, desires to possess her sexually, and views his father as a rival. At the same time, however, these feelings arouse strong guilt and a fear that the father might castrate him, hence the term *castration anxiety. This conflictual situation involving love for the mother and hostility toward the father is the* **Oedipus complex,** named for the Greek character Oedipus, who unknowingly killed his father and married his mother. Girls, meanwhile, discover that they lack a penis, blame the mother for their lack of what Freud considered the more desirable sex organ, and wish to bear their father's child as a substitute for the penis they lack. *The female counterpart of the Oedipus complex was termed the* **Electra complex.**

Freud believed that the phallic stage is a major milestone in the development of gender identity, for children normally resolve these conflicts by repressing their sexual impulses and moving from a sexual attachment to the opposite-sex parent to *identification* with the same-sex parent. Boys take on the traits of their fathers and girls those of their mothers. Identification allows the child to possess the opposite-sex parent indirectly, or vicariously, and also helps form the superego as children internalize the parent's values and moral beliefs.

As the phallic stage draws to a close at about 6 years of age, children enter the *latency stage*, during which sexuality becomes dormant for about 6 years. Sexuality normally reemerges in adolescence as the beginning of a lifelong *genital stage*, in which erotic impulses find direct expression in sexual relationships.

Research on Psychoanalytic Theory

Freud was committed to testing his ideas through case studies and clinical observations. He believed that careful observations of everyday behavior and clinical phenomena were the best source of evidence. He opposed experimental research, believing that the complex phenomena he had identified could not be studied under controlled conditions (Rosenzweig, 1992). Most modern psychologists do not believe that clinical observations are sufficient proof, but they do acknowledge the difficulty of studying psychoanalytic concepts under controlled laboratory conditions (Carver & Scheier, 2003; Mischel et al, 2004). Indeed, a major shortcoming of psychoanalytic theory is that many of its concepts are ambiguous and difficult to measure or even to define operationally. How, for example, can we measure the strength of an individual's id impulses and unconscious ego defenses, or study processes that are by definition unconscious and inaccessible to the person?

Fortunately, cognitive psychologists have developed new methods to identify and measure unconscious processing of information, and a growing body of research supports Freud's notion that much of our moment-to-moment mental and emotional life occurs outside of awareness (Bargh & Chartrand, 1999). On the biological front, cognitive neuroscience has provided methods for tapping into mental processes as they occur by measuring brain activity (D'Esposito, 2003). Increasingly, researchers are using these tools to test hypotheses derived from psychoanalytic theory with greater scientific precision.

In one study, researchers focused on patients who sought therapy for anxiety disorders or depression (Shevrin et al., 1996). The patients received psychiatric workups based on interviews and psychological tests designed to discover each patient's underlying unconscious conflicts. The researchers then created individualized sets of words for each patient. Some of the words were relevant to the patient's consciously experienced symptoms (e.g., *tension, sadness*). Other words were based on the patient's hypothesized underlying conflict (*rage, father*). Two other sets of word lists contained positive and negative words unrelated to the patient's symptoms or conflicts (e.g., *puppy, stench*). The words were then presented to the patients subliminally, too briefly to be consciously recognized but capable of being processed by the brain.

The researchers measured the patients' EEG brain response to each word and found that the words related to unconscious conflicts evoked different patterns of electrical brain responses than the other three types of words. They concluded that the psychodynamic conflict words were being processed differently in the brain, possibly through activated defensive processes designed to keep the concepts in the unconscious. This study is an intriguing illustration of how new scientific approaches may permit experimental tests of psychoanalytic hypotheses. Perhaps this is the kind of research Freud foresaw when he wrote, "Let the biologists go as far as they can, and let us go as far as we can. One day the two will meet" (Freud, 1900/1965, p. 276).

Neoanalytic and Object Relations Approaches

▶ 11. How do neoanalytic and object relations theories depart from and build on Freudian theory?

Freud's ideas were so revolutionary that they generated disagreement even within his circle of disciples. **Neoanalytic theorists** *were psychoanalysts who disagreed with certain aspects of Freud's thinking and developed their own theories.* Among them were Alfred Adler, Karen Horney, Erik

Erikson, and Carl Jung. The neoanalysts believed that Freud did not give social and cultural factors a sufficiently important role in the development and dynamics of personality. In particular, they believed that he stressed infantile sexuality too much (Kurzweil, 1989). The second major criticism was that Freud laid too much emphasis on the events of childhood as determinants of adult personality. Neoanalytic theorists agreed that childhood experiences are important, but some of them, such as Erikson, believed that personality development continues throughout the life span as individuals confront challenges that are specific to particular phases in their lives.

In contrast to Freud's assertion that behavior is motivated by inborn sexual and aggressive instincts and drives, Alfred Adler (1870–1937) insisted that humans are inherently social beings who are motivated by *social interest*, the desire to advance the welfare of others. They care about others, cooperate with them, and place general social welfare above selfish personal interests (Figure 11.8). In contrast, Freud seemed to view people as savage animals caged by the bars of civilization. Perhaps influenced by his own struggles to overcome childhood illnesses and accidents, Adler also postulated a general motive of *striving for superiority*, which drives people to compensate for real or imagined defects in themselves (the *inferiority complex*) and to strive to be ever more competent in life.

FIGURE 11.8

In Alfred Adler's theory, people have an inborn social interest that can cause them to put society's welfare above personal interests.

Like Adler, Carl Jung (1875–1961) was Freud's friend and associate before he broke away and developed his own theory. Jung expanded Freud's notion of the unconscious in unique directions. For example, he believed that humans possess not only a **personal unconscious** *based on their life experiences* but also a **collective unconscious** *that consists of memories accumulated throughout the entire history of the human race*. These memories are represented by **archetypes,** *inherited tendencies to interpret experiences in certain ways*. Archetypes find expression in symbols, myths, and beliefs that appear across many cultures, such as the image of a god, an evil force, the hero, the good mother, and the quest for self-unity and completeness (Figure 11.9). Jung's ideas bear some similarities to those of contemporary evolutionary theorists who emphasize innate cognitive processes.

Following Freud's death in 1939, Melanie Klein (1975), Otto Kernberg (1984), Margaret Mahler (1968), and Heinz Kohut (1971) developed a new psychodynamic emphasis. **Object relations theories** *focus on the images or mental representations that people form of themselves and other people as a result of early experiences with caregivers*. Whether realistic or distorted, these internal representations of important adults—for example, of the mother as kind or malevolent, the father as protective or abusive—become lenses, or "working models," through which later social interactions are viewed, and these relational themes exert an unconscious influence on a person's relationships throughout life (Westen, 1998). People who have difficulties forming and maintaining intimate relationships tend to mentally represent themselves and others in negative ways, expecting painful interactions and attributing malevolence or rejection to others (Kernberg, 1984; Nigg et al., 1992). These working models often create self-fulfilling prophesies, influencing the recurring relationships people form with others.

John Bowlby's (1969) attachment theory, which we discussed in Chapter 10, is an outgrowth of the object relations approach. Correlational research relating early attachment experiences to later adult relationships is yielding provocative results. For example, college students with a history of positive early attachments tend to have longer and more satisfying romances (Shaver & Clark, 1996). In contrast, child-abusing parents often have mental representations of their own parents as punitive, rejecting, and abusive (van Ijzendoorn, 1995). Table 11.7 shows descriptive statements that characterize people who manifest "secure," "avoidant," and "anxious-ambivalent" adult attachment styles. Today, a large proportion of psychodynamic theorists and clinicians claim to rely more heavily on object relations concepts than on classical psychoanalytic theory (Aron, 1996; Westen, 1998). The concepts in object relations theories are also easier to operationally define and measure, making them more amenable to research.

Evaluating the Psychodynamic Approach

Although psychoanalytic theory has profoundly influenced psychology, psychiatry, and other fields, it has often been criticized on scientific grounds. One reason is that many of its specific propositions have not held up under the scrutiny of research (Fisher & Greenberg, 1996). To some critics, psychoanalytic theory seems to be more science fiction than science. A great drawback of the theory is that it is hard to test, not because it doesn't explain enough, but because it often explains too much to allow clear-cut behavioral predictions (Meehl, 1995). For example, suppose we predict on the basis of psychoanalytic theory that participants in an experimental condition will behave aggressively but they behave instead in a loving manner. Is the theory wrong, or is the aggression being masked by the operation of a defense mechanism such as reaction formation (which produces exaggerated behaviors that are the opposite of the impulse)? The difficulties in making clear-cut behavioral predictions mean that some psychoanalytic hypotheses are untestable, and this detracts greatly from the theory's scientific usefulness.

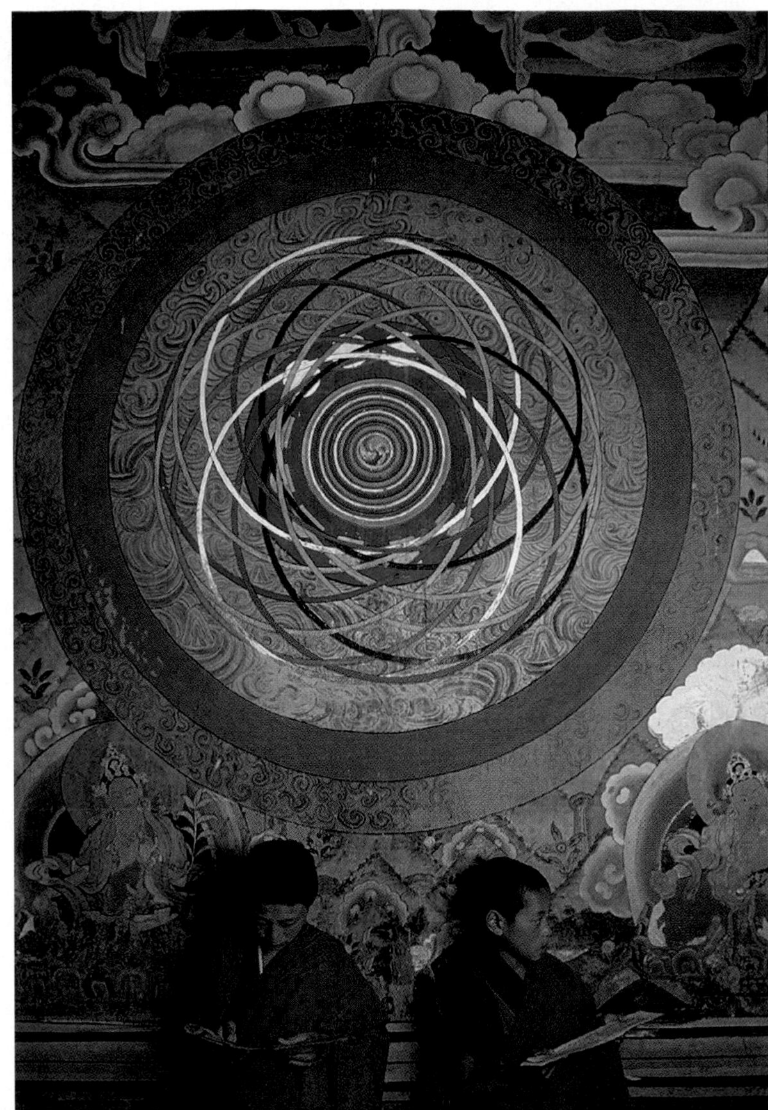

FIGURE 11.9

One of Carl Jung's archetypes, the notion of a holistic self, is expressed in this Tibetan mandala *(Sanskrit for "circle"),* which symbolizes wholeness and completion. *The mandala symbol occurs within numerous cultures and religions of the world, suggesting to Jung that it is a reflection of the collective unconscious.*

Freud's emphasis on the unconscious was scorned by a Victorian society that emphasized rationality, and later generations of personality psychologists with a behaviorist orientation condemned it as unscientific. However, research over the past 20 years has vindicated Freud's belief in unconscious psychic events by showing that nonconscious mental and emotional phenomena do indeed occur and can affect our behavior (Chartrand & Bargh, 2002; Erdelyi, 2001). On the other hand, the unconscious processes that have been demonstrated experimentally are by no means as exotic as those described by Freud (Kihlstrom, 1999). Rather than a seething cauldron of forbidden wishes and desires, current research is unearthing what one theorist describes as "a kinder, gentler unconscious" (Greenwald, 1992).

Freud's ideas about psychosexual development are the most controversial feature of his theory. Although many theorists reject Freud's assertions about childhood sexuality and the notion of specific psychosexual stages, there is strong evidence that childhood experiences do indeed influence the development of personality (Lewis, 1999). The previously wide gulf between psychodynamic theories and other psychological

TABLE 11.7 Attachment Styles in Adult Relationships

Question: Which of the following best describes your feelings?*

1. I find it relatively easy to get close to others and am comfortable depending on them and having them depend on me. I don't often worry about being abandoned or about someone getting too close to me. (secure)
2. I am somewhat uncomfortable being close to others; I find it difficult to trust them completely, difficult to allow myself to depend on them. I am nervous when anyone gets too close, and often, love partners want me to be more intimate than I feel comfortable being. (avoidant)
3. I find that others are reluctant to get as close as I would like. I often worry that my partner doesn't really love me or won't want to stay with me. I want to merge completely with another person, and this desire sometimes scares people away. (anxious-ambivalent)

*The first type of attachment style is described as "secure," the second as "avoidant," and the third as "anxious-ambivalent."

SOURCE: Based on Shaver et al., 1988.

perspectives is starting to narrow, due largely to the development of new methods for studying unconscious mental processes.

Can the psychodynamic perspective offer possible insights into Charles Whitman's personality and his eventual eruption into violence? Although born into a family of means and showered with material goods, Whitman grew up within a chaotic home environment. His father was a self-made but brutal man who ruled his house with an iron hand and frequently beat his wife. He brooked no weakness from his sons and viciously belittled them for any perceived failures. Whitman was very close to his mother and deeply resented his father's treatment of her, which, according to Freud, would only enhance any unresolved Oedipal hostility toward the father. In his suicide note, he wrote,

> The intense hatred I feel for my father is beyond description. My mother gave that man the 25 best years of his life and because she finally took enough of his beatings, humiliation, degredation [sic], and tribulations that I am sure that no one but she and he will ever know—to leave him. (Lavergne, 1997, p. 168)

These hostile feelings were bottled up and were revived on an almost daily basis by phone calls from his father begging him to convince his mother (who had moved to Austin after leaving her husband) to return home. Lacking a good paternal model with whom to identify, Whitman seemed to have a poorly developed superego and constantly wrote himself notes about how to behave appropriately, using the notes as a substitute for his tenuous inner controls. A friend describing Whitman said he was "like a computer. He would install his values into the machine, then program the things he had to do, and out would come the results" (Lavergne, 1997).

Object relations theories also have applicability to Whitman. Despite his hatred for his father, his own family experiences caused him to enter his marriage with an internal working model of "abusive husband" and "submissive wife." To his later regret, he beat his own wife on two occasions in the early years of his marriage. He was determined not to repeat this behavior and kept a journal in which he constantly wrote self-instructions about how to be a good husband. For the most part, these external constraints were effective in keeping his intense hostility under control—until the accumulation of severe life stressors caused his controls to disintegrate. "Unusual and irrational thoughts" began to intrude into consciousness as his defenses were strained to the breaking point, and he eventually exploded into violence. The psychiatrist at the Student Health Center who interviewed him several months before the tower incident (referred to in Whitman's letter at the opening of this chapter as "the doctor") found that he "had something about him that expressed the all-American boy," but "seemed to be oozing with hostility." Whitman told the psychiatrist that he had frequent fantasies about "going up on the tower with a deer rifle and shooting people," but the psychiatrist did not take them seriously because of his nonviolent history (Lavergne, 1997).

? *What Do You Think?*

SHOULD A PSYCHOTHERAPIST REPORT A PATIENT'S VIOLENT FANTASIES?

Should Whitman's report of his violent fantasies have alerted the psychiatrist about his penchant for violence and caused the psychiatrist to contact authorities? What is a mental health professional's responsibility in cases like this? What is the appropriate balance between client confidentiality and community safety? Think about it, then read the discussion on page 462.

IN REVIEW

- *Freud's psychoanalytic theory views personality as an energy system. Personality dynamics involve modifications and exchanges of energy within this system. Mental events may be conscious, preconscious, or unconscious.*
- *Freud divided the personality into three structures: id, ego, and superego. The id is irrational and seeks immediate instinctual gratification on the basis of the pleasure principle. The ego operates on the reality principle, which requires it to test reality and to mediate between the demands of the id, the superego, and reality. The superego is the moral arm of the personality.*
- *The dynamics of personality involve continuous conflict between impulses of the id and counterforces of the ego and superego. When dangerous id impulses threaten to get out of control or when the environment poses dangers, the result is anxiety. To deal with threat, the ego may develop defense mechanisms to ward off anxiety and permit instinctual gratification in disguised forms.*
- *Freud's psychosexual theory of personality development held that adult personality traits are molded by how children deal with instinctual urges and social reality during the oral, anal, and phallic stages.*
- *Neoanalytic theorists modified and extended Freud's ideas in important ways, stressing social and cultural factors in personality development. Modern object relations theorists focus on the mental representations that people form of themselves, others, and relationships.*

THE HUMANISTIC-PHENOMENOLOGICAL PERSPECTIVE

Humanistic theories were in part a reaction to Freud's conception of the human as being driven by "those half-tamed demons that inhabit the human beast" (Freud, 1900/1965, p. 202). Instead, humanists embrace a positive view that affirms the inherent dignity and goodness of the human spirit. They emphasize the central role of conscious experience *(phenomenology)*, as well as the individual's creative potential and inborn striving for **self-actualization,** *the total realization of one's human potential* (Figure 11.10). As described in Chapter 9, humanist Abraham Maslow considered self-actualization to be the ultimate human need and the highest expression of human nature.

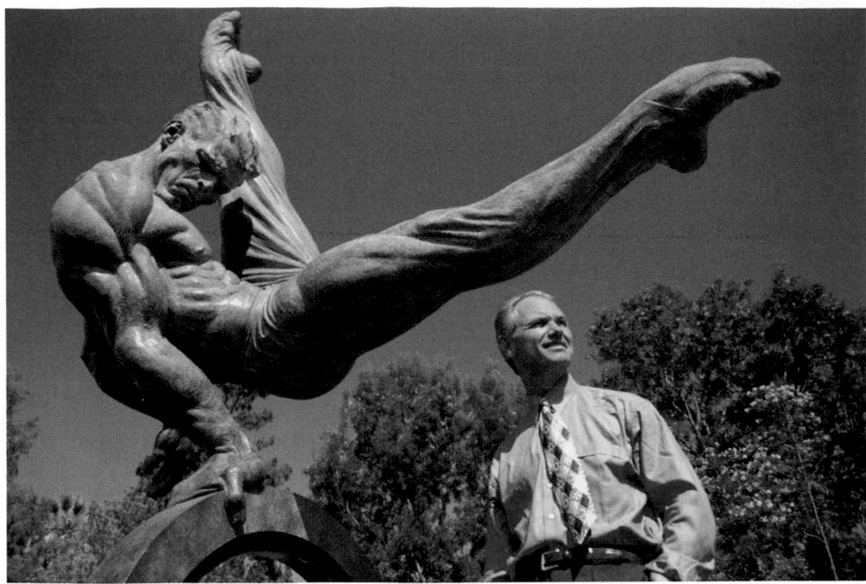

FIGURE 11.10

The motivations underlying behavior are much different for humanistic theorists than they are for Freudians. In the view of humanistic theorists such as Maslow and Rogers, creative and artistic accomplishments are not a product of intrapsychic conflict and sublimation but rather an expression of an innate tendency toward self-actualization.

Carl Rogers's Theory of the Self

Carl Rogers (1902–1987) was one of the most influential humanistic theorists. In contrast to Freud, Rogers believed that our behavior is not a reaction to unconscious conflicts but rather a response to our immediate conscious experience of self and environment (Rogers, 1951). This *emphasis on the primacy of immediate experience is known as* **phenomenology,** and it focuses our attention on the present instead of the past. As a humanist, Rogers believed that the forces that direct behavior are within us and that when they are not distorted or blocked by our environment, they can be trusted to direct us toward self-actualization.

The Self

The central concept in Rogers's theory is the **self,** *an organized, consistent set of perceptions of and beliefs about oneself* (Rogers, 1959). Once formed, the self plays a powerful role in guiding our perceptions and directing our behavior. The self thus has two facets: it is an object of perception (the self-concept), as well as an internal entity that directs behavior.

"I can't say I like the looks of that bunch."

FIGURE 11.11

Tendencies to behave in accordance with one's self-concept can at times have ominous implications.

Rogers theorized that at the beginning of their lives, children cannot distinguish between themselves and their environment. As they interact with their world, children begin to distinguish between the "me" and the "not-me." The self-concept continues to develop in response to our life experiences, though many aspects of it remain quite stable over time.

▶ 12. Describe the roles of self-consistency, congruence, threat, and conditions of worth in Rogers's self theory.

Once the self-concept is established, there is a tendency to maintain it, for it helps us to understand our relationship to the world around us. We therefore have needs for **self-consistency,** *an absence of conflict among self-perceptions,* and **congruence,** *consistency between self-perceptions and experience.* Any experience we have that is inconsistent, or incongruous, with our self-concept, including our perceptions of our own behavior, evokes **threat,** *or anxiety.* Well-adjusted individuals can respond to threat adaptively by modifying the self-concept so that the experiences are congruent with the self. But other people choose to deny or distort their experiences to remove the incongruence, a strategy that can lead to what Rogers termed "problems in living."

Suppose that an important aspect of Kevin's self-concept is the belief that he is so charming and handsome that every woman finds him irresistible. He meets Margot, whom he finds very attractive but who shows a total lack of interest in him. This incongruence between Kevin's self-concept and his experience produces threat and anxiety because his basic view of himself is challenged. Kevin could react adaptively by modifying his self-concept to acknowledge that he is not, after all, irresistible to *all* women. Alternatively, he might resolve the incongruence by distorting reality. He might deny Margot's lack of interest ("She's just playing hard to get"), or he might distort his perception of her ("She would have to be crazy not to appreciate how special I am—thank heaven I found out in time").

The self-consistency knife can cut in both directions, however. At the other extreme, consider Paul, who believes that he is totally unattractive to women. If a desirable woman expresses interest, Paul might appropriately revise his self-concept in a positive direction. But it is often as difficult for people with negative self-concepts to accept success as it is for those with unrealistically positive self-concepts to accept failure (Rogers, 1959). Thus Paul might find it necessary to give a congruent explanation ("She's just trying to be nice. She doesn't really like me"). Such interpretations will allow Paul to maintain his negative image of himself.

To preserve their self-concept, people not only interpret situations in self-congruent ways, but they also behave in ways that will lead others to respond to them in a self-confirming fashion (Brown, 1998). If Camille has an image of herself as unlovable and certain to be rejected if she lets people get close enough to hurt her, she may behave in ways that distance others. When her behavior is successful, others pull away from her, confirming in her mind that she is indeed unlovable. As Rogers frequently noted, people are pushed by self-consistency needs to behave in accord with their self-concept (Figure 11.11).

According to Rogers, the degree of congruence between self-concept and experience helps define one's level of adjustment. The more rigid and inflexible people's self-concepts are, the less open they will be to their experiences and the more maladjusted they will become (Figure 11.12a). If there is a significant degree of incongruence between self and experience and if the experiences are forceful enough, the defenses used to deny and distort reality may collapse, resulting in extreme anxiety and a temporary disorganization of the self-concept.

The Need for Positive Regard

Rogers believed that we are born with an innate **need for positive regard**—*for acceptance, sympathy, and love from others.* Rogers viewed positive regard as essential for healthy development.

Ideally, positive regard received from the parents is unconditional—that is, independent of how the child behaves. **Unconditional positive regard** *communicates that the child is inherently worthy of love, regardless of accomplishments or behavior.* In contrast, *conditional positive regard* is dependent on how the child behaves. In the extreme case, love and acceptance are given to the child *only* when the child behaves as the parents want.

People need positive regard not only from others but also from themselves. Thus a **need for positive self-regard,** *the desire to feel good about ourselves,* also develops. Lack of unconditional positive regard from parents and other significant people in the past teaches people that they are worthy of approval and love only when they meet certain standards. This fosters the development of **conditions of worth** *that dictate the circumstances under which we approve or disapprove of ourselves.* A child who experienced parental approval when behaving in a friendly fashion but disapproval whenever she became angry or aggressive may come to disapprove of her own "angry" feelings, even when they are justified. As an adult, she may deny in herself all feelings of anger and struggle to preserve a self-image of being totally loving. Rogers believed that conditions of worth can tyrannize people and cause major incongruence between self and experience, as well as a need to deny or distort important aspects of experience. Conditions of worth are similar to the "shoulds" and "musts" that populate Freud's concept of superego.

Fully Functioning Persons

Toward the end of his career, Rogers became particularly interested in **fully functioning persons,** *individuals who were close to achieving self-actualization.* As Rogers viewed them, such people do not hide behind masks or adopt artificial roles. They feel a sense of inner freedom, self-determination, and choice in the direction of their growth. They have no fear of behaving spontaneously, freely, and creatively. Because they are fairly free of conditions of worth, they can accept inner and outer experiences as they are, without modifying them defensively to suit a rigid self-concept or the expectations of others. Thus a fully functioning unmarried woman would be able (1) to state quite frankly that her career is more important to her than a role as wife and mother (*if* she truly felt that way), even if others did not approve of her choice, and (2) to act comfortably on those feelings. In this sense, she could be true to herself (Figure 11.12b).

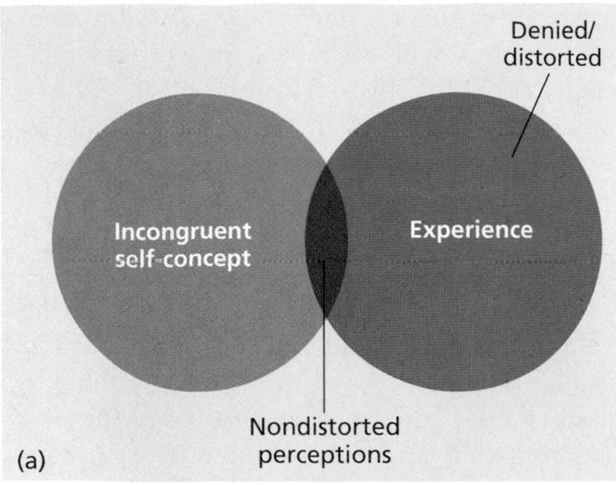

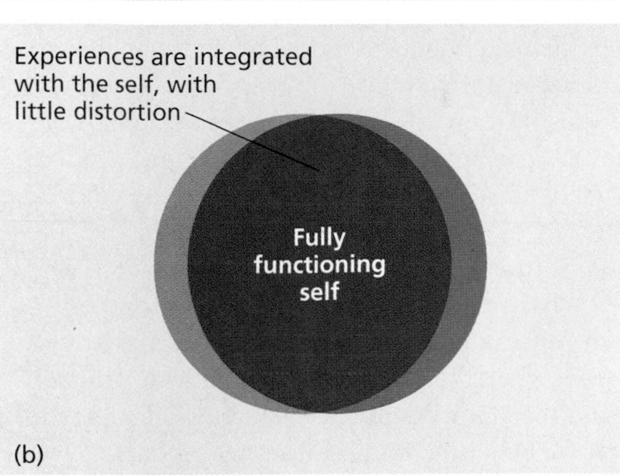

FIGURE 11.12

Rogers defined psychological adjustment in terms of the degree of congruence between self-concept and experience. (a) Maladjustment occurs when a person faced with incongruities between self and experience distorts or denies reality to make it consistent with the self-concept. (b) In contrast, extremely well adjusted, or fully functioning, people integrate experiences into the self with minimal distortion so that they are able to profit fully from their experiences.

What Do You Think?

IS SELF-ACTUALIZATION A USEFUL SCIENTIFIC CONSTRUCT?

Self-actualization is a central concept for humanistic theorists such as Maslow and Rogers. Consider what you have learned about formulating a psychological construct and evaluating a theory according to scientific principles. Can you see any problems with establishing the existence of this core motivation from a scientific perspective? Think about it, then see page 462 for a discussion.

Research on the Self

▶ 13. How does self-esteem develop? Describe the roles of self-verification and self-enhancement as motivational forces.

By giving the self a central place in his theory, Rogers helped stimulate a great deal of research on the self-concept. Two topics at the forefront are (1) the development of self-esteem and its effects on behavior, and (2) the roles played by self-enhancement and self-consistency motives.

Self-Esteem

Self-esteem, *how positively or negatively we feel about ourselves,* is a very important aspect of personal well-being, happiness, and adjustment

(Brown, 1998; Diener, 2000). Level of self-esteem is quite stable over the life span, with correlations from .50 to .70 from childhood to old age (Trzesniewski et al., 2003). Men and women do not differ in overall level of self-esteem (Brown, 1998; Maccoby & Jacklin, 1974).

High self-esteem is related to many positive behaviors and life outcomes. People with high self-esteem are happier with their lives, have fewer interpersonal problems, achieve at a higher and more consistent level, are less susceptible to social pressure, and are more capable of forming satisfying love relationships (Brown, 1998). In contrast, people with a poor self-image are less likely to try to make themselves feel better when they experience negative moods in response to perceived failures in their lives (Heimpel et al., 2002). This may be one reason why they are more prone to psychological problems such as anxiety and depression, to physical illness, and to poor social relationships and underachievement (Brown, 1998).

What conditions foster the development of high self-esteem? Children develop higher self-esteem when their parents communicate unconditional acceptance and love, establish clear guidelines for behavior, and reinforce compliance while giving the child freedom to make decisions and express opinions within those guidelines (Coopersmith, 1967). Beginning in early childhood, success in achieving positive outcomes builds a sense that one is an effective person (Hawley & Little, 2002). Feedback received from other people also has an impact on the child's sense of self. One study showed that when low-self-esteem children were exposed to highly supportive sport coaches who gave them high levels of positive reinforcement and encouragement, the children's self-esteem increased significantly over the course of the sport season (Smoll et al., 1993). Apparently, the positive feedback caused the children to revise their self-concepts in a positive direction.

Self-Verification and Self-Enhancement Motives

Rogers proposed that people are motivated to preserve their self-concept by maintaining self-consistency and congruence. **Self-verification** *refers to this need to confirm the self-concept.* In one study, researchers asked college students to describe themselves in order to measure their self-concept. In a later and supposedly unrelated experiment, the students interacted with other participants and received fake feedback from them in the form of adjectives that were either consistent or inconsistent with their self-concept. Later, when the students were asked to recall and identify the adjectives that had been attributed to them, they showed greater recall for the consistent adjectives, suggesting that people selectively attend to and recall self-consistent information (Suinn et al., 1962).

Self-verification needs are also expressed in people's tendency to seek out self-confirming relationships. One study found that if people with firmly held negative self-views marry spouses who appraise them favorably, they tend to eventually withdraw from the marriage. Such people are more likely to remain with spouses who agree with the negative image they have of themselves. In contrast, people with positive self-concepts prefer spouses who share their positive view of themselves (Swann et al., 1992).

Rogers (1959) also suggested that people have a need to regard themselves positively, and research confirms the existence of **self-enhancement,** *a strong and pervasive tendency to gain and preserve a positive self-image.* Self-enhancement needs have been demonstrated across many cultures (Sedikides et al., 2003), and several self-enhancement strategies have been identified. For example, people show a marked tendency to attribute their successes to their own abilities and effort but to attribute their failures to environmental factors. Furthermore, most people rate themselves as better than average on virtually any socially desirable characteristic that is subjective in nature (Steele, 1988). The vast majority of businesspeople and politicians rate themselves as more ethical than the average. In defiance of mathematical possibility, about 80 percent of high-school students rate themselves in the top 10 percent in their ability to get along with others. Even people who have been hospitalized after causing auto accidents rate themselves as more skillful than the average driver (Greenberg et al., 1997). Indeed, as evidence on self-serving biases in self-perception continues to accumulate, researchers are concluding that positive illusions of this sort are the rule rather than the exception in well-adjusted people and that these self-enhancement tendencies, or "positive illusions," contribute to people's psychological well-being (Taylor & Brown, 1988; Taylor et al., 2003). Particularly for people low in self-esteem, self-enhancement needs sometimes override self-verification tendencies. In a series of experimental studies, Tiffiny Bernichon and coworkers (2003) found that low-self-esteem individuals have a strong tendency to seek out positive feedback about themselves even when it is not self-verifying. Likewise, children low in self-esteem show an especially strong desire to play for sport coaches who provide a great deal of positive feedback and encouragement, and their global self-esteem increases when they play for these nonverifying coaches (Smith & Smoll, 1990).

Evaluating the Humanistic-Phenomenological Approach

Humanistic-phenomenological theorists focus on the individual's subjective experiences. What matters most is how people view themselves and the world. Some critics believe that the humanistic view relies too heavily on individuals' reports of their personal experiences. For example, psychoanalytic theorists maintain that accepting what a person says at face value can easily lead to erroneous conclusions because of the always present influence of unconscious defenses.

Although humanism may indeed seem nonscientific to some, Rogers (1959) dedicated himself to developing a theory whose concepts could be measured and its laws tested. One of his most notable contributions was a series of groundbreaking studies on the process of self-growth that can occur in psychotherapy. To assess the effectiveness of psychotherapy, Rogers and his coworkers measured the discrepancy between clients' *ideal selves* (how they would like to be) and their *perceived selves* (their perceptions of what they are actually like). The studies revealed that when clients first enter therapy, the discrepancy is typically large but that it gets smaller as therapy proceeds, suggesting that therapy may help the client become more self-accepting and perhaps also more realistic. Rogers and his coworkers also discovered important therapist characteristics that either aid or impede the process of self-actualization in therapy. We will describe this research in Chapter 14.

Let us consider what kinds of insights the humanistic-phenomenological perspective might contribute to Charles Whitman's violent outburst. The obvious starting point is Whitman's self-concept. Despite the successful facade of achievement and exemplary behavior erected during his childhood and adolescent years, the abuse and denigration Whitman received from his father took a heavy toll on his self-concept. After years of being belittled, he was anxious to prove himself as a man when he enlisted in the Marines. He worked hard and successfully at being a good soldier, but things began to deteriorate after he enrolled at the University of Texas on the Marine Corps scholarship. In the absence of the disciplinary structure provided first by his father and then by the Marines, he began to get into trouble, and his grades suffered to the point that his scholarship was withdrawn. He was ordered to return to his former Marine unit, where he now found military life oppressive. His conduct deteriorated, and he was court-martialed for gambling and for threatening the life of a fellow Marine with a pistol. This proved to be an early indication of his potential for violence.

Eventually, thanks to his father's political influence, Whitman was honorably discharged and returned to the University of Texas. Academic difficulties there left him riddled with self-doubt, and he struggled desperately to reduce the discrepancy between his ideal self and his perceived self. He wrote numerous self-improvement journals filled with instructions designed to program himself into behaving as a good husband, scholar, and citizen. He frequently studied all night and took amphetamines to stay awake, but the drugs made him even less efficient. Soon he began to despair of ever being the person he wanted to be, and failure to live up to his conditions of worth undermined his self-esteem even further. A note written after he killed his wife while she slept professed his love for her and his desire to relieve her of the shame she would experience if she were still alive after what he planned to do the next day at the top of the tower.

IN REVIEW

- *Humanistic theories emphasize the subjective experiences of the individual and thus deal with perceptual and cognitive processes. Self-actualization is viewed as an innate positive force that leads people to realize their positive potential if not thwarted by the environment.*
- *Rogers's theory attaches central importance to the role of the self. Experiences that are incongruous with the established self-concept produce threat and may result in a denial or distortion of reality. Conditional positive regard may result in unrealistic conditions of worth that can conflict with self-actualization. Rogers described a number of characteristics of the fully functioning person.*
- *Rogers's theory helped stimulate a great deal of research on the self-concept, including studies on the origins and effects of differences in self-esteem, self-enhancement and self-verification motives, and self-concept change.*

▶ 14. Describe the major features of social-cognitive theories, and the importance of reciprocal determinism.

▶ 15. Describe Rotter's concepts of expectancy, reinforcement value, and locus of control.

SOCIAL-COGNITIVE THEORIES

The psychology of learning has great relevance for understanding personality. Many behaviors ascribed to personality are acquired through classical conditioning, operant conditioning, and modeling (Bandura, 1999). However, the learner is not simply a passive reactor to environmental forces. Instead, as the cognitive perspective tells us, the human is a perceiver, a thinker, and a planner who mentally interprets events, thinks about the past, anticipates the future, and decides how to behave. Environmental effects are filtered through these cognitive processes and are influenced—even changed—by them. **Social-cognitive theories** *combine the behavioral and cognitive perspectives into an approach to personality that stresses the interaction of a thinking human with a social environment that provides learning experiences.*

To understand behavior, psychodynamic, humanistic, and trait theorists emphasize internal personal causes of behavior, such as unconscious conflicts, self-actualization tendencies, and personality traits. In a sense, they account for behavior from "the inside out." In contrast, radical behaviorists emphasize environmental causes and view humans as reactors to external events (Parker et al., 1998). To them, behavior is to be explained from "the outside in." Social-cognitive theorists take an intermediate position, focusing on both internal and external factors. They believe that the debate on whether behavior is more strongly influenced by personal factors or by the person's environment is basically a meaningless one. Instead, according to the social-cognitive principle of **reciprocal determinism,** *the person, the person's behavior, and the environment all influence one another in a pattern of two-way causal links* (Bandura, 1986; Figure 11.13).

As an example, let us consider how these interactions or linkages might operate in the case of a hostile and disagreeable man we'll call Tom. Tom's disagreeableness trait manifests itself in an irritable, cynical, and uncooperative behavior pattern (his personality influences his behavior). Tom's disagreeable behaviors tend to evoke negative responses from others (his behavior causes his social environment to respond to him in kind). These negative social consequences reinforce and strengthen still further his personality trait (including his expectations that others will eventually reject him), and they also strengthen his disagreeable behavior tendencies (his environment influences both his personality trait and his social behavior). Thus Tom's personality, his behavior, and his environment all influence one another.

FIGURE 11.13

A key concept in social-cognitive theory is reciprocal determinism, in which characteristics of the person, the person's behavior, and the environment all affect one another in reciprocal, or two-way, causal relations.

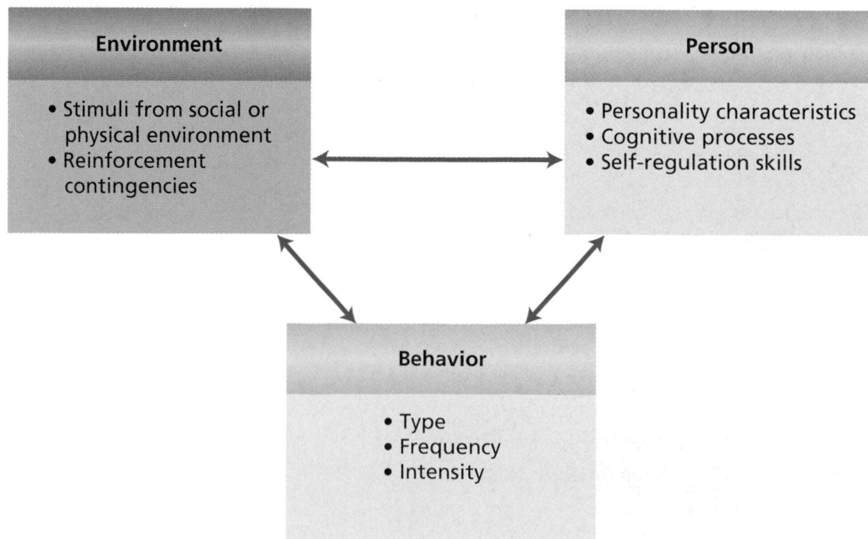

Julian Rotter: Expectancy, Reinforcement Value, and Locus of Control

In 1954, Julian Rotter (whose name rhymes with *motor*) laid the foundation for today's social-cognitive approaches. According to Rotter, the likelihood that we will engage in a particular behavior in a given situation is influenced by two factors: expectancy and reinforcement value. *Expectancy* is our perception of how likely it is that certain consequences will occur if we engage in a particular behavior within a specific situation. *Reinforcement value* is basically how much we desire or dread the outcome that we expect the behavior to produce. Thus a student who strongly values academic success and also expects that studying will result in high grades is likely to study (Rotter, 1954). Note that this approach makes use of *reinforcement*, a central behaviorist concept, but views its effects within a cognitive framework that emphasizes how we think about our behavior and its expected outcomes.

Locus of Control

One of Rotter's most influential concepts is **internal-external locus of control,** *an expectancy concerning the degree of personal control we have in our lives.* People with an *internal* locus of control believe that life outcomes are largely under personal control and depend on their own behavior

(Figure 11.14). In contrast, people with an *external* locus of control believe that their fate has less to do with their own efforts than with the influence of external factors, such as luck, chance, and powerful others. Table 11.8 contains items from Rotter's (1966) *Internal-External (I-E) Scale,* used to measure individual differences in locus of control. Locus of control is called a *generalized expectancy* because it is applies across many life domains as a general worldview.

Locus of control is a highly researched personality variable. Quite consistently, people with an internal locus of control behave in a more self-determined fashion (Burger, 2004). In the 1960s, African Americans who actively participated in the civil rights movement were more internal on the I-E Scale than were those who did not (Rotter, 1966). "Internal" college students achieve better grades than do "external" students of equal academic ability, probably because they link their studying to degree of success and work harder. Internals are more likely to actively seek out the information needed to succeed in a given situation (Ingold, 1989). Interpersonally, internals are more resistant to social influence, whereas externals tend to give in to high-status people who they see as powerful. Because they believe that their health is in large part under their control, internals are more likely than externals to engage in health-promoting behaviors, such as exercising regularly, maintaining a healthy diet, using seat belts, abstaining from smoking, and adhering to medical regimens (Wallston, 1993). When they do become ill, internals seek out more information about their illness in the hope of taking steps to speed their recovery.

Internal locus of control is positively related to self-esteem and feelings of personal effectiveness, and internals tend to cope with stress in a more active and problem-focused manner than do externals (Jennings, 1990). They are also less likely to experience psychological maladjustment in the form of depression or anxiety (Hoffart & Martinson, 1991).

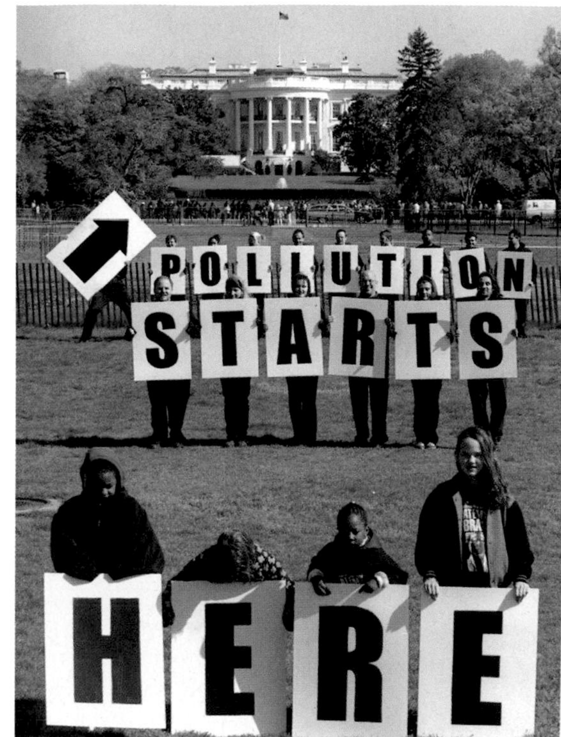

FIGURE 11.14

Research shows that people with an internal locus of control are more likely to take an active role in social change movements.

Albert Bandura: Social Learning and Self-Efficacy

Albert Bandura has made major contributions to the development of the social-cognitive approach. His early studies of modeling, described in Chapter 6, helped combine the psychology of learning with the cognitive perspective. Bandura's social learning analyses of aggression, moral behavior, and behavioral self-control demonstrated the wide applicability of the social-cognitive approach (Bandura, 1986). Perhaps his most influential contribution, however, is his theory and research on self-efficacy.

Self-Efficacy

▶ 16. Describe four determinants of self-efficacy. Which procedures in goal setting help enhance self-efficacy?

According to Bandura (1997), a key factor in how people regulate their lives is their sense of **self-efficacy,** *their beliefs concerning their ability to perform the behaviors needed to achieve desired outcomes.* People whose self-efficacy is high have confidence in their ability to do what it takes to overcome obstacles and achieve their goals.

TABLE 11.8 Sample Items From Rotter's Internal-External Scale

Choose statement a or b from each numbered choice.

1. (a) Many times I feel that I have little influence over the things that happen to me.
   (b) It is impossible for me to believe that chance or luck plays an important part in my life.
2. (a) The average citizen can have an influence in government decisions.
   (b) The world is run by the few people in power, and there isn't much the little guy can do about it.
3. (a) In the long run, people get the respect they deserve in this world.
   (b) Unfortunately, an individual's worth often passes unrecognized no matter how hard one tries.

NOTE: 1b, 2a, and 3a are the internal alternatives.
SOURCE: Adapted from Rotter, 1966.

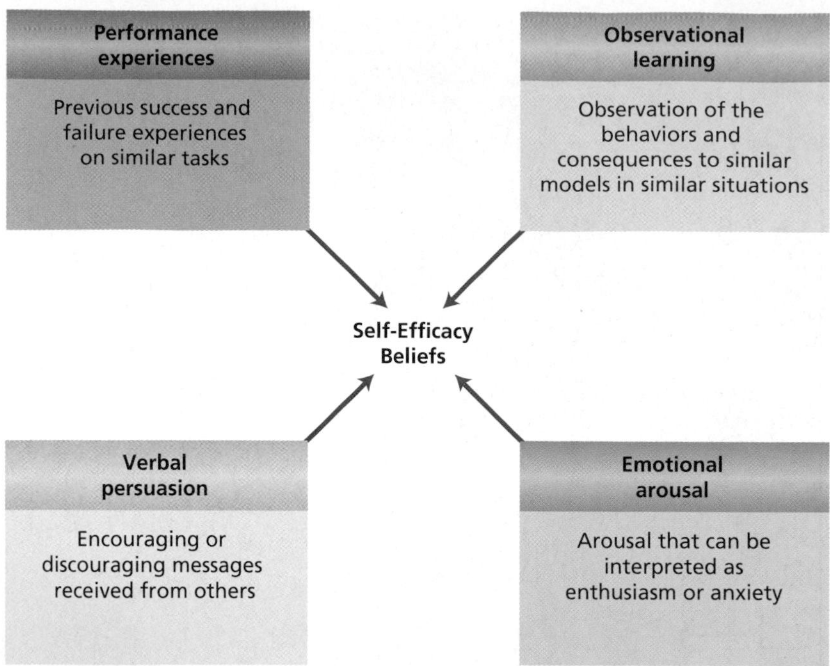

FIGURE 11.15

Four classes of information that affect self-efficacy beliefs. SOURCE: Based on Bandura, 1997.

A good deal of research has been done on the factors that create differences in self-efficacy (Figure 11.15). Four important determinants have been identified (Bandura, 1997). First, the most important is our previous *performance experiences* in similar situations. Such experiences shape our beliefs about our capabilities. For example, as shown in Figure 11.16, college women who felt that they had mastered the martial arts and emotional-control skills taught in a physical self-defense training program showed dramatic increases in their belief that they could escape from or disable a potential assailant or rapist (Weitlauf et al., 2000). Bandura stresses that self-efficacy beliefs are always specific to particular situations. Thus we may have high self-efficacy in some situations and low self-efficacy in others. For example, the women who mastered the physical self-defense skills did not feel more generally capable in all areas of their lives, despite their enhanced self-defense efficacy.

A second source of information comes from *observational learning*—that is, observing others' behaviors and their outcomes. If you observe a person similar to yourself accomplish a particular goal, then you are likely to believe that if you perform those same behaviors you will also succeed. A striking example of how powerful such expectations can be comes from the world of sports. At one time, physiologists insisted that it was physically impossible for a human being to run a mile in less than 4 minutes, and no one in the history of track and field had ever done it. When the Englishman Roger Bannister broke the 4-minute barrier in 1954, that limiting belief was shattered. The impact on other runners' performance was immediate and dramatic. In the year following Bannister's accomplishment, 37 other runners broke the barrier, and the year after that, nearly 300 runners did the "impossible." Apparently, a great many people came to believe that "if he can do it, so can I," and their new sense of self-efficacy enhanced their performance.

Third, self-efficacy can be increased or decreased by *verbal persuasion*. The messages we get from other people who affirm our abilities or downgrade them affect our efficacy beliefs. Thus inspirational teachers who convey high standards and a "you can do it" conviction can inspire their students to great accomplishments, as exemplified in the true-life story of Jaime Escalante, the mathematics teacher featured in the movie *Stand*

FIGURE 11.16

(a) Physical self-defense training has dramatic effects on women's self-efficacy to perform the behaviors needed to defend themselves. (b) The physical defense self-efficacy scores in this study could extend from 6 to 60. SOURCE: Based on Weitlauf et al., 2000.

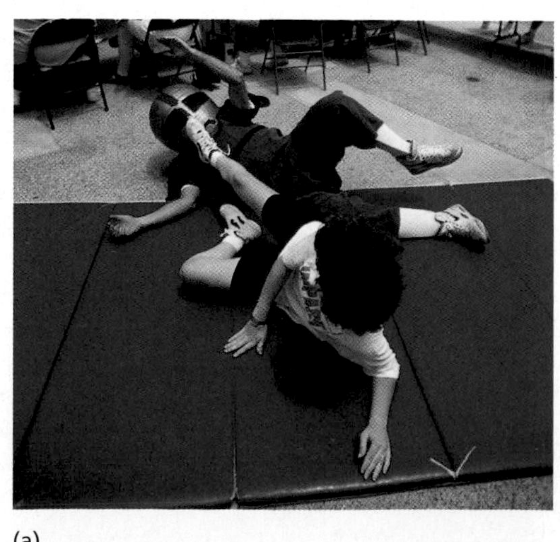

(a)

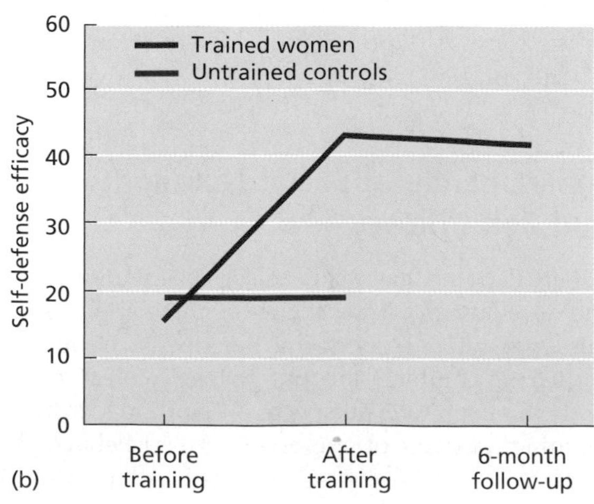

(b)

and Deliver (Figure 11.17). By convincing inner-city minority students who had trouble doing simple arithmetic that they were capable of much more, and by helping them prove their hidden competencies to themselves, Escalante helped them achieve award-winning success in calculus.

Fourth, high *emotional arousal* that is interpreted as anxiety or fatigue tends to decrease self-efficacy. However, if we find ourselves able to control such arousal, it may enhance efficacy beliefs and subsequent performance. For example, test-anxious college students who were given training in stress-management relaxation techniques showed increases in their belief that they could remain relaxed and focused during tests, and their test performance and grade point average improved significantly (Smith, 1989).

Efficacy beliefs are strong predictors of future performance and accomplishment (Bandura, 1997). They become a kind of self-fulfilling prophecy. In the words of Henry Ford, "Whether you believe you can do something or you believe you can't, you're probably right."

FIGURE 11.17

The film Stand and Deliver *depicts the extraordinary accomplishments of math teacher Jaime Escalante, who inspired his inner-city students to exceptional achievements in calculus. His stated faith in their potential and their own performance accomplishments enhanced their sense of self-efficacy.*

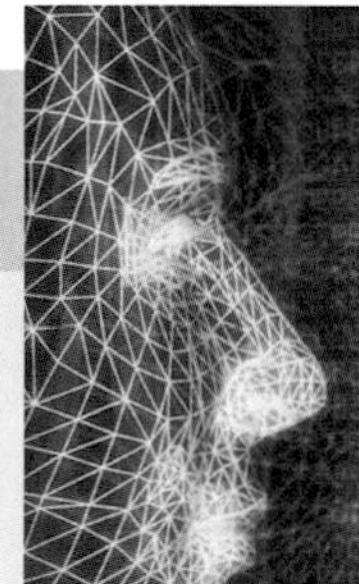

APPLYING PSYCHOLOGICAL SCIENCE

INCREASING SELF-EFFICACY THROUGH SYSTEMATIC GOAL SETTING

In Chapter 9, we described motivation as the impetus for goal-directed behavior. Because positive self-efficacy beliefs are consistently related to success in behaving effectively and achieving goals, Bandura and other social-cognitive theorists have been strongly interested in practical measures for enhancing self-efficacy. When people are successful and when they attribute their success to their own competencies (internal locus of control), their self-efficacy increases and assists them in subsequent goal-directed efforts. Moreover, successful people have usually mastered the skills involved in setting challenging and realistic goals, figuring out what they need to do on a day-by-day basis to achieve them, and making the commitment to do what is required. As they achieve each goal they have set, they become more skillful and increase their sense of personal efficacy (Bandura, 1997).

Not all goal-setting procedures are created equal, and it is important to apply the principles that make goal-setting programs most effective (Locke & Latham, 2002). Here are some research-derived guidelines for effective goal setting.

- *Set specific, behavioral, and measurable goals.* The first step in changing some aspect of your life is to set a goal. The kind of goal you set is very important, because certain kinds of goals encourage us to work harder, enjoy success, and increase self-efficacy. Studies show that specific and fairly narrow goals are far more effective than general "do your best" goals (Locke & Latham, 2002). A general goal like "improve my tennis game" is less helpful than "increase the number of serves I put in play by 20 percent." The latter goal refers to a specific behavior that you can focus on and measure.

One of the most important aspects of goal setting is systematically measuring progress toward the goal. This was shown in a study by Bandura and Daniel Cervone (1983) in which participants worked on a strenuous bicycle-pedaling task over a number of sessions. Two independent variables were manipulated: (1) whether the participants were given specific improvement goals before each session after the first (baseline) session, and (2) whether the participants were given feedback about their performance during the previous session. A control condition got neither goals nor feedback and provided a basis for evaluating

Continued

the effects of goals and feedback, either alone or in combination. The dependent variable was the speed and power with which the participants pedaled.

As shown in Figure 11.18, simply having goals was not enough, nor was feedback effective by itself. But having both goals and feedback was a powerful combination, resulting in by far the greatest improvement. This shows how important it is to find a way to measure your progress toward the goal so that you get performance feedback and can see your improvement. Visible movement toward realistic goals builds self-efficacy.

- *Set behavioral, not outcome, goals.* Many of our goals relate to outcomes in the future, such as "getting an A in this course." You are more likely to achieve such goals if you use the means-end heuristic discussed in Chapter 8 and think about the specific things you must *do* to achieve that outcome goal. Behavioral goals (what one has to do) work better than outcome goals because they keep the focus on the necessary behaviors. A behavioral goal might be "read and outline the textbook and outline the lecture notes for 1 hour each day." Achieving this behavioral goal can also be measured quickly and repeatedly, giving you constant feedback. Many people focus on outcome goals and forget what has to be done day-to-day to achieve them. It has been said that there are three kinds of people in this world: those who make things happen, those who wait for things to happen, and those who wonder what happened. Make sure you're someone who makes things happen.
- *Set difficult but realistic goals.* Moderately difficult goals challenge and motivate us and give us a sense of hope. When reached, they increase self-efficacy. Easy goals do not provide a sense of accomplishment, and extremely difficult or unattainable goals do not provide the success experiences you need to increase your self-efficacy.
- *Set positive, not negative, goals.* In Chapter 6 we discussed the advantages of positive reinforcement over punishment. Working toward positive goals, such as "study for 1 hour before breakfast" is better than avoiding a negative consequence, as in "don't sleep in." Again, positive goals keep you focused on the positive steps that you need to take to achieve them.
- *Set short-range as well as long-range goals.* Short-range goals are important because they provide the opportunity for immediate mastery experiences, and they keep you working positively. A long-range goal like "take all the courses for a double major" can easily be divided into a series of subgoals that you can be working toward right now. Short-range goals are like the steps on a staircase leading to the long-range goal. As each step is accomplished, you enjoy mastery experiences that also lead you toward your ultimate goal. In reaching any goal, "divide and conquer" is a cliché that works.
- *Set definite time spans for achievement.* To keep your goal-setting program on track, it is important to specify the dates by which you will meet specific performance goals or subgoals, as well as the behaviors needed to attain them in that time span.

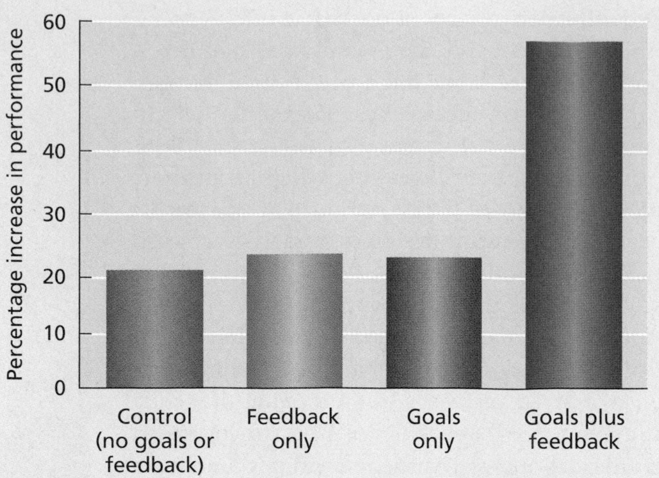

FIGURE 11.18

The effects of goals and feedback on performance improvement in a grueling bicycling task. Clearly, the combination of explicit goals and feedback resulted in the greatest improvement in performance.
SOURCE: Based on Bandura & Cervone, 1983.

Most of the preceding guidelines can be summarized in the acronym SMART: specific, measurable, action-oriented, realistic, and time-based. And it is true that systematic goal setting is one of the smartest ways to work toward goals.

Goal setting is a motivational technique that has resulted in remarkable improvements in productivity in many work, social, and academic settings (Locke & Latham, 2002). Moreover, for purposes of increasing self-efficacy, it has the added advantage of providing the repeated mastery experiences that are the most powerful sources of efficacy information.

Walter Mischel and Yuichi Shoda: The Cognitive-Affective Personality System

Walter Mischel, who studied under Julian Rotter at Ohio State and was a colleague of Albert Bandura's at Stanford, is a third key figure in social-cognitive theory. Like Bandura, Mischel was attracted by the scientific rigor of behaviorism, but he found radical behaviorism's focus on external stimuli and responses deficient for understanding personality. Behaviorists were interested in general laws of behavior and rejected cognitive and other "unseeable" factors. Personality theorists were interested in understanding differences between people and believed that this required an understanding of internal processes.

Bandura and Mischel became part of the "cognitive revolution" that began in the 1960s. They believed that a more cognitive approach to personality was required, one that takes into account not only the power of situational learning factors but also how people characteristically deal mentally and emotionally with experiences. Mischel set out to identify the important "person variables" that could help account for individual differences in personality.

In the most recent formulation of social-cognitive theory, Mischel and his former student Yuichi Shoda describe a **cognitive-affective personality system (CAPS),** *an organized system of five variables that interacts continuously with the environment, generating the distinctive patterns of behavior that characterize the person* (Mischel, 1999). The dynamic interplay among these five factors, together with the characteristics of the situation, accounts for individual differences between people, as well as differences in people's behavior across different situations.

The processes represented within the CAPS are summarized in Table 11.9. The fact that these "person variables" can affect one another in complex ways not only helps account for stable personality differences among people but also links their behaviors to characteristics of the particular situation that confronts them.

TABLE 11.9 Psychological Components of the Cognitive-Affective Personality System

1. What is my perception of the situation? ***Encoding strategies*** help us categorize and understand events.
2. How likely is it that certain outcomes will occur if I behave in manner X? In manner Y? How likely am I to succeed/how much personal control do I have? These are the person's ***expectancies and beliefs***.
3. How much do I want to experience, or to avoid, those outcomes? This relates to the person's ***goals and values***, or the person's motivational structure.
4. How do I feel about this? These emotional responses constitute the person's ***affects***, or feelings.
5. Do I have the behavioral skills needed to deal with this situation? What should I do? ***Personal competencies and self-regulatory processes*** affect behavior as well.

SOURCE: Based on Mischel, 1999.

Encoding Strategies

We respond to the world as perceived. People differ greatly in how they customarily *encode* (mentally represent, categorize, interpret) situations. An unkempt man dressed in a caveman-style loincloth who steps onto an elevator carrying a large snake might be labeled as "dangerous" by one fellow passenger and as "an intriguing person I'd like to get to know" by another. These different encodings will affect the other elements of the CAPS, including emotions, expectancies, and motivation to exit the elevator.

Our encodings determine how we respond emotionally and behaviorally to situations. For example, studies of highly aggressive youth reveal that they have a strong tendency to perceive others as having disrespect and hostile intent toward them. Thus they are primed to react to an innocuous event, such as being unintentionally brushed against on a stairway at school, with a violent response (Dodge, 1986). Other individuals tend to encode ambiguous interpersonal events, such as not being greeted by a fellow student, as instances of personal rejection and to become depressed as a result (Downey & Feldman, 1996). As object relations theorists have suggested, the mental representations or working models we have of relationships influence how we perceive (encode) and respond to others in our later relationships. This is an example of how the social-cognitive approach can incorporate concepts and insights from other theories, including psychodynamic ones.

▶ 17. Describe the 5 "person variables" in Mischel and Shoda's Cognitive-Affective Personality System (CAPS).

Expectancies and Beliefs

As Rotter emphasized, what we expect will happen if we behave in a particular way is a strong determinant of our behavioral choices. **Behavior-outcome expectancies** *represent the "if-then" links between alternative behaviors and possible outcomes. If* I take that course in organic chemistry, *then* what will happen to my grade point average? How likely is it that I'll be forgiven *if* I apologize? Will I make enough money to support myself *if* I become a teacher? Different people may have very different answers to such questions and therefore vary in their response to the same situation. For example, some people believe that assertively approaching someone they desire romantically is most likely to pay off, so they do so. Others may believe that to be assertive in this way is to court disaster and possible rejection, so they do not take the initiative.

In addition to behavior-outcome expectancies, beliefs about our competencies and about the degree of personal control we have influence our actions. Thus, the CAPS model also includes Bandura's self-efficacy and Rotter's locus of control as important expectancy variables.

Goals and Values

Motivation plays a central role in attempts to understand behavior, and it is represented in the CAPS system as goals and values that guide our behavior, cause us to persist in the face of barriers, and determine the outcomes and situations we seek and our reactions to them (Higgins, 1996). People differ in the goals that are important to them and the values that guide their lives. These differences can cause people to behave very differently in situations that are relevant to these important personality factors.

Affects (Emotions)

Anything that implies important consequences for us, whether beneficial or harmful, can trigger an emotional response (Lazarus, 2001). Once aroused, emotions color our perceptions and influence our behavior. For example, if you are already feeling bad due to an argument with a friend and you then get negative feedback in the form of a poor grade on a test, it is easy to become demoralized for a time.

Research shows that people exhibit stable individual differences in emotionality. For example, people who are high on Eysenck's trait of instability (neuroticism) have a tendency to experience negative *affect*, or emotion, in an intense fashion, a factor that influences many of their perceptions and behaviors. Other people seem predisposed to experience mainly positive affect in their lives (Watson & Clark, 1992).

Self-Regulatory Processes and Competencies

▶ 18. How does Mischel's theory reconcile the paradox of personality coherence and behavioral inconsistency?

Social-cognitive theorists stress that people extensively control, or regulate, their own behavior. One form of self-regulation is our ability to choose goals and develop action plans to achieve those goals. Thus people who know how to use the goal-setting procedures described earlier have an important self-regulation skill. The ability to delay gratification is another important self-regulation skill. We often need to put aside short-term rewards or endure great sacrifices to work toward a goal that lies far in the future. To succeed in this, we need to overcome the allure of short-term rewards in favor of the long-term goal (Fishbach et al., 2003). Emotional-control skills are another form of self-regulation. When we are angry with someone, we may feel like screaming at them, but it is usually more adaptive to take a deep breath and speak to the person calmly.

People clearly differ in their self-regulation capabilities. Some people are able to adhere to stringent diets, stop smoking after many years, and persist in the face of adversity and negative outcomes, whereas others are not. By the end of January each year, about 45 percent of New Year's resolutions have been abandoned, but 55 percent of people are still persisting (Norcross et al., 1989). People's ability to control their own behavior is a distinguishing aspect of personality, as are the competencies they develop that allow them to adapt to life successfully and pursue important goals. Some of these competencies are cognitive problem-solving methods that allow them to plan successful strategies, whereas others involve the ability to exert personal control over thoughts, emotions, and behaviors. People who score high on measures of self-esteem tend to have better self-regulation abilities and to enjoy more positive outcomes (Di Paula & Campbell, 2002). These successes undoubtedly contribute to their positive feelings about themselves.

One important way people regulate their own behavior is through self-administered consequences. **Self-reinforcement processes** *refer to internal, self-administered rewards and punishments* (Bandura, 1999; Mischel, 1999). In response to our own behaviors, we generate positive evaluations and emotions such as pride, self-approval, and the conviction that we did "the right thing." In contrast, we may respond with negative responses such as self-reproach, shame, and guilt when we violate our personal standards. Self-reinforcement processes often override external consequences, making us more autonomous and self-directed.

Reconciling Personality Coherence with Behavioral Inconsistency

As noted in our earlier discussion of the trait perspective, people's behavior often shows a notable lack of consistency across situations, a fact that has caused some to call the traditional concept of personality into question. How can we have a coherent and stable personality yet show such inconsistency across different situations? Does personality really matter? Recent social-cognitive research and theoretical advances may provide the answer to this paradox of personality coherence and inconsistent behavior.

In CAPS theory, personality is defined in terms of the cognitive-affective person variables and the interactions among them that produce the person's *behavioral signatures.* The CAPS model is assumed to be highly stable and consistent, although it can surely be modified by significant experiences. Behavior, however, need not be consistent. How a person behaves depends on many factors, including the features of the situation, how these features are encoded, the expectancies and beliefs that are activated, the goals that are relevant, the emotions that might occur, and the plans and self-regulatory processes that help determine the behavior. Thus it is entirely possible for people to behave inconsistently across situations that seem very similar to an outside observer. People will behave similarly in situations that, to them, have important characteristics in common, but they will behave inconsistently in situations that differ in ways that evoke different responses from the CAPS (Shoda & Mischel, 2000).

As a result of interactions between situations and the personality system, people exhibit distinctive **behavioral signatures,** *consistent ways of responding in particular classes of situations.* These behavioral signatures are the outward manifestation of personality that establish a person's unique identity (Mischel et al., 2002). Research shows that people can have very distinctive behavioral signatures. For example, Figure 11.19 shows the behavioral patterns of two verbally aggressive children in a residential summer camp (Shoda et al., 1994). The children's behaviors were systematically observed and coded for more than 150 hours per child. Overall, these two children were quite similar in the overall number of verbally aggressive responses they made. However, inspection of the *situational patterns* of aggression reveals that Child A reacted very aggressively toward adults, whether they were behaving toward the child in a warm or a punitive fashion. In contrast, this child showed relatively little aggression toward peers. Child B showed quite a different pattern, consistently reacting with low levels of aggression toward adults or when being teased by peers. On the other hand, a consistently high level of aggression occurred when peers approached this child in a friendly manner. An important lesson here is that if we simply averaged the aggressive behavior counts across the five situations, the two children would look equally "aggressive." But in so doing, we would mask the distinctive and consistent behavioral signatures that define each child's individuality.

Thus personality coherence is not necessarily incompatible with inconsistency in behavior across situations. The stability and coherence of personality is shown by consistent behavior patterns in the same or very similar situations. For example, researchers observed conscientious behaviors of college students in specific situations, such as turning in class projects on time, arriving at work on time, and keeping one's dorm room orderly. As in earlier studies, students were not similarly conscientious across these different situations. A student might be conscientious in getting academic work done on time but frequently be tardy for work. However, they were far more consistent within particular classes of situations, such as academic or employment settings (Mischel & Peake, 1982). Thus the coherence of personality is shown not at the level of individual behaviors but at the level of behavioral signatures.

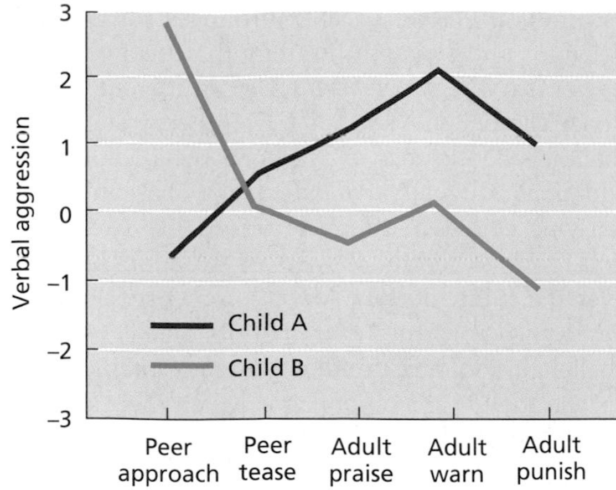

FIGURE 11.19

Aggressive responses of two children, A and B, in five different summer camp situations, showing the manner in which they have distinctive behavioral signatures for aggressive responding even though their aggression scores averaged across the five settings are quite similar. The zero point on the vertical axis represents the average amount of verbal aggression shown in each situation by all the children in the study. SOURCE: Adapted from Shoda et al., 1994.

Evaluating Social-Cognitive Theories

A strength of the social-cognitive approach is its strong scientific base. It brings together two perspectives that have strong research traditions: the behavioral and the cognitive. The constructs of social-cognitive theory can be defined, measured, and researched with considerable precision. As a result, the social-cognitive approach has advanced our understanding of how processes within the person and characteristics of the situation interact with one another to influence behavior. Another strength is its ability to translate insights derived from other perspectives into cognitive-behavioral concepts (Mischel et al., 2004).

Social-cognitive theory also helps resolve an apparent contradiction between the central assumption that personality produces stability in behavior and research findings that people's behavior is not very consistent across different situations. Mischel and Shoda's CAPS theory suggests that the inconsistency of a person's behavior across situations is actually a manifestation of a stable underlying cognitive-affective personality structure that reacts to certain features of situations. However, the ability of the CAPS to predict specific behavior needs further examination, and it will be challenging to measure the numerous interactions among the CAPS components. Much more needs to be learned about how the CAPS operates, but this question is being explored by many current researchers (Cervone & Shoda, 1999a; Mischel et al., 2004). Another major challenge will be to find out what "active ingredients" cause people to encode certain situations in similar ways, thereby producing the consistencies in behavior that constitute behavioral signatures (Ten-Berge et al., 2002).

To conclude our analysis of Charles Whitman, let's view him from a social-cognitive perspective. The behavioral aspect of the social-cognitive perspective would focus on past learning experiences that predisposed him to violence. These are not hard to find in his history. First, his father provided an aggressive model during his formative years, controlling his wife and children with physical abuse. His father was also a gun enthusiast, and there were guns hanging in virtually every room of the Whitman home. Family photos show young Charles holding guns when he was only 2 years old, and his father made sure he received plenty of training in using them. Long before he enlisted in the Marines, Whitman was an expert marksman, and the Marines built upon this expertise with sniper training that earned him a sharpshooter's badge. As other aspects of his life were crumbling, Whitman's marksmanship was a continuing and positive part of his personal self-identity, and he told several University of Texas acquaintances how easy it would be to pick off people from the tower. His expertise made him a deadly killer as he fired from the tower with stunning accuracy, killing people up to a half mile away.

How might Charles Whitman be represented within the CAPS model? At the level of encoding processes, Mischel and Shoda would focus on how he viewed himself and his world. Aggression is fueled by perceptions that we have been wronged and that the provocation was intentional (Lazarus, 2001). Clearly, Whitman felt victimized both by his father and by the Marines, and he saw the world as so malevolent that he regarded killing his wife and mother as an act of mercy. Moreover, his view of himself became increasingly negative as his life's fortunes declined. He saw his life going nowhere as failures piled one upon another. His outcome and self-efficacy expectancies were also quite negative. One source of self-efficacy that remained unchanged was his exceptional marksmanship, and it became the medium for the expression of his rage, as well as his entreé to the death he desired.

Whitman's values involved success in his career, in academics, and as a husband. Success was nowhere in sight, producing feelings of frustration and creating unbearable stress (negative affect) in his life. He felt unworthy of his wife and deeply regretted the two incidents early in their marriage when he had beaten her.

At the level of affect, what also stands out is Whitman's internal rage. In the words of the psychiatrist who saw him shortly before his outburst, he was "fairly oozing" with generalized hostility. Whitman tried to achieve his goals and exercise self-control with elaborate manuals filled with specific self-instructions about how to act, what to say, and how to inhibit his hostility. Eventually, though, in the absence of adequate self-regulation skills, these external controls failed, with tragic consequences.

Applying the concept of behavioral signatures to Charles Whitman, it is clear that Whitman's behavior differed dramatically across situations. Most of the time, he was an "all-American boy," charming, witty, agreeable, and a loving husband. However, when under stress, his defenses against his inner rage began to crumble and he became hostile and aggressive, capable of abusing his wife and threatening to shoot a fellow Marine. When stress reached a sufficiently severe level, his controls broke down completely and he committed the murderous acts. In the *if-then* language of behavioral signatures, we might summarize this aspect of his personality as: *if* not under stress, *then* friendly and well controlled; but *if* under stress and facing severe failure, *then* hostile and impulsive.

Having now described the various perspectives on personality, we have seen that each presents us with a different picture of human nature and that each focuses on particular determinants of human individuality. Clearly, each perspective provides us with different pieces of the puzzle that was Charles Whitman.

Figure 11.20 summarizes the determinants emphasized by the various theories at the biological, psychological, and environmental levels of analysis.

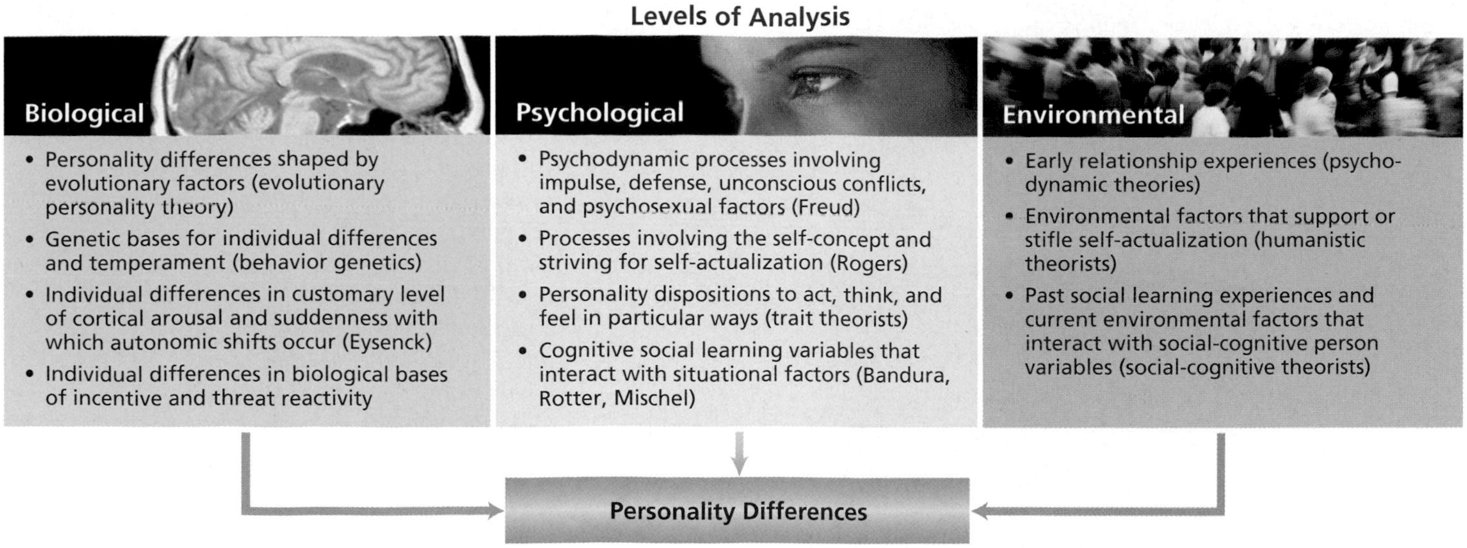

Levels of Analysis

Biological	Psychological	Environmental
• Personality differences shaped by evolutionary factors (evolutionary personality theory) • Genetic bases for individual differences and temperament (behavior genetics) • Individual differences in customary level of cortical arousal and suddenness with which autonomic shifts occur (Eysenck) • Individual differences in biological bases of incentive and threat reactivity	• Psychodynamic processes involving impulse, defense, unconscious conflicts, and psychosexual factors (Freud) • Processes involving the self-concept and striving for self-actualization (Rogers) • Personality dispositions to act, think, and feel in particular ways (trait theorists) • Cognitive social learning variables that interact with situational factors (Bandura, Rotter, Mischel)	• Early relationship experiences (psychodynamic theories) • Environmental factors that support or stifle self-actualization (humanistic theorists) • Past social learning experiences and current environmental factors that interact with social-cognitive person variables (social-cognitive theorists)

Personality Differences

FIGURE 11.20

Understanding Behavior: Personality differences.

IN REVIEW

- *Social-cognitive theories are concerned with how social relationships, learning experiences, and cognitive processes jointly contribute to behavior. A key concept is reciprocal determinism, relating to two-way causal relations between people, their behavior, and the environment.*
- *Rotter's theory viewed behavior as influenced by expectancies and the reinforcement value of potential outcomes. His concept of locus of control is a generalized belief in the extent to which we can control the outcomes in our life.*
- *Bandura's concept of self-efficacy relates to our self-perceived ability to carry out the behaviors necessary to achieve goals in a particular situation. It is influenced by past performance attainments, verbal persuasion, observation of others' attainments, and perceived emotional arousal. Self-efficacy can be enhanced through the application of systematic goal-setting procedures.*
- *According to Mischel and Shoda, situational features activate the person's cognitive-affective personality system (CAPS). The CAPS involves individual differences in encoding strategies, expectancies and beliefs, goals and values, affects, and competencies and self-regulatory processes. The CAPS interacts with features of the environment, helping to explain why people have specific behavioral signatures and do not necessarily behave consistently across situations.*

CULTURAL INFLUENCES ON PERSONALITY

As we have seen, personality is a product of interacting biological and environmental influences. Environment exists at many different levels, ranging from the physical surroundings in which we develop to the increasingly global social contexts shown in Figure 11.21. Among the most important, yet unappreciated, environmental influences is the culture in which we develop. We are often unaware of these influences because they serve as an amorphous background against which the specific events of our lives unfold. Culture encompasses unstated assumptions (including assumptions about the very nature of reality), norms, values, sex roles, and habitual ways of behaving that are shared by members of a social group. It influences what we perceive, how we perceive, how we relate to ourselves and others, and how we behave.

Dimensions of Cultural Variation

▶ 19. In what three ways can cultures differ, thereby influencing personality? What personality and gender differences occur within individualistic and collectivistic cultures?

Cultures differ along a number of dimensions that can affect personality development (Triandis & Suh, 2002). One is *complexity*. Consider how much more complex a Western information-age culture is than a hunter-gatherer culture in a remote region of an undeveloped country. Consider also how much more potential for diversity and conflict of values and behavioral norms exists in a highly complex culture.

A second dimension is a culture's *tightness*. In tight cultures, there are many rules about behavior, and those who deviate from the cultural norms, even in minor ways, are likely to be

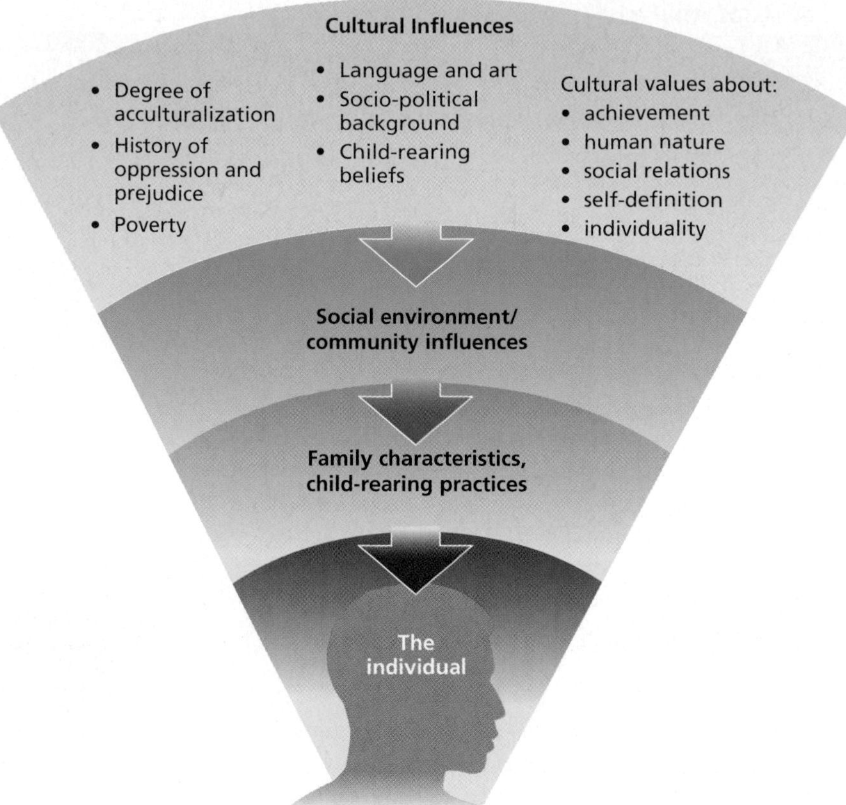

FIGURE 11.21

A model showing how cultural elements are transmitted to the individual through the medium of social environment and family influences.

punished. In Singapore, for example, adolescents are expected to adhere strictly to social norms that forbid experimenting with alcohol, tobacco, or sexual intercourse (Ball & Mosselle, 1995). As a result of explicit norms, people tend to differ less from one another in tight cultures than they do in loose cultures, where diversity in beliefs, values, and "doing your own thing" is permitted or even encouraged. Loose cultures are most likely to occur where people within a social group are not highly dependent on one another and where diversity is tolerated or even encouraged. Thus we would expect American adolescents to show greater diversity and feelings of individuality than those in Singapore. They might also experience more conflicts in deciding which values to embrace and what type of a person to be.

The cultural dimension that has received the greatest attention from psychologists is *individualism-collectivism.* Individualistic cultures such as those in the United States and Canada and northern Europe place an emphasis on independence and personal attainment, whereas collectivistic cultures such as those found in many parts of Asia, Africa, and South America emphasize connectedness among people and the achievement of group goals (Cross & Markus, 1999; Triandis, 1989).

Important personality differences have been found between people in individualistic and collectivistic cultures, although we should emphasize that significant variation can be found within any given culture because on average, only about 40 percent of the people strongly embrace individualistic or collectivistic goals (Triandis & Suh, 2002). In general, however, people in collectivistic cultures tend to see the environment as fixed (i.e., having rigid rules and expectations) and themselves as changeable, with a great capacity to fit in. In contrast, members of individualistic cultures are more likely to see themselves and their personalities as relatively stable and the environment as malleable, so that if they don't like their situation, they can leave it or change it (Hong et al., 2001). Interestingly, personality trait measures do not predict behavior as well in collectivistic cultures as they do in individualistic cultures, possibly because environmental factors play a stronger role in the behavior of collectivistic individuals (Church & Katigbak, 2000).

Self-enhancement needs are equally strong in individualistic and collectivistic cultures, but they are satisfied in different ways. Individualists enhance the self through personal successes, whereas collectivists feel better about themselves when their group succeeds (Sedikides et al., 2003). In individualistic cultures, personal success also serves to increase people's motivation, whereas in collectivistic cultures, motivation increases after failure as the person attempts to change the self and conform to the demands of the situation (Heine et al., 2000). Even emotional lives differ. In a study of cultural differences in experienced emotions, Americans reported more positive "socially disengaged" emotions, such as self-pride and personal happiness, whereas Japanese reported more positive interpersonally oriented emotions, such as closeness, friendliness, and respect (Kitayama et al., 2000).

Finally, let us consider the Big Five personality factors. As we noted earlier, some personality researchers view the Five Factor Model as universally applicable, showing impressive consistency across many cultures (John & Srivastava, 1999). Yet other evidence suggests some degree of cultural variation as well. The Conscientiousness, Agreeableness, Neuroticism, and Extraversion factors seem to hold up better than the Openness factor does, and researchers have found more or fewer personality dimensions—from three to seven—in some cultures (Triandis & Suh, 2002). Sometimes, a new dimension with elements of several Big Five factors will appear, such as one consisting of a mixture of Extraversion and Agreeableness. Clearly, more research is needed not only to establish where the Five Factor Model does not fit and why but also to compare mean scores of men and women on the Five Factor personality measures across different cultures.

Culture, Gender, and the Self

Culture provides a learning context in which the self develops. What kinds of self-concept differences would you predict in people from individualistic and collectivistic cultures?

In one study, American and Japanese college students were given a self-concept questionnaire on which they listed their five most important attributes. The researchers then classified each statement according to whether it referred to a personal attribute (e.g., "I am honest," "I am smart"), a social identity (e.g., "I am an oldest son," "I am a student"), or something else, such as a physical trait. As Figure 11.22 shows, the Americans were far more likely than the Japanese to list personal traits, abilities, or dispositions, whereas the Japanese more frequently described themselves in social identity terms. Thus the social embeddedness of the collectivistic Japanese culture was reflected in their self-perceptions, as was cultural individualism in the Americans' self-concepts (Cousins, 1989).

Other differences in self-descriptions also are found. Compared with a U.S. sample, people from a collectivistic Filipino culture rated themselves lower on individualistic traits such as independence, assertiveness, and pleasure seeking (Grimm et al., 1999). In another study, 84 percent of Japanese students applied the term *ordinary* to themselves, compared with only 18 percent of American students (Markus & Kitayama, 1998).

Gender-role socialization provides us with **gender schemas,** *organized mental structures that contain our understanding of the attributes and behaviors that are appropriate and expected for males and females* (Bem, 1981). Within a given culture, gender schemas tell us what the typical man or woman "should" be like. In Western cultures, men tend to prize attributes related to achievement, emotional strength, athleticism, and self-sufficiency, whereas women prize interpersonal competencies, kindness, and helpfulness to others (Beyer, 1990; Marsh, 1990). In this sense, men in Western cultures tend to develop more of an individualistic self-concept, emphasizing achievement and separateness from others, whereas women's self-concepts tend to be more collectivistic, emphasizing their social connectedness with others (Kashima et al., 1995). Nonetheless, we should keep in mind that significant individual differences exist within each gender group, with many women being individualists and many men collectivists (Triandis & Suh, 2002).

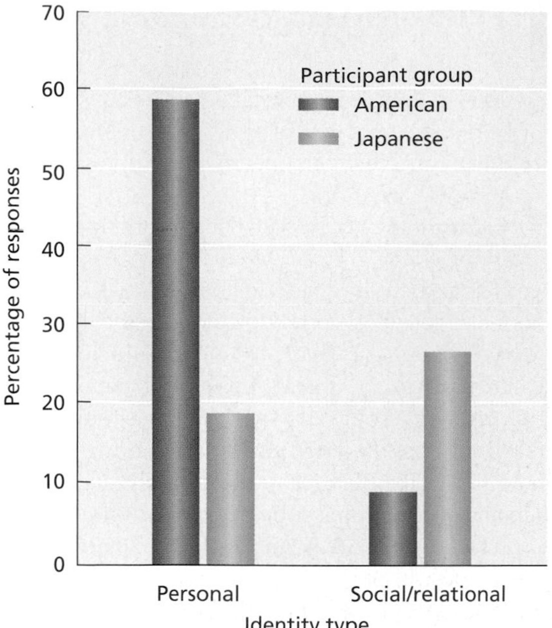

FIGURE 11.22

Cultural differences in the self-concept. Percentages of personal identity and social-relational self-attributes given by Japanese and American college students as key aspects of their self-concept. SOURCE: Adapted from Cousins, 1989.

IN REVIEW

- *Cultures differ along several important dimensions, including complexity, tightness, and individualism-collectivism, all of which can affect personality development.*
- *People in collectivistic cultures tend to see the environment as fixed (i.e., having rigid rules and expectations) and themselves as changeable, with a capacity to fit in. In contrast, members of individualistic cultures are more likely to see themselves and their personalities as relatively stable and the environment as malleable.*
- *Culture influences self-concept development. People from individualistic cultures tend to describe themselves in terms of personal traits, abilities, or dispositions, whereas those from individualistic cultures are more likely to describe themselves in social identity terms.*
- *Gender schemas are organized mental structures that contain our understanding of the attributes and behaviors that are appropriate and expected for males and females. In Western cultures, men tend to value achievement, emotional strength, and self-sufficiency, whereas women prize interpersonal skills, kindness, and helpfulness to others.*

PERSONALITY ASSESSMENT

If you were to be introduced to Jennifer, a woman you had never met before, and given one week to provide a complete personality description of her, what would you do?

Chances are, you would seek information in a variety of ways. You might start by interviewing Jennifer and finding out as much as you could about her. Based on your knowledge of the theories we have discussed, what questions would you ask? Would you ask about early childhood experiences and dreams? About how she sees herself and others? Would you be interested in the kinds of traits embodied in the Big Five model or in Eysenck's dimension of Introversion-Extraversion? Would you want to know how Jennifer customarily feels and responds in various situations? Your answers to these questions and your other assessment decisions would in some sense reflect your own theory of what is important in describing personality.

▶ 20. Define two characteristics that personality measures must have in order to be scientifically useful.

You probably would not be content simply to interview Jennifer. You might also decide to interview other people who know her well and get their views of what she is like. You might even ask them to rate her on a variety of traits, such as those found in Cattell's model of personality or in the Five Factor Model, and you could ask Jennifer to rate herself on the same measures to see if her self-concept agrees with how others see her.

▶ 21. How are interviews, behavioral assessment, and remote behavioral sampling used to assess personality?

Finally, you might decide that it would be useful to actually observe how Jennifer behaves in a variety of situations. You would want to observe her in a way that would allow you to get as "natural" and characteristic a sample of her behavior as possible. This information, together with that obtained from Jennifer and from those who know her best, might provide a reasonable basis for a personality description.

FIGURE 11.23

Measurement approaches used to assess personality.

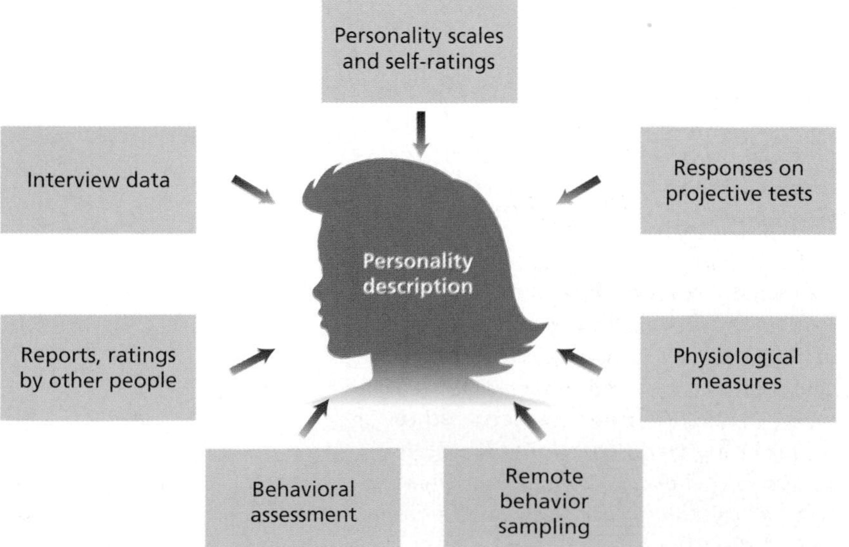

Figure 11.23 shows the major methods that psychologists use to assess personality characteristics. As you can see, they use some of the same methods you might have chosen: the interview; trait ratings and behavior reports; and behavioral assessment, or direct observation and measurement of the subject's behavior. In addition, they have developed several types of psychological tests, including objective self-report measures and "projective" tests that ask respondents to interpret ambiguous stimuli, such as inkblots or pictures. Finally, physiological measures can be used to measure various aspects of personality, such as emotional reactivity or levels of cortical arousal.

The task of devising valid and useful personality measures is anything but simple, and it has taxed the ingenuity of psychologists for nearly a century. To be useful from either a scientific or a practical perspective, personality tests must conform to the standards of reliability and validity discussed in Chapter 8. *Reliability*, or consistency of measurement, takes several forms. A test that measures a stable personality trait should yield similar scores when administered to the same individuals at different times (test-retest reliability). Another aspect of reliability is that different professionals should score and interpret the test in the same way (interjudge reliability). *Validity* refers to the most important question of all: Is the test actually measuring the personality variable that it is intended to measure? A valid test allows us to predict behavior that is influenced by the personality variable being measured. Research on test reliability and validity is an important activity of personality psychologists, and good measures of personality are an absolute must for scientific research on personality and for ethical clinical application (Domino, 2000).

Interviews

Interviews are one of the oldest methods of assessment. Long before the invention of writing, people undoubtedly made judgments about others by observing them and talking with them. Interviewers can obtain information about a person's thoughts, feelings, and other internal states, as well as information about current and past relationships, experiences, and behavior.

Structured interviews *contain a set of specific questions that are administered to every participant.* An attempt is made to create a standardized situation so that interviewees' responses to more-or-less identical stimuli can be interpreted and compared. Such interviews are frequently used to collect research data or to make a psychiatric diagnosis. Other interviews are unstructured, with interviewers tailoring their questions to the particular individual and situation.

Good interviewers do not limit their attention to what an interviewee says; they also look at how she or he says it. They note interviewees' general appearance and grooming, their voice and speech patterns, the content of their statements, and their facial expressions and posture. Sometimes, attitudes that are not expressed verbally can be inferred from behavior, as in this instance:

> During the interview she held her small son on her lap. The child began to play with his genitals. The mother, without looking directly at the child, moved his hand away and held it securely for a while. . . . Later in the interview the mother was asked what she ordinarily did when the child masturbated. She replied that he never did this—he was a very "good" boy. She was evidently entirely unconscious of what had transpired in the very presence of the interviewer. (Maccoby & Maccoby, 1954, p. 484)

The interview is valuable for the direct personal contact it provides, but it has some limitations. First, characteristics of the interviewer may influence how the interviewee responds in ways that can affect the validity of the information. In addition, the validity of information obtained in an interview depends on the interviewee's desire to cooperate, to respond honestly, and to report accurately what the interviewer is trying to assess. Some interview data may be valid, others invalid.

Despite its limitations, the face-to-face interview is essential for certain purposes. For example, a clinical psychologist needs to observe and converse with a person who is being considered for admission to a mental hospital. Interviews are often used in research as well. The challenge is to design and conduct interviews in ways that maximize the validity of the data obtained from the respondent.

Behavioral Assessment

Personality psychologists can sometimes observe the behaviors they are interested in rather than asking people about them. In **behavioral assessment,** *psychologists devise an explicit coding system that contains the behavioral categories of interest.* Then they train observers until they show high levels of agreement (interjudge reliability) in using the coding categories to record behavior (Figure 11.24). Behavioral assessment can provide valuable information about how frequently and under what conditions certain classes of behavior occur (Haynes, 2000). Social-cognitive researchers used this method to measure the "behavioral signatures" of the verbally aggressive children in the summer camp environment discussed earlier.

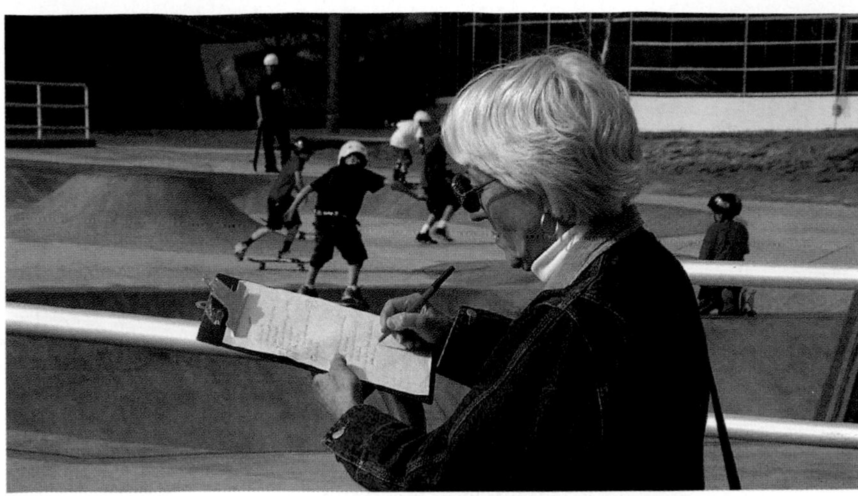

FIGURE 11.24

In behavioral assessment, carefully trained observers code specific classes of behavior and the conditions under which they occur.

Behavioral assessment requires precision in defining the behaviors of interest and the conditions under which they occur. For example, observers studying a young child who is having problems in school do not simply say, "Jerry is disruptive." Instead, they try to answer the question, "What, specifically, does Jerry *do* that causes disruption?" Once they have identified Jerry's specific behaviors, the next questions are, "How often and under what conditions does the disruptive behavior occur?" and "What kinds of outcomes do the behaviors produce?" Answers to these questions can be particularly important not only in measuring differences in people's personality characteristics but also in identifying potential situational causes of their behavior (Greene & Ollendick, 2000).

Remote Behavior Sampling

It is not practical or possible for behavioral assessors to follow people around from situation to situation on a daily basis. In addition, assessors are frequently interested in unobservable events, such as emotional reactions and thinking patterns, that may shed considerable light on personality functioning. Through **remote behavior sampling,** *researchers and clinicians can collect self-reported samples of behavior from respondents as they live their daily lives.* A tiny computerized device carried by respondents pages them at randomly determined times of the day. When the "beeper" sounds, respondents record their current thoughts, feelings, or behaviors, depending on what the researcher or therapist is assessing (Stone et al., 2000). Respondents may also report on aspects of the situation they are in so that situation-behavior interactions can be examined. The data can either be stored in the computer or transmitted directly to the assessor. Methodology like this was used in the Chapter 10 *Research Close-Up* (page 405) on adolescents' emotions.

Remote sampling procedures can be used over weeks or even months to collect a large behavior sample across many situations. This approach to personality assessment holds great promise, for it enables researchers and clinicians to detect patterns of personal functioning that might not be revealed by other methods.

Personality Scales

▶ 22. Compare the rational-theoretical and empirical approaches to developing personality scales.

Personality scales, or inventories, are widely used for assessing personality in both research and clinical work. Personality scales are considered *objective* measures because they include standard sets of questions, usually in a true-false or rating-scale format, that are scored using an agreed-upon scoring key (Nezami & Butcher, 2000). Their advantages include (1) the ability to collect data from many people at the same time, (2) the fact that all people respond to the same items, and (3) ease of scoring. Their major disadvantage is the possibility that some people will choose not to answer the items truthfully, in which case their scores will not be valid reflections of the trait being measured. To combat this threat to validity, some widely used tests have special *validity scales* that detect tendencies to respond in a socially desirable manner or to present an overly negative image of oneself.

The items on personality scales are developed in two major ways. In the **rational-theoretical approach,** *items are based on the theorist's conception of the personality trait to be measured.* For example, to develop a measure of introversion-extraversion, we would ask ourselves what introverts and extraverts often say about themselves, and then we would write items that captured those kinds of self-descriptions (e.g., "I love to be at large social gatherings" or "I'm very content to spend time by myself"). One frequently used measure developed according to the rational approach is the **NEO-PI,** *which measures the Big Five personality traits of Openness, Conscientiousness, Extraversion, Agreeableness, and Neuroticism* (Costa & McCrae, 1992). Other scales developed in this fashion are the measures of optimism-pessimism, self-monitoring, and locus of control, described earlier in the chapter (see Tables 11.2, 11.3, and 11.8).

In a different approach to personality test development known as the **empirical approach,** *items are chosen not because their content seems relevant to the trait on rational grounds, but because each item has been answered differently by groups of people (for example, introverts and extraverts) known to differ in the personality characteristic of interest.* The **Minnesota Multiphasic Personality Inventory (MMPI-2)** *is a widely used personality test developed according to the empirical approach.* The MMPI was originally designed to provide an objective basis for psychiatric diagnosis. Its 567 true-false items consist of statements that were answered by groups of patients diagnosed with specific psychiatric disorders (e.g., hysteria, paranoia, and schizophrenia) in ways different from the answers given by respondents in a nonpsychiatric comparison sample. The items vary widely in content; some are concerned with attitudes and emotions, others relate to overt behavior and symptoms, and still others refer to the person's life history.

The MMPI-2 has 10 clinical scales and 3 validity scales (Table 11.10). The validity scales are

TABLE 11.10 The Validity and Clinical Scales of the Minnesota Multiphasic Personality Inventory-2 (MMPI-2) and the Behavioral Characteristics Associated With High Scores on the Scales

Scale	Abbreviation	Behavioral Correlates
Validity Scales		
Lie	L	Lies or highly conventional
Frequency	F	Exaggerates complaints, answers haphazardly
Correction	K	Denies problems
Clinical Scales		
Hypochondriasis	Hs	Expresses bodily concerns and complaints
Depression	D	Is depressed, pessimistic, guilty
Hysteria	Hy	Reacts to stress with physical symptoms, lacks insight into negative feelings
Psychopathic deviate	Pd	Is impulsive, in conflict with the law, involved in stormy relationships
Masculinity, femininity	Mf	Has interests characteristic of the opposite sex
Paranoia	Pa	Is suspicious, resentful
Psychasthenia	Pt	Is anxious, worried, high-strung
Schizophrenia	Sc	Is confused, disorganized, disoriented, and withdrawn from others
Hypomania	Ma	Is energetic, active, restless
Social introversion	Si	Is introverted, with little social contact

used to detect tendencies to present either an overly positive picture or to exaggerate the degree of psychological disturbance. The clinical scales were originally intended to measure severe personality deviations such as schizophrenia, depression, and psychopathic personality, and they still do. In addition, however, the pattern, or *profile*, of scores obtained on the various scales also reveals important aspects of personality functioning even in people who do not display such disorders. Thus the MMPI-2 is used not only as an aid to psychiatric diagnosis but also for personality description and as a screening device in industrial and military settings.

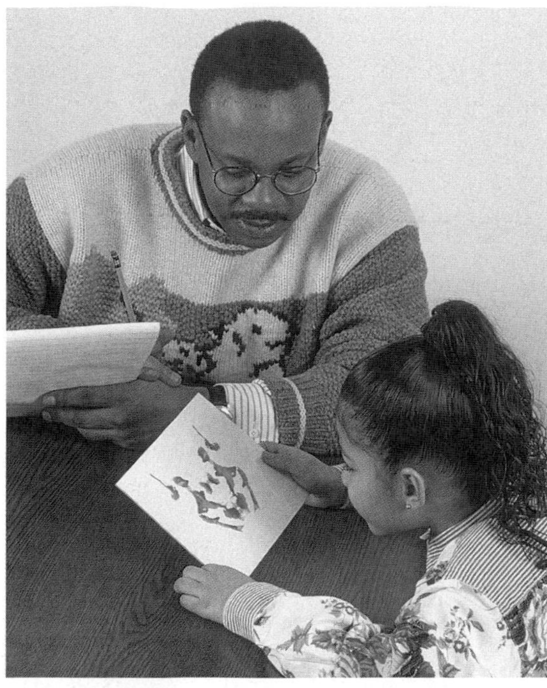

FIGURE 11.25

During a Rorschach test, the subject is presented with 10 inkblots and asked to indicate what each resembles and what feature of the stimulus (for example, its shape or its color) makes it appear that way.

Projective Tests

▶ 23. How do projective tests differ from objective measures? Describe and compare two projective tests.

Freud and other psychodynamic theorists emphasized the importance of unconscious factors in understanding behavior. By definition, however, people are unaware of unconscious dynamics, so they cannot report them to interviewers or on self-report tests like the NEO-PI or the MMPI-2. Other methods were therefore needed to assess them.

Projective tests *present subjects with ambiguous stimuli and ask for some interpretation of them.* The assumption is that because the meaning of the stimulus is unclear, the subject's interpretation will have to come from within, reflecting the "projection" of inner needs, feelings, and ways of viewing the world onto the stimulus.

The following fictional story helps illustrate the rationale for projective techniques. During the administration of a set of Rorschach inkblots, the man being tested saw every one of the inkblots as either sex organs or people engaging in sexual acts. After the last inkblot, the psychologist declared, "I've never in my entire career seen anyone as obsessed with sex as you seem to be." The man responded indignantly, "What do you mean, *I'm* obsessed with sex? *You're* the one with all the dirty pictures!"

Rorschach Inkblots

The ***Rorschach test*** *consists of 10 inkblots.* The person being tested is shown each one in succession and asked, "What does this look like? What might it be?" (Figure 11.25). After responding, the person is asked to explain what specific feature of the inkblot (e.g., its shape or its color) makes it seem that way. Examiners write down the responses word for word. They also carefully note the person's behavior during testing, including gestures, mannerisms, and expressed attitudes. They categorize and score responses in terms of the kinds of objects reported, the features attended to (e.g., the whole blot, colored portions, tiny details), and the emotional tone associated with particular types of responses (Erdberg, 2000).

Interpretations made by Rorschach examiners are often based on what the responses seem to symbolize. For example, people who see peering eyes and threatening figures in the inkblots are likely to be viewed as projecting their own paranoid fears and suspicions onto the stimuli. One drawback of the Rorschach is that different examiners may interpret the same response very differently, producing unreliability among examiners. In an attempt to minimize clinician subjectivity in interpreting Rorschach responses, John Exner (1991) developed a scoring system with specific coding categories and scoring criteria. Although this system created greater uniformity in scoring, many of the personality interpretations derived from the Rorschach lack research support, so the usefulness of the test for predicting behavior is dubious (Lilienfeld et al., 2000). Nonetheless, many psychodynamic clinicians maintain their faith in the Rorschach, insisting that they find

FIGURE 11.26

A picture from the Thematic Apperception Test. Subjects are asked to make up a story about the picture, covering specific questions such as those listed in the text. These stories are analyzed for recurrent themes that are assumed to reflect significant aspects of personality.
Reprinted by permission of the publisher from Henry A. Murray, *Thematic Apperception Test*, Plate 12 F. Cambridge, MA: Harvard University Press. Copyright © 1943 by the President and Fellows of Harvard College; Copyright © 1971 by Henry A. Murray.

it useful for gaining insight into unconscious processes.

Thematic Apperception Test

The ***Thematic Apperception Test (TAT)*** *consists of a series of pictures derived from paintings, drawings, and magazine illustrations*. In general, the pictures are less ambiguous than the Rorschach inkblots, but they still require an interpretation. To illustrate, look at the picture in Figure 11.26, and then write a story that addresses the following questions:

> What is happening? Who are the people involved?
>
> What has led up to this situation?
>
> What is being thought, felt, and wanted, and by whom?
>
> What will happen? How will the story turn out?

The stories told in response to a set of 10 to 20 pictures are analyzed for recurrent themes that are assumed to reflect important aspects of the respondent's personality. These might include the kinds of relationships depicted in the stories, the types of motives and feelings that are attributed to the characters, whether positive or negative outcomes occur, and factors that produce these outcomes such as personal weaknesses or forces in the environment.

The TAT, like the Rorschach, has the problem of nonstandardized or subjective interpretation of responses, which can result in different interpretations of the same stories. Since not everyone can be right, the possibility of erroneous interpretations is obvious. Where specific systems have been developed to score stories, the TAT has proven to be a useful and valid test (Atkinson, 1958). As discussed in Chapter 9, this method is used by researchers to measure motivational variables such as the needs for achievement, affiliation, and power. The TAT appears to provide a more valid measure of these needs than do objective self-report measures of the same motives, showing stronger relations with motivated behavior (Ferguson, 2000). Despite such exceptions, however, objective measures of personality have generally been found to have better reliability and validity than projective measures (Lilienfeld, 2000; Nezami & Butcher, 2000).

Personality Theory and Personality Assessment

Personality assessment is intimately related to theory. Theories provide us with a framework that specifies how thoughts, feelings, and bodily processes relate to one another and to behavior. Assessment provides tools for measuring personality variables and testing the theory. A clinician's or researcher's theoretical perspective therefore influences which assessment approach he or she is likely to use.

Projective techniques are favored by psychodynamic theorists who believe that people's responses to tests such as the Rorschach and TAT reveal unconscious processes. Humanistic theorists favor self-report measures of the self-concept and personal aspirations. Social-cognitive researchers use behavioral assessments and ask people to rate their expectations about what will happen in the future and how well they will do in particular situations. Remote behavior sampling is also useful in studying interactions between the person and the situation. Paper-and-pencil inventories including the MMPI and the NEO-PI are favored by trait theorists, who want to measure specific personality traits, and by behavior geneticists, who want to estimate genetic contributions to traits through twin or adoption studies. Researchers interested in biological processes that underlie personality functioning, such as emotional reactivity or brain processes, use physiological measures. All of these assessment methods have their place in studying personality and can help illuminate important aspects of individuality.

IN REVIEW

- *Methods used by psychologists to assess personality include the interview, behavioral assessment, remote behavior sampling, objective personality scales, and projective tests.*
- *The major approaches to constructing personality scales are the rational approach, in which items are written on an intuitive basis, and the empirical approach, in which items that discriminate between groups known to differ on the trait of interest are chosen. The MMPI-2 is the best-known test developed with the empirical approach. The NEO-PI, reflecting the rational approach, measures individual differences in the Big Five factors.*
- *Projective tests present ambiguous stimuli to people. It is assumed that interpretations of such stimuli give clues to important internal processes. The Rorschach inkblot test and the Thematic Apperception Test are the most commonly used projective tests.*

A Closing Thought

The topic of personality has captured the imagination of humans throughout history. The first systematic theory of personality was formulated by the Greek physician Hippocrates in the 5th century B.C. Personality dynamics and individuality have been celebrated and explored in the great literatures of many cultures, including the Bible and the Quran. In psychology, the study of personality has contributed to the development of all of our diverse perspectives on behavior. Yet, in its second century as a formal subject of scientific study, it remains one of the most vibrant areas in psychology. The fascinating topic of human diversity continues to attract theorists and researchers, who forge new understandings each day. Moreover, the field of personality is seeing increased collaboration among experts from diverse areas of psychology, including social, developmental, physiological, cognitive, and evolutionary psychology.

In the following chapters, we will build upon what we have learned about personality. We will see that personality factors influence health and people's responses to life stress. As we explore the behavior disorders, we will see what happens when personality development goes awry, resulting in deviant and maladaptive behavior patterns. We will explore the various disorders from the perspectives and theories you have read about in this chapter. Then we will see how our knowledge of personality development and personality change is being applied to the treatment of psychological disorders and how personality is both shaped by and influences our social behavior.

KEY TERMS AND CONCEPTS

Each term has been boldfaced and defined in the chapter on the page indicated in parentheses.

? What Do You Think?

SHOULD A PSYCHOTHERAPIST REPORT A PATIENT'S VIOLENT FANTASIES? p. 438

In some cases, critical thinking requires the balancing of competing demands. In the case of Charles Whitman, the psychiatrist who interviewed him needed to balance the competing demands of traditional patient confidentiality and public safety. In hindsight, we might conclude that the therapist should have sacrificed confidentiality and warned university security personnel. But the issue is clouded by the fact that, in general, mental health professionals have a very poor record of success in predicting violent behavior (Monahan, 1992).

In 1966, when the Whitman incident occurred, it was solely up to the therapist to decide whether a breach of confidentiality was warranted. Following the Whitman tragedy, a formal inquiry was held, and although many professionals questioned his judgment in not alerting authorities, the psychiatrist who saw Whitman was exonerated of professional misconduct. But three years later, at the University of California, a college student murdered his estranged girlfriend after telling his therapist he intended to do so. Although the therapist notified campus police, who released the assailant after questioning him, the victim's family sued the university and the therapist, claiming that he should also have warned the victim and her family. The family won the case. Thereafter, most jurisdictions passed laws requiring mental health professionals to violate confidentiality and report threats of violence in order to protect potential victims. The "duty to protect" is granted precedence over the seal of confidentiality. Had today's standards existed in 1966, the tragedy in Texas might have been averted. Still, legal mandates call for the therapist to exercise professional judgment as to whether a given client and a given set of circumstances constitute a clear and present danger. Therapists are hesitant to break the seal of confidentiality unless they are confident in their judgment of imminent danger to the community. In Whitman's case, a professional may well have concluded that his stated fantasies were not a compelling danger signal in the absence of a previous history of violent behavior. Thus it is part of a psychologist's professional responsibility to have the training and expertise to make such judgments. ■

IS SELF-ACTUALIZATION A USEFUL SCIENTIFIC CONSTRUCT? p. 441

Self-actualization is a centerpiece of some humanistic theories, but it is troublesome from a scientific perspective. Some critics believe that it is impossible to define an individual's actualizing tendency except in terms of the behavior that it supposedly produces. This would be an example of circular reasoning: Why did the person achieve such success? Because of self-actualization. How do we know self-actualization was at work? Because the person achieved great success.

Unless a construct can be operationally defined in a manner independent of the phenomena it is supposed to cause, it is not scientifically useful. A construct must also be measurable. While it is true that concepts related to the self-actualization motive (such as people's beliefs that they are fulfilling their potential) could potentially be measured, most psychologists suggest that rather than being a scientific construct, self-actualization is better considered a philosophical concept. ■

12

ADJUSTING TO LIFE
Stress, Coping, and Health

CHAPTER OUTLINE

Life is largely a process of adaptation
to the circumstances in which we exist.
—Hans Selye

Priscilla, now 18, had anything but an idyllic childhood. She grew up in an impoverished inner-city home with an alcoholic father who physically and sexually abused her and her younger sister. Priscilla's mother, too helpless and fearful to protect her children, was hospitalized twice for "nervous breakdowns." When Priscilla was 8 years old, a neighbor who suspected the sexual abuse reported the father to Child Protective Services. Upon being notified of the impending investigation, Priscilla's father called his family together in the living room and told them, "You drove me to this." He then put a gun to his head and committed suicide as his wife and children watched in horror. From that point on, Priscilla had to work after school to help support her family. For a time, the family was homeless and lived in a shelter. Her mother became increasingly disturbed and sometimes beat her.

Given her life circumstances, how could Priscilla become anything except an unhappy, maladjusted person, her emotional life dominated by anxiety, anger, and depression? Instead, she grew into a delightful and popular young woman who was emotionally well adjusted, president of her high school class, a talented singer, and an honor student who was awarded a scholarship to an Ivy League university.

■■■

In his book Persuasion and Healing, *psychiatrist Jerome Frank (1961) describes a treatment performed by the German physician Hans Rheder on three bedridden patients. One patient had an inflamed gall bladder and chronic gallstones. The second was having difficulty recovering from pancreatic surgery and had experienced such severe weight loss that Rheder described her as "skeletal." The third patient was dying from a painful uterine cancer that had spread throughout her body.*

Since conventional medicine had done all that was possible for the women, Rheder decided to try the unconventional: He told the women that he had discovered a powerful faith healer who could cure with remarkable success simply by directing his healing power to a particular place. Rheder told each woman that he had arranged for this healing power to be projected to her room on a specific day and hour. In truth, he had already tried the healer without telling the women, and there had been no change in their condition.

Within a few days after the appointed healing date, the woman who had been wasting away began to eat and subsequently gained 30 pounds. The patient with gallstones lost all of her symptoms, returned home, and remained symptom-free for a year. The patient with cancer was already a terminal case, but her bloated body soon excreted excess fluids, she gained strength, and her blood count improved. She was able to return home and lived for 3 months in relative comfort.

These cases illustrate some of the intriguing phenomena studied in an area known as *health psychology.* Children like Priscilla have been termed "invulnerable" or "resilient" youngsters because they somehow develop normally or even exceptionally in the face of great adversity (Garmezy, 1983; Masten, 2001). What allows resilient people to rise above extraordinarily stressful environments while other individuals, blessed with more benign life histories, collapse under the weight of relatively minor stresses? And what are we to think of the dramatic physical changes that followed Rheder's invocation of the faith healer's curative powers? How can mind triumph over matter to such a degree? Can a simple belief that one will be healed stop illness in its tracks? The answers to these questions will show us that adapting to the demands and challenges in our lives involves complex interactions between the person, the environment, and behavior. Figure 12.1 previews some of the biological, psychological, and environmental factors that influence our health and well-being.

Health psychology *addresses factors that influence well-being and illness, as well as measures that can be taken to promote health and prevent illness.* It therefore confronts many of the leading problems of our times. For example, because stress has negative effects on both physical and psychological well-being, the study of stress and coping is a central focus of health psychology. Pain is another important topic because it is a central feature of many illnesses. Health psychologists explore factors that influence pain perceptions and develop psychological interventions to reduce people's suffering. As we will see, they also develop and evaluate health-promotion and disease-prevention programs.

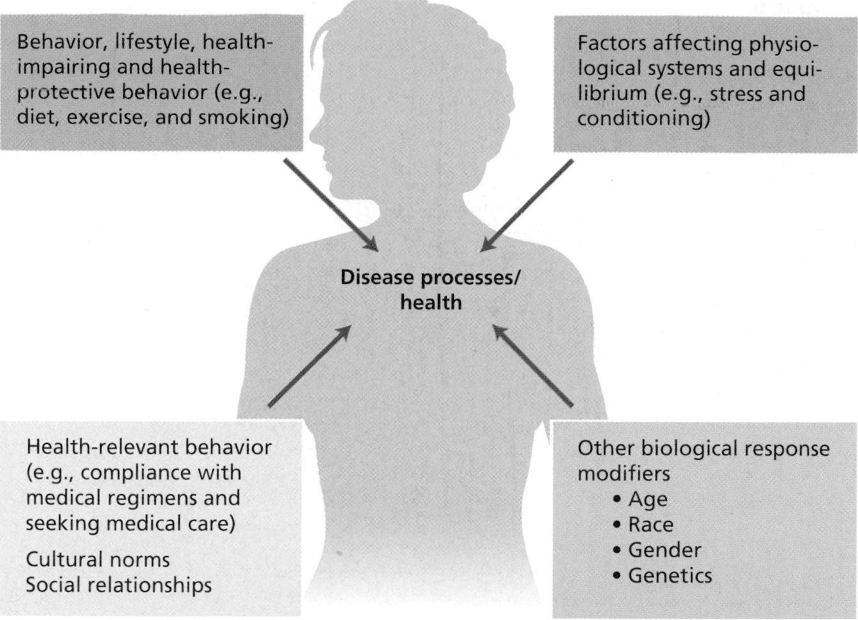

FIGURE 12.1

Biological, psychological, and environmental factors that contribute to disease processes and health. Source: Adapted from Baum, 1994.

STRESS AND WELL-BEING

The term *stress* appears regularly in our everyday discourse. It is also a leading topic of study in psychology. What, exactly, is stress?

Psychologists have viewed stress in three different ways: as a *stimulus*, as a *response*, and as an ongoing *interaction* between an organism and its environment. Some scientists define stress as events that place strong demands on us. These *demanding or threatening situations are* **stressors.** We refer to stress as a *stimulus* when we make statements such as, "I've got a lot of stress in my life right now. I have three exams next week, I lost my class notes, my fiancé just announced a vow of eternal celibacy, and my car broke down."

Stress can also be a *response* that has cognitive, physiological, and behavioral components. Thus a person might say, "I'm feeling all stressed out. I'm tensed up, I'm having trouble concentrating on things, and I've been flying off the handle all week." The presence of negative emotions is an important feature of the stress response and links the study of stress with the field of emotion (Zautra, 2003).

A third way of thinking about stress combines the stimulus and response definitions into a more inclusive model. Here stress is viewed as a *person-situation interaction*, or, more formally, as an ongoing *transaction* between the organism and the environment (Lazarus, 1991, 1998). This conception of stress is the basis for the model shown in Figure 12.2, and it will guide our discussion of stress. Note that this model incorporates both the stimulus and response aspects of stress. From this perspective, **stress** can be defined as *a pattern of cognitive appraisals, physiological responses, and behavioral tendencies that occurs in response to a perceived imbalance between situational demands and the resources needed to cope with them.*

▶ 1. Describe three ways that theorists have defined the term *stress*.

As we explore the topic of stress, we begin by describing different types of stressors, as well as the methods that scientists have developed to measure life stress. Then we explore the mind-body interaction that constitutes our response to stressors and the manner in which stress affects our psychological and physical health. Next we examine factors that influence the relations between stress and health. Finally, we describe the process of coping with stress.

Stressors

To explore the topic of stress, let us begin with the situational component. Stressors are specific kinds of stimuli. Whether physical or psychological, they place demands on us that endanger our well-being and require us to adapt in some manner. The more the demands of a situation outweigh

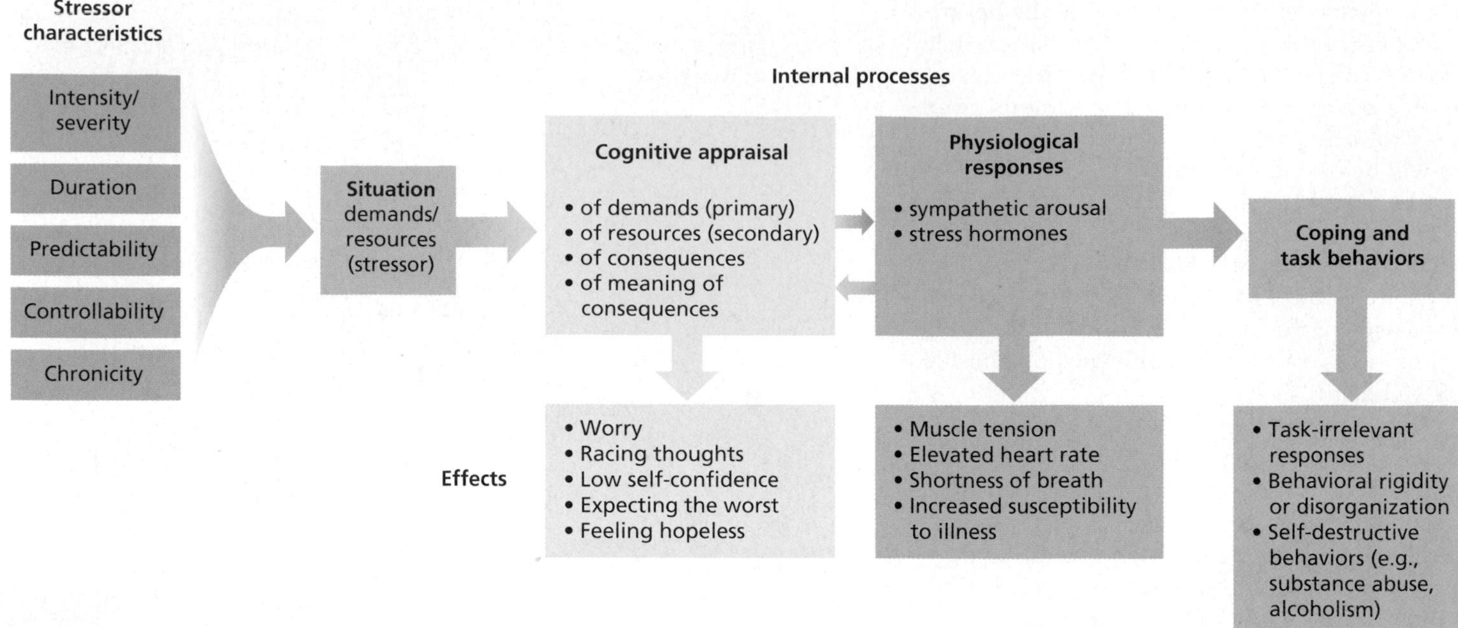

FIGURE 12.2

Stress involves complex interactions among situational (stressor) characteristics, cognitive appraisal processes, physiological responses, and behavioral attempts to cope with the situational demands. Stressor characteristics that influence stress responses are shown. The lower panels show potential cognitive, physiological, and behavioral stress responses that can interfere with well-being.

the resources we have to deal with them, the more stressful a situation is likely to be.

Stressors differ in their severity (Figure 12.3). They can range from *microstressors*—the daily hassles and minor annoyances we encounter at school, on the job, and in our family relationships—to more severe stressors. *Major negative events* such as the death or loss of a loved one, an academic or career failure, a serious illness, or being the victim of a serious crime, place strong demands on us and require major efforts to cope. *Catastrophic events* tend to occur unexpectedly and typically affect large numbers of people. They include traumatic natural disasters, acts of war or terrorism, physical or psychological torture, and concentration camp confinement. As we shall see, all three classes of stressors can have significant negative effects on psychological and physical well-being (van Praag, 2004; Zautra, 2003).

In addition to intensity or severity, other characteristics that make situations more or less stressful are listed at the far left of Figure 12.2. In general, events over which a person has little or no control, which occur suddenly and unpredictably, and which impact a person over a long period of time seem to take the greatest toll on physical and psychological well-being (Lazarus & Folkman, 1984; Taylor, 2003).

Measuring Stressful Life Events

Researchers have attempted to study the relation between life events and well-being. Sometimes the life events a person has experienced are verifiable. We may know, for example, that a person has lived through a natural disaster or lost a loved one to death. In other cases, researchers may have to rely on people's self-reports, using *life event scales* to quantify the amount of life stress that a person has experienced over a given period of time (e.g., the past 3 months or the past year). The life event scale shown in Table 12.1 asks people to indicate not only whether a particular event occurred but also their appraisal of whether the event was positive or negative and whether it was a major event (defined as having a significant and long-term impact on the person's life) or a minor event (Smith et al., 1990). We can thus score the scale for the number of specific kinds of events that occurred (for example, "minor negative," "major negative," "major positive"). We could obtain additional information by asking respondents to rate the predictability, controllability, and duration of each event they experienced, permitting an analysis of these factors as well. Life event scales have been widely used in life stress research. Like other self-report measures, however, we know that they are subject to possible distortion and failures of memory (Smith et al., 1999).

For more on stress and life events, see Interactive Segment 12.1.

Some early theorists believed that any life event that requires significant life adjustments, whether negative or positive, is a stressor (Holmes & Rahe, 1967; Selye, 1976). Because later research showed that only negative life changes consistently predicted adverse health and behavioral outcomes, most modern researchers now define stress in terms of negative

FIGURE 12.3

Stressful life events can vary from catastrophic ones to microstressors, or "daily hassles." Both classes of stressor take their toll on physical and psychological well-being.

▶ 2. What four types of appraisals occur in response to a potential stressor? Contrast primary and secondary appraisal.

life changes only (Cohen et al., 1995; Lazarus, 1998). Indeed, positive life events sometimes counter or even cancel out the impact of negative events (Thoits, 1983).

The Stress Response: A Mind-Body Link

Having considered the stimulus characteristics of stressors, we now consider how an organism responds to these situational demands. Like the emotional responses discussed in Chapter 9, the **stress response** *has cognitive, physiological, and behavioral components.*

Cognitive Appraisal

We respond to situations as we perceive them. The starting point for the stress response is therefore our cognitive appraisal of the situation and its implications for us. As Figure 12.2 indicates, four aspects of the appraisal process are particularly significant:

- Appraisal of the *nature and demands* of the situation (*primary appraisal*);
- Appraisal of the *resources* available to cope with it (*secondary appraisal*);
- Judgments of what the *consequences* of the situation could be; and

TABLE 12.1 Sample Items From a Self-Report Measure of Positive and Negative Life Events for Adolescents

Experience	Happened in Last 6 Months?		Good or Bad?		"Minor" or "Major"?	
Parents discover something you didn't want them to know	No	Yes	Good	Bad	Minor	Major
Pressures or expectation by parents	No	Yes	Good	Bad	Minor	Major
Receiving a gift	No	Yes	Good	Bad	Minor	Major
Having plans fall through (not going on a trip, etc.)	No	Yes	Good	Bad	Minor	Major
Losing job (quitting, getting fired, laid off, etc.)	No	Yes	Good	Bad	Minor	Major
Making honor roll or other school achievement	No	Yes	Good	Bad	Minor	Major
Making love or sexual intercourse	No	Yes	Good	Bad	Minor	Major
Something good happens to a friend	No	Yes	Good	Bad	Minor	Major
Work hassles (rude customers, unpleasant jobs, etc.)	No	Yes	Good	Bad	Minor	Major
Death of a friend or family member	No	Yes	Good	Bad	Minor	Major

SOURCE: Adapted from Smith et al., 1990.

- Appraisal of the *personal meaning*, that is, what the outcome might imply about us.

Let us apply these appraisal steps to a real-life situation. You are about to have an important job interview. According to Richard Lazarus (1991), a leading stress researcher, you will first engage in a **primary appraisal,** *interpreting the situation as either benign, neutral/irrelevant, or threatening in terms of its demands* (how difficult the interview will be) *and its significance for your well-being* (how badly you want or need the job). At the same time, through the process of **secondary appraisal,** *you will be appraising your perceived ability to cope with the situation, that is, the resources you have to deal with it.* Coping resources include your knowledge and abilities, your verbal skills, and your social resources, such as people who will give you emotional support and encouragement. If you believe that the demands of the interview greatly exceed your resources, you will likely experience stress.

▶ 3. Describe the three stages of Selye's GAS and their effects on health.

You will also take into account *potential consequences* of failing to cope successfully with the situation, including both the seriousness of the consequences and the likelihood that they will occur. Will you be able to pay your tuition if you perform poorly in the interview and don't get the job? How likely is it that you will fail? Appraising the consequences of failing as very costly and very likely to occur increases the perceived stressfulness of the situation.

Finally, the *psychological meaning of the consequences* may be related to your basic beliefs about yourself or the world. Certain beliefs or personal standards can make people vulnerable to particular types of situational demands. For example, if your feelings of self-worth depend on how successful you are in situations like this one, you may regard doing poorly during the interview as evidence that you are a worthless failure.

Distortions and mistaken appraisals can occur at any of the four points in the appraisal process, causing inappropriate stress responses. People may overestimate the difficulty of the demands, they may underestimate their own resources, they may exaggerate the seriousness of the consequences and the likelihood that they will occur, or they may have irrational self-beliefs that confer inappropriate meaning on the consequences (e.g., "If I don't succeed at this, it means I am a total loser and always will be"). The fact that appraisal patterns can differ from person to person in so many ways helps us understand why there can be so much variation in how people respond to the same event or situation, and it also helps us understand why some people are particularly vulnerable to certain types of demands.

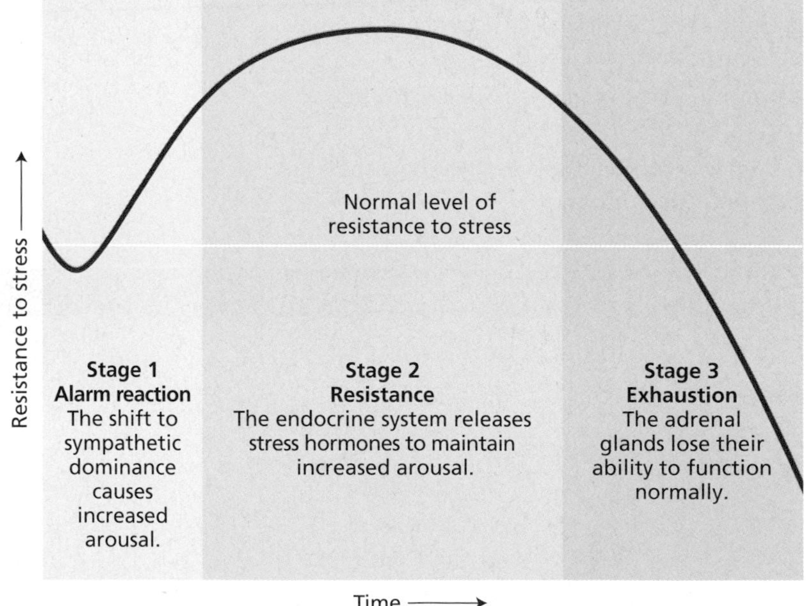

FIGURE 12.4

Hans Selye described the general adaptation syndrome. When a person is exposed to a stressor, the body's resistance is temporarily reduced by a state of shock until the alarm reaction mobilizes the body's resources. During the stage of resistance, stress hormones maintain the body's defensive changes, and the body signs that are characteristic of the alarm reaction virtually disappear. But if the stress persists over a long time, the body's resources become depleted, and exhaustion occurs; the organism can no longer cope and is highly vulnerable to breakdown.
SOURCE: Selye, 1976.

Physiological Responses

As soon as we make appraisals, the body responds to them (Borod, 2000; McEwen, 2001). Although appraisals begin the process, appraisals and physiological responses affect one another. Sensory feedback from our body's response can cause us to reappraise how stressful a situation is and whether our resources are sufficient to cope with it. Thus if you find yourself trembling and your heart pounding as you enter the interview room, you may appraise the situation as even more threatening than you did initially. The two-way arrows between the cognitive and physiological elements in Figure 12.2 illustrate this.

Endocrinologist Hans Selye (1976) was a pioneer in studying the body's response to stress. He described a physiological response pattern to strong and prolonged stressors. The **general adaptation syndrome (GAS)** *consists of three phases: alarm, resistance, and exhaustion* (Figure 12.4).

In response to a physical or psychological stressor, organisms exhibit an immediate increase in physiological arousal as the body mobilizes itself to respond to the threat. This *alarm* reaction occurs because of the sudden activation of the sympathetic nervous system and the release of stress hormones by the endocrine system. The alarm stage cannot last indefinitely, however, and the body's natural tendency to maintain the balanced internal state of homeostasis causes activity in the parasympathetic nervous system, which reduces arousal. The body continues to remain on "red alert," however, responding with the second stage, resistance.

During *resistance,* the body's resources are mobilized by the continued outpouring of stress hormones by the endocrine system, particularly the adrenal glands. Resistance can last for a relatively long time, but the body's resources are being depleted and immune system functioning is being partially suppressed by the stress hormones (Chiappelli, 2000). If the stressor is intense and persists too long, the body will eventually reach a stage of *exhaustion,* in which there is increased vulnerability to disease and, in some extreme cases, collapse and death. Selye theorized that whichever body system is weakest (e.g., cardiovascular, respiratory, gastrointestinal) will be the one most affected.

Effects of Stress on Well-Being

From a biological perspective, it seems that a high-arousal fight-or-flight biological mechanism sculpted by evolution to help us survive life-threatening *physical* stressors, such as attacks by marauding predators, may be maladaptive for dealing with the *psychological* stressors of modern life. In terms of survival, taking a final exam or sitting in rush-hour traffic is not equivalent to an attack by a hungry saber-toothed tiger, where high arousal could facilitate fighting or fleeing. In Selye's view, our physiological responses may thereby take an unnecessary toll on our physical and psychological well-being. Selye's work inspired a generation of psychological and medical researchers to explore the effects of stress on psychological and physical well-being.

Stress and Psychological Well-Being

Effects of stress on psychological well-being are clearest and most dramatic among people who have experienced catastrophic life events. Anthony Rubonis and Leonard Bickman (1991) surveyed the results of 52 studies of victims of catastrophic floods, hurricanes, and fires. In the wake of natural disasters, they found an average increase of 17 percent in rates of psychological disorders such as anxiety and depression.

Some stressors are so traumatic that they can have a strong and long-lasting psychological impact. More than 50 years after the horrors of the Holocaust, psychological scars remain for Jewish survivors of Nazi concentration camps (Nadler & Ben-Slushan, 1989; Valent, 2000). Many survivors are still troubled by high levels of anxiety and recurrent nightmares about their traumatic experiences. Children who lost their parents and siblings continue to experience sudden fears that something terrible will happen to their spouses or children whenever they are out of sight. Depression and crying spells are also common, as are feelings of insecurity and difficulties in forming close relationships. As one researcher reported, "child survivors (now in their 50s and 60s) . . . despite their outward normalcy, remain entrapped in this survival mode" (Valent, 1998, p. 751).

Long-lasting psychological symptoms have also been found among American soldiers who experienced the trauma of combat during the Vietnam War. Paula Schnurr and her coworkers (1998) found a significantly greater number of stress symptoms in Vietnam veterans who experienced combat than in veterans from the same era who did not experience combat.

As we will see in Chapter 13, some women who experience the trauma of rape have psychological scars that are intense and long-lasting. In one long-term study of female rape victims, one fourth of the women felt that they had not recovered psychologically 6 years after the rape (Meyer & Taylor, 1986).

Fortunately, most people do not experience stressors as severe as concentration camp confinement, combat, or rape. How do more typical but less serious stressors affect psychological well-being? To answer this question, researchers have examined relations between self-reported life events and measures of psychological well-being. Findings consistently show that the more negative life events people report on measures such as the one shown in Table 12.1, the more likely they are to also report symptoms of psychological distress, which include anxiety, depression, and unhappiness (Holahan & Moos, 1990; Monroe & Peterman, 1988). Many medical and psychological researchers have therefore concluded that "stress causes distress," and this conclusion has been widely accepted among the general public and in the mass media.

> **What Do You Think?**
>
> **DO STRESSFUL EVENTS CAUSE PSYCHOLOGICAL DISTRESS?**
>
> A consistent statistical relation has been shown between stressful life events and psychological distress; the greater the number of stressful events people have experienced, the more distress they are likely to report. Based on these results, are you willing to accept the conclusion that life stress causes distress, or can you think of other possible reasons for this relation? Think about it, then see page 504 for a commentary.

Stress and Illness

▶ 4. Describe physiological and behavioral mechanisms through which stress can contribute to illness.

There are indications that stress can combine with other physical and psychological factors to influence the entire spectrum of physical illnesses, from the common cold to cancer, heart disease, diabetes, and sudden death (Cohen et al., 1998; Suls & Wallston, 2003). Sometimes the effects are immediate. On the day of the 1994 Northridge, California, earthquake, the number of sudden deaths due to heart attacks in the greater Los Angeles area nearly tripled from an average of 35.7 per day during the previous seven days to 101 (Leor et al., 1996).

▶ 5. What kinds of psychosocial factors have been shown to affect immune functioning?

Other effects of major stressors on physical well-being are less immediate but no less severe. Within a month following the death of a spouse, bereaved widowers and widows begin to show a higher mortality rate than married people of the same age who have not lost a spouse (Kaprio et al., 1987). Stressful life events have also been linked to a higher risk of developing cancer (Sklar & Anisman, 1981).

A traumatic life event can worsen an already existing medical condition, as in this case of a 7-year-old African American girl with sickle-cell anemia:

> This little girl was bused to a new elementary school in a white neighborhood. . . . She and other black children were met with cries by angry whites to "go back to where you belong!" The little girl was quite upset by the incident. After some time at the school she went to the principal's office crying and complaining of chest pains. She died later that day in the hospital, apparently from a sickle-cell crisis brought on by stress. As she died, she kept repeating "go back where you belong." (Friedman & DiMatteo, 1989, p. 169)

Linkages between long-term stress and illness are not surprising, for physiological responses to stressors can directly harm other body systems. For example, the secretion of stress hormones, such as epinephrine, norepinephrine, and cortisol, is a major part of the stress response. These hormones affect the activity of the heart, and excessive secretions can damage the lining of the arteries. By reducing fat metabolism, the stress hormones can also contribute to the fatty blockages in arteries that cause heart attacks and strokes (McCabe et al., 2000; Willenberg et al., 2000).

Stress can also contribute to health breakdowns by causing people to behave in ways that increase the risk of illness. For example, people with diabetes can frequently control their disease through medication, exercise, and diet. When under stress, however, diabetics are less likely to regulate their diets and take their medication, resulting in an increased risk of serious medical consequences (Brantley & Garrett, 1993). People are also more likely to quit exercising when under stress, even if the primary reason they began exercising in the first place was to reduce stress (Stetson et al., 1997). Stress may also lead to smoking, alcohol and drug use, sleep loss, undereating or overeating, and other health-compromising behaviors.

Stress and the Immune System

Considerable evidence suggests that life stress can weaken immune functioning (Suls & Wallston, 2003; Taylor, 2003). Research by Ronald Glaser, Janet Kiecolt-Glaser, and their coworkers at Ohio State University has shown that reduced immune system effectiveness is one possible reason for increased risk of illness (Kiecolt-Glaser et al., 2002; Marsland et al., 2001). In one study, researchers closely followed medical students over a 1-year period. They collected blood samples from the students during three stressful academic examination periods in order to measure immune cell activity. The researchers found that immune system effectiveness was reduced during the stressful exam periods and that this reduction was linked to the likelihood of becoming ill. Other studies showed that stress hormones released into the bloodstream by the adrenal glands as part of the stress response can suppress the activity of specific immune system cells, increasing the likelihood of illness (Cohen & Herbert, 1996; Maier & Watkins, 1999).

Stress produced by interpersonal conflict and hostility can also cause breakdowns in immune system functioning. Janice Kiecolt-Glaser and her coworkers (1998) brought 90 newly married

FIGURE 12.5

Research has shown that the stress produced by marital conflict can decrease immune system functioning.

couples into a laboratory and asked them to discuss areas of conflict in their relationship. The researchers coded the couples' behavior during the discussions and measured their physiological and immune responses. Among those couples whose interactions became hostile during the conflict discussions, measurable decreases in immune functioning occurred within 24 hours (Figure 12.5).

School examinations and conflicts in close relationships are stressful, but they pale in comparison with some other life stressors, such as the death of a loved one. Within 1 year after the death of their spouse, about two thirds of bereaved people decline in health (Irwin et al., 1987). An increased rate of mortality is found particularly in men, who tend to respond to the death of their spouse with relatively greater distress and health declines than do women (Stroebe et al., 2001). These severe stressors are life-disrupting in many ways, and they can also reduce immune functioning (Suls & Wallston, 2003). To study the impact of bereavement on immune system functioning, Michael Irwin and coworkers (1987) monitored the immune cell activity of women before and after the death of their husbands. They found a decrease in immune cell activity only in women who reacted to the death of their husband with strong depressive symptoms.

Other studies also point to stress-produced depression and distress as factors that can weaken the immune system. Among people who survived the 1994 Northridge, California earthquake, those who reacted with the highest levels of distress showed a notable decline in immune system functioning over the next 4 months (Solomon et al., 1997). Researchers have also found that a reduction in immune system functioning caused by distress or depression can increase the body's vulnerability to viral diseases and, possibly, to cancer (Chiappelli, 2000; Kiecolt-Glaser et al., 2002).

Obviously, the immune system does not "know" that a feared examination is at hand, that a family member has died, or that an earthquake has occurred. But the brain knows, and what the brain knows and does can affect how well our immune system protects us.

IN REVIEW

- *Various theorists view stress as a stimulus; as a response having cognitive, physiological, and behavioral components; or as an interaction (i.e., transaction) between the person and the environment. The latter view incorporates the stimulus and response conceptions into a more dynamic model.*
- *Stressors are events that place physical or psychological demands on organisms. The stressfulness of a situation is defined by the balance between demands and resources. Life events can vary in terms of how positive or negative they are and how intense they are. Other dimensions that affect their impact include predictability, controllability, and chronicity.*
- *Cognitive appraisal processes play an essential role in people's responses to stressors. People appraise the nature of the demands, the resources available to deal with them, their possible consequences, and the personal meaning of these consequences. Distortions at any of these levels can result in inappropriate stress responses.*
- *The physiological response to stressors is mediated by the autonomic and endocrine systems and involves a pattern of arousal that mobilizes the body to deal with the stressor. Selye described a General Adaptation Syndrome (GAS), which involves the stages of alarm, resistance, and exhaustion.*
- *Measures of both major negative life events and microstressors are associated with negative psychological outcomes, such as anxiety and depression. Life stress also is related to negative health changes. It can worsen preexisting medical conditions and increase the risk of illness and death. Reduced immune system functioning may underlie some negative health effects caused by stress.*

FIGURE 12.6

Social support is one of the strongest protective factors against stress.

Factors That Influence Stress-Health Relations

As we saw with Priscilla at the opening of the chapter, some highly resilient individuals seem to tolerate extremely demanding stressors over a long period of time without negative effects. Others appear to quickly fall prey to relatively minor stressors. The fact that people differ so dramatically in their responses to stressful events has prompted many health psychologists to search for personal and environmental factors that make people more or less reactive to stressful events. **Vulnerability factors** *increase people's susceptibility to stressful events.* They include lack of a social support network, poor coping skills, tendencies to become anxious or pessimistic, excessive bottling-up of feelings, and other factors that reduce stress resistance. In contrast, **protective factors** *are environmental or personal resources that help people cope more effectively with stressful events.* They include a biological response pattern called *physiological toughness,* social support, effective coping skills, and cognitive factors such as hardiness, coping self-efficacy, optimism, and an ability to find meaning in stressful events.

Social Support

▶ 6. In what ways can social support protect against stressful events?

Social support is one of the most important environmental resources (Suls & Wallston, 2003). The knowledge that we can rely on others for help and support in a time of crisis helps blunt the impact of stress (Figure 12.6). In contrast, lack of social support is a significant vulnerability factor. Studies carried out in the United States, Finland, and Sweden carefully tracked the well-being of some 37,000 people for up to 12 years. Even after taking into account medical risk factors such as age, smoking, high blood pressure, high cholesterol levels, obesity, and lack of physical exercise, the researchers found that people with weak social ties were twice as likely to die during the period of the study as those with strong ties to others (House et al., 1988). The relation between social isolation and poor health was stronger for men than for women.

One way that social support protects against stress is by enhancing immune system functioning. Robert Baron and his coworkers (1990) studied people whose spouses were being treated for cancer and who were experiencing psychological distress. The participants agreed to be injected with an allergen so that their immune system responses could be measured. In response to the injections, the immune systems of the spouses who rated themselves as high in social support produced more immune cells, particularly at high levels of the allergen, than did the immune systems of those who indicated lower social support in their lives. These results may help explain why people who have high levels of social support are more disease-resistant when they are under stress (House et al., 1988).

Many other studies show that social support decreases psychological distress in people who are dealing with stressful life events of all kinds (Holahan & Moos, 1986, 1990; Schwarzer, 1998). In one such study, 86 women undergoing breast cancer treatment at Stanford Medical School were randomly assigned either to a weekly psychotherapy group designed to increase social support and strengthen their coping skills or to a control condition that received just the medical center's regular cancer treatment. As shown in Figure 12.7, those in the therapy groups survived nearly twice as long as did the controls (Spiegel et al., 1989). A later study using a similar intervention failed to find greater longevity among breast cancer patients, but it did find significant quality-of-life benefits, such as lowered depression, feelings of closeness with other group members, and a positive reordering of life priorities (Goodwin et al., 2001). Peer support groups appear especially helpful to breast cancer victims who lack support from their spouse and physician (Helgeson et al., 2000).

Besides enhancing immune system functioning, social support has a number of other stress-buffering benefits. People who feel that they are part of a social system experience a greater sense of identity and meaning in their lives, which in turn results in greater psychological well-being (S. Cohen, 1988; Rodin & Salovey, 1989). Social

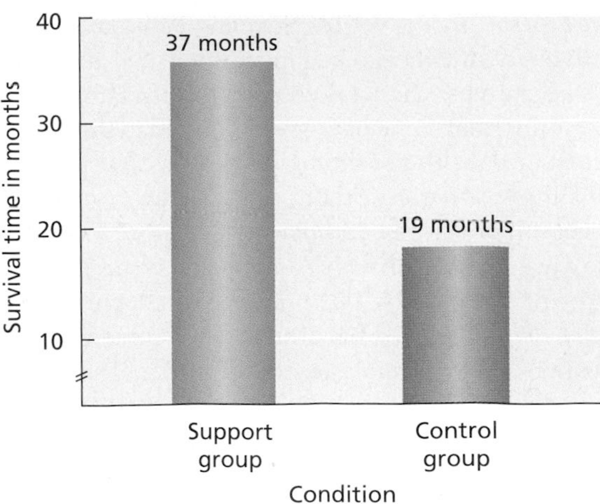

FIGURE 12.7

Mean survival time for breast cancer patients who received a coping skills and social support intervention compared with control patients who received normal cancer treatment. SOURCE: Based on Spiegel et al., 1989.

networks also reduce exposure to other risk factors, such as loneliness. Third, having the backing of others can increase one's sense of control over stressors. Finally, true friends can apply social pressure to prevent people from coping with stressors in maladaptive ways (e.g., through alcohol or drug use). Any of these buffering effects can help counteract the impact of stressful life events.

Physiological Reactivity

Responses of the autonomic and endocrine systems appear to underlie many of the negative psychological and health consequences of stress (McEwen, 2001). The fact that people differ widely in the pattern and intensity of their physiological responses makes people more or less vulnerable to stressors. As we saw in Chapter 11, people high in neuroticism, who tend to have intense and prolonged autonomic responses, seem more vulnerable to stress than are people low in this personality factor (Eysenck, 1990; Snyder, 2001).

Physiological toughness, a particular stress hormone pattern, appears to be a protective factor (Dienstbier, 1989). **Physiological toughness** *involves relations between two classes of hormones secreted by the adrenal glands in the face of stress.* Both *catecholamines* (which include epinephrine and norepinephrine) and *corticosteroids* (particularly cortisol) mobilize the body's fight-or-flight response in the face of stressors, but they have somewhat different effects on the body. Cortisol's arousal effects last much longer and seem to be more damaging than those produced by the catecholamines (unless the catecholamines are secreted at high levels over a long period of time). For example, cortisol reduces immune system functioning and helps create fatty deposits in the arteries that lead to heart disease. In contrast, catecholamine secretion increases immune system functioning (Taylor, 2003).

▶ 7. Describe the physiological toughness endocrine pattern.

Physiological toughness consists of (1) a low resting level of cortisol and low levels of cortisol secretion in response to stressors and (2) a low resting level of catecholamines but a quick and strong catecholamine response when the stressor occurs, followed by a quick decline in catecholamine secretion and arousal when the stressor is over (Figure 12.8). This hormonal pattern seems to provide maximum short-term mobilization of resources needed to deal with the stressor but prevents the eventual depletion of catecholamines and the wear and tear on the body that Selye identified with the exhaustion phase of GAS (Dienstbier, 1989). Increased vulnerability to bodily breakdowns occurs when the person responds to stress with high levels of cortisol instead of catecholamines. The fact that physical exercise entails catecholamine-produced arousal may help account for exercise's health-enhancing effects and its ability to promote physiological toughness and stress resistance (Ehrman, 2003; Morgan, 1997).

Type A Behavior Pattern

The Type A behavior pattern is said to have been discovered by an upholsterer working on the chairs in the office of a physician who specialized in treating heart attack victims. The upholsterer

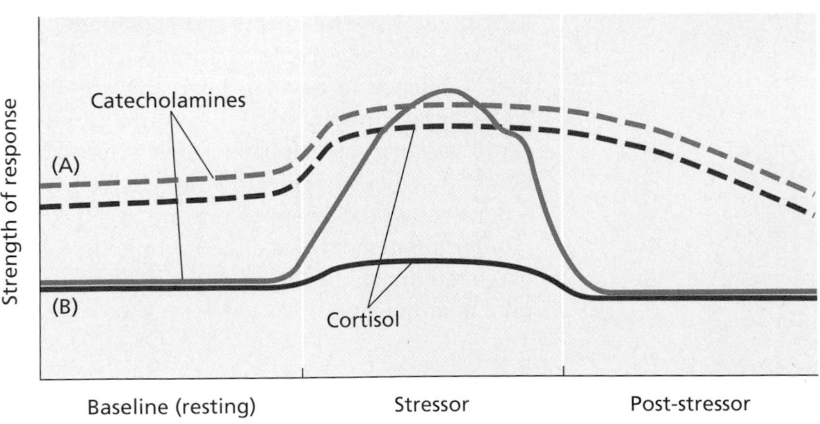

FIGURE 12.8

Hormonal patterns of response to stress. When a stressor occurs, a typical response (pattern A) is a strong, long-lasting rise in corticosteroid (cortisol) and catecholamine (epinephrine, norepinephrine) hormones. In physiologically tough individuals, however, cortisol secretion remains low, and there is a strong catecholamine response followed by a quick return to baseline (pattern B). This response, as well as low baseline levels of the hormones involved, seems to protect the body from damage.

▶ 8. Describe the Type A behavior pattern and how it can contribute to coronary heart disease.

For more on Type A behavior, see Interactive Segment 12.2.

noticed an unusual wear pattern at the front of the seats, not the back, indicating that the patients were constantly sitting on the edges of their seats and moving about.

This edge-of-the-seat pattern typifies the behaviors seen in people with the **Type A behavior pattern,** *who tend to live under great pressure and demand much of themselves and others.* Many Type A people are workaholics, continually striving to get more done in less time. Type A people are also characterized by high levels of competitiveness and ambition, which can foster aggressiveness and hostility when things get in their way. Several large-scale studies suggest that even when other physical risk factors, such as obesity and smoking, are taken into account, Type A men and women have about double the risk for coronary heart disease (CHD) compared with less driven people (Haynes et al., 1980; Rosenman et al., 1975).

However, research indicates that not all components of the Type A pattern increase vulnerability to CHD. The Type A person's fast-paced, time-conscious lifestyle and high ambition apparently are not the culprits. Rather, the crucial component seems to be negative emotions. The Type A behavior pattern virtually guarantees that these people will encounter many stressful situations, such as time pressures of their own making and barriers that anger them. A cynical hostility marked by suspiciousness, resentment, frequent anger, distrust, and antagonism seems particularly important (Barefoot et al., 1989). This aspect of the Type A pattern is likely to alienate others, produce interpersonal stress and conflict, and reduce the amount of social support the person receives. In addition, Type A people tend to overreact physiologically to stressful events and take longer to recover, a biological factor that may contribute to their tendency to develop heart disease (Taylor, 2003). John Hunter, an 18th-century pioneer in cardiovascular medicine, recognized his own vulnerability when he said, "My life is in the hands of any rascal who chooses to put me in a passion." Hunter's statement was all too prophetic; he died of a heart attack during an angry debate at a hospital board meeting.

The Importance of Beliefs

▶ 9. How do hardiness, coping self-efficacy, optimism-pessimism, and spiritual beliefs affect stress outcomes?

The mind as well as the body can make people more or less vulnerable to stressors. Considering the important role that appraisal processes play in emotions and stress, we should not be surprised that our beliefs, or ways of thinking about situations and ourselves, are significant protective and vulnerability factors.

Hardiness In the 1970s, Suzanne Kobasa of the University of Chicago began an intensive study of 200 executives who worked in highly stressful jobs. She found that some of them responded to their circumstances with psychological distress and physical illness, whereas others continued to function well both physically and psychologically. How did the two groups differ? The answer came in the form of *three beliefs, comprising a stress-protective factor that she termed* **hardiness.** The "three Cs" of hardiness are *commitment, control,* and *challenge.*

Hardy people are committed to their work, their families, and their other involvements, and they believe that what they are doing is important. Second, they view themselves as having control over their outcomes, as opposed to feeling powerless to influence events. Finally, they appraise the demands of the situations as challenges, or opportunities, rather than as threats. As a result, demanding situations not only become less stressful, but they can actually stimulate higher levels of performance (Kobasa et al., 1985).

Of these three hardiness components, control is apparently the strongest active ingredient in buffering stress (Funk, 1992; Steptoe, 2000). A 5-year longitudinal study showed that women who felt in control of their lives did not show increases in future illness when stress increased, whereas those low in perceived control did (Lawler & Schmied, 1992).

Coping Self-Efficacy When confronted by a stressor, one of the most significant appraisals we make is whether we have sufficient resources to cope with the demands (Bandura, 1997). Small wonder, then, that **coping self-efficacy**—*the belief that we can perform the behaviors necessary to cope successfully*—is an important protective factor (Bandura, 1989). As hardiness research shows, even events that are appraised as extremely demanding may generate little stress if we believe that we have the skills to deal with them.

Self-efficacy is always specific to the particular situation: "Can I handle *these* demands?" As noted in Chapter 11, previous successes in similar situations increase efficacy; failures undermine it (Bandura, 1997). People can also increase efficacy expectancies by observing others cope successfully and through social persuasion and encouragement from others. The teacher who befriended Priscilla constantly gave her the message "I believe in you. You can do it!" Finally, experiencing a low level of physiological arousal in the face of a stressor can convey a sense of strength and ability to cope, demonstrating another way in which arousal can affect appraisal.

Feelings of self-efficacy may fortify our bodies as well our minds against stressful events. An intriguing finding came from a laboratory study in which people with phobias confronted a feared object. When participants reported high self-efficacy while confronting the stressful situation, their immune systems actually begin to function more effectively. In contrast, those who reported low coping efficacy showed a drop in immune system functioning (Wiedenfeld et al., 1990).

Optimistic Expectations Our beliefs about how things are likely to turn out also play an important role in dealing with stressors. Recent research indicates that optimistic people are at lowered risk for anxiety and depression when they confront stressful events. Edward Chang (1998) found that people with optimistic beliefs felt less helpless in the face of stress and adjusted better to negative life events than did pessimists. In one year-long study, optimists had about half as many infectious illnesses and visits to doctors as did pessimists (Peterson & Seligman, 1987). In another study, researchers followed women who came to the National Cancer Institute for breast cancer treatment for 5 years. On average, women who were optimistic about their recovery lived longer than pessimists, even when the physical severity of the disease was the same at the beginning of the 5-year period (Levy et al., 1988).

Finding Meaning in Stressful Life Events Humanistic theorists emphasize the human need to find meaning in one's life and the psychological benefits of doing so (May, 1961; Watson & Greenberg, 1998). Some people find personal meaning through spiritual beliefs, which can be a great comfort in the face of crises. Daniel McIntosh and coworkers (1993) studied 124 parents who had lost their babies to sudden infant death syndrome. They found that grieving parents whose religious beliefs provided some higher meaning to their loss experienced greater well-being and less distress 18 months later. In another study, researchers found that people who were able to find meaning in the death of a family member experienced less distress during the year following the loss. Finding a sense of meaning from their own process of coping with the loss (e.g., the sense that the event helped them grow spiritually) had even longer-term positive effects (Davis et al., 1998).

Religious beliefs can be a two-edged sword, however: They can either decrease or increase stress, depending on their nature and the type of stressor to which they are applied. In one study of elderly people with medical problems, poorer physical and psychological adjustment occurred in patients who viewed God as punishing them; saw themselves as the victims of demonic forces; expressed anger toward God, clergy, or church members; or questioned their faith (Koenig et al., 1998). Religious beliefs may have positive effects in dealing with some types of stressors but not with others. Such beliefs seem to help people cope more effectively with losses, illnesses, and personal setbacks. In contrast, they can increase the negative impact of other stressors such as marital problems and abuse, perhaps by inducing guilt or placing internal pressures on individuals to remain in the stressful relationship (Strawbridge et al., 1998).

Resilient Children: "Superkids" or "Ordinary Magic"?

At the beginning of this chapter we described Priscilla, a child who grew up in a terrible home environment with a psychotic mother and a father who abused her and committed suicide in her presence. Somehow, despite these experiences, Priscilla grew into a highly successful young woman.

What factors matter in the lives of resilient children like Priscilla, who rise far above what their environments would predict for them? Are they "superkids," as a *New York Times* writer referred to them? After reviewing many studies of unusually resilient children and adolescents, Ann Masten (2001) concluded that such children are a monument to the ordinary adaptive processes that occur in the lives of most children, factors she termed "ordinary magic." Masten and J. Douglas Coatsworth (1998) found that these children have certain characteristics that contribute to a positive outcome even in the face of stressful life events (Table 12.2). These characteristics include adequate intellectual functioning, social skills, self-efficacy, and faith (optimism and hope), as well as environmental factors such as a relationship with at least one caring, prosocial adult.

To be resilient, a child need not have all of the characteristics listed in Table 12.2, but he or she must have some of them. Good intellectual functioning and a supportive relationship with a caring adult seem to be the most important (Masten & Coatsworth, 1998). In Priscilla's case, this positive adult relationship did not exist with either parent. Instead, the critical relationship was provided by a loving elementary school teacher who befriended, encouraged, and guided her during the critical formative period of middle childhood. This key relationship, combined with Priscilla's obvious intelligence, allowed her to develop self-esteem, a belief in

TABLE 12.2 Personal and Environmental Factors That Contribute to Stress-Resilience in Children

Source	Characteristic
Individual	Good intellectual functioning
	Appealing, sociable, easygoing disposition
	Self-efficacy, self-confidence, high self-esteem
	Talents
	Faith
Family	Close relationship to caring parent figure
	Authoritative parenting: warmth, structure, high expectations
	Socioeconomic advantages
	Connections to extended supportive family networks
Extrafamilial context	Bonds to prosocial adults outside the family
	Connections to prosocial organizations
	Attending effective schools

SOURCE: Masten & Coatsworth, 1998.

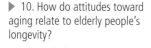

▶ 10. How do attitudes toward aging relate to elderly people's longevity?

her own capabilities, and the will to nurture her talents.

In Priscilla, then, we have an example of what can happen even in the face of great adversity when certain critical protective factors are present. As Masten (2001) concluded,

> What began as a quest for the extraordinary has revealed the power of the ordinary. Resilience does not come from rare and special qualities, but from the everyday magic of ordinary, normative human resources in the minds, brains, and bodies of children, in their families and relationships, and in their communities (p. 235)

Aging and Adaptation

The process of aging is a background stressor in many people's lives. People's reactions differ considerably as their hair thins, wrinkles deepen, physical and sexual capacity diminish, health declines, acquaintances begin to die, and a sense of mortality becomes more salient. Some dread the aging process, whereas others accept or even find value in it. Do such differences affect physical well-being? Our *Research Close-Up* suggests that the answer is yes.

RESEARCH CLOSE-UP

CAN ATTITUDES TOWARD AGING INFLUENCE HOW LONG WE LIVE?

Introduction

Although aging is a natural part of life, most people do not welcome the aging process as it occurs beyond midlife. In a culture that emphasizes youth, negative stereotypes concerning the physical and cognitive capacities of aged people abound, and most members of our culture internalize these beliefs to varying degrees. There are also some positive stereotypes attached to aging, such as an increase in wisdom. When people reach their later years, these internalized stereotypes become self-relevant. Depending on which beliefs about aging they have adopted, and the extent to which they have internalized them, aging people may have different self-perceptions. A preponderance of negative self-beliefs may have harmful psychological and physical effects on the person, whereas positive self-perceptions may serve as protective factors that support health and well-being. This study was designed to study the possible role of self-perceptions on the longevity of aging adults.

Method

In 1975, researchers recruited residents from Oxford, Ohio to participate in a longitudinal study of the aging process. The sample consisted of 338 men and 332 women who ranged in age from 50 to 94, with a mean age of 63 years. They completed a series of questionnaires concerning their physical health, health-related habits, and psychological variables such as loneliness

SOURCE: Becca R. Levy, Martin D. Slade, Suzanne R. Kunkel, and Stanislav V. Kasl (2002). Longevity increased by positive self-perceptions of aging. *Journal of Personality and Social Psychology, 83,* 261–270.

and various self-perceptions. One of the measures, the Attitudes Toward Own Aging Scale, consisted of the following 5 items:

1. Things keep getting worse as I get older.
2. I have as much pep as I did last year.
3. As you get older, you are less useful.
4. I am as happy now as when I was younger.
5. As I get older, things are [better, worse] than I thought they would be.

Respondents answered the first four items "yes" or "no" and chose the appropriate word for the fifth item. Researchers assigned each participant a score of 1 to 5 ("no" responses on items 1 and 3, "yes" responses on items 2 and 4, and the "better" choice on item 5 contributed to a positive score); a high score indicated a more positive attitude toward one's aging. The mean score for all participants was 3.67.

Twenty-two years later, researchers reviewed mortality records on all of the participants to see which ones were still alive and the age at which the deceased people had died. They then used the scores on the aging attitudes scale to create two groups: (1) those whose scores on the Attitude Toward Own Aging Scale were above the group mean and (2) those whose scores were below the mean, indicating more negative perceptions of their aging. The researchers then compared these two groups in terms of the number of days they stayed alive after the measures were collected in 1975, taking into account with statistical adjustments such factors as age, physical health, and loneliness at the 1975 baseline.

Results

Not surprisingly, the age of the participant at the beginning of the study was the strongest predictor of longevity: One doesn't expect 80-year-olds to live longer than 50-year-olds. Beyond that, however, attitudes toward aging were the strongest predictor of longevity, being actually more important than physical health. Figure 12.9 shows survival curves for the two attitude groups.

The curves represent the probability that a group member would still be alive in each of the 23 years of follow-up. On average, those people with positive attitudes toward their aging lived 7.6 years longer than those with negative attitudes. This survival advantage persisted even when the effects of age, sex, socioeconomic status, physical health, and loneliness were statistically controlled, so that their contributions to longevity were subtracted from the overall effect. The survival advantage also existed among age bands, that is, among positive- versus negative-attitude people who were in their 50s, 60s, 70s, or 80s when the study began. Within every age group, the positive-attitude people lived significantly longer.

Discussion

The results provide evidence that positive and negative attitudes toward one's aging process have a rather striking relation to longevity. This psychological factor made an overall difference of 7.6 years in longevity in this sample, and it related far more strongly to longevity than did physical health at the time the study began. In fact, the effect of attitudes on longevity was stronger than the typical findings for such health factors as lowered cholesterol or lowered blood pressure, which typically increase one's life span by an estimated 4 years; and nonsmoking, exercise, or weight loss, which add 1 to 3 years to one's life (Suls & Wallston, 2003; Taylor, 2003).

Had the investigators simply compared the positive- and negative-attitude groups with one another, the results would have been hard to interpret. For example, it would be expected that 80-year-olds would have less positive attitudes about aging than 50-year-olds, and they'd also have a lower life expectancy, which could by itself account for the overall result. The researchers dealt with this possibility in two ways. First, they were able to control statistically for the age effect, thereby removing its influence from the results. Second, they showed that, at every age level, positive attitude was related to longevity. Moreover, the results of this study mirror those of a study in Germany that found attitudes toward aging to be one of the strongest predictors of

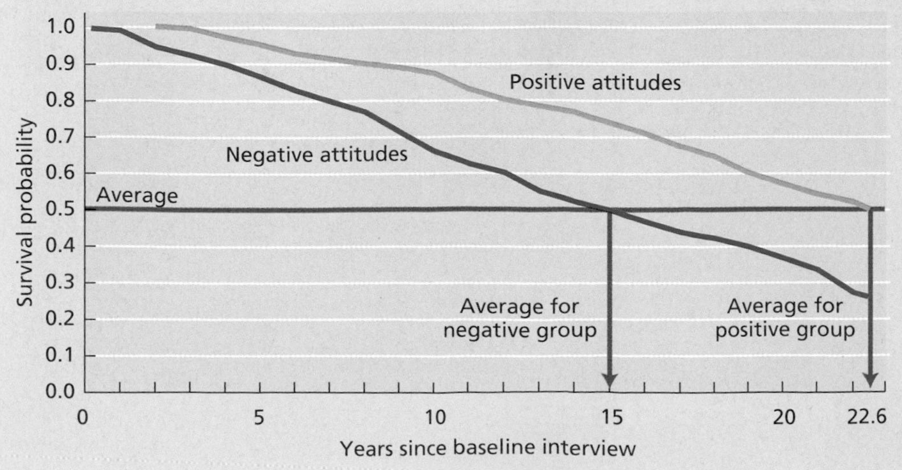

FIGURE 12.9

Relation between positive or negative self-perceptions of one's aging and subsequent longevity. These survival curves show the likelihood that a randomly selected group member would still be alive in a given year after the beginning of the study. The graph shows that the median number of years until death was 15 in the group with negative self-attitudes and 22.6 among positive-attitude participants. SOURCE: Adapted from Levy et al., 2002.

Continued

longevity in 70-year-olds. This similarity in results suggests that the finding is replicable in other samples.

What lies behind the attitude-longevity relationship? It may be that negative attitudes toward aging are a source of stress that takes a toll on the body. The authors also suggest that the "will to live" is an important factor. In 1977, the investigators administered a measure of this variable to the sample and found that those who valued their lives and wanted to live longer actually did so. Like other evidence, this study indicates the importance of cognitive and motivational factors in physical well-being. Future research will undoubtedly teach us more about the role of psychological processes in how long we live.

As we have now seen, a variety of biological, cognitive, and environmental factors influence stress and its effects on us. Figure 12.10 summarizes these important influences.

COPING WITH STRESS

▶ 11. Describe the three major classes of coping strategies. How does stressor controllability influence their outcomes?

> My courage sank, and with each succeeding minute it became less possible to resist this horror. My cue came, and on I went to that stage where I knew with grim certainty I would not be capable of remaining more than a few minutes. . . . I took one pace forward and stopped abruptly. My voice had started to fade, my throat closed up and the audience was beginning to go giddily round. (Aaron, 1986, p. 24)

This account of "stage fright" was given not by a novice actor in his first play but by Sir Laurence Olivier, considered by many the greatest actor of his generation. Few people were aware that for most of his career, Olivier experienced a private hell before every performance. His audiences saw only what happened once he stepped onto the stage: another flawless performance. Olivier had a remarkable ability to purge the terror from his mind, relax his body, and concentrate fully on his role once showtime arrived (Aaron, 1986).

Although there are countless ways people might respond to a stressor, coping strategies can be divided into the three broad classes shown in Figure 12.11. **Problem-focused coping** *strategies attempt to confront and directly deal with the demands of the situation or to change the situation so that it is no longer stressful.* Examples of problem-focused strategies might include studying for a test, going directly to another person to work out a misunderstanding, or signing up for a course to improve one's time-management skills.

Rather than dealing directly with the stressful situation, **emotion-focused coping** *strategies attempt to manage the emotional responses that result from it.* As Figure 12.11 shows, some forms of emotion-focused coping involve appraising the situation in a manner that minimizes its emotional impact. A person might deal with the stress from an interpersonal conflict by denying

FIGURE 12.10

Understanding Behavior: Biological, psychological, and environmental factors that affect the stress response.

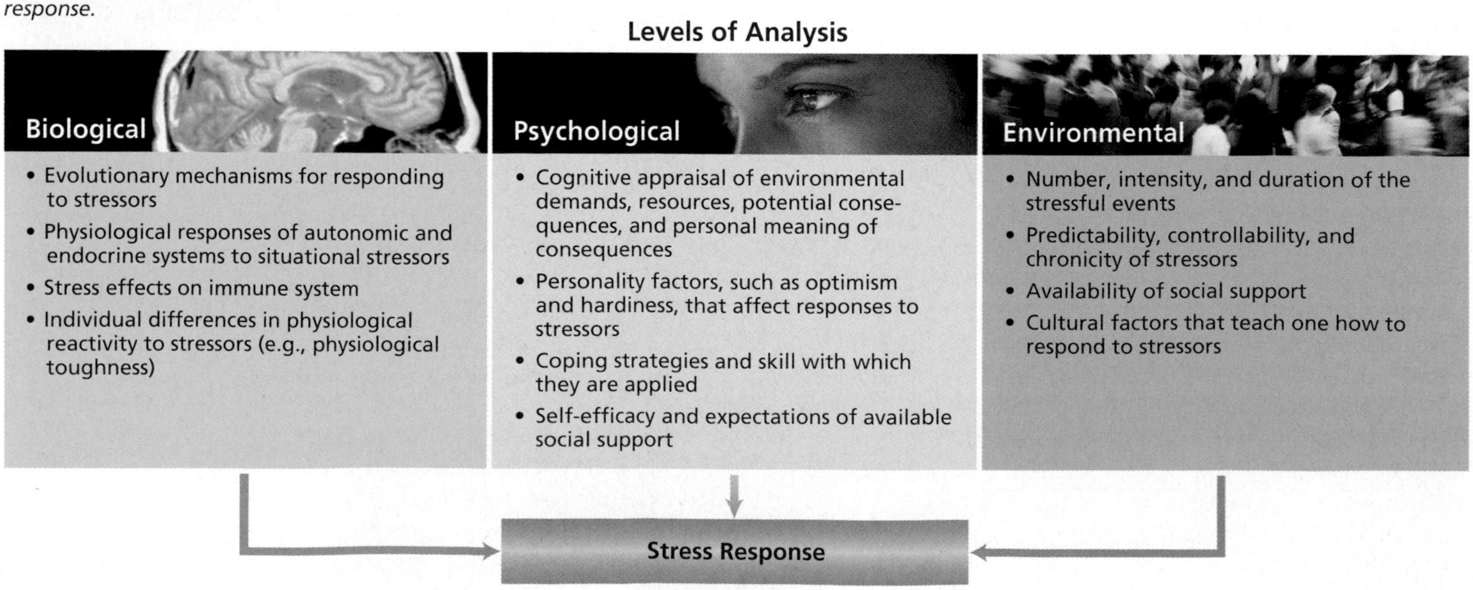

Levels of Analysis

Biological	Psychological	Environmental
• Evolutionary mechanisms for responding to stressors • Physiological responses of autonomic and endocrine systems to situational stressors • Stress effects on immune system • Individual differences in physiological reactivity to stressors (e.g., physiological toughness)	• Cognitive appraisal of environmental demands, resources, potential consequences, and personal meaning of consequences • Personality factors, such as optimism and hardiness, that affect responses to stressors • Coping strategies and skill with which they are applied • Self-efficacy and expectations of available social support	• Number, intensity, and duration of the stressful events • Predictability, controllability, and chronicity of stressors • Availability of social support • Cultural factors that teach one how to respond to stressors

Stress Response

that any problem exists. Other forms involve avoidance or acceptance of the stressful situation. Thus a student might decide to deal with anxiety about an upcoming test by going to a party and forgetting about it. Informed that he has a terminal illness, a man might decide that nothing can be done about the situation and simply accept this unwelcome reality—or he might use the avoidance strategy of discontinuing medical treatment and keeping the illness a secret, even from close family members.

A third class of coping strategies involves **seeking social support,** *that is, turning to others for assistance and emotional support in times of stress.* Thus the student might seek the help of a classmate in preparing for the test, and the man with the terminal illness choose to join a support group for the terminally ill. Priscilla accepted and benefited from the social support provided by the teacher who befriended her.

Effectiveness of Coping Strategies

Which of the three general classes of coping strategies would you expect to be most generally effective? Whenever we ask this question in our classes, the majority of our students vote for problem-focused coping. This response is understandable, for many people, particularly in Western cultures, approach problems with the attitude that if something needs fixing, we should fix it.

What does the research literature say? Charles Holahan and Rudolf Moos (1990) studied coping patterns and psychological outcomes in more than 400 California adults over a 1-year period. Although people often used several coping methods in dealing with a stressor, problem-focused coping methods and seeking social support were most often associated with favorable adjustment to stressors. In contrast, emotion-focused strategies that involved avoiding feelings or taking things out on other people predicted depression and poorer adjustment. Other studies have yielded similar results. In children and adults and across many different types of stressors, emotion-focused strategies that involve avoidance, denial, and wishful thinking seem to be related to less effective adaptation (Snyder, 2001). On the other hand, there are adaptive emotion-focused strategies, such as identifying and changing irrational negative thinking and learning relaxation skills to control arousal. These emotion-focused methods can reduce stress responses without avoiding or distorting reality, and they can be effective ways of dealing with stress (DeLongis, 2000; Meichenbaum, 1985).

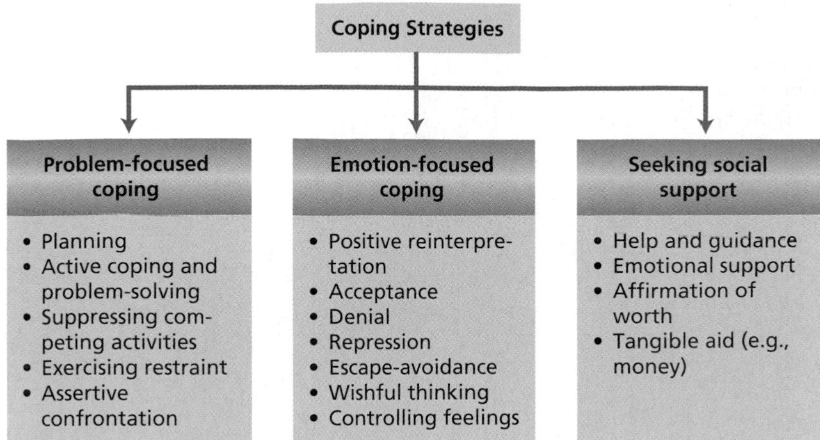

FIGURE 12.11

Coping strategies fall into three general categories: (1) problem-focused coping, consisting of active attempts to respond to situational demands; (2) emotion-focused coping, directed at minimizing emotional distress; and (3) seeking or accepting social support.

Controllability and Coping Efficacy

Despite the evidence generally favoring problem-focused coping, attempts to change the situation are not always the most adaptive way to cope with a stressor. There are situations that we cannot influence or modify, and in those cases problem-focused coping may not help much. It may even do more harm than good. Instead, emotion-focused coping may be the most adaptive approach we can take, for while we cannot master the situation, we may be able to prevent or control maladaptive emotional responses to it (Auerbach, 1989). Of course, reliance on emotion-focused coping is likely to be maladaptive if it prevents us from acting to change situations in which we actually *do* have control.

Thomas Strentz and Stephen Auerbach (1988) demonstrated the effectiveness of emotion-focused coping in adapting to a stressful situation with limited personal control. As part of an FBI (Federal Bureau of Investigation) program to deal with potential airline hijackings, airline employees volunteered to participate in a training exercise. The employees were randomly assigned to one of two experimental conditions or to a control condition. In one experimental condition, employees were trained in problem-focused techniques that hostages can use to actively deal with their predicament. They were shown how to interact with captors and maintain a facade of dignity and composure through appearance and behavior. They also learned ways of supporting one another nonverbally and communicating with one another by using a prisoner-of-war tap code.

Training for the second experimental group focused on the emotional reactions the hostages would likely experience and techniques they could use to minimize their stress responses. These emotion-focused techniques included deep

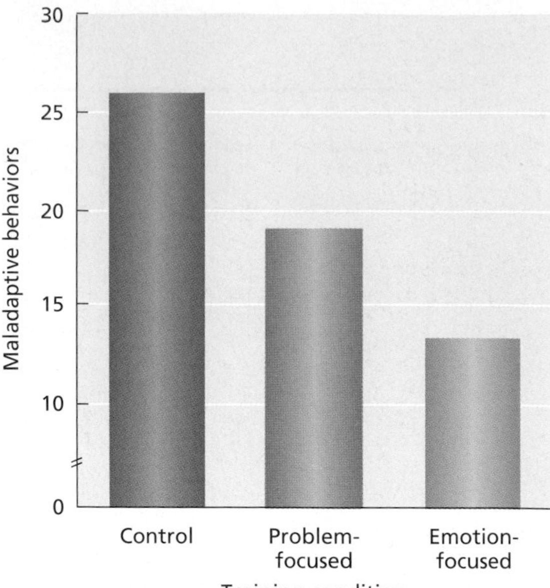

FIGURE 12.12

Behavioral ratings of adjustment to the stress of captivity by participants trained in problem- and emotion-focused coping techniques. The control group received no coping skills instruction. Higher scores indicate more disturbed behaviors. SOURCE: Based on Strentz & Auerbach, 1988.

▶ 12. How do trauma disclosure and emotional constraint affect well-being?

breathing, muscle relaxation, stopping unwanted thoughts, and generating pleasant fantasies. Hostages in the control condition were given no coping skills training.

Weeks later, the employees were unexpectedly abducted by FBI agents posing as terrorists and held hostage for 4 days under very realistic and stressful conditions. During their captivity, the hostages completed self-report measures of emotional distress and psychiatric symptoms. In addition, trained observers rated the adaptiveness of their behavior. Results indicated that the hostage groups trained in either problem-focused or emotion-focused strategies fared better than did the untrained employees on both the self-report and the behavioral measures. However, employees who had received emotion-focused training adapted better to the largely uncontrollable conditions of captivity than did those who had received problem-focused coping instruction (Figure 12.12).

The important conclusion from this and many other studies is that no coping strategy or technique is equally effective in all situations. Instead, effectiveness depends on the characteristics of the situation, the appropriateness of the technique, and the skill with which it is carried out. People are likely to adapt well to the stresses of life if they have mastered a variety of coping techniques and know how and when to apply them most effectively. The importance of controllability in the choice of techniques recalls the wisdom in theologian Reinhold Niebuhr's famous prayer that asks for the courage to change those things that can be changed, the forbearance to accept those that cannot be changed, and the wisdom to discern the difference.

Trauma Disclosure and Emotional Release

Is there any truth to the popular wisdom that when we are stressed out and upset, it's good to talk with someone about it? James Pennebaker (1995, 1997) conducted several studies in which college students talked about past traumas to an experimenter in an adjoining room, or they tape-recorded or wrote about the experiences. Many tearfully recounted incidents of personal failure, family tragedies, shattered relationships, sexual or physical abuse, and traumatic accidents. Participants in a control group were asked to talk or write about trivial everyday matters. A comparison of blood samples taken from the students before and after the session indicated enhanced immune system functioning in those who had "purged" themselves of negative emotions but not in those who had not. Moreover, the students who had disclosed the traumatic incidents had 50 percent fewer visits to the campus health center over the next 6 months compared with the control group. Pennebaker's results are intriguing, but more research is needed to determine when this type of emotional purging is helpful and whether there are circumstances when it is not. Likewise, because participants in these studies could choose whether or not to express their emotions, it is possible that some other factor, such as a personality trait, contributes to both the emotional disclosure and the health consequences.

Bottling Up Feelings: The Possible Costs of Emotional Constraint

You can probably think of several people in your life who differ greatly in how they express their negative emotions in response to stress. While constantly venting strong negative feelings may not be a good way to make friends and influence people, an inability to express negative feelings can also have its costs. Some studies have reported relations between cancer development and the use of denial or repressive coping strategies, but others have not (McKenna et al., 1999). In one long-term European study, people who were experiencing high stress levels but were too emotionally restrained to express negative feelings, even when appropriate, had a significantly higher likelihood of developing cancer than did highly stressed people who were not so emotionally restrained. Seeking to reduce this potential vulnerability factor, the researchers designed a treatment program to help stress-ridden but emotionally constrained people who had not yet developed cancer. The program focused on teaching participants how to express their emotions in an adaptive fashion and on building stress-coping skills to manage their feelings without bottling them up. A control group of similar people did not receive the training. Thirteen years later, a follow-up study revealed that 90 percent of the trained participants were still alive, whereas 62 percent of the control group participants had died from cancer and other ailments (Eysenck, 1994; Eysenck & Grossarth-Marticek, 1991).

The question of whether there is indeed a "cancer-prone personality" remains a topic of scientific study and debate (Suls & Wallston, 2003; Taylor, 2003). Nonetheless, in the eyes of many researchers, there is enough evidence to suggest that severe emotional constraint can have negative effects on health.

Gender, Culture, and Coping

▶ 13. How do gender and cultural factors affect the tendency to use particular coping strategies?

Many factors, including gender roles and culture, influence our tendency to favor one coping strategy over another. Although men and women both use problem-focused coping, men are more likely to use it as the first strategy when they confront a stressor (Ptacek et al., 1992). Women, who tend to have larger support networks and higher needs for affiliation than men, are more likely to seek social support (Billings & Moos, 1984; Schwarzer, 1998). Women also are somewhat more likely than men to report using emotion-focused coping (Carver et al., 1989; Pearlin & Schooler, 1978). This general pattern of coping preferences is consistent with the socialization that boys and girls traditionally experience. In most cultures, boys are pushed to be more independent, assertive, and self-sufficient, whereas girls are expected to be more emotionally expressive, supportive, and dependent (Eccles, 1991; Lytton & Romney, 1991). In the words of stress researcher Shelley Taylor (2003), the common male response is "fight or flight," whereas women are more likely than men to "tend and befriend." *Tending* involves nurturant activities designed to protect the self, offspring, and significant others. These behaviors promote safety and reduce distress. *Befriending* is the creation and maintenance of social networks that may aid in this process.

Taylor and coworkers (2000) speculate that the tend-and-befriend pattern is a product of biological mechanisms that underlie attachment and caregiving behavioral tendencies in women. The female hormone oxytocin, acting in conjunction with female reproductive hormones and endorphin mechanisms, may be a key player in this biological system.

Researchers have also found cultural differences in coping. North Americans and Europeans show a tendency to use problem-focused coping more than do Asian and Hispanic people, who tend to favor emotion-focused coping and social support (Essau & Trommsdorff, 1996; Jung, 1995). Asians also show a greater tendency to avoid stressful situations involving interpersonal conflict, perhaps reflecting their culture's emphasis on interpersonal harmony (Chang, 1996). In a study of how American married couples deal with marital stress, African Americans reported a greater tendency than Caucasian Americans to seek social support (Sistler & Moore, 1996). The manner in which particular coping strategies affect well-being under differing cultural conditions is an important topic for future research.

? *What Do You Think?*

WHY DO WOMEN OUTLIVE MEN?

The World Health Organization reported that, worldwide, women live an average of about 7 years longer than men do. A leading news magazine suggested that the difference is probably caused by the fact that men live more stressful lives. Given what you've learned so far, could you think of alternative explanations for the longevity difference? What would you need to know in order to rule out the life-stress explanation? (Think about it, then see the discussion on page 504.)

Stress Management Training

▶ 14. Which stress management skills can be used to control cognitive and physiological stress responses?

Because stress takes a toll on people's physical and psychological well-being, much effort has gone into developing methods for reducing stress. The model shown in Figure 12.2 suggests that we can reduce stress by modifying any of its major components. Thus we can change the situation that constitutes the stressor, modify cognitive appraisals that trigger the rest of the stress response, or learn ways to control the physiological arousal. Finally, we can adopt more effective behaviors for meeting the demands of the situation.

In many coping skills programs, people learn to modify habits of thought that trigger inappropriate emotional responses and to control

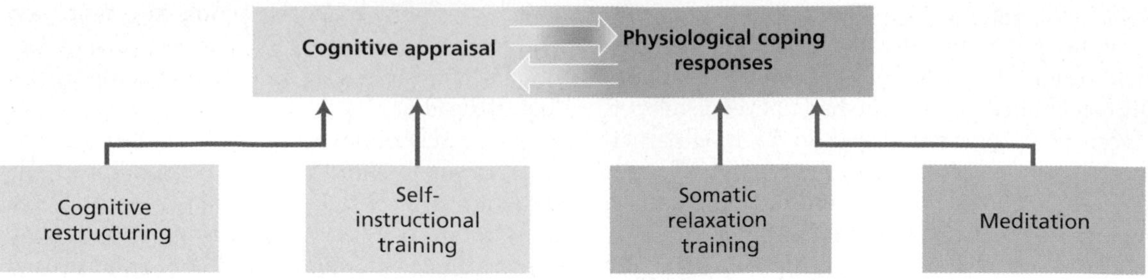

FIGURE 12.13

Many stress management coping skills programs teach self-modification techniques, such as cognitive restructuring and self-instructional training, to alter cognitive appraisals; as well as somatic relaxation techniques and meditation to counter physiological arousal.

physiological arousal responses through relaxation skills (Barlow & Rapee, 1991; Smith, 2003). Figure 12.13 previews the most common stress management techniques taught by psychologists.

Cognitive Coping Skills

Because cognitive appraisal processes play a central role in generating stress, Richard Lazarus, Albert Ellis, and other cognitive theorists maintain that the most powerful means of regulating feelings is by controlling how we think about stressful situations and about ourselves. Ellis (1962) suggests that a relatively small number of "irrational" core beliefs lie at the root of most maladaptive negative feelings. For example, we tell ourselves that we *must* achieve and be approved of in virtually every respect if we are to consider ourselves worthwhile people; that it is terrible, awful, and *catastrophic* when life or other people are not the way that we demand they be; that people who do not behave as we wish are bad and therefore deserving of punishment. In Ellis's terms, these "*must*urbation" and "catastrophizing" tendencies, together with other irrational ideas, generate unnecessary anxiety, despair, and anger. When people use the technique of **cognitive restructuring** *to systematically detect, challenge, and replace these irrational ideas,* their feelings can change dramatically, as in the following case:

> Whenever I find myself getting guilty or upset, I immediately tell myself that there must be some silly sentence that I am saying to myself to cause this upset; and almost immediately . . . I find this sentence. . . . [It] invariably takes the form of "Isn't it terrible that . . ." or "Wouldn't it be awful if . . ." And when I look at and question these sentences and ask myself, "How is it really terrible that . . . ?" or "Why would it actually be awful if . . . ?" I always find that it isn't terrible or wouldn't be awful, and I get over being upset very quickly. . . . I can hardly believe it, but I seem to be getting to the point, after so many years of worrying over practically everything and thinking I was a slob no matter what I did, of now finding that nothing is so terrible or awful, and I now seem to be recognizing this in advance rather than after I have seriously upset myself (Ellis, 1962, pp. 31–32).

Another approach to changing cognitions does not involve attacking irrational ideas that cause disturbance. In **self-instructional training,** *people learn to "talk to themselves" and guide their behavior in ways that help them cope more effectively* (Meichenbaum, 1985). They prepare different self-instructions to use at four critical stages of the stressful episode: preparing for the stressor, confronting the stressor, dealing with the feeling of being overwhelmed, and appraising coping efforts after the stressful situation. Table 12.3 provides examples of self-instructions that can be used at these stages of the coping process.

TABLE 12.3 Self-Instructional Training: Examples of Adaptive Self-Statements That Can Be Applied at Various Stages of the Coping Process

Phase of Coping Process	Self-Statements
Preparing for the stressor	• What do I have to do? • I can work out a plan to deal with it. • Remember, stick to the issues and don't take it personally. • Stop worrying. Worrying won't help anything.
Confronting and handling the stressor	• As long as I keep my cool, I'm in control of the situation. • I can meet this challenge. This tenseness is just a cue to use my coping techniques. • Don't think about stress, just about what I have to do. • Take a deep breath and relax. Ah, good.
Coping with the feeling of being overwhelmed	• Keep my focus on the present. What is it I have to do? • Relax and slow things down. • Don't try to eliminate stress totally; just keep it manageable. • Let's take the issue point by point.
Evaluation and self-reinforcement	• OK, what worked and what didn't? • I handled it pretty well. • It didn't work, but that's OK. I'll do better next time. • Way to go! You did it!

SOURCE: Adapted from Meichenbaum, 1985.

Relaxation Techniques

Coping skills training can also help people control their physiological responses in stressful situations. Because relaxation is incompatible with arousal, **somatic relaxation training** *provides a means of voluntarily reducing or preventing high levels of arousal.* To learn this skill, people typically tense the various muscle groups of their body and pair tension release with a trigger word (e.g., "Relax") and the exhalation (relaxing) phase of the breathing cycle. The goal is to condition relaxation to the trigger word and to exhalation so that a state of relaxation can be immediately produced in stressful situations by exhaling and mentally saying the trigger word. Most people can learn this technique with about a week of practice. Somatic relaxation training is a cornerstone of most stress-management training programs.

Another type of relaxation can be produced through meditation. Meditation not only relaxes the body, but also produces **cognitive relaxation,** *a peaceful, mind-clearing state.* In one approach, the person sits quietly in a comfortable position with eyes closed and mentally concentrates on the word "one" with each exhalation. This procedure is continued for about 20 minutes and, when mastered, quickly relaxes both body and mind (Benson & Klipper, 1976). One key difference between meditation and somatic relaxation is that the latter can be applied at any time during the stressful situation, whereas the former is best done in a quiet, private space. Many people who meditate practice their technique daily as a means of counteracting ongoing stressors in their lives and preventing short-term stressors from taking a toll.

IN REVIEW

- *Vulnerability and protective factors make people more or less susceptible to stressors. Social support is an important protective factor, having both direct and buffering effects that help people cope with stress.*
- *Individual differences in physiological reactivity also affect well-being. People who exhibit strong and prolonged arousal responses are more susceptible to negative psychological and health effects. Physiological toughness refers to a stress hormone pattern that involves (1) a low resting level of cortisol and low levels of cortisol secretion in response to stressors and (2) a quick, strong catecholamine response when the stressor occurs, followed by a quick decline in arousal when the stressor is over. The Type A behavior pattern increases vulnerability to coronary heart disease.*
- *Hardiness is a protective factor against stress. Hardy individuals are characterized by commitment, feelings of personal control, and a tendency to perceive stressful situations as challenges. Other cognitive protective factors are self-efficacy and optimism. Spiritual beliefs often help people cope more effectively with stressful life events, but certain religious beliefs seem capable of increasing stress.*
- *Studies of highly resilient children reveal important characteristics that contribute to positive outcomes as children mature, such as good intellectual functioning, social skills, self-efficacy, and hope, usually nurtured by social support from at least one caring adult in the child's life.*
- *Three major ways of coping with stressors are problem-focused coping, emotion-focused coping, and seeking social support. Problem-focused coping and seeking social support generally relate to better adjustment than emotion-focused coping. However, in situations involving low personal control, emotion-focused coping may be the most appropriate and effective strategy.*
- *Trauma disclosure has shown positive effects on physical and psychological well-being. Severe emotional constraint may be a risk factor for cancer and perhaps other disorders.*
- *Stress management training teaches people adaptive coping skills for handling stressful situations. Cognitive restructuring and self-instructional training can be used to develop adaptive cognitive coping responses; somatic relaxation training and meditation can be used to develop greater control of physiological arousal.*

PAIN AND PAIN MANAGEMENT

▶ 15. How does gate control theory explain pain perception and control?

Physical pain surely is one of the most unpleasant realities of life, and most of us do our best to avoid it. Hundreds of thousands seek relief from unbearable pain, and one third of all people experience pain that requires medical attention at some time in their lives. Half of all adult Americans suffer from back pain and 10 percent from severe headaches (Baum et al., 1997). Pain is a significant feature of many illnesses, and some form of pain is responsible for 80 percent of all medical complaints in North America and Europe (Salovey et al., 2000).

Pain, however, is a two-edged sword. Despite its unpleasantness, pain also has important survival functions. It serves as a warning signal when the body is being threatened or damaged, and it can trigger a variety of behavioral reactions that help us cope with the threat, such as jerking back from a hot skillet or going to see a doctor.

On the surface, we might think that pain is a purely sensory phenomenon and wonder why it is of interest to psychologists. When we examine it more carefully, however, we see that pain is a complex perceptual phenomenon that involves the operation of numerous psychological processes. For example, it is possible for people to experience excruciating pain in the absence of tissue damage (Melzack, 1998). Conversely, people may suffer severe physical damage and experience no pain, as has occurred in soldiers engaged in combat who were unaware for several hours that they had been wounded (Fordyce, 1988).

FIGURE 12.14

Acupuncture is a proven pain-reduction procedure. Gate control theory attributes its effects to the stimulation of thick sensory fibers. There is also evidence that acupuncture stimulates endorphin release.

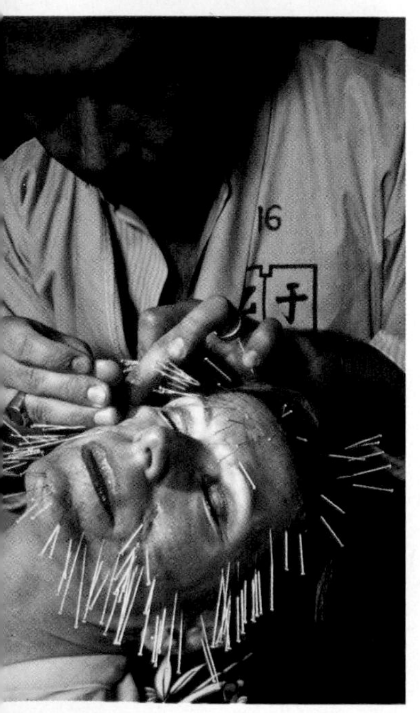

Biological Mechanisms of Pain

With the exception of the brain, bones, hair, nails, and nonliving parts of the teeth, pain receptors are found in all body tissues. Nerve endings in the skin and internal organs respond to intense mechanical, thermal, or chemical stimulation, and then send nerve impulses into the spinal cord, where sensory tracts carry pain information to the brain. Once in the brain, the sensory information about pain intensity and location is relayed by the thalamus to the somatosensory and frontal areas of the cerebral cortex (Zubieta & Stoller, 2002). Other tracts from the thalamus direct nerve impulses to the limbic system, which is involved in motivation and emotion. These tracts seem to control the emotional component of pain (Melzack, 1998). Thus pain has both a sensory and an emotional component. *Suffering* occurs when both painful sensations and a negative emotional response are present (Fordyce, 1988; Turk, 2001).

Gate Control Theory

Gate control theory, developed by Canadian psychologist Ronald Melzack and physiologist Patrick Wall (1982), was a major advance in the study of pain. **Gate control theory** *proposes that the experience of pain results from the opening and closing of "gating mechanisms" in the nervous system.* Briefly, sensations from two types of sensory fibers enter the spinal cord, where they can activate neurons that travel up toward the brain regions responsible for our perception of pain. Some of the sensory fibers are very thin in diameter, whereas others are thicker. The thin fibers carry sharp-pain impulses; the thick fibers convey dull-pain and touch information. Whether we experience pain depends partly on the ratio of thin-to-thick fiber transmission. Relatively high levels of thin-fiber activity open a system of spinal cord "gates" and allow the nerve impulses to travel toward the brain, whereas thick-fiber activity closes the gates.

It follows, then, that our perception of pain can be decreased by increasing thick-fiber nerve impulses. This explains why rubbing a bruise or scratching an itch, both of which stimulate primarily thick fibers, produces relief. Gate control theorists also suggest that acupuncture achieves its pain-relieving effects because the acupuncture needles stimulate mostly thick fibers, thereby closing the pain gates (Figure 12.14).

From a psychological perspective, perhaps the most intriguing feature of gate control theory is that nerve impulses in fibers descending from the brain can also influence the spinal gates, thereby increasing or decreasing the flow of "pain" stimulation to the brain. This *central control mechanism* allows thoughts, emotions, and beliefs to influence the experience of pain and helps explain why pain is a psychological phenomenon as well as a physical one. Gate control theory has been valuable in suggesting techniques for pain control and in stimulating research on psychological factors in pain (Turk & Melzack, 2001).

The Endorphins

In 1680 an English physician wrote, "Among the remedies which it has pleased Almighty God to give man to relieve his suffering, none is so universal and so efficacious as opium" (quoted in Snyder, 1977). Opiates (such as opium, morphine, and heroin) have been used for centuries to relieve pain, and they strongly affect the brain's pain and pleasure systems. In the 1970s, scientists discovered that opiates produce their effects by locking into specific receptor sites in brain regions associated with pain perception.

But why would the brain have built-in receptors for opiates unless there was some natural chemical in the brain for the receptor to receive? Later research disclosed what had to be true: The nervous system has its own built-in analgesics (painkillers) with opiate-like properties. These natural opiates were named **endorphins** (meaning *endogenous, or internally produced, morphines*). Endorphins exert some of their pain-killing effects by inhibiting the release of neurotransmitters involved in the synaptic transmission of pain impulses from the spinal cord to the brain (Fessler, 1989). Some endorphins are enormously potent. One of the brain endorphins isolated by scientists is more than 200 times more powerful than morphine (Franklin, 1987). Endorphins are of great interest to psychologists because they may help explain how psychological factors "in the head" can have such strong effects on pain and suffering.

In 2001, John-Kar Zubieta and coworkers published a landmark study that showed the endorphins in action within the brain. They injected a radioactive form of an endorphin into volunteer participants, then stimulated them with painful injections of salt water into the jaw muscles. Brain scans allowed the researchers to see which areas of the brain "lit up" from endorphin activity and to relate this activity to pain reports given by the participants every 15 seconds. The scans revealed a surge of endorphin activity within several brain regions, including the thalamus (the sensory "switchboard"), the amygdala (an emotion center), and a sensory area of the cortex. As the endorphin surge continued over 20 minutes of pain stimulation, participants reported decreased sensory and emotional ratings of pain.

Two other findings were noteworthy. First, people differed in their pain experiences despite identical pain stimulation. Second, these differences were linked to variations in (1) the number of opioid receptors the participants had for the endorphins to bind to and (2) their own ability to release endorphins. Thus biological as well as psychological factors seem to underlie differences in people's ability to tolerate pain (Zubieta et al., 2001).

Acupuncture is a pain-reduction technique that may ultimately be understood in terms of endorphin mechanisms. Injections of *naloxone,* a drug that counteracts the effects of endorphins, greatly decrease the pain-reducing effects of acupuncture (Oleson, 2002). This suggests that acupuncture normally releases endorphins.

Another phenomenon attributable to endorphins is **stress-induced analgesia,** *a reduction in—or absence of—perceived pain that occurs under stressful conditions.* For example, research has shown that about 65 percent of soldiers wounded during combat report having felt no pain at the time of their injury (Warga, 1987). Likewise, people involved in accidents are sometimes unaware of serious injuries until the crisis is over. This analgesic response could be highly adaptive. In a life-threatening situation, fight-or-flight defensive behavior must be given immediate priority over normal responses to pain, which typically involve immobility. By reducing or preventing pain sensations through the mechanism of endorphin release, stress-induced analgesia helps suppress these pain-related behaviors so that the person or animal can get on with the actions that are needed for immediate survival, such as fleeing, fighting, or getting help (Fanselow, 1991). As an example, consider the report of a man who was so severely bitten during an attack by a grizzly bear that he required more than 200 stitches:

▶ 16. How do endorphins influence pain perception and physical well-being?

> I had read the week before about someone who was killed and eaten by a grizzly bear. So I was thinking that this bear was going to eat me unless I got away. I did not have time for pain. I was fighting for my life. It was not until the next day that I started feeling pain and fear. (Kolb & Whishaw, 2001, p. 386)

The release of endorphins seems to be part of the body's natural response to stress, but we may pay a price for this temporary relief from pain. It appears that chronically high levels of endorphin release help block the activity of immune system cells that recognize and selectively kill tumor cells. This may be one way in which stress makes us more susceptible to serious illnesses such as cancer (Shavit, 1990).

Cultural and Psychological Influences on Pain

As a complex perception, pain is influenced by numerous factors. Cultural learning, meanings attributed to pain, beliefs, and personality factors all affect our experiences of pain.

Cultural Factors

▶ 17. How do cultural factors influence pain experience and behavior?

Our interpretation of pain impulses sent to the brain depends in part on our experiences and beliefs, and both of these factors are influenced by the culture in which we develop (Rollman, 1998). Consider, for example, the experience of childbirth. This event is widely perceived as a

FIGURE 12.15

Illustration of a hook-hanging ceremony practiced in remote villages in India. After blessing all the children and farm fields in a village, the celebrant leaps from the cart and hangs suspended by the hooks in a state of ecstasy, showing no sign of pain. SOURCE: Based on Kosambi, 1967.

painful ordeal in Western cultures, and many women express considerable anxiety about going through it (Blechman & Brownell, 1998). Yet in some cultures, women show virtually no distress during childbirth. Indeed, in one culture studied by anthropologists, it was customary for the woman's husband to get into bed and groan as if he were in great pain while the woman calmly gave birth to the child. The husband stayed in bed with the baby to recover from his terrible ordeal while the mother returned to work in the fields almost immediately (Kroeber, 1948).

Certain societies in India practice an unusual hook-hanging ritual. A holy person, chosen to bless children and crops, travels from village to village on a special ceremonial cart. Large steel hooks, attached by ropes to the top of the cart, are shoved under the skin and muscles on each side of the holy person's back. At the climax of the ceremony, he leaps from the cart and swings free, hanging only by the hooks embedded in his back (Figure 12.15). Incredibly, though hanging from the hooks with his entire body weight, the celebrant shows no evidence of pain during the ritual; on the contrary, he appears to be in a state of ecstasy. When the hooks are removed, the wounds heal rapidly and are scarcely visible within two weeks (Kosambi, 1967).

Although ethnic groups do not appear to differ in their ability to discriminate among pain stimuli, members of different cultural groups may differ greatly in their interpretation of pain and the amount of suffering they experience (Rollman, 1998; Zatzick & Dimsdale, 1990). In the Indian hook-hanging ceremony, for example, the religious meanings attached to the act seem to transform the interpretations and meaning of the sensory input from the hooks. Likewise, childbearing mothers in cultures where the pain of childbirth is not feared do not attach strong negative emotions to the associated sensations, and they therefore suffer far less.

The role of cultural factors in pain perception is found even within modern Western subcultures. In a study done in Massachusetts, researchers studied pain perception in 372 medical patients who represented six different ethnic groups: "Old Americans" (at least third-generation U.S.-born Caucasians who identified with no ethnic group except "Americans"), Hispanic Americans, Italian Americans, Irish Americans, French Canadians, and Polish Americans. All of the patients suffered from chronic pain conditions that had persisted for at least 3 months and were beyond the point of healing. The patients completed self-report measures about their pain experiences.

The ethnic groups did not differ overall in type of physical affliction, how long they had had it, or the kinds of treatments and medications they were receiving. They did differ, however, in the pain levels they reported, and these differences were associated with different attitudes and beliefs about their pain. The Hispanic American and Italian American patients believed most strongly that they had no control over their pain, reported feeling worried and angry about it, and believed that they would be unhappy as long as they experienced it. They also believed that it is appropriate to express one's pain openly. These two ethnic groups reported the highest levels of pain and suffering. In contrast, the Old American and Polish American patients felt it best to suppress the outward expression of pain, reported feeling less upset about their pain sensations, and believed that they had greater personal control over their lives. These attitudinal differences were associated with much lower levels of reported suffering (Bates et al., 1993).

▶ 18. How do cognitive and personality factors affect people's responses to pain stimuli?

Meanings and Beliefs

Differences exist not only between cultural groups but also within them, as physician Henry Beecher (1959) observed while working at Anzio Beachhead in World War II and later at Massachusetts General Hospital. At Anzio, Beecher found that only about 25 percent of the severely wounded soldiers he observed required pain medication, compared with 80 percent of civilian men who had received similarly serious "wounds" from surgeons at Massachusetts General. Why the difference? Beecher concluded that for the soldiers, the wounds had a fundamentally positive meaning: They spelled evacuation from the war zone and a socially acceptable "ticket back home" to their loved ones. For the civilian surgical patients, on the other hand, the operations meant a major life disruption and possible complications. The different meanings attributed to the pain stimuli resulted in very different levels of suffering and, consequently, different needs for pain relief.

Perhaps nowhere is the influence of belief on pain perception more evident than in the effects of **placebos,** *substances that have no medicinal value but are thought by the patient to be helpful* (Shapiro & Shapiro, 1997). At the beginning of this chapter we described the observations made by German physician Hans Rheder, whose female patients responded with startling improvements in their symptoms to the news that he had invoked the healing powers of a powerful faith healer. Similar observations have been made in pain research. In one classic study by Henry Beecher (1959), either a placebo or a morphine injection was given to 122 surgical patients who were suffering postoperative pain. All were told they were receiving pain medication. Of those who received morphine, 67 percent reported relief, but 42 percent of those given placebos reported equal relief. More recent medical studies of placebo effects have yielded even higher rates of pain relief, as high as 100 percent in some studies (Turner et al., 1994). However, it is also clear that placebos work only if people *believe* they are going to work. Research using PET-scan technology at the Karolinska Institute in Sweden indicates that given a positive belief in the placebo's effectiveness, the brain sends messages that result in the release of endorphins to reduce pain (Petrovic et al., 2002).

Where pain is concerned, the statement "I can control it" may be more than an idle boast or an empty reassurance. In one experiment, patients suffering from the prolonged pain of a bone-marrow transplant were randomly assigned to one of two conditions. One group was allowed to directly control the amount of pain medication that they received intravenously. The other patients were given prescribed amounts of the same medication by the hospital staff (and told they could request additional medication if needed). The patients who had direct control over their medication not only rated their pain as less intense but also gave themselves less pain medication (Zucker et al., 1998). As in the case of placebo effects, beliefs about personal control apparently exert their effects by increasing endorphin release. Naloxone injections, which counteract endorphin activity, sharply reduce the ability of people to endure intensely painful stimuli, no matter how high their confidence in their pain tolerance (Bandura et al., 1987).

Personality Factors and Social Support

Beginning with Sigmund Freud, personality theorists have suggested that emotional and personality factors can play a role in experiencing and responding to pain. Pain and suffering can be a way of attaining certain goals. For some bitter and deprived people, pain can be a way of dramatizing their unhappiness; eliciting caring, sympathy, or guilt from others; or gaining favors. Pain may also be a way of escaping from or avoiding threatening situations. For example, an athlete who dreads the possibility of failing may avoid the feared competition by experiencing severe pain that prevents participation. This coping process can occur at a subconscious level that is different from consciously faking being hurt (May & Sieb, 1987).

People who have the personality trait of *neuroticism,* the tendency to experience negative emotions such as anxiety and depression, report higher levels of physical pain, both in relation to medical conditions and in controlled laboratory administrations of painful stimuli such as heat, cold, electrical shock, or pressure (Turner & Aaron, 2001). In contrast, personality styles that include optimism and a sense of personal control over one's life are associated with lower pain perception and less suffering (Pellino & Ward, 1998). Moreover, patients with chronic pain conditions who are able to simply accept the pain rather than bemoaning their fate and responding emotionally to it have less disability, better social adjustment, and higher work performance (McCracken, 1998). Thus it seems clear that psychological factors play important roles in pain perception and adaptation.

Further evidence that one's emotional state and social support network are associated with one's experience of pain comes from a study by Carmen Alonso and Christopher Coe (2001). In a sample of 184 college women, the researchers found that self-reported depression and anxiety were strongly associated with ratings of menstrual pain. More significantly, perhaps, the greatest pain and distress occurred in women who had recently lost a significant source of social support.

The fact that psychological processes are so central to the experience of pain has stimulated many health psychologists to research methods that can be used to control or reduce pain and suffering. The following feature highlights this important area of application.

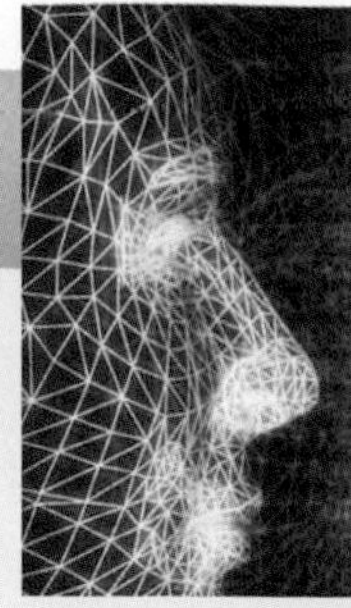

APPLYING PSYCHOLOGICAL SCIENCE

PSYCHOLOGICAL TECHNIQUES FOR CONTROLLING PAIN AND SUFFERING

We all occasionally experience physical pain, and for some people, pain is a never-ending nightmare. In recent years, psychological pain-control strategies have received increasing attention from health psychologists (Turk, 2001).

Cognitive Strategies

Recent attention has focused on two classes of cognitive strategies known as *dissociation* and *association.* A *dissociative strategy* involves dissociating, or distracting, oneself from the painful sensory input. This can be done in a variety of ways: by directing your attention to some other feature of the external situation, by vividly imagining a pleasurable experience, or by repeating a word or thought to yourself. Research has shown that dissociative strategies are most effective when they require a great deal of concentration or mental activity, thereby directing attention away from the painful stimuli.

If you are a recreational jogger or a long-distance runner, you may be familiar with the discomfort of extending yourself. Endurance running seems an ideal real-life task to use in the study of cognitive strategies. William Morgan and coworkers (1983) gave this simple dissociate strategy to participants who were running on a treadmill to exhaustion: "Focus your attention on a spot in front of you on the treadmill and say 'Down' each time your right foot comes down on the treadmill." A control group also ran the treadmill but did not receive the strategy. Although the two groups did not differ physiologically while running the treadmill, the mental-strategy group was able to tolerate the discomfort of treadmill running 32 percent longer than the control group.

A more dramatic, high-tech dissociative strategy is being tested in the burn center at the Harborview Medical Center in Seattle, Washington. There children and adults with burns covering up to 60 percent of their bodies are donning virtual-reality goggles during the often agonizing processes of wound cleansing and physical therapy. The goggles take patients into a visually compelling world of shapes and colors. Pain ratings are significantly lower when these patients are immersed in virtual reality than when they are in a nondistracted condition (Hoffman et al., 2001).

Associative strategies are just the opposite of dissociative ones. Here you focus your attention on the physical sensations and study them in a detached and unemotional fashion, taking care not to label them as painful or difficult to tolerate. It appears that when pain is intense, associative strategies become more effective than dissociative ones (McCaul & Malott, 1984). There seems to be a point at which pain stimuli become too intense to ignore and dissociative strategies become ineffective. Thus one strategy is to use dissociation as long as possible and then shift to an associative mode when the pain becomes too intense to permit distraction.

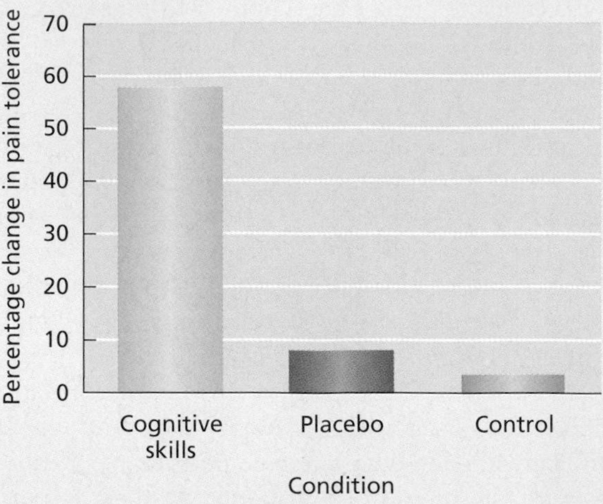

FIGURE 12.16

Increases in pain tolerance (ice water hand-immersion task) shown by a cognitive-skills training group, a placebo condition, and a control group that repeated the task with no intervention. SOURCE: Based on Bandura et al., 1987.

Combined dissociative and associative strategies can be quite effective in dealing with acute pain. In one study, participants' pain tolerance was tested by measuring how long they could keep their hand immersed in ice water. One group of participants was then trained and practiced a number of dissociative coping strategies (such as attention diversion and the use of distracting imagery) and associative strategies (such as imagining that the hand immersed in the ice water was detached from the body and focusing nonemotionally on the pain sensations). Two control groups equated in initial pain tolerance were given either no strategies or a placebo "pain reducer." Then their ice-water pain tolerance was tested a second time. As shown in Figure 12.16, the cognitive skills training resulted in a large increase in pain tolerance (Bandura et al., 1987).

Hospital Interventions: Giving Patients Informational Control

Having relevant information about a challenging environment and event is also a kind of cognitive control, since it tells us what to expect. In the medical setting of the past, doctors typically gave patients no more information than "needed" about the

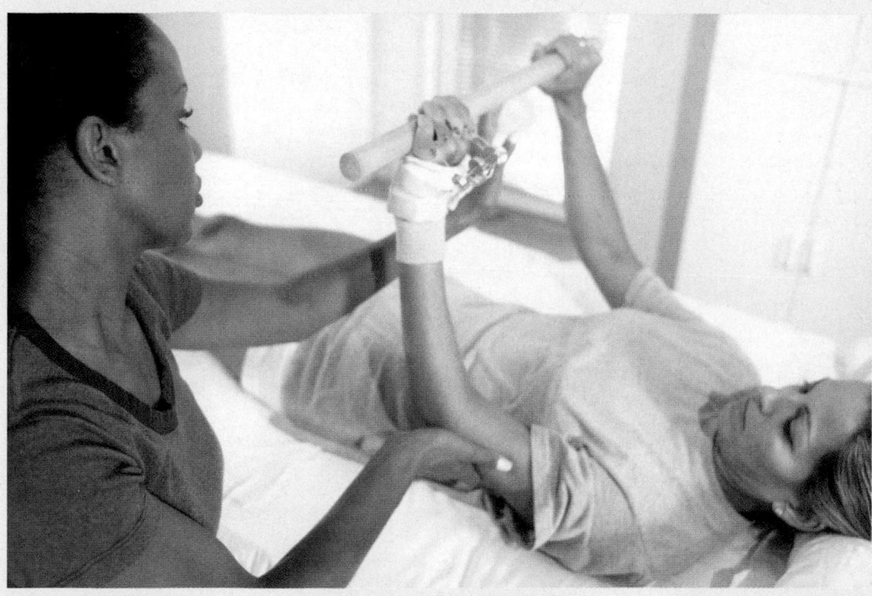

FIGURE 12.17

A key to preventing chronic pain and disability is to begin physical activity again as soon as possible.

medical procedure and its aftermath. However, psychological research on how certain types of information reduce anxiety and contribute to positive medical outcomes has ushered in a new era in many medical settings.

Imagine that you're in the hospital for major surgery. You know that this surgical procedure entails risk and that your recovery will be painful. What kinds of information would help you cope and recuperate more easily?

You might profit from *sensory information* about what you will feel after the operation. Knowing, for example, that patients often have shooting pains in their stomach after the surgery could prevent surprise or fear if it occurred to you. You would see the pain as a normal consequence of the surgery and the recovery process rather than as a sign of danger.

Second, *procedural information* on the surgery itself would help you understand what exactly is going to be done and why. You might be shown a model of the body part to demonstrate what will be done in the surgery, or you may see a video describing the procedure. This kind of information would give you a sense of predictability and control and reassure you that precautions were being taken to anticipate and reduce possible hazards.

Third, you could profit from *coping guidance* about handling the pain or other complications from the surgery. For example, you might learn breathing exercises designed to reduce pain by helping you relax (Tollison et al., 2002). You might also be taught some of the cognitive strategies previously described to get through sieges of acute pain during the recovery process.

Informational interventions have proved helpful in many medical settings. Surgical patients show better courses of recovery and require less pain medication than those treated in a traditional fashion (Faust, 1991). Such interventions have proven particularly successful in decreasing distress in hospitalized children, who are likely to find major medical procedures particularly frightening (Christopherson & Mortweet, 2001).

A Key Behavioral Strategy: Becoming Active Again

Recovering patients who avoid activity and become overly protective of an injured body part are at risk for developing a chronic pain condition (Turk, 2001). It is important to return to activity after an injury as soon as the healing process will allow (Figure 12.17). A key to successfully treating chronic pain patients who have "shut themselves down" is to decrease their guarding and resting behaviors and to modify their belief that their pain signals body damage. Such interventions produce significant decreases in patient disability (Jensen et al., 2001).

Wilbert Fordyce, a leader in the behavioral treatment of pain, emphasizes the negative effects that unnecessary rest and disuse of a body part can have on recovery:

> The lavish prescription of rest virtually ensures adverse disuse effects. With disuse in the musculoskeletal system, movement then becomes painful. But pain from disuse risks being interpreted by patient and professional as an indication of lack of healing. The result may become more prescribed rest or practical disuse and yet more pain with movement. . . . Pain problems originating in tissue injury but in which healing has occurred are made better by use. Patients must be helped to understand the dictum "To make it better, use it." . . . People who have something better to do don't suffer as much (Fordyce, 1988, p. 282).

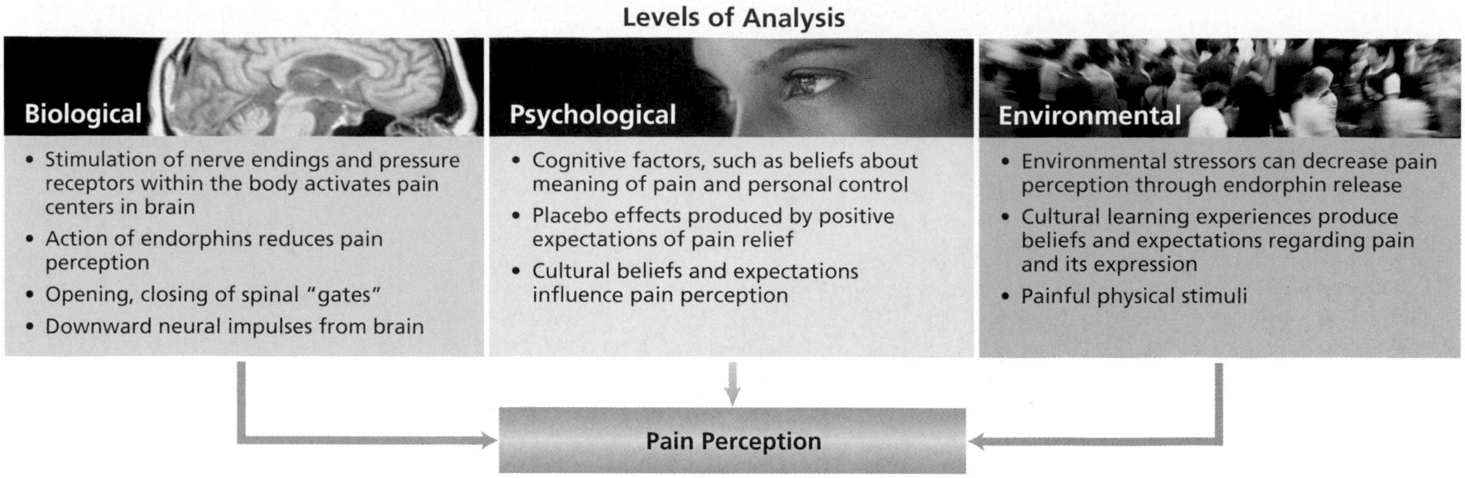

Levels of Analysis

Biological	Psychological	Environmental
• Stimulation of nerve endings and pressure receptors within the body activates pain centers in brain • Action of endorphins reduces pain perception • Opening, closing of spinal "gates" • Downward neural impulses from brain	• Cognitive factors, such as beliefs about meaning of pain and personal control • Placebo effects produced by positive expectations of pain relief • Cultural beliefs and expectations influence pain perception	• Environmental stressors can decrease pain perception through endorphin release • Cultural learning experiences produce beliefs and expectations regarding pain and its expression • Painful physical stimuli

Pain Perception

FIGURE 12.18

Understanding Behavior: Pain perception.

▶ 19. Describe cognitive, informational, and behavioral interventions for pain reduction.

Pain is an intriguing and complex biological, psychological, and social phenomenon. Figure 12.18 provides a levels-of-analysis summary of the factors we've discussed.

IN REVIEW

- *Pain is a complex perception influenced by biological, psychological, and sociocultural factors. At the biological level, the major pain receptors appear to be free nerve endings. Gate control theory attributes pain to the opening and closing of gates in the spinal cord and to influences from the brain. The nervous system contains endorphins, which play a major role in pain reduction.*
- *Expectations of relief produced by placebos can markedly reduce medical symptoms and pain. Cultural factors also influence the appraisal and response to painful stimuli, as do control beliefs. Negative emotional states increase suffering and decrease pain tolerance.*
- *Psychological techniques for pain control include (1) cognitive strategies, such as dissociative and associative techniques; (2) providing medical patients with sensory and procedural information to increase cognitive control and support; and (3) increasing activity level to counter chronic pain.*

HEALTH PROMOTION AND ILLNESS PREVENTION

In 1979, the Surgeon General of the United States issued a report entitled *Healthy People* (U.S. Public Health Service, 1979). The report concluded that improvements in the health of Americans are more likely to result from efforts to prevent disease and promote health than from new drugs and medical technologies.

That conclusion is borne out by comparing the leading modern causes of death in the United States and Europe with those in 1900. As Figure 12.19 shows, the leading culprits have changed from influenza, pneumonia, tuberculosis, and gastroenteritis to heart disease, cancer, and stroke. The major killers of the early 1900s have been largely controlled by medical advances. In contrast, the death rate has doubled for heart disease and tripled for cancer since 1900. As shown in Table 12.4, these diseases and today's other killers are strongly influenced by behavioral factors. Health authorities estimate that half the cases of early mortality (deaths occurring prior to the life expectancy age within a culture) from the 10 leading causes of death can be traced to risky behaviors, such as cigarette smoking, excessive alcohol consumption, insufficient exercise, poor dietary habits, use of illicit drugs, failure to adhere to doctors' instructions, unsafe sex practices, and failure to wear automobile seat belts (Centers for Disease Control and Prevention [CDC], 1994; Taylor, 2003).

Recognition of the crucial role that behavior plays in health maintenance has prompted much

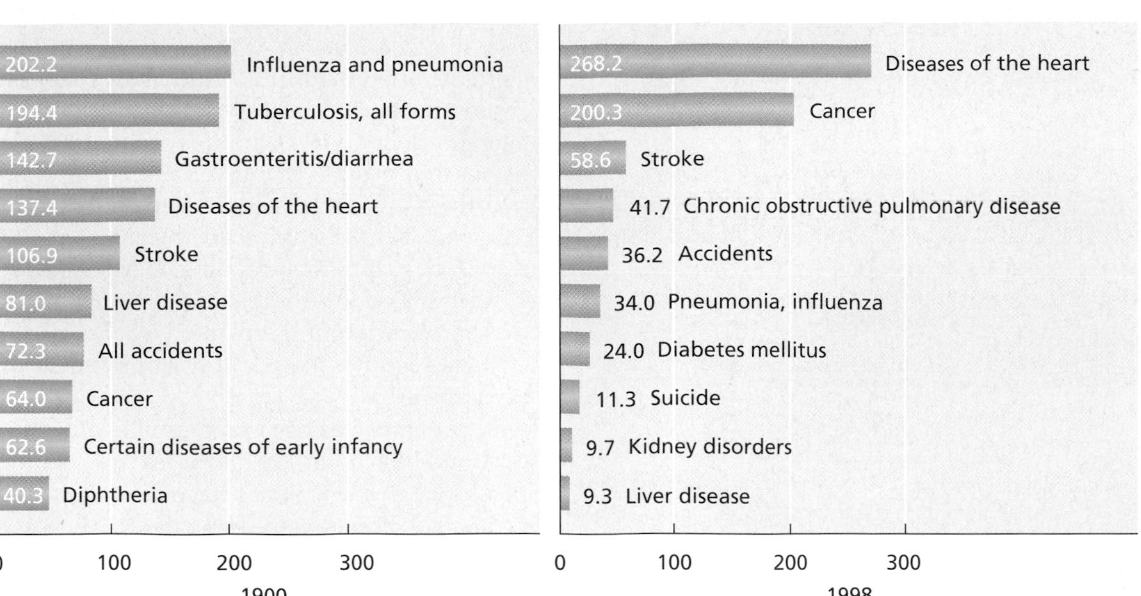

FIGURE 12.19

Causes of death in 1900 versus 1998. Modern causes of death are far more attributable to health-endangering behaviors.
SOURCES: Based on Sexton, 1979; Murphy, 2000; and Centers for Disease Control, 2002a.

research in the field of health psychology. Psychologists have helped identify many of the psychological and social causes for risky health behaviors, and the clear need for lifestyle interventions has spurred attempts around the world to promote positive changes in such behaviors (Suls & Wallston, 2003; Taylor, 2003). Modifying people's health behaviors as a form of illness prevention can reduce medical costs and avert the physical and psychological distress that illness produces.

Health-related behaviors fall into two main categories. *Health-enhancing behaviors* serve to maintain or increase health. Such behaviors include exercise, healthy dietary habits, safe sexual practices, regular medical checkups, and breast and testicular self-examination. *Health-impairing behaviors* promote the development of illness. They include tobacco use, fatty diets, a sedentary lifestyle, and unprotected sexual activity. Psychologists have developed programs that are focused on both classes of behavior.

How People Change: The Transtheoretical Model

In order to increase health-enhancing behaviors and reduce health-impairing ones, we need to understand the processes that underlie behavior change in general. In the 1980s, psychologists James Prochaska and Carlo DiClemente began to study the process that occurs as people modify their thoughts, feelings, and behaviors in positive ways, either on their own or with professional help. Their research resulted in a **transtheoretical model** *that identified six major stages in the change process* (DiClemente, 2003; Prochaska & DiClemente, 1984). The model, shown in Figure 12.20, does not assume that people go through the stages in a smooth sequence. Longitudinal studies have shown that many people move forward and backward through the stages as they try to change their behavior over time, and many people make repeated efforts to change before they finally succeed (Davidson, 1998; Evers et al., 1998). It is assumed, however, that failure at a given stage is likely to occur if the previous stages have not been mastered.

▶ 20. Describe the transtheoretical model and the rationale for stage-matched interventions.

The first stage is *precontemplation*. In this stage, people have no desire to change their

TABLE 12.4 Behavioral Risk Factors for the Leading Causes of Death in the United States

Disease	Risk Factors
Heart disease	Tobacco, obesity, elevated blood pressure, cholesterol, sedentary lifestyle
Cancer	Tobacco, improper diet, alcohol, environmental exposure
Cerebrovascular disease (stroke)	Tobacco, elevated blood pressure, cholesterol, sedentary lifestyle
Accidental injuries	Safety belt nonuse, alcohol, home hazards
Chronic lung disease	Tobacco, environmental exposure

SOURCE: Based on McGinnis, 1994.

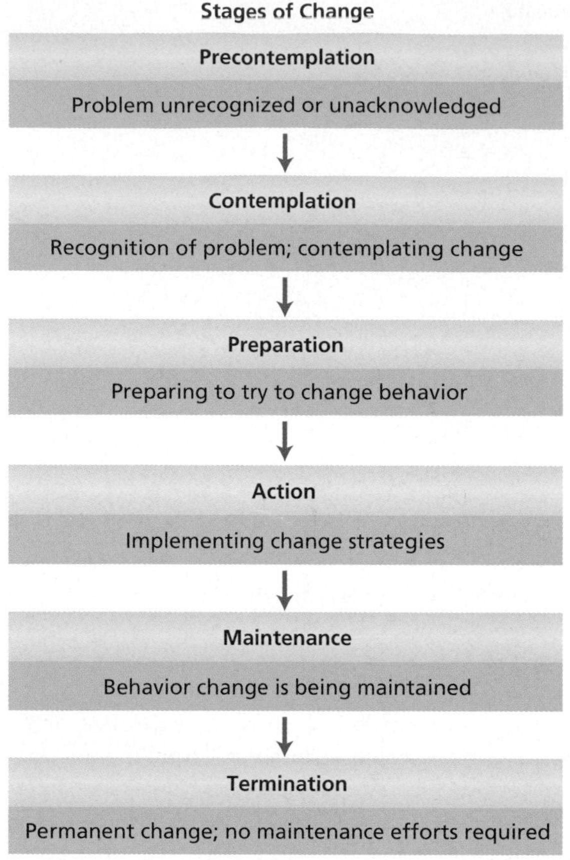

FIGURE 12.20

The transtheoretical model identifies a series of phases through which people pass as they modify their behavior. People may move up and down through the stages several times before they reach the final stage of termination. SOURCE: Prochaska et al., 1998.

behavior. Often they don't perceive themselves as having a problem, or they deny that their behavior has negative consequences. For example, public opinion polls suggest that there may be as many as 10 million people in the United States who still refuse to believe that smoking leads to premature death (Prochaska et al., 1994). Some precontemplators who do perceive a problem feel powerless to change their behavior, so they have no inclination to try.

Some precontemplators move on to the stage of *contemplation.* Here the person perceives a problem or the desirability of a behavior change but has not yet decided to take action. Thus some smokers are well aware of the health risks of their habit, yet they are not ready to make a decision to quit. Until the perceived benefits of changing outweigh the costs or effort involved, contemplators will not take action.

In the *preparation* stage, people have decided that they want to change their behavior but have not actively begun to do so. Typically, they are developing a plan to take action within the next month to accomplish the change. People in this stage have often begun making small changes, such as reducing the number of cigarettes they are smoking or identifying conditions that affect the behavior they want to change.

In the *action* stage, people actively begin to modify their behavior and their environment. For example, they stop smoking altogether. Success at this stage hinges on the behavior control skills necessary to carry out the plan of action. The action stage requires the greatest commitment of effort and energy.

If the person has been successful in avoiding relapse and has controlled the target behavior for 6 months, he or she is in the stage of *maintenance.* This does not mean that the struggle is over. Many people lapse back into their former behavior pattern at various times, as would be expected when one is trying to change deeply ingrained habits. The big challenge is not to give up when a lapse occurs and abandon the change program. It typically takes smokers three to five cycles through the action stage before they finally beat the habit, and New Year's resolutions are typically made for 5 or more consecutive years before they are finally carried out successfully (Prochaska et al., 1994; Schachter, 1982). The message is clear: If at first you don't succeed, don't give up. Instead, acquire the behavioral skills you need in order to succeed.

The final stage, *termination,* occurs when the change in behavior is so ingrained and under personal control that the original problem behavior will never return. It is the ultimate goal for all people who seek change.

The transtheoretical model is important because it helps us understand how people change and it has important applied implications. For example, we know that different intervention procedures are needed for people at various stages. Psychologists have therefore developed ways of determining what stage people are in so that they can apply *stage-matched interventions* designed to move the person toward the action, maintenance, and termination stages. Precontemplators need consciousness-raising information that finally convinces them that there is a problem, as well as social support to change (De Vries et al., 1998). Contemplators often need a "wakeup" emotional experience that increases their motivation to change or causes them to reevaluate themselves in relation to the behavior. For example, a serious auto accident while intoxicated may finally convince a problem drinker that this behavior has to change. In the preparation stage, the person needs to develop a specific plan (ideally based on the goal-setting procedures described in Chapter 11) and have the skills to carry it out before action is likely to be successful. Only when the person is ready for the action stage are change techniques, however powerful, likely to have their intended effect.

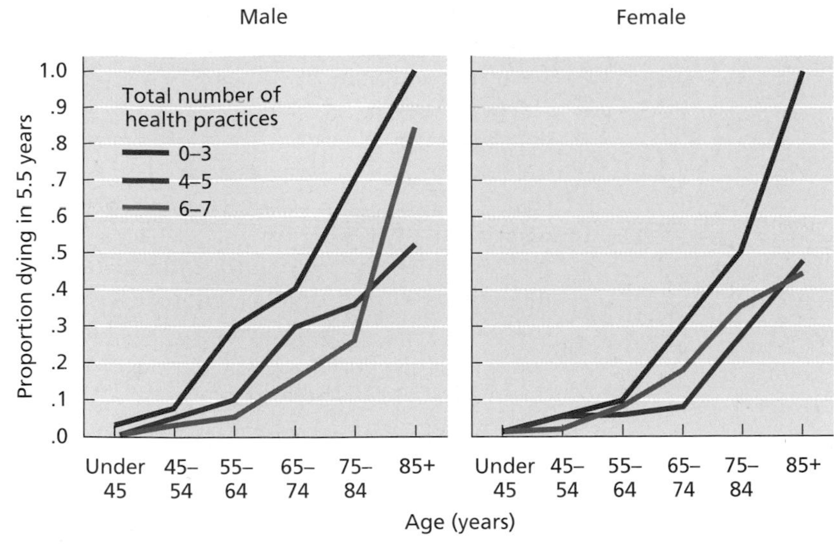

FIGURE 12.21

Relation between the number of positive health practices and longevity in men and women. Those who adhered to few of the health practices experienced earlier mortality, with the pattern appearing earlier for men than for women. SOURCE: Adapted from Belloc, 1973.

Increasing Behaviors That Enhance Health

During the 1970s, the role of behavior in maintaining health and living longer became evident as researchers began to study the effects of lifestyle. Figure 12.21 shows the results of one longitudinal study of nearly 7,000 adults. The researchers studied the relation of seven good-health practices to life expectancy. These included sleeping 7 to 8 hours per day, eating breakfast, not smoking, rarely eating between meals, being at or near one's prescribed body weight, engaging in regular physical activity, and drinking only small to moderate amounts of alcohol. For men and women alike, these behaviors predicted a longer life. A higher mortality rate among those with poor health practices began to appear in men between the ages of 45 and 64 and in women between 55 and 64 (Belloc, 1973). Let's examine some of these health-enhancing behaviors and what can be done to encourage them.

Exercise

The couch potato lives! (But apparently not as long.) A sedentary lifestyle is a significant risk factor for health problems, including coronary heart disease and obesity (Rodin & Salovey, 1989; Taylor, 2003). Despite this widely publicized fact, about 70 percent of Americans are inactive (Baum et al., 1997; Ehrman, 2003). As fewer people now engage in vigorous manual labor, inactivity has helped double the rate of obesity since 1900 despite a 10-percent decrease in daily caloric intake over the same period (Friedman & DiMatteo, 1989).

Aerobic exercise *is sustained activity, such as jogging, swimming, and bicycling, that elevates the heart rate and increases the body's need for oxygen.* This kind of exercise has many physical benefits. In a body that is well conditioned by regular aerobic exercise, the heart beats more slowly and efficiently, oxygen is better utilized, slow-wave sleep increases, cholesterol levels may be reduced, faster physiological adaptation to stressors occurs, and more calories are burned (Baum & Posluszny, 1999; deGeus, 2000).

Exercise is associated with physical health and longevity (Figure 12.22). A study that followed 17,000 Harvard undergraduates into middle age revealed that death rates were one quarter

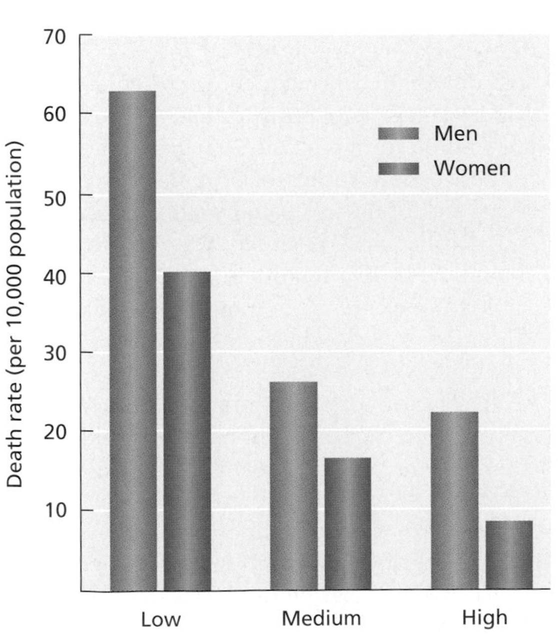

FIGURE 12.22

Aerobic exercise is an important health-enhancing behavior, contributing to physical well-being. Significantly higher death rate occur for both men and women who are low in physical fitness. SOURCE: Based on Blair et al., 1989.

▶ 21. What is aerobic exercise? What evidence exists that it promotes health and longevity?

to one third lower among moderate exercisers than among those in a less active group of the same age. Surprisingly, perhaps, extremely high levels of exercise were not associated with enhanced health; instead, moderate exercise (burning 2,000 to 3,500 calories per week) on a regular basis produced the best health benefits (Paffenbarger et al., 1986). Performing at 70 to 85 percent of maximal heart rate nonstop for 15 minutes three times a week significantly reduces risk for coronary heart disease (Dishman, 1982). Such exercise also has positive psychological effects, reducing depression and anxiety (Morgan, 1997).

Findings such as these have inspired behavioral interventions designed to promote regular exercise. Typically, these programs have an educational component that provides information on the benefits of regular exercise and the best ways to exercise. They may also include other components of behavior change, such as setting goals, writing explicit contracts that specify an exercise regimen, monitoring one's exercise behavior on a daily basis, and increasing social support by choosing an exercise partner or group.

▶ 22. How large are exercise drop-out rates? What factors do and do not predict dropout?

▶ 23. What are the behavior-change techniques used in behavioral weight control programs?

FIGURE 12.23

An alarmingly large percentage of adults and children are overweight and thus face increasing health risks.

Despite the demonstrated benefits of regular exercise, people in developed countries have a strong tendency either to avoid it or to discontinue it after a short period. In the United States, for example, only one fourth of the adult population exercises at levels high enough to maintain cardiorespiratory fitness and reduce the risk of premature death (Ehrman, 2003). When employers offer exercise programs to their employees, it is uncommon for more than 30 percent to participate, and dropout rates of 50 percent within 6 months are found in virtually all exercise programs that have been studied (Chenoweth, 2002; Dishman, 1994). On the other hand, people who are able to persist for 3 to 6 months are likely to continue as exercise becomes a healthy habit (McAuley, 1992).

What factors predict dropout? This is an important research question, for if we can identify the risk factors, we can take measures to counteract them. Research has shown that general attitudes toward physical fitness do *not* predict adherence or dropout; the exercise-related attitudes of dropouts and people who adhere to their exercise programs are equally favorable (Suls & Wallston, 2003). However, low self-efficacy for success in exercising regularly ("I can't do this"), Type A behavior pattern ("Sorry, too busy to exercise"), inflated estimates of current physical fitness ("I'm already in great shape from walking from my couch to the refrigerator"), and inactive leisure-time pursuits (such as watching television and walking to the refrigerator) all predict dropout (Martin & Dubbert, 1985; Wilcox & Storandt, 1996). The strongest social-environmental factor related to dropout is lack of social support from friends, family, or other exercisers (Ehrman, 2003).

Psychologists have been able to increase compliance by helping exercisers identify these impediments and prepare specific strategies to deal with them before they occur (Rosen, 2000; Simkin & Gross, 1994). For example, a person who anticipates feeling "too tired" to work out at the end of the day might prepare a set of self-statements about how much better she will feel after exercising. If she is not receiving social support and encouragement from others, she could also arrange for a pleasurable activity after her workout to positively reinforce her exercising (Courneya, 1995).

Weight Control

Health statistics indicate that nearly 30 percent of the adult American population is obese, defined as being more than 20 percent overweight (Figure 12.23). Since 1980, the average American adult's body weight has increased by about 8 pounds, and the upward trend continues (Suls & Wallston, 2003). A significant proportion of children (13.7 percent) and adolescents (11.5 percent) are also obese (Buet & Harris, 1994).

Obesity is a risk factor for a variety of chronic diseases, such as cardiovascular disease, kidney disease, and diabetes (Baum & Posluszny, 1999). Women who are 30 percent overweight are more than 3 times more likely to develop heart disease than normal-weight women (Manson et al., 1990). For reasons yet unknown, fat that is localized in the abdomen is a far greater risk factor for cardiovascular disease, diabetes, and cancer than is excessive fat in the hips, thighs, or buttocks (Taylor, 2003). Accumulation of abdominal fat is increased by *yo-yo dieting* that results in big weight fluctuations. Such dieting markedly increases the risk of dying from cardiovascular disease, an excellent reason to avoid this practice (Hafen & Hoeger, 1998; Rodin et al., 1990).

Were you to enroll in a behavioral intervention program for weight loss, here is what would happen: The program would begin with a period of self-monitoring, during which you would keep careful records of what you eat, how much you eat, and under what circumstances. This is designed to make you more aware of your eating habits and to identify situational factors (antecedents) that affect your food intake. You would then learn to take control over those antecedents. For example, you would learn to make low-calorie foods such as raw vegetables freely available and to limit high-calorie foods in the house. You would then learn stimulus-control techniques, such as confining your eating to one location in the house and eating only at certain times of the day. Because overeaters tend to wolf down their food and overload their stomachs, you would also learn to slow down your eating by putting down eating utensils until each bite is chewed and swallowed, and you would learn to pause between mouthfuls. These behaviors reduce food intake and help you learn to pay attention to how full you are. You would also be told to savor each mouthful of food. The goal is to eat less but enjoy it more. Finally, you would learn to chart the amount of food you eat to provide constant feedback, and you would arrange to positively reinforce yourself for successful performance. These behavioral practices would be combined with nutritional guidelines to help you eat a healthier diet. Table 12.5 shows specific guidelines from a highly successful weight-reduction program developed by Yale psychologist Kelly Brownell (1994).

TABLE 12.5 A Sample of Effective Behavioral Weight-Control Techniques

Keep an eating diary	Keep problem foods out of sight
Examine your eating patterns	Serve and eat one portion at a time
Prevent automatic eating	Use gradual shaping for behavior change
Examine triggers for eating	Distinguish hunger from cravings
Do nothing else while eating	Focus on behavior, not weight loss
Eat in one place	Cope positively with slips, lapses
Put fork down between bites	Keep an exercise diary
Pause during the meal	Understand benefits of exercise
Shop on a full stomach	Know calorie values of various exercise activities
Buy foods that require preparation	Program exercise activity

SOURCE: Based on Brownell, 1994.

Research shows that the addition of an exercise program increases the positive effects of behavioral eating-control programs (Jeffery & Wing, 1995; Wadden et al., 1997). High levels of physical activity are associated with initial weight loss and maintenance of the weight loss, and exercise adds to the effectiveness of other weight-loss methods, such as dietary change. Research results indicate that many overweight people are able to attain gradual weight loss of about 2 pounds per week for up to 20 weeks and to keep the weight off for 2 years and beyond (Jackson et al., 1999; Taylor, 2003).

Teaching people how to control their health-related programs can have dramatic benefits even for those who are already afflicted with serious illnesses. William Haskell and coworkers (1994) randomly divided a sample of patients suffering from coronary artery disease into two groups. Both groups received the usual high-quality medical care from their physicians at Stanford University Medical School. In addition, the experimental group received a behavioral self-regulation program that targeted health factors such as smoking, exercise, weight, nutrition, and medication adherence.

A 4-year follow-up revealed dramatic results. Those receiving the usual medical care showed either no improvement or a worsening of their condition, and their health habits had not improved. In contrast, those who also received the behavioral self-regulation program showed significant positive changes in their health habits. They reduced their intake of dietary fat, lowered their bad (LDL) cholesterol and raised their good (HDL) cholesterol, increased their exercise, and raised their cardiovascular capacity. The program also influenced the progression of the disease, as the self-management group had 47 percent less buildup of blockage material on artery walls. During the 4-year follow-up period, 45 percent of the control patients either died or had nonfatal heart attacks or other cardiac emergencies, compared with only 24 percent in the behavior self-regulation group. This study, like the others we've discussed, demonstrates the value of psychologically based health-promotion efforts.

Reducing Behaviors That Impair Health

We now turn our attention to several types of health-impairing behaviors. We begin with a class of behaviors that two decades ago was not considered a major health threat. Although a number of serious diseases can be transmitted through sexual contact, the majority of them can be successfully treated. In the early 1980s, however, a mysterious and lethal sexually transmitted disease emerged.

Psychology and the AIDS Crisis

On June 5, 1981, the Centers for Disease Control reported the first case of *acquired immune deficiency syndrome (AIDS)*. In the decades that followed, AIDS grew from an unknown disease into a

▶ 24. Describe the use and effectiveness of behavior change principles in AIDS prevention projects.

devastating worldwide epidemic for which no medical cure has been found. According to the World Health Organization (2002), about 16,000 new infections occur each day. Worldwide, 1 in every 100 adults between the ages of 15 and 49 is infected with the AIDS virus, and the disease has so far claimed the lives of nearly 20 million people. Of the 3 million people who died from AIDS in 2001, 37 percent were women and 20 percent were children. In some countries of southern Africa, 25 to 40 percent of the population is infected, including a third of all pregnant women. Globally, only 5 to 10 percent of the cases now occur in homosexual men (the population typically identified with the affliction), and women now make up half of all HIV cases (United Nations, 2002). In the early 2000s, the rates of infection began to rise again among homosexual men in North America, Europe, and Australia due to increases in risky sexual behavior (CDC, 2003). The AIDS epidemic threatens to overwhelm the world's health-care financing and delivery systems.

AIDS is caused by the *human immunodeficiency virus (HIV),* which cripples the immune system. The patient then becomes vulnerable to invading viruses, bacteria, and tumors, which are the actual killers. Because the AIDS virus evolves rapidly, vaccines are at present ineffective in preventing its spread. Moreover, the incubation period between initial infection and the appearance of the disease may be as long as 10 years, meaning that an infected person may unknowingly pass the virus on to many other people. The major modes of transmission are direct exposure to infected semen, vaginal fluids, and blood through either heterosexual or homosexual contact; the sharing of infected needles in intravenous drug use; and exposure to infected blood through transfusion or in the womb.

In the absence of a vaccine or cure, the only existing means of controlling the AIDS epidemic is by changing the high-risk behaviors that transmit the virus. In this respect, AIDS is as much a psychological problem as a medical one. Prevention programs are typically designed to (1) educate people concerning the risks that attend certain behaviors, such as unprotected sex; (2) motivate people to change their behavior and convince them that they can do so; (3) provide specific guidelines for changing the risky behaviors and teach the skills needed for change; and (4) give support and encouragement for the desired changes (O'Leary et al., 2001).

Early AIDS interventions were directed at homosexual men, who were originally the major at-risk group. In this population, a primary mechanism of HIV transmission is anal intercourse without the use of a condom. In one successful prevention study (Kelly et al., 1989), 42 homosexual men went through a program that instructed them on the risks accompanying unprotected intercourse, helped them develop and rehearse strategies for avoiding high-risk situations (such as sexual relations with strangers), and taught them how to be more assertive in refusing to engage in high-risk behaviors. Another group of 43 homosexual men also completed the program after initially serving as an untreated control group.

Both groups were assessed before and after the first group went through the program and then were followed for 8 months after completing the program to assess long-term behavior changes. As Figure 12.24 shows, the intervention program resulted in a substantial and lasting increase in the use of condoms during sexual activity. Similar programs are now being conducted with adolescent populations, where unprotected heterosexual intercourse is resulting in a surge of new infections (Jemmott et al., 1998). Another target for interventions is heterosexual women, who not only are the fastest-growing segment of the HIV population but also have the potential to infect their babies if they become pregnant.

Even when something as urgent as AIDS prevention is involved, research has shown that the success of prevention programs depends on the extent to which the individual's social system supports the desired changes. When sexual abstinence or the use of condoms runs contrary to the values of an individual or cultural group, people may continue to engage in high-risk behaviors even though they have been informed of the dangers involved (Herdt & Lindenbaum, 1992; Huff et al., 1999). Likewise, within both homosexual

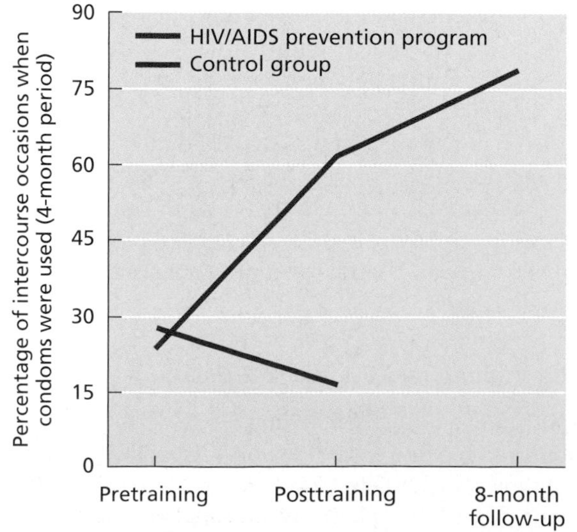

FIGURE 12.24

Effects of an HIV/AIDS prevention program for homosexual men on their use of condoms during sexual activity. The program educated the men on the risks involved in sexual behaviors (especially unprotected sex), promoted the use of condoms, and taught them coping skills to deal with high-risk situations.
SOURCE: Based on Kelly et al., 1989.

and heterosexual populations, and particularly among adolescents and young adults, many individuals continue to have an irrational sense of invulnerability to infection, and this belief contributes to a failure to abstain from sex or to engage in protected sexual practices (Kelly, 2001). Counteracting these barriers to safe sexual behavior is a major challenge for health psychologists.

One promising approach to cultural attitude change was inspired by Albert Bandura's social-cognitive theory. It involves the use of modeling procedures to change attitudes and behavior in some of the poorest and most hopeless parts of the world (Bandura, 2000). The strategy is to produce highly engaging "entertainment-education" radio dramas to increase awareness and counteract false beliefs. In Tanzania, for example, many people erroneously believe that AIDS is transmitted by mosquitoes and that using a condom while having sex could actually cause the disease.

In 1993, a new radio serial began in parts of that country. It was based on Bandura's findings that people learn from role models whose behavior they admire, and it was designed to have a compelling story line whose purpose was to encourage protected sex and to reduce soaring population growth. The program features three types of characters: positive role models whose behaviors have positive consequences, negative role models whose behaviors lead to disaster, and transitional models who start out behaving negatively and then change for the better and enjoy positive outcomes. For example, one soap opera character is a long-distance truck driver who has unprotected sex with multiple partners. His long-suffering wife finally leaves him and, with help from the community, establishes a business to support herself and her children. The promiscuous husband eventually develops AIDS and dies an agonizing death, while the woman becomes a successful businesswoman.

The program attracted many thousands of listeners in the regions where it was broadcast. Within 2 years, evaluations of the program showed that listeners were more likely to believe that unprotected sex could result in HIV infection. They also discussed AIDS more among themselves, reduced their number of sexual partners, increased condom use, developed more positive attitudes toward family-planning methods and a later age for women to marry, and desired smaller families. Control regions of Tanzania where the program was not aired showed no changes until the program was aired there, after which changes in their attitudes and behaviors also occurred (Rogers et al., 1996). Similar programs are now being aired in other developing countries. This social-cognitive approach may someday be referred to as "the theory that saved a million lives."

Combating Substance Abuse

Substance abuse exacts a fearsome toll on society. Tobacco use harms smokers and those who breathe their secondhand smoke. Smoking ranks as the single largest cause of preventable death, killing more than half a million Americans each year (American Cancer Society, 2000). Although tobacco use has leveled off in the United States since 1985, tobacco products have been aggressively marketed in other countries, and sales have nearly doubled over the past 15 years. The coming decades will therefore witness an appalling increase in the diseases caused by smoking, particularly in developing countries that are ill equipped to provide good medical treatment.

Alcohol abuse also contributes enormously to human suffering. In the United States alone, alcohol abuse costs over $100 billion a year in decreased work productivity and treatment costs and $13.8 billion in alcohol-related automobile accidents (Pedersen-Pietersen, 1997). Alcohol is implicated in half of all fatal automobile accidents and is a leading factor in industrial and farm accidents (Figure 12.25). Alcohol abuse is also highly damaging to one's health. Death rates among those who abuse alcohol are 2 to 4 times higher for men and 3 to 7 times higher for women, depending on the disease in question. Life expectancy is 10 to 12 years less (CDC, 2002). Alcohol affects the welfare of others as well. Some children are born with fetal alcohol syndrome, and others are subjected to disrupted family relationships, including domestic violence. For every person who has a problem with alcohol, an average of four other people's lives are adversely affected on a daily basis (Levinthal, 1996).

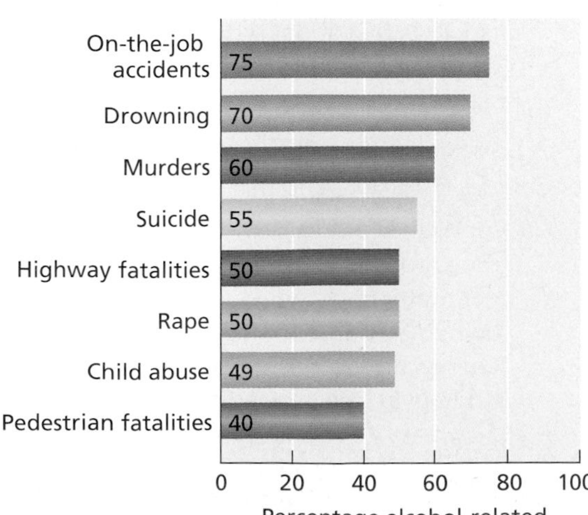

FIGURE 12.25

Societal costs of alcohol abuse, showing the percentage of common alcohol-related events. SOURCE: Based on Carroll, 1993.

Other varieties of substance abuse also have adverse effects. Many crimes are committed by users of illicit drugs in order to support their habit (Kendall, 1998). Moreover, substance abuse is highly associated with psychological disorders, often being part of a larger pattern of maladjustment in both adolescents and adults (Miller & Brown, 1997).

Psychological principles discussed in earlier chapters have been successfully applied to the treatment of smoking, problem drinking, and drug use (Taylor, 2003). As the transtheoretical model has shown, however, even the best programs are unlikely to be utilized effectively by people until they are ready to change. In recent years, there has been an emphasis on bringing precontemplators and contemplators to the point where they are ready to engage themselves in a change process.

▶ 25. What are the major goals and techniques in motivational interviewing?

▶ 26. What kinds of behavior-change procedures are employed in multimodal treatments for substance abuse?

Motivational Interviewing If smokers, problem drinkers, drug abusers, and others who practice self-defeating behaviors are to change, they must increase their awareness of their problems, have a desire to take action, and believe that they can change (Miller & Rollnick, 2002; Miller, 1996). Rather than confronting the person with his or her problem (which often drives away people who need help), the technique of **motivational interviewing** *leads the person to his or her own conclusion by asking questions that focus on discrepancies between the current state of affairs and the individual's ideal self-image, desired behaviors, and desired outcomes.* Focusing on these discrepancies may help motivate change. Consider the following exchange:

Client: I really don't believe I have a drinking problem.

Counselor: You're the best judge of that. May I ask how many drinks you have a day?

Client: Oh, it varies. Probably 5 or 6.

Counselor: Is that about what you'd like to be drinking?

Client: Well, I'd probably be better off if I cut down a little—maybe to 3 or 4.

Counselor: How would that be helpful to you?

Client: Well, I could study better and reduce the arguments with my roommate. I can get pretty nasty when I'm buzzed. I hate being nasty. I'm not that kind of person. Our relationship is going downhill, and I'd hate to lose a friend.

Counselor: Well, you know, you don't have to have a big problem in order to want to make a change. I'm sure you could do so if you really want to.

Client: I can see that I'd be more the person I want to be if I worked on this.

Counselor: And I'd be happy to help you make your change.

Following a client's decision to pursue behavior change, the counselor helps the client set specific goals and select from a menu of behavior-change strategies the ones he or she would like to employ. Thereafter the counselor provides feedback and support for the client's efforts.

Motivational interviewing has proven to be an effective and low-cost treatment approach for substance abusers (Miller & Rollnick, 2002). In one large-scale study of alcohol abuse patients, a 4-session motivational interviewing intervention proved to be as effective as a 12-session program modeled on Alcoholics Anonymous (Project MATCH Research Group, 1997).

Multimodal Treatment Approaches All substance-abuse behaviors are resistant to change, and for good reason. Some people may be more vulnerable than others because of genetic factors (Crabbe, 2002). Craving, caused by either psychological need or physical dependence, is a huge barrier to overcome. Negative emotions, such as anxiety, irritability, or depression, that are temporary results of abstinence cause many who quit successfully to have relapses. Past conditioning may create stimuli that trigger the behavior in certain common situations. For example, coffee drinking or social situations are linked with smoking for many individuals, thus encouraging lapses in behavioral control when those stimuli are present. The numerous factors that encourage smoking, drinking, or drug abuse make these behaviors very hard to change.

Psychologists are therefore willing to combine anything that has proven effective into what they hope will be a more powerful behavior-change "package" to apply when people are ready to make a change. These **multimodal treatments** *often include biological measures (for example, the use of nicotine patches to help smokers who are trying to quit), together with psychological measures* such as the following:

- Aversion therapy, in which the undesired behavior is associated with an aversive stimulus, such as electric shock or a nausea-producing drug, in an attempt to create a negative emotional response to the currently pleasurable substance;
- Relaxation and stress-management training, which help the person adapt to and deal with stressful situations;

- Self-monitoring procedures that help the person identify the antecedents and consequences of the abuse behaviors;
- Coping and social skills training for dealing with high-risk situations that trigger abuse;
- Marital and family counseling to reduce conflicts and increase social support for change; and
- Positive reinforcement procedures to strengthen change.

This broad-based multimodal approach appears to produce favorable outcomes for many people who have substance addictions. For example, in one of the more successful multimodal treatment outcome studies, 427 alcoholic patients were followed for 12 to 20 months after completing an inpatient program that included aversion therapy (using a drug that produces nausea when alcohol is consumed), personal counseling, and coping skills training. Follow-up assessments revealed that 65 percent were totally abstinent for 1 year after treatment. The best outcome occurred in cases where urges to drink had been eliminated (presumably by aversion therapy) and alternate coping skills were increased through the use of cognitive-behavioral techniques such as those just described (Smith & Frawley, 1993). Despite these encouraging results, typical treatment results are less favorable: Long-term maintenance of behavior changes often occurs in fewer than 30 percent of treated individuals, whether the target behavior is smoking, drinking, or some other substance abuse (Ockene et al., 2001). The goal of many researchers is therefore to develop increasingly more effective treatment packages.

▶ 27. How serious are the consequences of heavy drinking among college students?

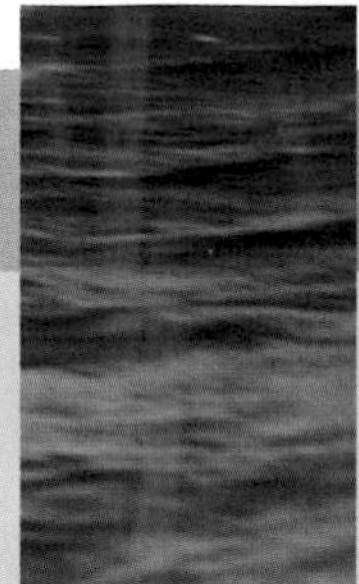

BENEATH THE SURFACE

COLLEGE-AGE DRINKING: HARMLESS FUN OR RUSSIAN ROULETTE?

The harmful problems that result from the behaviors of alcoholics and drug addicts are self-evident. But because college students view themselves as different from these populations, many fail to realize the extent to which they place themselves in harm's way through their use of alcohol. Many students view parties featuring heavy drinking as a natural part of college life, like going to classes or athletic events. Studies have found that many heavy-drinking students, who average 40 to 50 drinks per week, do not view their behavior as either abnormal or problematic (Marlatt, 1998).

Beneath this surface of complacency lies evidence that heavy-drinking students are placing themselves at considerable risk. In one national study carried out by the Harvard School of Public Health, binge drinking was defined as having more than 4 (for women) or 5 (for men) drinks at a time on at least three occasions during the previous 2 weeks (Wechsler et al., 1994). Data from 18,000 students at 140 U.S. colleges revealed that 50 percent of the males and 40 percent of the women met this bingeing criterion, yet fewer than 1 percent saw themselves as having an alcohol problem. However, the dangerous consequences of their drinking became clear when binge drinkers were asked about alcohol-related problems (Table 12.6). Frequent binge drinkers were 7 to 10 times more likely than moderate drinkers to engage in unplanned and unprotected sexual intercourse, to suffer injuries, to drive under the influence of alcohol, to damage property, and to get into trouble with the law. At schools with the highest alcohol-consumption rates, nondrinkers and moderate drinkers were 2 to 3 times more likely to report physical assault, sexual harassment, destruction of their property, and interruption of their sleep and studying by heavy drinkers. Some college women (sound sleepers, apparently) complained that they woke up Sunday after Sunday to find a strange man in bed with their roommate (and all too frequently the heavy-drinking roommate didn't know him either). Common belief may have it that heavy drinking is harmless fun, but scientific findings suggest otherwise.

Table 12.6 Percentage of Binge-Drinking College Students Who Reported Drinking-Related Problems

Problem	Percentage
Missed a class	61%
Forgot where they were or what they did	54%
Engaged in unplanned sex	41%
Got hurt	23%
Had unprotected sex	22%
Damaged property	22%
Got into trouble with campus or local police	11%
Had 5 or more alcohol-related problems in school year	47%

SOURCE: Based on Wechsler et al., 1994.

Harm-Reduction Approaches to Prevention

▶ 28. What is a harm reduction approach, and how does it differ from an abstinence-based one?

Substance abuse not only has negative effects on physical well-being but often results in other severe consequences, such as self-defeating sexual and aggressive behaviors. **Harm reduction** *is a prevention strategy that is designed not to eliminate a problem behavior but rather to reduce the harmful effects of that behavior when it occurs* (MacCoun, 1998; Weingardt & Marlatt, 1998). In the area of drug abuse, harm-reduction approaches include needle and syringe exchange programs to reduce the spread of HIV infections. Another example is methadone maintenance programs for heroin addicts that are targeted at reducing their need to engage in criminal activity to feed their heroin habit. The reasoning is that even if an addictive behavior cannot be eliminated, it is possible to modify how often and under what conditions it occurs and thereby minimize its harmful effects on the person and society.

The harm that can befall college students who abuse alcohol has inspired a new generation of intervention programs focused on helping problem drinkers control how much and under what circumstances they drink. The goal is to reduce harmful consequences to the problem drinkers and others (Marlatt et al., 2001). In one harm-reduction project carried out at a large western-U.S. university, incoming freshmen were screened for alcohol problems before they arrived on campus (Marlatt et al., 1998). Once on campus, those identified as problem drinkers were randomly assigned to either an intervention condition or to a no-treatment control condition. Over the next 2 years, the students in both conditions regularly reported on their alcohol consumption and alcohol-related problems. People who knew them well also furnished reports, and high agreement between the two sources of data indicated that the students were being truthful and accurate.

The intervention, occurring in the winter of the freshman year, was a brief one based on the motivational interviewing approach described earlier. The goal was to prevent or reduce harmful consequences of drinking by increasing motivation to make constructive changes, rather than to stop students' drinking. Clinical psychologists met with each student individually for one session. The interviewer reviewed the drinking data submitted by the student over the previous academic term and gave individualized feedback in graphic form. The graph compared his or her drinking rate with college student averages, which were invariably much lower. The interviewers listed the potential risks for heavy college drinkers (such as those shown in Table 12.6) and discussed environmental risk factors, such as being in a fraternity or sorority or having heavy-drinking friends, if relevant. The interviewers were never confrontational but instead helped students to evaluate their situation ("What do you make of this? Are you surprised?"), to think about present and possible future problems ("Would you be worried about something like this happening to you? What impact would it have on your life?"), and to consider the possibility of change. Specific goals of behavior change were left to the student and not imposed by the interviewer.

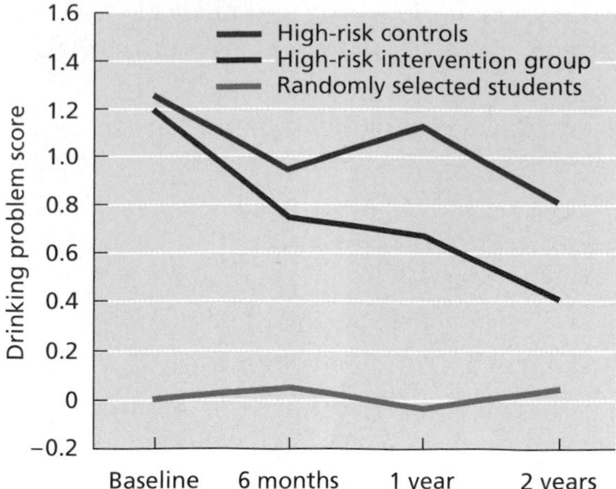

FIGURE 12.26

Effects of a brief motivational interviewing intervention on alcohol-related problems. At 1 year and 2 years after the intervention, high-risk drinkers who underwent the harm-reduction program still reported more alcohol-related problems than the average college student but fewer problems than the high-risk drinkers in the control group. SOURCE: Adapted from Marlatt et al., 1998.

At the end of 2 years, the students in the intervention group were still drinking more than the average college student, and although they continued to have more alcohol-related problems than the average student, the intervention group had far fewer alcohol-related problems than did the untreated high-risk group (Figure 12.26). Thus despite the lack of an explicit focus on reducing drinking, the brief one-session intervention had significant positive effects. In particular, students learned to moderate their drinking in potentially hazardous situations, thereby reducing harmful consequences.

Relapse Prevention: Maintaining Positive Behavior Change

▶ 29. Which factors increase or decrease relapse? How does relapse-prevention training address these factors?

Despite the availability of highly effective methods for changing behavior, high dropout rates and failure to maintain positive behavior changes are

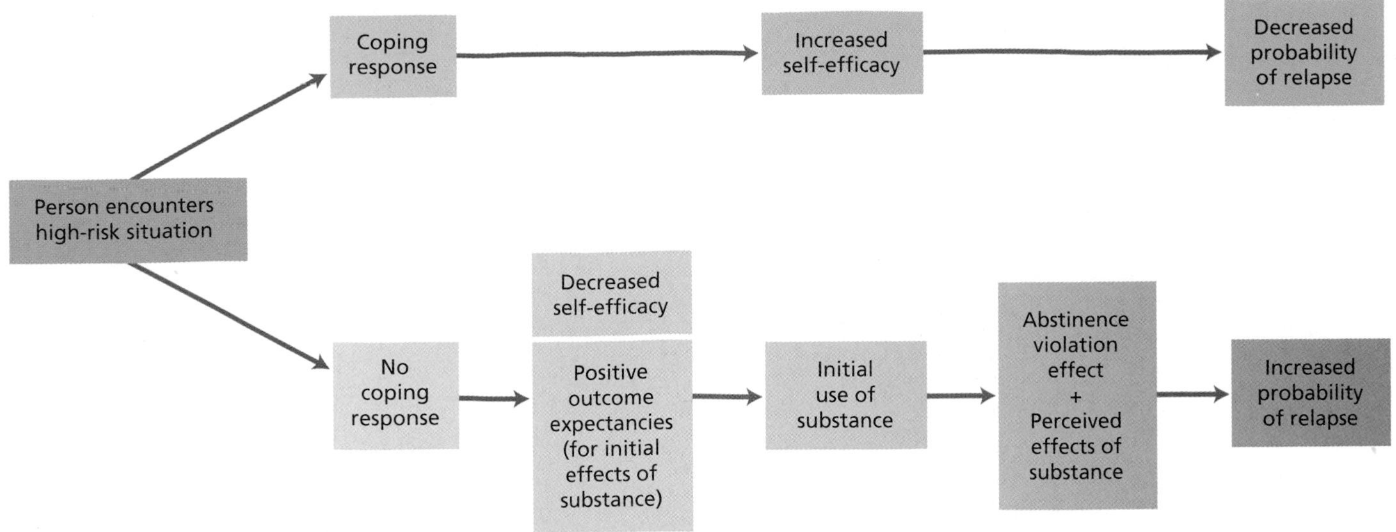

FIGURE 12.27

A model of relapse prevention. Relapse is most likely to occur as a result of inadequate coping skills for dealing with high-risk situations, a focus on anticipated positive effects of engaging in the behavior, and a resulting abstinence violation effect that causes the person to feel incapable of successful change and to abandon attempts at behavior control. SOURCE: Marlatt & Gordon, 1985.

a major problem in every health-relevant behavior we've discussed, from exercise maintenance to weight control to ending substance abuse. Why do people relapse into their problem behaviors, and what can be done to prevent this?

Research on these questions has led to a better understanding of the relapse process and an intervention known as **relapse prevention** *that is designed to reduce the risk of relapse* (Marlatt & Gordon, 1985). Research with substance abusers showed that most *relapses* (a full-fledged return to the undesirable behavior pattern) tended to occur after the person had suffered one or more *lapses* (occasional "slips") in response to high-risk situations. High-risk situations included stressful events, interpersonal conflicts, social pressure to perform the undesirable behavior, being in the company of other individuals using the substance, and experiencing negative emotions (Marlatt, 1996).

The path to relapse is shown in the bottom portion of Figure 12.27. Increased likelihood of relapse occurred when people had not developed strong enough coping skills to deal successfully with the high-risk situations. As a result, they experienced low self-efficacy, believing that they were not strong enough to resist the temptation, or they allowed expected positive benefits (such as enjoyment of the substance or anticipated stress reduction) to influence their decision to perform the undesirable behavior. A lapse would then occur, followed by a critically important reaction called the **abstinence violation effect,** *in which the person became upset and self-blaming over the lapse and viewed it as proof that he or she would never be strong enough to resist temptation.* This sense of hopelessness placed people at great risk to abandon all attempts to change, and in many cases a total relapse would occur.

Relapse resistance is shown in the upper portion of Figure 12.27. When confronting high-risk situations, people who have effective coping skills feel confident in their ability to handle them and are far less likely to relapse, even if they slip once in a while. To develop this adaptive process, relapse-prevention specialists tell people that a lapse means only that they've encountered a situation that exceeded their current coping skills. Moreover, the lapse has given them valuable information about the specific situational, cognitive, and emotional antecedents that they must learn to handle more effectively. When they master the needed skills, they will be better able to resist high-risk situations. Attention is then directed at learning and practicing the required skills so that self-efficacy improves. The continuing focus is on "progress, not perfection."

Relapse-prevention training is increasingly being incorporated into many behavior-change programs. It is an important complement to the transtheoretical model, which tells us that many people regress from the action and even maintenance stages back into a previous stage because they are not prepared to deal with the lapses that almost inevitably occur as they try to alter ingrained behavior patterns. Being prepared for occasional lapses helps people move more smoothly from the preparation stage to the action and maintenance stages (DiClemente, 2003). Building in relapse-prevention training appears to increase the effectiveness of many behavior-change programs (Taylor, 2003). The ultimate goal is to help people cope more successfully with life's challenges and to be more successful in their attempts to achieve their goals of health and happiness.

IN REVIEW

- *The transtheoretical model identifies six stages through which people may move during the process of successful long-term behavioral change: precontemplation, contemplation, preparation, action, maintenance, and termination. The model has inspired stage-matched interventions focused on the individual's current stage, with the intent of moving the person to the action, maintenance, and termination stages.*
- *Exercise is an important health-enhancing behavior that affects both physical and psychological well-being. Numerous behavioral interventions have been developed to promote exercise, but many people fail to adhere to exercise programs. One factor that influences adherence is social support. People who are able to stick with it for 3 to 6 months have a better chance of adhering thereafter.*
- *About a third of the American population is obese, as are 1 in 6 children and adolescents. Behavioral weight-control programs feature self-monitoring, stimulus control procedures, and eating procedures designed to help people eat less but enjoy it more. The addition of an exercise program to weight-control procedures enhances weight loss.*
- *Because HIV infection is caused by high-risk sexual and drug-abuse behaviors (e.g., sharing needles), a prevention approach is essential. Behavioral changes have been accomplished in homosexual populations, and efforts are centering on high-risk heterosexual populations, such as teenagers. Cultural factors sometimes conflict with safe sex practices, increasing the challenges of reducing health-endangering behaviors.*
- *Substance abuse is highly associated with other disorders and is often part of a larger pattern of maladjustment. Multimodal treatments combine a number of techniques, including aversion training, stress-management and coping-skills training, and positive reinforcement for change. A promising new approach is motivational interviewing, a nonconfrontational procedure designed to engage the person's own motivation to change self-defeating behaviors.*
- *Harm-reduction approaches attempt to reduce the negative consequences that a behavior produces rather than to focus on stopping the behavior itself. Examples include needle exchange programs for drug addicts and programs designed to reduce the destructive consequences of binge drinking in college students.*
- *Relapse prevention is designed to keep lapses from becoming relapses by building effective coping skills to deal with high-risk situations and countering the abstinence violation effect when lapses occur. This approach enhances the effects of many behavior-change programs.*

A Concluding Thought

The enterprise of living involves a constant process of adjusting to environmental demands. When those demands exceed our personal and social resources, we experience stress and may attempt to reduce it by changing our environment or our own behavior. Thus stress can be a catalyst for growth and change, or it can drag us down physically and psychologically, depending on how effectively we respond to it. Psychologists have been at the forefront of stress research and have developed interventions to help people cope more effectively.

We have also seen that people's behavior contributes strongly to both illness and physical well-being. The field of health psychology focuses on psychological and behavioral processes that affect physical well-being. Health psychologists have made important contributions to helping people reduce health-impairing behaviors and acquire healthier lifestyles, but many challenges remain.

Unfortunately, people do not always have the resources to cope with life's demands. As a result, they may engage in thought processes, emotional responses, and behaviors that are hurtful to themselves or to society. In the next chapter, we consider the behavior disorders that can result from failures to adapt successfully.

KEY TERMS AND CONCEPTS

Each term has been boldfaced and defined in the chapter on the page indicated in parentheses.

abstinence violation effect (p. 501)
aerobic exercise (p. 493)
cognitive relaxation (p. 482)
cognitive restructuring (p. 482)
coping self-efficacy (p. 474)
emotion-focused coping (p. 478)
endorphins (p. 485)
gate control theory (p. 484)
general adaptation syndrome (GAS; p. 468)
hardiness (p. 474)
harm reduction (p. 500)
health psychology (p. 465)
motivational interviewing (p. 498)
multimodal treatments (p. 498)
physiological toughness (p. 473)
placebo (p. 487)
primary appraisal (p. 468)
problem-focused coping (p. 478)
protective factors (p. 472)
relapse prevention (p. 501)
secondary appraisal (p. 468)
seeking social support (p. 479)
self-instructional training (p. 482)
somatic relaxation training (p. 483)
stress (p. 465)
stress-induced analgesia (p. 485)
stressors (p. 465)
stress response (p. 467)
transtheoretical model (p. 491)
Type A behavior pattern (p. 474)
vulnerability factors (p. 472)

? What Do You Think?

DO STRESSFUL EVENTS CAUSE PSYCHOLOGICAL DISTRESS? p. 470

As we noted, the relation between stress and distress is correlational. Now let's think critically and challenge the causal interpretation. Certainly, it's possible that life stress causes psychological distress—and there are other kinds of evidence to suggest that it does. But it is also possible that, for example, distress may be the causal factor. That is, distressed people may be more likely than nondistressed people to remember and report negative things that have happened to them. Or they may tend to view more events as negative, resulting in higher negative life-change scores. Moreover, psychological distress could actually cause people to believe in ways that produce more negative events. For example, research has shown that anxious and depressed people often evoke negative reactions from others because of their gloomy outlook and their tendency to frustrate others' attempts to help them feel better.

And that's not all: A third causal possibility is that some other variable causes both negative life events *and* psychological distress to go up or down, thus creating the relation between them. The Big Five personality trait of neuroticism, discussed in Chapter 11, might be such a "third variable." We know that people who are high in neuroticism have a tendency to experience lots of negative emotions *and* to get themselves into stressful situations through their self-defeating behaviors. Differences in neuroticism could thus cause the relation between stress and distress. These different causal possibilities do serve to remind us that stressful life events are part of a network of causal relations and that stressful life events can function as either a cause or an effect. ■

WHY DO WOMEN OUTLIVE MEN? p. 481

According to the World Health Organization, women live an average of 5 to 8 years longer than men in most industrialized countries of the world. Only in underdeveloped countries, where many women die in childbirth, do men live longer. Is stress the reason? The media interpretation is contradicted by research results showing that women report as many stressful events as men do and are, in fact, more susceptible to a variety of stress-related psychological disorders. What other factors could be at work?

One possibility is that biological factors make women more fit than men. Although more males than females are conceived, more male children are miscarried or stillborn, and more males die in infancy and at every age thereafter. Some biological survival factors may be genetic, some hormonal. One possibility is that females' XX chromosomal structure may protect them against certain diseases that afflict males. Another suggestion is that the female hormones estrogen and prolactin may help protect them against some major diseases, including heart disease.

Other explanations focus on behavioral and social differences between the sexes. Men engage in more risky and health-impairing behaviors. They are more likely to die in accidents and more likely to smoke and drink heavily. In fact, smoking differences may account for as much as 40 percent of the mortality difference between adult men and women. Finally, men are more likely to have physically hazardous occupations than are women.

At the environmental level, explanations focus on the important protective functions of social support on health and well-being. On average, women have larger and more active social support networks and more intimate relationships than do men. Whether this difference contributes to women's greater longevity is not known. Once again, however, we see the usefulness of considering potential causal factors at biological, psychological, and environmental levels of analysis.

Which of these sex differences do you think might be particularly important? Can you think of other differences that might matter? Finally, do you think that the diminishing differences in sex roles, which place increasingly more women into traditionally male work settings and lifestyles, might reduce the longevity difference in coming decades? ■

13

PSYCHOLOGICAL DISORDERS

CHAPTER OUTLINE

Why is it that when we talk to God we're praying,
but when God talks to us we're schizophrenic?

—Thomas Szasz, psychiatrist

Mark has been depressed for several years, but things are even worse now. He feels totally inadequate and inferior. The future looks hopeless, and he cannot sleep at night. During the day, he can barely function, and his moods alternate between deadening depression and intense anxiety. A friend has suggested that he seek professional counseling, but Mark is convinced that he has slipped too deeply into the black hole of despair to ever feel good again. He wonders how long he wants to go on living in his private hell.

Naomi was walking across campus the first time it happened. Suddenly, her heart began pounding and skipping beats. She grew weak and shaky, began sweating profusely, and felt an indescribable sense of impending doom. She was sure she was either going insane or was about to die on the spot. Gathering all her strength, she made it to her dormitory room and began to feel better. Now, after several such incidents while on campus, she is afraid to leave her dorm.

Unwashed, unshaven, and wearing tattered clothes, Eddie lives in the downtown area of the city. He often sits in a park mumbling to himself. Occasionally, he covers his ears and yells, "Shut up!" to try to still the voices in his head. Some nights he eats and sleeps at a shelter, but more often he rolls himself in a filthy blanket and sleeps under a freeway overpass. Eddie has been committed to a state mental hospital more than 10 times. In the hospital, he responds quickly to antipsychotic drugs and begins to behave more normally. But soon after being released back into the community, he stops taking his medication and gradually slides once again into a deteriorated mental state. Today a social service caseworker notices him and asks how he's doing. Staring vacantly into space, he replies, "Life is trouble, bubble, double, zubble."

These three people could very well live in your city or town. Mark or Naomi could be students at your college. Many people are unaware of how common psychological disorders are. In December 1999, the surgeon general of the United States issued a comprehensive report that summarized the results of hundreds of mental health studies (Satcher, 1999). Among the conclusions were the following:

- At any given time, 22 percent of the U.S. population suffers from a diagnosable mental disorder.
- Nearly half of all Americans between the ages of 15 and 54 will experience a psychological disorder at some point in their lives.
- Psychological disorders are the second leading cause of disability, after heart disease.
- Medications used to treat anxiety and depression are among the most frequently prescribed drugs in the United States.
- One adolescent commits suicide every 90 seconds.
- Each year, more than a million students withdraw from college because of emotional problems.
- One in four Americans will have a substance-abuse disorder during his or her lifetime. Alcohol abuse alone costs the U.S. economy about $117 billion a year.

These cold statistics, startling though they may be, cannot possibly capture the intense suffering that they reflect. They cannot communicate the confusion and alienation felt by the schizophrenic patient whose psychological world is

FIGURE 13.1

Abraham Lincoln and Winston Churchill suffered from severe depression during their lifetimes. Billionaire Howard Hughes had a debilitating obsessive-compulsive disorder involving fears of contamination that kept him isolated and bedridden for many years.

disintegrating, the intense personal misery of a depressed person who is sinking into a quagmire of hopelessness, the terror experienced by someone with a panic disorder, or the frustration endured by the families and friends of those who have psychological disorders.

This chapter is therefore not just about the problems of "someone else." Even if you are fortunate enough never to experience a psychological disorder in your lifetime, statistics suggest that you'll amost surely have a family member, friend, or acquaintance who does.

Psychological disorders are not just a modern problem. The pages of history are filled with accounts of prominent people who suffered from psychological disorders. The Bible describes King Saul's mad rages and terrors. The 18th-century French philosopher Jean-Jacques Rousseau developed marked paranoid symptoms in the latter part of his life and was plagued by fears of secret enemies. Mozart was convinced he was being poisoned during the time he was composing his *Requiem*. Abraham Lincoln was on one occasion so depressed that he failed to show up for his own wedding; although he did subsequently marry, he suffered recurrent bouts of depression throughout his life. Winston Churchill also periodically suffered from severe depression, referring to it as his "black dog." The billionaire Howard Hughes became so terrified of being infected with germs that he became a bedridden recluse for the last decade of his life (Figure 13.1).

Dysfunctional behaviors such as these do not go unnoticed. Throughout history, human societies have explained and responded to abnormal behavior in different ways at different times, based on their values and assumptions about human life and behavior. Psychological disorders have been viewed as the work of demons, as physical diseases, as products of psychological conflicts, as learned maladaptive behaviors, and as products of disordered perceptions of the world.

The belief that abnormal behavior is caused by supernatural forces goes back to the ancient Chinese, Egyptians, and Hebrews, all of whom attributed deviance to the work of the devil. One ancient "treatment" was based on the notion that bizarre behavior reflected an evil spirit's attempt to escape from a person's body. In order to "release" the spirit, a procedure called *trephination* was carried out. A sharp tool was used to chisel a hole in the skull about 2 centimeters in diameter (Figure 13.2). It seems likely that in many cases trephination successfully eliminated abnormal behaviors by putting an end to the patient's life.

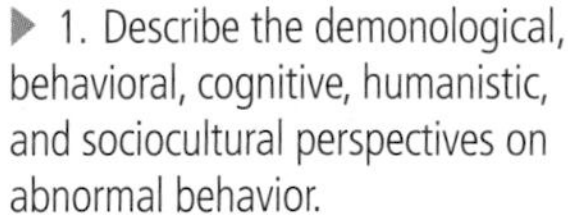

▶ 1. Describe the demonological, behavioral, cognitive, humanistic, and sociocultural perspectives on abnormal behavior.

FIGURE 13.2

An early treatment for disordered behavior was trephination, in which a hole was chiseled through the skull to release the evil spirit thought to be causing the abnormal behavior. Some people survived the operation, but many died from it.

FIGURE 13.3

This painting by Francisco de Goya reflects the widespread belief that disordered people were possessed by the devil. Sabbath *portrays the weekly gathering of Satan and the witches he possessed.*

In medieval Europe, the *demonological model* of abnormality reigned supreme. Religious dogma held that disturbed people either were possessed involuntarily by the devil or had voluntarily made a pact with the forces of darkness (Figure 13.3).

▶ 2. How does the vulnerability-stress model illustrate person-situation interactions?

Vulnerability factors
- Genetic factors
- Biological characteristics
- Psychological traits
- Previous maladaptive learning
- Low social support

Stressors
- Economic adversity
- Environmental trauma
- Interpersonal stresses or losses
- Occupational setbacks or demands

Current vulnerability **Currently experienced stress**

Psychological disorders

FIGURE 13.4

The vulnerability-stress model views behavior disorders as resulting from an interaction between personal vulnerability factors and life stressors. Personal vulnerability factors contribute to maladaptive efforts to cope with life's challenges.

The killing of witches was justified on theological grounds, and various "diagnostic" tests were devised. One was to bind a woman's hands and feet and throw her into a lake or pond. Based on the notion that impurities float to the surface, a woman who sank and drowned could be posthumously declared pure. Of course, a woman who floated was in *real* trouble. During the 16th and 17th centuries, more than 100,000 people with psychological disorders were identified as witches, hunted down, and executed.

Centuries earlier, about the 5th century B.C., the Greek physician Hippocrates suggested that mental illnesses are diseases just like physical disorders. Anticipating the modern viewpoint, Hippocrates believed that the site of mental illness was the brain. Hippocrates' belief that a mental or behavioral disorder could be caused by a physical dysfunction is today reflected in the biological perspective on psychological disorders.

By the 1800s, Western medicine had returned to viewing mental disorders as being biologically based and was attempting to extend medical diagnoses to them. The biological emphasis was given impetus by the discovery that *general paresis,* a disorder characterized in its advanced stages by mental deterioration and bizarre behavior, resulted from massive brain deterioration caused by the sexually transmitted disease syphilis. This was a breakthrough: the first demonstration that a psychological disorder was caused by an underlying physical malady.

In the early 1900s, Sigmund Freud's theory of psychoanalysis ushered in psychological interpretations of disordered behavior. As we shall see, psychodynamic theories of abnormal behavior were soon joined by other models based on behavioral, cognitive, and humanistic conceptions. These various conceptions focus on different classes of causal factors and help capture the complex determinants of abnormal behavior. The importance of cultural factors has also received increasing attention. Although many questions remain, these perspectives have given us a deeper understanding of how biological, psychological, and environmental factors can combine to cause psychological disorders.

Today, many psychologists find it useful to incorporate these factors into a more general framework. According to the **vulnerability-stress model** (Figure 13.4), *each of us has some degree of vulnerability (ranging from very low to very high) for developing a psychological disorder, given sufficient stress.* The *vulnerability,* or predisposition, can have a biological basis, such as our genotype, over- or underactivity of a neurotransmitter system in the brain, a hair-trigger autonomic nervous system, or a hormonal factor. It could also be due to a personality factor, such as low self-esteem or extreme pessimism, or to previous environmental factors such as poverty or a severe trauma or loss earlier in life. Likewise, cultural factors can create vulnerability to certain kinds of disorders (Ingram & Price, 2001).

But vulnerability is only part of the equation. In most instances, a predisposition creates a disorder only when a *stressor*—some recent or current event that requires a person to cope—combines with a vulnerability to trigger the disorder (van Praag, 2004). Thus a person who has a genetic predisposition to depression or who suffered a traumatic loss of a parent early in life may be primed to develop a depressive disorder *if* faced with the stress of another loss later in life. As we shall see, the biological, psychological, and environmental levels of analysis have all contributed to the vulnerability-stress model and to our understanding of behavior disorders and how they develop.

DEFINING AND CLASSIFYING PSYCHOLOGICAL DISORDERS

So far, we have discussed historical and contemporary accounts of abnormal behavior without actually defining what we mean by *abnormal.* Doing so is not as easy as it might at first appear.

What Is "Abnormal"?

Defining what is normal and what is abnormal is problematic. Judgments about where the line between normal and abnormal should be drawn differ depending on the time and the culture. For example, cannibalism has been practiced in many cultures around the world (Walker, 2001). In contemporary Western culture, however, such behavior would be viewed as extraordinarily pathological. In the 1940s, a woman who decided to forsake marriage and children in favor of a career in engineering would have been viewed by some segments of society, including many mental health professionals, as deviant and possibly in need of psychotherapy. Today most people would consider her choice a valid one. Until December 15, 1973, homosexuality was officially considered to be a form of mental illness. On that day, the trustees of the American Psychiatric Association voted unanimously to remove homosexuality from the psychiatric classification system—surely the quickest and most widespread "cure" in the history of psychiatry. Despite this formal change in the psychiatric status of this sexual orientation, many people in our society continue to view homosexuality as an indicator of psychological disturbance (Herek, 2002).

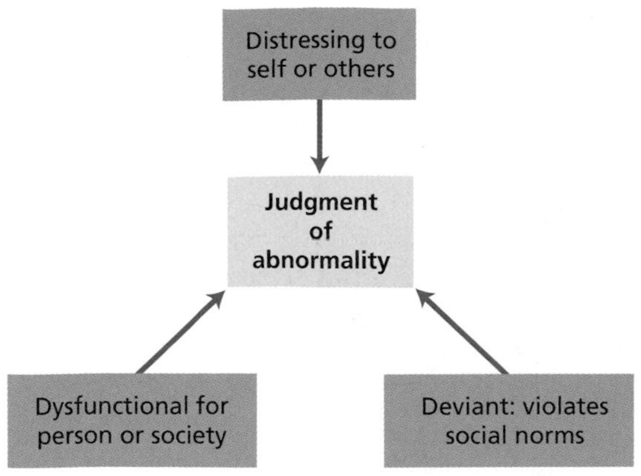

FIGURE 13.5

Whether a behavior is considered abnormal involves a social judgment made on the basis of the "three Ds," distress, dysfunction, and deviance.

▶ 3. Cite the "three Ds" that typically underlie judgments that behavior is abnormal.

Despite the arbitrariness of time, place, and value judgments, three criteria—distress, dysfunction, and deviance—seem to govern decisions about abnormality, and one or more of them seem to apply to virtually any behavior regarded as abnormal (Figure 13.5).

First, we are likely to label behaviors as abnormal if they are intensely *distressing* to the individual. People who are excessively anxious, depressed, dissatisfied, or otherwise seriously upset about themselves or about life circumstances may be viewed as disturbed, particularly if they seem to have little control over these reactions. On the other hand, personal distress is neither necessary nor sufficient to define abnormality. Some seriously disturbed mental patients are so out of contact with reality that they seem to experience little distress, and yet their bizarre behaviors are considered very abnormal. And although all of us experience suffering as a part of our lives, our distress is not likely to be judged abnormal unless it is disproportionately acute or long-lasting relative to the situation.

Second, most behaviors judged abnormal are *dysfunctional* either for the individual or for society. Behaviors that interfere with a person's ability to work or to experience satisfying relationships with other people are likely to be seen as maladaptive and self-defeating, especially if the person seems unable to control such behaviors. Some behaviors are labeled as abnormal because they interfere with the well-being of society. But even here, the standards are not cut and dried. For example, is a suicide bomber who detonates a bomb in a public market psychologically disturbed, a criminal, or a patriot?

▶ 4. What is meant by reliability and validity of diagnostic classification systems? Describe the features of DSM-IV.

The third criterion for abnormality is society's judgments concerning the *deviance* of a given behavior. As we have seen, conduct within every society is regulated by *norms*, behavioral rules that specify how people are expected to behave. Some norms are explicitly codified as laws, and violation of these norms defines criminal behavior. Other norms, however, are far less explicit. For example, it is generally expected in our culture that one should not carry on animated conversations with people who are not present, nor should one face the rear of an elevator and stare intently into the eyes of a fellow passenger (don't try this unless you want to see an elevator empty out quickly). People are likely to be viewed as psychologically disturbed if they violate these unstated norms, especially if the violations make others uncomfortable and cannot be attributed to environmental causes.

To summarize, both personal and social judgments of behavior enter into considerations of what is abnormal. Thus we may define **abnormal behavior** as *behavior that is personally distressing, personally dysfunctional, and/or so culturally deviant that other people judge it to be inappropriate or maladaptive.*

Table 13.1 A Sample of Major Diagnostic Categories in DSM-IV

1. *Anxiety disorders:* Intense, frequent, or inappropriate anxiety, but no loss of reality contact; includes phobias, generalized anxiety reactions, panic disorders, obsessive-compulsive disorders, and posttraumatic stress disorders
2. *Mood (affective) disorders:* Marked disturbances of mood, including depression and mania (extreme elation and excitement)
3. *Somatoform disorders:* Physical symptoms, such as blindness, paralysis, or pain, that have no physical basis and are assumed to be caused by psychological factors; also, excessive preoccupations and worry about health (hypochondriasis)
4. *Dissociative disorders:* Psychologically-caused problems of consciousness and self-identification, including amnesia and multiple personalities (dissociative identity disorder)
5. *Schizophrenic and other psychotic disorders:* Severe disorders of thinking, perception, and emotion that involve loss of contact with reality and disordered behavior
6. *Substance-abuse disorders:* Personal and social problems associated with the use of psychoactive substances, such as alcohol, heroin, or other drugs
7. *Sexual and gender identity disorders:* Inability to function sexually or enjoy sexuality (sexual dysfunctions); deviant sexual behaviors, such as child molestation and arousal by inappropriate objects (fetishes); strong discomfort with one's gender accompanied by the desire to be a member of the other sex
8. *Eating disorders:* Includes anorexia nervosa (self-starvation) and bulimia nervosa (patterns of bingeing and purging)
9. *Personality disorders:* Rigid, stable, and maladaptive personality patterns, such as antisocial, dependent, paranoid, and narcissistic disorders

SOURCE: Based on American Psychiatric Association, 1994.

Diagnosing Psychological Disorders

Classification is a necessary first step toward introducing order into discussions of the nature, causes, and treatment of psychological disorders. To be scientifically and practically useful, a classification system must meet standards of reliability and validity. **Reliability** *means that clinicians using the system should show high levels of agreement in their diagnostic decisions.* Because professionals with different types and amounts of training—including psychologists, psychiatrists, social workers, and physicians—make diagnostic decisions, the system should be couched in terms of observable behaviors that can be reliably detected in order to minimize subjective judgments (American Psychiatric Association, 2000). **Validity** *means that the diagnostic categories should accurately capture the essential features of the various disorders.* Thus if research and clinical observations show that a given disorder has four behavioral characteristics, the diagnostic category for that disorder should also have those four features. Moreover, the diagnostic categories should allow us to differentiate one psychological disorder from another.

The *Diagnostic and Statistical Manual of Mental Disorders, Fourth Edition* (DSM-IV; American Psychiatric Association, 1994), is the most widely used diagnostic classification system in the United States. For each of its more than 350 diagnostic categories, DSM-IV contains detailed lists of observable behaviors that must be present in order for a diagnosis to be made. Table 13.1 samples the range of major DSM-IV categories.

Reflecting an awareness of interacting personal and environmental factors, the DSM-IV allows diagnostic information to be represented along five dimensions, or *axes,* that take both the person and her or his life situation into account. Axis I, the primary diagnosis, represents the person's primary clinical symptoms, that is, the deviant behaviors or thought processes that are occurring at the present time. Axis II reflects long-standing personality or developmental disorders, such as ingrained, inflexible aspects of personality that can influence the person's behavior and response to treatment. Axis III notes any physical conditions that might be relevant, such as high blood pressure or a recent concussion. Reflecting the vulnerability-stress model discussed earlier, the clinician also rates the intensity of environmental stressors in the person's recent life on Axis IV and the person's coping resources, as reflected in recent adaptive functioning, on Axis V. Figure 13.6 shows how the axes are represented in a sample DSM-IV diagnosis.

Although the reliability and validity of DSM-IV are still being evaluated, the highly specific behavioral criteria in the DSM-IV categories clearly have improved Axis I reliability over earlier versions (Brown et al., 2001; Nathan & Lagenbucher, 1999). One trade-off, however, is that the criteria are so detailed and specific that many people don't fit neatly into the categories. Moreover, debate continues over the reliability and validity of certain categories, particularly some of the Axis II personality disorders, whose characteristics overlap extensively with one another and with some Axis I disorders (Beutler & Malik, 2002). Such overlap leads to diagnostic disagreements and concerns about how "different" these disorders really are from one another (Widiger & Sankis, 2000). An important goal in the development of the next version of the DSM is to develop categories with less overlap (Helzer & Hudziak, 2002).

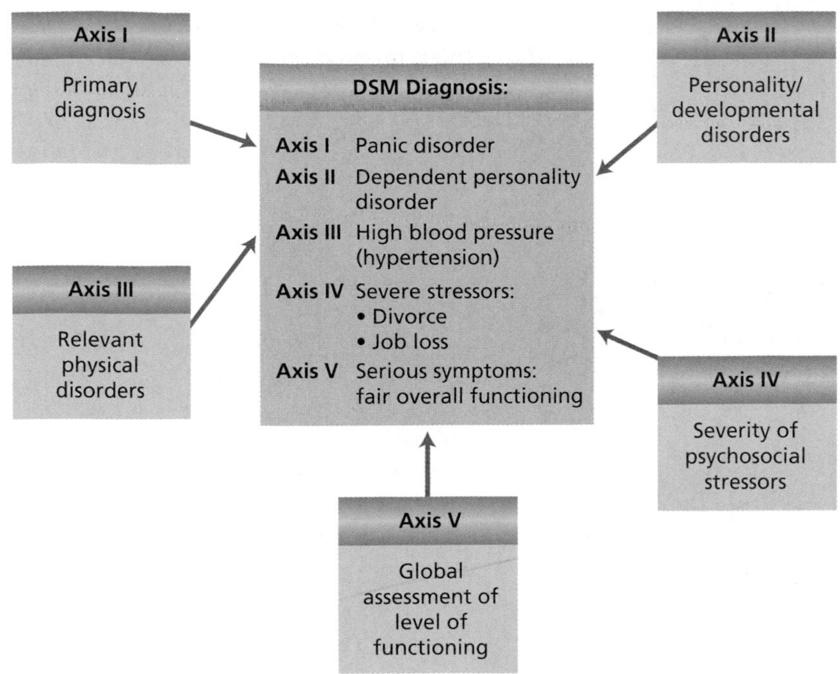

FIGURE 13.6

The DSM-IV uses a five-axis system to arrive at a comprehensive diagnosis that takes into account not only deviant behaviors but also other relevant personal and environmental factors. SOURCE: Based on American Psychiatric Association, 1994.

Social, Personal, and Legal Consequences of Diagnostic Labeling

Beyond their clinical and scientific utility, diagnostic labels can have important personal, social, and legal consequences for people who receive them. Once a diagnostic label is attached to a person, it becomes all too easy to accept the label as an accurate description of the *individual* rather than of the *behavior.* It then becomes difficult to look at the person's behavior objectively, without preconceptions about how he or she will act. It is also likely to affect how we will interact with that person. Consider for a moment how you might react if you were told that your new next-door neighbor had been diagnosed as a "sexual psychopath." It would be surprising indeed if this label did not influence your perceptions and interactions with that person, whether or not the label was accurate.

In one famous study, eight normal individuals, including psychologist David Rosenhan (1973), got themselves admitted to psychiatric hospitals in five different states by telling mental health workers that they were hearing strange voices. Not surprisingly, they received diagnoses of schizophrenia upon admission. Once in the hospitals, however, they acted completely normal for the duration of their stay. When they were discharged after intervals ranging from 7 to 52 days, they typically received the diagnosis "schizophrenia, in remission." This label means that the disorder was still presumed to be present, though not currently active. Once attached, diagnostic labels are not easily shed.

Diagnostic labels may also play a role in creating or worsening psychological disorders (Matorin, 2002). When people become aware that a psychiatric label has been applied to them, they may accept the new identity implied by the label and develop the expected role and outlook. Because psychiatric labels often carry degrading and stigmatizing implications, the effects on morale and self-esteem can be devastating. Moreover, a person may despair of ever changing and therefore give up trying to deal with life circumstances that may be responsible for the problems. In this way, the expectations that accompany a label may result in a self-fulfilling prophecy, in which expectation becomes reality. Many people with psychological disorders do not seek treatment because of the stigma attached to "mental illness."

▶ 5. How can psychiatric labels affect social and self-perceptions?

Psychiatric diagnoses also have important legal consequences. Individuals judged to be dangerous to themselves or others may be involuntarily committed to mental institutions under certain circumstances. When so committed, they lose some of their civil rights and may be detained indefinitely if their behavior does not improve.

▶ 6. Contrast the legal concepts of competency and insanity. What is the current burden of proof in insanity hearings?

The law tries to take into account the mental status of individuals accused of crimes. Two particularly important legal concepts are competency and insanity. **Competency** *refers to a defendant's state of mind at the time of a judicial hearing* (not at the time the crime was committed). A defendant

FIGURE 13.7

Both John Hinckley (top), who shot Ronald Reagan and his press secretary, James Brady, and the mass murderer Jeffrey Dahmer (bottom) pleaded not guilty by reason of insanity. Hinckley won his plea, whereas Dahmer's was rejected. These cases focused considerable attention on the insanity defense.

judged to be too disturbed to understand the nature of the legal proceedings may be labeled "not competent to stand trial" and institutionalized until judged competent.

Insanity *relates to the presumed state of mind of the defendant at the time the crime was committed.* Defendants may be declared "not guilty by reason of insanity" if they are judged to have been so severely impaired during the commission of a crime that they lacked the capacity either to appreciate the wrongfulness of their acts or to control their conduct. It is important to understand that insanity is a legal term, not a psychological one.

Despite the fact that the insanity plea is entered in only 1 of every 500 felony cases and that in 85 percent of those cases the prosecution agrees that the person was indeed insane, the insanity defense has long been hotly debated. There was an uproar upon the acquittal of John Hinckley, who attempted to assassinate President Ronald Reagan in 1981 (Figure 13.7). Instead of going to prison, Hinckley was committed to a mental hospital. Twelve years later, Jeffrey Dahmer, accused of the grisly murders and mutilations of 17 men, also entered a plea of not guilty by reason of insanity. The defense contended that no sane person could have committed the shocking acts that Dahmer freely admitted to doing, which included cutting up his victims and eating their body parts. Diagnostic interview and psychological test results also indicated severe psychological disturbance. Yet the insanity plea was rejected, and Dahmer was found guilty.

Both defendants clearly had serious mental disorders. Why the different verdicts? An important change had occurred in the legal requirement for proving sanity or insanity. At the time Hinckley was tried, the law required that the prosecution prove that Hinckley was *sane.* They could not do so beyond a reasonable doubt, and Hinckley was acquitted, provoking widespread public outrage. Partly in response to Hinckley's acquittal, the law was changed, and the burden of proof was shifted from the prosecution to the defense. Dahmer's attorneys were not able to convince the jury that their client was *insane* at the time he committed his crimes, so Dahmer was convicted of murder.

To balance punishment for crimes with concerns about a defendant's mental status and possible need for treatment, Canada and an increasing number of U.S. jurisdictions have adopted a verdict of "guilty but mentally ill." This verdict imposes a normal sentence for a crime but sends the defendant to a mental hospital for treatment. Defendants who are considered to have recovered before serving out their time are sent to prison for the remainder of the sentence.

What Do You Think?

"DO I HAVE THAT DISORDER?"

When people read descriptions of disorders, whether physical or psychological, they often see some of those symptoms or characteristics in themselves. In medical education, this is sometimes termed "medical students' disease." If you should experience such concerns as you read about the various psychological disorders in this chapter, how would you decide whether you have a problem worthy of professional attention? After thinking about this, compare your standards with those discussed on page 549.

IN REVIEW

- *Abnormality is largely a social judgment. Behavior that is judged to reflect a psychological disorder typically is (1) distressing to the person or to other people; (2) dysfunctional, maladaptive, or self-defeating; and/or (3) socially deviant in a way that arouses discomfort in others and cannot be attributed to environmental causes.*
- *The major psychiatric classification system in the United States is the DSM-IV, which describes the current status of the individual using five different dimensions, or axes, that capture personal and environmental factors. Reliability (diagnostic agreement) and validity are important issues in diagnostic classification systems.*
- *Among the important issues in psychiatric diagnosis are the potential negative effects of labeling on social perceptions and self-perceptions. Legal implications of competency and insanity judgments are also receiving attention. Competency to stand trial means that the individual is in sufficient contact with reality to understand the legal proceedings. Insanity refers to an inability to appreciate the wrongfulness of one's act and control one's behavior at the time the crime was committed.*

ANXIETY DISORDERS

▶ 7. Describe the four components of anxiety.

We have all experienced **anxiety,** *the state of tension and apprehension that is a natural response to perceived threat.* In **anxiety disorders,** *the frequency and intensity of anxiety responses are out of proportion to*

For a test to measure your level of anxiety, see Interactive Segment 13.1.

the situations that trigger them, and the anxiety interferes with daily life.

Anxiety responses have four components: (1) a *subjective-emotional* component, including feelings of tension and apprehension; (2) a *cognitive* component, including worrisome thoughts and a sense of inability to cope; (3) *physiological* responses, including increased heart rate and blood pressure, muscle tension, rapid breathing, nausea, dry mouth, diarrhea, and frequent urination; and (4) *behavioral* responses, such as avoidance of certain situations and impaired task performance (Barlow, 2002; Figure 13.8). Anxiety disorders take a number of different forms, including phobic disorders, generalized anxiety disorders, panic disorders, obsessive-compulsive disorders, and posttraumatic stress disorders.

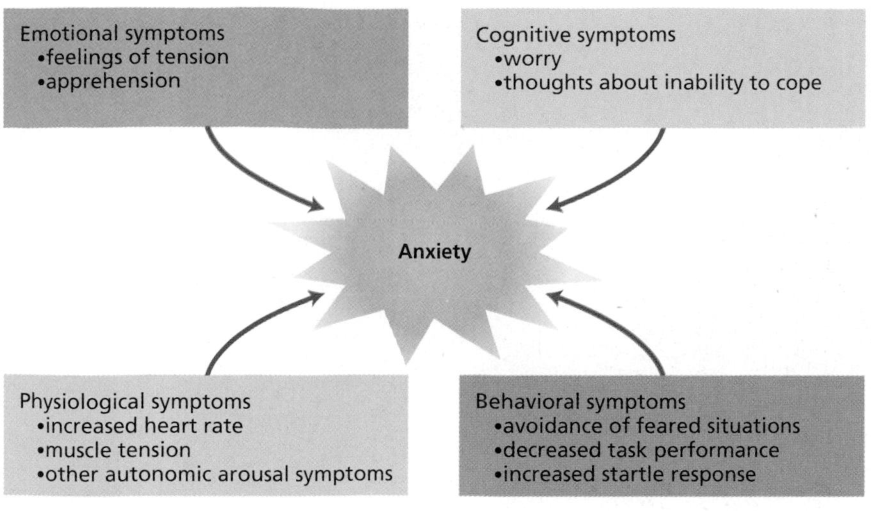

FIGURE 13.8

Anxiety consists of subjective-emotional, cognitive, physiological, and behavioral components.

Prevalence refers to the number of people who have a disorder during a specified period of time. Large-scale population studies indicate that anxiety disorders are the most prevalent of all psychological disorders in the United States, affecting 17.6 percent of Americans during their lifetimes (Kessler et al., 1994; Robins & Regier, 1991). Figure 13.9 shows lifetime prevalence rates for the various anxiety disorders, each of which occurs more frequently in females than in males. In more than 70 percent of cases, anxiety disorders are considered *clinically significant,* meaning that they interfere significantly with life functions or cause the person to seek medical or psychological treatment (Narrow et al., 2002).

Phobic Disorder

> Laura's fear of the water dates back to her childhood. She recalls that on several occasions her mother, who had a similar fear, vividly described seeing a schoolmate drown at a school picnic. Laura's fear of water intensified after she inhaled some water and panicked when a playmate "dunked" her at a swimming pool. She floundered and was sure she was going to drown until a lifeguard pulled her to safety. Although she took swimming lessons as a child, she now dreads the thought of swimming or even wading. For the past 15 years, Laura has avoided outings that would take her near the ocean, a lake, or even a pool. She once turned down a free trip to Hawaii because of the anxiety she knew she would experience flying over the ocean.

Phobias *are strong and irrational fears of certain objects or situations.* The word is derived from *Phobos,* the Greek god of fear, whose likeness was painted on masks and shields to frighten enemies in battle. Today's phobic individual fights a different kind of battle, with fears of a less realistic but no less intense nature.

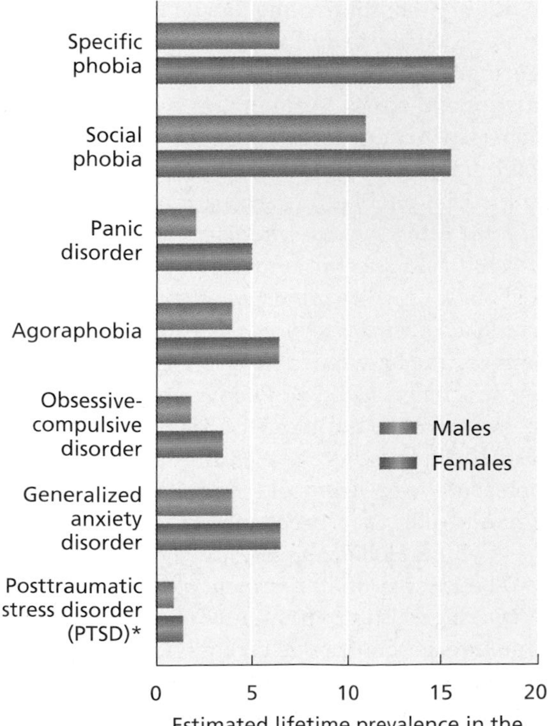

*Prevalence of PTSD is much higher in samples of individuals who have experienced traumatic events such as rape or combat.

FIGURE 13.9

Lifetime prevalence rates for the anxiety disorders in men and women. All of the disorders occur more frequently in women.

SOURCES: Based on Kessler et al., 1994; Robins & Regier, 1991.

▶ 8. Describe the features of phobic, generalized anxiety, panic, and obsessive-compulsive disorders.

FIGURE 13.10

People who suffer from phobic disorders cope in different ways. One famous figure, TV sports announcer John Madden (left), has such an intense fear of flying that he travels to his weekly assignments, sometimes separated by thousands of miles, in this specially equipped motor home. In contrast, Jenny Dibley's (right) acrophobia *(fear of heights) has not prevented her from operating the glass-walled elevator to the top of Seattle's Space Needle for more than 20 years. She never looks out the window or through the narrow crack between her elevator door and the observation deck. Away from her job, Ms. Dibley is afraid to climb a ladder or stand on a chair.*

People with phobias realize that their fears are out of proportion to the danger involved, but they feel helpless to deal with these fears. Instead, they make strenuous efforts to avoid the phobic situation or object. Among the most common phobias in Western society are **agoraphobia,** *a fear of open or public places from which escape would be difficult;* **social phobias,** *excessive fear of situations in which the person might be evaluated and possibly embarrassed;* and **specific phobias,** *such as a fear of dogs, snakes, spiders, airplanes, elevators, enclosed spaces, water, injections, or germs.* Animal fears are common among women; fear of heights, among men (Curtis et al., 1998). Phobias can develop at any point in life, but many of them arise during childhood, adolescence, and early adulthood. Once phobias develop, they seldom go away on their own, and they may broaden and intensify over time (Stein & Hollander, 2002).

The degree of impairment produced by a phobia depends in part on how often the phobic stimulus is encountered in the individual's normal round of activities. For example, fear of flying is a common phobia that occurs in some 25 million Americans (Bruce & Sanderson, 1998). An airplane phobia may be a relatively minor inconvenience for a person who never needs to fly, but it would be a serious handicap for a sales representative whose job requires extensive travel. Some people, such as TV sports announcer John Madden, simply refuse to fly despite great personal inconvenience (Figure 13.10).

Generalized Anxiety Disorder

> On initial assessment, Dr. J, who is manifestly tense, complains of never being entirely free of a sense of impending disaster, although he cannot further specify the nature of this anticipated catastrophe. He notes a number of signs of autonomic hyperarousal that he experiences on virtually a daily basis, emphasizing in particular excessive sweating, which has become a source of embarrassment. He is medicating himself for persistent attacks of diarrhea. He complains of an inability to attain a refreshing level of sleep even on those rare occasions when he can count on a few uninterrupted off-duty hours, and his very few waking "leisure" hours are filled with restless irritability. (Carson et al., 1988, p. 195)

Dr. J is suffering from a **generalized anxiety disorder,** *a chronic state of diffuse, or "free-floating," anxiety that is not attached to specific situations or objects.* In such cases, the anxiety may last for months, with the signs almost continually present. Emotionally, Dr. J feels jittery, tense, and constantly on edge. Cognitively, he expects something awful to happen but doesn't know what. Physically, he experiences a mild chronic emergency reaction. Dr. J sweats, his stomach is usually upset, he has diarrhea, and so forth.

As we might expect, this disorder can markedly interfere with daily functioning, even if the symptoms are not continually present for the 6 months required for a formal diagnosis (Kessler & Wittchen, 2002). The person may find it hard to concentrate, to make decisions, and to remember commitments. One large-scale study found that 5 percent of people between the ages of 15 and 45 reported having experienced the symptoms of generalized anxiety disorder. Onset tends to occur in childhood and adolescence (Wittchen et al., 1994).

Panic Disorder

In contrast to generalized anxiety disorder, which involves chronic tension and anxiety, **panic disorders** *occur suddenly and unpredictably, and they are much more intense.* The symptoms of panic attacks can be terrifying. As in the case of Naomi, the college student described at the beginning of the chapter, it is not unusual for victims to believe that they are dying (Ballenger, 2000).

> Ms. Watson reported that until the onset of her current problems two years ago, she had led a normal and happy life. She was returning from work one night when suddenly she felt that she couldn't catch her breath. Her heart began to pound, and she broke out into a cold sweat. Things began to seem unreal, her legs felt leaden, and she became sure she would die or faint before she reached home. She asked a passerby to help her get a taxi and went to a nearby hospital emergency room. (Spitzer et al., 1983, pp. 7–8)

As in Naomi's and Ms. Watson's cases, panic attacks usually occur out of the blue and in the absence of any identifiable stimulus. It is this unpredictable quality that makes panic attacks so mysterious and terrifying to their victims. About 60 percent of people with daytime panic disorders also experience attacks during their sleep. Their symptoms awaken them, and they fear that they are dying (Craske & Rowe, 1997).

Many people who suffer recurrent panic attacks develop agoraphobia, an aversion to public places, because they fear that they will have an attack in public. In extreme cases, they may fear leaving the familiar setting of the home, and some have been known to remain housebound for years at a time because of their "fear of fear" (Milrod et al., 1997). Ms. Watson developed an agoraphobic pattern:

> As the attacks continued, Ms. Watson began to dread going out of the house alone. She feared that while out she would have an attack and would be stranded and helpless. She stopped riding the subway to work out of fear she might be trapped in a car between stops when an attack struck, preferring instead to walk the 20 blocks between her home and work. Social and recreational activities, previously frequent and enjoyed, were severely curtailed because an attack might occur. (Spitzer et al., 1983, pp. 7–8)

Panic disorders with or without agoraphobia tend to appear in late adolescence or early adulthood and affect about 3.5 percent of the population (Kessler et al., 1994). Even more common are occasional panic attacks. In one survey of Canadian students, 34 percent reported having had at least one unexpected panic attack within the previous year, usually during periods of extreme stress (Norton et al., 1985). Under DSM-IV criteria, these students would *not* be diagnosed as having a panic disorder unless they developed an inordinate fear of having future attacks.

Obsessive-Compulsive Disorder

> A 38-year-old mother of one child had been obsessed by fears of contamination during her entire adult life. Literally hundreds of times a day, thoughts of being infected by germs would occur to her. Once she began to think that either she or her child might become infected, she could not dismiss the thought. The constant concern about infection resulted in a series of washing and cleaning rituals that took up most of her day. Her child was confined to one room only, which the woman tried to keep entirely free of germs by scrubbing it—floor to ceiling—several times a day. Moreover, she opened and closed all doors with her feet, in order to avoid contaminating her own hands. (Rachman & Hodgson, 1980)

This woman was diagnosed as having an *obsessive-compulsive disorder.* Such disorders usually consist of two components, one cognitive, the other behavioral, although either can occur alone. **Obsessions** *are repetitive and unwelcome thoughts, images, or impulses that invade consciousness, are often abhorrent to the person, and are very difficult to dismiss or control.* This mother was tyrannized by thoughts and images of contamination. **Compulsions** *are repetitive behavioral responses*—like the woman's cleaning rituals—*that can be resisted only with great difficulty.* Compulsions are often responses to obsessive thoughts; they function to reduce the anxiety associated with the thoughts (De Silva & Rachman, 1998). Once the mother performed her compulsive cleaning acts, she was relatively free from anxiety, at least until the thoughts of contamination intruded once more.

In this case, the woman's germ obsession clearly interfered with her life, as well as her daughter's. One man's obsession resulted in a far more favorable outcome: Louis Pasteur's discovery of a process for eliminating destructive microorganisms and limiting fermentation in milk, beer, and other liquids. His tireless work on this invention was fueled in part by his own obsession about contamination and infection. Pasteur refused to shake hands with others and had a ritual of vigorously wiping his plate and glass before dining (Asimov, 1997).

▶ 9. Describe the four major features of PTSD.

Behavioral compulsions are extremely difficult to control. They often involve checking things repeatedly (e.g, whether the door was locked or the gas burners on the stove were turned off), cleaning or hand washing, and repeating tasks endlessly. If the person does not perform the compulsive act, he or she may experience tremendous anxiety, perhaps even a panic attack. Like phobic avoidance responses, compulsions are strengthened through a process of negative reinforcement because they allow the person to avoid anxiety (Jenike, 1998).

Recent studies have found the lifetime prevalence of obsessive-compulsive disorder in the United States and Canada to be about 2.5 per 100 people. Onset typically occurs in the 20s (Robins & Regier, 1991; Weissman et al., 1994).

FIGURE 13.11

The violent destruction of September 11, 2001, traumatized many people, both in New York City and around the United States. One effect of the trauma was the development of posttraumatic stress disorder in many people, particularly those who lived near the destruction.

Posttraumatic Stress Disorder (PTSD)

Posttraumatic stress disorder (PTSD) *is a severe anxiety disorder that can occur in people who have been exposed to traumatic life events.* Four major symptoms commonly occur in this anxiety disorder:

- The person experiences severe symptoms of anxiety, arousal, and distress that were not present before the trauma.
- The person relives the trauma recurrently in "flashbacks," in dreams, and in fantasy (Pitman et al., 2000).
- The person becomes numb to the world and avoids stimuli that serve as reminders of the trauma.
- The individual experiences intense "survivor guilt" in instances where others were killed and the individual was somehow spared (Valent, 2000).

The PTSD category arose in part from studies of soldiers who had been subjected to the horrors of war. One study found the incidence of PTSD to be 7 times more likely for Vietnam veterans who spent significant time in combat and were wounded than for other Vietnam-era veterans (Centers for Disease Control, [CDC], 1988). Another study reported a 12-month PTSD rate of 27.8 percent following combat exposure (Prigerson et al., 2002). Civilian war victims may be even more vulnerable than soldiers. Amy Ai and coworkers (2002) found a PTSD rate of 60.5 percent in a sample of refugees from the bloody civil war in Kosovo. On average, the refugees reported having experienced 15 war-related traumatic events. Traumas caused by human actions, such as war, rape, and torture, tend to precipitate more severe PTSD reactions than do natural disasters, such as hurricanes or earthquakes (O'Donohue & Elliot, 1992). Compared with men, women exhibit twice the rate of PTSD following exposure to traumatic events (Kimerling et al., 2003).

Terrorist acts can exact a heavy toll in PTSD (Figure 13.11). Interviews with 1,008 adult residents of Manhattan revealed that 7.5 percent manifested symptoms consistent with a PTSD diagnosis in the 5 to 8 weeks following the September 11, 2001, destruction of the World Trade Center. In those living closest to the World Trade Center, the PTSD rate was 20 percent (Galea et al., 2002).

The psychological wreckage caused by PTSD may increase vulnerability to the later development of other disorders. One study found that women who experienced PSTD had double the risk of developing a depressive disorder and 3 times the risk of developing alcohol-related problems in the future (Bresalau et al., 1997). Such findings highlight the importance of prompt post-trauma intervention aimed at preventing the development of PTSD (Sorenson, 2002). This chapter's *Research Close-Up* focuses on such an approach.

For a personal account of PTSD, see Video Segment 13.1.

RESEARCH CLOSE-UP

RAPE, TRAUMA, AND PTSD

Introduction

The aftermath of being raped can be nearly as traumatic as the incident itself. For months or even years after the rape, victims may feel nervous and may fear another attack or retaliation by the rapist. They may experience sudden flashbacks or nightmares that force them to relive the traumatic experience. Many victims change their place of residence but continue to have nightmares and to be frightened when they are alone, outdoors, or in crowds. Victims frequently report decreased enjoyment of sexual activity long after the rape, even when they are still capable of having orgasms (Burgess & Holmstrom, 1974; Holmes & St. Lawrence, 1983). Follow-up studies have shown that over 70 percent of rape victims meet DSM criteria for PTSD 3 weeks after the trauma, as do nearly half of the victims after 3 months (Foa et al., 1995). In one long-term follow-up of rape victims, one quarter of the women felt that they had not recovered psychologically after 6 years (Meyer & Taylor, 1986).

Relatively little is known about the course of symptoms and recovery from rape because most studies have only assessed symptoms at one or two time periods, and no previous studies have compared the effects of being raped with other traumas. Clinicians who treat rape victims have found that the peak PTSD symptoms can occur at different times. Because of the importance of dealing emotionally with trauma as early as possible, many clinicians believe that women who show peak PTSD symptoms immediately after the trauma have a more favorable recovery than those who don't react emotionally until weeks later. This study addressed all of these issues.

SOURCE: Eva Gilboa-Schechtman and Edna Foa (2001). Patterns of recovery from trauma: The use of intraindividual analysis. *Journal of Abnormal Psychology, 110,* 392–400.

Method

Participants were 101 women who had been physically assaulted. Sixty-three of the women had been raped, and 38 were victims of nonsexual assault durings robberies or domestic violence. The women were seen on a weekly basis by trained clinicians for 12 consecutive weeks, during which time they were administered a DSM-based interview designed to assess PTSD symptoms. The interviewer rated each of 15 symptoms (e.g., flashbacks, nightmares, increased fearfulness, increased startle response, reduced leisure activities, concentration difficulties) on a scale of 0 ("not present") to 3 ("severe symptoms") and then assigned a total PTSD score that varied from 0 to 45.

Results

Figure 13.12a shows the PTSD scores for the sexual and nonsexual assault victims at the first assessment, after 1 month, and after 3 months. Sexual assault produced higher PTSD scores than did nonsexual assaults at every assessment point. The hypothesis that early onset of PTSD would result in better recovery was tested by comparing women whose PTSD symptoms peaked within the first 2 weeks of assessment (67 percent) with those whose peaks did not occur until the 3rd through 6th weeks. As illustrated in Figure 13.12b, the early responders showed significantly more improvement by the end of the 3-month assessment period than did those with delayed responses.

Discussion

This study is noteworthy from both scientific and practical perspectives. It is the first to track the course of PTSD symptoms over an extended period of time and to compare two different types of trauma. The results indicate that rape is a more

Continued

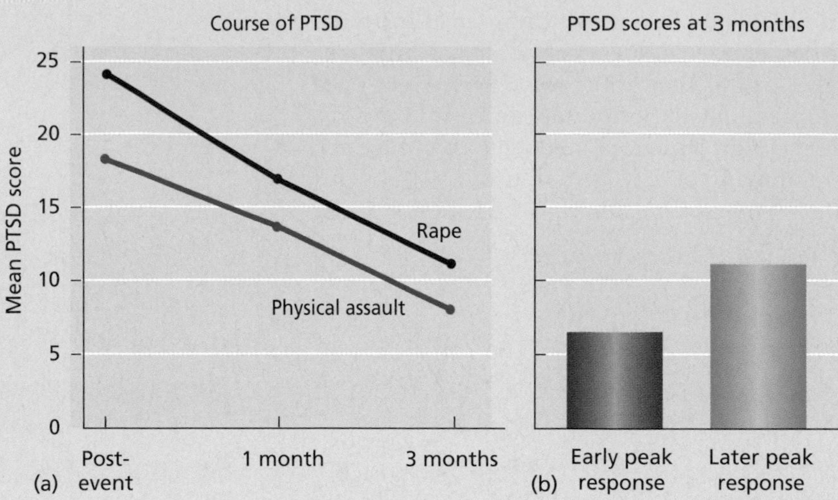

FIGURE 13.12

(a) Symptoms of PTSD reported over 3 months in women who were raped or who suffered a nonsexual assault. (b) PTSD symptoms at 3 months for women who had either immediate (1–2 weeks) or delayed (3–6 weeks) emotional reactions to their traumatic experiences. (These data are based on only those victims who had their peaks within the first 6 weeks. Those who peaked beyond 6 weeks had even higher PTSD scores at the 3-month assessment.) SOURCE: Based on Gilboa-Schechtman & Foa, 2001.

traumatic experience than other types of physical assault. The researchers expected that rape victims would also show a slower rate of recovery, but the recovery slopes of the two assault groups were quite similar over the 3-month period. However, in a follow-up replication study with a 6-month assessment, the researchers did find that the nonsexual assault victims recovered more quickly between the 3rd and 6th months.

Of special clinical significance is the finding that delayed onset of PTSD symptoms is associated with a poorer course of recovery. Apparently, a lack of emotional engagement with the traumatic event leads to a bottling-up of feelings that impedes recovery. This finding suggests the importance of immediate intervention with victims of traumatic events so that they can begin to emotionally process the experience they had. It is possible that "delayed reactors" eventually recover as fully as "early reactors," but that the process takes longer. Future studies of this kind can teach us more about individual differences in dealing with trauma and how such differences influence recovery and later adjustment.

This study also shows the value of repeated assessment over time. The researchers were able to track the course of recovery for each victim and to identify different patterns of adaptation to the traumatic events. Wide individual differences were observed among the women in their reaction to both the trauma and to the course of treatment. Such differences invite further research on how personality and coping strategies affect the course of adaptation. Although longitudinal studies like this are time- and effort-intensive, they yield a wealth of data that cross-sectional studies cannot reveal.

Causal Factors in Anxiety Disorders

Anxiety is a complex phenomenon having biological, psychological, and environmental causes. Within the vulnerability-stress model presented earlier, any of these factors can create predispositions to respond to stressors with an anxiety disorder.

Biological Factors

▶ 10. What are the possible roles of genetic, evolutionary, and biochemical factors in anxiety disorders?

Genetic factors may create a vulnerability to anxiety disorders (Blackwood, 2000). David Barlow (2002) suggests that such vulnerability may take the form of an autonomic nervous system that overreacts to perceived threat, creating high levels of physiological arousal. Hereditary factors may cause overreactivity of neurotransmitter systems involved in emotional responses (Mineka et al., 1998). Other evidence suggests that trauma-produced overactivity in the emotional systems of the right hemisphere (whose activity underlies negative emotional states) may produce vulnerability to PTSD (Schore, 2002).

Twin studies provide important clues to the importance of genetic causes. Identical twins are far more similar to one another in scores on psychological tests that measure anxiety than are fraternal twins, even when the identical twins were separated early in life and raised in different families. Heritability estimates based on these samples indicate that about 50 to 60 percent of the variation in anxiety scores can be attributed to genetic factors, with the remaining 40 to 50 percent attributable to personal life experiences (Blackwood, 2000;

Tellegen et al., 1988). Where clinical levels of anxiety are concerned, identical twins have a concordance rate (i.e., if one twin has it, so does the other) of about 40 percent for anxiety disorders, compared with a 4 percent concordance rate in fraternal twins (Carey & Gottesman, 1981). Although such findings indicate a genetic predisposition, the concordance rate even in identical twins is far from 100 percent, indicating the significance of psychological and environmental factors.

The search for biological processes associated with anxiety disorders has focused on several neurotransmitters in the brain. One such transmitter is GABA (gamma-aminobutyric acid), an inhibitory transmitter that reduces neural activity in the amygdala and other brain structures that trigger emotional arousal. Some researchers believe that abnormally low levels of inhibitory GABA activity in these arousal areas may cause some people to have highly reactive nervous systems that quickly produce anxiety responses to stressors (Bremner, 2000). Such people could also be more susceptible to classically conditioned phobias because they already have a strong unconditioned arousal response in place, ready to be conditioned to new stimuli. In support of this hypothesis, brain scans showed that patients with a history of panic attacks had a 22 percent lower concentration of GABA in the occipital cortex than age-matched controls without panic disorder (Goddard et al., 2001). Other transmitter systems may also be involved in the anxiety disorders.

As noted earlier, women exhibit anxiety disorders more often than men do. In a large-scale study of adolescents, Peter Lewinsohn and coworkers (1998) found that this sex difference emerges as early as 7 years of age. Even when the researchers applied statistical methods to control for sex differences in 11 psychosocial factors (including negative life events, self-esteem, and social support), a large sex difference in anxiety disorders remained. Such findings suggest a sex-linked biological predisposition for anxiety disorders, but social conditions that give women less power and personal control may also contribute (Craske, 2003). As in other instances of sex differences, it seems likely that biological, psychological, and environmental factors combine in complex ways.

Finally, we should recall the possible role of evolutionary factors in predisposing people to fear certain types of stimuli that might have had survival significance in the past, such as snakes, spiders, storms, and heights. As discussed in Chapter 6, evolutionary theorists believe that biological preparedness makes it easier for us to learn to fear certain stimuli and may explain why phobias seem to center on certain classes of "primal" stimuli, such as heights and potentially dangerous animals, and not on modern objects that are potentially more dangerous, such as guns, automobiles, and electrical power stations (Öhman, 1993).

Psychological Factors

▶ 11. Compare psychoanalytic and cognitive explanations of anxiety disorders.

Psychodynamic Theories Anxiety is a central concept in psychoanalytic conceptions of abnormal behavior. According to Freud, **neurotic anxiety** *occurs when unacceptable impulses threaten to overwhelm the ego's defenses and explode into consciousness or action.* How the ego's defense mechanisms deal with neurotic anxiety determines the form of the anxiety disorder. Freud believed that in phobic disorders, neurotic anxiety is displaced onto some external stimulus that has symbolic significance in relation to the underlying conflict. For example, in one of Freud's most celebrated cases, a 5-year-old boy named Hans suddenly developed a fear of horses and the possibility of being bitten. Seeing a horse fall down near his home worsened his fear, and Little Hans began to dread leaving his home. To Freud, the phobia resulted from the boy's unresolved Oedipus complex. The powerful horse represented Hans's father, and the fear of being bitten symbolized Hans's unconscious fear of being castrated by his father if he acted on his sexual desire for his mother; the falling horse symbolized Hans's forbidden triumph over his father.

Psychoanalysts believe that obsessions and compulsions are also ways of handling anxiety. According to Freud, the obsession is symbolically related to, but less terrifying than, the underlying impulse. A compulsion is a way of "taking back," or undoing, one's unacceptable urges, as when obsessive thoughts about dirt and compulsive hand washing are used to deal with one's "dirty" sexual impulses. Finally, generalized anxiety and panic attacks are thought to occur when one's defenses are not strong enough to control or contain neurotic anxiety but are strong enough to hide the underlying conflict.

Although psychoanalytic theory has stimulated considerable thinking about the causes and treatment of the anxiety disorders, the notion of anxiety disorder symptoms as symbolic expressions of underlying conflicts has not received much research support (Fisher & Greenberg, 1996). Cognitive and behavioral approaches are far more influential today in guiding research on anxiety disorders and their treatment.

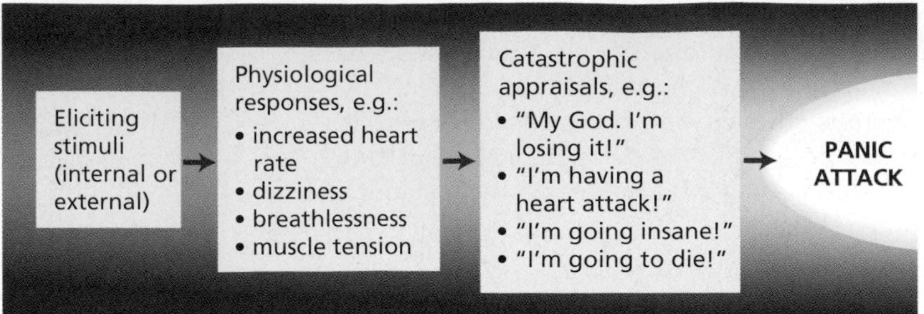

FIGURE 13.13

Cognitive explanations of panic attacks describe a process in which normal manifestations of anxiety are appraised catastrophically, increasing anxiety to a level that ultimately results in a full-blown panic attack.

Cognitive Factors Cognitive theorists stress the role of maladaptive thought patterns and beliefs in anxiety disorders. Anxiety-disordered people "catastrophize" about demands and magnify them into threats. They anticipate that the worst will happen and feel powerless to cope effectively (Clark, 1988; Mineka et al., 1998). Edna Foa and coworkers (1996) asked social phobics (1) how likely it was that they would embarrass themselves in a social situation and (2) how serious and costly the consequences of performing poorly would be for them. Compared with nonphobics, the social phobics judged both the likelihood and the costs to be much higher. Interestingly, these judgments were restricted to social situations. The social phobics did not differ in their likelihood and cost judgments in nonsocial situations, such as task-performance domains.

Cognitive processes also play an important role in panic disorders. According to David Barlow (2002), panic attacks are triggered by exaggerated misinterpretations of normal anxiety symptoms, such as heart palpitations, dizziness, and breathlessness. The panic-disordered person appraises these as signs that a heart attack or a psychological loss of control is about to occur, and these catastrophic appraisals create even more anxiety until the process spirals out of control, producing a full-blown state of panic (Figure 13.13). Helping panic patients replace such "mortal-danger" appraisals with more benign interpretations of their bodily symptoms (e.g., "It's only a bit of anxiety, not a heart attack") results in a marked reduction in panic attacks (Barlow, 1997; Craske, 1999).

▶ 12. Explain anxiety disorders in terms of classical conditioning, negative reinforcement, and observational learning.

Anxiety as a Learned Response From the behavioral perspective, anxiety disorders result from emotional conditioning (Öhman, 2000; Rachman, 1998). Some fears are acquired as a result of traumatic experiences that produce a classically conditioned fear response. For example, a person who has suffered a traumatic fall from a high place may develop a fear of heights (CR) because the high place (CS) was associated with the pain and trauma of the fall (UCS).

Classical conditioning cannot be the whole story, however, because many phobic people have never had a traumatic experience with the phobic object or situation that they now fear (Bruce & Sanderson, 1998; Menzies & Clarke, 1995). Most people who are afraid to fly have never been in an airplane crash. So how did they learn their fear? Clearly, phobias can also be acquired through observational learning. For example, televised images of airplane crashes evoke high levels of fear in some people. Yet most people do not develop phobias under these conditions, so there must be still more going on. It may be that biological dispositions and cognitive factors help determine whether a person develops a phobia from observing or even hearing about a traumatic event. Recall, for example, how Laura's fear of the water began with her mother's description of her classmate's drowning. Thus if a person has a biological disposition toward intense fear and if the person comes to believe that "sooner or later the same thing will happen to me," the likelihood of developing a phobia on the basis of observational learning may increase.

Once anxiety is learned, it may be triggered either by cues from the environment or by internal cues, such as thoughts and images (Pitman et al., 2000). In phobic reactions, the cues tend to be external ones relating to the feared object or situation. In panic disorders, the anxiety-arousing cues tend to be internal ones, such as bodily sensations (e.g., one's heart rate) or mental images (such as the image of collapsing and having a seizure in a public place; Craske, 1999).

People are highly motivated to avoid or escape anxiety because it is such an unpleasant emotional state. Here is where operant conditioning enters the picture. Behaviors that are successful in reducing anxiety, such as compulsions or phobic avoidance responses, become stronger through negative reinforcement. Thus the obsessive-compulsive mother's scrubbing ritual reduces anxiety about contamination, and Laura's avoidance of swimming prevents her from experiencing anxiety. In the case of agoraphobia, remaining at home also serves as a *safety signal,* a place where the person is unlikely to experience a panic attack (Seligman & Binik, 1977). Again, anxiety reduction reinforces the response of staying at home (Figure 13.14). Unfortunately, successful avoidance prolongs the problem because it prevents the learned anxiety response from being extinguished, which would occur eventually if these people exposed themselves to the feared stimuli enough times without experiencing the feared consequence.

Sociocultural Factors

Social and cultural factors also play a role in the development of anxiety disorders (Lopez & Guarnaccia, 2000). The role of culture is most dramatically shown in **culture-bound disorders** *that occur only in certain locales.* We may think of these disorders as existing only in non-Western cultures, but one culturally based anxiety disorder common in our own society is *anorexia nervosa.* Although formally classified as an eating disorder, anorexia nervosa has a strong phobic component, namely the fear of getting fat. This eating disorder is found almost exclusively in developed countries, where being thin has become a cultural obsession (Becker et al., 1999).

Another culture-specific disorder, found in Japan, is a social phobia called *Taijin Kyofushu* (Tanaka-Matsumi, 1979). People with this disorder are pathologically fearful of offending others by emitting offensive odors, blushing, staring inappropriately, or having a blemish or improper facial expression. Taijin Kyofushu has been attributed to the Japanese cultural value of extreme interpersonal sensitivity and to cultural prohibitions against expressing negative emotions or causing discomfort in others (Kleinknecht et al., 1997). *Koro* is a Southeast Asian anxiety disorder in which a man fears that his penis is going to retract into his abdomen and kill him. *Windigo* is an anxiety disorder found among certain North American Indians in which people are fearful of being possessed by monsters that will turn them into homicidal cannibals.

As we have seen, the causes of anxiety disorders are complex. They often interact with one another and can be analyzed at several levels of analysis (Figure 13.15).

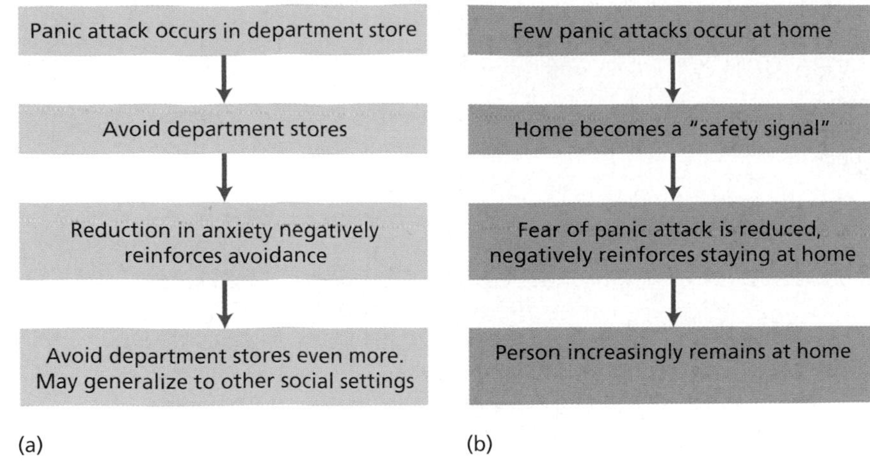

Panic attack occurs in department store
Avoid department stores
Reduction in anxiety negatively reinforces avoidance
Avoid department stores even more. May generalize to other social settings
Few panic attacks occur at home
Home becomes a "safety signal"
Fear of panic attack is reduced, negatively reinforces staying at home
Person increasingly remains at home
(a)
(b)

FIGURE 13.14

How panic disorders contribute to the development of agoraphobia. Negative reinforcement through anxiety reduction fosters avoidance of feared situations (a), as well as an attraction to safety signals, such as one's own home (b), where panic does not occur.

FIGURE 13.15

Understanding Behavior: Causal factors in anxiety disorders.

Levels of Analysis

Biological

- Evolutionary preparedness to fear certain stimuli
- Genetic predisposition
- Overreactive autonomic nervous system
- Greater relative right-hemisphere activation
- Low levels of inhibitory transmitter GABA
- Other possible neurotransmitter dysfunctions

Psychological

- Displacement of neurotic anxiety (e.g., phobia, obsessions)
- "Catastrophizing" appraisals of threatening events
- Exaggerated appraisals of anxiety symptoms (panic disorder)
- Classically conditioned fear responses
- Observationally learned fear responses
- Negatively reinforced avoidance responses

Environmental

- Previous exposure to aversive unconditioned stimuli
- Traumatic experiences (PTSD)
- Avoidable fear-inducing conditioned stimuli
- Exposure to fearful models or to other's traumatic experiences
- Fear-inducing media exposure
- Cultural learning experiences (culture-bound disorders)

Anxiety Disorders

IN REVIEW

- *Anxiety involves four components: (1) subjective-emotional feelings of tension and discomfort; (2) cognitive processes involving worry, perceptions of threat, and lack of control; (3) excessive physiological arousal; and (4) behaviors that reflect the anxious state and often are designed to escape or avoid the feared object or situation.*
- *Anxiety disorders include phobic disorder (an irrational fear of a specific object or situation), generalized anxiety disorder (recurrent anxiety reactions that are difficult to link to specific environmental stimuli), panic disorder, obsessive-compulsive disorder (which involves uncontrollable and unwelcome thoughts and repetitive behaviors), and posttraumatic stress disorder.*
- *Biological factors in anxiety disorders include both genetic and biochemical processes, possibly involving the action of neurotransmitters, such as GABA, within parts of the brain that control emotional arousal.*
- *Psychoanalytic theorists believe that neurotic anxiety results from the inability of the ego's defenses to deal with internal psychological conflicts. The cognitive perspective stresses the role of cognitive distortions, including the tendencies to magnify the degree of threat and danger and, in the case of panic disorder, to misinterpret normal anxiety symptoms in ways that can evoke panic.*
- *The behavioral perspective views anxiety as a learned response established through classical conditioning or vicarious learning. The avoidance responses in phobias and compulsive disorders are seen as operant responses that are negatively reinforced through anxiety reduction.*
- *Sociocultural factors are also involved in anxiety disorders, as illustrated by certain culture-bound anxiety disorders. The greater prevalence of anxiety disorders in women has been explained in both biological and sociocultural terms.*

SOMATOFORM AND DISSOCIATIVE DISORDERS

The anxiety disorders just considered involve anxiety and stress reactions that are vividly experienced by the sufferer. In some other disorders, however, anxiety is largely inferred rather than outwardly expressed. In somatoform and dissociative disorders, for example, the person may not consciously feel any anxiety because the function of the disorders is to protect the person from strong psychological conflicts (Rosenhan & Seligman, 1989). Psychodynamic theorists believe that whatever distress the person may experience in such disorders is less stressful than the underlying anxiety that is being defended against.

Somatoform Disorders

▶ 13. Describe three kinds of somatoform disorders. What causal factors might be involved?

Somatoform disorders *involve physical complaints or disabilities that suggest a medical problem but that have no known biological cause and are not produced voluntarily by the person* (Finell, 1997). In **hypochondriasis,** *people become unduly alarmed about any physical symptom they detect and are convinced that they have or are about to have a serious illness.* People with **pain disorder** *experience intense pain that either is out of proportion to whatever medical condition they might have or for which no physical basis can be found.* Somatoform disorders differ from *psychophysiological disorders,* in which psychological factors cause or contribute to a real medical condition, such as migraine headaches, asthma, hypertension (chronic high blood pressure), or cardiac problems.

Perhaps the most fascinating of the somatoform disorders is **conversion disorder,** *in which serious neurological symptoms, such as paralysis, loss of sensation, or blindness suddenly occur.* People with conversion disorders often exhibit *la belle indifference,* a strange lack of concern about their symptom and its implications (Pajer, 2000). In some cases, the complaint itself is physiologically impossible. An example is *glove anesthesia,* in which a person loses all sensation below the wrist. As Figure 13.16 shows, the hand is served by nerves that also provide sensory input above the hand, making glove anesthesia anatomically impossible.

Conversion disorders are relatively rare; they occur in about 3 in 1,000 Americans during peacetime (American Psychiatric Association, 1994, 2000), but they occur more frequently under wartime conditions (Slavney, 1990). In some cases, a soldier about to return to the trauma of combat

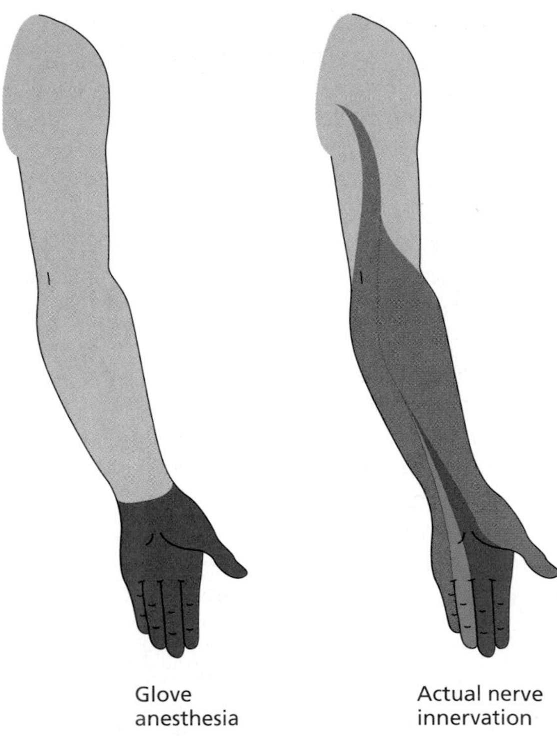

FIGURE 13.16

Glove anesthesia is a conversion disorder in which all feeling is lost below the wrist. The skin areas served by nerves in the arm make this symptom physiologically impossible.

may suddenly develop blindness or paralysis for which no physical cause can be found.

Although *psychogenic blindness* is rare in the general population, researchers have discovered the largest known civilian group of people in the world having trauma-induced blindness. They are Cambodian refugees who escaped from their country and settled in Long Beach, California. These survivors of the "killing fields" of Cambodia were subjected to unspeakable horror at the hands of the Khmer Rouge in the years following the Vietnam War (Cooke, 1991). More than 150 of them became functionally blind, even though their eyes appeared intact and electrophysiological monitoring shows that visual stimuli register in their visual cortex (Figure 13.17). Many of the victims reported that their blindness occurred suddenly after witnessing traumatic scenes of murder. Were the sights from the outer world so painful that the visual system involuntarily shut down? An intriguing but as yet unanswered question is how cultural factors might have affected the development of this response to trauma.

To Freud, such symptoms were a symbolic expression of an underlying conflict that aroused so much anxiety that the ego kept the conflict in the unconscious by converting the anxiety into a physical symptom. In one of Freud's cases, a young woman who was forced to take care of her hostile, verbally abusive, and unappreciative father suddenly developed paralysis in her arm. According to Freud, this occurred when her repressed hostile impulses threatened to break through and cause her to strike him using that arm (Freud, 1935). Contemporary psychodynamic theorists continue to accept explanations consistent with Freud's beliefs (Phillips, 2001).

FIGURE 13.17

A physician examines a Cambodian refugee who appears to be suffering from psychologically induced blindness. There is nothing wrong with his eyes, but he cannot see.

A predisposition to somatoform disorders may involve a combination of biological and psychological vulnerabilities. Somatoform disorders tend to run in families, though it is not clear whether this reflects the role of genetic factors, environmental learning and social reinforcement for bodily symptoms, or both (Trimble, 2003). Additionally, some people may experience internal sensations more vividly than others, or they may focus more attention on them. Somatoform patients are also very suggestible. One study found them to be far more responsive to hypnotic suggestions than were matched controls, and conversion patients' hypnotic susceptibility scores were significantly correlated with the number of conversion symptoms they reported (Roelofs et al., 2002).

The incidence of somatoform disorders tends to be much higher in cultures that discourage open discussion of emotions or that stigmatize psychological disorders (Tanaka-Matsumi & Draguns, 1997). Even within our culture, there are subgroups, such as the police force and military, where open discussion of feelings and self-disclosure of psychological problems are frowned upon. In such settings, somatic symptoms may be the only acceptable outlet for emotional distress. The same may occur in people who are so emotionally constricted that they cannot acknowledge their emotions or communicate them to others verbally (Trae & Deighton, 2000).

Dissociative Disorders

▶ 14. What is the central feature of dissociative disorders? Describe the three major dissociative disorders.

Ordinarily, personality has unity and coherence, and the many facets of the self are integrated so that people act, think, and feel with some degree of consistency. Memory plays a critical role in this integration, for it connects past with present and provides a sense of personal identity that extends over time. **Dissociative disorders** *involve a breakdown of normal personality integration, resulting in significant alterations in memory or identity.* Three forms that such disorders can take are psychogenic amnesia, psychogenic fugue, and dissociative identity disorder.

In **psychogenic amnesia,** *a person responds to a stressful event with extensive but selective memory loss.* Some people can remember nothing about their past. Others can no longer recall specific events, people, or places, although other contents of memory, such as cognitive, language, and motor skills remain intact.

Psychogenic fugue *is a more profound dissociative disorder in which a person loses all sense of personal identity, gives up his or her customary life, wanders to a new faraway location, and establishes a new identity.* Usually the fugue (derived from the Latin word *fugere,* "to flee") is triggered by a highly stressful event or trauma, and it may last from a few hours or days to several years. Some adolescent runaways have been found to be in a fugue state, and married fugue victims may wed someone else and start a new career (Loewenstein, 1991). Typically the fugue ends when the person suddenly recovers his or her original identity and "wakes up," mystified and distressed at being in a strange place under strange circumstances.

Dissociative Identity (Multiple Personality) Disorder

▶ 15. Summarize the trauma-dissociation theory of DID. On what grounds do critics challenge and explain DID?

In **dissociative identity disorder (DID)** (formerly called *multiple personality disorder*), *two or more separate personalities coexist in the same person.* DID is the most striking and widely publicized of the dissociative disorders, and several celebrated cases have been the topic of books and movies, such as *Sybil* and *The Three Faces of Eve* (Figure 13.18). In DID, a primary personality, or *host personality,* appears more often than the others (called *alters*), but each personality has its own integrated set of memories and behaviors. The personalities may or may not know about the existence of the others. They can differ in age, and one can be male, another female. The personalities can differ not only mentally and behaviorally but also physiologically, as in the following case.

FIGURE 13.18

Chris Sizemore, the actual person depicted in the book and movie, The Three Faces of Eve. *This movie and the later production of* Sybil *aroused considerable interest in dissociative identity (multiple personality) disorder and may be partly responsible for a dramatic increase in reported cases.*

> A 38-year-old woman named Margaret was admitted to a hospital with paralysis of her legs following a minor car accident. During the course of her interview the woman, a member of an ultrareligious sect, reported that she sometimes heard a strange voice inside her threatening to "take over completely." The physician suggested that she let the voice "take over." Here is his report of what happened:
>
> The woman closed her eyes, clenched her fists, and grimaced for a few moments during which she was out of contact with those in the room. Suddenly she opened her eyes and one was in the presence of another person. Her name, she said, was "Harriet." Whereas Margaret had been paralyzed, and complained of fatigue, headache, and backache, Harriet felt well and she at once proceeded to walk around the room unaided. She spoke scornfully of Margaret's religiousness, her invalidism, and her puritanical life, professing that she herself liked to drink and "go partying" but that Margaret was always going to church and reading the Bible. . . . At length, at the interviewer's suggestion, Harriet reluctantly agreed to "bring Margaret back" and after more grimacing and fist clenching, Margaret reappeared paralyzed, complaining of her headache and backache, and completely amnesic for the brief period of Harriet's release from her prison. (Nemiah, 1978, pp. 179–180)

Mental health workers have frequently reported dramatic physical differences among the alternate personalities of DID patients. The differences include physical health differences, voice changes, and even changes in right- and left-handedness. Some patients had severe allergies when one personality was present but no allergies when the others were active. One patient nearly died of a violent allergic reaction to a bee sting; a week later, when an alternate personality was active, another sting produced no reaction. Female patients frequently have different menstrual cycles for each female personality; one patient had three periods per month. Other patients need eyeglasses with different prescriptions for different personalities; one may be farsighted, another nearsighted (Miller et al., 1991). Epileptic patients with DID often have their seizures in one personality but not another (Drake et al., 1988).

What Causes DID?

According to **trauma-dissociation theory,** *the development of new personalities occurs in response to severe stress.* For the vast majority of patients, this begins to occur in early childhood, frequently in response to physical or sexual abuse. Frank Putnam (1989) studied the life histories of 100 diagnosed DID cases and found that 97 of them reported severe abuse and trauma in early and middle childhood, a time when children's identities are not well established and it is quite easy for them to dissociate. Putnam believes that in response to the trauma and their helplessness to resist it, children may engage in something akin to self-hypnosis and dissociate from reality. They create a new alternate identity to detach themselves from the trauma, to transfer what is happening to someone else who can handle it, and to blunt the pain. Over time, it is theorized, the protective functions served by the new personality remain separate in the form of an alternate personality rather than being integrated into the host personality (Meyer & Osborne, 1987; Putnam, 2000).

DID has become a controversial topic, and some critics question its very existence (Beahrs, 1994; Spanos, 1994). They wonder if DID is, in reality, a therapist-produced phenomenon. They point out that prior to 1970, only about 100 cases had been reported worldwide. Even today, DID is virtually unknown in many cultures, including Japan (Takahashi, 1990). But after the disorder was highly publicized in popular books and movies therapists began to report many additional cases until they numbered in the tens of thousands by the mid-1990s. The number of alternate personalities also increased from 2 or 3 to an average of about 15 (Spanos, 1994). Could this dramatic increase in the prevalence of DID and number of alters be the result of publicity and therapist expectations?

Some critics of DID believe that many features of the cases, including the memories of previous abuse and the multiple personalities themselves, could result from suggestions unintentionally implanted by overzealous therapists. The widespread use of hypnosis in treatment only adds to the danger of a therapist-induced clinical picture that is based on susceptibility to suggestion. In some instances, clients have filed lawsuits against therapists, charging them with creating the disorder in them. In one case, a Wisconsin woman and her insurance company successfully sued a psychiatrist who used hypnosis to allegedly unearth 120 different personalities in her, including Satan and a duck. The woman charged the therapist with implanting false memories of sexual abuse, rape, being pushed into an open grave, and aborting a baby. She maintained that she had never had any of those memories before beginning therapy and that the false memories caused nightmares, flashbacks, suicidal impulses, and, eventually, the need for hospitalization (Associated Press, December 12, 1997). As we noted in our discussion of hypnosis in Chapter 5, people can become so immersed in an imagined role that it becomes quite real to them, and they act accordingly (Spanos, 1996). The controversy that swirls around DID is inspiring research that may advance our understanding of factors that can produce alterations in memory, physiological responses, and behavior.

What Do You Think?

IS DID DISSOCIATION OR ROLE PLAYING?

Suppose you knew of several experimental studies that convincingly demonstrated that average people could, by means of role playing, produce all of the DID phenomena described in this section. What would this tell you about the validity of the dissociation cases described by mental health workers? Think about it, then see the discussion on page 549.

IN REVIEW

- *Somatoform disorders involve physical complaints that do not have a physiological explanation. They include hypochondriasis, pain disorders, and conversion disorders in which a physical symptom or disability occurs in the absence of physical pathology.*
- *Familial similarities in somatoform disorders may have a biological basis, or they may be the result of environmental shaping through attention and sympathy. Somatoform patients may be highly vigilant and reactive to somatic symptoms. Such disorders tend to occur with greater frequency in cultures that discourage open expression of negative emotions.*
- *Dissociative disorders involve losses of memory and personal identity. The major dissociative disorders are psychogenic amnesia, psychogenic fugue, and dissociative identity disorder (DID).*
- *The trauma-dissociation theory holds that DID emerges when children dissociate to defend themselves from severe physical or sexual abuse. This model has been challenged by other theorists who believe that multiple personalities result from role immersion and therapist suggestion.*

MOOD (AFFECTIVE) DISORDERS

Another set of emotion-based disorders are **mood disorders,** *which involve depression and mania (excessive excitement).* Together with anxiety disorders, mood disorders are the most frequently experienced psychological disorders. About half

▶ 16. Describe the four classes of symptoms that characterize (a) depression, and (b) mania. What sex differences exist?

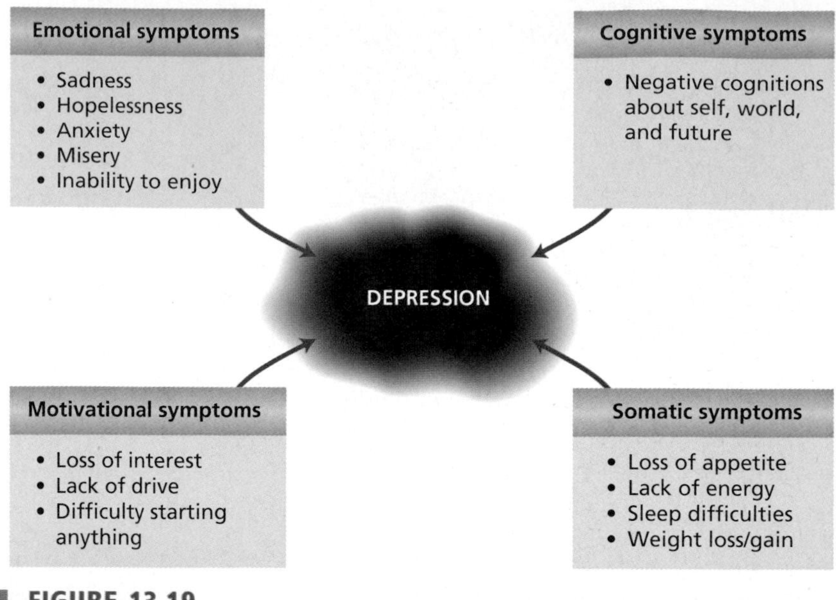

FIGURE 13.19

Depression includes emotional, cognitive, motivational, and somatic features.

of all depressed people also experience an anxiety disorder.

Depression

Almost everyone has experienced depression, at least in its milder and more temporary forms. Loss and pain are inevitable parts of life, and when they occur, most of us feel blue, sad, discouraged, apathetic, and passive. The future looks bleak, and some of the zest goes out of living. Such reactions are normal; at any point in time, 25 to 30 percent of college undergraduates experience mild depression (Seligman, 1991). These feelings usually fade away after the event has passed or as the person becomes accustomed to the new situation. In clinical depression, however, the frequency, intensity, and duration of depressive symptoms are out of proportion to the person's life situation. Some people may respond to a minor setback or loss with **major depression,** *an intense depressed state that leaves them unable to function effectively in their lives.* Mark, the young man described at the beginning of the chapter, suffers from a major depression. Other people exhibit **dysthymia,** *a less intense form of depression that has less dramatic effects on personal and occupational functioning.* Dysthymia is, however, a more chronic and long-lasting form of misery, occurring for years on end with some intervals of normal mood that never last more than a few weeks or months.

Although depression is primarily a disorder of mood, there are three other types of symptoms: cognitive symptoms, motivational symptoms, and somatic (physical) symptoms (Figure 13.19).

The *negative mood state* is the core feature of depression. When depressed people are asked how they feel, they most commonly report sadness, misery, and loneliness. Whereas people with anxiety disorders retain their capacity to experience pleasure, depressed people lose it (Mineka et al., 1998). Activities that used to bring satisfaction and happiness feel dull and flat. Even biological pleasures, such as eating and sex, lose their appeal.

Cognitive symptoms are also a central part of depression. Depressed people have difficulty concentrating and making decisions. They usually have low self-esteem, believing that they are inferior, inadequate, and incompetent. When setbacks occur in their lives, depressed people tend to blame themselves; when failure has not yet occurred, they expect that it will and that it will be caused by their own inadequacies. Depressed people almost always view the future with great pessimism and hopelessness (Clark et al., 1999).

Motivational symptoms in depression involve an inability to get started and to perform behaviors that might produce pleasure or accomplishment. A depressed student may be unable to get out of bed in the morning, let alone go to class or study. Everything seems too much of an effort. In extreme depressive reactions, the person may have to be prodded out of bed, clothed, and fed. In some cases of severe depression, the person's movements slow down and she or he walks or talks slowly and with excruciating effort.

Somatic (bodily) *symptoms* often include loss of appetite and weight loss in moderate and severe depression, whereas in mild depression, weight gain sometimes occurs as a person eats compulsively. Sleep disturbances, particularly insomnia, are common. Sleep disturbance and weight loss lead to fatigue and weakness, which tend to add to the depressed feelings. Depressed people also may lose sexual desire and responsiveness.

Bipolar Disorder

When a person experiences only depression, the disorder is called *unipolar depression.* In a **bipolar disorder,** *depression (which is usually the dominant state) alternates with periods of* **mania,** *a state of highly excited mood and behavior that is quite the opposite of depression.* In a manic state, mood is euphoric and cognitions are grandiose. The person sees no limits to what he or she can accomplish and fails to consider negative consequences that may ensue if grandiose plans are acted upon. At a motivational level, manic behavior is hyperactive. The manic person engages in frenetic activity, be it in work, in sexual relationships, or elsewhere. The 19th-century composer Robert Schumann produced 27 works during one manic year, but his productivity ground to a halt when he sank back into the depressive phase of his bipolar disorder (Jamison, 1995). Manic people can become very irritable when their momentary goals are frustrated in any way.

In a manic state, speech is often rapid or pressured, as if the person must say as many words as possible in the time allotted. With all this flurry of activity comes a greatly lessened need for sleep. A person may go for several days without sleeping, until exhaustion inevitably sets in and the mania slows down. The following case illustrates a severe manic episode:

> Robert B, a 56-year-old dentist, awoke one morning with the idea that he was the most gifted dental surgeon in his tri-state area; his mission then was to provide service for as many persons as possible so that they could benefit from his talents. Consequently, he decided to enlarge his 2-chair practice to a 20-chair one, and his plan was to reconstruct his two dental offices into 20 booths so that he could simultaneously attend to as many patients. That very day he drew up the plans for this arrangement and telephoned a number of remodelers and invited them to submit bids for the work.
>
> Toward the end of that day he became irritated with the "interminable delays" and, after he attended to his last patient, rolled up his sleeves and began to knock down the walls of his dental offices. When he discovered that he couldn't manage this chore with the sledge hammer he had purchased for this purpose earlier, he became frustrated and proceeded to smash his more destructible tools, washbasins, and X-ray equipment. He justified this behavior in his own mind by saying, "This junk is not suitable for the likes of me; it'll have to be replaced anyway."
>
> He was in perpetual motion and his speech was "overexcited." When Robert was later admitted to a hospital, he could not sit in his chair; instead he paced the office floor like a caged animal. (Kleinmuntz, 1980, pp. 309–310)

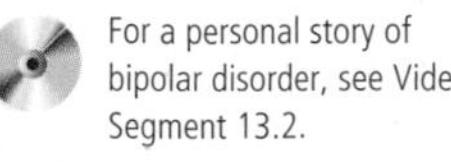
For a personal story of bipolar disorder, see Video Segment 13.2.

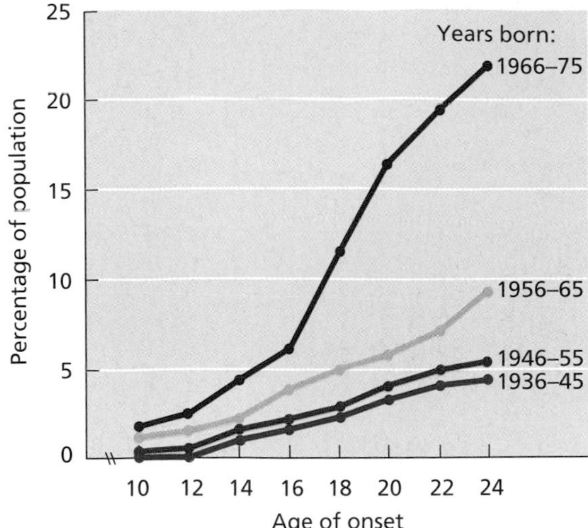

FIGURE 13.20

Depression rates in the United States have increased every decade from the 1930s to the 1990s.
SOURCE: U.S. Department of Health and Human Services, 2002.

Prevalence and Course of Mood Disorders

Epidemiological studies in the United States suggest that at this moment, about 1 in 20 Americans is severely depressed (Narrow et al., 2002). Statistically, the chances are nearly 1 in 5 that an American will have a depressive episode of clinical proportions at least once in his or her lifetime. No age group is exempt from depression. It appears in infants as young as 6 months who have been separated from their mothers for prolonged periods. The rate of depressive symptoms in children and adolescents is as high as the adult rate (Essau & Petermann, 1999).

Data from numerous studies indicate that depression is on the rise in young groups, with the onset of depression increasing dramatically in 15- to 19-year-olds (Burke et al., 1991). Figure 13.20 shows that the lifetime prevalence of major depression in the United States has increased in every decade since the 1930s, and the steepness of the curve indicates an earlier onset in those born after 1966.

Prevalence of depressive disorders is similar across socioeconomic and ethnic groups, but there is a major sex difference in our culture. Although men and women do not differ in prevalence of bipolar disorder, women appear to be about twice as likely as men to suffer unipolar depression

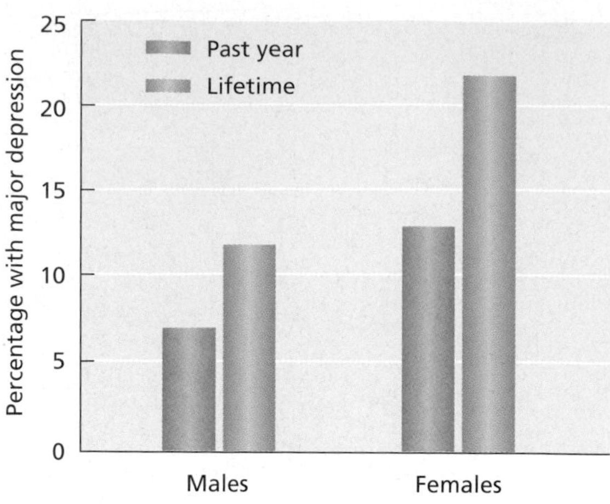

FIGURE 13.21

Prevalence rates for major depression in men and women. SOURCE: Based on Kessler et al., 1994.

(Figure 13.21). Women are most likely to suffer their first episode of depression in their 20s; men, in their 40s. Biological theories suggest that genetic factors, biochemical differences in the nervous system, or the premenstrual depression that many women experience may increase vulnerability to depressive disorders (Donaldson, 1998). Environmental theories focus on possible cultural causes. One environmentally based suggestion is that the traditional sex role expectation for women in Western cultures is to be passive and dependent in the face of stress or loss and to focus on their feelings, whereas men are more likely to distract themselves through physical activity and drinking (Nolen-Hoeksema, 1990).

Many people who suffer depressive episodes never seek treatment. What is likely to happen to such people? Perhaps the one positive thing that can be said about depression is that it usually dissipates over time. After the initial episode, which typically comes on suddenly after a stressful experience, depression typically lasts an average of 5 to 10 months when untreated (Tollefson, 1993).

Once a depressive episode has occurred, one of three patterns may follow. In perhaps 40 percent of all cases, clinical depression will not recur following recovery. Many other cases show a second pattern: recovery with recurrence. On average, these people will remain symptom-free for perhaps 3 years before experiencing another depressive episode of about the same severity and duration. The time interval between subsequent episodes of depression tends to become shorter over the years (Rubin, 2000). Finally, about 10 percent of people who have a major depressive episode will not recover and will remain chronically depressed (Figure 13.22).

Manic episodes, though less common than depressive reactions, are far more likely to recur. Fewer than 1 percent of the population experiences mania, but more than 90 percent of those who do have a recurrence (American Psychiatric Association, 2000; Kessler et al., 1994).

▶ 17. What evidence exists for genetic and biochemical factors in depression and mania?

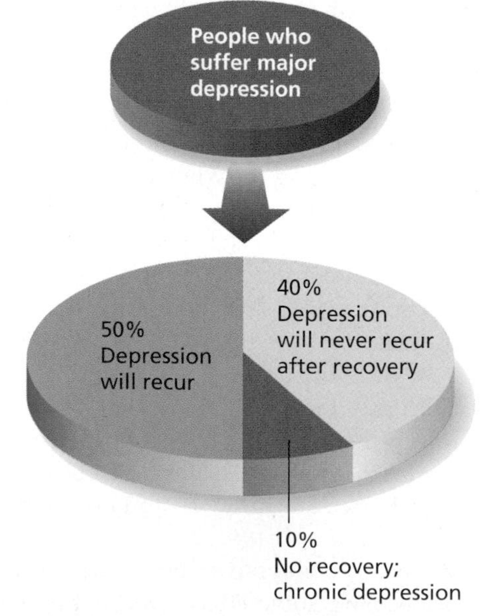

FIGURE 13.22

Course of outcome following a major depressive episode. About 40 percent never have a recurrence, perhaps 50 percent have a recurrence, and about 10 percent suffer chronic (ever-present) depression.

Causal Factors in Mood Disorders

Biological Factors

Both genetic and neurochemical factors have been linked to depression (Donaldson, 1998). Genetic factors surface in both twin and adoption studies. Identical twins have a concordance rate of about 67 percent for experiencing clinical depression, compared with a rate of only 15 percent for fraternal twins (Gershon et al., 1989). Among adopted people who develop depression, biological relatives are about 8 times more likely than adoptive relatives to also suffer from depression (Wender et al., 1986). What is likely inherited is a predisposition to develop a depressive disorder, given certain kinds of environmental factors such as significant losses and low social support (Barondes, 1999).

Increasingly, biological research has focused on the possible role of brain chemistry in depression. One influential theory holds that depression is a disorder of motivation caused by underactivity in a family of neurotransmitters that include norepinephrine, dopamine, and serotonin (Davidson,

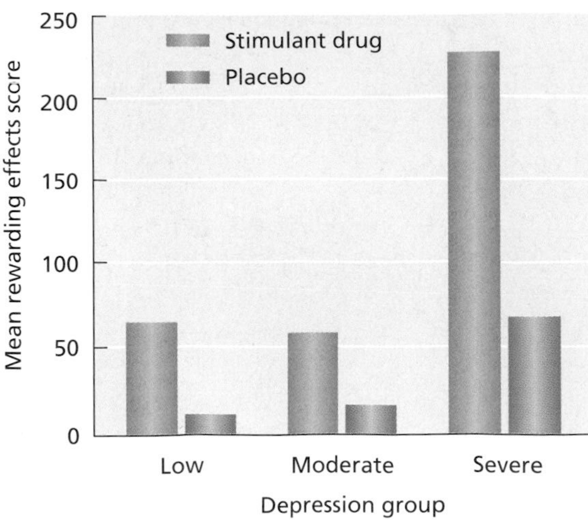

FIGURE 13.23

Increase in pleasure ratings produced by a stimulant drug or a placebo in nondepressed, moderately depressed, and severely depressed males and females. The magnitude of the increase in pleasure reported by severely depressed people suggests a normally underactive reward system in the brain. Source: Adapted from Tremblay et al., 2002.

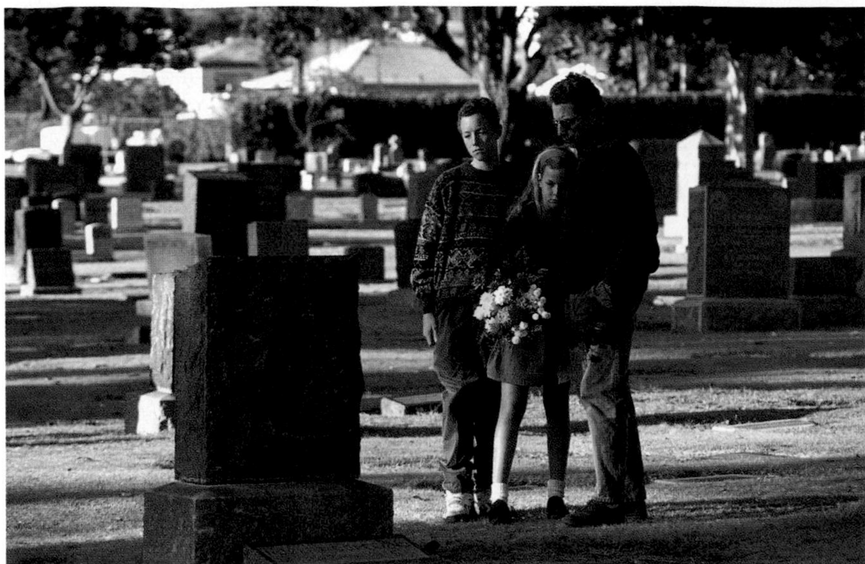

FIGURE 13.24

Psychoanalysts believe that early catastrophic losses increase vulnerability to later depressive disorders.

1998). These transmitters play important roles in several brain regions involved in experiencing reward and pleasure. When neural transmission decreases in these brain regions, the result is the lack of pleasure and loss of motivation that characterize depression (Donaldson, 1998; White & Milner, 1992). Also in support of this theory, several highly effective antidepressant drugs operate by increasing the activity of these neurotransmitters, thereby further stimulating the neural systems that underlie positive mood and goal-directed behavior. A study by Lescia Tremblay and coworkers (2002) tested the amount of reward experienced by depressed patients when these centers were activated by a stimulant drug, reasoning that an enhanced pleasure response would reflect a normally underactive reward system. As shown in Figure 13.23, severely depressed individuals showed a much stronger pleasure response to the drug, supporting the hypothesis of a "pleasure deficit" in the brain.

Bipolar disorder, in which depression alternates with less frequent periods of mania, has been studied primarily at the biological level because it appears to have a stronger genetic basis than does unipolar depression (Young & Joffe, 1997). Among both men and women, the lifetime risk of developing a bipolar disorder is just below 1 percent. Yet about 50 percent of patients with bipolar disorder have a parent, grandparent, or child with the disorder (Barondes, 1999; Rubin, 2000). The concordance rate for bipolar disorder is 5 times higher in identical twins than in fraternal twins, suggesting a genetic link.

Manic disorders may stem from an overproduction of the same neurotransmitters that are underactive in depression. This might explain the symptom picture that is quite the opposite of that seen in depression. Significantly, lithium chloride, the drug most frequently used to calm manic disorders, works by decreasing the activity of these transmitters in the brain's motivational/pleasure activation system (LeMoal, 1999; Robinson, 1997).

Psychological Factors

Biological factors seem to increase vulnerability to certain types of psychological and environmental events that can then trigger the disorders. Other perspectives specify what those events might be.

Personality-Based Vulnerability Psychoanalysts Karl Abraham (1911) and Sigmund Freud (1917/1957) believed that early traumatic losses or rejections create vulnerability for later depression by triggering a grieving and rage process that becomes part of the individual's personality (Figure 13.24). Subsequent losses and rejection reactivate the original loss and cause a reaction not only to the current event but also to the unresolved loss from the past.

Were he alive today, Freud would surely point to research by the British sociologists

George Brown and Terrill Harris (1978) to support his theory of early loss. Brown and Harris interviewed women in London and found that the rate of depression among women who had lost their mothers before age 11 and who had also experienced a severe recent loss was almost 3 times higher than the rate of depression among women who had experienced a similar recent loss but had not lost their mothers before age 11. Other research has shown that experiencing the death of a father while a young child is also associated with a greatly increased risk of later depression (Barnes & Prosen, 1985; Bowlby, 2000).

The humanistic perspective also addresses causes of depression. In attempting to explain the dramatic increase in depression among people born after 1960, Martin Seligman (1989) has suggested that the "me" generation, with its overemphasis on individuality and personal control, has sown the seeds for its own depression. Because people define their self-worth in terms of individual attainment and have fewer commitments to traditional values of family, religion, and the common good, they are likely to react much more strongly to failures, to view negative events as reflecting their own inadequacies, and to experience a sense of meaninglessness in their lives.

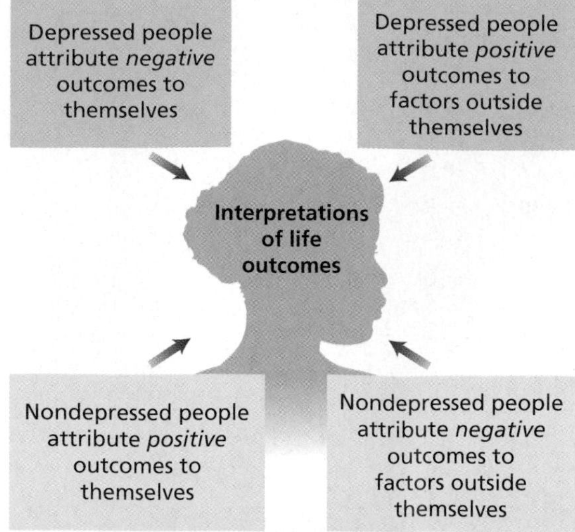
Depressive attributional pattern
Depressed people attribute *negative* outcomes to themselves
Depressed people attribute *positive* outcomes to factors outside themselves
Interpretations of life outcomes
Nondepressed people attribute *positive* outcomes to themselves
Nondepressed people attribute *negative* outcomes to factors outside themselves
Self-enhancement attributional pattern (nondepressed people)

FIGURE 13.25

Cognitive theorists believe that the attributional patterns of depressed people are the opposite of the self-enhancing patterns that characterize nondepressed people. In the depressive attributional pattern, people attribute negative outcomes to themselves and positive outcomes to factors outside themselves.

▶ 18. Relate the cognitive triad, the depressive attributional pattern, and learned helplessness to depression.

Cognitive Processes According to Aaron Beck (1976), depressed people victimize themselves through their own beliefs that they are defective, worthless, and inadequate. They also believe that whatever happens to them is bad and that negative things will continue happening because of their personal defects (Clark et al., 1989). This **depressive cognitive triad** *of negative thoughts concerning (1) the world, (2) oneself, and (3) the future* seems to pop into consciousness automatically, and many depressed people report that they cannot control or suppress the negative thoughts (Wenzlaff et al., 1988). Depressed people also tend to recall most of their failures and few of their successes, and they tend to focus much of their attention on their perceived inadequacies (Clark et al., 1999; Haaga et al., 1991). Such thoughts can trigger depressed affect.

As noted in the discussion of self-enhancement tendencies in Chapter 11, most people tend to take personal credit for the good outcomes in their lives and to blame their misfortunes on factors outside themselves, thereby maintaining and enhancing their self-esteem. According to Beck, depressed people do exactly the opposite: They exhibit a **depressive attributional pattern,** *attributing successes or other positive events to factors outside the self while attributing negative outcomes to personal factors* (Figure 13.25). Beck believes that taking no credit for successes but blaming themselves for failures helps depressed people maintain low self-esteem and their belief that they are worthless failures. Quite literally, they can't win, even when they do!

Another prominent cognitive account of depression, **learned helplessness theory,** *holds that depression occurs when people expect that bad events will occur and that there is nothing they can do to prevent or cope with them* (Abramson et al., 1978; Seligman & Isaacowitz, 2000). The depressive attributional pattern plays a central role in the learned helplessness model, but learned helplessness theorists take it a step further by specifying what the negative attributions for failures are like. They suggest that chronic and intense depression occurs as the result of negative attributions for failures that are personal ("It's all *my* fault"), stable ("I'll *always* be this way"), and global ("I'm a *total* loser"). Thus people who attribute negative events in their lives to factors such as low intelligence, physical repulsiveness, or an unlovable personality tend to believe that their personal defects will render them helpless to avoid negative events in the future, and their sense of hopelessness places them at significantly greater risk for depression.

Learning and Environmental Factors The behavioral perspective also has important things to say about depression. Peter Lewinsohn and his colleagues (1985) believe that depression is usually triggered by a loss, some other punishing event, or by a drastic decrease in the amount of positive reinforcement that the person receives from her or his environment. As the depression begins to take hold, people stop performing behaviors that previously provided reinforcement, such as hobbies and socializing. Moreover, depressed people tend to make others feel anxious, depressed, and hostile (Joiner & Coyne, 1999). Eventually, these other people begin to lose patience, failing to understand why the person doesn't "snap out of it." This diminishes social support still further and may eventually cause depressed people to be abandoned by those who are most important to them (Nezlek et al., 2000). Figure 13.26 shows the cyclical course of depression.

Behavioral theorists believe that to begin feeling better, depressed people must break this vicious cycle by initially forcing themselves to engage in behaviors that are likely to produce some degree of pleasure. Eventually, positive reinforcement produced by this process of *behavioral activation* will begin to counteract the depressive affect, undermine the sense of hopelessness that characterizes depression, and increase feelings of personal control over the environment.

Environmental factors may also help explain why depression tends to run in families. Constance Hammen (1991) studied the family histories of depressed people and concluded that children of depressed parents often experience poor parenting and many stressful experiences as they grow up. As a result, they may fail to develop good coping skills and a positive self-concept, making them more vulnerable later in life to stressful events that can trigger depressive reactions. This conclusion is supported by findings that children of depressed parents exhibit a significantly higher incidence of depression and other disorders as adolescents and young adults (Lieb et al., 2002).

Sociocultural Factors

Although depression exists in virtually all cultures, its prevalence, symptom pattern, and causes reflect cultural variation (Lopez & Guarnaccia, 2000). For example, the prevalence of depressive disorders is far lower in Hong Kong and Taiwan than in Western nations. People in these societies tend to have strong social support from family and other groups, which helps reduce the negative impact of loss and disappointments when they occur (Tseng et al., 1990).

▶ 19. How does Lewinsohn's learning theory explain the spiraling course downward that occurs in depression?

Cultural factors also can affect the ways in which depression is manifested. Feelings of guilt and personal inadequacy seem to predominate in North American and western European countries, whereas somatic symptoms of fatigue, loss of appetite, and sleep difficulties are more often reported in Latin, Chinese, and African cultures (Manson, 1994).

Finally, cultural factors may influence who develops depression. As noted earlier, women are about twice as likely as men to report feeling depressed in technologically advanced countries such as Canada, the United States, and other Western nations. Yet this sex difference is not found in developing countries (Culbertson, 1997; Nolen-Hoeksema, 1990). At present, we do not know why this pattern occurs, but attempts are underway to learn more about how the cultural environment influences the development of depression.

At one time or another, many depressed people consider suicide as a way to escape from the unhappiness of their lives. We now examine suicide, its causes, and what can be done to prevent this tragic event.

▶ 20. How are cultural factors related to prevalence, manifestations, and sex differences in depression?

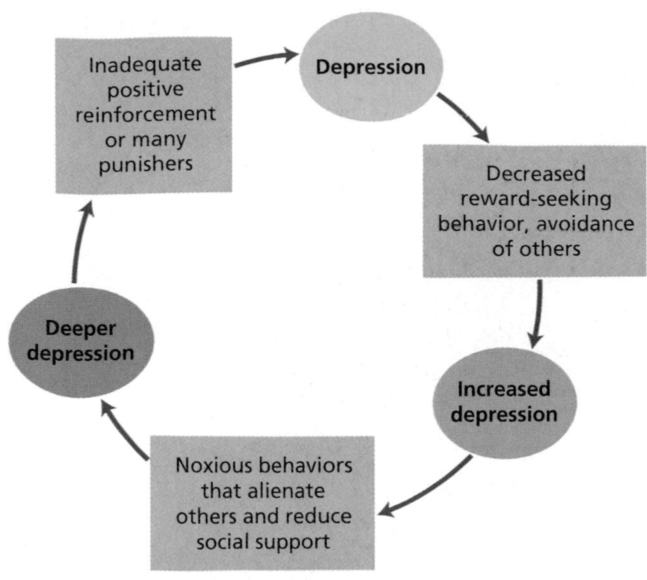

FIGURE 13.26

Lewinsohn's behavioral model of depression focuses on the environmental causes and effects of depression. Depression results from loss of positive reinforcement and produces further declines in reinforcement and social support in a vicious-cycle fashion.

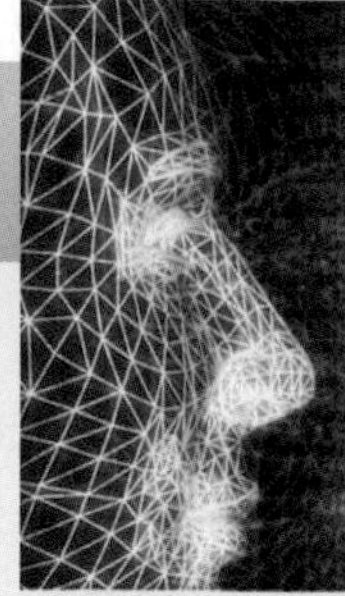

APPLYING PSYCHOLOGICAL SCIENCE

UNDERSTANDING AND PREVENTING SUICIDE

Suicide *is the willful taking of one's own life.* The World Health Organization estimates that worldwide, nearly 500,000 people commit suicide each year—nearly 1 per minute. Ten times that number engage in nonfatal suicide attempts. In the United States, suicide is the second most frequent cause of death (after accidents) among high school and college students, and suicide rates among 15- to 24-year-olds have tripled since 1960 (Figure 13.27; National Center for Health Statistics, 1995). More suicides (31,000) than homicides (23,000) occur in the United States each year (Centers for Disease Control [CDC], 2002).

Women attempt suicide about 3 times more often than men, but men are 3 times more likely to actually kill themselves. These differences may be due to (1) a higher incidence of depression in women and (2) men's choice of more lethal methods, such as shooting themselves or jumping off buildings. The suicide rate for both men and women is higher among those who have been divorced or widowed. Women's suicides are more likely to be triggered by failures in love relationships, whereas career failure more often prompts men's suicides (Shneidman, 1976). A history of sexual or physical abuse significantly increases the likelihood of later suicide attempts (Garnefski & Arends, 1998).

Depression is one of the strongest predictors of suicide. About 15 percent of clinically depressed individuals will eventually kill themselves, a rate that is 22 to 36 times higher than the suicide rate for the general population. An estimated 80 percent of suicidal people are significantly depressed. It is noteworthy, however, that suicides do not usually occur when depression is deepest. Instead, suicide often occurs unexpectedly as a depressed person seems to be emerging from depression and feeling better. The lifting of depression may provide the energy needed to complete the suicidal act but not reduce the person's underlying sense of hopelessness and despair.

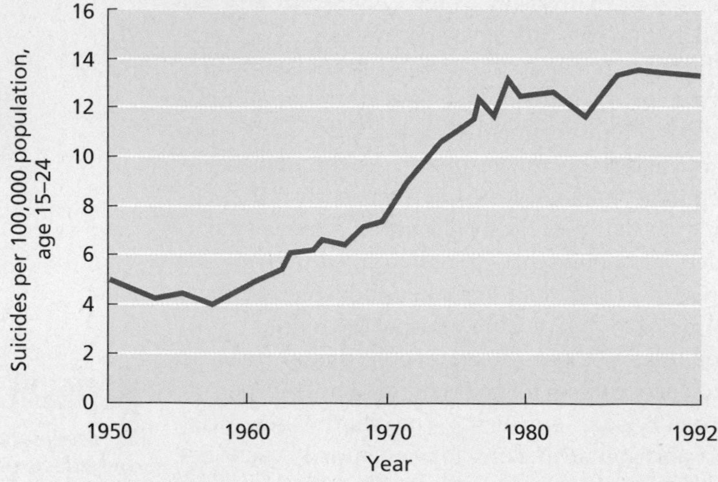

FIGURE 13.27

The rising suicide rate in young people. This graph illustrates the suicide rate per 100,000 persons age 15 to 24, from 1950 to 1992.
SOURCE: Based on National Center for Health Statistics, 1995.

Motives for Suicide

There appear to be two fundamental motivations for suicide: the desire to end one's life and the desire to manipulate and coerce other people into doing what the suicidal person wants (Beck et al., 1979). Those who wish to end their lives have basically given up. They see no other way to deal with intolerable emotional distress, and in death they see an end to their problems. In one study, 56 percent of suicide attempts were classified as having been motivated by the desire to die (Beck, 1976). These attempts were accompanied by high levels of depression and hopelessness, and they tended to be more lethal than other suicide attempts. In some instances, a suicide decision is based on a desire to stop being a burden to others.

The second primary motivation for suicide is manipulation of others. Many *parasuicides* (suicide attempts that do not end in death) are cries for help or attempts to coerce people to meet one's needs. Trying to prevent a lover from ending a relationship, induce guilt in others, or dramatize one's suffering are manipulative motives. Manipulative suicide attempters tend to use less lethal means (such as drug overdoses or wrist slashing) and to make sure help is available. In the study cited earlier (Beck, 1976), 13 percent of the suicide attempts were classified as manipulative. The remaining 31 percent combined the two types of motivation. A small minority of suicides result from altruistic decisions to sacrifice one's life for the survival of others: examples include the soldier who dives on a hand grenade to save his comrades' lives or the mother who elects to give birth rather than aborting her baby, knowing that she will die in the process.

Warning Signs for Suicide

The best predictor of suicide attempts in both men and women is a verbal or behavioral threat to commit suicide, and such threats should always be taken seriously. One of the most destructive myths about suicide is that people who talk openly about suicide are just seeking attention and don't actually intend to carry out the act. Yet research shows that a high proportion of suicide attempts—perhaps 80 percent—are preceded by some kind of warning (Bagley & Ramsay, 1997). Sometimes the warning is an explicit statement of intent, such as "I don't want to go on living" or "I won't be a burden much longer." Other times, the warnings are more subtle, as when a person expresses hopelessness about the future, withdraws from others or from favorite activities, gives away treasured possessions, or takes unusual risks. Other important risk factors are a history of previous suicide attempts and a detailed plan that involves a lethal method (Chiles & Strossahl, 1995; Shneidman, 1998).

Suicide Prevention: What You Can Do

Scientific research has taught us much about the dynamics and prevention of suicide. These findings provide guidelines for preventing this tragic answer to life's problems. Here are some guidelines for helping potentially suicidal people:

1. Another myth about suicide is that broaching the topic with a potentially suicidal person may prompt the person to carry out the act. In truth, the best first step if you suspect that someone may be suicidal is to ask the person directly whether he or she is considering suicide: "Have you thought about hurting yourself or ending your life?" If the person responds affirmatively, try to find out if he or she has a plan or a timetable in mind. Do not be hesitant to approach the person. *Diffusion of responsibility* (discussed in Chapters 2 and 15) could result in your assuming that someone else is helping a potentially suicidal person when in fact no one is (Goldsmith, 2003). Your ultimate goal should be to help the person receive assistance from a qualified professional as soon as possible, not to treat the person yourself. Nonetheless, you can take some immediate steps that may be helpful.
2. Many suicidal people feel alone in their misery. It is important to provide social support and empathy at this critical juncture. An expression of genuine concern can pave the way for other potentially helpful interventions (Barnett & Porter, 1998). For example, a frank discussion of the problem that is foremost in the person's life can be helpful. Suicidal people often feel totally overwhelmed by life, and focusing on a specific problem may help the person realize that it is not unsolvable and need not cloud his or her total perception of life.
3. When people are distressed and hopeless, their time orientation tends to narrow, and they have difficulty seeing beyond their current distress. Try to help the person see his or her present situation within a wider time perspective and to consider positive possibilities that might exist in the future. In particular, discuss reasons for continuing to live and focus on any doubts the person might have about electing suicide. For example, if the person indicates that his or her family will suffer greatly from the suicide, adopt this as one of your arguments for finding a different solution to the problem. Many suicidal people would like to feel that they do not have to commit suicide. Capitalize on such feelings.
5. If a person is suicidal, stay with him or her and seek professional assistance. Most cities have suicide-prevention centers that offer 24-hour services, including telephone and direct counseling. These centers are usually listed under *suicide* or *crisis* in the phone book.

▶ 21. What are the major motives and risk factors for suicide? Provide five guidelines for helping a suicidal person.

What Do You Think?

ADVOCATING SUICIDE EDUCATION

You are a student senator at a university whose counseling center has proposed a campuswide suicide education program. You favor adding the program because you believe it will decrease the risk of suicide among students, even though your school has not had any suicides in several years. Other campus officers and administrators are opposed to instituting the program. What might their concerns be, and how would you counter them? Think about it, then see the discussion on page 549.

IN REVIEW

- *Mood disorders include several depressive disorders and bipolar disorder, in which intermittent periods of mania (intense mood and behavior activation) occur. Depression has four sets of symptoms: emotional, cognitive, motivational, and somatic. The symptoms of negative emotions and thoughts, loss of motivation, and behavioral slowness are reversed in mania.*

- *Both genetic and neurochemical factors have been linked to depression. One prominent biochemical theory links depression to an underactivity of neurotransmitters (norepinephrine, dopamine, and serotonin) that activate brain areas involved in pleasure and positive motivation. Drugs that relieve depression increase the activity of these transmitters. Bipolar disorder seems to have an even stronger genetic component than unipolar depression does.*
- *Psychoanalytic theorists view depression as a long-term consequence of traumatic losses and rejections early in life that create a personality vulnerability pattern.*
- *Cognitive theorists emphasize the role of negative beliefs about the self, the world, and the future (the depressive triad) and describe a depressive attributional pattern in which negative outcomes are attributed to personal causes and successes to situational causes. Seligman's theory of learned helplessness suggests that attributing negative outcomes to personal, stable, and global causes fosters depression.*
- *The behavioral approach focuses on the vicious cycle in which depression-induced inactivity and aversive behaviors reduce reinforcement from the environment and thereby increase depression still further.*
- *Manipulation and a desire to escape distress are the two major motives for suicide. The risk for suicide increases if the person is depressed and has a lethal plan and a past history of parasuicide.*

SCHIZOPHRENIA

▶ 22. What is meant by the term schizophrenia? What are its major cognitive, behavioral, emotional, and perceptual features?

Of all the psychological disorders, schizophrenia is the most bizzarre and, in many ways, the most puzzling. It is also one of the most challenging disorders to treat effectively (Hogarty, 2003). Despite many theories of schizophrenia and thousands of research studies, a complete understanding of this disorder continues to elude us.

Schizophrenia *includes severe disturbances in thinking, speech, perception, emotion, and behavior* (Herz & Marder, 2002). The term *schizophrenia* was introduced by the Swiss psychiatrist Eugen Bleuler in 1911. Literally, the term means "split mind," which has often led people to confuse schizophrenia with dissociative identity disorder ("split personality") or with a Dr. Jekyll–Mr. Hyde phenomenon. But multiple personalities are not what Bleuler had in mind when he coined the term. Instead, Bleuler intended to suggest that certain psychological functions, such as thought, language, and emotion, which are joined together in normal people, are somehow split apart or disconnected in schizophrenia.

Characteristics of Schizophrenia

A diagnosis of schizophrenia requires evidence that a person misinterprets reality and exhibits disordered attention, thought, or perception. In addition, she or he typically withdraws from social interactions, communicates in strange or inappropriate ways, neglects personal grooming, and behaves in a disorganized fashion (American Psychiatric Association, 1994, 2000).

The schizophrenic thought disorder sometimes entails delusions. **Delusions** *are false beliefs that are sustained in the face of evidence that normally would be sufficient to destroy them.* A schizophrenic person may believe that his brain is being turned to glass by ray guns operated by his enemies from outer space (a *delusion of persecution*) or that Jesus Christ is one of his special agents (a *delusion of grandeur*).

Several aspects of the thought disorder were described by a schizophrenic patient during a period of recovery:

> The most wearing aspect of schizophrenia is the fierce battle that goes on inside my head in which conflicts become unresolvable. I am so ambivalent that my mind can divide on a subject, and those two parts subdivide over and over until my mind feels like it is in pieces, and I am totally disorganized. At other times, I feel like I am trapped inside my head, banging against its walls, trying desperately to escape while my lips can utter only nonsense. (*New York Times,* March 18, 1986, p. C12)

Perceptual disorganization and disordered thought become more pronounced as people progress into a schizophrenic condition (McKenna & Oh, 2003). What the world might come to look like from inside the schizophrenic mind is illustrated in art created by schizophrenic patients during periods of disturbance (Figure 13.28). Some experience **hallucinations,** *false perceptions that have a compelling sense of reality.* Auditory hallucinations (typically voices speaking to the patient) are most common, although visual and tactile hallucinations may also occur. This person describes his hallucinations:

FIGURE 13.28

These pictures, drawn by patients diagnosed with schizophrenia, may offer insights into the subjective world of individuals afflicted with this disorder.

> Recently, my mind has played tricks on me, creating The People inside my head who sometimes come out to haunt me and torment me. They surround me in rooms, hide behind trees and under the snow outside. They taunt me and scream at me and devise plans to break my spirit. The voices come and go, but The People are always there, always real. (*New York Times*, March 18, 1986, p. C12)

The language of people with schizophrenia is often disorganized and may contain strange words.

> I am here from a foreign university . . . and you have to have a "plausity" of all acts of amendment to go through for the children's code . . . and it is no mental disturbance or "putenance" . . . it is an "amorition" law . . . it is like their "privatilinia." (Vetter, 1969, p. 189)

Patients' language sometimes contains word associations that are based on rhymes or other associations rather than meaning. Consider the following conversation between a psychologist and a hospitalized schizophrenic:

> After two weeks, the psychologist said to him: "As you say, you are wired precisely wrong. But why won't you let me see the diagram?" Carl answered: "Never, ever will you find the lever, the eternalever that will sever me forever with my real, seal, deal, heel. It is not on my shoe, not even on the sole. It walks away." (Rosenhan & Seligman, 1989, p. 369)

Schizophrenia can affect emotions in a number of ways. Many people with schizophrenia have *blunted affect,* manifesting less sadness, joy, and anger than most people. Others have *flat affect,* showing almost no emotions at all. Their voices are monotonous, their faces impassive. *Inappropriate affect* can also occur, as in the following case:

> The psychologist noted that Carl "smiles when he is uncomfortable, and smiles more when in pain. He cries during television comedies. He seems angry when justice is done, frightened when someone compliments him, and roars with laughter on reading that a young child was burned in a tragic fire." (Rosenhan & Seligman, 1989, p. 369)

For an interview with a schizophrenia patient, see Video Segment 13.3.

Subtypes of Schizophrenia

▶ 23. Describe the four major subtypes of schizophrenic disorders.

Schizophrenia has cognitive, emotional, and behavioral facets that can vary widely from case to case. DSM-IV differentiates among four major subtypes of schizophrenia:

- **Paranoid schizophrenia,** *whose most prominent features are delusions of persecution, in which people believe that others mean to harm them, and*

FIGURE 13.29

The woman pictured here exhibits catatonic rigidity. She might hold this position for several hours. If someone were to move her limbs into another position, she would maintain that position, a phenomenon known as waxy flexibility.

▶ 24. Contrast positive and negative schizophrenia symptoms and their relation to patient history and prognosis.

delusions of grandeur, in which they believe they are enormously important. Suspicion, anxiety, or anger may accompany the delusions, and hallucinations may also occur in this subtype.

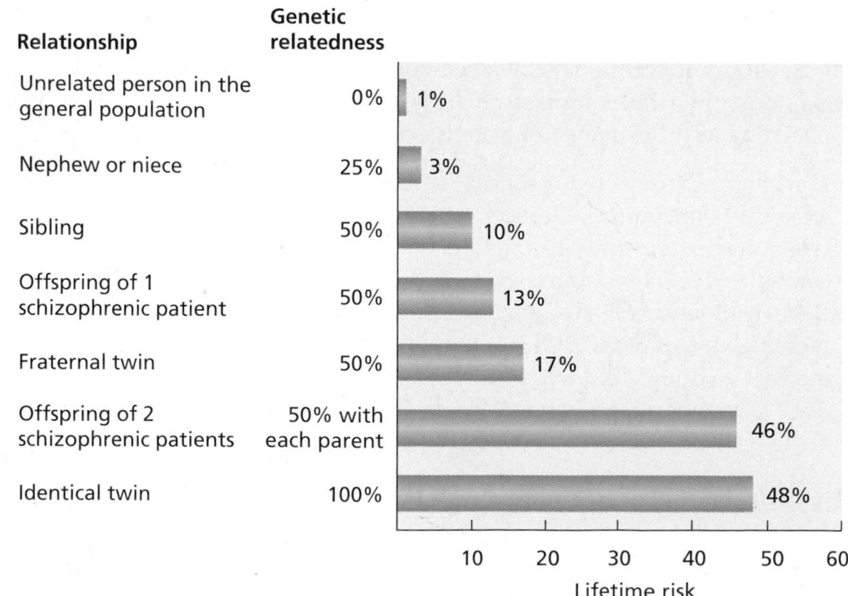

FIGURE 13.30

The degree of risk for developing schizophrenia in one's lifetime correlates highly with the degree of genetic relationship with someone who has that disorder. These data summarize the results of 40 concordance studies conducted in many countries. Source: Based on Gottesman, 1991.

- **Disorganized schizophrenia,** *whose central features are confusion and incoherence, together with severe deterioration of adaptive behavior, such as personal hygiene, social skills, and self-care.* Thought disorganization is often so extreme that it is difficult to communicate with these individuals. Their behavior often appears silly and childlike, and their emotional responses are highly inappropriate. People with disorganized schizophrenia are usually unable to function on their own.
- **Catatonic schizophrenia,** *characterized by striking motor disturbances ranging from muscular rigidity to random or repetitive movements.* People with catatonic schizophrenia sometimes alternate between stuporous states, in which they seem oblivious to reality, and agitated excitement, during which they can be dangerous to others. While in a stuporous state, they may exhibit a *waxy flexibility,* in which their limbs can be molded by another person into grotesque positions that they will then maintain for hours (Figure 13.29).
- **Undifferentiated schizophrenia,** *a category assigned to people who exhibit some of the symptoms and thought disorders of the above categories but who do not have enough of the specific criteria to be diagnosed in those categories.*

In addition to these formal DSM-IV categories, many mental health workers and researchers divide schizophrenic reactions into two main categories on the basis of two classes of symptoms. One type is characterized by a predominance of **positive symptoms,** *bizarre behaviors such as delusions, hallucinations, and disordered speech and thinking.* These symptoms are called *positive* because they represent pathological extremes of normal processes. The second type features **negative symptoms**—*an absence of normal reactions—such as lack of emotional expression, loss of motivation, and an absence of speech* (Herz & Marder, 2002).

The distinction between positive- and negative-symptom subtypes seems to be an important one. Researchers have found differences in brain function between schizophrenics having positive symptoms and those with primarily negative symptoms (Gur et al., 1998; Zakzanis, 1998). The subtypes also show differences in life history and prognosis. Negative symptoms are likely to be associated with a long history of poor functioning prior to diagnosis and with a poor outcome following treatment (McGlashan & Fenton, 1992). In contrast, positive symptoms, especially those associated with a diagnosis of paranoid schizophrenia, are associated with good functioning prior to breakdown and a better prognosis for eventual recovery, particularly if the symptoms came on suddenly and were preceded by a history of relatively good adjustment (Fenton & McGlashan, 1991a, 1991b).

Schizophrenia afflicts only 1 to 2 percent of the population, yet schizophrenic patients occupy about half of all psychiatric hospital beds in the United States. Many who are not hospitalized, such as Eddie, the man described at the beginning of the chapter, barely function as homeless "street people" in large cities (Herman et al., 1998). About 10 percent of people with schizophrenia remain permanently impaired, and 65 percent show intermittent periods of normal functioning. The other 25 percent recover from the disorder (American Psychiatric Association, 2000).

Causal Factors in Schizophrenia

Because of the seriousness of the disorder and the many years of anguish and incapacitation that its victims are likely to experience, schizophrenia is perhaps the most widely researched of the Axis I psychological disorders. There is a growing consensus that schizophrenia results from a biologically-based vulnerability factor that is set into motion by psychological and environmental events (Green, 1997; Herz & Marder, 2002).

Biological Factors

Genetic Predisposition Strong evidence exists for a genetic predisposition to schizophrenia, though the specific genes involved and their roles in creating the disposition are still unknown. As Figure 13.30 shows, the closer the biological relationship to a person diagnosed with schizophrenia, the greater the risk for developing the disorder during one's lifetime (Gottesman, 1991). Twin studies show that identical twins have higher concordance rates than fraternal twins, and adoption studies show much higher concordance with biological parents than with adoptive parents (Kety, 1988; Wahlberg et al., 1997). But, again, genetics do not by themselves account for the development of schizophrenia. If they did, the concordance rate in identical twins would be 100 percent, not 48 percent.

Brain Abnormalities Brain scans have indicated a number of structural abnormalities in the brains of schizophrenic patients. According to the *neurodegenerative hypothesis,* destruction of neural tissue can cause schizophrenia (Weinberger & McClure, 2002). MRI studies have shown mild to moderate *brain atrophy,* a general loss or deterioration of neurons in the cerebral cortex and limbic system, together with enlarged ventricles (cavities that contain cerebrospinal fluid). The atrophy is centered in brain regions that influence cognitive processes and emotion, which may help explain the thought disorders and inappropriate emotions that are seen in such patients (Figure 13.31). Likewise, MRI images of the thalamus, which collects and routes sensory input to various parts of the brain, reveal abnormalities. This may help account for the disordered attention and perception reported by schizophrenic patients whose cerebral cortex may be getting garbled or unfiltered information from the thalamus (Andreason et al., 1994). All of these structural differences are more common in patients who exhibit the negative-symptom pattern (Herz & Marder, 2002). As we have seen, these patients have a poorer chance of recovery than those with the positive-symptom pattern.

▶ 25. Describe the evidence for genetic, neurological, and biochemical factors in schizophrenia.

Biochemical Factors Dopamine, a major excitatory neurotransmitter, may play a key role in schizophrenia. According to the **dopamine hypothesis,**

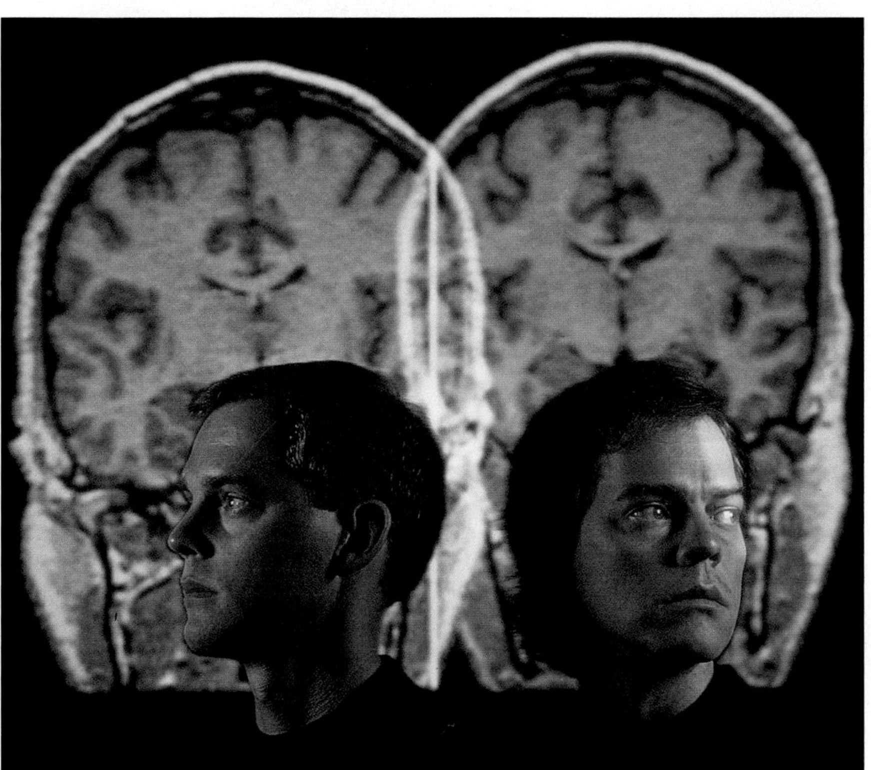

FIGURE 13.31

Not so-identical twins. The brother on the right is schizophrenic, whereas the man on the left has no disorder. As indicated in the MRIs in the background, the schizophrenic brother's brain shows atrophy and has enlarged ventricles (the butterfly-shaped spaces seen in the middle of the MRIs). Findings like these support the position that brain abnormalities play a role in schizophrenia.

the symptoms of schizophrenia—particularly positive symptoms—are produced by overactivity of the dopamine system in areas of the brain that regulate emotional expression, motivated behavior, and cognitive functioning (Heinrichs, 2001). People diagnosed with schizophrenia have more dopamine receptors on neuron membranes than do nonschizophrenics, and these receptors seem to be overreactive to dopamine stimulation (Black et al., 1988; Wong et al., 1986). Additional support comes from the finding that the effectiveness of antipsychotic drugs used to treat schizophrenia is positively related to their ability to reduce dopamine-produced synaptic activity (Creese et al., 1976; Green, 1997). Other neurotransmitter systems are probably involved in this complex disorder as well.

The biochemical and brain findings concerning schizophrenia are intriguing. What is not clear is whether they cause the disorder or are caused by it. Future research is almost certain to reveal other biological bases for the complex disorders of schizophrenia.

Psychological Factors

▶ 26. How do psychoanalytic and cognitive theorists explain the symptoms of schizophrenia?

Freud and other psychoanalytic thinkers viewed schizophrenia as a retreat from unbearable stress and conflict. For Freud, schizophrenia represented an extreme example of the defense mechanism of **regression,** *in which a person retreats to an earlier and more secure (even infantile) stage of psychosocial development in the face of overwhelming anxiety.* Other psychodynamic thinkers, focusing on the interpersonal withdrawal that is an important feature of schizophrenia, view the disorder as a retreat from an interpersonal world that has become too stressful to deal with. Although Freud's regression explanation has not received much direct research support (Fisher & Greenberg, 1996), the belief that life stress is a causal factor is generally accepted today (Crook & Copolov, 2000).

Some cognitive theorists believe that schizophrenics have a defect in the attentional mechanism that filters out irrelevant stimuli, so that they are overwhelmed by both internal and external stimuli. Sensory input thus becomes a chaotic flood, and irrelevant thoughts and images flash into consciousness. The stimulus overload produces distractability, thought disorganization, and the sense of being overwhelmed by disconnected thoughts and ideas. As one schizophrenic noted, "Everything seems to come pouring in at once . . . I can't seem to keep anything out" (Carson et al., 1988, p. 329). The recent MRI findings of thalamic abnormalities described earlier may help explain how this stimulus overload could occur through malfunction of the brain's "switchboard."

Schizophrenic thought processes may be linked to deficits in the executive functions of the frontal lobe (Kerns & Berenbaum, 2002). In one study, schizophrenic patients pressed a key to signal the experimenter when they were hearing voices or experiencing a strange visual experience. PET scans performed at these times showed that the auditory or visual areas of the cortex were highly active, but there was no activity in the prefrontal cortex, whose functioning helps us distinguish reality from fantasy (Silbersweig et al., 1995).

Environmental Factors

Stressful life events seem to play an important role in the emergence of schizophrenic behavior. These events tend to cluster in the 2 or 3 weeks preceding the "psychotic break" when the acute signs of the disorder appear (Day et al., 1987). Stressful life events seem to interact with biological or personality vulnerability factors. A highly vulnerable person may require little in the way of life stress to reach the breaking point (van Praag, 2004). In one study, psychotic and nonpsychotic people rated their emotional responses as they encountered stressful events in their daily lives. Psychotic individuals reacted to their stressors with more intense negative emotions, suggesting that emotional overreactivity may be a vulnerability factor (Myin-Germeys et al., 2002).

Family dynamics have long been a prime suspect in the origins of schizophrenia, but the search for parent or family characteristics that might cause the disorder has been largely unsuccessful. Significantly, children of biologically normal parents who are raised by schizophrenic adoptive parents do not show an increased risk of developing schizophrenia (Kety, 1988). Although persons with schizophrenia often come from families with problems, the nature and seriousness of those problems are not different from those of families in which nonschizophrenics are raised.

This does not mean that family dynamics are not important; rather, it may mean that an individual must have a biological vulnerability factor in order to be damaged by stressful family events to such a degree. Indeed, there is evidence that this vulnerability factor may appear early in life. In one study, researchers analyzed home movies showing preschizophrenic children (those who were later to develop schizophrenic behaviors) and their nonschizophrenic brothers and sisters. Even at these early ages—sometimes as young as 2 years of age—preschizophrenic children tended to show more odd and uncoordinated movements and less emotional expressiveness, especially for positive emotions (Grimes & Walker, 1994). These behavioral oddities may not only reflect a vulnerability factor, but they may also help create environmental stress by evoking negative reactions from others.

Although researchers have had difficulty pinpointing family factors that contribute to the *initial* appearance of schizophrenia, one consistent finding is that previously hospitalized schizophrenics are more likely to relapse if they return to a home environment that is high in a factor called *expressed emotion* (Vaughn & Leff, 1976). **Expressed emotion** *involves high levels of criticism* ("All you do is sit in front of that TV"), *hostility* ("We're getting sick and tired of your craziness"), *and overinvolvement* ("You're not going out unless I go with you"). One review of 26 studies showed that within 9 to 12 months of their return home, an average relapse rate of 48 percent occurred in patients whose families were high in expressed emotion, compared with a relapse rate of 21 percent when families were low in this factor (Kavanagh, 1992). Before we conclude that high expressed emotion causes patients to relapse, however, we should note a finding from another study in which researchers videotaped actual interactions involving patients and their families (Rosenfarb et al., 1995). Analyses of the videotapes revealed that families high in expressed emotion did indeed make more negative comments to patients when they engaged in strange behaviors, but they also showed that the patients in these families engaged in about 4 times as many strange and disruptive behaviors, clouding the issue of what causes what. Thus high expressed emotion may be either a cause of or a response to patients' disordered behaviors.

Sociocultural Factors

Sociocultural factors are undoubtedly linked to schizophrenia (Murray et al., 2003). Many studies have found that the prevalence of schizophrenia is highest in lower-socioeconomic populations (Figure 13.32). Why is this? Is poverty a cause of schizophrenia, or is it an effect of the disorder? Two views give opposite answers. The *social causation hypothesis* attributes the higher prevalence of schizophrenia to the higher levels of stress that low-income people experience, particularly within urban environments. In contrast, the *social drift hypothesis* proposes that as people develop schizophrenia, their personal and occupational functioning deteriorates, so that they drift down the socioeconomic ladder into poverty and migrate to economically depressed urban environments. Perhaps social causation and social drift are both at work, for the factors that link poverty, social and environmental stressors, and schizophrenia are undoubtedly complex.

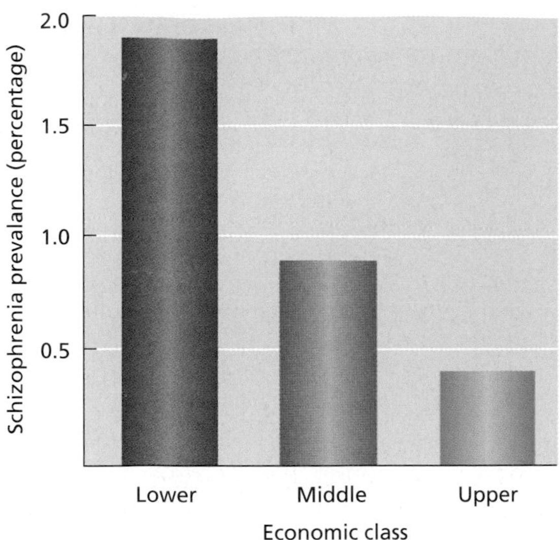

FIGURE 13.32

Relation between economic status and prevalence of schizophrenia. Is economic status a cause or an effect of schizophrenia? Or, does some other factor cause both? SOURCE: Based on Keith et al., 1991.

In contrast to most of the disorders we have described so far, schizophrenia may be a "culture-free" disorder. A worldwide epidemiological study sponsored by the World Health Organization indicated that the prevalence of schizophrenia is not dramatically different throughout the world (Jablensky et al., 1992). However, researchers have found that the likelihood of recovery is greater in developing countries than in the developed nations of North America and western Europe. This may reflect a stronger community orientation and greater social support extended to disturbed people in developing countries (Tanaka-Matsumi & Draguns, 1997).

Schizophrenia reflects complex interactions among biological, psychological, and environmental factors. Figure 13.33 presents prominent causal factors identified at these levels of analysis.

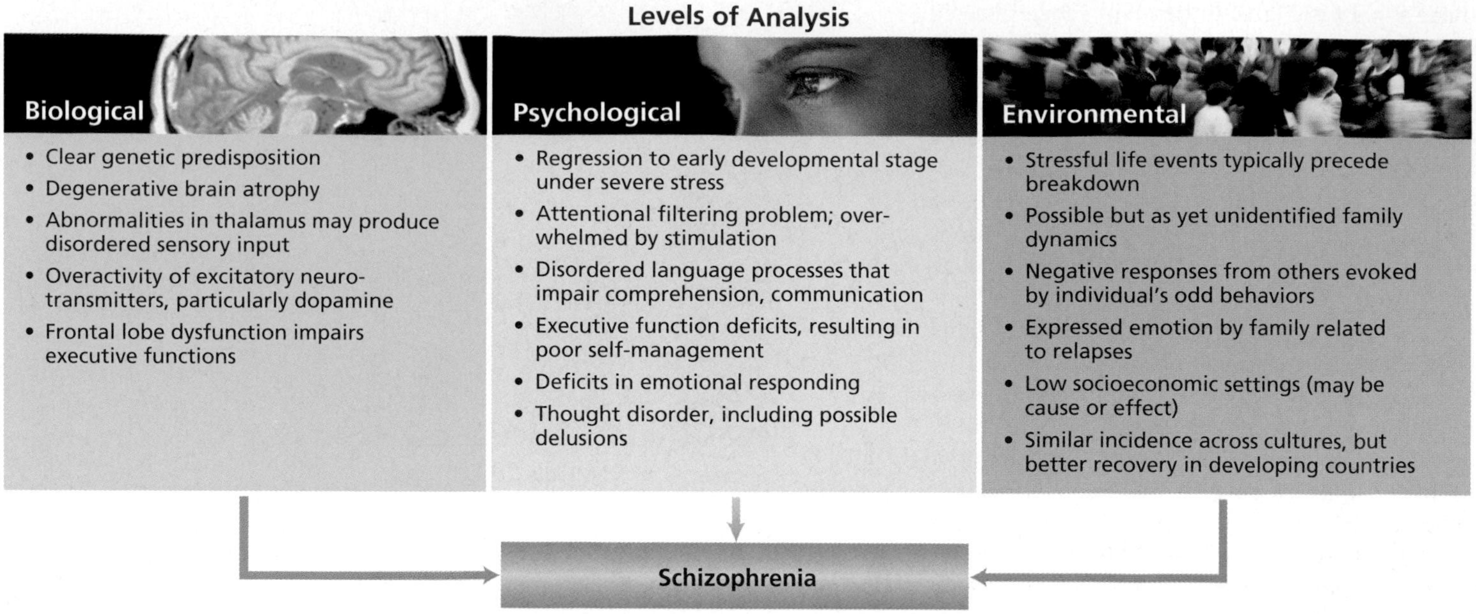

Levels of Analysis

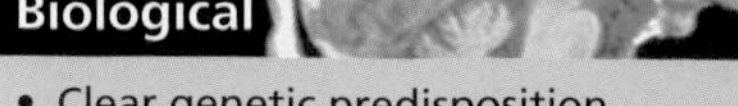

Biological	Psychological	Environmental
• Clear genetic predisposition • Degenerative brain atrophy • Abnormalities in thalamus may produce disordered sensory input • Overactivity of excitatory neurotransmitters, particularly dopamine • Frontal lobe dysfunction impairs executive functions	• Regression to early developmental stage under severe stress • Attentional filtering problem; overwhelmed by stimulation • Disordered language processes that impair comprehension, communication • Executive function deficits, resulting in poor self-management • Deficits in emotional responding • Thought disorder, including possible delusions	• Stressful life events typically precede breakdown • Possible but as yet unidentified family dynamics • Negative responses from others evoked by individual's odd behaviors • Expressed emotion by family related to relapses • Low socioeconomic settings (may be cause or effect) • Similar incidence across cultures, but better recovery in developing countries

Schizophrenia

FIGURE 13.33

Understanding Behavior: Biological, psychological, and environmental factors in schizophrenia.

IN REVIEW

- *Schizophrenia is a psychotic disorder featuring disordered thinking and language; poor contact with reality; flat, blunted, or inappropriate emotion; and disordered behavior. The cognitive portion of the disorder can involve delusions (false beliefs) or hallucinations (false perceptions).*
- *Schizophrenias have been categorized in a number of ways. The DSM-IV lists four subtypes: paranoid, disorganized, catatonic, and undifferentiated. Another categorization is based on the nature of the symptoms: a positive versus negative. Positive symptoms, such as delusions or hallucinations, predict a better outcome than negative symptoms, such as lack of emotional expression.*
- *There is strong evidence for a genetic predisposition to schizophrenia that makes some people particularly vulnerable to stressful life events. The dopamine hypothesis states that schizophrenia involves overactivity of the dopamine system, resulting in too much stimulation.*
- *Psychoanalytic theorists regard schizophrenia as a profound regression to a primitive stage of psychosocial development in response to unbearable stress, particularly within the family. Stressful life events do often precede a schizophrenic episode, but researchers have not been successful in identifying a family pattern related to the onset of schizophrenia. However, negative expressed emotion is a family variable related to relapse among formerly hospitalized schizophrenic individuals.*
- *Cognitive theorists focus on the thought disorder that is central to schizophrenia. One idea is that people with schizophrenia have a defect in their attentional filters, so that they are overwhelmed by internal and external stimuli and become disorganized. Deficiencies may also exist in the executive functions needed to organize behavior.*

PERSONALITY DISORDERS

People diagnosed with **personality disorders** *exhibit stable, ingrained, inflexible, and maladaptive ways of thinking, feeling, and behaving.* When they encounter situations in which their typical behavior patterns do not work, they are likely to intensify their inappropriate ways of coping, their emotional controls may break down, and unresolved conflicts tend to reemerge (Millon et al., 1998).

Personality disorders are an important part of the DSM system because they increase the likelihood of acquiring several Axis I (symptom) disorders, particularly anxiety, depression, and substance-abuse problems, and they are associated with a poorer course of recovery from these disorders. Ann Massion and coworkers (2002) followed people suffering from anxiety disorders for 5 years and found that those also diagnosed with personality disorders were 30 to 40 percent less likely to recover from their anxiety disorders.

Table 13.2 briefly describes the 10 personality disorders in Axis II of DSM-IV. The disorders are divided into three clusters that capture important commonalities: dramatic and impulsive behaviors, anxious and fearful behaviors, and odd and eccentric behaviors. As many as 10 to 15 percent of adults in the United States and European countries may have personality disorders. A study in Norway found a rate of 13.4 percent, equally distributed among men and women. The most frequently encountered were avoidant, paranoid, histrionic, and obsessive-compulsive disorders (Torgerson et al., 2001).

Among the personality disorders, the most destructive to society is the *antisocial personality disorder* (Livesley, 2003). We will focus on this personality disorder because of its social relevance and because it has received by far the greatest attention from clinicians and researchers over the years.

Table 13.2 DSM-IV Axis II Personality Disorders and Their Major Features

Dramatic/Impulsive Cluster

Antisocial personality disorder: Severe irresponsible and antisocial behavior beginning in childhood and continuing past age 18; impulsive need gratification and lack of empathy for others; often highly manipulative and seem to lack conscience

Histrionic personality disorder: Excessive, dramatic emotional reactions and attention seeking; often sexually provocative; highly impressionable and suggestible; out of touch with negative feelings

Narcissistic personality disorder: Grandiose fantasies or behavior, lack of empathy, and oversensitivity to evaluation; constant need for admiration from others; proud self-display

Borderline personality disorder: Pattern of severe instability of self-image, interpersonal relationships, and emotions, often expressing alternating extremes of love and hatred toward the same person; high frequency of manipulative suicidal behavior

Anxious/Fearful Cluster

Avoidant personality disorder: Extreme social discomfort and timidity; feelings of inadequacy and fearfulness of being negatively evaluated

Dependent personality disorder: Extreme submissive and dependent behavior; fears of separation from those who satisfy dependency needs

Obsessive-compulsive personality disorder: Extreme perfectionism, orderliness, and inflexibility; preoccupied with mental and interpersonal control

Odd/Eccentric Cluster

Schizoid personality disorder: Indifference to social relationships and a restricted range of experiencing and expressing emotions

Schizotypal personality disorder: Odd thoughts, appearance, and behavior, and extreme discomfort in social situations

Paranoid personality disorder: An unwarranted tendency to interpret the behavior of other people as threatening, exploiting, or harmful

SOURCE: Based on DSM-IV Axis II, American Psychiatric Association, 1994.

Antisocial Personality Disorder

In the past, individuals with antisocial personality disorder have been referred to as *psychopaths* or *sociopaths*. In the 19th century, such people were sometimes referred to as "moral imbeciles." People with antisocial personality disorder are among the most interpersonally destructive and emotionally harmful individuals. Males outnumber females 3 to 1 in this diagnostic group (American Psychiatric Association, 1994).

People with **antisocial personality disorder** *seem to lack a conscience; they exhibit little anxiety or guilt and tend to be impulsive and unable to delay gratification of their needs.* They also exhibit a lack of emotional attachment to other people, as suggested in this report by a man diagnosed as having an antisocial personality:

> When I was in high school my best friend got leukemia and died and I went to his funeral. Everybody else was crying . . . (but) . . . I suddenly realized I wasn't feeling anything at all. . . . That night I thought about it some more and found I wouldn't miss my mother and father if they died and that I wasn't too nuts about my brothers and sisters for that matter. I figured there wasn't anybody I really cared for but, then, I didn't need any of them anyway so I rolled over and went to sleep. (McNeil, 1967, p. 87)

▶ 27. Describe the major characteristics of the antisocial personality disorder.

A lack of capacity to care about others can make antisocial individuals a danger to society (Black, 1999). For example, murderers Charles Manson, Ted Bundy, and Jeffrey Dahmer failed to show any remorse for their crimes or sympathy for their victims. Although antisocial individuals often verbalize feelings and commitments with great sincerity, their behaviors indicate otherwise. They often appear very intelligent and charming, and they have the ability to rationalize their inappropriate behavior so that it appears reasonable and justifiable. Consequently, they are often virtuosos at manipulating others and talking their way out of trouble.

The characteristics we've discussed often are reflected in psychological test responses as well as in social behavior. Figure 13.34 shows the Minnesota Multiphasic Personality Inventory (MMPI)

FIGURE 13.34

The Minnesota Multiphasic Personality Inventory (MMPI) profile of serial killer Jeffrey Dahmer reveals severe antisocial tendencies. Scores beyond the dotted line are assumed to reflect pathological tendencies. Dahmer's extraordinarily elevated score on the Psychopathic Deviate scale reflects a callous disregard for other people and is consistent with his pattern of unrestrained and vicious victimization of others.
SOURCE: Caldwell, 1994.

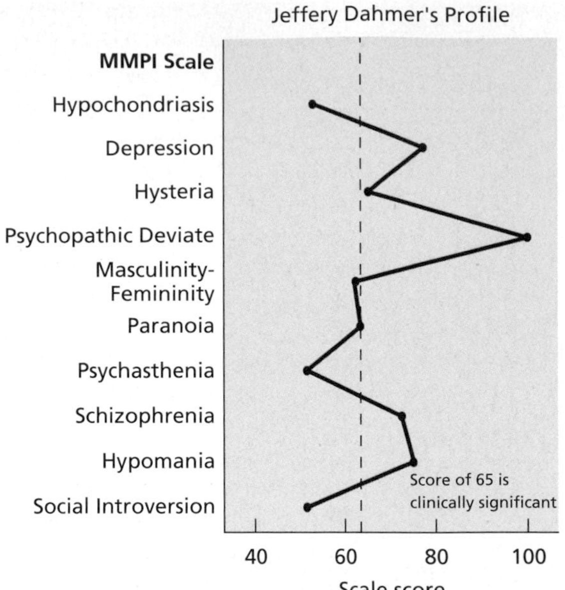

▶ 28. How do biological, psychoanalytic, and behavioral theorists account for antisocial personality disorder?

profile of Milwaukee serial killer Jeffrey Dahmer. Over a 3-year period, he killed and dismembered at least 17 male victims. He slept with the dead bodies, engaged in sex acts with them, stored body parts in jars, and cannibalized many of them. He was convicted of the serial murders and sentenced to 1,070 years in prison.

According to MMPI expert Alex B. Caldwell (1994), several aspects of this profile help explain Dahmer's bizarre and destructive behavior. The extraordinarily high score on the Psychopathic Deviate scale reflects an extreme antisocial impulsiveness coupled with a total lack of capacity for compassion and empathy. His victims were in all likelihood regarded as little more than objects to satisfy his perverse needs. Caldwell viewed the marked discrepancy between the Depression and Psychasthenia (anxiety) scales—rarely seen on the MMPI—as reflecting Dahmer's sense of being fated or doomed to repeat his acts until he would be caught (the high Depression score), together with an absence of fear that, in normal people, might inhibit murderous behavior (the low Psychasthenia score). Although the profile clearly indicates his high level of psychological disturbance, it also reflects an ability to mask his pathology and put up the normal facade that for years fooled law enforcement officials. Indeed, Dahmer's general demeanor was so normal-appearing that despite the horror of his acts and the level of psychopathology shown in his test results, his plea of not guilty by reason of insanity was rejected by the jury.

People with antisocial personalities also display a perplexing failure to respond to punishment. Because of their lack of anxiety (seen, for example, in Dahmer's MMPI profile), the threat of punishment does not deter them from engaging in self-defeating or illegal acts again and again. As a result, some of them develop imposing prison records.

To be diagnosed with antisocial personality disorder, a person must be at least 18 years of age. However, the diagnostic criteria also require substantial evidence of antisocial behavior before the age of 15, including such acts as habitual lying, early and aggressive sexual behavior, excessive drinking, theft, vandalism, and chronic rule violations at home and school. Thus antisocial personality disorder is the culmination of a deviant behavior pattern that typically begins in childhood (Kernberg, 2000).

Causal Factors

Biological Factors Biological research on antisocial personality disorder has focused on both genetic and physiological factors. Evidence for a genetic predisposition is shown in consistently higher rates of concordance for antisocial behavior among identical twins than among fraternal twins (Rutter, 1997). Adoption studies suggest a similar conclusion. In one study, researchers compared the criminal records of men who had been adopted early in life with those of their biological fathers and their adoptive fathers. Men whose biological fathers had no criminal record showed a low incidence of criminal behavior themselves, even if their adoptive fathers were criminal offenders. In contrast, the criminality rate was nearly twice as high if the biological father had a criminal record and the adoptive father did not, clearly suggesting the operation of genetic factors. However, the rate of criminality in the sons was still greater when both the biological and the adoptive fathers were criminals. These sons probably inherited a tendency toward criminality from their biological fathers and learned criminal behaviors from their adoptive fathers, showing the additive influences of genetic and environmental factors (Cloninger & Gottesman, 1987).

How might genetic factors predispose individuals to engage in antisocial behavior? One clue might lie in the relative absence of anxiety and guilt that seems to characterize antisocial personality disorder. Many researchers have suggested that the physiological basis for the disorder might be some dysfunction in brain structures that govern behavioral self-control and emotional arousal. This results in behavioral impulsiveness and a chronically underaroused state that impairs avoidance learning, causes boredom, and encourages a search for excitement (Arnett, 1997; Ishikawa et al., 2001). In support of a physiological basis, MRIs reveal that antisocial individuals have subtle neurological deficits in the prefrontal lobes—the seat of executive functions such as planning, reasoning, and behavioral inhibition; these neurological deficits are associated with reduced autonomic activity (Raine et al., 2000). It thus appears, as long suspected, that severely antisocial individuals may indeed be "wired" differently at a neurological level.

Psychological and Environmental Factors Psychodynamic theorists regard antisocial personalities as people without a conscience. Psychoanalytic theorists suggest that such people lack anxiety and guilt because they did not develop an adequate superego (Gabbard, 1990). In the absence of a well-developed superego, the restraints on the id are reduced, resulting in impulsive and hedonistic behavior. The failure to develop a strong superego is thought to result from inadequate identification with appropriate adult figures because these figures were either physically or psychologically unavailable to the child (Kernberg, 2000). In support of this position, father absence from the home is related to a higher incidence of antisocial symptoms in children, even when socioeconomic status is equated (Pfiffner et al., 2001).

Like some biological theories, learning explanations suggest that persons with the disorder lack impulse control. Learning theorists believe that poor impulse control occurs in these individuals because of an impaired ability to develop conditioned fear responses when punished. This results in a deficit in avoidance learning. Hans Eysenck (1964) maintained that developing a conscience depends on the ability to learn fear and avoidance responses through classical conditioning, and people who fail to do so will be less able to inhibit their behavior.

In accord with this hypothesis, Adrian Raine and coworkers (1996) did a 14-year follow-up of males who had been subjected at age 15 to a classical conditioning procedure in which a soft tone was used as the CS and a loud, aversive tone as the UCS. Conditioned fear was measured by the participant's skin conductance response when the CS occurred after a number of pairings with the loud UCS. The researchers found that men who accumulated a criminal record by age 29 had shown much poorer fear conditioning at age 15 than had those with no criminal record.

Learning through modeling may also play an important role. Many antisocial individuals come from homes where parents exhibit a good deal of aggression and are inattentive to their children's needs (Rutter, 1997). Such parents provide role models for both aggressive behavior and disregard for the needs of others. Another important environmental factor is exposure to deviant peers. Children who become antisocial often learn some of their deviant behaviors from peer groups who both model antisocial behavior and reinforce it with social approval (Bandura, 1997). It is easy to see how such environmental factors, combined with a possible genetic predisposition for antisocial behavior, would encourage the development of deviant behavior patterns.

Cognitive theorists believe that another deficit in antisocial individuals is their consistent failure to think about or anticipate the long-term negative consequences of their acts. As a result, they behave impulsively, thinking only of what they want at that moment (Bandura, 1997). From this perspective, a key to helping these individuals avoid getting into trouble is to help them to develop the cognitive controls (i.e., the executive functions) needed to think before acting.

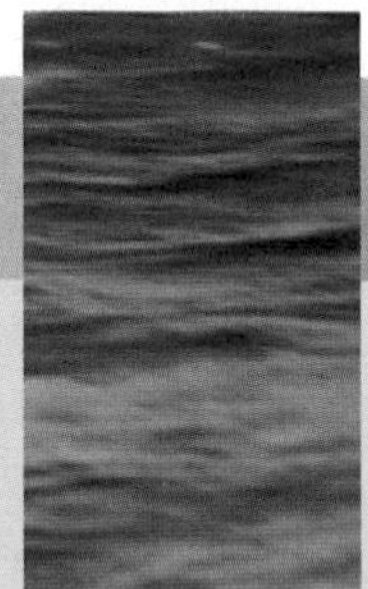

BENEATH THE SURFACE

HOW DANGEROUS ARE PEOPLE WITH PSYCHOLOGICAL DISORDERS?

When they occur, violent acts committed by mentally ill people or former mental patients often are sensationalized in the media. Fictional depictions of psychologically disturbed individuals often involve violent behavior. One analysis of prime-time TV programs revealed that 73 percent of mentally ill characters committed violent acts, compared with 40 percent of normal characters (Gerbner et al., 1981). Part of the stigma attached to psychological disorders is the widespread belief that such people are especially prone to commit violent acts (Monahan, 1992). How valid are such concerns?

The preceding discussion of antisocial personality disorder notes characteristics that can make such people prone to violence. Individuals such as Ted Bundy, Jeffrey Dahmer, and Charles Manson represent extreme examples of how destructive a mentally ill individual can be. Other subgroups with elevated violence potential are people with paranoid and catatonic schizophrenia who have stopped taking their medications (Torrey & Zdanowicz, 2001). The fact is, however, that the vast majority of people with

Continued

psychological disorders do not fall into these categories. The two largest diagnostic groups, people with anxiety disorders and depression, are likely to be no more dangerous than the average person, and severely depressed people in particular are of greater danger to themselves than they are to others.

As we've seen, severe disorders such as schizophrenia are more common in lower socioeconomic groups, and violent behavior is also more common at lower socioeconomic levels. In a study designed to control for this factor, people with mental disorders were followed for 1 year following their discharge from psychiatric hospitals (Steadman et al., 1998). The frequency with which they, family members, or police records revealed violent acts was compared with the frequency of similar acts in "normal" people from the same neighborhoods where the former patients lived.

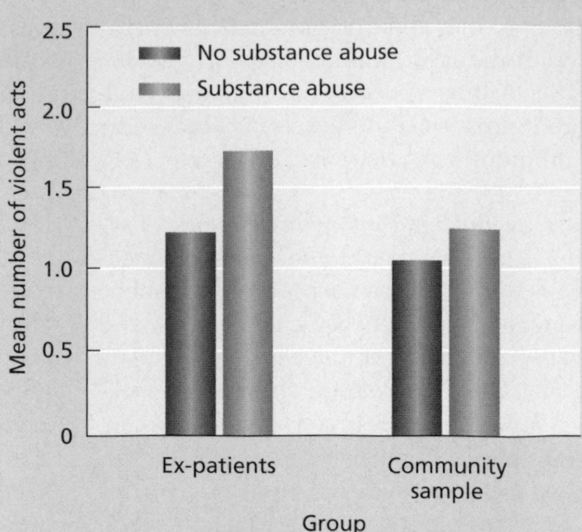

FIGURE 13.35

Mean number of violent acts committed by former psychiatric inpatients during the year following their discharge, compared with similar acts committed by nonpatients living in their neighborhoods. No difference was found between former patients and other community members who did not engage in substance abuse. Substance abuse was associated with more violence in both patient and nonpatient samples. SOURCE: Based on Steadman et al., 1998.

As shown in Figure 13.35, former inpatients without substance-abuse problems differed little in violence rates from nonpatients without substance-abuse problems during the yearlong period. However, substance abuse (which occurred more often among the former patients) was associated with a significant increase in the mean number of violent acts in both the patient and nonpatient groups. The researchers also found that violent acts by the former mental patients were most frequently directed toward family members and acquaintances. Nonpatients were actually more likely than former patients to commit the kinds of violent acts outside of the home that most frighten the public.

Based on this and other research, the following conclusion appears reasonable:

> To date, nearly every modern study indicates that public fears are way out of proportion to the empirical reality. The magnitude of the violence risk associated with mental illness is comparable to that associated with age, educational attainment, and gender, and is limited to only some disorders and symptom constellations. Furthermore, because serious mental illness is relatively rare and the excess risk modest, the contribution of mental illness to overall levels of violence in our society is miniscule. (Link & Steuve, 1998, p. 403)

IN REVIEW

- *Personality disorders are rigid, maladaptive patterns of behavior that characterize an individual's behavior over a long time. They fall on Axis II of DSM-IV. Personality disorders can contribute to the development of Axis I disorders and reduce the chances of recovery from those disorders.*
- *Antisocial personality disorder is the most studied of the Axis II disorders. It is characterized by an egocentric and manipulative tendency toward immediate self-gratification, a lack of empathy for others, a tendency to act out impulsively, and a failure to profit from punishment.*
- *Research on antisocial personality disorder suggests that genetic and physiological factors that result in underarousal may contribute to the disorder's causes. Psychoanalysts view the disorder as a failure to develop a superego, which might otherwise restrain the individual's impulsive self-gratification. Learning explanations focus on the failure of punishment to inhibit maladaptive behaviors and exposure to aggressive, uncaring models. It seems likely that there is a genetic predisposition that increases the risk of antisocial behavior, especially if the person is exposed to deviant models.*
- *It appears that the majority of people with psychological disorders are not a danger to others. Research is identifying the subgroups who are more dangerous, and substance abuse is an important risk factor.*

DISORDERS OF CHILDHOOD AND OLD AGE

Although we often tend to think of "the mentally ill" as young to middle-aged adults, the reality is that psychological disorders can occur at any point in the life span. Mental health professionals have observed symptoms resembling clinical depression in infants, and older children exhibit a wide range of problem behaviors (Mash & Barkley, 2003). Elderly adults can experience any of the disorders discussed in this chapter; in fact, people over age 65 are at greater risk for depression, and commit suicide in proportionately higher numbers, than any other age group (American Psychiatric Association, 2000). In addition, changes in brain functioning associated with the aging process or disease can create a state of deteriorated cognitive functioning known as *dementia*.

Childhood Disorders

Because emotional and social development occurs at different rates in individual children, it is often more difficult to diagnose a child with a behavior disorder than it is with an adult. An adult who has frequent, violent temper tantrums is likely to be judged as having a problem—but what about a 5-year-old who behaves in the same way? Does this behavior reflect a disorder, or is the child simply lagging in emotion-regulation skills? Children are also less able than adults to verbalize their feelings and thought processes, creating additional problems in judging the internal causes of their behavior.

Epidemiological studies indicate that psychological disorders are relatively common between infancy and age 17 (Mash & Barkley, 2003). In one study of several thousand children between the ages of 2 and 5, researchers diagnosed over 20 percent of the children with a DSM-IV disorder and considered half of them to be significantly affected by their symptoms (Lavigne et al., 1996). Similar levels of incidence and impairment exist in children between the ages of 9 and 17 (Satcher, 1999). Other studies show that only about 40 percent of children with psychological disorders receive professional attention, and only half of this group is seen by qualified mental health professionals (Satcher, 1999). In contrast, 74 percent of children with physical handicaps receive professional treatment (U.S. Office of Behavior Technology, 1990). Failure to treat childhood behavior disorders not only results in needless distress for children and families, but such disorders tend to continue into adulthood as psychological problems. In one New Zealand study, 4 in 5 adults with diagnosed DSM disorders also had histories of childhood or adolescent problems that met DSM criteria (Newman et al., 1996).

Externalizing Disorders

Externalizing disorders *are directed toward the environment in the form of behaviors that are disruptive and often aggressive.* In **attention-deficit/hyperactivity disorder (ADHD)**, *problems may take the form of attentional difficulties, hyperactivity-impulsivity, or a combination of the two that results in impaired functioning.* Ratings by teachers and parents indicate that 7 to 10 percent of American children meet DSM criteria for the disorder, making ADHD the most common childhood disorder. The disorder occurs at least 4 times more frequently in boys than in girls; boys are more likely to exhibit aggressive and impulsive behaviors, whereas girls are more likely to be primarily inattentive. Some professionals believe that the diagnosis is applied too liberally, since normal children also exhibit the behaviors in question. They worry that some children may be inappropriately labeled and medicated (Carlson, 2000).

▶ 29. Compare the types, causes, and consequences of internalizing and externalizing disorders in children.

It may be tempting to assume that children routinely "outgrow" ADHD, but follow-up studies of individuals diagnosed with the disorder suggest that in 50 to 80 percent the problems persist into adolescence and, for 30 to 50 percent, into adulthood (Biederman, 1998). Overall, adults with ADHD have more occupational, family, emotional, and interpersonal problems.

Despite many years of research, the precise causes of ADHD are unknown. Genetic factors are probably involved, as concordance is higher in identical than fraternal twins. In adoption studies of ADHD children, the children's biological parents are more likely to have ADHD than the adoptive parents (Smalley, 2000). Experts have long suspected that the disorder has a biological basis, but EEG studies of electrical brain activity and imaging studies of brain structures and neurotransmitters have failed to reveal consistent differences between people with ADHD and control groups (Green, 1999). This may be due to the fact that ADHD is a multifaceted disorder with several subcategories of biological patterns. Environmental factors are also involved, perhaps in complex combinations with biological factors.

Two other externalizing disorders have features in common with the hyperactive-impulsive

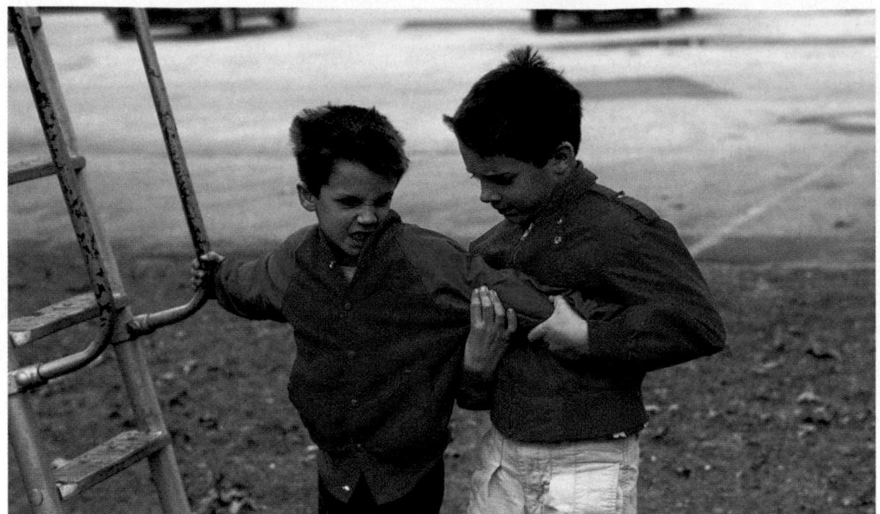

FIGURE 13.36

A history of rule breaking and aggressive behavior in childhood may predict the development of a clinically significant conduct disorder.

component of ADHD. Children with **oppositional defiant disorder (ODD)** *consistently behave in a disobedient, defiant, and hostile manner that interferes with the child's functioning and interpersonal relationships* (Figure 13.36; McMahon & Forehand, 2004). Unlike ADHD, the incidence of ODD does not differ for boys and girls, and the diagnosis is most likely to be applied during adolescence. ODD is more common in children with at least one parent having a history of ODD, antisocial behavior, mood disorder, or substance abuse. Both genetic and social learning factors may produce ODD in children. Serious marital conflict and harsh parental discipline are often associated with ODD.

In a small number of cases, ODD leads to a more severe pattern of misbehavior. Children with **conduct disorder** *violate important social norms and show disregard for the rights of others.* They exhibit a persistent pattern of behavior that may cause or threaten harm to other people and animals. They lie and steal and may commit serious rule violations. Boys are much more likely to receive this diagnosis than are girls. The incidence of the disorder in boys peaks at about age 10 and then declines, whereas girls are more likely diagnosed in their mid-teens. Conduct disorder is associated with poverty, family stress, and antisocial behavior in parents (McMahon & Forehand, 2004).

Internalizing Disorders

Unlike externalizing disorders, internalizing disorders are easy to overlook because the behaviors are not disruptive to others. **Internalizing disorders** *involve maladaptive thoughts and emotions. They include anxiety and mood disorders.* About 13 percent of children between the ages of 9 and 17 have a diagnosable anxiety disorder, and 9 percent have a mood disorder (Satcher, 1999).

Childhood internalizing disorders may take a toll on self-esteem and self-efficacy and interfere with the development of effective coping and interpersonal skills. In addition, having an anxiety or depressive disorder as a child increases the likelihood of similar problems as an adult (Kovacs & Devlin, 1998). This may be due to a genetically caused deficit in emotional regulation, the development of thinking styles that foster anxiety or depression, or classical conditioning of severe anxiety responses that persist into adulthood (as in the case of some childhood phobias).

Childhood anxiety disorders may take any of the forms discussed earlier in the chapter, including phobias, generalized anxiety disorder, panic disorder, and obsessive-compulsive disorder. Of the anxiety disorders, *separation anxiety disorder,* in which children experience anxiety or panic when separated from their caregivers or familiar environment, is the only DSM-IV category that is specific to children. The causal factors for these anxiety and mood disorders appear to be the same as those discussed for adult disorders.

Dementia in Old Age

I fear I am not in my perfect mind.

Methinks I should know you, and know this man; Yet I am doubtful, for I am mainly ignorant

What place this is, and all the skill I have

Remembers not these garments; nor I know not

Where I did lodge last night.

(Shakespeare, *King Lear,* Act IV, Scene 7)

In his characterization of the elderly King Lear, William Shakespeare captured the onset of **dementia,** *the gradual loss of cognitive abilities that accompanies brain deterioration and interferes with normal functioning.* In people with dementia, a progressive atrophy, or degeneration, of brain tissue occurs as a result of disease or injury. Depending on the cause, dementia can occur at any point in the life span, but elderly people are at greater risk than the general population. More than a dozen types and causes of dementia exist, the most common being Alzheimer's disease, Parkinson's disease, Huntington's disease, and Creutzfeldt-Jakob disease. Complications from high blood pressure and stroke may also be causes.

Regardless of the specific diagnosis, when dementia begins after age 65, it is labeled *senile dementia.* A large Canadian study indicated an overall rate of senile dementia of about 8 percent, and a female-to-male ratio of about 2 to 1. The prevalence rates were 2.4 percent between ages 65 and 74, 11 percent for those between 75 and 84, and 34.5 percent for those 85 and older (Costa, 1996). More than half of those over 65 living in institutions had dementia.

The onset of dementia is typically gradual, as is the appearance of symptoms. Memory impairment, poor judgment, confusion, language problems, and disorientation may appear gradually or sporadically. Memory for recent events is particularly affected, and the person may seem to live in the past because those memories are largely intact.

It is important to recognize that simple forgetfulness is not necessarily a symptom of dementia. Individuals who are developing dementia typically have episodes of distress because they feel confused; they may make nonsensical remarks, lose the procedural ability to perform familiar tasks, or even undergo marked personality change. Over half the cases diagnosed as senile dementia show various combinations of depression, anxiety, agitation, paranoid reactions, and disordered thinking that may resemble schizophrenia (American Psychiatric Association, 1994).

Alzheimer's disease *is the leading cause of dementia in the elderly,* accounting for about 60 percent of senile dementias. The disorder is caused by deterioration in the frontal and temporal lobes of the brain, including the hippocampus, a subcortical structure involved in memory. Medical and mental health professionals typically diagnose Alzheimer's by observing and interviewing the patient, but a postmortem microscopic examination of brain tissue is necessary to determine whether the patient had the tangled clumps of neurons and patches of disintegrating nerve cell branches called *plaques* that characterize the disease. A key to Alzheimer's disease is the destruction of cells that produce acetylcholine, a neurotransmitter that is critically involved in the neural processes underlying memory. One focus of current research is the development of drugs that might prevent the destruction of acetylcholine, enhance acetylcholine production, or directly stimulate acetylcholine receptors.

As people live longer lives, finding a cure for Alzheimer's disease and other forms of senile dementia becomes more urgent. Until then, many of us can expect our own family members to become Alzheimer's patients. Being a caregiver or watching the disease develop in a loved one is a painful and frustrating experience. In the advanced stages of the disease, the patient may not recognize even close family members. In addition, he or she may lose the ability to speak, walk, and control bladder and bowel functions. People with Alzheimer's also experience considerable stress as they feel their minds slipping away and their environment becoming more confusing.

IN REVIEW

- *Psychological disorders can occur at any point in the life span, and epidemiological data show that both children and aged people are at high risk for a variety of disorders. Moreover, many childhood disorders are precursors for psychological disorders in adulthood.*
- *Childhood disorders are divided into externalizing disorders, characterized by inattentive, disruptive, or aggressive behavior; and internalizing disorders, typically characterized by anxiety or depression. Attention-deficit/hyperactivity disorder, oppositional defiance disorder, and conduct disorder are externalizing disorders.*
- *Cognitive deterioration, or dementia, can occur at any point in life but is especially prevalent in old age. Alzheimer's disease accounts for more than half of senile dementias. Other diseases, brain damage, and strokes also produce dementias.*

A Closing Thought

All of us do the best we can to adapt to the many demands we face during the course of our lives. In this chapter, we have seen the intense personal and societal suffering that occurs when biologically and experientially produced vulnerabilities combine with stressful demands to create psychological disorders. It is our hope that this discussion has increased your understanding and compassion for those who suffer from these disorders. No one wills to be dysfunctional and miserable, and everyone deserves the opportunity to live a meaningful and fulfilling life. In the next chapter, we focus on what can be done through psychological and biological treatments to ease the suffering that results from psychological disorders.

KEY TERMS AND CONCEPTS

Each term has been boldfaced and defined in the chapter on the page indicated in parentheses.

abnormal behavior (p. 510)
agoraphobia (p. 514)
Alzheimer's disease (p. 547)
antisocial personality disorder (p. 541)
anxiety (p. 512)
anxiety disorders (p. 512)
attention-deficit/hyperactivity disorder (ADHD; p. 545)
bipolar disorder (p. 526)
catatonic schizophrenia (p. 536)
competency (p. 511)
compulsion (p. 515)
conduct disorder (p. 546)
conversion disorder (p. 522)
culture-bound disorders (p. 521)
delusions (p. 534)
dementia (p. 546)
depressive attributional pattern (p. 530)
depressive cognitive triad (p. 530)
disorganized schizophrenia (p. 536)
dissociative disorders (p. 523)
dissociative identity disorder (DID; p. 524)
dopamine hypothesis (p. 537)
dysthymia (p. 526)
expressed emotion (p. 539)
externalizing disorders (p. 545)
generalized anxiety disorder (p. 514)
hallucinations (p. 534)
hypochondriasis (p. 522)
insanity (p. 512)
internalizing disorders (p. 546)
learned helplessness theory (p. 530)
major depression (p. 526)
mania (p. 526)
mood disorders (p. 525)
negative symptoms (p. 536)
neurotic anxiety (p. 519)
obsession (p. 515)
oppositional defiant disorder (ODD; p. 546)
pain disorder (p. 522)
panic disorder (p. 515)
paranoid schizophrenia (p. 535)
personality disorder (p. 540)
phobia (p. 513)
positive symptoms (p. 536)
posttraumatic stress disorder (PTSD; p. 516)
psychogenic amnesia (p. 524)
psychogenic fugue (p. 524)
regression (p. 538)
reliability (p. 510)
schizophrenia (p. 534)
social phobia (p. 514)
somatoform disorder (p. 522)
specific phobia (p. 514)
suicide (p. 532)
trauma-dissociation theory (p. 524)
undifferentiated schizophrenia (p. 536)
validity (p. 510)
vulnerability-stress model (p. 508)

? What Do You Think?

"DO I HAVE THAT DISORDER?" p. 512

Wondering if one has a psychological disorder when reading about their features is quite understandable. We all experience problems in living at various times, and we may react in ways that bear similarities to the disorders described in this chapter. Logically, seeing such a similarity does not necessarily mean that you have the disorder at a clinically significant level. On the other hand, if you find that maladaptive behaviors such as those described in this chapter are interfering with your happiness or personal effectiveness, then you should not hesitate to seek professional assistance in changing these behaviors. In addition to the "three D's" discussed earlier (distress, dysfunction, and deviance), you will want to consider the frequency with which the particular behaviors or experiences occur, their intensity, and their duration. When problem behaviors occur frequently, are intense, and/or last for a long time, they are more likely to be clinically significant. In such a case, it is important not to let any stigma you might attach to having a psychological problem keep you from acting in your best interest and discussing your problem with a mental health professional. ■

IS DID DISSOCIATION OR ROLE PLAYING? p. 525

If a person asked to role-play different people could exhibit radically different behavioral and physiological features, could we conclude that the trauma-dissociation model of DID is disproven or that DID does not exist? A critical thinker will reframe this as follows: Does the fact that one explanation of a given phenomenon is supported prove that all other potential explanations are impossible? Not at all, as supporters of the trauma-dissociation theory would correctly maintain. Indeed, a compelling depiction of a schizophrenic person by a skilled actor such as Jack Nicholson (as in the 1976 movie *One Flew Over the Cuckoo's Nest*) does not prove that all cases of schizophrenia involve nothing more than acting. However, from a scientific perspective, the principle of parsimony dictates that if two different theories can each account for *all* the phenomena, then we should choose the simpler of the two theories. Although intriguing, our view is that the role theory explanation has not yet achieved the scientific support needed to displace other DID theories. ■

ADVOCATING SUICIDE EDUCATION p. 533

You could be dealing with several different issues in those who are resisting a campus suicide education program. Because no recent suicides have occurred, some may believe that such education is an unnecessary expense in a time of tight budgets. One of the difficulties in justifying prevention programs is that it can be hard to demonstrate effectiveness, since their success depends on something *not* happening. In this case, the status quo is no suicides. The question to ask is how costly in human terms even a single future suicide would be, particularly if it could be prevented. To support your position, you might want to look up research that shows reductions in attempted suicides at universities that have incorporated such education.

The other issue that could underlie resistance to such education is the misconception that bringing suicide out into the open might "give students ideas," or encourage suicide. This argument is easier to counter. As noted in *Applying Psychological Science* on page 532, there is much evidence that talking about suicide does not increase its likelihood of occurrence and may instead encourage a troubled student who is contemplating ending his or her life to discuss the topic with others. ■

14

TREATMENT OF PSYCHOLOGICAL DISORDERS

CHAPTER OUTLINE

It is a process, a thing-in-itself, an experience,
a relationship, a dynamic.

—Carl Rogers

I fought my way through Harvard in the midst of psychosis and "spaciness." . . . There is no doubt in my mind that therapy helped me get through school. . . . For so long I wondered why my therapist insisted on talking about my relationship with him. He was not my problem; the problem was my life—my past, my fears, what I was going to do tomorrow, how I would handle things, sometimes just how to survive. . . . It took a long time, but finally I saw why it was important to explore my relationship with my therapist—it was the first real relationship I had ever had: that is, the first I felt safe enough to invest myself in. I rationalized that it was all right because I would learn from this relationship how to relate to other people and maybe even one day leave behind the isolation of my own world. . . . I often felt at odds with my therapist until I could see that he was a real person and he related to me and I to him, not only as patient and therapist, but as human beings. Eventually I began to feel that I too was a person, not just an outsider looking in on the world.

Medication or superficial support is not a substitute for the feeling that one is understood by another human being. For me, the greatest gift came the day I realized that my therapist really had stood by me for years and that he would continue to stand by me and help me achieve what I wanted to achieve. With that realization, my viability as a person began to grow. ("A Recovering Patient," 1986, pp. 68–70)

In this poignant account, written by a person who had suffered from schizophrenia for much of her life, we see that even in this most serious of behavior disorders, humans can reach out and help one another. This chapter explores the many approaches that are being taken to treat psychological disorders, as well as the critical issue of their effectiveness. Although first-person reports, like this one offered by the "recovering patient," suggest that many people derive considerable benefit from psychotherapy, psychologists demand much more in the way of evidence. Nearly 40 years of research on psychological treatments has taught us that the question of efficacy, or treatment outcome, is a tremendously complex one that has no simple answers. Yet as we shall see, much has been learned about the effectiveness of these various therapeutic approaches and about the factors that influence treatment outcome.

PSYCHOLOGICAL TREATMENTS

▶ 1. Which two elements combine as prime ingredients in the treatment process?

The basic goal of all psychotherapy approaches is to help people change maladaptive thoughts, feelings, and behavior patterns so that they can live happier and more productive lives. As the remarks of the "recovering patient" suggest, the relationship between the client and the person providing help is a prime ingredient of psychotherapeutic success (Binder & Strupp, 1997; Norcross, 2003). Within that helping relationship, therapists use a variety of treatment techniques to promote positive changes in the client. These techniques vary widely, depending on the therapists' own theories of cause and change, and they may range from biomedical approaches (such as administering psychoactive drugs) to a wide range of psychological treatments. Both of

FIGURE 14.1

The process of therapy involves a relationship between a client and a therapist who applies the techniques dictated by his or her approach to treatment.

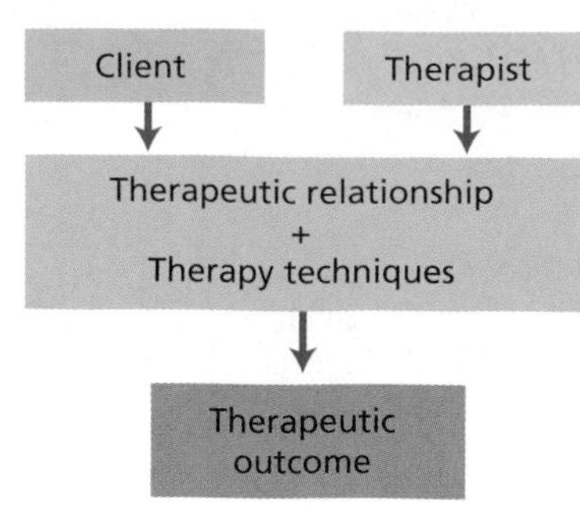

these elements—relationship and techniques—are important to the success of the treatment enterprise (Figure 14.1).

A majority of people with mental health problems first seek help not from mental health professionals but from family members, physicians, members of the clergy, acquaintances, or self-help groups (Seligman, 1995). Often, however, these sources of psychological support are not enough, and distressed people are increasingly seeking help from professional counselors and therapists. Surveys indicate that nearly 30 percent of Americans have sought psychological counseling from professionals at some point in their lives, a dramatic rise from the 13 percent who had done so in the mid-1950s (Meredith, 1986). These people receive treatment from mental-health professionals who fall into several categories.

Clinical and counseling psychologists make up one group. These psychologists, who typically hold a Ph.D. (Doctor of Philosophy) or Psy.D. (Doctor of Psychology) degree, have received 5 or more years of intensive training and supervision in a variety of psychotherapeutic techniques, as well as training in research and psychological assessment techniques. A second group, *psychiatrists,* are medical doctors who specialize in psychotherapy and in biomedical treatments, such as drug therapy.

▶ 2. What is the major therapeutic goal in psychoanalysis?

In addition to psychologists and psychiatrists, a number of other professionals provide treatment. These professionals typically receive a master's degree based on 2 years of highly focused and practical training. They include *psychiatric social workers,* who often work in community agencies; *marriage and family counselors,* who specialize in problems arising from family relationships; *pastoral counselors,* who tend to focus on spiritual issues; and *abuse counselors,* who work with substance and sexual abusers and their victims.

Having previewed the nature of therapy and those who provide it, we now consider the therapeutic approaches that have developed within the major perspectives on human behavior. Figure 14.2 provides an overview of the therapies we will consider.

Psychodynamic Therapies

Of the many psychotherapeutic approaches, psychodynamic treatments have the longest tradition. Their historical roots lie in Sigmund Freud's psychoanalytic theory. Although both the theory and the techniques of therapy were later modified by his followers and by those who defected to pursue rival approaches, the psychodynamic principles underlying Freud's approach continue to exert a major influence today. Psychodynamic approaches have in common a focus on internal conflicts and unconscious factors that underlie maladaptive behavior.

Psychoanalysis

The term *psychoanalysis* refers not only to Freud's theory of personality but also to the specific approach to treatment that he developed. The goal of psychoanalysis is to help clients achieve **insight,** *the conscious awareness of the psychodynamics that underlie their problems.* Such awareness permits clients to adjust their behavior to their current life situations, rather than repeating the maladaptive routines learned in childhood. Analysts believe that as the client repeatedly encounters and deals with long-buried emotions, motives, and conflicts within and outside of therapy, the

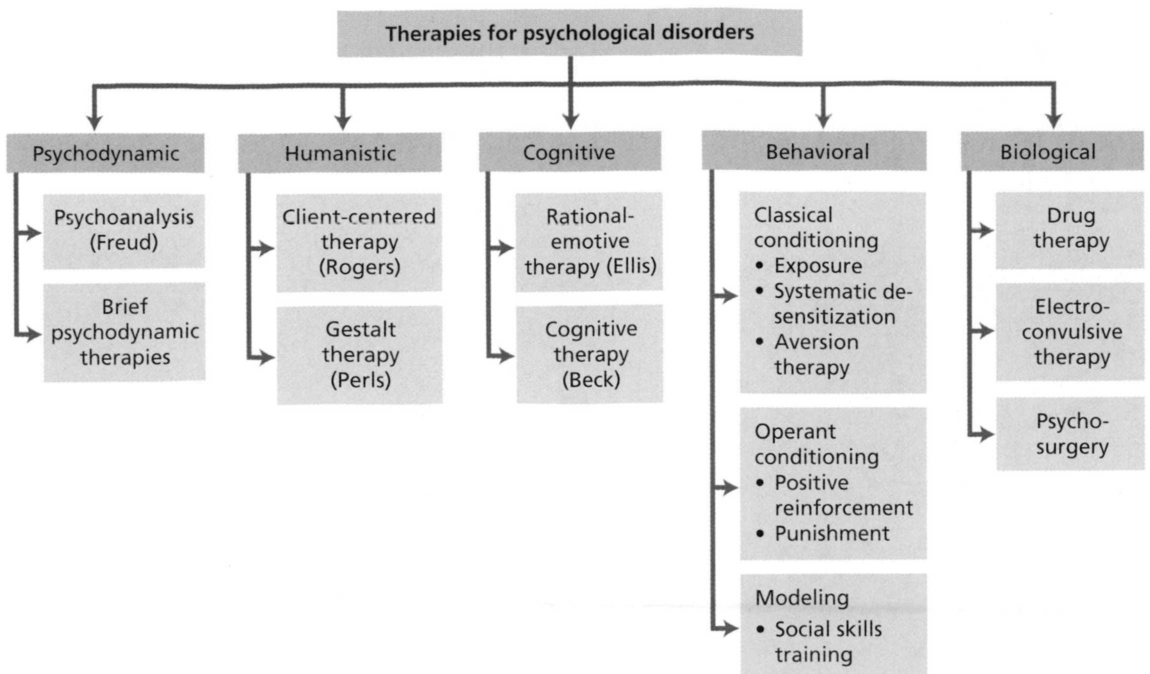

FIGURE 14.2

An overview of the major treatment approaches to the behavior disorders.

psychic energy that was previously devoted to keeping unconscious conflicts under control can be released and redirected to more adaptive ways of living. We now consider the methods and concepts that Freud developed to achieve the end-product of successful therapy: "Where there was id, there shall ego be" (Freud, 1923, p. 148).

Free Association Freud believed that mental events are meaningfully associated with one another, so that clues to the contents of the unconscious can be found in the ongoing stream of thoughts, memories, images, and feelings that we experience. In his technique of **free association,** *clients recline on a couch and verbally report without censorship any thoughts, feelings, or images that enter their awareness.* Analysts sit out of sight behind the client so that the client's thought processes will be determined primarily by internal factors (Figure 14.3).

The analyst does not expect that free association will necessarily lead directly to unconscious material but rather that it will provide clues concerning important themes or issues. For example, a client's stream of thoughts may suddenly stop after she mentions her father, suggesting the possibility that she was approaching a loaded topic that activated repressive defenses.

Dream Interpretation Psychoanalysts believe that dreams express impulses, fantasies, and wishes that the client's defenses keep bottled up in the unconscious during waking hours (Glucksman, 2001). Even in dreams, which Freud termed "the royal road to the unconscious," defensive processes usually disguise the threatening material to protect the dreamer from the anxiety that the material might evoke. In dream interpretation, the analyst tries to help the client search for the unconscious material contained in the dreams. One means of doing so is to ask the client to free-associate to each element of the dream. The analyst then tries to help the client arrive at an understanding of

▶ 3. Describe the roles of free association, dream analysis, resistance, transference, and interpretation in psychoanalysis.

FIGURE 14.3

In classical Freudian psychoanalysis, the client reclines on a couch while the analyst sits out of view to minimize external stimuli that might influence the client's thought processes.

"HAVE A COUPLE OF DREAMS, AND CALL ME IN THE MORNING."

FIGURE 14.4

Dream analysis is a central technique in psychoanalysis. © 2003 by Sidney Harris.

what the symbols in the dream might really represent (Figure 14.4).

Resistance Although clients come to therapists for help, they also have an unconscious investment in maintaining the status quo. After all, underlying their problems are unconscious conflicts so threatening and painful that the ego has resorted to maladaptive defensive patterns to deal with them. These avoidance patterns emerge in the course of therapy as **resistance,** *defensive maneuvers that hinder the process of therapy.* Resistance can appear in many different forms. A client may suddenly experience difficulty in free-associating, come late or "forget about" a therapy appointment, or avoid talking about certain topics. Resistance is a sign that anxiety-arousing material is being approached. An important task of analysis is to explore the reasons for resistance, both to promote insight and to guard against the ultimate resistance: the client's decision to drop out of therapy prematurely.

Transference As noted earlier, the analyst sits out of view of the client and reveals nothing to the client about herself or himself. Eventually, Freud discovered, clients begin to project onto the "blank screen" of the therapist important perceptions and feelings related to their underlying conflicts. **Transference** *occurs when the client responds irrationally to the analyst as if she or he were an important figure from the client's past.* Transference is considered a most important process in psychoanalysis, for it brings into the open repressed feelings and maladaptive behavior patterns that both the therapist and client can discover and explore.

Transference takes two basic forms. *Positive transference* occurs when a client transfers feelings of intense affection, dependency, or love to the analyst, whereas *negative transference* involves irrational expressions of anger, hatred, or disappointment. Analysts believe that until transference reactions are analyzed and resolved, there can be no full resolution of the client's problems. In the following excerpt from a psychoanalytic session, a client traces her transference reaction to its source and then recognizes the operation of similar reactions in other relationships.

Client: I don't want to like you. I'd rather not like you.

Therapist: I wonder why?

Client: I feel I'll be hurt. Liking you will expose me to being hurt.

Therapist: But how do you feel about me?

Client: I don't know. I have conflicting emotions about you. Sometimes I like you too much and sometimes I get mad at you for no reason. I often can't think of you, even picture you. . . . Yes, I don't want to like you. If I do, I won't be able to help myself. I'll get hurt. But why do I feel or insist that I'm in love with you?

Therapist: Are you?

Client: Yes. And I feel so guilty and upset about it. At night I think of you and get sexual feelings and it frightens me.

Therapist: Do I remind you of anyone?

Client: Yes. (Pause) There are things about you that remind me of my brother. (Laughs) I realize this is silly.

Therapist: Mmhmm.

Client: My brother Harry, the one I had the sex experiences with when I was little. He made me do things I didn't want to. I let him fool with me because he made me feel sorry for him.

Therapist: Do you have any of the same feelings toward me?

Client: It's not that I expect that anything will really happen, but I just don't want to have feelings for you. . . . I know it's the same thing. I'm afraid of you taking advantage of me. If I tell you I like you, that means you'll make me do what you want.

Therapist: Just like Harry made you do what he wanted.

Client: Yes. I didn't want to let him do what he did, but I couldn't help myself. I hated myself. That's why. I know it now because there is no reason why I should feel you are the same way. That's why I act that way with other people too. . . . I don't like to have people get too close to me. The whole thing is the same as happens with you. It's all so silly and wrong. You aren't my brother and the other people aren't my brother. I never saw the connection until now. (Wolberg, 1967, pp. 660–661)

In this interchange, we see both positive and negative transference reactions based on an important past relationship. The client's feelings about her brother continue to play out in her fear of getting close to others and becoming vulnerable to being exploited once again.

Interpretation How can analysts help clients detect and understand resistances, the meaning of dream symbols, and transference reactions? The analyst's chief therapeutic technique for these purposes is interpretation of the material the client presents. An **interpretation** *is any statement by the therapist intended to provide the client with insight into his or her behavior or dynamics.* An interpretative statement confronts clients with something that they have not previously admitted into consciousness, for example, "It's almost as if you're angry with me without realizing it."

A general rule in psychoanalytic treatment is to interpret what is already near the surface and just beyond the client's current awareness. Offering "deep" interpretations of strongly defended unconscious dynamics is considered poor technique because, even if they are correct, such interpretations are so far removed from the client's current awareness that they cannot be informative or helpful (Levy, 2002). This is one reason that even after the analyst fully understands the causes of the client's problems, psychoanalysis may require several more years of treatment. It is the client who must eventually arrive at the insights, then translate them into behavior changes within important life domains and relationships.

BENEATH THE SURFACE

IS THERAPY TOO LENGTHY AND EXPENSIVE?

Public attitudes and beliefs about psychotherapy have been influenced by literary and media descriptions of psychoanalysis that describe it as a long, arduous process of unearthing unconscious dynamics. As a result, many people believe that any psychotherapy experience will be a lengthy and expensive proposition, resulting in reluctance to seek treatment (Berkley, 1998). It's true that classical psychoanalysis as practiced by Freud (and by a declining number of contemporary analysts) is an expensive and time-consuming process, for the goal is no less than rebuilding the client's personality. In classical psychoanalysis, it is not uncommon for a client to be seen 5 times a week for 5 years or more, at fees exceeding $100 per session.

Today, however, many therapists consider this level of client and therapist commitment both impractical and unnecessary. Their conclusion is supported by psychotherapy studies in which researchers and clients rated the degree of improvement that occurred by the end of therapy. Figure 14.5 plots the amount of improvement in relation to the number of sessions the clients were seen for treatment. As you can see, about half of the clients improved markedly within 8 sessions, and most therapeutic effects occurred within 26 sessions.

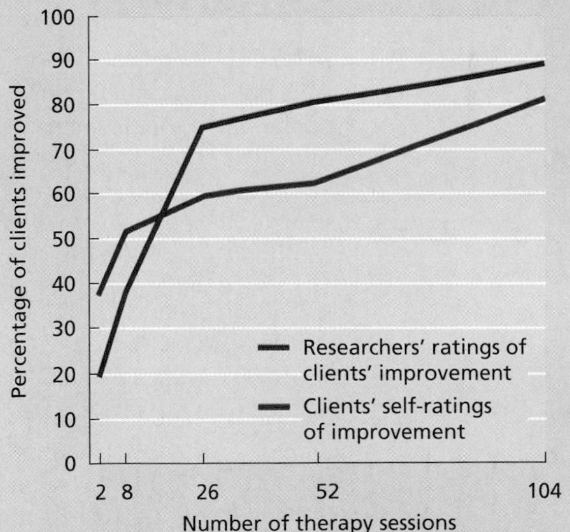

FIGURE 14.5

Percentage of clients improved (based on researchers' and clients' ratings) in relation to the number of sessions of psychotherapy the clients received. These data suggest that many improve within 8 sessions and that most improvement occurs within the first 26 sessions. Source: Adapted from Howard et al., 1986.

Continued

Other studies have also shown sudden gains early in treatment (Stiles et al., 2003). Moreover, as we shall see, there is no evidence that positive psychotherapeutic change requires the client to explore and resolve unconscious dynamics and childhood conflicts. To counter misconceptions that might discourage people from seeking needed treatment, some psychologists provide prospective clients with educational materials to orient them to the shorter and more affordable way in which therapy is practiced today (e.g., McCullough, 2003).

Brief Psychodynamic and Interpersonal Therapies

▶ 4. How do brief psychodynamic therapies differ from classical psychoanalysis? Which research results support their use?

Scientific research shows not only that therapeutic change can occur with surprisingly few sessions but also that classical analysis is not more effective than shorter forms of psychodynamic therapy (Fisher & Greenberg, 1996). To an increasing extent, psychodynamic theorists are adopting briefer and more economical approaches. Like psychoanalysis, brief psychodynamic psychotherapies focus on understanding the maladaptive influences of the past and relating them to current patterns of self-defeating behavior. Many of these brief therapies utilize basic concepts from psychoanalysis, such as the importance of insight and the use of interpretation, but they employ them in a more focused and active fashion (Levenson, 2002). The therapist and client are likely to sit facing one another, and conversation typically replaces free association. Clients are seen 1 or 2 times a week rather than daily, and the goal is typically limited to helping the client deal with specific life problems rather than attempting a complete rebuilding of the client's personality. Therapy is therefore more likely to focus on the client's current life situations than on past childhood experiences and may teach the client specific interpersonal and emotion-control skills (Benjamin, 2003).

One brief therapy with psychodynamic roots, **interpersonal therapy,** *focuses almost exclusively on clients' current relationships with important people in their lives* (Weissman & Markowitz, 1994). This therapy, designed in part for psychotherapy research, is highly structured and seldom takes longer than 15 to 20 sessions. Therapeutic goals include resolving role disputes such as marital conflict, adjusting to the loss of a relationship or to a changed relationship, and identifying and correcting deficits in social skills that make it difficult for the client to initiate or maintain satisfying relationships. The therapist collaborates very actively with the client in finding solutions to these problems and may invite the client to link issues in current relationships with those in important past relationships, thereby showing that what happened in the past need not be carried into the present. In controlled outcome studies, interpersonal therapy has proven to be an effective therapy for several disorders, particularly depression (Chambless & Hollon, 1998; DeRubeis & Crits-Christoph, 1998). Its relative brevity appeals not only to clinicians but also to insurance companies and health maintenance organizations that are interested in reducing therapy costs.

IN REVIEW

- *Psychodynamic therapists view maladaptive behaviors as symptoms of an underlying conflict that needs to be resolved if behavior is to change.*
- *The goal of Freudian psychoanalysis is to help clients achieve insight into the unconscious dynamics that underlie their behavior disorders so that they can deal adaptively with their current environment.*
- *The chief means for promoting insight in psychoanalysis are the therapist's interpretations of free associations, dream content, resistance, and transference reactions.*
- *Brief psychodynamic therapies have become increasingly popular alternatives to lengthy psychoanalysis. Their goal is also to promote insight, but they tend to focus more on current life events. Interpersonal therapy is a structured therapy that focuses on addressing current interpersonal problems and enhancing interpersonal skills.*

Humanistic Psychotherapies

▶ 5. How does the objective of humanistic therapies differ from psychodynamic therapies?

In contrast to psychodynamic theorists, who view behavior as a product of unconscious processes, humanistic theorists view humans as capable of consciously controlling their actions and taking responsibility for their choices and behavior. These theorists also believe that everyone possesses inner resources for self-healing and personal growth and that disordered behavior reflects a blocking of the natural growth process. This blocking is brought about by distorted perceptions, lack of awareness about feelings, or a negative self-image.

When these assumptions about human nature are applied to psychotherapy, they inspire treatments that are radically different from psychoanalysis. Humanistic psychotherapy is seen as a human encounter between equals. The therapist's goal is to create an environment in which clients can engage in self-exploration and remove the barriers that block their natural tendencies toward personal growth (Greenberg & Rice, 1997). These barriers often result from childhood experiences that fostered unrealistic or maladaptive standards for self-worth. When people try to live their lives according to the expectations of others rather than in terms of their own desires and feelings, they often feel unfulfilled and empty, and unsure about who they really are.

In contrast to classical psychoanalytic therapy, humanistic approaches focus primarily on the present and future instead of the past. Therapy is directed at helping clients to become aware of feelings as they occur rather than to achieve insights into the childhood origins of those feelings.

Client-Centered Therapy

The best-known and most widely used humanistic therapy is the *client-centered* (now sometimes called *person-centered*) *approach* developed by Carl Rogers (1959, 1980; Figure 14.6).

In the 1940s, Rogers began to depart from psychoanalytic methods. He became convinced that the important "active ingredient" in therapy is the relationship that develops between client and therapist, and he began to focus his attention on the kind of therapeutic environment that seemed most effective in fostering self-exploration and personal growth (Bozarth et al., 2002). Rogers's research and experiences as a therapist identified three important and interrelated therapist attributes:

- **Unconditional positive regard** *is communicated when therapists show clients that they genuinely care about and accept them, without judgment or evaluation.* The therapist also communicates a sense of trust in clients' ability to work through their problems. In part, this sense of trust is communicated in the therapist's refusal to offer advice or guidance.
- **Empathy,** *the willingness and ability to view the world through the client's eyes,* is a second vital factor. In a good therapeutic relationship, the therapist comes to sense the feelings and meanings experienced by the client and communicates this understanding to the client. The therapist does this by *reflecting* back to the client what she or he is communicating—perhaps by rephrasing something the client has just said in a way that captures the meaning and emotion involved.
- **Genuineness** *refers to consistency between the way the therapist feels and the way he or she behaves.* Therapists must be open enough to express their own feelings honestly, whether positive or negative. In the case of negative feelings, this may seem to be contradictory to the attribute of unconditional positive regard, but that is not necessarily the case. Indeed, the most striking demonstrations of both attributes occur when a therapist can express displeasure with a client's behavior and at the same time communicate acceptance of the client as a person. For example, a therapist might say, "I feel frustrated with the way you handled that situation because I want things to work out better than that for you."

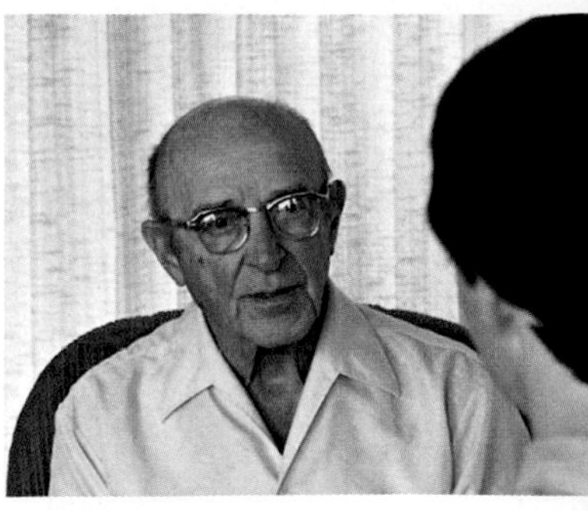

FIGURE 14.6

"Psychotherapy is the releasing of an already existing capacity in a potentially competent individual, not the expert manipulation of a more or less passive personality."—Carl Rogers

Rogers believed that when therapists can express these three key therapeutic attributes, they create a climate in which the client feels accepted, understood, and free to explore basic attitudes and feelings without fear of being judged or rejected. Within such a climate, clients experience the courage and freedom to grow.

▶ 6. What three therapist attributes did Rogers find to be crucial to therapeutic success?

These therapeutic attitudes are exhibited in the following excerpt from one of Rogers's therapy sessions:

Client: I cannot be the kind of person I want to be. I guess maybe I haven't the guts or the strength to kill myself, and if someone else would relieve me of the responsibility or I would be in an accident, I—just don't want to live.

Rogers: At the present time things look so black that you can't see much point in living. (Note the use of empathic reflection and the absence of any criticism.)

Client: Yes, I wish I'd never started this therapy. I was happy when I was living in my dream world. There I could be the kind of person I wanted to be. But now there is such a wide, wide gap between my ideal and what I am. . . . (Notice how the client responds to reflection with more information.)

Rogers: It's really tough digging into this like you are and at times the shelter of your dream world looks more attractive and comfortable. (Reflection.)

Client: My dream world or suicide. . . . So I don't see why I should waste your time coming in twice a week—I'm not worth it—what do you think?

Rogers: It's up to you. . . . It isn't wasting my time. I'd be glad to see you whenever you come, but it's how you feel about it. . . . (Note the genuineness in stating an honest desire to see the client and the unconditional positive regard in trusting her capacity and responsibility for choice.)

Client: You're not going to suggest that I come in oftener? You're not alarmed and think I ought to come in every day until I get out of this?

Rogers: I believe you're able to make your own decision. I'll see you whenever you want to come. (Trust and positive regard.)

Client: (Note of awe in her voice.) I don't believe you are alarmed about—I see—I may be afraid of myself but you aren't afraid for me. (She experiences the therapist's confidence in her.)

Rogers: You say you may be afraid of yourself and are wondering why I don't seem to be afraid for you. (Reflection.)

Client: You have more confidence in me than I have. I'll see you next week, maybe. (Based on Rogers, 1951, p. 49) [The client did not attempt suicide.]

Rogers believed that as clients experience a constructive therapeutic relationship, they exhibit increased self-acceptance, greater self-awareness, enhanced self-reliance, increased comfort with other relationships, and improved life functioning (Rogers, 1959). Research does indicate that therapists' characteristics have a strong effect on the outcome of psychotherapy. Therapy is most likely to be successful when the therapist is perceived as genuine, warm, and empathic (Sachse & Elliott, 2002).

Gestalt Therapy

Frederick S. (Fritz) Perls, a European psychoanalyst who was trained in Gestalt psychology, developed another humanistic approach to treatment. As noted in Chapter 4, the term *gestalt* ("organized whole") refers to perceptual principles through which people actively organize stimulus elements into meaningful "whole" patterns. Ordinarily, in whatever we perceive, whether external stimuli, ideas, or emotions, we concentrate on only part of our whole experience—the figure—while largely ignoring the background against which the figure appears. For people who have psychological difficulties, that background includes important feelings, wishes, and thoughts that are blocked from ordinary awareness because they would evoke anxiety. Gestalt therapy's goal is to bring them into immediate awareness so that the client can be "whole" once again.

Gestalt therapy is often carried out in groups, and Gestalt therapists have developed a variety of imaginative techniques to help clients "get in touch with their inner selves." These methods are much more active and dramatic than client-centered approaches, and sometimes even confrontational in nature. Therapists often ask clients to role-play different aspects of themselves so that they may directly experience their inner dynamics. In the *empty-chair technique,* a client may be asked to imagine his mother sitting in the chair, then carry on a conversation in which he alternatively role-plays his mother and himself, changing chairs for each role and honestly telling her how he feels about important issues in their relationship. These techniques can evoke powerful feelings and make clients aware of unresolved issues that affect other relationships in their lives as well.

Despite their common commitment to humanistic principles, Rogers and Perls differed sharply in their attitudes toward doing research on humanistic therapies. Rogers was committed to research that would help identify the factors that contribute to therapeutic success. He was a pioneer in tape-recording therapy sessions and analyzing them to study what went on in therapy (Rogers & Dymond, 1954). In contrast, Perls had a strongly antiscientific attitude that kept him and his followers from doing systematic research on the effectiveness of Gestalt therapy. As a result, the influence of the Gestalt movement began to wane following Perls's death in 1970. More recently, however, some clinical researchers have begun assessing the effects of Gestalt techniques.

In one recent study, Leslie Greenberg and Wanda Malcolm (2002) tested the effects of the empty-chair technique in helping clients resolve "unfinished business" with significant others in their past lives. The clients were seen for 12 to 14 hourly sessions. One client was a submissive middle-aged man who had felt humiliated and emotionally rejected by his mother's hurtful teasing and public humiliation of him as a child. Here is an sample of the client's (C) empty-chair statements to his mother (M) over several sessions:

C: You were self-centered and you didn't care too much about me and the way I was brought up as far as my emotions go.

M: (as client occupies her chair) What are you talking about? What do you mean? I gave you the best years of my life. Somebody had to look after you. I did the best I could.

C: I was hurt so much. I carry that. I lost some of that warmth inside me. It affects the way I have relationships. The way I relate to myself. The way I feel about myself. All these years I thought I was a joke. This is what I carry (crying). I'm ashamed of myself.

M: Yes, I know I did some of those things you said. And I could have been a better mother, but I guess I was young. I was still a child myself. I couldn't give you the emotional stability you wanted. . . . I'm sorry that it had an effect on you.

C: As a little boy I couldn't tell you "Stop it. Don't do it. Keep away." But I can tell you now that I resent you for it and I won't forgive you. . . . I'm not going to dance around you any more. I'm going to stand up for myself. I think it's about time. (p. 408)

Greenberg and Malcolm then had clinicians listen to tapes of these sessions. The clinicians judged 13 of 32 clients to have completely resolved their unfinished business, as evidenced by affirmation of the self as worthwhile and either an increased understanding, empathy, or forgiveness of the other person or the ability to hold the other accountable for wrongdoing. Compared to those who did not reach complete resolution, resolved clients expressed more intense emotions during the empty-chair exercise and had significantly better treatment outcomes on measures of psychological distress, self-esteem, and improvement in interpersonal problems. Figure 14.7 shows pre- and posttreatment scores on a measure of interpersonal problems for the resolved and unresolved clients. Although both groups showed therapeutic gains, only those shown by the resolved group were statistically significant. Today, the empty-chair exercise is one of several Gestalt techniques being incorporated into nonhumanistic therapies as well (Cain, 2002; A. Lazarus, 1995).

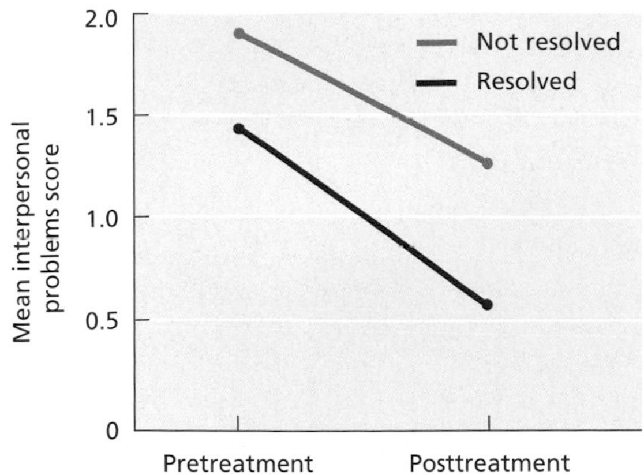

FIGURE 14.7

Use of the Gestalt therapy empty-chair technique to facilitate the resolution of unfinished business with significant others. Those clients judged to have achieved a full resolution of the past conflicts over the course of treatment showed a significant reduction in scores on a self-report measure of current interpersonal difficulties. SOURCE: Based on Greenberg & Malcolm, 2002.

IN REVIEW

- *Humanistic psychotherapies attempt to liberate the client's natural tendency toward self-actualization by establishing a growth-inducing therapeutic relationship.*
- *Rogers's client-centered therapy emphasizes the importance of three therapist characteristics: unconditional positive regard, empathy, and genuineness.*
- *The goal of Gestalt therapy is to remove blockages to clients' awareness of the wholeness of immediate experience by making them more aware of their feelings and the ways in which they interact with others.*

▶ 7. How is the ABCD model used in rational-emotive therapy? Which disorders respond well to Beck's cognitive therapy?

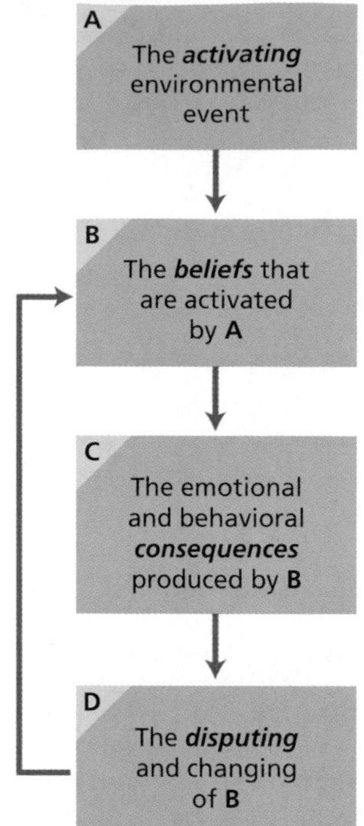

FIGURE 14.8

Albert Ellis's ABCD model describes his theory of the cause—and remediation—of maladaptive emotional responses and behaviors. In therapy, the goal is to discover, dispute, and change the client's maladaptive beliefs.

FIGURE 14.9

"The essence of effective therapy according to rational-emotive therapy is full tolerance of people as individuals combined with a ruthless campaign against their self-defeating ideas. . . . These can be easily elicited and demolished by any scientist worth his or her salt; and the rational-emotive therapist is exactly that: an exposing and nonsense-annihilating scientist."—Albert Ellis

Cognitive Therapies

As we have seen, many behavior disorders involve maladaptive ways of thinking about oneself and the world. Cognitive approaches to psychotherapy focus on the role of irrational and self-defeating thought patterns, and therapists who employ this approach try to help clients discover and change the cognitions that underlie their problems.

In contrast to psychoanalysts, cognitive therapists do not emphasize the importance of unconscious psychodynamic processes. They do, however, point out that because our habitual thought patterns are so well practiced and ingrained, they tend to "run off" almost automatically, so that we may be only minimally aware of them and may simply accept them as reflecting "reality" (Clark et al., 1999). Consequently, clients often need help in identifying the beliefs, ideas, and self-statements that trigger maladaptive emotions and behaviors. Once identified, these cognitions can be challenged and, with practice and effort, changed. Albert Ellis and Aaron Beck are the most influential figures in the cognitive approach to therapy.

Ellis's Rational-Emotive Therapy

Ellis's theory of emotional disturbance and his rational-emotive therapy are embodied in his ABCD model (Figure 14.8).

- *A* stands for the *activating event* that seems to trigger the emotion.
- *B* stands for the *belief system* that underlies the way in which a person appraises the event.
- *C* stands for the emotional and behavioral *consequences* of that appraisal.
- *D* is the key to changing maladaptive emotions and behaviors: *disputing*, or challenging, an erroneous belief system.

Ellis (Figure 14.9) points out that people are accustomed to viewing their emotions (C) as being caused directly by events (A). Thus a young man who is turned down for a date may feel rejected and depressed. However, Ellis would insist that the woman's refusal is *not* the true reason for the emotional reaction. Rather, the reaction is caused by the young man's irrational belief that "She doesn't want to be with me. I'm worthless, and no one will ever want me." If the young man does not want to feel depressed and rejected, this belief must be countered and replaced by a more rational interpretation (e.g., "It would have been nice if she had accepted my invitation, but I don't need to turn it into a catastrophe. It doesn't mean other women will never care about me").

Rational-emotive therapists introduce clients to commonly held irrational beliefs (Table 14.1) and then train them to ferret out the particular ideas that underlie their maladaptive emotional responses. Clients are given homework assignments to help them analyze and change self-statements. They may be asked to place themselves in challenging situations and practice control over their emotions by using new self-statements. For example, a shy person might be required to go to a party and practice rational thoughts that counteract social anxiety. Ellis reports that he overcame his own fears of rejection by going to Central Park in New York, practicing anxiety-reducing self-statements, and striking up conversations with more than 100 different women. He reports that he got only one date, but he overcame his anxiety without being either assaulted or arrested. By learning and practicing cognitive coping responses, clients can eventually modify underlying belief systems in ways that enhance well-being (Dryden, 2002).

TABLE 14.1 Irrational Ideas That Cause Disturbance and Alternatives That Might Be Offered by a Rational-Emotive Therapist

Irrational Belief	Rational Alternative
It is a dire necessity that I be loved and approved of by virtually everyone for everything I do.	Although we might prefer approval to disapproval, our self-worth need not depend on the love and approval of others. Self-respect is more important than giving up one's individuality to buy the approval of others.
I must be thoroughly competent and achieving to be worthwhile. To fail is to be a *failure.*	As imperfect and fallible human beings, we are bound to fail from time to time. We can control only effort; we have incomplete control over outcome. We are better off focusing on the process of doing rather than on demands that we do well.
It is terrible, awful, and catastrophic when things are not the way I demand that they be.	Stop catastrophizing and turning an annoyance or irritation into a major crisis. Who are we to demand that things be different from what they are? When we turn our preferences into dire necessities, we set ourselves up for needless distress. We had best learn to change those things we can control and accept those that we can't control (and be wise enough to know the difference).
Human misery is externally caused and forced on us by other people and events.	Human misery is produced not by external factors but rather by what we tell ourselves about those events. We feel as we think, and most of our misery is needlessly self-inflicted by irrational habits of thinking.
Because something deeply affected me in the past, it must continue to do so.	We hold ourselves prisoner to the past because we continue to believe philosophies and ideas learned in the past. If they are still troubling us today, it is because we are still propagandizing ourselves with irrational nonsense. We *can* control how we think in the present and thereby liberate ourselves from the "scars" of the past.

Beck's Cognitive Therapy

Like Ellis, Aaron Beck's goal is to point out errors of thinking and logic that underlie emotional disturbance and to help clients identify and reprogram their overlearned "automatic" thought patterns (Figure 14.10). In treating depressed clients, a first step is to help clients realize that their thoughts, and not the situation, cause their maladaptive emotional reactions. This sets the stage for identifying and changing the self-defeating thoughts.

Client: I get depressed when things go wrong. Like when I fail a test.

Beck: How can failing a test make you depressed?

Client: Well, if I fail, I'll never get into law school.

Beck: So failing a test means a lot to you. But if failing a test could drive people into clinical depression, wouldn't you expect everyone who failed a test to have a depression? Did everyone who failed get depressed enough to require treatment?

Client: No, but it depends on how important the test was to the person.

Beck: Right, and who decides the importance?

Client: I do.

Beck: Now what did failing mean?

Client: (Tearful) That I couldn't get into law school.

Beck: And what does that mean to you?

Client: That I'm just not smart enough.

Beck: Anything else?

Client: That I can never be happy.

Beck: And how do those thoughts make you feel?

Client: Very unhappy.

Beck: So it is the *meaning* of failing a test that makes you very unhappy. In fact, believing that you can never be happy is a powerful factor in producing unhappiness. So you get yourself into a trap—by definition, failure to get into law school equals "I can never be happy." (Beck et al., 1979, pp. 145–146 [italics added])

Beck's contributions to understanding and treating depression have made his cognitive therapy a psychological treatment of choice for that disorder (Moorey, 2003). Cognitive therapy has also been extended to the treatment of anger and anxiety disorders (Rush et al., 1998). As we shall see, cognitive therapy is also being combined with other therapeutic techniques to form highly effective treatment "packages" for certain disorders.

FIGURE 14.10

"The formula for treatment may be stated in simple terms: The therapist helps the patient to identify his warped thinking and to learn more realistic ways to formulate his experience."—Aaron Beck

Behavior Therapies

▶ 8. Which classical and operant conditioning principles underlie exposure therapy? What problems is it applied to?

In the 1960s, behavioral approaches emerged as a dramatic departure from the assumptions and methods that characterized psychoanalytic and humanistic therapies. The new practitioners of behavior therapy denied the importance of inner dynamics. Instead, they insisted that (1) maladaptive behaviors are not merely "symptoms" of underlying problems but rather *are* the problem; (2) problem behaviors are learned in the same ways normal behaviors are; and (3) maladaptive behaviors can be unlearned by applying principles derived from research on classical conditioning, operant conditioning, and modeling. Behaviorists demonstrated that these learning procedures could be applied effectively to change the behaviors of schizophrenia, to treat anxiety disorders, and to modify many child and adult behavior problems that seemed resistant to traditional therapy approaches (Hersen, 2002).

Classical conditioning procedures have been used in two major ways. First, they have been used to reduce, or decondition, anxiety responses. Second, they have been used in attempts to condition aversive emotional responses to a particular class of stimuli, such as alcohol or inappropriate sexual objects. The most commonly used classical conditioning procedures are exposure therapies, systematic desensitization, and aversion therapy.

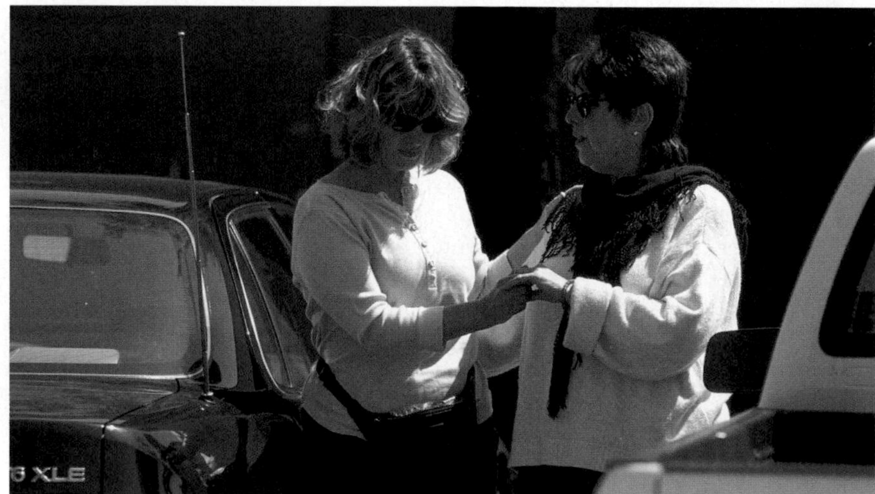

FIGURE 14.11

Exposure to feared stimuli can extinguish phobic behavior. In this photo, a therapist (right) is accompanying a client with severe agoraphobia during an exposure session in a public place. The client's anxiety is clearly evident, but it will dissipate as extinction occurs.

Exposure: An Extinction Approach

From a behavioral point of view, phobias and other fears result from classically conditioned emotional responses. The conditioning experience is assumed to involve a pairing of the phobic object (the neutral stimulus) with an aversive unconditioned stimulus (UCS). As a result, the phobic stimulus becomes a conditioned stimulus (CS) that elicits the conditioned response (CR) of anxiety. According to the two-factor learning theory discussed in Chapters 6 and 13, avoidance responses to the phobic situation are then reinforced by anxiety reduction (operant conditioning based on negative reinforcement). Thus a person who is bitten by a dog may subsequently be afraid of dogs. Moreover, each time he avoids a dog, his avoidance response is strengthened through anxiety reduction.

According to this formulation, the most direct way to reduce the fear is through a process of classical extinction of the anxiety response. This requires **exposure** *to the feared CS in the absence of the UCS* while using **response prevention** *to keep the operant avoidance response from occurring*. This is the theoretical basis for the exposure approach (Marks, 1991; Zinbarg et al., 1992). The client may be exposed to real-life stimuli (Figure 14.11) or asked to imagine scenes involving the stimuli. These stimuli will, of course, evoke considerable anxiety, but the anxiety will extinguish in time if the person remains in the presence of the CS and the UCS does not occur.

Some critics of exposure treatment are concerned that intense anxiety created by the treatment may worsen the problem or cause clients to flee from treatment (Bruce & Sanderson, 1998). In a study of women being treated for posttraumatic stress disorder with imaginal exposure, 15.4 percent did indeed showed a temporary increase in PTSD symptom intensity when exposure began. However, this increase did not impair treatment effectiveness or increase the likelihood of withdrawal from treatment (Foa et al., 2002).

Exposure has proved to be a highly effective technique for extinguishing anxiety responses in both animals and humans (Spiegler & Guevremont, 2003). Both real-life (*in vivo*) and imaginal exposure are effective. An additional advantage is that clients can administer exposure treatment to themselves under a therapist's direction with high success rates (Marks, 1991).

Computer technology has provided a new method for delivering exposure treatments.

Virtual reality (VR) *involves the use of computer technology to create highly realistic "virtual environments" that simulate actual experience so vividly that they evoke many of the same reactions that a comparable real-world environment would.* Observers typically wear helmets containing two small video monitors (one for each eye) attached to a high-speed computer. The image to each eye is slightly different, producing binocular depth perception cues that result in a 3-D image. With the aid of position-tracking devices, the computer monitors the person's physical movements and adjusts the images and sounds accordingly (Figure 14.12). Observers thus have a vivid sense of being present in a different place when navigating through the virtual world. This power to immerse the user in a simulated environment derives not so much from the realism of the displays as from the fact that perception and action are integrated as they are in real life (North et al., 2002). The following *Research Close-Up* describes the use of VR in treating patients with a fear of flying.

FIGURE 14.12

Virtual reality was used to treat this woman with a phobia of spiders. The client views a virtual "spider world" inside the helmet as she handles a realistic spider whose movements inside the virtual environment are linked to her manipulation of the toy spider. The monitor shows the scene being experienced by the client.

RESEARCH CLOSE-UP

EXPOSURE TREATMENT FOR FEAR OF FLYING USING VIRTUAL REALITY

Introduction

Approximately 25 million Americans suffer from a fear of flying in airplanes. They cope with their fear by flying under the influence of drugs or alcohol or by avoiding flying altogether. These coping methods can have negative medical, social, and occupational consequences.

Exposure therapy based on classical extinction principles offers a proven anxiety-reduction approach. In this study, exposure therapy using virtual reality (VR) was compared with a standard exposure approach having in vivo and imaginal components and with a waiting-list control condition that did not immediately receive treatment. If effective, VR can be an economical method for treating people with a variety of fear-based conditions, for the stimuli can be easily tailored to the specific problem and client.

Method

Forty-nine people who replied to an advertisement offering treatment for severe fear of flying were randomly assigned to three conditions: VR exposure therapy, a standard exposure therapy, and a waiting-list (WL) control group that was offered its choice of the two exposure therapies after the exposure groups were treated. Forty-five clients completed the study.

The VR and standard exposure treatments consisted of 8 individual sessions over a 6-week period. In the first 4 sessions, clients were oriented to the program and learned to reduce anxiety using deep breathing and to counter irrational thoughts, such as "This plane is going to crash. I'm doomed." Exposure therapy was carried out in the final 4 sessions. In the VR condition, clients donned a head-mounted display like that shown in Figure 14.12 and sat in specially equipped airplane seats. Stereo earphones piped in realistic recorded sounds of takeoffs and

Continued

SOURCE: Barbara O. Rothbaum, Larry Hodges, Page L. Anderson, Larry Price, and Samantha Smith (2002). Twelve-month follow-up of virtual reality and standard exposure therapies for the fear of flying. *Journal of Consulting and Clinical Psychology, 70,* 428–432.

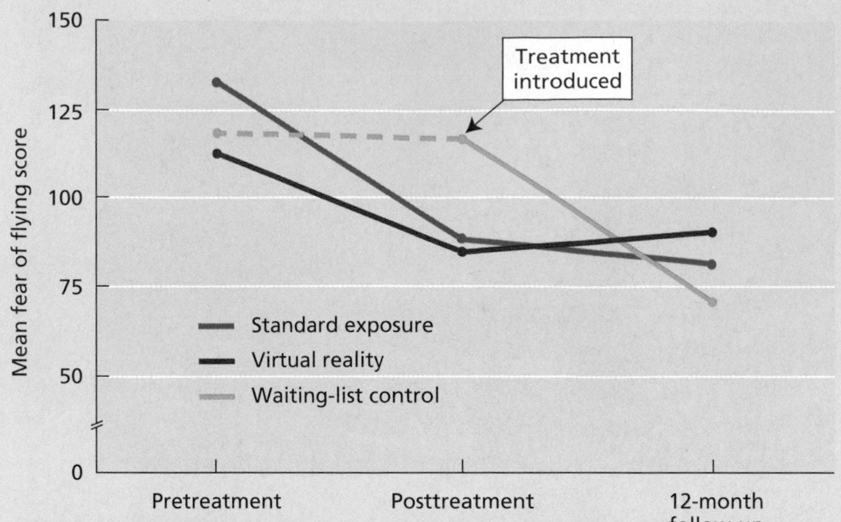

FIGURE 14.13

Effects of exposure treatment on self-reported fear of flying. Exposure was carried out in a two ways. Standard exposure involved in vivo and imaginal exposure, whereas virtual reality presented airline-related stimuli. Both exposure methods resulted in significant fear reduction that was maintained over a 12-month follow-up, and the waiting-list control group showed similar improvement when given the treatment. SOURCE: Based on Rothbaum et al., 2000, 2002.

landings and flying in both clear and stormy weather. Woofers under the seats provided realistic sounds and vibrations to simulate flight stimuli and turbulence. The therapist encouraged the clients to continue their exposure to the stimuli until their anxiety diminished.

In the standard exposure condition, clients were taken to the Atlanta airport and went through ticketing and security checks, rode a train to a remote gate, sat in a gate area with passengers, then boarded an empty airliner, where they were seated and asked to imagine scenes like those experienced by the VR clients.

After the treatments were completed, all clients in the three groups were offered the opportunity to take a round-trip commercial flight from Atlanta to Houston. Later, clients in the WL control condition were offered their choice of the two exposure treatments. All but one of the 15 chose the VR treatment.

Results

After randomly assigning participants to experimental and control conditions, the researchers assessed the clients before treatment began, at the end of the exposure treatments (Rothbaum et al., 2000), and 12 months after the completion of treatment. Outcome measures included both a self-report measure of fear of flying and a behavioral measure of actually flying in an airliner.

Figure 14.13 shows the intensity of clients' fear of flying at the three assessment periods. At the end of treatment, both exposure groups showed significant fear reduction, whereas the WL group showed no reduction. Treatment gains were maintained over the next 12 months, indicating that the treatment provides long-term benefits. After they received treatment, the control clients exhibited similar improvement on the fear measure.

On the behavioral measure of flying, 8 of 15 VR clients, 10 of 15 standard exposure clients, and only 1 of 15 WL clients accepted the invitation to take the posttreatment flight to Houston. By the 12-month follow-up, however, over 90 percent of the clients in the two exposure conditions had taken at least one commercial airline flight. No differences were found between the exposure groups on overall self-ratings of improvement or on satisfaction with the treatments they received.

Discussion

This study affirms the usefulness of short-term exposure treatments for anxiety-based problems, an effect shown in many previous studies. More significantly, results indicate that VR was similar in effectiveness to the traditional in vivo and imaginal exposure treatment, both in its initial effects at posttreatment and in the maintenance of therapy gains over the following 12 months. This is the first VR outcome study to conduct a follow-up assessment of treatment gains over such an extended period of time.

Conducting exposure treatment using VR may have some practical advantages. If the VR program is standardized for a particular fear, as in this study, then once the software has been developed, many therapists can apply the treatment to clients in their offices. Standard exposure treatments may require the therapist to leave the office and accompany the client to remote sites, an added treatment expense. With VR, a client may be able to experience many takeoffs and landings per hour, whereas repeated experiences on real airplanes would be prohibitively expensive. Another advantage of VR is the degree of control that is possible in the stimuli presented. Such control may not be possible in the real world, where the desired stimuli are not always available on demand. On the other hand, customizing stimuli for a client may require extensive programming that could be very expensive. It thus appears that standardized VR presentations for specific fears (e.g., driving, heights, exposure to various animals) may be most feasible at this time. Future research is certain to provide more information about the effectiveness, advantages, and possible limitations of VR for a variety of other disorders.

Systematic Desensitization: A Counterconditioning Approach

In 1958, Joseph Wolpe introduced **systematic desensitization,** *a learning-based treatment for anxiety disorders.* Wolpe also presented impressive outcome data for 100 phobic patients he had treated with the technique. Systematic desensitization remains a widely used treatment today. In many controlled studies, its success rate in treating a wide range of phobic disorders has been 80 percent or better (Rachman, 1998; Spiegler & Guevremont, 2003).

Wolpe viewed anxiety as a classically conditioned emotional response. His goal was to eliminate the anxiety by using a procedure called **counterconditioning,** *in which a new response that is incompatible with anxiety is conditioned to the anxiety-arousing CS.* The difference between extinction and counterconditioning is that extinction requires only exposure to the CS; it does not require a substitute response to counter the anxiety response.

The first step in systematic desensitization is to train the client in the skill of voluntary muscle relaxation, using an approach similar to that described in Chapter 10. Next the client is helped to construct a **stimulus hierarchy** *of 10 to 20 scenes arranged in roughly equal steps from low-anxiety scenes to high-anxiety ones.* Table 14.2 shows a stimulus hierarchy that was used in treating a college student with high test anxiety.

TABLE 14.2 A Stimulus Hierarchy Used in the Systematic Desensitization Treatment of a Test-Anxious College Student

Scene	Hierarchy of Anxiety-Arousing Scenes
1	Hearing about someone else who has a test
2	Instructor announcing that a test will be given in 3 weeks
3	Instructor reminding class that there will be a test in 2 weeks
4	Overhearing classmates talk about studying for the test, which will occur in 1 week
5	Instructor reminding class of what it will be tested on in 2 days
6	Leaving class the day before the exam
7	Studying the night before the exam
8	Getting up the morning of the exam
9	Walking toward the building where the exam will be given
10	Walking into the testing room
11	Instructor walking into the room with the tests
12	Tests being passed out
13	Reading the test questions
14	Watching others finish the test
15	Seeing a question I can't answer
16	Instructor waiting for me to finish the test

In the desensitization sessions, the therapist deeply relaxes the client and then asks the client to vividly imagine the first scene in the hierarchy (the least anxiety-arousing one) for several seconds. The client can't be both relaxed and anxious at the same time, so if the relaxation is strong enough, it replaces anxiety as the CR to that stimulus—the counterconditioning process. When the client can imagine that scene for increasingly longer periods without experiencing anxiety, the therapist proceeds to the next scene. When low-arousal scenes have been deconditioned, some of the total anxiety has been reduced and the person is now able to imagine more anxiety-arousing ones without becoming anxious. Therapists can also accomplish desensitization through carefully controlled exposure to a hierarchy of real-life situations (e.g., having a person with a phobia of heights actually stand on a step stool and, eventually, walk across a suspension bridge while voluntarily relaxed). Both imaginal and real-life desensitization approaches are highly effective in reducing anxiety (Hersen, 2003).

Although both exposure therapy based on extinction and systematic desensitization are very effective in reducing fear responses, there are practical tradeoffs. Systematic desensitization is sometimes preferred over exposure therapy because it produces far less anxiety for the client during the treatment. Exposure, however, often achieves the desired reduction in anxiety with a briefer course of therapy than does systematic desensitization (Bruce & Sanderson, 1998).

▶ 9. How does systematic desensitization differ from exposure in terms of its underlying principle and techniques?

For more on treatment for phobias, see Interactive Segment 14.1.

What Do You Think?

ARE CONDITIONING TECHNIQUES COMPATIBLE WITH PSYCHOANALYTIC THEORY?

Conditioning techniques such as exposure and systematic desensitization are highly effective in treating fears and phobias. Assume, however, that you are a psychoanalyst. From your theoretical perspective, what concerns would you have about using these behavioral techniques? Think about it, then see the discussion on page 589.

Aversion Therapy

For some clients, the therapeutic goal is not to reduce anxiety but to condition anxiety to a particular stimulus so as to reduce deviant approach behaviors. In **aversion therapy,** *the therapist pairs a*

▶ 10. Which learning principles underlie aversion therapy? What are its limitations and how can its effects be enhanced?

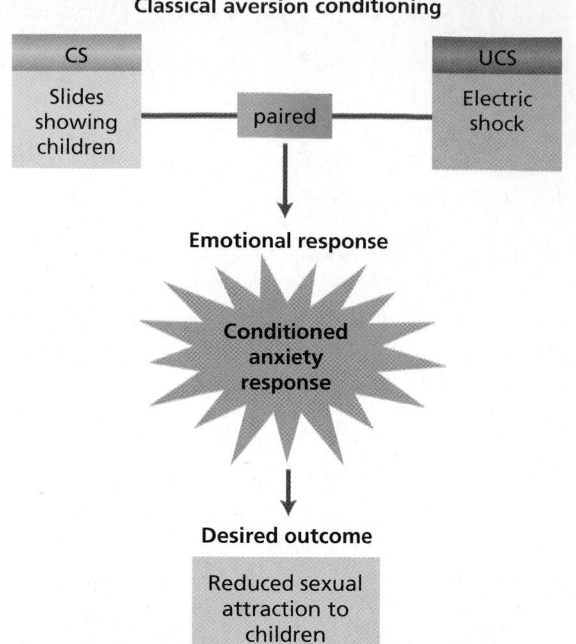

▶ 11. How are positive reinforcement and punishment used therapeutically? What evidence exists for their effectiveness?

FIGURE 14.14

The classical conditioning that occurs in aversion therapy is illustrated in the treatment of pedophiles who receive electric shocks as they view pictures of children. The goal of the treatment is the development of a conditioned aversion to reduce sexual attraction to children.

stimulus that is attractive to the client and stimulates deviant or self-defeating behavior (the CS) with a noxious UCS in an attempt to condition an aversion to the CS. For example, aversion treatment for alcoholics may involve injecting the client with a nausea-producing drug, then having him or her drink alcohol (the CS) as nausea (the UCS) develops. Electric shock may also be paired with alcohol ingestion. Similarly, pedophiles (child molesters) have undergone treatment in which strong electric shock is paired with slides showing children similar to those the offenders sexually abused (Figure 14.14). To measure the effects of the treatment for males, therapists can use a physiological recording device that measures penile blood volume responses to the slides; the therapists can then compare the readings before and after treatment (Sandler, 1986).

Aversion therapies have been applied to a range of disorders, with variable results. In one study of 278 alcoholics who underwent aversion therapy, 190 (63 percent) were still abstinent a year after treatment had ended. Three years later, a third of the patients were still abstinent, an impressive result given the traditionally high relapse rate in chronic alcoholics (Wiens & Menustik, 1983). Unfortunately, treatment gains from aversion therapies often fail to generalize from the treatment setting to the real world. A recovering alcoholic or drug addict who goes to a party where friends abuse the substance is likely to have difficulty resisting the temptation to relapse. Some experts believe that aversion therapy is most likely to succeed if it is part of a more comprehensive treatment program in which the client also learns specific coping skills for avoiding relapses (Marlatt & Gordon, 1985).

Operant Conditioning Treatments

The term **behavior modification** *refers to treatment techniques that apply operant conditioning procedures in an attempt to increase or decrease a specific behavior.* These techniques may use any of the operant procedures for manipulating the environment that we discussed in Chapter 6: positive reinforcement, extinction, negative reinforcement, or punishment. The focus in behavior modification is on externally observable behaviors, and measurement of the behaviors targeted for change occurs throughout the treatment program. This measurement allows the therapist to track the progress of the treatment program and to make modifications if behavior change begins to lag.

Behavior modification techniques have been successfully applied to many different behavior disorders. They have yielded particularly impressive results when applied to populations that are difficult to treat with more traditional therapies, such as chronic hospitalized schizophrenic patients, profoundly disturbed children, and mentally retarded individuals (Ayllon & Azrin, 1968; DeRubeis & Crits-Christoph, 1998; Lovaas, 1977). We now consider the use of positive reinforcement and punishment in two of these populations.

Positive Reinforcement One of the dangers of long-term psychiatric hospitalization is the gradual loss of social, personal-care, and occupational skills needed to survive outside the hospital. Such deterioration is common among chronic schizophrenic patients who have been hospitalized for an extended period. Verbal psychotherapies have very limited success in rebuilding such skills.

In the 1960s, Teodoro Ayllon and Nathan Azrin (1968) introduced a revolutionary approach to the treatment of hospitalized schizophrenics. The **token economy** *is a system for strengthening desired behaviors*—such as personal grooming, appropriate social responses, housekeeping behaviors, working on assigned jobs, and participation in vocational training programs—*through the systematic application of positive reinforcement.* Rather than being given reinforcers such as food or grounds privileges directly, patients earn a specified number of plastic tokens for the performance of each desired behavior listed on a kind of "menu." Patients can then redeem the tokens for a wide range of tangible reinforcers, such as a private room, exclusive rental of a radio or TV set, selection of personal furniture, freedom to leave the ward and walk around the grounds, recreational activities, and items from the hospital commissary. The long-term goal of token economy programs is to get the desired behaviors started with tangible reinforcers until they eventually come under the control of social reinforcers and self-reinforcement processes (such as self-pride), which the patient will need to get along in the world outside the hospital. When this begins to occur, the tokens can be phased out and the desired behaviors will continue (Kazdin, 2003). Using this technique, Ayllon and Azrin reported remarkable increases in adaptive behavior in patients for whom change seemed hopeless.

Token economy programs have proven highly effective with some of the most challenging populations. In one study, a token economy program was carried out over a 4-year period with severely disturbed schizophrenic patients who had been hospitalized an average of more than 17 years. During the course of the program, 98 percent of the patients from the behavioral treatment program were able to be released from the hospital (most to shelter-care facilities in the community), compared with only 45 percent of a control group that received the normal hospital treatments (Paul & Lentz, 1977). Token economies have also been applied successfully within business, school, prison, and home environments to increase desirable behaviors (Sullivan & O'Leary, 1990).

In one recent study, researchers used a positive reinforcement program to reduce cocaine and opium use among drug addicts receiving methadone treatment. Patients received weekly urine tests for drug detection. Those who had negative tests were eligible to draw a piece of paper from a bowl. Half of the papers earned them prizes ranging in value from $1 to $100. Bonus draws were given for extended periods of abstinence (for example, 2 consecutive weeks of negative urine tests earned six bonus draws). The patients randomly assigned to the positive reinforcement program had a significantly higher percentage of negative urine tests over the 12-week period. By abstaining from drugs, the patients had a greater opportunity to build coping responses to avoid relapse following treatment (Petry & Martin, 2002).

Therapeutic Application of Punishment As we saw in Chapter 6, punishment is the quickest way to stop a behavior from occurring, but most psychologists regard it as the least preferred way to control behavior because of its aversive qualities and potential negative side effects. Therefore, before deciding to use punishment as a therapy technique, therapists ask themselves two important questions: (1) Are there alternative, less painful approaches that might be effective? (2) Is the behavior to be eliminated sufficiently injurious to the individual or to society to justify the severity of the punishment?

Sometimes the answers to these questions lead to a decision to use punishment. For example, some of the most startling self-destructive behaviors occur in certain severely disturbed autistic children. Such children may strike themselves repeatedly, bang their heads on sharp objects, bite or tear pieces of flesh from their bodies, or engage in other self-mutilating behaviors. O. Ivar Lovaas (1977), a UCLA psychologist who pioneered the use of operant conditioning techniques in the treatment of such children, successfully eliminated such behaviors with a limited number of contingent electric shocks. One 7-year-old boy had been self-injurious for 5 years and had to be kept in physical restraints. During one 90-minute period when his restraints were removed, he struck himself more than 3,000 times. With the consent of his parents, shock electrodes were attached to the boy and he was given a painful electric shock each time he struck himself. Only 12 shocks were needed to virtually eliminate the self-destructive behavior. In another case, 15 shocks eliminated self-destructive behavior in a severely disturbed girl with a history of banging her head against objects. Punishment is never employed without consent of the client or the client's legal guardian in cases when the client is a minor or is mentally incompetent to give consent.

Modeling and Social Skills Training

▶ 12. How is modeling used in social skills training? How is self-efficacy involved in its effectiveness?

Modeling is one of the most important and effective learning processes in humans, and modeling procedures have been used to treat a variety of behavioral problems. One of the most widely used applications is designed to teach clients social skills that they lack.

In **social skills training,** *clients learn new skills by observing and then imitating a model who performs* *a socially skillful behavior.* In the following example, a therapist served as a model for his client, a socially anxious college student who had great difficulty asking women for dates. The client began by pretending to ask for a date over the telephone:

Client: By the way (pause), I don't suppose you want to go out Saturday night?

Therapist: Up to actually asking for the date you were very good. However, if I were the girl, I might have been offended when you said, "By the way." It's like asking her out is pretty casual. Also, the way you posed the question, you are kind of suggesting to her that she doesn't want to go out with you. Pretend for the moment I'm you. Now, how does this sound: "There's a movie at the Varsity Theater that I want to see. If you don't have other plans, I'd very much like to take you."

Client: That sounded good. Like you were sure of yourself and like the girl, too.

Therapist: Why don't you try it? (Rimm & Masters, 1979, p. 74).

Social skills training has been used with many populations, including individuals who have minor deficits in social skills, delinquents who need to learn how to resist negative peer pressures, and even hospitalized schizophrenic patients who need to learn social skills in order to function adaptively outside the hospital. It is often used in conjunction with other psychological or biological treatments to jump-start new adaptive behaviors that can then be strengthened by natural reinforcers in the client's everyday environment.

Research demonstrates that a key factor underlying the effectiveness of social skills training is increased self-efficacy. When clients come to believe that they are capable of performing the desired behaviors, they succeed in doing so (Bandura, 1997; Maddux, 1999). Observing successful models also increases self-efficacy by encouraging the view, "If she can do that, so can I."

Integrating and Combining Therapies

We have now surveyed a variety of therapeutic orientations. To an increasing extent, clinicians are embracing **eclecticism,** *a willingness to combine treatments and use whatever orientations and therapeutic techniques seem appropriate for the particular client they are treating* (Lazarus, 1995; Snyder & Ingram, 2000). For example, many therapists now label themselves *cognitive-behavioral therapists* because their techniques include elements of both perspectives. In recent years, Albert Ellis and other rational-emotive therapists have renamed their technique *rational-emotive behavior therapy* (Dryden, 2002).

In part, this tendency toward eclecticism reflects a responsiveness to research findings that certain approaches to therapy are well suited for some problems and ill suited for others. For example, Gestalt techniques are highly effective for helping people discover underlying feelings, but a behavioral approach would be the treatment of choice for treating a phobia, and cognitive therapy is highly effective for depression. A therapist could choose to use any combination of techniques for a client who has multiple problems. Also prompting the move toward eclecticism is the fact that modern therapists are being trained in a variety of perspectives and therapy approaches, so that they emerge as professionals with a wider range of therapeutic competencies (Norcross, 1991). One national survey of eclectic therapists revealed that 72 percent included psychodynamic principles within their version of treatment, 54 percent included cognitive approaches, 45 percent used behavioral techniques, and a smaller percentage used various humanistic techniques (Jensen et al., 1990).

The move toward eclecticism has resulted in some integrations that would have been unthinkable 30 years ago. For example, **psychodynamic behavior therapy** *involves an integration of psychoanalysis and behavior therapy.* These would appear to be strange bedfellows indeed, but Paul Wachtel (1997), originally trained as a psychoanalyst, has skillfully blended them into an approach that seems capable of being applied to a wide range of problems. For example, consider a highly submissive man who is unaware of his unresolved anger. Wachtel might treat this client with psychodynamic techniques to help him achieve insight into his unconscious anger and its origins in his early life. When the client achieves such insight, the irrational aspects of his anger may disappear, but he may still find himself unable to be assertive even when it would be appropriate. At this point, the therapist might decide that psychoanalysis has reached its limits of therapeutic effectiveness and switch to a behavioral social skills training program to allow the client to develop and practice assertiveness skills.

IN REVIEW

- *Cognitive and behavior therapies are among the most popular and effective approaches to psychological treatment.*
- *Ellis's rational-emotive therapy and Beck's cognitive therapy focus on discovering and changing maladaptive beliefs and logical errors of thinking that underlie maladaptive emotional responses and behaviors.*
- *Behavioral treatments based on classical conditioning are directed at modifying emotional responses. Exposure to a CS and prevention of avoidance responses promote extinction. Exposure may be provided in vivo (real life), through imagination, or through virtual reality (VR) technology.*
- *Systematic desensitization is designed to countercondition a response to anxiety-arousing stimuli that is incompatible with anxiety, such as relaxation. Aversion therapy is used to establish a conditioned aversion response to an inappropriate stimulus that attracts the client.*
- *Operant procedures have been applied successfully in many behavior modification programs. The token economy is a positive reinforcement program designed to strengthen adaptive behaviors. Punishment has been used to reduce self-destructive behaviors in disturbed children.*
- *Modeling is an important component of social skills training programs, which help clients learn and rehearse more effective social behaviors.*
- *Psychotherapy today shows a growing trend toward eclecticism—the combination of perspectives and techniques from several different therapies. There is also a movement to develop more effective therapies by combining different forms of therapy into new therapeutic techniques.*

Group, Family, and Marital Therapies

Most of the therapeutic approaches we have discussed so far can be carried out with groups of clients as well as with individuals (Beck & Lewis, 2000). Therapy groups typically include 6 to 8 clients and a single therapist. Within a group, clients can experience acceptance, support, and a sense of belonging. They soon see that other people also struggle with problems, a realization that helps counter feelings of isolation and deviance. Clients can also observe how others approach problems, and the interpersonal relations that develop within the group can be a training ground for learning new interpersonal skills. Furthermore, clients can gain insight into how they are perceived by others.

Family Therapy

Sometimes the group being treated is a family. Family therapy arose from the clinical observation that many clients who had shown marked improvement in individual therapy—often in institutional settings—suffered relapses when they returned home and began interacting with their families. This observation led to an important concept in the field of psychotherapy, namely, that the disorder shown by the "identified patient" may reflect disordered relationships within the family system and that permanent change in the client may require that the entire family system be the focus of therapy (Minuchin, 1974). Family therapists therefore try to help the family understand how it functions and how its unique patterns of interactions contribute to conflicts and to the problems of one or more members (Figure 14.15):

FIGURE 14.15

Family therapists focus on the total pattern of family interactions, and they include the entire family in treatment.

▶ 13. What principles underlie family and marital therapy? What is the importance of acceptance in marital therapy?

In one family, Jessica, an anorexic 14-year-old girl, was the identified patient. However, as the therapist worked with the family, he saw a competitive struggle for the father's attention and observed that the girl was able to compete and get "cuddly" affection from her father only when she presented herself to him as a "sick" person. To bring the hidden dynamics out into the open, the therapist worked at getting the family members to express their desires more directly—in words instead of through hidden behavioral messages. In time, Jessica became capable of expressing her need for affection directly to her father, and her anorexia disappeared. (Based on Aponte & Hoffman, 1974)

Marital Therapy

Today's soaring divorce rate is a stark reflection of the difficulties that exist in many marriages. Nearly half of all first marriages end in divorce, and the divorce rate is even higher among people who remarry (Hetherington, 1998). Couples frequently seek marital therapy because they are troubled by their relationship or because they are contemplating separation or divorce. Typically, the therapist works with both partners together, and therapy focuses on clarifying and improving the interactions between them. Research has shown that happily married couples differ from distressed couples in that they talk more to one another, keep channels of communication open, show more sensitivity to each other's feelings and needs, and are more skilled at solving problems (Gottman & Levinson, 1992). Marital therapy targets improvement in these areas.

▶ 14. What barriers to therapy exist for ethnic minorities? What characteristics are found in culturally competent and gender-sensitive therapists?

Distressed couples frequently have faulty communication patterns, as demonstrated in the following case:

Husband: She never comes up to me and kisses me. I am always the one to make the overtures.

Therapist: Is this the way you see yourself behaving with your husband?

Wife: Yes, I would say he is the demonstrative one. I didn't know he wanted me to make the overtures.

Therapist: Have you told your wife you would like this from her—more demonstration of affection?

Husband: Well, no. You'd think she'd know.

Wife: No, how would I know? You always said you didn't like aggressive women.

Husband: I don't, I don't like dominating women.

Wife: Well, I thought you meant women who make the overtures. How am I to know what you want?

Therapist: You'd have a better idea if he had been able to tell you. (Satir, 1967, pp. 72–73)

An important recent addition to marital therapy is a focus on *acceptance* (Jacobson & Christensen, 1996). This addition was based on findings that in well-functioning couples, as well as those who profit from treatment, partners make a decision to accept those aspects of the partner's behavior that probably are too ingrained to change. For example, it makes little sense to demand that a person with a highly introverted personality style suddenly become a social gadfly and life of the party. The therapeutic emphasis is on helping couples work toward change in those areas where change is possible and helping them learn to accept aspects of the partner and the relationship that seem unlikely to change. Doing so reduces frustration, lessens demands on the other spouse, and allows the couple to focus on and enjoy the positive aspects of their relationship. The addition of acceptance training to the other elements of marital therapy has improved treatment outcomes (Jacobson et al., 2000).

CULTURAL AND GENDER ISSUES IN PSYCHOTHERAPY

Psychological treatments reflect the cultural context in which they develop. Within the dominant cultures of western Europe and North America, personal problems are seen as originating within people in the form of dysfunctional thinking, conflict, and stress responses. People are assumed capable of expressing their feelings and taking personal responsibility for improving themselves. We can easily see these values and assumptions reflected in the therapies we have discussed. Psychodynamic, humanistic, and cognitive treatments all focus on changing these internal factors.

These values are not shared by all cultures and ethnic groups, however. For example, people from some Asian cultures might view the "therapeutic" expression of hostility toward one's parents as unthinkable (Hall & Okazaki, 2003). Likewise, the suggestion that assertiveness training would be helpful in competing more successfully with others and standing up for one's rights might be appalling to a person from a collectivistic culture (Cooper & Denner, 1998). Given diverse cultural norms and values, we should not be surprised that some individuals from non-Western cultures view psychotherapy as a totally inappropriate, and even shameful, option for the solution of their problems in living (Foulks et al., 1995).

Cultural Factors in Treatment Utilization

Although overall rates of psychopathology do not differ greatly among ethnic groups in the United States, utilization of mental health services is far less for minority groups than it is for the majority White population (Wang et al., 2002). Even when minority group members seek out mental health services, they often fail to stay in treatment. As a result, many problems that could benefit from psychological treatment go untreated (Sue, 1998; Wang et al., 2002). The growing cultural diversity in North America and Europe has important implications for the practice of psychotherapy, and researchers are trying to identify the barriers to psychological treatment and what can be done to lower them.

Psychologists Derald Sue and David Sue (1990) have identified several of these barriers. One of them is a cultural norm against turning to professionals outside one's own culture for help. Instead these individuals turn to family, clergy, acupuncturists, herbalists, and folk healers for assistance. Moreover, for many minority members, a history of frustrating experiences with White bureaucracies makes them unwilling to approach a hospital or mental health center. There may also be language barriers.

Sometimes access to treatment is a major problem. Because many minority groups suffer high rates of unemployment and poverty, they may not have health insurance and be unable to afford therapy. Likewise, many community mental health agencies and professional therapists are located outside the areas where the underserved populations live.

But according to Stanley Sue and Nolan Zane (1987), the biggest problem of all is that there are too few skilled counselors who could provide culturally responsive forms of treatment. Therapists often have little familiarity with the cultural backgrounds and personal characteristics of ethnic groups other than their own. Sometimes they operate on the basis of inaccurate stereotypes. This can result in unrealistic and possibly inappropriate goals and expectations on the part of a therapist, as well as great difficulty in establishing the positive client-therapist relationship that has been shown to be a powerful factor in therapeutic success.

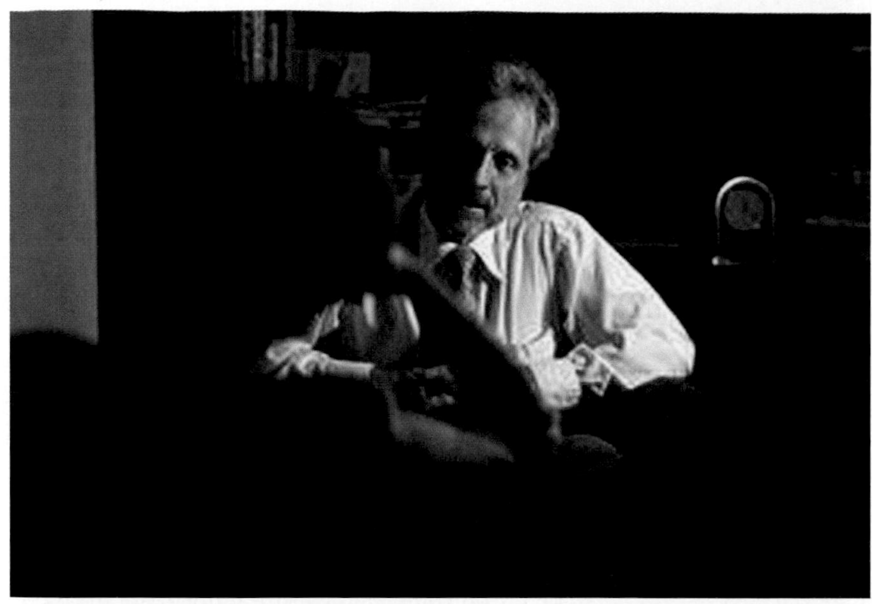

FIGURE 14.16

Research suggests that the outcome of therapy with minority populations is affected more by the cultural sensitivity and competency of the therapist than it is by the ethnic similarity of therapist and client.

What can be done to increase access of culturally diverse groups to psychological treatment? One answer is to take therapy to the people. Studies have shown that establishing mental health service agencies in minority population areas increases utilization of mental health services, particularly if agencies are staffed by culturally skilled counselors (S. Sue, 1998). Another solution might be to train more therapists from these ethnic groups. Stanley Sue and his coworkers (1991) found that dropout rates were reduced and the number of therapy sessions increased when clients saw ethnically similar therapists. However, for clients who elect to remain in therapy, it has *not* been demonstrated that treatment outcomes are better for clients who work with therapists from their own ethnic group. What seems more important than an ethnic match is for the therapist and client to form a good relationship and to share similar viewpoints regarding goals for treatment and preferred means for resolving problems (Figure 14.16).

Stanley Sue (1998) suggests that **culturally competent therapists** *are able to use knowledge about the client's culture to achieve a broad understanding of the client.* At the same time, they are attentive to how the client may differ from the cultural stereotype, thereby balancing cultural understanding with the individual characteristics and needs of the client. They are also able to introduce *culture-specific elements* into the therapy.

Thus a therapist might draw on some of the techniques used by folk healers within that culture (e.g., prayer or a specific ritual) to effect changes in the client. Obviously, this would require a good working knowledge of the culture from which the client comes, plus a willingness to take advantage of what "works" in that culture (Mishne, 2002).

Can therapists be trained to be more culturally sensitive? Indeed they can. In one study, experienced African American and White therapists were assigned to either a 4-hour cultural sensitivity training program or to a control condition that received no training. The therapists then treated African American clients from the community. The outcome of therapy was carefully assessed and the results showed that exposure to the ethnic training was more important to therapeutic outcome than was the ethnicity of the therapist. Clients rated the therapists who had received training (whether African American or White) as having greater empathy and expertise, and these clients also attended more therapy sessions (Wade & Bernstein, 1991). It thus appears that therapists can acquire cultural sensitivity and use it to enhance therapy for members of minority cultures.

Gender Issues in Therapy

Even within the same culture, the lives of men and women can differ in many ways, as can the life demands they are called upon to cope with. As we saw in Chapter 13, psychological disorders, particularly those involving anxiety and depression, occur more frequently among women in Western cultures. This may reflect the impact of specific stressors that women face, such as poverty (women are overrepresented at the poverty level); lack of opportunity fostered by sexism; strains created by the demanding multiple roles of mother, worker, and spouse among married women; and the violence and histories of abuse that many women experience. In many instances, psychological problems arise not so much from internal problems and conflicts but from oppressive elements in the family, social, and political worlds. As women strive for more egalitarian relationships with men and for equal opportunity to develop their potential, they often meet external barriers that are deeply embedded in their culture's traditional sex roles (Worell & Remer, 2003).

In the eyes of many therapists, it may be more important to focus on what can be done to change women's life circumstances than to help them adapt to sex-role expectations that constrain them (Brown, 1994). It is important for both men and women therapists to support people in making choices that meet their needs, whether it be a man who wishes to stay at home and care for children or a woman who wants a career in the military. Consistent with the research on cultural similarity between therapist and client, research on therapy with female clients indicates that they can work successfully with either female or male therapists. Whether the therapist is a man or a woman, what seems important is the therapist's sensitivity to gender issues.

IN REVIEW

- *Group approaches offer clients a number of advantages, including opportunities to form close relationships with others, to gain insights into how they interact with others and are perceived by them, and to observe how others approach problems.*
- *Family therapy is based on the notion that individuals' problems are often reflections of dysfunctional family systems. Such systems should be treated as a unit.*
- *Marital therapies help couples improve their communication patterns and resolve difficulties in their relationships. The recent addition of acceptance training has improved outcomes.*
- *Research has shown that members of minority groups underutilize mental health services. Barriers include lack of access to therapists who can provide culturally responsive forms of treatment. More important to outcome than a cultural match is a therapist who can understand the client's cultural background and share viewpoints on therapy goals and the means used to achieve them. Culturally competent therapists take into account both cultural and individual factors to understand and treat the client.*
- *For female clients, the most helpful therapist is one who is aware of oppressive environmental conditions and is willing to support life goals that do not necessarily conform to gender expectations. Whether the therapist is a man or a woman seems less important to outcome than gender sensitivity.*

EVALUATING PSYCHOTHERAPIES

Given the human suffering created by psychological disorders, the effects of psychotherapy have both personal and societal implications. Practicing clinicians and clinical researchers want to know which approaches are most effective against which kinds of problems and what the "active ingredients" of each treatment are that produce its effects.

Today the basic question "Does psychotherapy work?" is viewed as a gross oversimplification of a much more involved question known as the **specificity question:** *"Which types of therapy, administered by which kinds of therapists to which kinds of clients having which kinds of problems, produce which kinds of effects?"* After nearly a half century of psychotherapy research involving many hundreds of studies, this complex question is still not fully answered (Kazdin, 2003). Nonetheless, for many reasons, this question demands answers. Selecting and administering the most appropriate kind of intervention is vital in human terms. It is also important for economic reasons. Billions of dollars are spent each year on psychological treatments, with an increasing share of these costs paid by so-called third parties such as insurance companies, health maintenance organizations, and government agencies. As the costs rise, those who bear the financial burden increase their demands for accountability and for demonstrations that the treatments are useful.

Designing good psychotherapy research is one of the most challenging tasks in all of psychology because there are so many variables that cannot be completely controlled. In contrast to laboratory studies, in which the experimental conditions can be highly standardized, therapist-client interactions are by their nature infinitely varied. Another difficulty involves measuring the effects of psychotherapy. Figure 14.17 shows some of the typical ways of measuring change. These measures differ in the outcome variable assessed (emotions, thoughts, or behaviors) and in the source of the data (the client, the therapist, or other informants). Which measures of change are most important or valid? A behaviorist will insist that direct observations of behavior are the best measures, whereas a psychodynamic therapist may be most interested in how clients feel and how much insight they have achieved into the childhood roots of their problems. A humanistic therapist may place the greatest stock in self-concept changes. What if one set of measures indicates improvement, another indicates no change, and a third suggests that the client is worse off than before treatment? How should we evaluate the effects of the therapy? These are just a few of the vexing issues that can arise in psychotherapy research.

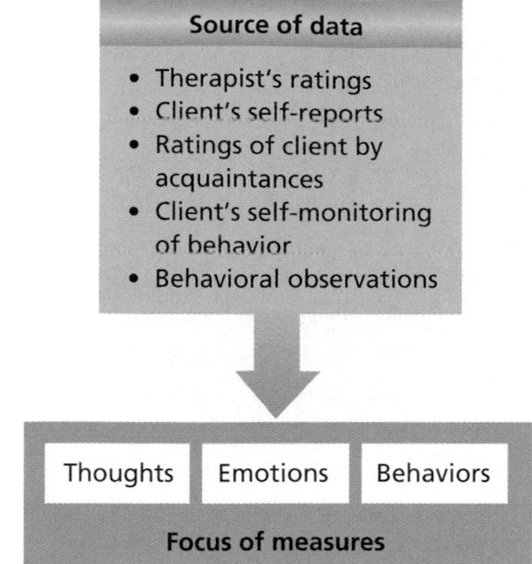

FIGURE 14.17

The measures used to assess the outcome of psychotherapy may come from a variety of data sources, and they may measure different aspects of the client's functioning.

▶ 15. What is the "specificity question" in psychotherapy research?

Psychotherapy Research Methods

In the 1930s and 1940s, individual case studies provided most of the psychotherapy outcome data. Indeed, Freud and other psychoanalysts opposed the use of experimental methods to evaluate psychoanalysis, insisting that case studies left no doubt regarding its effectiveness (Fisher & Greenberg, 1996). They assumed that without therapy, patients would not improve, and they saw plenty of people who did improve in analysis.

▶ 16. What types of outcome measures are used in psychotherapy research?

In 1952, British psychologist Hans Eysenck mounted a frontal assault on this assumption. Using recovery data from insurance companies on people who applied for disability because of psychological problems, Eysenck (1952) concluded that the rate of **spontaneous remission**—*symptom reduction in the absence of any treatment*—was as high as the success rates reported by psychotherapists. He therefore concluded that troubled people who receive psychotherapy are no more likely to improve than are those who go untreated. He also pointed out, quite correctly, that virtually all of the existing outcome data were based on therapists' evaluations of their clients' improvement, and he suggested that these evaluations could be biased by therapists' needs to see themselves as competent and successful.

Eysenck's conclusions sparked intense debate—even outrage—among clinicians, but they provided an important wake-up call that could not be ignored. Eysenck's challenge triggered a vigorous increase in psychotherapy research and stimulated the development of more sophisticated methods for evaluating treatment outcomes. Fifty years and many hundreds of studies later, we have reached the point where the Division of Clinical Psychology of the American Psychological Association (APA) has taken the lead in reviewing this research to identify **empirically supported therapies** *that have proven effective for specific disorders* (DeRubeis & Crits-Christoph, 1998; Kazdin & Weisz, 2003).

What Is a Good Psychotherapy Research Design?

▶ 17. Summarize good psychotherapy research techniques with regard to design, treatment standardization, and follow-up.

For many of the reasons mentioned in Chapter 2, where we discussed the value of experimental methods for drawing conclusions about causality, most psychotherapy researchers favor **randomized clinical trials** *in which participants who have well-defined psychological disorders and are similar on other variables that might affect response to treatment (e.g., age and ethnic status) are randomly assigned to either an experimental condition that gets treatment or to a control condition* (Kazdin, 2003). The control group may be either a no-treatment condition (typically, a waiting-list condition) or a **placebo control group** *that gets an intervention that is not expected to work.* The placebo condition is designed to control for client expectations of improvement and for being seen by a therapist. (For ethical reasons, clients in the control group, whether it be a no-treatment or placebo condition, are given the real treatment later.)

Another research design, which avoids the ethical dilemma of withholding or delaying treatment for some participants, involves randomly assigning participants to either the treatment being studied or to another kind of treatment that has proven effective for that disorder. If the new treatment being tested in the experimental condition is found to be at least as effective as the established treatment, then its value is supported. Sometimes, the design of a study involves a group in which the treatment is combined with another intervention such as a drug treatment. It is then possible to see if the group that received the drug *plus* psychotherapy does better as the groups that got only the drug or only the therapy (Hollon, 1996).

To standardize a research treatment, much as one would do in a laboratory experiment, the APA treatment evaluation group recommended issuing a manual containing procedures that the therapists have to follow exactly and evaluating therapists' compliance with these procedures by observing them or taping their sessions. This procedure is designed to ensure that participants in a particular treatment condition are truly receiving the same kind of therapy. The committee also recommended that at least some of the measures of improvement be behavioral in nature. To minimize experimenter bias in evaluating change during interviews or behavioral observations following treatment, interviewers and observers should not know whether a given client was in the control group or the experimental group.

Finally, researchers should collect follow-up data. This is extremely important, for we want to know not only how the treatment conditions differ at the end of the clinical trial but also how long-lasting the effects are. For example, in some studies comparing psychotherapy for depression with the effects of antidepressant drugs, the drug treatment effects occurred more quickly and were stronger at the end of the treatment period, suggesting a superiority for drug therapy. But follow-up data showed psychotherapy to be more effective in the long term. Because clients had learned specific psychological skills that they could apply after therapy ended, there were fewer relapses into depression (Hollon & Beck, 1994; Weissman & Markowitz, 1994).

Meta-Analysis: A Look at the Big Picture

▶ 18. What have meta-analyses shown about the effectiveness of different forms of therapy?

As discussed in Chapter 2, the technique of **meta-analysis** *allows researchers to combine the statistical results of many studies to arrive at an overall conclusion.* In the psychotherapy research literature they can compute an effect size statistic that represents a common measure of treatment effectiveness. The **effect size** *tells researchers what percentage of clients who received therapy had a more favorable outcome than that of the average control client who did not receive the treatment.*

In 1977, Mary Ann Smith and Gene Glass used meta-analysis to combine the effects of 375 studies of psychotherapy involving 25,000 clients and 25,000 control participants. These studies differed in many ways, but they all compared a treatment condition with a control condition. The results indicated that the average therapy client had a more favorable outcome than 75 percent of the untreated cases. These results prompted Smith and Glass to dispute Eysenck's earlier conclusion, maintaining that therapy does indeed have positive effects beyond spontaneous remission. More recent therapy meta-analyses support this conclusion.

What about differences among therapies? Smith and Glass broke down their meta-analysis in terms of many of the therapies described in this chapter. As shown in Figure 14.18, psychodynamic, client-centered, and behavioral approaches were quite similar in their effectiveness, and all of them seemed to yield somewhat more positive effects than Gestalt therapy. A more recent meta-analysis of brief-psychodynamic-therapy outcome studies supports a similar conclusion: Brief psychodynamic therapy yielded significantly better outcomes than did no-treatment or placebo control conditions, but it did not differ in efficacy from other forms of therapy with which it was compared (Anderson & Lambert, 1995). *This finding of similar efficacy for widely differing therapies has been termed the* **dodo bird verdict,** after the dodo bird's statement in *Alice in Wonderland* that "Everybody has won and all must have prizes" (Luborsky et al., 2002). Other researchers challenge this conclusion, maintaining that lumping together studies involving different kinds of clinical problems may mask *differential effectiveness,* i.e., the fact that specific therapies might be highly effective for treating some clinical disorders but not others (Beutler, 2002; Westen & Morrison, 2001).

The very definition of therapy "success" is a topic of debate. How much do clients have to improve in order to have a successful outcome? Is therapy successful if deeply depressed clients show a statistically significant decrease in self-report scores of depression following therapy but their scores still fall within the clinically depressed range? According to Neil Jacobson and coworkers (1996), **clinical significance** *would require that at the end of therapy, clients' depression scores fall within the range for nondepressed people.* This is, of course, a more stringent definition of therapeutic success than the one used in most meta-analyses (i.e., greater positive change in a treatment group than in a control group of similarly depressed clients) and would undoubtedly indicate lower levels of therapeutic success for most treatments.

In evaluating the results of meta-analyses, we should remember that the studies lumped together in a meta-analysis can differ in many ways, including the nature and severity of the problems that were treated, the outcome measures that were used, and the quality of the methodology. Psychotherapy researchers point out that combining good studies with less adequate ones can

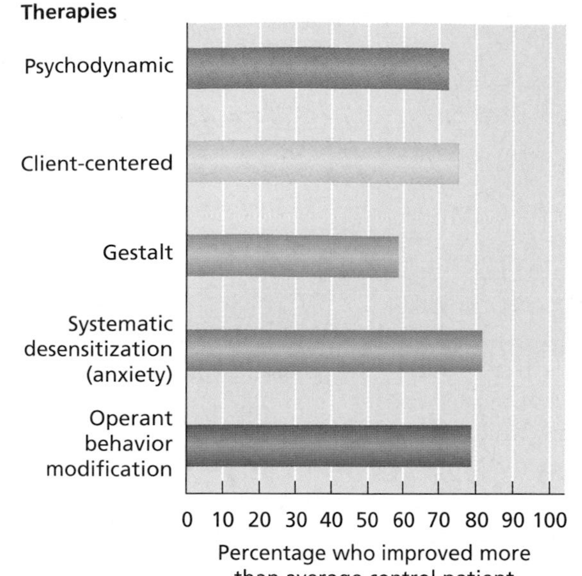

FIGURE 14.18

This meta-analysis of 375 studies of psychotherapy outcome yielded effectiveness data on various types of psychotherapy. The bars indicate the percentage of treated clients who improved more than the average control client.
SOURCE: Based on Smith & Glass, 1977.

produce misleading results (Kazdin, 2003). When studies that meet rigorous research standards are compared in meta-analyses with less rigorous studies, the rigorous studies tend to yield more favorable outcomes for therapy conditions (Matt & Navarro, 1997). Apparently, the rigorous methods used in such studies allow effective therapies to show their true effects.

Client Evaluations of Treatment

▶ 19. What were the major findings of the *CR* survey? On what bases were its conclusions criticized?

Randomized clinical trials are considered the gold standard of psychotherapy research, but they are not without their critics. Martin Seligman (1995) suggested that highly controlled efficacy studies may not provide a true indication of psychotherapy's effectiveness in real-life clinical practice. He therefore assisted the periodical *Consumer Reports (CR)* in a large-scale survey of its readership to assess consumers' evaluations of their therapy experiences and the professionals they worked with. One form of *CR*'s 1994 annual survey, mailed to 184,000 randomly selected subscribers, contained a section on stress and mental health. Readers were asked to complete the mental health section if they had sought help for emotional problems in the past three years. A total of 22,000 readers responded to the questionnaire—a 13 percent response rate that is typical of *CR* surveys. Of these, 35 percent reported that they had a mental health problem, and 40 percent (approximately 2,900 respondents) of this latter group reported that they had sought professional help from a psychologist, psychiatrist, social worker, or marriage counselor. The respondents were asked to

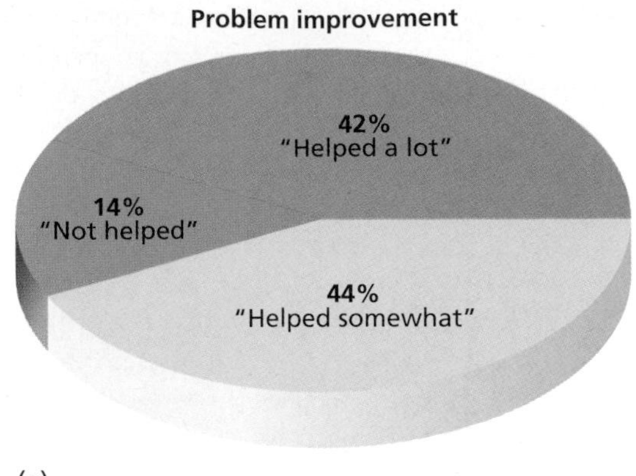

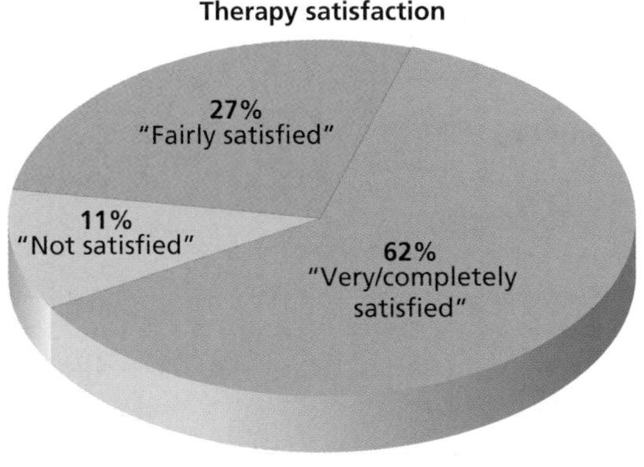

FIGURE 14.19

Ratings of (a) self-perceived improvement and (b) satisfaction with therapy outcome made by 2,900 subscribers of Consumer Reports *who had been in psychotherapy for the treatment of psychological disorders.* SOURCE: Based on Seligman, 1995.

▶ 20. What client, therapist, technique, and common factors influence treatment outcome?

indicate how much they improved as a result of treatment and how satisfied they were with the treatment they received.

As shown in Figure 14.19, the majority of clients said that they had improved as a result of treatment and that they were satisfied with their therapist. No overall outcome differences were found among mental health professionals, but clients were less satisfied with marriage counselors than with psychologists, psychiatrists, and social workers. As in the meta-analyses described earlier, the *CR* survey found no effectiveness differences between the various types of psychotherapy the clients said they had received. Seligman concluded that "*CR* has provided empirical validation of the effectiveness of therapy" (1995, p. 974). Further, he concluded that the survey method used in this study might actually have provided data that are more representative of real-life outcomes than data yielded by highly controlled clinical trials.

What Do You Think?

ARE "REAL-WORLD" CLIENTS' REPORTS MORE VALID THAN RESULTS FROM CLINICAL TRIALS?

Based on what you've learned about psychotherapy research standards, do you agree with Seligman's conclusion that his data may be a more valid reflection of therapy success than data from randomized clinical trials? Can you think of any aspects of the *CR* methods that might limit your ability to conclude how effective psychotherapy is? Compare your thoughts with the issues discussed on page 589.

Factors Affecting the Outcome of Therapy

Clearly, not everyone who enters therapy profits from it. There is even evidence that some clients—perhaps 10 percent—may get worse as a result of treatment (Binder & Strupp, 1997; Lambert et al., 1986). What, then, are the factors that influence treatment outcome? Research to answer this question has focused on three sets of variables: client variables, therapist variables, and technique variables (Figure 14.20).

Where client variables are concerned, three important factors are the client's openness to therapy, self-relatedness, and the nature of the problem. **Openness** *involves clients' general willingness to invest themselves in therapy and take the risks required to change themselves.* **Self-relatedness** *refers to their ability to experience and understand internal states such as thoughts and emotions, to be attuned to the processes*

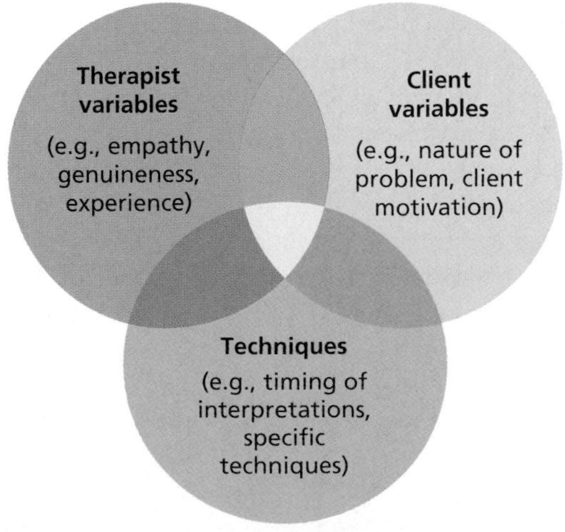

FIGURE 14.20

Research on factors that influence therapy outcome has focused on three sets of interacting variables: client variables, therapist variables, and technique variables.

that go on in their relationship with their therapist, and to apply what they learn in therapy to their lives outside of treatment (Howard et al., 1993). The third important client factor is the nature of the problem and its degree of "fit" with the therapy being used. For example, specific problems such as phobias may respond best to a behavioral anxiety-reduction treatment such as systematic desensitization or exposure, whereas a more global problem, such as a search for self-discovery and greater meaning in life, may respond better to a psychodynamic, cognitive, or humanistic approach.

Among therapist variables, perhaps the most important is the quality of the relationship that the therapist is able to establish with the client (Teyber & McClure, 2000). Carl Rogers's emphasis on the importance of therapist qualities such as empathy, unconditional acceptance of the client as a person, and genuineness has been borne out in a great many studies (Beutler et al., 1994; Norcross, 2003). An empathic, trusting, and caring relationship forms the foundation upon which the specific techniques employed by the therapist can have their most beneficial effects.

When therapists do not manifest these behaviors, the effects of therapy are not simply null; clients can actually get worse. For example, hostile interchanges between therapist and client can contribute to a *deterioration effect* in therapy (Binder & Strupp, 1997).

Assuming the therapy relationship is a positive one, there is still the consideration of technique variables. A therapist needs to be skilled and knowledgeable in selecting and implementing the appropriate techniques for each client and situation. For example, a large-scale study at the University of Pennsylvania revealed that the correctness of the interpretations made by psychoanalytic therapists, as measured by expert ratings, was related to more positive treatment outcome (Crits-Christoph et al., 1988). Likewise, in a detailed analysis of the audiotaped therapy sessions of 21 psychotherapists, Enrico Jones and coworkers (1988) found that the most effective therapists adjusted their techniques to the specific needs of their clients. They concluded that "general relationship factors, such as therapeutic alliance, are closely bound with the skillful selection and application of psychotherapeutic techniques" (p. 55).

If therapy is to be effective, clients must remain in treatment long enough for the therapeutic relationship and techniques to have their effects. For this reason, new research is focusing on the **dose-response effect,** *the relation between the amount of treatment received and the quality of the outcome.* One recent review of 29 randomized controlled clinical trials primarily involving cognitive and behavioral treatments found that between 58 and 67 percent of clients showed clinically significant improvement within an average of 13 sessions (Hansen et al., 2002). These rates are quite consistent with those typically found in research settings. The reviewers then turned to what occurs in the "real world" of clinical practice, examining the treatment records of 6,072 clients seen in a variety of naturalistic settings, including employee assistance programs, community and university counseling centers, and health maintenance organizations. Here they found that the average number of treatment sessions given was fewer than 5, and the rate of improvement in this sample was only about 20 percent. These results suggest that many clients seen in these naturalistic settings do not remain in therapy long enough to realize its potential benefits. One possible reason is that many insurance plans limit their coverage to a number of treatment sessions that is too low to expect meaningful improvement.

Despite dramatic differences in the techniques they employ, various therapies tend to enjoy similar success rates, perhaps because people who differ on the client variables are lumped together within studies. This finding has led many experts to search for **common factors,** *characteristics shared by these diverse forms of therapy that might contribute to their success.* These common factors include:

- clients' faith in the therapist and a belief that they are receiving help;
- a pausible explanation for clients' problems and an alternative way of helping them look at themselves and their problems;
- a protective setting where clients can experience and express their deepest feelings within a supportive relationship;
- an opportunity for clients to practice new behaviors; and
- clients' achieving increased optimism and self-efficacy.

How important these common factors are in comparison with specific therapeutic techniques is currently unknown, and the dodo bird verdict described earlier may reflect a failure to identify specific factors that underlie therapeutic success (Beutler, 2002). The complexities of psychotherapy pose a formidable challenge for clinical researchers. Despite decades of research on the efficacy of psychotherapy techniques, there is still much to learn. We know that some techniques are very effective for certain problems. Yet in the words of the eminent British psychotherapy researcher Isaac Marks, "Little is known about which treatment components produce improvement, how they do so, and why they do not help all sufferers" (Marks, 2002, p. 200).

IN REVIEW

- *Eysenck challenged the effectiveness of psychotherapy and stimulated the use of increasingly more sophisticated research methods to evaluate the outcomes of various therapies. The randomized clinical trial is the most powerful approach to researching the effects of therapy, and a number of standards have been established for conducting psychotherapy research.*
- *Meta-analysis is a method for combining the results of many studies into an effect size statistic. Meta-analyses of treatment outcome studies found more improvement in therapy clients than in 70 to 75 percent of control clients and little difference in effectiveness among various therapies (the so called dodo bird verdict). The* Consumer Reports *study of client self-report suggested high levels of client satisfaction.*
- *Three sets of interacting factors affect the outcome of treatment: client characteristics (including the nature of the problem), therapist characteristics, and therapy techniques.*
- *Client variables that contribute to therapy success include openness, self-relatedness, and a good match between the nature of the problem and the kind of therapy being received.*
- *A crucial factor in the success of various therapies is the quality of the relationship that the therapist establishes with the client. The three therapist characteristics suggested by Rogers—empathy, unconditional positive regard, and genuineness—are particularly important.*
- *Factors common to many therapies, such as faith in the therapist, a protected environment for self-exploration, and the ability to try out new behaviors, contribute to therapeutic outcome.*

BIOLOGICAL APPROACHES TO TREATMENT

In the previous chapter, we found that biological factors play an important role in many psychological disorders. Thus a direct biological approach designed to alter the brain's functioning is an alternative (or an addition) to psychological treatment.

Drug Therapies

Drug therapies are the most commonly used biological interventions. Discoveries in the field of psychopharmacology (the study of how drugs affect cognitions, emotions, and behavior) have revolutionized the treatment of the entire range of behavior disorders. Each year in the United States alone, doctors ranging from primary care physicians to psychiatrists to psychopharmacologists write more than 200 million prescriptions for drugs that affect mood, thought, and behavior (Lieberman, 1998). The most commonly prescribed drugs fall into three major categories: antianxiety drugs, antidepressant drugs, and antipsychotic drugs. Effective drugs (e.g., lithium) also exist for the treatment of mania. Many experts recommend using such drugs in conjunction with psychotherapy to achieve a higher level of long-term success (Hollon, 1996; Thase et al., 1997).

Antianxiety Drugs

▶ 21. How do antianxiety drugs achieve their effects? Do they have any drawbacks?

Surveys have shown that more than 15 percent of Americans between the ages of 18 and 74 use antianxiety or tranquilizing drugs such as those with the brand names Valium, Xanax, and BuSpar. These drugs are designed to reduce anxiety as much as possible without affecting alertness or concentration. Sometimes antianxiety drugs are used in combination with psychotherapy to help clients cope successfully with problematic situations (Stahl, 1998). A temporary reduction in anxiety from the use of a drug may allow a client to enter anxiety-arousing situations and learn to cope more effectively with them.

Antianxiety drugs can have a variety of undesirable side effects, such as drowsiness, lethargy, and concentration difficulties. A more serious drawback is psychological and physical dependence that can result from their long-term use. People who have developed physiological dependence can experience characteristic withdrawal symptoms, such as intense anxiety, nausea, and restlessness when they stop taking the drug (Lieberman, 1998). In addition, anxiety symptoms often return when people stop taking the drugs.

Antianxiety drugs work by slowing down excitatory synaptic activity in the nervous system. For example, *buspirone* (BuSpar) functions by blocking receptors of the excitatory transmitter serotonin and by enhancing the postsynaptic activity of GABA, an inhibitory transmitter that reduces neural activity in areas of the brain associated with emotional arousal (Gorman, 2002; Pies, 1998).

Antidepressant Drugs

Antidepressant drugs fall into three major categories: *tricyclics* (e.g., Elavil, Tofranil); *monoamine oxidase (MAO) inhibitors* (e.g., Nardil, Parnate); and *selective serotonin reuptake inhibitors*, or *SSRIs* (e.g., Prozac, Zoloft, Paxil). The first two classes increase the activity of the excitatory neurotransmitters norepinephrine and serotonin, whose lowered level of activity in brain regions involved in positive emotion and motivation is related to depression. The tricyclics work by preventing reuptake of the excitatory transmitters into the presynaptic neurons, allowing them to continue stimulating postsynaptic neurons. The MAO inhibitors reduce the activity of monoamine oxidase, an enzyme that breaks down the neurotransmitters in the synapse.

MAO inhibitors have more severe side effects than the tricyclics. They can cause dangerous elevations in blood pressure when taken with certain foods, such as cheeses and some types of wine. Many patients have abandoned their antidepressant medications because of severe side effects. The SSRIs were designed to decrease side effects by increasing the activity of just one transmitter, serotonin (Marangell, 2002). Like the other antidepressants, however, SSRIs do have side effects. For example, about 30 percent of patients on Prozac report nervousness, insomnia, sweating, joint pain, or sexual dysfunction (Hellerstein et al., 1993). Nonetheless, the SSRIs are gradually replacing the tricyclics because, in addition to milder side effects, they reduce depressive symptoms more rapidly and also reduce anxiety symptoms that often accompany depression (Lieberman, 1998). Figure 14.21 shows how the SSRIs produce their effects.

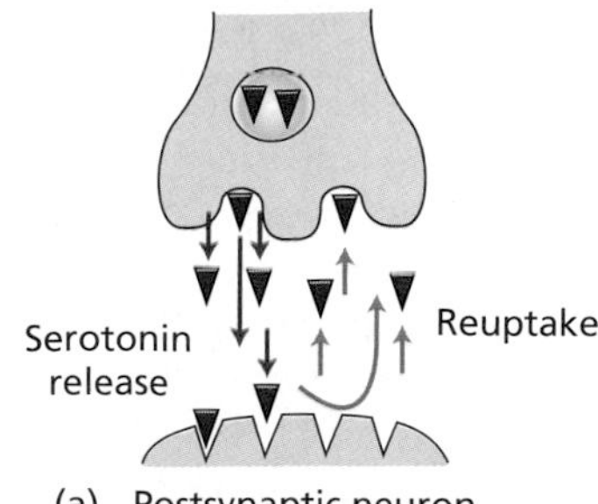

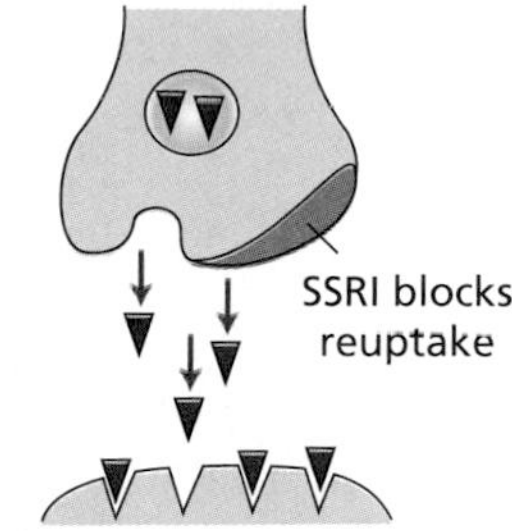

FIGURE 14.21

(a) When a presynaptic neuron releases serotonin into the synaptic space, a reuptake mechanism begins to pull neurotransmitter molecules back into the "sending" neuron, limiting the stimulation of the postsynaptic neuron. (b) Selective serotonin reuptake inhibitors (SSRIs) allow serotonin, whose activity is reduced in depressed clients, to continue its stimulation of postsynaptic neurons by inhibiting the reuptake of serotonin into the presynaptic neuron.

Increasingly, depression researchers are studying the effects of combining drugs and psychotherapy. A meta-analysis of such studies revealed that recovery rates for psychotherapy and the combined treatments did not differ for less severely depressed people. However, the combination of psychotherapy and drug treatment yielded the best recovery rates in more severe cases of depression (Thase et al., 1997).

▶ 22. How do antidepressant drugs achieve their effects? How effective are they compared and combined with therapy?

For more on the causes of and treatments for depression, see Video Segment 14.1.

Antipsychotic Drugs

Perhaps the most dramatic effects of drug therapy have occurred in the treatment of severely disordered people, permitting many of them to function outside of the hospital setting (Shorter, 1998). As shown in Figure 14.22, a sharp decline

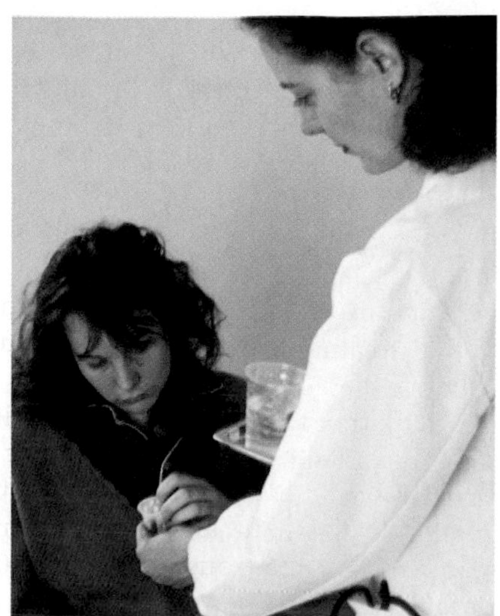

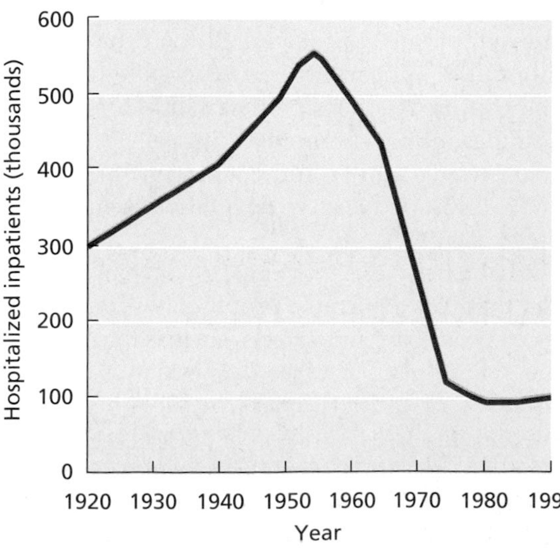

FIGURE 14.22

Antipsychotic drugs have revolutionized the treatment of severely disturbed individuals, allowing many of them to leave mental hospitals. Note the decline that occurred following the introduction of antipsychotic drugs in the mid-1950s. Source: National Institute of Mental Health, 1992.

in the number of inpatients in public mental hospitals has occurred since 1955, when antipsychotic drugs were first introduced on a wide scale.

The revolution in drug therapy for severe psychological disorders began in the early 1950s when it was accidentally discovered that *reserpine,* a drug derived from the root of the snakeroot plant, calmed psychotic patients. This discovery resulted in the development of synthetic *antipsychotic drugs* (also called *major tranquilizers*) used today to treat schizophrenic disorders. The primary effect of the major tranquilizers is to decrease the action of dopamine, the neurotransmitter whose overactivity is thought to be involved in schizophrenia (Schatzberg et al., 2002). These drugs have dramatic effects in reducing positive symptoms, such as hallucinations and delusions. However, they have little effect on negative symptoms, such as apathy and withdrawal. Antipsychotic drugs are now so widely used that nearly all schizophrenic patients living in the United States, Canada, and western Europe have received them at one time or another. Because patients often relapse very quickly if they stop taking the drugs, it is common practice to recommend that the medication be continued indefinitely once the individual has returned to the community.

▶ 24. Which disorders do and do not respond favorably to ECT and psychosurgery? What are their drawbacks?

▶ 23. What is tardive dyskinesia, and what causes it?

Antipsychotic drugs have reduced the need for padded cells, straitjackets, and other restraints that were formerly used to control the disordered behavior of hospitalized patients. Although they allow many patients to be released from hospitals, these drugs can produce **tardive dyskinesia,** *a severe movement disorder* (Kane, 1992). Uncontrollable and grotesque movements of the face and tongue are especially prominent in this disorder, and sometimes the patient's arms and legs flail uncontrollably. Tardive dyskinesia can be more debilitating than the psychotic symptoms that prompted the drug treatment, and it appears to be irreversible once it develops. One study found that within 4 years of beginning antipsychotic medications, 18.5 percent of young adults and 31 percent of those over 55 developed tardive dyskinesia symptoms (Saltz et al., 1991).

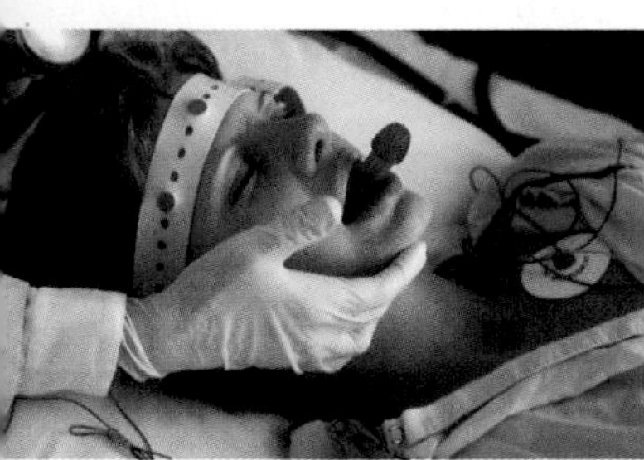

FIGURE 14.23

A severely depressed and possibly suicidal patient is prepared for electroconvulsive therapy. The patient has been sedated and given a muscle relaxant to minimize limb movements during the brief electrical stimulation of the brain. The rubber object in her mouth prevents her from biting her tongue or damaging her teeth during the convulsion.

Researchers are working to develop new drugs that can control schizophrenic symptoms without producing side effects, such as the devastating symptoms of tardive dyskinesia. A newer drug called *clozapine* (Clozaril) reduces not only positive symptoms but negative ones as well, and it appears not to produce tardive dyskinesia (Marangell, 2002). Unfortunately, it produces a fatal blood disease in 1 to 2 percent of people who take it, requiring expensive weekly blood tests for patients who use the medication.

Antipsychotic drugs can often be used effectively in conjunction with psychotherapy. For example, drugs may be used to bring psychotic symptoms under control so that the patient can benefit from other approaches such as social skills training, family therapy, and group therapy.

Electroconvulsive Therapy (ECT)

Another biologically based treatment, *electroconvulsive therapy (ECT),* was based on the observation by a Hungarian physician that schizophrenia and epilepsy rarely occur in the same person. (Apparently, he didn't stop to consider the fact that the probability of epilepsy and *any* other disorder occurring together is very low.) The physician therefore suggested that seizure induction might be useful in the treatment of schizophrenia. In 1938, two Italian physicians, Ugo Cerletti and Lucio Bini, began to treat schizophrenic patients by attaching electrodes to their skulls and inducing a seizure by means of an electric current administered to the brain. In early applications of ECT, a wide-awake patient was strapped to a table, electrodes were attached to the patient's scalp, and a current of roughly 100 volts was applied to the brain, producing violent convulsions and loss of consciousness. Sometimes the seizures were so violent that patients fractured their arms or legs.

Today the procedure is quite different (Figure 14.23). A patient is first given a sedative and a muscle relaxant to prevent injuries from the convulsions. The patient is then placed on a well-padded mattress, and electrodes are attached to his or her scalp. A modified procedure in which electrodes are placed on only one side of the head is often used. The duration of the shock is less than a second, causing a seizure of the central nervous system. There is little observable movement in the patient, other than a twitching of the toes and a slight facial grimace. The patient wakes up 10 to 20 minutes after ECT, possibly with a headache, sore muscles, and some confusion. Recently, scientists have been able to calibrate the amount of electric current a patient needs so that treatments can be individualized, and research is being carried out to determine whether certain drugs can further reduce seizure-induced confusion and amnesia.

When ECT was first introduced in the 1930s, it was applied to a wide range of disorders, but later research revealed that it cannot relieve anxiety disorders and is of questionable value for schizophrenic patients (Herrington & Lader, 1996). However, ECT can be useful in treating severe depression, particularly if there is a high risk of suicide. In such cases, the use of antidepressant drugs may be impractical because they will likely take several weeks to begin reducing the depression. In contrast, the effects of ECT can be immediate. Controlled studies indicate that 60 to 70 percent of severely depressed people given ECT improve, but no one knows why ECT works (Rey & Walter, 1997).

ECT has many critics. Some note that even when the effects are dramatically positive, the possibility of a depressive relapse is high, perhaps 85 percent (Swartz, 1995). Concerns have been raised about the safety of ECT because in some instances permanent memory loss has been reported, and there are also concerns about the possibility of permanent brain damage when ECT is used repeatedly. Today the number of ECT treatments is limited to fewer than 10, and scientific evidence suggests that today's ECT is a safer treatment than previous forms were. For example, MRI studies of patients who received brief pulse treatment to both sides of the brain revealed no evidence of brain damage (Coffey et al., 1991). After reviewing both sides of the issue, the American Psychiatric Association (1990) concluded that this therapy should be regarded as a useful procedure for major depression in patients who cannot take or do not respond to medication.

Psychosurgery

Psychosurgery *refers to surgical procedures that remove or destroy brain tissue in an attempt to change disordered behavior.* It is the least used of the biomedical procedures, but such was not always the case. In the 1930s, before the advent of antipsychotic drugs, Portuguese surgeon Egas Moniz reported that cutting the nerve tracts that connect the frontal lobes with subcortical areas of the brain involved in emotion resulted in a calming of psychotic and uncontrollably violent patients. The operation eliminated emotional input from the limbic system into the areas of the brain connected with executive functions of planning and reasoning. Walter Freeman developed a 10-minute *lobotomy* operation performed by inserting an ice pick–like instrument with sharp edges through the eye socket into the brain, then wiggling it back and forth to sever the targeted nerve tracts. During the 1930s and 1940s, tens of thousands of patients—50,000 in the United States alone—underwent the operation. Moniz received a Nobel prize for his discovery.

Initial enthusiasm for lobotomy was soon replaced by a sober recognition that the massive neural damage it caused had severe side effects on mental and emotional functioning. Seizures, stupor, memory and reasoning impairments, and listlessness occurred frequently. With the development of antipsychotic drugs in the 1950s, lobotomies decreased and are hardly ever used today. However, more precise and limited psychosurgery procedures are sometimes used in the most extreme cases and when every other avenue has been tried. One procedure called *cingulotomy* involves cutting a small fiber bundle near the corpus callosum that connects the frontal lobes with the limbic system. Cingulotomy has been used successfully in treating severe depressive and obsessive-compulsive disorders that failed to improve with drug treatment or psychotherapy. However, this more limited procedure can also produce side effects, including seizures (Pressman, 1998). Appropriately, cingulotomy and other forms of psychosurgery are considered to be last-resort procedures.

Mind, Body, and Therapeutic Interventions

The impact of drug and electroconvulsive therapies on psychological disorders illustrates once again the important interactions between biological and psychological phenomena. In the final analysis, both psychological and biological treatments affect brain functioning in ways that can change disordered thoughts, emotions, and behavior. Moreover, they may constitute different routes to the same changes, as illustrated in a recent study by Tomas Furmark and coworkers (2002) at Uppsala University in Sweden. The researchers randomly assigned patients with social phobia to 9-week treatments that involved either drug therapy with an SSRI or a course of cognitive and behavioral psychotherapy involving exposure to feared social situations and cognitive modification of anxiety-arousing thoughts. Before and after treatment, the participants received PET scans while they gave a hastily prepared speech to a group of 6 to 8 persons standing around the scanner bed. They also provided subjective ratings of their anxiety during the procedure. Uniformly high anxiety scores were reported by all participants prior to treatment.

In general, both treatments were effective, although overall the psychological treatment produced a stronger reduction in fear and social phobia symptoms than did the drug treatment.

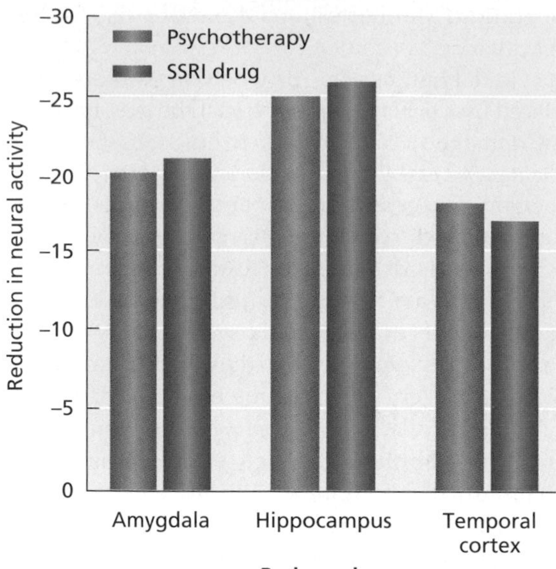

FIGURE 14.24

Effects of psychotherapy and drug therapy on brain activity in clients treated for social phobia. Clients who responded to the treatments with reduced anxiety showed nearly identical changes in PET-scan recordings of neural activity in three areas of the brain whose activation is thought to underlie anxiety. SOURCE: Based on Furmark et al., 2002.

Nonetheless, when the researchers compared the pre- and posttreatment PET scans of those participants who responded to the two treatments with reduced social anxiety, the psychotherapy and drug groups showed basically the same changes in cerebral blood flow from the first speech situation to the second. These changes involved reduced neural activity in an "anxiety circuit" involving the amygdala, the hippocampus, and areas of the temporal cerebral cortex (Figure 14.24).Treatment nonresponders did not show these brain changes. Thus different forms of therapy, whether "psychological" or "biological" in nature, may result in similar changes at a neurological level and, ultimately, at a behavioral level.

An important factor to keep in mind is that drug treatments, however effective they may be in modifying some disordered behaviors in the short term, do not "cure" the disorder. They suppress symptoms but do not teach the client coping and problem-solving skills to deal with stressful life situations (DeLongis et al., 2000; Nezu et al., 2000). They may even prevent people from taking steps to confront the real causes of their problems. Many therapists believe that one of the major benefits of psychological treatments is their potential not only to help clients deal with current problems but also to increase their personal resources so that they might enjoy a higher level of adjustment and life satisfaction in the future (Hollon, 1996).

We have now considered a wide spectrum of approaches to treating abnormal behavior. Figure 14.25 summarizes biological, psychological, and environmental mechanisms for therapeutic change.

FIGURE 14.25

Understanding Behavior: Mechanisms of therapeutic behavior change.

Levels of Analysis

Biological

- Changes in neurotransmitter, autonomic, or hormonal activity brought about by drug treatment, psychotherapy, or surgical procedures
- Structural changes in brain circuitry and synaptic networks produced by cognitive, emotional, and behavioral changes.

Psychological

- Cognitive and emotional changes brought about by cognitive therapies
- Modification of conditioned emotional responses by deconditioning procedures such as exposure, desensitization, and aversion therapy
- Behavioral changes produced by operant procedures
- Self-concept changes brought about by psychotherapy (e.g., client-centered, Gestalt therapy)
- Insight into unconscious dynamics and development of more mature defenses brought about by short- and long-term psychodynamic therapies

Environmental

- Life situation changes resulting from constructive behavior changes learned in therapy or produced by biological means
- Exposure to specific therapeutic techniques administered by a mental-health expert
- A positive therapeutic relationship that helps promote change and allows therapy techniques to be effective
- Cultural factors that affect access to therapy, type of therapy, and exposure to a culturally competent therapist

Therapeutic Behavior Change

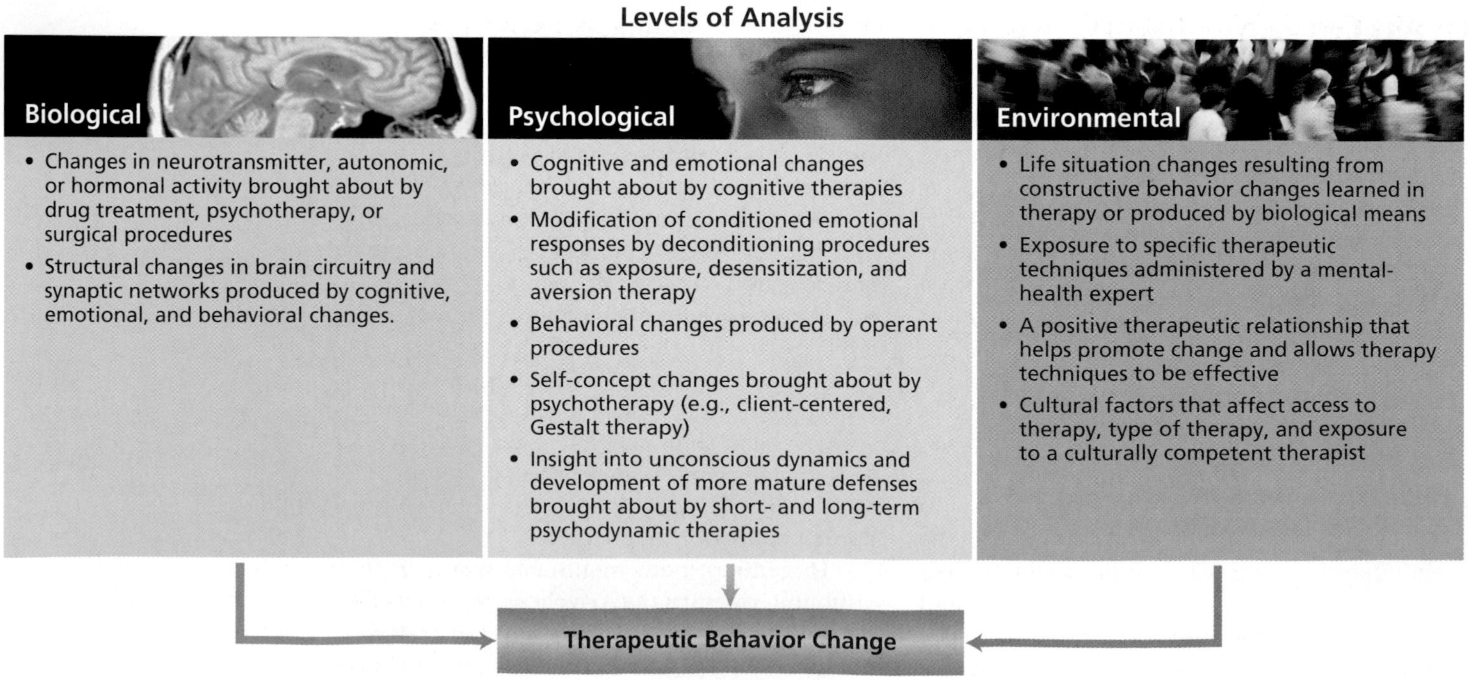

IN REVIEW

- *Drugs have revolutionized the treatment of many behavior disorders and have permitted many hospitalized patients to function outside of institutions. Drugs and psychotherapy may be combined to hasten the relief of symptoms while establishing more effective coping responses to deal with the sources of the disorder. Effective drug treatments exist for anxiety, depression, schizophrenia, and mania. Some of these drugs have undesirable side effects and can be addictive. All of them affect neurotransmission within the brain, and they work on specific classes of neurotransmitters.*
- *Electroconvulsive therapy is used less frequently than in the past, and its safety has been increased. It is used primarily to treat severe depression, particularly when a strong threat of suicide exists.*
- *Psychosurgery techniques have become more precise, but they are still generally used only after all other treatment options have failed.*
- *Studies have shown similar alterations of brain functioning in successful treatment, whether the treatment involves drug treatment or psychotherapy.*

PSYCHOLOGICAL DISORDERS AND SOCIETY

Since the days of insane asylums, first established in the 16th century to segregate the insane from society, severe behavior disorders have been treated in institutional settings. In the United States, a national network of nearly 300 state-funded mental hospitals was built between 1845 and 1945. Many private facilities were also built. The number of patients being treated in public mental hospitals increased steadily from about 250,000 in 1920 to more than 500,000 in 1950. By 1955, psychiatric patients occupied half of all hospital beds in the United States. However, it was readily apparent to mental health experts that although there were some high-quality institutions, many public mental hospitals were not fulfilling their intended role as treatment facilities. They were overcrowded, understaffed, and underfinanced. Many of them could provide little more than minimal custodial care and a haven from the stresses and demands of the outside world. Moreover, people who were admitted to such hospitals often sank into a chronic "sick" role in which passive dependence and "crazy" behavior were not only tolerated, but expected (Goffman, 1961; Scheff, 1966). They lost the self-confidence, motivation, and skills needed to reenter and adapt to the outside world and had little chance of surviving outside the hospital.

Deinstitutionalization

▶ 25. What is the rationale for deinstitutionalization? What prevents achievement of its goals?

By the 1960s, the stage was set for a new approach to the treatment of behavior disorders. Concerns about the inadequacies of mental hospitals, together with the ability of antipsychotic drugs to "normalize" patients' behavior, resulted in a **deinstitutionalization movement** *to transfer the primary focus of treatment from the hospital to the community.*

In 1963, Congress passed the Community Mental Health Centers Act, which provided for the establishment of one mental health center for every 50,000 people. Community mental health centers are designed to provide outpatient psychotherapy and drug treatment so that clients can remain in their normal social and work environments. The centers can also arrange for short-term inpatient care, usually at a local general hospital, when clients are acutely disturbed. Many have crisis centers and telephone hotlines to respond to emergency situations encountered by people in the community. Finally, community mental health centers provide education and consultation for their communities. For example, staff members may provide drug education programs to local schools or educate police officers on how to deal with seriously disturbed people they might encounter in the line of duty.

Combined with the development of effective drug treatments, the impact of deinstitutionalization on the treatment of behavior disorders has been dramatic. According to the National Institute of Mental Health, 77.4 percent of all patients were being treated as inpatients in public and private hospitals in 1955. By 1990, the inpatient figure had shrunk to 27.1 percent. As Figure 14.26 indicates, the average length of hospitalization for patients having severe (typically schizophrenic) disorders has also decreased markedly.

The concept of community treatment is a good one, for it allows people to remain in their social and work environments and to be treated with minimal disruption of their lives. However,

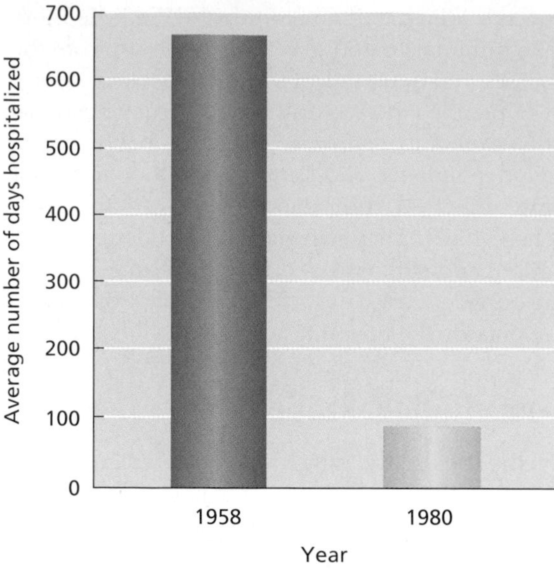

FIGURE 14.26

Average length of psychiatric hospitalization at Veterans Administration Hospitals in 1958 and 1980.
SOURCE: Based on National Institute of Mental Health, 1992.

▶ 26. What therapeutic issues exist in managed-care environments?

it requires the availability of high-quality mental health care in community clinics, halfway houses, sheltered workshops, and other community facilities. When these facilities are available, deinstitutionalization can work. Unfortunately, many communities never were able to fund the needed facilities, and the 1980s saw sharp cutbacks in federal funding of community mental health centers. As a result, many patients are being released into communities that are ill prepared to care for their needs. The result is a *revolving door phenomenon* involving repeated rehospitalizations. Nearly three fourths of all hospital admissions involve formerly hospitalized patients. Eddie, the homeless man described at the beginning of Chapter 13, is one such person. While in the hospital, he responds well to antipsychotic medications and is soon released back into a community that cannot offer him the care he requires. Following his release, he stops taking his medication, his condition deteriorates to the point where he must be rehospitalized, and the cycle begins again.

This revolving door has produced a growing population of disturbed and homeless people who have nowhere to go for help (Figure 14.27). In some states with large urban populations, the largest mental wards exist not in hospitals but on city streets. There are as many as 1 million homeless people in the United States, and approximately one third have a severe mental disorder, typically schizophrenia (Torrey, 1997). One large-scale public health survey study revealed that only 15.3 percent of people with serious mental disorders had received minimally adequate treatment during the previous year (Wang et al., 2002).

Deinstitutionalization can work only if society commits to making it work. Time will tell if funding will be provided for the community programs needed to slow the revolving door phenomenon and provide the help so desperately needed by the many people who are being left without treatment and without hope.

Mental Health Treatment in a Managed-Care Environment

Rising medical and insurance costs have swelled the rolls of health maintenance organizations (HMOs), and managed care has altered the mental health treatment landscape dramatically. The desire of HMOs and insurance providers to contain health costs translates into a strong preference for drug treatments and short-term versus more costly long-term forms of psychotherapy. Third-party providers are also demanding evidence that the treatments they are paying for are effective. These pressures have had some positive results, including the stimulation of research on treatment outcomes and the development of some effective short-term therapies.

There are, however, some serious negative effects as well. To many psychologists, the most serious is that decisions about type and duration of therapy are being made by untrained representatives of insurers or HMOs rather than by

FIGURE 14.27

The revolving door phenomenon created by inadequate funding of community-based treatment facilities has produced a large population of severely disturbed homeless people who live on our nation's streets.

the client or a mental health professional. In some instances, the number of sessions permitted may be woefully inadequate to treat a serious disorder (Figure 14.28). Although many psychologists concede that some of the more effective treatments are short-term cognitive-behavioral and interpersonal therapies, they do not believe that these treatments are best for every problem and client. Current data suggest that about 12 to 18 sessions are required to achieve a 50 percent recovery rate for most disorders (Hansen et al., 2002). Managed-care plans frequently limit payment to fewer sessions than this, so that many managed-care subscribers do not receive the level of care that they need. Likewise, the preference for drug treatments that require minimal contact between the patient and a professional may provide short-term improvement at the cost of a more satisfactory long-term result that could occur with psychological treatments that allow the development of better coping skills.

"IT'S YOUR INSURANCE COMPANY,
THEY SAY YOU'RE CURED."

FIGURE 14.28

In today's managed-care environment, treatment decisions may be made by untrained representatives of an insurance company instead of a health-care professional. Cartoon by Ron Delgado, *The Wall Street Journal*, 1997. By permission of Cartoon Features Syndicate.

Preventive Mental Health

Up to now, we have focused entirely on what can be done to help people once they have developed a behavior disorder. Successful treatment is one way to reduce the toll of human suffering produced by failures to adapt. Another way is to try to *prevent* the development of disorders through psychological intervention. In terms of economic, personal, and societal costs, it may indeed be the case that "an ounce of prevention is worth a pound of cure." If current efforts to enhance personal well-being and to slow the rise of health-care costs are to be successful, the prevention of behavior disorders must be a focal point of social policy. In some cases, this may involve treating psychological disorders during childhood in an attempt to prevent their continuation into adult life. School-based intervention programs have proven effective in preventing and reducing aggressive behaviors in children (Wilson et al., 2003). Both internalizing (e.g., anxiety, depression) and externalizing (e.g., conduct, attention-deficit/hyperactivity) disorders have responded positively to interventions applied in childhood (Compton et al., 2002; Farmer, 2002), but additional research is needed to see if the positive treatment effects persist into adulthood.

People may become vulnerable to psychological disorders as the result of situational factors, personal factors, or both. Thus prevention can be approached from two perspectives (Figure 14.29).

Situation-focused prevention *is directed at either reducing or eliminating the environmental causes of behavior disorders or enhancing situational factors that help prevent the development of disorders.* Psychologist George Albee (1996), who champions this approach, insists that prevention must focus on efforts to reduce the stresses of unemployment, economic exploitation, discrimination, and poverty. Programs designed to enhance the functioning

▶ 27. Describe two major approaches to prevention, and provide an example of each.

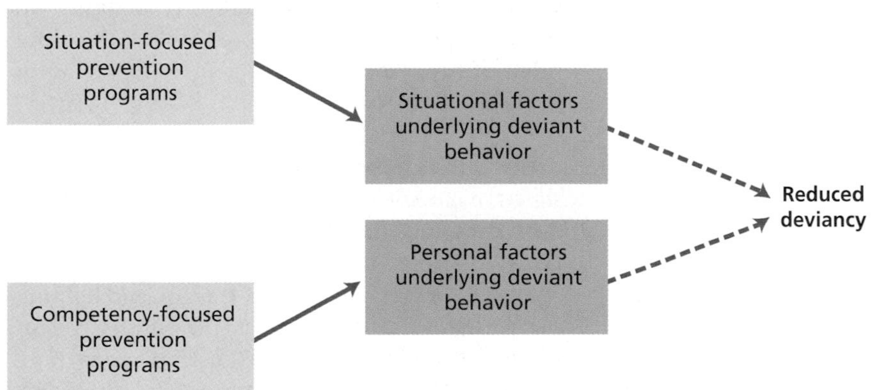

FIGURE 14.29

Two approaches to the prevention of psychological disorders, based on the principle that deviant behavior represents the interaction of personal and situational factors. Situation-focused approaches increase situational protective factors or reduce vulnerability factors in the environment. Competency-focused approaches reduce personal vulnerability factors or strengthen personal competencies and coping skills.

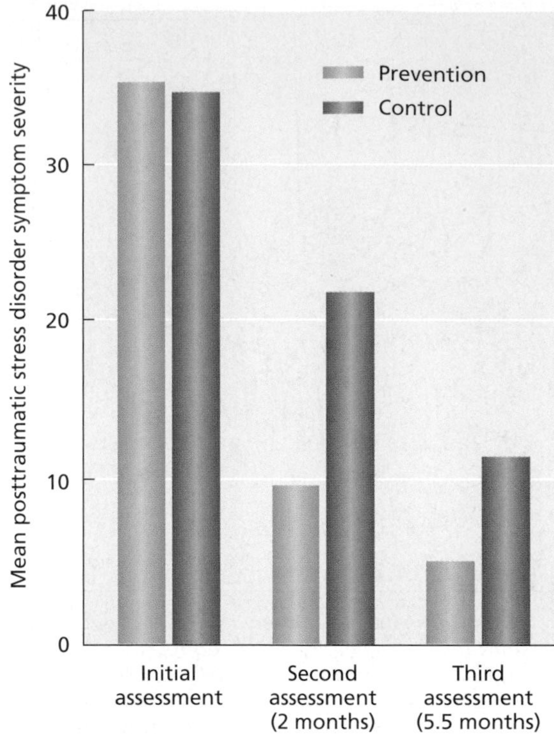

FIGURE 14.30

Results of a competency-based prevention project designed to prevent PTSD in women who were victims of rape and assault. The program, which combined a number of behavioral and cognitive therapy techniques to increase stress-management coping skills, sharply reduced the likelihood of developing PTSD. SOURCE: Foa et al., 1995.

of families, reduce stress within organizations, provide better educational opportunities for children, and develop a sense of "connection" to other people and the community at large all have the potential to help prevent the development of behavior disorders (Albee, 1997; Taylor & Wang, 2000).

The personal side of the equation is addressed by **competency-focused prevention,** *designed to increase personal resources and coping skills.* Such programs may focus on strengthening resistance to stress, improving social and vocational competencies, enhancing self-esteem, and helping people gain the skills needed to build stronger social support systems. One illustrative program, developed by Edna Foa and her coworkers (1995), focused on preventing posttraumatic stress disorder in women who had recently been raped or assaulted.

The victims were randomly assigned to either a treatment condition or to a nontreatment control condition. Over a 4-week period, the women in the treatment group underwent a posttrauma psychoeducational program. They learned about the common psychological reactions to being raped, helping them understand that their responses were understandable given the circumstances. They also relived their trauma through guided imagery to help defuse their lingering fears through exposure, learned stress-management coping skills such as relaxation, and went through a cognitive therapy procedure to replace stress-producing cognitions with more realistic appraisals.

The results of the prevention program are shown in Figure 14.30. The women exposed to the prevention treatment had less severe symptoms at both the 2-month and 5.5-month assessments. Moreover, 2 months after their trauma, diagnostic interviews with the women in the two groups revealed that 70 percent of the women in the control condition met the DSM-IV criteria for PTSD compared with only 10 percent of the women who had received the prevention program. Thus for many of the women, an efficient 4-hour program prevented what might have been a PTSD disorder that would have created tremendous personal misery and required a far more expensive and time-consuming course of therapy.

Although many mental health experts believe that more resources need to be focused on the prevention of maladaptive behavior, they also recognize that prevention presents its own challenges. For one, we cannot develop an intervention program until we understand the causes of the disorder we want to reduce. Even when causal factors are known, we also need to understand what kinds of interventions will be successful in modifying them. This requires careful research into which types of programs are most effective in preventing which types of problems in which types of people—our old specificity question.

Another practical problem is that the effects of prevention are usually not immediately obvious. It may take years for their effects to become evident. Moreover, their effects (which usually involve the *absence* of a disorder) can be hard to measure. For these reasons, prevention programs can be difficult to justify when funding priorities are being set, even though the programs may, in the long run, have greater positive impact than programs that focus on treating disorders that have already developed.

Having described the nature and benefits of treatments, we end this chapter with some research-derived guidelines for seeking and profiting from therapy.

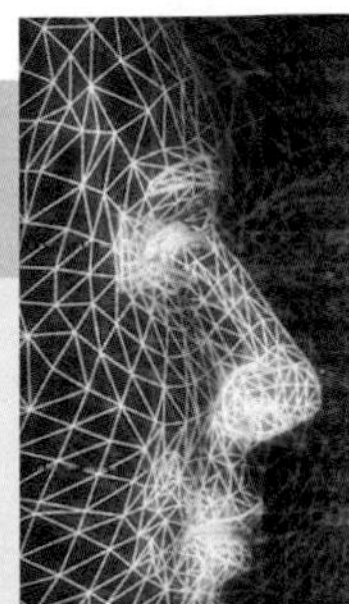

APPLYING PSYCHOLOGICAL SCIENCE

WHEN AND WHERE TO SEEK THERAPY

No one is immune to the problems of living. Every day, each of us does the best we can to balance our personal and social resources against the demands created by our life circumstances. We all have certain vulnerabilities, and if environmental demands and our vulnerabilities combine to exceed our resources, we may experience psychological problems for which professional assistance would be helpful. Here are some general guidelines for seeking such help and profiting from it.

First is the issue of when to seek help. In general terms, you should consider seeking professional assistance if any of the following apply:

- You are experiencing serious emotional discomfort, such as feelings of depression or anxiety, that are adversely affecting your personal, work, or family life.
- You are encountering a serious problem or life transition that you feel unable to handle on your own.
- A problem that has interfered with your life or personal happiness in the past is worsening or has suddenly resurfaced.
- You have experienced some traumatic event, either in the past or recently, that you find yourself frequently thinking about, dreaming about, or responding to with negative emotions.
- You are preoccupied with your weight or body image and are taking extreme steps, such as not eating or purging yourself by vomiting or taking laxatives.
- You have severe and recurring conflicts with other people.
- You hear voices telling you what to do, or you feel that others are controlling your thoughts.

How does one go about getting help in dealing with psychological problems? Help may be sought at a college counseling center, at a community agency, at an HMO, or from a professional in private practice. The campus counseling center is often a good place for a college student to start, for it can provide direct help or an appropriate referral to a reputable mental health professional. If you are at a larger university that has a graduate program in clinical or counseling psychology, there may also be an on-campus psychology training clinic administered by that program. There you would typically work with a graduate student who is being closely supervised by a licensed clinician.

How expensive is treatment? For students it is often offered free or at a nominal fee at a campus facility or HMO. Community agencies typically have a sliding-fee scale based on the client's income so financial considerations need not be a barrier to seeking professional assistance. A private practitioner may charge as much as medical doctors, dentists, and attorneys, often exceeding $100 per 50-minute session. As a prospective client, you should always ask beforehand about the fee. You should also check into the mental health benefits provided by your health insurance policy, including what kinds of treatments and the number of sessions it covers, and whether it will reimburse your chosen treatment provider. Student insurance plans usually cover on-campus treatment.

In choosing a therapist, what should you look for? It is important that your therapist be well-trained and competent. Ask the therapist about her or his degree, license, training, therapeutic orientation, and the problems in which she or he specializes. This chapter has provided an overview of the major theoretical orientations, and one or more of them may seem especially attractive to you or suited to the problems you wish to address.

As we've seen, the relationship between client and therapist is of the utmost importance. You will want a therapist who can create a good working relationship with you. The degree of "value similarity" between you and the therapist can be important. Timothy Kelly and Hans Strupp (1992) found that the most positive therapeutic outcomes were achieved when the client and therapist were neither very similar nor very dissimilar in values. High similarity may result in a failure to explore value-related issues that should be explored, whereas too much dissimilarity may interfere with building a good therapeutic relationship. One exception to this general rule may occur in the area of religious values. Clients who have strong and committed religious values may profit most from a therapy that supports those values and uses them to help change problem behaviors (Probst et al., 1992).

Some clients prefer to work with either a male or female therapist, or one who is heterosexual or gay or lesbian, depending in part on the nature of the personal issues that have caused them to seek counseling. As we have seen, research has shown that personal warmth, sincere concern, and empathy are important therapist characteristics. You should like and feel comfortable with your therapist, and you should feel at ease with the methods the therapist uses. Under no circumstances should your therapeutic relationship involve physical intimacy of any kind; if a therapist should ever engage in such behavior, you should immediately terminate treatment with that therapist and notify the appropriate professional organization, such as the state psychological or medical association. Such conduct is a serious breach of professional ethics and cannot be condoned under any circumstances.

You and your therapist should have explicit, agreed-on goals for the treatment program. If therapy proceeds well, you will experience beneficial changes that indicate movement toward your

Continued

goals. It may take some time for these changes to occur, however, since long-standing personal vulnerabilities are not easily changed, and significant change seldom occurs overnight. If you do not see any progress after several months, or if you seem to be functioning less well than before, you should discuss your progress with the therapist. The therapist may be more satisfied with your progress than you are. However, if you continue to be dissatisfied with your progress or with the therapeutic relationship, you may at some point decide to terminate it. This should not prevent you from seeking help from another therapist.

Entering a helping relationship is a courageous step, and resolving problems in living may involve taking risks and experiencing pain. However, many clients look back on the pain and risks and feel that the process was a valuable one that enabled them to live happier lives than they otherwise could have. Here is a reflection by Dr. Sandra L. Harris, a prominent clinical psychologist, on the course of therapy she undertook as a college student:

> When I think about the girl I was in my freshman year at the University of Maryland and the young woman I was when I graduated four years later, it is clear that it was not only the issues Jim and I discussed, but how we talked that made the difference. The intangibles of trust, respect, and caring were at least as important as the active problem solving that transpired in our weekly meetings. It was not a dramatic transformation, rather it was a slight shifting of a path by a few degrees on the compass. Over the years that shift has had a cumulative effect and I walk a very different road than I would have without him. (Harris, 1981, p. 3)

IN REVIEW

- *The introduction of drug therapies that normalize disturbed behavior, as well as concerns about the deterioration of life skills during hospitalization, have helped stimulate a move toward deinstitutionalization—the treatment of people in their communities.*
- *Research has shown that deinstitutionalization can work when adequate community treatment is provided. Unfortunately, many communities have been unable to fund the needed facilities, resulting in a "revolving door" of release and rehospitalization, as well as a new generation of homeless people who live on the streets and do not receive needed treatment.*
- *Managed care is requiring therapists to demonstrate the efficacy of their techniques and to develop shorter, more economical treatments. An issue of concern is that decisions about the type and duration of treatment are increasingly being taken out of the hands of trained professionals.*
- *Prevention programs may be classified as either situation-focused or competency-focused, depending on whether they are directed at changing environmental conditions or personal factors.*

KEY TERMS AND CONCEPTS

Each term has been boldfaced and defined in the chapter on the page indicated in parentheses.

aversion therapy (p. 565)
behavior modification (p. 566)
clinical significance (p. 575)
common factors (p. 577)
competency-focused prevention (p. 586)
counterconditioning (p. 565)
culturally competent therapist (p. 571)
deinstitutionalization movement (p. 583)
dodo bird verdict (p. 575)
dose-response effect (p. 577)
eclecticism (p. 568)
effect size (p. 574)
empathy (p. 557)
empirically supported therapies (p. 574)
exposure (p. 562)
free association (p. 553)
genuineness (p. 557)
insight (p. 552)
interpersonal therapy (p. 556)
interpretation (p. 555)
meta-analysis (p. 574)
openness (p. 576)
placebo control group (p. 574)
psychodynamic behavior therapy (p. 568)
psychosurgery (p. 581)
randomized clinical trial (p. 574)
resistance (p. 554)
response prevention (p. 562)
self-relatedness (p. 576)
situation-focused prevention (p. 585)
social skills training (p. 567)
specificity question (p. 573)
spontaneous remission (p. 573)
stimulus hierarchy (p. 565)
systematic desensitization (p. 565)
tardive dyskinesia (p. 580)
token economy (p. 566)
transference (p. 554)
unconditional positive regard (p. 557)
virtual reality (VR; p. 563)

What Do You Think?

ARE CONDITIONING TECHNIQUES COMPATIBLE WITH PSYCHOANALYTIC THEORY? p. 565

Behaviorists and psychoanalytic theorists have very different viewpoints about psychological symptoms, such as a phobia. For the behaviorist, the phobia *is* the problem, period. Decondition it and the problem is resolved. In contrast, the psychodynamic view is based on a "medical model" analogy that distinguishes between symptoms and underlying causes. As noted in Chapter 13, a psychoanalyst would view a phobia as a behavioral manifestation of some underlying, probably unconscious, conflict. Simply treating the observed symptom does nothing to resolve the psychodynamic issues assumed to cause it, in much the same way that reducing a malaria victim's fever with aspirin does nothing to cure the underlying disease. The analyst would therefore maintain that the goal of therapy should be to treat the underlying dynamics, after which the phobia should disappear on its own. Even if the phobia were successfully treated with behavioral conditioning therapies, the underlying problem remains unresolved, and some new symptom may well appear in place of the phobia. This prediction of *symptom substitution* was frequently raised by psychodynamic critics of behavior therapies, but no indisputable evidence of new symptoms popping up after behavior therapy treatment has ever materialized (Paul, 2001). In instances when new symptoms appeared, they could be attributed to new posttreatment learning experiences. ■

ARE "REAL-WORLD" CLIENTS' REPORTS MORE VALID THAN RESULTS FROM CLINICAL TRIALS? p. 576

Seligman's conclusions that clinical trials underestimate the effects of psychotherapy are provocative, but before you accept them, you should consider some shortcomings of the data on which they were based. First, consider the nature of the *CR* sample. Only 1.6 percent of the original 184,000 people contacted described their therapy experience. Is it possible that among the other 98.4 percent are a significant number of people who had been in therapy with unfavorable results and chose not to share their experiences? If so, the effectiveness of therapy could be exaggerated in this self-selected sample.

Second, what about the nature and quality of the data? We have only global after-the-fact reports from clients. There is no way to corroborate respondents' reports with other sources of data. How do we know that they are not biased by memory distortions or by rationalizing their investment ("If I spent that much time and money, I must have gotten better")? Rationalization could also account for the apparent superiority of long-term therapy, where more time and money were expended, as well as the tendency to return the questionnaire and share the success story.

Third, what has the *CR* study told us about the more important specificity question? We don't know if some matches of clinical problems with specific forms of therapy yielded better outcomes than others. In fact, we can't even be sure what kinds of therapy were administered because respondents didn't describe their treatments in detail.

Fourth, how about the absence of a control group? Can we rule out spontaneous remission of symptoms? As we saw in Chapter 13, many mental health problems (e.g., depression and anxiety) fluctuate or improve with time. People who are assessed at their low points, when they are most likely to seek therapy, are almost certain to improve, with or without therapy (Mintz et al., 1996). Could this factor alone explain the respondents' perceptions that they had improved? As Seligman himself conceded, "Because there are no control groups, the *CR* . . . study cannot tell us directly whether talking to sympathetic friends or merely letting time pass would have produced just as much improvement as treatment by a mental-health professional" (1995, p. 972). ■

15

SOCIAL THINKING AND BEHAVIOR

CHAPTER OUTLINE

Without the human community,
one single human being cannot survive.
—The Dalai Lama

The prison had become a living hell. Hidden behind their mirrored sunglasses, the guards asserted their total authority over the prisoners. They made the prisoners ask permission to do virtually anything, including going to the toilet. The guards conducted roll calls in the middle of the night to assert their power and disrupt the prisoners' sleep, and they forced prisoners to do push-ups, sometimes with their foot pushing down on the prisoner's back. For their part, the prisoners became increasingly passive and depressed. They hated the guards but were powerless against them. After a few days, one prisoner cracked emotionally. Soon another broke down. Before long, the demoralized prisoners became nothing more than what the guards expected them to be: piteous objects of scorn and abuse.

This prison was not in some brutal dictatorship, the prisoners were not hardened criminals, nor were the guards sadistic psychopaths. Instead, this prison was in the basement of the psychology building at Stanford University, and the guards and prisoners were college students who had volunteered for a study of "prison life." Before the study, screening questionnaires, interviews, and psychological tests showed the participants to be well adjusted.

Philip Zimbardo, the social psychologist who designed the study, watched in disbelief as scenes of callous inhumanity unfolded before him. What began as a 2-week simulation of prison life had to be halted after only 6 days. Afterward, Zimbardo and his associates held several sessions with the participants to help them work through their powerful emotional reactions, and they maintained contact over the following year to minimize the risk that participants would experience lasting negative effects.

What transformed normal college students into people they would not have recognized a week earlier? As one guard recalled, "I was surprised at myself. I made them . . . clean out the toilets with their bare hands. I practically considered the prisoners cattle. . . ." (Zimbardo et al., 1973, p. 42). Decades later, the Stanford prison study remains a landmark for dramatically illustrating a basic concept: Behavior is determined not only by our biological endowment and past learning experiences but also by the power of the immediate social situation (Haney & Zimbardo, 1998).

For more on the Stanford prison study, see Video Segment 15.1.

As social creatures, we spend our days in an ever changing series of social environments that profoundly shape how we behave, think, and feel. This chapter explores the field of social psychology, which studies how we think about our social world (*social thinking*), how other people influence our behavior (*social influence*), and how we relate toward other people (*social relations*).

SOCIAL THINKING

In your judgment, why did some guards in the Stanford prison study act so brutally? Did you form any impressions of the guards or prisoners as you read about the study? Do you feel that the study was worthwhile? These questions focus on three key aspects of social thinking: attributions, impressions, and attitudes.

Attribution: Perceiving the Causes of Behavior

In everyday life we often make **attributions,** *judgments about the causes of our own and other people's behavior and outcomes* (Figure 15.1). Was my A on the midterm due to hard work and ability, or was it just an easy test? Did Bill criticize Linda because he is a rude person, or was he provoked? Did the guards' brutal behavior reflect their personalities or some aspect of the situation? In the courtroom, jurors' attributions about a defendant's behavior influence their decisions about guilt versus innocence.

Personal Versus Situational Attributions

▶ 1. What types of information lead us to make situational rather than personal attributions?

Fritz Heider (1958), a pioneer of attribution theory, maintained that our attempts to understand why people behave as they do typically involve either personal attributions or situational attributions. *Personal (internal) attributions* infer that people's behavior is caused by their characteristics: "Bill insulted Linda because he is a rude person." "My A on the midterm exam reflects my high ability." *Situational (external) attributions* infer that aspects of the situation cause a behavior: "Bill was provoked into insulting Linda." "I received an A because the test was easy."

▶ 2. Describe the fundamental attribution error and the self-serving bias, and discuss how they are affected by culture.

FIGURE 15.1

"He's been under a lot of stress lately." "He only thinks about himself. What a jerk!" Depending on which attribution she makes for her husband's outburst, this woman may respond with understanding or anger.

How do we decide whether a behavior is caused by personal or situational factors? Suppose you ask Kim for advice on whether to take a particular course (say, Art 391) and she tells you that the course is terrible. Is Art 391 really poor (a situational attribution), or is it something about Kim (a personal attribution) that led to this response? According to Harold Kelley (1973), three types of information determine the attribution we make: *consistency, distinctiveness,* and *consensus.* First, is Kim's response consistent over time? If you ask Kim again two weeks later and she still says that Art 391 is terrible, then consistency is high. Second, is her response distinctive? If Kim dislikes only Art 391, then distinctiveness is high; if she thinks that most of her courses are terrible, then distinctiveness is low. Finally, how do other people respond? If other students agree with Kim that Art 391 is poor, then consensus is high, but if they disagree with her, then consensus is low.

As Figure 15.2 illustrates, when consistency, distinctiveness, and consensus are all high, we are likely to make a situational attribution: "The course is bad." But when consistency is high and the other two factors are low, we make a personal attribution: "Perhaps Kim is overly critical or just doesn't like college." Humans, however, are often not so logical when making decisions and judgments (Shafir & LeBoeuf, 2002). Our emotions may influence our judgments, and we often take mental shortcuts and make snap judgments that bias our attributions.

Attributional Biases

Social psychology teaches us that the immediate social environment profoundly influences behavior, yet at times we seem to ignore this and conclude that a behavior reflects not the situation but the individual's personal qualities (Ross, 2001). This tendency is most often called the **fundamental attribution error:** *We underestimate the impact of the situation and overestimate the role of personal factors when explaining other people's behavior.*

Imagine that as part of a course assignment you write an essay on whether physicians should be allowed to help terminally ill patients commit suicide. The professor gives you the choice of writing in favor of or against physician-assisted suicide. Your classmates read the essay, and because they know you had a choice, they logically assume that the essay's content reflects your personal views. Thus if the essay supports rather than opposes physician-assisted suicide, your

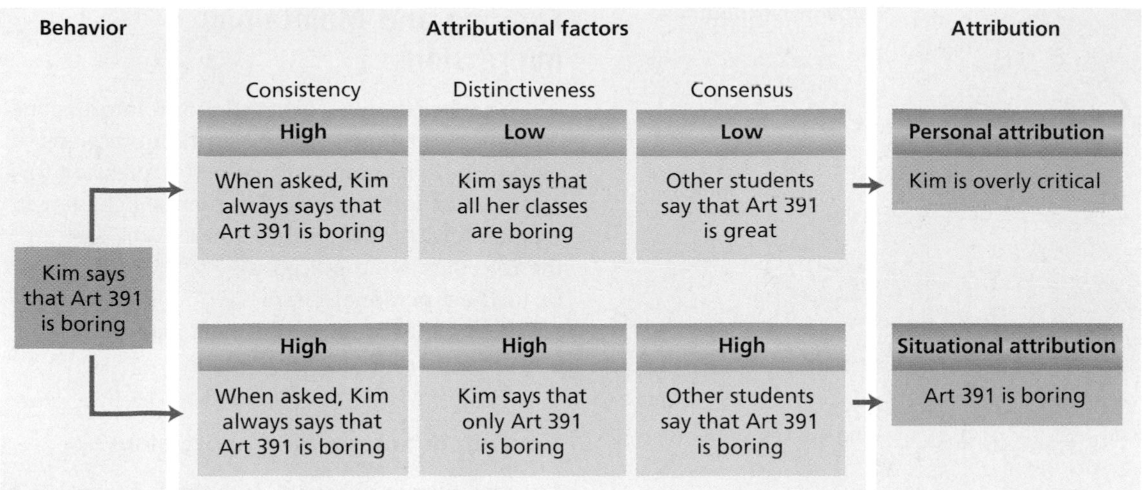
Behavior
Attributional factors
Attribution
Consistency
Distinctiveness
Consensus
High
Low
Low
Personal attribution
When asked, Kim always says that Art 391 is boring
Kim says that all her classes are boring
Other students say that Art 391 is great
Kim is overly critical
Kim says that Art 391 is boring
High
High
High
Situational attribution
When asked, Kim always says that Art 391 is boring
Kim says that only Art 391 is boring
Other students say that Art 391 is boring
Art 391 is boring

FIGURE 15.2

Consistency, distinctiveness, and consensus information help us determine whether to make personal or situational attributions for someone else's behavior. Note that in both examples consistency is high. If Kim's behavior has low consistency (sometimes she says Art 391 is boring, and other times she says it's interesting), we typically attribute the behavior to transient conditions (e.g., changes in Kim's mood) rather than to stable personal or situational factors. SOURCE: Based on Kelley, 1973.

classmates will conclude that you are in favor of this practice.

But suppose that instead of giving you a choice the professor assigns you to write a supportive essay or assigns you to write an opposing essay. Your classmates know that you were told to express either pro or con views. Logically, the content of the essay reflects the situation to which you were assigned. After all, perhaps you are against physician-assisted suicide but were told to write an essay in favor of it, or perhaps the reverse occurred. You likely would not want your classmates to make assumptions about your personal attitudes based on a viewpoint you were told to express. Yet experiments indicate that the content of the essay will still influence your classmates' perception of whether you support or oppose the issue (Jones & Harris, 1967). Figure 15.3 provides another example.

Psychologists debate the causes and strength of the fundamental attribution error, but everyone agrees that it's not inevitable (Sabini et al., 2001). When people have time to reflect on their judgments or are highly motivated to be careful, the fundamental attribution error is reduced. Moreover, keep in mind that the fundamental attribution error applies to how we perceive other people's behavior rather than our own. As comedian George Carlin once noted, the slow driver ahead of us is a "moron," and the fast driver trying to pass us is a "maniac." Yet we don't think of ourselves as a moron or a maniac when we do these things, perhaps because we are more aware of situational factors impinging on us (such as being on an unfamiliar road). After the Stanford prison study ended, guards who had acted cruelly toward the prisoners were quick to attribute their behavior to the role that they had been in rather than to their personal qualities.

Indeed, when it comes to explaining our own behavior, we often make attributions that protect or enhance our self-esteem by displaying a **self-serving bias,** *the tendency to make personal attributions for successes and situational attributions for failures* (Ross & Nisbett, 1991). The strength of this bias, however, depends on many factors. For example, depressed people often display the opposite attributional pattern—taking too little credit for successes and too much credit for failures—a pattern that helps keep them depressed.

FIGURE 15.3

Unlike Mr. Spock, the logical and emotionless Vulcan from the series Star Trek, *actor Leonard Nimoy has feelings just like the rest of us. TV and movie fans make the fundamental attribution error when they expect media stars to have the same traits as the characters they play. The title of Nimoy's autobiography,* I Am Not Spock, *emphasizes this point.*

Culture and Attribution

Just as culture influences how we perceive the physical world, it affects how we perceive the social world. Consider the fundamental attribution error. Many studies suggest that the tendency to attribute other people's behavior to personal factors may reflect a Westernized emphasis on individualism (Triandis, 2001). In a study by J. G. Miller (1984), participants of varying ages from India and the United States attributed causality

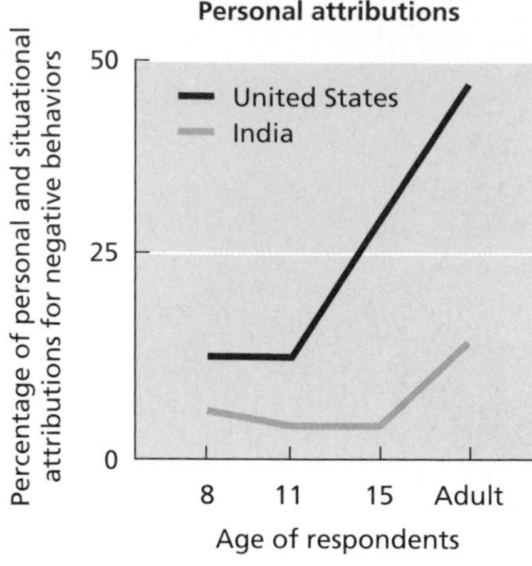

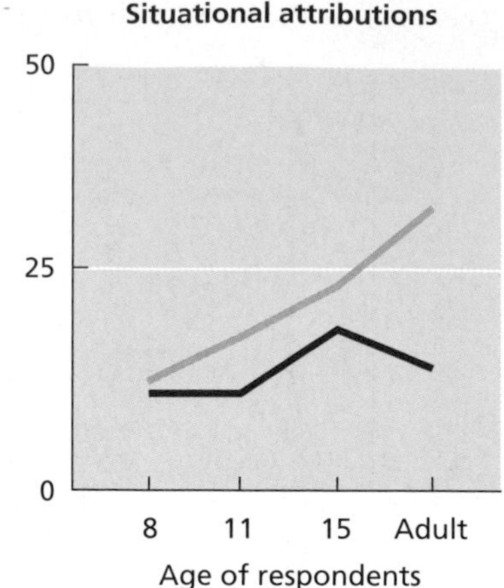

FIGURE 15.4

With increasing age from childhood to adulthood, Americans show a greater tendency to make personal attributions for other people's behaviors. In contrast, participants from India show an increased tendency to make situational attributions. SOURCE: Adapted from Miller, 1984.

▶ 3. Discuss how the primacy effect, stereotypes, and self-fulfilling prophecies influence impression formation.

for several behaviors. As Figure 15.4 shows, with increasing age, participants from India made more situational attributions, whereas those from America made more personal attributions. Culture also influences attributions for our own behavior. For example, modesty is highly valued in China's collectivistic culture. Chinese college students take less personal credit for successful social interactions than do American students and accept more responsibility for their failures (Anderson, 1999).

Beyond influencing the types of attributions that we make, our cultural background also seems to affect the way we go about making attributions. Consider that East Asians, in general, tend to hold a more holistic view of the universe than Westerners (Nisbett et al., 2001). This view, reflected in the belief that all events are interconnected and therefore cannot be understood in isolation, leads East Asians to develop more complex views about the causes of behavior. Accordingly, Incheol Choi and coworkers (2003) predicted and found that compared to European American college students, Korean college students scored higher overall on measures of holistic thinking and also took a greater amount of information into account when making causal attributions for other people's behavior.

Importantly, this relation between holistic thinking and the use of information was also found within each culture. Among the American students and among the Korean students, those who thought more holistically than their peers took more information into account when making attributions (Choi et al., 2003). Thus the *same underlying psychological principle*—a link between holistic thinking and beliefs about causality—seems to account for information-seeking differences between cultures as well as among individuals within each culture.

Forming and Maintaining Impressions

As social beings, we constantly form impressions of other people, just as they form impressions of us. Attributions play a key role in impression formation: Do you attribute the guards' behavior in the Stanford prison study to the role they were placed in or to their personal characteristics? Other factors, however, also affect how we form and maintain impressions.

For more on impression formation, see Interactive Segment 15.1.

How Important Are First Impressions?

Try this simple exercise. Tell some people that you know a person who is "intelligent, industrious, impulsive, critical, stubborn, and envious." Tell some others that you know a person who is "envious, stubborn, critical, impulsive, industrious, and intelligent." Then ask for their quick impression of how much they might like this person. Solomon Asch (1946) found that the person in the first description is perceived more positively—as being more sociable and happier—than the person in the second description, even though (as you may have noticed) both groups received identical information but in reverse order.

When forming impressions, the **primacy effect** *refers to our tendency to attach more importance to the initial information that we learn about a person.* New information can change our opinion, but it has to "work harder" to overcome that initial impression for two reasons. First, we tend to be most alert to information we receive first. Second, initial information may shape how we perceive subsequent information. Imagine an athlete who gets off to a great start in training camp. The coach attributes high ability to the athlete. But as time goes on, the athlete's performance declines. To maintain this positive initial impression, the coach need only attribute the performance decline to fatigue, a drop in motivation, or a string of bad breaks.

Primacy is the rule of thumb in impression formation, especially for people who dislike ambiguity and uncertainty (Kruglanski & Webster, 1996). We seem to have a remarkable capacity for forming snap judgments based on small amounts of initial information, and some evolutionary psychologists propose that evaluating stimuli quickly (such as rapidly distinguishing friend from foe) was adaptive for our survival (Krebs & Denton, 1997). But we are not slaves to primacy. Primacy effects decrease—and *recency effects* (giving greater weight to the most recent information) may occur—when we are asked to avoid making snap judgments, reminded to consider the evidence carefully, and made to feel accountable for our judgments (Webster et al., 1996).

Seeing What We Expect to See

Imagine that we are going to a party and I tell you that the host, Max, is a distant, aloof, cold person. You meet him and try to make conservation, but Max doesn't say much, avoids eye contact, and doesn't ask you about your life. A bit later, you say to me, "You were right, he's really a cold fish." Now let's roll back this scene. Suppose I describe Max as nice but extremely shy. Later when you try to make conservation, he doesn't say much, avoids eye contact, and doesn't ask you about your life. You say to me, "You were right, he's really shy." Same behavior, different impression. This example reminds us of a basic perceptual principle highlighted in Chapter 4. Whether perceiving objects or people, the same stimulus can be "seen" in different ways. Our *mental set,* which is a readiness to perceive the world in a particular way, powerfully shapes how we interpret a stimulus.

What creates our mental sets? One important factor that we have encountered throughout the book is *schemas,* mental frameworks that help us organize and interpret information. By telling you that our host is "cold" or "shy," I activate a set of concepts and expectations (your schema) for how such a person is likely to behave. Although the host's behavior can be interpreted in multiple ways, you fit his behavior into the particular schema that is already activated.

A **stereotype,** *which is a generalized belief about a group or category of people,* represents a powerful type of schema. In one study, participants watched a videotape of a 9-year-old girl named Hannah and then judged her academic potential (Darley & Gross, 1983). The randomly assigned participants were told either that Hannah came from an upper-middle-class environment and had parents with white-collar careers or that she came from a poor neighborhood and had parents who were blue-collar workers. On the videotape, Hannah displayed average performance, answering some questions and missing others. All participants saw the same performance, but those who thought Hannah came from a disadvantaged background rated her as having less ability. This study illustrates how our stereotypes (e.g., about social class) can bias the way we perceive other people's behavior.

Creating What We Expect to See

Seeing what we expect to see is only one way we confirm our initial impressions. Usually without conscious awareness, a **self-fulfilling prophecy** *occurs when people's erroneous expectations lead them to act toward others in a way that brings about the expected behaviors, thereby confirming their original impression.* Returning to our party example, if you expect the host to be cold and aloof, your behavior toward him may change in subtle ways. You make conversation, but perhaps you smile less, stand farther away, and give up a little earlier than you would have if I had simply told you that Max was a great guy. His reserved response, in part, could be a reaction to *your* behavior (Figure 15.5).

Self-fulfilling prophecies have been demonstrated in hundreds of studies across different countries and settings, including schools, businesses, the military, sports, close relationships, and general interactions with strangers (McNatt, 2000; Snyder, 2001). In interacting with other people, our initially unfounded expectations can influence how we behave toward them, thereby shaping other people's behavior in a way that ultimately confirms our expectations.

Attitudes and Attitude Change

▶ 4. What is an attitude? Describe three conditions under which people's attitudes best predict their behavior.

Beyond attributions and impressions, much of our social thinking involves the attitudes that we hold. Indeed, from political elections and war to the latest fashion craze, attitudes help steer the course of world events. An **attitude** *is a positive or negative evaluative reaction toward a stimulus,* such as a person, action, object, or concept (Tesser & Shaffer, 1990). Whether agreeing or disagreeing with a governmental policy or a friend's opinion of a movie, you are expressing an evaluative reaction (Figure 15.6). Our attitudes help define our identity, guide our actions, and influence how we judge people (Maio & Olson, 2000).

Do Our Attitudes Influence Our Behavior?

If we tell you that, according to research, people's attitudes strongly guide their behavior, you might reply "So what? That's just common sense." But consider a classic study by Richard LaPiere (1934). In the 1930s, he toured the United States with a young Chinese couple, stopping at 251 restaurants, hotels, and other establishments. At the time, prejudice against Asians was widespread, yet the couple—who often entered the establishment before LaPiere did—were refused service only once.

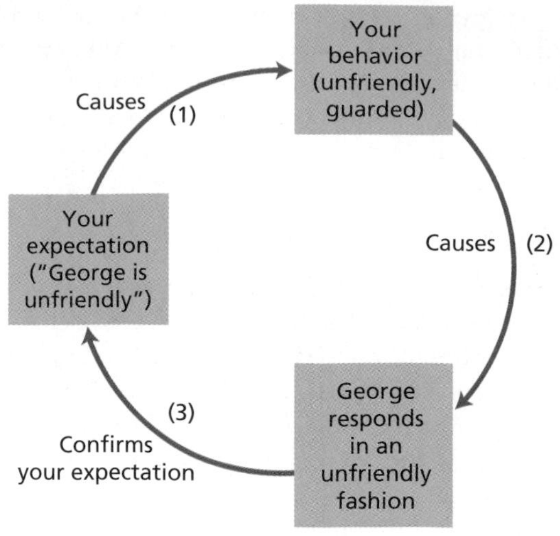

FIGURE 15.5

What first impressions will these people form of each other? How might these impressions influence their behavior and possibly create a self-fulfilling prophecy?

Later LaPiere wrote to all of these establishments, asking if they would provide service to Chinese patrons. More than 90 percent of those who responded stated that they would not.

In LaPiere's study, we cannot be sure that the people who expressed negative attitudes in the survey were the same individuals who, months earlier, had actually served the Chinese couple. Yet the discrepancy between stated prejudicial attitudes and nondiscriminatory behavior seemed so overwhelming that it called the "commonsense" assumption of attitude-behavior consistency into question. Decades of better-controlled research, however, indicate that attitudes do predict behavior to a modest degree (Kraus, 1995). Most important, we now understand three factors that help explain why the attitude-behavior relationship is strong in some cases but weak in others.

First, *attitudes influence behavior more strongly when counteracting situational factors are weak.* For example, conformity and obedience pressures may lead us to behave in ways that are at odds with our inner convictions. According to the **theory of planned behavior** and similar models (Ajzen, 1991), *our intention to engage in a behavior is strongest when we have a positive attitude toward that behavior, when subjective norms (our perceptions of what other people think we should do) support our attitudes, and when we believe that the behavior is under our control.* Researchers have used this theory to predict successfully whether people will become smokers, exercise regularly, attend church, donate blood, and perform many other behaviors (Blanchard et al., 2002).

Second, *attitudes have a greater influence on behavior when we are aware of them and when they are strongly held.* Sometimes we seem to act without thinking, out of impulse or habit. Attitude-behavior consistency increases when people consciously think about or are reminded of their attitudes before acting (Powell & Fazio, 1984; White et al., 2002).

Third, *general attitudes do best at predicting general classes of behavior, and specific attitudes do best at predicting specific behaviors.* For example, Martin Fishbein and Icek Ajzen (1974) found almost no relation between people's general attitudes toward religion and 70 specific religious behaviors (such as the frequency of praying before meals or attending services). However, when they combined the 70 specific behaviors into a single global index of religious behavior, the relation between

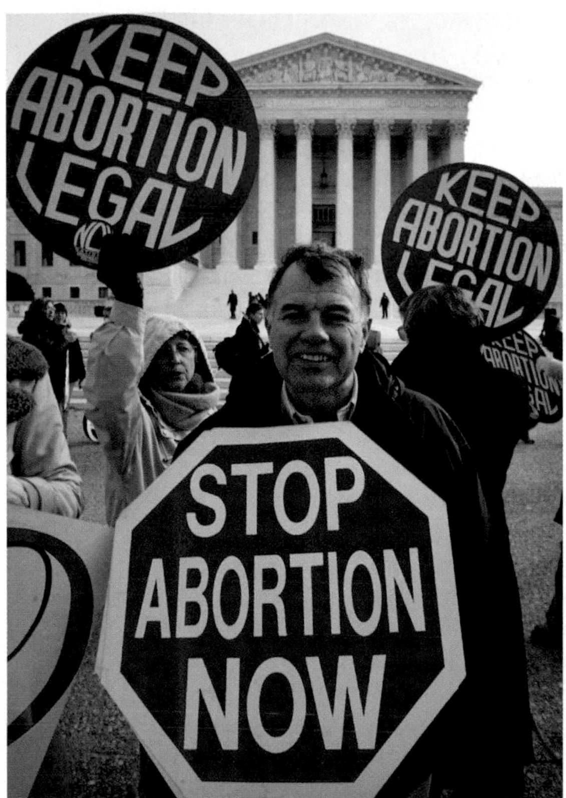

FIGURE 15.6

Attitudes represent an important form of social thinking. They help define who we are, and they affect the way people judge one another. Do the attitudes expressed by these protestors influence your impression of them?

general religious attitudes and overall religious behavior was substantial.

Does Our Behavior Influence Our Attitudes?

As we have just seen, under the proper conditions people's attitudes guide their behavior. But attitude-behavior consistency is not a one-way street: We also come to develop attitudes that are consistent with how we behave. In the Stanford prison study, as the guards slipped into their roles and began mistreating the prisoners, they began to view the prisoners as little more than animals. Why should this be?

Self-Justification Imagine that you volunteer for an experiment, arrive at the laboratory, and repeatedly perform two extremely boring tasks: emptying and filling a tray with spools and turning 48 pegs stuck into holes. After you endure 60 minutes of sheer boredom, the experimenter enters, thanks you for participating, and asks for your help: It is important for the next student to begin the study with a "positive attitude" about the tasks, and all you have to do is tell the student that the boring tasks are interesting. Depending on the condition to which you have been randomly assigned, the experimenter offers to pay you either $1 or $20 for, essentially, lying to the next participant. You agree to do so. Afterward, you go to the psychology department's main office to collect your money and fill out a "routine form" that asks how much you enjoyed the tasks in the experiment.

Make a prediction: Comparing participants who lied for $1 and who lied for $20 with a control group that simply rated the boring tasks without telling any lie beforehand, which of the three groups rated the task most positively? Why?

Common sense might suggest that participants paid $20 would feel happiest about the experiment and rate the tasks most highly. However, as Leon Festinger and J. Merrill Carlsmith (1959) predicted, participants who were paid $1 gave the most positive ratings. Indeed, they actually rated the boring tasks as "slightly enjoyable"!

▶ 5. Explain the causes of cognitive dissonance and how it produces attitude change.

According to Festinger's (1957) **theory of cognitive dissonance,** *people strive for consistency in their cognitions.* When two or more cognitions contradict one another (such as "I am a truthful person" and "I just told another student that those boring tasks were interesting"), the person experiences an uncomfortable state of tension, which Festinger calls *cognitive dissonance,* and becomes motivated to reduce this dissonance. The theory predicts that to reduce dissonance and restore a state of cognitive consistency, people will change one of their cognitions or add new cognitions. Participants who received $20 could justify their behavior by adding a new cognition—"Who wouldn't tell a little lie for $20?"—and there was little reason for them to change their attitude toward the boring tasks. Those who had lied for only $1 could not use this trivial monetary gain to justify their behavior. But if they could convince themselves that the tasks actually were enjoyable, then they wouldn't have been lying after all. Thus they changed their attitude about the task to bring it more in line with how they had behaved.

Behavior that is inconsistent with one's attitude is called *counterattitudinal behavior,* and it produces dissonance only if we perceive that our actions were freely chosen rather than coerced. Freely chosen behaviors that produce foreseeable negative consequences or that threaten our sense of self-worth are especially likely to arouse dissonance. Once the behavior occurs, argue Jeff Stone and Joel Cooper (2001), people start to consider the meaning of what they have done, and this produces dissonance. Recall the statement by one of the guards

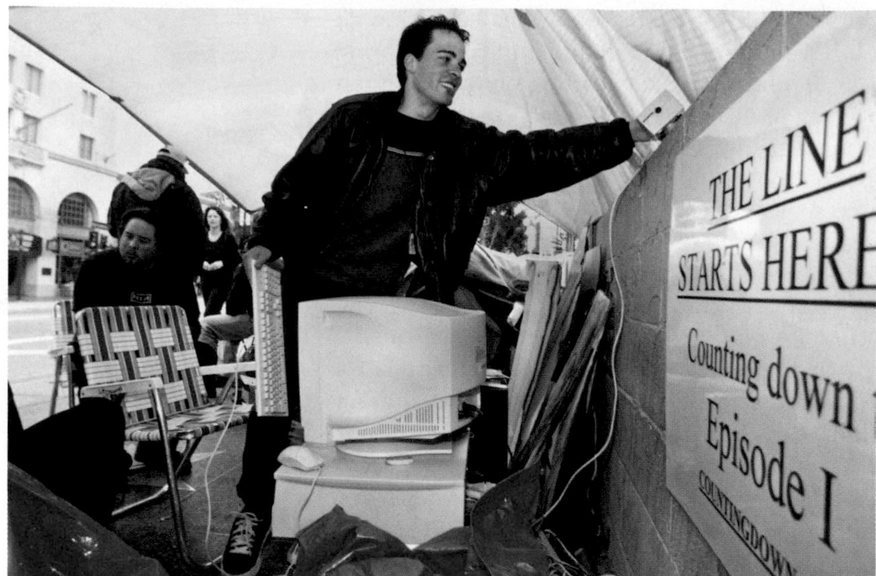

FIGURE 15.7

Effort justification: "May the force (of dissonance) be with you!" Some fans began camping out days in advance to see Star Wars: The Phantom Menace. *Most critics and many moviegoers found the movie disappointing, but fans who waited in line for days said the movie was "awesome." No doubt, a major reason for their positive attitude is that they are hard-core fans. But might cognitive dissonance have played a role? Experiments show that when people invest a lot of time and energy toward a goal, finding out that the goal wasn't all it was cracked up to be creates cognitive dissonance. To justify their effort and thus reduce dissonance, people may convince themselves that the goal (e.g., the movie) is more attractive or worthwhile than it really is.*

in the Stanford prison study regarding his treatment of the prisoners: "I was surprised at myself." If the guard thought of himself as a good, moral person, then his callous behavior toward the prisoners should create dissonance. Changing one's attitude toward the prisoners—essentially coming to see them as "cattle" who did not have the same rights as humans—would reduce dissonance.

Dissonance, however, does not always lead to attitude change. People can reduce dissonance by finding external justifications or by making other excuses (Buunk & Dijkstra, 2001). In surveys of over 3,300 Scandinavian adolescents and adults, people who drank alcohol despite having negative attitudes toward drinking often emphasized that "Other people drink more than I do." As researcher Klaus Mäkelä (1997) noted, the general rationalization seemed to be "I may not be perfect, but other people are still worse." Despite the many ways to reduce dissonance, the theory helps explain many interesting aspects of human behavior (Figure 15.7).

▶ 6. Evaluate dissonance versus self-perception theory views of why counterattitudinal behavior produces attitude change.

Self-Perception If we see someone campaigning for a political candidate, we will likely assume that this person has a positive attitude toward the candidate. If we see someone exerting great effort to achieve a goal, we will logically judge that the goal is important to that person. In short, we infer what other people's attitudes must be by watching how they behave. According to Daryl Bem's (1972) **self-perception theory,** *we make inferences about our own attitudes in much the same way: by observing how we behave.* Knowing that for very little external justification ($1) you have told a fellow student that the boring experimental tasks are enjoyable, you logically conclude that "deep down" you must feel that the tasks were at least somewhat enjoyable. In Bem's view, your attitude is not produced by a mysterious concept called *cognitive dissonance;* rather you simply observe how you have acted and infer how you must have felt to have behaved in this fashion.

Self-perception theory and cognitive dissonance theory both predict that counterattitudinal behavior produces attitude change. How, then, can we determine which theory more accurately explains the reason behind such attitude change? One key difference is that only dissonance theory assumes that we experience heightened physiological arousal (tension produced by dissonance) when we engage in counterattitudinal behavior. Do we? At least in some instances it appears so. In one study, college students consumed an unpleasant-tasting drink and were then asked to write a sentence stating that they liked the taste. Students who were given a high degree of choice whether to write this counterattitudinal statement showed higher arousal (measured by sweat gland activity) and greater attitude change than participants who were simply told to write the statement (Harmon-Jones et al., 1996).

These and other findings indicate that dissonance theory best explains why people change their views after behaving in ways that openly contradict their clearly defined attitudes, especially when such behaviors threaten their self-image. Lying to someone for a measly dollar threatens our self-image of honesty, and acting inhumanely toward prisoners threatens our self-image of being a "good, decent person"—unless we can somehow justify those actions (such as by convincing ourselves that the task is enjoyable and the prisoners are worthless cattle). However, in situations where counterattitudinal behavior does not threaten self-worth and we have weak attitudes to begin with, such behavior is less likely to create significant arousal—yet people may still alter their attitudes to be more consistent with how they have behaved. In this case, self-perception theory may provide the better explanation. Thus both dissonance theory and self-perception theory appear to be correct, but under different circumstances

FIGURE 15.8

Fear appeals are a common approach to persuasion. They are most effective when people believe that a feared event could occur ("Driving after drinking can increase my risk of an accident"), that the consequences would be aversive ("I could lose my license, or be killed), that there is an effective way to reduce the risk ("If I drink, I won't drive"), and that they can carry out this behavior without great cost ("Have a designated driver; call a friend").

(Tesser & Shaffer, 1990). Both theories, however, agree that *our behaviors can influence our attitudes.*

Persuasion

Whether through political speeches, advertisements, or discussions with family and friends, persuasion is a fact of everyday life (Maio & Olson, 2000). The topic of persuasion represents a broad intersection of social thinking and social influence. Persuaders typically try to influence our beliefs and attitudes so that we, in turn, will vote for them, buy their products, or otherwise behave as they want us to. Here we briefly examine three aspects of the persuasion process.

▶ 7. Describe how communicator, message, and audience characteristics affect the persuasion process.

The Communicator **Communicator credibility**—*how believable we perceive the communicator to be*—is often a key to effective persuasion. In fact, audience members who do not enjoy thinking deeply about issues may pay little attention to the content of a message and simply go along with the opinions of a highly credible source. Credibility has two major components: *expertise* and *trustworthiness* (Hovland et al., 1953). The most effective persuader is one who appears to be an expert and to be presenting the truth in an unbiased manner. We are especially likely to perceive communicators as trustworthy when they advocate a point of view that is contrary to their own self-interest (Petty et al., 2001). Communicators who are physically attractive, likable, and similar to us (such as in interests or goals) may also gain a persuasive edge, which is why advertisers spend millions of dollars hiring attractive, likable stars to promote their products.

The Message In trying to persuade someone, is it more effective to present only your side of the issue or to also present the opposition's arguments and then refute them? Overall, research indicates that the *two-sided refutational approach* is most effective (Allen, 1991). Especially if an audience initially disagrees with the communicator's viewpoint or is aware that there are two sides to the issue, a two-sided message will be perceived as less biased.

Many messages, such as those in Figure 15.8, attempt to persuade by arousing fear. Does it work? Or do people reduce their fear simply by denying the credibility of the message or the communicator? Overall, fear arousal seems to work best when the message evokes moderate to strong fear and also provides people with effective, feasible (i.e., low-cost) ways to reduce the threat (Johnson, 1991; Witte & Allen, 2000). High-fear messages accompanied by inadequate information about "what to do" typically lead to denial.

The Audience A message loaded with logical arguments and facts may prove highly persuasive to some people yet fall flat on its face with others. One reason is that people differ in their *need for cognition.* Some enjoy analyzing issues; others prefer not to spend much mental effort.

According to Richard Petty and John Cacioppo (1986), there are two basic routes to persuasion. The **central route to persuasion** *occurs when people think carefully about the message and are influenced because they find the arguments compelling.* The **peripheral route to persuasion** *occurs when people do not scrutinize the message but are influenced mostly* *by other factors* such as a speaker's attractiveness or a message's emotional appeal. Attitude change that results from the central route tends to last longer and to predict future behavior more successfully.

People who have a high need for cognition tend to follow the central route to persuasion. In forming attitudes about consumer services and products, for example, they pay attention to information about the service and product (Wood & Swait, 2002). In contrast, people with a low need for cognition are more strongly influenced by peripheral cues, such as the attractiveness of the person who endorses a product.

IN REVIEW

- *Consistency, distinctiveness, and consensus information jointly influence whether we make a personal or situational attribution for a particular act.*
- *The fundamental attribution error is the tendency to attribute other people's behavior to personal factors while underestimating the role of situational factors. The self-serving bias is the tendency to attribute one's successes to personal factors and one's failures to situational factors.*
- *Although our impressions of people may change over time, our first impression generally carries extra weight. Stereotypes and schemas create mental sets that powerfully shape our impressions.*
- *Through self-fulfilling prophecies, our initially false expectations shape the way we act toward someone. In turn, this person responds to our behavior in a way that confirms our initially false belief.*
- *Attitudes are evaluative judgments. They predict behavior best when situational influences are weak, when the attitude is strong, and when we consciously think about our attitude.*
- *Our behavior also influences our attitudes. Counterattitudinal behavior is most likely to create cognitive dissonance when the behavior is freely chosen and has negative implications for our sense of self-worth or produces foreseeable negative consequences.*
- *To reduce dissonance, we may change our attitude to become more consistent with how we have behaved. In situations where our attitudes are weak and counterattitudinal behavior doesn't threaten our self-worth, we may change our attitudes through self-perception.*
- *Communicator, message, and audience characteristics influence the effectiveness of persuasion. Communicator credibility is highest when the communicator is perceived as expert and trustworthy. Fear-arousing communications may be effective if they arouse moderate to strong fear and suggest how to avoid the feared result. The central route to persuasion works best with listeners who have a high need for cognition; for those with a low cognition need, the peripheral route works better.*

SOCIAL INFLUENCE

Patricia, a novice piano player, makes more mistakes after her parents enter the room to listen to her practice. Brad, a "guard" in the Stanford prison study, starts treating prisoners harshly after witnessing several of his fellow guards do the same. These diverse situations share a basic ingredient: They involve social influence.

▶ 8. When does the mere presence of others enhance performance and impair performance? Why?

The Mere Presence of Others

Norman Triplett (1898) helped launch the field of social psychology by testing a deceptively simple hypothesis: The presence of others energizes performance. Triplett, who loved bicycle racing, analyzed the records from numerous competitions. In some races, cyclists performed individually against the clock; in other races of similar distance, they performed together in a pack. As Triplett predicted, cyclists' average speed per mile was much faster in group races than in individual races, but from experience he knew that other factors (e.g., racers riding behind one another to cut wind resistance) could also explain this finding. To test the effect of others' presence in a laboratory experiment, Triplett had children perform a simple physical task as rapidly as they could, either alone or in the

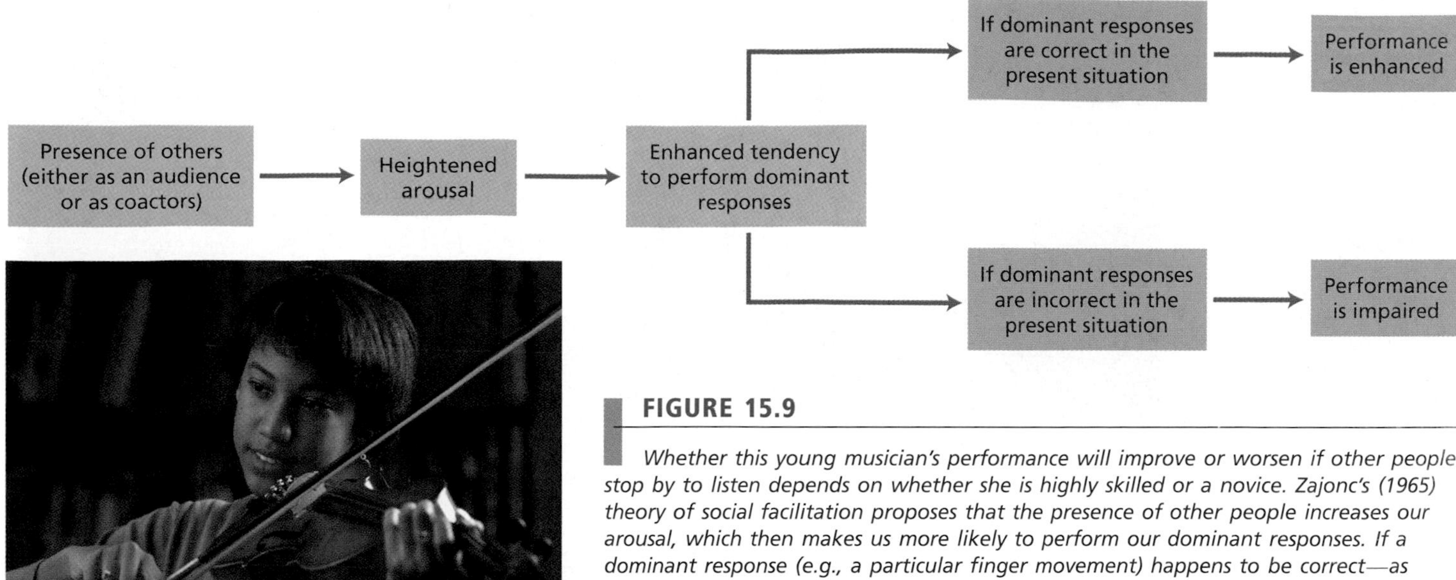

FIGURE 15.9

Whether this young musician's performance will improve or worsen if other people stop by to listen depends on whether she is highly skilled or a novice. Zajonc's (1965) theory of social facilitation proposes that the presence of other people increases our arousal, which then makes us more likely to perform our dominant responses. If a dominant response (e.g., a particular finger movement) happens to be correct—as typically occurs on simple tasks or complex tasks that have been mastered—then performance will be enhanced. But if a dominant response is incorrect—as often occurs when a novice is trying to learn a complex task—then the presence of other people most likely will impair performance.

presence of another child (called a *coactor*) who independently performed the same task. Again, performance improved when people were in each other's presence.

Many early studies replicated this finding, revealing that the *mere presence* of coactors or of a passive, silent audience enhanced performance. Even ants carried more dirt when in the presence of other ants (Chen, 1937). Yet other experiments found that performance on some tasks worsened when coactors or an audience were present.

In 1965, Robert Zajonc proposed a theory to explain this seeming paradox. First, the mere physical presence of another person (or member of the same species) increases our arousal. Second, as arousal increases, we become more likely to perform whatever behaviors happen to be our *dominant responses* (i.e., most typical responses) to that specific situation. When a task is complex and we are first trying to learn it, our dominant responses are likely to be incorrect ones, so we make errors. Therefore performing in front of other people will impair performance. But when a task is either simple or complex but well learned, our dominant responses usually are correct ones. In these situations, performing in the presence of others will enhance performance (Figure 15.9). This phenomenon is called **social facilitation,** *an increased tendency to perform one's dominant responses in the mere presence of others.*

Social facilitation occurs in species ranging from cockroaches and fruit flies to hens and humans (Thomas et al., 2002). It is a basic form of social influence, and overall it produces small but reliable effects on human performance. Social facilitation also has an important practical implication: When learning complex tasks, minimize the presence of other people.

Norms, Conformity, and Obedience

Years ago, a professor on our campus gave his class an unusual assignment: Without doing anything illegal, each student was to violate some "unspoken rule" of social behavior and observe how others reacted. One student licked her plate clean at a formal dinner, receiving cold stares from the other guests. Another boarded a nearly empty city bus, sat down next to the only other passenger, and said "Hi!" The passenger sat up stiffly and stared out the window.

Social norms *are shared expectations about how people should think, feel, and behave,* and they are the cement that binds social systems together (Morris et al., 2001). Some norms are formal laws and regulations, but many—as illustrated by the two preceding examples—are implicit and unspoken. Such norms powerfully regulate daily behavior without our conscious awareness; we usually take them for granted until they are violated.

A **social role** *consists of a set of norms that characterizes how people in a given social position ought to behave.* The social roles of "college student," "professor," "police officer," and "spouse" carry different

(a)

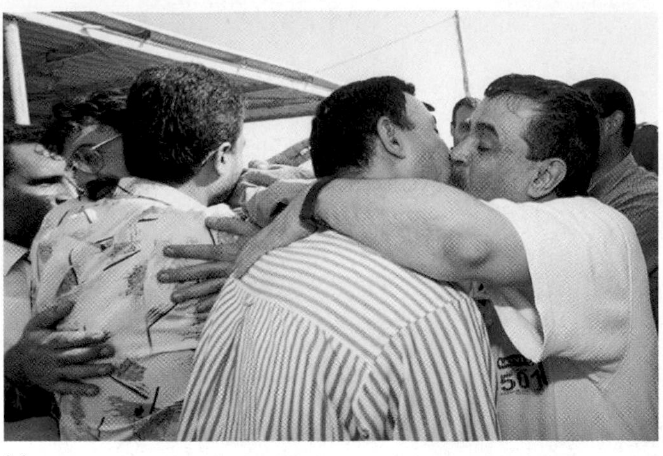

(b)

FIGURE 15.10

Norms may vary over time and across cultures. (a) A century ago it was not "normal" for many Western women to have the right to vote or to become doctors, business managers, and police officers. (b) Among men who are relatives or close friends, what type of greeting seems "normal" to you? A handshake? A bow? A hug? A kiss? Norms governing forms of greeting vary across cultures.

sets of behavior expectations. Because we may wear many hats in our daily life, *role conflict* can occur when the norms accompanying different roles clash. College students who hold jobs and have children often experience role conflict as they try to juggle the competing demands of school, work, and parenthood.

Norms and roles can influence behavior so strongly that they compel a person to act uncharacteristically. The guards in the Stanford prison study were well-adjusted students, yet norms related to the role of "guard" seemed to override their values, leading to their dehumanizing treatment of the prisoners.

Norm Formation and Culture

Social norms lose invisibility not only when they are violated but also when we examine behavior across cultures and historical periods. In doing so, we see that many social customs we take for granted as "normal"—from gender roles and child rearing to views about love and marriage—are arbitrary (Figure 15.10). Norms even regulate such subtle aspects of social behavior as the amount of *personal space* that we prefer when interacting with people (Li, 2001). For example, Japanese sit farther apart when conversing than Venezuelans do, and Americans prefer an intermediate distance (Sussman & Rosenfeld, 1982).

▶ 9. Use the concepts of informational and normative social influence to explain how social norms and roles guide behavior.

It is difficult to imagine any society, organization, or social group functioning well without norms. In a classic experiment, Muzafer Sherif (1935) found that even randomly created groups develop norms. The task involved an optical illusion called the *autokinetic effect:* When people stare at a dot of light projected on a screen in a dark room, they begin to perceive the dot as moving, even though it really is stationary. When Sherif tested college students individually over several trials, each student perceived the light to move a different amount, from an inch or two to almost a foot.

Later the students were randomly placed into groups of 3 and made further judgments. As the members within each group heard one another's judgments over several sessions, their judgments converged and a group norm evolved. The participants did not explicitly communicate or "decide" to develop a group norm. It just happened. Moreover, just as norms vary across cultures, the norm that evolved for the autokinetic effect varied from group to group, and it was not the simple average of the original judgments.

Sherif's finding has been replicated in other countries and with different types of tasks (Khoury, 1985). Whether at a cultural level or in small random groups, humans placed together seem to develop common standards for behavior and judgment.

Why Do People Conform?

Norms can influence behavior only if people conform to them. Without *conformity*—the adjustment of individual behaviors, attitudes, and beliefs to a group standard—we would have social chaos. It is no accident, therefore, that all social systems exert overt and subtle pressures on their members to conform.

As Figure 15.11 illustrates, at times we conform due to **informational social influence,** *following the opinions or behavior of other people because we believe they have accurate knowledge and what they are doing is "right."* We also may succumb to **normative social influence,** *conforming to obtain the rewards that come from being accepted by other people while at the same time avoiding their rejection* (Deutsch & Gerard, 1955).

Solomon Asch's (1951, 1956) landmark conformity experiments illustrated both types of

"Well, heck! If all you smart cookies agree, who am I to dissent?"

FIGURE 15.11

Often we conform to a majority because we believe that their opinion "must be right."

influence. In the experimental condition, groups of college students performed several trials of a simple visual task (Figure 15.12a) in which they were asked—for various sets of lines—which of the 3 lines on the right was the same length as Line A. Only one member of the group, however, actually was a participant. The rest were accomplices of the experimenter. Group members sat around a table and were called on in order. The real participant sat next to last. According to plan, every accomplice intentionally gave the same wrong answer on some trials. Imagine yourself hearing the first group member choose Line 1. (You think to yourself, "Huh?") Then the next four members also say "Line 1." (You're wondering, "Can this really be?") Now it is your turn.

Would anybody conform to the group's incorrect judgments? Asch found that overall, participants conformed 37 percent of the time, compared with a mere 1 percent error rate in a control condition where people judged the lines by themselves. This finding stunned many scientists because the task was so easy and the confederates did not overtly pressure participants to conform.

After the task was over, some participants told the experimenter that they felt the group was wrong but went along to avoid "making waves" and possible rejection. This reflects normative social influence. After several trials, other participants yielded to informational social influence and began to doubt their eyesight and judgment (Figure 15.12b).

For more on the study of conformity, see Video Segment 15.2.

Factors That Affect Conformity

▶ 10. Describe situational factors that influence conformity to the group. When will minority influence be strongest?

Asch demonstrated that complex social behavior could be studied scientifically under controlled conditions. In subsequent experiments, he manipulated different independent variables and measured their effects on conformity. Consider two examples:

- *Group size.* Conformity increased from about 5 to 35 percent as group size increased from 1 to about 4 or 5 confederates, but contrary to what we might expect, further increases in group size did not increase conformity.
- *Presence of a dissenter.* When one confederate (according to plan) disagreed with the others (e.g., the majority says "Line 3," and the dissenter says "Line 2"or even "Line 1"), this greatly reduced real participants' conformity. When someone else dissents, this serves as a model for remaining independent from the group.

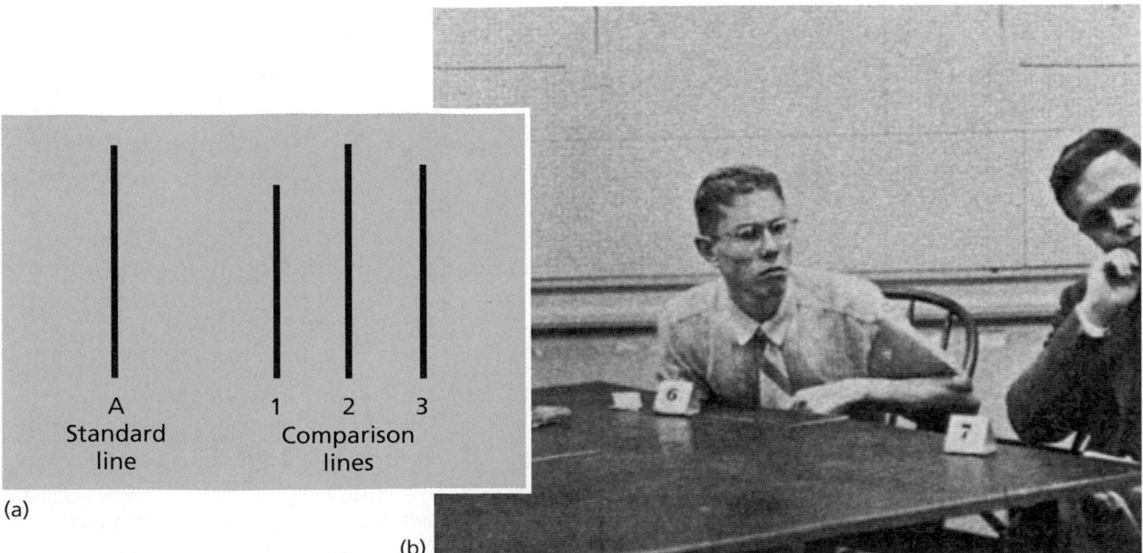

FIGURE 15.12

(a) In Asch's (1956) conformity experiments, students were asked to judge which of three comparison lines was the same length as the standard line. They performed this task for multiple trials, using a different set of standard and comparison lines each time. (b) Upon hearing other group members unanimously say that "Line 1" is the correct match, this participant wonders whether his own judgment (Line 2) is correct.

▶ 11. Describe Milgram's research, factors that increase and decrease obedience, and implications for society.

Reviewing 97 conformity experiments conducted in the United States from 1951 to 1990, Rod Bond and Peter Smith (1996) found that the overall level of conformity decreased slightly over this time period. Around the globe, conformity tends to be greater among research participants from collectivistic cultures, where group harmony is valued more highly than in individualistic cultures.

Minority Influence

Although majority influence is powerful, in political, business, and other real-world contexts, dissenting information presented by the minority may cause majority members to change their view, particularly when it comes from several minority members rather than just one (R. D. Clark, 2001). Serge Moscovici (1985) proposes that to maximize its influence, the minority must be highly committed to its point of view and remain independent and consistent in the face of majority pressure, yet appear to keep an open mind. Indeed, reviewing almost 100 studies, Wendy Wood and coworkers (1994) found that minority influence is strongest when the minority maintains a highly consistent position over time. However, if the minority appears too unreasonable, deviant, or negative, it may cause the majority to become entrenched.

Obedience to Authority

Like conformity to a group, obedience to an authority figure is inherently neither good nor bad. As an airplane passenger, you would not be amused if the copilot disregarded the pilot's commands simply because he or she "didn't feel like obeying," putting the flight and your life at risk. Without obedience, society would face chaos. But obedience can also produce tragic results. After World War II, the famous Nuremberg trials were held to judge Nazi war criminals who had slaughtered millions of innocent people in concentration camps. In many instances, the defendants argued that they had "only followed orders." In the massacre of men, women, and children at My Lai during the Vietnam War, American soldiers accused of atrocities gave the same explanation. No doubt we will continue to hear the cry "I was just following orders" as accountability is judged for more recent mass atrocities around the globe.

Just as the Nuremberg court did, many of us reject justifications based on obedience to authority as mere rationalizations, secure in our conviction that we would behave more humanely in such situations. But would we? Our *Research Close-Up*—part of the most famous series of studies ever conducted in social psychology—suggests some provocative answers.

RESEARCH CLOSE-UP

THE DILEMMA OF OBEDIENCE: WHEN CONSCIENCE CONFRONTS MALEVOLENT AUTHORITY

Background

Fueled by a scientific interest in social influence and a desire to understand the horrors of the Holocaust, psychologist Stanley Milgram (1974) asked a disturbing question: Would ordinary citizens obey the orders of an authority figure if those orders meant physically harming an innocent person? He conducted 18 studies between 1960 and 1963 to answer this question and to identify factors that increased or decreased obedience to authority.

SOURCE: Stanley Milgram, 1974. *Obedience to Authority*. New York: Harper & Row.

Method

Forty men, ranging in from age 20 to 50 and representing a cross section of occupations and educational backgrounds, participated in the study. At the laboratory, each participant met a middle-aged man who was introduced as another participant but who was actually a confederate. Participants were told that the experiment examined the effects of punishment on memory. Then through a supposedly random draw (it was rigged), the real participant became the "teacher" and the confederate became the "learner." The teacher presented a series of memory problems to the learner through a two-way intercom system. Each time the learner made an error, the teacher was instructed to administer an electric shock using a machine that had 30 switches, beginning with 15 volts and increasing step-by-step to 450 volts (Figure 15.13a). As the teacher watched, the experimenter strapped the learner into a chair in

(a)

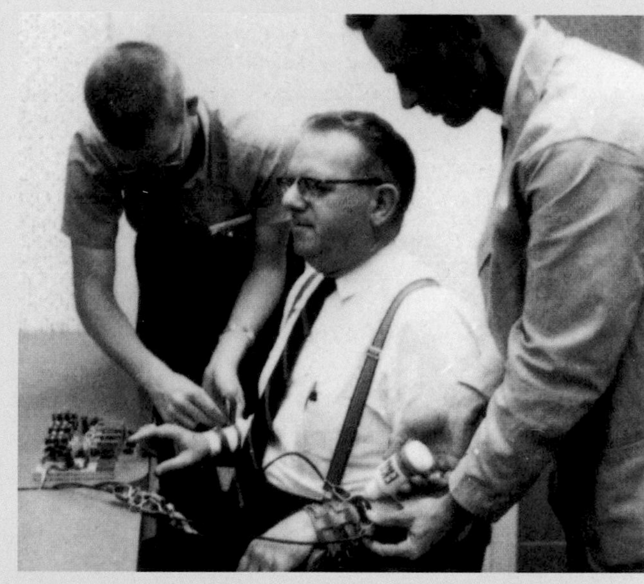

(b)

FIGURE 15.13

(a) Switches on the shock generator ranged from 15 volts ("slight shock") to 450 volts ("XXX"). (b) The participant (teacher) saw the learner being strapped into the chair.

an adjoining room and hooked him up to wires from the shock generator (Figure 15.13b). The learner expressed concern about the shocks and mentioned that he had a slight heart problem.

Returning to the main room, the experimenter gave the teacher a sample shock (45 volts) and then ordered the experiment to begin. Unbeknownst to the teacher, the learner intentionally committed many errors, and he did *not* actually receive any shock. The learner made verbal protests that were standardized on a tape recorder, so that they were the same for all participants.

As the learner's errors mounted, the teacher increased the shock. If the teacher balked at continuing, the experimenter issued one or more escalating commands, such as "Please continue," "You must continue," and "You have no other choice." At 75 volts, the learner moaned when the teacher threw the switch. At 150 volts, the learner's reaction was "Ugh!!! Experimenter! That's all. Get me out of here. I told you I had heart trouble. My heart's starting to bother me now. Get me out of here, please. . . . I refuse to go on. Let me out." Beyond 200 volts, he emitted agonized screams every time a shock was delivered, yelling "Let me out! Let me out!" At 300 volts, the learner refused to answer and continued screaming to be let out. At 345 volts and beyond, there was only silence. Full obedience was operationally defined as continuing to the maximum shock level of 450 volts.

Results

Participants wrestled with a dilemma. Should they continue to hurt this innocent person, as the experimenter commanded, or should they stop the learner's pain by openly disobeying? Most participants became distressed. Some trembled, sweated, laughed nervously, or, in a few cases, experienced convulsions. But would they obey? Make a prediction: What percentage of people obeyed to 450 volts?

When Milgram asked psychiatrists, professors, university students, and middle-class adults to predict the outcome, they estimated a 1-percent obedience rate. Indeed, most participants balked or protested at one time or another and said they would not continue. But ultimately, 26 of the 40 men (65 percent) obeyed all the way to the end (Figure 15.14).

For more on obedience to authority, see Video Segment 15.3.

Discussion

Milgram's research has generated controversy for decades (Blass, 2000). Its ethics were harshly criticized because participants were deceived, were exposed to substantial stress, and risked long-lasting negative effects to their self-image (Baumrind, 1964). Milgram countered that the research was so socially significant as to warrant the deception, that participants were carefully debriefed afterward, and that psychiatric follow-ups of a sample of obedient participants suggested no long-term ill effects. Weighing the costs and benefits, do you believe that this research was justified?

Researchers also debate why obedience was high, but many agree with Milgram's view that participants psychologically transferred much of the "responsibility" for the teacher's fate to the experimenter. Participants viewed the experimenter as an expert, legitimate authority figure (Blass & Schmitt, 2001). While administering the shock, some participants stated that they "were

Continued

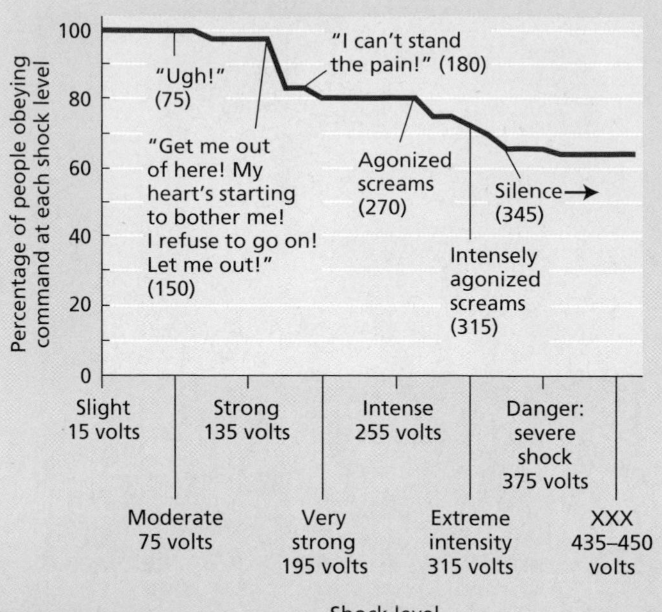

FIGURE 15.14

This graph shows the percentage of male participants who continued to shock the learner through various voltage levels. SOURCE: Based on Milgram, 1974.

not responsible" for what happened. Others asked, "Who is responsible if something happens to the learner?" When the experimenter replied, "I am responsible," participants felt greater freedom to continue. Yet they were the ones flipping the switch.

Would similar results occur today? We suspect so. For 25 years after Milgram's research, experiments in different countries, in "real-world" settings, and with children, adolescents, and adults, yielded consistent results. In the 1980s, Dutch researchers Wim Meeus and Quinten Raaijmakers (1986, 1995) conducted 19 obedience studies. In one, 92 percent of participants completely obeyed an experimenter's orders to repeatedly disrupt the performance of a job applicant (actually a confederate) taking an important job screening test. The applicant pleaded with participants to stop, to no avail.

How would you have responded? Almost all of our students say they would have disobeyed. So suppose we conduct an obedience study today but with real electric shock and with you as the learner. The teacher will be a randomly selected student from your class. Are you confident that this student will disobey the experimenter and stop giving you shocks if you yell in protest? Few of our students express such confidence. In short, virtually all of us are confident that *we* would not obey, but we are not so sure about *other* people—and they in turn are not so sure about *us*.

Factors That Influence Destructive Obedience

By manipulating the following aspects of the laboratory situation, Milgram and other researchers obtained obedience rates ranging from 0 to over 90 percent:

- *Remoteness of the victim.* Obedience was greatest when the learner was out of sight. When the teacher and learner were placed in the same room, obedience dropped to 40 percent. Further, when the teacher had to make physical contact and force the learner's hand onto a "shock plate," obedience dropped to 30 percent (Figure 15.15).
- *Closeness and legitimacy of the authority figure.* Obedience was highest when the authority figure was close by and perceived as legitimate. When the experimenter left the scene and gave orders by phone, or when an "ordinary person" (a confederate) took over and gave the orders, obedience dropped to about 20 percent.
- *Cog in a wheel.* When another "participant" (actually a confederate) flipped the shock switch and real participants only had to perform another aspect of the task, 93 percent obeyed. In short, *obedience increases when someone else does the "dirty work."* In contrast, when Harvey Tilker (1970) made participants feel fully responsible for the learner's welfare, not a single person obeyed to the end.
- *Personal characteristics.* Milgram compared the political orientation, religious affiliation,

FIGURE 15.15

In one of Milgram's studies (touch proximity), the teacher was ordered to physically force the learner's hand onto a shock plate after the learner refused to continue. Here, 30 percent of participants obeyed fully to 450 volts. Although touch proximity strongly reduced obedience, that a significant minority still obeyed raises considerable concern.

occupations, education, length of military service, and psychological characteristics of obedient versus disobedient participants. Differences were weak or nonexistent.

What Do You Think?

DO WOMEN DIFFER FROM MEN IN OBEDIENCE?

Suppose that the participants in Milgram's featured study had been women. Keeping everything else constant (i.e., the same male experimenter and male learner) would you expect women to be more or less obedient than the men, or equally obedient? Why? Think about it, then see page 631.

Lessons Learned

What lessons shall we draw from this research? Certainly, it is *not* that people are apathetic or evil. Participants became stressed precisely because they did care about the learner's welfare. Neither is the lesson that we are sheep. If we were, obedience would be high across all situations, which is not the case. Rather, Milgram sums up a key lesson as follows:

> It would be a mistake . . . to make the simple-minded statement that kindly and good persons disobey while those who are cruel do not . . . often, it is not so much the kind of person a man is as the kind of situation in which he finds himself that determines how he will act. (Milgram, 1974, p. 205)

Thus by arranging the situation appropriately, most people—ordinary, decent citizens—can be induced to follow orders from an authority figure they perceive as legitimate, even when doing so contributes to harming an innocent person. The applicability of this principle to the Holocaust and other atrocities seems clear (Saltzman, 2000). During the Holocaust, obedience was made easier because most of the personnel working at the concentration camps were cogs in a horrendous wheel: They didn't pull the switch to flood the chambers with gas but instead performed other tasks. Their victims also were "remote" at the moment of their murder. Further, to lessen concentration camp workers' feelings of responsibility, Hitler's subordinate Heinrich Himmler told them in manipulative speeches that only he and Hitler were personally responsible for what took place (Dawidowicz, 1975).

Does obedience research suggest that we are not responsible for following orders? This is a moral and legal question, not a scientific one. But if anything, this research should heighten our responsibility for being aware of the pitfalls of blind obedience and prevent us from being so smug or naive as to feel that such events "could never happen here."

Detecting and Resisting Compliance Techniques

▶ 12. Identify four common compliance techniques and explain how they work.

From telemarketers and salespeople to TV and Internet advertisements, would-be persuaders often come armed with special *compliance techniques:* strategies that may manipulate you into saying yes when you really want to say no. By learning to identify these techniques, you will be in a better position to resist them.

The powerful **norm of reciprocity** *involves the expectation that when others treat us well, we should respond in kind.* Thus to get you to comply with a request, I can do something nice for you now—such as an unsolicited favor—in hopes that you will feel pressure to reciprocate later when I present you with my request (Cialdini, 1988). As Figure 15.16 illustrates, the Hare Krishna Society (a religious group) cleverly used "flower power" to manipulate the norm of reciprocity and raise millions of dollars in donations.

Now consider the **door-in-the-face technique:** *A persuader makes a large request, expecting you to reject*

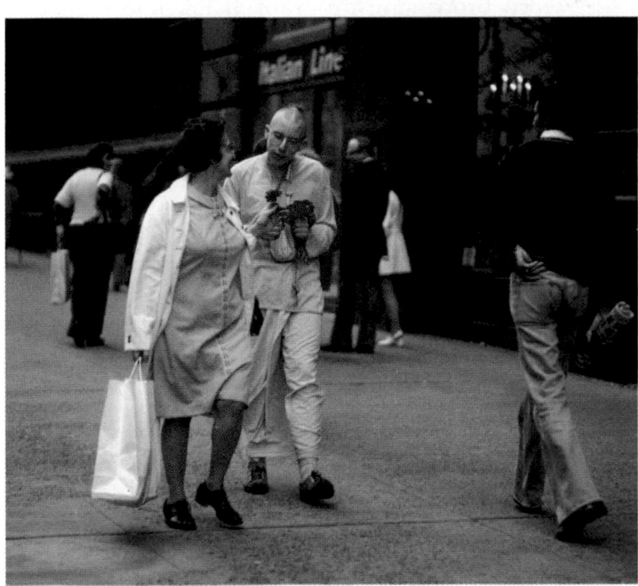

FIGURE 15.16

In the 1970s, members of the Hare Krishna Society approached passersby and gave them a small flower. If a passerby refused, the member said "Please. It is a gift for you." Reluctantly, people often accepted. Then the member asked for a donation. People felt pressure to reciprocate, donated money, and often threw the flower away.

it (you "slam the door" in the persuader's face), and then presents a smaller request. Telemarketers feast on this technique. Rather than ask you directly for a modest monetary contribution to some organization or cause, they first ask for a much larger contribution, knowing that you will say no. After you politely refuse, they ask for the smaller contribution. In one experiment, after people declined an initial request to donate $25 to a charity, they were more likely to donate $2 than were participants who were directly asked for $2 (Wang et al., 1989). To be effective, the same persuader must make both requests. The persuader "compromises" by making the second, smaller request, so we feel pressure to reciprocate by complying. Refusing the first request also may produce guilt, and complying with the smaller request may help us reduce guilt or feel socially responsible (Tusing & Dillard, 2000).

Using the **foot-in-the-door technique,** *a persuader gets you to comply with a small request first (getting the "foot in the door") and later presents a larger request.* Imagine receiving an E-mail message from a stranger requesting help. It's a student who needs to collect data for a class project and asks if you would fill out a 20-minute online questionnaire about your dietary habits. Would you do it? In an experiment with French college students, 44 percent complied (Guéguen, 2002). Now let's turn to a different condition of this experiment. Imagine receiving an E-mail from a stranger who asks for simple advice about a word processing program. It takes less than 1 minute to reply, and you do (as did all the participants in this condition of the experiment). Once the person gets the foot in the door, a second E-mail appears minutes later, asking if you would help with a class project by filling out a dietary questionnaire. In this condition many more students—76 percent—complied. Although hypotheses abound, researchers are not sure why the foot-in-the-door technique is effective.

▶ 13. Describe social loafing, social compensation, and the causes and consequences of group polarization and groupthink.

With a final technique, **lowballing,** *a persuader gets you to commit to some action and then—before you actually perform the behavior—he or she increases the "cost" of that same behavior.* Imagine negotiating to buy a used car for $8,000, a "great price." The salesperson says, "I need to confirm this with my manager," comes back shortly, and states, "I'm afraid my manager says the price is too low. But you can have the car for only $400 more. It's still a great price." At this point, you are more likely to go through with the deal than you would have been, had the "real" $8,400 price been set at the outset.

Both lowballing and the foot-in-the-door technique involve moving from a smaller request to a larger, more costly one. But with the foot-in-the-door approach, the smaller and larger requests often involve different acts (e.g., giving advice, filling out a questionnaire) and the larger request is made after you finish complying with the smaller request. In lowballing, the stakes for the *same behavior* are raised after you commit to it but *before* you consummate the behavior. Having made a commitment, you may find it easier to rationalize the added costs or may feel obligated to the person to whom you made the commitment.

By recognizing when compliance techniques are being used to manipulate your behavior, you are in a better position to resist them. Consider the norm of reciprocity. Robert Cialdini (1988), an expert on influence techniques, suggests that the key is not to resist the initial gift or favor; instead, accept the unsolicited "favor," but if the person then asks you for a favor in return, recognize this as a manipulative technique. As Cialdini notes, "The rule says that favors are to be met with favors; it does not require that tricks be met with favors" (1988, p. 53). Similarly, if a telemarketer asks you to agree to a large request and then after you decline immediately asks for a smaller commitment, respond by thinking or even saying, "I see; the door-in-the-face technique." Of course, you can still choose to comply if you believe it is the right thing to do. The goal is not to automatically reject every social influence attempt but to avoid feeling coerced into doing something you don't want to do.

Behavior in Groups

Much of human behavior occurs in groups. From sports teams and social clubs to volunteer boards and work committees, people often form groups to share interests and activities, and to perform tasks and achieve goals that are too complex or demanding to be accomplished by one person (Figure 15.17).

Social Loafing

In 1913, Max Ringelmann, a French agricultural engineer, measured the force that men exerted while pulling on a rope as hard as they could. Individually, the men averaged 63 kilograms (kg) of pull. Thus you might expect that 8 men pulling in unison would exert a combined force of about 504 kg (i.e., 8 × 63 kg). Surprisingly, group performance was 51 percent below expectations. Part of the reason may have been that the men didn't coordinate the timing of their pull precisely and

FIGURE 15.17

Whether for recreational, volunteer, or work activities, much of human behavior occurs in groups.

there was a loss of mechanical efficiency. But another contributing factor is **social loafing,** *the tendency for people to expend less individual effort when working in a group than when working alone.* In contrast to social facilitation experiments, in which a person performs a task individually (in front of an audience or with a coactor) and does not pool her or his effort with anyone, social loafing involves collective performance. Social loafing also occurs on cognitive tasks, as when groups have to evaluate written materials or make decisions. Why does social loafing occur? Steven Karau and Kipling Williams (1993, 2001) propose a *collective effort model:* On a collective task, people will put forth effort only to the extent that they expect their effort to contribute to obtaining a valued goal. In support of this model, studies reveal that social loafing is *more* likely to occur when

- people believe that individual performance within the group is not being monitored;
- the task (goal) or the group has less value or meaning to the person; and
- the task is simple and the person's input is redundant with that of other group members (Karau & Williams, 1993).

Social loafing also depends on gender and culture. It occurs more strongly in all-male groups than in all-female or mixed-sex groups, possibly because women may be more concerned about group outcomes than are men. Participants from individualistic cultures (e.g., Canada and the United States) exhibit more social loafing than people from collectivistic cultures (e.g., China, Japan, Taiwan), in which group goals are especially valued.

Social loafing suggests that in terms of group performance, "the whole is less than the sum of its parts." But this is not always the case. Social loafing may disappear when individual performance is monitored or when members highly value their group or the task goal. In fact, to achieve a highly desired goal, some people may engage in **social compensation,** *working harder in a group than alone to compensate for other members' lower output* (Hart et al., 2001).

Group Polarization

Educational institutions, corporations, and other organizations often develop policies through committees. Key decisions are often entrusted to groups because they are assumed to be more conservative than individuals and less likely to "go off the deep end." Is this assumption correct? It is, as long as the group is generally conservative to begin with. In such cases, the group's final opinion or attitude will likely be even *more conservative.* But if the group members lean toward a more liberal or risky viewpoint to begin with, the group's decision will tend to become *more liberal or riskier.* This principle is called **group polarization:** *When a group of like-minded people discusses an issue, the "average" opinion of group members tends to become more extreme* (Moscovici & Zavalloni, 1969).

Why does group polarization occur? One reason, reflecting normative social influence, is that individuals who are attracted to a group may be motivated to adopt a more extreme position to gain the group's approval. A second reason, reflecting informational social influence, is that during group discussions people hear arguments supporting their positions that they had not previously considered. These new arguments tend to make the initial positions seem even more valid (Sia et al., 2002).

FIGURE 15.18

Antecedents, symptoms, and negative effects of groupthink on decision making. SOURCE: Adapted from Janis, 1982.

Antecedent conditions

1. High stress to reach a decision
2. Insulation of the group
3. Directive leadership
4. High cohesiveness

Some symptoms of groupthink

1. Illusion of invulnerability (group overestimates itself)
2. Direct pressure on dissenters
3. Self-censorship
4. Illusion of unanimity
5. Self-appointed mind guards

↓

Groupthink increases risk of defective decision making

1. Incomplete survey of alternatives
2. Incomplete survey of objectives
3. Failure to examine risks of preferred choice
4. Poor information search
5. Failure to reappraise alternatives

Groupthink

After the U.S. military ignored warning signs of imminent attack by Japan in 1941, the fleet at Pearl Harbor was destroyed in a "surprise" attack. In 1961, President Kennedy and his advisors launched the hopelessly doomed Bay of Pigs invasion of Cuba. In 1972, five men working for the Republican campaign broke into Democratic Party offices at the Watergate Hotel, and the following cover-up ultimately forced President Nixon to resign. According to Yale social psychologist Irving Janis (1982), the decision makers involved in each of these historical blunders fell victim to a process called **groupthink,** *the tendency of group members to suspend critical thinking because they are striving to seek agreement.*

Janis developed the concept of groupthink, shown in Figure 15.18, after analyzing historical accounts of group deliberations that resulted in disastrous decisions. He proposed that groupthink is most likely to occur when a group

- is under *high stress* to reach a decision;
- is *insulated* from outside input;
- has a *directive leader* who promotes a personal agenda; and
- has *high cohesiveness,* reflecting a spirit of closeness and ability to work well together.

Under these conditions, the group is so committed to reaching consensus, and remaining loyal and agreeable, that members suspend their critical judgment. In the business world, groupthink can contribute to poor management decisions that adversely affect the financial value and public reputation of the company (Eaton, 2001).

Various symptoms signal that groupthink is at work. For example, group members who express doubt are faced with *direct pressure* to stop "rocking the boat." Some members serve as *mind guards* by preventing negative information from reaching the group. Ultimately, members display *self-censorship* and withhold their doubts, creating a potentially disastrous *illusion of unanimity* in which each member comes to believe that "everyone else seems to agree with the decision" (Figure 15.19).

Many aspects of groupthink were present during the decision process leading up to the fatal launch of the space shuttle *Challenger* in 1986 (Esser & Lindoerfer, 1989). The engineers who designed the rocket boosters had strongly opposed the launch, fearing that subfreezing weather would make the rubber seals too brittle to contain hot gasses from the rocket. NASA, however, was under high stress and leadership was directive. This shuttle mission was carrying America's first civilian into space, there had been several delays, and NASA didn't want another one. To foster an illusion of unanimity, a key NASA executive polled only management officials, excluding the engineers from the final decision-making process (Magnuson, 1986). Thanks to mind guarding, the NASA official who gave the final go-ahead was never informed of the concerns expressed by the engineers.

In the days leading up to the fiery disintegration of the space shuttle *Columbia* as it reentered earth's atmosphere in 2003, engineers, supervisors, and some NASA officials intensely debated whether *Columbia*'s left wing had sustained damage due to a mishap during launch. But as the Columbia Accident Investigation Board found, tragically, "dangerous aspects of NASA's 1986 culture... remained unchanged" (2003, p. 198). For example, stress was high, key managers were isolated from outside expert opinion, and a "need to produce consensus at each level" filtered out dissenting information on safety risks (p. 198).

Can groupthink be prevented? Janis suggested that it might, if the leader remains impartial during discussions, encourages critical thinking, brings in outsiders to offer their opinions, and divides the larger group into subgroups—to see if each subgroup independently reaches the same decision. Of course, while critical debate may enhance the odds

"All those in favor say 'aye'."
"Aye." "Aye." "Aye." "Aye." "Aye."

FIGURE 15.19

(left) The illusion of unanimity occurs when group members collectively fail to speak their true minds. © The New Yorker Collection 1979 Henry Martin from cartoonbank.com. All Rights Reserved. *(right) The illusion of unanimity also contributed to the ill-fated decision to launch the space shuttle* Challenger *on January 28, 1986. The* Challenger *exploded shortly after takeoff, killing all the astronauts onboard.*

of making a good decision, it does not guarantee a positive outcome and in some cases may cause the group to become deadlocked (Kowert, 2002).

Deindividuation

Years ago in New York City, a man sat perched on the ledge of an upper-story window for an hour while a crowd of nearly 500 people on the street below shouted at him to jump. Fortunately, police managed to rescue the man. New York is hardly alone, as Australian psychologist Leon Mann (1981) found when he analyzed newspaper reports of incidents in which crowds were present when a person threatened to jump off a building. In 10 of 21 cases, the crowd had encouraged the person to jump.

What could prompt people to encourage distraught human beings to end their lives? In crowds, people may experience **deindividuation,** *a loss of individuality that leads to disinhibited behavior* (Festinger et al., 1952). The concept of deindividuation has been applied to diverse types of antisocial behavior, from cheating and stealing to riots by sports fans to acts of genocide (Figure 15.20).

But what is the primary aspect of deindividuation that disinhibits behavior? Tom Postmes and Russell Spears (1998) meta-analyzed 60 deindividuation studies and determined that *anonymity to outsiders* was the key. Conditions that make an individual less identifiable to people *outside* the group reduce feelings of accountability and, slightly but consistently, increase the risk of antisocial actions. Postmes and Spears suggest that being anonymous to outsiders enhances the individual's tendency to focus on her or his identity with the group and makes the person more responsive to emerging group norms.

During the Stanford prison study, no names were used and prisoners had to address guards as "Mr. Correctional Officer." All guards wore identical uniforms and reflecting sunglasses that prevented the prisoners from making direct eye contact. The guards were unaware that their behavior was being monitored by the experimenters, and antisocial norms evolved from the role of "tough prison guard" adopted by participants who spontaneously took over leadership roles (Zimbardo et al., 1973). These factors led Zimbardo to conclude that deindividuation was a key factor in the cruelty exhibited by the guards. Reducing anonymity—and thereby increasing public accountability—may be the most basic approach to counteracting deindividuation.

▶ 14. Describe deindividuation, its main cause, and how conditions in the Stanford prison study may have fostered it.

FIGURE 15.20

Deindividuation can lead to a loss of restraint that causes people to engage in uncharacteristic behaviors.

IN REVIEW

- *A social norm is a shared rule or expectation about how group members should think, feel, and behave. A social role is a set of norms that defines a particular position in a social system.*
- *People conform to a group because of informational social influence and normative social influence. The size of the majority and the presence or absence of dissenters influence the degree of conformity. Minority influence is strongest when the minority maintains a consistent position over time but does not appear too deviant.*
- *Milgram's obedience research raised strong ethical concerns and found unexpectedly high percentages of people willing to obey destructive orders. Such obedience is stronger when the victim is remote and when the authority figure is close by, legitimate, and assumes responsibility for what happens.*
- *People often use special techniques to get us to comply with their requests. These compliance techniques include the norm of reciprocity, the door-in-the-face technique, the foot-in-the-door technique, and lowballing.*
- *Social loafing occurs when people exert less individual effort when working as a group than when working alone. Social loafing decreases when the goal or group membership is valued highly and when people's performance within the group can be individually monitored.*
- *When the members of a decision-making group initially share the same conservative or liberal viewpoint, the group's final decision often reflects a polarization effect and becomes more extreme than the average opinion of the individual members.*
- *Cohesive decision-making groups that have directive leaders, are under high stress, and are insulated from outside input, may display groupthink, a suspension of critical thinking to maintain cohesion and loyalty to the leader's viewpoint.*
- *Deindividuation is a temporary lowering of restraints that can occur when a person is immersed in a group. Anonymity to outsiders appears to be the key factor in producing deindividuation.*

SOCIAL RELATIONS

People like and love, and dislike and hate. They help one another and harm one another. As we now explore, social relations take many forms.

Attraction: Liking and Loving Others

Commenting on friendship and love, humorist Mason Cooley once quipped, "Friendship is love minus sex and plus reason. Love is friendship plus sex and minus reason" (Columbia, 1996). Alas, the difference between *liking* and *loving* may not be so simple, but attraction is indeed the first phase of most friendships and romantic relationships. What causes us to "connect" with some people but not others?

▶ 15. Discuss how proximity, mere exposure, similarity, and beauty play a role in initial attraction.

Initial Attraction: Proximity, Mere Exposure, and Similarity

People cannot develop a relationship unless they first meet, and proximity (nearness) is the best predictor of who will cross paths with whom. In today's increasingly "wired" world, friendships and even romantic relationships sometimes develop after long-distance strangers make initial contact through Internet chat rooms or E-mail. Still, *physical proximity* matters. We tend to interact most with people who are physically closer. Residents in married-student apartments are most likely to form friendships with other residents who live close by; students assigned specific classroom seats are most likely to become friends with students seated nearby; and many adults meet their future spouse or dating partner at school, work, or a place of worship (Michael et al., 1994).

Proximity increases the chance of frequent encounters, and over 200 experiments in different countries provide evidence of a **mere exposure effect:** *Repeated exposure to a stimulus typically increases our liking for it.* No matter the stimuli—college classmates, photographs of faces, random geometric shapes, and so on—as long as they are not unpleasant and we are not oversaturated, exposure generally enhances liking (Monahan et al., 2000).

After two people meet, then what? When it comes to attraction, folk wisdom covers all the bases. On the one hand, "opposites attract." On the other hand, "birds of a feather flock together." So which is it? The evidence overwhelmingly supports the role of *similarity:* from fourth-graders to retirees, from Asia to Europe to North America, people most often are attracted to others who are similar to themselves. For psychological attributes, similarity of attitudes and values seems to matter the most (Buss, 1985).

In the laboratory, college students' degree of liking for a stranger can be predicted accurately simply by knowing the proportion of similar attitudes that they share (Byrne, 1997). Outside the laboratory, Donn Byrne and coworkers (1970) matched college students on a brief 30-minute date, pairing people with partners who had either highly similar or dissimilar attitudes. Students were more attracted to similar partners, talked with them more during the rest of the semester, and had a stronger desire to date them. One reason we like people with similar attitudes is that they validate our view of the world.

Like mismatched roommates Felix Unger (an uptight neatnik) and Oscar Madison (a carefree slob) in the classic movie *The Odd Couple,* do opposites ever attract? At times, of course. But much more often, opposites repel (Krueger & Caspi, 1993). When choosing potential friends or mates, we typically screen out people who are dissimilar to us. And when dissimilar people do form relationships, they tend not to last as long. As Diane Felmlee (1998) found, dissimilarity increases the risk of "fatal attractions." We initially find some characteristic of another person appealing, but over time we come to dislike it.

Spellbound by Beauty

It may be shallow and unfair, but most people seem drawn to beauty like moths to a flame (Figure 15.21). In many studies, when men and women rate the desirability of short-term dating partners, their judgments are influenced most strongly by how good-looking the person is (Wiederman & Dubois, 1998).

In a classic study, Elaine Walster and coworkers (1966) randomly paired over 700 first-year University of Minnesota students on blind dates for a "Welcome Week" dance. Earlier, the researchers had given all the participants a battery of personality, intelligence, and social skills tests, and had other students rate each participant's physical attractiveness. During an intermission at the dance, students rated how desirable they found their partner. Did any of the psychological characteristics predict who would like whom? No. Only one factor did. Women and men who dated physically attractive partners liked them more and had a stronger desire to date them again. Similarly, among 100 gay men whom researchers paired together for a date, men's liking for their partner and desire to date him again were most strongly influenced by the partner's physical attractiveness (Sergios & Cody, 1985–1986).

What motivates the desire to affiliate with attractive people? One factor may be the widespread stereotype that "what is beautiful is good"; we often assume that attractive people have more positive personality characteristics than unattractive people. The popular media reinforce this stereotype. Analyzing 5 decades of top-grossing U.S. movies, Stephen Smith and coworkers (1999) found that good-looking male and female characters were portrayed as more intelligent, moral, and sociable than less attractive characters. Because we are often judged by the company we keep, we also may prefer to associate with attractive people to buttress our self-esteem (Richardson, 1991).

Lest you conclude that beauty is the key to happiness, we should note that physical attractiveness during the college years is unrelated to life satisfaction in middle age (Kaner, 1995). And physically attractive people do not necessarily have the highest levels of self-esteem. Beauty is sometimes linked with self-doubt, because highly attractive individuals may attribute the positive responses of others solely to their surface beauty rather than to their inner personal qualities.

Although we are attracted to "beautiful people," romantic relationships typically reveal a **matching effect:** *We are most likely to have a partner whose level of physical attractiveness is similar to our own* (Feingold, 1988). In this case, "birds of equally attractive feathers flock together." One reason for this is that the most attractive people may match up first and are "taken," then the next most attractive people match up, and so on. Another factor is that people may refrain from approaching potential dating partners who are more attractive than they are to lessen the risk of rejection.

As Attraction Deepens: Close Relationships

How do close relationships grow? People may share an initial attraction, but have different goals regarding what form they want a relationship to take. Among two people who are getting to know one another, one may desire a closer friendship than the other. Among newly dating partners, one

FIGURE 15.21

Hey good lookin'! The way that both sexes initially judge someone is influenced by that person's attractiveness and other physical features. We are not alone. Many species, such as these frigate birds (male on the left), have evolved distinct features and ritualized mating displays to attract a potential mate's attention.

may desire greater emotional commitment in the relationship while the other seeks greater physical intimacy.

▶ 16. Based on social penetration and social exchange theories, what factors determine whether a relationship will deepen?

▶ 17. Contrast evolutionary and sociocultural explanations for sex differences in mate preferences.

According to **social penetration theory,** *relationships progress as interactions between people become broader (involving more areas of their lives) and deeper (involving more intimate and personally meaningful areas;* Altman & Taylor, 1973). Partners may share activities, other experiences, or physical intimacy, but *self-disclosure*—the sharing of innermost thoughts and feelings—plays a key role in fostering close relationships (Dindia, 2002). In friendships, dating relationships, and marriages, more extensive and intimate self-disclosure is associated with greater emotional involvement and relationship satisfaction. This relation is reciprocal. Self-disclosure fosters intimacy and trust, and intimacy and trust encourage self-disclosure.

Social exchange theory *proposes that the course of a relationship is governed by rewards and costs that the partners experience* (Thibaut and Kelley, 1959). Rewards include companionship, emotional support, and the satisfaction of other needs. Costs may include the effort spent to maintain the relationship, arguments, conflicting goals, and so forth. The overall *outcome* (rewards minus costs) in a relationship can be positive or negative.

Outcomes are evaluated against two standards (Figure 15.22). The first, called the *comparison level,* is the outcome that a person has grown to expect in relationships, and it influences the person's *satisfaction* with the present relationship. Outcomes that meet or exceed the comparison level are satisfying; those that fall below this standard are dissatisfying. The second standard, called the *comparison level for alternatives,* focuses on potential alternatives to the relationship, and it influences the person's degree of *commitment.* Even when a relationship is satisfying, partners may feel low commitment if they perceive that something even better is available. In turn, the partners' sense of commitment to the relationship helps predict whether they will remain together or end their relationship in the future (Sprecher, 2001).

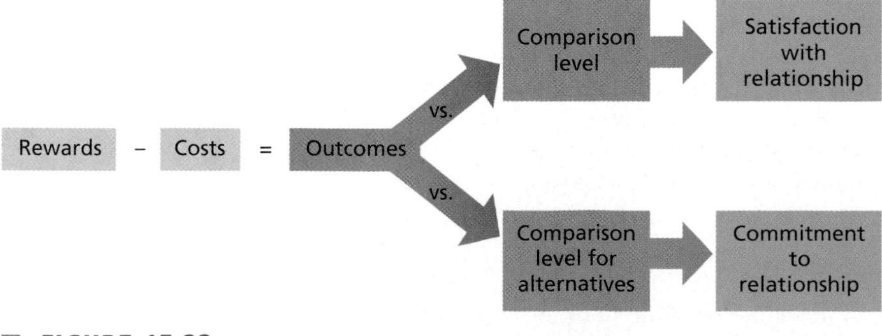

FIGURE 15.22

According to Thibaut and Kelley's social exchange theory, rewards minus costs equal the outcome of a relationship. Comparing our outcomes with two standards, the comparison level and the comparison level for alternatives, determines our satisfaction and commitment to the relationship, respectively.

Sociocultural and Evolutionary Views

According to social exchange theory, a partner's desirable characteristics can be viewed as rewards, whereas undesirable characteristics represent costs. But what specific characteristics do people typically desire in a partner? In a massive cross-cultural study involving about 10,000 men and women from 37 cultures around the world, evolutionary psychologist David Buss and coworkers asked participants to identify the qualities they sought in an ideal long-term mate (Buss, 1989; Buss et al., 1990). Overall, for men as well as women, the characteristics of mutual attraction/love, dependable character, emotional stability/maturity, and pleasing disposition emerged (in that order) as the most highly rated of 18 characteristics that participants were asked to evaluate. Both sexes also placed education/intelligence, sociability, good health, and a desire for home/children among the next most important traits.

The importance attached to many qualities, however, varied considerably across cultures. For example, whereas American men and women viewed "refinement/neatness" as having only modest importance, Iranian men and women viewed it as the most important quality they desired in a mate. In many cultures, a mate's chastity (no previous experience in sexual intercourse) was viewed as last or near-last in importance, but in China and India, men viewed chastity as one of the most important qualities in a mate, and women also felt it was important for their mate to be chaste.

There also are remarkably consistent sex differences in mate preferences across cultures. Men tend to place greater value on a potential mate's physical attractiveness and domestic skills, whereas women place greater value on a potential mate's earning potential, status, and ambitiousness. Men tend to desire a mate who is a few years younger, whereas women desire a mate who is a few years older. Men also are more likely to desire and pursue a greater number of short-term romantic encounters than are women (Schmitt et al., 2001).

As we discussed in detail in Chapter 9, some evolutionary psychologists argue that these sex differences reflect inherited predispositions, shaped by natural selection in response to different adaptive problems that men and women have faced over the ages (Buss & Schmitt, 1993; Schmitt et al.,

2001). According to the *sexual strategies theory*, ancestral men who were predisposed to have sex with more partners increased the likelihood of fathering more children and passing on their genes. Such men may have perceived a woman's youth and attractive appearance as signs that she was fertile and had many years left to bear children (Buss, 1989). Ancestral women, however, maximized their reproductive success by selecting mates who were willing and able to commit time, energy, and other resources (e.g., food, shelter, protection) to the family (Buss, 1989).

Do men and women have different biological wiring when it comes to romantic attraction and relationships? *Social structure theory* proposes that most of these sex differences in mating strategies and preferences occur because society directs men into more advantaged social and economic roles (Eagly & Wood, 1999). As this theory predicts, in cultures with less gender inequality, many of the sex differences in mate preferences shrink. Women place less emphasis, for example, on a mate's earning power and status, and men and women seek mates more similar in age. Men's tendency to attach greater importance than women to having a physically attractive mate does not decrease in such cultures, but it is still a leap, say critics, to conclude that sex differences in mating preferences reflect a hereditary predisposition rather than some other aspect of gender socialization that may be consistent across cultures.

This issue is far from settled, but perhaps the most important point for you to realize is that the notion that men and women come from "different planets" when it comes to attraction, romance, and close relationships is more pop psychology than reliable science. Sex differences exist, but cross-cultural differences tend to be stronger. That is, men and women within the same culture are typically more similar to one another than are men from different cultures or women from different cultures (Buss et al., 1990). As some evolutionary psychologists emphasize, overall "men and women are basically similar in what they seek in a mate [and in] the processes by which they become attached to a mate" (Hazan & Diamond, 2000, p. 194).

Love

Love must be powerful, for as a common adage says, it "makes the world go round." Indeed Buss and coworkers (1990) found that, across cultures, mutual attraction/love was among the most consistently valued mate characteristics. In North and South America, eastern and western Europe, Scandinavia and the United Kingdom, Australia and New Zealand, and most Asian countries they studied, mutual attraction/love ranked as first or second in importance. But what is love?

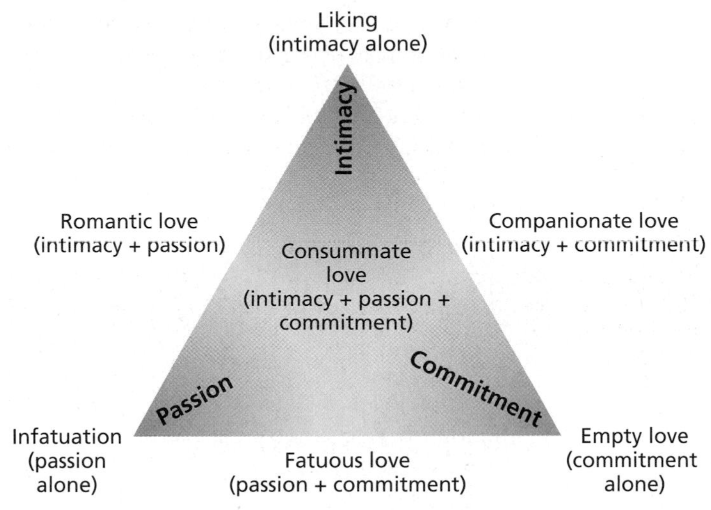

FIGURE 15.23

According to Sternberg, different types of love involve varying combinations of intimacy, commitment, and passion. Consummate love involves the presence of all three factors, whereas nonlove represents the absence of all three.

When it comes to romantic relationships, many psychologists identify two basic types of love: passionate and companionate (Hatfield, 1988). **Passionate love** *involves intense emotion, arousal, and yearning for the partner.* We may ride an emotional roller coaster that ranges from ecstasy when the partner is present to heartsickness when the person is absent. **Companionate love** *involves affection and deep caring about the partner's well-being.* At least when studied in Westernized countries, both types of love contribute to satisfaction in long-term romantic relationships (Sprecher & Regan, 1998). In general, passionate love is less stable and declines more quickly over time than companionate love, but this does not mean that the flames of passionate love inevitably extinguish.

Psychologist Robert Sternberg (1988, 1997), however, views love as more complex. His **triangular theory of love** *proposes that love involves three major components: passion, intimacy, and commitment. Passion* refers to feelings of physical attraction and sexual desire; *intimacy* involves closeness, sharing, and valuing one's partner; and *commitment* represents a decision to remain in the relationship. Research suggests that these three components do a good job of capturing the way people commonly think about love (Aron & Westbay, 1996).

▶ 18. Describe types of love, and discuss research-based principles that may help enhance relationship quality.

Figure 15.23 shows that different combinations of these components characterize seven types of love (plus *nonlove*, which is the absence of all three). Sternberg proposes that the ultimate form of love between people—*consummate love*—occurs when intimacy, passion, and commitment are all present. Clearly, for close relationships to develop and endure, they need more than passion alone. Intimacy and commitment provide a basis for the friendship and trust that sustain and increase love. As our *Applying Psychological Science* feature highlights, other behaviors also help make close relationships successful.

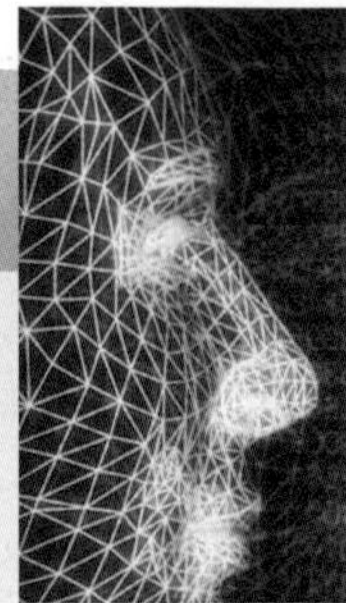

APPLYING PSYCHOLOGICAL SCIENCE

MAKING CLOSE RELATIONSHIPS WORK: LESSONS FROM PSYCHOLOGICAL RESEARCH

Close relationships go through good times and bad, persisting or dissolving over time. Consider marriage. Although highly intimate, this union is often fragile, and many marriages end in divorce. How can people make their close relationships more satisfying and stable? Research on marriage suggests several answers that also can be applied to dating relationships and friendships.

For decades, most marital research simply asked people about their marriages. But as Figure 15.24 shows, researchers are now bringing couples into laboratories to videotape their interactions and chart their facial reactions, stress hormones, and other physiological responses as they discuss emotionally charged issues (Kiecolt-Glaser et al., 2003). Rather than focusing only on unhappy couples to find out what is going wrong in their relationships, researchers are also studying happy couples to discover the secrets of their success.

Using these methods, psychologists have predicted with impressive accuracy whether marriages will last or dissolve. In one laboratory study, John Gottman and coworkers (1998) collected behavioral and physiological data from 130 newlywed couples as they discussed areas of marital conflict (e.g., in-laws, finances, sex) during the first 6 months of their marriage. Six years later, participants reported being happily married, unhappily married, or divorced. Using data collected while the couples were newlyweds, the researchers predicted which marriages would end in divorce with 83-percent accuracy and the degree of marital satisfaction in still-married couples with 80-percent accuracy.

Surprisingly, the amount of anger expressed by husbands and wives in their laboratory interactions predicted neither stability nor happiness 6 years later. Instead, the crucial factor was the manner in which couples dealt with their anger. Four behaviors were particularly important: *criticism, contempt, defensiveness,* and *stonewalling* (listener withdrawal and nonresponsiveness).

Couples headed for unhappiness or divorce often exhibit these behaviors while discussing conflict, thereby escalating their conflict and negative emotions. When the wife criticizes the husband, he often responds defensively or stonewalls and withdraws from her attempts to reach some resolution. Her resulting

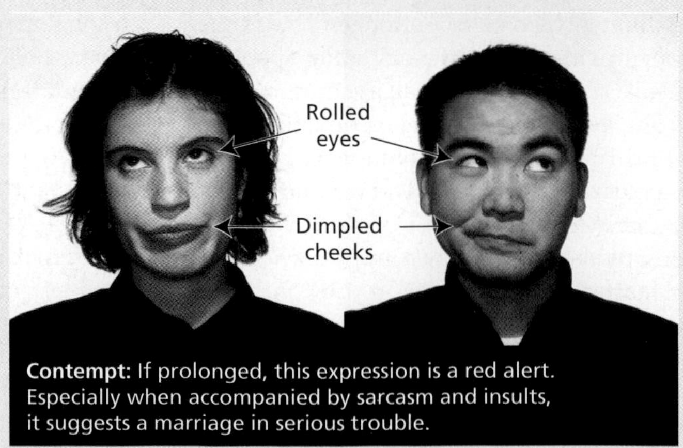

Contempt: If prolonged, this expression is a red alert. Especially when accompanied by sarcasm and insults, it suggests a marriage in serious trouble.

FIGURE 15.24

In John Gottman's "love lab," married couples (husband shown in rear) are filmed while interacting. Researchers record facial expressions, actions, heart rate, breathing rate, perspiration, fidgeting, and other responses.

frustration leads to stronger emotional displays and criticism, and the interaction degenerates into exchanges of contempt in which the partners tear each other down. Once this negative cycle develops, even positive overtures by one spouse are likely to evoke a negative response from the other (Margolin & Wampold, 1981).

Happily married couples also experience conflict and anger but do not allow the spiral of negativity to get out of control. Instead, they make frequent "repair attempts" to resolve their differences in a spirit of mutual respect and support. Gottman and his coworkers (1998) found that in happy marriages, the wife often introduced the conflict topic in a softened or low-intensity manner, rather than with sarcasm, criticism, and strong emotion. Next a key factor occurred: The husband responded to the issues she raised in a concerned and respectful manner that de-escalated negative emotion. A husband who turns off the TV and listens to his wife or who says, "I can see you're upset, so let's work this out," demonstrates that her concerns are important to him. In happy marriages, after the husbands' responsiveness de-escalated the conflict, couples tended to "soothe" one another (and themselves) with positive comments and humor, resulting in more emotionally positive interchanges and lowered physiological arousal.

Happily married couples maintain a much higher ratio of positive to negative interactions than couples headed for divorce, and this history provides a positive "emotional bank account" that helps them repair and recover from their immediate anger and conflict (Wilson & Gottman, 2002). They also make the effort to get to know each other's psychological world—their fears and dreams, philosophy of life, attitudes, and values—and they continually update their knowledge. This "love map," as Gottman calls it, allows each partner be more responsive to the other's needs and to navigate around relationship roadblocks (Gottman & DeClaire, 2002). Such behavior contributes to an essential aspect of happy marriages: a deep and intimate friendship between the partners. The lessons of happy marriages can be applied to other types of close relationships, and affirmative answers to the questions in Table 15.1 suggest that such relationships are on solid psychological ground.

Table 15.1 How Strong Is Your Relationship?

Answer each question True (T) or False (F):

I can tell you about some of my partner's dreams.	T	F
We just love talking to each other.	T	F
My partner is one of my best friends.	T	F
My partner listens respectfully, even when we disagree.	T	F
We generally mesh well on basic values and goals in life.	T	F
I feel that my partner knows me pretty well.	T	F

The greater the number of "True" answers, the stronger your relationship. Source: Courtesy of John Gottman.

Prejudice: Bias Against Others

Walk into a party, classroom, job interview—any social situation—and just by looking at your body build and facial attractiveness people will start to form an impression of you (Crandall et al., 2001). Children and adults tend to form less favorable impressions of people who are less attractive. They expect them to have less desirable personality traits and to achieve less success and happiness in life, even though correlational studies typically find that such variables are unrelated or only weakly related to attractiveness and other facial features (Zebrowitz et al., 1996).

Perhaps above all characteristics, ethnicity and gender matter the most in impression formation. They are likely to be the first characteristics someone notices about you and, like so many other personal qualities, can be the basis for prejudice and discrimination (Fiske, 2002). **Prejudice** *refers to a negative attitude toward people based on their membership in a group.* Thus we *prejudge* people—dislike them or hold negative beliefs about them—simply because they are female or male, belong to one ethnic group or religion rather than to another, are gay or straight, and so on. **Discrimination** *refers to overt behavior that involves treating people unfairly based on the group to which they belong.*

Conscious and Unconscious Prejudice

Even in this day and age, overt prejudice and discrimination are in abundant supply (Figure 15.25). Armed conflicts based on ethnic or religious divisions continue across the globe; supremacist groups and hate crimes persist; and people's race,

FIGURE 15.25

Prejudice reveals itself in many subtle and not-so-subtle forms.

▶ 19. How can unconscious prejudice be measured? Describe cognitive and motivational roots of prejudice.

gender, religion, and sexual orientation spark unfair treatment (Herek, 2000). In some ways, however, the most blatant forms of prejudice and discrimination have decreased in many countries. Racial segregation is no longer sanctioned by government policy in the United States or South Africa, and opinion polls indicate that fewer people express prejudiced attitudes toward other ethnic groups than was the case decades ago.

Although prejudiced attitudes truly seem to have faded a bit, in many ways modern racism, sexism, and other forms of prejudice have gone underground and are more difficult to detect. Many people intentionally hide their prejudices, expressing them only when they feel it is safe or socially appropriate. In other cases, people may display unconscious (also called *implicit*) prejudice. They may honestly believe that they are not prejudiced but still show biases when tested in sophisticated ways (Fazio et al., 1995).

Can unconscious prejudice be measured? Anthony Greenwald and his coworkers (1998) developed the *Implicit Association Test (IAT)* in which a series of word pairs, such as "black-pleasant" and "white-pleasant" are flashed on a computer screen. As soon as you see each pair, your task is to press a computer key as quickly as you can, and this represents your reaction time. The principle underlying this test is that people react more quickly when they perceive that the two words in each pair "fit" together than when they don't. Thus *without conscious control,* a person prejudiced against Blacks will react more slowly to the "black-pleasant" pair than to the "white-pleasant" pair. The larger the discrepancy in reaction times, the stronger are the person's underlying negative attitudes.

Psychologists have used the IAT to reveal many types of unconscious prejudice (Greenwald et al., 2002). Large reaction time differences occur even among White males who claim—in response to standard questions—to have no prejudice against Blacks. Likewise, Japanese and Koreans, whose nations have a history of conflict, react differently toward pairs such as "Japanese-pleasant" and "Korean-pleasant."

Cognitive Roots of Prejudice

Whether overt or subtle, prejudice and discrimination are caused by a constellation of factors. These include historical and cultural norms that legitimize differential treatment of various groups and socialization processes through which parents and other adults transmit values and beliefs to their children. Let's examine several cognitive and motivational causes of prejudice.

Categorization and "Us-Them" Thinking To organize and simplify our world, we have a tendency to categorize people and objects. At times, this helps us predict other people's behavior and react quickly to environmental stimuli (Ito & Cacioppo, 2000). But our tendency to categorize people also helps lay a foundation for prejudice.

Categorization leads to the perception of "in-groups" and "out-groups," groups to which we do and do not belong, respectively. In turn, in-group versus out-group distinctions spawn several common biases. *In-group favoritism* represents the tendency to favor in-group members and attribute more positive qualities to "us" than to "them," whereas *out-group derogation* reflects a tendency to attribute more negative qualities to "them" than to "us." Although people may display both biases, especially when they feel threatened, in-group favoritism is usually the stronger of the two (Hewstone et al., 2002).

People also display an *out-group homogeneity bias.* They generally view members of out-groups as being more similar to one another than are members of in-groups (Brauer, 2001). In other words, we perceive that "they are all alike" but recognize that "we are diverse." The mere fact that we identify people as "Asian," "Hispanic," "Black," and "White" reflects such a bias, because each of these ethnic categories contains many subgroups. In one study, Anglo-American college students were less likely to distinguish among "Hispanic" subgroups than were Cuban American, Mexican American, and Puerto Rican American college students (Huddy & Virtanen, 1995). But just like Anglo-American students, the Cuban American, Mexican American, and Puerto Rican American students also engaged in us-them thinking: They saw their own subgroup as distinct from the others but did not differentiate between the other two Hispanic subgroups.

Stereotypes and Attributional Distortions. Categorization and in-group biases enhance the tendency to judge other people based on their perceived group membership rather than their individual characteristics. Whether at a conscious or unconscious level, category labels pertaining to people's race, gender, and other attributes seem to activate stereotypes about them (Fiske, 2002). Figure 15.26 illustrates two ways in which racial categorization and gender categorization activate stereotypes and affect our perceptions.

What happens when we encounter individual members of out-groups whose behavior clearly contradicts our stereotypes? One possibility is that we may change our stereotype; but if we

(a)

(b)

FIGURE 15.26

(a) Who is holding the razor knife? Allport and Postman (1947) showed this picture to one person, who then described it while looking at it. A second person listened to this description and was asked to repeat it "as exactly as possible" to another person, who repeated this description to another person, and so on (up to six or seven tellings). In over half of the trials following this procedure, at some point the Black man was erroneously described as holding the knife. (b) Which person contributes most strongly to this research team? When the drawing shows an all-male group, all-female group, or mixed-sex group with a man at the head of the table (seat 3), participants say that the person in seat 3 is the strongest member. But in this mixed-gender drawing, most male and female participants do not pick the woman in seat 3. Instead, they pick one of the two men. SOURCE: Based on Porter & Geis, 1981.

are motivated to hold on to our prejudiced belief, we may explain away discrepant behavior in several ways. For example, the out-group member may be seen as an exceptional case or as having succeeded at a task not because of high ability but because of tremendous effort, good luck, or special advantage (Pettigrew, 1979).

Motivational Roots of Prejudice

People's ingrained ways of perceiving the world—categorizing, forming in-groups and out-groups, and so forth—appear to set the wheels of prejudice in motion, but motivational factors affect how fast those wheels spin.

Competition and Conflict According to **realistic conflict theory,** *competition for limited resources fosters prejudice.* In the United States and Europe, hostility toward minority groups increases when economic conditions worsen (Pettigrew & Meertens, 1995). Originally, it was believed that a threat to one's personal welfare (as in the fear of losing one's job to a minority worker) was the prime motivator of prejudice, but research suggests that prejudice is triggered more strongly by a *perceived threat to one's in-group* (Tajfel & Turner, 1986). As the Robber's Cave summer camp experiment illustrated in Chapter 1, competition between groups can breed hostility and derogation of the out-group (Sherif et al., 1961). Likewise, among Whites, prejudice against Blacks is not related to personal resource gains and losses but to the belief that White people as a group are in danger of being "overtaken" (Bobo, 1988).

Enhancing Self-Esteem According to **social identity theory,** *prejudice stems from a need to enhance our self-esteem.* Some experiments find that people express more prejudice after their self-esteem is threatened (such as by receiving negative feedback about their abilities) and that the opportunity to derogate others helps restore self-esteem (Fein & Spencer, 1997). Self-esteem, however, is based on two components: a personal identity and a group identity (Tajfel & Turner, 1986). We can raise self-esteem not only by acknowledging our own virtues but also by associating ourselves with our in-group's accomplishments. Conversely, threats to our in-group threaten our self-esteem and may prompt us to derogate the out-group that constitutes the threat (Perdue et al., 1990).

How Prejudice Confirms Itself

▶ 20. How do self-fulfilling prophecies and stereotype threat perpetuate prejudice? How can prejudice be reduced?

Self-fulfilling prophecies are one of the most invisible yet damaging ways of maintaining prejudiced beliefs. An experiment by Carl Word and his colleagues (1974) illustrates this point. The researchers began with the premise—supported by research at the time—that Whites held several negative stereotypes of Blacks. In the experiment, White male college students interviewed White and Black high school students who were seeking admission into a special group. The participants used a fixed set of interview questions provided by the experimenter, and unknown to them, each applicant was an accomplice who had been trained to respond in a standard way to the questions. The findings indicated that these White participants sat farther away, conducted shorter interviews, and made more speech errors when the applicants were Black. In short, their behavior was discriminatory.

But this is only half the picture. In a second experiment—a job interview simulation—White male undergraduates served as *job applicants.* Through random assignment, they were treated either as the White applicants had been treated in the first experiment or as the Black applicants had been treated. Thus for half the participants, the interviewer sat farther away, held a shorter interview, and made more speech errors. The findings revealed that White participants who were treated more negatively performed worse during the job interview, were less composed, made more speech errors, and rated the interviewer as less friendly. In short, these experiments suggest that an interviewer's negative stereotypes can lead to discriminatory treatment during a job interview, and this discriminatory behavior can cause the applicant to perform more poorly—ultimately confirming the interviewer's initial stereotype.

Stanford psychologist Claude Steele (1997) has demonstrated another debilitating way that prejudice ends up confirming itself. As described in Chapter 8, his concept of **stereotype threat** *proposes that stereotypes create self-consciousness among stereotyped group members and a fear that they will "live up" to other people's stereotypes.* For example, in a study comparing female and male college students who major in various fields, women majoring in the traditionally "male" fields of math, science, and engineering reported the highest level of stereotype threat (J. Steele et al., 2002). They were more likely to feel that they (as well as other women in their major) had been targets of sex discrimination and that because of their gender, other people (including their professors) expected them to have less ability and do more poorly.

Stereotype threat can occur even if group members do not accept the stereotype themselves, and experiments reveal its debilitating consequences. Given the stereotype that "Blacks are not as intelligent as Whites." Black college students who take a difficult verbal ability test perform more poorly when it is described as "an intelligence test" than when it is described merely as a laboratory task. In contrast, the "intelligence test" description does not decrease White students' performance. Similar results were found for other stereotypes relating to mathematical ability, namely, "Whites are inferior to Asians," "Latinos are inferior to Whites," and "women are inferior to men." When a difficult standardized math test is given in situations that activate these stereotypes, Whites, Latinos, and women perform more poorly than when the test is presented in a more neutral way (Aronson et al., 1999; Gonzales et al., 2002).

For more on stereotype threat, see Video Segment 15.4.

Reducing Prejudice

Psychologists are interested not only in the causes of prejudice but also in identifying ways to reduce it. With some success, they have implemented many techniques aimed at changing the way people categorize one another and think about in-groups and out-groups (Hewstone et al., 2002).

The best-known approaches to prejudice reduction are based on a principle called **equal status contact:** *Prejudice between people is most likely to be reduced when they (1) engage in sustained close contact, (2) have equal status, (3) work to achieve a common goal that requires cooperation, and (4) are supported by broader social norms* (Allport, 1954; Figure 15.27).

In 1954, the United States Supreme Court handed down a momentous decision in the case of *Brown v. Board of Education,* ruling that school segregation based solely on race violates the constitutional rights of racial minorities. Providing key testimony, several psychologists stated that segregation contributed to racial prejudice and hostility.

Did school desegregation reduce prejudice? Walter Stephan (1990) reviewed more than 80 evaluation studies of desegregation programs and concluded that increasing direct contact through desegregation did not, in and of itself, consistently reduce racial prejudice. Indeed, some studies found that prejudice increased after desegregation.

Why weren't the results more positive? First, the condition of equal status contact was often not met, and contact when status is unequal serves only to perpetuate both groups' negative stereotypes of one another. Second, in many integrated school situations, close and personal contact between group members did not occur. Black and White students were sometimes placed in different "learning tracks" that minimized in-class contact, and they tended to associate only with members of their own ethnic group outside of class. Third, classroom experiences focused on individual rather than cooperative learning. And finally, intergroup contact was often not supported by broader social norms. In the early years of desegregation, many White politicians, parents, teachers, and school officials militantly opposed school integration.

When intergroup contact takes place under proper conditions, however, prejudice often decreases (Pettigrew & Tropp, 2000). In school settings, *cooperative learning programs* (such as the "jigsaw classroom" program described in Chapter 1) place children into multiracial learning groups. Contact is close and sustained, each child is accorded equal status, and each has responsibility for learning and then teaching other group members one piece of the information that is needed for the group to succeed in its assignment (Aronson et al., 1978). Overall, such programs reduce prejudice and promote appreciation of ethnic group differences (Johnson, 2000).

Beyond equal status contact, cooperative learning programs enable children to forge a common group identity, much as athletes on a team or members of a military unit form a group identity. Adopting a common identity is another factor that helps reduce prejudice among group members (Dovidio et al., 2000).

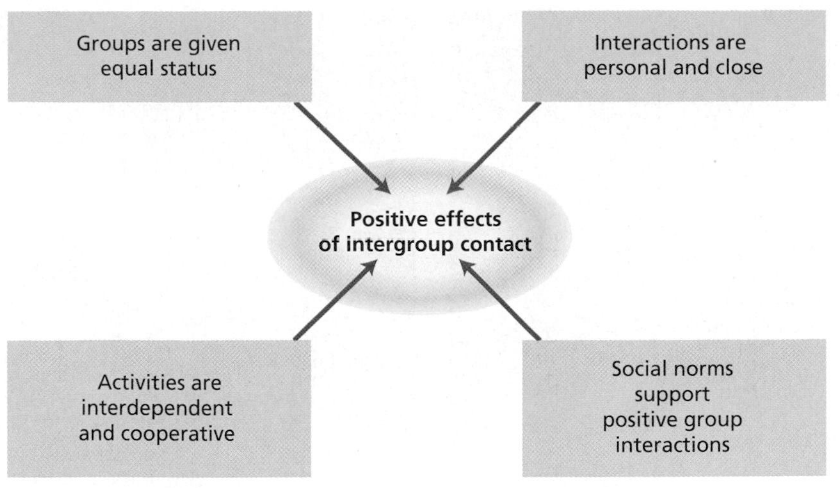

FIGURE 15.27

Prejudice between two people or groups is most likely to decrease when contact between them occurs under these four conditions.

Prosocial Behavior: Helping Others

Helping, or *prosocial behavior*, comes in many forms, from performing heroic acts of bravery to donating to charity and tutoring a classmate. Acts of violence often dominate the headlines, but we should not lose sight of the mountains of good deeds performed by people around the world each day (Figure 15.28).

Why Do People Help?

What motivates prosocial behavior? The debate over this question has practical consequences and profound implications for our conception of human nature.

▶ 21. Discuss evolutionary, social learning, and empathy-altruism explanations for helping behavior.

Evolution and Prosocial Behavior Prosocial behavior occurs throughout the animal kingdom. Evolutionary psychologists and sociobiologists (biologists who study species' social behavior) propose that helping has a genetic basis, shaped by evolution (Hamilton, 1964). According to the principle of **kin selection,** *organisms are most likely to help others with whom they share the most genes, namely, their offspring and genetic relatives.* By protecting their

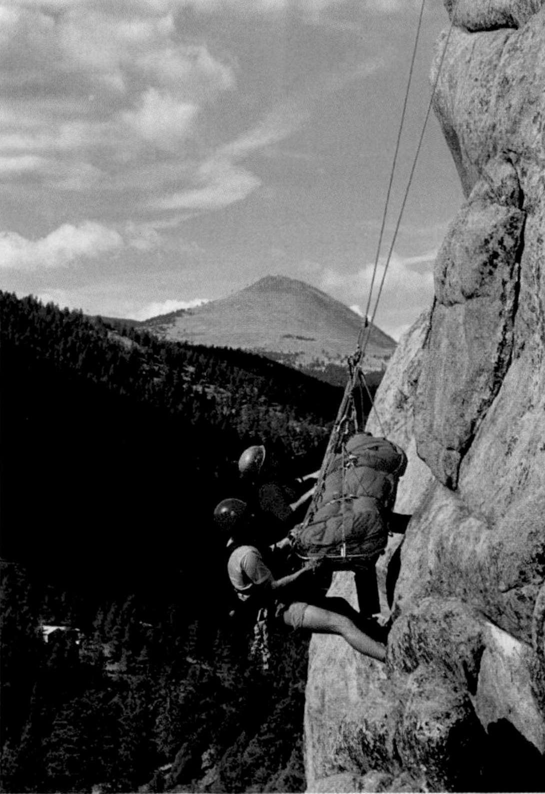

FIGURE 15.28

Like this rescue worker, many people seek careers or join volunteer organizations that allow them to help other people.

FIGURE 15.29

(a) Spotting a predator, this female ground squirrel may sound an "alarm call" that warns other squirrels. Is the call truly a prosocial act, much like a human yelling "Look out!"? Perhaps it simply indicates the squirrel's own sense of alarm, much as we might scream out of fear for our own safety. But if this is the case, why is she more likely to sound this call when her own kin—rather than other squirrels—are nearby? (b) Some species of animals regularly display prosocial behavior toward other members who are not kin, but do animals also display prosocial behavior toward members of other species? What factors might explain this dog's behavior?

kin, prosocial individuals increase the odds that their genes will survive across successive generations, and the gene pool of the species increasingly represents the genes of its prosocial members (West et al., 2002). In this manner, over the course of evolution, helping became a biologically predisposed response to certain situations. To support their view that genetics influence helping behavior, sociobiologists note that identical twins are more similar in the behavioral trait of helpfulness than fraternal twins or nontwin siblings (Rushton, 1989).

But what accounts for the abundant helping and care that humans display toward friends and strangers, and that even some animal species display toward nonrelatives (Clutton-Brock, 2002; Figure 15.29)? Sociobiologists propose the concept of *reciprocal altruism:* Helping others increases the likelihood that they will help us or our kin in return, thereby enhancing the survival of our genes (Trivers, 1971).

Critics question sociobiologists' generalizations from nonhumans to humans, and in some cases kin selection and reciprocal altruism do not adequately explain why people or animals cooperate (Clutton-Brock, 2002). Sociobiologists note that other biological tendencies may play a role and, even so, that genetic factors only predispose us to act in certain ways. Experience also shapes helping behavior.

Social Learning and Cultural Influences Socialization, modeling, and reinforcement play key roles in fostering prosocial behavior and attitudes. Beginning in childhood, we are exposed to helpful models and taught prosocial norms.

Two social norms are especially relevant to helping behavior (De Cremer & van Lange, 2001). First, the *norm of reciprocity* states that we should reciprocate when others treat us kindly. Second, the *norm of social responsibility* states that people should help others and contribute to the welfare of society. Throughout childhood we receive approval for adhering to these norms, receive disapproval for violating them, and observe other people receiving praise for following these norms. Eventually, we internalize prosocial norms and values as our own, enabling powerful *self-reinforcers* such as pride, self-praise, and feelings of satisfaction to maintain prosocial behaviors even in the absence of external reinforcement.

Studies in Europe, Asia, and North America confirm that socialization matters (Eisenberg &

Valiente, 2002). Children are more likely to act prosocially when they have been raised by parents who have high moral standards, who are warm and supportive, and who encourage their children to develop empathy and "put themselves in other people's shoes" (Krevans & Gibbs, 1996). However, there also are cross-cultural differences in beliefs about when and why we should help. For example, Joan Miller and coworkers (1990) found that Hindu children and adults in India believe that one has a moral obligation to help friends and strangers, whether their need is serious or mild. In contrast, when a person's need for assistance is mild, American children and adults view helping as more of a choice than an obligation.

Empathy and Altruism C. Daniel Batson (Batson et al., 2002) proposes that prosocial behavior can be motivated by altruistic as well as egoistic goals. *Altruism* refers to unselfishness, or helping another for the ultimate purpose of enhancing that person's welfare. In contrast, *egoistic goals* involve helping others to improve our own welfare. For example, we might help others to increase our self-esteem, to avoid feeling guilty for not helping, to obtain approval or praise, or to alleviate the distress we feel when seeing someone else suffer. Do humans truly have a capacity to help others without any concern for themselves? Batson believes that true altruism does exist, and according to his **empathy-altruism hypothesis,** *altruism is produced by empathy—the ability to put oneself in the place of another and to share what that person is experiencing* (Batson, 1991).

What Do You Think?

DOES PURE ALTRUISM REALLY EXIST?

Do you believe that people ever help one another for purely altruistic reasons? Or is even a small degree of egoism always involved? Think about it, then see page 631.

When Do People Help?

Ordinary citizens often go to great lengths to help strangers, yet at times bystanders fail to assist people who are clearly in distress (Figure 15.30). Recall the infamous Kitty Genovese murder discussed in Chapter 2. Genovese was stabbed and raped by an assailant outside her New York City apartment. It was about 3 A.M., the attack lasted for half an hour, and 38 of her neighbors heard her screams and pleas for help. Yet no one even called the police until it was too late, and Genovese died. What, then, influences whether a bystander will invervene?

FIGURE 15.30

Why do bystanders sometimes fail to assist a person in need?

Many situational and personal factors, such as a lack of time pressure (i.e., not being in a hurry), recently observing a prosocial role model, and being in a good mood, increase the likelihood that we will intervene when someone needs help (Eisenberg, 2000).

Bibb Latané and John Darley (1970) view bystander intervention as a 5-step process (Figure 15.31). First, a bystander will not help unless she or he notices the situation. Imagine that as you walk along a street, you hear two people yelling and then hear a single scream coming from inside

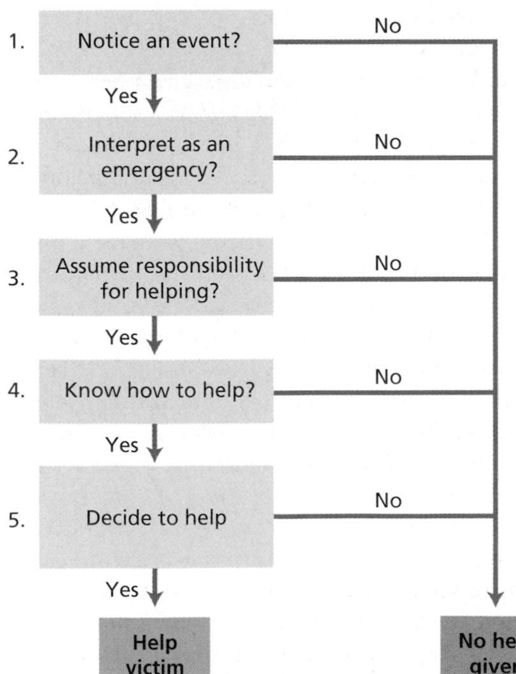

FIGURE 15.31

Bystander intervention in an emergency situation can be viewed as a 5-step process. If the answer at each step is yes, help is given. SOURCE: Based on Latané & Darley, 1970.

▶ 22. When and whom are people most likely to help? How can prosocial behavior be increased?

a house. You've noticed the situation, but now what? In everyday life, many social situations are ambiguous, and step 2 involves deciding whether this is an emergency. Is someone really in danger? To answer this question, we often engage in *social comparison:* We look around to see how other people are responding. You might say to yourself, "No one else seems concerned, so it mustn't be anything too serious." In Kitty Genovese's murder, some bystanders mistakenly thought that because nobody else intervened they were merely witnessing a "lovers' quarrel" that didn't warrant their "butting in" (Darley & Latané, 1968).

If you conclude that a situation is an emergency, then you move to step 3: assuming responsibility to intervene. If you are the only person to hear someone screaming, then responsibility for helping falls squarely on you. But if others are present, there may be a *diffusion of responsibility*—"If I don't help, someone else will"—and if each bystander has this thought, the victim won't receive help. In the Kitty Genovese murder, many bystanders who *did* interpret the incident as an emergency failed to intervene because they were certain that someone must already have called the police (Darley & Latané, 1968). Similarly, in a experiment where college students were isolated in individual cubicles and listened to another student who indicated he was having a seizure, participants were less likely to assist the seizure victim if they believed that other bystanders were present (Darley & Latané, 1968).

If you do take responsibility, then whether you actually intervene still depends on two more steps. Step 4 involves your self-efficacy (confidence) in dealing with the situation. Sometimes, we fail to help because we don't know how to or don't believe our help will be effective. But even if you know what to do and your self-efficacy is high, in step 5 you still may decide not to intervene. For example, you may perceive that the costs of helping outweigh the benefits (Fritzsche et al., 2000). Potential costs include not only possible physical danger but also negative social consequences, such as appearing foolish by trying to help inappropriately.

As this model indicates, the commonsense adage "there is safety in numbers" is not always true when it comes to receiving help. Many experiments find a **bystander effect:** *The presence of multiple bystanders inhibits each person's tendency to help, largely due to social comparison or diffusion of responsibility.* This inhibition is more likely to occur when the bystanders are strangers rather than friends; it even occurs when communicating over the Internet. Over a 30-day period, P. M. Markey (2000) sent a general request for help ("Can anyone tell me how to look at someone's profile?") to 200 chat groups. Assistance came more slowly from larger chat groups than from smaller ones.

▶ 23. Describe how biological factors, environmental stimuli, learning, and psychological factors influence aggression.

Whom Do People Help?

Some people are more likely to receive help than others for the following reasons:

- *Similarity.* Whether in attitudes, nationality, or other characteristics, perceiving that a person is similar to us increases our willingness to provide help (Dovidio, 1984).
- *Gender.* Male bystanders are more likely to help a woman than a man in need, whereas female bystanders are equally likely to help women and men (Eagly & Crowley, 1986).
- *Perceived fairness and responsibility.* Beliefs about fairness influence people's willingness to help others (Blader & Tyler, 2002). For example, people are more likely to help someone if they perceive that the person is not responsible for causing his or her own misfortune.

Increasing Prosocial Behavior

Can prosocial behavior be increased? One approach, consistent with social learning theory, is to expose people to prosocial models. Psychologists have used prosocial modeling as part of a nationwide program to increase blood donations (Sarason et al., 1991). Students in 66 high schools watched an audiovisual program showing high school donors giving blood. Compared with a control condition presented with a standard appeal from the local blood bank, the prosocial video increased blood donations by 17 percent.

Research suggests that developing feelings of empathy and connectedness with others also may make people more likely to help (Eisenberg, 2000), and simply learning about factors that hinder bystander intervention may increase the tendency to help someone in distress. Arthur Beaman and coworkers (1978) exposed some college students to information about the bystander effect. Control participants did not receive this information. Two weeks later, more than half of the students who had learned about the bystander effect provided aid to the victim of an accident (staged by the researchers), compared with only about one fourth of the control group participants.

Aggression: Harming Others

We love. We nurture. We help. But as current events and the history of humankind attest, we also harm. In humans, *aggression* represents any

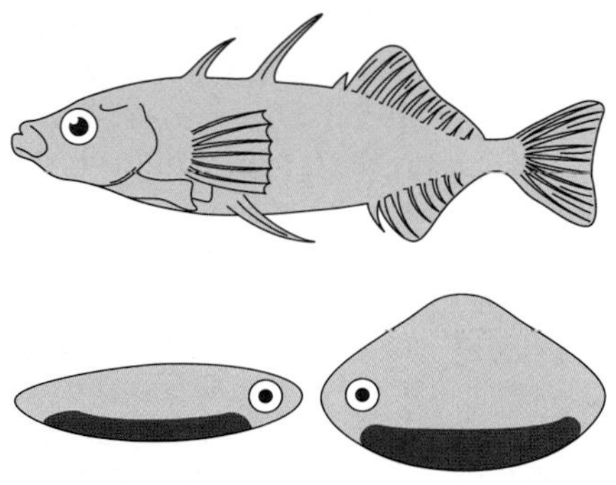

FIGURE 15.32

During the mating season, the male stickleback fish develops a red belly. The sight of another red-bellied male—a potential rival for a mate—reflexively triggers an attack by the first male. The key releaser stimulus for this fixed action pattern is the red marking. A male stickleback will not attack a realistic-looking male model that has no red belly, but it will attack unrealistic fish models that have this red marking. SOURCE: Based on Tinbergen, 1951.

form of behavior that is intended to harm another person. What causes people to aggress?

Biological Factors in Aggression

From household dogs and barnyard bulls to laboratory rats and mice, animals can be selectively bred over generations to be more or less aggressive (Lagerspetz et al., 1968). In some species, certain aggressive behaviors are reflexively triggered by specific environmental stimuli (Figure 15.32). Humans do not display such rigid, inborn aggressive responses, but heredity partly determines why some people are more aggressive than others. Identical twins are more similar in their aggressive behavior patterns than are fraternal twins, even when the identical twins are raised in different homes (Beatty et al., 2002).

Some theorists propose that, as in other species, a genetic predisposition toward aggression can be traced to evolutionary adaptation. Aggression at the proper time, they argue, helped our ancestors to compete successfully for mates, food, and shelter and to survive against attack. This increased the odds that individuals who were predisposed to such aggression would pass their genes on to the next generation (Rushton, 1989).

The search for biological causes of aggression has led researchers deep within the brain. Electrically stimulate certain neural pathways in a cat's hypothalamus, and it will arch its back and attack. Surgically destroy areas of the amygdala—an approach that has been used with some violent human criminals—and in many species, defensive aggression will decrease (Aggleton, 1993). Especially in humans, aggression also involves activity in the frontal lobes—the seat of reasoning and impulse control. Deficient frontal lobe activity makes it more difficult to regulate aggressive impulses generated by deeper brain regions (Raine, 2002).

Just as there is no single brain center for aggression, there is no one "aggression chemical." Atypically low levels of serotonin activity appear to play a role in impulsive aggression, as when people lash out from emotional rage (Moore et al., 2002). In many species of mammals, higher levels of the sex hormone testosterone (found in males and females) contribute to greater *social aggression,* unprovoked aggressive acts that establish a dominance hierarchy among members of the same species. Injecting adult males with testosterone increases social aggression, whereas castration decreases it. But in humans and other primates, the association between testosterone and aggression is weaker and less consistent (O'Connor et al., 2002).

Environmental Stimuli and Learning

Aggression is also influenced by our present environment and past learning experiences. *Frustration,* which occurs when some event interferes with our progress toward a goal, increases the risk of verbal and physical aggression. But we do not always respond to frustration by acting aggressively. Inhibited by our internal moral standards, we may simply "control ourselves" and find nonaggressive ways of dealing with conflict (Anderson & Bushman, 2002).

Many other aversive events, including painful stimuli, extreme heat, provocation, and crowding also increase the risk of aggression in humans and other species (Anderson, 2001). For some motorists, increasingly congested roads and being trapped in inescapable traffic jams set the stage for high stress and aggressive acts of "road rage" (Figure 15.33).

Aggression, like other behaviors, is influenced by learning (Anderson & Bushman, 2002).

FIGURE 15.33

Increasingly crowded roads and stressed drivers have made road rage a national problem in the United States.

Nonaggressive animals can be trained to become vicious aggressors if reinforcement is arranged so that they are consistently victorious in fights with weaker animals. Such operant conditioning also affects human aggression. Preschool children become increasingly aggressive when their aggressive behavior produces positive outcomes for them, such as when they successfully force another child to give up a desired toy (Patterson et al., 1967).

As Albert Bandura's (1965) classic "Bobo doll" experiments (see Chapter 6) clearly demonstrated, aggression also can be learned by observing others. Children learn how to aggress even when they witness an aggressive model being punished. Later, if the punishing agent is not present or if rewards are available for aggressing, children are likely to reproduce the model's actions. Correlational studies, while not establishing cause and effect, find that aggressive and delinquent children tend to have parents who often behave aggressively (Stormshak et al., 2000).

Psychological Factors in Aggression

Many psychological factors influence whether we behave aggressively in a particular situation (Anderson & Bushman, 2002). From gang violence to rape and war, people may employ several types of *self-justification* to make it psychologically easier to harm other people (Lanier, 2001). Aggressors may blame the victim for imagined wrongs or otherwise convince themselves that the victim "deserves it." They may also "dehumanize" their victims by stripping them of human qualities, as the guard in the Stanford prison study did when he began to view the prisoners as "cattle."

Our *attribution of intentionality* and degree of empathy also affect how we respond to provocation. When we believe that someone's negative behavior toward us was intentional or controllable, we are more likely to become angry and retaliate (Graham et al., 1992). And when someone offends us and then apologizes, whether we will forgive the person depends in part on how well we can empathize and understand his or her viewpoint (McCullough et al., 1997).

▶ 24. Discuss catharsis and social learning views on effects of media violence. Do violent video games promote aggression?

Sigmund Freud believed that impulses from aggressive instincts build up inside us over time, eventually have to be released, and then build up again in a never ending cycle. His principle of **catharsis** *stated that performing an act of aggression discharges aggressive energy and temporarily reduces our impulse to aggress.* But how does one do this in a world where violence is discouraged and punished? Freud proposed that we can channel aggressive impulses into socially acceptable behaviors (such as competitive sports) and discharge aggressive impulses *vicariously* by watching and identifying with other people who behave aggressively.

If people cannot express their aggressive impulses, will the unreleased pressures build up to an explosion point? In some cases, seemingly meek or unassertive people do commit shocking and brutal crimes. These individuals, whom psychologist Edwin Megargee (1966) describes as having *overcontrolled hostility,* show little immediate reaction to provocations. Instead, they bottle up their anger and, after provocations accumulate, suddenly erupt into violence. The final provocation that triggers their destructive outburst is often trivial. For example, one 10-year-old boy with no previous history of aggression stabbed his sister more than 80 times with an ice pick after she changed the channel during his favorite TV show. After the aggressive outburst, such people typically revert to their former passive, unassertive state. Among female prison inmates, those who score high on a psychological test measuring overcontrolled hostility are more likely to have committed a one-time violent crime than a nonviolent crime or repeated violent crimes (Verona & Carbonell, 2000; Figure 15.34).

Cases of overcontrolled hostility seem to be consistent with the concept of catharsis, but much research is not. For example, hitting a punching bag while thinking about someone who has just angered them increases—not decreases—people's subsequent aggressive behavior toward that person (Bushman, 2002). And what about watching violent movies and TV programs? Do these activities help people "blow off steam," as some stars in the entertainment industry claim?

Media Violence: Catharsis Versus Social Learning

Many movies, as well as fiction and nonfiction TV programs, are saturated with violence. According to psychodynamic theory, movie and TV violence should be a cathartic pot of gold. But social learning theorists argue that by providing numerous aggressive models—including many who are reinforced—media violence is more likely to increase viewers' aggressive behavior than to reduce it.

Headline-making "copycat" acts of violence clearly illustrate social learning effects. Still, hundreds of millions of people are entertained by

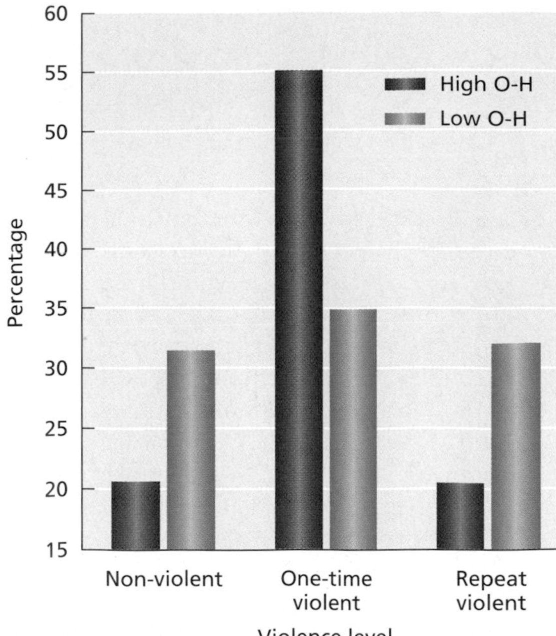

FIGURE 15.34

Female inmates at a state prison completed psychological tests that identified whether they had high overcontrolled hostility (High O-H) or low overcontrolled hostility (Low O-H). Inmates with high overcontrolled hostility—but not inmates with low overcontrolled hostility—were much more likely to have committed a one-time violent crime than a nonviolent crime or multiple violent crimes. Source: Adapted from Verona & Carbonell, 2000.

media violence and, fortunately, few of them commit copycat crimes. What then are the more general effects of media violence on aggression? Over the past 30 years, hundreds of experiments and correlational studies have shed light on the "catharsis versus social learning" debate.

To most experts, the verdict is clear: The evidence favors the social learning view (Johnson et al., 2002). Exposure to TV and movie violence is related to the tendency of children, adolescents, and adults to behave aggressively. For example, American children who watch greater amounts of TV violence are more likely than their peers to display physical aggression when they become young adults (Eron, 1987; Huesmann et al., 2003). This association is not simply due to the fact that children who watch the most TV violence are already more aggressive to begin with. Moreover, boys and girls who perceive TV violence to be highly realistic and identify strongly with same-sex aggressive TV characters are most likely to act aggressively as adults (Huesmann et al., 2003).

Experiments in laboratory and field settings suggest a clearer causal link between watching media violence and behaving more aggressively. In an experiment in Belgium, Jacque Leyens and coworkers (1975) went into a facility for high school–age juvenile delinquents and held a special "movie week" in which they showed different groups of boys either violent or nonviolent movies each night. The result: Among boys who watched the violent films, physical and verbal aggression increased during that week.

Media violence appears to exert its effects through multiple avenues (Huesmann, 1997):

- Viewers learn new aggressive behaviors through modeling.
- Viewers come to believe that aggression usually is rewarded, or at least rarely punished.
- Viewers become desensitized to the sight and thought of violence and to the suffering of victims.

Beyond movies and TV, the question of whether violent video games promote aggression also has raised public and scientific concern (Figure 15.35). In July, 2000, the St. Louis County Council passed an ordinance—since challenged in the courts—to penalize businesses that allow people under the age of 18 to play violent video games without parental consent (Jurkowitz, 2002). Political reaction or overreaction? What does science have to say?

FIGURE 15.35

Do children who play graphically violent video games become desensitized to violence and more likely to behave aggressively toward other people?

BENEATH THE SURFACE

DO VIOLENT VIDEO GAMES PROMOTE AGGRESSION?

"I think the issue has been vastly overblown and overstated. . . . There is absolutely no evidence, none, that playing a violent video game leads to aggressive behavior." —Doug Lowenstein, President, Interactive Digital Software Association (Interviewed on CNN, May 12, 2000; Quoted in Anderson & Bushman, 2001, p. 353).

"The results clearly support the hypothesis that exposure to violent video games poses a public-health threat to children and youths, including college-age individuals." —Craig Anderson and Brad Bushman, social psychologists, Iowa State University (2001, p. 358).

In his book *On Killing: The Psychological Cost of Learning to Kill in War and Society*, psychologist David Grossman (1996) argues that in order to kill, we must learn to overcome a natural inhibition against killing members of our own species. And, he proposes, violent video games can be a powerful disinhibitor and teacher.

Grossman, a psychologist and retired U.S. Army officer, points to a history of warfare in which soldiers have been reluctant to kill the enemy face-to-face. In World War II, the U.S. Army found that for every 100 soldiers who had a clear shot at the enemy, only 15 percent fired at their target: a 15-percent so-called "kill rate." To counteract this, the Army trained soldiers by using operant and classical conditioning principles. A "shooting" response was gradually shaped via increasingly realistic target practice, progressing from bull's-eye targets, to human silhouettes and "pop-up" human figures, and finally to video combat simulations. Over time, soldiers became desensitized to shooting at human forms; by the Korean and Vietnam Wars, the kill rates increased to 55 and 90 percent, respectively. Police departments and other law enforcement agencies also condition their personnel to shoot—and to discern when not to shoot—using video simulations (Cummins, 1999).

Experiments on Video Game Violence

Does evidence support Grossman's view? In one of the better studies to date, Roland Irwin and Alan Gross (1995) randomly assigned sixty 7- and 8-year-old boys to play either a violent or nonviolent video game for 20 minutes. In the violent game, *Double Dragon*, a player assumed the role of a martial arts hero who kicks, punches, and uses a rope or chain to whip and defeat ruthless street gang members. In the nonviolent game, *Excitebike*, the player races a motorcycle against the clock.

After playing one of the games, each child engaged in a 10-minute "free-play" period with another boy (an accomplice). Next, as each participant competed against this boy on a task for a prize, the boy (according to plan) cheated. Compared with participants who had played *Excitebike*, those who played *Double Dragon* displayed more physical and verbal aggression toward inanimate objects (e.g., toys), more verbal aggression toward the other boy during the free-play period, and more physical aggression toward the other boy during the frustrating competition.

Let's think critically about this result. Did *Double Dragon*'s violent content increase participants' aggression, or was it simply a more exciting game? If so, perhaps it was only greater arousal that led to more aggression? Irwin and Gross measured participants' heart rate both before and during the video game play. The result: no heart rate differences between the two video game conditions, strengthening the conclusion that the content of the violent game was the key factor.

To date, of 4 studies (including this one) employing this procedure, 3 have found that children's aggression while playing with peers increases immediately after playing violent video games (Bensley & Van Eenwyk, 2001). More recently, Bruce Bartholow and Craig Anderson (2002) found that among college students, briefly playing a violent video game (*Mortal Kombat*) increased women's and especially men's aggressive behavior toward a female student (actually a confederate) who had earlier aggressed against them.

The Big Picture

Three extensive reviews of experiments and real-world correlational studies on violent video games suggest that

- for both sexes, there is a weak but positive relation between playing violent video games and increased aggressive behavior;
- the relation between playing video games and aggression is strongest for games that involve violent fantasy action;
- evidence does not support the catharsis hypothesis that playing violent video games will decrease people's aggression by letting them "blow off steam"; and
- we cannot draw conclusions about long-term consequences because research has focused on the short-term effects of playing video games (Anderson & Bushman, 2001; Bensley & Van Eenwyk, 2001; Sherry, 2001).

Are these findings cause for worry? We know how the video game industry feels (this is no surprise), but how do you interpret the evidence?

Clearly, the overwhelming majority of children and adults who play violent video games do not go out and assault or kill people. But aggression comes in many forms, physical and verbal, obvious and subtle. It is also noteworthy that the more recent studies, examining participants who are exposed to more graphically violent video games, find stronger effects than older studies (Sherry, 2001). Still, continued research focusing on long-term effects is needed to pinpoint how strongly children and adults are affected by a world full of *Mortal Kombat* and *Doom*.

As we close this section on social relations, Figure 15.36 highlights some of the biological, psychological, and environmental factors that contribute to human aggression.

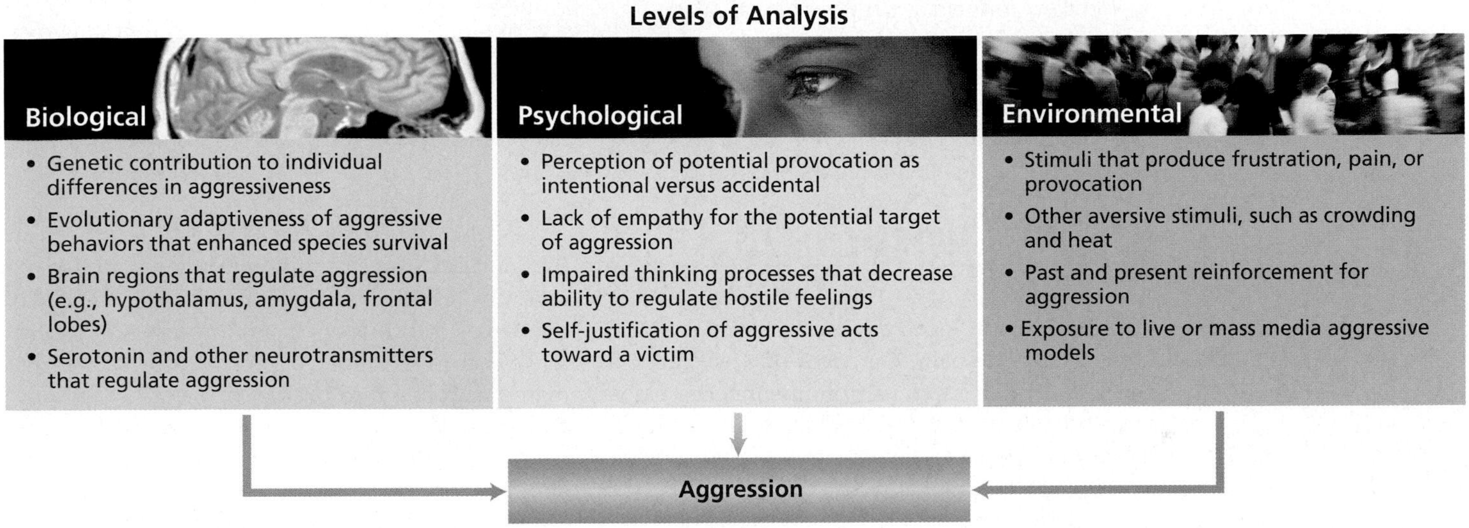

Levels of Analysis

Biological

- Genetic contribution to individual differences in aggressiveness
- Evolutionary adaptiveness of aggressive behaviors that enhanced species survival
- Brain regions that regulate aggression (e.g., hypothalamus, amygdala, frontal lobes)
- Serotonin and other neurotransmitters that regulate aggression

Psychological

- Perception of potential provocation as intentional versus accidental
- Lack of empathy for the potential target of aggression
- Impaired thinking processes that decrease ability to regulate hostile feelings
- Self-justification of aggressive acts toward a victim

Environmental

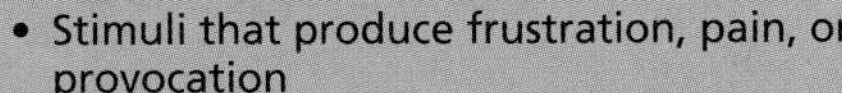

- Stimuli that produce frustration, pain, or provocation
- Other aversive stimuli, such as crowding and heat
- Past and present reinforcement for aggression
- Exposure to live or mass media aggressive models

Aggression

FIGURE 15.36

Understanding Behavior: Why do people aggress?

IN REVIEW

- *Proximity, mere exposure, similarity of attitudes, and physical attractiveness typically enhance our attraction toward someone. Relationships deepen as partners self-disclose and exchanges between them become more intimate and broader. Social exchange theory analyzes relationships in terms of the rewards and costs experienced by each partner.*
- *The qualities that people find most attractive in a mate vary somewhat across cultures. Evolutionary theorists propose that gender difference in mate preferences reflect inherited biological tendencies, whereas sociocultural theorists believe that these differences result from socialization and gender inequities in economic opportunities.*
- *Partners are more likely to remain happily married when they understand each other and deal with conflicts by de-escalating their emotions and providing mutual support.*
- *Overt prejudice has decreased in some ways, but people may hide their prejudice or be unaware of subtle prejudices they harbor.*
- *Prejudice stems partly from our tendency to perceive in-groups and out-groups. People typically display in-group favoritism and an out-group homogeneity bias. Perceived threats to one's in-group and a need to enhance one's self-esteem can motivate prejudice.*
- *Prejudice often is reduced when in-group and out-group members work closely together, with equal status, on tasks involving common goals and under conditions of broader institutional support.*
- *Some theorists propose that through kin selection and reciprocal altruism, evolution has helped shape a genetic predisposition toward prosocial behavior among humans. Social learning theorists emphasize how social norms, modeling, and reinforcement shape prosocial attitudes and behavior.*

- *The presence of multiple bystanders may decrease bystander intervention through social comparison processes and a diffusion of responsibility for helping. We are most likely to help others when we perceive that they are similar to us and are not responsible for their plight.*
- *Prosocial behavior can be increased by enhancing people's feelings of empathy for victims and providing prosocial models.*
- *Heredity influences the strength of an organism's tendency to aggress. The hypothalamus, amygdala, and frontal lobes play especially important roles in certain types of aggression.*
- *Provocation, heat, crowding, and stimuli that cause frustration or pain increase the risk of aggression. Learning experiences help shape a tendency to behave more or less aggressively. People are more likely to aggress when they find ways to justify and rationalize their aggressive behavior, perceive provocation as intentional, and have little empathy for others.*
- *Most research supports the social learning theory prediction that watching movie and TV violence, and playing video games, increase the risk that children and adults will act aggressively.*

A FINAL WORD

In Chapter 1, we began a shared journey through the sprawling domain of modern-day psychology. That journey has taken us from the inner recesses of the human mind to the social world in which we spend our lives. We have examined the intricate workings of the brain and the biological processes that underlie our thoughts, feelings, and behaviors. We have also explored the learning mechanisms that enable us to profit from our experiences and adapt to our environment. We have seen how the environment in which we live, including our culture, exerts powerful influences over who we become and how we behave. We have achieved greater understanding of the cognitive processes that, more than anything else about us, define our humanity. We have also gained insights into the processes by which we develop from a single cell at the moment of conception into the most psychologically complex creature on our planet, and we have explored the personality processes that help make each of us unique. We have learned about the many ways in which people cope, both adaptively and maladaptively, with the demands of living, as well as the many interventions that help people live happier and more fulfilling lives. As we have found in every area of psychological study, the brain, mind, and environment interact in complex ways to influence our behavior.

We are privileged to have been your guides in this psychological journey. We hope that your introductory psychology course has influenced your conception of human nature, your understanding of yourself and others, your capacity to think critically about your world, and your ability to utilize psychological principles to enrich your life.

KEY TERMS AND CONCEPTS

Each term has been boldfaced and defined in the chapter on the page indicated in parentheses.

What Do You Think?

DO WOMEN DIFFER FROM MEN IN OBEDIENCE? p. 607

After we describe Milgram's research to our own students, one of the first questions they usually ask is, "Did Milgram study women?" The answer is yes. After conducting the study described in the *Research Close-Up*, Milgram repeated the identical procedure with 40 women who, like the prior male participants, varied in age and occupation.

What was your hypothesis about sex differences in obedience? A few of our students predict no sex differences, but almost all expect women to differ from men.

About half of them predict that women would be more likely to obey the experimenter's orders and keep shocking the learner all the way to the 450-volt level. Their rationale: Given the traditional sex-role expectation that men are more dominant than women, and especially given how strong this expectation was at the time of Milgram's research (the early 1960s), women would be less likely to defy the authority of a male experimenter.

The other half of our class usually disagrees, predicting that women would be less obedient because they have more empathy than men for people who are suffering. Thus the learner's screams and pleas to stop would affect women more, and they would stop giving the shocks.

Are either of these hypotheses similar to yours? They both sound plausible, highlighting once again that different people have different "common sense," leading to opposite predictions that cover all the bases. And what did Milgram find? In the study with men, 26 of 40 (65 percent) obeyed fully. Among the women, the results were identical: 26 of 40 (65 percent) obeyed fully.

Using procedures similar to Milgram's, other researchers also failed to find consistent sex differences in obedience rates. Occasionally, a particular study would find that women were more obedient than men, another would show that men were more obedient, while others—including Milgram's—found no sex differences in obedience rates.

One study, conducted in Jordan, examined three age groups of boys and girls (6- to 8-year-olds, 10- to 12-year-olds, and 14- to 16-year-olds) who were placed in the role of "teacher" (Shanab & Yahya, 1977). The experimenter was female, and the "learner" was a confederate matched in age and sex to each participant (e.g., 10- to 12-year-old girls administered shock to a similarly aged girl). Overall, 73 percent of the participants were fully obedient, and neither their sex nor age significantly influenced the results. In sum, the most reasonable conclusion is that there are no consistent sex differences in obedience rates in studies like those conducted by Milgram. ■

DOES PURE ALTRUISM REALLY EXIST? p. 623

Do you believe that people ever help others for purely altruistic reasons? Perhaps your initial response is to say, "Sure. Good Samaritans sometimes care only about the other person's welfare and even help someone at a cost to themselves." Certainly, people make anonymous donations to charity and may help strangers in situations where no one (including the recipient) finds out. In such cases we can seemingly rule out motives for helping based on gaining recognition or others' approval. But still, doesn't helping someone else make us feel good about ourselves?

Moreover, by helping someone, don't we feel better knowing that the person's plight has been reduced? According to the *negative state relief model,* high empathy causes us to feel distress when we learn of others' suffering, so by helping them we reduce our own personal distress—a self-focused, egoistic goal, not an altruistic one (Cialdini et al., 1987). As you can see, the issue is more complicated than it first seemed.

Based on two decades of additional research, Batson and many other psychologists believe that while egoistic motives account for some prosocial behavior, at times people do help others for purely altruistic reasons (Batson et al., 1997, 2002). Yet other psychologists remain unconvinced, arguing for example that some negative state relief is always involved (Cialdini et al., 1997). Thus, the scientific debate about altruism and its relation to empathy continues (Eisenberg, 2000).

Finally, beyond the question of whether true altruism exists, why do you think people do good deeds for one another? Of the explanations for prosocial behavior you have read, which views seem most credible to you and why? Consider the six major psychological perspectives discussed in Chapter 1 (psychodynamic, behavioristic, humanistic, cognitive, sociocultural, and biological) and how they each might account for prosocial behavior. ■

Appendix: Statistics in Psychology

At various points throughout the text we have briefly described statistical procedures to help you understand the information being presented. This appendix discusses statistics in greater detail and focuses on the concepts underlying these procedures. Our goal is to help you understand how psychologists use statistics in their research.

For some students, the prospect of studying statistics evokes visions of complex higher mathematics. You will find, however, that if you can add, subtract, multiply, and divide, you can easily perform basic statistical operations.

DESCRIPTIVE STATISTICS

Psychological research often involves a large number of measurements. Typically, it is difficult to make sense of the data merely by examining the individual scores of each participant. **Descriptive statistics** *summarize and describe the characteristics of a set* (also called a *distribution*) *of scores.*

To summarize a set of scores, we might first construct a **frequency distribution,** *which shows how many participants received each score.* For example, suppose that 50 college students took a 32-item psychological test that measured their level of self-esteem. The frequency distribution in Table A.1 tells us that two participants had scores of 30, 31, or 32; one had a score of 27, 28, or 29; eleven had scores of 15, 16, or 17, and so on. Note that the researcher chose to use *intervals* of three points (e.g., 30–32) rather than to show the number (frequency) of participants who obtained each of the 33 possible (0–32) scores. She could have done the latter if she had wished to break down the scores even further. The number of intervals chosen is somewhat arbitrary, but frequency distributions often contain 10 to 12 categories.

This frequency distribution tells us at a glance about certain characteristics of the data, such as whether scores tend to cluster in one region of the distribution or are scattered throughout. We can easily convert these data into a **histogram,** *which is a graph of a frequency distribution.* Typically, the scores (or in this case, score intervals) are plotted along the horizontal axis (i.e., *x-axis*, or *abscissa*), and the frequencies are plotted on the vertical axis (i.e., *y-axis* or *ordinate*). This produces a column or bar above each score or score interval that shows how frequently the score occurred. Figure A.1 represents a histogram of the self-esteem scores for our sample of 50 college students.

TABLE A.1 Frequency Distribution of Self-Esteem Scores

Self-Esteem Scores	Frequency
30–32	2
27–29	1
24–26	4
21–23	6
18–20	9
15–17	11
12–14	8
9–11	3
6–8	4
3–5	1
0–2	1

Measures of Central Tendency

Frequency distributions and histograms give us a general picture of how scores are distributed. **Measures of central tendency** *describe a distribution in terms of a single statistic that is in some way "typical" of the sample as a whole.* There are three commonly used measures of central tendency: the *mode*, the *mean*, and the *median*. For example, Table A.2 shows the salaries of the 10 employees who work at Honest Al's Savings and Loan Corporation. Our task is to arrive at a single number that somehow typifies the salaries of the group as a whole.

The **mode** *is the most frequently occurring score in a distribution.* At Honest Al's, the modal salary is $205,000, because it is the only salary received by more than one person. Although the mode is easy to identify in a distribution, it is not always the most representative score, particularly if it falls far from the center of the distribution. Clearly, $205,000 is not the "typical" salary of the 10 employees, because 8 of them receive $20,000 or less.

The most commonly used measure of central tendency, the **mean,** *represents the arithmetic average of a set of scores.* The mean is calculated by adding up all the scores and dividing by the number of scores. The statistical formula for computing the mean is:

$$M = \frac{\Sigma X}{N}$$

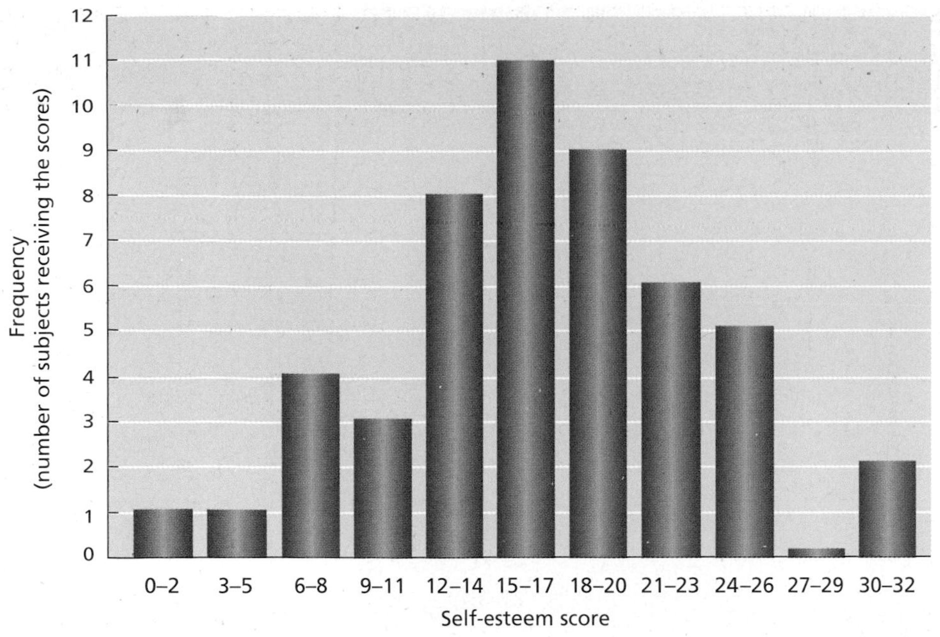

FIGURE A.1

A histogram of the self-esteem distribution shown in Table A.1.

X is the symbol for an individual score, N denotes the number of scores, and M is the symbol for the mean of the individual scores. The Greek letter Σ (sigma) means "the sum." Thus to compute the mean of the salaries at Honest Al's, we simply add up the individual salaries and divide the total by 10, the number of salaries. As Table A.2 shows, the mean salary at Honest Al's is $55,350.

Would you be tempted to go to work at Honest Al's if, during a job interview, Al told you that "our average salary is $55,350 per year"? Your negative answer to this question illustrates a shortcoming of the mean as a measure of central tendency. The mean can be strongly affected by one or more extremely high or low scores that are not representative of the group as a whole. In this case, the high salaries of Honest Al and his mother increased the mean to a figure more than twice as great as the salary of the next highest paid employee (i.e., Johnson). Thus we cannot consider the mean to be representative of the salaries of Honest Al's employees.

Our third measure of central tendency, the **median,** *is the point that divides the distribution in half when the individual scores are arranged in order from lowest to highest.* In other words, half of the remaining scores lie above the median and half below it. If there is an odd number of scores, there will be one score that is exactly in the middle. If there were 11 salaries in Table A.2, the sixth-ranked score would be the median, because 5 scores would fall above and 5 below. In a distribution having an even number of scores, the median is halfway between the 2 middle scores. In our salary distribution, the median is the point halfway between employee 5 ($19,000) and employee 6 ($18,000), or $18,500.

TABLE A.2 Annual Salaries of 10 Employees

Employee	Annual Salary (X)
1. Honest Al	$205,000
2. Honest Al's mother	205,000
3. Johnson	20,000
4. Rodriguez	19,500
5. Jones	19,000
6. Chen	18,000
7. Brown	17,500
8. Carter	17,000
9. Mullins	16,500
10. Watson	16,000
$N = 10$	$\Sigma X = \$553,500$

Mode = The score that occurs most often—in this case, $205,000.

Mean = The arithmetic average, computed by the following formula:

$$M = \frac{\Sigma X}{N} = \frac{553,500}{10} = 55,350$$

Median = The point above and below which there is an equal number of scores. In this case, because there is an even number of scores, the median is midway between the 5th- and 6th-ranked salaries—that is, $18,500.

TABLE A.3 Computation of the Variance and Standard Deviation for Two Distributions of Scores with Identical Means ($M = 10$)

X (score)	Distribution A $X - M = x$	x^2	X (score)	Distribution B $X - M = x$	x^2
12	+2	4	18	+8	64
12	+2	4	18	+8	64
11	+1	1	15	+5	25
11	+1	1	15	+5	25
10	0	0	10	0	0
10	0	0	10	0	0
9	−1	1	5	−5	25
9	−1	1	5	−5	25
8	−2	4	2	−8	64
8	−2	4	2	−8	64
$\Sigma X = 100$	$\Sigma x = 0$	$\Sigma x^2 = 20$	$\Sigma X = 100$	$\Sigma x = 0$	$\Sigma x^2 = 356$
$N = 10$			$N = 10$		
$M = 10.00$			$M = 10.00$		

x (deviation) $= X - M$

$$\text{variance} = \frac{\Sigma x^2}{N} = \frac{20}{10} = 2.00 \qquad \text{variance} = \frac{\Sigma x^2}{N} = \frac{356}{10} = 35.6$$

$$SD \text{ (standard deviation)} = \sqrt{2.00} = 1.414 \qquad SD = \sqrt{35.6} = 5.967$$

The median has an important property that the mean does not have: It is unaffected by extreme scores. Whether Honest Al makes $205,000 or $500,000, the median remains the same. Therefore the median is more representative of the group as a whole in instances when there are very extreme scores. In Honest Al's case, the median figure of $18,500 is more representative of the "typical" employee's salary than is the mean figure of $55,350 or the modal figure of $205,000. The median, however, can fail to capture important information. For example, suppose that employee 3 (Johnson) and employee 4 (Rodriguez) each received an $80,000 raise. In this case the median would not change, because the "middle score" would still be the midpoint between employees 5 (Jones) and 6 (Chen). The mean, however, would increase to $71,350 ($713,500/10) and reflect the fact that Honest Al is being more generous in paying some of his employees.

Measures of Variability

Measures of central tendency provide us with a single score that typifies the distribution. But to describe a distribution adequately, we need to know more. One key question concerns the amount of variability, or spread, that exists among scores. Do they tend to cluster closely about the mean, or do they vary widely? **Measures of variability** *provide information about the spread of scores in a distribution.*

The **range**, *which is the difference between the highest and the lowest score in a distribution*, is the simplest but least informative measure of variability. At Honest Al's, the range is $205,000 − $16,000 = $189,000. As another example, if we have a distribution of 20 IQ scores and the highest IQ is 150 and the lowest is 70, then the range is 150 − 70 = 80. But suppose the other 18 people all have IQs of 110. If we knew only the range of scores, we might be led to believe that the scores in this distribution vary far more than they actually do. Thus it would be more useful to know how much, on average, each IQ score varies or deviates from the mean of the distribution.

To do this we first create a *deviation score* (represented by a lowercase x) that measures the distance between each score (X) and the mean (M). To provide a simple example, suppose we have two distributions, A and B, each composed of 10 scores. Looking at the "X (score)" column in Table A.3 for each distribution, you can see that although each distribution has a mean of 10, the scores in distribution B are more spread out than in distribution A. Now for each score we compute how much it differs from the mean (i.e., $x = X - M$). At this stage, you might think that to measure the variability of each distribution we need only add up its deviation scores and then compute the average deviation. But we have a problem. Even though distribution B is more spread out than distribution A, adding up the deviation scores for each distribution yields a sum of zero ($\Sigma x = 0$).

TABLE A.5 Intercorrelations Among Six Ability Tests						
Test	1	2	3	4	5	6
1	1.00	.84	.71	.04	.11	−.07
2		1.00	.79	.12	.01	.00
3			1.00	−.05	.12	.08
4				1.00	.69	.74
5					1.00	.92
6						1.00

the patterns of correlations and perform a factor analysis in a few seconds. The term *factor* refers to the underlying characteristic that presumably accounts for why the measures within each cluster are linked together.

Factor analysis is complex, and for purposes of this discussion, we need not be concerned with its mathematical basis. Our interest is in how psychologists use it as a research tool, so consider a simple example. Let us assume that Table A.5 shows the correlations among only 6 of the 40 measures. Such a table is called a *correlation matrix.* The correlation coefficients of 1.00 along the diagonal of the matrix reflect the obvious fact that each variable correlates perfectly with itself. Because the bottom half of the matrix contains the same correlations as the top, we need concern ourselves only with the upper half.

Examining Table A.5 reveals two clusters of tests. Tests 1, 2, and 3 correlate strongly with one another. Likewise, tests 4, 5, and 6 correlate strongly with one another. Notice also that tests 1, 2, and 3 have low correlations with tests 4, 5, and 6, which indicates that the two clusters are measuring different things. But just what do these two clusters of tests measure? Factor analysis cannot answer this question directly; it can only identify the clusters for us. Now it is up to the psychologist to examine the nature of the tests in each cluster and decide what the underlying factors might be. Suppose that test 1 measures vocabulary, test 2 measures reading comprehension, and test 3 requires participants to fill in sentences having missing words. Because all three tasks involve the use of words, the psychologist might decide to name the underlying factor "verbal ability" or perhaps "word fluency." What matters in Table A.5 is that we have reduced 6 variables and 15 correlations to two underlying factors. In our complete example, with 40 tests and 780 correlations, a typical factor analysis might identify between two to six factors. In psychology, where researchers often attempt to identify basic dimensions of behavior, factor analysis is a valuable tool.

Inferential Statistics and Hypothesis Testing

Regardless of the type of research, psychologists rarely have access to the entire population of people they are interested in. Instead, they must be satisfied with studying relatively small samples of participants. Thus 80 introductory psychology students might participate in an experiment on bystander helping, and 400 adults recruited through newspaper advertisements might participate in a correlational study examining the relation between self-esteem and depression. On the basis of the results obtained from such samples, researchers seek to generalize their conclusions to the population as a whole.

In experiments, we are typically interested in overall differences between the various conditions. Suppose we find that participants randomly assigned to be alone help a victim more quickly than participants assigned to groups of two or four bystanders. Before concluding that the independent variable (number of bystanders) truly influenced the dependent variable (speed of helping), we must first ask whether this difference is "real" or is merely a "chance" finding. In other words, because our data are based only on a particular sample of people in each condition, how do we know that similar results would have occurred if we had tested other samples? Perhaps for one reason or another the participants we tested were not truly representative of the populations from which they were drawn. Perhaps, despite random assignment, participants assigned to be alone happened by chance to have more highly altruistic personalities than participants in the other conditions, and this (rather than "being alone") is the reason they helped more quickly.

Inferential statistics *tell us how confident we can be in drawing conclusions or inferences about a population based on findings obtained from a sample.* Thus if we observe differences in an experiment between experimental and control groups or find that there is a correlation between two variables, we use inferential statitistics to determine the likelihood that these results occurred by chance alone and thus do not reflect a genuine difference in the population from which the sample is drawn. When researchers analyze their data and conclude that a correlation or a difference in behavior between groups in an experiment is "statistically significant," the term **statistical significance** *means that it is unlikely that the particular finding occurred by chance alone.* Psychologists typically consider a result to be be statistically significant only if it could have occurred by chance alone less than 5 times in 100.

The logic underlying tests of statistical significance is related to our previous discussion of the normal curve and its statistical properties. Determining statistical significance is in many ways similar to the IQ problem presented earlier in the appendix: If IQ is normally distributed with a mean of 100 and a standard deviation of 15, what is the likelihood of randomly selecting a person with an IQ of 145? To answer that question, all we had to do was to determine what proportion of cases are 3 standard deviations above the mean in a normal distribution. We found that proportion to be about one tenth of 1 percent. Thus we would expect to randomly select a person with an IQ that high about 1 in 1,000 times—pretty small odds. With this example in mind, let us consider the logic of statistical inference in greater detail.

Suppose we are interested in the effects of a stress-management program on the academic performance of freshmen college students who are high in test anxiety. We hypothesize that learning to control anxiety during tests will result in better performance. We randomly assign 40 students who have received high scores on a self-report measure of test anxiety to either an experimental group (20 participants) that participates in a stress-management program for test anxiety, or to a control group (20 participants) that receives no guidance or treatment. All of the students take the same required courses, and at the end of the academic year we compare the mean grade point averages of the two groups. On a 0.0 (F) to 4.0 (A) scale, we find that the experimental group (training program condition) obtains a mean grade point of 3.17 and the control group has a mean grade point of 2.61. Thus the difference between the two groups is 3.17 − 2.61 = +0.56 grade points. How can we decide whether this difference between the two samples reflects a difference in the respective populations (i.e., all high-test-anxious students who might participate in a stress-management program and all who do not)?

If we repeated our experiment several times with different high-anxiety participants, we would find that the means for the two samples would vary in each experiment. For example, the next three times we performed the study the means might be 2.94 (experimental) versus 2.77 (control), 3.34 versus 2.31, and 2.89 versus 2.83, yielding differences between the groups of 0.17, 1.03, and 0.06, respectively. By repeating the experiment a great many times, we could create a distribution of experimental versus control difference scores, and mathematical theory tells us that this distribution would be a *normal* distribution. This gives us the key. Because we have a normal distribution, just as we previously assessed the exact likelihood of randomly selecting a person with an IQ of 145, we can now determine the likelihood of randomly obtaining a difference of any particular size between our sample means. But to do this, we must first know what the mean and standard deviation of our distribution of differences are. As we've seen, one way to determine these values would be to perform our experiment a large number of times. But, fortunately, we can estimate these values on the basis of a single experiment and thereby avoid the need for many replications.

To do this, we use an approach to statistical analysis that involves testing the **null hypothesis**, *which states that any observed differences between the samples are due to chance.* We begin by assuming that the null hypothesis is true—that there is no real difference, for example, in grade point average between the populations of trained and untrained test-anxious students. If the null hypothesis is true, then if we repeated our experiment a great many times, we would expect the mean of our distribution of difference scores to be zero. Therefore, the normal distribution of difference scores would cluster around this mean of zero. The standard deviation of this normal distribution can be estimated from the standard deviations of the two samples, although the mathematics need not concern us here.

In our hypothetical experiment, we obtained grade point means of 3.17 for the experimental group and 2.61 for the control group, a difference of +0.56. Let us now suppose that the standard deviation of our distribution of differences between means was estimated on the basis of our samples to be .25. Thus our obtained difference of +0.56 is slightly more than 2 SD above the mean (0) of the null hypothesis distribution. From the properties of the normal curve, we know that more than 95 percent of the cases fall in the area of the curve between -2 SD and +2 SD. Thus, *if the null hypothesis were true,* we would expect a difference in means as large as .56 (either above or below zero) less than 5 percent of the time on the basis of chance factors. This probability level meets the criterion for statistical significance described earlier. In view of this fact, we would reject the null hypothesis and conclude that there is a real difference in grade point average in the two populations. Thus our experimental hypothesis that the stress-management program resulted in a higher level of academic performance would be supported.

Note that we used the term *supported,* not *proven,* because we are making an inference based on a probability statement. There is, after all, some possibility (though less than 5 percent) that the null hypothesis is true and this really was a chance finding. Note also that this statistical analysis does not tell us why the stress-management group performed better (e.g., Did they perform better due to the program's content or the mere attention they received?). This is one reason why repeating or replicating research studies is so valuable. If another study—particularly one with more control groups—also yields statistically significant results, we can have more confidence that the difference we obtained reflects a real relation between the independent and dependent variables. But no matter how many times we repeat the experiment, we shall never move from the world of probability into the world of absolute truth.

IN REVIEW

- *Descriptive statistics summarize the characteristics of a set of data. A frequency distribution shows how many participants received each score. Histograms are graphs of frequency distributions.*
- *The mean, median, and mode are measures of central tendency, and each describes a distribution in terms of a single "typical" score. The range, variance, and standard deviation are measures of variability, and each describes how much variation there is within a set of scores.*
- *A normal curve is a theoretical, symmetrical bell-shaped curve. Fifty percent of the cases fall on each side of the mean, and the mean, median, and mode all have the same value. The standard deviation can be used to make probability estimates by dividing the normal distribution into areas containing known percentages of a population.*
- *Researchers seek to determine how much behavioral variance can be accounted for by relations between variables, including experimental manipulations, and how much is due to random, unmeasured, or uncontrolled factors.*
- *Two variables are correlated when changes in the scores of one variable correspond reliably with changes in the scores of the other variable. Correlations may be positive, negative, or zero, as well as weak or strong. Squaring the correlation coefficient tells us how much of the variance in one measure can be accounted for by differences in the other measure. Correlation does not allow us to assume causality, but it often gives us the basis for predictions.*
- *Factor analysis reduces a large number of measures to a smaller number of clusters. The measures within each cluster are highly intercorrelated and reflect the same underlying psychological dimension.*
- *Inferential statistics tell us how likely it is that differences between groups or correlations among variables are the result of chance alone. We need inferential statistics because most research is done with samples, and such statistics allow us to generalize conclusions to the population from which the sample was drawn.*
- *Typically, a result is considered statistically significant only if it could have occurred by chance alone less than 5 times in 100. Statistical analysis often involves testing the null hypothesis, which assumes that any observed difference between group means or correlation among variables is due to chance. Inferential statistics yield probability statements, not absolute proof.*

KEY TERMS AND CONCEPTS

descriptive statistics (A-1)
factor analysis (A-7)
frequency distribution (A-1)
histogram (A-1)
inferential statistics (A-8)
mean (A-1)
measures of central tendency (A-1)
measures of variability (A-3)
median (A-2)
mode (A-1)
normal curve (A-4)
null hypothesis (A-9)
Pearson product-moment correlation coefficient (A-6)
range (A-3)
standard deviation (SD; A-4)
statistical significance (A-8)
variance (A-4)

Credits

PHOTOGRAPHS

Chapter One

Opener: © Royalty-Free/CORBIS; **1.1** © Jeffrey W. Myers/Stock Boston; **1.3a** Courtesy of Neal E. Miller; **1.3b** © David Austin/Stock Boston LLC 119; **1.4** Public Domain; **1.5** © Archives of the History of American Psychology—The University of Akron; **1.6** © SCIENCE PHOTO LIBRARY/Photo Researchers; **1.7** © Archives of the History of American Psychology; **1.8** © Leo Baeck Institute; **1.9** © Culver Pictures, Inc.; **1.10** © Sam Falk/Photo Researchers; **1.11** © Reuters NewMedia Inc./CORBIS; **1.12** © Eric Lessing/Art Resource; **1.13** © Yerkes National Primate Research Center, Emory University; **1.14** © Bill Anderson/Photo Researchers; **1.15** © SINER JEFF/CORBIS SYGMA; **1.16** Library of Congress Image #LC-USZ62-112521; **1.17** © Archives of the History of American Psychology; **1.18** © Michael Phelps; **1.19** © Thomas Nebbia/Woodfin Camp & Associates; **1.20** © Granger Collection; **1.21** © Michael W. Tweedie/Photo Researchers; **1.23a** © Bettmann/CORBIS; **1.23b** © Reuters NewMedia Inc./CORBIS; **1.23c** © Leif Skoogfors/CORBIS.

Chapter Two

Opener: © David Young-Wolff/PhotoEdit; **2.1** © New York Times Pictures; **2.2a** © Apeiron/Corbis-Sygma; **2.2b** © Steve Nickerson/Detroit Free Press; **2.7a** © David Buffington/Getty; **2.7b** © Richard T. Nowitz/Photo Researchers; **2.7c** © Spencer Grant/PhotoEdit; **2.8** © Bettmann/Corbis; **2.9** © Penelope Breese/Liaison Agency; **2.15** © Mark R. Rosenzweig; **2.16** © Jonathan Nourok/PhotoEdit; **2.19** © Will & Deni McIntyre/Photo Researchers; **2.21** © Royalty-Free/CORBIS; **2.22** © Michael Newman/PhotoEdit; **2.23a** © Lawrence Migdale/Photo Researchers; **2.23b** © Will & Deni McIntyre/Photo Researchers; **2.24** Used by permission of the Skeptical Inquirer magazine (www.csicop.org).

Chapter Three

Opener: MEHAU KULYK/PHOTO RESEARCHERS, INC.; **3.1a** © Michael Nichols/Magnum; **3.1b** © Michael Nichols/Magnum; **3.2** From: Damasio H., Grabowski, T., Frank R., Galaburda A.M., Damasio A.R.: The return of Phineas Gage: Clues about the brain from the skull of a famous patient. Science, 264:1102-1105, 1994. Departments of Neurology and Image Analysis Facility, University of Iowa.; **3.4a** © Ryan McVay/Getty; **3.4b** © David Bartruff/Stock Boston; **3.4c** © Owen Franken/CORBIS; **3.7a** © L. Clarke/CORBIS; **3.7b** © Jim Whitmer; **3.12** © Joe Raedle/Newsmakers/Getty; **3.17a** © Larry Mulvehill/Science Source/Photo Researchers; **3.17c** © RICHARD PRICE/Getty; **3.17d** © Clinique Ste. Catherine/CNRI/SPL/Photo Researchers; **3.17e** © Dan McCoy/Rainbow; **3.17f** © Lester Lefkowitz/CORBIS; **3.18** © Martin M.Rotker/Science Source/Photo Researchers; **3.19** © Richard Hutchings/CORBIS; **3.20b** © Arthur Leipzig; **3.28** © Manfred Kage/Peter Arnold, Inc.

Chapter Four

Opener: © Sylvain Grandadam/Getty; **4.1** © AP/Wide World Photos; **4.10** © Matthew McVay/Stone/Getty; **4.16** Fritz Goro, Life Magazine © Time, Inc; **4.20** © Culver Pictures; **4.21** Robert E. Preson, Courtesy of Prof. J. E. Hawkins, Kresge Hearing Research Institute, U of MI; **4.24** Courtesy of Evelyn Glennie; **4.25** © AP Photo/Lee Chuan-hsien; **4.26** Courtesy of the Department of Veterans Affairs; **4.27** © Jeff Miller/UW-Madison University Communications; **4.30a** © R. Benson/RobertStock; **4.30b** The Advertising Archive Ltd.; **4.32** © Crockett Photography and Design; **4.33** *Pinto* by Bev Doolittle, 1979. The Greenwich Workshop Inc., Trumbull, CT.; **4.36** © 11/1/1900 by the New York Times Co. Reprinted by permission; **4.38** © Jeffery Grosscup; **4.39** © Reuters NewMedia Inc./CORBIS; **4.40** © 1948 M.C. Escher Foundation/Baarn-Holland, All Rights Reserved; **4.41** © Ted Spiegel/CORBIS; **4.42** © Holway & Lobel Globus/Stock Market/Corbis; **4.44** © Baron Wolman/Woodfin Camp & Associates; **4.46** © Dawson Jones/Stock Boston; **4.49** © Jack Deutsch/Innervisions; **4.50** © K. Rice/RobertStock.

Chapter Five

Opener: © Jonathan Nourok/PhotoEdit; **5.1a** © David Bartruff/Stock Boston; **5.1b** © A. Ramey/PhotoEdit; **5.2a** © Anne Dowie; **5.2b** Photo by Donna T. Biershwale. Courtesy of the Cognitive Evolution Group at University of Louisiana Lafayette.; **5.5a** © Tom Ives/Corbis-Sygma; **5.5b** © Tom Ives/Corbis-Sygma; **5.9** © Najlah Feanny/Stock Boston; **5.10** © ED YOUNG/PHOTO RESEARCHERS, INC.; **5.14** © James Holland/Stock Boston; **5.18a** © Louis Psihoyos/Matrix; **5.18b** © Louis Psihoyos/Matrix; **5.19** The Kobal Collection; **5.28a** The Advertising Archive Ltd.; **5.28b** © CORBIS; **5.29** © Dr. G. A. Ricaurte, Johns Hopkins University School of Medicine. Reprinted with Permission from Elsevier Science (The Lancet. 1998, Vol. 352. pp 1433–1437); **5.30** © Claudia Andujar/Photo Researchers, Inc.; **5.31** © 1997 Newsweek, Inc. All rights reserved. Reprinted by permission.; **5.33** © SCIENCE PHOTO LIBRARY/PHOTO RESEARCHERS, INC; **5.34** © AP/Wide World Photos; **5.35** © Bettmann/Corbis; **5.36** Courtesy News and Publications Service, Stanford University.

Chapter Six

Opener: © Peter Beck/CORBIS; **6.2a** © Wayne R. Bilenduke/Stone/Getty; **6.2b** Steve McCurry/National Geographic Society; **6.4** © Bettmann/Corbis; **6.7a** © Zuma Press/CORBIS; **6.10** Courtesy of Professor Benjamin Harris; **6.11** © Bill Aron/PhotoEdit; **6.14** Nina Leen, Life Magazine © Time, Inc.; **6.16** © Roy Morsch/CORBIS; **6.17** Courtesy of Elizabeth Thompson Gershoff, Ph.D.; **6.18** © Brian Bahr/ALLSPORT/Getty; **6.19a, 6.19b, 6.19c, 6.19d** Robert W. Kelley, Life Magazine © Time, Inc; **6.21** © Michael Okoniewski/The Image Works; **6.25a** © Jose Azel/Aurora; **6.25b** © Luc Marescot/Gamma; **6.28a** Courtesy of Albert Bandura, Stanford University; **6.28b** Courtesy of Albert Bandura, Stanford University; **6.28c** Courtesy of Albert Bandura, Stanford University; **6.30a** © Lincoln P. Brower; **6.30b** © Lincoln P. Brower; **6.31** © Monte S. Buchsbaum, M.D., Mt. Sinai School of Medicine, New York, NY; **6.32a, 6.32b, 6.32c** © SuperStock.

Chapter Seven

Opener © Bob Krist/CORBIS; **7.4** © Mark Gibson/Gibson Stock Photography; **7.5a** © Michael Newman/PhotoEdit; **7.9** © Robbie Jack/CORBIS; **7.11b** © Steve Skjold/PhotoEdit; **7.14a** © Peter C. Brandt/Getty Images; **7.14b** © Ezra Shaw/Getty Images; **7.15** © Richard Herrmann/Visuals Unlimited; **7.16** Photofest; **7.18** © Bettmann/Corbis; **7.21** © James McLoughlin/AGE Fotostock; **7.24a** Intraub, H., Gottesman, C.V., Willey, E.V., & Zuk, I.J. (1996), Boundary extension for briefly glimpsed pictures: Do common perceptual processes result in unexpected memory distortions? Journal of Memory and Language, 35, 118–134; **7.26a** © Bettmann/Corbis; **7.26b** © Bettmann/Corbis; **7.28** © Shahn-Kermani/Liaison Agency; **7.29a** © Hideo Haga/HAGA/The Image Works; **7.31** © Ralph A. Clevenger/CORBIS.

Chapter Eight

Opener © Premium Stock/CORBIS; **8.1** © James Cachero/Corbis–Sygma; **8.3** © Kay Smith; **8.5** Marcus Raichle, Washington University, St. Louis, McDonnell Center for High Brain Function; **8.6** Sex differences . . . . Brain and Language, 80, 97-105, Fig. 1, p. 102 "Rossell, S.L. et al. (2002). Sex differences in functional brain activation during a lexical visual field task. Brain and Language, 80, 97-105 Figure 1, p. 102; Brain and Language Copyright © 2003 Elsevier Science (USA). All rights reserved"; **8.7** © Ariel Skelley/CORBIS; **8.10** Courtesy of Sue Savage-Rumbaugh; **8.11** © Amy Etra/PhotoEdit; **8.18** © Mark Junak/Getty; **8.19** © AP/Wide World Photos; **8.25a** Sir Francis Galton Hulton Archive/Getty Images; **8.25b** © Bettmann/CORBIS; **8.27** © Lew Merrim/Photo Researchers; **8.31a** © Mark Wilson/Getty Images; **8.31b** © AFP/CORBIS; **8.31c** © Bruce Ayres/Getty; **8.37** © Richard Hutchings/CORBIS.

Chapter Nine

Opener © Look/eStock Photo; **9.4** Copyright 1995 Amgen Inc.; **9.6a** © Museo del Prado, Madrid/Peter Willi/Superstock; **9.6b** © The Granger Collection; **9.6c** © ImageState; **9.8** © Michael Freeman/CORBIS; **9.11a** © William Thompson/Index Stock Imagery; **9.11** © William Thompson/Powerstock/Zefa/Index Stock Imagery; **9.12b** © Cheryl Maeder/CORBIS; **9.13** "The New Virginity" from Newsweek, Dec. 23, 2002 © 2002 Newsweek, Inc. All rights reserved. Reprinted by permission.; **9.15a** © David Young-Wolff/Photo Edit; **9.15b** © MILNER MOSHE/CORBIS SYGMA; **9.18** © Donna Day/Stone/Getty; **9.20** © Irvington Publishers; **9.21** © A Ramey/Stock Boston LLC 109; **9.24a** © Photo News/GAMMA; **9.24b** © Jed Jacobson/Allsport/Getty; **9.26** © ATABOY/Getty; **9.28** Polygraph test © Michael L. Abramson/Woodfin Camp & Associates; **9.29a** © Thomas Kitchin & Victoria Hurst; **9.29b** © The beauty archive/eStock Photo; **9.30** © P. Ekman and W.V. Friesen, "Pictures of Facial Affect." Consulting Psychologists Press, Palo Alto, CA, 1976; **9.31b** © AFP/CORBIS; **9.31c** © TempSport/CORBIS; **9.33a** © Tony Freeman/PhotoEdit; **9.34b** © Tony Freeman/ PhotoEdit.

Chapter Ten

Opener © Richard Hutchings/Photo Researchers; **10.1** © The British Library; **10.3a** © David M. Phillips/The Population Council/Photo Researchers; **10.3b** © Biophoto Associates/Photo Researchers; **10.3c** © John Watney Photo Library/Photo Researchers; **10.4** © CNRI/SPL/Photo Researchers; **10.5a** © George Steinmetz; **10.5b** © Streissguth, A.P., & Little, R.E. (1994). "Unit 5: Alcohol, Pregnancy, and the Fetal Alcohol Syndrome: Second Edition" of the Project Cork Institute Medical School Curriculum (slide lecture series) on Biomedical Education: Alcohol Use and Its Medical Consequences, produced by Dartmouth Medical School; **10.6a, 10.6b, 10.6c** © Dr. Charles A. Nelson; **10.8a** © Michael Siluk; **10.8b** © Dr. Melanie Spence, University of Texas, Dallas; **10.9** Courtesy of Dr. Andrew Meltzoff; **10.15** © Steven Raymer/National Geographic Image Collection; **10.14a** © Goodman/Photo Researchers; **10.14b** © Goodman/Photo Researchers; **10.15a, 10.15b, 10.15c** © Tony Freeman/PhotoEdit; **10.20a** © Bob Daemmrich/Stock, Boston LLC; **10.20b** © Carroll E. Izard; **10.21a** Courtesy of Bill Lishman; **10.21b** © Myrleen Ferguson Cate/PhotoEdit; **10.22** © Harlow Primate Laboratory; **10.24** © Myrleen Ferguson Cate/PhotoEdit; **10.27a** © Michael Keller/CORBIS; **10.27b** © Rosanne Olson/Stone/Getty; **10.29** © Darama/CORBIS; **10.30** © Bill Gillette/Stock Boston; **10.31a** © Bob Daemmrich/Stock, Boston LLC; **10.34** © Cameron/CORBIS; **10.35** © Figaro Magazine/Liaison Agency; **10.36a** © NASA; **10.36b** © Cameron/CORBIS;

10.39 © Lawrence Migdale/Stock, Boston LLC; **10.40** National Geographic Society/James L. Stanfield.; **10.43** © Owen Franken/CORBIS.

Chapter Eleven

Opener © Mehau Kulyk/Photo Researchers; **11.1a, 11.11b** © Bettmann/CORBIS; **11.5a** © Mary Evans/John Cutten Collection; **11.6** © CORBIS; **11.8** © AFP/CORBIS; **11.9** © Paul Chesley/Photographers Aspen/Picture Quest; **11.10** © Gregg Mancuso/Stock Boston; **11.14** © AFP/CORBIS; **11.16a** © Spencer Grant/Stock Boston; **11.17** The Kobal Collection; **11.24** © Spencer Grant/PhotoEdit; **11.25** © Laura Dwight/Corbis

Chapter Twelve

Opener © Bill Varie/CORBIS; **12.3a** © David Hamilton/Getty; **12.3b** © PhotoDisc Blue/Getty; **12.5** © Oscar Burriel/Latin Stock/SPL/Photo Researchers; **12.6** © Jennie Woodcock; Reflections Photolibrary/CORBIS; **12.14** © J.P. Laffont/Corbis-Sygma; **12.17** © Ronnie Kaufman/CORBIS; **12.23** © Bruce Ayers/Stone/Getty.

Chapter Thirteen

Opener © Tom & Dee Ann McCarthy/CORBIS; **13.1a, 13.1b, 13.1c** © Bettmann/CORBIS; **13.2** © Kjell Sandved/Visuals Unlimited, Inc.; **13.3** Witches' Sabbath: The He-Goat. 1798 Museo Lazaro Galdiano, Madrid, Spain. Giraudon/Art Resource, NY 13-07; **13.7 top** © Bettmann/Corbis; **13.7 bottom** © AP/Wide World Photos; **13.10a** © AP Photo/G. Paul Burnette; **13.10b** © JIMI LOTT/THE SEATTLE TIMES; **13.11** © Reuters NewMedia Inc./CORBIS; **13.17** © Steve Smith; **13.18** © AP/Wide World Photos; **13.24** © David Young-Wolff/Photo Edit; **13.28** © Bettmann/CORBIS; **13.29** © Grunnitus/Photo Researchers; **13.31** © Joe McNally **13.36** © Dennis MacDonald/PhotoEdit.

Chapter Fourteen

Opener © Royalty-Free/CORBIS; **14.1** © Will Hart/PhotoEdit; **14.3** © Bruce Ayres/Stone/Getty; **14.6** Courtesy of Natalie Rogers; **14.9** Courtesy of Dr. Albert Ellis; **14.10** Courtesy of Dr. Aaron T. Beck; **14.11** © Bonnie Kamin/PhotoEdit; **14.12** Courtesy of Hunter Hoffman; photo by Mary Levin, University of Washington.; **14.15** © David Kelly Crow/PhotoEdit; **14.16** © Ed Lallo/Index Stock; **14.22** © Michael Newman/PhotoEdit; **14.23** © Will & Deni McIntyre/Photo Researchers; **14.27** © David Young-Wolff/Photo Edit.

Chapter Fifteen

Opener © Mary Kate Denny/PhotoEdit; **15.1** © Bruce Ayres/Getty; **15.3** The Kobal Collection; **15.5a** © Spencer Grant/PhotoEdit; **15.6** © Mark Wilson/Getty Images; **15.7** © AFP/CORBIS; **15.8a** © Momatiuk Eastcott/Image Works; **15.8b** © A. Ramey/PhotoEdit; **15.9** © Flash! Light/Stock Boston; **15.10a** © Robert E Daemmrich/Getty; **15.10b** © KOREN ZIV/CORBIS SYGMA; **15.12b** William Vandivert, Scientific American, November 1955, Vol. 193, Issue 5, pp. 31-35.; **15.13a** © 1965 by Stanley Milgram. From the film OBEDIENCE, distributed by Penn State, Media Sales; **15.13b** © 1965 by Stanley Milgram. From the film OBEDIENCE, distributed by Penn State, Media Sales; **15.15** © 1965 by Stanley Milgram. From the film OBEDIENCE, distributed by Penn State, Media Sales; **15.16** © Owen Franken/Stock, Boston LLC; **15.17a** © Michael Newman/PhotoEdit; **15.17b** © Science VU/NASA/Visuals Unlimited, Inc.; **15.19b** © NASA; **15.20** © Reuters NewMedia Inc./CORBIS; **15.21a** © Richard Lord/PhotoEdit; **15.21b** © Sid Bahrt/Photo Researchers; **15.24a** © Andrew Brusso; **15.24b** © Andrew Brusso; **15.25** © AFP/CORBIS; **15.28** © Ed Kashi/IPN/Aurora; **15.29a** © Richard R. Hansen/Photo Researchers; **15.29b** © David Gray/Reuters NewMedia Inc./CORBIS; **15.30** © Viviane Moos/CORBIS; **15.33** © Jose Luis Pelaez, Inc./CORBIS; **15.35** © Johathan Nourok/PhotoEdit.

LINE ART AND TEXT

Chapter One

Table 1.2 Levine, R., Sato, S., Hashimoto, T., & Verma, J. (1995). Love and marriage in eleven cultures. *Journal of Cross-Cultural Psychology, 26,* 554–571. Copyright © 1995 by Western Washington University. Reprinted by permission of Sage Publications, Inc.; **Figure 1.24** From data in table. American Psychological Association Research Office (2001). Employment characteristics of APA members by membership status, 2000 (Table 4). In *2000 APA Directory Survey*. Copyright © 2000 by the American Psychological Association. Adapted with permission. Note: The data in this graph have been derived from the APA membership and as such may not accurately represent the distribution of employment settings in which the larger population of doctoral-level psychologists is found in the United States.

Chapter Two

Figure 2.4 Adapted from Latané, B., & Darley, J. M. (1970). *The unresponsive bystander: Why doesn't he help?* p. 98. Copyright © 1970 Appleton-Century-Crofts. Reprinted by permission of Pearson Education, Inc., Upper Saddle River, NJ.; **Figure 2.5** © 2004 by Sidney Harris; **Table 2.1** Courtesy of National Sleep Foundation, 2002.; **Figure 2.17** Wilson, G. T., & Lawson, D. M. (1976). Expectancies, alcohol, and sexual arousal in male social drinkers. *Journal of Abnormal Psychology, 85,* 591, Table 1. Copyright © 1976 by the American Psychological Association. Adapted with permission.; **Figure 2.18** © 2004 by Sidney Harris.; **Figure 2.20** © 2004 by Sidney Harris.

Chapter Three

Page 64 Cartoon by Don Wright, © 2001. All Rights Reserved. Reprinted with permission of Tribune Media Services.; **Figure 3.7a, 3.7c** Smith, B. D. (1998). *Psychology: Science and understanding,* Figure 10.4. Copyright © 1998 by The McGraw-Hill Companies, Inc.

Chapter Four

Figure 4.5 Adapted from Pritchard, R. M. (1961, June). Stabilized images on the retina. *Scientific American,* p. 75. Reprinted with permission of Eric Mose, Jr.; **Figure 4.23** Adapted from Smith, B. D. (1998). *Psychology: Science and understanding*; Figure 4.33. Copyright © 1998 by The McGraw-Hill Companies, Inc.; **Figure 4.43** Smith, B. D. (1998). *Psychology: Science and understanding,* Fig. 4.21. Copyright © 1998 by The McGraw-Hill Companies, Inc.; **Figure 4.51a** Adapted from Gregory, R. L., & Gombrich, E. H. (1973). *Illusion in nature and art.* Reprinted by permission of Duckworth Publishers.; **Figure 4.51b** Adapted from Hudson, W. (1960). Pictorial depth perception in sub-cultural groups in Africa. *Journal of Social Psychology, 52,* 183–208. Copyright © 1960. Published by Heldref Publications, 1319 Eighteenth Street, NW, Washington, DC 20036–1802. Reprinted with permission of the Helen Dwight Reid Educational Foundation.; **Figure 4.53** Adapted from Blakemore, C., & Cooper, G. F. (1970). Development of the brain depends on visual environment. *Nature, 228,* 477–478. Copyright © 1970 Macmillan Publishers Ltd. Reprinted with permission.

Chapter Five

Figure 5.3 Adapted from Monk, T. H., Folkard, S., & Wedderburn, A. I. (1996). Maintaining safety and high performance on shift work. *Applied Ergonomics, 27,* 18, Fig. 1. Copyright © 1996 Elsevier. Reprinted with permission from Elsevier.; **Table 5.1** Smith, C. S., Folkard, S., Schmieder, R. A., Parra, L. F., Spelten, E., & Almiral, H. (2002). Investigation of morning-evening orientation in six countries using the preferences scale. *Personality and Individual Differences, 32,* 949–968. Reprinted with permission from Elsevier.; **Figure 5.7** Adapted from Kogi, K. (1985). Introduction to the problems of shift work. In S. Folkard & T. H. Monk, (Eds.). *Hours of Work,* p. 184. Copyright © 1985 John Wiley & Sons Limited. Used with permission.; **Figure 5.8** Data adapted from Mersch, P. P. A., Middendorp, H. M., Bouhuys, A. L., Beersma, D. G. M., & van den Hoofdakker, R. H. (1999). Seasonal affective disorder and latitude: A review of the literature. *Journal of Affective Disorders, 53,* 35–48. Copyright © 1999 Elsevier. Reprinted with permission. Map graphic of U. S. reproduced with permission from *The New York Times,* December 29, 1993, p. B7. Copyright © 1993 *The New York Times;* **Figure 5.15** Adapted from Roffwarg, H. P., Muzio, J. N., & Dement, W. C. (1966). Ontogenetic development of human dream-sleep cycle. *Science, 152,* 604, Fig. 1. Copyright © 1966 American Association for the Advancement of Science. Reprinted with permission.; **Figure 5.17** Reproduced with permission of authors and publisher from: Agnew, H. W., Jr., Webb, W. B., & Williams, R. L. Comparison of Stage Four and 1-REM sleep deprivation. *Perceptual and Motor Skills* 1967, 24, 851–858. © Southern Universities Press 1967.; **Figure 5.20** Adapted from Fosse, R., Stickgold, R., & Hobson, J. A. (2001). Brain-mind states: Reciprocal variation in thoughts and hallucinations. *Psychological Science, 12, No.1,* 33, Fig. 3. Copyright © 2001 American Psychological Society. Reprinted by permission of Blackwell Publishing.; **Figure 5.27** MacDonald, T. K., Zanna, M. P., & Fong, G. T. (1995). Decision making in altered states: Effects of alcohol on attitudes toward drinking and driving. *Journal of Personality and Social Psychology, 68* (6), 979, Fig. 1. Copyright © 1995 by the American Psychological Association. Reprinted with permission.; **Figure 5.37** Adapted from Kosslyn, S. M., Thompson, W. L., Costantini-Ferrando, M. F., Alpert, N. M., & Spiegel, D. (2000). Hypnotic visual illusion alters color processing in the brain. *American Journal of Psychiatry, 157,* 1279–1284, Fig. 1. Copyright © 2000 American Psychiatric Association. *http://psychiatryonline.org.* Reprinted with permission.

Chapter Six

Figure 6.1 Adapted from Hailman, J. P. (1969, December). How an instinct is learned. *Scientific American, 221,* 98–106. Reprinted with permission of Eric Mose, Jr.; **Figure 6.3** The Far Side ® by Gary Larson © 1984 FarWorks, Inc. All Rights Reserved. Distributed by Creators Syndicate.

Used with permission.; **Figure 6.22** © Zits Partnership. Reprinted with Special Permission of King Features Syndicate. **Figure 6.29** Adapted from Garcia, J., & Koelling, R. A. (1966). The relation of cue to consequence in avoidance learning. *Psychonomic Science, 4,* 123–124. Reprinted by permission of Psychonomic Society Inc.; **Figure 6.34** Cartoon by H. Mazzeo & P. Gardner from *Columbia Jester* (1951). Reprinted with permission of *Jester of Columbia*, Columbia University.

Chapter Seven

Figure **7.1b** Adapted from Milner, B. (1965). Memory disturbances after bilateral hippocampal lesions. In Peter Milner and S. G. Glickman (Eds.), *Cognitive processes and the brain,* p. 108, Fig. 6. Princeton, NJ: Van Nostrand Co., Inc. Reproduced by permission of Brenda Milner.; **Figure 7.2** Adapted from Atkinson, R. C., & Shriffrin, R. M. (1968). Human memory: A proposed system and its control processes. In K. W. Spence & J. T. Spence (Eds.) *Advances in the psychology of learning and motivation: Research and theory, Vol. 2.* Copyright © 1968 Academic Press. Reprinted with permission from Elsevier.; **Figure 7.6** Adapted from Glanzer, M., & Cunitz, A. (1966). Two storage mechanisms in free recall. *Journal of Verbal Learning and Verbal Behavior* (now *Journal of Memory and Language), 5,* 358, Fig. 2. Reprinted with permission from Elsevier.; **Figure 7.7** Cartoon by Ed Fisher. © The New Yorker Collection 1983. All Rights Reserved. Used with permission of cartoonbank.com.; **Figure 7.12** Collins, A. M., & Loftus, E. F. (1975). A spreading activation theory of semantic processing. *Psychological Review, 82,* 412, Fig. 1. Copyright © 1975 by the American Psychological Association. Adapted with permission.; **Figure 7.15** Adapted from Godden, D. R., & Baddeley, A. D. (1975). Context-dependent memory in two natural environments: On land and under water. *British Journal of Psychology, 66,* 325-331. Reprinted by permission of Alan Baddeley.; **Figure 7.20** Adapted from Nickerson, R. S., & Adams, M. J. (1979). Long-term memory for a common object. *Cognitive Psychology, 11,* 287–307. Copyright © 1979 Academic Press. Reprinted with permission from Elsevier.; **Figure 7.23** Adapted from Bahrick, H. P., Hall, L. K., & Berger, S. A. (1996). Accuracy and distortion in memory for high school grades. *Psychological Science, 7,* 265–271. Reprinted by permission of Blackwell Publishing.; **Figure 7.24** Courtesy of Helene Intraub.

Chapter Eight

Figure 8.2 © 2004 by Sidney Harris.; **Figure 8.9** © 2004 by Sidney Harris.; **Figure 8.10 b** Savage-Rumbaugh, E. S., McDonald, K., Sevcik, R. A., Hopkins, W. D., & Rupert, E. (1986). Spontaneous symbol acquisition and communicative use by pygmy chimpanzees (*Pan paniscus). Journal of Experimental Psychology: General, 115,* 220, Fig. 1. Copyright © 1986 by the American Psychological Association. Adapted with permission.; **Table 8.2** Copyright © 1972 by The Riverside Publishing Company. All rights reserved. Reproduced from the Stanford-Binet Intelligence Scales, Form L-M, by L. M. Terman and M. A. Merrill, with permission of the publisher. Note: these items are not from the current edition of Stanford-Binet.; **Table 8.4** Thurstone, L. L. (1938). *Primary mental abilities.* Reprinted by permission of the University of Chicago Press.; **Table 8.5** Schutte, N. S., Malouff, J. M., Hall, L. E., Haggerty, D. J., Cooper, J. T. , Golden, C. J., & Dornheim, L. (1998). Development and validation of a measure of emotional intelligence. *Personality and Individual Differences, 25,* 167–177. Reprinted with permission from Elsevier.; **Figure 8.35** Kimura, D. (1992). Sex differences in the brain. *Scientific American, 267* (3), 121–122, Fig. 1. Adapted by permission of Jared Schneidman Design.; **Figure 8.36a, 8.36b** Steele, C. M. (1997). A threat in the air: How stereotypes shape intellectual identity and performance. *American Psychologist, 52,* 620–621, Figures 1 and 2. Copyright © 1997 by the American Psychological Association. Reprinted with permission.; **Table 8.7** Reprinted with permission from the *Diagnostic and statistical manual of mental disorders, fourth edition.* Copyright © 1994 American Psychiatric Association.

Chapter Nine

Figure 9.12a Adapted from Michael, R. T., Gagnon, J. H., Laumann, E. O., & Kolata, G. (1994). *Sex in America.* Copyright © 1994 by C. S. G. Enterprises, Inc. Reprinted with permission of Little, Brown & Company, Inc. (US) and Time Warner Books UK.; **Figure 9.16** Adapted from Michael, R. T., Gagnon, J. H., Laumann, E. O., & Kolata, G. (1994). *Sex in America.* Copyright © 1994 by C. S. G. Enterprises, Inc. Reprinted with permission of Little, Brown & Company, Inc. (US) and Time Warner Books UK.; **Figure 9.17** Adapted from Blanchard, R., & Bogaert, A. F. (1996). Homosexuality in men and number of older brothers. *American Journal of Psychiatriy, 153,* 27-31. Copyright © 1996 the American Psychiatric Association; *http://ajp.psychiatryonline.org.* Reprinted with permission.; **Figure 9.19** Adapted from Pedersen, W. C., Miller, L. C., Putcha-Bhagavatula, A. D., & Yang, Y. (2002, March). Evolved sex differences in the number of partners desired? The long and short of it. *Psychological Science, 13,* 159, Fig. 1. Reprinted by permission of Blackwell Publishing.; **Figure 9.22** The Far Side © by Gary Larson (1985 FarWorks, Inc. All Rights Reserved. Distributed by Creators Syndicate. Used with permission.; **Figure 9.34** Speisman, J., Lazarus, R. S., Mordkoff, A., & Davidson, L. (1964). Experimental reduction of stress based on ego-defense theory. *Journal of Abnormal and Social Psychology, 68,* 373, Fig. 1. Copyright © 1964 by the American Psychological Association. Reprinted with permission.

Chapter 10

Figure 10.12 Reprinted by permission of the publisher from *The postnatal development of the human cerebral cortex, Vols. I-VIII* by Jesse LeRoy Conel. Cambridge, MA: Harvard University Press. Copyright © 1939, 1975 by the President and Fellows of Harvard College.; **Figure 10.17** Baillargeon, R. (1987). Object permanence in 3 _- and 4 _-month-old infants. *Developmental Psychology, 23,* 656, Fig. 1. Copyright © 1987 by the American Psychological Association. Adapted with permission.; **Figure 10.18** Adapted from Vurpillot, E. (1968). The development of scanning strategies and their relation to visual differentiations. *Journal of Experimental Child Psychology, 6,* 632–650. Copyright © 1968. Reprinted with permission from Elsevier.; **Figure 10.19** Adapted from Kail, R. (1988). Development functions for speeds of cognitive processes. *Journal of Experimental Child Psychology, 45,* 339–364. Copyright © 1988. Reprinted with permission from Elsevier.; **Figure 10.25** Adapted from Maccoby, E. E., & Martin, J. A. (1983). Socialization in the context of the family: Parent-child interaction. In E. M. Hetherington (Ed.), *Handbook of Child Psychology*, 4th Ed. Used by permission of John Wiley & Sons, Inc.; **Figure 10.26** Jaffee, S. R., Moffitt, T. E., Caspi, A., & Taylor, A. (2003). Life with (or without) father: The benefits of living with two biological parents depend on the father's antisocial behavior. *Child Development, 74,*118, Fig. 2. Reprinted by permission of Blackwell Publishing.; **Figure 10.28** Adapted from Crowley, K., Callanan, M. A., Tenenbaum, H. R., & Allen, E. (2001). Parents explain more often to boys than to girls during shared scientific thinking. *Psychological Science, 12,* 258–261. Reprinted by permission of Blackwell Publishing.; **Table 10.3** Adapted from Kohlberg, L. (1984). *The psychology of moral development: Essays on moral development, Vol. 2,*176–177, Table 2. . Copyright © 1984 Harper & Rowe. Reprinted by permission of Pearson Education, Inc.; **Figure 10.31b** Adapted from Inhelder, B., & Piaget, J. (1958). *The growth of logical thinking from childhood to adolescence.* Copyright © 1958 by Basic Books, Inc. Reprinted by permission of Basic Books, a member of Perseus Books, L.L.C., and by permission of Thomson Publishing Services for Routledge & Kegan Paul Ltd.; **Figure 10.32** © Zits Partnership. Reprinted with Special Permission of King Features Syndicate.; **Figure 10.34** Adapted from Larson, R. W., Moneta, G., Richards, M. H., & Wilson, S. (2002). Continuity, stability, and change in daily emotional experience across adolescence. *Child Development, 73,* 1158, Fig. 1. Reprinted by permission of Blackwell Publishing.; **Figure 10.37** Schaie, K. W. (1994). The course of adult intellectual development. *American Psychologist, 49,* 307–308, Figures 5 and 6. Copyright © 1994 by the American Psychological Association. Adapted with permission. **Figure 10.41** Bengtson, V. L. (2001, Feb.). Beyond the nuclear family: The increasing importance of multigenerational bonds. *Journal of Marriage and Family, 63 (1),* 1–16, Fig. 2. Copyright © 2001 by the National Council on Family Relations, 3989 Central Ave., NE, Suite 550, Minneapolis, MN 55421. Reprinted with permission.

Chapter 11

Table 11.2 Scheier, M. F., Carver, C. S., & Bridges, M. W. (1994). Distinguishing optimism from neuroticism (and trait anxiety, self-mastery, and self-esteem): A reevaluation of the Life Orientation Test. *Journal of Personality and Social Psychology, 67,* 1073, Table 6. Copyright © 1994 by the American Psychological Association. Adapted with permission.; **Figure 11.5b** From Eysenck, H. J. (1967). *The biological basis of personality,* Fig. 13. Courtesy of Charles C. Thomas Publisher, Ltd., Springfield, IL.; **Table 11.4** Carver, C. S., & White, T. L. (1994). Behavioral inhibition, behavioral activation, and affective responses to impending rewards and punishments: The BIS/BAS scales. *Journal of Personality and Social Psychology, 67,* 323, Table 1. Copyright © 1994 by the American Psychological Association. Adapted with permission.; **Table 11.5** Tellegen, A., Lykken, D. T., Bouchard, T. J., Wilcox, K. L., Segal, N. L., & Rich, S. (1988). Personality similarity in twins reared apart and together. *Journal of Personality and Social Psychology, 54,* 1036, Table 5. Copyright © 1988 by the American Psychological Association. Adapted with permission.; **Figure 11.7** Adapted from Smith, B. D. (1998). *Psychology: Science and understanding.* Fig. 14.2. Copyright © 1998 by The McGraw-Hill Companies, Inc.; **Figure 11.11** Cartoon by Dana Fradon. © The New Yorker Collection 1971. All Rights Reserved. Used with permission from cartoonbank.com.; **Table 11.8** Rotter, J. B. (1966). Generalized expectancies for internal versus external control of reinforcement. *Psychological Monographs, 80,* (Whole No. 609), 11–12, Table 1. Copyright © 1966 by the American Psychological Association. Adapted with permission.; **Figure 11.19** Shoda, Y., Mischel, W., & Wright, J. C. (1994). Intra-individual stability and patterning of behavior: Incorporating psychological situations into the idiographic analysis of personality. *Journal of Personality and Social Psychology, 67,* 678, Fig. 1, panels 2 & 3. Copyright © 1994 by the American Psychological Association. Adapted with permission.; **Figure 11.22** Cousins, S. D. (1989).

Culture and self-perception in the United States and Japan. *Journal of Personality and Social Psychology, 56,* 124–131, Fig. 1. Copyright © 1989 by the American Psychological Association. Adapted with permission.; **Figure 11.26** Reprinted by permission of the publisher from Henry A. Murray, *Thematic Apperception Test,* Plate 12F. Cambridge, MA: Harvard University Press. Copyright © 1943 by the President and Fellows of Harvard College, Copyright © 1971 by Henry A. Murray.

Chapter 12

Table 12.1 Smith, R. E., Smoll, F. L., & Schultz, R. W. (1990). Measurement and correlates of sport-specific cognitive and somatic trait anxiety: The Sports Anxiety Scale. *Anxiety, Stress & Coping* (formerly *Anxiety Research), 2,* 263-280. Copyright © 1990 Brunner-Routledge. Adapted by permission of the publisher: http://www.tandf.co.uk.; **Figure 12.4** Selye, H. (1976). *The stress of life, 2/e,* p. 476. Copyright © 1976 by The McGraw-Hill Companies, Inc.; **Table 12.2** Masten, A. S., & Coatsworth, J. D. (1998). The development of competence in favorable and unfavorable environments: Lessons from research on successful children. *American Psychologist, 53,* 212, Table 2. Copyright © 1998 by the American Psychological Association. Reprinted with permission.; **Figure 12.9** Levy, B. R., Slade, M. D., Kinkel, S. R., & Kasl, S. V. (2002). Longevity increased by positive self-perceptions of aging. *Journal of Personality and Social Psychology, 83,* 264, Fig. 1. Copyright © 2002 by the American Psychological Association. Adapted with permission.; **Table 12.3** Adapted from Meichenbaum, D. (1985). *Stress inoculation training.* Copyright © 1985 Pergamon. Reprinted with permission of Donald Meichenbaum, Ph.D., Distinguished Professor Emeritus, University of Waterloo, Ontario, Canada; **Figure 12.15** Drawings based on photographs by Kosambi, D. D. (1967, February). Living prehistory in India. *Scientific American, 216,* 110-111.; **Figure 12.20** Prochaska, J. O., Johnson, S., & Lee, P. (1998). The transtheoretical model of behavior change. In S. A. Shumaker & E. B. Schron (Eds.), *The handbook of health behavior change (2nd ed.).* Copyright © 1998 Springer Publishing Company, Inc., New York, NY 10012. Reprinted with permission.; **Figure 12.21** Adapted from Belloc, N. B. (1973). Relationship of health practices and mortality. *Preventive Medicine, 2,* 67-81. Copyright © 1973 by Academic Press. Reprinted with permission from Elsevier.; **Figure 12.26** Marlatt, G. A., Baer, J. S., Kivlahan, D. R., et al. (1998). Screening and brief intervention for high-risk college student drinkers: Results from a 2-year follow-up assessment. *Journal of Consulting and Clinical Psychology, 66,* 611, Fig. 2. Copyright © 1998 by the American Psychological Association. Adapted with permission.; **Figure 12.27** Marlatt, G. A., & Gordon, J. R. (1985). *Relapse prevention: Maintenance strategies in the treatment of addiction.* p. 38, Fig. 1-4. Copyright © 1985 by Guilford Publications, Inc. Reprinted with permission.

Chapter 13

P. 524 Excerpt from John C. Nemiah (1978). Psychoneurotic disorders. Reprinted by permission of the publisher from *Harvard guide to modern psychiatry,* edited by Armand M. Nicholi, Jr., pp. 179–180. Cambridge, MA: The Belknap Press of Harvard University Press. Copyright © 1978 by the President and Fellows of Harvard College.; **P. 527** Excerpt from Kleinmuntz, B. (1980). *Essentials of abnormal psychology* (2nd ed.). Copyright © 1980 Harper & Rowe. Reprinted by permission of Benjamin Kleinmuntz.; **Figure 13.23** Adapted from Tremblay, L. K., Naranjo, C. A., Cardenas, L., Hermann, N., & Busto, U. E. (2002). Probing brain reward system function in major depressive disorder. *Archives of General Psychiatry, 59,* 412, Fig. 2. Used by permission of the American Medical Association.; **Pp. 534-535** Excerpt from "I Feel Like I'm Trapped . . . " *The New York Times,* March 18, 1986, p. C12. Copyright © 1986 by The New York Times Co. Reprinted with permission.; **Figure 13.34** Caldwell, A. B. (1994). The profile of Jeffrey Dahmer (videotape). Published by Caldwell Report, Inc. Reproduced with permission.

Chapter 14

P. 551 Excerpt from: A recovering patient (1986). "Can we talk?" The schizophrenic patient in psychotherapy. *American Journal of Psychiatry, 143,* 68–70. Copyright © 1986 by the American Psychiatric Association; *http://ajp.psychiatryonline.org.* Reprinted by permission.; **Figure 14.4** © 2003 by Sidney Harris.; **Pp. 554–555** Excerpt from Wolberg, L. R. (1967). *The technique of psychotherapy* (2nd ed.), pp. 660-661. Copyright © 1967 Grune and Stratton. Reprinted with permission from Elsevier.; **Figure 14.5** Howard, K. I., Kopta, S. M., Krause, M. S., & Orlinsky, D. E. (1986). The dose-effect relationship in psychotherapy. *American Psychologist, 41,*160, Fig. 1. Copyright © 1986 by the American Psychological Association. Adapted with permission.; **Pp. 557–558** Excerpt from Rogers, C. R. (1951). *Client-centered therapy,* p. 49. Copyright © 1951 by Houghton Mifflin Co. Used with permission.; **P. 561** Excerpt from Beck, A. T., Rush, A. J., Shaw, B. F., & Emery, G. (1979). *Cognitive therapy of depression,* pp. 145–146. Copyright © 1979 by Guilford Publications, Inc. Reprinted with permission.; **Figure 14.28** Drawing by Ron Delgado from *The Wall Street Journal* (1997). By permission of Cartoon Features Syndicate.; **Figure 14.30** Foa, E. B., Hearst-Ikeda, D., & Perry, K. J. (1995). Evaluation of a brief cognitive-behavioral program for the prevention of PTSD in recent assault victims. *Journal of Consulting and Clinical Psychology, 63,* 952, Fig. 1. Copyright © 1995 by the American Psychological Association. Reprinted with permission.

Chapter 15

Figure 15.4 Miller, J. G. (1984). Culture and the development of everyday social explanation. *Journal of Personality and Social Psychology, 46,* 961–978. Copyright © 1984 by the American Psychological Association. Adapted with permission.; **Figure 15.11** Cartoon by J.B. Handelsman. © New Yorker Collection 1972. All Rights Reserved. Used with permission from cartoonbank.com.; **Figure 15.18** Janis, I. L. (1982). *Groupthink: Psychological studies of policy decisions and fiascos (2nd ed.).* Copyright © 1982 by Houghton Mifflin Company. Adapted with permission.; **Figure 15.19a** Cartoon by Henry Martin. © The New Yorker Collection 1979. All Rights Reserved. Used with permission from cartoonbank.com.; **Figure 15.26a** Allport, G. W., & Postman, L. (1947). *The psychology of rumor.* Copyright © 1947 Henry Holt & Co.; **Figure 15.34** Adapted from Verona, E., & Carbonell, J. L. (2000, April). Female violence and personality: Evidence for a pattern of overcontrolled hostility among one time violent female offenders. *Criminal Justice and Behavior, 27 (2)* 187, Fig. 1. Copyright © 2000 by American Association for Correctional Psychologists. Reprinted by permission of Sage Publications.

Glossary

A

abnormal behavior Behavior that is personally distressful, personally dysfunctional, and/or so culturally deviant that other people judge it to be inappropriate or maladaptive.

absolute refractory period The brief time interval following an action potential when a neuron is incapable of being stimulated to another impulse.

absolute threshold The lowest intensity at which a stimulus can be detected 50 percent of the time.

abstinence violation effect A response to a lapse in which a person blames himself or herself and concludes that he or she is incapable of resisting high-risk situations.

accommodation In cognitive development, the process by which new experiences cause existing schemas to change.

acetylcholine (ACh) An excitatory neurotransmitter that operates at synapses with muscles and is also the transmitter in some neural networks involved in memory.

achievement test A measure of an individual's degree of accomplishment in a particular subject or task based on a relatively standardized set of experiences.

action potential A nerve impulse resulting from the depolarization of an axon's cell membrane.

activation-synthesis theory Maintains that dreams represent the brain's attempt to interpret random patterns of neural activation triggered by the brain stem during sleep.

adaptations Biological and behavioral changes that allow organisms to meet recurring environmental challenges to their survival, thereby increasing their reproductive ability.

adaptive significance The manner in which a particular behavior enhances an organism's chances of survival and reproduction.

adolescent egocentrism Highly self-focused thinking, particularly in the early teenage years.

adoption study A research method in behavior genetics in which adopted people are compared on some characteristic with both their biological and adoptive parents in an attempt to determine the strength of a characteristic's genetic component.

adrenal glands Endocrine glands that release stress hormones, including catecholamines and corticosteroids.

aerobic exercise Sustained activity that elevates the heart rate and increases the body's need for oxygen.

agonist A drug that increases or mimics the activity of a neurotransmitter.

agoraphobia A fear of being in places or situations (e.g., on a bridge or a bus, in crowds or wide open spaces) from which escape might be difficult in the event of sudden incapacitation.

alcohol myopia When intoxicated, a "shortsightedness" in thinking (a failure to consider consequences) caused by an inability to pay attention to as much information as when sober.

algorithms Procedures, such as mathematical formulas, that automatically generate correct solutions to problems.

all-or-none law An action potential is not proportional to the intensity of stimulation; a neuron either fires with maximum intensity or it does not fire (compare with *graded potential*).

alpha waves A brain-wave pattern of 8 to 12 cycles per second that is characteristic of humans in a relaxed waking state.

Alzheimer's disease A brain disorder, typically but not always occurring in old age, whose prominent features are memory loss and confused thinking.

amphetamine psychosis Schizophrenia-like hallucinations and delusions that occur when the brain's dopamine activity is artificially increased far beyond normal levels by continuous, heavy amphetamine use.

amplitude The vertical size of the sound wave, which gives rise to perception of loudness and is measured in terms of decibels.

amygdala A limbic system structure that helps organize emotional response patterns.

anorexia nervosa An eating disorder involving a severe and sometimes fatal restriction of food intake.

antagonist A drug that inhibits or decreases the action of a neurotransmitter.

anterograde amnesia Memory loss for events that occur after the initial onset of amnesia.

anticipatory nausea and vomiting (ANV) Classically conditioned nausea and vomiting that occur when cancer patients are exposed to stimuli associated with their treatment.

antigens Literally, antibody generators, or foreign substances that activate the cells of the immune system.

antisocial personality disorder A long-term stable disorder characterized by a lack of conscience, defects in empathy, and a tendency to act out in an impulsive manner that disregards future consequences.

anxiety An emotional state characterized by apprehension accompanied by physiological arousal and fearful behavior.

anxiety disorders A group of behavior disorders in which anxiety and associated maladaptive behaviors are the core of the disturbance.

aphasia The loss of ability to understand speech (receptive aphasia) or to produce it (productive aphasia).

applied behavior analysis A process in which operant conditioning is combined with scientific data collection to solve individual and societal problems.

applied research Research that is designed to solve or examine specific, practical problems.

approach-approach conflict A conflict in which an individual is simultaneously attracted to two incompatible positive goals.

approach-avoidance conflict A conflict in which an individual is simultaneously attracted to and repelled by the same goal.

aptitude test A measure of a person's ability to profit from further training or experience in an occupation or skill; usually based on a measure of skills gained over a person's lifetime rather than during a specific course of study.

archetypes In Jung's theory, innate concepts and memories (e.g., God, the hero, the good mother); memories that reside in the collective unconscious.

archival measures Records or past documents that contain information about some type of behavior.

artificial intelligence (AI) The field within cognitive science aimed at developing computer simulations of human mental processes.

assimilation In cognitive development, the process by which new experiences are incorporated into existing schemas.

association cortex The areas of the cerebral cortex that do not have sensory or motor functions but are involved in the integration of neural activity that underlies perception, language, and other higher-order mental processes.

associative network The view that long-term memory is organized as a massive network of associated ideas and concepts.

attachment The strong emotional bond that develops between children and their primary caregivers.

attention-deficit/hyperactivity disorder (ADHD) A disorder, usually originating in childhood, that may take the form of attentional difficulties, hyperactivity-impulsivity, or a combination of the two that results in impaired functioning.

attitude A positive or negative evaluative reaction toward a stimulus (e.g., toward a person, action, object, or concept).

attribution A judgment about the causes of our own and other people's behavior.

authoritarian parents Caregivers who exert control over their children within a cold, unresponsive, or rejecting relationship.

authoritative parents Caregivers who are controlling but warm; they establish and enforce clear rules within a caring, supportive atmosphere.

autoimmune reactions Immune disorders in which the immune system mistakenly identifies part of the body as an antigen and attacks it.

automatic processing Mental activities that occur with minimal or no conscious control or awareness.

autonomic nervous system The branch of the peripheral nervous system that stimulates the body's involuntary muscles (e.g., heart) and internal organs.

availability heuristic A rule of thumb used to make likelihood judgments based on how easily examples of that category of events come to mind or are "available" in memory.

aversion therapy A form of therapy in which a conditioned stimulus that currently evokes a positive but maladaptive response is paired with a noxious, unpleasant unconditioned stimulus, in an attempt to condition a repulsion toward the conditioned stimulus.

aversive punishment (punishment by application) A type of punishment in which an operant response is weakened by the subsequent presentation of a noxious stimulus.

avoidance conditioning Through conditioning, an organism learns to perform a response to avoid an undesirable consequence.

avoidance-avoidance conflict A conflict in which an individual must choose between two alternatives, both of which she or he wishes to avoid.

axon An extension from one side of the neuron cell body that conducts nerve impulses to other neurons, muscles, or glands.

B

basic research Research designed to obtain knowledge for its own sake.

basilar membrane A membrane that runs the length of the cochlea and contains the organ of Corti and its sound receptor hair cells.

behavior genetics The scientific study of the role of genetic inheritance in behavior.

behavior modification Therapeutic procedures based on operant conditioning principles, such as positive reinforcement, operant extinction, and punishment.

behavioral assessment The measurement of behavior through direct observation and application of a coding system.

behavioral neuroscience A subfield of psychology that examines brain processes and other physiological functions that underlie our behavior, sensory experiences, emotions, and thoughts.

behavioral perspective A view that emphasizes how the environment and learning experiences shape and control behavior.

behavioral signatures Consistent ways of responding in particular classes of situations.

behaviorism A school of psychology that emphasizes the effects of learning and environmental control on behavior and maintains that the proper subject matter of psychology is observable behavior.

behavior-outcome expectancy The subjective likelihood that a particular consequence will follow a particular behavior in a given situation.

belief bias The tendency to abandon logical rules and to form a conclusion based on one's existing beliefs.

beta waves A brain-wave pattern of 15 to 30 cycles per second that is characteristic of humans who are in an alert waking state.

binocular depth cues Depth cues that require the use of both eyes.

binocular disparity The binocular depth cues produced by the projection of slightly different images of an object on the retinas of the two eyes.

biological perspective A view that focuses on the role of biological factors in behavior, including biochemical and brain processes, as well as genetic and evolutionary factors.

biologically based mechanisms Evolved biological structures that receive input from the environment, process the information, and respond to it.

bipolar disorder A mood disorder in which intermittent mania appears against a background of depression.

blood-brain barrier A specialized lining of cells in the brain's blood vessels that screens out foreign substances while letting nutrients pass through to neurons.

bottom-up processing Perceptual processes that begin with the analysis of individual elements of the stimulus and work up to the brain's integration of them into a unified perception.

brain stem The portion of the brain formed by the swelling of the spinal cord as it enters the skull; its structures regulate basic survival functions of the body, such as heart rate and respiration.

British empiricism A 17th-century school of philosophy championed by Locke, according to which all the contents of the mind are gained experientially through the senses.

Broca's area A region of the left frontal lobe involved in speech production.

bulimia nervosa An eating disorder that involves a repeated cycle of binge eating followed by purging of the food.

bystander effect The principle that the presence of multiple bystanders inhibits each person's tendency to help, largely due to social comparison or diffusion of responsibility.

C

Cannon-Bard theory A theory of emotion that proposed that the thalamus sends simultaneous messages to the cortex (producing our experience of emotion), and to the viscera and skeletal muscles, producing actions and physiological responses.

case study An in-depth analysis of an individual, group, or event.

catatonic schizophrenia A schizophrenic reaction characterized by alternating stuporous states and agitated excitement, during which the person can be quite dangerous.

catharsis The idea that performing an act of aggression discharges aggressive energy and temporarily reduces our impulse to aggress.

Cholecystokinin (CCK) A peptide that appears to decrease eating and thereby helps regulate food intake during a meal.

central nervous system The portion of the nervous system that includes the brain and the spinal cord.

central route to persuasion Occurs when people think carefully about a message and are influenced because they find the arguments compelling.

cephalocaudal principle The tendency for physical development to proceed in a head-to-foot direction.

cerebellum A convoluted hindbrain structure involved in motor coordination and some aspects of learning and memory.

cerebral cortex The gray, convoluted outer covering of the brain that is the seat of higher-order sensory, motor, perceptual, and mental processes.

cerebrum The most advanced portion of the brain, containing the cerebral cortex and underlying structures.

chaining An operant conditioning procedure used to develop a sequence (chain) of responses by reinforcing each response with the opportunity to perform the next response.

chromosomes Tightly coiled strands of deoxyribonucleic acid (DNA) and protein that contain the genes.

chunking Combining individual items into larger units of meaning.

circadian rhythms Biological cycles within the body that occur on an approximately 24-hour cycle.

classical conditioning A procedure in which a formerly neutral stimulus (the conditioned stimulus) comes to elicit a conditioned response by virtue of being paired with an unconditioned stimulus that naturally elicits a similar response (the unconditioned response).

clinical significance As distinguished from statistical significance, the extent to which clients who undergo treatments return to a normal level of functioning rather than simply becoming less maladjusted.

cochlea A small coil-shaped structure of the inner ear that contains the receptors for sound.

cognitive appraisal The process of making judgments about situations, personal capabilities, likely consequences, and personal meaning of consequences.

cognitive behaviorism A behavioral approach that incorporates cognitive concepts, suggesting that the environment influences our behavior by affecting our thoughts and giving us information.

cognitive map A mental representation of the spatial layout of an area.

cognitive neuroscience An area of psychology that intersects the subfields of cognitive psychology and physiological psychology and examines brain processes that underlie mental activity.

cognitive perspective A view that emphasizes humans as rational information processors and problem solvers, and that focuses on the mental processes that influence behavior.

cognitive process theories Approaches to intelligence that analyze the mental processes that underlie intelligent thinking.

cognitive relaxation A state of mental quiescence produced by meditation and other methods.

cognitive restructuring A cognitive stress-reduction approach that involves attempts to detect, dispute, and change maladaptive or irrational ideas that trigger negative emotions.

cognitive-affective personality system (CAPS) A model that organizes five person variables that account for how a person might respond to a particular situation; the dynamic interplay among these five factors, together with the characteristics of the situation, accounts for individual differences between people, as well as differences in people's behavior across different situations.

cognitive-process dream theories Approaches that focus on how (rather than why) we dream, and propose that dreaming and waking thought are produced by the same mental systems in the brain.

collective unconscious Jung's notion of an unconscious that consists of innate ancestral memories.

collectivism A cultural orientation that emphasizes the achievement of group rather than individual goals and in which personal identity is largely defined by ties to the larger social group (compare with *individualism*).

common factors Therapeutic elements that are possessed by virtually any type of therapy and that may contribute to the similar positive effects shown by many different treatment approaches.

communicator credibility The degree to which an audience views a communicator as believable, largely based on the communicator's expertise and trustworthiness.

companionate love An affectionate relationship characterized by commitment and caring about the partner's well-being; sometimes contrasted with passionate love, which is more intensely emotional.

compensatory response A bodily response that opposes a drug's effects and occurs in an attempt to restore homeostasis.

competency A legal decision that a defendant is mentally capable of understanding the nature of the charges, participating meaningfully in the trial, and consulting with his or her attorney.

competency-focused intervention Prevention programs that are designed to enhance personal resources needed to cope with situations that might otherwise cause psychological disorders.

compulsion A repetitive act that the person feels compelled to carry out, often in response to an obsessive thought or image.

computerized axial tomography (CT or **"CAT") scan** A method of scanning the brain with narrow beams of X rays that are then analyzed and combined by a computer to provide pictures of brain structures from many different angles.

concept A mental category containing similiar objects, people, and events.

concordance The likelihood that two people share a particular characteristic.

concrete operational stage In Piaget's theory, the stage of cognitive development during which children can perform basic mental operations concerning problems that involve tangible (i.e., "concrete") objects and situations.

conditioned response (CR) In classical conditioning, a response to a conditioned stimulus; the conditioned response is established by pairing a conditioned stimulus with an unconditioned stimulus that evokes a similar response.

conditioned stimulus (CS) A neutral stimulus that comes to evoke a conditioned response after being paired with an unconditioned stimulus.

conditioned taste aversion A learned repulsion to a food that formerly was neutral or desired, by virtue of pairing the food with an aversive unconditioned stimulus.

conditions of worth Internalized standards for self-worth fostered by conditional positive regard from others.

conduct disorder A pattern of abnormal behavior in which children violate important social norms and show disregard for the rights of others.

conduction deafness Hearing loss caused by damage to the mechanical system that conducts sound waves to the cochlea.

cones Photoreceptors in the retina that function best in bright light and are differentially sensitive to red, green, or blue wavelengths; the retina's color receptors.

confirmation bias The tendency to seek and favor information that reinforces our beliefs rather than to be open to disconfirming information.

confounding of variables In experiments, a situation in which the independent variable is intertwined or mixed up with another, uncontrolled variable; thus, we cannot tell which variable is responsible for changes in the behavior of interest (i.e., in the dependent variable).

congruence Consistency between self-perceptions and experience.

consciousness Our moment-to-moment awareness of ourselves and our environment; consciousness involves selective attention to ongoing thoughts, perceptions, and feelings.

conservation The principle that basic properties of objects, such as their mass or quantity, stay the same (are "conserved") even though their outward appearance may change.

construct validity The extent to which a test measures the psychological construct (e.g., intelligence, anxiety) that it is purported to measure.

content validity The extent to which test items adequately sample the domain that the test is supposed to measure (e.g., intelligence, mathematical reasoning).

context-dependent memory The phenomenon that it is typically easier to remember something in the same environment in which it was originally learned or experienced.

continuous reinforcement schedule A reinforcement schedule in which each correct response is followed by reinforcement.

control group In an experiment, the group that either is not exposed to the treatment or receives a zero level of the independent variable.

controlled (effortful) processing Mental processing that requires volitional control and attentiveness.

conventional moral reasoning According to Kohlberg, the stage at which moral judgments are based on conformity to social expectations, laws, and duties.

convergence A binocular depth cue produced by the muscles that rotate the eyes as they focus on nearby objects.

conversion disorder A disorder in which serious neurological symptoms, such as paralysis, loss of sensation, or blindness suddenly occur without physical cause.

coping self-efficacy Beliefs relating to our ability to deal effectively with a stressful stimulus or situation, including pain.

corpus callosum A broad band of white, myelinated fibers that connect the left and right cerebral hemispheres and allow the two hemispheres to communicate with one another.

correlation coefficient A statistic that indicates the direction and strength of a relation between two variables; values can range from +1.00 to −1.00.

correlational research Research that measures two or more naturally occurring variables and examines whether they are statistically related.

counterconditioning The process of conditioning an incompatible response to a particular stimulus to eliminate a maladaptive response (e.g., anxiety), as occurs in systematic desensitization.

creativity The ability to produce something that is both new and valuable.

critical periods Limited time periods during which plasticity can occur as a result of experience or in response to injury; in development, a time period in which exposure to particular kinds of stimulation is required for normal growth to occur.

cross-sectional design A research design that simultaneously compares people of different ages at a particular point in time.

crystallized intelligence Intellectual abilities that depend on a store of information and the acquisition of particular skills (compare with *fluid intelligence*).

cultural display rules Cultural norms that regulate when and how emotions are expressed.

cultural psychology An area of psychology, sometimes called *cross-cultural psychology,* that explores how culture is transmitted to its members and examines psychological similarities and differences that occur between people from diverse cultures.

culturally competent therapists Practitioners who have a set of therapeutic skills, including scientific mindedness, the ability to consider both cultural and individual factors, and the capacity to introduce culture-specific elements into therapy with people from minority cultures.

culture The enduring values, beliefs, behaviors, and traditions that are shared by a large group of people and passed from one generation to the next.

culture-bound disorders Behavior disorders whose specific forms are restricted to one particular cultural context.

D

dark adaptation The progressive increase in brightness sensitivity that occurs over time as photopigments regenerate themselves during exposure to low levels of illumination.

decay theory Maintains that with time and disuse, the physical memory trace in the nervous system fades away.

decibel A logarithmic measure of sound intensity.

decision criterion In signal detection theory, the potentially changing standard of how certain a person must be that a stimulus is present in order to report its presence.

declarative memory Our memory for factual knowledge, which comprises two subcategories: knowledge pertaining to personal experiences (episodic memory) and knowledge of general facts and language (semantic memory).

deductive reasoning Reasoning from a general principle to a specific case.

deep structure A linguistic term that refers to the underlying meaning of a spoken or written sentence; the meanings that make up deep structure are stored as concepts and rules in long-term memory.

defense mechanisms Unconscious processes that help us cope with anxiety and the pain of traumatic experiences. Defense mechanisms prevent the expression of anxiety-arousing impulses or allow them to appear in disguised forms.

deindividuation A state of increased anonymity in which a person, often as part of a group or crowd, engages in disinhibited behavior.

deinstitutionalization movement The attempt to move the primary locus of treatment from mental hospitals to the community.

delta waves Low-frequency, high-amplitude brain waves that occur in stage 3 sleep and predominate in stage 4 sleep.

delusions False beliefs, often involving themes of persecution or grandeur, that are sustained in the face of evidence that normally would be sufficient to destroy them.

demand characteristics Cues used by research participants to guess the purpose or hypothesis of a study, thereby causing them to alter their behavior.

dementia The gradual loss of cognitive abilities that accompanies brain deterioration and interferes with normal functioning.

dendrites Small branching fibers that extend from the soma of a neuron and receive messages from adjacent neurons.

dependent variable In an experiment, the factor measured by the researcher that presumably is influenced by the independent variable.

depressants Drugs—including alcohol, barbiturates, and tranquilizers—that reduce neural activity and can decrease feelings of tension and anxiety.

depressive attributional pattern The tendency of depressed people to attribute negative outcomes to their own inadequacies and positive outcomes to factors outside of themselves.

depressive cognitive triad A pattern of negative evaluations of the self, the world, and the future often found in depressed people.

descriptive research Research in which the main goal is to carefully describe how organisms behave, particularly in natural settings.

descriptive statistics Statistics that summarize and describe the characteristics of a set of scores.

difference threshold The smallest difference between two similar stimuli that people can detect; also called the *just noticeable difference (jnd).*

discourse The combining of sentences into larger language units, such as paragraphs, articles, novels, and so on.

discrimination (classical conditioning) The occurrence of a conditioned response to one stimulus but not to another stimulus.

discrimination (social behavior) Treating people unfairly based on the group to which they belong.

discriminative stimulus An antecedent stimulus that signals the likelihood of certain consequences if a response is made.

disorganized schizophrenia A schizophrenic disorder marked by verbal incoherence, disordered thought processes, disorganized behavior, and inappropriate emotional responses.

displacement The capacity of language to represent objects and conditions that are not physically present.

dissociation theories (of hypnosis) Views that focus on hypnosis as an altered state involving a division ("dissociation") of consciousness; one theory proposes that the hypnotized person simultaneously experiences two streams of consciousness that are cut off from one another.

dissociative disorders Disorders that involve a major dissociation of personal identity or memory.

dissociative identity disorder (DID) A dissociative disorder in which two or more separate identities or personalities coexist within an individual.

divergent thinking A creative form of thinking that involves generating novel ideas that diverge from the normal ways of thinking about something.

divided attention The ability to perform more than one activity at the same time.

dodo bird verdict The conclusion reached by some psychotherapy researchers that virtually all treatment approaches have similar success rates.

domain-specific adaptations Evolutionary adaptations designed to solve a particular problem, such as selecting a suitable mate, choosing safe foods to eat, and avoiding certain environmental hazards.

door-in-the-face technique A manipulation technique in which a persuader makes a large request, expecting you to reject it, and then presents a smaller request.

dopamine hypothesis States that the symptoms of schizophrenia are produced by overactivity of the dopamine system in areas of the brain that regulate emotional expression, motivated behavior, and cognitive functioning.

dose-response effect The relation between the degree of improvement shown and the amount of treatment (or medication) administered to a client.

double-blind procedure A procedure in which both the participant and the experimenter are kept unaware of the research condition to which the participant has been assigned.

downward comparison Comparing oneself or one's situation with less positive alternatives.

drive A state of internal tension that motivates an organism to behave in ways that reduce this tension.

dual coding theory Maintains that if we encode information using both verbal and imagery codes, the chances improve that at least one of the two codes will be available later to support recall.

dual-process theory A modern theory of color vision that combines the trichromatic and opponent process theories. Light waves are coded by red-, blue-, and green-sensitive cones at the retina and by opponent processes thereafter in the visual system.

dysthymia A depressive mood disorder of moderate intensity that occurs over a long period of time but does not disrupt functioning as a major depression does.

E

eclecticism An approach to therapy that incorporates principles and procedures from multiple therapies to provide the most suitable treatment to a client.

effect size In meta-analysis, a measure of treatment effectiveness that indicates what percentage of treated clients improve more than the average untreated client.

ego The "executive" of the personality that is partly conscious and that mediates between the impulses of the id, the prohibitions of the superego, and the dictates of reality.

egocentrism Difficulty in viewing the world from someone else's perspective.

elaborative rehearsal Focusing on the meaning of information or relating it to other things we already know.

Electra complex The female version of the Oedipus complex in which the female child experiences erotic feelings toward her father, desires to possess him sexually, and views her mother as a rival.

electroencephalograph (EEG) A device used to record the simultaneous activity of many thousands of neurons through electrodes attached to the scalp.

eliciting stimuli Internal or external cues that evoke an emotional response.

embryo A scientific term for the prenatal organism during the 2nd week through the 8th week after conception.

emotion A pattern of cognitive, physiological, and behavioral responses to situations and events that have relevance to important goals or motives.

emotion regulation The processes by which a person evaluates and modifies her or his emotional reactions.

emotional intelligence The ability to respond adaptively in the emotional realm by reading and responding appropriately to others' emotions, to be aware of and have the ability to control one's own emotions, and to delay gratification.

emotion-focused coping Coping strategies directed at minimizing or reducing emotional responses to a stressor.

empathy The capacity for experiencing the same emotional response being exhibited by another person; in therapy, the ability of a therapist to view the world through the client's eyes and to understand the client's emotions.

empathy-altruism hypothesis The view that pure altruism does exist and that it is produced by the capacity to empathize with the person in need of aid.

empirical approach An approach to test construction in which items (regardless of their content) are chosen that differentiate between two groups that are known to differ on a particular personality variable.

empirically supported therapies Psychotherapy and behavior-change techniques that have been shown to be efficacious in controlled clinical trials.

encoding Getting information into the memory system by translating it into a neural code that the brain processes and stores.

encoding specificity principle States that memory is enhanced when conditions present during retrieval match those that were present during encoding.

endocrine system The body's system of glands that secrete hormones into the bloodstream and thereby affect many bodily functions.

endorphins Natural opiate-like substances that are involved in pain reduction.

episodic memory Our store of factual knowledge concerning personal experiences—when, where, and what happened in the episodes of our lives.

equal status contact The principle that prejudice between people is most likely to be reduced when they engage in sustained close contact, have equal status within the context of their interaction, work to achieve a common goal that requires cooperation, and are supported by broader social norms that encourage prejudice reduction.

escape conditioning A form of learning in which the organism learns to perform a behavior to escape from an aversive stimulus.

evolution A change over time in the frequency with which particular genes, and the characteristics they produce, occur within an interbreeding population.

evolutionary personality theory A recently developed attempt to account for personality traits such as the Big Five in terms of the evolutionary history of the human species; these traits are thought to develop from processes of natural selection.

evolutionary psychology A field of study that focuses on the role of evolutionary processes (especially natural selection) in the development of adaptive psychological mechanisms and social behavior in humans.

evolutionary/circadian sleep models The view that in the course of evolution, each species developed an adaptive circadian sleep-wake pattern that increased its chances of survival in relation to its environmental demands.

expectancy × value theory A cognitive theory stating that goal-directed behavior is jointly influenced by (1) the person's expectancy that a particular behavior will contribute to reaching the goal and (2) how positively or negatively the person values the goal.

experiment A research method in which the researcher manipulates an independent variable under controlled conditions and measures whether this produces changes in a dependent variable.

experimental group In an experiment, the group that receives a treatment or is exposed to an active level of the independent variable.

experimenter expectancy effects Subtle and unintentional ways in which an experimenter influences participants to behave in a way that will confirm the experimenter's hypothesis.

explicit memory Conscious or intentional memory retrieval.

exposure (therapies) Therapeutic techniques designed to extinguish anxiety responses by exposing clients to anxiety-arousing stimuli or situations while preventing escape or avoidance.

expressed emotion A family interaction pattern, involving criticism, hostility, and overinvolvement, that is associated with relapse in formerly hospitalized schizophrenic patients who return home.

expressive behaviors Observable behavioral indications of subjectively experienced emotions.

external validity The degree to which the results of a study can be generalized to other people, settings, and conditions.

externalizing disorder Childhood disorders that involve oppositional and aggressive behaviors.

extinction (classical conditioning) Occurs when a conditioned stimulus is presented without the unconditioned stimulus, causing the conditioned response to weaken and eventually stop occurring.

extinction (operant conditioning) Occurs when the absence of reinforcement for a previously reinforced response causes that response to weaken and eventually stop.

extrinsic motivation Motivation to perform a behavior to obtain external rewards and reinforcers, such as money, status, attention, and praise.

F

facial feedback hypothesis States that somatic feedback from facial muscles provides feedback to the brain and influences emotional experience.

factor analysis A statistical technique that permits a researcher to reduce a large number of measures to a small number of clusters or factors; it identifies the clusters of behavior or test scores that are highly correlated with one another.

fantasy-prone personality The tendency of some people to spend much of their waking time living in a vivid, rich fantasy world that they control.

feature detectors Sensory neurons that respond to particular features of a stimulus, such as its shape, angle, or color.

fetal alcohol syndrome (FAS) A severe group of abnormalities that results from prenatal exposure to alcohol.

fetus A scientific term for the prenatal organism from the 9th week after conception until birth.

figure-ground relations Perceptual organization in which a focal stimulus is perceived as a figure against a background of other stimuli.

fixation A state of arrested development due to unresolved conflicts at a particular earlier psychosexual stage.

fixed action pattern An unlearned response that is automatically triggered by a simple (releaser) stimulus.

fixed-interval (FI) schedule A reinforcement schedule in which the first correct response occurring after a constant time interval is reinforced.

fixed-ratio (FR) schedule A reinforcement schedule in which reinforcement is given after a constant number of correct responses.

flashbulb memories Recollections that seem so vivid and clear that we can picture them as if they were snapshots of moments in time.

fluid intelligence The ability to deal with novel problem-solving situations for which personal experience does not supply a solution (compare with *crystallized intelligence*).

foot-in-the-door technique A manipulation technique in which the persuader gets you to comply with a small request first and later presents a larger request.

forebrain Brain structures above the midbrain, including the thalamus, hypothalamus, limbic system, and the cerebral hemispheres; involved in higher-order sensory, motor, and cognitive functions.

formal operational stage In Piaget's theory, the period in which individuals are able to think logically and systematically about both concrete and abstract problems, form hypotheses, and test them in a thoughtful way.

fovea A small area in the center of the retina that contains only cones and where visual acuity is greatest.

free association In psychoanalysis, the procedure of verbalizing all thoughts that enter consciousness without censorship.

frequency In audition, the number of cycles per second in a sound wave that is responsible for the pitch of the sound; the measure of frequency is the hertz (Hz), which equals one cycle per second.

frequency distribution For a set of data, a table that shows how frequently each score value has occurred for a particular variable.

frequency theory of pitch perception Maintains that the number of nerve impulses sent to the brain by the hair cells of the cochlea corresponds to the frequency of the sound wave; this theory is accurate at low frequencies.

fully functioning persons Rogers's term for self-actualized people who are free from unrealistic conditions of worth and who exhibit congruence, spontaneity, creativity, and a desire to develop still further.

functional fixedness A phenomenon often found in problem-solving tasks in which the customary use of an object interferes with its use in a novel situation.

functional MRI (fMRI) A brain scanning procedure that produces pictures of blood flow in the brain taken less than a second apart.

functionalism An early school of American psychology that focused on the functions of consciousness and behavior in helping organisms adapt to their environment and satisfy their needs.

fundamental attribution error The tendency to underestimate the impact of the situation and overestimate the role of personal factors when explaining other people's behavior.

fundamental emotional patterns Basic emotional response patterns that are believed to be innate.

G

gate control theory A theory of pain that postulates the existence of gating mechanisms in the spinal cord and brain that can increase or decrease the experience of pain by regulating the flow of pain impulses to the brain.

gender constancy The understanding that being male or female is a permanent part of a person.

gender identity The sense of "femaleness" or "maleness" that is an integral part of our identity.

gender schemas Organized mental structures that contain our understanding of the attributes and behaviors that are appropriate and expected for males and females.

general adaptation syndrome (GAS) Selye's description of the body's responses to a stressor, which includes successive phases of alarm, resistance, and exhaustion.

generalized anxiety disorder A chronic state of diffuse, or "free-floating," anxiety that is not attached to specific situations or objects.

genes The biological units of heredity, located on the chromosomes.

genotype The specific genetic makeup of the individual, which may or may not be expressed in the observable phenotype.

genuineness The ability of a therapist to honestly express her or his feelings to a client.

Gestalt laws of perceptual organization The notion that people group and interpret stimuli in accordance with similarity, proximity, closure, and continuity.

Gestalt psychology A German school of psychology that emphasized the natural organization of perceptual elements into wholes, or patterns, as well as the role of insight in problem solving.

glucose A simple sugar that is the body's (and especially the brain's) major source of immediately usable fuel.

goal-setting programs An approach to increasing employee performance that rests on the premise that motivation increases when people consciously pursue goals that they value and expect they can reach.

graded potential A change in the electrical potential of a neuron that is proportional to the intensity of the incoming stimulation but not sufficient to produce an action potential.

group polarization When a group of like-minded people discusses an issue, the "average" opinion of group members tends to become more extreme.

groupthink The tendency of group members to suspend critical thinking because they are motivated to seek agreement.

gustation The sense of taste.

H

habituation A decrease in the strength of a response to a repeated stimulus.

hallucinations False perceptions that have a compelling sense of reality.

hallucinogens Drugs, such as LSD and PCP, that distort or intensify sensory experiences and evoke hallucinations and disordered thought processes.

hardiness A stress-resistant personality pattern that involves the factors of commitment, control, and challenge.

harm reduction A prevention strategy that is designed not to eliminate a problem behavior but to reduce its harmful consequences.

health psychology The study of psychological and behavioral factors in the prevention and treatment of illness and in enhancement of health.

Hering's opponent-process theory The color vision theory stating that the retina contains three sets of color receptors that respond differentially to red-green, blue-yellow, and black-white; the opponent processes that result can produce a perception of any hue.

heritability coefficient A numerical estimate of the percentage of group variability in a particular characteristic that can be attributed to genetic factors.

hertz (Hz) The measure of sound wave frequency as cycles per second.

heuristics A method of problem solving characterized by quick and easy search procedures similar to rules of thumb.

higher-order conditioning In classical conditioning, a neutral stimulus becomes a conditioned stimulus after it is paired with another conditioned stimulus (rather than with the original unconditioned stimulus).

hindbrain The part of the brain situated immediately above the spinal cord that contains the brain stem and cerebellum.

hippocampus A structure of the limbic system that plays a key role in the formation and storage of memories.

histogram A graph of a frequency distribution.

homeostasis The maintenance of biological equilibrium, or balance, within the body.

hormones Chemical substances secreted by the glands of the endocrine system that travel in the bloodstream and affect bodily organs, psychological functions, and development.

humanistic perspective (humanism) A psychological view that emphasizes personal freedom, choice, and self-actualization.

hypnosis A condition of enhanced suggestibility in which some people are able to experience imagined situations as if they were real.

hypnotic susceptibility scale A set of induction procedures and test questions that enable researchers to measure a person's responsiveness to hypnotic suggestions.

hypochondriasis A somatoform disorder characterized by an overreaction to physical symptoms and a conviction that one has or is on the verge of a serious illness.

hypothalamus A forebrain structure located below the thalamus and above the pituitary gland that controls autonomic and hormonal processes and plays a major role in many aspects of motivation and emotional behavior.

hypothesis A tentative explanation or prediction about some phenomenon.

I

id The primitive and unconscious part of the personality that contains the instincts.

illusions Incorrect perceptions based on false perceptual hypotheses that often result from constancies that do not apply to the stimuli in question.

imaginal thought A form of thinking that uses images that can be from any sense modality.

implicit memory Occurs when memory influences our behavior without conscious awareness.

imprinting In some species, a sudden, biologically primed form of attachment.

incentive An environmental stimulus or condition that motivates behavior.

incentive programs Based on learning theory, an approach that seeks to enhance employees' performance by making reinforcement contingent on productivity.

incubation A phenomenon in which the solution to a problem suddenly appears in consciousness after a problem solver has stopped thinking about it for a while.

independent variable In an experiment, the factor that is manipulated by the researcher.

individualism A cultural orientation, characteristic of many Western nations, that favors the achievement of individual over group goals; self-identity is based primarily on one's own attributes and achievements (compare with *collectivism*).

inductive reasoning Reasoning that proceeds from a set of specific facts to a general conclusion or principle.

indulgent parents Caregivers who have warm and caring relationships with their children but do not provide much guidance and discipline.

infantile amnesia An inability to remember personal experiences from the first few years of our lives.

inferential statistics Statistics that tell us how confident we can be in drawing conclusions or inferences about a population based on findings obtained from a sample.

informational social influence Following the opinions or behavior of other people because we believe that they have accurate knowledge and that what they are doing is "right."

informed consent The principle that prior to agreeing to participate in research, a person should be fully informed about the procedures, the risks involved, and the right to withdraw at any time without penalty.

insanity A legal decision that a defendant was so severely impaired at the time a crime was committed that he or she was incapable of appreciating the wrongfulness of the act or controlling his or her behavior.

insight In Gestalt psychology, the sudden perception of a useful relation or solution to a problem; in psychoanalysis, the conscious awareness of unconscious dynamics that underlie psychological problems.

insomnia A sleep disorder involving chronic difficulty in falling asleep, staying asleep, or experiencing restful sleep.

instinct An inherited characteristic, common to all members of a species, that automatically produces a particular response when the organism is exposed to a particular stimulus.

instinctive drift The tendency for instinctive behaviors to override a conditioning procedure, thus making it difficult to create or maintain a conditioned response.

instrumental behaviors Emotional coping behaviors that are directed at achieving the goal or performing the task that is relevant to the emotion.

intelligence A concept that refers to individual differences in the ability to acquire knowledge, to think and reason effectively, and to deal adaptively with the environment.

intelligence quotient (IQ) Originally defined as mental age (MA) divided by chronological age (CA) multiplied by 100 (IQ = (MA/CA) × 100); an IQ of 100 indicates that an individual is average for his or her age group. IQ scores today are based on norms derived from people of various ages.

interaction In analyzing causal factors, an interaction occurs when the way in which one factor influences behavior depends on the presence of another factor.

interjudge reliability The extent to which different observers or scorers agree in their scoring of a particular test or observed behavior.

internal consistency The extent to which items within a psychological test correlate with one another, indicating that they are measuring a common characteristic.

internal validity The degree to which an experiment produces clear causal conclusions; internal validity is high when there is no confounding of variables.

internal-external locus of control In Rotter's theory, a generalized expectancy that one's outcomes are under personal versus external control.

internalizing disorder Childhood disorders in which anxiety and depression are the major feature.

interneurons Neurons that are neither sensory nor motor neurons but that perform associative or integrative functions within the nervous system.

interpersonal therapy A form of brief therapy that focuses on the client's interpersonal problems and seeks to develop new interpersonal skills.

interpretation In psychoanalysis, a statement made by the analyst that is intended to promote insight in the client.

intrinsic motivation The motivation to perform a task simply because one finds it interesting or enjoyable for its own sake.

J

James-Lange theory A theory of emotion that proposed that emotional experience is based on a person's perception of her or his bodily responses.

job enrichment An approach to increasing employees' intrinsic motivation by making their jobs more fulfilling and providing them with opportunities for growth.

K

kin selection The view that organisms are most likely to help others with whom they share the most genes—namely, their offspring and genetic relatives.

kinesthesis The body sense that provides feedback on the position and movements of our body parts.

L

language A system of symbols and rules for combining them that can produce an infinite number of possible messages and meanings.

language acquisition device (LAD) In Chomsky's theory, an innate, biologically based mechanism that facilitates the learning of language.

language acquisition support system (LASS) The social learning opportunities involved in learning a language.

latent learning Learning that occurs in the absence of reinforcement but is not displayed until reinforcement is later introduced into the situation.

lateralization The localization of a function in either the right or the left cerebral hemisphere.

law of effect Thorndike's concept that a response followed by satisfying consequences will become more likely to occur, whereas a response followed by unsatisfying consequences will become less likely to occur.

learned helplessness theory A theory of depression maintaining that if people are unable to control life events, they develop a state of helplessness that leads to depressive symptoms.

learning A relatively enduring change in an organism's behavior or performance capabilities that occurs as a result of experience.

lens The transparent structure behind the pupil that changes its shape to focus images on the retina.

leptin A hormone secreted by fat cells that decreases general appetite.

levels of processing The concept that the more deeply we process information, the better it will be remembered.

limbic system A group of subcortical structures, including the hippocampus and amygdala, that are involved in organizing many goal-directed and emotional behaviors.

linguistic relativity hypothesis The idea, suggested by Whorf, that people's language determines the ways in which they perceive and think about their world.

longitudinal design A research approach in which the same people are repeatedly tested as they grow older.

long-term memory Our vast library of more durable stored memories.

long-term potentiation An enduring increase in synaptic strength that occurs after a neural circuit is rapidly stimulated.

lowballing A manipulation technique in which a persuader gets you to commit to some action and then—before you actually perform the behavior—she or he increases the "cost" of that same behavior.

M

magnetic resonance imaging (MRI) A brain-scanning procedure that produces a highly detailed image of living tissue based on the tissue's response to a magnetic field; can be used to study both structure and, in the case of functional MRI (fMRI), brain functions as they occur.

maintenance rehearsal The simple rote repetition of information.

major depression A mood disorder characterized by intense depression that interferes markedly with functioning.

mania A state of intense emotional and behavioral excitement in which a person feels very optimistic and energized.

mastery goals Achievement goals that focus on the desire to master a task and learn new knowledge or skills.

matching effect In romantic relationships, the tendency for partners to have a similar level of physical attractiveness.

maturation A genetically programmed biological process that governs our growth.

mean A statistic that represents the arithmetic average of a set of scores.

means-end analysis A heuristic problem-solving device in which people first define a subgoal that they hope to achieve (an "end"), compare that subgoal with their present state of knowledge, and, if there is a discrepancy between them, try to find the means to reduce the difference.

measures of central tendency Statistics that describe a distribution (a set of data) in terms of a single number that is in some way "typical" of the distribution as a whole.

measures of variability Statistics that provide information about the spread of scores in a distribution.

median In a set of data, the point that divides the distribution in half when the individual scores are arranged in order from lowest to highest.

medulla A brain stem structure that controls vital functions, including heartbeat and respiration.

melatonin A hormone, secreted by the pineal gland, that has a relaxing effect on the body and promotes a readiness for sleep.

memory The processes that allow us to record, store, and later retrieve experiences and information.

memory codes Mental representations of some type of information or stimulus.

memory consolidation The creation and binding together of neural codes that allow information to be transferred from working memory into long-term memory.

menstrual synchrony The tendency for some women who live together to become more similar to one another in the timing of their menstrual cycles over time.

mental representations Cognitive representations of the world, including images, ideas, concepts, and principles, that are the foundations of thinking and problem solving.

mental set The tendency to stick to problem-solving strategies or solutions that have worked in the past.

mere exposure effect The tendency to evaluate a stimulus more favorably after repeated exposure to it.

meta-analysis A statistical procedure for combining the results of different studies that examine the same topic.

metabolism The rate of energy expenditure by the body.

method of loci A memory aid in which pieces of information (e.g., items in a list) are each associated with a mental image of a different physical location.

midbrain Brain structures above the hindbrain that are involved in sensory and motor functions and in attention and states of consciousness.

mind-body dualism The philosophical position that the mind is a nonphysical entity that is not subject to physical laws and therefore cannot be reduced to physical processes; body and mind are separate entities.

Minnesota Multiphasic Personality Inventory (MMPI-2) A widely used personality test whose items were developed using the empirical approach of comparing various kinds of psychiatric patients with a nonpsychiatric sample.

misinformation effect The distortion of a memory by misleading postevent information.

mnemonic device A strategy or technique that aids memory.

mnemonist (memorist) A person who displays extraordinary memory skills.

mode A statistic that represents the most frequently occurring score in a distribution of data.

monism The philosophical position that mental events are reducible to physical events in the brain, so that mind and body are one and the same.

monocular depth cues Depth cues that require only one eye; include linear perspective, decreasing size, height in the horizontal plane, texture, clarity, light and shadow, motion parallax, and interposition.

mood disorders Psychological disorders whose core conditions involve maladaptive mood states, such as depression or mania.

mood-congruent recall The tendency to recall information or events that are congruent with our current mood.

morpheme The smallest unit of meaning in a given language; English morphemes include whole words, prefixes, and suffixes. There are over 100,000 English morphemes.

motivation A process that influences the direction, persistence, and vigor of goal-directed behavior.

motivational interviewing A treatment approach that avoids confrontation and leads clients to their own realization of a problem and increases their motivation to change.

motor cortex The cortical area in the rear portion of the frontal lobes that controls voluntary movements on the opposite sides of the body.

motor neurons Specialized neurons that carry neural messages from the brain and spinal cord to the muscles and glands.

motoric thought Mental representations of motor movements, such as throwing an object.

multimodal treatments Substance-abuse interventions that combine a number of treatments, such as aversion therapy and coping skills training.

myelin sheath A fatty insulating substance on the axon of some neurons that increases the speed of neural transmission.

N

narcolepsy A sleep disorder that involves extreme daytime sleepiness and sudden, uncontrollable sleep attacks during waking hours.

natural selection The evolutionary process through which characteristics that increase the likelihood of survival and reproduction are preserved in the gene pool and thereby become more common in a species over time.

naturalistic observation A method in which the researcher observes behavior in a natural setting and tries to avoid influencing the participants being observed.

need for achievement The desire to accomplish tasks and attain standards of excellence.

need for positive regard In Rogers's personality theory, an innate need to be positively evaluated by significant others, which enhances survival potential and need satisfaction.

need for positive self-regard In Rogers's personality theory, the psychological need to feel positively about oneself that underlies self-enhancement behaviors.

negative correlation As scores on one variable change, scores on a second variable tend to change in the opposite direction.

negative reinforcement A response is strengthened by the subsequent removal of a noxious stimulus.

negative symptoms Schizophrenic symptoms that reflect a lack of normal reactions, such as emotions, speech, or social behaviors.

neglectful parents Caregivers who provide neither warmth nor rules or guidance.

neoanalytic theorists Former followers of Freud, such as Adler and Jung, who developed their own psychodynamic theories that generally deemphasized psychosexual factors in favor of social ones and gave increased emphasis to ego functioning.

NEO-PI An objective personality test that measures the Big Five personality factors.

nerve deafness Hearing loss caused by damage to the cochlear receptor cells or to the auditory nerve.

neural network A model in which each concept stored in memory is represented by a unique pattern of distributed and simultaneously activated nodes that process information in parallel; also known as a *parallel distributed processing model*.

neural plasticity The ability of neurons to modify their structure and function in response to experiential factors or injury.

neural stem cells Immature "uncommitted" cells that can mature into any type of neuron or glial cell needed by the brain.

neuromodulators Neurotransmitter substances that are released by neurons and circulate within the nervous system to affect the sensitivity of many neurons to their natural transmitter substances.

neurons Nerve cells that constitute the basic building blocks of the nervous system.

neurotic anxiety In psychoanalytic theory, a state of anxiety that arises when impulses from the id threaten to break through into behavior.

neurotransmitters Chemical substances that are released from the axons of one neuron, travel across the synaptic space, and bind to specially keyed receptors in another neuron, where they produce a chemical reaction that is either excitatory or inhibitory.

night terrors A disorder in which a sleeper—often feeling a strong sense of dread or danger—becomes aroused to a near panic state; the sleeper may suddenly sit up, let out a blood-curdling scream, and thrash about or flee to another room, as if trying to escape.

norm of reciprocity The tendency to respond in kind when other people treat us well.

normal curve A symmetrical bell-shaped curve that represents a theoretical distribution of scores in the population.

normal distribution A frequency distribution in the shape of a symmetrical or bell-shaped curve that satisfies certain mathematical conditions deduced from the theory of probability.

normative social influence Conformity motivated by gaining social acceptance and avoiding social rejection.

norms (cultural or group) Rules (often unwritten) that specify what behavior is acceptable and expected for members of a particular culture or group.

norms (test) Test scores derived from a relevant sample used to evaluate individuals' scores.

null hypothesis The hypothesis that any observed differences between samples on the variable(s) of interest are due to chance (i.e., in an experiment, the hypothesis that the independent variable had no effect on the dependent variable).

O

object permanence The recognition that an object continues to exist even when it no longer can be seen.

object relations theories The view that people form images or mental representations of themselves and other people as a result of early experiences with caregivers.

observational learning Learning through observing the behavior of a model.

obsession an unwanted and disturbing thought or image that invades consciousness and is very difficult to control.

Oedipus complex The male child experiences erotic feelings toward his mother, desires to possess her sexually, and views his father as a rival.

olfaction The sense of smell.

olfactory bulb A forebrain structure that receives input from the receptors for the sense of smell.

openness The client's willingness to become personally invested in the process of therapy that predicts favorable therapeutic outcomes.

operant conditioning A type of learning in which behavior is modified by its consequences, such as by reinforcement and punishment.

operant discrimination An operant response occurs when a particular antecedent stimulus is present but not when another antecedent stimulus is present.

operant generalization An operant reponse occurs to a new antecedent stimulus that is similar to the original antecedent stimulus.

operational definition Defining a concept or variable in terms of the specific procedures used to produce or measure it.

opiates A category of drugs consisting of opium and drugs derived from it, such as morphine, codeine, and heroin.

oppositional defiant disorder (ODD) A disorder in which children consistently behave in a disobedient, defiant, and hostile manner that interferes with the child's functioning and interpersonal relationships.

optic nerve The bundle of ganglion cell axons that carries information from the visual receptors to the visual area of the thalamus.

organ of Corti Structures embedded in the basilar membrane that contain the hair cell receptors for sound.

overconfidence The pervasive tendency to overestimate one's degree of knowledge and predictive ability.

overlearning Continued rehearsal past the point of initial learning that significantly improves performance on memory tasks.

P

pain disorder A somatoform disorder in which the person's complaints of pain cannot be accounted for in terms of degree of physical damage.

panic disorder An anxiety disorder characterized by unpredictable panic attacks and a pervasive fear that another will occur; may also include a resulting agoraphobia.

paranoid schizophrenia A schizophrenic disorder marked by delusional thinking and suspiciousness.

parasympathetic nervous system The branch of the autonomic nervous system that slows down bodily processes to conserve energy and reduce arousal.

paraventricular nucleus (PVN) A cluster of neurons in the hippocampus packed with receptor sites for transmitters that stimulate or reduce appetite.

partial (intermittent) reinforcement A schedule in which only a portion of correct responses are followed by a reinforcer.

passionate love A form of love that involves intense emotional arousal and yearning for one's partner.

pearson product-moment correlation coefficient A statistic that reflects the direction and strength of the relation between two variables; can range in magnitude from -1.00 to $+1.00$.

perception The process of organizing stimulus input and giving it meaning.

perceptual constancies The ability to recognize stimulus characteristics—size, color, and so on—under varying conditions.

perceptual schemas Internal representations that contain the essential features of an object of perception.

perceptual set A readiness to perceive a stimulus in a particular way based on expectations, motives, emotions, or beliefs.

performance-approach goals Achievement goals that reflect a competitive orientation (i.e., goals that focus on being judged favorably relative to other people).

performance-avoidance goals Achievement goals that focus on the avoidance of being judged negatively.

peripheral nervous system All of the neurons that connect the central nervous system with the sensory receptors, the muscles, and the glands.

peripheral route to persuasion Occurs when people do not scrutinize a message but are influenced mostly by other factors such as a speaker's attractiveness or a message's emotional appeal.

personal unconscious According to Jung, those aspects of the unconscious that arise from the individual's life experiences.

personality Those biologically and environmentally determined characteristics within the person that account for distinctive and relatively enduring patterns of thinking, feeling, and acting.

personality disorders Stable, inflexible, and maladaptive ways of thinking, feeling, and acting.

personality traits Relatively stable cognitive, emotional, and behavioral characteristics that help establish people's individual identities.

phenomenology A philosophical approach that focuses on immediate subjective experience.

phenotype The observable characteristics produced by one's genetic endowment.

pheromones Chemical signals found in natural body scents.

phobias Strong and irrational fears of particular objects or circumstances.

phoneme The smallest unit of sound in a language; the vowel and consonant sounds that are recognized in any given language. English has 45 phonemes.

photopigments Protein molecules within the rods and cones whose chemical reactions when absorbing light result in the generation of nerve impulses.

physiological toughness A protective stress hormone pattern involving (1) a low resting level of cortisol and low levels of cortisol secretion in response to stressors and (2) a low resting level of catecholamines but a quick and strong catecholomine response when the stressor occurs, followed by a quick decline in catecholamine secretion and arousal when the stressor is over.

place theory of pitch perception States that sound frequencies are coded in terms of the portion of the basilar membrane where the fluid wave in the cochlea peaks; this theory accounts for perception of frequencies above 4,000 hertz.

placebo An inactive or inert substance.

placebo control group A control group that receives an intervention that is assumed to have no therapeutic value.

placebo effect A change in behavior that occurs because of the expectation or belief that one is receiving a treatment.

pleasure principle The drive for instant need gratification that is characteristic of the id.

polygenic transmission A number of genes working together to create a particular phenotypic characteristic.

polygraph A research and clinical instrument that measures a wide array of physiological responses.

pons A brain stem structure having sensory and motor tracts whose functions are involved in sleep and dreaming.

population In a survey, the entire set of individuals about whom we wish to draw a conclusion.

positive correlation As scores on one variable change, scores on a second variable tend to change in the same direction.

positive psychology movement A view that emphasizes the study of human strengths, fulfillment, and optimal living.

positive reinforcement A response is strengthened by the subsequent presentation of a stimulus.

positive symptoms Schizophrenic symptoms such as delusions, hallucinations, and disordered speech and thinking.

positron emission tomography (PET) scan A procedure that provides a visual display of the absorption of a radioactive substance by neurons, indicating how actively they are involved as the brain performs a task.

postconventional moral reasoning According to Kohlberg, the stage at which moral judgments are based on a system of internalized, well-thought-out moral principles.

posttraumatic stress disorder (PTSD) A pattern of distressing symptoms, such as flashbacks, nightmares, avoidance, and anxiety responses that recur after a traumatic experience.

preconventional moral reasoning According the Kohlberg, the stage at which moral judgments are based on anticipated punishments or rewards.

predictive validity The ability of a test to predict future outcomes (e.g., academic performance) that are influenced by the characteristic measured by the test (e.g., intelligence).

prefrontal cortex The area of the frontal lobe just behind the eyes and forehead that is involved in the executive functions of planning, self-awareness, and responsibility.

prejudice A negative attitude toward people based on their membership in a group.

preoperational stage In Piaget's theory, the stage of cognitive development in which children represent the world symbolically through words and mental images but do not yet understand basic mental operations or rules.

preparedness The notion that through evolution, animals have become biologically predisposed to learn some associations more readily than other associations.

primacy effect (impression formation) Our tendency to attach more importance to the initial information that we learn about a person.

primary appraisal The initial appraisal of a situation as benign, irrelevant, or threatening; a perception of the severity of demands.

primary reinforcer A positive reinforcer that satisfies a biological need, such as food or water.

priming The activation of one concept (or one unit of information) by another.

proactive interference Occurs when material learned in the past interferes with the recall of newer material.

problem-focused coping Coping strategies that involve direct attempts to confront and master a stressful situation.

problem-solving dream models The view that dreams can help us find creative solutions to our problems and conflicts because they are not constrained by reality.

problem-solving schemas Step-by-step scripts for selecting information and solving specialized classes of problems.

procedural (nondeclarative) memory Memory that is reflected in learned skills and actions.

projective tests Tests, such as the Rorschach and the Thematic Apperception Test, that present ambiguous stimuli to the subject; the responses are assumed to be based on a projection of internal characteristics of the person onto the stimuli.

proposition A statement that expresses an idea in subject-predicate form.

propositional thought A form of linguistically based thought that expresses a statement in subject-predicate thought.

prospective memory Remembering to perform an activity in the future.

protective factors Environmental or personal resources that help people fare better in the face of stress.

prototype The most typical and familiar member of a class that defines a concept.

proximodistal principle The tendency for physical development to begin along the innermost parts of the body and continue toward the outermost parts.

psychoactive drugs Chemicals that produce alterations in consciousness, emotion, and behavior.

psychoanalysis A psychological theory, developed by Freud, that emphasizes internal and primarily unconscious psychological causes of behavior.

psychodynamic behavior therapy An integration of psychoanalysis and behavior therapy.

psychodynamic perspective A psychological perspective that focuses on how personality processes—including unconscious impulses, defenses, and conflicts—influence behavior.

psychogenic amnesia An extensive but selective memory loss that occurs after a traumatic event.

psychogenic fugue A dissociative phenomenon in which a person loses all sense of personal identity and may wander to another place and establish a new identity.

psychological test A method for measuring individual differences related to some psychological construct, based on a sample of relevant behavior obtained under standardized conditions.

psychology The scientific study of behavior and the mind.

psychometrics The study of statistical properties of psychological tests; the psychometric approach to intelligence focuses on the number and nature of abilities that define intelligence.

psychophysics The study of relations between the physical characteristics of stimuli and the sensory experiences they evoke.

psychosexual stages Stages of development in which psychic energy is focused on certain body parts. The major childhood stages are the oral, anal, and phallic stages; experiences during these stages are assumed to shape personality development.

psychosocial stages A sequence of eight developmental stages proposed by Erikson, each of which involves a different "crisis" (i.e., conflict) over how we view ourselves in relation to other people and the world.

psychosurgery Surgical procedures, such as lobotomy or cingulotomy, in which brain tissue involved in a behavior disorder is removed or destroyed.

puberty A period of rapid biological maturation in which the person becomes capable of sexual reproduction.

punishment A response is weakened by an outcome that follows it.

R

random assignment A procedure in which each participant has an equal likelihood of being assigned to any one group within an experiment.

random sampling In survey research, a method of choosing a sample in which each member of the population has an equal probability of being included in the sample.

randomized clinical trial A research design that involves the random assignment of clients having specific problems to an experimental (therapy) group or to a control condition so as to draw sound causal conclusions about the therapy's efficacy.

range A statistic that represents the difference between the highest and the lowest score in a distribution.

rational-theoretical approach An approach to test construction in which test items are made up on the basis of a theorist's conception of a construct.

reaction range The genetically influenced limits within which environmental factors can exert their effects on an organism.

realistic conflict theory Maintains that competition for limited resources fosters prejudice.

reality principle The ego's tendency to take reality factors into account and to act in a rational fashion in need satisfaction.

receptor sites Protein molecules on neurons' dendrites or soma that are specially shaped to accommodate a specific neurotransmitter molecule.

reciprocal determinism Bandura's model of two-way causal relations between the person, behavior, and the environment.

recombinant DNA procedures Gene-splicing procedures that can be used to produce new life forms, such as bacteria that can produce scarce chemical materials like human growth hormone.

reflexes Automatic, inborn behaviors triggered by specific stimuli.

regression A psychoanalytic defense mechanism in which a person retreats to an earlier stage of development in response to stress.

reinforcement A response is strengthened by an outcome that follows it.

relapse prevention A treatment approach designed to teach coping skills, increase self-efficacy, and counter the abstinence violation effect thus reducing the likelihood of relapse.

reliability In psychological testing, the consistency with which a measure assesses a given characteristic or different observers agree on a given score.

REM sleep A recurring sleep stage characterized by rapid eye movements, increased physiological arousal, paralysis of the voluntary muscles, and a high rate of dreaming.

REM sleep behavior disorder (RBD) A sleep disorder in which the loss of muscle tone that causes normal REM-sleep paralysis is absent, thereby enabling sleepers to move about—sometimes violently—and seemingly "act out" their dreams.

remote behavior sampling A method of collecting samples of behavior from respondents as they live their daily lives.

replication The process of repeating a study to determine whether the original findings can be duplicated.

representative sample A sample that accurately reflects the important characteristics of the population.

representativeness heuristic A rule of thumb in estimating the probability that an object or event belongs to a certain category based on the extent to which it represents a prototype of that category.

repression The basic defense mechanism that actively keeps anxiety-arousing material in the unconscious.

resistance Largely unconscious maneuvers that protect clients from dealing with anxiety-arousing material in therapy.

response cost (punishment by removal) A type of punishment in which an operant response is weakened by the subsequent removal of a stimulus that was not the cause of the original response (e.g., TV privileges are taken away from a child who is misbehaving in order to gain attention).

response prevention The prevention of escape or avoidance responses during exposure to an anxiety-arousing conditioned stimulus so that extinction can occur.

resting potential The voltage differential between the inside and outside of a neuron (about −70 mv) caused by the unequal distribution of ions inside the neuron's membrane and outside in the fluid surrounding the neuron when the neuron is at rest.

restoration model The theory that sleep recharges our run-down bodies and allows us to recover from physical and mental fatigue.

reticular formation A structure extending from the hindbrain into the lower forebrain that plays a central role in consciousness and attention, in part by alerting and activating higher brain centers (ascending portion) and by selectively blocking some inputs to higher regions in the brain (descending portion).

retina The light-sensitive back surface of the eye that contains the visual receptors.

retrieval The process of accessing information in long-term memory.

retrieval cue Any stimulus, whether internal or external, that triggers the activation of information stored in long-term memory.

retroactive interference Occurs when newly acquired information interferes with the ability to recall information learned at an earlier time.

retrograde amnesia Memory loss for events that occurred prior to the onset of amnesia.

reuptake The process whereby transmitter substances are taken back into the presynaptic neuron so that they do not continue to stimulate postsynaptic neurons.

rods Visual receptors that function under low levels of illumination and do not give rise to color sensations.

S

sample In a survey, a subset of individuals drawn from the population.

scatterplot A graph commonly used to examine correlational data; each pair of scores on variable X and variable Y is plotted as a single point.

schema A "mental framework"; an organized pattern of thought about some aspect of the world, such as a class of people, events, situations, or objects.

schizophrenia A psychotic disorder involving serious impairments of attention, thought, language, emotion, and behavior.

seasonal affective disorder (SAD) A disorder in which depressive symptoms appear or worsen during certain seasons of the year (most typically, fall and winter) and then improve during the other seasons.

secondary appraisal One's judgment of the adequacy of personal resources needed to cope with a stressor.

secondary (conditioned) reinforcer A stimulus that acquires reinforcing qualities by being associated with a primary reinforcer.

seeking social support Turning to others for assistance or emotional support in times of stress.

self In Rogers's theory, an organized, consistent set of perceptions and beliefs about oneself.

self-actualization In humanistic theories, an inborn tendency to strive toward the realization of one's full potential.

self-consistency An absence of conflict among self-perceptions.

self-efficacy The conviction that we can perform the behaviors necessary to produce a desired outcome.

self-enhancement Processes whereby one enhances positive self-regard.

self-esteem How positively or negatively we feel about ourselves.

self-fulfilling prophecy Occurs when people's erroneous expectations lead them to act toward others in a way that brings about the expected behaviors, thereby confirming the original impression.

self-instructional training A cognitive coping approach of giving adaptive self-instructions to oneself at crucial phases of the coping process.

self-monitoring A personality trait that reflects people's tendencies to regulate their social behavior in accord with situational cues, as opposed to internal values, attitudes, and needs.

self-perception theory Maintains that we make inferences about our own attitudes by observing how we behave.

self-reinforcement processes Self-administered rewards and punishments that are contingent on meeting certain standards for behavior that are an important basis for self-regulation of behavior.

self-relatedness A client's ability to be flexible to change, to listen carefully to the therapist, and to constructively use what is learned in therapy.

self-serving bias The tendency to make relatively more personal attributions for success and situational attributions for failures.

self-verification The tendency to try to verify or validate one's existing self-concept (i.e., to satisfy congruence needs).

semantic memory General factual knowledge about the world and language, including memory for words and concepts.

semantics The linguistic rules for connecting symbols in language to what they represent.

sensation The process by which stimuli are detected, transduced into nerve impulses, and sent to the brain.

sensitive period An optimal age range for certain experiences, but if those experiences occur at another time, normal development will still be possible.

sensorimotor stage In Piaget's theory, the stage of cognitive development in which children understand their world primarily through sensory experiences and physical (motor) interactions with objects.

sensory adaptation Diminishing sensitivity to an unchanging stimulus with the passage of time as sensory neurons habituate to the stimulation.

sensory memory Memory processes that retain incoming sensory information just long enough for it to be recognized.

sensory neurons Specialized neurons that carry messages from the sense organs to the spinal cord and brain.

sensory prosthetic device A device for providing sensory input that can, to some extent, substitute for what cannot be supplied by the person's own sensory receptors.

separation anxiety Distress experienced by infants when they are separated from a primary caregiver, peaking between ages 12 and 16 months and disappearing between ages 2 and 3 years.

sequential design A research approach that involves repeatedly testing several age cohorts as they grow older.

serial position effect The finding that recall is influenced by a word's position in a series of items.

set point A biologically determined standard around which body weight (or more specifically, our fat mass) is regulated.

sex-typing Treating other people differently based on whether they are female or male.

sexual dysfunction Chronic, impaired sexual functioning that distresses a person.

sexual orientation A person's emotional and erotic preference for partners of a particular sex.

sexual response cycle A physiological response to sexual stimulation that involves stages of excitement, plateau, orgasm, and resolution.

sexual strategies theory Maintains that sex differences in mating strategies and mating preferences reflect inherited biological predispositions that have been shaped in women and men over the course of evolution.

shaping An operant conditioning procedure in which reinforcement begins with a behavior that the organism can already perform and then is made contingent upon behaviors that increasingly approximate the final desired behavior.

short-term memory A memory store that temporarily holds a limited amount of information.

signal detection theory A theory that assumes that stimulus detection is not based on a fixed absolute threshold but rather is affected by rewards, punishments, expectations, and motivational factors.

situation-focused intervention Prevention efforts that focus on altering environmental conditions that are known to promote the development of psychological disorders.

Skinner box An experimental chamber in which animals learn to perform operant responses, such as pressing a bar or pecking, so that the learning process can be studied.

sleep apnea A disorder characterized by a repeated cycle in which the sleeper stops breathing, momentarily awakens gasping for air, and then returns to sleep.

slow-wave sleep Stages 3 and 4 of sleep, in which the EEG pattern shows large, slow brain waves called delta waves.

social clock A set of cultural norms concerning the optimal age range during which work, marriage, parenthood, and other major life experiences should occur.

social comparison The act of comparing one's personal attributes, abilities, and opinions with those of other people.

social compensation Working harder when in a group than when alone to compensate for other members' lower output.

social constructivism The view that people construct their reality and beliefs through their cognitions.

social exchange theory A theory proposing that a social relationship can best be described in terms of exchanges of rewards and costs between the two partners.

social facilitation An increased tendency to perform one's dominant response in the mere presence of others.

social identity theory Maintains that prejudice stems from a need to enhance our self-esteem.

social loafing The tendency for people to expend less individual effort when working collectively in a group than when working alone.

social norms Shared expectations about how people should think, feel, and behave.

social penetration theory Maintains that as a relationship deepens, exchanges (including self-disclosure) become broader and more intimate.

social phobia An excessive and inappropriate fear of social situations in which a person might be evaluated and possibly embarrassed.

social role A set of norms that characterizes how people in a given social position (e.g., "the college student," "the police officer") ought to behave.

social skills training A technique in which a client learns more effective social behaviors by observing and imitating a skillful model.

social structure theory Maintains that men and women behave differently, such as expressing different mate preferences, because society directs them into different social and economic roles.

social-cognitive theories (of hypnosis) The view that hypnotic experiences occur because people are highly motivated to assume the role of being "hypnotized"; the person develops a readiness to perceive hypnotic experiences as real and involuntary.

social-cognitive theory A cognitive-behavioral approach to personality developed by Bandura and Mischel that emphasizes the role of social learning, cognitive processes, and self-regulation.

socialization The process by which culture is transmitted to new members and internalized by them.

sociocultural perspective A view that emphasizes the role of culture and the social environment in understanding commonalities and differences in human behavior.

somatic nervous system The branch of the peripheral nervous system that provides input from the sensory receptors and output to the voluntary muscles of the body.

somatic relaxation training A means of voluntarily reducing or preventing high arousal using muscle relaxation.

somatic sensory cortex Cortical strips in the front portions of the parietal lobes that receive sensory input from various regions of the body.

somatoform disorder A disorder in which a person complains of bodily symptoms that cannot be accounted for in terms of actual physical damage or dysfunction.

source confusion The tendency to recall something or recognize it as familiar but to forget where it was encountered.

specific phobia An irrational and excessive fear of specific objects or situations that pose little or no actual threat.

specificity question The ultimate question of psychotherapy research: "Which types of therapy administered by which kinds of therapists to which kinds of clients having which kinds of problems produce which kinds of effects?"

spontaneous recovery In classical conditioning, the reappearance of a previously extinguished conditioned response after a period of time has passed following extinction.

spontaneous remission Improvements in symptoms in the absence of any therapy.

standard deviation (SD) A statistic that represents the square root of the variance of a distribution.

standardization In psychological testing, refers to (1) creating a standard set of procedures for administering a test or making observations and (2) deriving norms with which an individual's performance can be compared.

state-dependent memory The enhanced ability to retrieve information when our internal state at the time of retrieval matches our original state during learning.

statistical significance In research, a term that means it is unlikely that a particular finding occurred by chance alone. Psychologists typically consider a result to be statistically significant only if it could have occurred by chance alone less than 5 times in 100.

stereotype A generalized belief about a group or category of people.

stereotype threat The anxiety created by the perceived possibility that one's behavior or performance will confirm a negative stereotype about one's group.

stimulants Drugs that stimulate neural activity, resulting in a state of excitement or aroused euphoria.

stimulus control The occurrence of an operant behavior in response to a discriminative stimulus.

stimulus generalization A conditioned response occurs to stimuli other than the original conditioned stimulus, based on the similarity of these stimuli to the conditioned stimulus.

stimulus hierarchy In systematic desensitization, the creation of a series of anxiety-arousing stimuli that are ranked in terms of the amount of anxiety they evoke.

storage The retention of information in memory over time.

strange situation A standardized procedure used to determine the type of emotional attachment between an infant and a caregiver.

stranger anxiety Distress over contact with strangers that typically develops in the first year of infancy and dissipates in the second year.

stress A term variously used to refer to (1) situations that place strong demands on an organism, (2) the cognitive, physiological, and behavioral responses to such situations, and (3) the ongoing transaction between individuals and demanding situations.

stress response The pattern of cognitive, physiological, and behavioral reactions to demands that exceed a person's resources.

stress-induced analgesia A reduction in pain sensitivity that occurs when endorphins are released under stressful conditions.

stressors Situations that place demands on organisms that tax or exceed their resources.

stroboscopic movement The illusory movement produced when adjacent lights are illuminated and extinguished at specific time intervals.

structuralism An early German school of psychology established by Wundt that attempted to study the structure of the mind by breaking it down into its basic components, which were believed to be sensations.

structured interview A standardized interview protocol in which specific questions are asked.

subgoal analysis A problem-solving heuristic in which people attack a large problem by formulating subgoals, or intermediate steps toward a solution.

subjective well-being Happiness; the overall degree of satisfaction with one's life.

sublimation The channeling of unacceptable impulses into socially accepted behaviors, as when aggressive drives are expressed in violent sports.

subliminal stimuli Weak stimuli below the perceptual threshold that are not consciously perceived.

substance dependence A maladaptive pattern of substance use that causes a person significant distress or substantially impairs that person's life; substance dependence is diagnosed as occurring "with physiological dependence" if drug tolerance or withdrawal symptoms have developed.

suicide The willful taking of one's own life.

superego In psychonalysis, the moral arm of the personality that internalizes the standards and values of society and serves as the person's conscience.

suprachiasmatic nuclei (SCN) The brain's master "biological clock," located in the hypothalamus, that regulates most circadian rhythms.

surface structure A linguistic term for the words and organization of a spoken or written sentence. Two sentences may have quite different surface structure but still mean the same thing.

survey research A method using questionnaires or interviews to obtain information about many people.

sympathetic nervous system The branch of the autonomic nervous system that has an arousal function on the body's internal organs, speeding up bodily processes and mobilizing the body.

synapse The biochemically-mediated transmission of nerve impulses from one neuron to another.

synaptic vesicles Chambers within the axon that contains the neurotransmitter substance.

synesthesia A condition in which stimuli are experienced not only in the normal sensory modality but in others as well.

syntax The rules for the combination of symbols within a given language.

systematic desensitization An attempt to eliminate anxiety using counterconditioning, in which a new response that is compatible with anxiety is conditioned to the anxiety-arousing conditioned stimulus.

T

tardive dyskinesia An irreversible motor disorder that can occur as a side effect of certain antipsychotic drugs.

taste buds The receptors for taste in the tongue and in the roof and back of the mouth that are sensitive to the qualities of sweet, sour, salty, and bitter.

temperament A biologically based general style of reacting emotionally and behaviorally to the environment.

teratogens Environmental (nongenetic) agents that cause abnormal prenatal development.

test-retest reliability The extent to which scores on a presumably stable characteristic are consistent over time.

thalamus A major sensory integration and relay center in the forebrain, sometimes referred to as the brain's sensory switchboard.

THC (tetrahydrocannabinol) The major active ingredient in marijuana.

theory A set of formal statements that explains how and why certain events or phenomena are related to one another.

theory of cognitive dissonance States that people strive to maintain consistency in their beliefs and actions and that inconsistency creates dissonance (i.e., unpleasant arousal) that motivates people to restore balance by changing their cognitions.

theory of mind A person's beliefs about the "mind" and ability to understand other people's mental states.

theory of planned behavior Maintains that our intention to engage in a behavior is strongest when we have a positive attitude toward that behavior, when subjective norms (our perceptions of what other people think we should do) support our attitudes, and when we believe that the behavior is under our control.

threat In Roger's theory, any experience we have that is inconsistent with our self-concept, including our perceptions of our own behavior.

tip-of-the-tongue (TOT) state The experience of being unable to recall something but feeling that you are on the verge of remembering it.

token economy A procedure in which desirable behaviors are reinforced with tokens or points that can later be redeemed for other reinforcers.

tolerance A condition in which increasingly larger doses of a drug are required to produce the same level of bodily responses; caused by the body's compensatory responses, which counter the effects of the drug.

top-down processing Perceptual processing in which existing knowledge, concepts, ideas, or expectations are applied in order to make sense of incoming stimulation.

transduction The conversion of one form of energy into another; in sensation, the process whereby physical stimuli are translated into nerve impulses.

transference The psychoanalytic phenomenon in which a client responds irrationally to the analyst as if the latter were an important person from the client's past who plays a significant role in the client's dynamics.

transtheoretical model A model of behavior change that includes the phases of precontemplation, contemplation, preparation, action, maintenance, and termination.

trauma-dissociation theory A theory that accounts for the development of dissociative identity disorder in terms of dissociation as a defense against severe childhood abuse or trauma.

triangular theory of love Maintains that various types of love result from different combinations of three core factors: intimacy, commitment, and passion.

triarchic theory of intelligence Sternberg's theory of intelligence that distinguishes between analytical, practical, and creative forms of mental ability.

twin study A research method in behavior genetics in which identical (monozygotic) and fraternal (dizygotic) twins are compared on some characteristic; this method is particularly informative if the twins have been raised in different environments.

two-factor theory of avoidance learning Maintains that avoidance learning first involves the classical conditioning of fear, followed by learning operant responses that avoid an anticipated aversive stimulus and thus are reinforced by anxiety reduction.

two-factor theory of emotion Schachter's theory stating that intensity of physiological arousal determines perceived intensity of emotion, whereas appraisal of environmental cues tells us which emotion we are experiencing.

Type A behavior pattern A sense of time urgency, pressured behavior, and hostility that appears to be a risk factor in coronary heart disease.

U

unconditional positive regard A communicated attitude of total and unconditional acceptance of another person that conveys the person's intrinsic worth.

unconditioned response (UCR) A response (usually reflexive or innate) that is elicited by a specific stimulus (the unconditioned stimulus) without prior learning.

unconditioned stimulus (UCS) A stimulus that elicits a particular reflexive or innate response (the unconditioned response) without prior learning.

undifferentiated schizophrenia A residual category of schizophrenia for people who show some of the symptoms of paranoid, disorganized, and catatonic types but not enough to be placed in one of those diagnostic categories.

upward comparison Comparing oneself or one's current situation with more positive alternatives.

V

validity The extent to which a test actually measures what it is supposed to measure; the degree to which a diagnostic system's categories contain the core features of the behavior disorders and permit differentiation among the disorders.

variable Any characteristic of an organism or situation that can vary.

variable-interval (VI) schedule A reinforcement schedule in which reinforcement follows the first correct response that occurs after an average but variable time interval following the last reinforced response.

variable-ratio (VR) schedule A reinforcement schedule in which reinforcement is based on an average but variable number of correct responses.

variance A statistic that measures the average of the squared deviation scores about the mean of a distribution.

vestibular sense The sense of body orientation or equilibrium.

virtual reality (VR) Computer-produced virtual environments that immerse an individual and produce experiences similar to those of a corresponding real environment.

visual acuity The ability to see fine detail.

vulnerability factors Situational or physical factors that increase susceptibility to the negative impact of stressful events.

vulnerability-stress model Explains behavior disorders as resulting from predisposing biological or psychological vulnerability factors that are triggered by a stressor.

W

Weber's law States that to perceive a difference between two stimuli, the stimuli must differ by a constant percentage or ratio.

Wernicke's area An area of the left temporal lobe that is involved in speech comprehension.

wish fulfillment In Freudian theory, the partial or complete satisfaction of a psychological need through dreaming or waking fantasy.

withdrawal The occurrence of compensatory responses after drug use is discontinued, causing the person to experience physiological reactions opposite to those that had been produced by the drug.

working memory A "mental workspace" that temporarily stores information, actively processes it, and supports other cognitive functions.

Y

Young-Helmholtz trichromatic theory The color vision theory stating that there are three types of color receptors in the retina—one for red, one for blue, and one for green—and that combinations of activation of these receptors can produce perception of any hue in the visible spectrum.

Z

zone of proximal development The difference between what a child can do independently and what the child can do with assistance from adults or more advanced peers.

zygote The fertilized egg.

References

Aamodt, M. G. (1991). *Applied industrial/organizational psychology.* Belmont, CA: Wadsworth.

Aaron, S. (1986). *Stage fright.* Chicago: University of Chicago Press.

Abdul-Rahim, H. F., Holmboe-Ottesen, G., Stene, L. C. M., Husseini, A., Giacaman, R., Jervell, J., & Bjertness, E. (2003). Obesity in a rural and an urban Palestinian West Bank population. *International Journal of Obesity, 27,* 140–146.

Abel, T., & Kandel, E. (1998). Positive and negative regulatory mechanisms that mediate long-term memory storage. *Brain Research Reviews, 26,* 360–378.

Abraham, K. (1911). Notes on the psychoanalytic investigation and treatment of manic-depressive insanity and allied conditions. In *Selected papers of Karl Abraham.* New York: Basic Books, 1968.

Abramov, I., & Gordon, J. (1994). Color appearance: On seeing red—or yellow, or green, or blue. *Annual Review of Psychology, 45,* 451–485.

Abramson, L. Y., Seligman, M. E. P., & Teasdale, J. D. (1978). Learned helplessness in humans: Critique and reformulation. *Journal of Abnormal Psychology, 87,* 49–74.

Achter, J., Lubinski, D., & Benbow, C. P. (1996). Multipotentiality among the intellectually gifted: "It was never there and already it's vanishing." *Journal of Counseling Psychology, 43,* 65–76.

Adair, R. K. (1990). *The physics of baseball.* New York: Harper & Row.

Adams, P. R., & Cox, K. J. A. (2002). Synaptic Darwinism and neocortical function. *Neurocomputing, 42,* 197–214.

Adelmann, P. K., & Zajonc, R. B. (1989). Facial efference and the experience of emotion. *Annual Review of Psychology, 40,* 249–280.

Ader, R. (2001). Psychoneuroimmunology. *Current Directions in Psychological Science, 10,* 94–98.

Ader, R., & Cohen, N. (1975). Behaviorally conditioned immunosuppression. *Psychosomatic Medicine, 37,* 333–340.

Ader, R., & Cohen, N. (1982). Behaviorally conditioned immunosuppression and murine systemic lupus erythematosus. *Science, 215*(4539), 1534–1536.

Ader, R., Cohen, N., & Felten, D. (1995). Psychoneuroimmunology: Interactions between the nervous system and the immune system. *Lancet, 345,* 99–103.

Aggleton, J. P. (1993). The contribution of the amygdala to normal and abnormal emotional states. *Trends in Neurosciences, 16,* 328–333.

Agnew, H. W., Jr., Webb, W. B., & Williams, R. L. (1967). Comparison of stage four and 1-REM sleep deprivation. *Perceptual and Motor Skills, 24,* 851–858.

Aguiar, A., & Baillargeon, R. (2002). Developments in young infants' reasoning about occluded objects. *Cognitive Psychology, 45,* 267–336.

Ahadi, S. & Diener, E. (1989). Multiple determinants and effect size. *Journal of Personality and Social Psychology, 56,* 398–406.

Ai, A. K., Peterson, C., & Ubelhor, D. (2002). War-related trauma and symptoms of posttraumatic stress disorder among adult Kosovar refugees. *Journal of Traumatic Stress, 15,* 157–160.

Aiello, R. (Ed.). (1994). *Musical perceptions.* London: Oxford University Press.

Aiken, L. R. (1999). *Psychological testing and assessment.* Needham Heights, MA: Allyn & Bacon.

Ainsworth, M. (1989). Attachments beyond infancy. *American Psychologist, 44,* 709–716.

Ainsworth, M., Blehar, M. C., Waters, E., & Wall, S. (1978). *Patterns of attachment: A psychological study of the strange situation.* Hillsdale, NJ: Erlbaum.

Aitchison, J. (1998). *The articulate mammal: An introduction to psycholinguistics.* Florence, KY: Taylor & Francis/Routledge.

Aitken, S., & Bower T. G. (1982). Intersensory substitution in the blind. *Journal of Experimental Child Psychology, 33,* 309–323.

Ajzen, I. (1991). The theory of planned behavior. *Organizational Behavior and Human Decision Processes, 50,* 179–211.

Akerstedt, T., Kecklund, G., & Hoerte, L. G. (2001). Night driving, season and the risk of highway accidents. *Sleep: Journal of Sleep and Sleep Disorders Research, 24,* 401–406.

Albee, G. W. (1996). Revolutions and counterrevolutions in prevention. *American Psychologist, 51,* 1130–1133.

Albee, G. W. (1997). Speak no evil? *American Psychologist, 52,* 1143–1144.

Alcock, J. (2002). *Animal behavior: An evolutionary approach.* New York: Sinauer.

Aldridge, S. (1998). *The thread of life: The story of genes and genetic engineering.* New York: Cambridge University Press.

Alfieri, T., Ruble, D. N., & Higgins, E. T. (1996). Gender stereotypes during adolescence: Developmental changes and the transition to junior high school. *Developmental Psychology, 32,* 1129–1137.

Allen, M. (1991). Meta-analysis comparing the persuasiveness of one-sided and two-sided messages. *Western Journal of Speech Communication, 55,* 390–404.

Allen, M., D'Alessio, D., & Brezgel, K. (1995). A meta-analysis summarizing the effects of pornography: II. Aggression after exposure. *Human Communication Research, 22,* 258–283.

Allen, M., D'Alessio, D., & Emmers-Sommer, T. M. (2000). Reactions of criminal sexual offenders to pornography: A meta-analytic summary. In M. Roloff (Ed.), *Communication Yearbook 22.* Thousand Oaks, CA: Sage Publications.

Allport, G. W. (1937). *Personality: A psychological interpretation.* New York: Holt, Rinehart & Winston.

Allport, G. W. (1954). *The nature of prejudice.* Reading, MA: Addison-Wesley.

Allport, G. W., & Odbert, H. S. (1936). Trait names: A psycho-lexical study. *Psychological Monographs, 47*(Whole No. 211).

Allport, G. W., & Postman, L. (1947). *The psychology of rumor.* New York: Holt.

Alonso, C., & Coe, C. J. (2001). Disruptions of social relationships accentuate the association between emotional distress and menstrual pain in young women. *Health Psychology, 20,* 411–416.

Altman, I., & Taylor, D. A. (1973). *Social penetration: The development of interpersonal relationships.* New York: Holt, Rinehart & Winston.

Altman, J., & Bayer, S. A. (1996). *Development of the cerebellar system: In relation to its evolution, structure and functions.* Boca Raton, FL: CRC-Press.

Amato, P. R., & Keith, B. (1991). Parental divorce and the well-being of children: A meta-analysis. *Psychological Bulletin, 110,* 26–46.

American Cancer Society. (2000). *Smoking facts and figures.* New York: Author.

American Psychiatric Association. (1990). *The practice of ECT: Recommendations for treatment, training, and privileging.* Washington, DC: American Psychiatric Press.

American Psychiatric Association. (1994). *Diagnostic and statistical manual of mental disorders* (4th ed.). Washington, DC: Author.

American Psychiatric Association. (2000). *DSM-IV text revision.* Washington, DC: Author.

American Psychological Association. (2003). *APA divisions.* http://www.apa.org/about/division.html

American Psychological Association Research Office. (2001). Employment characteristics of

APA members by membership status, 2000 (Table 4). In *2000 APA Directory Survey*. Washington, DC: American Psychological Association.

American Psychological Society. (2003). *History of APS*. Available online: http://www.psychologicalscience.org/about/history.html

Anand, B. K., & Brobeck, J. R. (1951). Hypothalamic control of food intake in rats and cats. *Yale Journal of Biology and Medicine, 24*, 123–140.

Anderson, C. A. (1999). Attributional style, depression, and loneliness: A cross-cultural comparison of American and Chinese students. *Personality and Social Psychology Bulletin, 25*, 482–499.

Anderson, C. A. (2001). Heat and violence. *Current Directions in Psychological Science, 10*, 33–38.

Anderson, C. A., & Bushman, B. J. (2001). Effects of violent video games on aggressive behavior, aggressive cognition, aggressive affect, physiological arousal, and prosocial behavior: A meta-analytic review of the scientific literature. *Psychological Science, 2*, 353–359.

Anderson, C. A., & Bushman, B. J. (2002). Human aggression. *Annual Review of Psychology, 53*, 27–51.

Anderson, E. M., & Lambert, M. J. (1995). Short-term dynamically oriented psychotherapy: A review and meta-analysis. *Clinical Psychology Review, 15*, 503–514.

Anderson, J. R. (1980). *Cognitive psychology and its implications*. San Francisco: W. H. Freeman.

Anderson, J. R. (1985). *Cognitive psychology and its implications* (2nd ed.). New York: Freeman.

Anderson, J. R. (1991). The adaptive nature of human categorization. *Psychological Review, 98*, 409–429.

Anderson, M. C., & Neely, J. H. (1996). Interference and inhibition in memory retrieval. In E. L. Bjork & R. A. Bjork (Eds.), *Memory. Handbook of perception and cognition* (2nd ed.). San Diego: Academic Press.

Anderson, N. D., & Craik, F. I. M. (2000). Memory in the aging brain. In E. Tulving & F. I. M. Craik (Eds.), *The Oxford handbook of memory*. New York: Oxford University Press.

Anderson, S. R., & Lightfoot, D. W. (1999). The human language faculty as an organ. *Annual Review of Physiology, 62*, 697–722.

Andreasen, N. C., Arndt, S., Swayze, V., Cizadlo, T., et al. (1994). Thalamic abnormalities in schizophrenia visualized through magnetic resonance image averaging. *Science, 266*, 294–298.

Andrews, F. M. (1991). Stability and change in levels and structure of subjective well-being: USA 1972 and 1988. *Social Indicators Research, 25*, 1–30.

Ankney, C. D. (1992). Sex differences in relative brain size: The mismeasure of women, too? *Intelligence, 16*, 329–336.

Anthony, J. C., Warner, L. A., & Kessler, R. C. (1997). Comparative epidemiology of dependence on tobacco, alcohol, controlled substances, and inhalants: Basic findings from the National Comorbidity Survey. In G. A. Marlatt & G. R. VandenBos (Eds.), *Addictive behaviors: Readings on etiology, prevention and treatment*. Washington, DC: American Psychological Association.

Anton, R. F. (2001). Pharmacologic approaches to the management of alcoholism. *Journal of Clinical Psychiatry, 62*, 11–17.

Antonov, I., Antonova, I., Kandel, E. R., & Hawkins, R. D. (2001). The contribution of activity dependent synaptic plasticity to classical conditioning in *Aplysia*. *Journal of Neuroscience, 21*, 6413–6422.

Antrobus, J. (1991). Dreaming: Cognitive processes during cortical activation and high afferent thresholds. *Psychological Review, 98*, 96–121.

APA Monitor (1997, December). *APA Monitor, 28*(12). Author.

Aponte, H., & Hoffman, L. (1973). The open door. A structural approach to a family with an anorectic child. *Family Process, 12*, 1–44.

Arendt, J., Skene, D. J., Middleton, B., Lockley, S. W., & Deacon, S. (1997). Efficacy of melatonin treatment in jet lag, shift work, and blindness. *Journal of Biological Rhythms, 12*, 604–617.

Argyle, M. (1999). Causes and correlates of happiness. In D. Kahneman, E. Diener, & N. Schwarz (Eds.), *Well-being: The foundations of hedonic psychology*. New York: Russell Sage Foundation.

Ariznavarreta, C., Cardinali, D. P., Villanua, M. A., Granados, B., Martin, M., Chiesa, J. J., et al. (2002). Circadian rhythms in airline pilots submitted to long-haul transmeridian flights. *Aviation, Space, and Environmental Medicine, 73*, 445–455.

Arnett, J. J. (1999). Adolescent storm and stress, reconsidered. *American Psychologist, 54*, 317–326.

Arnett, P. A. (1997). Autonomic responsivity in psychopaths: A critical review and theoretical proposal. *Clinical Psychology Review, 17*, 903–936.

Aron, A., & Westbay, L. (1996). Dimensions of the prototype of love. *Journal of Personality and Social Psychology, 70*, 535–551.

Aron, L. (1996). *A meeting of minds: Mutuality in psychoanalysis*. Hillsdale, NJ: Analytic Press.

Aronson, E. (1997). *The jigsaw classroom: Building cooperation in the classroom*. Reading, MA: Good Year Books.

Aronson, E., Stephan, C., Sikes, J., Blaney, N., & Snopp, M. (1978). *The jigsaw classroom*. Beverly Hills, CA: Sage Publications.

Aronson, J., Lustina, M. J., Good, C., Keough, K., Steele, C. M., & Brown, J. (1999). When White men can't do math: Necessary and sufficient factors in stereotype threat. *Journal of Experimental Social Psychology, 35*, 29–46.

Arrigo, J. M., & Pezdek, K. (1997). Lessons from the study of psychogenic amnesia. *Current Directions in Psychological Science, 6*, 148–152.

Asch, S. E. (1946). Forming impressions of personality. *Journal of Abnormal and Social Psychology, 41*, 258–290.

Asch, S. E. (1951). Effects of group pressure upon the modification and distortion of judgment. In H. Guetzkow (Ed.), *Groups, leadership, and men*. Pittsburgh: Carnegie Press.

Asch, S. E. (1956). Studies of independence and conformity: A minority of one against a unanimous majority. *Psychological Monographs, 70*, 416.

Asimov, I. (1997). *Isaac Asimov's book of facts*. New York: Random House/Wings Books.

Aspinwall, L. G., & Staudinger, U. M. (Eds.). (2003). *A psychology of human strengths: Fundamental questions and future directions for a positive psychology*. Washington, DC: American Psychological Association.

Assanand, S. P., John, P. J., & Lehman, D. R. (1998). Teaching theories of hunger and eating: Overcoming students' misconceptions. *Teaching of Psychology, 25*, 44–46.

Atkinson, J. W. (1964). *An introduction to motivation*. Princeton, NJ: Van Nostrand.

Atkinson, J. W. (Ed.). (1958). *Motives in fantasy, action, and society*. Princeton, NJ: Van Nostrand.

Atkinson, J. W., & Birch, D. (1978). *An introduction to motivation*. New York: Van Nostrand.

Atkinson, R. C., & Shiffrin, R. M. (1968). Human memory: A proposed system and its control processes. In K. W. Spence & J. T. Spence (Eds.), *Advances in the psychology of learning and motivation: Research and theory* (Vol. 2). New York: Academic Press.

Auerbach, S. M. (1989). Stress management and coping research in the health care setting: An overview and methodological commentary. *Journal of Consulting and Clinical Psychology, 57*, 388–395.

Austin, M., & Leader, L. (2000). Maternal stress and obstetric and infant outcomes: Epidemiological findings and neuroendocrine mechanisms. *Australian and New Zealand Journal of Obstetrics and Gynaecology, 40*, 331–337.

Ayllon, T., & Azrin, N. H. (1965). The measurement and reinforcement of behavior of psychotics. *Journal of the Experimental Analysis of Behavior, 8*, 357–383.

Ayllon, T., & Azrin, N. H. (1968). *The token economy: A motivational system for therapy and rehabilitation*. New York: Appleton-Century-Crofts.

Ayres, J. J. B. (1998). Fear conditioning and avoidance. In W. T. O'Donohue (Ed.), *Learning and behavior therapy*. Boston: Allyn & Bacon.

Baars, B. J. (1997). In the theatre of consciousness: Global workspace theory, a rigorous scientific theory of consciousness. *Journal of Consciousness Studies, 4*, 292–309.

Bachman, J. G., Johnson, L. D., & O'Malley, P. M. (1987). *Monitoring the future: Questionnaire responses from the nation's high school seniors*. Ann Arbor, MI: Institute for Social Research, University of Michigan.

Backhaus, W. G., Kliegl, R., & Werner, J. S. (Eds.). (1998). *Color vision: Perspectives from different disciplines*. New York: Walter De Gruyter.

Baddeley, A. D. (2002). Is working memory still working? *European Psychologist, 7*, 85–97.

Baddeley, A. D., & Hitch, G. J. (1974). Working memory. In G. H. Bower (Ed.), *The psychology of learning and motivation* (Vol. 8). New York: Academic Press.

Baddeley, A. D., & Hitch, G. J. (2000). Development of working memory: Should the Pascual-Leone and the Baddeley and Hitch models be merged? *Journal of Experimental Child Psychology, 77*, 128–137.

Baehr, E. K. (2001). Circadian phase-delaying effects of nocturnal exercise in older and young adults. *Dissertation Abstracts International: Section B: The Sciences and Engineering, 62* (4-B), 2105.

Bagley, C., & Ramsay, R. (1997). *Suicidal behaviour in adolescents and adults: Research, taxonomy and prevention*. Ashgate, England: Ashgate Publishing.

Bahrick, H. P. (1984). Semantic memory content in permastore: Fifty years of memory for Spanish learned in school. *Journal of Experimental Psychology: General, 113*, 1–29.

Bahrick, H. P., Hall, L. K., & Berger, S. A. (1996). Accuracy and distortion in memory for high school grades. *Psychological Science, 7*, 265–271.

Bailey, J. M., Dunne, M. P., & Martin, N. G. (2000). Genetic and environmental influences on sexual orientation and its correlates in an Australian twin sample. *Journal of Personality and Social Psychology, 78*, 524–536.

Bailey, J. M., & Pillard, R. C. (1991). A genetic study of male sexual orientation. *Archives of General Psychiatry, 48*, 1089–1096.

Bailey, J. M., Pillard, R. C., Neale, M. C., & Agyei, Y. (1993). Heritable factors influence sexual orientation in women. *Archives of General Psychiatry, 50*, 217–223.

Baillargeon, R. (1987). Object permanence in 3 ½- and 4 ½-month-old infants. *Developmental Psychology, 23*, 655–664.

Baldwin, E. (1993). The case for animal research in psychology. *Journal of Social Issues, 49*, 121–131.

Ball, H. L., Hooker, E., & Kelly, P. J. (2000). Parent-infant co-sleeping: Fathers' roles and perspectives. *Infant and Child Development, 9*, 67–74.

Ball, J., & Mosselle, K. (1995). Health risk behaviors of adolescents in Singapore. *Asian Journal of Psychology, 1*, 54–62.

Ballard, C. G. (2002). Advances in the treatment of Alzheimer's disease: Benefits of dual cholinesterase inhibition. *European Neurology, 47*, 64–70.

Ballenger, J. C. (2000). Panic disorder and agoraphobia. In G. Fink (Ed.), *Encyclopedia of stress*. San Diego, CA: Academic Press.

Baltes, P., & Staudinger, U. M. (2000). Wisdom: A metaheuristic (pragmatic) to orchestrate mind and virtue toward excellence. *American Psychologist, 55*, 122–136.

Bandura, A. (1965). Influence of models' reinforcement contingencies on the acquisition of imitated responses. *Journal of Personality and Social Psychology, 1*, 589–595.

Bandura, A. (1969). *Principles of behavior modification*. New York: Holt, Rinehart & Winston.

Bandura, A. (1977). *Social learning theory*. Englewood Cliffs, NJ: Prentice Hall.

Bandura, A. (1986). *Social foundations of thought and action: A social-cognitive theory*. Englewood Cliffs, NJ: Prentice Hall.

Bandura, A. (1989). Social cognitive theory. *Annals of Child Development, 6*, 3–58.

Bandura, A. (1997). *Self-efficacy: The exercise of control*. New York: W. H. Freeman.

Bandura, A. (1999). Social cognitive theory of personality. In D. Cervone & Y. Shoda (Eds.), *The coherence of personality*. New York: Guilford Press.

Bandura, A. (2000). Health promotion from the perspective of social cognitive theory. In P. Norman, C. Abraham, & M. Conner (Eds.), *Understanding and changing health and behaviour*. Reading, England: Harwood.

Bandura, A. (2002). Growing primacy of human agency in adaptation and change in the electronic era. *European Psychologist, 7*, 2–16.

Bandura, A., & Cervone, D. (1983). Self-evaluative and self-efficacy mechanisms governing the motivational effects of goal systems. *Journal of Personality and Social Psychology, 45*, 1017–1028.

Bandura, A., O'Leary, A., Taylor, C., et al. (1987). Perceived self-efficacy and pain control: Opioid and nonopioid mechanisms. *Journal of Personality and Social Psychology, 53*, 563–571.

Barber, J. (1998). The mysterious persistence of hypnotic analgesia. *International Journal of Clinical and Experimental Hypnosis, 46*, 28–43.

Barber, T. X. (1961). Death by suggestion. *Psychosomatic Medicine, 23*, 153–155.

Bardo, M. T. (1998). Neuropharmacological mechanisms of drug reward: Beyond dopamine in the nucleus accumbens. *Critical Reviews in Neurobiology, 12*, 37–67.

Bargh, J. A. (1997). The automaticity of everyday life. In R. S. Wyer, Jr. (Ed.), *The automaticity of everyday life: Advances in social cognition* (Vol. 10). New York: Guilford Press.

Bargh, J. A., & Chartrand, T. L. (1999). The unbearable automaticity of being. *American Psychologist, 54*, 462–479.

Barlow, D. H. (1997). Cognitive-behavioral therapy for panic disorder: Current status. *Journal of Clinical Psychiatry, 58*(Suppl. 2), 32–36.

Barlow, D. H. (2002). *Anxiety and its disorders*. New York: Guilford Press.

Barlow, D. H., Raffa, S. D., & Cohen, E. M. (2002). Psychosocial treatments for panic disorders, phobias, and generalized anxiety disorder. In P. E. Nathan & J. M. Gorman (Eds.), *A guide to treatments that work* (2nd ed.). London: Oxford University Press.

Barlow, D. H., & Rapee, R. M. (1991). *Mastering stress: A lifestyle approach*. Dallas, TX: American Health Publishing.

Barnes, G. E., & Prosen, H. (1985). Parental death and depression. *Journal of Abnormal Psychology, 94*, 64–69.

Barnett, J. E., & Porter, J. E. (1998). The suicidal patient: Clinical and risk management strategies. In L. VandeCreek & S. Knapp (Eds.), *Innovations in clinical practice: A source book* (Vol. 16). Sarasota, FL: Professional Resource Press.

Baron, A., & Perone, M. (2001). Explaining avoidance: Two factors are still better than one. *Journal of the Experimental Analysis of Behavior, 75*, 357–361.

Baron, R. S., Cutrona, C. E., Hicklin, D., Russell, D. W., & Lubaroff, D. M. (1990). Social support and immune responses among spouses of cancer patients. *Journal of Personality and Social Psychology, 59*, 344–352.

Barondes, S. H. (1999). *Mood genes: Hunting for origins of mania and depression*. New York: Oxford University Press.

Barrett, G. V., & Depinet, R. L. (1991). A reconsideration of testing for competence rather than intelligence. *American Psychologist, 46*, 1012–1024.

Barrow, C. J. (2003). *Environmental change and human development: The place of environmental change in human evolution*. New York: Oxford University Press.

Bartholow, B. D., & Anderson, C. A. (2002). Effects of violent video games on aggressive behavior: Potential sex differences. *Journal of Experimental Social Psychology, 38*, 283–290.

Bartlett, F. C. (1932). *Remembering: A study in experimental and social psychology*. New York: Cambridge University Press.

Basedow, H. (1925). *The Australian aboriginal*. Adelaide, Australia: F. W. Preece.

Bastik, T. (1982). *Intuition: How we think and act*. New York: Wiley.

Bates, M. S., Edwards, W. T., & Anderson, K. O. (1993). Ethnocultural influences on variation in chronic pain percpetion. *Pain, 52*, 101–112.

Batson, C. D., Ahmad, N., Lishner, D. A., & Tsang, J. A. (2002). Empathy and altruism. In C. R. Snyder & S. J. Lopez (Eds.), *Handbook of positive psychology*. London: Oxford University Press.

Batson, C. D., Sager, K., Garst, E., & Kang, M. (1997). Is empathy-induced helping due to self-other merging? *Journal of Personality and Social Psychology, 73*, 495–509.

Batson, G. D. (1991). *The altruism question: Toward a social-psychological answer*. Hillsdale, NJ: Erlbaum.

Baum, A. (1994). Disease processes: Behavioral, biological, and environmental interactions in disease processes. In S. J. Blumenthal, K. Matthews, & S. M. Weiss (Eds.), *New research frontiers in behavioral medicine: Proceedings of the national conference*. Washington, DC: NIH Publications.

Baum, A., Krantz, D. S., & Gatchel, R. J. (1997). *An introduction to health psychology* (3rd ed.). Boston: McGraw-Hill.

Baum, A., & Posluszny, D. M. (1999). Health psychology: Mapping biobehavioral contributions to health and illness. *Annual Review of Psychology, 50,* 137–164.

Baumeister, R. F., & Leary, M. R. (1995). The need to belong: Desire for interpersonal attachments as a fundamental human motivation. *Psychological Bulletin, 117,* 497–529.

Baumeister, R. F., & Tice, D. M. (1990). Anxiety and social exclusion. *Journal of Social and Clinical Psychology, 9,* 165–195.

Baumrind, D. (1964). Some thoughts on ethics of research: After reading Milgram's behavioral study of "obedience." *American Psychologist, 19,* 421–423.

Baumrind, D. (1967). Child care practices anteceding three patterns of preschool behavior. *Genetic Psychology Monographs, 75,* 43–88.

Baumrind, D. (1991). Parenting styles and adolescent development. In J. Brooks-Gunn, R. Lerner, & A. C. Petersen (Eds.), *The encyclopedia of adolescence.* New York: Garland.

Baumrind, D., Larzelere, R. E., & Cowan, P. A. (2002). Ordinary physical punishment: Is it harmful? Comment on Gershoff (2002). *Psychological Bulletin, 128,* 580–589.

Bauserman, R. (1996). Sexual aggression and pornography: A review of correlational research. *Basic and Applied Social Psychology, 18,* 405–427.

Bayley, T. M., Dye, L., Jones, S., DeBono, M., & Hill, A. J. (2002). Food cravings and aversions during pregnancy: Relationships with nausea and vomiting. *Appetite, 38,* 45–51.

Beahrs, J. O. (1994). Dissociative identity disorder: Adaptive deception of self and others. *Bulletin of the American Academy of Psychiatric Law, 22,* 223–237.

Beaman, A. L., Barnes, P. J., Klentz, B., & McQuirk, B. (1978). Increasing helping rates through information dissemination: Teaching pays. *Personality and Social Psychology Bulletin, 4,* 406–411.

Beatty, M. J., Heisel, A. D., Hall, A. E., Levine, T. R., & La France, B. H. (2002). What can we learn from the study of twins about genetic and environmental influences on interpersonal affiliation, aggressiveness, and social anxiety? A meta-analytic study. *Communication Monographs, 69,* 1–18.

Beauchamp, G. K., & Bartoshuk L. (Eds.). (1997). *Tasting and smelling.* Philadelphia: Academic Press.

Beck, A. P., & Lewis, C. M. (Eds.). (2000). *The process of group psychotherapy: Systems for analyzing change.* Washington, DC: American Psychological Association.

Beck, A. T. (1976). *Cognitive therapy and the emotional disorders.* New York: International Universities Press.

Beck, A. T. (2002). Cognitive patterns in dreams and daydreams. *Journal of Cognitive Psychotherapy, 16,* 23–28.

Beck, A. T., Rush, A. J., Shaw, B. F., & Emery, G. (1979). *Cognitive therapy of depression.* New York: Guilford Press.

Becker, A. E., Grinspoon, S. K., Klibanski, A., & Herzog, D. B. (1999). Current concepts: Eating disorders. *New England Journal of Medicine, 340,* 1092–1098.

Bedard, J., & Chi, M. T. (1992). Expertise. *Current Directions in Psychological Science, 4,* 135–139.

Beecher, H. K. (1959). Generalization from pain of various types and diverse origins. *Science, 130,* 267–268.

Beilcock, S. L., & Carr, T. H. (2001). On the fragility of skilled performance: What governs choking under pressure? *Journal of Experimental Psychology: General, 130,* 701–725.

Bekesy, G. von. (1957). The ear. *Scientific American, 230,* 66–78.

Bell, A. P., Weinberg, M. S., & Hammersmith, S. K. (1981). *Sexual preference: Its development in men and women.* Bloomington: Indiana University Press.

Belloc, N. B. (1973). Relationship of health practices and mortality. *Preventive Medicine, 2,* 67–81.

Bem, D. J. (1972). Self-perception theory. In L. Berkowitz (Ed.), *Advances in experimental social psychology* (Vol. 6). New York: Academic Press.

Bem, D. J. (1996). Exotic becomes erotic: A developmental theory of sexual orientation. *Psychological Review, 103,* 320–335.

Bem, D. J. (2001). Exotic becomes erotic: Integrating biological and experiential antecedents of sexual orientation. In A. R. D'Augelli & C. J. Patterson (Eds.), *Lesbian, gay, and bisexual identities and youth: Psychological perspectives.* London: Oxford University Press.

Bem, D. J., & Honorton, C. (1994). Does psi exist? Replicable evidence for an anomalous process of information transfer. *Psychological Bulletin, 115,* 4–18.

Bem, S. L. (1981). Gender schema theory: A cognitive account of sex typing. *Psychological Review, 88,* 354–364.

Benedito-Silva, A. A., Menna-Barreto, I. S., Cipolla-Neto, J., Marques, N., & Tenreiro, S. (1989). A self-evaluation questionnaire for the determination of morningness-eveningness types in Brazil. *Chronobiologia, 16,* 311.

Bengtson,V. L. (2001). Beyond the nuclear family: The increasing importance of multigenerational bonds. *Journal of Marriage and the Family, 63,* 1–16.

Benjamin, A. S., & Bjork, R. A. (2000). On the relationship between recognition speed and accuracy for words rehearsed via rote versus elaborative rehearsal. *Journal of Experimental Psychology: Learning, Memory, and Cognition, 26,* 638–648.

Benjamin, L. S. (2003). *Interpersonal reconstructive therapy: Promoting change in nonresponders.* New York: Guilford Press.

Benjamin, L. T., Cavell, T. A., & Shallenberger, W. R. (1984). Staying with initial answers on objective tests: Is it a myth? *Teaching of Psychology, 11,* 133–141.

Bennett, H. L. (1983). Remembering drink orders: The memory skills of cocktail waitresses. *Human Learning, 2,* 157–169.

Benski, C., & Scientists from CRSSA. (1998). Testing new claims of dermo-optical perception. *Skeptical Inquirer, 22*(1), 21–26.

Bensley, L., & Van Eenwyk, J. (2001). Video games and real life aggression: Review of the literature. *Journal of Adolescent Health, 29,* 244–257.

Benson, H., & Klipper, M. Z. (1976). *The relaxation response.* New York: Morrow.

Berg, K. M., & Boswell, A. E. (1998). Infants' detection of increments in low- and high-frequency noise. *Perception and Psychophysics, 60,* 1044–1051.

Berkley, M. (1998). *Writing towards change: Changing public attitudes about psychotherapy.* Unpublished doctoral dissertation, Massachusetts School of Professional Psychology, Boston.

Bernichon, T., Cook, K. E., & Brown, J. D. (2003). Seeking self-evaluative feedback: The interactive role of global self-esteem and specific self-views. *Journal of Personality and Social Psychology, 84,* 194–204.

Berntsen, D. (2001). Involuntary memories of emotional events: Do memories of traumas and extremely happy events differ? *Applied Cognitive Psychology, 5,* S135–S158.

Berry, J. W., Poortinga, Y. H., Segall, M. H., & Dasen, P. (1992). *Cross-cultural psychology: Research and application.* New York: Cambridge University Press.

Berry, L. M. (1998). *Psychology at work* (2nd ed.). Boston: McGraw-Hill.

Berthoud, H. R. (2002). Multiple neural systems controlling food intake and body weight. *Neuroscience and Biobehavioral Reviews, 26,* 393–428.

Beutler, L. E. (2002). The dodo bird is extinct. *Clinical Psychology: Science and Practice, 9,* 30–34.

Beutler, L. E., Machado, P. P., & Neufeldt, S. A. (1994). Therapist variables. In A. E. Bergin & S. L. Garfield Sol Louis (Eds.), *Handbook of psychotherapy and behavior change* (4th ed.). New York: Wiley.

Beutler, L. E., & Malik, M. L. (2002). *Rethinking the DSM: A psychological perspective.* Washington, DC: American Psychological Association.

Beyer, S. (1990). Gender differences in the accuracy of self-evaluations of performance. *Journal of Personality and Social Psychology, 59,* 960–970.

Biederman, J. (1998). Attention-deficit/hyperactive disorder: A life-span perspective. *Journal of Clinical Psychology, 59,* 1–13.

Billings, A. G., & Moos, R. H. (1984). Coping, stress, and social resources among adults with unipolar depression. *Journal of Personality and Social Psychology, 46,* 877–891.

Binder, J. L., & Strupp, H. H. (1997). "Negative process": A recurrently discovered and underestimated facet of therapeutic process and outcome in the individual psychotherapy of adults. *Clinical Psychology: Science & Practice, 4,* 121–139.

Bjorklund, D. F., & Pellegrini, A. D. (2002). Evolutionary perspectives on social development. In P. K. Smith & C. H. Hart (Eds.), *Blackwell handbook of childhood social development.* Malden, MA: Blackwell.

Black, D. W. (1999). *Bad boys, bad men: Confronting antisocial personality disorder.* New York: Oxford University Press.

Black, D. W., Yates, W. R., & Andreasen, N. C. (1988). Schizophrenia, schizophreniform disorder, and delusional paranoid disorders. In J. A. Talbott, R. E. Hales, & S. C. Yudofsky (Eds.), *Textbook of psychiatry.* Washington, DC: American Psychiatric Press.

Blackwood, D. (2000). Genetic predispositions to stressful conditions. In G. Fink (Ed.), *Encyclopedia of stress.* San Diego, CA: Academic Press.

Blader, S. L., & Tyler, T. R. (2002). Justice and empathy: What motivates people to help others? In M. Ross & D. T. Miller (Eds.), *The justice motive in everyday life.* New York: Cambridge University Press.

Blair, S. N., Kohl, H. W., III, Paffenbarger, R. S., et al. (1989). Physical fitness and all-cause mortality: A prospective study of healthy men and women. *Journal of the American Medical Association, 262,* 2395–2401.

Blakemore, C., & Cooper, G. G. (1970). Development of the brain depends on visual environment. *Nature, 228,* 477–478.

Blanchard, C. M., Courneya, K. S., Rodgers, W. M., Daub, B., Knapik, G. (2002). Determinants of exercise intention and behavior during and after phase 2 cardiac rehabilitation: An application of the theory of planned behavior. *Rehabilitation Psychology, 47,* 308–323.

Blanchard, R. (2001). Fraternal birth order and the maternal immune hypothesis of male homosexuality. *Hormones and Behavior, 40,* 105–114.

Blanchard, R., & Bogaert, A. F. (1996). Homosexuality in men and number of older brothers. *American Journal of Psychiatry, 153,* 27–31.

Blanke, O., Ortigue, S., Landis, T., & Seeck, M. (2002). Stimulating illusory own-body perceptions. *Nature, 419*(6904), 269–270.

Blanton, H., Pelham, B., DeHart, T., & Carvallo, M. (2001). Overconfidence as dissonance reduction. *Journal of Experimental Social-Psychology, 37,* 373–385.

Blass, T. (Ed.). (2000). *Obedience to authority: Current perspectives on the Milgram paradigm.* Mahwah, NJ: Erlbaum.

Blass, T., & Schmitt, C. (2001). The nature of perceived authority in the Milgram paradigm: Two replications. *Current Psychology: Developmental, Learning, Personality, Social, 20,* 115–121.

Blechman, E., & Brownell, K. D. (1998). *Behavioral medicine and women: A comprehensive handbook.* New York: Guilford Press.

Blessing, W. W. (1997). *The lower brainstem and bodily homeostasis.* New York: Oxford University Press.

Block, N. (2002). How heritability misleads about race. In J. M. Fish (Ed.), *Race and intelligence: Separating science from myth.* Mahwah, NJ: Erlbaum.

Blodgett, H. C. (1929). The effect of the introduction of reward on the maze performance of rats. *University of California Publications in Psychology, 4*(8), 114–126.

Blodgett, R. (1986, May). Lost in the stars: Psychics strike out (again). *People Expression,* 32–35.

Bloomfield, K., Greenfield, T. K., Kraus, L., & Augustin, R. (2002). A comparison of drinking patterns and alcohol-use-related problems in the United States and Germany, 1995. *Substance Use and Misuse, 37,* 399–428.

Bobo, L. (1988). Attitudes toward the black political movement: Trends, meaning, and effects of racial policy preferences. *Social Psychology Quarterly, 51,* 287–302.

Boehm, S. L., Reed, C. L., McKinnon, C. S., & Phillips, T. J. (2002). Shared genes influence sensitivity to the effects of ethanol on locomotor and anxiety-like behaviors, and the stress axis. *Psychopharmacology, 161,* 54–63.

Boesch, C. (1995). Innovation in wild chimpanzees (*Pan troglodytes*). *International Journal of Primatology, 16,* 1–16.

Bolles, R. C., & Beecher, M. D. (Eds.). (1988). *Evolution and learning.* Hillsdale, NJ: Erlbaum.

Bond, R., & Smith, P. B. (1996). Culture and conformity: A meta-analysis of studies using Asch's (1952b, 1956) line judgment task. *Psychological Bulletin, 119,* 111–137.

Boneva, B., Frieze, I. H., Ferligoj, A., Pauknerova, D., & Orgocka, A. (1998). Achievement, power, and affiliation motives as clues to (e)migration desires: A four-countries comparison. *European Psychologist, 3,* 247–254.

Bonnel, A. M., & Hafter, E. R. (1998). Divided attention between simultaneous auditory and visual signals. *Perception & Psychophysics, 60,* 179–190.

Bonson, K. R., Grant, S. J., Contoreggi, C. S., Links, J. M., Metcalfe, J., Weyl, H. L., et al. (2002). Neural systems and cue-induced cocaine craving. *Neuropsychopharmacology, 26,* 376–386.

Bonvillian, J. D., & Patterson, F. G. P. (1997). Sign language acquisition and the development of meaning in a lowland gorilla. In C. Mandell & A. McCabe (Eds.), *The problem of meaning: Behavioral and cognitive perspectives.* Amsterdam: North-Holland/Elsevier Science.

Booth, A., & Amato, P. R. (2001). Parental predivorce relations and offspring postdivorce well-being. *Journal of Marriage and the Family, 63,* 197–212.

Bootzin, R. R. (2002). Cognitive-behavioral treatment of insomnia: Knitting up the ravell'd sleeve of care. In D. T. Kenny, J. G. Carlson, F. J. McGuigan, & J. L. Sheppard (Eds.), *Stress and health: Research and clinical applications.* Amsterdam: Harwood.

Borod, J. C. (2000). *The neuropsychology of emotion.* New York: Oxford University Press.

Boschker, M. S., Baker, F. C., & Michaels, C. F. (2002). Memory for the functional characteristics of climbing walls: Perceiving affordances. *Journal of Motor Behavior, 34,* 25–36.

Bouchard, T. J., Lykken, D. T., McGue, M., Segal, N. L., & Tellegen, A. (1990). Sources of human psychological differences: The Minnesota study of twins reared apart. *Science, 250,* 223–228.

Bouchard, T. J., & McGue, M. (1981). Familial studies of intelligence: A review. *Science, 212,* 1055–1059.

Boulos, Z. (1998). Bright light treatment for jet lag and shift work. In R. Lam & W. Raymond (Eds.), *Seasonal affective disorder and beyond: Light treatment for SAD and non-SAD conditions.* Washington, DC: American Psychiatric Press.

Boutros, N. N., Gelernter, J., Gooding, D. C., Cubells, J., Young, A., Krystal, J. H., & Kosten, T. (2002). Sensory gating and psychosis vulnerability in cocaine-dependent individuals: Preliminary data. *Biological Psychiatry, 51,* 683–686.

Bower, G. H., Clark, M. C., Lesgold, M. A., & Winzenz, D. (1969). Hierarchical retrieval schemes in recall of categorized word lists. *Journal of Verbal Learning and Verbal Behavior, 8,* 323–343.

Bowers, K. S. (1992). Imagination and dissociation in hypnotic responding. *International Journal of Clinical and Experimental Hypnosis, 40,* 253–275.

Bowlby, J. (1969). *Attachment and loss: Vol. 1. Attachment.* New York: Basic Books.

Bowlby, J. (1973). *Attachment and loss: Vol. 2. Separation: Anxiety and anger.* London: Hogarth.

Bowlby, J. (2000a). *Loss: Sadness and depression.* New York: Basic Books.

Bowlby, J. (2000b). *Separation: Anxiety and anger.* New York: Basic Books.

Bozarth, J. D., Zimring, F. M., & Tausch, R. (2002). Client-centered therapy: The evolution of a revolution. In D. J. Cain (Ed.), *Humanistic psychotherapies: Handbook of research and practice.* Washington, DC: American Psychological Association.

Brandon, S., Boakes, J., Glaser, D., & Green, R. (1998). Recovered memories of childhood sexual abuse: Implications for clinical practice. *British Journal of Psychiatry, 172,* 296–307.

Bransford, J. D., & Johnson, M. K. (1972). Contextual prerequisites for understanding: Some investigations of comprehension and recall. *Journal of Verbal Learning and Verbal Behavior, 11,* 717–726.

Brantley, P., & Garrett, V. D. (1993). Psychobiological approaches to health and disease. In P. B Sutker & H. E. Adams, *Comprehensive handbook of psychopathology* (2nd ed.). New York: Plenum.

Brauer, M. (2001). Intergroup perception in the social context: The effects of social status and group membership on perceived out group homogeneity and ethnocentrism. *Journal of Experimental Social Psychology, 37,* 15–31.

Bray, J. H., & Berger, S. H. (1993). Developmental issues in Step Families Research Project: Family relationships and parent-child interactions. *Journal of Family Psychology, 7,* 76–90.

Brehm, J. W., & Self, E. A. (1989). The intensity of motivation. *Annual Review of Psychology, 40,* 109–131.

Breland, K., & Breland, M. (1961). The misbehavior of organisms. *American Psychologist, 16,* 681–684.

Breland, K., & Breland, M. (1966). *Animal behavior.* New York: Macmillan.

Bremner, J. D. (2000). Neurobiology of posttraumatic stress disorder. In G. Fink (Ed.), *Encyclopedia of stress.* San Diego, CA: Academic Press.

Brickman, P., Coates, D., & Janoff-Bulman (1978). Lottery winners and accident victims: Is happiness relative? *Journal of Personality and Social Psychology, 36,* 917–927.

Bridis, T. (2003, February 27). NASA engineers feared a disaster—then it happened. *Seattle Post-Intelligencer,* p. A1.

Briere, J., & Lanktree, C. (1983). Sex role–related effects of sex bias in language. *Sex Roles, 9,* 625–632.

Broberg, D. J., & Bernstein, I. L. (1987). Candy as a scapegoat in the prevention of food aversions in children receiving chemotherapy. *Cancer, 60,* 2344–2347.

Bronzaft, A. L., Ahern, K. D., McGinn, R., O'Connor, J., & Savino, B. (1998). Aircraft noise: A potential health hazard. *Environment and Behavior, 30,* 101–113.

Brooks-Gunn, J., Han, W. J., & Waldfogel, J. (2002). Maternal employment and child cognitive outcomes in the first three years of life: The NICHD study of early child care. *Child Development, 73,* 1052–1072.

Brown, E., Deffenbacher, K., & Sturgill, W. (1977). Memory for faces and the circumstances of encounter. *Journal of Applied Psychology, 62,* 311–318.

Brown, G. W., & Harris, T. O. (1978). *Social origins of depression.* London: Tavistock Press.

Brown, J. A. (1958). Some tests of the decay theory of immediate memory. *Quarterly Journal of Experimental Psychology, 10,* 12–21.

Brown, J. D. (1998). *The self.* Boston: McGraw-Hill.

Brown, L. S. (1994). *Subversive dialogues: Theory in feminist therapy.* New York: Basic Books.

Brown, N. O. (1959). *Life against death.* New York: Random House.

Brown, R. (1973). *A first language: The early stages.* Cambridge, MA: Harvard University Press.

Brown, R., & Kulik, J. (1977). Flashbulb memories. *Cognition, 5,* 73–99.

Brown, T. A., Di-Nardo, P. A., Lehman, C. L., & Campbell, L. A. (2001). Reliability of DSM-IV anxiety and mood disorders: Implications for the classification of emotional disorders. *Journal of Abnormal Psychology, 110,* 49–58.

Brown, T. S., & Wallace, P. (1980). *Physiological psychology.* New York: Academic Press.

Brownell, K. D. (1994). *The LEARN program for weight control.* Dallas, TX: American Health Publishing.

Bruce, T. J., & Sanderson, W. C. (1998). *Specific phobias: Clinical applications of evidence-based psychotherapy.* Northvale, NJ: Jason Aronson.

Bruck, M., Ceci, S. J., & Hembrooke, H. (1998). Reliability and credibility of young children's reports: From research to policy and practice. *American Psychologist, 53,* 136–151.

Bruederl, J., Diekmann, A., & Engelhardt, H. (1997). Erhoeht eine Probeehe das Scheidungrisiko? Eine empirische Untersuchung mit dem Familiensurvey [Does a trial marriage increase divorce risk? Empirical study of the Families Survey]. *Koelner Zeitschrift fuer Soziologie und Sozialpsychologie, 49,* 205–222.

Bruunk, B., & Gibbons, F. X. (Eds.). (1997). *Health, coping, and well-being: Perspectives from social comparison theory.* Mahwah, NJ: Erlbaum.

Bryan, J., III. (1986). *Hodgepodge: A commonplace book.* New York: Ballantine.

Buck, L., & Axel, R. (1991). A novel multigene family may encode odorant receptors: A molecular basis for odor recognition. *Cell, 65,* 175–187.

Buckworth, J., & Dishman, R. (2002). *Exercise psychology.* Champaign, IL: Human Kinetics.

Buet, V. I., & Harris, T. (1994). The third national health and nutrition examination survey: Contributing data. *Gerontologist, 34,* 486–490.

Bullier, J. (2002). Neural basis of vision. In H. Pashler & S. Yantis (Eds.), *Steven's handbook of experimental psychology: Vol. 1. Sensation and perception* (3rd ed.). New York: Wiley.

Bureau of the Census. (2002). *Demographic Trends in the 20th Century: Census 2000 Special Reports, CENSR-4, November.* Available online: http://www.census.gov/population/www/cen2000/briefs.html

Bureau of the Census. (2003). Married-couple and unmarried-partner households: 2000. *Census 2000 Special Reports, CENSR-5.* Available online: http://www.census.gov/population/www/cen2000/briefs.html

Burger, J. M. (2004). *Personality* (6th ed.). Belmont, CA: Wadsworth.

Burgess, A. W., & Holmstrom, L. I. (1974). Rape trauma syndrome. *American Journal of Psychiatry, 131,* 981–986.

Burgess, C. A., & Kirsch, I. (1999). Expectancy information as a moderator of the effects of hypnosis on memory. *Contemporary Hypnosis, 16,* 22–31.

Burgwyn-Bailes, E., Baker-Ward, L., Gordon, B. N., & Ornstein, P. A. (2001). Children's memory for emergency medical treatment after one year: The impact of individual difference variables on recall and suggestibility. *Applied Cognitive Psychology, 15,* S25–S48.

Burke, K. C., Burke, J. D., Rae, D. S., & Regier, D. A. (1991). Comparing age at onset of major depression and other psychiatric disorders by birth cohorts in five U.S. community populations. *Archives of General Psychiatry, 48,* 789–795.

Burns, M. O., & Seligman, M. E. P. (1991). Explanatory style, helplessness, and depression. In C. R. Snyder & D. R. Forsyth (Eds.), *Handbook of social and clinical psychology: The health perspective.* New York: Pergamon Press.

Busey, T. A., Tunnicliff, J. J., Loftus, G. R., & Loftus, E. F. (2000). Accounts of the confidence-accuracy relation in recognition memory. *Psychonomic Bulletin and Review, 7,* 26–48.

Bushman, B. J. (2002). Does venting anger feed or extinguish the flame? Catharsis, rumination, distraction, anger and aggressive responding. *Personality and Social Psychology, 28,* 724–731.

Bushman, B. J., & Bonacci, A. M. (2002). Violence and sex impair memory for television ads. *Journal of Applied Psychology, 87,* 557–564.

Bushnell, I. W. R. (2001). Mother's face recognition in newborn infants: Learning and memory. *Infant and Child Development, 10,* 67–74.

Buske-Kirschbaum, A., Kirschbaum, C., & Hellhammer, D. H. (1994). Conditioned modulation of NK cells in humans: Alteration of cell activity and cell number by conditioning protocols. *Psychologische Beitraege, 36,* 100–111.

Buske-Kirschbaum, A., Kirschbaum, C., Stierle, H., & Lehnert, H. (1992). Conditioned increase of natural killer cell activity (NKCA) in humans. *Psychosomatic Medicine, 54,* 123–132.

Buss, D. M. (1985). Human mate selection. *American Scientist, 73,* 47–51.

Buss, D. M. (1989). Sex differences in human mate preferences: Evolutionary hypotheses tested in 37 cultures. *Behavioral and Brain Sciences, 12,* 1–49.

Buss, D. M. (1991). Evolutionary personality theory. *Annual Review of Psychology, 42,* 459–491.

Buss, D. M. (1995). Evolutionary psychology: A new paradigm for psychological science. *Psychological Inquiry, 6,* 1–30.

Buss, D. M. (1999). Human nature and individual differences: The evolution of human personality. In L. A. Pervin & O. P. John (Eds.), *Handbook of personality: Theory and research.* New York: Guilford Press.

Buss, D. M., Abbott, M., Angleitner, A., Asherian, A., Biaggio, A., Blanco-Villasenor, A., et al. (1990). International preferences in selecting mates: A study of 37 cultures. *Journal of Cross-Cultural Psychology, 21,* 5–47.

Buss, D. M., & Schmitt, D. P. (1993). Sexual Strategies Theory: An evolutionary perspective on human mating. *Psychological Review, 100,* 204–232.

Buunk, B. P., & Dijkstra, P. (2001) Rationalizations and defensive attributions for high-risk sex among heterosexuals. *Patient Education and Counseling, 45,* 127–132.

Byer, C. O., Shainberg, L. W., & Galliano, G. (2002). *Dimensions of human sexuality* (6th ed.). Boston: McGraw-Hill.

Byrd, M. R., Richards, D. F., Hove, G., & Frima, P. C. (2002). Treatment of early onset hair pulling as a simple habit. *Behavior Modification, 26,* 400–411.

Byrne, D. (1997). An overview (and underview) of research and theory within the attraction paradigm. *Journal of Social and Personal Relationships, 14,* 417–431.

Byrne, D., Ervin, C. R., & Lamberth, J. (1970). Continuity between the experimental study of attraction and real-life computer dating. *Journal of Personality and Social Psychology, 16,* 157–165.

Byrne, D., & Greendlinger, V. (1989). *Need for affiliation as a predictor of classroom friendships.* Unpublished manuscript, State University of New York at Albany.

Cacioppo, J. T., Berntson, J. T., Poehlmann, K. M., & Ito, T. A. (2000). The psychophysiology of emotion. In M. Lewis & J. M. Haviland-Jones (Eds.), *Handbook of emotions* (2nd ed.). New York: Guilford Press.

Cacioppo, J. T., & Gardner, W. L. (1999). Emotion. *Annual Review of Psychology, 50,* 101–124.

Cain, D. J., & Seeman, J. (Eds.). (2002). *Humanistic psychotherapies: Handbook of research and practice.* Washington, DC: American Psychological Association.

Cairns, H. (1952). Disturbances of consciousness in lesions of the mid-brain and diencephalon. *Brain, 75,* 107–114.

Caldwell, A. B. (1994). *The profile of Jeffrey Dahmer* [Videotape]. Los Angeles: Caldwell Report.

Camilleri, C., & Malewska-Peyre, H. (1997). Socialization and identity strategies. In J. W. Berry, P. R. Dasen, & T. S. Saraswathi (Eds.), *Handbook of cross-cultural psychology: Basic processes and human development: Vol. 2. Handbook of cross-cultural psychology* (2nd ed.). Boston: Allyn & Bacon.

Campbell, S. S. (1993). Seasonal effects on sleep. In M. A. Carskadon (Ed.), *Encyclopedia of sleep and dreaming.* New York: Macmillan.

Campfield, L. A. (1997). Metabolic and hormonal controls of food intake: Highlights of the last 25 years: 1972–1997. *Appetite, 29,* 135–152.

Candido, A., Maldonado, A., Rodriguez, A., & Morales, A. (2002). Successive positive contrast in one-way avoidance learning. *Quarterly Journal of Experimental Psychology: Comparative and Physiological Psychology, 55,* 171–184.

Canivez, G. L., & Watkins, M. W. (1998). Long-term stability of the Wechsler Intelligence Scale for Children—Third Edition. *Psychological Assessment, 10,* 285–291.

Cannon, W. B. (1929). *Bodily changes in pain, hunger, fear, and rage.* New York: Appleton-Century.

Cannon, W. B. (1942). "Voodoo" death. *American Anthropologist, 44,* 169–181.

Cannon, W. B., & Washburn, A. L. (1912). An explanation of hunger. *American Journal of Physiology, 29,* 441–454.

Caporeal, L. R. (2000). Evolutionary psychology: Toward a unifying theory and a hybrid science. *Annual Review of Psychology, 52,* 607–628.

Cardeña, E., Lynn, S. J., & Krippner, S. (2000). Introduction: Anomalous experiences in perspective. In E. Cardeña, S. J. Lynn, & S. Krippner (Eds.), *Varieties of anomalous experience: Examining the scientific evidence.* Washington, DC: American Psychological Association.

Carey, F. (1977). The child as a word learner. In M. Halle, J. Bresnan, & G. Miller (Eds.), *Linguistic theory and psychological reality.* Cambridge, MA: MIT Press.

Carey, G., & Gottesman, I. I. (1981). Twin and family studies of anxiety, phobic, and obsession disorders. In D. F. Klein & J. Rabkin (Eds.), *Anxiety: New research and changing concepts.* New York: Raven Press.

Carlson, C. (2000). ADHD is overdiagnosed. In R. L. Atkinson, R. C. Atkinson, E. E. Smith, D. J. Bem, & S. Nolen-Hoeksema, *Hilgard's introduction to psychology* (13th ed.). Ft. Worth, TX: Harcourt Brace.

Carlson, J. G., & Hatfield, E. (1992). *Psychology of emotion.* Ft. Worth, TX: Harcourt Brace Jovanovich.

Carlson, S. M., Moses, L. J., & Hix, H. R. (1998). The role of inhibitory processes in young children's difficulties with deception and false belief. *Child Development, 69,* 672–691.

Carney, L. H. (2002). Neural basis of audition. In H. Pashler & S.Yantis (Eds.), *Steven's handbook of experimental psychology: Vol. 1. Sensation and perception* (3rd ed.). New York: Wiley.

Carnicero, J. A. C., Perez-Lopez, J., Salinas, M. D. C. G., & Martinez-Fuentes, M. T. (2000). A longitudinal study of temperament in infancy: Stability and convergence of measures. *European Journal of Personality, 14,* 21–37.

Carpenter, R., & Robson, J. (Eds.). (1999). *Vision research: A practical guide to laboratory methods.* New York: Oxford University Press.

Carroll, C. R. (1993). *Drugs in modern society.* Madison, WI: Brown & Benchmark.

Carson, R. C., Butcher, J. N., & Coleman, J. C. (1988). *Abnormal psychology and modern life* (8th ed.). Glenview, IL: Scott, Foresman.

Carter, S. J., & Cassaday, H. J. (1998). State dependent retrieval and chlorpheniramine. *Human Psychopharmacology: Clinical and Experimental, 13,* 513–523.

Cartwright, R. D. (1977). *Night life: Explorations in dreaming.* Englewood Cliffs, NJ: Prentice Hall.

Carver, C. S., & Scheier, M. F. (2003). *Perspectives on personality* (5th ed.). Boston: Allyn & Bacon.

Carver, C. S., Scheier, M. F., & Weintraub, J. K. (1989). Assessing coping strategies: A theoretically based approach. *Journal of Personality and Social Psychology, 56,* 267–283.

Carver, C. S., Sutton, S. K., & Scheier, M. F. (1999). Action, emotion, and personality: Emerging conceptual integration. *Personality and Social Psychology Bulletin, 26,* 741–751.

Carver, C. S., & White, T. L. (1994). Behavioral inhibition, behavioral activation, and affective responses to impending rewards and punishments: The BIS/BAS scales. *Journal of Personality and Social Psychology, 67,* 319–333.

Case, R. (1987). The structure and process of intellectual development. *International Journal of Psychology, 22,* 571–607.

Case, R., Demetriou, A., Platsidou, M., & Kazi, S. (2001). Integrating concepts and tests of intelligence from the differential and developmental traditions. *Intelligence, 29,* 307–336.

Caspi, A., Elder, G. H., & Bem, D. J. (1988). Moving away from the world: Life course patterns of shy children. *Developmental Psychology, 24,* 824–831.

Caspi, A., & Roberts, B. W. (1999). Personality continuity and change across the life course. In L. A. Pervin & O. P. John (Eds.), *Handbook of personality: Theory and research.* New York: Guilford Press.

Catania, A. C. (2001). Positive psychology and positive reinforcement. *American Psychologist., 56,* 86–87.

Catania, C. A. (1998). *Learning* (4th ed.). Upper Saddle River, NJ: Prentice Hall.

Catchpole, C. K., & Rowell, A. (1993). Song sharing and local dialects in a population of the European wren *Troglodytes troglodytes. Behaviour, 125,* 67–78.

Catrambone, R. (1998). The subgoal learning model: Creating better examples so that students can solve novel problems. *Journal of Experimental Psychology: General, 127,* 355–376.

Cattell, R. B. (1965). *The scientific analysis of personality.* Chicago: Aldine.

Cattell, R. B. (1971). *Abilities: Their growth, structure, and action.* Boston: Houghton Mifflin.

Cattell, R. B. (1998). Where is intelligence? Some answers from the triarchic theory. In J. J. McArdler et al. (Eds.), *Human cognitive abilities in theory and practice.* Mahwah, NJ: Erlbaum.

Caudill, W., & Plath, D. W. (1966). Who sleeps by whom? Parent-child involvement in urban Japanese families. *Psychiatry: Journal for the Study of Interpersonal Processes, 29,* 344–366.

Ceci, S. J. (1996). *On intelligence: A bioecological treatise on intellectual development.* Cambridge, MA: Harvard University Press.

Ceci, S. J., Bruck, M., & Battin, D. B. (2000). The suggestibility of children's testimony. In D. F. Bjorklund (Ed.), *False-memory creation in children and adults: Theory, research, and implications.* Mahwah, NJ: Erlbaum.

Centers for Disease Control and Prevention. (1988). *Posttraumatic stress disorders.* Atlanta, GA: Author.

Centers for Disease Control and Prevention. (1994). *Addressing emerging infectious disease threats: A prevention strategy for the United States.* Washington, DC: Author.

Centers for Disease Control and Prevention. (1997). *Fertility, family planning, and women's health: New data from the 1995 National Survey on Family Growth* (Series 23, No. 19). Washington DC: Author.

Centers for Disease Control and Prevention. (2002a). *Causes of death in the United States.* Atlanta, GA: Author.

Centers for Disease Control and Prevention. (2002b). *Statistics on addictive behaviors.* Atlanta, GA: Author.

Centers for Disease Control and Prevention. (2002c). Youth risk behavior surveillance—United States, 2001. *Morbidity and Mortality Weekly Report, 51*(SS04), 1–64. Washington, DC: Author.

Centers for Disease Control and Prevention. (2003). *HIV/AIDS statistics.* Atlanta, GA: Author.

Cervone, D. (1999). Bottom-up explanation in personality psychology: The case of cross-situational consistency. In D. Cervone & Y. Shoda (Eds.), *The coherence of personality.* New York: Guilford Press.

Cervone, D., & Shoda, Y. (1999a). *The coherence of personality: Social-cognitive bases of consistency, variability, and organization.* New York: Guilford Press.

Cervone, D., & Shoda, Y. (1999b). Social-cognitive theories and the coherence of personality. In D. Cervone & Y. Shoda (Eds.), *The coherence of personality: Social-cognitive bases of consistency, variability, and organization.* New York: Guilford Press.

Chalmers, D. J. (1995). The puzzle of conscious experience. *Scientific American, 273*(6), 80–86.

Chambless, D. L., & Hollon, S. D. (1998). Defining empirically supported therapies. *Journal of Consulting and Clinical Psychology, 66,* 7–18.

Chan, Z. C. Y., & Ma, J. L. C. (2002). Family themes of food refusal: Disciplining the body and punishing the family. *Health Care for Women International, 23,* 49–58.

Chang, E. C. (1996). Cultural differences in optimism, pessimism, and coping: Predictors of subsequent adjustment in American and Caucasian American college students. *Journal of Counseling Psychology, 43,* 113–123.

Chang, E. C. (1998). Dispositional optimism and primary and secondary appraisal of a stressor: Controlling for confounding influences and relations to coping and psychological and physical adjustment. *Journal of Personality and Social Psychology, 74,* 1109–1120.

Chapell, M. S., & Overton, W. F. (1998). Development of logical reasoning in the context of parental style and test anxiety. *Merrill Palmer Quarterly, 44,* 141–156.

Chappell, M., & Humphreys, M. S. (1994). An auto-associative neural network for sparse representations: Analysis and application to models of recognition and cued recall. *Psychological Review, 101,* 103–128.

Chartrand, T. L., & Bargh, J. A. (2002). Nonconscious motivations: Their activation, operation, and consequences. In A. Tesser, D. A. Stapel, & J. V. Wood (Eds.), *Self and motivation: Emerging psychological perspectives.* Washington, DC: American Psychological Association.

Chartrand, T. L., Bargh, J. A., & van Baaren, R. (2002). *Consequences of automatic evaluation for mood.* Manuscript submitted for publication.

Chase, W. G., & Simon, H. A. (1973). Perception in chess. *Cognitive Psychology, 4,* 55–81.

Cheasty, M., Clare, A. W., Collins, C. (2002). Child sexual abuse: A predictor of persistent depression in adult rape and sexual assault victims. *Journal of Mental Health UK, 11,* 79–84.

Chen, C., Greenberger, E., Lester, J., Dong, Q., & Guo, M. S. (1998). A cross-cultural study of family and peer correlates of adolescent misconduct. *Developmental Psychology, 34,* 770–781.

Chen, H., Charlat, O., Tartaglia, L. A., Woolf, E. A., Weng, X., & Ellis, S. J. (1996). Evidence that the diabetes gene encodes the leptin receptor: Identification of a mutation in the leptin receptor gene in db/db mice. *Cell, 84,* 491–495.

Chen, H., & Lan, W. (1998). Adolescents' perceptions of their parents' academic expectations: Comparison of American, Chinese-American, and Chinese high school students. *Adolescence, 33,* 385–390.

Chen, S. C. (1937). Social modification of the activity of ants in nest-building. *Physiological Zoology, 10,* 420–436.

Chenoweth, D. (2002). *Evaluating worksite health promotion.* Champaign, IL: Human Kinetics.

Chi, M. T. H. (1997). Creativity: Shifting across ontological categories flexibly. In T. B. Ward et al. (Eds.), *Creative thought: An investigation of conceptual structures and processes.* Washington, DC: American Psychological Association.

Chiappelli, F. (2000). Immune suppression. In G. Fink (Ed.), *Encyclopedia of stress.* San Diego, CA: Academic Press.

Chiles, J. A., & Strosahl, K. D. (1995). *The suicidal patient: Principles of assessment, treatment, and case management.* Washington, DC: American Psychiatric Press.

Chiriboga, D. A. (1989). Mental health at the midpoint: Crisis, challenge, or relief? In S. Hunter & M. Sundel (Eds.), *Midlife myths: Issues, findings, and practice implications.* Newbury Park, CA: Sage Publications.

Choi, I., Dalal, R., Kim Prieto, C., & Park, H. (2003). Culture and judgement of causal relevance. *Journal of Personality and Social Psychology, 84,* 46–59.

Chomsky, N. (1965). *Aspects of a theory of syntax.* Cambridge, MA: MIT Press.

Chomsky, N. (1972). *Language and mind.* New York: Harcourt.

Chomsky, N. (1987). Language in a psychological setting. *Sophia Linguistic Working Papers in Linguistics, 22,* Sophia University, Tokyo.

Christianson, S. A., & Nilsson, L. G. (1989). Hysterical amnesia: A case of aversively motivated isolation of memory. In T. Archer & L. G. Nilsson (Eds.), *Aversion, avoidance, and anxiety: Perspectives on aversively motivated behavior.* Hillsdale, NJ: Erlbaum.

Christopherson, E. R., & Mortweet, S. L. (2001). *Treatments that work with children: Empirically supported strategies for managing childhood problems.* Washington, DC: American Psychological Association.

Church, A. T., & Katigbak, M. S. (2000). Trait psychology in the Philippines. *American Behavioral Scientist, 44,* 73–94.

Chwalisz, K., Diener, E., & Gallagher, D. (1988). Autonomic arousal feedback and emotional experience: Evidence from the spinal cord injured. *JPSP, 54,* 820–828.

Chwilla, D. J., & Kolk, H. H. J. (2002). Three step priming in lexical decision. *Memory and Cognition, 30,* 217–225.

Cialdini, R. B. (1988). *Influence: Science and practice* (2nd ed.). Glenview, IL: Scott, Foresman.

Cialdini, R. B., Brown, S. L., Lewis, B. P., & Luce, C. (1997). Reinterpreting the empathy-altruism relationship: When one into one equals oneness. *Journal of Personality and Social Psychology, 73,* 481–494.

Cialdini, R. B., Schaller, M., Hoolihan, D., Arps, K., Fultz, J., & Beaman, A. L. (1987). Empathy-based helping: Is it selflessly or selfishly motivated? *Journal of Personality and Social Psychology, 52,* 749–758.

Cianelli, S. N., & Fouts, R. S. (1998). Chimpanzee to chimpanzee American Sign Language. *Human Evolution, 13,* 147–159.

Cicirelli, V. G. (1998). Personal meanings of death in relation to fear of death. *Death Studies, 22,* 713–733.

Cigales, M., Field, T., Lundy, B., Cuadra, A., & Hart, S. (1997). Massage enhances recovery from habituation in normal infants. *Infant Behavior and Development, 20,* 29–34.

Clancy, S. A., McNally, R. J., Schacter, D. L., Lenzenweger, M. F., & Pitman, R. K. (2002). Memory distortion in people reporting abduction by aliens. *Journal of Abnormal Psychology, 111,* 455–461.

Claparède, E. (1911). Recognition et moiïté. *Archives de Psychologies, 11,* 79–90.

Clark, A. E. (1998). *The positive externalities of higher unemployment: Evidence from household data.* Working paper, Universite d'Orleans, Orleans, France.

Clark, D. A., Beck, A. T., & Alford, B. A. (1999). *Scientific foundations of cognitive theory and therapy of depression.* New York: Wiley.

Clark, D. A., Beck, A. T., & Brown, G. (1989). Cognitive mediation in general psychiatric outpatients: A test of the content-specificity hypothesis. *Journal of Personality and Social Psychology, 56,* 958–964.

Clark, D. M. (1988). A cognitive model of panic attacks. In S. Rachman & J. D. Maser (Eds.), *Panic: Psychological perspectives.* Hillsdale, NJ; Erlbaum.

Clark, K. B., & Clark, M. P. (1947). Racial identification and preference in negro children. In T. N. Newcomb & E. L. Hartley (Eds.), *Readings in Social Psychology.* New York: Holt.

Clark, R. D., III. (2001). Effects of majority defection and multiple minority sources on minority influence. *Group Dynamics, 5,* 57–62.

Clarke, A. M., & Clarke, A. D. B. (2000). *Early experience and the life path.* London: Jessica Kingsley.

Clay, R. A. (2002). Advertising as science. *Monitor on Psychology, 33*(9), 38–41.

Cloninger, C. R. (1987). A systematic method for clinical description and classification of personality variants: A proposal. *Archives of General Psychiatry, 44,* 573–588.

Cloninger, C. R., & Gottesman, I. I. (1989). Genetic and environmental factors in antisocial behavior disorders. In S. Mednick, T. Moffitt, & S. Strack (Eds.), *The causes of crime: New biological approaches.* Cambridge, England: Cambridge University Press.

Clutton-Brock, T. (2002). Breeding together: Kin selection and mutualism in cooperative vertebrates. *Science, 296,* 69–72.

Coffey, C., Carlin, J. B., Degenhardt, L., Lynskey, M., Sanci, L., & Patton, G. C. (2002). Cannabis dependence in young adults: An Australian population study. *Addiction, 97,* 187–194.

Coffey, C. E., Weiner, R. D., Djang, W. T., et al. (1991). Brain anatomic effects of electroconvulsive therapy: A prospective magnetic resonance imaging study. *Archives of General Psychiatry, 48,* 1013–1020.

Cohen, K. M. (2002). Relationships among childhood sex-atypical behavior, spatial ability, handedness, and sexual orientation in men. *Archives of Sexual Behavior, 31,* 129–143.

Cohen, S. (1988). Psychosocial models of the role of social support in the etiology of physical disease. *Health Psychology, 7,* 269–297.

Cohen, S., Frank, E. D., Doyle, W. J., Skoner, D. P., Rabin, B. S., & Gwaltney, J. M., Jr. (1998). Types of stressors that increase susceptibility to the common cold in healthy adults. *Health Psychology, 17,* 214–223.

Cohen, S., & Herbert, T. B. (1996). Health psychology: Psychological factors and physical disease from the perspective of human psychoneuroimmunology. *Annual Review of Psychology, 47,* 113–142.

Cohen, S., Kessler, R. C., & Gordon, L. U. (1995). *Measuring stress.* New York: Oxford University Press.

Cohen, S. I. (1985). Psychosomatic death: Voodoo death in a modern perspective. *Integrative Psychiatry, 3,* 46–51.

Collings, P. (2001). If you got everything, it's good enough: Perspectives on successful aging in a Canadian Inuit community. *Journal of Cross-Cultural Gerontology, 16,* 127–155.

Collins, A. M., & Loftus, E. F. (1975). A spreading activation theory of semantic processing. *Psychological Review, 82,* 407–428.

Collins, D. W., & Kimura, D. (1997). A large sex difference on a two-dimensional mental rotation task. *Behavioral Neuroscience, 111,* 845–849.

Collins, W. A., Maccoby, E. E., Steinberg, L., & Hetherington, E. M. (2000). Contemporary research on parenting: The case for nature and nurture. *American Psychologist, 55,* 218–232.

Columbia. (1996). *The Columbia world of quotations.* Retrieved March 21, 2003, from http://www.bartleby.com

Columbia Accident Investigation Board (2003). *Report* (Vol. 1). Accessed October 2, 2003 from http://www.nasa.gov/columbia/home/index.html.

Compton, S., Burns, B. J., Egger, H. L., & Robertson, E. (2002). Review of the evidence base for treatment of childhood psychopathology: Internalizing disorders. *Journal of Consulting and Clinical Psychology, 71,* 1240–1266.

Comuzzie, A. G., & Allison, D. B. (1998). The search for human obesity genes. *Science, 280,* 1374–1377.

Conel, J. L. (1939–1975). *The postnatal development of the human cerebral cortex* (Vols. 1–8). Cambridge, MA: Harvard University Press.

Conrad, R. (1964). Acoustic confusions in immediate memory. *British Journal of Psychology, 55,* 75–84.

Cooke, P. (1991, June 23). They cried until they couldn't see. *New York Times Magazine,* 25, 43.

Cooper, C. R., & Denner, J. (1998). Theories linking culture and psychology: Universal and community-specific processes. *Annual Review of Psychology, 49,* 559–584.

Coopersmith, S. (1967). *The antecedents of self-esteem.* San Francisco: Freeman.

Core Institute. (2002). *Statistics on substance use by college students.* Carbondale, IL: Author.

Cosmides, L., & Tooby, J. (2002). Unraveling the enigma of human intelligence: Evolutionary psychology and the multimodular mind. In R. J. Sternberg & J. C. Kaufman (Eds.), *The evolution of intelligence.* Mahwah, NJ: Erlbaum.

Costa, L. (1996). Lifespan neuropsychology. *Clinical Neuropsychologist, 10,* 365–374.

Costa, P. T., & McCrae, R. R. (1992). The five-factor model of personality and its relevance to personality disorders. *Journal of Personality Disorders, 6,* 343–359.

Costa, P. T., & McCrae, R. R. (2002). Looking backward: Changes in the mean levels of personality traits from 80 to 12. In D. Cervone & W. Mischel (Eds.), *Advances in personality science.* New York: Guilford Press.

Courneya, K. S. (1995). Understanding readiness for regular physical activity in older individuals: An application of the theory of planned behavior. *Health Psychology, 14,* 80–87.

Cousins, S. D. (1989). Culture and self-perception in the United States and Japan. *Journal of Personality and Social Psychology, 56,* 124–131.

Cowan, C. P., & Cowan, P. A. (2000). *When partners become parents: The big life change for couples.* Mahwah, NJ: Erlbaum.

Crabbe, J. C. (2002). Genetic contributions to addiction. *Annual Review of Psychology, 53,* 435–462.

Craik, F. I. M., & Lockhart, R. S. (1972). Levels of processing: A framework for memory research. *Journal of Verbal Learning and Verbal Behavior, 11,* 671–684.

Craik, F. I. M., & Salthouse, T. A. (Eds.). (2000). *The handbook of aging and cognition.* Mahwah, NJ: Erlbaum.

Craik, F. I. M., & Tulving, E. (1975). Depth of processing and the retention of words in episodic memory. *Journal of Experimental Psychology: General, 104,* 268–294.

Crandall, C. S., D'Anello, S., Sakalli, N., Lazarus, E., Wieczorkowska, G., & Feather, N. T. (2001). An Attribution-Value model of prejudice: Anti-fat attitudes in six nations. *Personality and Social Psychology Bulletin, 27,* 30–37.

Craske, M. (1999). *Anxiety disorders: psychological approaches to theory and treatment.* Boulder, CO: Westview Press.

Craske, M. (2003). *Origins of phobias and anxiety disorders: Why more women than men?* New York: Elsevier Science.

Craske, M. G., & Rowe, M. K. (1997). Nocturnal panic. *Clinical Psychology: Science and Practice, 4,* 153–174.

Crawford, M., & Chaffin, R. (1997). The meanings of difference: Cognition in social and cultural context. In P. J. Caplan & M. Crawford (Eds.), *Gender differences in human cognition. Counterpoints: Cognition, memory, and language.* New York: Oxford University Press.

Crawford, M., Stark, A. C., & Renner, C. H. (1998). The meaning of Ms.: Social assimilation of a gender concept. *Psychology of Women Quarterly, 22,* 197–208.

Creese, I., Burd, D. R., & Snyder, S. H. (1976). Dopamine receptor binding predicts clinical and pharmocological potencies of antischizophrenic drugs. *Science, 192,* 481–483.

Crits-Christoph, P., Cooper, A., & Luborsky, L. (1988). The accuracy of therapists' interpretations and the outcome of dynamic psychotherapy. *Journal of Consulting and Clinical Psychology, 56,* 490–495.

Crook, J. M., & Copolov, D. L. (2000). Schizophrenia. In G. Fink (Ed.), *Encyclopedia of stress.* San Diego, CA: Academic Press.

Cross, S. E., & Markus, H. R. (1999). The cultural constitution of personality. In L. A. Pervin & O. P. John (Eds.), *Handbook of personality: Theory and research.* New York: Guilford Press.

Crowe, L. C., & George, W. H. (1989). Alcohol and human sexuality: Review and integration. *Psychological Bulletin, 105,* 374–386.

Crowley, K., Callanan, M. A., Tenenbaum, H. R., & Allen, E. (2001). Parents explain more often to boys than to girls during shared scientific thinking. *Psychological Science, 12,* 258–261.

Culbertson, F. M. (1997). Depression and gender: An international review. *American Psychologist, 52,* 25–31.

Cull, W. L. (2000). Untangling the benefits of multiple study opportunities and repeated testing for cued recall. *Applied Cognitive Psychology, 14,* 215–235.

Cummins, H. J. (1999, March 2). Kids learn to kill like soldiers do, author says. *Seattle Post-Intelligencer,* p. E4.

Curtis, G. C., Magee, W. J., Eaton, W. W., Wittchen, H.-U., & Kessler, R. C. (1998). Specific fears and phobias: Epidemiology and classification. *British Journal of Psychiatry, 173,* 112–117.

Curtiss, S. (1977). *Genie: A psychological study of a modern day "wild child."* New York: Academic Press.

Cytowic, R. E. (2002). *Synesthesia: A union of the senses* (2nd ed.). Boston: MIT Press.

Dalton, P. (2002). Olfaction. In H. Pashler & S. Yantis (Eds.), *Steven's handbook of experimental psychology: Vol. 1. Sensation and perception* (3rd ed.). New York: Wiley.

Daly, M., & Wilson, M. (1988). *Homicide.* New York: Aldine de Gruyter.

Daniels, C. W. (2002). Legal aspects of polygraph admissibility in the United States. In M. Kleiner (Ed.), *Handbook of polygraph testing.* San Diego, CA: Academic Press.

Darley, J. M., & Gross, P. H. (1983). A hypothesis-confirming bias in labeling effects. *Journal of Personality and Social Psychology, 44,* 20–33.

Darley, J. M., & Latané, B. (1968). Bystander intervention in emergencies: Diffusion of responsibility. *Journal of Personality and Social Psychology, 8,* 377–383.

Dasen, P. R., Barthélémy, D., Kan, E., Kouamé, K., Daouda, K., Adjéi, K. K., & Assandé, N. (1985). N'glouele, l'intelligence chez les Baoulé [N'glouele, intelligence according to the Baoulé]. *Archives de Psychologie, 53,* 293–324.

Davidson, R. J. (1998). *Neuropsychological perspectives on affective and anxiety disorders.* Chicago: Psychology Press.

Davidson, R. J., & Fox, N. A. (1988). Cerebral asymmetry and emotion: Developmental and individual differences. In D. L. Molfese & S. J. Segalowitz (Eds.), *Brain lateralization in children: Developmental implications.* New York: Guilford Press.

Davis, C. G., Nolen, H. S., & Larson, J. (1998). Making sense of loss and benefiting from the experience: Two construals of meaning. *Journal of Personality and Social Psychology, 75,* 561–574.

Davis, S., Jenkins, G., & Hunt, R. (Eds.). (2002). *The pact: Three young men make a promise and fulfill a dream.* New York: Riverhead.

Dawidowicz, L. S. (1975). *The war against the Jews, 1933–1945.* New York: Holt, Rinehart & Winston.

Dawood, K., Pillar, R. C., Horvath, C., Revelle, W., & Bailey, J. M. (2000). Familial aspects of male homosexuality. *Archives of Sexual Behavior, 29,* 155–163.

Day, R., Nielsen, J. A., Korten, A., et al. (1987). Stressful life events preceding the acute onset of schizophrenia. *Culture, Medicine, and Psychiatry, 11,* 123–205.

DeCasper, A. J., & Spence, M. J. (1986). Prenatal maternal speech influences newborns' perceptions of speech sounds. *Infant Behavior and Development, 9,* 133–150.

deCastro, J. M. (2002). Age-related changes in the social, psychological, and temporal influences on food intake in free-living, healthy, adult humans. *Journals of Gerontology: Series A. Biological Sciences and Medical Sciences, 57A,* 368–377.

De Cremer, D., & van Lange, P. A. M. (2001). Why prosocials exhibit greater cooperation than proselfs: The roles of social responsibility and reciprocity. *European Journal of Personality, 15,* 5–18.

Deese, J. (1959). Influence of inter-item associative strength upon immediate free recall. *Psychological Reports, 5,* 305–312.

Degen, L., Matzinger, D., Drewe, J., & Beglinger, C. (2001). The effect of cholecystokinin in controlling appetite and food intake in humans. *Peptides, 22,* 1265–1269.

deGeus, E. J. C. (2000). Aerobics in stress reduction. In G. Fink (Ed.), *Encyclopedia of stress.* San Diego, CA: Academic Press.

Dehaene, S., & Naccache, L. (2001). Towards a cognitive neuroscience of consciousness: Basic evidence and a workspace framework. *Cognition, 79,* 1–37.

Dekker, E., & Groen, J. (1956). Reproducible psychogenic attacks of asthma. *Journal of Psychosomatic Research, 1,* 56–67.

DeLongis, A. (2000). Coping skills. In G. Fink (Ed.), *Encyclopedia of stress.* San Diego, CA: Academic Press.

Demarest, J., & Allen, R. (2000). Body image: Gender, ethnic, and age differences. *Journal of Social Psychology, 140,* 465–472.

Dement, W. C. (1974). *Some must watch while some must sleep.* San Francisco: Freeman.

DeMoranville, B. M., Jackson, I., Ader, R., Madden, K. S., Felten, D. L., & Bellinger, D. L. (2000). Endocrine and immune systems. In B. S. Fogel, R. B. Schiffer, & S. M. Rao (Eds.), *Synopsis of neuropsychiatry.* Philadelphia: Lippincott-Raven.

Denham, S. A, Blair, K. A, DeMulder, E., Levitas, J., Sawyer, K., Auerbach Major, S., & Queenan, P. (2003). Preschool emotional competence: Pathway to social competence? *Developmental Psychology, 74,* 238–256.

Depue, R. A., & Collins, P. F. (1999). Neurobiology of the structure of personality: Dopamine, facilitation of incentive motivation, and extraversion. *Behavioral and Brain Sciences, 22,* 491–569.

DeRegnier, R. A., Wewerka, S., Georgieff, M. K., Mattia, F., & Nelson, C. A. (2002). Influences of postconceptional age and postnatal experience on the development of auditory recognition memory in the newborn infant. *Developmental Psychobiology, 41,* 216–225.

Derogatis, L. R. (1986). *Clinical psychopharmacology.* Menlo Park, CA: Addison-Wesley.

DeRubeis, R. J., & Crits-Christoph, P. (1998). Empirically supported individual and group psychological treatments for adult mental disorders. *Journal of Consulting and Clinical Psychology, 66,* 37–52.

De Silva, P., & Rachman, J. (1998). *Obsessive-compulsive disorders.* New York: Oxford University Press.

D'Esposito, M. D. (2003). *Neurological Foundations of Cognitive Neuroscience.* Boston: MIT Press.

Deutsch, M., & Gerard, H. B. (1955). A study of normative and informational social influence upon individual judgment. *Journal of Abnormal and Social Psychology, 51,* 629–636.

DeValois, R. L., & DeValois, K. K. (1988). *Spatial vision.* New York: Oxford University Press.

Devane, W. A., Hanus, L., Breuer, A., Pertwee, R. G., Stevenson, L. A., & Griffin, G. (1992). Isolation and structure of a brain constituent that binds to the cannabinoid receptor. *Science, 18,* 1946–1949.

DeVries, H., Mudde, A. N., Dijkstra, A., & Willemsen, M. C. (1998). Differential beliefs, perceived social influences, and self-efficacy expectations among smokers in various motivational phases. *Preventive Medicine, 27,* 681–689.

Dewsbury, D. A. (1997). In celebration of the centennial of Ivan P. Pavlov's (1897/1902) *The Work of the Digestive Glands. American Psychologist, 52,* 933–935.

Diaz, J. (1997). *How drugs influence behavior: A neuro-behavioral approach.* Upper Saddle River, NJ: Prentice Hall.

DiClemente, C. C. (2003). *Addiction and change: How addictions develop and addicted people recover.* New York: Guilford Press.

Diener, E. (2000). Subjective well-being: The science of happiness and a proposal for a national index. *American Psychologist, 55,* 34–43.

Diener, E., & Diener, C. (1996). Most people are happy. *Psychological Science 7,* 181–185.

Diener, E., Diener, M., & Diener, C. (1995). Factors predicting the well-being of nations. *Journal of Personality and Social Psychology, 69,* 851–864.

Diener, E., Gohm, C. L., Suh, E., Oishi, S. (2000). Similarity of the relations between marital status and subjective well-being across cultures. *Journal of Cross-Cultural Psychology, 31,* 419–436.

Diener, E., & Seligman, M. E. P. (2002). Very happy people. *Psychological Science, 13,* 81–84.

Diener, E., Suh, E., Lucas, R. E., & Smith, H. L. (1999). Subjective well-being: Three decades of progress. *Psychological Bulletin, 125,* 276–302.

Dienstbier, R. A. (1989). Arousal and physiological toughness: Implications for mental and physical health. *Psychological Review, 96,* 84–100.

Dimberg, U. (1997). Psychophysiological reactions to facial expressions. In U. C. Segerstrale et al. (Eds.), *Nonverbal communication: Where nature meets culture.* Mahwah, NJ: Erlbaum.

Dindia, K. (2002). Self-disclosure research: Knowledge through meta-analysis. In M. Allen, R. W. Preiss, B. M. Gayle, & N. A. Burrell (Eds.), *Interpersonal communication research: Advances through meta-analysis.* Mahwah, NJ: Erlbaum.

Di Paula, A., & Campbell, J. D. (2002). Self-esteem and persistence in the face of failure. *Journal of Personality and Social Psychology, 83,* 711–724.

Dishman, R. K. (1982). Compliance/adherence in health-related exercise. *Health Psychology, 1,* 237–267.

Dishman, R. K. (1994). *Advances in exercise adherence.* Champaign, IL: Human Kinetics.

Dixon, N. F. (1981). *Preconscious processing.* New York: Wiley.

Dobson, V., & Teller, D. Y. (1978). Visual acuity in human infants: A review and comparison of behavioral and electrophysiological studies. *Vision Research, 18,* 1469–1483.

Dodge, K. A. (1986). A social information processing model of social competence in children. *Cognitive perspectives on children's social behavioral development. The Minnesota symposium on child psychology, 18,* 77–125.

Doka, K. J. (1995). Coping with life-threatening illness: A task model. *Omega: Journal of Death and Dying, 32,* 111–122.

Domhoff, G. W. (1999). Drawing theoretical implications from descriptive empirical findings on dream content. *Dreaming: Journal of the Association for the Study of Dreams, 9,* 201–210.

Domhoff, G. W. (2001). A new neurocognitive theory of dreams. *Dreaming: Journal of the Association for the Study of Dreams, 11,* 13–33.

Domino, G. (2000). *Psychological testing.* Upper Saddle River, NJ: Prentice Hall.

Domjan, M. (2000a). *The essentials of conditioning and learning* (2nd ed.). Belmont, CA: Wadsworth/Thomson.

Domjan, M. (2000b). General process learning theory: Challenges from response and stimulus factors. *International Journal of Comparative Psychology, 13,* 101–118.

Donaldson, D. (1998). *Psychiatric disorders with a biochemical basis.* New York: Parthenon Publishing Group.

Donnerstein, E., & Malamuth, N. (1997). Pornography: Its consequences on the observer. In L. B. Schlesinger & E. Revitch (Eds.), *Sexual dynamics of anti-social behavior* (2nd ed.). Springfield, IL: Charles C Thomas.

Doppelt, J. E., & Wallace, W. L. (1955). Standardization of the Wechsler Adult Intelligence Scale for older persons. *Journal of Abnormal and Social Psychology, 51,* 312–330.

Dossenbach, M., & Dossenbach H. D. (1998). *All about animal vision.* Chicago: Blackbirch Press.

Dovidio, J. F. (1984). Helping behavior and altruism: An empirical and conceptual overview. In L. Berkowitz (Ed.), *Advances in experimental social psychology* (Vol. 17). New York: Academic Press.

Dovidio, J. F., Kawakami, K., & Gaertner, S. L. (2000). Reducing contemporary prejudice: Combatting bias at the individual and intergroup levels. In S. Oskamp (Ed.), *Reducing prejudice and discrimination.* Mahwah, NJ: Erlbaum.

Downey, G., & Feldman, S. L. (1996). Implications of rejection sensitivity for intimate relationships. *Journal of Personality and Social Psychology, 70,* 1327–1343.

Drake, M. E., Pakalnis, A., & Denio, L. C. (1988). Differential diagnosis of epilepsy and multiple personality: Clinical and EEG findings in 15 cases. *Neuropsychiatry, Neuropsychology, and Behavioral Neurology, 1,* 131–140.

Drigotas, S. M. (2002). The Michelangelo phenomenon and personal well-being. *Journal of Personality, 70,* 59–77.

Driskell, J. E., Willis, R. P., & Copper, C. (1992). Effect of overlearning on retention. *Journal of Applied Psychology, 77,* 615–622.

Drukin, K. (1998). Implicit content and implicit processes in mass media use. In K. Kirsner et al. (Eds.), *Implicit and explicit mental processes.* Mahwah, NJ: Erlbaum.

Dryden, W. (Ed.). (2002). *Handbook of individual therapy.* Thousand Oaks, CA: Sage.

Duffy, J. F., Rimmer, D. W., Czeisler, C. A. (2001). Association of intrinsic circadian period with morningness-eveningness, usual wake time, and circadian phase. *Behavioral Neuroscience, 115,* 895–899.

Duncan, P. M., Alici, T., & Woodward, J. D. (2000). Conditioned compensatory response to ethanol as indicated by locomotor activity in rats. *Behavioural Pharmacology, 11,* 395–402.

Dunn, J., & Plomin, R. (1990). *Separate lives: Why siblings are so different.* New York: Basic Books.

Dunne, M. P., Bailey, J. M., Kirk, K. M., & Martin, N. G. (2000). The subtlety of sex-atypicality. *Archives of Sexual Behavior, 29,* 549–565.

Durrant, J. E. (2000). Trends in youth crime and well-being since the abolition of corporal punishment in Sweden. *Youth and Society, 31,* 437–455.

Duvander, A. Z. E. (1999). The transition from cohabitation to marriage: A longitudinal study of the propensity to marry in Sweden in the early 1990s. *Journal of Family Issues, 20,* 698–717.

Dying to be thin [Television series program]. (2000). *Nova,* WGBH: Boston.

Eacott, M. J., & Crawley, R. A. (1998). The offset of childhood amnesia: Memory for events that occurred before age 3. *Journal of Experimental Psychology: General, 127,* 22–33.

Eagly, A. H., & Carli, L. L. (1981). Sex of researcher and sex-typed communications as determinants of sex differences in influenceability: A meta-analysis of social influence studies. *Psychological Bulletin, 90,* 1–20.

Eagly, A. H., & Crowley, M. (1986). Gender and helping behavior: A meta-analytic review of the social psychological literature. *Psychological Bulletin, 100,* 283–308.

Eagly, A. H., & Wood, W. (1999). The origins of sex differences in human behavior: Evolved dispositions versus social roles. *American Psychologist, 54,* 408–423.

Eagly, A. H., Wood, W., & Diekman, A. B. (2000). Social role theory of sex differences and similarities: A current appraisal. In T. Eckes & H. M. Trautner (Eds.), *The developmental social psychology of gender.* Mahwah, NJ: Erlbaum.

Eaton, J. (2001). Management communication: The threat of groupthink. *Corporate Communications, 6,* 183–192.

Ebbinghaus, H. (1964). *Über das Gedächtnis: Untersuchungen Zur Experimentellen Psychologie [Memory: A contribution to experimental psychology].* (H. A. Ruger & C. E. Bussenius, Trans.). New York: Dover. (Original work published 1885)

Eccles, J. (1991). Gender-role socialization. In R. M. Baron, W. G. Graziano, & C. Stangor (Eds.), *Social psychology.* Ft. Worth, TX: Holt, Rinehart & Winston.

Echt, K. V., Morrell, R. W., & Park, D. C. (1998). Effects of age and training formats on basic computer skill acquisition in older adults. *Educational Gerontology, 24,* 3–25.

Eckensberger, L. H., & Zimba, R. F. (1997). The development of moral judgment. In J. W. Berry, P. R. Dasen, & T. S. Saraswathi (Eds.), *Handbook of cross-cultural psychology* (2nd ed., Vol. 2). Boston: Allyn & Bacon.

Edser, S. J. (2002). Hypnotically facilitated counter conditioning of anticipatory nausea and vomiting associated with chemotherapy: A case study. *Australian Journal of Clinical Hypnotherapy and Hypnosis, 23,* 18–30.

Edwards, A. E. (1962). A demonstration of the long-term retention of a conditioned galvanic skin response. *Psychosomatic Medicine, 24,* 459–463.

Efran, J. F., & Greene, M. A. (2000). The limits of change: Heredity, environment, and family influence. In W. C. Nichols & M. A. Pace-Nichols (Eds.), *Handbook of family development and intervention.* New York: Wiley.

Ehrman, J. (2003). *Clinical exercise psychology.* Champaign, IL: Human Kinetics.

Eisenberg, N. (2000). Emotion, regulation, and moral development. *Annual Review of Psychology, 51,* 665–697.

Eisenberg, N. (2002). Emotion related regulation and its relation to quality of social functioning. In W. Hartup & R. A. Weinberg (Eds.), *Child psychology in retrospect and prospect: In celebration of the 75th anniversary of the Institute of Child Development. The Minnesota symposia on child psychology* (Vol. 32). Mahwah, NJ: Erlbaum.

Eisenberg, N., & Valiente, C. (2002). Parenting and children's prosocial and moral development. In M. H. Bornstein (Ed.), *Handbook of parenting: Vol. 5. Practical issues in parenting* (2nd ed.). Mahwah, NJ: Erlbaum.

Eisenstein, E. M., Eisenstein, D., & Smith, J. C. (2001). The evolutionary significance of habituation and sensitization across phylogeny: A behavioral homeostasis model. *Integrative Physiological and Behavioral Science, 36,* 251–265.

Ekman, P. (1999a). Basic emotions. In T. Dalgleish & M. J. Power (Eds.), *Handbook of cognition and emotion.* Chichester, England: Wiley.

Ekman, P. (1999b). Facial expressions. In T. Dalgleish & M. J. Power (Eds.), *Handbook of cognition and emotion*. Chichester, England: Wiley.

Ekman, P., & Friesen, W. V. (1987). *Facial Action Coding System*. Palo Alto, CA: Consulting Psychologists Press.

Ekman, P., Friesen, W. V., & Ellsworth, P. (1972). *Emotion in the human face: Guidelines for research and an integration of findings*. Oxford, England: Pergamon Press.

Elbert, T., Pantev, C., Wienbruch, C., Rockstroh, B., & Taub, E. (1995). Increased cortical representation of the fingers of the left hand in string players. *Science, 270*, 305–307.

Elkind, D. (1967). Egocentrism in adolescence. *Child Development, 38*, 1025–1034.

Elliot, A. J., & Church, M. A. (1997). A hierarchical model of approach and avoidance achievement motivation. *Journal of Personality and Social Psychology, 72*, 218–232.

Elliot, A. J., McGregor, H. A., & Gable, S. (1999). Achievement goals, study strategies, and exam performance: A mediational analysis. *Journal of Educational Psychology, 91*, 549–563.

Elliot, A. J., & Thrash, T. M. (2002). Approach-avoidance motivation in personality: Approach and avoidance temperaments and goals. *Journal of Personality and Social Psychology, 82*, 804–818.

Ellis, A. (1962). *Reason and emotion in psychotherapy*. New York: Lyle Stuart.

Ellis, L., & Ames, M. A. (1987). Neurohormonal functioning and sexual orientation: A theory of homosexuality-heterosexuality. *Psychology Bulletin, 101*, 233–258.

Elsey, B., & A. Fujiwara (2000). Kaizen and technology transfer instructors as work-based learning facilitators in overseas transplants: A case study. *Journal of Workplace Learning, 12*, 333–342.

Emerson, R. M. (1966). Mount Everest: A case study of communication feedback and sustained group goalstriving. *Sociometry, 29*, 213–227.

Emery, C. E., Jr. (2001, January/February). Cracked crystal balls? Psychics' predictions for past year a litany of prognostive failures *The Skeptical Inquirer, 25*(1), 7–8.

Emlen, S. T. (1975, August). The stellar-orientation system of a migratory bird. *Scientific American*, 102–111.

Epstein, M. A., & Bottoms, B. L. (2002). Explaining the forgetting and recovery of abuse and trauma memories: Possible mechanisms. *Child Maltreatment: Journal of the American Professional Society on the Abuse of Children, 7*, 210–225.

Epstein, R., Kirshnit, C. E., Lanza, R. P., & Rubin, L. C. (1984). "Insight" in the pigeon: Antecedents and determinants of an intelligent performance. *Nature, 308*, 61–62.

Epstein, S. (1983). Aggregation and beyond: Some basic issues on the production of behavior. *Journal of Personality, 51*, 360–392.

Epstein, S. (1998). *Constructive thinking: The key to emotional intelligence*. Westport, CT: Praeger.

Erdberg, P. (2000). Rorschach assessment. In G. Goldstein & M. Hersen (Eds.), *Handbook of psychological assessment* (3rd ed.). New York: Elsevier.

Erdelyi, M. H. (2001). Defense processes can be conscious or unconscious. *American Psychologist, 56*, 761–762.

Ericsson, K. A., & Chase, W. G. (1982). Exceptional memory. *American Scientist, 70*, 607–615.

Ericsson, K. A., Chase, W. G., & Faloon, S. (1980). Acquisition of a memory skill. *Science, 208*, 1181–1182.

Ericsson, K. A., Krampe, R. T., & Tesch R. C. (1993). The role of deliberate practice in the acquisition of expert performance. *Psychological Review, 100*, 363–406.

Ericsson, K. A., & Polson, P. G. (1988). An experimental analysis of the mechanisms of a memory skill. *Journal of Experimental Psychology: Learning, Memory, and Cognition, 14*, 305–316.

Erikson, E. H. (1968). *Identity, youth and crisis*. New York: W. W. Norton.

Erikson, E. H. (1980). *Identity and the life cycle*. New York: W. W. Norton. (Original work published 1959)

Erikson, E. H., Erikson, J. M., & Kivnick, H. Q. (1986). *Vital involvement in old age*. New York: W. W. Norton.

Eriksson, P. S., Perfilieva, E., Bjork-Erikkson, T., Alborn, A. M., Nordborg, C., Peterson, D. A., & Gage, F. H. (1998). Neurogenesis in the adult human hippocampus. *Nature-Medicine, 4*(11), 1313–1317.

Ernst, M., Moolchan, E. T., & Robinson, M. L. (2001). Behavioral and neural consequences of prenatal exposure to nicotine. *Journal of the American Academy of Child and Adolescent Psychiatry, 40*, 630–641.

Eron, L. D. (1987). The development of aggressive behavior from the perspective of a developing behaviorism. *American Psychologist, 42*, 435–442.

Eron, L. D. (2000). A psychological perspective. In V. B. Van Hasselt & M. Hersen (Eds.), *Aggression and violence: An introductory text*. Boston: Allyn & Bacon.

Esparza, J., Fox, C., Harper, I. T., Bennett, P. H., Schulz, L. O., Valencia, M. E., & Ravussin, E. (2000). Daily energy expenditure in Mexican and USA Pima Indians: Low physical activity as a possible cause of obesity. *International Journal of Obesity and Related Metabolic Disorders, 24*, 55–59.

Essau, C., & Petermann, F. (1999). *Depressive disorders in children and adolescents: Epidemiology, risk factors, and treatment*. Northvale, NJ: Jason Aronson.

Essau, C., & Trommsdorff, G. (1996). Coping with university-related problems: A cross-cultural comparison. *Journal of Cross-Cultural Psychology, 27*, 315–328.

Esser, J. K., & Lindoerfer, J. S. (1989). Groupthink and the space shuttle Challenger accident: Toward a quantitative case analysis. *Journal of Behavioral Decision Making, 2*, 167–177.

Estes, T. H., & Vaughn, J. L. (1985). *Reading and learning in the content classroom: Diagrams and instructional strategies* (3rd ed.). Boston: Allyn & Bacon.

Evers, K. E., Harlow, H. L., Redding, C. A., & LaForge, R. G. (1998). Longitudinal changes in stages of change for condom use in women. *American Journal of Health Promotion, 13*, 19–25.

Exner, J. E. (1991). *The Rorschach—A comprehensive system: Assessment of personality and psychopathology* (Vol. 2). New York: Wiley.

Eysenck, H. J. (1952). The effects of psychotherapy: An evaluation. *Journal of Consulting Psychology, 16*, 319–324.

Eysenck, H. J. (1964). *Crime and personality*. Boston: Houghton Mifflin.

Eysenck, H. J. (1967). *The biological basis of personality*. Springfield, IL: Charles C. Thomas.

Eysenck, H. J. (1990). Biological dimensions of personality. In L. A. Pervin (Ed.), *Handbook of personality: Theory and research*. New York: Guilford Press.

Eysenck, H. J. (1994). Cancer, personality, and stress: Prediction and prevention. *Advances in Behaviour Research and Therapy, 16*, 167–215.

Eysenck, H. J., & Grossarth-Marticek, R. (1991). Creative novation behavior therapy as a prophylactic treatment for cancer and coronary heart disease: II. Effects of treatment. *Behavior Research and Therapy, 29*, 17–31.

Fagley, N. S. (1987). Positional response bias in multiple-choice tests of learning: Its relation to testwiseness and guessing strategy. *Journal of Educational Psychology, 79*, 95–97.

Fagot, B. I., Leinbach, M. D., & O'Boyle, C. (1992). Gender labeling, gender stereotyping, and parenting behaviors. *Developmental Psychology, 28*, 225–230.

Faith, M. S., Matz, P. E., Jorge, M.A. (2002). Obesity depression associations in the population. *Journal of Psychosomatic Research, 53*, 935–942.

Fallon, A. E., & Rozin, P. (1985). Sex differences in perceptions of desirable body shape. *Journal of Abnormal Psychology, 94*, 102–105.

Fanselow, M. S. (1991). Analgesia as a response to aversive Pavlovian conditional stimuli: Cognitive and emotional mediators. In M. R. Denny (Ed.), *Fear, avoidance, and phobias: A fundamental analysis*. Hillsdale, NJ: Erlbaum.

Fantz, R. L. (1961, May). The origin of form perception. *Scientific American, 204*, 66–72.

Farmer, E. M. Z., Compton, S. N., Burns, B. J., & Robertson, E. (2002). Review of the evidence base for treatment of childhood psychopathology: Externalizing disorders. *Journal of Consulting and Clinical Psychology, 71*, 1267–1302.

Faust, J. (1991). Same-day surgery preparation: Reduction of pediatric patient arousal and distress through participant modeling. *Journal of Consulting and Clinical Psychology, 59*, 473–478.

Fazio, R. H., Jackson, J. R., Dunton, B. C., & Williams, C. J. (1995). Variability in automatic activation as an unobstrusive measure of racial attitudes: A bona fide pipeline? *Journal of Personality and Social Psychology, 69,* 1013–1027.

Federal Interagency Forum on Aging-Related Statistics. (2000). Older Americans 2000: *Key indicators of well-being.* Available online: http://www.agingstats.gov/chartbook2000

Feeny, N. C., & Foa, E. B. (2000). Sexual assault. In G. Fink (Ed.), *Encyclopedia of stress.* San Diego, CA: Academic Press.

Fein, S., & Spencer, S. J. (1997). Prejudice as self-image maintenance: Affirming the self through derogating others. *Journal of Personality and Social Psychology, 73,* 31–44.

Feingold, A. (1988). Matching for attractiveness in romantic partners and same-sex friends: A meta-analysis and theoretical critique. *Psychological Bulletin, 104,* 226–235.

Feingold, A., & Mazzella, R. (1998). Gender differences in body image are increasing. *Psychological Science, 9,* 190–195.

Felmlee, D. H. (1998). "Be careful what you wish for . . .": A quantitative and qualitative investigation of "fatal attractions." *Personal Relationships, 5,* 235–253.

Felton, D. L., & Maida, M. E. (2000). Neuroimmunomodulation. In G. Fink (Ed.), *Encyclopedia of stress.* San Diego, CA: Academic Press.

Fenton, W. S., & McGlaskan, T. H. (1991a). Natural history of schizophrenia subtypes: I. Longitudinal study of paranoid, hebephonic, and undifferentiated schizophrenia. *Archives of General Psychiatry, 48,* 969–977.

Fenton, W. S., & McGlaskan, T. H. (1991b). Natural history of schizophrenia subtypes: II. Positive and negative symptoms and long-term course. *Archives of General Psychiatry, 48,* 978–986.

Ferguson, E. D. (2000). *Motivation: A biosocial and cognitive integration of motivation and emotion.* New York: Oxford University Press.

Fernald, A., Taeschner, T., Dunn, J., Papousek, M., De Boysson-Bardies, B., & Fukui, I. (1989). A cross-cultural study of prosodic modification in mothers' and fathers' speech to preverbal infants. *Journal of Child Language, 16,* 477–501.

Ferster, C. B., & Skinner, B. F. (1957). *Schedules of reinforcement.* Englewood Cliffs, NJ: Prentice Hall.

Fessler, R. G. (1989). Physiology, anatomy and pharmacology of pain perception. In P. M. Camic & F. D. Brown (Eds.). *Assessing chronic pain: A multidisciplinary approach.* New York: Springer-Verlag.

Festinger, L. (1954). A theory of social comparison processes. *Human Relations, 2,* 117–140.

Festinger, L. (1957). *A theory of cognitive dissonance.* Stanford, CA: Stanford University Press.

Festinger, L., & Carlsmith, J. M. (1959). Cognitive consequences of forced compliance. *Journal of Abnormal and Social Psychology, 58,* 203–210.

Festinger, L., Pepitone, A., & Newcomb, T. (1952). Some consequences of deindividuation in a group. *Journal of Abnormal and Social Psychology, 47,* 382–389.

Fetterman, D. M. (1988). *Excellence and equality: A qualitatively different perspective on gifted and talented education.* Albany: State University of New York Press.

Fiedler, K., Nickel, S., Muehlfriedel, T., & Unkelbach, C. (2001). Is mood congruency an effect of genuine memory or response bias? *Journal of Experimental Social Psychology, 37,* 201–214.

Field, T. (2000). Infant massage therapy. In C. H. Zeanah, Jr. (Ed.), *Handbook of infant mental health* (2nd ed.). New York: Guilford Press.

Field, T. (2001). Massage therapy facilitates weight gain in preterm infants. *Current Directions in Psychological Science, 10,* 51–54.

Field, T. M., Schanberg, S. M., Scafidi, F., Bauer, C. R., Vega-Lahr, N., Garcia, R., Nystrom, J., & Kuhn, C. M. (1986). Tactile/kinesthetic stimulation effects on preterm neonates. *Pediatrics, 77,* 654–658.

Filogamo, G. (1998). *Brain plasticity: development and aging: Advances in neurobiology: plasticity and regeneration.* New York: Plenum.

Finell, J. S. (1997). *Mind-body problems: Psychotherapy with psychosomatic disorders.* Northvale, NJ: Jason Aronson.

Fishbach, A., Friedman, R. S., & Kruglanski, A. W. (2003). Leading us not unto temptation: Momentary allurements elicit overriding goal activation. *Journal of Personality and Social Psychology, 84,* 296–309.

Fishbein, M., & Ajzen, I. (1974). Attitudes toward objects as predictors of single and multiple behavioral criteria. *Psychological Review, 81,* 59–74.

Fisher, C., Kahn E., Edwards, A., Davis, D. M., & Fine, J. (1974). A psychophysiological study of nightmares and night terrors: III. Mental content and recall of stage 4 night terrors. *Journal of Nervous and Mental Disease, 158,* 174–188.

Fisher, S., & Greenberg, R. P. (1996). *Freud scientifically reappraised: Testing the theories and therapy.* New York: Wiley.

Fiske, S. T. (2002). What we know about bias and intergroup conflict, the problem of the century. *Current Directions in Psychological Science, 11,* 123–128.

Flavell, J. H. (1970). Developmental studies of mediated behavior. In H. W. Reese and L. P. Lipsett (Eds.), *Advances in child development and behavior* (Vol. 5). New York: Academic Press.

Flegal K. M., Carroll, M. D., Ogden, C. L., & Johnson, C. L. (2002). Prevalence and trends in obesity among U.S. adults, 1999–2000. *Journal of the American Medical Association, 288,* 1723–1727.

Flynn, J. R. (1987). Massive IQ gains in 14 nations: What IQ tests really measure. *Psychological Bulletin, 101,* 171–191.

Flynn, J. R. (1998). IQ gains over time: Toward finding the causes. In U. Neisser et al. (Eds.), *The rising curve: Long-term gains in IQ and related measures.* Washington, DC: American Psychological Association.

Foa, E. B., Franklin, M. E., Perry, K., & Herbert, J. D. (1996). Cognitive biases in generalized social phobia. *Journal of Abnormal Psychology, 105,* 433–439.

Foa, E. B., & Meadows, E. A. (1997). Psychosocial treatments for posttraumatic stress disorder: A critical review. *Annual Review of Psychology, 48,* 449–480.

Foa, E. B., Riggs, D. S., & Gershuny, B. S. (1995). Arousal, numbing, and intrusion: Symptom structure of post traumatic stress disorder following assault. *American Journal of Psychology, 152,* 116–120.

Foa, E. B., Zoellner, L. A., Feeny, N. C., Hembree, E. A., & Alvarez-Conrad, J. (2002). Does imaginal exposure exacerbate PTSD symptoms? *Journal of Consulting and Clinical Psychology, 70,* 1022–1028.

Folkard, S., & Monk, T. H. (Eds.). (1985). *Hours of work: Temporal factors in work scheduling.* New York: Wiley.

Fordyce, W. E. (1988). Pain and suffering: A reappraisal. *American Psychologist, 43,* 276–283.

Fosse, R., Stickgold, R., & Hobson, J. A. (2001). Brain-mind states: Reciprocal variation in thoughts and hallucinations. *Psychological Science, 2001, 12,* 30–36.

Foulkes, D. (1982). REM-dream perspectives on the development of affect and cognition. *Psychiatric Journal of the University of Ottawa, 7,* 48–55.

Foulkes, D. (1999). *Children's dreaming and the development of consciousness.* Cambridge, MA: Harvard University Press.

Foulks, F. F., Bland, I. J., & Shervington, D. (1995). Psychotherapy across cultures. *Review of Psychiatry, 14,* 511.

Fouts, D. H. (1994). The use of remote video recordings to study the use of American Sign Language by chimpanzees when no humans are present. In R. A. Gardner, B. T. Gardner, A. B. Chiarelli, & F. X. Plooij (Eds.), *The ethological roots of culture.* Dordrecht, Netherlands: Kluwer.

Fouts, R. S., Fouts, D. H., & Van Cantfort, T. E. (1989). The infant Loulis learns signs from other cross-fostered chimpanzees. In R. A. Gardner, B. T. Gardner, & T. E. Van Cantfort (Eds.), *Teaching sign language to chimpanzees.* Albany: State University of New York Press.

Fowles, D. C., & Kochanska, G. (2000). Temperament as a moderator of pathways to conscience in children: The contribution of electrodermal activity. *Psychophysiology, 37,* 788–795.

Fox, D. K., Hopkins, B. L., & Anger, W. K. (1987). The long-term effects of a token economy on safety performance in open-pit mining. *Journal of Applied Behavior Analysis, 20,* 215–224.

Frank, N. C., Spirito, A., Stark, L., & Owens-Stively, J. (1997). The use of scheduled awakenings to eliminate childhood sleepwalking. *Journal of Pediatric Psychology, 22,* 345–353.

Frankenberger, K. D. (2000). Adolescent egocentrism: A comparison among adolescents and adults. *Journal of Adolescence, 23,* 343–354.

Franklin, J. (1987). *Molecules of the mind: The brave new science of molecular psychology.* New York: Atheneum.

Franklin, T. R., Acton, P. D., Maldjian, J. A., Gray, J. D., Croft, J. R., Dackis, C. A., O'Brien, C. P., & Childress, A. R. (2002). Decreased gray matter concentration in the insular, orbitofrontal, cingulate, and temporal cortices of cocaine patients. *Biological Psychiatry, 51,* 134–142.

Frayser, S. G. (1985). *Varieties of sexual experience: An anthropological perspective on human sexuality.* New Haven, CT: HRAF.

Fredrickson, B. L. (1998). What good are positive emotions? *Review of General Psychology, 2,* 300–319.

French, S. J., & Cecil, J. E. (2001). Oral, gastric and intestinal influences on human feeding. *Physiology and Behavior, 74,* 729–734.

Freud, S. (1917). Mourning and melancholia. In J. Strachey (Ed.), *The standard edition of the complete psychological works of Sigmund Freud,* (Vol. 14). London: Hogarth, 1957.

Freud, S. (1923). *The ego and the id.* New York: W. W. Norton.

Freud, S. (1935). *A general introduction to psychoanalysis.* New York: Washington Square Press.

Freud, S. (1953). The interpretation of dreams. In J. Strachey (Ed.), *The standard edition of the complete psychological works of Sigmund Freud* (Vols. 4 and 5). London: Hogarth. (Original work published 1900)

Freud, S. (1965). *The interpretation of dreams.* New York: Avon. (Original work published 1900)

Friedman, H., & DiMatteo, M. R. (1989). *Health psychology.* New York: Prentice Hall.

Frisco, M. L., & Williams, K. (2003). Perceived housework equity, marital happiness, and divorce in dual earner households. *Journal of Family Issues, 24,* 51–73.

Fritsch, J. (1999, May 25). 95% Regain Lost Weight. Or Do They? *New York Times,* p. F7.

Fritzsche, B. A., Finkelstein, M. A., & Penner, L. A. (2000). To help or not to help: Capturing individuals' decision policies. *Social Behavior and Personality, 28,* 561–578.

Fuligni, A. J. (1998). Authority, autonomy, and parent-adolescent conflict and cohesion: A study of adolescents from Mexican, Chinese, Filipino, and European backgrounds. *Developmental Psychology, 34,* 782–792.

Funk, S. C. (1992). Hardiness: A review of theory and research. *Health Psychology 11,* 335–345.

Furmark, T., Tillfors, M., Marteinsdottir, I., Fischer, H., Pissiota, A., Langstroem, B., Fredrikson, M. (2002). Common changes in cerebral blood flow in patients with social phobia treated with citalopram or cognitive-behavioral therapy. *Archives of General Psychiatry, 59,* 425–433.

Gabbard, G. O. (1990). *Psychodynamic psychiatry in clinical practice.* Washington, DC: American Psychiatric Press.

Gabrieli, J. D. E. (1998). Cognitive neuroscience of human memory. *Annual Review of Psychology, 49,* 87–115.

Gabrieli, J. D. E., Desmond, J. E., Demb, J. B., & Wagner, A. D. (1996). Functional magnetic resonance imaging of semantic memory processes in the frontal lobes. *Psychological Science, 7,* 278–283.

Gainotti, G. (1972). Emotional behavior and hemispheric side of lesion. *Cortex, 8,* 41–55.

Galanter, E. (1962). Contemporary psychophysics. In R. Brown (Ed.), *New directions in psychology.* New York: Holt, Rinehart & Winston.

Galati, D., & Lavelli, M. (1997). Neonate and infant emotion expression perceived by adults. *Journal of Nonverbal Behavior, 21,* 57–83.

Galea, S., Ahern, J., Resnick, H., Kilpatrick, D., Bucuvalas, M., Gold, J., & Vlahov, D. (2002). Psychological sequelae of the September 11 terrorist attacks in New York City. *New England Journal of Medicine, 346,* 982–987.

Gallup, G. G., Jr. (1970). Chimpanzees: Self-recognition. *Science, 167*(3914), 86–87.

Gallup Organization (1988). *America's youth 1977–1988.* Princeton, NJ: Author.

Garbarino, S., Beelke, M., Costa, G., Violani, C., Lucidi, F., Ferrillo, F., et al. (2002). Brain function and effects of shift work: Implications for clinical neuropharmacology. *Neuropsychobiology, 45,* 50–56.

Garcia, J., & Koelling, R. A. (1966). The relation of cue to consequence in avoidance learning. *Psychonomic Science, 4,* 123–124.

Garcia, J., Lasiter, P. S., Bermudez, R. F., & Deems, D. A. (1985). A general theory of aversion learning. *Annals of the New York Academy of Sciences, 443,* 8–21.

Gardner, H. (2000). *Multiple intelligences: The theory in practice.* New York: Basic Books.

Gardner, H. (2003). Three distinct meanings of intelligence. In R. J. Sternberg, J. Lautrey, & T. I. Lubart (Eds.), *Models of intelligence: International perspectives.* Washington, DC: American Psychological Association.

Gardner, R. A., & Gardner, B. T. (1969). Teaching language to a chimpanzee. *Science, 165,* 664–672.

Garland, D. J., & Barry, J. R. (1991). Cognitive advantage in sport: The nature of perceptual structures. *American Journal of Psychology, 104,* 211–228.

Garmezy, N. (1983). *Stress, coping and development in children.* New York: McGraw-Hill.

Garnefski, N., & Arends, E. (1998). Sexual abuse and adolescent maladjustment: Differences between male and female victims. *Journal of Adolescence, 21,* 99–107.

Gathercole, S. E. (1998). The development of memory. *Journal of Child Psychology and Psychiatry and Allied Disciplines, 39,* 3–27.

Gazzaniga, M. S. (1985). *The social brain.* New York: Basic Books.

Gazzaniga, M. S., & Smylie, C. S. (1983). Facial recognition and brain asymmetries: Clues to underlying mechanisms. *Annals of Neurology, 13,* 536–540.

Ge, X., Conger, R. D., & Elder, G. H., Jr. (1996). Coming of age too early: Pubertal influences on girls' vulnerability to psychological distress. *Child Development, 67,* 3386–3400.

Geary, D. (1995). Reflections of evolution and culture in children's cognition: Implications for mathematical instruction and development. *American Psychologist, 50,* 24–37.

Geiger, M. A. (1991). Changing multiple choice answers: A validation and extension. *College Student Journal, 25,* 181–186.

Geldard, F. A. (1972). *The human senses.* New York: Wiley.

George, W. H., Stoner, S. A., Norris, J., Lopez, P. A., & Lehman, G. L. (2000). Alcohol expectancies and sexuality: A self-fulfilling prophecy analysis of dyadic perceptions and behavior. *Journal of Studies on Alcohol, 61,* 168–176.

Geracioti, T. D., Loosen, P. T., Ebert, M. H., & Schmidt, D. (1995). Fasting and postprandial cerebrospinal fluid glucose concentrations in healthy women and in an obese binge eater. *International Journal of Eating Disorders, 18,* 365–369.

Gerbner, G., Gross, L., Morgan, M., & Signiorelli, N. (1981). Health and medicine on television. *New England Journal of Medicine, 305,* 901–904.

Gergen, K. (2000). *An invitation to social constructivism.* Thousand Oaks, CA: Sage Publications.

Gershoff, E. T. (2002a). Corporal punishment by parents and associated child behaviors and experiences: A meta-analytic and theoretical review. *Psychological Bulletin, 128,* 539–579.

Gershoff, E. T. (2002b). Corporal punishment, physical abuse, and the burden of proof: Reply to Baumrind, Larzelere, and Cowan (2002), Holden (2002), and Parke (2002). *Psychological Bulletin, 128,* 602–611.

Gershon, E. S., Berrettini, W. H., & Golden, L. E. (1989). Mood disorders: Genetic aspects. In H. I. Kaplan & B. J. Sadock (Eds.), *Comprehensive textbook of psychiatry/V.* Baltimore: Williams & Wilkins.

Gerwirtz, J. C., & Davis, M. (2000). Using Pavlovian higher order conditioning paradigms to investigate the neural substrates of emotional learning and memory. *Learning and Memory, 7,* 257–266.

Ghetti, S., Qin, J., & Goodman, G. S. (2002). False memories in children and adults: Age, distinctiveness, and subjective experience. *Developmental Psychology, 38,* 705–718.

Gibson, J. J. (1979). *The ecological approach to visual perception.* Boston: Houghton Mifflin.

Gilbert, P. (2001). Evolutionary approaches to psychopathology: the role of natural defences. *Australian and New Zealand Journal of Psychiatry, 35,* 17–29.

Gilboa-Schechtman, E., & Foa, E. B. (2001). Patterns of recovery from trauma: The use of intraindividual analysis. *Journal of Abnormal Psychology, 110,* 392–400.

Gilligan, C. (1982). *In a different voice: Psychological theory and women's development.* Cambridge, MA: Harvard University Press.

Glanzer, M. (1972). Storage mechanisms in recall. In G. H. Bower (Ed.), *The psychology of learning and motivation: Advances in research and theory* (Vol. 5). New York: Academic Press.

Glanzer, M., & Cunitz, A. R. (1966). Two storage mechanisms in free recall. *Journal of Verbal Learning and Verbal Behavior, 5,* 351–360.

Glaser, R., & Bassok, M. (1989). Learning theory and the study of instruction. *Annual Review of Psychology, 40,* 631–666.

Glaser, R., & Kiecolt-Glaser, J. (Eds.). (1995). *Handbook of human stress and immunity.* New York: Academic Press.

Gleason, J.-B., & Ely, R. (2002). Gender differences in language development. In A. McGillicuddy-De Lisi & R. De Lisi (Eds.), *Biology, society, and behavior: The development of sex differences in cognition. Advances in applied developmental psychology* (Vol. 21). Westport, CT: Ablex Publishing.

Glucksman, M. L. (2001). The dream: A psychodynamically informative instrument. *Journal of Psychotherapy Practice and Research, 10,* 223–230.

Gobet, F., & Simon, H. A. (2000). Five seconds or sixty? Presentation time in expert memory. *Cognitive Science, 24,* 651–682.

Goddard, A. W., Mason, G. F., Almai, A., et al. (2001). Reductions in occipital cortex GABA levels in panic disorder detected with sup-1H-magnetic resonance spectroscopy. *Archives of General Psychiatry, 58,* 556–561.

Goddard, H. H. (1917). Mental tests and immigrants. *Journal of Delinquency, 2,* 243–277.

Godden, D. R., & Baddeley, A. D. (1975). Context-dependent memory in two natural environments: On land and under water. *British Journal of Psychology, 66,* 325–332.

Goffman, E. (1961). *Asylums: Essays on the social situation of mental patients and other inmates.* New York: Doubleday.

Goldberg, L. R. (1981). Unconfounding situational attributions from uncertain, neutral, and ambiguous ones: A psychometric analysis of descriptions of oneself and various types of others. *Journal of Personality and Social Psychology, 41,* 517–552.

Goldsmith, S. K. (2003). *Reducing suicide: A national imperative.* Washington, DC: National Academy Press.

Goldstein, B. (2002). *Sensation and perception* (6th ed.). Belmont, CA: Wadsworth.

Goldstein, G. (2000). Comprehensive neuropsychological assessment batteries. In G. Goldstein & M. Hersen (Eds.), *Handbook of psychological assessment* (3rd ed.). New York: Elsevier.

Goldstein, J. H., Cajko, L., Oosterbroek, M., Michielsen, M., Houten, O., & Salverda, F. (1997). Video games and the elderly. *Social Behavior and Personality, 25,* 345–352.

Gonzales, P. M., Blanton, H., & Williams, K. J. (2002). The effects of stereotype threat and double minority status on the test performance of Latino women. *Personality and Social Psychology Bulletin, 28,* 659–670.

Gonzalez, R. A., & Jaworski, J. N. (1997). Alcohol and glutamate. *Alcohol Health and Research World, 21,* 120–127.

Goodall, J. (1986). *The chimpanzees of Gombe: Patterns of behavior.* Cambridge, MA: Harvard University Press.

Goode, W. J. (1959). The theoretical importance of love. *American Sociological Review, 24,* 38–47.

Goodman, G. S., Quas, J. A., Batterman-Faunce, J. M., Riddlesberger, M. M., & Kuhn, J. (1994). Predictors of accurate and inaccurate memories of traumatic events experienced in childhood. *Consciousness and Cognition: An International Journal, 3,* 269–294.

Goodman, W. (1982, August 9). Of mice, monkeys and men. *Newsweek,* 61.

Goodwin, P. J., Leszcz, M., Ennis, M., et al. (2001). The effect of group psychosocial support on survival in metastatic breast cancer. *New England Journal of Medicine, 34,* 1719–1726.

Gorman, J. M. (2002). Treatment of generalized anxiety disorder. *Journal of Clinical Psychiatry, 63*(Suppl. 8), 17–23.

Gottesman, I. I. (1991). *Schizophrenia genesis: The origins of madness.* New York: Freeman.

Gottfried, A. E., Fleming, J. S., & Gottfried, A. W. (1998). Role of cognitively stimulating home environment in children's academic intrinsic motivation: A longitudinal study. *Child Development, 69,* 1448–1460.

Gottman, J. M., Coan, J., Carrere, S., & Swanson, C. (1998). Predicting marital happiness and stability from newlywed interactions. *Journal of Marriage and the Family, 60,* 5–22.

Gottman, J. M., & DeClaire, J. (2002). *The relationship cure: A five-step guide to strengthening your marriage, family, and friendships.* New York: Three Rivers Press.

Gottman, J. M., & Levenson, R. (1992). Marital processes predictive of later dissolution: Behavior, psychology and health. *Journal of Personality and Social Psychology, 63,* 221–233.

Gould, E., Reeves, A. J., Graziano, M. S. A., & Gross, C. G. (1999, October 15). Neurogenesis in the neocortex of adult primates. *Science,* 548–552.

Gracely, R. H., Farrell, M. J., & Grant, M. A. B. (2002). Temperature and pain perception. In H. Pashler & S.Yantis, (Eds.), *Steven's handbook of experimental psychology: Vol. 1. Sensation and perception* (3rd ed.). New York: Wiley.

Graham, S., Hudley, C., & Williams, E. (1992). Attributional and emotional determinants of aggression among African-American and Latino young adolescents. *Developmental Psychology, 28,* 731–740.

Grant, H. M., Bredahl, L. C., Clay, J., Ferrie, J., Groves, J. E., McDorman, T. A., & Dark, V. J. (1998). Context-dependent memory for meaningful material: Information for students. *Applied Cognitive Psychology, 12,* 617–623.

Graw, P., Werth, E., Kraeuchi, K., Gutzwiller, F., Cajochen, C., & Wirz-Justice, A. (2001). Early morning melatonin administration impairs psychomotor vigilance. *Behavioural Brain Research, 121,* 167–172.

Green, G., Brennan, L. C., & Fein, D. (2002). Intensive behavioral treatment for a toddler at high risk for autism. *Behavior Modification, 26,* 69–102.

Green, J. T., & Woodruff-Pak, D. S. (2000). Eyeblink classical conditioning: Hippocampal formation is for neutral stimulus associations as cerebellum is for association-response. *Psychological Bulletin, 126,* 138–158.

Green, M. (1999). Diagnosis of attention-deficit/hyperactivity disorder. *Technical Review Number 3, Publication No. 99-0050.* Rockville, MD: Agency for Health Care Policy and Research.

Green, M. F. (1997). *Schizophrenia from a neurocognitive perspective: Probing the impenetrable darkness.* Boston: Allyn & Bacon.

Greenberg, J., Solomon, S., & Pyszynski, T. (1997). Terror management theory of self-esteem and cultural worldviews: Empirical assessments and conceptual refinements. In M. P. Zanna (Ed.), *Advances in experimental social psychology* (Vol. 29). San Diego: Academic Press.

Greenberg, L. S., & Malcolm, W. (2002). Resolving unfinished business: Relating process to outcome. *Journal of Consulting and Clinical Psychology, 70,* 406–416.

Greenberg, L. S., & Rice, L. N. (1997). Humanistic approaches to psychotherapy. In P. L. Wachtel & S. B. Messer (Eds.), *Theories of psychotherapy: Origins and evolution.* Washington, DC: American Psychological Association.

Greene, K., Krcmar, M., Walters, L. H, Rubin, D. L. & Hale, J. L. (2000). Targeting adolescent risk-taking behaviors: The contribution of egocentrism and sensation seeking. *Journal of Adolescence, 23,* 439–461.

Greene, R. L. (1992). *Human memory: Paradigms and paradoxes.* Hillsdale, NJ: Erlbaum.

Greene, R. W., & Ollendick, T. H. (2000). Behavioral assessment of children. In G. Goldstein & M. Hersen (Eds.), *Handbook of psychological assessment* (3rd ed.). New York: Elsevier.

Greenfield, P. M. (1997). Culture as process: Empirical methods for cultural psychology. In J. W. Berry, Y. H. Poortinga, & J. Pandey (Eds.), *Cross-cultural psychology: Theory and method* (2nd ed., Vol. 1). Boston: Allyn & Bacon.

Greenleaf, E. (1973). "Senoi" dream groups. *Psychotherapy: Theory, Research and Practice, 10,* 218–222.

Greenwald, A. G. (1992). New look 3: Unconscious cognition reclaimed. *American Psychologist, 47,* 766–779.

Greenwald, A. G., & Banaji, M. R. (1995). Implicit social cognition: Attitudes, self-esteem, and stereotypes. *Psychological Review, 102,* 4–27.

Greenwald, A. G., Banaji, M. R., Rudman, L. A., Farnham, S. D., Nosek, B. A., & Mellott, D. S. (2002). A unified theory of implicit attitudes, stereotypes, self-esteem, and self-concept. *Psychological Review, 109,* 3–25.

Greenwald, A. G., McGhee, D. E., & Schwartz, J. (1998). Measuring individual differences in implicit cognition: The implicit association test. *Journal of Personality and Social Psychology, 74,* 1464–1480.

Greenwald, A. G., Spangenberg, E. R., Pratkanis, A. R., & Eskenazi, J. (1991). Double-blind tests of subliminal self-help tapes. *Psychological Science, 2,* 119–122.

Greer, H. S., Morris, T., & Pettingale, K. W. (1979). Psychological response to breast cancer: Effect on outcome. *Lancet, 2,* 785–787.

Gregory, R. J. (1998). *Foundations of intellectual assessment: The WAIS-III and other tests in clinical practice.* Boston: Allyn & Bacon.

Gregory, R. L., & Gombrich, E. H. (1973). *Illusion in nature and art.* London: Duckworth.

Grigorenko, E. L. (2003). Selected links between nutrition and the mind. In R. J. Sternberg, J. Lautrey, & T. I. Lubart (Eds.), *Models of intelligence: International perspectives.* Washington, DC: American Psychological Association.

Grimes, K., & Walker, E. F. (1994). Childhood emotional expressions, educational attainment, and age at onset of illness in schizophrenia. *Journal of Abnormal Psychology, 103,* 784–790.

Grimm, S. D., Church, A. T., Katigbak, M. S., & Reyes, J. A. (1999). Self-described traits, values, and moods associated with individualism and collectivism: Testing I-C theory in an individualistic (U.S.) and collectivistic (Philippine) culture. *Journal of Cross-Cultural Psychology, 30,* 466–500.

Gross, A. M., Bennett, T., Sloan, L., Marx, B. P., & Juergens, J. (2001). The impact of alcohol and alcohol expectancies on male perception of female sexual arousal in a date rape analog. *Experimental and Clinical Psychopharmacology, 9,* 380–388.

Grossman, D. (1996). *On killing: The psychological cost of learning to kill in war and society.* Boston: Little, Brown.

Groth-Marnat, G. (1999). *Handbook of psychological assessment.* New York: Wiley.

Guéguen, N. (2002). Foot in the door technique and computer mediated communication. *Computers in Human Behavior, 18,* 11–15.

Guilford, J. P. (1959). Three faces of intellect. *American Psychologist, 14,* 469–479.

Guilford, J. P. (1967). *The nature of human intelligence.* New York: McGraw-Hill.

Guilleminault, C., Poyares, D., Abat, F., & Palombini, L. (2001). Sleep and wakefulness in somnambulism: A spectral analysis study. *Journal of Psychosomatic Research, 51,* 411–416.

Guinness book of records. (2000). Stamford, CT: Guinness Media.

Gulevich, G., Dement, W., & Johnson, L. (1966). Psychiatric and EEG observations on a case of prolonged (264 hours) wakefulness. *Archives of General Psychiatry, 15,* 29–35.

Gump, L. S., Baker, R. C., & Roll, S. (2000). Cultural and gender differences in moral judgment: A study of Mexican Americans and Anglo-Americans. *Hispanic Journal of Behavioral Sciences, 22,* 78–93.

Gupta, P., & Cohen, N. J. (2002). Theoretical and computational analysis of skill learning, repetition priming, and procedural memory. *Psychological Review, 109,* 401–448.

Gur, R. E., Cowell, P., Turetsky, B. I., Gallacher, F., Cannon, T., Bilker, W., & Gur, R. B. (1998). A follow-up magnetic resonance imaging study of schizophrenia: Relationship of neuroanatomical changes to clinical and neurobehavioral measures. *Archives of General Psychiatry, 55,* 145–152.

Gustavson, C. R., Garcia, J., Hankins, W. G., & Rusiniak, K. W. (1974). Coyote predation control by aversive conditioning. *Science, 184,* 581–583.

Guthrie, J. P., Ash, R. A., & Bendapudi, V. (1995). Additional validity evidence for a measure of morningness. *Journal of Applied Psychology, 80,* 186–190.

Haaga, D. A. F., Dyck, M. J., & Ernst, D. (1991). Empirical status of cognitive theory of depression. *Psychological Bulletin, 110,* 215–236.

Hackman, J. R., & Lawler, E. E. (1971). Employee reactions to job characteristics. *Journal of Applied Psychology, 55,* 259–286.

Hafen, B. Q., & Hoeger, W. W. K. (1998). *Wellness: Guidelines for a healthy lifestyle.* Englewood, CO: Morton Publishing.

Haier, R. J., Siegel, B. V., Crinella, F. M., & Buchsbaum, M. S. (1993). Biological and psychometric intelligence: Testing an animal model in humans with positron emission tomography. In D. K. Detterman (Ed.), *Individual differences and cognition: Current topics in human intelligence* (Vol. 3). Norwood, NJ: Ablex.

Hailman, J. P. (1967). The ontogeny of an instinct. *Behaviour Supplements, 15,* 1–159.

Hailman, J. P. (1969). How an instinct is learned. *Scientific American, 221,* 98–106.

Hall, C. S., & Van de Castle, R. (1966). *The content analysis of dreams.* New York: Appleton-Century-Crofts.

Hall, D. R., & Zhao, J. Z. (1995). Cohabitation and divorce in Canada: Testing the selectivity hypothesis. *Journal of Marriage and the Family, 57,* 421–427.

Hall, G. C. N., & Okazaki, S. (2003). *Asian American psychology: The science of lives in context.* Washington, DC: American Psychological Association.

Hall, G. S. (1904). *Adolescence* (Vols. 1 and 2). New York: Appleton-Century-Crofts.

Hall, N. R. S., Anderson, J. A., & O'Grady, M. P. (1994). Stress and immunity in humans: Modifying variables. In R. Glaser & J. K. Kiecolt-Glaser (Eds.), *Handbook of human stress and immunity.* San Diego, CA: Academic Press.

Halpern, B. (2002). Taste. In H. Pashler & S. Yantis (Eds.). *Steven's handbook of experimental psychology: Vol. 1. Sensation and perception* (3rd ed.). New York: Wiley.

Halpern, D. F. (2000). *Sex differences in cognitive abilities* (3rd ed.). Mahwah, NJ: Erlbaum.

Halpern, D. F., & Tan, U. (2001). Stereotypes and steroids: Using a psychobiosocial model to understand cognitive sex differences. *Brain and Cognition, 45,* 392–414.

Hamann S., & Mao, H. (2002). Positive and negative emotional verbal stimuli elicit activity in the left amygdala. *Neuroreport, 13* (1), 15–19.

Hamer, D. H., & Copeland, P. (1998). *Living with our genes: Why they matter more than you think.* New York: Doubleday.

Hamilton, W. D. (1964). The genetical theory of social behaviour, I, II. *Journal of Theoretical Biology, 12,* 12–45.

Hammen, C. (1991). *Depression runs in families: The social context of risk and resilience in children of depressed mothers.* New York: Springer-Verlag.

Hampson, E., & Kimura, D. (1992). Sex differences and hormonal influences on cognitive functions in humans. In J. B. Becker, S. M. Breedlove, & D. Crews (Eds.), *Behavioral endocrinology.* Cambridge, MA: MIT Press.

Haney, C., & Zimbardo, P. (1998). The past and future of U.S. prison policy: Twenty-five years after the Stanford Prison Experiment. *American Psychologist, 53,* 709–727.

Hankin, B. L., Abramson, L. Y., Moffit, T. E., Silva, P. A., McGee, R., & Angell, K. E. (1998). Development of depression from preadolescence to young adulthood: Emerging gender differences in a 10-year longitudinal study. *Journal of Abnormal Psychology, 107,* 128–140.

Hanley, S. J., & Abell, S. C. (2002). Maslow and relatedness: Creating an interpersonal model of self-actualization. *Journal of Humanistic Psychology, 42,* 37–56.

Hansen, C. H., & Hansen, R. D. (1988). Finding the face in the crowd: An anger superiority effect. *Journal of Personality and Social Psychology, 54,* 917–924.

Hansen, N. B., Lambert, M. J., & Forman, E. M. (2002). The psychotherapy dose-response effect and its implications for treatment delivery services. *Clinical Psychology: Science and Practice, 9,* 329–343.

Happé, F. G. E., Winner, E., & Brownell, H. (1998). The getting of wisdom: Theory of mind in old age. *Developmental Psychology, 34,* 358–362.

Harackiewicz, J. M., Barron, K. E., Tauer, J. M., & Elliot, A. J. (2002). Predicting success in college: A longitudinal study of achievement goals and ability measures as predictors of interest and performance from freshman year through graduation. *Journal of Educational Psychology, 94,* 562–575.

Hardy, M. A., & Quadagno, J. (1995). Satisfaction with early retirement: Making choices in the auto industry. *Journals of Gerontology: Psychological Sciences and Social Sciences, 50B,* S217–S228.

Harley, K., & Reese, E. (1999). Origins of autobiographical memory. *Developmental Psychology, 35,* 1338–1348.

Harlow, H. F. (1958). The nature of love. *The American Psychologist, 13,* 673–685.

Harlow, H. F., & Suomi, S. J. (1970). The nature of love-simplified. *American Psychologist, 25,* 161–168.

Harlow, J., & Roll, S. (1992). Frequency of day residue in dreams of young adults. *Perceptual and Motor Skills, 74,* 832–834.

Harlow, J. M. (1868). Recovery from the passage of an iron bar through the head. *Massachusetts Medical Society, 2,* 327.

Harmon-Jones, E., Brehm, J. W., Greenberg, J., Simon, L., & Nelson, D. E. (1996). Evidence that the production of aversive consequences is not necessary to create cognitive dissonance. *Journal of Personality and Social Psychology, 70,* 5–16.

Harris, C. (2002, August 27). Amazing memory for digits still loses track of car keys. *Naples Daily News.*

Harris, R. J. (1977). Comprehension of pragmatic implications in advertising. *Journal of Applied Psychology, 62,* 603–608.

Harris, S. L. (1981). A letter from the editor on loss and trust. *Clinical Psychologist, 34*(3), 3.

Harrison, J. E., & Baron-Cohen, S. C. (1997). Synaesthesia: A review of psychological theories. In S. C. Baron et al. (Eds.), *Synaesthesia: Classic and contemporary readings.* Oxford, England: Blackwell.

Hart, J. W., Bridgett, D. J., & Karau, S. J. (2001). Coworker ability and effort as determinants of individual effort on a collective task. *Group Dynamics, 5,* 181–190.

Hartigan, J. A., & Wigdor, A. K. (Eds.). (1989). *Fairness in employment testing.* Washington, DC: National Academy Press.

Hartmann, E., Kunzendorf, R., Rosen, R., & Grace, N. G. (2001). Contextualizing images in dreams and daydreams. *Dreaming: Journal of the Association for the Study of Dreams, 11,* 97–104.

Hartshorne, H., & May, A. (1928). *Studies in the nature of character: Vol. 1. Studies in deceit.* New York: Macmillan.

Hasegawa, I., & Myashita, Y. (2002). Categorizing the world: Expert neurons look into key features. *Nature: Neuroscience, 5,* 90–91.

Hasher, L., & Zacks, R. T. (1979). Automatic and effortful processes in memory. *Journal of Experimental Psychology: General, 108,* 356–388.

Haskell, W. L., Alderman, E. L., Fair, J. M., et al. (1994). Effects of intensive multiple risk factor reduction on coronary atherosclerosis and clinical cardiac events in men and women with coronary artery disease. *Circulation, 89,* 975–990.

Hatfield, E. (1988). Passionate and companionate love. In R. J. Sternberg & M. L. Barnes (Eds.), *The psychology of love.* New Haven, CT: Yale University Press.

Hauri, P. (1982). *The sleep disorders* (2nd ed.). Kalamazoo, MI: Upjohn.

Hawley, P., & Little, T. D. (2002). Evolutionary and developmental perspectives on the agentic self. In D. Cervone & W. Mischel (Eds.), *Advances in personality science.* New York: Guilford Press.

Haynes, S. N. (2000). Behavioral assessment of adults. In G. Goldstein & M. Hersen (Eds.), *Handbook of psychological assessment* (3rd ed.). New York: Elsevier.

Hayslip, B., & Panek, P. E. (1989). *Adult development and aging.* New York: Harper & Row.

Hazan, C., & Diamond, L. M. (2000). The place of attachment in human mating. *Review of General Psychology, 4,* 186–204.

Hearold, S. (1986). A synthesis of 1043 effects of television on social behavior. In G. Comstock (Ed.), *Public communications and behavior* (Vol. 1). New York: Academic Press.

Heath, A. C., Bucholz, K. K., Madden, P. A. F., Dinwiddie, S. H., Slutske, W. S., & Bierut, L. J. (1997). Genetic and environmental contributions to alcohol dependence risk in a national twin sample: Consistency of findings in women and men. *Psychological Medicine, 27,* 1381–1396.

Heath, A. C., Kendler, K. S., Eaves, L. J., & Martin, N. G. (1990). Evidence for genetic influences on sleep disturbance and sleep pattern in twins. *Sleep, 13,* 318–335.

Heath, R. G. (1972). Pleasure and brain activity in man. *Journal of Nervous and Mental Disease, 154,* 3–18.

Heaton, T. B. (2002). Factors contributing to increasing marital stability in the U.S. *Journal of Family Issues, 23,* 392–409.

Hebb, D. O. (1949). *The organization of behavior.* New York: Wiley.

Heider, F. (1958). *The psychology of interpersonal relations.* New York: Wiley.

Heiman, J. R. (1977). A psychophysiological exploration of sexual arousal patterns in females and males. *Psychophysiology, 14,* 266–274.

Heimpel, S. A., Wood, J. V., Marshall, M. A., & Brown, J. D. (2002). Do people with low self-esteem really want to feel better? Self-esteem differences in motivation to repair negative moods. *Journal of Personality and Social Psychology, 82,* 128–147.

Heine, S. J., Kitayama, S., Lehman, D. R., Takata, T., Ide, E., et al. (2000). *Divergent consequences of success and failure in Japan and North America: An investigation of self-improving motivations and malleable selves.* Vancouver: University of British Columbia.

Heinrichs, R. W. (2001). *In search of madness: Schizophrenia and neuroscience.* New York: Oxford University Press.

Helgeson, V. S., Cohen, S., Schultz, R., & Yasko, J. (2000). Group support interventions for women with breast cancer: Who benefits from what? *Health Psychology, 19,* 107–114.

Heller, M. A., & Schiff, W. (Eds.). (1991). *The psychology of touch.* Hillsdale, NJ: Erlbaum.

Heller, W., Schmidke, J. I., Nitschke, J. B., Koven, N. S., & Miller, G. A. (2002). States, traits, and symptoms: Investigating the neural correlates of emotion, personality, and psychopathology. In D. Cervone & W. Mischel (Eds.), *Advances in personality science.* New York: Guilford Press.

Hellerstein, D., Yankowitch, P., Rosenthal, J., et al. (1993). A randomized double-blind study of fluoxetine versus placebo in the treatment of dysthymia. *American Journal of Psychiatry, 150,* 1169–1175.

Helson, R., Jones, C., & Kwan, V. S. Y. (2002). Personality change over 40 years of adulthood: Hierarchical linear modeling analyses of two longitudinal samples. *Journal of Personality and Social Psychology, 83,* 752–766.

Helzer, J. E., & Hudziak, J. J. (Eds). (2002). *Defining psychopathology in the 21st century: DSM-V and beyond.* Washington, DC: American Psychiatric Publishing.

Hendy, H. M., & Raudenbush, B. (2000). Effectiveness of teacher modeling to encourage food acceptance in preschool children. *Appetite, 34,* 61–76.

Herdt, G., & Lindenbaum, S. (Eds.). (1992). *Social analysis in the time of AIDS.* Newbury Park, CA: Sage Publications.

Herek, G. M. (2000). The psychology of sexual prejudice. *Current Directions in Psychological Science, 9,* 19–22.

Herek, G. M. (2002). Gender gaps in public opinion about lesbians and gay men. *Public Opinion Quarterly, 66,* 40–66.

Herman, D. B., Susser, E. S., Jandorf, L., Lavelle, J., & Bromet, E. J. (1998). Homelessness among individuals with psychotic disorders hospitalized for the first time: Findings from the Suffolk County Mental Health Project. *American Journal of Psychiatry, 155,* 109–113.

Herrington, R., & Lader, M. H. (1996). *Biological treatments in psychiatry* (2nd ed.). New York: Oxford University Press.

Hersen, M. (2002). *Clinical behavior therapy: Adults and children.* New York: Wiley.

Hersen, M. (2003). *Effective brief therapies.* New York: Academic Press.

Herskovits, M. J. (1948). *Man and his works.* New York: Knopf.

Herz, M., & Marder, S. (2002). *Schizophrenia: A comprehensive text.* New York: Williams & Wilkins.

Hess, E. H. (1959). Imprinting. *Science, 130,* 133–141.

Hess, W. R. (1965). Sleep as phenomenon of the integral organism. In K. Akert, C. Bally, & J. P. Schade (Eds.), *Sleep mechanisms.* New York: Elsevier.

Hetherington, E. M. (1998). Relevant issues in developmental science: Introduction to the special issue. *American Psychologist, 53,* 93–94.

Hetherington, E. M., Bridges, M., & Insabella, G. M. (1998). What matters? What does not? Five perspectives on the association between marital transitions and children's adjustment. *American Psychologist, 53,* 167–184.

Hetherington, E. M., & Stanley-Hagan, M. (2002). Parenting in divorced and remarried families. In M. H. Bornstein (Ed.), *Handbook of parenting: Being and becoming a parent* (2nd ed., Vol. 3). Mahwah, NJ: Erlbaum.

Hewstone, M., Rubin, M., & Willis, H. (2002). Intergroup bias. *Annual Review of Psychology, 53,* 575–604.

Heylighen, F. (1992). A cognitive-systemic reconstruction of Maslow's theory of self-actualization. *Behavioral Science, 37,* 39–58.

Higgins, E. T. (1996). The "self digest": Self-knowledge serving self-regulatory functions. *Journal of Personality and Social Psychology, 71,* 1062–1083.

Hilgard, E. R. (1977). *Divided consciousness: Multiple controls in human thought and action.* New York: Wiley.

Hilgard, E. R. (1991). A neodissociation interpretation of hypnosis. In S. J. Lynn & J. W. Rhue (Eds.), *Theories of hypnosis: Current models and perspectives.* New York: Guilford Press.

Hill, C. A. (1987). Affiliation motivation: People who need people but in different ways. *Journal of Personality and Social Psychology, 52,* 1008–1018.

Hill, M. M., Dodson, B. B., Hill, E. W., & Fox, J. (1995). An infant sonicguide intervention program for a child with a visual disability. *Journal of Visual Impairment and Blindness, 89,* 329–336.

Hill, W. F. (1963). *Learning: A survey of psychological interpretations.* San Francisco: Chandler.

Hillman, D. C., Siffre, M., Milano, G., & Halberg, F. (1994). Free-running psycho-physiologic circadians and three-month pattern in a woman isolated in a cave. *New Trends in Experimental and Clinical Psychiatry, 10,* 127–133.

Hinze, S. W. (2000). Inside medical marriages: The effect of gender on income. *Work and Occupations, 27,* 464–499.

Hobson, J. A. (1996). *Chemistry of conscious states: How the brain changes its mind.* Boston: Little, Brown.

Hobson, J. A., Pace-Schott, E. F., & Stickgold, R. (2000). Dreaming and the brain: Toward a cognitive neuroscience of conscious states. *Behavioral and Brain Sciences, 23,* 793–842.

Hodges, J., & Tizard, B. (1989). Social and family relationships of ex-institutional adolescents. *Journal of Child Psychology and Psychiatry, 30,* 77–97.

Hoffart, A., & Martinson, E. W. (1991). Mental health locus of control in agoraphobia and depression: A longitudinal study of inpatients. *Psychological Reports, 68,* 1011–1018.

Hoffman, H. G., Patterson, D. R., Canougher, G. J., & Sharar, S. R. (2001). Effectiveness of virtual reality-based pain control with multiple treatments. *Clinical Journal of Pain, 17,* 229–235.

Hoffman, M. L. (1994). Discipline and internalization. *Developmental Psychology, 30,* 26–28.

Hofman, M. A. (2001). Seasonal rhythms of neuronal activity in the human biological clock: A mathematical model. *Biological Rhythm Research, 32,* 17–34.

Hofmann, A. (1980). *LSD, my problem child.* New York: McGraw-Hill.

Hofstede, G., Arrindell, W. A., Best, D. L., De Mooij, M., Hoppe, M. H., et al. (1999). *Masculinity and femininity: The taboo dimensions of national cultures.* Thousand Oaks, CA: Sage Publications.

Hogan, R. (1983). A socioanalytic theory of personality. In M. Page & R. Dienstbier (Eds.), *Nebraska Symposium on Motivation, 1982.* Lincoln: University of Nebraska Press.

Hogarty, G. E. (2003). *Personal therapy for schizophrenia and related disorders.* New York: Guilford Press.

Hogue, M. E., Beaugrand, J. P., & Lauguee, P. C. (1996). Coherent use of information by hens observing their former dominant defeating or being defeated by a stranger. *Behavioural Processes, 38,* 241–252.

Holahan, C. J., & Moos, R. H. (1986). Personality, coping, and family resources in stress resistance: A longitudinal analysis. *Journal of Personality and Social Psychology 51,* 389–395.

Holahan, C. J., & Moos, R. H. (1990). Life stressors, resistance factors, and improved psychological functioning: An extension of the stress resistance paradigm. *Journal of Personality and Social Psychology, 58,* 909–917.

Holden, G. W. (2002). Perspectives on the effects of corporal punishment: Comment on Gershoff (2002). *Psychological Bulletin, 128,* 590–595.

Holland, J. L. (1985). *Making vocational choices: A theory of vocational personalities and work environments* (2nd ed.). Englewood Cliffs, NJ: Prentice Hall.

Hollis, K. L. (1997). Contemporary research on Pavlovian conditioning: A "new" functional analysis. *American Psychologist, 52,* 956–965.

Hollon, S. D. (1996). The efficacy and effectiveness of psychotherapy relative to medications. *American Psychologist, 51,* 1025–1030.

Hollon, S. D., & Beck, A. T. (1994). Cognitive and cognitive-behavioral therapies. In A. E. Bergin & S. L. Garfield (Eds.), *Handbook of psychotherapy and behavior change.* New York: Wiley.

Holmes, D. S. (1990). The evidence for repression: An examination of sixty years of research. In J. L. Singer (Ed.), *Repression and dissociation.* Chicago: University of Chicago Press.

Holmes, M. R., & St.-Lawrence, J. S. (1983). Treatment of rape-induced trauma: Proposed behavioral conceptualization and review of the literature. *Clinical Psychology Review, 3,* 417–433.

Holmes, T. H., & Rahe, R. H. (1967). The Social Readjustment Rating Scale. *Journal of Psychosomatic Research, 11,* 213–218.

Hong, Y., Ip, G., Chiu, C., & Morris, M. W. (2001). Cultural identity and dynamic construction of the self: Collective duties and individual rights in Chinese and American cultures. *Social Cognition, 19,* 251–268.

Honts, C. R., & Perry, M. V. (1992). Polygraph admissibility: Changes and challenges. *Law and Human Behavior, 16,* 357–379.

Hooper, J., & Teresi, M. (1986). *The three-pound universe.* New York: Macmillan.

Horn, J. (1985). Remodeling old models of intelligence. In B. B. Wolman (Ed.), *Handbook of intelligence: Theory, measurement, and application.* New York: Wiley.

Horn, J. L., & Cattell, R. C. (1966). Refinement and test of the theory of fluid and crystallized general intelligences. *Journal of Educational Psychology, 57,* 253–270.

Horn, J. L., & Masunaga, H. (2000). On the emergence of wisdom: Expertise development. *Understanding wisdom: Sources, science, & society.* Philadelphia: Templeton Foundation Press.

Houpt, T. A., Boulos, Z., Moore, E., & Martin, C. (1996). MidnightSun: Software for determining light exposure and phase-shifting schedules during global travel. *Physiology and Behavior, 59,* 561–568.

House, J. S., Landis, K. R., & Umberson, D. (1988). Social relationships and health. *Science, 241,* 540–545.

Hovland, C. I., Janis, I., and Kelley, H. H. (1953). *Communication and persuasion.* New Haven, CT: Yale University Press.

Howard, I. P. (2002). Depth perception. In H. Pashler & S.Yantis (Eds.), *Steven's handbook of experimental psychology: Vol. 1. Sensation and perception* (3rd ed.). New York: Wiley.

Howard, K. I., Kopta, S. M., Krause, M. S., & Orlinsky, D. E. (1986). The dose-effect relationship in psychotherapy. *American Psychologist, 41,* 159–164.

Howard, K. I., Lueger, R. J., Maling, M. S., & Martinovich, Z. (1993). A phase model of psychotherapy outcome: Causal mediation of change. *Journal of Consulting and Clinical Psychology, 61,* 678–685.

Hubbard, K., O'Neill, A. M., & Cheakalos, C. (1999, April 12). Out of control. *People,* 52–72.

Hubel, D. H., & Wiesel, T. N. (1979). Brain mechanisms of vision. *Scientific American, 241,* 150–162.

Hublin, C., Kaprio, J., Partinen, M., Heikkila, K., Koskenvuo, M. (1997). Prevalence and genetics of sleepwalking: A population-based twin study. *Neurology, 48,* 177–181.

Hublin, C., Kaprio, J., Partinen, M., & Koskenvuo, M. (2001). Parasomnias: Co-occurrence and genetics. *Psychiatric Genetics, 11,* 65–70.

Huddy, L., & Birtanen, S. (1995). Subgroup differentiation and subgroup bias among Latinos as a function of familiarity and positive distinctiveness. *Journal of Personality and Social Psychology, 68,* 97–108.

Hudson, W. (1960). Pictorial depth perception in sub-cultural groups in Africa. *Journal of Social Psychology, 52,* 183–208.

Huesmann, L. R. (1997). Observational learning of violent behavior: Social and biosocial processes. In A. Raine, P. A. Brennan, D. P. Farrington, & S. A. Mednick (Eds.), *Biosocial bases of violence.* New York: Plenum.

Huesmann, L. R., Moise, Titus, J., Podolski, C. L., & Eron, L. D. (2003). Longitudinal relations between children's exposure to TV violence and their aggressive and violent behavior in young adulthood: 1977–1992. *Developmental Psychology, 39,* 201–221.

Huff, R. M., Kline, M. V. (Eds.). (1999). *Promoting health in multicultural populations: A handbook for practitioners.* Thousand Oaks, CA: Sage Publications.

Hui, C. H., Yee, C., & Eastman, K. L. (1995). The relationship between individualism-collectivism and job satisfaction. *Applied Psychology: An International Review, 44,* 276–282.

Hull, C. L. (1943). *Principles of behavior, an introduction to behavior theory.* New York: Appleton-Century.

Human Genome Project Information (2003). http://www.ornl.gov/techresources/HumanGenome

Hunt, E. (1997). The status of the concept of intelligence. *Japanese Psychological Research, 39,* 1–11.

Hunt, E., & Agnoli, F. (1991). The Whorfian hypothesis: A cognitive psychology perspective. *Psychological Review, 98,* 377–389.

Hunter, J. E., & Hunter, R. F. (1984). Validity and utility of alternative predictors of job performance. *Psychological Bulletin, 96,* 72–98.

Huon, G. F., Mingyi, Q., Oliver, K., & Xiao, G. (2002). A large-scale survey of eating disorder symptomatology among female adolescents in the people's Republic of China. *International Journal of Eating Disorders, 32,* 192–205.

Huttenlocher, P. R. (1979). Synaptic density in human frontal cortex: Developmental changes and effects of aging. *Brain Research, 163,* 195–205.

Huttenlocher, P. R. (2002). *Neural plasticity.* Cambridge, MA: Harvard University Press.

Hyde, J. S., & DeLamater, J. (2003). *Understanding human sexuality* (8th ed.). Boston: McGraw-Hill.

Hyman, I. E., Husband, T. H., & Billings, F. J. (1995). False memories of childhood experiences. *Applied Cognitive Psychology, 9,* 181–197.

Hyman, R. (1994). Anomaly or artifact? Comments on Bem and Honorton. *Psychological Bulletin, 115,* 19–24.

Iervolino, A. C., Pike, A., Manke, B., Reiss, D., Hetherington, E. M., & Plomin, R. (2002). Genetic and environmental influences in adolescent peer socialization: Evidence from two genetically sensitive designs. *Child Development, 73,* 162–174.

Ikegaya, Y., Delcroix, I., Iwakura, Y., Matsuki, N., & Nishiyama, N. (2003). Interleukin-1 beta abrogates long-term depression of hippocampal CA1 synaptic transmission. *Synapse, 47,* 54–57.

Ikemi, Y., & Nakagawa, A. (1962). A psychosomatic study of contagious dermatitis. *Kyushu Journal of Medical Science, 13,* 335–350.

Ingelhart, R., & Rabier, J. R. (1986). Aspirations adapt to situations—but why are the Belgians so much happier than the French? A cross-cultural study of the quality of life. In F. M. Andrews (Ed.), *Research on the quality of life.* Ann Arbor, MI: Institute for Social Research, University of Michigan.

Ingold, C. H. (1989). Locus of control and use of public information. *Psychological Reports, 64,* 603–607.

Ingram, R. E., & Price, J. M. (2001). *Vulnerability to psychopathology: Risk across the lifespan.* New York: Guilford Press.

Inhelder, B., & Piaget, J. (1958). *The growth of logical thinking from childhood to adolescence.* New York: Basic Books.

Intraub, H. (2002). Anticipatory spatial representation of natural scenes: Momentum without movement? *Visual Cognition, 9,* 93–119.

Intraub, H., Gottesman, C. V., Willey, E. V., & Zuk, I. J. (1996). Boundary extension for briefly glimpsed photographs: Do common perceptual processes result in unexpected memory distortions? *Journal of Memory and Language, 35,* 118–134.

Ip, M. S. M., Tsang, W. T., Lam, W. K., & Lam, B. (1998). Obstructive sleep apnea syndrome: An experience in Chinese adults in Hong Kong. *Chinese Medical Journal, 111,* 257–260.

Irie, M., Maeda, M., & Nagata, S. (2001). Can conditioned histamine release occur under urethane anesthesia in guinea pigs? *Physiology and Behavior, 72,* 567–573.

Irwin, A. R., & Gross, A. M. (1995). Cognitive tempo, violent video games, and aggressive behavior in young boys. *Journal of Family Violence, 10,* 337–350.

Irwin, J. R., & McCarthy, D. (1998). Psychophysics: Methods and analyses of signal detection. In K. A. Lattal & M. Perone (Eds.), *Handbook of research methods in human operant behavior: Applied clinical psychology.* New York: Plenum.

Irwin, M., Daniels, M., & Weiner, H. (1987). Immune and neuroendocrine changes during bereavement. *Psychiatric Clinics of North America, 10,* 449–465.

Isaacs, K. S. (1998). *Uses of emotion: Nature's vital gift.* New York: Praeger.

Isaacson, R. L. (2002). Unsolved mysteries: The hippocampus. *Behavioral and Cognitive Neuroscience Reviews, 1,* 87–107.

Ishikawa, S. L., Raine, A., Lencz, T., Bihrle, S., & Lacasse, L. (2001). Autonomic stress reactivity and executive functions in successful and unsuccessful criminal psychopaths from the community. *Journal of Abnormal Psychology, 110,* 423–432.

Itard, J. M. G. (1962). *The wild boy of Aveyron* (G. Humphrey & M. Humphrey, Trans.). New York: Appleton-Century-Crofts. (Original work published 1894)

Ito, T. A., & Cacioppo, J. T. (2000). Electrophysiological evidence of implicit and explicit categorization processes. *Journal of Experimental Social Psychology, 36,* 660–676.

IUPsyS. (2003). Members in IUPsyS. *International Union of Psychological Science.* Available online: http://www.iupsys.org/

Iwasa, N. (2001). Moral reasoning among adults: Japan U.S. comparison. In H. Shimizu & R. A. LeVine (Eds.) *Japanese frames of mind: Cultural perspectives on human development.* New York: Cambridge University Press.

Iwasaki, Y. (2003). Roles of leisure in coping with stress among university students: A repeated-assessment field study. *Anxiety, Stress and Coping: An International Journal, 16,* 31–57.

Izard, C. (Ed.). (1982). *Measuring emotions in infants and children.* Cambridge, England: Cambridge University Press.

Izard, C. E. (1989). The structure and functions of emotions: Implications for cognition, motivation, and personality. In I. S. Cohen (Ed.), *The G. Stanley Hall Lecture Series* (Vol. 9). Washington, DC: American Psychological Association.

Jablensky, A., Sartorius, N., Enberg, C., Anker, M., Korten, A., et al. (1992). Schizophrenia: Manifestation, incidence, and course in different cultures: A World Health Organization ten country study. *Psychological Medicine Monograph Supplement 20.* Cambridge, England: Cambridge University Press.

Jackson, A., Morrow, J., Hill, D., & Dishman, R. (1999). *Physical activity for health and fitness.* Champaign, IL: Human Kinetics.

Jackson, N., & Butterfield, E. (1986). A conception of giftedness designed to promote research. In R. J. Sternberg & J. E. Davidson (Eds.), *Conceptions of giftedness.* New York: Cambridge University Press.

Jacobson, N. S., & Christensen, A. (1996). *Integrative couple therapy: Promoting acceptance and change.* New York: W. W. Norton.

Jacobson, N. S., Christensen, A., Prince, S. E., Cordova, J., & Eldridge, K. (2000). Integrative couple behavior therapy: An acceptance-based, promising new treatment for couple discord. *Journal of Consulting and Clinical Psychology, 68,* 351–355.

Jaffee, S. R., Moffitt, T. E., Caspi, A., & Taylor, A. (2003). Life with (or without) father: The benefits of living with two biological parents depend on the father's antisocial behavior. *Child Development, 74,* 109–126.

Jahoda, G. (1983). European "lag" in the development of an economic concept: A study in Zimbabwe. *British Journal of Developmental Psychology, 1,* 113–120.

James, W. (1879). Are we automata? *Mind, 4,* 1–22.

James, W. (1950). *Principles of psychology* (Vol. 2). New York: Dover Publications. (Original work published 1890)

Jamison, K. (1995, February). Manic-depressive illness and creativity. *Scientific American,* 63–67.

Janis, I. L. (1982). *Groupthink: Psychological studies of policy decisions and fiascos* (2nd ed.). Boston: Houghton Mifflin.

Jansma, J. M., Ramsey, N. F., Slagter, H. A., & Kahn, R. S. (2001). Functional anatomical correlates of controlled and automatic processing. *Journal of Cognitive Neuroscience, 13,* 730–743.

Janson, C., Lindberg, E., Gislason, T., Elmasry, A., & Boman, G. (2001). Insomnia in men: A 10-year prospective population based study. *Sleep: Journal of Sleep and Sleep Disorders Research, 24,* 425–430.

Janus, S. S., & Janus, C. L. (1993). *The Janus report on sexual behavior.* New York: Wiley.

Jeffery, R. W., & Wing, R. R. (1995). Long-term effects of interventions for weight loss using food provisions and money incentives. *Journal of Consulting and Clinical Psychology, 63,* 793–796.

Jemmott, J. B., Jemmott, L. S., & Fong, G. T. (1998). Abstinence and safer sex HIV risk-reduction interventions for African American adolescents. *Journal of the American Medical Association, 279,* 1529–1536.

Jencks, C., & Phillips, M. (Eds). (1998). *The Black-White test score gap.* Washington, DC: Brookings Institution.

Jenike, M. A. (1998). *Obsessive-compulsive disorders.* St. Louis, MO: Mosby.

Jennings, B. M. (1990). Stress, locus of control, social support, and psychological symptoms among head nurses. *Research in Nursing & Health, 13,* 393–401.

Jensen, A. R. (1998). The g factor and the design of education. In R. J. Sternberg & W. M. Williams (Eds.), *Intelligence, instruction, and assessment: Theory into practice.* Mahwah, NJ: Erlbaum.

Jensen, J. P., Bergin, A. E., & Greaves, D. W. (1990). The meaning of eclecticism: New survey and analysis of components. *Professional Psychology: Research and Practice, 21,* 124–130.

Jensen, M. P., Turner, J. A., & Romano, J. M. (2001). Changes in beliefs, catastrophizing, and coping are associated with improvement in multidisciplinary pain treatment. *Journal of Consulting and Clinical Psychology, 69,* 655–662.

Jéquier, E. (2002). Pathways to obesity. *International Journal of Obesity and Related Metabolic Disorders, 26,* 12–17.

Jimenez, L., & Mendez, C. (2001). Implicit sequence learning with competing explicit cues. *Quarterly Journal of Experimental Psychology: Comparative, and Physiological Psychology, 54,* 345–369.

John, O. P., & Srivastava, S. (1999). The Big Five trait taxonomy: History, measurement, and theoretical perspectives. In L. A. Pervin & O. P. John (Eds.), *Handbook of personality: Theory and research.* New York: Guilford Press.

Johnson, A. M., Wadsworth, J., Wellings, K., & Bradshaw, S. (1992). Sexual lifestyles and HIV risk. *Nature, 360,* 410–412.

Johnson, B. T. (1991). Insights about attitudes: Meta-analytic perspectives. *Personality and Social Psychology Bulletin, 17,* 289–299.

Johnson, D. W. (2000). Cooperative learning processes reduce prejudice. In S. Oskamp (Ed.), *Reducing prejudice and discrimination.* Mahwah, NJ: Erlbaum.

Johnson, J. G., Cohen, P., Smailes, E. M., Kasen, S., & Brook, J. S. (2002). Television viewing and aggressive behavior during adolescence and adulthood. *Science, 295,* 2468–2471.

Johnson, J. L., & Newport, E. L. (1989). Critical period effects in second language learning: The influence of maturational state on the acquisition of English as a second language. *Cognitive Psychology, 21,* 60–99.

Johnson, S. K. (2002). Hmong health beliefs and experiences in the Western health care system. *Journal of Transcultural Nursing, 13,* 126–132.

Johnson-Laird, P. N. (1997). An end to the controversy? A reply to Rips. *Minds & Machines, 7,* 425–432.

Johnston, L. D., O'Malley, P. M., & Bachman, J. G. (2002). *Monitoring the Future national survey results on drug use, 1975–2001: Vol. 2. College students and adults ages 19–40* (NIH Publication No. 02-5107). Bethesda, MD: National Institute on Drug Abuse.

Johnston, M. S., Kelley, C. S., Harris, F. F., & Wolf, M. M. (1966). An application of reinforcement principles to development of motor skills of a young child. *Child Development, 37,* 379–387.

Joiner, T. E., & Coyne, J. C. (Eds.). (1999). *The interactional nature of depression: Advances in interpersonal approaches.* Washington, DC: American Psychological Association.

Jones, E., Cumming, J. D., & Horowitz, M. J. (1988). Another look at the nonspecific hypothesis of therapeutic effectiveness. *Journal of Consulting and Clinical Psychology, 56,* 48–55.

Jones, E. E., & Harris, V. A. (1967). The attribution of attitudes. *Journal of Experimental Social Psychology, 3,* 2–24.

Jones, M. C. (1924). A laboratory study of fear: The case of Peter. *Pedagogical Seminary, 31,* 308–315.

Joseph, R. (2000). The evolution of sex differences in language, sexuality, and visual-spatial skills. *Archives of Sexual Behavior, 29,* 35–66.

Julien, R. M. (2001). *A primer of drug action: A concise nontechnical guide to the actions, uses, and side effects of psychoactive drugs* (9th ed.). New York: St. Martin's.

Jung, J. (1995). Ethnic group and gender differences in the relationship between personality and coping. *Anxiety, Stress & Coping: An International Journal, 8,* 113–126.

Jurkowitz, M. (2002, October 2). Appeals court holds key in battle over regulation of violent video games. *Boston Globe,* p. D1.

Kaas, J. (2002). Convergences in the modular and areal organization of the forebrain of mammals: Implications for the reconstruction of forebrain evolution. *Brain and Behavior Evolution, 59,* 262–272.

Kagan, J. (1989). Temperamental contributions to social behavior. *American Psychologist, 44,* 668–674.

Kagan, J., Kearsley, R. B., & Zelazo, P. (1978). *Infancy: Its place in human development.* Cambridge, MA: Harvard University Press.

Kagan, J., Reznick, S., & Snidman, N. (1988). Biological bases of childhood shyness. *Science, 240,* 167–171.

Kagitçibasi, C. (1997). Individualism and collectivism. In J. W. Berry, M. H. Segall, & C. Kagitçibasi (Eds.), *Handbook of cross-cultural psychology* (Vol. 3). Boston: Allyn & Bacon.

Kahn, S., Zimmerman, G., Csikszentmihalyi, M., & Getzels, J. W. (1985). Relations between identity in young adulthood and intimacy at midlife. *Journal of Personality and Social Psychology, 49,* 1316–1322.

Kahneman, D., & Tversky, A. (1979). Prospect theory: An analysis of decisions under risk. *Econometrica, 47,* 263–291.

Kahneman, D., & Tversky, A. (1982). On the study of statistical intuitions. *Cognition, 11,* 123–141.

Kail, R. (1991). Developmental change in speed of processing during childhood and adolescence. *Psychological Bulletin, 109,* 490–501.

Kail, R. (2002). Developmental change in proactive interference. *Child Development, 73,* 1703–1714.

Kampmann, K. M., Volpicelli, J. R., Mulvaney, F., Rukstalis, M., Alterman, A. I., Pettinati, et al. (2002). Cocaine withdrawal severity and urine toxicology results from treatment entry predict outcome in medication trials for cocaine dependence. *Addictive Behaviors, 27,* 251–260.

Kandel, E. R. (2001). The molecular biology of memory storage: A dialogue between genes and synapses. *Science, 294,* 1030–1038.

Kane, J. M. (Ed.). (1992). *Tardive dyskinesia: A task force report of the American Psychiatric Association.* Washington, DC: American Psychiatric Press.

Kaner, A. (1995). Physical attractiveness and women's lives: Findings from a longitudinal study. *Dissertation Abstracts International: Section B. The Sciences and Engineering, 56,* 2942.

Kanfer, F. H., & Goldstein, A. P. (Eds.). (1991). *Helping people change: A textbook of methods* (4th ed.). New York: Pergamon Press.

Kanwisher, N. (1998). The modular structure of human visual recognition: Evidence from functional imaging. In M. Sabourin et al. (Eds.), *Advances in psychological science: Vol. 2. Biological and cognitive aspects.* Hove, England: Psychology Press/Erlbaum (UK) Taylor & Francis.

Kaplan, H., & Dove, H. (1987). Infant development among the Ache of eastern Paraguay. *Developmental Psychology, 23,* 190–198.

Kaprio, J., Koskenvu, M., & Rita, H. (1987). Mortality after bereavement: A prospective study of 95,647 widowed persons. *American Journal of Public Health, 77,* 283–287.

Karau, S. J., & Williams, K. D. (1993). Social loafing: A meta-analytic review and theoretical integration. *Journal of Personality and Social Psychology, 65,* 681–706.

Karau, S. J., & Williams, K. D. (2001). Understanding individual motivation in groups: The collective effort model. In M. E. Turner (Ed.), *Groups at work: Theory and research. Applied social research.* Mahwah, NJ: Erlbaum.

Karon, B. P. (2002). Psychoanalysis: Legitimate and illegitimate concerns. *Psychoanalytic Psychology 19,* 564–571.

Kashima, Y., Yamaguchi, S., Kim, U., Choi, S., Gelfand, M., & Yuki, M. (1995). Culture, gender, and self: A perspective from individualism-collectivism research. *Journal of Personality and Social Psychology, 69,* 925–937.

Katz, J., & Melzack, R. (1990). Pain "memories" in phantom limbs: Review and clinical observations. *Pain, 43,* 319–336.

Kavanagh, D. (1992). Schizophrenia. In P. H. Wilson (Ed.), *Principles and practice of relapse prevention.* New York: Guilford Press.

Kay, L. (1982). *Spatial perception through an acoustic sensor.* Christchurch, New Zealand: University of Canterbury Press.

Kaye, W. H., Strober, M., & Klump, K. L. (2002). Serotonin neuronal function in anorexia nervosa and bulimia nervosa. In F. Lewis Hall et al. (Eds.). *Psychiatric illness in women: Emerging treatments and research.* Washington, DC: American Psychiatric Publishing.

Kazdin, A. E. (1975). The impact of applied behavior analysis on diverse areas of research. *Journal of Applied Behavior Analysis, 8,* 213–229.

Kazdin, A. E. (Ed.). (2003). *Methodological issues and strategies in clinical research* (3rd ed.). Washington, DC: American Psychological Association.

Kazdin, A. E., & Weisz, J. R. (2003). *Evidence-based psychotherapies for children and adolescents.* New York: Guilford Press.

Keefe, F. J., Lefebvre, J. C., Maixner, W., Salley, A. N., & Caldwell, D. S. (1997). Self-efficacy for arthritis pain: Relationship to perception of thermal laboratory pain stimuli. *Arthritis Care & Research, 10,* 177–184.

Keinan, G. (2002). The effects of stress and desire for control on superstitious behavior. *Personality and Social Psychology Bulletin, 28,* 102–108.

Keith, S. J., Regier, D. A., & Rae, D. S. (1991). Schizophrenic disorders. In L. N. Robins & D. S. Regier (Eds.), *Psychiatric disorders in America: The Epidemiological Catchment Area Study.* New York: Free Press.

Keller, H. (1955). *The story of my life.* New York: Doubleday.

Kelley, H. H. (1973). The process of causal attribution. *American Psychologist, 28,* 107–128.

Kelly, G. F. (2001). *Sexuality today: The human perspective* (7th ed.). Boston: McGraw-Hill.

Kelly, J. A., St. Lawrence, J. S., Hood, H. V., & Brasfield, T. L. (1989). Behavioral intervention to reduce AIDS risk activities. *Journal of Consulting and Clinical Psychology, 57,* 60–67.

Kelly, T. A., & Strupp, H. H. (1992). Patient and therapist values in psychotherapy: Perceived changes, assimilation, similarity, and outcome. *Journal of Consulting and Clinical Psychology, 60,* 34–40.

Keltner, D., & Ekman, P. (2000). Facial expression of emotion. In M. Lewis & J. M. Haviland-Jones (Eds.), *Handbook of emotions* (2nd ed.). New York: Guilford Press.

Kenardy, J., Brown, W. J., & Vogt, E. (2001). Dieting and health in young Australian women. *European Eating Disorders Review, 9,* 242–254.

Kendall, D. (1998). *Social problems in a diverse society.* Boston: Allyn & Bacon.

Kendler, K. S., Gardner, C. O., Neale, M. C., & Prescott, C. O. (2001). Genetic risk factors for major depression in men and women: Similar or different heritabilities and same or partly distinct genes? *Psychological Medicine, 31,* 605–616.

Kenrick, D. T., & Funder, D. C. (1988). Profiting from controversy: Lessons from the person-situation debate. *American Psychologist, 43,* 23–34.

Kensinger, E. A., Ullman, M. T., & Corkin, S. (2001). Bilateral medial temporal lobe damage does not affect lexical or grammatical processing: Evidence from amnesic patient H.M. *Hippocampus, 11,* 347–360.

Kernberg, O. F. (1984). *Severe personality disorders: Psychotherapeutic strategies.* New Haven, CT: Yale University Press.

Kernberg, O. F. (2000). *Personality disorders in children and adolescents.* Poulsbo, WA: H-R Press.

Kerns, J. G., & Berenbaum, H. (2002). Cognitive impairments associated with formal thought disorder in people with schizophrenia. *Journal of Abnormal Psychology, 111,* 211–224.

Kerr, M., Lambert, W. W., & Bem, D. J. (1996). Life course sequelae of childhood shyness in Sweden: Comparison with the United States. *Developmental Psychology, 32,* 1100–1105.

Kessler, R. C., McGonagle, K. A., Zhao, S., Nelson, C., et al. (1994). Lifetime and 12-month prevalence of DSM-III-R psychiatric disorder in the United States. *Archives of General Psychiatry, 51,* 8–19.

Kessler, R. C., & Wittchen, H. U. (2002). Patterns and correlates of generalized anxiety disorder in community samples. *Journal of Clinical Psychiatry, 63*(Suppl. 8), 4–10.

Ketellar, T. (1995). *Emotion as mental representations of fitness affordances: I. Evidence supporting the claim that the negative and positive emotions map onto fitness costs and benefits.* Paper presented at the annual meeting of the Human Behavior and Evolution Society, Santa Barbara, CA.

Kety, S. S. (1988). Schizophrenic illness in the families of schizophrenic adoptees: Findings from the Danish national sample. *Schizophrenia Bulletin, 14,* 217–222.

Kety, S. S., Rosenthal, D., Wender, P. H., Schulsinger, F., & Jacobson, B. (1978). The biological and adoptive families of adopted individuals who become schizophrenic: Prevalence of mental illness and other characteristics. In L. C. Wynne, R. L. Cromwell, & S. Matthysse (Eds.), *The nature of schizophrenia: New approaches to research and treatment.* New York: Wiley.

Khoury, R. M. (1985). Norm formation, social conformity, and the confederating function of humor. *Social Behavior and Personality, 13,* 159–165.

Kiecolt-Glaser, J., Bane, C., Glaser, R., & Malarkey, W. B. (2003). Love, marriage, and divorce: Newlyweds' stress hormones foreshadow relationship changes. *Journal of Consulting and Clinical Psychology, 71,* 176–188.

Kiecolt-Glaser, J., Glaser, R., Cacioppo, J. T., & Malarkey, W. (1998). Marital stress: Immunologic, neuroendocrine, and autonomic correlates. *Annals of the New York Academy of Sciences, 840,* 656–663.

Kiecolt-Glaser, J., McGuire, L., Robles, T. F., & Glaser, R. (2002). Emotions, morbidity, and mortality: New perspectives from psychoneuroimmunology. *Annual Review of Psychology, 53,* 83–107.

Kihlstrom, J. F. (1985). Posthypnotic amnesia and the dissociation of memory. *Psychology of Learning and Motivation, 19,* 131–178.

Kihlstrom, J. F. (1998). Dissociations and dissociation theory in hypnosis: Comment on Kirsch and Lynn. *Psychological Bulletin, 123,* 186–191.

Kihlstrom, J. F. (1999). The psychological unconscious. In L. A. Pervin & O. P. John (Eds.), *Handbook of personality: Theory and research.* New York: Guilford Press.

Kimble, D. P. (1992). *Biological psychology* (2nd ed.). Ft. Worth, TX: Harcourt Brace Jovanovich.

Kimerling, R., Ouimette, P., & Wolfe, J. (2003). *Gender and PTSD.* New York: Guilford Press.

Kimura, D. (1992). Sex differences in the brain. *Scientific American, 267*(3), 119–195.

Kimura, K., Tachibana, N., Aso, T., Kimura, J., & Shibasaki, H. (1997). Subclinical REM sleep behavior disorder in a patient with corticobasal degeneration. *Sleep, 20,* 891–894.

King, N. J., Dudley, A., Melvin, G., Pallant, J., & Morawetz, D. (2001). Empirically supported treatments for insomnia. *Scandinavian Journal of Behaviour Therapy, 30,* 23–32.

Kinsey, A. C., Pomeroy, W. B., & Martin, C. E. (1948). *Sexual behavior in the human male.* Philadelphia: Saunders.

Kinsey, A. C., Pomeroy, W. B., Martin, C. E., & Gebhard, P. H. (1953). *Sexual behavior in the human female.* Philadelphia: Saunders.

Kirk, K. M., Bailey, J. M., & Martin, N. G. (2000). Etiology of male sexual orientation in an Australian twin sample. *Psychology, Evolution, and Gender, 2,* 301–311.

Kirsch, I. (2001). The response set theory of hypnosis: Expectancy and physiology. *American Journal of Clinical Hypnosis, 44,* 69–73.

Kirsch, I., & Braffman, W. (2001). Imaginative suggestibility and hypnotizability. *Current Directions in Psychological Science, 10,* 57–61.

Kitayama, S., Markus, H. R., & Kurokawa, M. (2000). Culture, emotion, and well-being: Good feelings in Japan and the United States. *Cognition and Emotion, 14,* 93–124.

Klahr, D., & Simon, H. A. (2001). What have psychologists (and others) discovered about the process of scientific discovery? *Current Directions in Psychological Science, 10,* 75–79.

Klein, M. (1975). *The writings of Melanie Klein.* London: Hogarth Press.

Klein, S. B., & Mowrer, R. R. (1989). *Contemporary learning theories: Vol I. Pavlovian conditioning and the status of tradition.* Hillsdale, NJ: Erlbaum.

Kleiner, M. (Ed). (2002). *Handbook of polygraph testing.* San Diego, CA: Academic Press.

Kleinknecht, R. A., Dinnel, D. L., Kleinknecht, E. E., Hiruma, N., et al. (Eds.). (1997). Cultural factors in social anxiety: A comparison of social phobia symptoms and Taijin Kyofusho. *Journal of Anxiety Disorders, 2,* 157–177.

Kleinmuntz, B. (1980). *Essentials of abnormal psychology* (2nd ed.). New York: Harper & Row.

Kleinmuntz, B., & Szucko, J. J. (1984). Lie detection in ancient and modern times: A call for contemporary scientific study. *American Psychologist, 39,* 766–776.

Kleitman, N. (1963). *Sleep and wakefulness* (2nd ed.). Chicago: University of Chicago Press.

Kliegel, M., Martin, M., McDaniel, M. A., & Einstein, G. O. (2002). Complex prospective memory and executive control of working memory: A process model. *Psychologische Beitrage, 44,* 303–318.

Kluckhohn, C., & Murray, H. A. (1953). Personality formation: The determinants. In C. Kluckhohn, H. A. Murray, & D. M. Schneider (Eds.), *Personality in nature, society, and culture.* New York: Alfred A. Knopf.

Kluft, R. P. (1999). True lies, false truths, and naturalistic raw data: Applying clinical research findings to the false memory debate. In L. M. Williams & V. L. Banyard (Eds.), *Trauma and memory.* Thousand Oaks, CA: Sage Publications.

Knauth, P. (1996). Designing better shift systems. *Applied Ergonomics, 27,* 39–44.

Knoblauch, K. (2002). Color vision. In H. Pashler & S. Yantis (Eds.), *Steven's handbook of experimental psychology: Vol. 1. Sensation and perception* (3rd ed.). New York: Wiley.

Kobasa, S. C., Maddi, S. R., Puccetti, M. C., & Zola, M. A. (1985). Effectiveness of hardiness, exercise and social support as resources against illness. *Journal of Psychosomatic Research, 29,* 525–533.

Kochanska, G., Casey, R. J., & Fukumoto, A. (1995). Toddlers' sensitivity to standard violations. *Child Development, 66,* 643–656.

Kochanska, G., & Murray, K. (2000). Mother-child mutually responsive orientation and conscience development: From toddler to early school age. *Child Development, 71,* 417–431.

Kochanska, G., Murray, K., & Coy, K. C. (1997). Inhibitory control as a contributor to conscience in childhood: From toddler to early school age. *Child Development, 68,* 263–277.

Koenig, H. G., Pargament, K. L., & Nielsen, J. (1998). Religious coping and health status in medically ill hospitalized older adults. *Journal of Nervous & Mental Disease, 186,* 513–521.

Koestner, R., & McClelland, D. C. (1990). Perspectives on competence motivation. In L. A. Pervin (Ed.), *Handbook of personality theory and research.* New York: Guilford Press.

Kogi, K. (1985). Introduction to the problems of shift work. In S. Folkard & T. H. Monk (Eds.), *Hours of work.* West Sussex: Wiley.

Kohlberg, L. (1963). The development of children's orientations toward a moral order: I. Sequence in the development of moral thought. *Human Development, 6,* 11–33.

Kohlberg, L. (1984). *The psychology of moral development: Essays on moral development* (Vol. 2). New York: Harper & Row.

Köhler, W. (1925). *The mentality of apes* (Trans. from the 2nd rev. ed. by Ella Winter). New York: Harcourt.

Kohut, H. (1971). *Analysis of the self.* New York: International Universities Press.

Kohut, H. (1977). *The restoration of self.* New York: International Universities Press.

Kokko, K., & Pulkkinen, L. (2000). Aggression in childhood and long-term unemployment in adulthood: A cycle of maladaptation and some protective factors. *Developmental Psychology, 36,* 463–472.

Kolb, B. (1989). Brain development, plasticity, and behavior. *American Psychologist, 44,* 1203–1212.

Kolb, B., & Whishaw, I. Q. (2001). *An introduction to brain and behavior.* New York: Worth.

Kolb, B., & Whishaw, I. Q. (2003). *Fundamentals of human neuropsychology* (5th ed.). New York: Worth.

Kollar, E. J., & Fisher, C. (1980). Tooth induction in chick epithelium: Expression of quiescent genes for enamel synthesis. *Science, 207,* 993–995.

Koluchova, J. (1972). Severe deprivation in twins: A case study. *Journal of Child Psychology and Psychiatry, 13,* 107–114.

Koluchova, J. (1991). Severely deprived twins after 22 years of observation. *Studiea Psychologica, 33,* 23–28.

Koriat, A., Goldsmith, M., & Pansky, A. (2000). Toward a psychology of memory accuracy. *Annual Review of Psychology, 51,* 481–537.

Kortegaard, L., Hoerder, K., Joergensen, J., Gillberg, C., & Kyvik, K. O. (2001). A preliminary population-based twin study of self-reported eating disorder. *Psychological Medicine, 31,* 361–365.

Kosambi, D. D. (1967). Living prehistory in India. *Scientific American, 216,* 105.

Kosslyn, S. M., Thompson, W. L., Costantini-Ferrando, M. F., Alpert, N. M., & Spiegel, D. (2000). Hypnotic visual illusion alters color processing in the brain. *American Journal of Psychiatry, 157,* 1279–1284.

Kottak, C. P. (2000). *Cultural anthropology* (8th ed.). Boston: McGraw-Hill.

Kovacs, M., & Devlin, B. (1998). Internalizing disorders in childhood. *Journal of Child Psychology and Psychiatry, 39,* 47–63.

Kowert, P. A. (Ed.). (2002). *Groupthink or deadlock: When do leaders learn from their advisors? SUNY series on the presidency.* New York: State University of New York Press.

Kraft, C. L. (1978). A psychophysical contribution to air safety: Simulator studies of visual illusions in night visual approaches. In H. L. Pick, Jr., H. W. Leibowitz, J. E. Singer, A. Steinschneider, & H. W. Stevenson (Eds.), *Psychology: From research to practice.* New York: Plenum.

Kramsch, C. J. (2003). *Language acquisition and language socialization: Ecological perspectives.* New York: Continuum International Publishing Group.

Krasnegor, N. A., Lyon, G. R., & Goldman, R. P. S. (1997). *Development of the prefrontal cortex: Evolution, neurobiology, and behavior.* Baltimore, MD: Paul H. Brookes.

Kraus, S. J. (1995). Attitudes and the prediction of behavior: A meta-analysis of the empirical literature. *Personality and Social Psychology Bulletin, 21,* 58–75.

Krebs, D. L., & Denton, K. (1997). Social illusions and self-deception: The evolution of biases in person perception. In J. A. Simpson & D. T. Kenrick (Eds.), *Evolutionary social psychology.* Mahwah, NJ: Erlbaum.

Krech, D. (1978). Quoted in M. C. Diamond, The aging brain: Some enlightening and optimistic results. *American Scientist, 66,* 66–71.

Krevans, J., & Gibbs, J. C. (1996). Parents' use of inductive discipline: Relations to children's empathy and prosocial behavior. *Child Development, 67,* 3263–3277.

Kroeber, A. L. (1948). *Anthropology.* New York: Harcourt Brace Jovanovich.

Krosnick, J. A., Betz, A. L., Jussim, L. J., & Lynn, A. R. (1992). Subliminal conditioning of attitudes. *Personality and Social Psychology Bulletin, 18,* 152–162.

Krueger, R. F., & Caspi, A. (1993). Personality, arousal, and pleasure: A test of competing models of interpersonal attraction. *Personality and Individual Differences, 14,* 105–111.

Kruglanski, A. W., & Webster, D. M. (1996). Motivated closing of the mind: "Seizing" and "freezing." *Psychological Review, 103,* 263–283.

Kryger, M. H., Walld, R., & Manfreda, J. (2002). Diagnoses received by narcolepsy patients in the year prior to diagnosis by a sleep specialist. *Sleep: Journal of Sleep and Sleep Disorders Research, 25,* 36–41.

Kübler-Ross, E. (1969). *On death and dying.* New York: Macmillan.

Kuhn, C. M., & Schanberg, S. M. (1998). Responses to maternal separation: Mechanisms and mediators. *International Journal of Developmental Neuroscience, 16,* 261–270.

Kulik, J. A., & Mahler, H. I. M. (2000). Social comparison, affiliation, and emotional contagion under threat. In J. Suls & L. Wheeler (Eds.), *Handbook of social comparison: Theory and research.* Dordrecht, Netherlands: Kluwer.

Kulik, J. A., Mahler, H. I. M., & Moore, P. J. (1996). Social comparison and affiliation under threat: Effects of recovery from major surgery. *Journal of Personality and Social Psychology, 66,* 301–309.

Kunzendorf, R. G., Hartmann, E., Cohen, R., & Cutler, J. (1997). Bizarreness of the dreams and daydreams reported by individuals with thin and thick boundaries. *Dreaming: Journal of the Association for the Study of Dreams, 7,* 265–271.

Kunzman, U., & Baltes, P. B. (2003). Beyond the traditional scope of intelligence: Wisdom in action. In R. J. Sternberg, J. Lautrey, & T. I. Lubart (Eds.). *Models of intelligence: International perspectives.* Washington, D.C.: American Psychological Association.

Kurdek, L. A. (1999). The nature and predictors of the trajectory of change in marital quality for husbands and wives over the first 10 years of marriage. *Developmental Psychology, 35,* 1283–1296.

Kurzweil, E. (1989). *The Freudians: A comparative perspective.* New Haven, CT: Yale University Press.

LaBar, K. S., & Phelps, E. A. (1998). Arousal-mediated memory consolidation: Role of the medial temporal lobe in humans. *Psychological Science, 9,* 490–493.

Lagerspetz, K. Y., Tirri, R., & Lagerspetz, K. M. (1968). Neurochemical and endocrinological studies of mice selectively bred for aggressiveness. *Scandinavian Journal of Psychology, 9,* 157–160.

Laible, D., & Thompson, R. A. (2000). Mother-child discourse, attachment security, shared positive affect, and early conscience development. *Child Development, 71,* 1424–1440.

Lakein, A. (1973). *How to get control of your time and your life.* New York: Peter H. Wyden.

Lambert, M. J., Shapiro, D. A., & Bergin, A. E. (1986). The effectiveness of psychotherapy. In S. L. Garfield & A. E. Bergin (Eds.), *Handbook of psychotherapy and behavior change* (3rd ed.). New York: Wiley.

Lambert, W. E., Genesee, F., Holobow, N., & Chartrand, L. (1993). Bilingual education for majority English-speaking children. *European Journal of Psychology of Education, 8,* 3–22.

Lamble, D., Kauranen, T., Laakso, M., & Summala, H. (1999). Cognitive load and detection thresholds in car following situations: Safety implications for using mobile (cellular) telephones while driving. *Accident Analysis and Prevention, 31,* 617–623.

Lamborn, S. D., Mounts, N. S., Steinberg, L., & Dornbusch, S. M. (1991). Patterns of competence and adjustment among adolescents from authoritative, authoritarian, indulgent, and neglectful families. *Child Development, 62,* 1049–1065.

Landers, D. M., & Arent, S. (2001). Arousal-performance relations. In J. M. Williams (Ed.), *Applied sport psychology: Personal growth to peak performance* (4th ed.). Boston: McGraw-Hill.

Landesman, S., & Ramey, C. T. (1989). Developmental psychology and mental retardation: Integrating scientific principles with treatment practices. *American Psychologist, 44,* 409–415.

Lane, R. D., Reiman, E. M., Ahern, G. L., & Schwartz, G. E. (1997). Neuroanatomical correlates of happiness, sadness, and disgust. *American Journal of Psychiatry, 154,* 926–933.

Langer, E. (1989). *Mindlessness.* Reading, MA: Addison-Wesley.

Lanier, C. A. (2001). Rape accepting attitudes: Precursors to or consequences of forced sex. *Violence Against Women, 7,* 876–885.

LaPiere, R. T. (1934). Attitudes and actions. *Social Forces, 13,* 230–237.

Larivée, S., Normandeau, S., & Parent, S. (2000). The French connection: Some contributions of French language research in the post Piagetian era. *Child Development, 71,* 823–839.

Larroque, B., & Kaminski, M. (1998). Prenatal alcohol exposure and development at preschool age: Main results of a French study. *Alcoholism: Clinical and Experimental Research, 22,* 295–303.

Larsen, R., & Buss, D. M. (2002). *Personality psychology: Domains of knowledge about human nature.* Boston: McGraw-Hill.

Larsen, R., & Diener, E. (1985). A multitrait-multimethod examination of affect structure: Hedonic level and emotional intensity. *Personality and Individual Differences, 6,* 631–636.

Larson, R. W., Moneta, G., Richards, M. H., & Wilson, S. (2002). Continuity, stability, and change in daily emotional experience across adolescence. *Child Development, 73,* 1151–1165.

Lasco, M. S., Jordan, T. J., Edgar, M. A., Petito, C. K., Byne, W. (2002). A lack of dimorphism of sex or sexual orientation in the human anterior commissure. *Brain Research, 936,* 95–98.

Lashley, K. S. (1930). The mechanism of vision: 1. A method for rapid analysis of pattern-vision in the rat. *Journal of Genetic Psychology, 37,* 453–460.

Lashley, K. S. (1950). In search of the engram. *Symposia of the Society for Experimental Biology, 4,* 454–482.

Latané, B., & Bourgeois, M. J. (2001). Successfully simulating dynamic social impact: Three levels of prediction. In J. P. Forgas & K. D. Williams (Eds.), *Social influence: Direct and indirect processes. The Sydney symposium of social psychology.* Philadelphia, PA: Psychology Press.

Latané, B., & Darley, J. M. (1970). *The unresponsive bystander: Why doesn't he help?* New York: Appleton-Century-Crofts.

Latané, B., & Nida, S. (1981). Ten years of research on group size and helping. *Psychological Bulletin, 89,* 308–324.

Laumann, E. O., Gagnon, J. H., Michael, R. T., & Michaels, S. (1994). *The social organization of sexuality: Sexual practices in the United States.* Chicago: University of Chicago Press.

Lavergne, G. M. (1997). *A sniper in the tower: The Charles Whitman murders.* Denton: University of North Texas Press.

Lavie, P. (2000). Sleep-wake as a biological rhythm. *Annual Review of Psychology, 52,* 277–303.

Lavigne, J. V., Gibbons, R. D., Christoffel, K. K., & Arend, R. (1996). Prevalence rates and correlates of psychiatric disorders among preschool children. *Journal of the American Academy of Child and Adolescent Psychiatry, 35,* 204–214.

Lawler, K. A., & Schmied, L. A. (1992). A prospective study of women's health: The effects of stress, hardiness, locus of control, Type A behavior, and physiological reactivity. *Women and Health, 19,* 27–41.

Lazarus, A. A. (1995). Multimodal therapy. In R. J. Corsini & D. Wedding (Eds.), *Current psychotherapies* (5th ed.). Itasca, IL: Peacock.

Lazarus, R. S. (1991). Progress on a cognitive-motivational-relational theory of emotion. *American Psychologist, 46,* 819–834.

Lazarus, R. S. (1998). *Fifty years of the research and theory of R. S. Lazarus: An analysis of historical and perennial issues.* Mahwah, NJ: Erlbaum.

Lazarus, R. S. (2001). Relational meaning and discrete emotions. In B. K. Scherer et al. (Eds.), *Appraisal processes in emotion: Theory, methods, research.* New York: Oxford University Press.

Lazarus, R. S., & Folkman, S. (1984). *Stress, appraisal, and coping.* New York: Springer.

LeDoux, J. E. (1998). *The emotional brain.* New York: Simon & Schuster.

LeDoux, J. E. (2000). Emotion circuits in the brain. *Annual Review of Neuroscience, 23,* 155–184.

LeDoux, J. E., & Phelps, E. A. (2000). Emotional networks in the brain. In M. Lewis & J. M. Haviland-Jones (Eds.), *Handbook of emotions* (2nd ed.). New York: Guilford Press.

LeDoux, J. E., Wilson, D. H., & Gazzaniga, M. S. (1977). A divided mind: Observations on the conscious properties of the separated hemispheres. *Annals of Neurology, 2,* 417–421.

Lee, J. D. (1998). Which kids can "become" scientists? Effects of gender, self-concepts, and perceptions of scientists. *Social Psychology Quarterly, 61,* 199–219.

Lee, R. M. (2000). *Unobtrusive methods in social research.* Buckingham, England: Open University Press.

Lehmann-Haupt, C. (1988, August 4). Books of the times: How an actor found success, and himself. *New York Times,* p. 2.

Leichtman, M. D., & Ceci, S. J. (1995). The effects of stereotypes and suggestions on preschoolers' reports. *Developmental Psychology, 31,* 568–578.

LeMoal, H., (1999). *Dopamine and the brain: From neurons to networks.* New York: Academic Press.

Leon, G. R., & Roth, L. (1977). Obesity: Psychological causes, correlations, and speculations. *Psychological Bulletin, 84,* 117–139.

Leor, J., Poole, W. K., & Kloner, R. A. (1996). Sudden cardiac death triggered by an earthquake. *New England Journal of Medicine, 334*(7), 413–419.

LePage, M., Habib, R., & Tulving, E. (1998). Hippocampal PET activations of memory encoding and retrieval: The HIPER model. *Hippocampus, 8,* 313–322.

Leppämäki, S. J., Partonen, T. T., Hurme, J., Haukka, J. K., Lönnqvist, J. K. (2002). Randomized trial of the efficacy of bright-light exposure and aerobic exercise on depressive symptoms and serum lipids. *Journal of Clinical Psychiatry, 63,* 316–321.

Leppänen, J. M., & Hietanen, J. K. (2001). Emotion recognition and social adjustment in school aged girls and boys. *Scandinavian Journal of Psychology, 42,* 429–435.

Leslie, J. C. (2002). *Essential behaviour analysis.* London: Arnold.

Lester, D. (1972). Voodoo death: Some new thoughts on an old phenomenon. *American Anthropologist, 74,* 386–390.

Levenson, H. (2002). *Concise guide to brief dynamic and interpersonal therapy.* Washington, DC: American Psychiatric Press.

Levine, R., Sato, S., Hashimoto, T., & Verma, J. (1995). Love and marriage in eleven cultures. *Journal of Cross-Cultural Psychology, 26,* 554–571.

Levinson, D. J. (1986). A conception of adult development. *American Psychologist, 41,* 3–13.

Levinson, D. J. (1990). A theory of life structure development in adulthood. In C. N. Alexander & E. J. Langer (Eds.), *Higher stages of human development: Perspectives on adult growth.* New York: Oxford University Press.

Levinson, D. J., Darow, C. N., Klein, E. B., Levinson, M. H., & McKee, B. (1978). *The seasons of a man's life.* New York: Knopf.

Levinthal, C. F. (1996). *Drugs, behavior, and modern society.* Boston: Allyn & Bacon.

Levitsky, D. A. (2002). Putting behavior back into feeding behavior: A tribute to George Collier. *Appetite, 38,* 143–148.

Levy, B. R., Slade, M. D., Kunkel, S. R., & Kasl, S. V. (2002). Longevity increased by positive self-perceptions of aging. *Journal of Personality and Social Psychology, 83,* 261–270.

Levy, S. (2002). *Principles of interpretation: Mastering clear and concise interventions in psychotherapy.* New York: Jason Aronson.

Levy, S., Marrow, L., Bagley, C., & Lippman, M. (1988). Survival hazards analysis in first recurrent breast cancer patients: Seven-year follow-up. *Psychosomatic Medicine, 50,* 520–528.

Lewin, R. (1998). *The origin of modern humans.* New York: American Scientific Library.

Lewinsohn, P. M, Gotlib, I. H., Lewinsohn, M., Seeley, J. R., & Allen, N. B. (1998). Gender differences in anxiety disorders and anxiety symptoms in adolescents. *Journal of Abnormal Psychology, 107,* 109–117.

Lewinsohn, P. M., Hoberman, H., Teri, L., & Hantzinger, M. (1985). An integrative theory of depression. In S. Reiss & R. Bootzin (Eds.), *Theoretical issues in behavior therapy.* New York: Academic Press.

Lewis, C., O'Sullivan, C., & Barraclough, J. (Eds.). (1995). *The psychoimmunology of human cancer.* New York: Oxford University Press.

Lewis, M. (1999). On the development of personality. In L. A. Pervin & O. P. John (Eds.), *Handbook of personality: Theory and research.* New York: Guilford Press.

Lewis, M. (2000). The emergence of human emotions. In M. Lewis & J. M. Haviland-Jones (Eds.), *Handbook of emotions* (2nd ed.). New York: Guilford Press.

Leyens, J. P., Camino, L., Parke, R. D., & Berkowitz, L. (1975). Effects of movie violence on aggression in a field setting as a function of group dominance and cohesion. *Journal of Personality and Social Psychology, 32,* 346–360.

Lezak, M. (1995). *Neuropsychological assessment* (3rd ed.). New York: Oxford University Press.

Li, S. (2001). How close is too close? A comparison of proxemic reactions of Singaporean Chinese to male intruders of four ethnicities. *Perceptual and Motor Skills, 93,* 124–126.

Li, T. K. (2000). Pharmacogenetics of responses to alcohol and genes that influence alcohol drinking. *Journal of Studies on Alcohol, 61,* 5–12.

Lieb, R., Isensee, B., Hoefler, M., Pfister, H., & Wittchen, H. U. (2002). Parental major depression and the risk of depression and other mental disorders in offspring: A prospective-longitudinal community study. *Archives of General Psychiatry, 59,* 365–374.

Lieberman, J. A. (1998). *Psychiatric drugs.* Philadelphia: Saunders.

Lilienfeld, S. O., Wood, J. M., & Garb, H. N. (2000). The scientific status of projective techniques. *Psychological Science in the Public Interest, 1,* 25–62.

Link, B. G., & Steuve, A. (1998). New evidence on the violence risk posed by people with mental illness. *Archives of General Psychiatry, 55,* 403–404.

Linver, M. R., Brooks-Gunn, J., & Kohen, D. E. (2002). Family processes as pathways from income to young children's development. *Developmental Psychology, 38,* 719–734.

Linz, D., & Donnerstein, E. (1989). The effects of countertransformation on the acceptance of rape myths. In D. Zillmann & J. Bryant (Eds.), *Pornography: Research advances and policy considerations.* Hillsdale, NJ: Erlbaum.

Lippa, R. A. (2002). *Gender, nature, and nurture.* Mahwah, NJ: Erlbaum.

Lipsitt, L. P. (1990). Learning processes in the human newborn: Sensitization, habituation, and classical conditioning. *Annals of the New York Academy of Sciences, 608,* 113–127.

Livesley, W. J. (2003). *Practical management of personality disorder.* New York: Guilford Press.

Livingstone, M., & Hubel, D. (1994). Segregation of form, color, movement, and depth: Anatomy, physiology, and perception. In H. Gutfreund & G. Toulouse (Eds.), *Biology and computation: A physicist's choice. Advanced series in neuroscience.* Singapore: World Scientific Publishing.

Lobina, C., Agabio, R., Reali, R., Gessa, G. L., & Colombo, G. (1999). Contribution of GABA-sub(A) and GABA-sub(B) receptors to the discriminative stimulus produced by gamma-hydroxybutyric acid. *Pharmacology, Biochemistry and Behavior, 64*(2), 363–365.

Locke, E. A., & Latham, G. P. (2002). Building a practically useful theory of goal setting and task motivation: A 35-year odyssey. *American Psychologist, 57,* 705–717.

Loehlin, J. C. (1992). *Genes and environment in personality development.* Newbury Park, CA: Sage Publications.

Loehlin, J. C., Willerman, L., & Horn, J. M. (1988). Genetics and human behavior. *Annual Review of Psychology, 39,* 101–134.

Loewenstein, R. J. (1991). Psychogenic amnesia and psychogenic fugue: A comprehensive review. In A. Tasman & S. M. Goldfinger (Eds.), *American Psychiatric Press review of psychiatry* (Vol. 10). Washington, DC: American Psychiatric Association.

Loftus, E. F. (2000). Remembering what never happened. In E. Tulving (Ed.), *Memory, consciousness, and the brain: The Tallinn Conference.* Philadelphia: Psychology Press/Taylor & Francis.

Loftus, E. F. (2003). The dangers of memory. In R. J. Sternberg (Ed.), *Psychologists defying the crowd: Stories of those who battled the establishment and won.* Washington, DC: American Psychological Association.

Loftus, E. F., & Burns, T. E. (1982). Mental shock can produce retrograde amnesia. *Memory and Cognition, 10,* 318–323.

Loftus, E. F., & Loftus, G. R. (1980). On the permanence of stored information in the human brain. *American Psychologist, 35,* 409–420.

Loftus, E. F., & Palmer, J. C. (1974). Reconstruction of automobile destruction: An example of the interaction between language and memory. *Journal of Verbal Learning and Verbal Behavior, 13,* 585–589.

Logue, A. W. (1991). *The psychology of eating and drinking* (2nd ed.). New York: Freeman.

Lopez, S. R., & Guarnaccia, P. J. (2000). Cultural psychopathology: Uncovering the social world of mental illness. *Annual Review of Psychology, 51,* 571–598.

Lorenz, K. (1937). The companion in the bird's world. *Auk, 54,* 245–273.

Lovaas, O. I. (1977). *The autistic child.* New York: Irvington.

Luborsky, L., Rosenthal, R., Diguer, L., Andrusyna, T. P., Berman, J. S., Jeffrey, S., Levitt, J. T., Seligman, D. A., & Krause, E. D. (2002). The dodo bird verdict is alive and well—mostly. *Clinical Psychology: Science and Practice, 9,* 2–12.

Lucas, R. E., & Diener, E. (2001). Understanding extraverts' enjoyment of social situations: The importance of pleasantness. *Journal of Personality and Social Psychology, 81,* 343–356.

Luchins, A. J. (1942). Mechanization in problem solving: The effect of Einstellung. *Psychological Monographs, 54*(6, Whole No. 248).

Luciano, M., Wright, M. J., Smith, G. A., Geffen, G. M., Geffen, L. B., & Martin, N. G. (2001). Genetic covariance among measures of information processing speed, working memory, and IQ. *Behavior Genetics, 31,* 581–592.

Luck, S. J., & Vecera, S. P. (2002). Attention. In H. Pashler & S.Yantis (Eds.), *Steven's handbook of experimental psychology: Vol. 1. Sensation and perception* (3rd ed.). New York: Wiley.

Luria, A. R. (1968). *The mind of a mnemonist: A little book about a vast memory.* New York: Basic Books.

Lykken, D. T. (1981). *A tremor in the blood: Uses and abuses of the lie detector.* New York: Plenum.

Lykken, D. T. (1984). Polygraph interrogation. *Nature, 307,* 681–684.

Lykken, D. T., McGue, M., Tellegen, A., & Bouchard, T. J. (1992). Emergenesis: Genetic traits that may not run in families. *American Psychologist, 47,* 1565–1577.

Lykken, D. T., & Tellegen, A. (1996). Happiness is a stochastic phenomenon. *Psychological Science, 7,* 186–189.

Lynn, E. J. (1971). Amphetamine abuse: A "speed" trap. *Psychiatric Quarterly, 45,* 92–101.

Lynn, S. J., Neuschatz, J., Fite R., & Kirsch I. (2001). Hypnosis in the forensic arena. *Journal of Forensic Psychology Practice, 1,* 113–122.

Lytton, H., & Romney, D. M. (1991). Parents' differential socialization of boys and girls: A meta-analysis. *Psychological Bulletin, 109,* 267–296.

MacAndrew, C., & Edgerton, R. B. (1969). *Drunken comportment: A social explanation.* Chicago: Aldine.

Maccoby, E. E., & Maccoby, N. (1954). The interview: A tool of social science. In G. Lindzey (Ed.), *Handbook of social psychology.* Cambridge, MA: Addison-Wesley.

Maccoby, E. E., & Martin, J. A. (1983). Socialization in the context of the family: Parent-child interaction. In E. M. Hetherington (Ed.), *Handbook of child psychology: Socialization, personality, and social development.* New York: Wiley.

MacCoun, R. J. (1998). Toward a psychology of harm reduction. *American Psychologist, 53,* 1199–1208.

MacDonald, S., Uesiliana, K., & Hayne, H. (2000). Cross-cultural and gender differences in childhood amnesia. *Memory, 8,* 365–376.

MacDonald, T. K., Fong, G. T., Zanna, M. P., & Martineau, A. M. (2000). Alcohol myopia and condom use: Can alcohol intoxication be associated with more prudent behavior? *Journal of Personality and Social Psychology, 78,* 605–619.

MacDonald, T. K., Zanna, M. P., & Fong, G. T. (1995). Decision making in altered states: Effects of alcohol on attitudes toward drinking and driving. *Journal of Personality and Social Psychology, 68,* 973–985.

MacLeod, C. (1998). Implicit perception: Perceptual processing without awareness. In K. Kirsner et al. (Eds.), *Implicit and explicit mental processes.* Mahwah, NJ: Erlbaum.

Maddux, J. E. (1999). Personal efficacy. In V. J. Derlega, B. A. Winstead, & W. H. Jones (Eds.), *Personality: Contemporary theory and research.* Chicago: Nelson Hall.

Maes, H. H. M., Neale, M. C., & Eaves, L. J. (1997). Genetic and environmental factors in relative body weight and human adiposity. *Behavior Genetics, 27,* 325–351.

Magnuson, S. (1986, March 10). "A serious deficiency": The Rogers Commission faults NASA's "flawed" decision-making process. *Time* (Intl. ed.), 40–42.

Mahler, M. (1968). *On human symbiosis and the vicissitudes of individuation: Infantile psychosis.* New York: Basic Books.

Maier, S. F., & Watkins, L. R. (1999). Bidirectional communication between the brain and the immune system: Implications for behaviour. *Animal Behaviour, 57(4),* 741–751.

Maio, G. R., & Olson, J. M. (Eds.). (2000). *Why we evaluate: Functions of attitudes.* Mahwah, NJ: Erlbaum.

Major, B., Spencer, S., Schmader, T., Wolfe, C., & Crocker, J. (1998). Coping with negative stereotypes about intellectual performance: The role of psychological disengagement. *Personality and Social Psychology Bulletin, 24,* 34–50.

Mäkelä, K. (1997). Drinking, the majority fallacy, cognitive dissonance and social pressure. *Addiction, 92,* 729–736.

Malamuth, N. M., Addison, T., & Koss, M. (2000). Pornography and sexual aggression: Are there reliable effects and can we understand them? *Annual Review of Sex Research, 11,* 26–91.

Maldonado, R., & Rodriguez de Fonseca, F. (2002). Cannabinoid addiction: Behavioral models and neural correlates. *Journal of Neuroscience, 22,* 3326–3331.

Mann, L. (1981). The baiting crowd in episodes of threatened suicide. *Journal of Personality and Social Psychology, 41,* 703–709.

Manning, M. (2002, June 8). If you want to see a UFO, you first have to believe, Kreskin says. *Seattle Post-Intelligencer,* p. A8.

Manson, J. E., Colditz, G. A., Stampfer, M. J., et al. (1990). A prospective study of obesity and risk of coronary heart disease in women. *New England Journal of Medicine, 322,* 882–888.

Manson, S. M. (1994). Culture and depression: Discovering variations in the experience of illness. In W. J. Lonner & R. S. Malpass (Eds.), *Psychology and culture.* Boston: Allyn & Bacon.

Mäntylä, T. (1986). Optimizing cue effectiveness: Recall of 500 and 600 incidentally learned words. *Journal of Experimental Psychology: Learning, Memory, and Cognition, 12,* 66–71.

Marangell, L. B. (2002). Concise guide to psychopharmacology. Washington, DC: American Psychiatric Publishing.

Marcia, J. E. (1966). Development and validation of ego identity status. *Journal of Personality and Social Psychology, 3,* 551–558.

Marcia, J. E. (1994). The empirical study of ego identity. In H. A. Bosma, T. L. G. Graafsma, H. D. Grotevant, & D. J. de Levita (Eds.), *Identity and development: An interdisciplinary approach.* Thousand Oaks, CA: Sage Publications.

Margolin, G., & Wampold, B. E. (1981). Sequential analysis of conflict and accord in distressed and nondistressed marital partners. *Journal of Consulting and Clinical Psychology, 49,* 554–567.

Markey, P. M. (2000). Bystander intervention in computer mediated communication. *Computers in Human Behavior, 16,* 183–188.

Markham, S. E., Scott, K. D., & McKee, G. H. (2002). Recognizing good attendance: A longitudinal, quasi-experimental field study. *Personnel Psychology, 55,* 639–660.

Markovitz, H., & Nantel, G. (1989). The belief-bias effect in the production and evaluation of logical conclusions. *Memory and Cognition, 17,* 11–17.

Marks, I. M. (1977). Phobias and obsessions: Clinical phenomena in search of laboratory models. In J. Maser & M. E. P. Seligman (Eds.), *Psychopathology: Experimental models.* San Francisco: Freeman.

Marks, I. M. (1991). Self-administered behavioural treatment. *Behavioural Psychotherapy, 19,* 42–46.

Marks, I. M. (2002). The maturing of therapy: Some brief psychotherapies help anxiety/depressive disorders but mechanisms of action are unclear. *British Journal of Psychiatry, 180,* 200–204.

Markus, H. R., & Kitayama, S. (1991). Culture and the self: Implications for cognition, emotion, and motivation. *Psychological Review, 98,* 224–253.

Markus, H. R., & Kitayama, S. (1998). The cultural psychology of personality. *Journal of Cross-Cultural Psychology, 29,* 63–87.

Marlatt, G. A. (1987). Alcohol, the magic elixir: Stress, expectancy, and the transformation of emotional states. In E. Gottheil, K. A. Druley, S. Pashko, & S. P. Weinstein (Eds.), *Stress and addiction.* New York: Brunner/Mazel.

Marlatt, G. A. (1996). Taxonomy of high-risk situations for alcohol relapse: Evolution and development of a cognitive-behavioral model. *Addiction, 91*(Suppl.), S37–S49.

Marlatt, G. A. (Ed.). (1998). *Harm reduction: Pragmatic strategies for managing high-risk behaviors.* New York: Guilford Press.

Marlatt, G. A., Baer, J. S., Kivlahan, D. R., et al. (1998). Screening and brief intervention for high-risk college student drinkers: Results from a 2-year follow-up assessment. *Journal of Consulting and Clinical Psychology, 66,* 604–615.

Marlatt, G. A., Blume, A. W., & Parks, G. A. (2001). Integrating harm reduction therapy and traditional substance abuse treatment. *Journal of Psychoactive Drugs, 33,* 13–21.

Marlatt, G. A., & Gordon, J. R. (1985). *Relapse prevention: Maintenance strategies in the treatment of addiction.* New York: Guilford Press.

Marler, P. (1970). A comparative approach to vocal learning: Song development in white-crowned sparrows. *Journal of Comparative and Physiological Psychology, 71,* 1–25.

Marlowe, D. H. (2001). *Psychological and psychosocial consequences of combat and deployment: With special emphasis on the Gulf War.* Santa Monica, CA : RAND, 2001.

Marschark, M., & Mayer, T. S. (1998). Interactions of language and memory in deaf children and adults. *Scandinavian Journal of Psychology, 39,* 145–148.

Marsh, H. W. (1990). A multidimensional, hierarchical model of self-concept: Theoretical and empirical justification. *Educational Psychology Review, 2,* 77–172.

Marshall, L. H., & Magoun, H. W. (1997). *Discoveries in the human brain: Neuroscience prehistory, brain structure, and function.* New York: Humana Press.

Marsiglio, W., Amato, P., Day, R. D., Lamb, M. E. (2000). Scholarship on fatherhood in the 1990s and beyond. *Journal of Marriage and the Family, 62,* 1173–1191.

Marsland, A. L., Cohen, S., Rabin, B. S., & Manuck, S. B. (2001). Associations between stress, trait negative affect, acute immune reactivity, and antibody response to Hepatitis B injection in healthy young adults. *Health Psychology, 20,* 4–11.

Martin, J. E., & Dubbert, P. M. (1985). Adherence in exercise. In R. I. Terjung (Ed.), *Exercise and sport sciences review* (Vol. 13). New York: Macmillan.

Martin S. C., Leenders, K. L, Chevalley, A. F., Missimer, J., Kuenig, G., Magyar, S., et al. (2001). Reward mechanisms in the brain and their role in dependence: Evidence from neurophysiological and neuroimaging studies. *Brain Research Reviews, 36,* 139–149.

Martinez, J. L., Jr., Barea-Rodriguez, E. J., & Derrick, B. E. (1998). Long-term potentiation, long-term depression, and learning. In J. L. Martinez, Jr., & R. P. Kesner (Eds.), *Neurobiology of learning and memory.* San Diego: Academic Press.

Martinez, M., & Raul, E. (2000). Conducta sexual procesos psicologicos moduladores, en mujeres y hombres [Sexual behavior and modulating psychological processes in women and men]. *Archivos Hispanoamericanos de Sexologia, 6,* 133–152.

Mash, E. J., & Barkley, R. A. (2003). *Child psychopathology* (2nd ed.). New York: Guilford Press.

Maslow, A. H. (1954). *Motivation and personality.* New York: Harper.

Massion, A. O., Dyck, I. R., Shea, M. T., Phillips, K. A., Warshaw, M. G., & Keller, M. B. (2002). Personality disorders and time to remission in generalized anxiety disorder, social phobia and panic disorder. *Archives of General Psychiatry, 59,* 434–440.

Masten, A. S. (2001). Ordinary magic: Resilience processes in development. *American Psychologist, 56,* 227–238.

Masten, A. S., & Coatsworth, J. D. (1998). The development of competence in favorable and unfavorable environments: Lessons from research on successful children. *American Psychologist, 53,* 205–220.

Masters, W., & Johnson, V. (1966). *Human sexual response.* London: Churchill.

Masters, W. H., Johnson, V. E., & Kolodny, R. C. (1988). *Human Sexuality,* 3rd ed. Boston: Little, Brown.

Matorin, S. (2002). Stigma as a barrier to recovery. *Psychiatric Services, 53,* 629–630.

Matsumoto, D., & Hull, P. (1994). Cognitive development and intelligence. In D. Matsumoto (Ed.), *People: Psychology from a cultural perspective.* Pacific Grove, CA: Brooks/Cole.

Matt, G. E., & Navarro, A. M. (1997). What meta-analyses have and have not taught us about psychotherapy effects: A review and future directions. *Clinical Psychology Review, 17,* 1–32.

Matthews, R., & Blackmore, S. (1995). Why are coincidences so impressive? *Perceptual and Motor Skills, 80,* 1121–1122.

May, J. R., & Sieb, G. E. (1987). Athletic injuries: Psychosocial factors in the onset, sequellae, rehabilitation, and prevention. In J. R. May & M. J. Asken (Eds.), *Sport psychology: The psychological health of the athlete.* New York: PMA Publishing.

May, R. (1961). The emergence of existential psychology. In R. May (Ed.), *Existential psychology.* New York: Random House.

Mayer, J. D., & Salovey, P. (1997). What is emotional intelligence? In P. Salovey & D. J. Sluyter (Eds.), *Emotional development and emotional intelligence: Educational implications.* New York: Basic Books.

Mayes, L. C., Grillon, C., Granger, R., & Schottenfeld, R. (1998). Regulation of arousal and attention in preschool children exposed to cocaine prenatally. *Annals of the New York Academy of Sciences, 846,* 126–143.

McAdams, D. P., & de St. Aubin, E. (Eds.). (1998). *Generativity and adult development: How and why we care for the next generation.* Washington, DC: American Psychological Association.

McAdams, S., & Drake, C. (2002). Auditory perception and cognition. In H. Pashler & S. Yantis (Eds.), *Steven's handbook of experimental psychology: Vol. 1. Sensation and perception* (3rd ed.). New York: Wiley.

McArdle, J. J., Ferrer-Caja, E., Hamagami, F., & Woodcock, R. W. (2002). Comparative longitudinal structural analyses of the growth and decline of multiple intellectual abilities over the life span. *Developmental Psychology, 38,* 115–142.

McAuley, E. (1992). The role of efficacy cognitions in the prediction of exercise behavior in middle-aged adults. *Journal of Behavioral Medicine, 15,* 65–88.

McCabe, P. M., Schneiderman, N., & Field, T. (2000). *Stress, coping, and cardiovascular disease.* Mahwah, NJ: Erlbaum.

McCall, R. B. (1977). Childhood IQs as predictors of adult educational and occupational status. *Science, 197,* 482–483.

McCall, W. V., & Edinger, J. D. (1992). Subjective total insomnia: An example of sleep state misperception. *Sleep, 15,* 71–73.

McCarley, R. W. (1998). Dreams: Disguise of forbidden wishes or transparent reflections of a distinct brain state? In R. M. Bilder & F. F. LeFever (Eds.), *Neuroscience of the mind on the centennial of Freud's Project for a Scientific Psychology: Annals of the New York Academy of Sciences* (Vol. 843). New York: New York Academy of Sciences.

McCaul, K. D., & Malott, J. J. (1984). Distraction and coping with pain. *Psychological Bulletin, 95,* 516–533.

McClelland, D. C. (1989). *Human motivation.* New York: Cambridge University Press.

McClelland, D. C., Atkinson, J. W., Clark, R. A., & Lowell, E. L. (1953). *The achievement motive.* New York: Appleton-Century-Crofts.

McClelland, D. C., & Cheriff, A. D. (1997). The immunoenhancing effects of humor on secretory IgA and resistance to respiratory infections. *Psychology and Health, 12,* 329–344.

McConnell, J. V. (1962). Memory transfer through cannibalism in planarians. *Journal of Neuropsychiatry, 3*(Suppl. 1), 542–548.

McCracken, L. M. (1998). Learning to live with pain: Acceptance of pain predicts adjustment in persons with chronic pain. *Pain, 74,* 21–27.

McCrae, R. R., & Costa, P. T. (1990). *Personality in adulthood.* New York: Guilford Press.

McCrae, R. R., & Costa, P. T. (2003). *Personality in adulthood: A Five-Factor Theory perspective.* New York: Guilford Press.

McCullough, J. P. (2003). *Patient manual for the cognitive behavioral analysis system of psychotherapy (BBASP).* New York: Guilford Press.

McCullough, M. E., Worthington, E. L., Jr., & Rachal, K. C. (1997). Interpersonal forgiving in close relationships. *Journal of Personality and Social Psychology, 73,* 321–336.

McEwen, B. S. (2001). *Coping with the environment: Neural and endocrine mechanisms.* New York: Oxford University Press.

McGinnis, M. (1994). The role of behavioral research in national health policy. In S. J.

Blumenthal, K. Matthews, & S. M. Weiss (Eds.), *New research frontiers in behavioral medicine: Proceedings of the national conference.* Washington, DC: NIH Publications.

McGinty, D. (1993). Energy conservation. In M. A. Carskadon (Ed.), *Encyclopedia of sleep and dreaming.* New York: Macmillan.

McGlaskan, T. H., & Fenton, W. S. (1992). The positive-negative distinction in schizophrenia: Review of natural history validators. *Archives of General Psychiatry, 49,* 63–72.

McGregor, H. A., & Elliot, A. J. (2002). Achievement goals as predictors of achievement-relevant processes prior to task engagement. *Journal of Educational Psychology, 94,* 381–395.

McIntosh, D. N., Silver, R. C., & Wortman, C. B. (1993). Religion's role in adjustment to a negative life event: Coping with the loss of a child. *Journal of Personality and Social Psychology, 65,* 812–821.

McKenna, P., & Oh, T. (2003). *Formal thought disorder in schizophrenia.* New York: Cambridge University Press.

McMahon, R. J., & Forehand, R. L. (2004). *Helping the noncompliant child: Family-based treatment for oppositional behavior.* New York: Guilford Press.

McMillan, T. M., Robertson, I. H., & Wilson, B. A. (1999). Neurogenesis after brain injury: Implications for neurorehabilitation. *Neuropsychological Rehabilitation, 9,* 129–133.

McNatt, D. B. (2000). Ancient Pygmalion joins contemporary management: A meta-analysis of the result. *Journal of Applied Psychology, 85,* 314–322.

McNeil, E. B. (1967). *The quiet furies: Man and disorder.* Englewood Cliffs, NJ: Prentice Hall.

Mead, M. (1935). *Sex and temperament in three primitive societies.* New York: Morrow.

Meaney, M. J., Mitchell, J. B., Aitken, D. H., & Bhatnagar, S. (Eds.). (1991). The effects of neonatal handling on the development of the adrenocortical response to stress: Implications for neuropathology and cognitive deficits in later life. *Psychoneuroendocrinology, 16,* 85–103.

Mechan, A. O., Moran, P. M., Elliot, J. M., Young, A. M. J., Joseph, M. H., & Green, A. R. (2002). A study of the effect of a single neurotoxic dose of 3,4 methylenedioxymethamphetamine (MDMA; "ecstasy") on the subsequent long-term behaviour of rats in the plus maze and open field. *Psychopharmacology, 159,* 167–175.

Meddis, R., Pearson, A. J., & Langford, G. (1973). An extreme case of healthy insomnia. *Electroencephalography and Clinical Neurophysiology, 35,* 213–214.

Medin, D. L., Coley, J. D. (1998). Concepts and categorization. In H. Julian et al. (Eds.), *Perception and cognition at century's end. Handbook of perception and cognition* (2nd ed.). San Diego, CA: Academic Press.

Meehl, P. E. (1995). "Is psychoanalysis one science, two sciences, or no science at all? A discourse among friendly antagonists": Comment. *Journal of the American Psychoanalytic Association, 43,* 1015–1023.

Meeus, W. H. J., & Raaijmakers, Q. A. W. (1986). Administrative obedience: Carrying out orders to use psychological-administrative violence. *European Journal of Social Psychology, 16,* 311–324.

Meeus, W. H. J., & Raaijmakers, Q. A. W. (1995). Obedience in modern society: The Utrecht studies. *Journal of Social Issues, 51,* 155–175.

Megargee, E. I. (1966). Undercontrolled and overcontrolled personality types in extreme anti-social aggression. *Psychological Monographs, 80*(Whole No. 611).

Mehnert, T., Krauss, H. H., Nadler, R., & Boyd, M. (1990). Correlates of life satisfaction in those with disabling conditions. *Rehabilitation Psychology, 35,* 3–17.

Meichenbaum, D. (1985). *Stress inoculation training.* New York: Pergamon Press.

Meier, R. P. (1991). Language acquisition by deaf children. *American Scientist, 79,* 61–70.

Meleski, M. E., & Damato, E. G. (2003). HIV exposure: neonatal considerations. *Journal of Obstetric, Gynecologic, and Neonatal Nursing, 32,* 109–116.

Meltzoff, A. N. (2002). Elements of a developmental theory of imitation. In A. N. Meltzoff, N. Andrew, & W. Prinz (Eds.), *The imitative mind: Development, evolution, and brain bases. Cambridge studies in cognitive perceptual development.* New York: Cambridge University Press.

Meltzoff, A. N., & Moore, M. K. (1977). Imitation of facial and manual gestures by human neonates. *Science, 198,* 75–78.

Melzack, R. (1998). Pain and stress. Clues toward understanding chronic pain. In M. Sabourin et al. (Eds.), *Advances in psychological science.* Hove, England: Psychology Press/ Erlbaum.

Melzack, R., & Wall, P. D. (1982). *The challenge of pain.* New York: Basic Books.

Mendelson, W. B. (2000). Sleep-inducing effects of adenosine microinjections into the medial preoptic area are blocked by flumazenil. *Brain Research, 852,* 479–481.

Menzies, R. G., & Clarke, J. C. (1995). The etiology of acrophobia and its relationship to severity and individual response patterns. *Behaviour Research and Therapy, 33,* 795–803.

Meredith, N. (1986). Testing the talking cure. *Science, 232,* 31–37.

Merikle, P. M., & Daneman, M. (1998). Psychological investigations of unconscious perception. *Journal of Consciousness Studies, 5,* 5–18.

Mersch, P. P. A., Middendorp, H. M., Bouhuys, A. L., Beersma, D. G. M., & van den Hoofdakker, R. H. (1999). Seasonal affective disorder and latitude: A review of the literature. *Journal of Affective Disorders, 53,* 35–48.

Mesquita, B., Frijda, N. H., & Scherer, K. R. (1997). Culture and emotion. In J. W. Berry et al. (Eds.), *Handbook of cross-cultural psychology: Vol. 2. Basic processes and human development* (2nd ed.). Boston: Allyn & Bacon.

Methot, L. L., & Huitema, B. E. (1998). Effects of signal probability on individual differences in vigilance. *Human Factors, 40,* 78–90.

Meyer, C. B., & Taylor, S. E. (1986). Adjustment to rape. *Journal of Personality and Social Psychology, 50,* 1226–1234.

Meyer, R. G. & Osborne, Y. H. (1987). *Case studies in abnormal behavior* (2nd ed.). Boston: Allyn & Bacon.

Meyer, T. A., Svirsky, M. A., Kirk, K. I., & Miyamoto, R. T. (1998). Improvements in speech perception by children with profound prelingual hearing loss: Effects of device, communication mode, and chronological age. *Journal of Speech, Language, and Hearing Research, 41,* 846–858.

Michael, R. T., Gagnon, J. H., Laumman, E. O., & Kolata, G. (1994). *Sex in America: A definitive survey.* Boston: Little, Brown.

Mignot, E. (1998). Genetic and familial aspects of narcolepsy. *Neurology, 50,* S16–S22.

Miles, C., & Hardman, E. (1998). State dependent memory produced by aerobic exercise. *Ergonomics, 41,* 20–28.

Miles, H. L., Mitchell, R. W., & Harper, S. E. (1996). Simon says: The development of imitation in an enculturated orangutan. In A. E. Russon & K. A. Bard (Eds.), *Reaching into thought: The minds of the great apes.* Cambridge, England: Cambridge University Press.

Milgram, S. (1974). *Obedience to authority: An experimental view.* New York: Harper & Row.

Miller, B. C., Fan, X., Christensen, M., Grotevant, H. D., & van Dulmen, M. (2000). Comparisons of adopted and nonadopted adolescents in a large, nationally representative sample. *Child Development, 71,* 1458–1473.

Miller, G. A. (1956). The magical number seven, plus or minus two: Some limits on our capacity for processing information. *Psychological Review, 63,* 81–97.

Miller, G. E., & Cohen, S. (2001). Psychological interventions and the immune system: A meta-analytic review and critique. *Health Psychology, 20,* 47–63.

Miller, J. G. (1984). Culture and the development of everyday social explanation. *Journal of Personality and Social Psychology, 46,* 961–978.

Miller, J. G., Bersoff, D. M., & Harwood, R. L. (1990). Perceptions of social responsibility in India and in the United States: Moral imperatives or personal decisions? *Journal of Personality and Social Psychology, 58,* 33–47.

Miller, K. F., & Stigler, J. F. (1987). Counting in Chinese: Cultural variation in a basic cognitive skill. *Cognitive Development, 2,* 279–305.

Miller, L., & Budd, J. (1999). The development of occupational sex-role stereotypes, occupational preferences and academic subject preferences in children at ages 8, 12, and 16. *Educational Psychology, 19,* 17–35.

Miller, L. S., & Rohling, M. L. (2001). A statistical interpretive method for neuropsychological test data. *Neuropsychology Review, 11*(3), 143–169.

Miller, N. E. (1944). Experimental studies of conflict. In J. McV. Hunt (Ed.), *Personality and the behavior disorders* (Vol. 1). New York: Ronald Press.

Miller, N. E., & Dollard, J. (1941). *Social learning and imitation.* New Haven, CT: Yale University Press.

Miller, S. D., Blackburn, T., Scholes, G., White, G. L., & Mamales, N. (1991). Optical differences in multiple personality disorder: A second look. *Journal of Nervous and Mental Disease, 179,* 132–135.

Miller, W. R. (1996). Motivational interviewing: Research, practice, and puzzles. *Addictive Behaviors, 21,* 835–842.

Miller, W. R., & Brown, S. A. (1997). Why psychologists should treat alcohol and drug problems. *American Psychologist, 52,* 1269–1279.

Miller, W. R., & Rollnick, S. (1991). *Motivational interviewing: Preparing people to change addictive behavior.* New York: Guilford Press.

Miller, W. R., & Rollnick, S. (2002). *Motivational interviewing* (2nd ed.). New York: Guilford Press.

Millon, T., Simonsen, E., Birket-Smith, M., & Davis, R. D. (Eds.). (1998). *Psychopathy: Antisocial, criminal and violent behavior.* New York: Guilford Press.

Milner, B. (1965). Memory disturbances after bilateral hippocampal lesions. In P. Milner & S. Glickman (Eds.), *Cognitive processes and the brain.* Princeton, NJ: Van Nostrand.

Milner, B. R. (1970). Memory and medial temporal regions of the brain. In K. H. Pribram & D. R. Broadbent (Eds.), *Biology of memory.* Orlando, FL: Academic Press.

Milrod, B., Busch, F., Cooper, A., & Shapiro, T. (1997). *Manual of panic-focused psychodynamic psychotherapy.* Washington, DC: American Psychiatric Press.

Milton, J., & Wiseman, R. (1999). Does psi exist? Lack of replication of an anomalous process of information transfer. *Psychological Bulletin, 125,* 387–391.

Milton, J., & Wiseman, R. (2001). Does psi exist? Reply to Storm and Ertel. *Psychological Bulletin, 127,* 434–438.

Mineka, S., Watson, D., & Clark, L. A. (1998). Comorbidity of anxiety and unipolar mood disorder. *Annual Review of Psychology, 49,* 377–412.

Mintz, J., Drake, R. E., & Crits-Christoph, P. (1996). Efficacy and effectiveness of psychotherapy: Two paradigms, one science. *American Psychologist, 51,* 1084–1085.

Minuchin, S. (1974). *Families and family therapy.* Cambridge, MA: Harvard University Press.

Mischel, W. (1984). Convergences and challenges in the search for consistency. *American Psychologist, 39,* 351–364.

Mischel, W. (1999). Personality coherence and dispositions in a cognitive-affective personality system (CAPS) approach. In D. Cervone & Y. Shoda (Eds.), *The coherence of personality.* New York: Guilford Press.

Mischel, W., & Peake, P. K. (1982). In search of consistency: Measure for measure. In M. P. Zanna, E. T. Higgins, & C. P. Herman (Eds.), *Consistency in social behavior: The Ontario Symposium* (Vol. 2). Hillsdale, NJ: Erlbaum.

Mischel, W., Shoda, Y., & Mendoza-Denton, R. (2002). Situation-behavior profiles as a locus of consistency in personality. *Current Directions in Psychological Science, 11,* 50–54.

Mischel, W., Shoda, Y., & Smith, R. E. (2004). *Introduction to personality: Toward an integration.* New York: Wiley.

Mishne, J. (2002). *Multiculturalism and the therapeutic process.* New York: Guilford.

Mistlberger, R. E., Antle, M. C., Glass, J. D., & Miller, J. D. (2000). Behavioral and serotonergic regulation of circadian rhythms. *Biological Rhythm Research, 31,* 240–283.

Mitchell, K. J., & Zaragoza, M. S. (2001). Contextual overlap and eyewitness suggestibility. *Memory and Cognition, 29,* 616–626.

Moen, P., Kim, J. E., & Hofmeister, H. (2001). Couples' work/retirement transitions, gender, and marital quality. *Social Psychology Quarterly, 64,* 55–71.

Molfese, D. L., & Molfese, V. J. (2002). *Developmental variations in learning: Applications to social, executive function, language, and reading skills.* Mahwah, NJ: Erlbaum.

Monahan, J. (1992). Mental disorder and violent behavior: Attitudes and evidence. *American Psychologist, 47,* 511–521.

Monahan, J. L., Murphy, S. T., & Zajonc, R. B. (2000). Subliminal mere exposure: Specific, general, and diffuse effects. *Psychological Science, 11,* 462–466.

Monk, T. H., Buysse, D. J., Welsh, D. K., Kennedy, K. S., & Rose, L. R. (2001). A sleep diary and questionnaire study of naturally short sleepers. *Journal of Sleep Research, 10,* 173–179.

Monk, T. H., Folkard, S., & Wedderburn, A. I. (1996). Maintaining safety and high performance on shiftwork. *Applied Ergonomics, 27,* 17–23.

Monroe, S. M., & Peterman, A. M. (1988). Life stress and psychopathology. In L. H. Cohen (Ed.), *Life events and psychological functioning: Theoretical and methodological issues.* Newbury Park, CA: Sage Publications.

Montgomery, G. H., DuHamel, K. N., & Redd, W. H. (2000). A meta-analysis of hypnotically induced analgesia: How effective is hypnosis? *International Journal of Clinical and Experimental Hypnosis, 48,* 138–153.

Moody, M. S. (1997). Changes in scores on the Mental Rotations Test during the menstrual cycle. *Perceptual and Motor Skills, 84,* 955–961.

Moon, C., & Fifer, W. P. (1990). Syllables as signals for 2-day-old infants. *Infant Behavior and Development, 13,* 377–390.

Moore, T. M., Scarpa, A., & Raine, A. (2002). A meta-analysis of serotonin metabolite 5 HIAA and antisocial behavior. *Aggressive Behavior, 28,* 299–316.

Moorey, S. (2003). *Cognitive behaviour therapy for people with cancer.* Oxford, England: Oxford University Press.

Moreland, J. L., Dansereau, D. F., & Chmielewski, T. L. (1997). Recall of descriptive information: The roles of presentation format, annotation strategy, and individual differences. *Contemporary Educational Psychology, 22,* 521–533.

Morgan, W. (1997). *Physical activity and mental health.* Philadelphia: Taylor & Francis.

Morgan, W. P., Horstman, D. H., Cymerman, A., & Stokes, J. (1983). Facilitation of physical performance by means of a cognitive strategy. *Cognitive Therapy and Research, 7,* 251–264.

Morrell, M. J., Dixen, J. M., Carter, C. S., & Davidson, J. M. (1984). The influence of age and cycling status on sexual arousability in women. *American Journal of Obstetrics and Gynecology, 148,* 66–71.

Morris, D., Collett, P., Marsh, P., & O'Shaughnessy, M. (1979). *Gestures.* New York: Stein & Day.

Morris, M. W., Podolny, J. M., & Airel, S. (2001). Culture, norms and obligations: Cross national differences in patterns of interpersonal norms and felt obligations toward coworkers. In W. Wosinska, R. B. Cialdini, D. W. Barrett, & J. Reykowski (Eds.), *The practice of social influence in multiple cultures.* Mahwah, NJ: Erlbaum.

Morrison, D. C. (1988). Marine mammals join the navy. *Science, 242,* 1503–1504.

Moscovici, S. (1985). Social influence and conformity. In G. Lindzey & E. Aronson (Eds.), *Handbook of social psychology* (3rd ed.). New York: Random House.

Moscovici, S., & Zavalloni, M. (1969). The group as a polarizer of attitudes. *Journal of Personality and Social Psychology, 12,* 124–135.

Mowrer, O. H. (1947). On the dual nature of learning: A reinterpretation of "conditioning" and "problem solving." *Harvard Educational Review, 17,* 102–150.

Muchinsky, P. M. (2000). *Psychology applied to work* (6th ed.). Pacific Grove, CA: Brooks/Cole.

Müller M. M., & Hübner, R. (2002). Can the spotlight of attention be shaped like a doughnut? *Psychological Science, 13,* 119–124.

Murdoch, H. (1984). Maternal rubella: The implications. *Association of Educational Psychologists Journal, 6,* 3–6.

Murphy, S. L. (2000). Deaths: Final data for 1998. *National Vital Statistics Reports* (NCHS), pp. 26, 73.

Murray, H. A. (1971). *Thematic Apperception Test.* Cambridge, MA: Harvard University Press.

Murray, R., Jones, P., Van Oss, J., et al. (2003). *The epidemiology of schizophrenia.* New York: Cambridge University Press.

Myin-Germeys, I., van Os, J., Schwartz, J. E., Stone, A. A., & Delespaul, P. A. (2001). Emotional reactivity to daily life stress in psychosis. *Archives of General Psychiatry, 58,* 1137–1144.

Nadler, A., & Ben-Slushan, D. (1989). Forty years later: Long-term consequences of massive traumatization as manifested by holocaust survivors from the city and the Kibbutz. *Journal of Consulting and Clinical Psychology, 57*, 287–293.

Nakayama, K., & Tyler, C. W. (1981). Psychophysical isolation of movement sensitivity by removal of familiar position cues. *Vision Research, 21*, 427–433.

Narrow, W. E., Rae, D. S., Robins, L. N., & Regier, D. A. (2002). Revised prevalence based estimates of mental disorders in the United States: Using a clinical signficance criterion to reconcile 2 surveys' estimates. *Archives of General Psychiatry, 59*, 115–123.

Nathan, P. E. (1985). Aversion therapy in the treatment of alcoholism: Success and failure. *Annals of the New York Academy of Sciences, 443*, 357–364.

Nathan, P. E. (1997). Substance use disorders in the DSM-IV. In G. A. Marlatt & G. R. VandenBos (Eds.), *Addictive behaviors: Readings on etiology, prevention and treatment*. Washington, DC: American Psychological Association.

Nathan, P. E., & Lagenbucher, J. W. (1999). Psychopathology: Description and classification. *Annual Review of Psychology, 50*, 79–107.

National Center for Education Statistics. (2001). *Postsecondary institutions in the United States: Fall 2000 and degrees and other awards conferred: 1999–2000*. Available online: http://nces.ed.gov/pubsearch/pubsinfo.asp?pubid=2002156

National Center for Health Statistics. (1995). *Healthy people 2000*. Washington, DC: Author.

National Highway Traffic Safety Administration. (2002). *Traffic Safety Facts 2000: Alcohol* (DOT HS 808 950). Available online: http://www.fars.nhtsa.dot.gov/pubs/2.pdf

National Institute of Child Health and Human Development. (2001a). Child care and children's peer interaction at 24 and 36 months: The NICHD study of early child care. *Child Development, 72*, 1478–1500.

National Institute of Child Health and Human Development. (2001b). Child care and family predictors of preschool attachment and stability from infancy. *Developmental Psychology, 37*, 847–862.

National Safety Council. (1992). *Blood alcohol level and risk of having an automobile accident*. Washington, DC: Author.

National Sleep Foundation. (2002). *2002 omnibus sleep in America poll*. Available online: http://www.sleepfoundation.org/publications/2002poll.html

Natsoulas, T. (1999). An ecological and phenomenological perspective on consciousness and perception: Contact with the world at the very heart of the being of consciousness. *Review of General Psychology, 3*, 224–245.

Nederhof, A. J. (1985). Methods of coping with social desirability bias: A review. *European Journal of Social Psychology, 15*, 263–280.

Needham, A., Barrett, T., & Peterman, K. (2002). A pick me up for infants' exploratory skills: Early simulated experiences reaching for objects using 'sticky' mittens enhances young infants' object exploration skills. *Infant Behavior and Development, 25*, 279–295.

Neisser, U., Bouchard, T. J., Jr., Boykin, A. W., Brody, N., Ceci, S. J., Halpern, D. F., Loehlin, J. C., Perloff, R., Sternberg, R. J., & Urbina, S. (1998). Intelligence: Knowns and unknowns. In M. E. Hertzig et al. (Eds.), *Annual progress in child psychiatry and child development: 1997*. Bristol, PA: Brunner/Mazel.

Neisser, U., & Harsch, N. (1993). Phantom flashbulbs: False recollections of hearing the news about Challenger. In E. Winograd & U. Neisser (Eds.), *Affect and accuracy in recall: Studies of "flashbulb" memories*. New York: Cambridge University Press.

Nelson, C. A., & Luciana, M. (Eds.). (2001). *Handbook of developmental cognitive neuroscience*. Cambridge, MA: MIT Press.

Nemiah, J. C. (1978). Psychoneurotic disorders. In A. M. Nicholi (Ed.), *Harvard guide to modern psychiatry*. Cambridge, MA: Harvard University Press.

Nesbitt, E. B. (1973). An escalator phobia overcome in one session of flooding in vivo. *Journal of Behavior Therapy and Experimental Psychiatry, 4*, 405–406.

Neugarten, B. L., & Hall, E. (1980, April). Acting one's age: New roles for old. *Psychology Today*, 66–80.

Neumäker, K. J. (2000). Mortality rates and causes of death. *European Eating Disorders Review, 8*, 181–187.

Neuschatz, J. S., Lampinen, J., Preston, E. L., Hawkins, E. R., & Toglia, M. P. (2002). The effect of memory schemata on memory and the phenomenological experience of naturalistic situations. *Applied Cognitive Psychology, 16*, 687–708.

Newell, A., & Simon, H. A. (1972). *Human problem solving*. Englewood Cliffs, NJ: Prentice Hall.

Newlin, D. B., & Thomson, J. B. (1997). Alcohol challenge with sons of alcoholics: A critical review and analysis. In G. A. Marlatt & G. R. VandenBos (Eds.), *Addictive behaviors: Readings on etiology, prevention and treatment*. Washington, DC: American Psychological Association.

Newman, D. L., Caspi, A., Moffitt, T. E., & Silva, P. A. (1997). Antecedents of adult interpersonal functioning: Effects of individual differences in age 3 temperament. *Developmental Psychology, 33*, 206–217.

Newman, D. L., Moffit, T. E., Caspi, A., Silva, P. A., & Stanton, W. R. (1996). Psychiatric disorder in a birth cohort of young adults: Prevalence, comorbidity, clinical significance, and new case incidence from ages 11–21. *Journal of Consulting and Clinical Psychology, 64*, 552–562.

Newport, F., & Strausberg, M. (2001, June). Americans' belief in psychic and paranormal phenomena is up over last decade. *Gallup Poll Monthly*, 14–17.

Nezami, E., & Butcher, J. N. (2000). Objective personality assessment. In G. Goldstein & M. Hersen (Eds.), *Handbook of psychological assessment* (3rd ed.). New York: Elsevier.

Nezlek, J. B., Hampton, C. P., & Shean, G. (2000). Clinical depression and day-to-day social interaction in a community sample. *Journal of Abnormal Psychology, 109*, 11–19.

Nezu, A. M., Nezu, C. M., & D'Zurilla, T. (2000). Problem-solving skills training. In G. Fink (Ed.), *Encyclopedia of stress*. San Diego, CA: Academic Press.

Nichols, C. D., & Sanders-Bush, E. (2002). A single dose of lysergic acid diethylamide influences gene expression patterns within the mammalian brain. *Neuropsychopharmacology, 26*, 634–642.

Nickerson, R. S., & Adams, M. J. (1979). Long-term memory for a common object. *Cognitive Psychology, 11*, 287–307.

Niehoff, B., Moorman, R. H., Blakely, G., & Fuller, J. (2001). The influence of empowerment and job enrichment on employee loyalty in a downsizing environment. *Group and Organization Management, 26*, 93–113.

Nigg, J. T., Lohr, N. E., Westen, D., & Gold, L. J. (1992). Malevolent object representation in borderline personality disorder and major depression. *Journal of Abnormal Psychology, 101*, 61–67.

Nisbett, R. E. (1998). Race, genetics, and IQ. In C. Jencks et al. (Eds.), *The Black-White test score gap*. Washington, DC: Brookings Institution.

Nisbett, R. E., Peng, K., Choi, I., & Norenzayan, A. (2001). Culture and systems of thought: Holistic vs. analytic cognition. *Psychological Review, 108*, 291–310.

Nishino, S., Mignot, E., & Dement, W. C. (2001). Sedative hypnotics. In A. F. Schatzberg & C. B. Nemeroff (Eds.), *Essentials of clinical psychopharmacology*. Washington, DC: American Psychiatric Association.

Noble, E. P. (1998). The D_2 dopamine receptor gene: A review of association studies in alcoholism and phenotypes. *Alcohol, 16*, 33–45.

Noice, T., & Noice, H. (2002a). The expertise of professional actors: A review of recent research. *High Ability Studies, 13*, 7–20.

Noice, T., & Noice, H. (2002b). Very long-term recall and recognition of well-learned material. *Applied Cognitive Psychology, 16*, 259–272.

Nolen-Hoeksema, S. (1990). *Sex differences in depression*. Stanford, CA: Stanford University Press.

Nolte, J. (1998). *The human brain: An introduction to its functional anatomy*. St. Louis, MO: Mosby.

Norcross, J. C. (1991). Prescriptive matching in psychotherapy: An introduction. *Psychotherapy, 28*, 439–443.

Norcross, J. C. (2003). *Psychotherapy relationships that work: Therapist contributions and responsiveness to patients*. New York: Oxford University Press.

Norcross, J. C., Karg-Bray, R. S., & Prochaska, J. O. (1995). *Clinical psychologists in the 1990s.* Unpublished manuscript, University of Scranton.

Norcross, J. C., Ratzin, A. C., & Payne, D. (1989). Ringing in the New Year: The change processes and reported outcomes of resolutions. *Addictive Behaviors, 14,* 205–212.

Normann, R. A., Maynard, E. M., Guillory, K. S., & Warren, D. J. (1996). Cortical implants for the blind. *IEEE Spectrum, 33,* 54–9.

Normann, R. A., Maynard, E. M., Rousche, P. J., & Warren, D. J. (1999). A neural interface for a cortical vision prosthesis. *Vision Research, 39,* 2577–2587.

Norris, J. (1994). Alcohol and female sexuality: A look at expectancies and risks. *Alcohol Health and Research World, 18,* 197–201.

North, M., North, S. M., & Coble, J. R. (2002). Virtual reality therapy: An effective treatment for psychological disorders. In K. M. Stanney (Ed.), *Handbook of virtual environments: Design, implementation, and applications. Human factors and ergonomics.* Mahwah, NJ: Erlbaum.

Norton, G. R., Harrison, B., Haunch, J., & Rhodes, L. (1985). Characteristics of people with infrequent panic attacks. *Abnormal Psychiatry, 94,* 216–221.

Nossal, C. J. V., & Hall, E. (1995). Choices following antigen entry: Antibody formation or immunologic tolerance? *Annual Review of Immunology, 13,* 171–204.

Nyberg, L., Forkstam, C., Petersson, K. M., Cabeza, R., & Ingvar, M. (2002). Brain imaging of human memory systems: Between-systems similarities and within-system differences. *Cognitive Brain Research, 13,* 281–292.

Ockene, J. K., et al. (2001). Relapse and maintenance issues for smoking cessation. *Health Psychology, 19,* 17–31.

O'Connor, D. B., Archer, J., Hair, W. M., & Wu, F. C. W. (2002). Exogenous testosterone, aggression, and mood in eugonadal and hypogonadal men. *Physiology and Behavior, 75,* 557–566.

O'Connor, S. C., & Rosenblood, L. K. (1996). Affiliation motivation in everyday experience: A theoretical comparison. *Journal of Personality and Social Psychology, 70,* 513–522.

O'Donohue, W., & Elliot, A. (1992). The current status of posttraumatic stress disorder as a diagnostic category: problems and proposals. *Journal of Traumatic Stress, 5,* 421–439.

Office of Applied Studies. (2002). *Results from the 2001 National Household Survey on Drug Abuse: Vol. 1. Summary of national findings* (DHHS Publication No. SMA 02–3758, NHSDA Series H–17). Rockville, MD: Substance Abuse and Mental Health Services Administration. Available online: http://www.samhsa.gov/oas/NHSDA/2k1NHSDA/vol1/Chapter2.htm

Ohayon, M. M., Guilleminault, C., & Priest, R. G. (1999). Night terrors, sleepwalking, and confusional arousals in the general population: Their frequency and relationship to other sleep and mental disorders. *Journal of Clinical Psychiatry, 60,* 268–276.

Öhman, A. (1993). Fear and anxiety as emotional phenomena: Clinical phenomenology, evolutionary perspectives, and information-processing mechanisms. In M. Lewis & J. M. Haviland (Eds.), *Handbook of emotions.* New York: Guilford Press.

Öhman, A. (2000). Anxiety. In G. Fink (Ed.), *Encyclopedia of stress.* San Diego, CA: Academic Press.

Öhman, A., & Mineka, S. (2001). Fears, phobias, and preparedness: Toward an evolved module of fear and fear learning. *Psychological Review, 108,* 483–522.

Öhman, A., & Soares, J. J. F. (1998). Emotional conditioning to masked stimuli: Expectancies for aversive outcomes following nonrecognized fear-relevant stimuli. *Journal of Experimental Psychology: General, 127,* 69–82.

Olds, J. (1958). Self-stimulation of the brain. *Science, 127,* 315–324.

O'Leary, A., & The National Institute of Mental Health Multisite HIV Prevention Trial Group. (2001). Social-cognitive theory mediators of behavior change in the National Institute of Mental Health Multisite HIV Prevention Trial. *Health Psychology, 20,* 369–376.

O'Leary, K. D., & Wilson, G. T. (1987). *Behavior therapy: Application and outcome.* Englewood Cliffs, NJ: Prentice Hall.

Oleson, T. (2002). Auriculotherapy stimulation for neuro-rehabilitation. *NeuroRehabilitation, 17,* 49–62.

Olness, K., & Ader, R. (1992). Conditioning as an adjunct in the pharmacotherapy of lupus erythematosus. *Journal of Developmental and Behavioral Pediatrics, 13,* 124–125.

Orbuch, T. L., House, J. S., Mero, R. P., & Webster, P. S. (1996). Marital quality over the life course. *Social Psychology Quarterly, 59,* 162–171.

Orne, M. T. (1959). The nature of hypnosis: Artifact and essence. *Journal of Abnormal and Social Psychology, 58,* 277–299.

Orne, M. T. (1962). On the social psychology of the psychological experiment: With particular reference to demand characteristics and their implications. *American Psychologist, 17,* 776–783.

Orne, M. T., & Evans, F. J. (1965). Social control in the psychological experiment: Antisocial behavior and hypnosis. *Journal of Personality and Social Psychology, 1,* 189–200.

Ornstein, R. (1997). *Right mind.* Ft. Worth, TX: Harcourt Brace.

Ost, J., Vrij, A., Costall, A., & Bull, R. (2002). Crashing memories and reality monitoring: Distinguishing between perceptions, imaginations and false memories. *Applied Cognitive Psychology, 16,* 125–134.

Ouellette, J. A., & Wood, W. (1998). Habit and intention in everyday life: The multiple processes by which past behavior predicts future behavior. *Psychological Bulletin, 124,* 54–74.

Owen, P. R., & Laurel-Seller, E. (2000). Weight and shape ideals: Thin is dangerously in. *Journal of Applied Social Psychology, 30,* 979–990.

Paffenbarger, R. S., Jr., Hyde, R. T., Wing, A. L., & Hsieh, C. C. (1986). Physical activity, all-cause mortality, and longevity of college alumni. *New England Journal of Medicine, 314,* 605–613.

Paivio, A. (1969). Mental imagery is associative learning and memory. *Psychological Review, 76,* 241–263.

Paivio, A., Khan, M., & Begg, I. (2000). Concreteness of relational effects on recall of adjective noun pairs. *Canadian Journal of Experimental Psychology, 54,* 149–160.

Pajer, K. (2000). Hysteria. In G. Fink (Ed.), *Encyclopedia of stress.* San Diego, CA: Academic Press.

Palfai, T., & Jankiewicz, H. (1991). *Drugs and human behavior.* Dubuque, IA: Wm. C. Brown.

Palmer, J. A., & Palmer, L. K. (Eds.). (2002). *Evolutionary psychology: The ultimate origins of human behavior* (Vol. 15). Needham Heights, MA.: Allyn & Bacon.

Palmer, S. E. (2002). Perceptual organization in vision. In H. Pashler & S. Yantis (Eds.), *Steven's handbook of experimental psychology: Vol. 1. Sensation and perception* (3rd ed.). New York: Wiley.

Palmere, M., Benton, S. L., Glover, J. A., & Ronning, R. (1983). Elaboration and recall of main ideas in prose. *Journal of Education Psychology, 75,* 898–907.

Papanicolaou, A. C. (1989). *Emotion: A reconsideration of the somatic theory.* New York: Gordon & Breach.

Papini, M. R. (2002). Pattern and process in the evolution of learning. *Psychological Review, 109,* 186–201.

Parchman, S. W., Ellis, J. A., Christinaz, D., & Vogel, M. (2000). An evaluation of three computer-based instructional strategies in basic electricity and electronics training. *Military Psychology, 12,* 73–87.

Park, D. C., Smith, A. D., & Cavanaugh, J. C. (1990). Metamemories of memory researchers. *Memory and Cognition, 18,* 321–327.

Parker, A. (2000). A review of the ganzfeld work at Gothenburg University. *Journal of the Society for Psychical Research, 64,* 1–15.

Parker, C. R., Bolling, M. Y., & Kohlenberg, R. J. (1998). Operant theory of personality. In D. F. Barone, M. Hersen, & V. B. Van Hasselt (Eds.), *Advanced personality.* New York: Plenum.

Parkinson, A. J., Parkinson, W. S., Tyler, R. S., Lowder, M. W., & Gantz, B. J. (1998). Speech perception performance in experienced cochlear-implant patients receiving the

SPEAK processing strategy in the Nucleus Spectra-22 cochlear implant. *Journal of Speech, Language, and Hearing Research, 41,* 1073–1087.

Parrott, A. C. (1999). Does cigarette smoking cause stress? *American Psychologist, 54,* 817–820.

Parrott, A. C. (2001). Human psychopharmacology of Ecstasy (MDMA): A review of 15 years of empirical research. *Human Psychopharmacology Clinical and Experimental, 16,* 557–577.

Pashler, H., & Yantis, S. (Eds.). (2002). *Steven's handbook of experimental psychology: Vol. 1. Sensation and perception* (3rd ed.). New York: Wiley.

Pasupathi, M., Staudinger, U. M., & Baltes, P. B. (2001). Seeds of wisdom: Adolescents' knowledge and judgment about difficult life problems. *Developmental Psychology, 37,* 351–361.

Patterson, G. R., Littman, R. A., & Bricker, W. (1967). Assertive behavior in children: A step toward a theory of aggression. *Monographs of the Society for Research in Child Development, 32*(Whole No. 5).

Pauk, W., & Fiore, J. P. (2000). *Succeed in college!* Boston: Houghton Mifflin.

Paul, G. L. (2001). The active unconscious, symptom substitution, and other things that went 'bump' in the night. In W. T. O'Donohue et al. (Eds.), *A history of the behavioral therapies: Founders' personal histories.* New York: Guilford Press.

Paul, G. L., & Lentz, R. J. (1977). *Psychosocial treatment of chronic mental patients: Milieu versus social learning programs.* Cambridge, MA: Harvard University Press.

Paulos, J. A. (1988). *Innumeracy.* New York: Hill & Wang.

Paunonen, S. V. (2003). Big Five factors of personality and replicated predictions of behavior. *Journal of Personality and Social Psychology, 84,* 411–424.

Pavlov, I. P. (1928). *Lectures on conditioned reflexes: Twenty-five years of objective study of the higher nervous activity (behaviour) of animals* (W. H. Gantt, Trans.). New York: International Publishers. (Original work published 1923)

Pearlin, L. I., & Schooler, C. (1978). The structure of coping. *Journal of Health and Social Behavior, 19,* 2–21.

Pedalino, E., & Gamboa, V. U. (1974). Behavior modification and absenteeism: Intervention in one industrial setting. *Journal of Applied Psychology, 59,* 694–698.

Pedersen, W. C., Miller, L. C., Putcha-Bhagavatula, A. D., & Yang, Y. (2002). Evolved sex differences in the number of partners desired? The long and short of it. *Psychological Science, 13,* 157–161.

Pedersen-Pietersen, L. (1997, January 12). You're sober at last: Now prove it to the boss. *New York Times,* p. F10.

Pedrotti, F. L., & Pedrotti, L. S. (1997). *Optics and vision.* Englewood Cliffs, NJ: Prentice Hall.

Pelletier, D. L., & Frongillo, E. A. (2003). Changes in child survival are strongly associated with changes in malnutrition in developing countries. *Journal of Nutrition, 133,* 107–119.

Pellino, T. A., & Ward, S. E. (1998). Perceived control mediates the relationship between pain severity and patient satisfaction. *Journal of Pain and Symptom Management, 15,* 110–116.

Penfield, W., & Perot, P. (1963). The brain's record of auditory and visual experience. *Brain, 86,* 595–696.

Pennebaker, J. W. (1995). *Emotion, disclosure and health.* Washington, DC: American Psychological Association.

Pennebaker, J. W. (1997). *Opening up: The healing power of expressing emotions.* New York: Guilford Press.

Peplau, L. A., Garnets, L. D., Spalding, L. R., Conley, T. D., & Veniegas, R. C. (1998). A critique of Bem's "Exotic Becomes Erotic" theory of sexual orientation. *Psychological Review, 105,* 387–394.

Perani, D., Paulesu, E., Galles, N. S., Dupoux, E., & Dehaene, S. (1998). The bilingual brain: Proficiency and age of acquisition of the second language. *Brain, 121,* 1841–1852.

Perdue, C. W., Dovidio, J. F., Gurtman, M. B., & Tyler, R. B. (1990). Us and them: Social categorization and the process of intergroup bias. *Journal of Personality and Social Psychology, 59,* 475–486.

Pert, C. B. (1986). The wisdom of the receptors: Neuropeptides, the emotions, and bodymind. *Advances, 3,* 8–16.

Pert, C. B. (1997). *Molecules of emotion: Why you feel the way you feel.* New York: Simon & Schuster.

Peterson, C., & Seligman, M. E. P. (1987). Explanatory style and illness. *Journal of Personality, 55,* 237–265.

Peterson, C., & Whalen, N. (2001). Five years later: Children's memory for medical emergencies. *Applied Cognitive Psychology 15,* 7–24.

Peterson, L. R., & Peterson, M. J. (1959). Short term retention of individual verbal items. *Journal of Experimental Psychology, 58,* 193–198.

Petrill, S. (2003). The development of intelligence: Behavior genetics approaches. In R. J. Sternberg, J. Lautrey, & T. I. Lubart (Eds.), *Models of intelligence: International perspectives.* Washington, DC: American Psychological Association.

Petrinovich, L. F. (1999). *Darwinian dominion: Animal welfare and human interests.* Cambridge, MA: MIT Press.

Petrovic, P., & Ingvar, M. (2002). Imaging cognitive modulation of pain processing. *Pain, 95,* 1–5.

Petrovic, P., Kalso, E., Petersson, M. K., & Ingvarm, M. (2002, February). Placebo and opioid analgesia: Imaging a shared neuronal network. *Science Express Reports,* pp. 17–22.

Petry, N., & Martin, B. (2002). Low-cost contingency management for treating cocaine- and opioid-abusing methadone patients. *Journal of Consulting and Clinical Psychology, 70,* 398–405.

Pettigrew, T. F. (1979). The ultimate attribution error: Extending Allport's cognitive analysis of prejudice. *Personality and Social Psychology Bulletin, 55,* 461–476.

Pettigrew, T. F., & Meertens, R. W. (1995). Subtle and blatant prejudice in western Europe. *European Journal of Social Psychology, 25,* 57–76.

Pettigrew, T. F., & Tropp, L. R. (2000). Does intergroup contact reduce prejudice: Recent meta-analytic findings. In S. Oskamp (Ed.), *Reducing prejudice and discrimination. The Claremont Symposium on Applied Social Psychology.* Mahwah, NJ: Erlbaum.

Petty, R. E., & Cacioppo, J. T. (1986). *Communication and persuasion: Central and peripheral routes to attitude change.* New York: Springer-Verlag.

Petty, R. E., Fleming, M. A., Priester, J. R., Feinstein, A. H. (2001). Individual versus group interest violation: Surprise as a determinant of argument scrutiny and persuasion. *Social Cognition, 19,* 418–442.

Pezdek, K. (2002). *Event memory and autobiographical memory for the events of September 11, 2001.* Manuscript submitted for publication.

Pfeifer, M., Goldsmith, H. H., & Davidson, R. R. M. (2002). Continuity and change in inhibited and uninhibited children. *Child Development, 73,* 1474–1485.

Pfiffner, L. J., McBurnett, K., & Rathouz, P. (2001). Father absence and familial antisocial characteristics. *Journal of Abnormal Child Psychology, 29,* 357–367.

Phillips, K. A. (2001). *Somatoform and factitious disorders.* Washington, DC: American Psychiatric Association.

Phillips, M., Brooks, G. J., Duncan, G. J., Klebanov, P., & Crane, J. (1998). Family background, parenting practices, and the Black-White test score gap. In C. Jencks & M. Phillips (Eds.), *The Black-White test score gap.* Washington, DC: Brookings Institution.

Piaget, J. (1926). *The language and thought of the child.* New York: Meridian Books.

Piaget, J. (1970). Piaget's theory. In P. H. Mussen (Ed.), *Carmichael's manual of child psychology* (Vol.1). New York: Wiley.

Piaget, J. (1977). *The development of thought: Equilibration of cognitive structure.* New York: Viking.

Piccione, C., Hilgard, E. R., & Zimbardo, P. G. (1989). On the degree of measured hypnotizability over a 25-year period. *Journal of Personality and Social Psychology, 56,* 289–295.

Pickering, A. D., & Gray, J. A. (1999). The neuroscience of personality. In L. A. Pervin & O. P. John (Eds.), *Handbook of personality: Theory and research.* New York: Guilford Press.

Pickrell, J. E., Bernstein, D., & Loftus, E. F. (2003). The misinformation effect. In R. Pohl (Ed.), *Cognitive illusions: Fallacies and biases in thinking, judgment, and memory.* London: Psychology Press.

Pies, R. W. (1998). *Handbook of essential psychopharmacology.* Washington, DC: American Psychiatric Press.

Pilbeam, D. (1984). The descent of hominoids and hominids. *Scientific American, 250,* 84–97.

Pilcher, J. J., & Huffcutt, A. J. (1996). Effects of sleep deprivation on performance: A meta-analysis. *Sleep, 19,* 318–326.

Pilcher, J. J., & Walters, A. S. (1997). How sleep deprivation affects psychological variables related to college students' cognitive performance. *Journal of American College Health, 46,* 121–126.

Pinker, S. (2000). *Words and rules: The ingredients of language.* New York: Basic Books.

Pion, G. M., Mednick, M. T., Astin, H. S., & Hall, C. C. I. (1996). The shifting gender composition of psychology: Trends and implications for the discipline. *American Psychologist, 51,* 509–528.

Pitman, R. K., Shalev, A. Y., & Orr, S. P. (2000). Posttraumatic stress disorder: emotion, conditioning, and memory. In M. S. Gazzaniga (Ed.), *The new cognitive neurosciences* (2nd ed.). Cambridge, MA: MIT Press.

Pitz, G. F., & Sachs, N. J. (1984). Judgment and decision: Theory and application. *Annual Review of Psychology, 35,* 139–163.

Plomin, R. (1997). *Behavioral genetics.* New York: St. Martin's.

Plomin, R., & Caspi, A. (1999). Behavior genetics and personality. In L. A. Pervin & O. P. John (Eds.), *Handbook of personality: Theory and research.* New York: Guilford Press.

Plomin, R., & Craig, I. (2002). "Genetic research on cognitive ability": Author's reply. *British Journal of Psychiatry, 180,* 185–186.

Plous, S. (1996a). Attitudes toward the use of animals in psychological research and education: Results from a national survey of psychologists. *American Psychologist, 51,* 1167–1180.

Plous, S. (1996b). Attitudes toward the use of animals in psychological research and education: Results from a national survey of psychology majors. *Psychological Science, 7,* 352–358.

Plutchik, R. (1994). *Psychology of emotion.* Reading, MA: Addison-Wesley.

Pool, R. (1994). *The dynamic brain.* Washington, DC: National Academy Press.

Porter, N. P., & Geis, F. L. (1981). Women and nonverbal leadership cues: When seeing is not believing. In C. Mayo & N. M. Henley (Eds.), *Gender and nonverbal behavior.* New York: Springer-Verlag.

Porter, R. H., & Winberg, J. (1999). Unique salience of maternal breast odors for newborn infants. *Neuroscience and Biobehavioral Reviews, 23,* 439–449.

Posada, G., Jacobs, A., Richmond, M. K., Carbonell, O. A., Alzate, G., Bustamante, M. R., & Quiceno, J. (2002). Maternal caregiving and infant security in two cultures. *Developmental Psychology, 38,* 67–78.

Posthuma, D., Neale, M. C., Boomsma, D. I., & de Geus, E. J. C. (2001). Are smarter brains running faster? Heritability of alpha peak frequency, IQ, and their interrelation. *Behavior Genetics, 31,* 567–579.

Postman, L., & Phillips, L. W. (1965). Short-term temporal changes in free recall. *Quarterly Journal of Experimental Psychology, 17,* 132–138.

Postman, L., & Underwood, B. J. (1973). Critical issues in interference theory. *Memory and Cognition, 1,* 19–40.

Postmes, T., & Spears, R. (1998). Deindividuation and antinormative behavior: A meta-analysis. *Psychological Bulletin, 123,* 238–259.

Powell, M. C., & Fazio, R. M. (1984). Attitude accessibility as a function of repeated attitudinal expression. *Personality and Social Psychology Bulletin, 10,* 139–148.

Powell, R. W., & Curley, M. (1976). Instinctive drift in nondomesticated rodents. *Bulletin of the Psychonomic Society, 8,* 175–178.

Powley, T. L., & Keesey, R. E. (1970). Relationship of body weight to the lateral hypothalamic feeding syndrome. *Journal of Comparative and Physiological Psychology, 70,* 25–36.

Pratkanis, A. R., Eskenazi, J., & Greenwald, A. G. (1994). What you expect is what you believe (but not necessarily what you get): A test of the effectiveness of subliminal self-help audiotapes. *Basic and Applied Social Psychology, 15,* 251–276.

Pressman, J. D. (1998). *Last resort: Psychosurgery and the limits of medicine.* New York: Cambridge University Press.

Preti, G., Cutler, W. B., Garcia, G. R., Huggins, G. R., & Lawley, J. J. (1986). Human axillary secretions influences women's menstrual cycles: The role of donor extract from females. *Hormones and Behavior,* 20, 473–480.

Prigerson, H., Maciejewski, P. K, & Rosenheck, R. A. (2002). Population attributable fractions of psychiatric disorders and behavioral outcomes associated with combat exposure among U.S. men. *American Journal of Public Health, 92*(1), 59–63.

Pritchard, R. M. (1961, June). Stabilized images on the retina. *Scientific American,* 72–78.

Probst, L. R., Ostrom, R., Watkins, P., Dean, T., & Mashburn, D. (1992). Comparative efficacy of religious and non-religious cognitive-behavioral therapy for the treatment of clinical depression in religious individuals. *Journal of Consulting and Clinical Psychology, 60,* 94–103.

Prochaska, J. O., Johnson, S., & Lee, P. (1998). The transtheoretical model of behavior change. In S. A. Shumaker & E. B. Schron (Eds.), *The handbook of health behavior change* (2nd ed.). New York: Springer.

Prochaska, J. O., Norcross, J. C., & DiClemente, C. C. (1994). *Changing for good.* New York: Avon Books.

Project MATCH Research Group. (1997). Matching alcoholism treatments to client heterogeneity: Project MATCH posttreatment drinking outcomes. *Journal of Studies on Alcohol, 58,* 7–29.

Ptacek, J. T., Smith, R. E., & Zanas, J. (1992). Gender, appraisal, and coping: A longtudinal analysis. *Journal of Personality, 60,* 747–769.

Pugh, G. E. (1977). *The biological origin of human values.* New York: Basic Books.

Punamäki, R. L., & Joustie, M. (1998). The role of culture, violence, and personal factors affecting dream content. *Journal of Cross-Cultural Psychology, 29,* 320–342.

Putnam, F. W. (1989). *Diagnosis and treatment of multiple personality disorder.* New York: Guilford Press.

Putnam, F. W. (2000). Dissociative disorders. In A. J. Sameroff & M. Lewis (Eds.), *Handbook of developmental psychopathology* (2nd ed.). New York: Cambridge University Press.

Pyszczynski, T., Hamilton, J. C., Greenberg, J., & Becker, S. E. (1991). Self-awareness and psychological dysfunction. In C. R. Snyder & D. O. Forsyth (Eds.), *Handbook of social and clinical psychology: The health perspective.* New York: Pergamon Press.

Qu, T., Brannen, C. L., Kim, H. M., & Sugaya, K. (2001). Human neural stem cells improve cognitive function of aged brain. *Neuroreport: For Rapid Communication of Neuroscience Research, 12*(6), 1127–1132.

Quintero, N. (1980, February). Coming of age the Apache way. *National Geographic, 157*(2), 262–271.

Rachman, S. (1998). *Anxiety.* Mahwah, NJ: Erlbaum.

Rachman, S. J., & Hodgson, R. J. (1980). *Obsessions and compulsions.* Englewood Cliffs, NJ: Prentice Hall.

Raichle, M. E. (1994). Images of the mind: Studies with modern imaging techniques. *Annual Review of Psychology, 45,* 333–356.

Raine, A. (2002). Annotation: The role of prefrontal deficits, low autonomic arousal and early health factors in the development of antisocial and aggressive behavior in children. *Journal of Child Psychology and Psychiatry and Allied Disciplines, 43,* 417–434.

Raine, A., Buchsbaum, M., & LaCasse, L. (1997). Brain abnormalities in murderers indicated by positron tomography. *Biological Psychiatry, 42,* 495–508.

Raine, A., Lencz, T., Bihrle, S., LaCasse, L., & Colletti, P. (2000). Reduced prefrontal gray matter volume and reduced autonomic activity in antisocial personality disorder. *Archives of General Psychiatry, 57,* 119–127.

Raine, A., Venables, P. H., & Williams, M. (1996). Better autonomic conditioning and faster electrodermal half-recovery time at age 15 years as possible protective factors against crime at age 29 years. *Developmental Psychology, 32,* 624–630.

Rakic, P. (2002). Neurogenesis in adult primate neocortex: An evaluation of the evidence. *National Review of Neuroscience,* 3(1), 65–71.

Ramaekers, J. G., Robbe, H. W. J., & O'Hanlon, J. F. (2000). Marijuana, alcohol and actual driving performance. *Human Psychopharmacology Clinical and Experimental, 15*, 551–558.

Rao, R. (2001). Cannabis: Some psychiatric aspects. *Primary Care Psychiatry, 7*, 101–105.

Ravussin, E., & Gautier, J. F. (1999). Metabolic predictors of weight gain. *International Journal of Obesity and Related Metabolic Disorders, 23*(Suppl. 1), 37–41.

Ray, O. S., & Ksir, C. J. (2002). *Drugs, society and human behavior* (9th ed.). Boston: McGraw-Hill.

Ray, W. J. (2000). Methods: Toward a science of behavior and experience (6th ed.). Belmont, CA: Wadsworth.

Raz, A., & Shapiro, T. (2002). Hypnosis and neuroscience: A cross talk between clinical and cognitive research. *Archives of General Psychiatry, 59*, 85–90.

Rechtschaffen, A., Bergmann, B. M., Gilliland, M. A., & Bauer, K. (1999). Effects of method, duration, and sleep stage on rebounds from sleep deprivation in the rat. *Sleep, 22*, 11–31.

"A Recovering Patient." (1986). "Can we talk?" The schizophrenic patient in psychotherapy. *American Journal of Psychiatry, 143*, 68–70.

Redelmeier, D. A., & Tibshirani, R. J. (1997). Association between cellular telephone calls and motor vehicle collisions. *New England Journal of Medicine, 336*, 453–458.

Reifman, A.,Villa, L. C., Amans, J. A., Rethinam, V., & Telesca, T. Y. (2001). Children of divorce in the 1990s: A meta-analysis. *Journal of Divorce and Remarriage, 36*, 27–36.

Reisberg, D. (1997). *Cognition: Exploring the science of the mind*. New York: W. W. Norton.

Rendell, P. G., & Thomson, D. M. (1999). Aging and prospective memory: Differences between naturalistic and laboratory tasks. *Journals of Gerontology: Series B: Psychological Sciences and Social Sciences, 54B*(4), 256–269.

Renzulli, J. S. (1986). The three-ring conception of intelligence: A developmental model for creative productivity. In R. J. Sternberg & J. E. Davidson (Eds.), *Conceptions of giftedness*. Cambridge, England: Cambridge University Press.

Rescorla, R. A. (1968). Probability of shock in the presence and absence of CS in fear. *Journal of Comparative and Physiological Psychology, 66*, 1–5.

Rescorla, R. A., & Solomon, R. L. (1967). Two-process learning theory: Relationships between Pavlovian conditioning and instrumental learning. *Psychological Review, 74*, 151–182.

Rescorla, R. A., & Wagner, A. R. (1972). A theory of Pavlovian conditioning: Variations in the effectiveness of reinforcement and nonreinforcement. In A. H. Black & W. F. Prokasky (Eds.), *Classical conditioning: II. Current research and theory*. New York: Appleton-Century-Crofts.

Rey, J. M., & Walter, G. (1997). Half a century of ECT use in young people. *American Journal of Psychiatry, 154*, 595–602.

Richard, S., Davies, D. C., & Faure, J. M. (2000). The role of fear in one-trial passive avoidance learning in Japanese quail chicks genetically selected for long or short duration of the tonic immobility reaction. *Behavioural Processes, 48*, 165–170.

Richardson, D. R. (1991). Interpersonal attraction and love. In R. M. Baron, W. G. Graziano, & C. Stangor (Eds.), *Social psychology*. Ft. Worth, TX: Holt, Rinehart & Winston.

Richter, C. P. (1957). Phenomenon of sudden death in animals and man. *Psychosomatic Medicine, 19*, 191–198.

Riedel, W. J., Klaassen, T., Griez, E., Honig, A., Menheere, P. P. C. A., & van Praag, H. M. (2002). Dissociable hormonal, cognitive and mood responses to neuroendocrine challenge: Evidence for receptor-specific serotonergic dysregulation in depressed mood. *Neuropsychopharmacology, 26*, 358–367.

Rilling, M. (1996). The mystery of the vanished citations: James McConnell's forgotten 1960s quest for planarian learning, a biochemical engram, and celebrity. *American Psychologist, 51*, 589–598.

Rimm, D. C., & Masters, J. C. (1979). *Behavior therapy: Techniques and empirical findings* (2nd ed.). New York: Academic Press.

Rips, L. J. (1994). *The psychology of proof: Deductive reasoning in human thinking*. Cambridge, MA: MIT Press.

Rips, L. J. (1997). Goals for a theory of deduction: Reply to Johnson-Laird. *Minds & Machines, 7*, 409–424.

Ritblatt, S. N. (2000). Children's level of participation in a false-belief task, age, and theory of mind. *Journal of Genetic Psychology, 161*, 53–64.

Roberts, B., Helson, R., & Klohnen, E. C. (2002). Personality development and growth in women across 30 years: Three perspectives. *Journal of Personality, 70*, 79–102.

Robins, L. N., & Regier, D. A. (Eds.). (1991). *Psychiatric disorders in America: The Epidemiological Catchment Area Study*. New York: Free Press.

Robins, R. W., Gosling, S. D., & Craik, K. H. (1999). An empirical analysis of trends in psychology. *American Psychologist, 54*, 117–128.

Robinson, D. (1997). *Neurobiology*. New York: Springer-Verlag.

Roche, A. F. (1979). Secular trends in human growth, maturation, and development. *Monographs of the Society for Research and Child Development, 44*(3–4, Serial No. 179).

Rodin, J., Bartoshuk, L., Peterson, C., & Schank, D. (1990). Bulimia and taste: Possible interactions. *Journal of Abnormal Psychology, 99*, 32–39.

Rodin, J., & Salovey, P. (1989). Health psychology. *Annual Review of Psychology, 40*, 533–579.

Rodrigues, S. M., Bauer, E. P., Farb, C. R., Shafe, G. E., & LeDoux, J. E. (2002). The group I metabotropic glutamate receptor mGluR5 is required for fear memory formation and long-term potentiation in the lateral amygdala. *Journal of Neuroscience, 22*, 5219–5229.

Roebers, C. M. (2002). Confidence judgments in children's and adults' recall and suggestibility. *Developmental Psychology, 38*, 1052–1067.

Roediger, H. L., III, & McDermott, K. B. (1995). Creating false memories: Remembering words not presented in lists. *Journal of Experimental Psychology: Learning, Memory, and Cognition, 21*, 803–814.

Roediger, H. L., III, & McDermott, K. B. (2000). Tricks of memory. *Current Directions in Psychological Science, 9*, 123–127.

Roelofs, K., Hoogduin, K. A. L., Keijsers, G. P. J., Naering, G. W. B, Moene, F. C., & Sandijck, P. (2002). Hypnotic susceptibility in patients with conversion disorder. *Journal of Abnormal Psychology, 111*, 390–395.

Roffwarg, H. P., Muzio, J. N., & Dement, W. C. (1966). Ontogenetic development of human dream-sleep cycle. *Science, 152*, 604–609.

Rogers, C. R. (1951). *Client-centered therapy*. Boston: Houghton Mifflin.

Rogers, C. R. (1959). A theory of therapy, personality and interpersonal relationships, as developed in the client-centered framework. In S. Koch (Ed.), *Psychology: A study of a science* (Vol. 3). New York: McGraw-Hill.

Rogers, C. R. (1980). *A way of being*. Boston: Houghton Mifflin.

Rogers, C. R. (Ed.). (1967). *The therapeutic relationship and its impact: A study of psychotherapy with schizophrenics*. Madison: University of Wisconsin Press.

Rogers, C. R., & Dymond, R. F. (1954). *Psychotherapy and personality change: Coordinated studies in the client-centered approach*. Chicago: University of Chicago Press.

Rogers, E. J., Vaughan, P. W., Swalahe, R. M. A., Rao, N., & Sood, S. (1996). *Effects of an entertainment-education radio soap opera on family planning and HIV/AIDS prevention behavior in Tanzania*. Unpublished manuscript, Department of Communication and Journalism, University of New Mexico at Albuquerque.

Rohsenow, D. J., & Marlatt, G. A. (1981). The balanced placebo design: Methodological considerations. *Addictive Behaviors, 6*, 107–122.

Roland, P. E. (1997). *Brain activation*. New York: Wiley.

Rollins, B. C., & Feldman, H. (1970). Marital satisfaction over the family life cycle. *Journal of Marriage and the Family, 32*, 20–28.

Rollman, G. (1998). Culture and pain. In S. S. Kazarian et al. (Eds.), *Cultural clinical psychology: Theory, research, and practice*. New York: Oxford University Press.

Rolls, B. J., Rolls, E. T., Rowe, E. A., & Sweeney, K. (1981). Sensory specific satiety in man. *Physiology and Behavior, 27*, 137–142.

Rolls, E. T. (2000). Memory systems in the brain. *Annual Review of Psychology, 5*, 599–630.

Rolls, E. T., & Deco, G. (2002). *Computational neuroscience of vision.* London: Oxford University Press.

Ron, M. A., & David, A. S. (1997). *Disorders of brain and mind.* Cambridge, England: Cambridge University Press.

Ronen, T., Rahav., G., & Rosenbaum, M. (2003). Children's reactions to a war situation as a function of age and sex. *Anxiety, Stress and Coping: An International Journal, 16*, 59–69.

Rosch, E. (1973). On the internal structure of perceptual and semantic categories. In T. E. Moore (Ed.), *Cognitive development and the acquisition of language.* New York: Academic Press.

Rosch, E. (1977). Human categorization. In N. Warren (Ed.), *Advances in cross-cultural psychology* (Vol. 1). London: Academic Press.

Rose, R. J. (1995). Genes and human behavior. *Annual Review of Psychology, 46*, 625–654.

Rosen, C. S. (2000). Integrating stage and continuum models to explain processing of exercise messages and exercise initiation among sedentary college students. *Health Psychology, 19*, 172–180.

Rosenfarb, I. S., Goldstein, M. J., Mintz, J., Nuechterlein, K. H. (1995). Expressed emotion and subclinical psychopathology observable within the transactions between schizophrenic patients and their family members. *Journal of Abnormal Psychology, 104*, 259–267.

Rosenhan, D. L. (1973). On being sane in insane places. *Science, 179*, 250–258.

Rosenhan, D. L., & Seligman, M. E. P. (1989). *Abnormal psychology* (2nd ed.). New York: W. W. Norton.

Rosenthal, N. E., & Wehr, T. A. (1987). Seasonal affective disorders. *Psychiatric Annals, 17*, 670–674.

Rosenthal, R. (1985). From unconscious experimenter bias to teacher expectancy effects. In J. B. Dusek, V. C. Hall, & W. J. Meyer (Eds.), *Teacher expectancies.* Hillsdale, NJ: Erlbaum.

Rosenthal, R., Archer, D., DiMatteo, M. R., Koivumaki, J. H., & Rogers, P. L. (1974). Body talk and tone of voice: The language without words. *Psychology Today, 8*, 64–71.

Rosenzweig, M. R. (1984). Experience, memory, and the brain. *American Psychologist, 39*, 365–376.

Rosenzweig, M. R., & Bennett, E. L. (1996). Psychobiology of plasticity: Effects of training and experience on brain and behavior. *Behavioural Brain Research, 78*, 57–65.

Rosenzweig, S. (1992). Freud and experimental psychology: The emergence of idiodynamics. In S. Koch & D. E. Leary (Eds.), *A century of psychology as science.* Washington, DC: American Psychological Association.

Ross, L. (2001). Getting down to fundamentals: Lay dispositionism and the attributions of psychologists. *Psychological Inquiry, 12*, 37–40.

Ross, L., & Nisbett, R. E. (1991). *The person and the situation: Perspectives of social psychology.* New York: McGraw-Hill.

Rossell, S. L., Bullmore, E. T., Williams, S. C. R., et al. (2002). Sex differences in functional brain activation during a lexical visual field task. *Brain and Language, 80*, 97–105.

Rotenberg, A., Abel, T., Hawkins, R. D., Kandel, E. R., & Muller, R. U. (2000). Parallel instabilities of long-term potentiation, place cells, and learning caused by decreased protein kinase A activity. *Journal of Neuroscience, 20*, 8096–8102.

Rothbaum, B. O., Hodges, L., Anderson, P. L., Price, L., & Smith, S. (2002). Twelve-month follow-up of virtual reality and standard exposure therapies for the fear of flying. *Journal of Consulting and Clinical Psychology, 70*, 428–432.

Rotter, J. B. (1954). *Social learning and clinical psychology.* Englewood Cliffs, NJ: Prentice Hall.

Rotter, J. B. (1966). Generalized expectancies for internal versus external control of reinforcement. *Psychological Monographs, 80*(Whole No. 609).

Rouhana, N. N., & Bar-Tal, D. (1998). Psychological dynamics of intractable ethnonational conflicts: The Israeli-Palestinian case. *American Psychologist, 53*, 761–770.

Rowe, D. C. (1999). Heredity. In V. J. Derlega, B. A. Winstead, & W. H. Jones (Eds.), *Personality: Contemporary theory and research.* Chicago: Nelson Hall.

Rowley, J. T., Stickgold, R., & Hobson, J. A. (1998). Eyelid movements and mental activity at sleep onset. *Consciousness and Cognition: An International Journal, 7*, 67–84.

Rozin, P., Dow, S., Moscovitch, M., & Rajaram, S. (1998). What causes humans to begin and end a meal? A role for memory for what has been eaten, as evidenced by a study of multiple meal eating in amnesic patients. *Psychological Science, 9*, 392–396.

Rubin, D. C., & Kozin, M. (1984). Vivid memories. *Cognition, 16*, 81–95.

Rubin, R. T. (2000). Depression and manic-depressive illness. In G. Fink (Ed.), *Encyclopedia of stress.* San Diego, CA: Academic Press.

Rubonis, A. V., & Bickman, L. (1991). Psychological impairment in the wake of disaster: The disaster-psychopathology relationship. *Psychological Bulletin, 109*, 384–399.

Ruffman, R., Perner, J., Naito, M., Parkin, L., & Clements, W. A. (1998). Older (but not younger) siblings facilitate false belief understanding. *Developmental Psychology, 34*, 161–174.

Rumbaugh, D. M. (1990). Comparative psychology and the great apes: Their competency in learning, language, and numbers. *Psychological Record, 40*, 15–39.

Rumstein, M. O., & Hunsley, J. (2001). Interpersonal and family functioning of female survivors of childhood sexual abuse. *Clinical Psychology Review, 21*, 471–490.

Rush, A. J., Crismon, M. L., Toprac, M. G., et al. (1998). Consensus guidelines in the treatment of major depressive disorder. *Journal of Clinical Psychiatry, 59*(Suppl. 20), 73–84.

Rushton, J. P. (1989). Genetic similarity, human altruism, and group selection. *Behavioral and Brain Sciences, 12*, 503–559.

Russell, J. A. (1994). Is there universal recognition of emotion from facial expressions? A review of the cross-cultural studies. *Psychological Bulletin, 115*, 102–141.

Russell, P. A., Deregowski, J. B., & Kinnear, P. R. (1997). Perception and aesthetics. In J. W. Berry, P. R. Dasen, & T. S. Saraswathi (Eds.), *Handbook of cross-cultural psychology: Vol. 2. Basic processes and human development* (2nd ed.). Boston, MA: Allyn & Bacon.

Ruttenber, A. J., Lawler, H. J., Yin, M., & Wetli, C. V. (1997). Fatal excited delirium following cocaine use: Epidemiologic findings provide new evidence for mechanisms of cocaine toxicity. *Journal of Forensic Sciences, 42*, 25–31.

Rutter, M. L. (1997). Nature-nurture integration: The example of antisocial behavior. *American Psychologist, 52*, 390–398.

Ryff, C. D., & Singer, B. (2003). Flourishing under fire: Resilience as a prototype of challenged thriving. In C. L. M. Keyes & J. Haidt (Eds.), *Flourishing: Positive psychology and the life well-lived.* Washington, DC: American Psychological Association.

Sabini, J., Siepmann, M., & Stein, J. (2001). The really fundamental attribution error in social psychological research. *Psychological Inquiry, 12*, 1–15.

Sachse, R., & Elliott, R. (2002). Process-outcome research on humanistic therapy variables. In D. J. Cain (Ed.), *Humanistic psychotherapies: Handbook of research and practice.* Washington, DC: American Psychological Association.

Sack, R. L., Hughes, R. J., Edgar, D. M., & Lewy, A. J. (1997). Sleep-promoting effects of melatonin: At what dose, in whom, under what conditions, and by what mechanisms? *Sleep, 20*, 908–915.

Sacks, O. (1985, 1986) *The man who mistook his wife for a hat and other clinical tales.* New York: Summit Books and Simon & Schuster.

Saczynski, J. S., Willis, S. L., & Schaie, K. W. (2002). Strategy use in reasoning training with older adults. *Aging, Neuropsychology and Cognition, 9*, 48–60.

Sage, C. E., Southcott, A. M., & Brown, S. L. (2001). The health belief model and compliance with CPAP treatment for obstructive sleep apnea. *Behaviour Change, 18*, 177–185.

Sagi, A., Koren-Karie, N., Gini, M., Ziv, Y., & Joels, T. (2002). Shedding further light on the effects of various types and quality of early child care on infant-mother attachment relationship: The Haifa Study of Early Child Care. *Child Development, 73*, 1166–1186.

Salovey, P., Mayer, J. D., Goldman, S. L., Turvey, C., & Palfai, T. P. (1995). Emotional attention, clarity, and repair: Exploring emotional intelligence using the Trait Meta-Mood Scale. In J. W. Pennebaker et al. (Eds.) *Emotion, disclosure & health*. Washington, DC: American Psychological Association.

Salovey, P., & Pizzaro, D. A. (2003). The value of emotional intelligence. In R. J. Sternberg, J. Lautrey, & T. I. Lubart (Eds.), *Models of intelligence: International perspectives*. Washington, DC: American Psychological Association.

Salovey, P., Rothman, A. J., Detweiler, J. B., & Steward, W. T. (2000). Emotional states and physical health. *American Psychologist, 55*, 110–121.

Saltz, B., Lieberman, J. A., Johns, C. A., et al. (1991). Prospective study of tardive dyskinesia incidence in the elderly. *Journal of the American Medical Association, 266*, 2402–2406.

Saltzman, A. L. (2000). The role of the obedience experiments in Holocaust studies: The case for renewed visibility. In T. Blass (Ed.), *Obedience to authority: Current perspectives on the Milgram paradigm*. Mahwah, NJ: Erlbaum.

Sandler, J. (1986). Aversion methods. In F. H. Kanfer & A. P. Goldstein (Eds.), *Helping people change: A textbook of methods* (3rd ed.). New York: Pergamon Press.

Saphier, D. (1992). Electrophysiological studies of the effects of interleukin-1 and interferon on the EEG and pituitary-adrenocortical activity. In J. J. Rothwell & R. D. Dantzer (Eds.), *Interleukin-1 in the brain*. Oxford, England: Pergamon Press.

Sarason, I. G., & Sarason, B. R. (1990). Test anxiety. In H. Leitenberg (Ed.), *Handbook of social and evaluation anxiety*. New York: Plenum.

Sarason, I. G., Sarason, B. R., Pierce, G. R., Shearin, E. N., & Sayers, M. H. (1991). A social learning approach to increasing blood donations. *Journal of Applied Social Psychology, 21*, 896–918.

Satcher, D. (1999). *Mental health: A report of the Surgeon General*. Washington, DC: U.S. Department of Health and Human Services.

Satir, V. (1967). *Conjoint family therapy*. Palo Alto, CA: Sciences and Behavior Books.

Savage-Rumbaugh, E. S., McDonald, K., Sevcik, R. A., Hopkins, W. D., & Rupert, E. (1986). Spontaneous symbol acquisition and communicative use by pygmy chimpanzees (*Pan paniscus*). *Journal of Experimental Psychology: General, 115*, 211–235.

Savage-Rumbaugh, E. S., Murphy, J., Sevcik, R. A., Brakke, K. E., et al. (1993). Language comprehension in ape and child. *Monographs of the Society for Research in Child Development, 58*(233), 1–254.

Savage-Rumbaugh, E. S., Pate, J. L., Lawson, J., Smith, S. T., & Rosenbaum, S. (1983). Can a chimpanzee make a statement? *Journal of Experimental Psychology: General, 112*, 457–492.

Scarr, S. (1998). American child care today. *American Psychologist, 53*, 95–108.

Scarr, S. (1992). Developmental theories for the 1990s: Development and individual differences. *Child Development, 63*, 1–19.

Schachter, S. (1959). *The psychology of affiliation: Experimental studies of the sources of gregariousness*. Stanford, CA: Stanford University Press.

Schachter, S. (1966). The interaction of cognitive and physiological determinants of emotional state. In C. D. Spielberger (Ed.), *Anxiety and behavior*. New York: Academic Press.

Schachter, S. (1982). Recidivism and self-cure of smoking and obesity. *American Psychologist, 37*, 436–444.

Schachter, S., & Wheeler, L. (1962). Epinephrine, chlorpromazine, and amusement. *Journal of Abnormal and Social Psychology, 65*, 121–128.

Schacter, D. L. (1992). Understanding implicit memory: A cognitive neuroscience approach. *American Psychologist, 47*, 559–569.

Schacter, D. L., & Badgaiyan, R. D. (2001). Neuroimaging of priming: New perspectives on implicit and explicit memory. *Current Directions in Psychological Science, 10*, 1–4.

Schafe, G. E., LeDoux, J. E. (2002). Emotional plasticity. In H. Pashler & R. Gallistel, (Eds.), *Steven's handbook of experimental psychology: Vol. 3. Learning, motivation, and emotion* (3rd ed.). New York: Wiley.

Schaie, K. W. (1994). The course of adult intellectual development. *American Psychologist, 49*, 304–313.

Schaie, K. W. (1998). The Seattle Longitudinal Studies of adult intelligence. In M. Lawton et al. (Eds.), *Essential papers on the psychology of aging. Essential papers in psychoanalysis*. New York: New York University Press.

Schatzberg, A. F., Cole, J. O., & DeBattista, C. (2002). *Manual of clinical psychopharmacology*. Washington, DC: American Psychiatric Publishing.

Scheff, T. J. (1966). *Being mentally ill: A sociological theory*. Chicago: Aldine.

Scheier, M. F., & Carver, C. S. (1985). Optimism, coping, and health: Assessment and implications of generalized outcome expectancies. *Health Psychology, 4*, 219–247.

Scheier, M. F., Carver, C. S., & Bridges, M. W. (1994). Distinguishing optimism from neuroticism (and trait anxiety, self-mastery, and self-esteem): A re-evaluation of the Life Orientation Test. *Journal of Personality and Social Psychology, 67*, 1063–1078.

Schenck, C. H., Hurwitz, T. D., Bundlie, S. R., & Mahowald, M. W. (1991). Sleep-related eating disorders: Polysomnographic correlates of a heterogeneous syndrome distinct from daytime eating disorders. *Sleep: Journal of Sleep Research and Sleep Medicine, 14*, 419–431.

Schenck, C. H., Milner, D. M., Hurwitz, T. D., & Bundlie, S. R. (1989). A polysomnographic and clinical report on sleep-related injury in 100 adult patients. *American Journal of Psychiatry, 146*, 1166–1173.

Schlegel, A., & Barry, H. (1991). *Adolescence: An anthropological inquiry*. New York: Free Press.

Schmader, T. (2002). Gender identification moderates stereotype threat effects on women's math performance. *Journal of Experimental Social Psychology, 38*, 194–201.

Schmitt, D. P., Shackelford, T. K., & Buss, D. M. (2001). Are men really more "oriented" toward short-term mating than women? A critical review of theory and research. *Psychology, Evolution and Gender, 3*, 211–239.

Schmolck, H., Buffalo, E. A., & Squire, L. R. (2000). Memory distortions develop over time: Recollections of the O. J. Simpson trial verdict after 15 and 32 months. *Psychological Science, 11*, 39–45.

Schneer, J. A., & Reitman, F. (1995). The impact of gender as managerial careers unfold. *Journal of Vocational Behavior, 47*, 290–315.

Schneer, J. A., & Reitman, F. (1997). The interrupted managerial career path: A longitudinal study of MBAs. *Journal of Vocational Behavior, 51*, 411–434.

Schneidman, E. S. (1976). *Suicidology: Contemporary developments*. New York: Grune & Stratton.

Schnurr, P. P., Spiro, A., III, Aldwin, C. M., & Stukel, T. A. (1998). Physical symptom trajectories following trauma exposure: Longitudinal findings from the Normative Aging Study. *Journal of Nervous & Mental Disease, 186*, 522–528.

Schoop, V. M., Gardziella, S., & Muller, C. M. (1997). Critical period-dependent reduction of the permissiveness of cat visual cortex tissue for neuronal adhesion and neurite growth. *European Journal of Neuroscience, 9*, 1911–1922.

Schore, A. N. (2002). Dysregulation of the right brain: a fundamental mechanism of traumatic attachment and the psychopathogenesis of posttraumatic stress disorder. *Australian and New Zealand Journal of Psychiatry, 36*, 9–30.

Schulz, R., & Aderman, D. (1980). Clinical research and the stages of dying. In R. A. Kalish (Ed.), *Death, dying, and transcending*. Farmingdale, NY: Baywood.

Schutte, N. S., Malouff, J. M., Hall, L. E., Haggerty, D. J., Cooper, J. T., Golden, C. J., & Dornheim, L. (1998). Development and validation of a measure of emotional intelligence. *Personality and Individual Differences, 25*, 167–177.

Schwartz, B. L. (2002). The phenomenology of naturally occurring tip of the tongue states: A diary study. In S. P. Shohov (Ed.), *Advances in psychology research* (Vol. 8). New York: Nova Science.

Schwartz, R. (1984). Body weight regulation. *University of Washington Medicine, 10*, 16–20.

Schwartz, S., & Maquet, P. (2002). Sleep imaging and the neuro-psychological assessment of dreams. *Trends in Cognitive Sciences, 6*, 23–30.

Schwarzer, R. (1998). Stress and coping from a social-cognitive perspective. *Annals of the New York Academy of Sciences, 851*, 531–537.

Scoboria, A., Mazzoni, G., Kirsch, I., & Milling, L. S. (2002). Immediate and persisting effects of misleading questions and hypnosis on memory reports. *Journal of Experimental Psychology: Applied, 8*, 26–32.

Scott, T. R. (1992). Taste, feeding, and pleasure. In A. N. Epstein et al. (Eds.), *Progress in psychobiology and physiological psychology.* San Diego, CA: Academic Press.

Scott, T. R., & Giza, B. K. (1993). Gustatory control of ingestion. In D. A. Booth et al. (Eds.), *Neurophysiology of ingestion. Pergamon studies in neuroscience.* Oxford, England: Pergamon Press.

Scott, W. D., & Cervone, D. (2002). The impact of negative affect on performance standards: Evidence for an affect as information mechanism. *Cognitive Therapy and Research, 26,* 9–37.

Sears, R. R. (1977). Sources of life satisfaction of the Terman gifted men. *American Psychologist, 32,* 119–128.

Sears, R. R., Maccoby, E. E., & Levin, H. (1957). *Patterns of child rearing.* Evanston, IL: Row, Peterson.

Seattle Times. (1997, December 11). Paralyzed woman is good Samaritan. Author, p. B3.

Sedikides, C., Gaertner, L., & Toguchi, Y. (2003). Pancultural self-enhancement. *Journal of Personality and Social Psychology, 84,* 60–79.

Segal, N. L. (1999). *Entwined lives: Twins and what they tell us about human behavior.* New York: Plume.

Segall, M. H., Campbell, D. T., & Herskowitz, M. J. (1966). *The influence of culture on visual perception.* New York: Pergamon Press.

Sekuler, R., Watamaniuk, S., & Blake, R. (2002). In H. Pashler & S. Yantis (Eds.), *Steven's handbook of experimental psychology: Vol. 1. Sensation and perception* (3rd ed.). New York: Wiley.

Seligman, M. E. P. (1970). On the generality of the laws of learning. *Psychological Review, 77,* 406–418.

Seligman, M. E. P. (1971). Phobias and preparedness. *Behavior Therapy, 2,* 307–320.

Seligman, M. E. P. (1975). *Helplessness: On depression, development, and death.* New York: Freeman.

Seligman, M. E. P. (1989). Research in clinical psychology: Why is there so much depression today? In I. S. Cohen (Ed.), *The G. Stanley Hall lecture series* (Vol. 9). Washington, DC: American Psychological Association.

Seligman, M. E. P. (1991). *Learned optimisim.* New York: Knopf.

Seligman, M. E. P. (1995). The effectiveness of psychotherapy: The *Consumer Reports* study. *American Psychologist, 50,* 965–974.

Seligman, M. E. P. (2002). *Authentic happiness: Using the new positive psychology to realize your potential for lasting fulfillment.* New York: Free Press.

Seligman, M. E. P., & Binik, Y. M. (1977). The safety signal hypothesis. In H. Davis & H. Hurvitz (Eds.), *Pavlovian-operant interactions.* Hillsdale, NJ: Erlbaum.

Seligman, M. E. P., & Isaacowitz, D. M. (2000). Learned helplessness. In G. Fink (Ed.), *Encyclopedia of stress.* San Diego, CA: Academic Press.

Seligman, M.E.P., & Peterson, C. R. (Eds.). (2004). *Human strengths: A classification manual.* New York: Oxford University Press.

Selye, H. (1976). *The stress of life* (Rev. ed.) New York: McGraw-Hill.

Senden, M. von. (1960). *Space and sight: The perception of space and shape in the congenitally blind before and after operation* (P. Heath, Trans.). New York: Free Press.

Sergios, P. A., & Cody, J. (1985/1986). Importance of physical attractiveness and social assertiveness skills in male homosexual dating behavior and partner selection. *Journal of Homosexuality, 12,* 71–84.

Seto, M. C., & Barbaree, H. E. (1995). The role of alcohol in sexual aggression. *Clinical Psychology Review, 15,* 545–566.

Sexton, M. M. (1979). Behavioral epidemiology. In O. F. Pomerleau & J. P. Brady (Eds.), *Behavioral Medicine: Theory and Practice.* Baltimore, MD: Williams & Wilkins.

Shaffer, D. R. (1989). *Developmental psychology: Childhood and adolescence* (2nd ed.). Pacific Grove, CA: Brooks/Cole.

Shafir, E., & LeBoeuf, R. A. (2002). Rationality. *Annual Review of Psychology, 53,* 491–517.

Shair, H. N., Barr, G. A., & Hofer, M. A. (Eds.). (1991). *Developmental psychobiology.* New York: Oxford University Press.

Shallice, T., & Burgess, P. (1991). Higher-order cognitive impairments and frontal-lobe lesions in man. In H. S. Levin, H. M. Eisenberg, & A. L. Benton (Eds.), *Frontal lobe function and dysfunction.* New York: Oxford University Press.

Shanab, M. E., & Yahya, L. A. (1977). A behavioral study of obedience in children. *Journal of Personality and Social Psychology, 35,* 530–536.

Shapiro, A. K., & Shapiro, E. (1997). *The powerful placebo: From ancient priest to modern physician.* Baltimore: Johns Hopkins University Press.

Shapiro, C. M., Bortz, R., Mitchell, D., Bartel, P., & Jooste, P. (1981). Slow-wave sleep: A recovery period after exercise. *Science, 214,* 1253–1254.

Shaver, P., Hazan, C., & Bradshaw, D. (1988). Love as attachment: The integration of three behavioral systems. In R. J. Sternberg & M. L. Barnes (Eds.), *The psychology of love.* New Haven, CT: Yale University Press.

Shaver, P. R., & Clark, C. L. (1996). Forms of adult romantic attachment and their cognitive and emotional underpinnings. In G. G. Noam et al. (Eds.), *Development and vulnerability in close relationships. The Jean Piaget symposium series.* Mahwah, NJ: Erlbaum.

Shavit, Y. (1990). Stress-induced immune modulation in animals: Opiates and endogenous opioid peptides. In R. Ader, N. Cohen, & D. L. Felten (Eds.), *Psychoneuroimmunology II.* New York: Academic Press.

Shaywitz, B. A., Shaywitz, S. E., Pugh, K. R., et al. (1995). Sex differences in the functional organization of the brain for language. *Nature, 373,* 607–609.

Sheehan, P. W., Green, V., & Truesdale, P. (1992). Influence of rapport on hypnotically induced pseudomemory. *Journal of Abnormal Psychology, 101,* 690–700.

Shek, D. T. L. (1998). A longitudinal study of the relations between parent-adolescent conflict and adolescent psychological well-being. *Journal of Genetic Psychology, 159,* 53–67.

Sheldon, K. M., & Kasser, T. (2001). Getting older, getting better? Personal strivings and psychological maturity across the life span. *Developmental Psychology, 37,* 491–501.

Shepherd, G. (1997). *The synaptic organizer of the brain.* New York: Oxford University Press.

Sherif, M. (1935). A study of some social factors in perception. *Archives of Psychology* (No. 187).

Sherif, M., Harvey, O., White, B., Hood, W., & Sherif, C. (1961). *Intergroup conflict and cooperation: The Robbers Cave experiment.* Norman: University of Oklahoma Press.

Sherry, J. L. (2001). The effects of violent video games on aggression: A meta-analysis. *Human Communication Research, 27,* 409–431.

Shevrin, H., Bond, J. A., Brakel, L. A. W., Hertel, R. K., & Williams, W. J. (1996). *Conscious and unconscious processes: Psychodynamic, cognitive, and neurophysiological convergences.* New York: Guilford Press.

Shiner, R. L. (1998). How shall we speak of children's personalities in middle childhood? A preliminary taxonomy. *Psychological Bulletin, 124,* 308–332.

Shneidman, E. S. (1998). *The suicidal mind.* New York: Oxford University Press.

Shoda, Y., & Mischel, W. (2000). Reconciling contextualism with the core assumptions of personality psychology. *European Journal of Personality, 14,* 407–428.

Shoda, Y., Mischel, W., & Wright, J. C. (1994). Intra-individual stability and patterning of behavior: Incorporating psychological situations into the idiographic analysis of personality. *Journal of Personality and Social Psychology, 67,* 674–687.

Shorter, E. (1998). *A history of psychiatry: From the era of the asylum to the age of Prozac.* New York: Wiley.

Shultz, K. S., Morton, K. R., & Weckerle, J. R. (1998). The influence of push and pull factors on voluntary and involuntary early retirees' retirement decision and adjustment. *Journal of Vocational Behavior, 53,* 45–57.

Sia, C. L., Tan, B. C. Y., & Wei, K. K. (2002). Group polarization and computer mediated communication: Effects of communication cues, social presence, and anonymity. *Information Systems Research, 13,* 70–90.

Siegel, S. (1984). Pavlovian conditioning and heroin overdose: Reports from overdose victims. *Bulletin of the Psychonomic Society, 22,* 428–430.

Siegel, S., & Allan, L. G. (1996). The widespread influence of the Rescorla-Wagner model. *Psychonomic Bulletin and Review, 3,* 314–321.

Siegel, S., Baptista, M. A. S., Kim, J. A., McDonald, R. V., & Weise-Kelly, L. (2000). Pavlovian psychopharmacology: The associative basis of tolerance. *Experimental and Clinical Psychopharmacology, 8,* 276–293.

Siegler, R. S. (1986). *Children's thinking.* Englewood Cliffs, NJ: Prentice Hall.

Siegler, R. S. (1996). *Emerging minds: The process of change in children's thinking.* New York: Oxford University Press.

Sigala, N., & Logothetis, N. K. (2002). Visual categorization shapes feature selectivity in the primate temporal cortex. *Nature, 415,* 318–320.

Sigelman, C. K., & Shaffer, D. R. (1991). *Life-span human development.* Pacific Grove, CA: Brooks/Cole.

Silbersweig, D. A., Stern, E., Strain, E. C., Frith, C., Cahill, C., et al. (1995). A functional neuroanatomy of hallucinations in schizophrenia. *Nature, 378*(6553), 176–179.

Simkin, L. R., & Gross, A. M. (1994). Assessment of coping with high risk situations for exercise relapse among healthy women. *Health Psychology, 13,* 274–277.

Simon, H. A. (1990). Invariants of human behavior. *Annual Review of Psychology, 41,* 1–20.

Simonton, D. K. (1999). Creativity and genius. In L. A. Pervin & O. P. John (Eds.), *Handbook of personality: Theory and research* (2nd ed). New York: Guilford Press.

Simpaio, E., Maris, S., & Bach-y-Rita, P. (2001). Brain plasticity: "Visual" acuity of blind persons via the tongue. *Brain Research, 908,* 204–207.

Sistler, A. B., & Moore, G. M. (1996). Cultural diversity in coping with marital stress. *Journal of Clinical Geropsychology, 2,* 77–82.

Skinner, B. F. (1938). *The behavior of organisms: an experimental analysis.* New York: Appleton-Century-Crofts.

Skinner, B. F. (1948). *Walden two.* New York: Macmillan.

Skinner, B. F. (1953). *Science and human behavior.* New York: Macmillan.

Skinner, B. F. (1957). *Verbal behavior.* New York: Prentice Hall.

Skinner, B. F. (1968). *The technology of teaching.* New York: Appleton-Century-Crofts.

Skinner, B. F. (1971). *Beyond freedom and dignity.* New York: Knopf.

Skinner, B. F. (1989a). The origins of cognitive thought. *American Psychologist, 44,* 13–18.

Skinner, B. F. (1989b). Teaching machines. *Science, 243,* 1535.

Skinner, B. F. (1990). Can psychology be a science of mind? *American Psychologist, 45,* 1206–1210.

Sklar, L. S., & Anisman, H. (1981). Stress and cancer. *Psychological Bulletin, 89,* 369–406.

Skoyles, J. R. (1997). Evolution's 'missing link': A hypothesis upon neural plasticity, prefrontal working memory and the origins of modern cognition. *Medical Hypotheses, 48,* 499–501.

Slavney, P. R. (1990). *Perspectives on "hysteria."* Baltimore, MD: Johns Hopkins University Press.

Slobin, D. I. (1996). From "thought and language" to "thinking for speaking." In J. J. Gumperz et al. (Eds.), *Rethinking linguistic relativity. Studies in the social and cultural foundations of language.* Cambridge, England: Cambridge University Press.

Slovic, P., Fischhoff, B., & Lichtenstein, S. (1988). Response mode, framing, and information-processing effects in risk assessment. In D. E. Bell & H. Raiffa (Eds.), *Decision making: Descriptive, normative, and prescriptive interactions.* New York: Cambridge University Press.

Smalley, S. L., McGough, J. J., Del'Homme, M., et al. (2000). Familial clustering of symptoms and disruptive behaviors in multiplex families with attention-deficit/hyperactivity disorder. *Journal of the American Academy of Child and Adolescent Psychiatry, 39,* 1135–1143.

Smetana, J. (1988). Adolescents' and parents' conceptions of parental authority. *Child Development, 59,* 321–335.

Smith, B. D. (1998). *Psychology: Science and understanding.* New York: McGraw-Hill.

Smith, C. S., Folkard, S., Schmieder, R. A., Parra, L. F., Spelten, E., Almiral, H., et al. (2002). Investigation of morning-evening orientation in six countries using the preferences scale. *Personality and Individual Differences, 32,* 949–968.

Smith, E. R., & Zarate, M. A. (1992). Exemplar-based model of social judgment. *Psychological Review, 99,* 3–21.

Smith, J. C. (2003). *Stress management: A comprehensive handbook of techniques and strategies.* New York: Springer.

Smith, J. W., & Frawley, P. J. (1993). Treatment outcome of 600 chemically dependent patients treated in a multimodal inpatient program including aversion therapy and pentothal interviews. *Journal of Substance Abuse Treatment, 10,* 359–369.

Smith, M. C., & Phillips, M. R., Jr. (2001). Age differences in memory for radio advertisements: The role of mnemonic. *Journal of Business Research, 53,* 103–109.

Smith, M. E. (1926). An investigation of the development of the sentence and the extent of vocabulary in young children. *University of Iowa Studies in Child Welfare, 3*(No. 5).

Smith, M. L., & Glass, G. V. (1977). Meta-analyses of psychotherapy outcome studies. *American Psychologist, 32,* 752–760.

Smith, R. E. (1989). Effects of coping skills training on generalized self-efficacy and locus of control. *Journal of Personality and Social Psychology, 56,* 228–233.

Smith, R. E. (1996). Performance anxiety, cognitive interference, and concentration enhancement strategies in sports. In I. G. Sarason, G. R. Pierce, & B. R. Sarason (Eds.), *Cognitive interference: Theories, methods, and findings.* Mahwah, NJ: Erlbaum.

Smith, R. E., Leffingwell, T. R., & Ptacek, J. T. (1999). Can people remember how they coped? Factors associated with discordance between same-day and retrospective reports. *Journal of Personality and Social Psychology, 76,* 1050–1061.

Smith, R. E., & Smoll, F. L. (1990). Self-esteem and children's reactions to youth sport coaching behaviors: A field study of self-enhancement processes. *Developmental Psychology, 26,* 987–993.

Smith, R. E., Smoll, F. L., & Ptacek, J. T. (1989). Conjunctive moderator variables in vulnerability and resiliency research: Life stress, social support and coping skills, and adolescent sport injuries. *Journal of Personality and Social Psychology, 58,* 360–370.

Smith, R. E., Smoll, F. L., & Schultz, R. W. (1990). Measurement and correlates of sport-specific cognitive and somatic trait anxiety: The Sports Anxiety Scale. *Anxiety Research* [now *Anxiety, Stress & Coping*], *2,* 263–280.

Smith, S. L., & Donnerstein, E. (1998). Harmful effects of exposure to media violence: Learning of aggression, emotional desensitization, and fear. In R. G. Geen & E. Donnerstein (Eds.), *Human aggression: Theories, research, and implications for social policy.* San Diego, CA: Academic Press.

Smith, S. M., McIntosh, W. D., & Bazzini, D. G. (1999). Are the beautiful good in Hollywood? An investigation of the beauty-and-goodness stereotype on film. *Basic and Applied Social Psychology, 21,* 69–80.

Smith, S. M., & Vela, E. (2001). Environmental context dependent memory: A review and meta-analysis. *Psychonomic Bulletin and Review, 8,* 203–220.

Smith, T. W., & Gallo, L. C. (2001). Personality traits as risk factors for physical illness. In A. Baum & T. A. Revenson (Eds.), *Handbook of health psychology.* Mahwah, NJ: Erlbaum.

Smoll, F. L., Smith, R. E., Barnett, N. P., & Everett, J. J. (1993). Enhancement of children's self-esteem through social support training for youth sport coaches. *Journal of Applied Psychology, 78,* 602–610.

Snow, M. E., Jacklin, C. N., & Maccoby, E. E. (1983). Sex-of-child-differences in father-child interaction at one year of age. *Child Development, 54,* 227–232.

Snyder, C. R. (Ed.). (2001). *Coping with stress: Effective people and processes.* New York: Oxford University Press.

Snyder, C. R., & Ingram, R. E. (Eds.). (2000). *Handbook of psychological change: Psychotherapy processes & practices for the 21st century.* Mahwah, NJ: Erlbaum.

Snyder, M. (1987). *Public appearances/private realities: The psychology of self-monitoring.* New York: Freeman.

Snyder, M. (2001). Self-fulfilling stereotypes. In A. Branaman (Ed.). *Self and society: Blackwell readers in sociology.* Malden, MA: Blackwell.

Snyder, M., Clary, E. G., & Stukas, A. A. (2000). The functional approach to volunteerism. In G. R. Maio & J. M. Olson. *Why we evaluate: Functions of attitudes.* Mahwah, NJ: Erlbaum.

Snyder, S. H. (1977). Opiate receptors and internal opiates. *Scientific American, 236,* 44–56.

Sober, E., & Wilson, D. S. (1998). *Unto others: The evolution and psychology of unselfish behavior.* Cambridge, MA: Harvard University Press.

Solms, M. (2002). Dreaming: Cholinergic and dopaminergic hypotheses. In E. Perry, H. Ashton, & A. Young (Eds.), *Neurochemistry of consciousness: Neurotransmitters in mind. Advances in consciousness research.* Amsterdam: Benjamins.

Solomon, G. F., Segerstrom, S. C., Grohr, P., Kemeny, M., & Fahey, J. (1997). Shaking up immunity: Psychological and immunologic changes after a natural disaster. *Psychosomatic Medicine, 59,* 114–127.

Solomon, R. L., & Wynne, L. C. (1953). Traumatic avoidance learning: Acquisition in normal dogs. *Journal of Abnormal and Social Psychology, 48,* 291–302.

Sorenson, S. B. (2002). Preventing traumatic stress: Public health approaches. *Journal of Traumatic Stress, 15,* 3–7.

Soussignan, R. (2002). Duchenne smile, emotional experience, and autonomic reactivity: A test of the facial feedback hypothesis. *Emotion, 2,* 52–74.

Sowell, E. R., Thompson, P. M., Tessner, K. D., & Toga, A. W. (2001). Mapping continued brain growth and gray matter density reduction in dorsal frontal cortex: Inverse relationships during postadolescent brain maturation. *Journal of Neuroscience, 21,* 8819–8829.

Spanos, N. P. (1986). Hypnotic behavior: A social-psychological interpretation of amnesia, analgesia, and "trance logic." *Behavioral and Brain Sciences, 9,* 449–467.

Spanos, N. P. (1991). A sociocognitive approach to hypnosis. In S. J. Lynn & J. W. Rhue (Eds.), *Theories of hypnosis: Current models and perspectives.* New York: Guilford Press.

Spanos, N. P. (1994). Multiple identity enactments and multiple personality disorder: A sociocognitive perspective. *Psychological Bulletin, 116,* 143–165.

Spanos, N. P. (1996). *Multiple identities and false memories: A sociocognitive perspective.* Washington, DC: American Psychological Association.

Spanos, N. P., & Chaves, J. F. (Eds.). (1988). *Hypnosis: The cognitive-behavioral perspective.* Buffalo, NY: Prometheus Books.

Spearman, C. (1923). *The nature of "intelligence" and the principles of cognition.* London: Macmillan.

Speisman, J., Lazarus, R. S., Mordkoff, A., & Davidson, L. (1964). Experimental reduction of stress based on ego-defense theory. *Journal of Abnormal and Social Psychology, 68,* 367–380.

Spencer, S. J., Steele, C. M., & Quinn, D. M. (1999). Stereotype threat and women's math performance. *Journal of Experimental Social Psychology, 35,* 4–28.

Sperling, G. (1960). The information available in brief visual presentations. *Psychological Monographs, 74*(Whole No. 11).

Sperling, G. (1984). A unified theory of attention and signal detection. In R. Parasuraman & D. R. Davies (Eds.), *Varieties of attention.* New York: Academic Press.

Sperry, R. W. (1970). Perception in the absence of neocortical commissures. In Association for Research in Nervous and Mental Disease, *Perception and its disorders.* New York: Williams & Wilkins.

Spiegel, D., Bloom, J. R., Kraemer, H. C., & Gottleib, E. (1989, October 14). Effect of psychoso- cial treatment on survival of patients with metastatic breast cancer. *The Lancet,* 888–891.

Spiegler, M. D., & Guevremont, D. C. (2003). *Contemporary behavior therapy.* Belmont, CA: Wadsworth.

Spielberger, C. D., & DeNike, L. D. (1966). Descriptive behaviorism versus cognitive theory in verbal operant conditioning. *Psychological Review, 73,* 306–326.

Spitzer, R. L., Skodol, A. E., Gibbon, M., & Williams, J. B. W. (1983). *Psychopathology: A casebook.* New York: McGraw-Hill.

Sporting News (1985, August 19). Author.

Sprafkin, J. N., Liebert, R. M., & Poulos, R. W. (1975). Effects of a prosocial televised example on children's helping. *Journal of Experimental Child Psychology, 20,* 119–126.

Sprecher, S. (2001). A comparison of emotional consequences of and change in equity over time using global and domain specific measures of equity. *Journal of Social and Personal Relationships, 18,* 477–501.

Sprecher, S., & Regan, P. C. (1998). Passionate and companionate love in courting and young married couples. *Sociological Inquiry, 68,* 163–185.

Springer, S. (1997). *Left brain, right brain.* San Francisco: Freeman.

Squier, L. H., & Domhoff, G. W. (1998). The presentation of dreaming and dreams in introductory psychology textbooks: A critical examination with suggestions for textbook authors and course instructors. *Dreaming: Journal of the Association for the Study of Dreams, 8,* 149–168.

Squire, L. R. (1987). *Memory and brain.* Oxford, England: Oxford University Press.

Squire, L. R., & Zola-Morgan, S. (1991). The medial temporal lobe memory system. *Science, 253,* 1380–1386.

Sroufe, L. (2002). From infant attachment to promotion of adolescent autonomy: Prospective, longitudinal data on the role of parents in development. In J. G. Borkowski, S. L. Ramey, & M. Bristol-Power (Eds.), *Parenting and the child's world: Influences on academic, intellectual, and social-emotional development. Monographs in parenting.* Mahwah, NJ: Erlbaum.

Staats, H., van Leeuwen, E., & Wit, A. (2000). A longitudinal study of informational interventions to save energy in an office building. *Journal of Applied Behavior Analysis, 33,* 101–104.

Stahl, S. M. (1998). *Essential psychopharmacology: Neuroscientific basis and clinical applications.* New York: Cambridge University Press.

Stajkovic, A. D., & Luthans, F. (2001). Differential effects of incentive motivators on work performance. *Academy of Management Journal, 44,* 580–590.

Stams, G. J. J. M., Juffer, F., & van IJzendoorn, M. H. (2002). Maternal sensitivity, infant attachment, and temperament in early childhood predict adjustment in middle childhood: The case of adopted children and their biologically unrelated parents. *Developmental Psychology, 38,* 806–821.

Stankow, L. (2003). Complexity in human intelligence. In R. J. Sternberg, J. Lautrey, & T. I. Lubart (Eds.), *Models of intelligence: International perspectives.* Washington, DC: American Psychological Association.

Stanley, B. G., Kyrkouli, S. E., Lampert, S., & Leibowitz, S. F. (1986). Neuropeptide Y chronically injected into the hypothalamus: A powerful neurochemical inducer of hyperphagia and obesity. *Peptides, 7,* 1189–1192.

Stark, E. (1989, May). Teen sex: Not for love. *Psychology Today,* 10–11.

Steadman, H. J., Mulvey, E. P., Monahan, J., Robbins, P. C., Appelbaum, P. S., Grisso, T., Roth, L., & Silver, E. (1998). Violence by people discharged from acute inpatient facilities and by others in the same neighborhoods. *Archives of General Psychiatry, 55,* 393–401.

Steele, C. M. (1988). The psychology of self-affirmation: Sustaining the integrity of the self. In L. Berkowitz (Ed.), *Advances in experimental social psychology* (Vol. 21). New York: Academic Press.

Steele, C. M. (1997). A threat in the air: How stereotypes shape intellectual identity and performance. *American Psychologist, 52,* 613–629.

Steele, C. M., & Aronson, J. (1995). Stereotype threat and the intellectual test performance of African Americans. *Journal of Personality and Social Psychology, 69,* 797–811.

Steele, C. M., & Josephs, R. A. (1990). Alcohol myopia: Its prized and dangerous effects. *American Psychologist, 45,* 921–933.

Steele, J., James, J. B., & Barnett, R. C. (2002). Learning in a man's world: Examining the perceptions of undergraduate women in male-dominated academic areas. *Psychology of Women Quarterly, 26,* 46–50.

Stein, D. J., & Hollander, E. (2002). *Textbook of anxiety disorders.* Washington, DC: American Psychiatric Press.

Steinberg, L., Lamborn, S. D., Darling, N., & Mount, N. S. (1994). Over-time changes in adjustment and competence among adolescents from authoritative, authoritarian, indulgent, and neglectful families. *Child Development, 65,* 754–770.

Steinberg, R. J. (1988). *The triarchic mind.* New York: Viking Press.

Stephan, W. G. (1990). School desegregation: Short-term and long-term effects. In H. Knopke (Ed.), *Opening doors: An appraisal of race relations in America.* Tuscaloosa: University of Alabama Press.

Steptoe, A. (2000). Control and stress. In G. Fink (Ed.), *Encyclopedia of stress.* San Diego, CA: Academic Press.

Sternberg, K. J., Lamb, M. E., Esplin, P. W., Opbach, Y., & Hershkowitz, I. (2002). Using a structure interview protocol to improve the quality of investigative interviews. In M. L. Eisen, (Ed.), *Memory and suggestibility in the forensic interview: Personality and Clinical Psychology Series.* Mahwah, NJ: Erlbaum.

Sternberg, R. J. (1988). Triangulating love. In R. J. Sternberg & M. L. Barnes (Eds.), *The psychology of love.* New Haven, CT: Yale University Press.

Sternberg, R. J. (1997). Construct validation of a triangular love scale. *European Journal of Social Psychology, 27,* 313–335.

Sternberg, R. J. (1998a). Applying the triarchic theory of human intelligence in the classroom. In R. J. Sternberg & W. M. Williams (Eds.), *Intelligence, instruction, and assessment: Theory into practice.* Mahwah, NJ: Erlbaum.

Sternberg, R. J. (1998b). Principles of teaching for succesful intelligence. *Educational Psychologist, 33,* 65–72.

Sternberg, R. J., Lautrey, J., & Lubart, T. I. (2003). *Models of intelligence: International perspectives.* Washington, DC: American Psychological Association.

Sternberg, R. J., Nokes, C., Geissler, P., Prince, R., Okatcha, F., Bundy, D. A., & Grigorenko, E. L. (2001). The relationship between academic and practical intelligence: A case study in Kenya. *Intelligence, 29,* 401–418.

Sternberg, R. J., Torff, B., & Grigorenko, E. L. (1998). Teaching triarchically improves school achievement. *Journal of Educational Psychology, 90,* 374–384.

Stetson, B. A., Rahn, J. M., Dubbert, P. M., Wilner, B. I., & Mercury, M. G. (1997). Prospective evaluation of the effects of stress on exercise adherence in community-residing women. *Health Psychology, 16,* 515–520.

Stewart, J. (2002). Modulation of the subjective and physiological effects of drugs by contexts and expectations—The search for mechanisms: Comment on Alessi, Roll, Reilly, and Johanson (2002). *Experimental and Clinical Psychopharmacology, 10,* 96–98.

Stiles, W. B., Leach, C., Barkham, M., et al. (2003). Early sudden gains in psychotherapy under routine clinic conditions: Practice-based evidence. *Journal of Consulting and Clinical Psychology, 71,* 14–21.

Stoddard, J., Raine, A., Bihrle, S., & Buchsbaum, M. (1997). Prefrontal dysfunction in murderers lacking psychosocial deficits. In A. Raine, P. A. Brennan, D. P. Farrington, & S. A. Mednick (Eds.), *Biosocial bases of violence.* New York: Plenum.

Stokols, D. (1995). The paradox of environmental psychology. *American Psychologist, 50,* 821–837.

Stone, A. A., Shiffman, S. S., & DeVries, M. (2000). Rethinking our self-report assessment methodologies: An argument for collecting ecologically valid, momentary measurements. In D. Kahneman, E. Diener, & N. Schwarz (Eds.), *Understanding quality of life: Scientific perspectives on enjoyment and suffering.* New York: Russel Sage.

Stone, J., & Cooper, J. (2001). A self standards model of cognitive dissonance. *Journal of Experimental Social Psychology, 37,* 228–243.

Stone, L. J., & Church, J. (1968). *Childhood and adolescence.* New York: Random House/Church & Stone.

Storm, L., & Ertel, S. (2001). Does psi exist? Comments on Milton and Wiseman's (1999) meta-analysis of Ganzfield research. *Psychological Bulletin, 12,* 424–433.

Stormshak, E. A., Bierman, K. L., McMahon, R. J., Lengua, L. J., & Conduct Problems Prevention Research Group. (2000). Parenting practices and child disruptive behavior problems in early elementary school. *Journal of Clinical Child Psychology, 29,* 17–29.

Stouffer, S. A., Lumsdaine, A. A., Lumsdaine, M. H., & Williams, R. M., Jr. (1949a). *The American soldier: Combat and its aftermath.* Princeton, NJ: Princeton University Press.

Stouffer, S. A., Suchman, E. A., De Vinney, L. C., Star, S. A., & Williams, R. M., Jr. (1949b). *The American soldier: Adjustments during army life.* Princeton, NJ: Princeton University Press.

Strack, F., Martin, L. L., & Stepper, S. (1988). Inhibiting and facilitating conditions of facial expressions: A non-obtrusive test of the facial feedback hypothesis. *Journal of Personality and Social Psychology, 54,* 768–777.

Straus, M. A., & Stewart, J. H. (1999). Corporal punishment by American parents: National data on prevalence, chronicity, severity, and duration, in relation to child and family characteristics. *Clinical Child and Family Psychology Review, 2*(2), 55–70.

Strawbridge, W. J., Shema, S. J., Cohen, R. D., Roberts, R. E., & Kaplan, G. A. (1998). Religion buffers effects of some stressors on depression but exacerbates others. *Journal of Gerontology, 53,* 118–126.

Strayer, D. L., & Johnston, W. A. (2001). Driven to Distraction: Dual Task Studies of Simulated Driving and Conversing on a Cellular Telephone. *Psychological Science, 12,* 462–466.

Streissguth, A. P. (1977). Maternal drinking and the outcome of pregnancy: Implications for child mental health. *American Journal of Orthopsychiatry, 47,* 422–431.

Streissguth, A. P. (2001). Recent advances in fetal alcohol syndrome and alcohol use in pregnancy. In D. P. Agarwal, H. K. Seitz, & K. Helmut (Eds.), *Alcohol in health and disease.* New York: Dekker.

Streissguth, A. P., Clarren, S. K., & Jones, K. L. (1985). Natural history of the fetal alcohol syndrome: A 10-year follow-up of eleven patients. *The Lancet, 2*(8446), 85–91.

Strentz, T., & Auerbach, S. M. (1988). Adjustment to the stress of simulated captivity: Effects of emotion-focused versus problem-focused preparation on hostages differing in locus of control. *Journal of Personality and Social Psychology, 55,* 652–660.

Striegel-Moore, R. H, McMahon, R. P., Biro, F. M., Schreiber, G., Crawford, P. B., & Voorhees, C. (2001). Exploring the relationship between timing of menarche and eating disorder symptoms in black and white adolescent girls. *International Journal of Eating Disorders, 30,* 421–433.

Strober, M., & Humphrey, L. L. (1987). Familial contributions to the etiology and course of anorexia nervosa and bulimia. *Journal of Consulting and Clinical Psychology, 55,* 654–659.

Stroebe, M., Stroebe, W., & Schut, H. (2001). Gender differences in adjustment to bereavement: An empirical and theoretical review. *Review of General Psychology, 5,* 62–82.

Strough, J., Berg, C. A., & Sandone, C. (1996). Goals for solving everyday problems across the life span: Age and gender differences in the salience of interpersonal concerns. *Developmental Psychology, 32,* 1106–1115.

Strupp, H. H. (1989). Psychotherapy: Can the practitioner learn from the researcher? *American Psychologist, 44,* 717–724.

Stryer, L. (1987). The molecules of visual excitation. *Scientific American, 257*(1), 42–50.

Subramanian, K. N. S., Yoon, H., & Toral, J. C. (2002, October 31). *Extremely low birth weight infant.* Available online: http://www.emedicine.com/ped/topic2784.htm

Sue, D. W., & Sue, D. (1990). *Counseling the culturally different: Theory and practice.* New York: Wiley.

Sue, S. (1998). In search of cultural competence in psychotherapy and counseling. *American Psychologist, 53,* 440–448.

Sue, S., Fujino, D., Hu, L., Takeuchi, D., & Zane, N. (1991). Community mental health services for ethnic minority groups: A test of the cultural responsiveness hypothesis. *Journal of Consulting and Clinical Psychology, 59,* 533–540.

Sue, S., & Zane, N. (1987). The role of culture and cultural techniques in psychotherapy. *American Psychologist, 42,* 37–45.

Suh, E., Diener, E., Oishi, S., & Triandis, H. (1998). The shifting basis of life satisfaction judgments across cultures: Emotions versus norms. *Journal of Personality and Social Psychology, 74,* 482–493.

Suinn, R. M., Osborne, D., & Winfree, P. (1962). The self-concept and accuracy of recall of inconsistent self-related information. *Journal of Clinical Psychology, 18,* 473–474.

Sullivan, M. A., & O'Leary, S. G. (1990). Maintenance following reward and cost token programs. *Behavior Therapy, 21,* 139–149.

Suls, J. M., & Wallston, K. A. (2003). *Social psychological foundations of health and illness.* New York: Blackwell.

Super, D. E. (1957). *The psychology of careers.* New York: Harper & Row.

Sussman, N. M., & Rosenfeld, H. M. (1982). Influence of culture, language, and sex on conversational distance. *Journal of Personality and Social Psychology, 42,* 66–74.

Sutton, S. K. (2002). Incentive and threat reactivity: Relations with anterior cortical activity. In D. Cervone & W. Mischel (Eds.), *Advances in personality science.* New York: Guilford Press.

Swain, J. C., & McLaughlin, T. F. (1998). The effects of bonus contingencies in a classwide token program on math accuracy with middle-school students with behavioral disorders. *Behavioral Interventions, 13,* 11–19.

Swann, W. B., Jr., Stein-Seroussi, A., & Giesler, R. B. (1992). Why people self-verify. *Journal of Personality and Social Psychology, 62,* 392-401.

Swartz, C. (1995). Setting the ECT stimulus. *Psychiatric Times, 12*(6). (Reprint addition)

Szkrybalo, J., & Ruble, D. N. (1999). "God made me a girl": Sex-category constancy judgments and explanations revisited. *Developmental Psychology, 35,* 392–402.

Tajfel, H., & Turner, J. C. (1986). The social identity theory of intergroup behavior. In S. Worchel & W. G. Austin (Eds.), *The psychology of intergroup relations* (2nd ed.). Chicago, IL: Nelson Hall.

Takahashi, Y. (1990). Is multiple personality disorder really rare in Japan? *Dissociation: Progress in the Dissociative Disorders, 3,* 57–59.

Tanaka-Matsumi, J. (1979). Taijin Kyofushu: Diagnostic and cultural issues in Japanese psychiatry. *Culture, Medicine, and Psychiatry, 3,* 231–245.

Tanaka-Matsumi, J., & Draguns, J. G. (1997). Culture and psychopathology. In J. W. Berry, M. H. Segall, & C. Kagitçibasi (Eds.), *Handbook of cross-cultural psychology* (Vol. 3). Boston: Allyn & Bacon.

Tarr, M. J., & Vuong, Q. C. (2002). Visual object recognition. In H. Pashler & S. Yantis (Eds.). *Steven's handbook of experimental psychology: Vol. 1. Sensation and perception* (3rd ed.). New York: Wiley.

Taylor, F. W. (1911). *The principles of scientific management.* New York: Harper.

Taylor, R. D., & Wang, M. C. (Eds.). (2000). *Resilience across contexts: Family, work, culture, and community.* Mahwah, NJ: Erlbaum.

Taylor, S. E. (2003). *Health psychology* (3rd ed.). Boston: McGraw-Hill.

Taylor, S. E., & Brown, J. D. (1988). Illusion and well-being: A social psychological perspective on mental health. *Psychological Bulletin, 103,* 193–210.

Taylor, S. E., Klein, L. C., Lewis, B., Gruenewald, T. L., Gurung, R. A. R., & Updegraff, J. A. (2000). Biobehavioral responses to stress in females: Tend-and-befriend, not fight-or-flight. *Psychological Review, 107,* 411–429.

Taylor, S. E., Lerner, J. S., Sherman, D. K., Sage, R. M., & McDowell, N. K. (2003). Portrait of the self-enhancer: Well adjusted and well liked or maladjusted and friendless? *Journal of Personality and Social Psychology, 84,* 165–176.

Teachman, B. A., Gapinski, K. D., Brownell, K. D., Rawlins, M., & Jeyaram, S. (2003). Demonstrations of implicit anti-fat bias: The impact of providing causal information and evoking empathy. *Health Psychology, 22,* 68–78.

Teachman, J. D. (2002). Childhood living arrangements and the intergenerational transmission of divorce. *Journal of Marriage and Family, 64,* 717–729.

Teghtsoonian, R. (1971). On the exponents in Stevens' law and the constant in Ekman's law. *Psychological Review, 78,* 71–80.

Tellegen, A., Lykken, D. T., Bouchard, T. J., Wilcox, K. J., Segal, N. L., & Rich, S. (1988). Personality similarity in twins reared apart and together. *Journal of Personality and Social Psychology, 54,* 1031–1039.

Ten-Berge, M. A., Maaike, A., & De-Raad, B. (2002). The structure of situations from a personality perspective. *European Journal of Personality, 16,* 81–102.

Tenenbaum, H. R., & Leaper, C. (2003). Parent-child conversations about science: The socialization of gender inequities? *Developmental Psychology, 39,* 34–47.

Terman, J. S., Terman, M., Lo, E. S., & Cooper, T. B. (2001). Circadian time of morning light administration and therapeutic response in winter depression. *Archives of General Psychiatry, 58,* 69–75.

Terman, L. M., & Merrill, M. A. (1972). *Stanford-Binet intelligence scale, third edition, form L–M.* Boston: Houghton Mifflin.

Terrace, H. S. (1979). *Nim.* New York: Knopf.

Tesser, A., & Shaffer, D. (1990). Attitudes and attitude change. *Annual Review of Psychology, 41,* 479–523.

Teyber, E., & McClure, F. (2000). Therapist variables. In C. R. Snyder & R. E. Ingram (Eds.), *Handbook of psychological change: Psychotherapy processes and practices for the 21st century.* New York: Wiley.

Thase, M. E., Greenhouse, J. B., Frank, E., et al. (1997). Treatment of major depression with psychotherapy or psychotherapy-pharmacotherapy combinations. *Archives of General Psychiatry, 54,* 1009–1015.

Thatch, W. T., Goodkin, H. P., & Keating, J. G. (1992). The cerebellum and the adaptive coordination of movement. *Annual Review of Neuroscience, 15,* 161–182.

Thibaut, J. W., & Kelley, H. H. (1959). *The social psychology of groups.* New York: Wiley.

Thoits, P. (1983). Dimensions of life events that influence psychological distress: An evaluation and synthesis of the literature. In H. B. Kaplan (Ed.), *Psychological stress: Trends in theory and research.* New York: Academic Press.

Thomas, A., & Chess, S. (1977). *Temperament and development.* New York: Brunner/Mazel.

Thomas, L. (1974). *The lives of a cell.* New York: Viking Press.

Thomas, S. A., & Palmiter, R. D. (1997). Disruption of the dopamine Beta-hydroxylase gene in mice suggests roles for norepinephrine in motor function, learning, and memory. *Behavioral Neuroscience, 111,* 579–589.

Thomas, S. L., Skitka, L. J., Christen, S., & Jurgena, M. (2002). Social facilitation and impression formation. *Basic and Applied Social Psychology, 24,* 67–70.

Thomas, W. P., & Collier, V. P. (1997). *School effectiveness for language minority students.* Washington, DC: National Clearinghouse for Bilingual Education.

Thompson, C. P., Cowan, T. M., & Frieman, J. (1993). *Memory search by a memorist.* Hillsdale, NJ: Erlbaum.

Thompson, R. F. (1985). *The brain: An introduction to neuroscience.* New York: Freeman.

't Hooft, G. (2000). Physics and the paranormal: A theoretical physicist's view. *Skeptical Inquirer, 24*(2), 27–33.

Thorndike, E. L. (1898). *Animal intelligence, an experimental study of the associative processes in animals.* New York: Macmillan.

Thorndike, E. L. (1911). *Animal intelligence; experimental studies.* New York: Macmillan.

Thurstone, L. L. (1938). *Primary mental abilities.* Chicago: University of Chicago Press.

Tienari, P., Wynne, L. C., Moring, J., Lahti, I., et al. (Eds.). (1994). The Finnish adoptive family study of schizophrenia: Implications for family research. *British Journal of Psychiatry, 164,* 20–26.

Tilker, H. A. (1970). Socially responsible behavior as a function of observer responsibility and victim feedback. *Journal of Personality and Social Psychology, 14,* 95–100.

Till, B. D., & Priluck, R. L. (2000). Stimulus generalization in classical conditioning: An initial investigation and extension. *Psychology and Marketing, 17,* 55–72.

Tinbergen, N. (1951). *The study of instinct.* Oxford, England: Clarendon Press.

Tizard, B., & Hodges, J. (1978). The effect of early institutional rearing on the development of eight-year-old children. *Journal of Child Psychology and Psychiatry, 19,* 99–118.

Tobin, J. J., & Friedman, J. (1983). Spirits, shamans, and nightmare death: Survivor stress in a Hmong refugee. *American Journal of Orthopsychiatry, 53,* 439–448.

Todorov, A., & Bargh, J. A. (2002). Automatic sources of aggression. *Aggression and Violent Behavior, 7,* 53–68.

Tollefson, G. D. (1993). Major depression. In D. L. Dunner (Ed.), *Current psychiatric therapy.* Philadephia: Saunders.

Tollison, C. D., Satterswaithe, J. R., & Tollison, J. W. (2002). *Practical pain management.* New York: Williams & Wilkins.

Tolman, E. C. (1948). Cognitive maps in rats and men. *Psychological Review, 55,* 189–208.

Tolman, E. C., & Honzik, C. H. (1930). Introduction and removal of reward and maze performance in rats. *University of California Publications in Psychology, 4,* 257–275.

Tomarken, A. J., & Keener, A. D. (1998). Frontal brain asymmetry and depression: A self-regulatory perspective. Special Issue: Neuropsychological perspectives on affective and anxiety disorders. *Cognition & Emotion, 12*(3), 387–420.

Tomkins, S. S. (1991). *Affect, imagery, and consciousness.* New York: Springer-Verlag.

Tooby, J., & Cosmides, L. (1992). The psychological foundations of culture. In J. H. Barkow, L. Cosmides, & J. Tooby (Eds.), *The adapted mind.* New York: Oxford University Press.

Torgersen, S., Kringlen, E., & Cramer, V. (2001). The prevalence of personality disorders in a community sample. *Archives of General Psychiatry, 58,* 590–596.

Torrey, E. F. (1997). *Out of the shadows: Confronting America's mental illness crisis.* New York: Wiley.

Torrey, E. F., & Zdanowicz, M. (2001). Outpatient commitment: What, why, and for whom. *Psychiatric Services, 52,* 337–341.

Toufexis, A. (1989, June 5). The times of your life. *Time,* 66–67.

Trae, H. C., & Deighton, R. M. (2000). Emotional inhibition. In G. Fink (Ed.), *Encyclopedia of stress.* San Diego, CA: Academic Press.

Tremblay, L. K., Naranjo, C. A., Cardenas, L., Hermann, N., & Busto, U. E. (2002). Probing brain reward system function in major depressive disorder: Altered response to dextroamphetamine. *Archives of General Psychiatry, 59,* 409–417.

Triandis, H. C. (1989). Cross-cultural studies of individualism and collectivism. In J. J. Berman (Ed.), *Nebraska Symposium on Motivation 1989* (Vol. 37). Lincoln: University of Nebraska Press.

Triandis, H. C. (2001). Individualism-collectivism and personality. *Journal of Personality, 69,* 907–924.

Triandis, H. C., & Suh, E. M. (2002). Cultural influences on personality. *Annual Review of Psychology, 53,* 133–160.

Trimble, M. (2003). *Somatoform disorders.* New York: Cambridge University Press.

Triplett, N. (1898). The dynamogenic factors in pace-making and competition. *American Journal of Psychology, 9,* 507–533.

Trivers, R. (1971). The evolution of reciprocal altruism. *Quarterly Review of Biology, 46,* 35–57.

Trivers, R. L. (1972). Parental investment and sexual selection. In B. Campbell (Ed.), *Sexual selection and the descent of man.* Chicago: Aldine-Atherton.

Trull, T. J., & Geary, D. C. (1997). Comparison of the Big-Five Factor structure across samples of Chinese and American adults. *Journal of Personality Assessment, 69,* 324–341.

Tryon, W. W. (2002). Network models contribute to cognitive and social neuroscience. *American Psychologist, 57,* 728.

Trzesniewski, K. H., Donnellan, M. B., & Robins, R. W. (2003). Stability of self-esteem across the life span. *Journal of Personality and Social Psychology, 84,* 205–220.

Tseng, W. S., Asai, M., Liu, J., Pismai, W., et al. (1990). Multi-cultural study of minor psychiatric disorders in Asia: Symptom manifestations. *International Journal of Social Psychiatry, 36,* 252–264.

Tucker, V. A. (2000). The deep fovea, sideways vision and spiral flight paths in raptors. *Journal of Experimental Biology, 203,* 3745–3754.

Tuiten, A., Van Honk, J., Koppeschaar, H., Bernaards, C., Thijssen, J., & Verbaten, R. (2000). Time course of effects of testosterone administration on sexual arousal in women. *Archives of General Psychiatry, 57,* 149–153.

Tulving, E. (2002). Episodic memory: From mind to brain. *Annual Review of Psychology, 53,* 1–25.

Tulving, E., & Psotka, J. (1971). Retroactive inhibition in free recall: Inaccessibility of information available in the memory store. *Journal of Experimental Psychology, 87,* 1–8.

Tulving, E., & Thomson, D. M. (1973). Encoding specificity and retrieval processes in episodic memory. *Psychological Review, 80,* 359–380.

Turk, D. C. (2001). Physiological and psychological bases of pain. In A. Baum & T. A. Revenson (Eds.), *Handbook of health psychology.* Mahwah, NJ; Erlbaum.

Turk, D. C., & Melzack, R. (2001). *Handbook of pain assessment* (2nd ed.). New York: Guilford Press.

Turner, J. A., & Aaron, L. A. (2001). Pain-related catastrophizing: What is it? *Clinical Journal of Pain, 17,* 65–71.

Turner, J. A., Deyo, R. A., Loeser, J. D., et al. (1994). The importance of placebo effects in pain treatment and research. *Journal of the American Medical Association, 271,* 1609–1614.

Tusing, K. J., & Dillard, J. P. (2000). The psychological reality of the door-in-the-face: It's helping, not bargaining. *Journal of Language and Social Psychology, 19,* 5–25.

Tversky, A., & Kahneman, D. (1982). Judgments of and by representativeness. In D. Kahneman, P. Slovic, & A. Tversky (Eds.), *Heuristics and biases.* Cambridge University Press.

Tversky, B., & Tuchin, M. (1989). A reconciliation of the evidence on eyewitness testimony: Comments on McCloskey and Zaragoza. *Journal of Experimental Psychology: General, 118,* 86–91.

Tyc, V. L., Mulhern, R. K., & Bieberich, A. A. (1997). Anticipatory nausea and vomiting in pediatric cancer patients: An analysis of conditioning and coping variables. *Journal of Developmental and Behavioral Pediatrics, 18,* 27–33.

Tyrka, A. R., Waldron, I., Graber, J. A., & Brooks-Gunn, J. (2002). Prospective predictors of the onset of anorexic and bulimic syndromes. *International Journal of Eating Disorders, 32,* 282–290.

Tzeng, J. M., & Mare, R. D. (1995). Labor market and socioeconomic effects on marital stability. *Social Science Research, 24,* 329–351.

Tzeng, O. J., Hung, W., Cohen, F. J., & Wang, P. (1979). Visual lateralization effect in reading Chinese characters. *Nature, 282,* 499–501.

Tzeng, S. F. (1997). Neural progenitors isolated from newborn rat spinal cords differentiate into neurons and astroglia. *Journal of Biomedical Science, 9*(1), 10–16.

Unverzagt, F. W., Gao, S., Baiyewu, O., Ogunniyi, A. O., Gureje, O., Perkins, A., et al. (2001). Prevalence of cognitive impairment: Data from the Indianapolis Study of Health and Aging. *Neurology, 57,* 1655–1662.

U.S. Department of Health and Human Services. (2002). *National Comorbidity Survey, 1990–92.* Available online: http://www.icpsr.umich.edu/SAMHDA/STUDIES/ncs.html (Substance Abuse and Mental Health Data Archive [SAMHDA]).

U.S. Office of Behavior Technology. (1990). *Provision of professional services to the physically handicapped.* Washington, DC: Author.

U.S. Public Health Service. (1979). *Healthy people: The Surgeon General's report on health promotion and disease prevention.* Washington, DC: U.S. Government Printing Office.

Valent, P. (1998). Effects of the Holocaust on Jewish child survivors: Traumas and latent disturbances 50 years later. *Psyche: Zeitschrift fuer Psychoanalyse und ihre Anwendungen, 52,* 751–771.

Valent, P. (2000a). Stress effects of the Holocaust. In G. Fink (Ed.), *Encyclopedia of stress.* San Diego, CA: Academic Press.

Valent, P. (2000b). Survivor guilt. In G. Fink (Ed.), *Encyclopedia of stress.* San Diego, CA: Academic Press.

Vallone, R. P., Griffin, D., Lin, S., & Ross, L. (1990). Overconfident prediction of future actions and outcomes by self and others. *Journal of Personality and Social Psychology, 58,* 582–592.

Valsiner, J., & Lawrence, J. A. (1997). Human development in culture across the life span. In J. W. Berry, P. R. Dasen, & T. S. Saraswathi (Eds.), *Handbook of cross-cultural psychology* (Vol. 2). Boston: Allyn & Bacon.

van Ijzendoorn, M. (1995). Adult attachment representations, parental responsiveness, and infant attachment: A meta-analysis of the Adult Attachment Interview. *Psychological Bulletin, 117,* 387–403.

van Praag, H. M. (2004). *Stress, vulnerability and depression.* New York: Cambridge University Press.

Van Zomeren, A. H., & Brouwer, W. H. (1994). *Clinical neuropsychology of attention.* New York: Oxford University Press.

Vargha-Khadem, F., Gadian, D. G., Watkins, K. E., Connelly, A., Van Paesschen, W., & Mishkin, M. (1997). Differential effects of early hippocampal pathology on episodic and semantic memory. *Science, 277,* 376–380.

Vartanian, L. R. (2000). Revisiting the imaginary audience and personal fable constructs of adolescent egocentrism: A conceptual review. *Adolescence, 35,* 639–661.

Vaughn, C., & Leff, J. (1976). The measurement of expressed emotion in the families of psychiatric patients. *British Journal of Social and Clinical Psychology, 15,* 157–165.

Verona, E., & Carbonell, J. L. (2000). Female violence and personality: Evidence for a pattern of overcontrolled hostility among one time violent female offenders. *Criminal Justice and Behavior, 27,* 176–195.

Verplanken, B., & Holland, R. W. (2002). Motivated decision making: Effects of activation and self centrality of values on choices and behavior. *Journal of Personality and Social Psychology, 82,* 434–447.

Vertes, R. P., & Eastman, K. E. (2000). The case against memory consolidation in REM sleep. *Behavioral and Brain Sciences, 23,* 867–876.

Vetter, H. J. (1969). *Language behavior and psychopathology.* Chicago: Rand McNally.

Villarreal, D. M., Do, V., Haddad, E., & Derrick, B. E. (2002). NMDA receptor antagonists sustain LTP and spatial memory: Active processes mediate LTP decay. *Nature Neuroscience, 5,* 48–52.

Vinden, P. G. (2002). Understanding minds and evidence for belief: A study of Mofu children in Cameroon. *International Journal of Behavioral Development, 26,* 445–452.

Vogels, W. W. A., Dekker, M. R., Brouwer, W. H., & deJong, R. (2002). Age-related changes in event-related prospective memory performance: A comparison of four prospective memory tasks. *Brain and Cognition, 49,* 341–362.

Vonk, R. (1997). Attitudes toward animal research. *American Psychologist, 52,* 1248–1249.

Vral, A., Thierens, H., Baeyens, A., & De Ridder, L. (2002). The micronucleus and g(2)-phase assays for human blood lymphocytes as biomarkers of individual sensitivity to ionizing radiation: Limitations imposed by intraindividual variability. *Radiation Research, 157,* 472–477.

Vurpillot, E. (1968). The development of scanning strategies and their relation to visual differentiations. *Journal of Experimental Child Psychology, 6,* 632–650.

Vygotsky, L. S. (1978). *Mind in society: The development of higher psychological processes.* Cambridge, MA: Harvard University Press. (Original work published 1935)

Wachs, T. D. (2000). *Necessary but not sufficient: The respective roles of single and multiple influences of individual development.* Washington, DC: American Psychological Association.

Wachtel, P. L. (1997). *Psychoanalysis, behavior therapy, and the relational world.* Washington, DC: American Psychological Association.

Wadden, T. A., Brownell, K. D., & Foster, G. D. (2002). Obesity: Responding to the global epidemic. *Journal of Consulting and Clinical Psychology, 70,* 510–525.

Wadden, T. A., Vogt, R. A., Andersen, R. E., et al. (1997). Exercise in the treatment of obesity: Effects of four interventions on body composition, resting energy expenditure, appetite, and mood. *Journal of Consulting and Clinical Psychology, 654,* 269–277.

Wade, N. J., & Swanston, M. (1991). *Visual perception: An introduction.* New York: Routledge.

Wade, P., & Bernstein, B. (1991). Culture sensitivity training and counselor's race: Effects on Black female client's perceptions and attrition. *Journal of Counseling Psychology, 38,* 9–15.

Wagman, M. (1997). *Cognitive science and the symbolic operations of human and artificial intelligence: Theory and research into the intellective processes.* Westport, CT: Praeger.

Wahlberg, K. E., Wynne, L. C., Oja, H., Keskitalo, P., et al. (1997). Gene-environment interaction in vulnerability to schizophrenia: Findings from the Finnish Family Study of Schizophrenia. *American Journal of Psychiatry, 154,* 355–362.

Wakefield, M., Reid, Y., Roberts, L., Mullins, R., & Gillies, P. (1998). Smoking and smoking cessation among men whose partners are pregnant: A qualitative study. *Social Science and Medicine, 47,* 657–664.

Walbott, H., & Scherer, K. (1988). How universal and specific is emotional experience? Evidence from 27 countries and five continents. In K. Scherer (Ed.), *Facets of emotion: Recent research.* Hillsdale, NJ: Erlbaum.

Walen, S. R., & Roth, D. (1987). A cognitive approach. In J. H. Geer & W. T. O'Donohue (Eds.), *Theories of human sexuality.* New York: Plenum.

Walker, P. L. (2001). A bioarchaeological perspective on the history of violence. *Annual Review of Anthropology, 30,* 573–596.

Walla, P., Hufnagl, B., Lindinger, G., Deecke, L., Imhof, H., & Lang, W. (2001). False recognition depends on depth of prior word processing: A magnetoencephalographic (MEG) study. *Cognitive Brain Research, 11,* 249–257.

Walling, D. P., Baker, J. M., & Dott, S. G. (1998). Scope of hypnosis education in academia: Results of a national survey. *International Journal of Clinical and Experimental Hypnosis, 46,* 150–156.

Wallston, K. A. (1993). Hocus-pocus, the focus isn't strictly on locus: Rotter's social learning theory modified for health. *Cognitive Therapy and Research, 16,* 183–199.

Walsh, B. T., & Devlin, M. J. (1998). Eating disorders: Progress and problems. *Science, 280,* 1387–1390.

Walster, E., Aronson, V., Abrahams, D., & Rottman, L. (1966). The importance of physical attractiveness in dating behavior. *Journal of Personality and Social Psychology, 4,* 508–516.

Walther, E. (2002). Guilty by mere association: Evaluative conditioning and the spreading attitude effect. *Journal of Personality and Social Psychology, 82,* 919–934.

Wang, A. Y., & Thomas, M. H. (2000). Looking for long-term mnemonic effects on serial recall: The legacy of Simonides. *American Journal of Psychology, 113,* 331–340.

Wang, P. S., Demler, O., & Kessler, R. C. (2002). Adequacy of treatment for serious mental illness in the United States. *American Journal of Public Health, 92,* 92–98.

Wang, Q. I. (2001). Culture effects on adults' earliest childhood recollection and self-description: Implications for the relation between memory and the self. *Journal of Personality and Social Psychology, 81,* 220–233.

Wang, T., Brownstein, R., & Katzev, R. (1989). Promoting charitable behaviour with compliance techniques. *Applied Psychology: An International Review, 38,* 165–183.

Ward, S. L., & Overton, W. F. (1990). Semantic familiarity, relevance, and the development of deductive reasoning. *Developmental Psychology, 26,* 488–493.

Warga, C. (1987). Pain's gatekeeper. *Psychology Today, 21,* 50–59.

Wasserman, D., & Wachbroit, R. (2001). *Genetics and criminal behavior.* New York: Cambridge University Press.

Waters, A., Hill, A., & Waller, G. (2001). Bulimics' responses to food cravings: Is binge-eating a product of hunger or emotional state? *Behaviour Research and Therapy, 39,* 877–886.

Watkins, L. R., & Maier, S. F. (2000). The pain of being sick: Implications of immune-to-brain communication for understanding pain. *Annual Review of Psychology, 51,* 29–57.

Watson, D., & Clark, L. A. (1992). Affects separable and inseparable: On the hierarchical arrangement of the negative affects. *Journal of Personality and Social Psychology, 62,* 489–505.

Watson, D. L., & Tharp, R. G. (1997). *Self-directed behavior: Self-modification for personal adjustment* (7th ed.) Belmont, CA: Brooks/Cole.

Watson, J. B. (1924). *Behaviorism.* New York: People's Institute.

Watson, J. B., & Rayner, R. (1920). Conditioned emotional reactions. *Journal of Experimental Psychology, 3,* 1–14.

Watson, J. C., & Greenberg, L. S. (1998). The therapeutic alliance in short-term humanistic and experiential therapies. In J. D. Safran & C. J. Muran (Eds.), *The therapeutic alliance in brief psychotherapy.* Washington, DC: American Psychological Association.

Webb, E. J., Campbell, D. T., Schwartz, R. D., & Sechrest, L. (1966). *Unobtrusive measures: Nonreactive research in the social sciences.* Chicago: Rand McNally.

Webb, W. B. (1974). Sleep as an adaptive response. *Perceptual and Motor Skills, 38,* 1023–1027

Webb, W. B. (1992). *Sleep: The gentle tyrant* (2nd ed.). Bolton, MA: Anker.

Webb, W. B. (1994). Prediction of sleep onset. In R. D. Ogilvie & J. R. Harsh (Eds.), *Sleep onset: Normal and abnormal processes.* Washington, DC: American Psychological Association.

Webster, D. M., Richter, L., & Kruglanski, A. W. (1996). On leaping to conclusions when feeling tired: Mental fatigue effects on impressional primacy. *Journal of Experimental Social Psychology, 32,* 181–195.

Wechsler, H., Davenport, A., Dowdall, G., Hoeykins, B., & Castillo, S. (1994). Health and behavioral consequences of binge drinking in college: A national survey of students at 140 campuses. *Journal of the American Medical Association, 272,* 1672–1677.

Weg, R. B. (1983). Changing physiology of aging: Normal and pathological. In D. S. Woodruff & J. E. Birren (Eds.), *Aging: Scientific perspectives and social issues* (2nd ed.). Monterey, CA: Brooks/Cole.

Weinberger, D. R., & McClure, R. K. (2002). Neurotoxicity, neuroplasticity, and magnetic resonance imaging morphometry: What is happening in the schizophrenic brain? *Archives of General Psychiatry, 59,* 553–559.

Weiner, B. (1992). *Human motivation: Metaphors, theories, and research.* Newbury Park, CA: Sage Publications.

Weinert, F. E., & Hany, E. A. (2003). The stability of individual differences in intellectual development. In R. J. Sternberg, J. Lautrey, & T. I. Lubart (Eds.), *Models of intelligence: International perspectives.* Washington, DC: American Psychological Association.

Weingardt, K. R., & Marlatt, G. A. (1998). Harm reduction and public policy. In G. A. Marlatt (Ed.), *Harm reduction: Pragmatic strategies for managing high-risk behaviors.* New York: Guilford Press.

Weingarten, H. P. (1983). Conditioned cues elicit feeding in sated rats: A role for learning in meal initiation. *Science, 220,* 431–433.

Weissman, M. M., Bland, R. C., Canino, G. J., et al. (1994). The cross-national epidemiology of obsessive-compulsive disorder: The Cross-National Collaborative Group. *Journal of Clinical Psychiatry, 55,* 5–10.

Weissman, M. M., Geshon, E. S., Kidd, K. K., Prusoff, B. A., Leckman, J. F., Dibble, E., Hamovit, J., Thompson, W. D., Pauls, D. L., & Guroff, J. J. (1984). Psychiatric disorders in the relatives of probands with affective disorders. *Archives of General Psychiatry, 41,* 13–21.

Weissman, M. M., & Markowitz, J. C. (1994). Interpersonal psychotherapy: Current status. *Archives of General Psychiatry, 51,* 599–606.

Weitlauf, J., Smith, R. E., & Cervone, D. (2000). Generalization effects of coping skills training: Influences of self-defense training on women's efficacy beliefs, assertiveness, and aggression. *Journal of Applied Psychology, 85,* 625–633.

Weitzenhoffer, A. M., & Hilgard, E. R. (1962). *Stanford Hypnotic Susceptibility Scale: Form C.* Palo Alto, CA: Consulting Psychologists.

Weller, A., & Weller, L. (1997). Menstrual synchrony under optimal conditions: Bedouin families. *Journal of Comparative Psychology, 111,* 143–151.

Weller, L., Weller, A., Koresh, H. K., & Shoshan, B. R. (1999). Menstrual synchrony in a sample of working women. *Psychoneuroendocrinology, 24,* 449–459.

Wender, P. H., Kety, S. S., Rosenthal, D., Schulsinger, F., Ortmann, J., & Lunde, I. (1986). Psychiatric disorders in the biological and adoptive families of adopted individuals with affective disorders. *Archives of General Psychiatry, 43,* 923–929.

Wenzlaff, R. M., Wegner, D. M., & Roper, D. W. (1988). Depression and mental control: The resurgence of unwanted negative thoughts. *Journal of Personality and Social Psychology, 55,* 882–892.

Wernig, M., & Brustle, O. (2002). Fifty ways to make a neuron: Shifts in stem cell hierarchy and their implications for neuropathology and CNS repair. *Journal of Neuropathology and Experimental Neurology, 61*(2), 101–110.

Werth, J. L., Jr., Blevins, D., Toussaint, K. L., & Durham, M. R. (2002). The influence of cultural diversity on end of life care and decisions. *American Behavioral Scientist, 46,* 204–219.

Wertheimer, M. (1912). Experimentelle studien über das Gesehen von Bewegung. *Zeitschrift für Psychologie, 61,* 161–265.

West, P. D., & Evans, E. F. (1990). Early detection of hearing damage in young listeners resulting from exposure to amplified music. *British Journal of Audiology, 24,* 89–103.

West, S. A., Pen, I., & Griffin, A. S. (2002). Cooperation and competition between relatives. *Science, 296,* 72–75.

Westen, D. (1998). The scientific legacy of Sigmund Freud: Toward a psychodynamically informed psychological science. *Psychological Bulletin, 24,* 333–371.

Westen, D., & Morrison, K. (2001). A multidimensional meta-analysis of treatments for depression, panic, and generalized anxiety disorder: An empirical examination of the status of empirically supported therapies. *Journal of Consulting and Clinical Psychology, 69,* 875–889.

Western, D. (1998). The scientific legacy of Sigmund Freud: Toward a psychodynamically informed psychological science. *Psychological Bulletin, 124,* 333–371.

Wethington, E. (2000a). Expecting stress: Americans and the "midlife crisis." *Motivation and Emotion, 24,* 85–103.

Wethington, E. (2000b). Life events scale. In G. Fink (Ed.), *Encyclopedia of stress.* San Diego, CA: Academic Press.

Wexley, K. N., & Yukl, G. A. (1977). *Organizational behavior and personnel psychology.* Homewood, IL: Irwin.

Wheeden, A., Scafidi, F. A., Field, T., & Ironson, G. (1993). Massage effects on cocaine-exposed preterm neonates. *Journal of Developmental and Behavioral Pediatrics, 14,* 318–322.

Wheeler, L., & Miyake, K. (1992). Social comparison in everyday life. *Journal of Personality and Social Psychology, 62,* 760–773.

Whitam, F. L., & Mathy, R. M. (1991). Childhood cross-gender behavior of homosexual females in Brazil, Peru, the Philippines, and the United States. *Archives of Sexual Behavior, 20,* 151–170.

Whitbourne, S. K. (1985). *The aging body: Physiological changes and psychological consequences.* New York: Springer-Verlag.

White, K. M., Hogg, M. A., & Terry, D. J. (2002). Improving attitude behavior correspondence through exposure to normative support from a salient ingroup. *Basic and Applied Social Psychology, 24,* 91–103.

White, L. (2003). *Second language acquisition and universal grammar.* New York: Cambridge University Press.

White, N. M., & Milner, P. M. (1992). The psychobiology of reinforcers. *Annual Review of Psychology, 43,* 443–472.

Whorf, B. L. (1956). Science and linguistics. In J. B. Carroll (Ed.), *Language, thought and reality: Selected writings of Benjamin Lee Whorf.* Cambridge, MA: MIT Press.

Whyte, J., & Kavey, N. B. (1990). Somnambulistic eating: A report of three cases. *International Journal of Eating Disorders, 9,* 577–581.

Widiger, T. A., & Sankis, L. M. (2000). Adult psychopathology: Issues and controversies. *Annual Review of Psychology, 51,* 377–405.

Wiebe, R. E., & McCabe, S. B. (2002). Relationship perfectionism, dysphoria, and hostile interpersonal behaviors. *Journal of Social and Clinical Psychology, 21,* 67–91.

Wiedenfeld, S. A., O'Leary, A., Bandura, A., Brown, S., Levine, S., & Raska, K. (1990). Impact of perceived self-efficacy in coping with stressors on components of the immune system. *Journal of Personality and Social Psychology, 59,* 1082–1094.

Wiederman, M. W., & Dubois, S. L. (1998). Evolution and sex differences in preferences for short-term mates: Results from a policy capturing study. *Evolution and Human Behavior, 19,* 153–170.

Wiens, A. N., & Menustik, C. E. (1983). Treatment outcome and patient characteristics in an aversion therapy program for alcoholism. *American Psychologist, 38,* 1089–1096.

Wilcox, S., & Storandt, M. (1996). Relations among age, exercise, and psychological variables in a community sample of women. *Health Psychology, 15,* 110–113.

Wilkins, A. J., & Baddeley, A. D. (1978). Remembering to recall in everyday life: An approach to absentmindedness. In M. M. Grueneberg, P. E. Morris, & R. N. Sykes (Eds.), *Practical aspects of memory.* London: Academic Press.

Willenberg, H. S., Bornstein, S. R., & Crousos, G. P. (2000). Stress-induced disease: Overview. In G. Fink (Ed.), *Encyclopedia of stress.* San Diego, CA: Academic Press.

Williams, L. M. (1995). Recovered memories of abuse in women with documented child sexual victimization histories. *Journal of Traumatic Stress, 8,* 649–673.

Williams, T. J., Pepitone, M. E., Christensen, S. E., Cooke, B. M., Huberman, A. D., & Breedlove, N. J. (2000). Finger length patterns and human sexual orientation. *Nature, 404,* 455–456.

Williamson, A. M., Feyer, A. M., Mattick, R. P., Friswell, R., & Finlay-Brown, S. (2001). Developing measures of fatigue using an alcohol comparison to validate the effects of fatigue on performance. *Accident Analysis and Prevention, 2001, 33,* 313–326.

Willingham, W. W., Rock, D. A., & Pollack, J. (1990). Predictability of college grades: Three tests and three national samples. In W. W. Willingham & C. Lewis (Eds.), *Predicting college grades: An analysis of institutional trends over two decades.* Princeton, NJ: Educational Testing Service.

Willis, S. L., & Schaie, K. W. (1986). Training the elderly on the ability factors of spatial orientation and inductive reasoning. *Psychology and Aging, 1,* 239–247.

Wilson, B. J., & Gottman, J. M. (2002). Marital conflict, repair, and parenting. In M. H. Bornstein (Ed.). *Handbook of parenting: Vol. 4. Social conditions and applied parenting* (2nd ed.). Mahwah, NJ: Erlbaum.

Wilson, G. T., & Lawson, D. M. (1976). Expectancies, alcohol, and sexual arousal in male social drinkers. *Journal of Abnormal Psychology, 85,* 587–594.

Wilson, S. C., & Barber, T. X. (1982). The fantasy-prone personality: Implications for understanding imagery, hypnosis, and parapsychological phenomena. *PSI-Research, 1,* 94–116.

Wilson, S. J., Lipsey, M. W., & Derzon, J. H. (2003). The effects of school-based intervention programs on aggressive behavior: A meta-analysis. *Journal of Consulting and Clinical Psychology, 71,* 136–149.

Windholz, G. (1997). Ivan P. Pavlov: An overview of his life and psychological work. *American Psychologist, 52,* 941–946.

Winkler, I., Korzyukov, O., Gumenyuk, V., Cowan, N., Linkenkaer, H. K., Ilmoniemi, R. J., Alho, K., & Naeaetaenen, R. (2002). Temporary and longer term retention of acoustic information. *Psychophysiology, 39,* 530–534.

Winnepenninckx, B., Rooms, L., & Kooy, R. F. (2003). Mental retardation: A review of the genetic causes. *British Journal of Developmental Disabilities, 49,* 29–44.

Winner, E. (2000). The origins and ends of giftedness. *American Psychologist, 55,* 159–169.

Winson, J. (1990). The meaning of dreams. *Scientific American, 260*(11), 86–96.

Winston, J. S., Strange, B. A., O'Doherty, J., & Dolan, R. J. (2002). Automatic and intentional brain responses during evaluation of trustworthiness of faces. *Nature Neuroscience, 5,* 277–283.

Witelson, S. F., Kigar, D. L., & Harvey, T. (1999). The exceptional brain of Albert Einstein. *Lancet, 353,* 2149–2153.

Wittchen, H. U., Zhao, S., Kessler, R. C., & Eaton, W. W. (1994). DSM-III-R generalized anxiety disorder in the National Comorbidity Survey. *Archives of General Psychiatry, 51,* 355–364.

Witte, K., & Allen, M. (2000). A meta-analysis of fear appeals: Implications for effective public health campaigns. *Health Education and Behavior, 27,* 591–615.

Wixted, J. T. (1991). Conditions and consequences of maintenance rehearsal. *Journal of Experimental Psychology: Learning, Memory, and Cognition, 17,* 963–973.

Woerzbicka, A. (1986). Human emotions: Universal or culture-specific? *American Anthropologist, 88,* 584–594.

Wolberg, L. R. (1967). *The technique of psychotherapy* (2nd ed.). New York: Grune & Stratton.

Wolken, J. J. (1995). *Light detectors, photoreceptors, and imaging systems in nature.* New York: Oxford University Press.

Wolpe, J. (1958). *Psychotherapy by reciprocal inhibition.* Stanford, CA: Stanford University Press.

Wolpe, J., & Plaud, J. J. (1997). Pavlov's contributions to behavior therapy: The obvious and the not so obvious. *American Psychologist, 52,* 966–972.

Wong, D. F., Wagner, H. N., Tune, L. E., et al. (1986). Positron emission tomography reveals elevated D_2 dopamine receptors in drug-naive schizophrenics. *Science, 234,* 1558–1563.

Wong, M. M., & Csikszentmihalyi, M. (1991). Affiliation motivation and daily experience: Some issues on gender differences. *Journal of Personality and Social Psychology, 60,* 154–164.

Wood, S. L., & Swait, J. (2002). Psychological indicators of innovation adoption: Cross classification based need for cognition and need for change. *Journal of Consumer Psychology, 12,* 1–13.

Wood, W., & Eagly, A. H. (2000). A call to recognize the breadth of evolutionary perspectives: Sociocultural theories and evolutionary psychology. *Psychological Inquiry, 11,* 52–55.

Wood, W., Lundgren, S., Ouellete, J. A., Busceme, S., & Blackstone, T. (1994). Minority influence: A meta-analytic review of social influence processes. *Psychological Bulletin, 115,* 323–345.

Wood, W., Rhodes, N., & Whelan, M. (1989). Sex differences in positive well-being: A consideration of emotional style and marital status. *Psychological Bulletin, 106,* 249–264.

Woodruff-Pak, D. S. (1993). Eyeblink classical conditioning in H. M.: Delay and trace paradigms. *Behavioral Neuroscience, 107,* 911–925.

Woods, S. C., & Seeley, R. J. (2002). Hunger and energy homeostasis. In H. Pashler & R. Gallistel (Eds.), *Steven's handbook of experimental psychology: Vol. 3. Learning, motivation, and emotion* (3rd ed.). New York: Wiley.

Word, C. O., Zanna, M. P., & Cooper, J. (1974). The nonverbal mediation of self-fulfilling prophecies in interracial interaction. *Journal of Experimental Social Psychology, 10,* 109–120.

Worell, J., & Remer, P. P. (2003). *Feminist perspectives in therapy: Empowering diverse women.* New York: Wiley.

World Health Organization. (2002). *AIDS epidemic update, December, 2001.* Geneva, Switzerland: Author.

Xu, Y., & Corkin, S. (2001). H. M. revisits the Tower of Hanoi Puzzle. *Neuropsychology, 15,* 69–79.

Xu, Y., Ehringer, M., Yang, F., & Sikela, J. M. (2001). Comparison of global brain gene expression profiles between inbred long-sleep and inbred short-sleep mice by high-density gene array hybridization. *Alcoholism: Clinical and Experimental Research, 25,* 810–818.

Yandava, B. D., Billinghurst, L. L., & Snyder, E. Y. (1999). "Global" cell replacement is feasible via neural stem cell transplantation: Evidence from the dysmyelinated shiverer mouse brain. *Proceedings of the National Academy of Sciences, 96,* 7029–7034.

Yerkes, R. M., & Dodson, J. D. (1908). The relation of strength of stimulus to rapidity of habit-formation. *Journal of Comparative and Physiological Psychology, 18,* 459–482.

Yin, T. C. T., & Kuwada, S. (1984). Neuronal mechanisms of binaural interaction. In G. M. Edelman, W. M. Cowan, & W. E. Gall (Eds.), *Dynamic aspects of neocortical function.* New York: Wiley.

Young, J. E., Klosko, J. S., & Weishaar, M. E. (2003). *Schema therapy: A practitioner's guide.* New York: Guilford Press.

Young, L. R., & Joffe, R. T. (1997). *Bipolar disorder: Biological models and their clinical application.* New York: Marcel Dekker.

Youngstedt, S. D., O'Connor, P. J., & Dishman, R. K. (1997). The effects of acute exercise on sleep: A quantitative synthesis. *Sleep, 20,* 203–214.

Yrizarry, N., Matsumoto, D., Imai, C., Kooken, K., & Takeuchi, S. (2001). Culture and emotion. In L. L. Adler & U. P. Gielen (Eds.), *Cross-cultural topics in psychology* (2nd ed.). Westport, CT: Praeger.

Zajonc, R. B. (1965). Social facilitation. *Science, 149,* 269–274.

Zajonc, R. B., Murphy, S. T., & Inglehart, M. (1989). Feeling and facial efference: Implications of a vascular theory of emotion. *Psychological Review, 96,* 395–416.

Zakzanis, K. K. (1998). Neuropsychological correlates of positive vs. negative schizophrenic symptomatology. *Schizophrenia Research, 29,* 227–233.

Zambelis, T., Paparrigopoulos, T., & Soldatos, C. R. (2002). REM sleep behaviour disorder associated with a neurinoma of the left pontocerebellar angle. *Journal of Neurology, Neurosurgery & Psychiatry, 72,* 821–822.

Zangari, W., & Machado, F. R. (1996). Survey: Incidence and social relevance of Brazilian university students' psychic experiences. *European Journal of Parapsychology, 12,* 75–87.

Zatzick, D. F., & Dimsdale, J. E. (1990). Cultural variations in response to painful stimuli. *Psychosomatic Medicine, 52,* 544–557.

Zautra, A. J. (2003). *Emotions, stress, and health.* New York: Oxford University Press.

Zebrowitz, L. A., Voinescu, L., & Collins, M. A. (1996). "Wide-eyed" and "crooked-faced": Determinants of perceived and real honesty across the life span. *Personality and Social Psychology Bulletin, 22,* 1258–1269.

Zhang, Y., Proenca, R., Maffei, M., Barone, M., Leopold, L., & Friedman, J. M. (1994). Positional cloning of the mouse obese gene and its human homologue. *Nature, 372,* 425–432.

Zhdanova, I. V., & Wurtman, R. J. (1997). Efficacy of melatonin as a sleep-promoting agent. *Journal of Biological Rhythms, 12,* 644–650.

Zimbardo, P. G., Haney, C., Banks, W. C., & Jaffe, D. (1973, April 8). The mind is a formidable jailer: A Pirandellian prison. *New York Times Magazine,* pp. 38–60.

Zinbarg, R. E., Barlow, D. H., Brown, T. A., & Hertz, R. M. (1992). Cognitive-behavioral approaches to the nature and treatment of anxiety disorders. *Annual Review of Psychology, 43, 235–268.*

Zinovieva, I. L. (2001). Why do people work if they are not paid? An example from Eastern Europe. In D. R. Denison (Ed.), *Managing organizational change in transition economies.* Mahwah, NJ: Erlbaum.

Zubieta, J.-K., Smith, Y. R., Bueller, J. A., et al. (2001). Regional mu opioid receptor regulation of sensory and affective dimensions of pain. *Science, 293,* 311–315.

Zubieta, J.-K., & Stohler, C. S. (2002, February 25). Response: Measuring our natural painkiller. *Trends in Neuroscience, 69,* 42–51.

Zucker, T. P., Flesche, C. W., Germing, U., Schroeter, S., Willers, R., Wolf, H. H., & Heyll, A. (1998). Patient-controlled versus staff-controlled analgesia with pethidine after allogeneic bone marrow transplantation. *Pain, 75,* 305–312.

Zuckerman, M. (1991). *Psychobiology of personality.* New York: Cambridge University Press.

Zuckerman, M., Hall, J. A., DeFrank, R. S., & Rosenthal, R. (1976). Encoding and decoding of spontaneous and posed facial expressions. *Journal of Personality and Social Psychology, 34,* 966–977.

Name Index

D

E

F

N

O

P

Subject Index

C

D

E

F

N

O

P

R

S

Selected Themes

SEX DIFFERENCES/GENDER ISSUES

CRITICAL THINKING/DISPELLING MISCONCEPTIONS

(* = ***BENEATH THE SURFACE*** **FEATURE**)